Informatik — Fachberichte

Band 195: I. S. Bátori, U. Hahn, M. Pinkal, W. Wahlster (Hrsg.), Computerlinguistik und ihre theoretischen Grundlagen. Proceedings. IX, 218 Seiten. 1988.

Band 197: M. Leszak, H. Eggert, Petri-Netz-Methoden und -Werkzeuge. XII, 254 Seiten. 1989.

Band 198: U. Reimer, FRM: Ein Frame-Repräsentationsmodell und seine formale Semantik. VIII, 161 Seiten. 1988.

Band 199: C. Beckstein, Zur Logik der Logik-Programmierung. IX, 246 Seiten. 1988.

Band 200: A. Reinefeld, Spielbaum-Suchverfahren. IX, 191 Seiten. 1989.

Band 201: A. M. Kotz, Triggermechanismen in Datenbanksystemen. VIII, 187 Seiten. 1989.

Band 202: Th. Christaller (Hrsg.), Künstliche Intelligenz. 5. Frühjahrsschule, KIFS-87, Günne, März/April 1987. Proceedings. VII, 403 Seiten, 1989.

Band 203: K. v. Luck (Hrsg.), Künstliche Intelligenz. 7. Frühjahrsschule, KIFS-89, Günne, März 1989. Proceedings. VII, 302 Seiten. 1989.

Band 204: T. Härder (Hrsg.), Datenbanksysteme in Büro, Technik und Wissenschaft. GI/SI-Fachtagung, Zürich, März 1989. Proceedings. XII, 427 Seiten. 1989.

Band 205: P. J. Kühn (Hrsg.), Kommunikation in verteilten Systemen. ITG/GI-Fachtagung, Stuttgart, Februar 1989. Proceedings. XII, 907 Seiten. 1989.

Band 206: P. Horster, H. Isselhorst, Approximative Public-Key-Kryptosysteme. VII, 174 Seiten. 1989.

Band 207: J. Knop (Hrsg.), Organisation der Datenverarbeitung an der Schwelle der 90er Jahre. 8. GI-Fachgespräch, Düsseldorf, März 1989. Proceedings. IX, 276 Seiten. 1989.

Band 208: J. Retti, K. Leidlmair (Hrsg.), 5. Österreichische Artificial-Intelligence-Tagung, Igls/Tirol, März 1989. Proceedings. XI, 452 Seiten. 1989.

Band 209: U. W. Lipeck, Dynamische Integrität von Datenbanken. VIII, 140 Seiten. 1989.

Band 210: K. Drosten, Termersetzungssysteme. IX, 152 Seiten. 1989.

Band 211: H. W. Meuer (Hrsg.), SUPERCOMPUTER '89. Mannheim, Juni 1989. Proceedings, 1989. VIII, 171 Seiten. 1989.

Band 212: W.-M. Lippe (Hrsg.), Software-Entwicklung. Fachtagung, Marburg, Juni 1989. Proceedings. IX, 290 Seiten. 1989.

Band 213: I. Walter, Datenbankgestützte Repräsentation und Extraktion von Episodenbeschreibungen aus Bildfolgen. VIII, 243 Seiten. 1989.

Band 214: W. Görke, H. Sörensen (Hrsg.), Fehlertolerierende Rechensysteme / Fault-Tolerant Computing Systems. 4. Internationale GI/ITG/GMA-Fachtagung, Baden-Baden, September 1989. Proceedings. XI, 390 Seiten. 1989.

Band 215: M. Bidjan-Irani, Qualität und Testbarkeit hochintegrierter Schaltungen. IX, 169 Seiten. 1989.

Band 216: D. Metzing (Hrsg.), GWAI-89. 13th German Workshop on Artificial Intelligence. Eringerfeld, September 1989. Proceedings. XII, 485 Seiten. 1989.

Band 217: M. Zieher, Kopplung von Rechnernetzen. XII, 218 Seiten. 1989.

Band 218: G. Stiege, J. S. Lie (Hrsg.), Messung, Modellierung und Bewertung von Rechensystemen und Netzen. 5. GI/ITG-Fachtagung, Braunschweig, September 1989. Proceedings. IX, 342 Seiten. 1989.

Band 219: H. Burkhardt, K. H. Höhne, B. Neumann (Hrsg.), Mustererkennung 1989. 11. DAGM-Symposium, Hamburg, Oktober 1989. Proceedings. XIX, 575 Seiten. 1989

Band 220: F. Stetter, W. Brauer (Hrsg.), Informatik und Schule 1989: Zukunftsperspektiven der Informatik für Schule und Ausbildung. GI-Fachtagung, München, November 1989. Proceedings. XI, 359 Seiten. 1989.

Band 221: H. Schelhowe (Hrsg.), Frauenwelt – Computerräume. GI-Fachtagung, Bremen, September 1989. Proceedings. XV, 284 Seiten. 1989.

Band 222: M. Paul (Hrsg.), GI – 19. Jahrestagung I. München, Oktober 1989. Proceedings. XVI, 717 Seiten. 1989.

Band 223: M. Paul (Hrsg.), GI – 19. Jahrestagung II. München, Oktober 1989. Proceedings. XVI, 719 Seiten. 1989.

Band 224: U. Voges, Software-Diversität und ihre Modellierung. VIII, 211 Seiten. 1989

Band 225: W. Stoll, Test von OSI-Protokollen. IX, 205 Seiten. 1989.

Band 226: F. Mattern, Verteilte Basisalgorithmen. IX, 285 Seiten. 1989.

Band 227: W. Brauer, C. Freksa (Hrsg.), Wissensbasierte Systeme. 3. Internationaler GI-Kongreß, München, Oktober 1989. Proceedings. X, 544 Seiten. 1989.

Band 228: A. Jaeschke, W. Geiger, B. Page (Hrsg.), Informatik im Umweltschutz. 4. Symposium, Karlsruhe, November 1989. Proceedings. XII, 452 Seiten. 1989.

Band 229: W. Coy, L. Bonsiepen, Erfahrung und Berechnung. Kritik der Expertensystemtechnik. VII, 209 Seiten. 1989.

Band 230: A. Bode, R. Dierstein, M. Göbel, A. Jaeschke (Hrsg.), Visualisierung von Umweltdaten in Supercomputersystemen. Karlsruhe, November 1989. Proceedings. XII, 116 Seiten. 1990.

Band 231: R. Henn, K. Stieger (Hrsg.), PEARL 89 – Workshop über Realzeitsysteme. 10. Fachtagung, Boppard, Dezember 1989. Proceedings. X, 243 Seiten. 1989.

Band 232: R. Loogen, Parallele Implementierung funktionaler Programmiersprachen. IX, 385 Seiten. 1990.

Band 233: S. Jablonski, Datenverwaltung in verteilten Systemen. XIII, 336 Seiten. 1990.

Band 234: A. Pfitzmann, Diensteintegrierende Kommunikationsnetze mit teilnehmerüberprüfbarem Datenschutz. XII, 343 Seiten. 1990.

Band 235: C. Feder, Ausnahmebehandlung in objektorientierten Programmiersprachen. IX, 250 Seiten. 1990.

Band 236: J. Stoll, Fehlertoleranz in verteilten Realzeitsystemen. IX, 200 Seiten. 1990.

Band 237: R. Grebe (Hrsg.), Parallele Datenverarbeitung mit dem Transputer. Aachen, September 1989. Proceedings. VIII, 241 Seiten. 1990.

Band 238: B. Endres-Niggemeyer, T. Hermann, A. Kobsa, D. Rösner (Hrsg.), Interaktion und Kommunikation mit dem Computer. Ulm, März 1989. Proceedings. VIII, 175 Seiten. 1990.

Band 239: K. Kansy, P. Wißkirchen (Hrsg.), Graphik und KI. Königswinter, April 1990. Proceedings. VII, 125 Seiten. 1990.

Band 240: D. Tavangarian, Flagorientierte Assoziativspeicher und -prozessoren. XII. 193 Seiten. 1990.

Band 241: A. Schill, Migrationssteuerung und Konfigurationsverwaltung für verteilte objektorientierte Anwendungen. IX, 174 Seiten. 1990.

Band 242: D. Wybranietz, Multicast-Kommunikation in verteilten Systemen. VIII, 191 Seiten. 1990.

Band 243: U. Hahn, Lexikalisch verteiltes Text-Parsing. X, 263 Seiten. 1990.

Band 244: B. R. Kämmerer, Sprecherunabhängigkeit und Sprecheradaption. VIII, 110 Seiten. 1990.

Band 245: C. Freksa, C. Habel (Hrsg.), Repräsentation und Verarbeitung räumlichen Wissens. VIII, 353 Seiten. 1990.

Informatik-Fachberichte 291

Herausgeber: W. Brauer
im Auftrag der Gesellschaft für Informatik (GI)

Subreihe Künstliche Intelligenz

Mitherausgeber: C. Freksa
in Zusammenarbeit mit dem Fachbereich 1
„Künstliche Intelligenz" der GI

W. Brauer D. Hernández (Hrsg.)

Verteilte Künstliche Intelligenz und kooperatives Arbeiten

4. Internationaler GI-Kongreß
Wissensbasierte Systeme

München, 23.-24. Oktober 1991

Proceedings

Springer-Verlag

Berlin Heidelberg New York London Paris
Tokyo Hong Kong Barcelona Budapest

Herausgeber

W. Brauer
D. Hernández
Institut für Informatik, Technische Universität München
Arcisstr. 21, W-8000 München 2

Veranstalter

Gesellschaft für Informatik e.V.
In Zusammenarbeit mit der Münchener Messegesellschaft mbH

Programmkomitee

W. Brauer, München
W. Büttner, München
B. Faltings, Lausanne
G. Gottlob, Wien
H. Helbig, Dresden
M. Jarke, Aachen
B. Neumann, Hamburg
C.-R. Rollinger, Osnabrück
W. Wahlster, Saarbrücken

CR Subject Classification (1991): I.2, I.2.11, H.5.3, H.1.2, H.4, I.2.4-7, I.2.1, J.1-2, J.7

ISBN-13:978-3-540-54617-7   e-ISBN-13:978-3-642-76980-1
DOI: 10.1007/978-3-642-76980-1

Satz: Reproduktionsfertige Vorlage vom Autor

33/3140-543210 – Gedruckt auf säurefreiem Papier

Vorwort

Wissensbasierte Systeme gehören mittlerweile schon fast zum Alltag – sowohl in der Forschung als auch in der Praxis. Sie wurden in den letzten Jahren zu wichtigen, gefragten Produkten der schnell wachsenden Informatik-Industrie. Die gewaltigen Steigerungen der Verarbeitungsgeschwindigkeit, der Speicherkapazität und der Parallelverarbeitungsmöglichkeit von Rechnern sowie die vielfältigen Verbesserungen im Bereich der Rechner-Rechner- und Mensch-Rechner-Interaktion, verbunden mit beträchtlichen Fortschritten in vielen anderen Bereichen der Informatik, erlauben die Entwicklung dieser Anwendungssysteme von ganz neuer Qualität.

Bisher sind wissensbasierte Systeme jedoch vornehmlich als Unterstützungssysteme für Einzelne entwickelt und eingesetzt worden. Die intelligente Lösung komplexer Aufgaben erfordert jedoch i.a. das Zusammenwirken verschiedener Partner. Rechnerunterstützung für verteilte Systeme von selbständig agierenden kooperativen Partnern ist mehr als bloße Zusammenschaltung von Rechnern in einem Netz. Denn es geht nicht nur um den Zugang Einzelner zu verteilten Rechnersystemen, sondern sowohl um die Rechnerunterstützung des kooperativen Arbeitens mehrerer Personen als auch um die Organisation der Zusammenarbeit von mehreren relativ selbständigen Rechnersystemen bei der Bearbeitung komplexer Aufgaben. In den letzten Jahren hat sich in der Informatik und speziell auch in der Künstlichen Intelligenz ein Wandel in der Auffassung vom Computer und seiner Verwendung vollzogen – von der Vorstellung von der sequentiell arbeitenden Funktionseinheit zum verteilten, interaktiven, parallel arbeitenden System von Agenten/Akteuren. Computer werden also nicht nur als persönliches Werkzeug, sondern als Medium für Kommunikation und als einer unter vielen intelligenten Partnern in einer verteilten Arbeitsumgebung verwendet. In der Bundesrepublik hat die rege Forschungsaktivität auf diesem Gebiet bereits zur Gründung einer neuen Fachgruppe "Verteilte KI" innerhalb des Fachbereichs 1 (KI) der Gesellschaft für Informatik geführt.

Der 4. Internationale GI-Kongreß "Wissensbasierte Systeme" befaßt sich hauptsächlich mit diesem für den praktischen Einsatz der Wissensverarbeitung äußerst wichtigen Themenkreis der Verteilten Künstlichen Intelligenz und der Unterstützung kooperativen Entscheidens und Handelns sowie mit eng verwandten Gebieten wie Wissensrepräsentation, Mensch-Maschine-Interaktion und natürlich-sprachlichen Systemen.

Einen größeren Raum als früher nimmt das immer enger mit der traditionellen Informatik und Künstlichen Intelligenz zusammenwachsende Gebiet der Theorie und Anwendung neuronaler Netze ein – die Ideen des Konnektionismus und des verteilten Lernens in wissensbasierten Systemen sind ja nicht nur über den Aspekt der Parallelverarbeitung verbunden. Dieser GI-Kongreß führt auch die Tradition fort, BMFT-Verbundprojekte vorzustellen; diesmal werden alle Projekte zur Neuroinformatik präsentiert.

Neu ins Programm gekommen ist das zwar schon fast klassische aber in letzter Zeit für die Modellierung technischer Systeme immer nützlicher gewordene Gebiet des qualitativen modellbasierten Schließens, das u.a. auch für den Einsatz neuronaler Netze zur Steuerung von Systemen sowie für die Kommunikation zwischen an der Steuerung eines Systems beteiligten Partnern von einiger Wichtigkeit ist. Wir hoffen, daß auch dieser GI-Kongreß wieder dazu beiträgt, die Kooperation zwischen verschiedenen Gebieten zu fördern.

Bei der Programmgestaltung wurde darauf Wert gelegt, daß alle Partner der "Arbeitsgemeinschaft der Deutschen KI-Institute" (AKI), der Sonderforschungsbereich "Künstliche Intelligenz" der DFG (Karlsruhe, Kaiserslautern, Saarbrücken), das LILOG-Projekt der IBM Deutschland und der Universitäten Hamburg, Osnabrück, Saarbrücken, Trier, das Frauenhofer Institut Karlsruhe sowie eine Reihe weiterer wichtiger in- und ausländischer Forschungsinstitutionen und Industrieprojekte vertreten sind. Wegen der Begrenzung des Kongreßprogramms konnten jedoch längst nicht alle wichtigen Forschungsgruppen berücksichtigt werden.

Wie auch beim letzten Mal fördern Informatik-Gesellschaften aus europäischen Nachbarländern den GI-Kongreß (afcet; BCS; NGI; OCG; SI), wobei – kennzeichnend für die gesellschaftlichen und politischen Veränderungen der letzten zwei Jahre – die ungarische "John von Neumann Informatik Gesellschaft" (NJSZT) erstmals dabei ist.

Wir danken der Münchener Messegesellschaft, insbesondere Frau Hein, sowie Herrn Benesch (Siemens AG) und seinen Mitarbeitern aus der Siemens AG und von der TU München für die Kongreßorganisation. Ebenso gilt unser Dank allen weiteren Mitgliedern des Programm- und Organisationskomitees und nicht zuletzt den Vortragenden für ihre Kooperation bei der rechtzeitigen Fertigstellung dieses Tagungsbandes.

München, Juli 1991   W. Brauer, D. Hernández

Inhaltsverzeichnis

Informationstechnik im Wandel
- Aufgaben staatlicher Förderung -

Werner Gries
Bundesministerium für Forschung und Technologie (BMFT)
Heinemannstr. 2
5300 Bonn 2

In der Informationstechnik tragen Halbleiter-Chips zwar nur 8 % zum Weltumsatz der Informationstechnik bei. Der Chip hat aber, ähnlich wie Öl im Energiemarkt, die entscheidende Rolle bei der Durchdringung der Informationstechnik in allen Bereichen der Wirtschaft. Der Rohstoff Information ist angewiesen auf den Chip. Vor diesem Hintergrund kommt es darauf an - ergänzend zu den Forschungszielen im Bereich Künstliche Intelligenz als das beherrschende Informatik-Thema des 4. Internationalen GI-Kongresses - den Blick über dieses Wissenschaftsgebiet hinaus auf einige grundsätzliche, industriepolitische Aspekte von erheblicher Tragweite zu richten.

1   Die Multiplikatorfunktion der Informationstechnik

Das Wort Informationstechnik wird als Sammelbegriff sehr häufig benutzt, ohne daß hinreichend verdeutlicht wird, was alles darunter verstanden wird. In der folgenden Betrachtung werden zur Informationstechnik gerechnet:

- Mikroelektronik
- Informationsverarbeitung
- Bürotechnik
- Kommunikationstechnik
- Unterhaltungselektronik
- Industrieelektronik
- Software

Das Volumen des Weltmarktes für Informationstechnik belief sich 1989 auf etwa 736 Mrd US-Dollar, hiervon entfielen auf die Informationsverarbeitungstechnik einschließlich Software und Computerdienstleistungen 43 % des Marktes, danach folgen Kommunikationstechnik mit 21 % und Unterhaltungselektronik mit 11 %. Etwa 8 % des Marktes entfallen auf Halbleiterbauelemente.

Die strategische industriepolitische Bedeutung der Informationstechnik besteht darin, daß sie erhebliche Auswirkungen in anderen Bereichen der Wirtschaft hat. In der Bundesrepublik Deutschland beeinflußt die Informationstechnik den Jahresumsatz der fünf exportstärksten Bereiche der Investitionsgüterindustrie, nämlich

- Maschinenbau,
- Straßen- und Fahrzeugbau,
- Elektrotechnik,
- Feinmechanik und Optik,
- Büro- und Datentechnik

in Höhe von 655 Mrd DM entscheidend.

Man kann es auch so ausdrücken: 1 DM Umsatz in der Informationstechnik beeinflußt 7 DM Umsatz in der Wirtschaft.

<u>Die Multiplikatorfunktion der Informationstechnik ist somit entscheidend.</u> Keine andere Technik durchdringt in diesem Ausmaß die gesamte Wirtschaft. Ausgangspunkt hierbei ist die Tatsache, daß es gelungen ist, Informationen komprimiert zu speichern und einer systematischen Auswertung zuzuführen. Ein Schlüssel hierzu bilden deshalb die Halbleiterbauelemente, die in der Mikroelektronik entwickelt werden. Sie gestatten die zunehmend kostengünstige Speicherung der Information auf einem sogenannten "Chip". Auf eine kurze Formel gebracht, heißt das:

<u>Was Rohöl für den Energiemarkt bedeutet, bedeutet das Halbleiterbauelement - der Chip - für die Informationstechnik. Der Rohstoff "Information" wird durch den Chip umfassend und effizient nutzbar.</u>

Mit dem Chip als Informationsspeicher wird es so möglich, die gesamte Anwendungspalette der Steuerung von Geräten und die benutzerfreudliche Handhabung einer Vielzahl von Produkten zu beeinflussen. Deshalb ist die Integration des Chip in die gesamte Wirtschaft ein wesentlicher Wettbewerbsfaktor. Beispielhaft sei nur verwiesen auf den Maschinenbau oder den Automobilsektor, der durch die Einbeziehung modernster Informationstechnik z.Zt. starken strukturellen Veränderungen unterworfen ist.

2 Konsequenzen für die Mikroelektronik

Die Chip-Herstellung ist geprägt durch überproportional steigende Kosten und kurze Innovationszyklen. Die Forschungs- und Entwicklungskosten sowie die Fertigung des 4-Megabit-Chips belaufen sich bei einer Monatsproduktion von 10 Millionen Stück DRAM (Dynamic Random Access Memory) auf 1,6 Mrd US-Dollar. Für die gleiche Fertigungsstückzahl braucht man im Falle von 64 Megabit-Speicherchips schon 6 Mrd US-Dollar. Schon aus diesen Zahlenrelationen erkennt man, daß nur noch große Unternehmen oder Zusammenschlüsse von großen Unternehmen überhaupt in der Lage sind, die notwendigen Investitionen zu tätigen. An dieser Entwicklung wird sich in absehbarer Zeit kaum etwas ändern. Vielleicht gelingt es in einem Jahrzehnt, neue Techniken für Informationsspeicher zu entwickeln, die diesen Teufelskreis durchbrechen.

Hinzu kommt, daß Geräte und Materialien für die Halbleiterfertigung teilweise nur von ein oder zwei Unternehmen angeboten werden. Da viele dieser Unternehmen zur Zeit von japanischem Kapital getragen werden, ist eine entscheidende Abhängigkeit von Japan im Bereich der Halbleiterfertigung und bei den Materialien und Ausrüstungen für die Halbleiterfertigung festzustellen.

Daraus ergeben sich folgende Überlegungen:

1. Entscheidend ist, daß bei Halbleiter-Chips der weltweite Wettbewerb, der durch die Dominanz japanischer Unternehmen bei Halbleiterproduktion, Materialien und Ausrüstungen für die Halbleiterproduktion gefährdet ist, aufrechterhalten und möglichst verstärkt wird. Dies kann geschehen durch

- Unterstützung von Unternehmenszusammenschlüssen außerhalb der japanischen Unternehmen, die als Konkurrenten der dominierenden japanischen Unternehmen auftreten,

- weltweite Kartellregulierungen, die beispielsweise von einer UNO-Kartellbehörde ausgeübt werden könnte, um die Marktwirtschaft weltweit zu sichern.

2. Wir müssen Abschied nehmen von einer rein nationalen oder europäischen Betrachtungsweise beim Bemühen um konkurrierende Unternehmen im Bereich der Halbleiter. Es geht nicht darum, eine europäische Halbleiterindustrie aufrechtzuerhalten oder zu unterstützen, sondern darum, in weltweitem Wettbewerb funktionsfähige Unternehmen zu bilden, die im Wettbewerb zu den dominierenden japanischen Unternehmen auftreten. Kriterium staatlicher Förderung der Unternehmen im Bereich Halbleiter muß deshalb sein:

- Erhöhung des weltweiten Wettbewerbs im Bereich Halbleiter,

- Schaffung inländischer oder europäischer Arbeitsplätze in Forschung und Produktion.

3 Staatlicher Handlungsrahmen

Der staatliche Handlungsrahmen bei der Informationstechnik ist sehr umfassend im Zukunftskonzept Informationstechnik der Bundesregierung dargelegt worden. Hier sind die allgemeinen Ziele wie folgt festgelegt:

1.	Rahmenbedingungen fortentwickeln, um der IT-Hersteller-industrie in Deutschland gute Entfaltungsmöglichkeiten zu bieten und der IT-Anwenderindustrie Zugang zum IT-Know-How zu sichern.

2.	Verstärkung der Grundlagenforschung; Kooperation zwischen Wirtschaft und Wissenschaft verbessern. Kleine und mittlere Unternehmen stärker einbeziehen.

3.	Alle Möglichkeiten des Einsatzes der Informationstechnik in Umwelt, Arbeitsbedingungen, rationeller Energieverwendung und Erfüllung staatlicher Aufgaben ausschöpfen.

4.	In Schule, Hochschule, Berufliche Bildung, Weiterbildung IT in den Bildungsauftrag integrieren.

Im Hinblick auf die Halbleiterfertigung besteht der Handlungsrahmen vor allem darin, dafür zu sorgen, daß keine Monopole den Wettbewerb beeinträchtigen. Dies bedeutet vor allem das Setzen staatlicher Rahmenbedingungen und nicht Einsatz von Steuergeldern.

Was die Forschungsförderung anbetrifft, so ist sie primär auf die Hochschulen, die außeruniversitären Forschungseinrichtungen und den Verbund zwischen Wirtschaft und Wissenschaft konzentriert. Die Einzelförderung eines Unternehmens ist in der Zwischenzeit zu einer Rarität geworden, im Gegensatz zur Praxis der früheren Jahre. Durch die Förderung des Humankapitals, durch die Finanzierung von Projekten zwischen Wirtschaft und Wissenschaft und durch die Mobilität dieses Humankapitals wird ein wichtiger Beitrag geleistet.

Kein Wunder ist es deshalb, daß in der Zwischenzeit die direkte Projektförderung der Wirtschaft beim Forschungsministerium nur noch 25 % der staatlichen Forschungsausgaben für die Informationstechnik ausmacht. Darüber hinaus ist innerhalb der verbleibenden Förderung der Wirtschaft in der Informationstechnik des BMFT eine Konzentration auf kleine und mittlere Unternehmen erfolgt, die dazu führt, daß 1990 etwa 50 % der Projektförderung auf diesen Bereich entfielen.

Der gesamte Forschungsaufwand des Staates für die Informationstechnik in Deutschland (alte Bundesländer) belief sich 1990 auf:

- 1,14 Milliarden insgesamt, darin 180 Mio EG vorrangig für die Wirtschaft,

- Anteil des Bundes 823 Mio DM, diese zu 75 % außerhalb der Wirtschaft.

Die EG konzentriert sich auf die grenzüberschreitenden Projekte und leistet damit einen wichtigen Beitrag zur Zusammenarbeit Europas in der Informationstechnik. Die EG-Programme sind aber auf große Breitenwirkung angelegt. Für die Konzentration der Mittel auf ausgewälte strategische Vorhaben wurde daher zusätzlich die EUREKA-Initiataive gestartet. Das größte strategische Programm im IT-Bereich ist das EUREKA-Vorhaben JESSI. Ein anderes, ebenfalls langfristig und mit strategischer Dimension angesetztes EUREKA-Projekt ist PROMETHEUS in der Verkehrstechnik, wobei es bei dem Teilverbund PRO-ART (PRO=PROMETHEUS, ART=Artificial Intelligence=Künstliche Intelligenz= KI) im Kern um Fortschritte in der KI-Teildisziplin Maschinensehen (Erkennen und Verstehen natürlicher, bewegter Szenen) geht, um im Kraftfahrzeug zur Unterstützung des Fahrers und zur Erhöhung der Verkehrssicherheit eingesetzt zu werden.

JESSI hat zum Ziel, die Beinträchtigung des Wettbewerbs bei Halbleitern, Ausrüstungen und Materialien zur Fertigung von Halbleitern und beim Aufbau von flexiblen Fertigungsverfahren in einer Gemeinschaftsaktion aufzuheben.

JESSI öffnet sich deshalb auch der US-Initiative SEMATECH, weil gemeinsam das Ziel verfolgt wird, den globalen Wettbewerb der Informationstechnik zu stärken.

Die Eigeninitiative der Wirtschaft wird in einem EUREKA-Projekt zusammengefaßt. Nationale Regierungen und die EG leisten finanzielle Beiträge in einem unterschiedlichen Umfang. Einen festen Fördersatz der öffentlichen Hand für JESSI-Projekte gibt es nicht; einzelne JESSI-Projekte sollten auch ohne staatliche Förderung durchgeführt werden.

4 Industriepolitische Folgerungen

<u>Der Stellenwert</u> der EG-Forschungsförderung für die Industriepolitik wird auch bei der EG-Kommission zunehmend erkannt. Sie hat deshalb im Februar 1991 neue Vorschläge zur Förderung der Informationstechnik vorgelegt, die einen Kurswechsel in Richtung Industriepolitik erkennen lassen.

Ein wichtiger Aspekt ist auch in der informationstechnischen Industrie die Globalisierung des Wirtschaftsgeschehens. Gerade in jüngster Zeit können wir beobachten, daß japanische Unternehmen die Kapitalmehrheit an klassischen europäischen Unternehmen (Beispiel ICL) erwerben oder daß große europäische Unternehmen (Beispiel Philips) Teile der Informationstechnik aufgeben. In der Regel sind dies auch Unternehmen, die in der Vergangenheit erhebliche Forschungsmittel seitens des Staates erhalten haben. Es stellt sich nun die Frage, ob der Wechsel des Kapitaleigners zu Konsequenzen bei der staatlichen Forschungsförderung führen muß. Hier ergibt sich für das BMFT folgende Position: Entscheidend dafür, ob ein Unternehmen durch staatliche Forschungsmittel gefördert wird, ist nicht die Verteilung des Kapitaleigentums, sondern sind die Kriterien,

-       ob damit der marktwirtschaftliche Wettbewerb weltweit ausgedehnt wird,

-       ob mit den nationalen Fördermitteln die inländischen Forschungskapazität und auch inländische Arbeitsplätze erhalten oder geschaffen werden.

Konkret bezogen auf die Fälle von Firmen in Deutschland, bei denen Japaner die Mehrheit übernommen haben, bedeutet dies, daß stets im Einzelfall zu prüfen ist, ob und wie der Wettbewerb sich darstellt und die inländische Forschung und Produktion sich entwickelt.

Gemeinsame Forschungsprojekte mit ausländischen Firmen und Forschungseinrichtungen sollten generell vom Prinzip der Gegenseitigkeit ausgehen. Darüber hinaus gilt als Kriterium aber auch die konkrete Verhaltensweise der Regierung des Kapitaleigners gegenüber deutschen Unternehmen.

Cooperating Agent Architectures to Manage Manufacturing Processes

Peter Raulefs
Intel Corporation
Artificial Intelligence Laboratory
Santa Clara, California

Abstract

Manufacturing has become one of the most challenging domains to drive both fundamental and applied research in Artificial Intelligence, and it is of far greater economic significance than any other domain. Combining recent advances in representation theory, distributed problem solving, and distributed system architectures, this paper describes an approach to Computational Manufacturing *as the new field that describes manufacturing as computation in symbolic models.*

1   Introduction

For several decades, automation and computer-integrated manufacturing have introduced computational approaches to manufacturing. Much emphasis of automation systems has been on automating design and material handling, and CIM systems have primarily focused on managing the integration of data across different manufacturing domains. Automated control systems had to adopt formal views that rely on more or less explicitly described models, usually expressed in terms of control models characterizing mathematical relationships between parameters allowing to set up plans for tracking observable data, and for actions to achieve desired conditions.

Recent advances in Artificial Intelligence open up opportunities to create *symbolic models* of manufacturing systems, describing manufacturing as a computational process of transforming symbolically described physical objects to become the manufactured artifacts. Also, we have learned how to build computational agents that reason about such models, acquire observed data and compare them with models to maintain consistency with the physical environment. Furthermore, computational agents make plans to achieve temporally extended goal structures, such as production schedules, and they induce the execution of their plans. **Computational Manufacturing (CM)** is the new field that describes manufacturing as computation in symbolic models.

These approaches lead to manufacturing system architectures that separate *virtual* from *physical factories*. A virtual factory consists of symbolic models and the computational agents performing reasoning tasks on the models that induce the actions carried out in the physical factory. To abbreviate, we call such architectures *CM architectures*.

Humans are key players in CM architectures. In fact, successful CM architectures are primarily designed to *assist and support* humans design, set up, and run factories. Automation is an issue that is orthogonal to the concerns of designing CM architectures, as automation is just about replacing well delineated functions, formerly done by humans, with machines. In CM architectures, humans are modeled as computational agents, acting via interfaces that constrain their effects within guidelines, but no explicit descriptions of how they achieve their goals are given.

Another key ingredient of CM architectures is that its entities are distributed, acting and interacting concurrently as organized and, to some extent, self-organizing, structures of agents and objects. This has led to an increasingly fruitful interaction between the fields of Distributed Artificial Intelligence and Distributed Processing.

This paper is intended to provide an introduction to, and an overview of a particular approach to CM that has evolved from applications in process industries, especially manufacturing of chemicals and integrated circuits (ICs). Section 2 gives a brief rationale of CM, and Section 3 discusses roots in Distributed Artificial Intelligence and Processing. Section 4 introduces some concepts of RPS *Representation of Physical Systems*, the representation system that underlies our CM architecture. Applications to IC manufacturing are discussed in Sections 5 and 6.

2 Computational Manufacturing

Manufacturing is a vast field extending beyond its core domains of product and (manufacturing) process design, and process operation to incorporate financial, economical, organizational, and many other issues. In this paper, we adopt a much narrower focus, where manufacturing is about fabricating physical artifacts, reducing it to engineered domains of physical manipulation of physical objects. Considering that manufacturing is about manipulating physical objects, it may seem strange to *view manufacturing as computation*. However, several reasons suggest that this is actually the only perspective possible.

First, it is impossible to speak of and reason about physical objects and manipulations *per se*. Instead, we form mental models and describe them with properties, such as geometrical dimensions, refraction indices, etc., and relations to other objects, such as applying a force, or conducting heat. A vocabulary together with its semantics is used to form a model of the domain. Manufacturing operations are described as transformations modifying, creating, and terminating objects in the model. With models being symbolic representations of the domain, manufacturing cannot but be described as an activity of manipulating symbolic representations. Describing such manipulations as transformations on symbolic representations of objects leaves no conceptual difference between carrying out a manufacturing procedure and computation.

Manufacturing is viewed from many different perspectives. Consider, for example, a plasma etcher used in semiconductor manufacturing. A safety expert may only be concerned about possible leakage of poisonous gases. He forms a *partial model*, describing the etcher as a device that may leak poisonous gases, together with conditions that lead to, or prevent leakage. A factory manager will have little interest in any detail at all, and form an *abstract model* of the etcher. The abstract model describes the etcher's main function, such as removing unmasked polysilicon film, the throughput capacity, and the main conditions to keep it working. On the other hand, a process engineer will have a *deep model* that describes, starting from basic principles, how the etcher works. Most properties of the partial and abstract models will be derivable from the deep model, but many such derivations will be extremely tedious and impractical, so that it is better to store their consequences as *compiled knowledge* directly with partial and abstract models.

Again, each of the people involved views a manufacturing operation in terms of particular models. Models are specialized to provide as direct support as possible for the job functions they are used for. Each person, in his job, deals with such models rather than with some unique physical reality. Of course, each person must ensure consistency between his models and the signals he receives from the domain. But consistency is constrained to the job function. For example, there is nothing wrong with a manager who thinks of etchant molecules as little animals eating polysilicon when activated by RF fields. This model is consistent with his views at the level of abstraction appropriate for his job. It is, however, inconsistent with the more detailed signals that a process engineer deals with.

Manufacturing systems are controlled by interpreting sensory observations in the context of models. For example, valves regulate gas flow rates determining the composition of etch gases in a manufacturing process for microprocessors. This composition determines etch selectivity which, in turn, influences the geometrical sizes of features on the wafer which, in turn, influence electrical properties of the device they are part of, etc. In other words, there is a relationship between gas flow rates and performance properties of a microprocessor built in the process. Understanding this relationship is achieved by a model that describes, in more or less intermediate detail, how one property influences another. In Computer Science terms, one is building a network of constraints, and uses constraint propagation techniques to see how properties influence each other.

In summary, we observe that people in manufacturing perform their job functions on the basis of models of the domain, and view manufacturing in terms of information processing activities in such models.

3 Distributed Artificial Intelligence and Distributed Processing

Distributed Artificial Intelligence (DAI) and Distributed Processing (DP) are two fields that are often confused with each other. In fact, they have fertile areas of overlap, and benefit from mutually complementing each other.

The main tenet of DAI is that machine entities actively plan, reason about, and interact with tasks performed by machine entities. The DP field studies how to construct and analyze properties of systems of distributed machine entities. In other words, DAI tries to add planning and reasoning capabilities to distributed systems. This poses new challenges to DP, while the DP field supplies the underlying computer and system architectures to build DAI systems. The main motivation for building distributed systems is exploiting the efficiency of concurrent computation, as well as utilizing already existing computing resources to perform tasks that none could do individually.

In contrast, the main motivation for DAI is to tackle inherently distributed problems, because of the structure of the domain or the structure of solution methods. For example, *distributed sensing and monitoring* [11] simply does not admit non-distributed solutions, as sensors are too distant to permit other than local interpretation when rapid responses are required. Another classical domain is speech understanding [5], requiring specialized problem-solving capabilities (acoustics, syntax, ...) with dynamically evolving interactions.

Another distinction is that DP assumes that problems are a priori partitioned, where DAI is concerned with building systems that partition the problems that they then set out to solve. This leads to somewhat complementary foci of the two fields: DP is primarily concerned with performing disparate tasks on interconnected machines (focusing, for example, on protection schemes), where DAI does typically not assume predefined roles of computing resources.

DAI has evolved along two main paradigms [18]. The first is *planning tasks for multiple, distributed agents*, with planning and task execution are performed by distinct entities. The main issue is achieving synchrony in centrally produced plans.

The second is *Distributed Problem Solving (DPS)*, where groups of agents collectively decompose problems into subproblems, construct plans to solve the problems, execute the tasks, and synthesize results from the outcomes of the tasks.

It will become apparent in Section 6 that the approach developed in this paper is DPS, including the first paradigm as a special case.

4 Agent-Object Structures

The notion of an agent is closely related to, and has evolved in conjunction with that of objects in object-oriented languages and modeling approaches. Unfortunately, many researchers in the DAI community have adopted views by which agents are rather loosely defined as entities that act in a more or less autonomous way. Such concepts are, in fact, often subordinated to the particular DAI paradigm that a project subscribes to.

For example, approaches to construct plans for concurrently executed tasks [18] take agents as resources to carry out either arbitrary, or specific tasks. This, in turn, leads to models of homogeneous agents in the former, and heterogeneous agents in the latter case. Agents are like encapsulated modules in distributed processing approaches.

The Distributed Problem Solving camp, however, has developed a quite different notion of agents. Instead of merely executing given plans, agents are active participants in decomposing problems, constructing plans, and executing plans (e.g., plans they have helped constructing before). When making *limited rationality* and *bounded perception* assumptions [21], agents not capable of solving their assigned (or self-appointed) problems dynamically find ways to enlist the cooperation of other agents, incurring resource allocation and control problems about timing, precedence, etc.

In RPS, we distinguish objects and agents. Objects are meant to model physical entities whose behavior is solely determined by physical laws (supposed to be modeled in classes that the objects are instances of). Actions must be licensed by particular conditions, and the actions establishing these conditions constitute the direct cause(s) for a subsequent action. Agents may to some extent behave like objects do. In addition, however, an agent maintains a *belief structure* that determines its behavior to achieve goals, based on assumptions, resources, and acquaintances with other agents. To achieve a goal, an agent may *decide* to perform an action even though there is no physical cause. For example, to flip a switch, an agent issues a command "On!" to have the same effect as applying a force to push a lever that physically moves the switch to its "on"-position. As deliberate, decision-based actions must be caused by such commands, agents cannot overturn physical laws.

Objects and agents are created as instances of classes, using the usual data abstraction, behavior ssharing, and inheritance machinery of object-oriented languages. Fig. 1 shows the main constituents of object and agent class definitions:

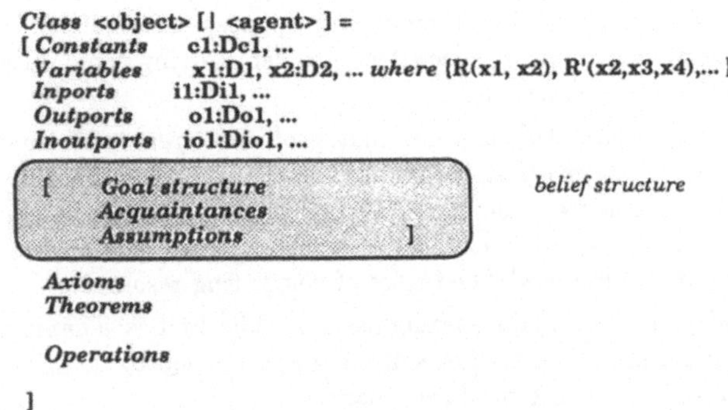

Figure 1: Object/Agent Class Definition

Objects and agents have local states that map local variables to values; some of the states may be designated as *(in, out, inout) ports* to indicate that these states may be shared with other objects and agents, where information flows in the direction indicated. The cartesian product of the variable and port domains make up a superset of the local state space, with the actual state space being a restriction imposed by constraints expressed in *where*-clauses and axioms (and theorems implied by axioms, listed to improve efficiency of reasoning). All state transitions, if not affected by external influences communicated through ports, result from executing *operations*.

Agents have a *belief structure*, consisting of three additional slots. Agent operations may change the belief structure. *Goal structures* define which goals the agent tries to achieve, given specified conditions. In other words, an agent's goals depend on an actual situation, and may change when the situation changes. One particular component of a current situation are an agent's *assumptions*, or retractable beliefs about its environment.

The communication structure of a system of agents is defined in terms of their *acquaintances* with other agents and objects. An acquaintance consists of a reference to an agent or object, and a set of operations allocated for use by the agent owning the acquaintance. *Request constraints* may restrict requests for operations. Request constraints are expressed as conditions under which requests get executed.

Unlike actor and earlier agent systems [1, 2], an acquaintance of agent A with agent B is known to agent B. This facility is used to implement *publish/subscribe services*, where subscribers own acquaintances to publishers (or data sources), and publishers provide their services to agents that subscribe to them. As acquaintances list operations, or services, provided by publishers, agents may *selectively subscribe* to different services provided by a publishing agent.

Another use of acquaintances is in *resource allocation*. An agent, such as a *scheduling agent*, allocates resources to an agent A by sending acquaintances to objects/agents ("resources") together with the services requested, and restrictions to limit the extent of the services rendered to A.

Fig. 2 shows an ontology of the concepts that we use to model a system. It distinguishes between a *component structure* that describes the objects and agents that constitute the entities in a factory, and a *process structure* that describes the patterns of activities performed by objects and agents. Component structures are arranged in part/subpart hierarchies that include classes with underlying scientific and technological theories governing the behavior of the objects and the non-deliberate behavior of the agents.

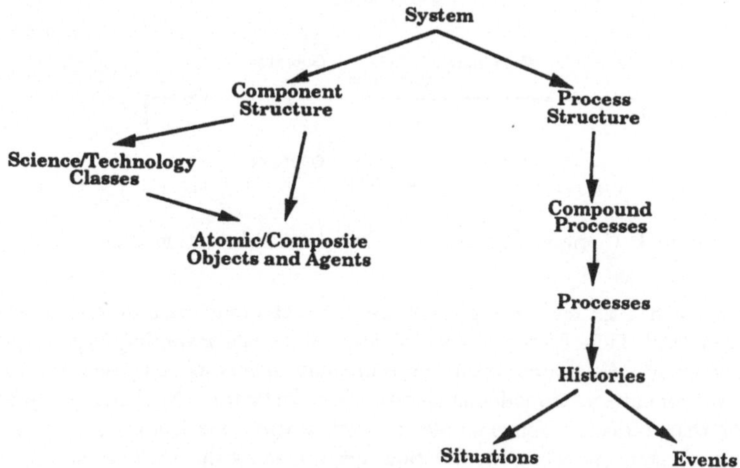

Figure 2: Factory Model Ontology

Both objects and processes are instants of classes, as familiar from object-oriented languages. Some classes will, in fact, not be instantiated at all, but serve to inherit theories they express to object classes. For examples, systems of physical laws, such as thermodynamics, are expressed in such classes. [16] describes an approach to account for continuous and mixed-view objects in this framework, using ensemble theory.

5 Virtual Factories

Next, we discuss how the above concepts are applied to construct models of factories. We call such models *virtual factories*, justified by not only having all the ingredients of a "real" factory, but also by having the agents and objects of the virtual factory behaving like the entities they are models of. Control agents manage what other objects and agents do. We can reason about agents achieving their goal structures, their efficiency, causes of failures, and plans to fix faults. The subsequent section shows, using an example, how a virtual factory interacts with its associated physical factory.

5.1 Factory Component Structures

Following the ontology outlined in Fig. 2, a virtual factory consists of a component and a process structure. The component structure is an architecture of factory entities, described by objects and agents. For example, Fig. 3 indicates the organization of a wafer fabrication facility. The factory acts as an agent, with a goal structure reflecting efficient use of its resources to meet business objectives, based on beliefs (listed under its *Assumptions*) of market conditions, technology trends, financial conditions, etc.

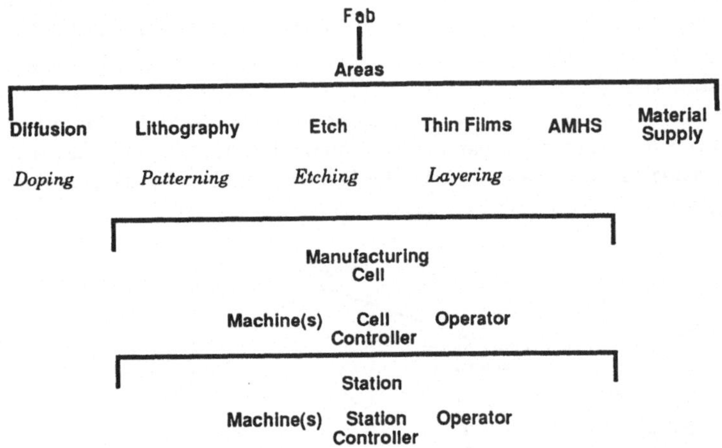

Figure 3: Component Structure of a Wafer Fabrication Plant (Fab)

The factory agent has six main component agents for the four main functional areas (Diffusion, Lithography, Etch, and Thin Films), an Automated Materials Handling System (AHMS), and a Materials Supply Agent. Each area agent has *equipment agents* as components. For example, the Etch agent has component agents modeling all etchers in the factory. Note that equipment is modeled as agents rather than objects. For example, an etch station consists of an object, modeling the physical machine, an agent modeling the functions performed by the workstation controlling the etch machine object, and an agent describing the functions of an operator that oversees the functions of the other two.

However, the hierarchy indicated in Fig. 3 applies different criteria to aggregate agents and objects into composites. Although the Etch area agent includes all the factory's etchers as components, the etchers are, in fact, components of Manufacturing Cell agents. Manufacturing Cell agents include components that are agents/objects of other areas, breaking the hierarchy that we started by introducing areas.

A manufacturing cell is meant to optimize on flow and control of material. For example, a patterning operation of a stepper in lithography, projecting and developing a circuit image onto a photoresist layer, is followed with an etching operation. Combining a diffusion furnace (for doping), a sputter machine (to spin photoresist onto wafers), a stepper, and an etcher into a manufacturing cell makes good sense to optimize process recipe parameters for controlling target parameters within narrow tolerances. However, a process engineer specialized on etching maintains a different view of the factory, aggregating all etchers to form the functional area he is responsible for.

Our component structures describe different *views*, aggregating the same agents and objects in different ways. Each view corresponds to a particular composite agent/object. The fact that their sets of components intersect imposes consistency constraints on views so that an etcher, when viewed as a component of an etch area agent, does not behave inconsistently with the etch agent viewed as a component of a Manufacturing Cell agent. The notion of *roles* [8] is simply the inverse of views: An agent/object A belonging to two different views V1 and V2 is also said to play roles in V1 and V2. As agents in V1 and V2 may own different acquaintances with A, using different services in A (or the same, but constrained with different conditions), the behavior of A viewed under its role in V1 may be different from its behavior when viewed from its V2 role.

5.2 Factory Process Structures

In RPS, a *process* describes a *temporally extended activity pattern* performed by agents and objects in a component model. The primitive elements of process descriptions are *situations* and *operations*.

A situation constrains the states of objects throughout some period of time. In other words, a situation consists of an assertion (proposition about states that may change its truth value over time), and a time interval constraint: Situation := [Assertion|TimeConstraint].

A time constraint denotes a set of time intervals throughout which the assertion persists (the assertion holds for every instant of the intervals). We describe time intervals in terms of clock times, interval expressions formed with the functions beg/end/dur (begin, end, duration of intervals), and Allen/Hayes' interval relations [19]. Time intervals are always taken to be open on both sides.

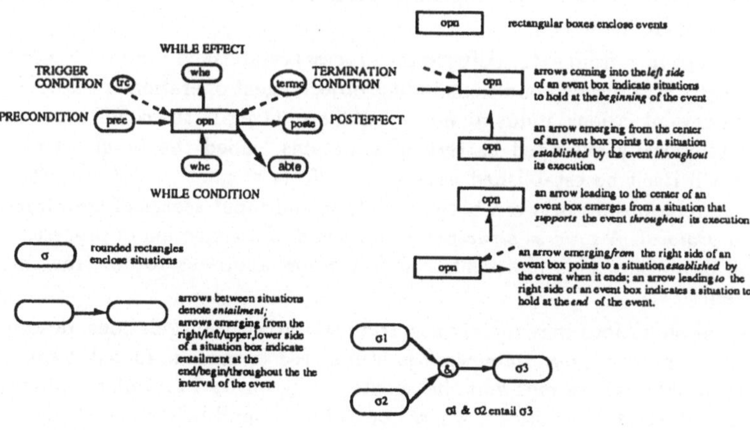

Figure 4: Operation

An *event* denotes a change that occurs over some period of time. An *operation* describes a mechanism which, when executed, brings about an event. An operation may bring about arbitrarily many events. Different events of an operation will occur over different time intervals, and they may differ in details. In other words, an operation can also be viewed as a *pattern* denoting a set of events that differ by properties determined by context conditions, such as initial values, starting time, and properties established while the operation executes.

Operations may denote both discrete and continuous events. For a discrete event, the time period of change is an instant, unless it is uncertain (see below). Continuous change is usually described in terms of time-dependent quantities, most often described with differential equations. Then, to describe a continuous event occurring over a time interval $(\$t_1,\$t_2)$ and making a quantity $x(t)$ change, we need an initial condition, an indication of the start time $\$t_1$, an indication of the end time $\$t_2$, a condition that enables the operation, and a condition that ensures it can proceed. To make references to time points, we use assertions about states. For example, a machine may start executing an operation exactly when its entry bay is loaded up. Such conditions, called *trigger* and *termination* conditions specify when events of an operation start and when they terminate. Initial and enabling conditions are rolled into a *precondition*, which must hold or just terminate when the trigger condition begins to hold. A *while condition* specifies state constraints that must be satisfied while the operation executes. Situations called *while effect* and *termination effect* specify the outcomes of events performed by the operation.

A *process* is described by a network of situations and operations. The arcs linking situations and operations are those explained above. *Executing a process* corresponds to an instant of the situation-operation network to a situation-event network, where state and time constraints in situations are substituted with states and specific time intervals, and operations are instantiated to events. The resulting situation-event network is a *history* of the process. One way of producing a process history is to pick start situations, and apply the constraints in the process to propagate start situations through the network. Depending on which start situations have been selected, and the order of propagation, process execution may correspond to *temporal projection* into the future, past, or even both. In this way, process execution generalizes *envisioning* [4].

In executing a process, the constraints propagated from start situations may not lead to unique situations throughout. Instead, propagation corresponds to constraint reasoning, leading to narrowed constraints on other situations throughout the process network. In other words, we obtain a partial instantiation that denotes a subset of original process extension (set of all its histories), admitting many more than a single history.

A process is determined from externally (to the process) established conditions and the component structure. Externally established conditions induce object/agent operations to execute events which, in turn, establish new situations, inducing new events, etc. Overall, the conditions making a process execute form a temporally extended pattern of situations, called the *input scene* of the process. An input scene will itself be established as a set of effects of another process, the other process' *output scene*. The relationship between between output and input scenes of two processes makes up their *interaction protocol*. A *process structure* is composed of a collection of processes, together with their interaction protocols. This representation framework allows us to describe and reason about distributed system.

As object/agent operations may merely constrain state transition relations, describing functional relations only in the extreme, our framework is well suited to provide mixed detailed and approximative accounts of physical systems and the agents acting on it. Particularly important are *specifications*, or approximative descriptions, where constraints bound behaviors without saying *how* the behavior is accomplished. RPS also supports probabilistic models, beyond the scope of this paper.

6 Distributed Monitoring and Diagnosis

As an example of the interaction between virtual and physical factory, we review distributed monitoring and diagnosis in a semiconductor factory.

IC fabrication proceeds according to process recipes of several hundred steps. A wafer fab may have some 1,000 machines on which several manufacturing processes are simultaneously performed, each process making 50-100 different products. Conceptually, we view a fab as a network of machines as illustrated in Fig. 5, where wafer lots traverse the network on fab trajectories, or paths whose nodes are machines. Monitoring is meant to detect processing problems, and diagnosis is to determine causes of detected problems. Distributed monitoring and diagnosis problems arise when processing faults occur that consist of temporally and spatially separated conditions in several machines, where particular conditions do not necessarily constitute faults when viewed at a local perspective. In other words, a distributed fault is a pattern of conditions extended in time and space, and across different elements in the factory.

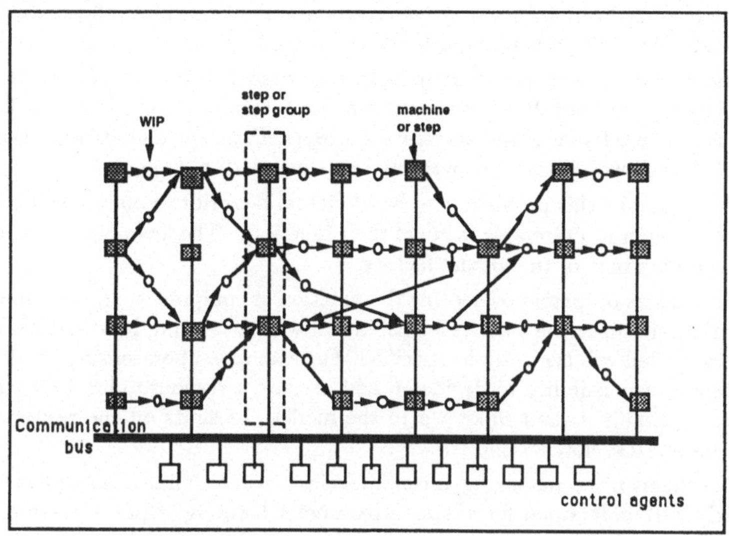

Figure 5: WIP Trajectories in a Wafer Factory

Faults are detected by observing fault symptoms. In the framework developed above, fault symptoms are observations establishing situations that are inconsistent with (a) a particular process supposed to be executed, or (b) with *any* process that may execute on the component structure modeling the factory, induced by appropriate situations. The first case (a) indicates a *process fault*, and the second (b) a *component model fault*. In this section, we consider process faults.

Detecting a process fault requires that situations are observed and interpreted as a fault symptom. Interpreting any observation requires a model. In our framework, a monitoring agent tries to explain observations, such as sensor data, as established by given situations, or by effects resulting from events that the process is assumed to be executing. If no such explanation for the observation can be found, the observation may hold regardless of whether or not the process is executed. If, however, the assumption that the process is executed establishes that the observed situation cannot hold, the monitoring agent has detected a process fault symptom.

Distributed fault symptoms, however, cannot be detected by any single monitoring agent. Time and space constraints prohibit that any single agent collects and interprets all observed data required. Instead, several agents collect and interpret observations from incomplete models, each raising the hypothesis that a distributed fault symptom may be indicated. Through a *negotiated interpretation protocol*, they will come to an overall interpretation, where each agent only draws on its own, incomplete view of the component and process structure.

A *diagnosis* is a modification of the process (and, possibly, component structure) model making it consistent with the fault symptoms. A *strong diagnosis* is a modified model that establishes the fault symptoms, while a *weak diagnosis* merely admits, but does not establish them. Similar to distributed fault detection, distributed diagnosis results from a negotiation protocol.

It is often the case that observed evidence is insufficient to confirm or disconfirm observations to constitute a fault symptom, or to reach a diagnosis. Monitoring and diagnosing agents need to bring about additional observations. Such observations may, in fact, induce process modifications. Such *diagnostic actions* are especially taken when they promise to simultaneously contribute to repairing the problem. In such cases, monitoring, diagnosis, and repair become an integrated procedure.

Monitoring proceeds in the virtual factory, based on interpreting observed sensor data in the context of models. Monitoring agents in the virtual factory devise and maintain *tracking plans* by which sensor data are acquired. Fault symptom hypotheses raised by monitoring agents, and fault hypotheses raised by diagnosis agents may require revisions of tracking plans, especially if such hypotheses are predictive, and prevention of faults is desired.

A critical issue of such a system is that models, i.e. virtual factories, will always lack realism. This results in faults that are not detected, because no fault symptoms are found, or data cannot be interpreted because the model lacks the necessary concepts. Deficient models will also prohibit that fault symptoms, if found, will always get properly explained with a diagnosis.

Our approach to manage this problem is to build virtual factories as *open systems* [10], meant to assist humans even though it automates many of their functions. The key point is to properly design *human agents* to become part of the virtual factory.

Human agents, such as operators overseeing the function of equipment, are described with behavioral constraints that circumscribe their responsibilities, without saying how humans achieve them, although resources needed will typically be specified. For example, upon sensing an alarm condition, it is a human agent's responsibility to decide on and execute a response plan that either results in fixing the problem (possibly a fault unknown to the model), or shuts off the respective equipment and routes work-in-progress flow around it.

The second mechanism for managing inconsistencies between virtual and physical factories is *model repair*, fairly well understood for adaptive parameter learning. Upon receiving observed data from the physical factory that are inconsistent with its model, the virtual factory modifies parametric constraints to achieve consistency. A fundamental open problem is repairing component structure deficiencies, such as missing objects or behaviors.

7 Remarks

Probabilistic models. The representation framework described in this paper ignores the fact that much of the data and the models in manufacturing is uncertain. However, a probabilistic extension of RPS provides an approach to address this issue. In this extension, state assertions become assertions about probability density functions on state variables. Situation entailment is described with conditional probability distributions. We have developed techniques to compile such models to *belief networks* [13] with both discrete and continuous variables, where continuous distributions are Gaussians or mixtures of Gaussians to admit symbolic reasoning procedures [3, 14, 17, 20].

Implementation. Our prototype implementation of a distributed agent/object architecture supporting a virtual factory interacting with a physical factory relies heavily on distributed system capabilities that become increasingly available commercially:

- A federated data base system.

- A uniform, high-level application programmatic interface (API) that shields *all* subsystems from implementation details, such as programming languages and operating systems.

- A communication network that supports all communication protocols, and provides client/server and publish/subscription services.

References

[1] Agha, G. *Actors: A Model of Concurrent Computation in Distributed Systems.* MIT Press, Cambridge, MA, 1986.

[2] Boehm, H.-P., H.-L. Fischer, P. Raulefs. CSSA. In Proc. ACM Conf. on Artificial Intelligence and Programming Languages, 1977, pp. 99-109.

[3] D'Ambrosio, B. Efficient Incremental Updating of Probabilistic Models. In AAAI 1989 Workshop on Uncertainty and AI. Detroit, 1989.

[4] De Kleer, J. and J. S. Brown. A Qualitative Physics Based on Confluences. In *Formal Theories of the Common Sense World,* eds. J. R. Hobbs and R. C. Moore, Ablex Publ. Co., 1986, pp. 109 - 184.

[5] L. D. Erman, F. Hayes-Roth, V. R. Lesser, and D. R. Reddy. The Hearsay-II speech understanding system: Integrating knowledge to resolve uncertainty. Computing Surveys, vol. 12, June 1980, pp. 213 - 253.

[6] Forbus, K. Qualitative Process Theory. in *Mental Models,* eds. D. Gentner and A. Stevens, Erlbaum Publ. Co., 1985.

[7] Fox, M. S. An Organizational View of Distributed Systems. *IEEE Trans. on Systems, Man and Cybernetics,* vol. 11,1981 pp. 70-80.

[8] Gasser, L., N. F. Rouquette, R. W. Hill, and J. Lieb. Representing and using organizational knowledge in DAI systems. In L. Gasser and M. N. Huhns, eds., *Distributed Artificial Intelligence,* vol. 2, 1989, pp. 55 - 78.

[9] Hayes-Roth, F., L. D. Erman, S. Fouse, J. S. Lark, J. Davidson. ABE: A Cooperative Operating System and Development Environment. In *AI Tools and Techniques,* ed. Mark Richer, Ablex Publ. Corp., 1988.

[10] Hewitt, C., C. Manning, J. Inman and G. Agha, eds. *Towards Open Information Systems Science.* MIT Press, Cambridge, MA, 1990.

[11] V. R. Lesser and L. D. Erman. Distributed interpretation: A model and experiment. IEEE Trans. Computers, vol. 29, no. 12, 1980, pp. 1144 - 1163.

[12] Pan, J. Y.-C., J. M. Tenenbaum, and J. Glicksman. A Framework for Knowledge-Based Computer-Integrated Manufacturing. IEEE Trans. on Semiconductor Manufacturing, vol. 2, No. 2, 1989, pp. 33 - 46.

[13] Pearl, J. *Probabilistic Reasoning in Intelligent Systems: Networks of Plausible Inference.* Morgan Kaufman Publ. co., 1988.

[14] Poland, W. Efficient Solution of Continuous-Variable and Discrete/Continuous Decision Problems. Memorandum, Dept. of Engineering-Economics Systems, Stanford Univ., Jan. 1991.

[15] Raulefs, P., B. D'Ambrosio, M. R. Fehling, S. Forrest, and B. M. Wilber. Real-Time Process Management for Materials Composition. Proc. 3rd IEEE Conf. on Artificial Intelligence Applications, Kissimmee, Fla., 1987, pp. 120 -125. Revised version published in IEEE Expert, Summer 1987.

[16] Raulefs, P. A Representation Framework for Continuous Dynamic Systems. Proc. 10th IJCAI, Milan, 1987.

[17] Raulefs, P. Communicating Influence Networks: Integrating Multiple Perspectives to Diagnose Manufacturing Problems. In *Workshop Notes, AAAI Spring Symposium on AI in Manufacturing*, Stanford Univ., April 1989.

[18] Rosenschein, J. S. Synchronization of multi-agent plans. Proc. AAAI-82:115-119, 1982.

[19] Allen, J. A., P. H. Hayes. A Common-Sense Theory of Time. 9th IJCAI, 1985, pp. 528 - 531.

[20] Shachter, Ross D. and C. R. Kenley. Gaussian Influence Diagrams. Management Science, vol. 35, no. 5, May 1989, pp. 527-550.

[21] Simon, H. A. *Models of Man.* Wiley Publ. Co., New York, 1957.

GROUPWARE: Overview and Perspectives

by
Clarence (Skip) Ellis
Department of Computer Science
University of Colorado
Boulder, Colorado 80309-0430

Groupware reflects a change in emphasis from using the computer to solve problems to using the computer to facilitate human interaction. This paper describes categories and examples of groupware and discusses some underlying groupware issues.

1. Introduction

Society acquires much of its character from the ways in which people interact. Although the computer in the home or office is now commonplace, how we interact with each other is more or less the same now as it was a decade ago. But as the technologies of computers and communications continue to converge, people have begun, and will continue, to interact in new and different ways.

One probable outcome of this technological marriage is the electronic workplace—an organization-wide system integrating information processing and communication activities. The study of such system is part of a new multidisciplinary field: Computer-Supported Cooperative Work (CSCW). Drawing on the expertise and collaboration of many specialists, including social scientists and computer scientists, CSCW looks at how groups work and seeks to discover how technology (especially computers) can help them work.

Commercial CSCW products, such as The Coordinator [7] and other PC-based software [20], are often referred to as examples of groupware. This term is frequently used almost synonymously with CSCW technology. Others define groupware as software for small or narrowly focused groups, not organization-wide support. We propose a somewhat broader view, suggesting that groupware be seen as the class of applications, for small groups and for organizations, arising from the merging of computers and large information bases and communications technology—applications that may or may not specifically support cooperation.

This paper explores groupware in this larger sense and delineates classes of design issues facing groupware developers. It is divided into three sections. First, the Overview defines groupware in terms of a group's common task and its need for a shared environment. Since our definition of groupware covers a range of systems, the second section provides taxonomies of groupware systems. The third describes the widely ranging perspectives of those who build these systems.

2. Overview

Most software systems support one form of interaction—that between a user and the system. Whether preparing a document, writing a program, querying a database, or even playing a video game, the user interacts solely with the computer. Even systems designed for multiuser applications, such as office information systems, provide minimal support for user-to-user interaction. This type of support is clearly needed; after all, much of a person's activity occurs in a group, rather than an individual, context. As we begin to focus on how to support this group interaction, we must attend to three key areas: communication, collaboration, and coordination.

The Importance of Communication, Collaboration, and Coordination

Computer-based or computer-mediated communication, such as electronic mail, is not fully integrated with other forms of communication. The primarily asynchronous world of electronic mail and bulletin boards exists quite separately from the synchronous world of telephone and face-to-face conversations. While applications such as voice mail or talk programs blur this distinction somewhat, there are still gaps between the asynchronous and the synchronous worlds. One cannot transfer a document between two arbitrary phone numbers, for example, and it is uncommon to originate a telephone conversation from a workstation. Integrating telecommunications and computer processing technologies will help bridge these gaps.

Like communication, collaboration is a cornerstone of group activity. Effective collaboration demands that people share information, and unfortunately, current information systems—database systems in particular—go to great lengths to insulate users from each other. As an example, consider two designers working with a CAD database. Seldom are they able to simultaneously modify different parts of the same object and be aware of each other's changes; rather, they must check the object in and out and tell each other what they have done. Many tasks require an even finer granularity of sharing. What is needed are shared environments that unobtrusively offer up-to-date group context and explicit notification of each user's actions when appropriate.

Communication and collaboration can be more effective if a group's activities are coordinated. Without coordination, for example, a team of programmers or writers will often engage in conflicting or repetitive actions. Coordination can be viewed as an activity in itself, as a necessary overhead when several parties are performing a task. While current database applications contribute somewhat to the coordination of groups—by providing multiple access to shared objects—most software tools offer only a single-user perspective and thus do little to assist this important function.

A Definition of Groupware

Groupware aims to assist groups in communicating, in collaborating, and in coordinating their activities. Specifically, we define groupware as: *computer-based systems that support groups of people engaged in a common task (or goal) and that provide an interface to a shared environment.*

The notions of a common task and a shared environment are crucial to this definition. This may exclude multiuser systems, such as time-sharing systems, whose users may not share a common task. Note also that the definition does not specify that the users be active simultaneously. Groupware that specifically supports simultaneous activity is called real-time groupware; otherwise, it is non-real-time groupware.

The term groupware was first defined by Johnson-Lentz [12] to refer to a computer-based system plus the social group processes. In his book on groupware [11], Johansen restricts his definition to the computer-based system. Our definition follows the line of reasoning of Johansen since this paper is primarily concerned with system level technical issues. It is acknowledged by us and all of the above authors that the system and the group are intimately interacting entities. Successful technological augmentation of a task or process depends upon a delicate balance between good social processes and procedures with appropriately structured technology.

The Groupware Spectrum

There is no rigid dividing line between systems that are groupware and those that are not. Since systems support "common tasks" and "shared environments" to varying degrees, it is appropriate to think of a groupware spectrum with different systems at different points on the spectrum. Of course, this spectrum is multi-dimensional; two dimensions are illustrated in Figure1.

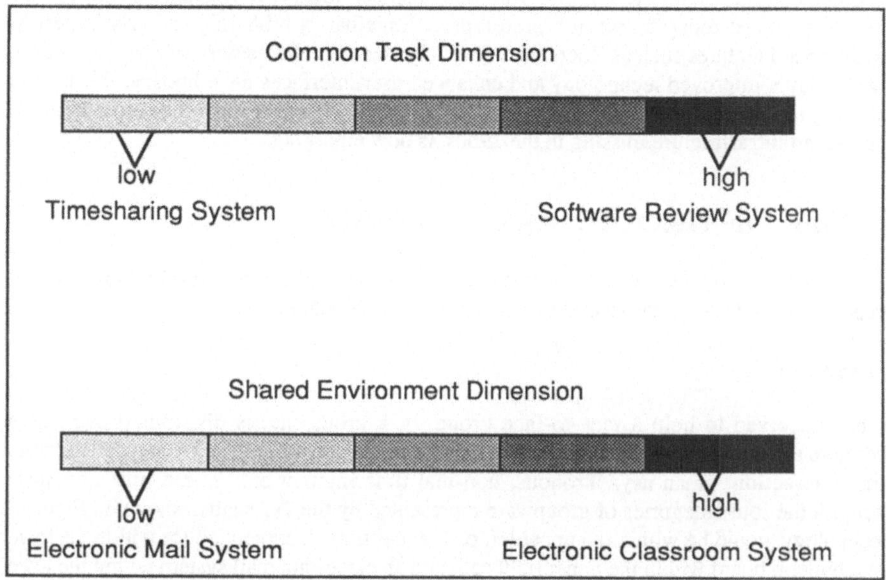

FIGURE 1. Two Dimensions of the Groupware Spectrum

Following are two examples of systems described according to our definition's "common task" dimension:

1.   A conventional time-sharing system supports many users concurrently performing their separate and independent tasks. Since they are not working in a tightly coupled mode on a common task, this system is usually low on the groupware spectrum.

2.   In contrast, consider a software review system that electronically allows a group of designers to evaluate a software module during a real-time interaction. This system assists people who are focusing on the same specific task at the same time, and who are closely interacting. It is high on the groupware spectrum.

Other systems, such as those described in the following examples, can be placed on the groupware spectrum according to how they fit the "shared environment" part of our definition—in other words, the extent to which they provide information about the people participating, the current state of the project, the social atmosphere, and so on.

1.   The typical electronic mail system transmit messages, but it provides few environmental cues. It is, therefore, rather low on the groupware spectrum.

2.   In contrast, the "electronic classroom" system uses multiple windows to post information about the subject being taught, and about the environment. Emulating a traditional classroom, this system allows an

instructor to present an on-line lecture to students at remote personal workstations. In addition to the backboard controlled by the teacher, windows display the attendance list, students' questions and comments, and the classroom status. Many commands facilitate lecture delivery and class interaction. This system is high on the groupware spectrum.

Over time, systems can migrate to higher points on the groupware spectrum. For example, Engelbart's pioneering work on augmenting the intellect in the 1960s demonstrated multiuser systems with groupware capabilities similar to some of today's research prototypes. Engelbart's NLS [6], an early hypertext system, contained advanced features such as filters for selectively viewing information, and support for on-line conferencing. Today's improved technology and enhanced user interfaces have boosted this type of system higher on the groupware spectrum. Additionally, the technological infrastructure required for groupware's wide use, an infrastructure missing in the 1960s, is now emerging.

3. TAXONOMY OF GROUPWARE SYSTEMS

This section presents two taxonomies useful for viewing the variety of groupware. The first taxonomy is based upon notions of time and space; the second on application level functionality.

Time Space Taxonomy

Groupware can be conceived to help a face-to-face group, or a group that is distributed over many locations. Furthermore a groupware system can be conceived to enhance communication and collaboration within a real-time interaction, or an asynchronous, non-real-time interaction. These time and space considerations suggest the four categories of groupware represented by the 2x2 matrix shown in Figure 2. Meeting room technology would be within the upper left cell; a real-time document editor within the lower left cell; a physical bulletin board within the upper right cell; and an electronic mail system within the lower right cell.

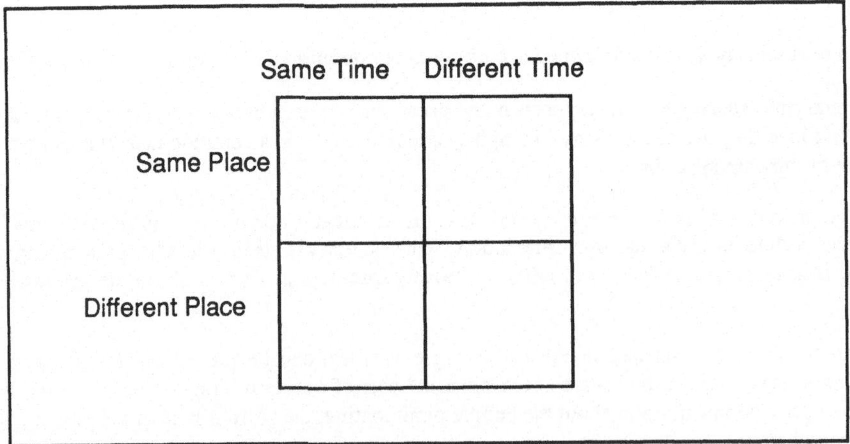

FIGURE 2. Groupware Time Space Matrix

A comprehensive groupware system might best serve the needs of all of the quadrants. For example, it would be quite helpful to have the same base functionality, and look and feel (a) while I am using a computer to edit a document in a meeting room with a group and (b) while I am alone editing in my office or home. Of course, there are other dimensions, such as group size, which can be added to this simple 2x2 matrix. Further details of this taxonomy are presented by Johansen [11].

Application Level Taxonomy

The second taxonomy presented in this section is based on application-level functionality and is not meant to be comprehensive; furthermore, many of the defined categories overlap. This taxonomy is intended primarily to give a general idea of the breadth of the groupware domain.

Message Systems

The most familiar example of groupware is the computer-based message system, which supports the asynchronous exchange of textual messages between groups of users. Examples include electronic mail and computer conferencing or bulletin board systems. The proliferation of such systems has led to the "information overload" phenomenon. Some recent message systems help manage information overload by easing the user's processing burden. "Intelligence" is sometimes added to the message delivery system; for example, the Information Lens [19] lets users specify rules that automatically file or reroute incoming messages depending on their content. Other systems add intelligence to the messages themselves; the Imail system [9], for example, has a language for attaching scripts to messages. Scripts are sender-specified programs that execute in the receiver's environment and that can, for example, query the receiver, report back to the sender, or cause the message to be reroute.

Multiuser Editors

Members of a group can use multiuser editors to jointly compose and edit a document. Some of these editors, such as ForComment [20], are for asynchronous use, and conveniently separate the text supplied by the author from the comments of various reviewers. Real-time group editors allow a group of people to edit the same object at the same time. The object being edited is usually divided into logical segments; for example, a document could be split into sections or a program into procedures or modules. Typically, a multiuser editor allows concurrent read access to any segment, but only one writer per segment. The editor transparently manages locking and synchronization, and users edit the shared object as they would a private object. Examples include Shared Book [18], and Quilt [17]

Some multiuser editors provide explicit notification of other users' actions. For example, Mercury [13], an editor intended for programming teams, informs users when their code needs to be changed because of program modifications made by others. The DistEdit system [15] tries to provide a toolkit for building and supporting multiple group editors.

Group Decision Support Systems and Electronic Meeting Rooms

Group decision support systems (GDSSs) provide computer-based facilities for the exploration of unstructured problems in a group setting. The goal is to improve the productivity of decision-making meetings, either by speeding up the decision-making process or by improving the quality of the resulting decisions. There are GDSS aids for decision structuring, such as alternative ranking and voting tools, and for idea generation or issue analysis.

Many GDSSs are implemented as electronic meeting rooms containing several networked workstations, large computer-controlled public displays, and audio/video equipment. Some of these facilities require a specially trained operator, others assume operational competence among the group members.

A well-known example is the PlexCenter Planning and Decision Support Laboratory at the University of Arizona [2]. The facility provides a large U-shaped conference table with eight personal workstations; a workstation in each of four break-out rooms; a video disk; and a large-screen projection system that can display screens of individual workstations or a compilation of screens. The conference table workstations are recessed to enhance the participants' line of sight and to encourage interaction. They communicate over a local area network and run software tools for electronic brainstorming, stakeholder identification and analysis, and issue analysis.

Unusually, the work at the University has concentrated upon the support of larger groups of more than eight people. This presents unique challenges and opportunities. The current Arizona large group facility has 24 IBM Personal System 2 computer workstations designed to support up to 48 people.

Computer Conferencing

The computer serves as a communications medium in a variety of ways. In particular, it has provided three new approaches in the way people carry out conferences: real-time computer conferencing, computer teleconferencing, and desktop conferencing.

Real-time Computer Conferencing

Real-time computer conferencing allows a group of users, who are either gathered in an electronic meeting room or physically dispersed, to interact synchronously through their workstations or terminals. When a group is physically dispersed, an audio link, such as a conference call, is often established.

There are two basic approaches to implementing real-time computer conferencing software. The first embeds an unmodified single-user application in conferencing environment that multiplexes the application's output to each participant's display. Input comes from one user at a time, and a "floor passing" protocol exchanges input control among users. Examples include terminal linking (a service found in some time-sharing systems) and replicated windows (typically implemented by a window server that drives a set of displays in tandem). The second approach is to design the application specifically to account for the presence of multiple users. Some examples are RTCAL [22], a meeting scheduling system, and Cognoter [23], a real-time group note-taking system.

Each approach has its advantages and disadvantages. While the first allows existing applications to be used, each user has an identical view of the application—there is no per-user context. The second approach offers the possibility of a richer interface, but the application must be built from the ground up or with considerable additional effort.

Computer Teleconferencing

Telecommunication support for group interaction is referred to as teleconferencing. The most familiar examples of teleconferencing are conference calls and video conferencing. Teleconferencing tends to be awkward, requiring special rooms and sometimes trained operators. Newer systems provide workstation-based interfaces to a conference and make the process more accessible.

Xerox, for example, established an audio/video link for use by a project team split between Portland, Oregon, and Palo Alto, California. Most video interactions occurred between large "Commons" areas at each site, but project members could also access video channels through their office workstations. A similar system, CRUISER [21], lets users electronically roam the hallways by "browsing" video channels.

Desktop Conferencing

Not only is teleconferencing relatively inaccessible, but it also does not let participants share text and graphics. Real-time computer conferencing does not offer video capabilities. A third type of computer-supported conferencing combines the advantages of teleconferencing and real-time conferencing while mitigating their drawbacks. Dubbed "desktop conferencing," this method still uses the workstation as the conference interface, but it also runs applications shared by the participants. Modern desktop conferencing systems support multiple video windows per workstation. This allows display of dynamic views of information, and dynamic video images of participants.

An example of desktop conferencing is the MMConf system [3]. MMConf provides a shared display of a multimedia document, as well as communications channels for voice and for shared pointers. Another example is the Rapport multimedia conferencing system [1]. Rapport is designed for workstations connected by a multimedia network (a network capable of transmitting data, voice, and video). The system supports various forms of interaction, from simple telephone-like conversations to multi-party shared-display interaction.

Intelligent Agents

Not all the participants in an electronic meeting need be people. Multiplayer computer games, for example, might automatically generate participants if the number of people is too low for a challenging game. Such non-human participants are a special case of intelligent agents (a similar concept is "surrogates"). In general, intelligent agents are responsible for some set of tasks, and the user interface makes their actions resemble those of other users.

As a specific example, we have developed a groupware toolkit which includes an agent named Liza [8]. One of the tools in the toolkit displays the pictures and locations of all session participants.

When Liza joins a session a picture of an intelligent-looking android is also displayed, indicating to the group that Liza is "participating." Liza's participation means that a set of rules owned by Liza become active; these rules monitor session activity and result in Liza suggesting changes of content or form.

Coordination Systems

The coordination problem is the "integration and harmonious adjustment of individual work efforts towards the accomplishment of a larger goal." Coordination systems address this problem in a variety of ways. Typically these systems allow individuals to view their actions, as well as the relevant actions of others, within the context of the overall goal. Systems may also trigger users' actions by informing users of the states of their actions and their wait conditions, or by generating automatic reminders and alerters. Coordination systems can be categorized by the type of model they embrace as being form, procedure, conversation, or communication structure oriented.

Form-oriented models typically focus on the routing of documents (forms) in organizational procedures. These systems address coordination by explicitly modeling organizational activity as fixed processes. In some of the more recent systems there is an effort to make process support more flexible. For example, in EFC [14], exception handling is addressed through migration specifications that describe all the possible task migration routes in terms of the steps to be carried out in processing organizational documents.

Procedure-oriented models view organizational procedures as programmable processes; hence the phrase "process programming." This approach was first applied to coordination problems in the software process domain and takes the view that software process descriptions should be thought of and implemented as software. The development of process programs is itself a rigorous process consisting of specification, design, implementation, and testing/ verification phases.

Conversation-oriented models are based on the observation that people coordinate their activities via their conversations. The underlying theoretical basis for many systems embracing the conversation model is speech act theory. For example, The Coordinator [7] is based on a set of speech acts (i.e., requests, promises, etc.) and contains a model of legal conversational moves (e.g., a request has to be issued before a promise can be made). As users make conversational moves, typically through electronic mail, the system tracks their requests and commitments.

Communication structure-oriented models describe organizational activities in terms of role relationships. For example, in the ITT approach [10], a person's electronic work environment is composed of a set of centers, where each center represents a function for which the person is responsible. Within centers are roles that perform the work and objects that form the work materials for carrying out the function of that center. Centers and roles have connections to other centers and roles, and the behavior of the connections is governed by the role scripts of the interacting roles.

Summary

As mentioned, there exist overlap in these categories. As the demand for integrated systems increases, we see more merging of these functionalities. Intelligent message systems can and have been used for coordination. Desktop conferencing systems can and have been used for group editing. Nevertheless, many systems can be categorized according to their primary emphasis and intent. This, in turn, may depend upon the perspectives of the system designers.

4. PERSPECTIVES

As the preceding section's taxonomy suggests, groupware relies on the approaches and contributions of many disciplines. In particular, there are at least five key disciplines or perspectives upon which successful groupware depends: distributed systems, communications, human-computer interaction, artificial intelligence, and social theory. It is important to note that the relationship between groupware and these five domains of study is mutually beneficial one. Not only does each discipline advance our understanding of the theory and practice of groupware, but groupware presents challenging topics of research for all five domains—topics that without groupware might never be explored.

Of equal importance is the notion that a given groupware system most often combines the perspectives of two or more of these disciplines. We can see the desktop conferencing paradigm, for example, as having been derived in either of two ways:.

• By starting with communications technology and enhancing this with further computing power and display devices at the phone receiver, or

• By starting with the personal workstation (distributed systems perspective) and integrating communications capabilities.

The rest of this section comments on how each perspective contributes to groupware and how groupware challenges each perspective with new problems.

Distributed Systems Perspective

Because their users are often distributed in time and/or space, many multiuser systems are naturally conceived as distributed systems. The distributed systems perspective explores and emphasizes this decentralization of data and control. Essentially, this type of system infers global system properties and maintains consistency of the global state by observing and manipulating local parameters.

The investigation of efficient algorithms for distributed operating systems and distributed databases is a major research area in distributed systems theory. Some of these research results are applicable to groupware systems. For example, implementing electronic mail systems evokes complex distributed systems issues related to robustness: recipients should be able to receive messages even when the mail server is unavailable. One solution is to replicate message storage on multiple server machines. Discovering and implementing the required algorithms—algorithms that will keep these servers consistent and maintain a distributed name look-up facility—is a challenging task.

Communications Perspective

This perspective emphasizes the exchange of information between remote agents. Primary concerns include increasing connectivity and bandwidth, and protocols for the exchange of many types of information—text, graphics, voice, video.

One of the commonly posed challenges of groupware to communications technology is how to make distributed interactions as effective as face-to-face interactions. Perhaps the correct view of native medium which will not replace face-to-face, but which may actually be preferable in some situations for some groups because certain difficulties, inconveniences, and breakdowns can be eliminated or minimized. This is analogous to findings on the usage of telephone, electronic mail, and other technologies. None of these replace face-to-face interaction, but each has its niche where it is a unique and useful mode of communication. The challenge, then, is to apply appropriate technological combinations to the classes of interactions that will benefit the most from the new medium.

Human-Computer Interaction Perspective

This perspective emphasizes the importance of the user interface in computer systems. Human computer interaction is itself a multidisciplinary field, relying on the diverse skills of graphics and industrial designers, computer graphics experts (who study display technologies, input devices, and interaction techniques), and cognitive scientists (who study human cognitive, perceptual, and motor skills).

Until recently, most user interface research has focused on single-user systems. Groupware challenges researchers to broaden this perspective, to address the issues of human-computer interaction within the context of multiuser or "group" interfaces. Since these interfaces are sensitive to such factors as group dynamics and organizational structure—factors not normally considered relevant to user interface design—it is vital that social scientists and end users play a role in the development of group interfaces.

Artificial Intelligence Perspective

With an emphasis on theories of intelligent behavior, this perspective seeks to develop techniques and technologies for imbuing machines with human-like attributes. The artificial intelligence approach is usually heuristic or augmentative, allowing information to accrue through user-machine interaction rather than being initially complete and structured.

This approach blends well with groupware's requirements. For example, groupware designed for use by different groups must be flexible and accommodate a variety of team behaviors and tasks: research suggests that two different teams performing the same task use group technology in very different ways; likewise, the same team doing two separate tasks use the technology differently for each task.

AI may, in the long run, provide one of the most significant contributions to groupware. This technology could transform machines from passive agents that process and present information to active agents that enhance interactions. The challenge is to ensure that the systems' activity enhances interaction in a way that is procedurally and socially desirable to the participants.

Social Theory Perspective

This perspective emphasizes social theory, or sociology, in the design of groupware systems. Systems designed from this perspective embody the principles and explanations derived from sociological research. The developers of Quilt [17], for example, conducted systematic research on the social aspects of writing, and from this research they derived the requirements for their collaborative editing environment. As a result, Quilt assigns document access rights according to interactions between users' social roles, the nature of the information, and the stage of the writing project.

Systems such as this ask people to develop a new or different awareness, an awareness that can be difficult to maintain until it is internalized. For example, Quilt users must be aware when their working styles— which are often based on informal agreements—change, so that the system can be reconfigured to provide appropriate access controls. With The Coordinator [7], users need to learn about the language implications of requests and promises, because the system makes these speech acts explicit by automatically recording them in a group calendar. Both these examples suggest the need for coaching. Perhaps the systems themselves could coach users, both by encouraging and teaching users the theories upon which the systems are based.

5. CONCLUDING REMARKS

We have shown how the conceptual underpinning of groupware—the merging of computer and communications technology—applies to a broad range of systems. We have indicated that there are significant technical problems associated with designing and building these systems; groupware casts a new light on some traditional computer science issues. Information sharing in the groupware context leads, for example, to unexplored problems in distributed systems and user interface design that emphasize group interaction.

Although the prospects for groupware appear bright, we must take into account a history of expensive and repetitive failure. Applications such as video conferencing and on-line calendars have largely been disappointments. These failures are not simply the result of poor technology, but can also be traced to designers' naive assumptions about the use of the technology.

Thus, an important area not covered in this paper is concerned with the social and organizational aspects of groupware design, introduction, usage, and evolution. It should be noted that a tool's effect on a group is frequently not easily predicted nor well understood. As mentioned earlier, the system and the group are intimately interacting entities. A substantial literature explores the impact of computer technology on organizations and individuals [16]. Ultimately, groupware should be evaluated along many dimensions in terms of its utility to groups, organizations and societies.

Groupware research and development should proceed as an interdisciplinary endeavor. We use the word "interdisciplinary" as opposed to "multidisciplinary" to stress that the contributions and approaches of the many disciplines, and of end users, must be integrated, and not simply considered. It is our belief that in groupware design, it is very difficult to separate technical issues from social concerns—and the methods and theories of the social sciences will prove critical to groupware's success.

6. ACKNOWLEDGEMENTS

This paper was excerpted from several documents written by the author, co-authored with Simon Gibbs, and Gail Rein. The author would like to acknowledge the work and inspiration of Simon and Gail. See following bibliography for papers. The work of putting together this paper was done at MCC (the Microelectronics and Computer Technology Corporation), and at IFTF (the Institute for the Future.) Appreciation is extended to both of these institutions for their generous support.

7. BIBLIOGRAPHY

[1] Ahuja, S.R., Ensor, J.R., and Horn, D.N. The Rapport multimedia conferencing system. In *Proceedings of the Conference on Office Automation Systems* (Palo Alto, CA, March 23-25). ACM, New York, 1988, pp. 1-8.

[2] Applegate, L.M., Konsynski, B.R., and Nunamaker, J.F. A group decision support system for idea generation and issue analysis in organization planning. In *Proceedings of the First Conference on Computer-Supported Cooperative Work* (Austin, TX, December 3-5). ACM, New York, 1986, pp. 16-34.

[3] Crowley, T. et. al. MMConf: An infrastructure for building shared multimedia applications. In *Proceedings of the Third Conference on Computer-Support Cooperative Work* (Los Angeles, CA, October 8-10). ACM, New York, 1990.

[4] Ellis, C.A., Gibbs, S.J., and Rein, G.L. Design and use of a group editor. In *Engineering for Human-Computer Interaction* (G. Cockton, editor), North-Holland, Amsterdam, 1990, 13-25.

[5] Ellis, C.A., Gibbs, S.J., and Rein G.L. Groupware: issues and experiences. In *Communications of the ACM*, 33, 1, January 1991.

[6] Engelbart, D.C., and English, W.K. A research center for augmenting human intellect. In *Proceedings of the Fall Joint Computer Conference* (San Francisco, California, December 9-11). AFIPS, Reston, VA, 1968, pp. 395-410.

[7] Flores, F., Graves, M., Hartfield, B., and Winograd, T. Computer systems and the design of organizational interaction. *ACM Transactions on Office Information Systems 6*, 2 (April 1988), 153-172.

[8] Gibbs, S.J. LIZA: An extensible groupware toolkit. In *Proceedings of the ACM SIGCHI Conference on Human Factors in Computing Systems* (Austin, TX, April 30-May 4). ACM, New York, 1989.

[9] Hogg, J. Intelligent message systems. In *Office Automation*, D. Tsichritzis, Ed. Springer-Verlag, New York, 1985, pp. 113-133.

[10] Holt, A.W. Diplans: A new language for the study and implementation of coordination. *ACM Transactions on Office Information Systems 6*, 2 (April 1988), 109-125.

[11] Johansen, R. *Groupware: Computer Support for Business Teams*. The Free Press, New York, 1988.

[12] Johnson-Lentz, P. and Johnson-Lentz, T. Groupware: The process and impacts of design choices. In *Computer-Mediated Communication Systems: Status and Evaluation* by Kerr, E.B. and Hiltz, S.R. Academic Press, New York, NY, 1982.

[13] Kaiser, G.E., Kaplan, S.M., and Micallef, J. Multiuser, distributed language-based environments. *IEEE Software 4*, 6 (November 1987), 58-67.

[14] Karbe, B., Ramsperger, N., Weiss, P. Support of cooperative work by electronic circulation folders. In *Proceedings of the Conference on Office Automation Systems* (Cambridge, MA, April 25-27). ACM, New York, 1990, pp. 109-117.

[15] Knister, M.J., Prakash, A. DistEdit: A distributed toolkit for supporting multiple group editors. In *Proceedings of the Third Conference on Computer-Supported Cooperative Work* (Los Angeles, California, October 8-10). ACM, New York, 1990.

[16] Kraut, R.E. Social issues and white-collar technology: an overview. *Technology and the Transformation of White-Collar Work*, Erlbaum Associates, Hillsdale, California, 1987, 1-21.

[17] Leland, M.D.P., Fish, R.S., and Kraut, R.E. Collaborative document production using Quilt. In *Proceedings of the Conference on Computer-Supported Cooperative Work* (Portland, OR, September 26-28). ACM, New York, 1988, pp. 206-215.

[18] Lewis, B.T., and Hodges J.D. Shared Books: Collaborative publication management for an office information system. In *Proceedings of the Conference on Office Information Systems* (Palo Alto, CA, March 23-25). ACM, New York, 1988, pp. 197-204.

[19] Malone, T., Grant, K., Turbak, F., Brobst, S., and Cohen, M. Intelligent information-sharing systems. *Communications of the ACM 30*, 5, (May 1987), 390-402.

[20] Opper, S. A groupware toolbox. *Byte*, December, 1988.

[21] Root, R.W. Design of a multi-media vehicle for social browsing. In *Proceedings of the Second Conference on Computer-Supported Cooperative Work* (Portland, OR, September 26-28). ACM, New York, 1988, pp. 25-38.

[22] Sarin, S., and Greif, I. Computer-based real-time conferencing systems. *IEEE Computer, 18*, 10 (October 1985), 33-45.

[23] Stefik, M., Foster, G., Bobrow, D.G., Kahn, K., Lanning, S., and Suchman, L. Beyond the chalkboard: Computer support for collaboration and problem solving in meetings. *Communications of the ACM 30*, 1 (January 1987), 32-47.

A multi-agents cooperating system
for on-line supervision
of Production Management activities

Jacqueline AYEL, Jean-Pierre LAURENT
Laboratoire d'Intelligence Artificielle
Université de Savoie
BP 1104 - 73 011 CHAMBERY (FRANCE)

In the CIM (Computer Integrated Manufacturing) field the problem of integrating Production Management activities is often viewed as nothing but a problem of Data Sharing between activities. However the integration of activities must take into account the management of conflicts between them. We propose an architecture in which the production management activities are grouped into "islands" of activities and in which the coordination and synchronization task (also called supervision task) of these activities is distributed at the level of each "island" in the form of Software called a Unit-Controller. Each Unit-Controller is a knowledge-based reactive system which uses a blackboard mechanism and which is able to dialogue with the other Unit-Controllers. General behavior models for any Unit-Controller have been defined, particularly cooperative behavior of Unit-Controllers with each other and cooperative behavior of any Unit-Controller within its island of activities. A Unit-Controller shell has been developed from which all Unit-Controllers are instantiated.

1   Introduction

In the CIM (Computer Integrated Manufacturing) field the problem of integrating Production Management activities is often viewed as nothing but a problem of Data Sharing between activities. However the integration of activities must take into account the management of conflicts between them. Insofar as production management activities are not built to cooperate, a specific production activity is needed to ensure on-line management of the coordination and synchronization of these activities. We will call it the supervision activity for production management activities.

We propose an architecture in which the production management activities are grouped into "islands" of activities and in which the coordination and synchronization task (i.e. supervision task) of these activities is distributed at the level of each "island" in the form of Software called a Unit-Controller. Thus the supervision task is carried out by a set of cooperating Unit-Controllers.

The first part of this article will be devoted to presenting the characteristics of a production management system, as well as the problem posed by supervision of these activities. The second part will present our conceptual model of supervision for production activities. This conceptual model especially serves to set up a taxonomy of general cooperative behavior between the Unit-Controllers and a taxonomy of the behavior of a Unit-Controller as concerns the activities in its island. Using this definition of general behavior, we have created a Unit-Controller shell called CIMES; each Unit-Controller is implemented by instantiating CIMES. The last part of the article presents the CIMES system and the way a Unit-Controller is instantiated.

2 Supervision of production management activities

2.1 The production management system

Managing production means making decisions at every level in the plant, decisions which will allow the production process to be organized with due account taken of all the various constraints relating to the production function. There are several methods for analyzing a production management system, one of which is the GRAI method developed at the University of Bordeaux's GRAI laboratory, especially focused on analysis of the decision-making system and on flows of information for decision-making within that system. This method demonstrates that production management activities can be divided along two axes, one functional and the other temporal.

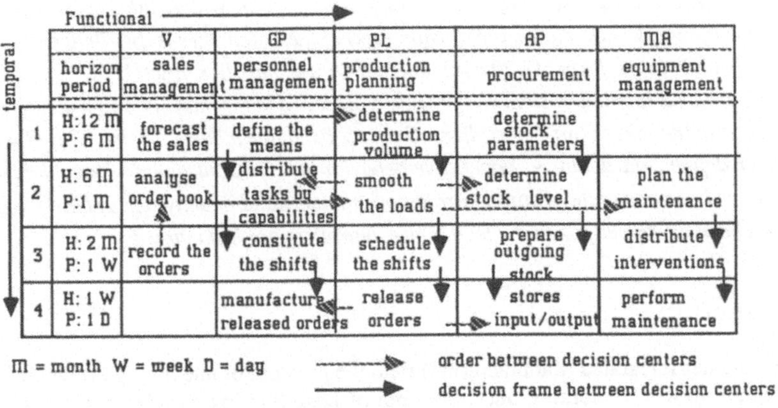

Figure 1- Example of GRAI décision grid

The functional axis refers to the functions in the plant (production planning, personnel management, quality control, etc) associated with the production management activities in question. The temporal axis refers to the period in which decisions made by the activities are updated (the decision period) and to the time interval in which the said decision is defined and a priori considered to be valid (the decision horizon). This latter axis makes it possible to define levels within the plant. One level groups activities associated with the same temporal criterion (period and horizon). In the GRAI method, the name "activity center" is given to the set of production management activities at the intersection of a function axis with a level. These activity centers are represented on a grid known as a GRAI decision grid (figure 1). Activities belonging to an activity center can therefore be said to take part in a particular decision-making at a given level of the plant and for a given function.

Among the information that can be exchanged between activity centers, The GRAI method points out two types of information : decision frames and orders. Exchanges of these types of information are represented on the GRAI decision grid by arrows linking the activity center supplying the information to the activity center using it. These arrows can be decision frame arrows or order arrows depending on the nature of the information exchanged.

Decision frame D1 stands for information provided by decision center C1 to activity center C2 in order to guide decision D2 made by C2. In fact, decision D2 is obtained by breaking down D1 (or a part thereof) according to time units, resources, and products specific to D2. Exchanges of decision frames between activity centers allows policy decisions from the highest levels of the company to be transmitted to the production level. Each activity center must respect its decision frame to ensure coherency between low and high level decisions.

Information O1 provided by decision center C1 to activity center C2 is an order for C2 if O1 is information D2 must take into consideration in making its decision, but it can request a modification of O1 from C1 if the information is too restrictive for D2 and prevents it from making its decision. For example, the head of activity center C1 may be responsible for weekly planning of production and simultaneously schedule in his production time-table reserved times for maintenance. Let us suppose that such time-slots represent an order for activity center C2 which is responsible for scheduling weekly maintenance. Should C2 be unable to schedule maintenance activities in the reserved time-slots, the head of activity center C2 can, in a first step, negotiate a modification of these time-slots with the head of activity center C1.

The information used by an activity center which is neither a decision frame nor an order cannot be negotiated. This is the case of information on execution follow-up or on the state of the production system.

2.2 Supervision

Integration of production management activities into a global system results in a need to synchronize, coordinate, and ensure communication between such activities ; this need cannot be satisfied merely by limiting the activities rights of access, in reading or writing, to a common database. Integration also implies a need for dialogue between the activities in order to solve the inevitable conflicts (between production and maintenance, between production and supply management, etc). Integration of production management activities consists in automating the cooperation and synchronization behavior of the various activities while preserving their individual views of the production management system, i.e. their own reasoning and representation models. As production management activities are carried out by isolated computer modules, with no knowledge of one another or of how to coordinate their action, such coordination incumbs on a specific system, a production management supervisor which we have called the 3M-System, short for Manufacturing Management Monitoring System.

The role of a 3M-System is to guarantee at any given moment that the decisions made at the various levels in the plant remain coherent ; these decisions must be coherent with each other but also with the state of the production system and with the production environment. A 3M-System must therefore be capable of :

- analyzing the current situation, i.e. detecting any conflicts that might arise between the decisions made by the production management activities, or between those decisions and the state of the production system, or between those decisions and the production environment

- trigger decision up-dates to solve conflicts or to account for evolution of the situation within the plant.

3 The Conceptual Supervision Model

The 3M-System is in charge of the cooperation and the synchronization of production management activities. it is therefore a system which takes care of cooperation between activities in a specific universe, the universe of production management. This universe cannot be compared to the human one in which cooperation between individuals is highly complex and the processes for solving conflicts can take on many forms that are difficult to model. In the relatively rigid and hierarchical universe of production management, the forms of cooperation between activities and the protocols for problem-solving must be relatively simple for reasons of efficiency. It should therefore be possible to automate them, providing that models of cooperative behavior appropriate to this universe. This is why we have defined a conceptual supervision model for production management activities, called CSM.

Here we will first present the organizational choice we have made for the supervision function, in favor of distributed supervision at the level of groups of activities (islands). Then, we will identify different types of interaction between islands and of interaction between activities within an island. These different types of interaction serve as a basis for the behavioral scripts in the 3M-System.

3.1 The organizational aspect of supervision

3.1.1 Supervision as a partially distributed activity

One of the first questions to ask in modeling the supervision task for production management activities is how to organize these activities in such a way as to allow the 3M-System to be set up. The supervision task could be seen as a centralized activity, carried out by a single computer module in charge of all the production management activities. We have rejected this solution for reasons of efficiency and safety. In the same way, the supervision task could be entirely distributed at the level of each production management activity. We have also eliminated this solution because too many interactions would have to be managed.

We have chosen to organize the supervision task as a partially distributed activity at the level of groups of activities called islands. The production management system is then made up of all of the activities of the islands.

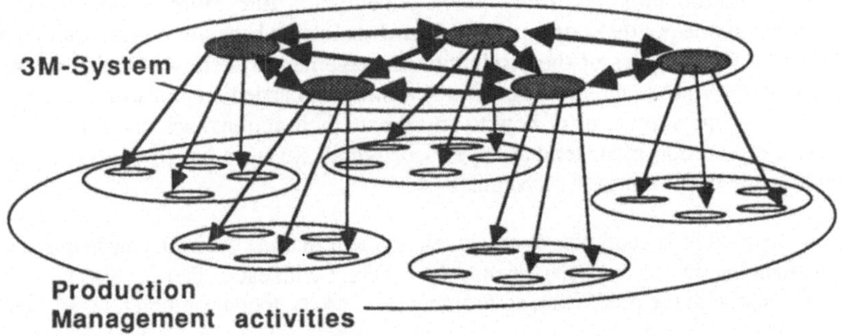

Figure 2 The integrated production management system

As we shall see further along, this type of organization makes it possible to take into account the knowledge provided by the GRAI method concerning interaction between production management activities.

The consequence of grouping production management activities into islands is that the supervision task must be distributed at the level of each island of activities. Each island will therefore be associated with a specific module known as a **Unit-Controller**.

Note : The integrated production management system is composed of all the activity islands and all of their Unit-Controllers.

Each Unit-Controller controls a group of production management activities in an island. At the level of the supervision system, it takes care of coordinating and synchronizing its own action with that of the other Unit-Controllers.

The Supervision task in the integrated production management system is carried out by the set of Unit-Controllers. This set of cooperating Unit-Controllers forms the 3M-System.

The criteria used to divide the activities into activity islands make use of both the physical characteristics of the plant and of considerations on the role of the activities in production management. In particular, each island must have a limited and clearly defined role in production management, i.e. each island will be responsible for solving a punctual and partial problem in production management, on request from the 3M-System. An island contains all the activities of a single activity center as obtained using the GRAI method. It is responsible for updating the decision associated with this activity center of the GRAI grid for a physical entity in the plant (workshop, workcell, etc.).

A supervision unit (SU) is the set made up of the activities of an island with the island's Unit-Controller.

3.1.2 The hierarchical structure of supervision units

The GRAI method brings out the hierarchical structure of decision-making in a plant. Indeed, the "decision frame" arrow allows a hierarchy to be defined between activity centers. In fact each center receives a decision frame from a single other activity center. Moreover, the role of activity center C2 using a decision frame provided by activity center C1 is limited to setting out in detail the information in the decision frame at its level of responsibility in the plant. It can therefore be said that the responsibility of any activity center in decision-making is limited by the decision frame it receives. Thus the set of activity centers defined via the GRAI analysis is organized in a tree hierarchy which corresponds to the hierarchy of decision-making responsibility in the plant's production management system.

The SUs are obtained from the activity centers resulting from the GRAI analysis of a plant. The hierarchy of the production management system, as revealed by the decision frame arrows, is repeated in the form of a hierarchy between supervision units. In this way each SU's responsibility is limited by one and only one other SU, i.e. the SU supplying the information it uses as a decision frame.

Definition: The decision frame arrow which, in the GRAI analysis, expresses the exchange of a decision frame between two activity centers, will be represented in the CSM formalism by a link between two SUs called a **control link**.

3.2 The cooperative aspect of the 3M-System

The result of the organizational choices we have made is that the 3M-System is a multi-agent one whose agents, called Unit-Controllers, manage cooperation with the activities of their island and are responsible for cooperation between supervision units. We will therefore identify the general cooperative behavior of Unit-Controllers with each other and of Unit-Controllers in terms of the activities of their islands.

3.2.1 Cooperation of a Unit-Controller in terms of its island's activities.

Separation of activities into islands makes it possible to associate a well defined role with each SU in the production management system. This role is to periodically update (or to update upon request from another SU) a certain decision in the production management system. We can therefore consider that the Unit-Controller manages a process of problem-solving by dynamically defining a problem-solving plan to update its decision and by implementing this update. Thus it cooperates with the activities in its SU by triggering activities according to its problem-solving plan and by recovering the results of the activities. No negotiation is possible between the Unit-Controller and the activities, as activities have no knowledge of cooperation. They are passive activities from the standpoint of cooperation.

Because of the limited number of activities within an SU, all the problem-solving strategies can be defined a priori for creation of a decision under the SU's responsibility. We have chosen to represent all these strategies by means of a graph called the graph of strategies by default.

The behavior of a Unit-Controller towards the activities within its SU consists in:

- detecting the situation which require updating of the decision the SU is in charge of;

- checking (before triggering an update properly speaking) that the information needed for an update is valid;

- if the information is not up to date, sending messages to request the information needed,

- waiting for a certain time for the information to arrive and if necessary giving up on them after a limited time to adopt extrapolated values in their place;

- setting up the problem-solving process with at each stage in the process the choice of either continuing the process, in which case a strategy to continue problem solving must be chosen from the strategy by default graph, or of interrupting problem-solving in order to resume it in a given place in the strategy by default graph;

- deciding to send the updated decision to the SUs concerned and to the common database.

Situations which imply updating of a decision must be identified. They may depend on messages received from other Unit-Controllers and in this case the problem-solving behavior of the Unit-Controller will interfere with its cooperative behavior with the other Unit-Controllers. They may also depend solely on the Unit-Controller itself (for example in the case of periodic updating of the decision).

Furthermore, for the concept of strategies by default, it will be necessary to define concepts of choices of arcs for continuation of a problem-solving strategy within the strategy by default graph, concepts of criteria for interruption of problem-solving in each node of the graph, and criteria for choosing nodes in the graph in the case of an interruption of the problem-solving process and resumption of it. Definition of all these concepts allows the Unit-Controller to know when to cooperate with the activities of its SU, with which activity to cooperate, and how to do so.

3.2.2 Cooperation between Unit-Controllers

Each SU has a certain autonomy in making its decision. The word "decision" translates a certain liberty in decision-making, with the understanding that some decisions will be more satisfactory than others and that some will be so bad as to be unacceptable. We can therefore say that each SU has a certain margin in order to make its decision but that this margin is limited. For each decision made by an SU, a degree of satisfaction can be assessed according to the margin it leaves.

Thus it can happen that an SU is so restrained in making its decision that it cannot make any while respecting its margin. This leads to a blocked situation, called a decision jam, which the SU must work its way out of by cooperating with the other SUs.

A Unit-Controller must cooperate with other Unit-Controllers when it finds itself in a decision jam or when it is needed to help another SU get out of a decision jam.

We must now define schemas for cooperation in order to answer the questions of how to cooperate and with whom? Three types of cooperation between Unit-Controllers have been defined to this end, associated with the three types of possible interaction between SUs.

The first type of interaction between SUs is associated with the existence of a control link between two SUs, one of which controls the other. This type of interaction is associated with the hierarchy of responsibility within the plant.

In the same way as we have associated a type of interaction between two SUs where one receives a decision frame from the other (represented by a control link), we have also associated a type of interaction between two SUs where one receives an order from another (the term "order" being used in the GRAI sense). Such interaction will be represented by an oriented dependency link from the SU giving the order to the SU receiving it.

3.2.2.1 Cooperation between supervision units linked by a control link

Let us first note that the control link is a static link between two SUs. Each SU has knowledge of the SU controlling it and of the SUs it controls. Moreover, it has knowledge of the information that can be part of any negotiating that can arise between SUs linked by a control link, i.e. decision frames and the parameters defining the margin the SU has in decision-making.

Let U_i be a supervision unit, U_j the supervision unit controlling U_i, and U_k the supervision unit controlling U_j.

Only U_j can relax U_i's decision frame or its margin. Cooperation between U_i and U_j can only concern relaxation of these two constraints. It is considered as a last resort for U_i to get out of a blocked situation. Therefore, U_j must propose relaxation relating to one of the two constraints, decision frame or margin.

Cooperation between U_i and U_j is marked by the fact that:

- U_i requests that U_j cooperate when U_i is in a decision jam situation and the efforts to solve the jam by cooperation with the SUs it depends on have failed.

- To solve U_i's jam situation, U_j must readjust its decision in order to relax U_i's decision frame or to relax the parameters defining U_i's margin. Such a readjustment may result in a decision jam situation for U_j which it must solve in order to make a proposal to U_i.

- Cooperation between U_i and U_j must unblock the situation. This may lead U_j to cooperate with U_k, up to the level of responsibility on which the conflict can be solved.

3.2.2.2 Cooperation between supervision units linked by dependency

Like the control link, the dependency link is a static one between two supervision units. Each SU has knowledge of the SUs with which it has dependency links, the direction of the links, and the order information concerned. The cooperation that can exist between two SUs linked by a dependency link relates to negotiation on the value of an order. In a case where a supervision unit U_i finds itself in a decision jam situation, it may make a request to supervision unit U_l which will give it an order relaxing that order, so that it can get out of this jam. Unlike the preceding case, U_l is not required to return an answer that will enable the situation to be unblocked. It must examine the relaxation request by triggering an update that will take the request into account. But if it cannot find a satisfactory solution which respects its own constraints, U_l can reply by refusing the relaxation.

Thus the cooperation between two supervision units linked by a dependency link is marked by the following facts:

- The cooperation process is triggered when a supervision unit is in a jam situation.

- It then chooses among the supervision units giving it orders (i.e. those with which it shares a dependency link directed toward it) whichever one has set up its order with the greatest possible margin. Let U_1 be the supervision unit in question and D_1 the order given by U_1 to U_i.

- Negotiation between U_i and U_1 commences upon a request from U_i to relax D_1.

- U_1 attempts to satisfy U_i by updating its decision and in particular D_1 (D_1 being a part of its decision).

- If U_1 can satisfy U_i it transmits the new value of D_1 to U_i and its new decision to the supervision units concerned.

- If satisfaction is not possible, U_1 transmits a refusal to relax to U_i.

- If U_i receives a refusal from a supervision unit it depends on, it begins negotiations with another supervision unit it depends on to obtain relaxation of another of its orders.

- If it receives only refusals to relax its orders, it can then begin negotiations with the supervision unit controlling it, with a view to obtaining relaxation of its decision frame. Such negotiation is carried out according to the negotiation schema attached to the control link and it must unblock U_i's situation.

4 The Unit-Controller shell: The CIMES system

Our starting point was the idea that the mechanisms involved in the supervision within a supervision unit or in coordination between one supervision unit and the others were sufficiently general to allow a general program to be designed (which we call the SUPERVISION KERNEL) implementing all of the mechanisms in question.

First of all the process of decision-making which is proper to an island is always the same. It is described by general scripts associated with each phase of the problem-solving process. Changes concern only the names of the tasks involved in problem-solving, the "strategy by default" graph, the criteria for choices of arcs and nodes in the graph, the initial data to be awaited at the beginning of the process, the maximum time to wait for them, etc. All these elements can be considered as parameters of a single mechanism. In the same way, from the standpoint of the behavior of a supervision unit towards other supervision units, the types of messages and the situations which require a message to be sent are the same. They are described in general scripts associated with the three types of links between supervision units. The mechanisms for interpretation and consideration of messages, the recognition of the situations calling for messages to be sent, and how the messages are set up only differ in their name and the predefined characteristics of the supervision units involved in the messages. These will be determined, for a given supervision unit, by the specification of its links with the other supervision units, data sharing between supervision units, network addresses of the supervision units and modules, etc. These elements can also be considered as parameters of a single mechanism.

It is therefore possible to implement separately the SUPERVISION KERNEL and the knowledge specific to a Unit-Controller's supervision unit. The set made up of the Supervision Kernel and the knowledge specific to a supervision unit constitutes the Unit-Controller of that supervision unit.

4.1 The Unit-Controller shell: The CIMES system

CIMES is made up of four parts: the supervision kernel, a knowledge base model relating to the supervision task (KB-SUP-MODEL), an acquisition tool for instantiation of the KB-SUP-MODEL for a given plant (this acquisition is made to complement the results of a GRAI analysis of the plant), and finally a generic communications interface to allow Unit-Controllers to communicate, both with each other and with their internal activities. The supervision kernel can be considered as a control mechanism for supervision (for a Unit-Controller) which in order to function uses an instantiation of the KB-SUP-MODEL on the island associated with the Unit-Controller.

4.1.1 The supervision kernel

We felt that the computer architecture that would be the best adapted to setting up within a single system the various abilities of a Unit-Controller was a blackboard architecture ([10] [11] [12] [13]).

The blackboard data structure allows us to store the situation on which the Unit-Controller is to work, i.e. the state of the problem-solving process and the state of the dialogues with the other Unit-Controllers. We have divided the blackboard in four : Result-blackboard, Control-blackboard, External-I/O-blackboard and Internal-I/O-blackboard, according to the type of data to be considered, respectively speaking the state of the problem-solving process, the state of the control decisions for the problem-solving process, the state of the dialogues with the other Unit-Controllers, and the state of the triggering orders for the internal activities of the supervision unit.

Knowledge sources allow the behavior of the Unit-Controllers in the situations described by the state of the blackboard to be expressed. They translate:

- The general supervision behavior as defined in the CSM (towards other SUs) by the scripts associated with the control, dependency, and triggering links;

- The behavior of the problem-solving mechanism towards the internal modules of the SU by using the scripts defined for each phase in the problem-solving process.

The condition part of a knowledge source is a predicate which matches to changes on the blackboard, i.e. modifications in the situation inside or outside the SU (the reactive aspect of a Unit-Controller).

The action part of a knowledge source matches (when it is triggered) both with the state of the blackboard, i.e. the current situation, and with the descriptors of the SU contained within the instantiation of the KB-SUP-MODEL. Its action is to change the state of the blackboard, meaning the situation. Thus the action part describes in a general manner the reaction of the Unit-Controller to a situation by creating a new situation.

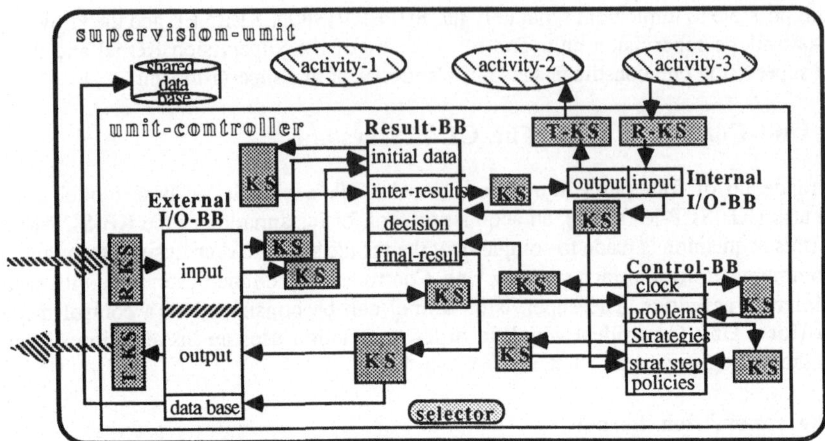

Figure 3 - The generic architecture of the Unit-Controllers

We have changed the classic control cycle of the blackboard (which we call a selector) in order to be able, on the one hand, to send and receive asynchronous messages with the other Unit-Controllers, and on the other hand, to send triggering orders to the internal modules and receive stays in execution from these modules. At each cycle, the "selector" examines the situation inside and outside the supervision unit through the state of the blackboard and it can choose which knowledge source to trigger in answer to the situation. This characteristic allows the Unit-Controller to react rapidly to changes since it re-analyses the situation upon each cycle of the selector.

4.2.2 The knowledge base model: KB-SUP-MODEL

We have seen that the "supervision kernel" uses knowledge specific to the SUs (names of the modules used, strategy by default graph, etc.). This knowledge can only be used by the "supervision kernel" if its structure is the same for all the SUs. Thus the SUPERVISION KERNEL's knowledge sources will be able to refer to this information as information associated with any SU whatsoever, like context variables.

The KB-SUP-MODEL's purpose is to provide a uniform reception structure for the knowledge specific to the SUs, in the form of object classes. The KB-SUP-MODEL takes the concepts of the CSM into account and is made up of a set of descriptors for supervision units.

Like the engine of an expert system, the SUPERVISION KERNEL is software which uses the instantiation of the KB-SUP-MODEL on a specific SU in order to set up the process of supervision in a given Unit-Controller. It is therefore unable to function alone and must be associated with an instantiation of the KB-SUP-MODEL on a specific supervision unit. Indeed the knowledge sources of the SUPERVISION KERNEL contain variables that match not only the facts on the blackboard, but also the knowledge contained in the instantiation of the KB-SUP-MODEL.

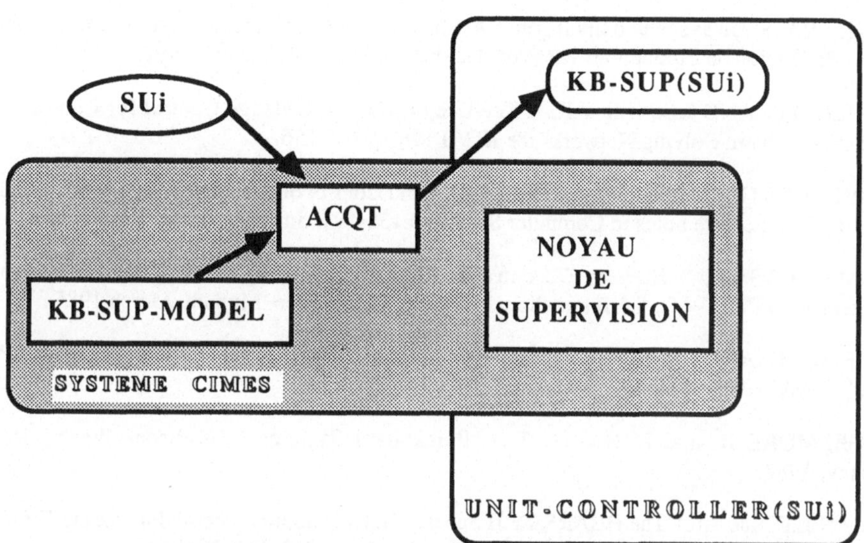

Figure 4 - The CIMES system and the instantiation of a Unit-Controller

5   Conclusion

We have created a simplified mock-up of a supervision network in order to validate our approach and to show that the mechanisms we have designed function properly. In order to do this, we have chosen to implement a partial centred network comprising six supervision units over two levels of the GRAI grid. In this implementation, in COMMON LISP (with FLAVORS) on a SUN4 workstation, the supervision units have been implemented using the CIMES system. The other units linked to them are simulated by means of various types of messages which arrive and to which the Unit-Controllers react.

Bibliography

[1] ALLEN J.F., "Towards a General Theory of Action and Time", Artificial Intelligence (23) pp 123-153 (1983)

[2] ALLEN J.F.,"Maintaining Knowledge about Temporal Intervals", Communication of A.C.M.(26) (1983)

[3] AYEL J. , "A conceptual supervision model in computer integrated manufacturing", European Conference on Artificial Intelligence, ECAI Munchen 1988 pp 427- 432

[4] AYEL J., LAURENT J.P. et al "Distributed Artificial Intelligence : A necessary paradigm for supervision production management activities", Second International Conference on Industrial & Engineering Applications of Artificial Intelligence & Expert Systems (IEA/AIE). UTSI Tullahoma, Tennessee USA , pp 326-335

[5] AYEL J., LAURENT J.P., PANET B.P., "D.A.I. for production supervision", Invited Conference, AAAI Spring Symposium, Stanford (USA), March 1989.

[6] AYEL J. CIMES, Un système d'Intelligence Artificielle Distribuée pour la Supervision en continu des activités de Gestion de Production. Thèse de doctorat Université de Savoie 1991.

[7] CORKILL D.D. AND LESSER V.R. , "The Use of Meta-Knowledge Control for Coordination in a Distributed Problem-Solving Network" 8e IJCAI 1983 p 747-756.

[8] DOUMEINGTS G., "Methodology to Design CIM and Control of Manufacturing Units", Methods and Tools for CIM, Lecture notes in Computer Science p.138-194, Springer verlag, Berlin 1984.

[9] DOUMEINGTS G., " How to Decentralize Decisions Through GRAI Model in Production Management" I.F.I.P.W.G. 5.7 International Working Conference, Munich, March 1985.

[10] DURFEE E.H. AND LESSER V.R.,"Incremental Planning to Control a Blackboard-Based Problem-Solver", AAAI 1986 p 58-64.

[11] ENGELMORE R. and MORGAN T. , "Blackboard Systems" , Addison- Wesley Publishing company, 1988.

[12] ERMAN L.D. and All, "The HEARSAY II Speech Understanding System : Integrating Knowledge to Resolve Uncertainty" , ACM Computing Surveys Vol. 12 pp 212-253 (1980).

[13] HAYES-ROTH B. " A Blackboard Architecture for Control ", Artificial Intelligence 26 pp 251 361. (1985).

[14] S. SMITH, M. FOX and P. OW, "Constructing and Maintaining Detailed Production Plans: Investigations into Development of Knowledge -Based Factory Scheduling Systems" , AI Magazine, 1986.

[15] S. SMITH, and P. OW, " The Use of Multiple Problem Decomposition in Time Constrained Planning Tasks", Proc 9th IJCAI, Los Angeles, 1985.

Structured Social Agents[*]

Jürgen Müller & Jörg Siekmann
National German Research Center for Artificial Intelligence (DFKI)
University of Saarbrücken
Stuhlsatzenhausweg 3
D-6600 Saarbrücken
Germany
Tel.: ++49 681 205 5275
e-mail: {mueller, siekmann}@dfki.uni-sb.de

Five essential capabilities of intelligent social agents are analysed. It is stipulated, that these abilities are crucial for the cooperativity of an agent society and it is argued that a maximum of cooperativity can be reached in the society in case all five features exist at the same time. From these five basic abilities we derive the model of a structured social agent as used in the multi-agent testbed RATMAN. The modeling of a society of intelligent agents is realized in RATMAN by specifying different knowledge bases (KBs), one for each agent. The KBs not only contain the agents´ world knowledge, but they take some of the fundamental mental capacities of the agents into account, like the degree of communication facilities, learning skills or self-reflection. We describe a prototypical model of such a KB, whose essential structure is derived from the five basic abilities an intelligent social agent is alledged to have. The different knowledge packages are structured hierarchically from simple propositional knowledge to highly abstract (meta-) knowledge. They are realized with various representation formalisms (i.e. different kinds of logics), which are mutually compatible.

1 Introduction

Using a society of autonomous cooperating agents to solve a problem or to perform some task has become an increasingly popular approach in Artificial Intelligence and the work on modeling such societies of agents grew rapidly in the last few years [2], [10], [11], [15], [16]. But what is an autonomous cooperating agent? Some authors suggest the notion of some kind of robot, thus stressing motion and action skills, while others have some expert system in mind, which cooperates with other systems of different expertise, thus stressing the reasoning skills. Bond and Gasser [2] speak of an agent as a computational process with a single locus of control and/or "intention", and they sketch the position of multi-agent (MA) systems as follows:

"Distributed artificial intelligence (DAI) is the subfield of AI, that is concerned with concurrency in AI at many levels. DAI branches into the area of distributed problem solving (DPS), which considers how the work of solving a particular problem can be divided among a number of cooperating and knowledge-sharing modules or nodes, on the one hand and into MA systems on the other. In MA systems the coordination of intelligent behavior of a collection of autonomous intelligent agents is the main concern. A third area - parallel artificial intelligence (PAI) - stresses more on performance problems than on conceptual

---

[*] The multi-agent project is sponsored by the German Ministry for Research and Technology under grant ITW 8903 0.

advances and is involved in the development of parallel computer architecture, parallel languages and algorithms. But a sharp distinction between these areas could not be drawn as there is no clear commonly accepted definition of "autonomous cooperating agents".

Essentially two paradigms of multi-agent systems can be identified in the literature, namely the *behavior-based* approach and the *knowledge-based* approach. The central idea of the behavior-based approach is that the agents react in response to environmental changes, where in the knowledge-based approach they act as a consequence of their reasoning about inner goals and intentions.

In the context of behavior-based systems Connah, Shiels, and Wavish [8] describe the structure of artificial agents from a cognitive point of view. They develop an integrated architecture, where abstract cognitive activities emerge from a concrete, situated activity. In a continuation paper the model of a testbed for cooperating agents is described in five parts [9] : Nature of the world, representation of position, shape, time, and causality. Steels [25] tackles the problem of cooperation between distributed agents and advocats a behavior-based approach to examplify self-organization as the main feature for establishing the emergent functionality. The interesting point of his approach is that there is no explicit, symbolic representation of the world nor explicitly defined communication between the agents. A similar approach is taken by Moyson and Manderick [21] who study the collective behavior of ants. The simulation of the emergence of self-organization is achieved by an intrinsically parallel algorithm. Furthermore they propose a mathematical model of the behavior, which is used to compute the parameters of the simulation. Finally Maes [18] gives an interesting approach to model the activation/inhibition of agents in an emergent, noncommunication agent environment. She represents the preconditions of activations as formulas. An agent becomes active if the precondition of a goal is proved to be valid.

The main ideas of the knowledge-based approach may be found in [7] where an introduction to the interaction of multi-agent systems in terms of actual questions from the point of view of a rational agent is given. The focus of the discussion is the communication between agents. Tennenholtz and Moses [28] present a theoretical foundation for a multi-agent planning environment. The set of goals of different agents defines the "cooperative goal of the system". The abstract "cooperative goal achievement decision problem" is then the question whether each of the goals can be fulfilled by the agent society. Myerson [24] discusses the communication activities between agents with different goals from a game theoretic point of view. By combining the "incentive constraints" of the partners an optimal plan between the different goals may be computed. A logic based approach is taken in the development of Mazer [19]. He studies commitment problems in distributed environments. The approach is based on "knowledge logic", a temporal modal logic to describe the interaction of processes, which can execute events, via a communication system. Communication abilities, negotiation and planning for multi-agent systems of this category are reported in [17], [30], [31], [32].

Standard computer systems are stand-alone machines that do not actively cooperate with their environment. Even if the programs are dialog oriented, they are usually not really cooperative. A current trend for really cooperative systems is CSCW (Computer Supported Cooperative Work) for example reported in [29], where the computer and the user together are supposed to form an effective problem solver unit. The synergy usually works, since humans can perfectly well react to the activities of the machine. The next step then is to connect different machines, such that *they* form "a society". This is the approach of DAI or more specifically the idea of Multi-Agent Systems

While the discussion thus far concentrates on the current approaches for a *computational realization* of a multi agent society it blurres the overall motivation for most of this work, a motivation and research interest that is most expicitely present in M. Minsky's "Society of Mind" [20], namely the fact, that a society of agents can perform much better than the total sum of its individual agents. The whole is more than the sum of its parts, provided there is the right communication structure as well as the right structure of each individual agent. This "synergy effect" can be seen in many disguises in nature, for example

- a DNA-molecule is more than the sum of its atoms

- an organism is more than its number of cells

- a state is more than its number of citizens etc.

In all cases, the cooperation of many independent components is suddenly capable of exhibiting new qualities that do not necessarily follow from the qualities of the components. The discovery in physics that thermal dynamics consists of uncoordinated movements of single atoms is a point in case: While single atoms are characterized by energy and impulse, the statistical movement of *many* atoms results in the notions of temperature and pressure as characteristic descriptive dimensions.

Even more surprising are societies of insects, for example the termites: Although a single termite is only capable of modest intelligence, a *colony* of termites is capable of achieving an astonishing level of intelligence, for example the development of climate control for their nests or the introduction of agriculture, such as the maintenance of plant lice.

We are still a long way from understanding the principles by which these new qualities arise from the cooperation of their single components. However there are promising approaches which utilize these effects in technical applications. The most prominent example is a neural network where the neurons are circuits with a simple functionality. The cooperation of millions of these elements can produce a system, which is able to solve rather complex problems, for instance to recognize a handwritten letter.

These examples, atoms, termites, neurons, are prototypical for many others and they show some similarities: It is impossible to recognize which components are responsible for the solution of the overall behaviour. Furthermore, one can often eliminate single components without a significant change. On the other hand, the whole system reacts very sensitively to a change of the communication structure. For example the communication structure of atoms is determined by the behaviour of the clashes. If both atoms would not have the same energy after a clash, but more energy, matter would heat up permanently. A society of termites would be very drastically affected, if one would change their signal scent through genetical manipulation. Working with neural nets one can change the communication structure by an alteration of weights and threshold values to obtain the desired behaviour.

The communication *structure*, not the individual communication of single components, is the obviously fundamental factor, which determines the overall behaviour. But currently there is no theory, which determines the overall behaviour given the description of the communication structure nor vice versa, i.e. that determines the communication structure from the given overall behaviour.

Although the overall communication structure appears to be the fundamental factor that determines the capabilities of a society of agents, surely this in turn is a function of the capabilities of each of the individual agents and its knowledge structure.

So in studying Multi-Agent Systems the first question to be answered is:

What are the main features artificial agents have to have in order to form a cooperative society?

Or in other words: What do we have to add to our computers and programs, to transform them from stand-alone systems to cooperative intelligent agent societies?

Once we have an answer for this, the second question is:

What is the appropriate internal strucure of a social agent?

In most multi agent testbeds the agents are organized either as *programs* or as *objects* in a database environment and in addition they are provided with a communication facility. In the Activation Framework (AF) [13], which is a tool for the implementation of AI programs on interconnected computers, each expert is a special program, e.g. an arithmetic expert, which performs a special task when asked for. In the MACE system [12] the agents are independent problem solvers. Apart from standard attributes like name, address etc. the agents receive their special knowledge from their creators, who fill in the appropriate attributes for the goals, skills and plans, which are arbitrary LISP functions. Similar to AF, AGORA [1] is an environment that supports the construction of programs distributed over parallel executing processors. The agents (Knowledge Sources) are sets of functions which are triggered by certain patterns. They have access to a shared knowledge base realized as a semantic net. Another promising approach is realized in the MAGES [3] testbed: Here the agents (Actors) are implemented as objects within an object oriented programming language. The different agents form an inheritance tree that ranges from basic kernel agents up to expert agents with more elaborate reasoning capabilities. The software architecture for autonomous agents, as described in [14], uses a special time logic to describe the agents, which are structured in several layers. In [26] the agents are realized as a composition of their functional parts. An agent consists of his Body, reflecting his functionality, his Head, containing his knowledge about the world and himself and the Mouth, which processes a message defined by the Head and gives the information packages to the communication channels. The agent (Akteur) architecture of [27] is also implemented in terms of the functional parts of the agents' knowledge, i.e. his intention, cognition, communication, sensors and actuators.

In the following we shall distinguish five basic abilities of an intelligent agent, which are crucial for the cooperativity of an agent society. From this we shall derive a model for the internal structure of a social agent.

2 The Socialization of Artificial Agents

What are the characteristics of an (artificial) agent to optimaly perform in a society and in particular what are the characteristics of each agent to induce a societal behaviour that is optimal for the society as such - although it may be less than optimal for the individual concerned?

Obviously the agent should be able to perform cooperatively, i.e. it has to have the appropriate facilities for communication, representation of the needs of others and so on. But of course it is not just the *ability* that is required, what is at least as important is the representational means to induce the *willingness* to actually use these abilities for the benefit of the whole society. In other words although each agent has its internal goals to achieve the task it is specialized for, it should always be willing to dispense of its own goals if there is some overall duty of the society that requires this. On the other hand complete insubordination and selflessness renders an agent almost useless for the society - the optimal socialization of an artificial agent requires the representational means to struck an optimal balance between selfishness with respect to achieving the agent's goals and selflessness if the society as such (or some other agent in need of help) thus requires.

In summary here are the five essential features each agent has to possess in order to perform in a society of cooperative agents:

<u>Axiom 1:</u>	The representational means to store its environment and to draw inferences from this knowledge. **(Rep)**

<u>Axion 2:</u>   The ability to communicate. **(Com)**

<u>Axiom 3:</u>   The willingness to help. **(WH)**

<u>Axiom 4:</u>   Knowledge about other Agents. **(KA)**

<u>Axiom 5:</u>   Knowledge about its personal goals and knowledge of
the global task of the society. **(KT)**

The ability to represent the environment (the physical environment or an abstract environment, in case of an abstract nonphysical task) and to draw conclusions from this representation is of course the prerequisit for any autonomous agent, cooperative or not.

The ability to communicate is a first step towards cooperativeness and thus an important point. Communication does not only mean verbal communication, but also gesticulation or even some physical reaction if one agent "sees" that an other agent needs help. If agents can communicate, potentially they can do things together. But if the agents should really become cooperative, (to be cooperative means to do always more than you are asked to do) there must be something like the will to help. Finally, in order to act cooperatively it is fundamental that the agent has at least partial information about the skills and local goals of the other agents in the society and also it has to know what the global goals of the society are. To sum up the last two features, we may say that knowing the tasks may induce optimal planning, knowing the skills of the other agents may induce optimal coordination and if we have both, then we can hope for optimal cooperative planning.

Of course what we have in mind is not a central planning agency but a distributed planning capability that derives its strength from the cooperative interaction of the individual agents concerned: Although in principle the values of a socialist planned economy may be superior to those of a free capitalist society, its failure to respond to the rapid technological changes as well as its inability to set free the initiative and creativity of the individuals concerned is but one of the contemporary indications for the superiority of a free agent society: If Karl Marx had known contemporary work in DAI and had thus been able to recognize the values of "autopoesis" and "emerging functionality" - who knows if things might have been different in the past.

However it may be advisable to turn our attention to a less ambitious but more concrete domain and to study the effects of our approach in the setting of a wellknown puzzle in AI research.

3 A Test Case

In order to isolate the essential features of cooperation we implemented a problem from early work in AI on planning: The Towers of Hanoi. However as opposed to the central assumption of AI-research in the sixties we do not presuppose the existence of a central planning device. Instead let the objects concerned do the job and the final plan will implicitly emerge (emerging functionality) from the communication structure as well as the structure of the individual agents. To this end each disc is an autonomous cooperating agent with the ability to hop from one stick to another. The world simply consists of agents (representing the discs) and places (representing the sticks).

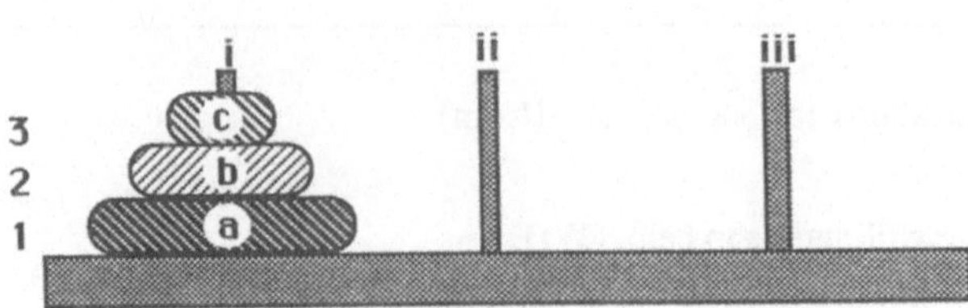

Each agent is able to hop to any other place, except if the place is occupied by a smaller agent. The classical task then is to rebuild the original tower on another stick by moving one disc at a time.

In our case the overall task is to reconstruct the tower say on stick (ii), and the agents can move in parallel (synchronized of course), i.e. all agents at the top of a stick, and only these, can change their position in one round. It is not allowed that a position is entered by more than one disc at a time (in one round). As a basis each agent is equipped with an agenda which contains its goal(s) to be reached. Initially the agenda of each agent consists of the same goal, namely "GOTO (ii)".

After some initial hopping and some further refinements of the agenda the task was solved and surprisingly the wellknown optimal "plan" emerged with far less resources spent (see [4] for details)

We shall now use this scenario that was actually implemented in RATMAN (Rational Agents Testbed for Multi Agent Networks) [5] to discuss our five axioms for cooperativity:

•   The representation assumption (**Rep**): Each agent (disc) knows about the places   (sticks) and the fact that it cannot hop on top of a smaller agent.

•   The ability to communicate (**Com**): Each agent can send and receive messages   to/from all other agents.

•   The willingness to help (**WH**): Each agent reacts upon a message by generating a new goal for its agenda that creates a favorable situation for another agent (provided   that it does not contradict the current goals).

•   Knowledge about the other agents (**KA**): The agents know about the goals of the   others,   their possibilities to move, etc.

•   Knowledge about the global tasks (**KT**): The agents not only know that they should   go to (ii), but also that the tower should probably be reconstructed, i.e. they know   the global goal.

In order to get a better feeling for what actually happend in this test scenario and also to further motivate our abstraction of the five axioms from this and other test cases, we like to go through a sequence of steps in more detail. For a more extensive discussion see [23] and [4]).

In our scenario the agents have their task (i.e. to move to stick (ii)) a priori. Thus **c** moves to (ii), while **a** and **b** are blocked and we arrive at the following situation (all these activities are covered by axiom 1, i.e. the knowledge that allows for the situatedness of each agent):

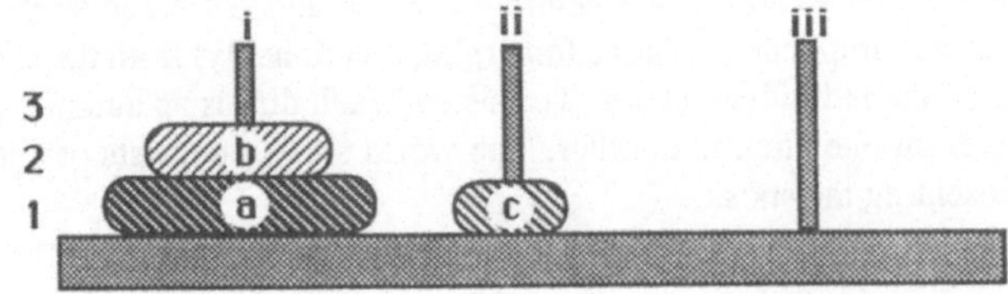

Now the agenda of **c** is empty, i.e. **c** does not want to move anymore. Since agent **a** is blocked and **b** can only move to (iii) (no larger discs on smaller ones), which is not its goal, and **c** does not want to leave (ii) (there is no reason for it to do so) the overall goal could never be achieved unless some communication (axiom 2) takes place now:

If the agents are able to communicate they would still just wait passively for a task. But if an agent can actively send a message to another agent to ask for support (axiom 4) and if in addition the agents are polite and willing to help (axiom 3), they may actually be able to perform the task together. Consider the situation of our scenario as above: In this situation **a** will broadcast a message to ask its top to be free. Now **c** still does not leave (ii), because this would contradict its goal. But **b** reacts to the message of **a** and it moves to (iii), since it cannot move to (ii).

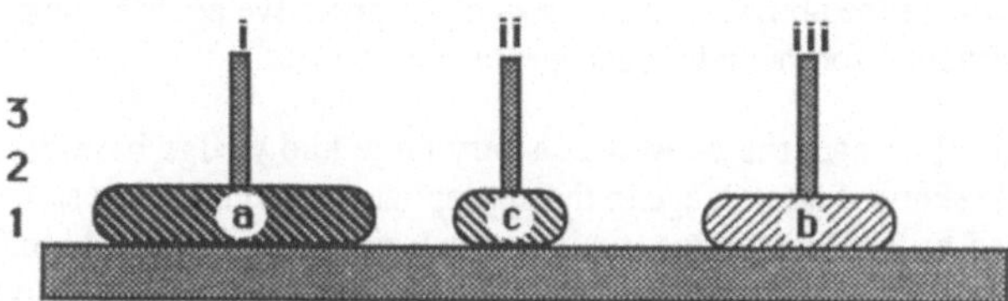

In a general setting where there are a lot of tasks, an agent would actively ask what to do next and it would try to integrate the others by giving them appropriate subtasks. In particular it would divide the task and distribute the subtasks to the most appropriate and idle fellow agents. Now **c** can swap its place with **a** on request by **a**. Of course this violates the goal of **c**, but this is done by some round of arbitration on the grounds of the global goal (subordination of its own goals if the overall plan/society thus requests), where **a** has to be on (ii) first. This leads to the following state:

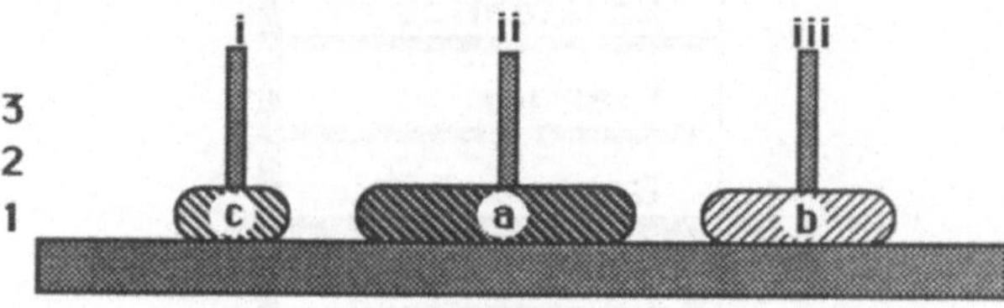

And then to:

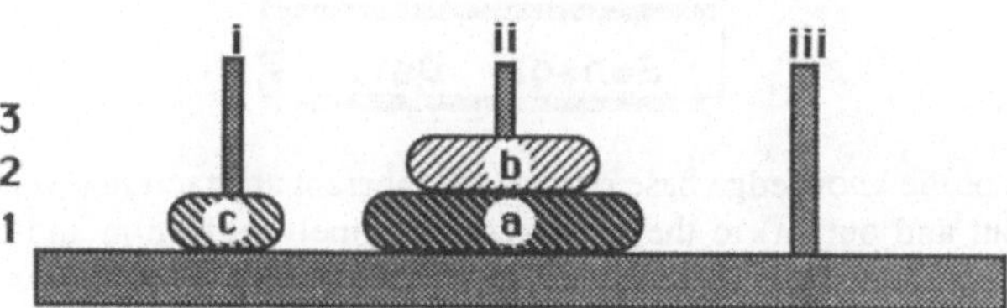

And now in one further step the final goal is achieved:

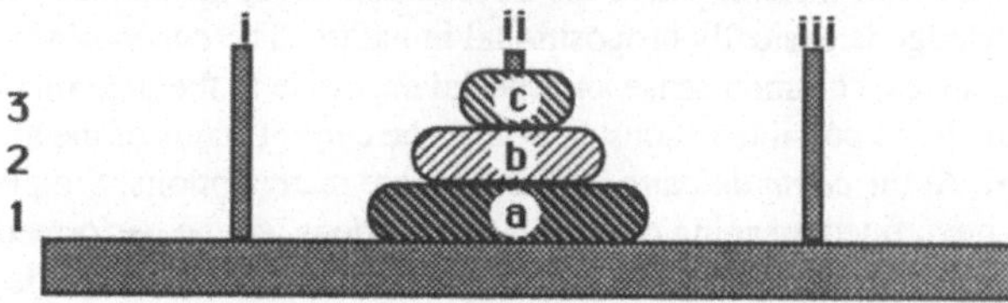

Note that in this case the final state is reached by a minimal number of steps (synchronized state changes).

We conclude by saying that if the agents fullfill all five axioms (full cooperation capacity), the society is perfect with respect to the cooperativity: Each agent acts as effective for the group as possible. This argument can be supported by some actual statistics: In our implementation [4], and with the ideas from above, the Tower of Hanoi problem with 10 discs and 4 places is solved after 50 to 229 moves and within 11.6 to 32.4 seconds depending on the variation of the features. Knowing that in this situation there are 4^{10} different states and up to 20^{50} moves of the agents (=nodes in the search tree) it is clear that the traditional approach with a central planning device is out of the question.

4 Agents as Hierarchically Structured Knowledge Bases

Given the five basic skills of the above axioms, a socially cooperative agent is supposed to posses, we shall now derive a layered structure for the individual agents themselves.

In RATMAN [5] [6] [22] an agent is viewed as a very large knowledge base that comprises all sorts of knowledge from simple sensoric knowledge to the approptiate communication skills and learning facilities. An agent is determined by his knowledge, which summarizes his skills and abilities. The size of these knowledge bases depend on the actual application, but in any real world scenario these knowledge bases tend to be very large (in the sense of "very large DBs") and hence must be structured. We use a hierarchical structure, where simple, propositional knowledge, for example sensory data, is stored at the lowest level and knowledge about knowledge as, for instance used for introspection and learning, will be found at the top levels. The following diagram shows the seven-layer model of the knowledge base.

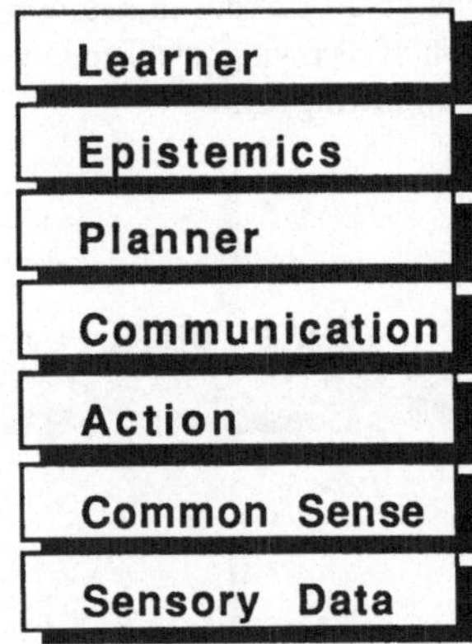

This layered structure of the knowledge base reflects the inherent abstraction levels from the least abstract data (the sensory input and output) to the most general namely reflection and learning facilities. It is understood that each layer has potential access to the one immediately below, but neither the knowledge contained in the layers above nor in layers of lesser abstraction is accesssible directely.

At the lowest level is the *sensory data*, where the information about the status of hands, feet, eyes, etc. is represented. This knowledge is basically propositional in nature. The *common sense level* basically holds knowledge about time, space, common sense and special expertise in the domain of interest. At the *action* level information about all the possible actions as well as the current status of the actions to be performed is stored and manipulated. At the *communication* level there are many options: Simple communication might use bit vectors (with a predefined meaning of the bits) and actions will be performed according to the status of these bits. In a little more elaborate situation, a dictionary of key words is stored and the agents communicate by sending and receiving single key words. The most elaborated situation relies on the generation and analysis of simple sentences in a predefined subset of natural language. The *planner* contains predefined plans that can be combined and executed in order to solve the current task (this is also the place where a planning device for distributed planning could be situated). At the meta knowledge level *(auto-)epistemic* knowledge, i.e. the agent's knowledge about its own knowledge and its partners' knowledge is recorded of course not just as copies of its own knowledge base or that of the partner agent, but by (auto-) epistemic models of the other knowledge bases. Finally there is the *learner* component – also a meta knowledge base – where all the agent's learning facilities are stored. This relies heavily on the introspection component, since the agent needs to know whether he already knows the "new" knowledge pieces or what he knows about these new things he is intended to learn.

5 Functional Aspects

The general principle underlying the structure is that a higher level knowledge layer is realized in terms of concepts, which are defined in detail at the lower level, which in turn may become more specific in a layer below. For example a predicate ASK_FOR_HELP is used at the planning level (see [5] for details). This predicate invokes the generation of an information block I and a new predicate ASK&WAIT(I) at the (lower) communication level. ASK&WAIT(I) is then given to the action level where it is decomposed into send and receive actions, which need information about the communication status from the sensory data and possibly knowledge about time for scheduling.

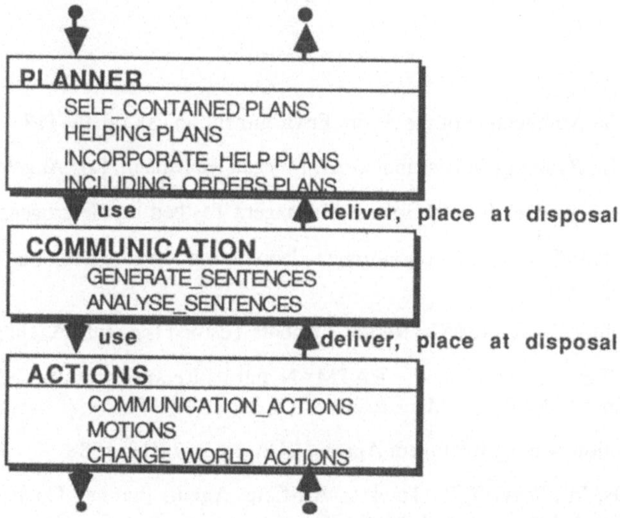

In other words, the level i places the defined predicates at the disposal of level i+1 (counting from the bottom) and delivers positive or negative answers to the next upper level. In our example, if the communication channels are open (the agent can speak and hear) the send receive actions are performed and the answers are given to the communication level, where they are analyzed. If there is a positive answer from another agent this information is passed to the planner level, where the ASK_FOR_HELP predicate becomes true and the respective arguments are instantiated by the necessary information (e.g. who can help).

The levels themselves have an internal structure that is realized by modules, such that different agents are implemented by choosing the appropriate modules at each level. If for example only propositions reflecting unidirectional communication channels are chosen at the lowest level (instead of bidirectional ones), then the corresponding agent can only "speak" or "hear", but not both.

For another case in point consider the planning level: If only the module SELF_CONTAINED PLANS is chosen, then no cooperation will take place, because the agent tries to fulfill its task without the collaboration of other agent. As a consequence, if a module is skipped at a lower level, modules at a higher level may be skipped automatically if they use predicates defined in the skipped one. Furthermore it is possible to define several general predefined settings, e.g. that each agent can communicate with *all* the others. Then for example the COMMUNICATION_ACTIONS are part of each agents action level and can not be removed by the designer.

6 Conclusion

Using a wellknown problem of early research in AI, the Towers of Hanoi, we have isolated five crucial features of a social agent that is supposed to perform cooperatively.

The emerging functionality of this simple test case was impressiv, in particular the comparatively little resources that were actually used came as a surprise.

We shall use the multiagent testbed RATMAN now for more elaborate "real world scenarios" such as a transportation company, where "planes", "cars" and "trains" are cooperating agents that strive for an optimal plan for the transportation of goods or passengers.

References

[1] Bisiani, R. et al.: The Architecture of the Agora Environment, in [8], pp. 99-117

[2] Bond, A., Gasser, L.: Readings in Distributed AI, Morgan Kaufmann, Los Angeles, 1988

[3] Bouron, T., Ferber, J.,Samuel, F.: MAGES: A Multiagent Testbed for Heterogeneous Agents, [11]

[4] Breuer, P.: Distibuted Planning for Autonomous Cooperating Agents, Diploma Thesis, University of Kaiserslautern, May 1991

[5] Bürckert, H.-J., Müller, J. , RATMAN: Rational Agents Testbed for Multi Agent Networks, in [11].

[6] Bürckert, H.J., Müller, J., Schupeta, A. : RATMAN and its Relation to Other Multi-Agent Testbeds, DFKI Research Report, RR-91-09, März 1991

[7] Coelho, H.: Interaction Among Intelligent Agents, ECAI88, 717-718, 1988

[8] Connah, D., Shiels, M., Wavish, P.: Towards Artificial Agents that can Cooperate, Technical Note 2643, Philips Research Labs, England, 1988

[9] Connah, D., Shiels, M., Wavish, P.: A Testbed for Research on Cooperating Agents, Technical Note 2644, Philips Research Labs, England, 1988, also short version in ECAI88

[10] Demazeau,Y., Muller, J.-P.: Decentralized Artificial Intelligence, Proc of the first workshop on Modelling Autonomous Agents in a Multi-Agent World, Elsevier Sc. Pub/North Holland, 1990

[11] Demazeau Y, Muller, J.P., Proceedings of the 2nd European Workshop "Modelizing Autonomous Agents in Multi-Agent Worlds", Saint-Quentin en Yvelines, Aug. 90, ELSEVIER Publishers, to appear 1991

[12] Gasser, L., Braganza, C., Herman, N.: MACE: A flexible Testbed for Distributed AI Research, in [15], pp. 119-152

[13] Green, P.E.: AF: A Framework for Real-Time Distributed Cooperative Problem Solving, in [15], pp. 153-175

[14] Hultman,J., Nyberg,A., Svensson,M., A Software Architecture for Autonomous Systems, Research Report LiTH-IDA-R-89-40, University of Linköping, Sweden, 1989

[15] Huhns, M.N.: Distributed Arificial Intelligence, Pitman/ Morgan Kaufmann Publ., San Mateo,CA, 1987

[16] Huhns, M.N. (ed.), Proceedings of the 10th Int. Workshop on Distributed Artificial Intelligence, Bandera, Texas, Oct 1990, MCC Tech. Rep. ACT-AI-355-90

[17] Konolige, K., Pollack, M. E.: Ascribing Plans to Agents, IJCAI89, 924-930, 1989

[18] Maes, P.: The Dynamics of Action Selection, IJCAI89, 991-997, 1989

[19] Mazer, M.S., A Knowledge Theoretic Account of Recovery in Distributed Systems: The Case of Negotiated Commitment, RAK88, 309-323, 1988

[20] Minsky, M.L.: The society of mind, New York, Simon and Schuster 1986

[21] Moyson, F., Manderick, B.: The Collective Behavior of Ants: An Example of Self-Organization in Massive Parallelism, AI Memo 88-7, Vrije Universiteit Brussel, 1988

[22] Müller, J.: Defining Rational Agents by Using Hierarchical Structured Knowledge Bases, Computing and Control Division Colloquium on "Intelligent Agents", Digest No. 1991/048, Feb. 91

[23] Müller, J. : From Silly Stand-Alone Systems to Cooperative Intelligent Agent Societies, Proc. of the Europea Simulation Multiconference 1991, Kopenhagen, June 1991

[24] Myerson, R.B., Incentive Constraints and Optimal Communication Systems, Proc. of the Reasoning about Knowledge (RAK 88) Conference, 179-193, 1988

[25] Steels, L.: Cooperation between Distributed Agents through Self-Organization, AI Memo 89-9, Vrije Universiteit Brussel, 1989

[26] Steiner, D., Mahling, D.E., Haugeneder, H., Human Computer Cooperative Work, in [16] chap.22.

[27] Sundermeyer, K., Modellierung von Szenarien kooperierender Akteure, 14th German Workshop on AI, Springer IFB 251,11-18

[28] Tennenholtz, M., Moses, Y.: On Cooperation in a Multi-Entity Model, IJCAI 89, 918-923, 1989

[29] Weihmayer, R., Brandau, R., Shinn, H.S.: Modes of Diversity: Issues in Cooperation Among Dissimilar Agents, In [16] Chap. 7.

[30] Werner, E.: Toward a Theory of Communication and Cooperation for Multi-agent Planning, RAK88, 129-143, 1988

[31] Werner, E.: Social Intentions, Proc. of the ECAI88, 719-723, 1988

[32] Zlotkin, G., Rosenschein, J.S.: Negotiation and Task Sharing Among Autonomous Agents in Cooperative Domains, IJCAI89, 912-917

Situated Adaptive Design: Toward a New Methodology for Knowledge Systems Development

Rolf Pfeifer*   Philip Rademakers
Artificial Intelligence Laboratory, Free University of Brussels
Pleinlaan 2, B-1050 Brussels, Belgium
E-mail: rolf/filip@arti.vub.ac.be
(On leave from: Institute for Informatics, University of Zurich)

In recent years there has been much criticism of knowledge systems technology and of artificial intelligence (AI) in general. In addition to arguments concerning brittleness and lack of noise and fault tolerance the main thrust of the criticism has been, in essence, that cognition is "situated" while most AI systems are not. "Situated" means that an intelligent system can only be understood in its interaction with the real world in a particular situation in which it has to act. Traditional non-situated AI systems which are strongly based on the notion of models tend to suffer from the notorious frame problem. In the first part the basic criticism and the issues involved are introduced and reasons for the pertinent problems of AI are given. It is then argued that by taking the criticisms seriously we cannot only gain theoretical insights but we can also derive guidelines on how to build better knowledge systems. This will lead to a methodology of "situated adaptive design". The methodology is illustrated with two successful examples. It is concluded that (a) the application of this methodology promises to resolve some of the basic problems, and (b) that research efforts in the area of knowledge systems should be re-directed.

1   Introduction

In recent years there has been much criticism of knowledge systems (KS) technology and of artificial intelligence (AI) in general. Points of criticism concern the brittleness of AI models, their lack of systematic learning and generalization capacities, their lack of fault and noise tolerance, and the fact that they are too much like digital computers and not sufficiently brain-like. For some time it seemed that progress in AI and KS was slow. Connectionism (or neural networks) was warmly welcomed by part of the AI community since it promised to resolve a number of fundamental problems. Indeed, connectionist models do not suffer as much from some of the shortcomings of traditional symbolic models: they propose interesting solutions to the problems of learning, generalization, and fault and noise tolerance. But after an initial phase of excitement it became clear that connectionism would not solve some of the more fundamental conceptual problems of AI, namely "situatedness" and the "frame problem" (see Section 2).

Our argument will be as follows. A significant number of knowledge systems projects have failed in the past. While general scepticism towards AI and management problems were important factors responsible for the failures, we argue that there are also some fundamental conceptual reasons.

Knowledge systems mostly build on the conceptual framework and the technology of traditional AI (logic-based symbolic representations, heuristics, etc.). AI has neglected the interaction with a real outside world and has thus largely failed to deal with some of the most important problems

---

*This research was partly supported by the Swift AI Chair, Free University of Brussels

of intelligence. Knowledge systems, by definition, do act in the real world. But the conceptual frameworks and the technology employed were not developed to cope with the problems involved. This is the bottom line why many KS projects failed.

In Section 2 some of the basic problems of AI are discussed. It is shown that if a system is to act in the real world, it must be *situated*. The crucial phrase here is "has to act in the real world". While in AI the system of interest which has to act is the *artificial system* (e.g. the robot), in KS it is the *user*, not the KS. So what is situated in the case of KS is not the KS itself but rather the human problem solver, i.e. the user.

In Section 3 the implications of strictly viewing the user as a situated problem solver for knowledge systems development are discussed. The results of this discussion is summarized as a number of steps of a new methodology (Section 4). The methodology is illustrated with two case studies (Section 5) and a number of preliminary conclusions are drawn (Section 6).

2 The basic problems

We start from the observation that a human expert or a user of an knowledge system has to solve a problem in the real world. The fact that problem solvers — human or artificial — typically have to interact continuously with the real world has not sufficiently been taken into account in traditional AI research.

2.1 Characteristics of the real world

The real world has a number of characteristics: it is constantly changing, intrinsically unpredictable, indefinitely rich and thus only partially knowable. Since we are interested in solving tasks in the real world, we need a way of characterizing their "difficulty". A systematic way in terms of *pragmatic features* has been suggested (Steels, 1990). For example, the input to a task can be characterized in terms of the amount, the quality, and the availability of data. In a real-world situation there is always too much but at the same time too little data available. There are always errors and noise in the data. There is always the potential for novel situations, i.e. situations the system has not encountered before. In addition there are epistemological limitations on the part of the agents (humans and computers) which are due to the fact that resources are always limited in terms of space and processing power, the search space may be very large, there are always costs associated with data acquisition, and the theoretical models, since they are all based on limited quality data and limited quality agents, will also be of limited quality. Moreover, decisions must be taken within a limited interval of time. If a decision takes too much time, the world may have changed in the meantime and the data on which the decision had been based may no longer be true[1].

This characterization of tasks defines a "difficulty" space: a "benign" world (high-quality data, small computational requirements, no changes, low costs associated with data acquisition, good models available, etc.) would be more easy to cope with and thus require less intelligence than a "tough" one (low quality data, large computational requirements, rapidly changing world, etc.). Since the epistemological limitations of humans and computers are different they will have optimal performance in different regions of the "difficulty" space.

2.2 The "frame-of-reference problem"

The "frame-of-reference problem" (Clancey, 1989) allows us to better conceptualize the relationship between an observer or a designer, a system and the environment. We will use the case of an knowledge system for purposes of illustration. There is a system to be modeled, e.g. a human expert, an observer (of the expert), a designer (of the knowledge system), a user, and the knowledge system

---

[1]Simon (1982) has applied the concept of *bounded rationality* to such decisions. It is important to note that bounded rationality is not a practical consequence but a fundamental one: there is no way around it.

itself. Frequently the observer and the designer are one and the same person: the knowledge engineer. For our argument it is not important whether the knowledge system reflects in a psychological sense the cognitive processes of the human expert.

The knowledge engineer observes the human expert and decides what parts of his behavior he will put into the system. Moreover, he defines — typically in collaboration with the human expert — a particular domain ontology (i.e. a categorization in terms the kinds of objects, relations, and actions of a domain). For example, a domain ontology for train scheduling may include schedules, train engines, rides, and the operation of connecting rides. This forms the basis for the representations (the models) to be developed. Normally the interaction of a KS with the real world is mediated by a human (the user)[2]. He interprets the representations and establishes the relation to the real world. Given the characteristics of the real world, the restrictions imposed by the domain ontology, as well as the subjectivity (and thus changeability) of such an interpretation, there is bound to be a mismatch, at some point, i.e. a situation not covered or a false conclusion by the model.

In discussing intelligent systems we must take care to specify whose point of view we are assuming: the one of the observer, designer, user or the one of the (artificial) system. For example, for the knowledge system the environment only consists of its input space which is given by the domain ontology which in turn is imposed onto the system by the designer. For the designer (and for humans in general) the environment and thus the input space is much richer.

We conjecture that the neglect of the frame-of-reference perspective is one of the reasons for the problems traditional AI has encountered.

2.3   Situatedness

The problem of situatedness can briefly be explained as follows (e.g. Agre & Chapman, 1987, Suchman, 1987, Winograd & Flores, 1986). Let us look at a traditional plan-based AI system. If such a system has to act in a particular situation in the real world, there will always be relevant factors which have not have been foreseen by its designer, again because the properties of the real world. In other words, no matter how detailed the models[3] may be, and no matter how large the library of models, there will always be relevant situations which have not been anticipated. This is the main reason for their brittleness. Trying to cover for all potential situations would lead to a so-called *model explosion cycle* (Gutknecht et al., 1991). Moreover, if the models are very detailed to cover potentially a large range of situations, this typically not only implies high computational costs but may also require a lot of interaction in order to supply the necessary information to the model to keep it up to date[4].

There is another problem involved with a modeling view. Normally only a small part of the world is relevant in a particular moment, and it is hard to decide beforehand which one it is without neglecting potentially important influences. This is the "frame problem" for which there are no satisfactory solutions (e.g. Pylyshyn, 1988).

If a system is *"situated"* it has direct access to all the relevant information in the situation it needs in order to act. The use of indexical/functional terms is also a feature of situatedness. They refer to the system's view of the current situation and its actions (e.g. "the direction in which I am going", "the ice cube in front of me" — Agre & Chapman, 1987). An important consequence is that the behavior of a "situated" system is largely *reactive* rather than purely plan or model-based. A situated system can take advantage of the fact that the world is, in a sense, its own model. This drastically reduces the need for detailed models. Situatedness can be easily understood by assuming the perspective of the system itself. Viewed from the system's perspective, the currently relevant information is determined by the situation the system is in, thereby minimizing the frame

---

[2]Although we think there is great potential for sensory-based knowledge systems we restrict our current discussion to systems without sensors.

[3]For the purposes of the present discussion we are using the terms "model" and "knowledge base" as synonyms.

[4]For lack of space we have not included any examples of the problems involved. Using a traditional approach in one of our own projects we ran precisely into this problem. The interested reader is referred to Gutknecht et al. (1991).

problem. Moreover, situated systems are more adaptive — and thus less brittle — since they can react appropriately in particular situations.

This view of systems as being situated sharply contrasts with the one of traditional AI where the designer tries to anticipate all potentially relevant situations.

2.4   The nature of expertise

Let us now assume a real expert's point of view who has to solve a problem. He is an expert because he can cope well with the epistemological problems posed by the real world. Moreover, an expert is situated, i.e. he continuously interacts with a particular situation and takes advantage of the information which is there.

A distinction has been made between routine expertise and adaptive expertise (Hatano & Inagaki, 1986). Routine expertise is only useful and applicable if the pragmatic features of a task are benign. If the only real pragmatic problem concerns the size of the search space, KS can be applied. They encode routine expertise. A case in point is the highly successful chess program *Deep Thought.* Chess is a formal game, it is completely knowable and there is no uncertainty in the data or the rules. The only difficulty is a large game tree. The tougher the pragmatic features of a problem, the more adaptive expertise there must be. Since the real world is never entirely benign routine expertise will never be sufficient.

But — given the problems discussed above — we cannot currently achieve adaptive expertise in AI systems. Thus we cannot expect to develop systems which solve problems on their own in the real world. This entails a significant change in our goals: instead of trying to develop problem solving systems we are aiming at developing problem solving support systems (When we use the term "knowledge system" in the following we mean problem solving support systems). Thus the human problem solver who is to be supported now becomes the focus of our interest. As pointed out in the introduction it is now *he* who has to be viewed as situated, not the system to be built. This provides us with a new perspective on knowledge systems design.

3   Implications for knowledge systems design

Our arguments are based on a number of premises. First, the user has to be viewed strictly as a situated problem solver. Second, care has to be taken to separate out the perspectives of the different parties involved in the development process, namely the end-user, the knowledge system itself, and the knowledge engineer. Third, since humans and computers have different epistemological limitations and thus perform differently in different regions of the "difficulty" space, it may be possible to take advantage of the capabilities of both.

3.1   The end-user perspective

From the end-user's perspective the goal is not to have a maximally "intelligent" system but rather one that will help him most in his day-to-day work. Our understanding of what users really find useful is fairly limited, largely anecdotal, and frequently based on designer's projections of what they themselves feel others must find useful. For example, problem solving behavior of human experts can conveniently be described using AI modeling techniques. However, it is a common misconception to conclude from this fact that the implementation of such a model will *automatically* be helpful to a user. Informal observation from our own experience suggests that this is indeed frequently not the case. While research on designing systems that users find really useful is still in its infancy, there is a simple evaluation criterion of usefulness: if the users keep using the system over extended periods of time, it is useful, if they don't, it is considered a failure.

To the situated user the system is part of the environment. Thus, as a new system is introduced his environment changes which causes the user to change his behavior. In fact the introduction of a system interacts with the user (and the larger environment) in highly complex ways which are currently only poorly understood. Experience teaches that the introduction of a new system also changes the sorts of problems the system is used for and consequently the ways in which it is put to use. This in turn implies a newly changed environment etc. The behavior of the user is extremely hard to predict because there is an interaction of his prior knowledge, the new situation, and the learning mechanisms. Even in the comparatively very simple case of autonomous robots, this interaction is hard to understand (Pfeifer & Verschure, 1991).

Since our understanding of how to build systems which users find truly useful is limited[5] we have to follow two paths. First, in our methodology we must take this limited understanding into account, and second we must include a way of improving our understanding over time. Concerning the first point, care should be taken to minimize the change entailed for the user by the introduction of a new system. The smaller the change the easier it will be to anticipate his behavior. This implies that one should start with systems that are transparent to the user and that relate to his previous way of working. But since the interaction of the user with his environment changes continuously it will be necessary to change the system continuously, too (see Section 4). In other words, the methodology must be *adaptive* or, more precisely, geared towards continuous adaptation. This has also been called "evolutionary system development" (Floyd, 1984). As to the second point we suggest the observation of users *over extended periods of time.* This includes, of course, the initial phase, but is not restricted to it. One of the few studies of this sort in the area of KS that we are aware of concerns the XCON-system (e.g. Soloway et al., 1987). A discussion of the results of this study is beyond the scope of the paper. But it definitely confirms the need for continuous adaptation. We hope that there will be additional studies along these lines: they could provide us with the empirical foundations needed to develop a methodology for evolutionary system development.

3.2   The knowledge engineer's perspective

Designing the end-user system: The knowledge engineer is one of the participants in the system development process and is normally at the same time observer and designer. His goal is to develop a system that the user community will find useful, i.e. one which will remain in use over long periods of time.

In traditional knowledge acquisition the knowledge engineer interacts with a human expert and develops a model of part of his problem solving behavior. This is typically done using knowledge level modeling frameworks such as KADS (e.g. Breuker & Wielinga, 1989) or the "componential framework" (Steels, 1990). While this may be a good way of understanding human expert behavior and the problems of the domain, the implementation of such models will not automatically lead to systems which appeal to a user[6]. Whether it will or not is essentially an empirical question. We are currently not aware of long-term studies investigating this problem in detail.

It is clear that in designing any support system the traditional insights concerning user-friendliness have — to the extent that they exist — to be taken into account. This aspect will not be further discussed.

Rather than focusing on the design of the initial systems, the designer's major task is to think of ways to maintain the attractiveness of the system. This implies taking change into account or, in other words, *designing for change.*

It is common knowledge in information technology that after some initial excitement users often get bored with their systems (though the opposite can happen as well). A case in point are video games, but it is true for other systems, too. Many reasons have been given and we will not discuss them here. Only the one case where the system does not function appropriately will be discussed (see below).

---

[5]The field of human computer interaction promises to yield insights in the near future.

[6]This may be one of the reasons why a number of knowledge systems which were initially conceived for user support, ended up in the training departments of the companies.

There are essentially two ways in which change can occur: the way in which the system is used changes, or the system changes (or both). System changes can be either automatic (the system changes itself) or manual (the system is changed by the knowledge engineer or the user).

Many approaches to provide for such changes have been tried. Examples are: designing systems to support different types of usages which may then change over time (such as tutoring, browsing, knowledge acquisition); developing user models which will adapt to the level of competence of the user; or systems that, in one way or another, incorporate experience about the problem domain over time. Many of the system which increase their expertise by incorporating new cases typically employ certain types of machine learning techniques. Gutknecht et al. (1991) suggest a kind of apprenticeship learning via a neural network which essentially picks up the user's control structure. Van de Velde (1988) shows how expertise can be augmented through a learning technique called "progressive refinement". While Gutknecht et al. (1991) present some informal evidence supporting the hypothesis that users find their adaptive neural network technique useful, there is generally little information available concerning the user perspective. Again, the fact that some of these methods look interesting to a knowledge engineer or to a scientist, does not imply much about their potential utility to end-users.

As the system is used over time the user's needs will change and he will want the system to do other things for him. While case coverage can to some extent be increased automatically, changing or extending the functionality has to be performed manually since this implies changing the domain ontology (which in turn changes the input space of the system).

Let us now turn to the example in which the system performs inappropriately, e.g. it proposes inappropriate tests in a troubleshooting domain or it connects inappropriate train rides in a scheduling task. From the considerations in the previous sections it is clear that this can and *will* happen whenever models are involved. Now, rather than refraining from employing models at all, their potential failure has to be taken into account. One obvious answer is to design the systems such that the user is always under control and that he can at any point easily introduce changes to the system's proposals. Again, this seems obvious to the designer, but whether the users find it useful is a different question. Moreover, it is not clear what the user's reactions will be if this happens frequently. Again, this is an empirical problem. In order to minimize such breakdowns we believe the kinds of models used should be as simple as possible. An additional advantage of simple models — in contrast to highly sophisticated ones — is that the interactional costs of keeping them up-to-date are smaller.

Designing the knowledge engineering tools: What are the means available to actually achieve adaptive design? To be concrete let us talk about the knowledge-level modeling tools we mentioned above, for example KADS and the componential framework. We can apply the same arguments that we applied to end-user systems to the knowledge engineering tools: they are the end-user system of the knowledge engineers. Because of the properties of the real world, not all the potential applications for knowledge engineering tools can be foreseen: there will always be cases which have not been anticipated. Thus, rather than trying to extend and refine highly sophisticated modeling libraries, it might be more beneficial to support the difficult process of applying the modeling frameworks to specific problems (Pfeifer et al., 1991). But even if this mapping process can be effectively supported the resulting end-user system will still be subject to intrinsic brittleness due to the properties of the real world.

In the next section we will try to summarize the points made in this section in a more systematic way.

4 Situated adaptive design

The following summary of the methodology of "situated adaptive design" consists of a number of important points to keep in mind, rather than a step-by-step methodology. Given its preliminary stage this would not have been possible.

1. During the whole system development process keep the following points in mind: (a) The end-user must be considered strictly as a situated problem solver. The to-be-developed system will be part of the user's environment with which he will interact just as he will interact with other parts of the environment. (b) Always clearly specify whose perspective or point of view is assumed, the end-user's, the system's, the designer's, or the human expert's. This will in particular help to separate designer claims about what the end-user finds useful from those of the end-user himself. (c) The goal is to develop a system that will be helpful to the end-user. This may or may not include a model of human expert problem solving. The evaluation criterion is whether the system will be used over extended periods of time.

2. Start with a small part of the system which can function on its own. This way the users can interact with a system which is transparent to them early on in the project. Extensions will come more natural. This enables us to study system-user interaction from almost the beginning. The results of these studies will be the basis for extending the system.

3. Focus on adaptivity and incremental development rather than trying to develop a full-fledged system from the very beginning. This has two aspects, the end-user system, and the knowledge engineering tools. For the *end-user system* this principle implies that it has to be foreseen in terms of system facilities but also in terms of project organization how the system will adapt to changes in the environment. This can be done in part automatically e.g. when adapting to a particular user, or to a "case environment" of the company, or it must be done manually, e.g. when extending the functionality of a system. The latter amounts to an extension of the system's input space. For the *knowledge engineering tools* the principle implies that the tool libraries should not be extended indefinitely but rather the process of their application to particular situations should be supported.

4. Account for failures. It was pointed out that since every model or knowledge base will always be incomplete, given the properties of the real world, the system is bound to fail at some point. Rather than refraining from employing models entirely it is suggested that the potential for failures be taken into account. In other words, facilities must be provided such that in spite of these failures, the user will find the support of the system useful.

5. Analyze the pragmatic features of the tasks. Since humans and computers are subject to different epistemological limitations, they will have their strengths in different regions of the "difficulty" space spanned by the pragmatic features. This analysis will give us an assessment of the feasibility of automating the tasks. However, feasibility should not be confounded with usefulness to the user.

6. Observe the interactions of the users with their systems over extended periods of time. (a) Record the activities of the users by automatic recording facilities (case recording, statistics) and by informal observation (needed to get a common-sense based impression of the performance of the system). (b) Is the system used regularly? What parts are used, how frequently? Do these distributions change over time? Do they stabilize? (c) Record the new requirements of the users. Through the use of the system they will come up with new ideas of what sort of support they would like to have. This will eventually lead to better understanding of how user behavior changes as a reaction to the introduction of systems. Although the initial phase is crucial for the interaction to start, the real test is a long-term one.

This methodology will now be illustrated with a scheduling and a troubleshooting example.

5   Case studies

The two applications were chosen because on the one hand they are quite different and on the other we are involved in both of them so that we have access to the pertinent information. SCHEDULE is a joint project between the Belgian railway company, Knowledge Technologies NV (Brussels), and the VUB AI Lab (Rademakers, 1991). The goal of the SCHEDULE system is, to support the scheduling of traction equipment (engines) given the trains which have been planned. DDT, a joint project between the AI Lab, University of Zurich, Switzerland, and TECAN AG, a hightech company manufacturing equipment for analytical chemistry and laboratory automation in the Zurich area. The goal of DDT is to support an expert at the company in troubleshooting of laboratory robots[7]. A significant difference between the two applications is that in SCHEDULE, the final product, the schedule, is constructed, whereas in DDT the final "product" is that the robot functions again.

Let us illustrate some points of the methodology with examples from the two projects.

Point 1: Conceptualization: We have found it extremely useful to follow the conceptual advice proposed. Some of the implications for the methodology have have been pointed out and are summarized below. An extensive discussion would be beyond the scope of this paper.

Point 2: Starting with a small part of the system: In SCHEDULE the user interface was put into place first. This was fairly straightforward since the interface more or less faithfully reproduces what the experts had been doing on paper before. Figure 1 illustrates part of a "schedule" the experts work with. Simple operations can be performed such as removing, or connecting trains. The fact that the schedules on the interface look the same as the schedules on paper implies that the initial disturbance introduced by this system is minimal. Therefore, the users could quickly work with the system on an everyday basis. The initial experiences were highly positive.

Point 3: Focusing on adaptivity: In the organization of the SCHEDULE project it is foreseen that extensions are successively introduced, i.e. the functionality is continuously augmented. There are currently no ways of automatically incorporating case experience. In DDT there is a pertinent adaptive facility (Gutknecht et al., 1991). One of the most difficult parts of the troubleshooting task is to determine the sequence in which hypotheses are to be pursued and observations and tests executed. Therefore this sequencing was not included in the initial design of the system, but rather, the decisions on what to do next was left to the user. Through a kind of apprenticeship learning in which the system learns from the user the system eventually picks up the control structure and comes up with increasingly better proposals over time. This way the system adapts to its own "case environment" and thus incorporates expertise. This is implemented such that the user chooses from a display of hypotheses, observations or tests. These decisions are stored and eventually a neural network is trained with these particular choices. To successively augment the functionality a manual adaptation loop is foreseen.

Point 4: Accounting for failures: Both SCHEDULE and DDT will make errors. In SCHEDULE the automatic train connecting facility may produce inappropriate connections, and in DDT inadequate tests may be proposed, e.g. tests which don't make sense in a particular situation. In both cases this is not fatal since the user can always override the system's proposals. However, only long-term tests will show whether the users find this acceptable.

Point 5: Task distribution: In DDT the analysis with pragmatic features was used for task distribution to humans and machine. For example control (e.g. the sequence of tests) requires a lot of experience (see point 3). It turned out that it was not possible to develop the models that would account for it. Thus, an important pragmatic feature in this case is the lack of theoretical models which implies that this task must be performed by the human. On the other hand the learning task is well-suited for computer implementation since the examples are provided to the system via the case-recording facility[8].

Point 6: Observation over extended periods of time: Continuous observation is currently under way in both projects. Although we are only at the beginning, first results can already be seen. In the SCHEDULE project several changes in the problem solving behavior of the experts could be observed. While earlier they were happy to find any solution at all, the availability of a tool enables them to get a global view of the problem. They are now beginning to take interactions between different parts of the problem into account which could not have been done before because the different parts

---

[7]A description of DDT can be found in Gutknecht et al. (1991) or in Stolze et al. (1991).

[8]The conditions under which this approach will work, are discussed in Gutknecht et al., (1991).

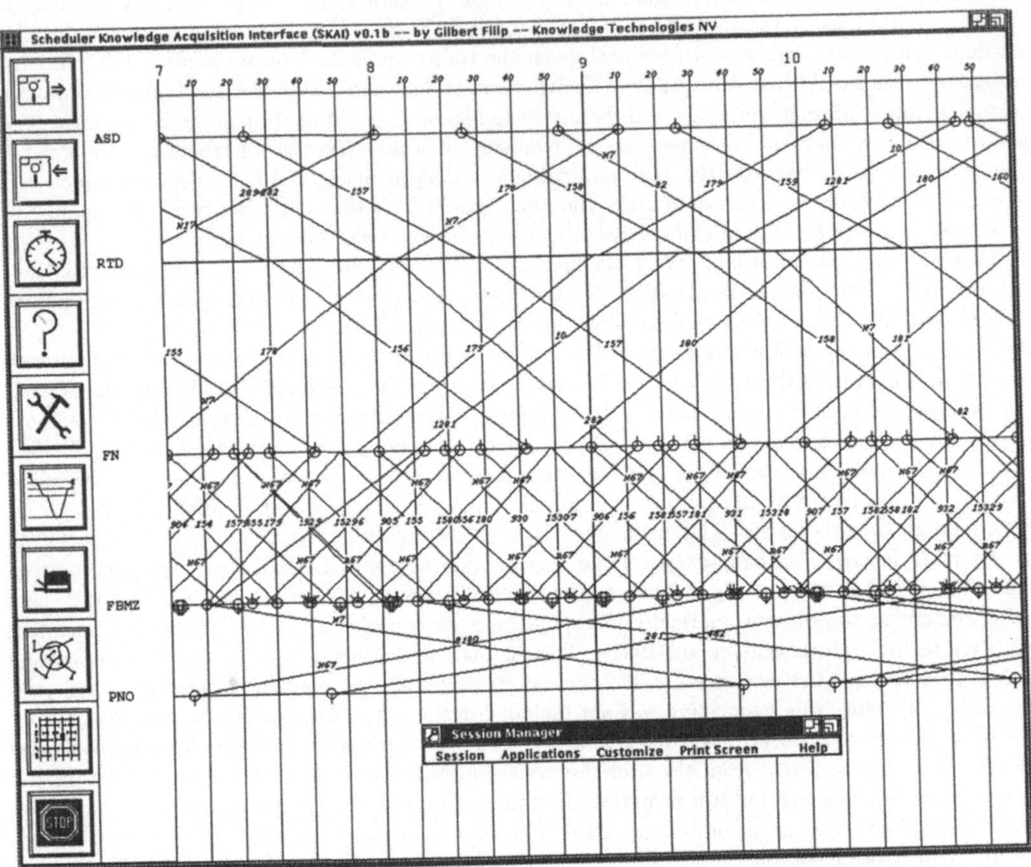

Figure 1: Interface to the SCHEDULE system (place-time diagram). The horizontal axis contains a timescale of 24 hours while the vertical axis contains a set of stations that have been selected from the station database (Amsterdam - Rotterdam - Antwerp - Brussels - Paris). The trains from the timetable database are represented as lines in this diagram (e.g. train 157 drives from Amsterdam to Brussels). The icons at the left of the screen are menus that contain commanda that invoke different kinds of operations (e.g. clicking on the "clock" icon allows the user to zoom in on the time dimension).

are performed by different users. This is supported by the possibility to put schedules together in the same drawing. In other words the problems they are interested in change.

An example of a change in functionality suggested by the users was the following. A basic operation is "connecting trains", i.e. reusing engines to drive other trains. In many cases this operation is fairly trivial but requires a lot of routine work. The users suggested that for the trivial cases this be done automatically. Thus such a facility was installed. Whether this facility will turn out to be useful will be seen in the future.

In DDT there is a case-recording facility which is used for the apprenticeship learning and in the performance evaluation by the experts. We are are also currently collecting statistical data to get a better idea of the frequency of use of the different parts of the system.

6 Discussion

We started from a number of fundamental problems of traditional AI. Using a characterization of the real world and taking into account the "frame-of-reference problem" we argued that any system that is to function appropriately in the real world must be situated. We analyzed the implications for knowledge systems design and arrived at the methodology of "situated adaptive design". We then illustrated some of the points using two successful knowledge systems projects.

In our methodology "situated" means that the human problem solver whom we are going to support is situated, not the system that we are building. Whether the system itself is situated or not is largely irrelevant. It is merely considered part of the user's environment. If the user finds the interaction with the system useful he will use it, otherwise he won't. We proposed an evaluation criterion which is based entirely on the user, namely whether a system is used in the long term. "Adaptive" means that, given the characteristics of the real world, not everything can be foreseen and therefore the system has to be designed for change, i.e. made adaptive. The user-centered view suggests a focus on cooperation between a human and a computer system, rather than trying to automate everything.

Our initial experiences with the methodology have been extremely positive[9]. But there are a few points of caution that should nevertheless be mentioned. First, the methodology starts with a simple but functioning part of the system. For the management this is on the one hand positive since something usable is quickly in place. On the other hand there is the difficulty that in this methodology it is hard or even impossible to predict at the outset what the final system will look like. This makes it, of course, difficult to sell the system to the management. In fact, if the methodology is applied, it will require a lot of re-thinking on the part of the management. They will have to think in terms of adaptive systems. However, that may be beneficial in the long run in any case. Second, the methodology is only in a preliminary state and not worked out in sufficient detail to be readily usable. Many points are left open and need to be further investigated. Third, applying the methodology will require that the participants are willing to depart from traditional ways of thinking.

Relation to other work: Some of what we have said seems obvious. For example, the need to take the user into account and to focus on cooperation has been widely recognized. However, we are not merely advocating cooperative systems. We argue that a principled analysis of the shortcomings of traditional systems is needed. The theoretical framework presented provides us with a systematic way of assessing the implications of the ontological commitments made by a designer on the system development process. This will help us to avoid making the same errors as in the past when developing new systems. Let us illustrate this with an example from a cooperative system. The process of negotiation about who could perform the task requires a dialog model. As in the case of problem solving models this implies a pre-categorization of the potential dialog situations and our arguments re-apply. Thus, cooperation will not automatically get us out of the problems; a thorough theoretical analysis is needed.

---

[9]The methodology is currently further elaborated in our AI Lab (e.g. Stolze et al., 1991).

The points that we made, though obvious, have until fairly recently, been neglected to a large extent. For example, in the field of knowledge-level modeling, there still seems to be the goal of developing sophisticated models in order to automate complex tasks. And normally there is a strong effort to cover potentially all situations that can occur. Only little reflections is given to the inherent problems of this way of proceeding. So, while perhaps not new for human-computer interaction, it may be somewhat new for knowledge systems.

It also seems obvious that the human problem solver interacts with his environment in order to solve a problem. However, viewing him strictly as situated in the sense discussed in the paper represents a major re-conceptualization of the system development process.

In summary "situated adaptive design" promises to resolve a number of basic problems. But it also implies that research efforts be re-directed.

References

[1] Agre, P.E., & Chapman, D. (1987). Pengi: An implementation of a theory of activity. *AAAI-87*, Seattle, WA, 268-272.

[2] Breuker, J., & Wielinga, B.J. (1989). Models of expertise in knowledge acquisition. In G. Guida, & C. Tasso (ed.). *Topics in expert system design*, 265-295.

[3] Clancey, W.J. (1989). The frame-of-reference problem in cognitive modeling. *Annual conference of the cognitive science society*, 107-114.

[4] Floyd, C. (1984). A systematic look at prototyping. In R. Budde, K. Kuhlenkamp, L. Mathiassen, & H. Zullinghoven (eds.). *Approaches to prototyping*. Berlin: Springer, 1-18.

[5] Gutknecht, M., Pfeifer, R., & Stolze, M. (1991). Cooperative hybrid systems. To appear in: *Proceedings IJCAI-91*.

[6] Hatano, G., & Inagaki, K. (1986). Two courses of expertise. In H. Stevenson, H. Azuma, & K. Hakuta (eds.). *Child development and education in Japan*. San Franciso: Freeman.

[7] Pfeifer, R., Rothenfluh, T., Stolze, M., & Steiner, F. (1991). Mapping expert behavior onto task-level frameworks: the need for "eco-pragmatic" approaches to knowledge engineering. To appear in: *Lecture Notes in Artificial Intelligence*. Berlin/Heidelberg: Springer.

[8] Pfeifer, R., & Verschure, P.F.M.J. (1991). Distributed adaptive control: a paradigm for designing autonomous agents. Techreport, AI Lab, Free University of Brussels.

[9] Pylyshyn, Z.W. (ed.). *The robot's dilemma. The Frame Problem in artificial intelligence*. Norwood, N.J.: Ablex.

[10] Rademakers, P. (1991). Task analysis of an equipment assignment problem. Techreport, AI-Lab, Free University of Brussels.

[11] Simon, H.A. (1982). *The sciences of the artificial*. Cambridge, Mass.: MIT Press (2nd edition).

[12] Soloway, E., Bachant, J., & Jensen, K. (1987). Assessing the Maintainability of XCON-in-RIME: Coping with the problems of a *very* large rule-based system. *Proceedings of the Sixth National Conference on Artificial Intelligence*, Seattle, Washington.

[13] Steels, L. (1990). Components of expertise. *AI Magazine, 11(2)*, 28-49.

[14] Stolze, M., Gutknecht, M., & Pfeifer, R. (1991). Integrated knowledge acquisition: toward adaptive expert system design. Techreport 91.04, Institut für Informatik, University of Zurich.

[15] Suchman, L.A. (1987). *Plans and situated actions*. Cambridge University Press.

[16] Van de Velde, W. (1988). Learning from experience. Techreport 88-1, AI Lab, Free University of Brussels.

[17] Winograd, T., & Flores, F. (1986). *Understanding computers and cognition*. Reading, Mass.: Addison-Wesley.

A Management System for Distributed Knowledge Base Applications

Günter KNIESEL, Mechthild ROHEN, Armin B. CREMERS
Universität Bonn
Institut für Informatik III
Römerstr. 164
5300 Bonn 1
e-mail: {gk,cremers}@uran.informatik.uni-bonn.de

EPSILON is a knowledge base management system (KBMS) integrating object oriented features, logic programming and databases in a uniform framework. Theories, containing knowledge in different representation formalisms, are the basic components of a knowledge base. Relationships among theories are expressed by various types of links, including inheritance links, which allow to combine the contents of existing theories. In a distributed environment it is possible to develop parts of an application separately on different nodes and to integrate them by defining suitable links as well as to split complex applications into a set of cooperating sub-applications running on different machines. Partitioning of a knowledge base and allocation of sub-knowledge bases to different nodes allow to exploit parallelism and make most efficient use of the resources of the network. Cooperation of autonomous problem solvers is supported by a communication subsystem with decentralized control.*

1. Introduction

During the short history of computer science, hundreds of programming languages and systems have been developed. Only few of them have been widely used for a long time, mostly due to a mismatch between their modeling power and the complexity of applications.

A series of different programming styles and paradigms have been proposed to improve this situation. During the past years AI researchers and practitioners have adopted the view of programming as *knowledge representation*. To avoid the dead end of ad hoc features, knowledge representation languages need a formal basis. Many researchers identified *logic* and its various extensions to be the natural basis for formalizing the semantics of a system and logic itself has even been 'discovered' as a powerful knowledge representation language. At the same time, based on theoretical work on abstract data types, *object oriented programming* emerged as another powerful paradigm, answering the need for a behavioural description of complex simulations. Soon, the following abundance of object oriented data models, languages and systems showed one main weakness of this approach: the lack of a common formal basis.

To create a system that offers both, a well-founded formal semantics and the power to describe highly complex interacting processes, an integration of (logic based) knowledge representation and object oriented programming appears promising, all the more so because both paradigms already share basic concepts like object-centered structuration of knowledge (/ programs) and reuse of knowledge (/ software) by inheritance mechanisms.

---

*	EPSILON is the acronym for ESPRIT I Project 530, "Advanced KBMS Based on the Integration of Logic Programming and Databases"

The aim to develop realistic models of the way humans interact in order to solve problems, naturally leads to modeling of distributed systems ([1], [2], [3]). From a more technical point of view, distribution of knowledge and control offers advantages related to reliability, efficiency and increased autonomy of the processing nodes. Nowadays, the exchange and management of information in a decentralized distributed system has become as essential for a company´s survival as the introduction of databases at the core of a company´s data management in the past years.

The design of advanced knowledge representation features integrating concepts from databases, logic programming and object oriented programming ([4], [5], [6]) and their use in distributed environments ([7], [8], [9], [10], [11]) have been the main topics of the EPSILON project, presented partly in this paper. The basic knowledge representation features of EPSILON are introduced and illustrated by short examples in chapter 2. Chapter 3 describes the distributed EPSILON prototype. To clarify our position related to what is usually called distributed artificial intelligence (DAI), EPSILON will be compared to some standard DAI concepts in chapter 4.

2. EPSILON: Basic Concepts

The EPSILON KBMS is built on top of a commercial Prolog and an available database management system (DBMS), running on standard UNIX environments. The main concepts underlying the EPSILON approach are ([4], [5]):
- the extension of Prolog with *theories* (objects / worlds) as a structuring mechanism,
- the explicit specification of relationships between theories using *links*,
- the definition of a transparent interface from Prolog to relational *DBMSs*,
- the use of *metaprogramming* as a basic technique to define new inference engines and tools,
- the use of *partial evaluation* as a systematic method to "compile" metaprograms.

2.1. Theories, engines and links

The basic component of an EPSILON knowledge base is a *theory* ([12]). Theories are similar to worlds in MULTILOG ([13]), to unit worlds and instances in MANDALA ([14]) and to units in Contextual Logic Programming ([15]). A knowledge base (KB) is a collection of theories together with relations on theories, defined by *links*. Each theory is accompanied by an inference engine (*theory processor*), which can itself be a metalevel theory, providing operations to query, update and search a class of theories. Theories can contain knowledge in different representation techniques, e.g. database tuples, relational algebra expressions, various logic languages. The logic languages are extensions or restrictions of Prolog. A given logic language is defined by a theory processor that implements the corresponding knowledge representation features (e.g. logic programming with certainty factors) and the inference control mechanism (e.g. forward reasoning or planning).

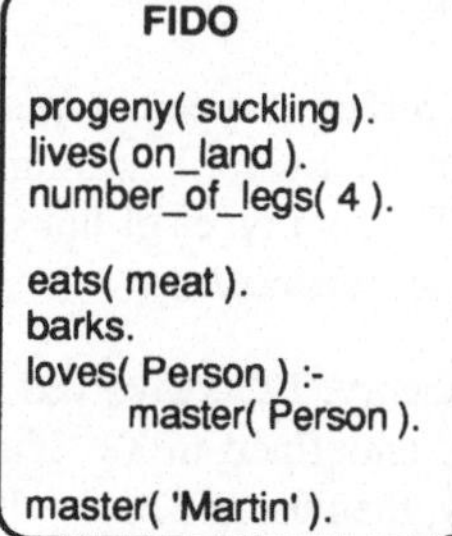

Fig. 1. Description of whales, beavers and a dog named Fido in the theories WHALE, DOG and FIDO

The example shown in fig. 1 gives an idea of the object-centered ([16]) representation of knowledge in theories. A theory can be regarded as an object, its contents as the properties of the object, e.g. 'lives(in_water)' in the theory WHALE simply states that a ("typical") whale lives in water. The rule 'loves...' in theory FIDO expresses that Fido loves his master. We will refine this example in the remainder of this chapter. In all the examples we will use Prolog syntax: arguments enclosed in simple quotes or starting with lower case letters denote constants and arguments starting with upper-case letters denote variables. The symbol ':-' separates head (consequent) and body (antecedent) of a clause (rule).

Besides their contents and their unique name, theories have two other important attributes: their 'class' and their 'type'. All theory processors are of type *engine*, while all other theories are of type *object[1]*. Every theory processor defines a *class[1]* of theories. All theories of one class have the same theory processor. The definition of the theory processor also includes the declaration of a set of tools available for all theories of this class (e.g. partial evaluator, tracer, explanator). Users can create theory processors of their own, either by writing a corresponding inference engine or by composing it from existing ones. In [17] a methodology for the definition and composition of engines is described, that is applicable to a large class of metainterpreters. Inference engines defined by metaprograms in turn need another inference engine. The inference engine at the root of the hierarchy of metainterpreters is Prolog extended with structuring of the knowledge base (theory handling primitives), which corresponds to the primitive *class kernel*. The *class database* is also a primitive class. EPSILON also provides a set of predefined though non-primitive classes (theory processors), defined by means of metaprogramming: *inheritance, constraints, planning* and *uncert*.

Relationships among theories are specified by the definition of different types of *links*. Some predefined types of links (dict and version) are handled by the system. A *dict link* from theory T1 to theory T2, expresses that T2 is a data dictionary, containing metainformation about T1. In the case that T1 is a database theory, T2 simply contains its schema definition. Dictionaries associated to theories of other classes may contain other types of metainformation, depending on the power of the corresponding theory processor. In the case of a *version link*, T2 is the result of the application of a tool (e.g. compiler / partial evaluator) to the theory T1.

The user can define his own types of links by writing corresponding theory processors. Predefined non-primitive theory processors that implement new types of links are *planning, constraint* and *inheritance*. A *constraint link* between theories T1 and T2 specifies that T2 contains the integrity constraints of T1. These are automatically checked every time T1 is updated. A parametric *'transition(_Action)' link* specifies an action that must be performed to reach a desired state. In this case T1 represents the initial state and T2 the desired state. The semantics of inheritance links is described in section 2.2.

Information about the structure of a KB (theories, their classes and types, links, tools) is stored in the *knowledge base dictionary (KBD)*. The operations for handling the KBD and the primitive classes (kernel, database) are included in the EPSILON kernel (fig. 6).

2.2 Inheritance links

The *inheritance* theory processor defines different types of *inheritance links* (*closed_copy, open_copy, closed_consultance, open_consultance*). An inheritance link from theory T1 to T2 defines that T1 (the heir) inherits knowledge from T2 (the parent). The four types of links result from the combination of two pairs of inheritance modalities, open/closed and consultance/copy.

If an inheritance link is *closed*, the parent theory, T2, is involved in the solution of a query addressed to the heir, T1, only if the queried predicate is undefined in T1. If an inheritance link is *open*, each query addressed to T1, is first solved in T1 only, then using T2, too. If T1 does not (re)define any predicate of

---

1 In EPSILON "object" and "class" have a different meaning than in object oriented languages.

T2, there is no difference between open and closed links. The (general) definitions in T2 can be regarded as defaults, which are either overridden or extended by the (more specific) definitions in T1.

There are some obvious weaknesses in the example given in figure 1. The fact that Fido barks and eats meat is not a specific property of Fido but typical for every dog and the fact that all represented animals have sucklings is a common typical property of all mammals. Therefore it would be better to define the properties of mammals and dogs in separate theories and specify the relationship(s) among mammals, whales, beavers, dogs and Fido in a way that allows the common properties of a species to be shared by subspecies (and individuals).

Figure 2 shows how the first example can be improved using open and closed inheritance links. Beavers have all the properties of mammals (they have sucklings, four legs and live on land) plus some additional properties (they *also* live in water). On the contrary, whales, although they have sucklings and thus are mammals, do not have legs and live *only* in water. Therefore we use an open link for beavers and a closed one for whales. We do not specify the type of the links between MAMMAL, DOG and FIDO, the effect of open and closed links being the same when the sets of properties defined in linked theories are disjunct.

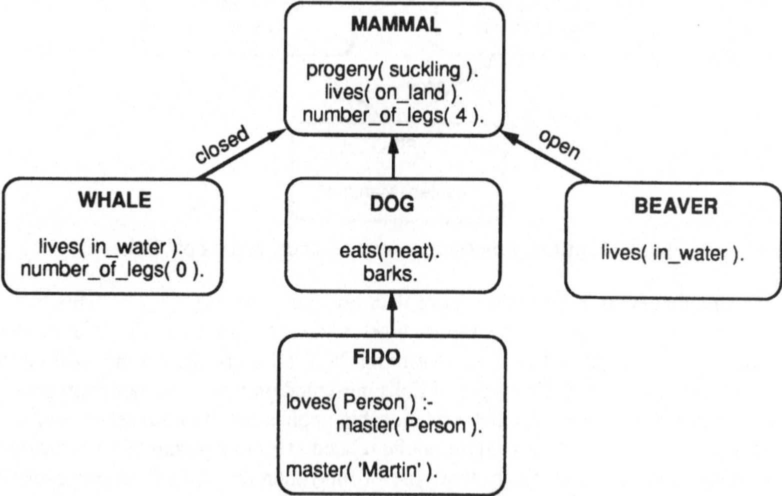

Fig. 2. Inheritance via 'closed' and 'open' links

Please note, that the use of inheritance only requires the specific properties of subspecies to be represented explicitly in the corresponding theories. How these properties relate to the general properties of mammals is specified by links.

In the example given in figure 2 only facts are inherited via the links. Therefore we could neglect the second pair of inheritance modalities, as the semantic difference of using a copy or a consultance link only manifestates if the parent theory contains rules that call predicates defined in the heir. A *copy* link defines inheritance of *clauses* between two theories using the same knowledge representation formalism, i.e. having the same theory processor. Queries addressed to the heir theory are solved in the program resulting from the union of the predicates of the heir and the visible[1] predicates of the parent. A *consultance* link defines that T1 inherits *results of queries* answered by T2´s inference engine using T2´s contents. Operationally this means that the theory processor of T2 can be called for solving a query addressed to T1. The two theories may have different theory processors.

---

[1] A predicate of a parent theory can be invisible to a heir theory either if there is a 'closed' link beetween them and the heir contains a definition of the predicate (fig. 2) or if the link has an associated import list that does not contain the predicate (fig. 4)

In figure 3 we have further refined Fido´s representation assuming that loving his master is a typical property of pets and that Fido only has this property because of being Martin´s pet. If we did not use a copy link, the semantics of FIDO would be different from the previous examples. Using a consultance link, the query 'loves(Person)' addressed to FIDO would be forwarded to PET and fail to produce an answer, because no definition for the predicate 'master' is available in PET. A 'copy' link makes the definition of the predicate 'loves' accessible in FIDO. The evaluation of the query in the context of FIDO therefore produces the intended result, Person = 'Martin'.

Summarizing, copy links allow clauses in parent theories to call predicates not defined in the parent theory itself but in a heir theory. Thus common predicates can be partially defined already in more general (parent) theories and this definition can be shared and completed as required by more specific (heir) theories. Consultance links are necessary if a (sub)query must be evaluated only in the context of a parent theory.

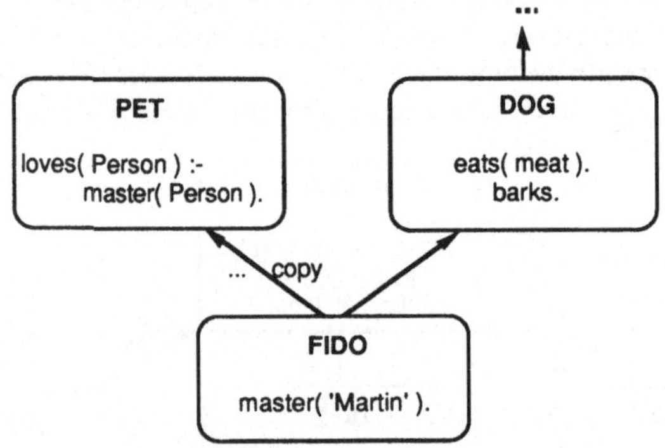

Fig. 3. Multiple inheritance, 'consultance' and 'copy' links.

EPSILON allows one theory to inherit from more than one parent theory (fig. 3). This feature is usually called *multiple inheritance*. Using multiple inheritance can lead to problems. If different definitions of a predicate exist in different theories that have a common heir, all these definitions will be inherited. But sometimes this might not be desired. The types of links presented until now are not appropriate handle such a case, since they do not allow to express that a relationship applies only to a subset of the properties of two theories. Some properties of a heir theory might not be related at all to a parent theory or they might have a different relationship (corresponding to another type of link) than the rest of the properties (fig. 4.). The situation that a theory with multiple parents should inherit a predicate only from some of its parents but not from the others, is a special case.

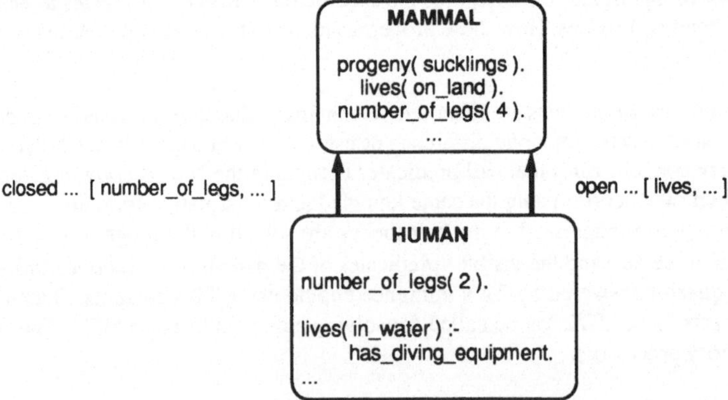

Fig. 4. Inheritance links with import-list

To allow a finer granularity of their scope, the introduced inheritance links have been extended by *import-lists* ([18]). The import-list of a link contains those predicates of the parent theory which may be visible to the heir. From a database perspective import-lists can be regarded as a view mechanism. In figure 4 we have used import lists to show how humans can be defined as mammals that only have two legs (*overriding* the default definition of the predicate 'number_of_legs') and live on land and in water (*extending* the default definition of the predicate 'lives'). The square brackets indicate the import lists.

In summary, the EPSILON architecture is essentially object-oriented. Its main feature is uniformity. All objects in the architecture (inference engines, tools, programs in different logic languages, data bases, integrity constraints, results of optimization) are represented in a uniform way by the theory feature. The link feature allows to define relationships between theories, including the definition of new inference engines in terms of existing ones (composition of interpreters). The declarative semantics of theories linked by inheritance links (including links with import lists, multiple inheritance and cyclic inheritance) is defined in [19].

3. DEP: The Distributed EPSILON Prototype

Distributed problem solving is a basic method for solving problems which are too complex to be solved by a single processor ([20]) or for organizing expert systems as a "cooperating community of specialists" ([21]) where each specialist contains its own knowledge base and corresponding inference mechanism, and where specialists must cooperate to solve problems outside of their own domain. Distributed problem solving in EPSILON is regarded as the *cooperative* solution of requests to the knowledge base by a *decentralized* and *loosely coupled* collection of knowledge sources, located on distinct nodes in a local area network (LAN). Cooperation is required because no node has sufficient information to solve an entire problem. Loosely coupled means that individual knowledge sources spend the greatest percentage of their time in computation rather than in communication. Decentralization refers to control and knowledge, which are both distributed.

An application, corresponding to one knowledge base (KB) defined as a collection of theories and links between theories, is decomposed into a set of sub-KBs, which are allocated to different nodes in a network. The actual allocation of sub-KBs is fully transparent to users, who work with one logically integrated application. Because distribution is transparent, it is possible to develop and test different parts of a KB separately on different nodes and to integrate them later simply by creating suitable links. Vice versa, every application initially designed and developed at only one node will run without changes even if some of its theories are allocated to other nodes.

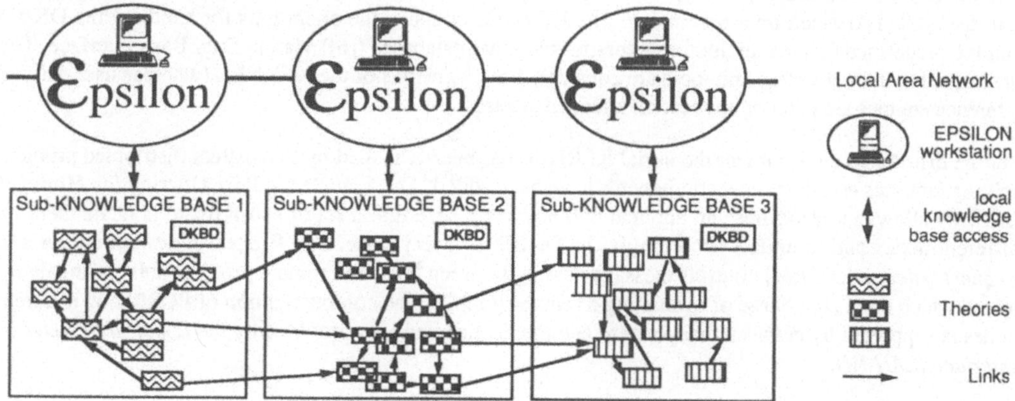

Fig. 5. Distributed EPSILON Environment

To free the user from details of distributed knowledge base management and distributed request evaluation, the KBD has been extended by knowledge about the locations of theories in the network. The resulting *distributed KBD (DKBD)* is redundantly stored on every node (fig. 5), due to safety and efficiency considerations. Redundant DKBD allocation avoids high network communication overhead caused otherwise by frequent remote DKBD access, as well as the risk of total system failure if the node holding the single copy of the DKBD fails.

Due to the cooperation facilities of EPSILON instances on different nodes, every node has access to all the knowledge stored on every other node (fig. 5). In order to let problem solvers cooperate an intranode and internode communication facility, based on a network independent communication protocol, is needed. Particular attention has been paid to control of internode communication. In order to avoid reliability and efficiency problems, no node plays a central role by providing special processing capabilities (e.g. DB-server) and there is no global control of network communication or distributed request evaluation. Based on the redundant allocation of the DKBD, control of communication and processing is distributed within the network, each node being able to execute requests, as well as to send requests to other nodes.

Distribution of the KB allows parallel processing on different nodes to take place. The overall performance of the distributed EPSILON depends on mechanisms to increase parallelism (parallel inferencing, parallel fact retrieval) and to reduce communication. Exploitation of potential parallelism is restricted by the allocation of knowledge to processing nodes of the network. The theory and link concept in EPSILON is well suited for a distributed environment, providing a knowledge base structuring mechanism which has been exploited for decomposition and distribution of knowledge bases. The additional information provided by import lists proved especially useful for efficient distribution of knowledge and for optimization of query evaluation, allowing to determine without (remote) access to a parent theory, whether it really contains a predicate definition that can be used to solve a subquery of a heir theory. Based on the information available in the DKBD, strategies have been developed to determine allocations of sub-KBs on different nodes, which use efficiently the resources of the network (processors, storage). Especially the trade-off between communication and parallelism has been considered. Decomposition and allocation strategies are implemented as an additional tool, the Knowledge Base Distribution Manager (KBDM), described in [11].

3.1. Architecture of Distributed EPSILON

The architecture of the distributed EPSILON has evolved from the single user implementation of EPSILON, called SUP (single user prototype). Readers interested in the SUP architecture are referred to [4] and [5]. Here we shall just summarize the actual state of the prototype.

The distributed EPSILON prototype (DEP) is implemented on SUN workstations. The existing User Interface (UI) is defined on a Macintosh. The KERNEL contains the operations for handling the DKBD and the predefined classes, including access to relational databases ([6]) via the Data Base Interface. The predefined metainterpreters and tools are considered as extensions of the KERNEL (whereas user defined inference engines are parts of application knowledge bases).

For the distributed environment the initial KERNEL has been extended by transparent distributed problem solving facilities and three new components have been added. The *Knowledge Base Distribution Manager (KBDM)* allows to decompose an application knowledge base into a set of sub-KBs, to allocate them on different nodes and to update accordingly the DKBD on every node. The *Process Communication and Request Manager (PCRM)* controls message passing between local and remote problem solvers and determines which one is in charge of evaluating a request (cf 3.2). The communication of PCRMs on different nodes is supported by network independent communication services provided by the *Local Area Network Interface (LAN-IF)*.

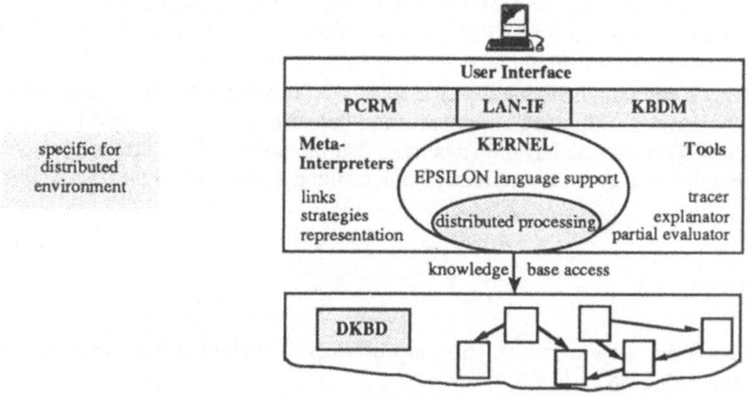

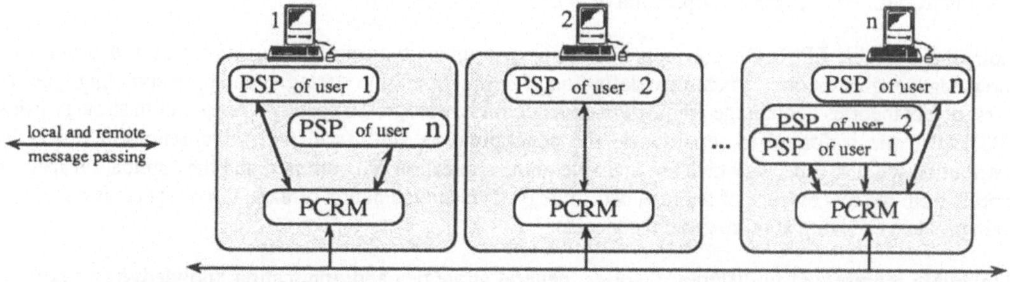

Fig. 6. Architecture of Distributed EPSILON Prototype (DEP)

3.2. Process Structure and Communication

Although efficiency considerations suggest to have as few processes as possible, the system is more reliable, if the overall control is separated from the problem solving facilities. If a problem solver loops or breaks down, the rest of the system (on the same node and on other nodes) can still continue its work, as long as the global control resides in another process. Therefore our approach distinguishes two different classes of processes: *problem solving processes (PSPs)*, which produce answers to requests and *communication processes*, responsible for passing requests and answers among the PSPs and for controling the PSPs.

A *Problem Solving Process* consists of the kernel together with the predefined metainterpreters and tools. The EPSILON communication processes are the *User Interface process* and the *PCRM process*, containing the PCRM, the LAN-IF and the KBDM. The PCRM[1] is responsible for the management (creation, deletion) of local PSPs, for the decision which PSP is in charge of evaluating a request and for the control of communication (connections, message passing) between local and remote processes.

Fig. 7. Management of problem solving processes and of communication by cooperating PCRMs

Evaluation of one user request may require access to different nodes in the LAN. On every accessed node there is one PSP assigned to the corresponding user. The local PCRM maps every (sub)request of the same user to the same problem solving process; for different users, different problem solving processes are created by the PCRM ('one PSP per user approach', fig. 7). We followed this approach in order to avoid errors of one user having undesirable side-effects on other users and to assure fair timesharing (since fair timesharing of different processes is automatically done by the operating system). Detailed descriptions of design and implementation of the PCRM can be found in [10] and [11].

---

[1] In the following we will simply say PCRM instead of PCRM-process, if the distinction is not relevant.

Different PCRM processes communicate using services provided by the LAN-IF. Network communication is implemented using stream sockets based on the TCP/IP protocol. Stream sockets guarantee reliable and efficient message passing between communicating processes. They offer a uniform interface to local communication as well as to network communication and provide the most flexible process communication facilities in the distributed environment, allowing communication between several unrelated processes. Having the communication based on sockets has the advantage that the process structure can easily be changed / extended. Exploiting this facility we are currently implementing a new process and communication management strategy.

4. EPSILON and DAI

In the following we will sketch our view of the relationship between "standard" distributed artificial intelligence (DAI) concepts and EPSILON.

DAI systems often concentrate on agent models and cooperation strategies suitable for a certain type of distributed application. It seems that, due to the existence of a large variety of applications, there are as many agent and cooperation models as research groups working in this field. In view of this situation we neither intended to add some more models nor to solve the very ambitious task of finding a general unifying model of agents or cooperation. We started "from the other side", by defining a knowledge representation formalism with a semantics that *abstracts* from distribution aspects. Regarding distribution, the main aim of EPSILON is to provide a tool that frees the user from caring about distribution issues.

Cooperation strategies essentially being inference procedures, they can simply be added to EPSILON by exploiting the possibility to define new engines. To define a cooperation strategy one only needs to know which objects exist and with which objects they can cooperate. This corresponds to knowing the theories and links of a knowledge base. A link defines that two objects can cooperate and its type defines the type of cooperation (i.e. the cooperation strategy). We denoted theories as objects and not as agents, because EPSILON does not impose a fixed agent model. One could regard a theory as an agent and the existing link types (inheritance, constraint, etc) as special types of cooperation, but many other models are possible. Just to give an example, it is as well possible to interpret a group of theories (linked by the existing types of links) as the knowledge base of an agent and to relate this group (/agent) to others by new types of links, specifically defined to express cooperation of agents.

Using the available EPSILON concepts one has to distinguish between general strategies and application knowledge: engine theories contain the definition of new cooperation strategies and corresponding types of links; object theories contain the application dependent knowledge. To specify a cooperation strategy using EPSILON, one is forced to separate, at the conceptual as well as at the implementation level, the distribution specific aspects (which are invisible to the applcation programmer) and the application specific aspects from the real essence of the intended strategy. The amalgamation of these three aspects is one of the main problems arriving at more general concepts.

Explicitely represented in different theories, general strategies and application knowledge can both be reused in another context, either by applying the same strategies to other applications, or by running the application under control of other strategies. Using one common application, the performance of different DPS approaches can be compared. A comparison of different concepts in a common framework is one more step towards their integration.

Being mainly concerned with knowledge representation and the management of distributed KBs, EPSILON is more closely related to the new area of cooperating knowledge base systems (CKBS) than to "classic" DAI. Anyway, as we have just described, EPSILON could be used as a tool for the implementation and evaluation of DAI concepts.

5. CONCLUSIONS

We have presented an advanced knowledge base management system architecture and its extension by a transparent interface to distributed knowledge bases, allowing decentralized cooperation of different inference engines within a local area network. The architecture makes a clear distinction between cooperative distributed problem solving and the process communication facilities, needed for its support. The separation of problem solving from communication management increases the reliability of the system and allows to use a flexible and easily extensible process communication model. Further we have sketched how DAI concepts can be implemented exploiting EPSILON´s features, especially its open, extensible architecture.

The current prototype is a solid basis for the investigation of further problems arising in distributed environments. Here are just some open questions: Is it possible to simplify the communication model, without restricting the functionality of the system? What has to be done, in order to efficiently support consistent updates of redundantly stored knowledge? Is it possible to define a general purpose protocol the integration of other systems into our communication framework? What is a good model for exploiting (large grain) parallelism? Which known DAI concepts can be implemented in EPSILON? Which cannot? Which extensions would be required to handle them too?

ACKNOWLEDGEMENTS

The results of the EPSILON project are very much a team effort and include work investigated by all partners (Systems & Management, University of Pisa, C.R.I.S.S., University C. Bernard of Lyon, Bense KG, University of Dortmund), presented in detail in many other project documents. We thank all our coworkers for their efforts which have made this a fruitful project. Special thanks are due to all the members of the EPSILON team who contributed to the specification, design and implementation of the distributed EPSILON environment, especially to Harald Hönig and Ralf Schlüter. For helpful comments on a draft of this paper we want to thank Thomas Lemke.

REFERENCES

[1] A.S. Cromarthy. Control of Process by Communication over Ports as a Paradigm for Distributed Knowledge-Based System Design. In L. Kershberg (ed.), Proc. of First Conference on Expert Data Base Systems, Charleston, South Carolina 1986, pp. 47-59.

[2] E.H. Durfee, V.R. Lesser, D.D. Corkill. Coherent Cooperation among Communicating Problem Solvers. In *IEEE Transact. on Computer*, C 36(11):1275-1291, 1987.

[3] R.G. Smith. The Contract Net Protocol: High-Level Communication and Control in a Distributed Problem Solver. In *IEEE Transactions on Comp.*, C-29(12):1104-1113, 1980.

[4] P. Coscia, S. Djennaoui, P. Franceschi, J. Kouloumdjian, G. Levi, L. Lei, G.H. Moll, I. De Saint Victor, G. Sardu, C. Simonelli, L. Torre. The EPSILON KBMS: Architecture and DB access optimization. Workshop on Integration of Logic Programming and Data Bases, Venice 1988.

[5] G. Levi, M. Modesti, J. Kouloumdjian. Status and Evolution of the EPSILON System. In Proc. of the 4th Annual ESPRIT Conference, North Holland 1987, pp. 593-610.

[6] J. Kouloumdjian, L. Lei, S. Djennaoui, G.H. Moll. The Communication Processor: Kernel - DBMS Communication, ESPRIT project 530, Report 15, 1986.

[7] M. Rohen, G. Kniesel, A.B. Cremers, H. Bense. Specification of an Architecture for Distributed Problem Solving in EPSILON. In Proceedings of the 5th annual ESPRIT Conference 1988, North Holland, pp. 659-673.

[8] G. Kniesel, A.B. Cremers. Cooperative Distributed Problem Solving in EPSILON. In Proceedings of the 7th annual ESPRIT Conference 1990, North Holland, pp. 177-193.

[9] M. Rohen, G. Kniesel. Specification of the Distributed EPSILON Architecture, ESPRIT project 530 Report 13, 1987.

[10] M. Rohen, G. Kniesel, R. Schlüter, H. Hönig, E. Moll. Design of the Distributed EPSILON KBMS, ESPRIT project 530 Report 2, 1988.

[11] G. Kniesel, M. Rohen, K.-U. Höffgen, R. Schlüter, R. Waschkowski. Implementation of the Distributed EPSILON Prototype, ESPRIT project 530 Report 10, 1990.

[12] K.A. Bowen, R.A. Kowalski. Amalgamating Language and Metalanguage in Logic Programming. In K.L. Clark, S.A. Tärnlund, (eds.), *Logic Programming*, Academic Press 1982, pp. 153-172.

[13] H. Kauffmann, A. Grumbach. Representing and Manipulating Knowledge within Worlds. In L. Kershberg (ed.), Proc. of First Conference on Expert Data Base Systems, Charleston, South Carolina, 1986, pp. 61-73.

[14] K. Furukawa, A. Takeuchi, S. Kunifuji, H. Yasukawa, M. Ohki, K. Ueda. MANDALA: A logic based knowledge programming system. In Proceedings of International Conf. on 5th Generation Computer Systems 1984, pp. 613-622.

[15] L. Monteiro, A. Porto. Contextual Logic Programming. In Proc. of sixth International Conference on Logic Programming, pp. 284-299. MIT Press 1989.

[16] N.J. Nilsson. Principles of Artificial Intelligence. Springer 1984.

[17] M. Degl'Innocenti, G. Levi, G. Sardu. A methodology for the Design and Automatic Composition of Structured Prolog Meta-Interpreters. ESPRIT project 530 Report, May 1988.

[18] G. Kniesel, M. Rohen. Das Theorien und Link-Konzept unter dem Aspekt der Verteilung (Distribution Aspects of the Theory and Link Concept). Internal paper, University of Dortmund, 1987.

[19] M. Rohen. Semantik von komponierten modularen logischen Programmen in einer Programmierumgebung mit integrierten objektorientierten Vererbungsmechanismen (Semantics of Composed Modular

Logic Programs in a Programming Environment with Object-Oriented Inheritance Mechanisms). Doctoral thesis at the Universiy of Dortmund, April 1991.

[20] B.A . Lambird, D. Lavine, L.N. Kanal. Distributed architecture and parallel non-directional search for knowledge based cartographic feature extraction systems. In M.J. Coombs (ed.), *Developments in expert systems*, Academic Press 1984, pp. 221-234.

[21] B. Chandrasekaran. Expert systems: Matching techniques to tasks. New York University Symposium on AI Applications for Business, 1983.

Planning and Uncertainty:
On the Logic of Multi-Agent Plans and their Entropy

Eric Werner *
University of Hamburg
Distributed Systems Research Group
Department of Computer Science, Bodenstedtstr. 16,
2000 Hamburg 50, West Germany
email: werner@rz.informatik.uni-hamburg.dbp.de

The logical foundations of plans in the context of uncertain knowledge about the state of the world and uncertain knowledge about the plans of other agents are investigated. The partial plans of single and groups of agents are formally defined and their properties are studied. The concept of entropy is extended through a mathematical definition of the control entropy of plan states. Furthermore, fuzzy plan states are defined. A tensed modal language, containing can and plan operators, is given a formal semantics. The relevance to communication and cooperation among multiple agents in distributed AI is discussed.

1 Introduction: The Social World

An agent acts not only in a physical, inanimate world but also in a social world of other agents. Multi-agent social worlds are essential for the emergence of cooperative activity. Furthermore, an agent will in general not be informed about the state of the inanimate world, nor about the state of the social world. In distributed artificial intelligence the generation of social activity between agents requires a theory of such uncertainties in order to give an account of communication, cooperation and multi-agent interaction. In this paper we attempt to define formally an agent's uncertainty in the context of a physical and social world. This characterization of uncertainty leads to a formal definition of control entropy extending the notion beyond its traditional use in the physical and biological sciences and communication theory [Khinchin 49, Shannon 48]. Along the way we define the plan states of single agents and groups. The formal definitions allow us to give a unified account of single and multi-agent action and planning in the context of a social world. Such an account is the basis of a formal theory of multi-agent communication, cooperation and social organization [Werner 89b].

We start with a discussion and then a formalization of types of uncertainty. Then, we apply the formal theory of uncertainty to define control entropy, to define fuzzy plan states and, finally, to give a semantics for a logic of plans and ability. The definition of control entropy is important because by extending the traditional concept of entropy to the social world, it allows the measurement of the entropy of a multi-agent system, such as, an organization. Thereby, it supports the study of the global dynamics of organizations. The definition of fuzzy plan states is of interest because it permits the formalization of fuzzy control (see below). Finally, the logic of abilities and plans will bring us closer to the goal of enabling agents to reason about plans and abilities in the context of uncertainty.

---

2 Types of Uncertainty

If we consider planning from the perspective of an agent A who is acting in an environment Ω in the context of a group G of other agents, then uncertainty can occur at several points:

State Uncertainty: The agent A may be uncertain about the actual state σ of the world H at time t. This uncertainty may include *temporal uncertainty* where the agent does not know the exact time. The agent may be uncertain about what other agents know about the world. By world H we mean the physical world and its events.

Action Uncertainty: The agent A may be uncertain about the consequences of an action. This uncertainty may have different causes. There may be *inherent action uncertainty* where the agent is uncertain about the consequences of an action because the world itself is indeterministic. State uncertainty may also result in action uncertainty because an action's consequences will normally depend upon the given state of the world. If the state of the world is not fully known, then the state following the action cannot be determined in advance. Finally, action uncertainty may also be due to a multi-agent setting. In a multi-agent social world a given agent's actions will never fully determine the next state, because this state is dependent on what the other agents do as well. Only control knowledge about the other agent's plan states, can reduce this kind of *socially induced action uncertainty*.

Plan Uncertainty: There are two cases to consider, single agent plan uncertainty and multi-agent plan uncertainty. In the case of *single agent plan uncertainty*, an agent A may be uncertain about the actions and plans that he A or another agent B intends to execute. Thus, A may know he intends to execute action a_1 as well as a_2 or a_3, but he may not know if he will do a_2 or a_3. This sort of uncertainty may hold for plans as well. Note, plan uncertainty differs from action uncertainty, for an agent may be certain about the consequences of each action but still not know which action he will perform. Similarly, an agent may know he will perform an action, such as going to the bank, but not know fully the consequences of that action.

In the case of *multi-agent plan uncertainty*, an agent A may also be uncertain about the plans of a group of agents. Since the group may include the agent himself, the agent may be uncertain about the plans of his group. Both single agent plan uncertainty and group plan uncertainty are a special case of plan uncertainty. With *plan uncertainty* the agent is uncertain about either his own plans or the plans of others or both.

Plan Consequence Uncertainty: An agent may be uncertain of the consequences of following a plan by self or others. This may be uncertainty about the consequences of an individual plan or the consequences of the plans of a set of agents. Like with action consequence uncertainty, state uncertainty may generate plan consequence uncertainty. Note, plan consequence uncertainty may hold even when there is no uncertainty about the consequences of individual actions. For the agent may know the consequences of each of his actions, and still not be able to compute the outcome of a plan.

Plan uncertainty is not always a bad thing. Indeed, having a *partial plan* is tantamount to having a well circumscribed plan uncertainty. Often an agent may not need or be able to have a total representation of what he intents to do. Instead, a partial plan may be sufficient. So too he need not have perfect information about the intentions (plans) of the group, as long as he has the information relevant to his planning for his goals. Furthermore, he may only be interested in the consequences that are relevant to his goals and interests.

States of Information and Uncertainty: Information and uncertainty are two sides of the same coin. For each of the above types of uncertainty (state, action, plan, etc.), an agent may be in two basic kinds of *states* of uncertainty or information. We will say an agent is in a *state of imperfect information* or, simply, the agent has *imperfect information* about the world, the consequences of an action, his own plans or the plans of others, or the consequences of a plan or set of plans, if that agent has state uncertainty, action uncertainty, plan uncertainty, or plan consequence uncertainty, respectively. Otherwise, the agent has *perfect information* about state, action consequences, or plans.

An agent in a state of imperfect information may either have some information or no information.

To say an agent has *total uncertainty* is equivalent to saying the agent has no information. If the agent has perfect information of some kind, it is equivalent to saying the agent has no uncertainty of the kind in question. Thus, we get the following equivalences: *No Information $\iff$ Total Uncertainty, Partial Information $\iff$ Partial Uncertainty, Perfect Information $\iff$ No Uncertainty.* A minimal requirement of any theory of information and uncertainty is that it be able to define and distinguish perfect information (no uncertainty), from imperfect information (partial uncertainty), and no information (total uncertainty). In what follows we will talk either of uncertainty or information depending which side of the coin we want to emphasize.

Next, we will formally define these different types of information and uncertainty by defining the different kinds of states of information and uncertainty of agents. This will make possible the investigation of the precise interrelationships between these types of uncertainty and information.

3 State Uncertainty

3.1 Possible Situations Over Time

Let Ψ be the set of time instants ordered by a relation $<$. Let TP be the set of time periods over Ψ. We will use t to represent instants and τ to represent time periods. Let s be a situation at a given instant. A situation is a partial representation of the state of the world [Barwise and Perry 83]. Let Sit be the set of all possible situations. An *event e* is a partial function from the set of times into the set of possible situations, $e : \Psi \to Sit$. Let EVENTS be the set of all possible events.

Let a *world state* σ be a total description of the state of the world at a given instant. Hence a world state will be a totally defined situation. Let Σ be a set of states. A *(total) history H* is a function from Ψ into Σ. A history is thus a series of complete situations over the time period Ψ. We will also refer to histories as possible worlds, possible past and futures, or as world lines. Let Ω be the set of all total histories each indexed by Ψ. If $H \in \Omega$, then let H_t be the value of the function H at $t \in \Psi$. H_t represents the state of the world H at time t. Ω then represents the set of all possible changes the system can undergo given the constraint that these changes are allowed by the rules or laws governing the system. A given history H *realizes* an event e over period $\tau \in TP$ iff $Domain(e) = \tau$ and $\forall t \in Domain(e), e_t \subseteq H_t$.

A *partial history H^t* of H is a partial function from Ψ into Σ such that $H^t_{t_0} = H_{t_0}$ if $t_0 \leq t$ and undefined if $t < t_0$. $V(\Omega)$ represents the class of all partial histories in Ω.

3.2 Information States

State information is that which reduces state uncertainty. By state information we mean information about the state of the world. For example, the state of the cards in a game of cards or the location of a robot in a room at a particular point in time gives state information. We distinguish it from strategic information which gives information about agent plans and intentions.

An information set or I-set on Ω is a nonempty class I of partial histories in Ω such that for any t, $t' \in \Psi$ and any $H \in \Omega$, if $H^t \in I$ and $H^{t'} \in I$ then $t = t'$. We will use the letter I, J with and without superscripts to denote information sets. For a given agent A the information set I_A represents the information state of the agent at some time in a given world. If I is any information set on Ω, let I^* be the class of worlds intersected by I. I^* is the set of histories allowed by the information I. $I^* =_{df} \{H : H \in \Omega$ and there is a $t \in \Psi$ such that $H^t \in I\}$. With each information set I we associate a set of alternatives $Alt(I)$. Alternatives are the choices available to the agent given the information I. Note, the alternatives leaving an information set are different from the possibilities H^t in the information set. Let INF be the class of all possible information states.

Information sets have an interesting property, which we call the *Entropy Principle*: The information available to an agent is inversely related to the number of possibilities in the information set. A corollary principle is the *Principle of Possibility Reduction PPR* which also holds for information sets: The more information becomes available the fewer the possibilities. To illustrate this principle consider an example: Mary, who is playing cards with Joe, knows Joe has the Queen of Hearts ($Q\heartsuit$), but she does not know if Joe has the King of Hearts ($K\heartsuit$) or the Jack of Spades ($J\spadesuit$). Mary's information state $I_1 = \{\sigma_1, \sigma_2\}$ is one where she does not know if Joe's hand is in state $\sigma_1 = <Q\heartsuit, J\spadesuit>$ or in state $\sigma_2 = <Q\heartsuit, K\heartsuit>$. The information that Joe has the King of Hearts reduces the information set I_1 (by the possibility reduction principle) to the information state $I_2 = \{\sigma_2\}$ where Mary knows with certainty (has perfect information) that Joe has the hand $\sigma_2 = <Q\heartsuit, K\heartsuit>$. Note, here information sets consist of states σ which are partial histories that are one instant of time in length (see [Werner 91] for further discussion about these and other principles.) Starting from very similar intuitions, a complementary approach to state information in planning is taken by Steel [Steel 91].

3.3 Temporal Uncertainty

Let $Time(I_A) = \tau$ be the time period specified by the information state I. It is the temporal information given by I. An information set I is *straight* if for any H, $K \in \Omega$, if $H^t \in I$ and $K^{t'} \in I$ then $t = t'$. An information set that is not straight will be said to be *slanted*. Straight information sets give perfect temporal information about the $Time(I)$ because any two partial histories in I pick out the same unique present time t. Slanted information sets give imperfect information about time. Formally, this means that for two partial histories H^t and $K^{t'}$ their present times t and t' may differ.

An information set is *thin* if $H^t \in I$ and $H^{t'} \in I$ then $t = t'$. Intuitively, this means that the for a given history H the agent has no uncertainty about time. In effect, perfect information about the history and state of the world gives the agent perfect information about time. The general restriction on information sets is that they are thin. But, one could imagine situations where the agent is uncertain about the time of the world even though he knows exactly what has occurred up to his range of uncertainty. He just does not know if he is in the future or in the past relative to his temporal uncertainty. This situation may hold if the world can have two successive states that are absolutely identical. The only difference is the time. An example might be an agent who sits passively in a room without a clock and who looses track of the time.

3.4 Information Conditions

The following is used to represent all possible information conditions of a given agent:

An *information ensemble* for Ω is a class Ξ of information sets on Ω such that the following conditions hold:

1. For any $H^t \in V(\Omega)$, there is an information set $I \in \Xi$ such that $H^t \in I$.

2. For any I, $J \in \Xi$, if $I \neq J$ then $I \cap J = \Lambda$, the null set.

We will use the symbols Ξ, Ξ' to denote information ensembles.

It follows immediately from the definition, that if Ξ is any ensemble for Ω, then for any partial history $H^t \in V(\Omega)$, there is a unique information set I in Ξ such that $H^t \in I$. Let this unique information set be denoted by $I(H^t)$. Let the *information history* $I(H)$ be a function from Ψ to Ξ where $I(H)(t) = I(H)_t =_{df} I(H^t)$ for each $t \in \Psi$.

An information set $I(H^t)$ represents the information available to an agent in the world H at time t. $I(H)$ represents the changing information conditions in H. An information ensemble Ξ then gives the information conditions for an observer for all possible developments of the given system. We interpret an ensemble as relativized to an observer-agent. The information conditions for n agents are then given by n information ensembles $\Xi_1, ..., \Xi_n$.

3.5 Nondiminishing Information

Let Ξ be any ensemble for Ω , then there is *nondiminishing information* in Ξ if for all $H \in \Omega$ and all $t, t' \in \Psi$, if $t \leq t'$ then $I(H^{t'})^* \subseteq I(H^t)^*$. If there is nondiminishing information in Ξ, we call Ξ

an *NDI-ensemble.* An increase in size of an information set $I(H)$ represents a decrease in available information. By insuring that the information set $I(H)$ does not expand in the future, the condition of nondiminishing information guarantees that no information is lost once it is stored.

3.6 Perfect State Information

The condition of nondiminishing information is the weakest information condition one can place on an ensemble and still have no loss of stored information. We now define the strongest condition one can place on the information.

Let Ξ be any ensemble for Ω, then there is *perfect state information* in Ξ if for each $I \in \Xi$, I is a unit set, i.e., if $\forall v, v_1 \in V(\Omega)$, if $v \in I$ and $v_1 \in I$ then $v = v_1$.

A decrease in the size of the information set represents an increase of information. When $I(H^t)$ is a unit set for some $H \in \Omega$, the observer has total knowledge of the history of the system up to and including the time t. Chess and checkers are examples of games with perfect information; most card games are games of imperfect information.

3.7 Definition of an Information Relation

The information conditions of an agent generate a Kripke like accessibility relation with the difference that it is a dynamic relation that varies with time and information. Given an ensemble Ξ for Ω, the variable *information relation* I^Ξ generated by Ξ is defined as follows: For any $H, K \in \Omega$ and any $t \in \Psi, HI_t^\Xi K$ iff $K \in I(H^t)^*$.

Intuitively, I^Ξ is a relation that varies with time. $HI_t^\Xi K$ says that K is a possible outcome of H given the information available in H at time t. K is an associated world of H, but need not be accessible to H in the sense of being an actual possibility. K may only appear to be possible because of the limited information available in H. We can abstract away from the reference to the information ensemble Ξ and state information conditions as properties of a temporal accessibility relation [Werner 88].

4 Action Uncertainty

4.1 Action Types

An action is a type of event. At the lowest level we have *token actions* that are sets of objects with properties and relations varying in time with a distinguished object called the agent. They are partial situations over time. An *action type* **a** is then a class of such token actions. A token action a is *realized* in a world H iff $a \subseteq H$. An action type **a** is *realized* in a world H iff for some token $a \in$ **a**, a is realized in H. With an action and an agent and given situation we associate a set of possible consequence events. An action type's uncertainty will be the union of all the possible consequences of each of its possible token actions.

4.2 Action Uncertainty from Indeterminism

In an indeterministic universe multiple possible consequences may be an objective feature of an action. But there is also a subjective aspect that results from the lack of information the agent has about the effects of the action given his computational limitations. This set of possible consequences represents one type of subjective action consequence uncertainty.

4.3 Action Uncertainty from State Uncertainty

However, even if we assume a deterministic universe, and no subjective uncertainty about an action's consequences for a given state, the agent may still be uncertain about the action's consequences since his information state I may not tell the agent his exact state in the world. And, since the action's effects depend on the given state, the agent will not know all the consequences of his action. This is represented formally by the fact that an alternative leaving an information set I is a whole set of token actions, one for each possible state of the world given the information I.

4.4 Multi-Agent Action Uncertainty

Socially induced action uncertainty is a natural part of our theory. For in a multi-agent world the state is determined only after all agents have made some choice. The do-nothing or null choice being, of course, always one of the options available to an agent. Formally, any given pure agent strategy π_A will not have a unique outcome in a multi-agent social world. Indeed, the more agents the less is the result of π_A determined.

4.5 The Interaction of Simultaneous Actions

Related to this point is the problem of simultaneous actions. Two or more agents will, in general, be acting simultaneously, all of the time, if we consider the null action as an action. An action's total effects will not be determined without knowledge of the actions of the other agents. Since an action can be viewed as a function from states to states, and since an information state is just a set of historic states, an action will take an information state to a new information state. In this sense, we can view an action a as a strategy, namely, the constant strategy that always picks the same action a. But, once we have made this generalization, actions of a given agent and of multiple agents can interact just like strategies (see below). This leads to a coherent account of actions and strategies as well as an account of the interaction of simultaneous actions. Given two actions a and b and their corresponding action-strategies π_a and π_b then their interaction is given by $\pi_a^* \cap \pi_b^*$.

5 Plan Uncertainty

5.1 Conceptual Foundations

An agent need not know everything he will do in advance. So too most of our plans for the future are only partial, subject to revision and default. Plans only guide our actions but do not determine them in all detail. This is consistent with the agent being a robot, a deterministic machine. The agent actions are ultimately determined by a *control structure* CS, or, viewed dynamically, a control process CP. The control structure CS consists of flexible (programmable, transformable) parts which may function analogous to distributed programs, and less flexible parts which are "hard-wired" (less easily transformable). These programs need not be explicit and their form may be quite different than what we know of programs today.

The control structure CS is the ultimate structure that governs a process that determines the agent's actions. For all we know its specification may require a hypertheory based on global plans, tactical strategies, low level reflexes, neural nets or even molecular processes. The low level control structure CS is a theoretical construct, a way of referring to and summing up all the internal influences on the agent's actions. The selection of action is, of course, dependent on the state of the world including the agent's state.

For any given information state I of the agent, the control structure CS generates an action response (including the do-nothing response). It follows that this low level control structure CS is associated with a pure strategy π_{CS} that indicates the effects of CS in terms of the agent's actions in the world. Let us refer to π_{CS} as the agent's *actual control strategy*. The agent's control structure CS is in part specified and determined by the agent's high level plans and intentions S. Ultimately, if the agent's plan state S and the agent's control state CS are to be coherent, S must be compiled (interpreted, translated) into CS.

Formally, we will define the agent A's *plan state* S_A as a class of pure strategies π. Any class of strategies S generates a unique partial strategy Π_S and any partial strategy Π generates a unique class of strategies S (see [Werner 91]). Thus, an agent's plan state S can be defined as a partial strategy or as a class of pure strategies. The plan state S if it is coherent with the control structure CS must be such that $\pi^*_{CS} \subseteq S^*$. The star operator $*$ denotes the set of possible histories (past, present, and future) allowed by the strategy or plan state. In other words, if the plan state is correct, then the consequences of the agent's actual control strategy π_{CS} must be contained within what is allowed by the agent's plan state S.

Since the agent does not know his control structure CS, he never has perfect information about his actual control strategy π_{CS}. But if his plan information S is correct then $\pi_{CS} \in S$. And, if this is so, we can prove that the agent's actions will cohere with his plans.

Just as state information reduces the agent's state uncertainty, so strategic information reduces the agent's plan uncertainty. An agent's plan state gives information and describes the uncertainty about the agent's plans.

5.2   Strategic Information

In order to formally define plan uncertainty, we need some formal preliminaries. A *pure strategy* π is a function from information sets I in INF to the alternatives at I. Thus, $\pi(I) \in Alt(I)$. $STRAT$ is the set of all possible strategies. If π is a pure strategy, let π^* be those histories H in Ω that are compatible with that strategy. We refer to the class X^* generated by the star operator $*$ on X as the potential of X. π^* is then the potential of a strategy π and consists of all those possible histories that are not excluded by the strategy π, i.e., $\pi^* =_{df} \{H : H \in \pi_A(I), \forall I \in \Xi_A(H)\}$ where $\Xi_A(H) =_{df} \{I : I \in \Xi_A \text{ and } \exists t \in \Psi, H^t \in I\}$.

Since, action occurs in the context of information I possessed by the agent, let $\pi^*[I]$ be the set of worlds allowed by the strategy π given the information I. Thus, $\pi^*[I] =_{df} \pi^* \cap I^*$.

5.3   Single Agent Plan Uncertainty

5.3.1   Given Perfect State Information

Recall when A has perfect information his information sets I are unit sets of the form $I(H^t) = \{H^t\}$. Given perfect information we need to describe the agent's plan state S_A for each of A's possible information states $I = \{H^t\}$, or, more simply, for each state H^t.

We describe an agent A's partial plans by a class of strategies S_A that govern that agent's actions. Any strategy π in S_A is one of the agent's possible strategies that may be guiding his actions. Analogous to information sets, if π is not in S_A, then it is known π is not guiding A's actions. We refer to $S_A(H^t)$ as the *plan state* of agent A at time t in the world H. More formally:

Let $STRAT_A$ be the set of all possible strategies of agent A. For each $H^t \in V(\Omega)$, let $S_A(H^t) \subseteq STRAT_A$. $S_A(H^t)$ is the set of A's possible strategies that are guiding A's actions at time t in the world H. $S_A(H^t)^* =_{df} \cup_{\pi \in S_A(H^t)} \pi^*$ describes the potential worlds, past, present and future, given strategic information S_A in the world H at time t. $S_A(H)$ is the *plan history* of the agent A. It describes the changing plan states in the world H.

$S_A^B(H^t) \subseteq STRAT_B$ is the strategic information that agent A has about agent B's plans in the world H at the time t. $S_B(H^t) \subseteq S_A^B(H^t)$ when A's strategic information is correct.

$S_A^B(H^t)^* =_{df} \cup_{\pi \in S_A^B(H^t)} \pi^*$ is the set of worlds that are possible given what agent A knows about B's plans in the world H at time t. Thus, $S_A^B(H^t)$ and $S_A^B(H^t)^*$ are two ways of representing A's strategic information about B's plans given there is perfect information about the state of the world up to time t.

84

5.3.2 Given Imperfect State Information

When an agent A has imperfect state information, we need to extend the above definitions of knowledge about plan states. Let $S_A(I) =_{df} \cup_{H^t \in I} S_A(H^t)$. This represents A's plan state given the partial state information I. Since each world state $H^t \in I$ is indistinguishable for A, each plan state $S_A(H^t)$ is identical for each state H^t in I. Hence, $S_A(I_A) = S_A(H^t)$ for H^t in I_A.

For A's strategic information about other agent's plan states, A may be able to distinguish B's plan states over different world states I^t in I. Let $S_A^B(I) =_{df} \cup_{H^t \in I} S_A^B(H^t)$. Then $S_A^B(I_A(H^t))$ represents A's strategic information about B's plans relative to A's state information $I_A(H^t)$.

$S_A^B(I_A(H^t))^* =_{df} \cup_{\pi \in S_A^B(I(H^t))} \pi^*$ describes the potential worlds (past and future) that are possible given agent A's strategic information about B's plans given A has imperfect state information about the world at time t.

5.4 Multi-Agent Plan Uncertainty

5.4.1 Given Perfect State Information

In order for an agent to determine what he can do, the agent must be able to represent the plans not just of other individual agents, but of whole groups of agents. Let Ag be a group of agents, $Ag = \{1, ..., n\}$. Then, $S_A^{Ag}(H^t) =_{df} \{S_A^i(H^t)\}_{i \in Ag} = \{< 1, S_A^1(H^t) >, ..., < n, S_A^n(H^t) >\}$. This represents the strategic knowledge that agent A has about the plans of other agents Ag in the world H at time t. It is the strategic information that A has given he has perfect information about the state of the world. The potential $S_A^{Ag}(H^t)^* =_{df} \{S_A^{Ag}(H^t)\}^* =_{df} \cap_{i \in Ag} S_A^i(H^t)^*$. Note, we take the set intersection of the potential strategy classes of the individual agents, because those are the worlds possible given the combined plans of the agents in Ag.

5.4.2 Given Imperfect State Information

The *plan state* $S_{Ag}(I_{Ag}(H^t))$ of a group of agents Ag given imperfect information $I_{Ag}(H^t) = \{I_1(H^t), ..., I_n(H^t)\}$ is defined as follows: $S_{Ag}(I_{Ag}(H^t)) = \{S_1(I_1(H^t)), ..., S_n(I_n(H^t))\}$. Here the potential $S_{Ag}(I_{Ag}(H^t))^* =_{df} \cap_{i \in Ag} S_i(I_i(H^t))^*$ is the set of possibilities allowed by the plan state S_{Ag} of the group given the state information I_{Ag} of the group.

To define strategic information an agent A has a group's plans given his imperfect state information we proceed as follows:

$S_A^{Ag}(I_A(H^t)) =_{df} \{S_A^i(I_A(H^t))\}_{i \in Ag} = \{< 1, S_A^1(I_A(H^t)) >, ..., < n, S_A^n(I_A(H^t)) >\}$. $S_A^{Ag}(I_A(H^t))$ describes agent A's information about the plans of all other agents given state information I in the world H at time t.

The potential $S_A^{Ag}(I_A(H^t))^* =_{df} \{S_A^{Ag}(I_A(H^t))\}^* =_{df} \cap_{i \in Ag} S_A^i(I_A(H^t))^*$. $S_A^{Ag}(I_A(H^t))^*$ represents the set of pasts, presents, and futures that are possible given what agent A knows about the plans S_A^{Ag} of the other agents Ag relative to A's state information I_A in the world H at time t. Intuitively, it describes the effects of plans of the other agents given the available information at the time t in the world H.

6 Plan Consequence Uncertainty

With any partial or total strategy Π we associate, relative to an agent A with information state I_A, a set Π^* of possible worlds that are possible consequences of the strategy. These are the actually possible consequence worlds of the strategy given the information available to the agent. An agent will in general not be able to compute Π^*. Instead the agent will associate expected consequences (a class of possible events) with the strategy. These expectations generate a set of possible futures $C_{A,I}(\Pi)$ thought possible by the agent A relative to information I. We say the agent's expectations for Π are *correct* iff $\Pi^* \subseteq C_{A,I}(\Pi)$. If an agent does not know the exact consequences of a strategy, his assessment is correct if it does not contradict the actual possible consequences of the strategy.

7 The Entropy of Plans and Organizations

Fascinating is the thought of being able to give a measure of the uncertainty of control in a multi-agent system. Put differently, can we come up with a measure of the control information in a multi-agent organization? Can we come up with measures of the entropy of an organization? We now take some preliminary steps that take us in the direction of measuring the entropy of multi-agent systems.

Beyond defining state uncertainty, we have also been able to define control uncertainty formally and explicitly. Historically, a formal account of state uncertainty made a formal definition of the *entropy* of a system possible. Thus, given a set of states $\sigma \in I$ and a probability distribution p over I we can define the entropy of I to be $H(I) = -\sum_{\sigma \in I} p(\sigma) \log p(\sigma)$. This definition was, in its essence, first given by Boltzmann in his statistical foundations of thermodynamics [Khinchin 49] and later by many others including Shannon [Shannon 48] in his mathematical theory of communication. Without probabilities the entropy is simply the log of the magnitude of the set I.

7.1 Control Entropy

Because, we have constructed a formal definition of plan or control uncertainty, we can now also give an analogous definition of *control entropy*:

$$H(S) = -\sum_{\pi \in S} p(\pi) \log p(\pi)$$

where $p(\pi)$ is the probability that the agent is following the strategy π and S is the control information of the agent[1]. This gives a mathematical measure of the control uncertainty of an agent. Alternatively, it gives a measure of the *control information content* if that control uncertainty were removed. To distinguish the new concept of control entropy from the traditional notion of entropy, we call the former *control entropy* (also, *plan entropy*) and the latter *state entropy* since it is concerned with measuring state uncertainty or, positively, the state information content if that uncertainty is removed. The plan state S may be for a single agent or for a whole multi-agent system.

7.2 Conditional Control Entropy

Given the definition of control entropy we can define other concepts concerning control information that are analogous to some of the traditional concepts in Shannon's communication theory. Thus, given two agents A and B[2], with plan states S_A and S_B, the *conditional control entropy* is defined as:

$$H_{S_A}(S_B) = \sum_{\pi \in S_A} p(\pi) H_\pi(S_B)$$

where

$$H_\pi(S_B) = -\sum_{\theta \in S_B} p_\pi(\theta) \log p_\pi(\theta)$$

where $p_\pi(\theta)$ is the conditional probability that B has plan θ when A has plan π. Expressed in terms of control information $H_A(B)$ indicates how much control information is contained on the average in the partial plan state S_B given it is known that agent A is following plan state S_A.

---

[1] The strategic information or plan state S is not to be confused with the "S" in the Boltzmann formula for state entropy: $S = k \ln P$ where P is the thermodynamic probability of the system being in a given state and k is the Boltzmann constant. Furthermore, it should be obvious from the context that the notation $H()$ for entropy and the notation H for world history are two very different things.

[2] It should be clear from the above that these may be groups as well.

7.3 Strategic Entropy Due to Multi-Agent Side Effects

We have already seen above that actions and strategies, in the context of a social world of other agents, are not fully determined. We can actually measure the entropy of a strategy due to multi-agent side effects.

$$H(\pi_A) = - \sum_{K \in \pi^*} p(K) \log p(K)$$

where π_A is a strategy of agent A and $p(K)$ is the probability of the future world K given the strategy π_A. This measures the uncertainty of the strategy given no information about the strategies of the other agents. The relations between state entropy, plan entropy and strategic entropy will be the subject of another paper.

7.4 Fuzzy Plan States

If we add a probability distribution over the strategies in a plan state S where, as usual, $\sum_{\pi \in S} p(\pi) = 1$, and where the probability $p(\pi)$ indicates the probability that a strategy π will be followed, then we can construct *restricted fuzzy plan states* μ_S. We let p represent degree of membership in the fuzzy set by letting

$$\mu_S(\pi) = \begin{cases} p(\pi) & \text{if } \pi \in S \\ 0 & \text{otherwise} \end{cases}$$

When π is not in S, then it is also not in the fuzzy plan state μ_S.

More generally, a *fuzzy plan state* or *fuzzy control state* is defined over the universe of possible strategies $STRAT_A$ of an agent A:

$$\mu_S(\pi) \in [0,1] \text{ for } \pi \in STRAT_A$$

It is a function that assigns a probability (in the closed interval $[0,1]$) of membership to any strategy π_A indicating the likelihood of its being in the fuzzy plan state of an agent A.

There are interesting relationships to what has been called *fuzzy control* [Mamdani 83]. In fuzzy control the system allows the use of partial control knowledge in terms of fuzzy rules to constrain the behavior of an agent. The result is often more efficient partially controlled action. The fuzzy control rules give a partial strategy for the system using probabilistic information. This amounts to giving a partial plan state S for the system together with associated probabilities for the pure (complete) strategies in S. What we have done is to give the notion of fuzzy control a precise foundation and a precise measure in terms of control entropy. The control entropy measures the degree of control uncertainty (fuzziness) in the agent or system.

8 The Language CANPLAN

To give some of the above concepts a focus, and a further application, we first define a tensed modal language that contains plan and can operators, and then, we give a semantics of this language in terms of the concepts developed above. A tensed modal language $CANPLAN$ contains, as primitive symbols: propositional variables $p, q, p_1, ...$; agent indices $A, B, A_1, ...$; group indices $Group, Group_1, ...$: the logical connectives $\neg$ (not), $\lor$ (or), tense operators F (It will be the case that...), P (It was the case that...) and modal operators $\Box_A$ (Given the information it is necessary for agent A that..., or, A has the information that ...), $\triangleright_A \alpha$ (Agent A intends, plans to α), $\triangleright_{Group} \alpha$ (The group $Group$ plans or intends to α), CAN_A (Agent A can achieve ...), $COCAN_A$ (Agent A can coordinate his actions with other agents to achieve ...), $COOPCAN_{Group} \alpha$ (A group of agents can cooperatively achieve ...). Formulas: The set of formulas of $CANPLAN$ is the smallest set meeting the following conditions: (1) Every propositional variable is a formula of $CANPLAN$; (2) If α and β are formulas of $CANPLAN$ then $\alpha \lor \beta$, $\neg \alpha$, $F\alpha$, $P\alpha$ and $\Box_A \alpha$, $\triangleright_A \alpha$, $\triangleright_{Group} \alpha$, $CAN_A \alpha$, $COCAN_A \alpha$, and $COOPCAN_{Group} \alpha$ are formulas of $CANPLAN$. $\Diamond_A$ (It is possible for A that ...) is defined in terms of the necessity operator, $\Diamond_A \alpha =_{df} \neg \Box_A \neg \alpha$. Material implication $\rightarrow$ is defined as usual: $\alpha \rightarrow \beta =_{df} \neg \alpha \vee \beta$.

We can express that "The group G plans to build the house" as $\rhd_G \theta$ where $\theta =$ "the group builds the house". $G =$ "the group". It says that relative to the joint interactions of the individual strategies of the agents in the group G, the house will be built. We can thus formalize a logic of single and multi-agent plan interactions. Furthermore, we can interpret statements of ability: Thus, in this language statements like "if agent A has the information that the table is in the room, then agent A can cooperate with B to move the table out of the room" can be expressed as $\Box_A \alpha \rightarrow COOPCAN_{A,B} F\beta$. This formula reads: "If A has the information that α then A and B can cooperatively achieve that it will be the case that β" where $\alpha =$ "the table is in the room" and $\beta =$ "A and B move the table out of the room".

9 Information-Plan-Based Semantics

An *information-plan-based model* Γ for a tensed modal language $CANPLAN$ is an ordered tuple $\Gamma = (\Sigma, (\Psi, <), \Omega, Ag, \Xi_i, S_i, \Phi)$ where Σ, $(\Psi, <)$, and Ω are defined as above, $Ag = \{1, ..., n\}$ is the set of agents, Ξ_i, $S_i = (\Xi_1, S_1, ..., \Xi_n, S_n)$ are the information and plan ensembles for agents $1, ..., n$ in Ag. Let Λ be the empty set. Φ is an evaluation function from the formulas of $CANPLAN$ onto $\{T, F\}$ defined as follows:

1. For propositional variables p of $CANPLAN$ and any $\sigma \in \Sigma$, $\Phi(p, \sigma) = \{^T_F$

2. If p is a propositional variable, $t \in \Psi$ and $H \in \Omega$ then $\Phi(p, t, H) = T$ iff $\Phi(p, H_t) = T$

   Given Φ is defined for formulas α and β of $CANPLAN$:

3. $\Phi(\neg \alpha, t, H) = T$ iff $\Phi(\alpha, t, H) = F$.

4. $\Phi(\alpha \vee \beta, t, H) = T$ iff $\Phi(\alpha, t, H) = T$ or $\Phi(\beta, t, H) = T$.

5. $\Phi(P\alpha, t, H) = T$ iff $\exists t_0 \in \Psi$ such that $t_0 < t$ and $\Phi(\alpha, t_0, H) = T$.

6. $\Phi(F\alpha, t, H) = T$ iff $\exists t' \in \Psi$ such that $t < t'$ and $\Phi(\alpha, t', H) = T$.

7. $\Phi(\Box_A \alpha, t, H) = T$ iff $\forall K \in \Omega$, if $H I_t^{\Xi} K$ then $\Phi(\alpha, t, K) = T$.

8. $\Phi(\rhd_A \alpha, t, H) = T$ iff $\forall K \in S_A(I_A(H^t))^*, \Phi(\alpha, t, K) = T$.

9. $\Phi(\rhd_{Group} \alpha, t, H) = T$ iff $\forall K \in S_{Group}(I_{Group}(H^t))^*, \Phi(\alpha, t, K) = T$.

10. $\Phi(CAN_A \alpha, t, H) = T$ iff $\exists \pi \in STRAT_A$ such that $\forall K \in \pi^*[I_A(H^t)], \Phi(\alpha, t, K) = T$.

11. $\Phi(COCAN_A \alpha, t, H) = T$ iff $\exists \pi \in STRAT_A$ such that $\pi^*[I_A(H^t)] \cap S_A^{Ag}(I_A(H^t))^* \neq \Lambda$ and $\forall K \in \pi^*[I_A(H^t)] \cap S_A^{Ag}(I_A(H^t))^*, \Phi(\alpha, t, K) = T$.

12. $\Phi(COOPCAN_{Group} \alpha, t, H) = T$ iff $\forall i \in Group, \exists \pi_i \in STRAT_i$ such that $\cap_{i \in Group} \pi_i^*[I_i(H^t)] \neq \Lambda$ and $\forall K \in \cap_{i \in Group} \pi_i^*[I_i(H^t)], \Phi(\alpha, t, K) = T$.

We read $\Phi(\alpha, t, H) = T$ as "α is true at time t in the world H". A formula α of a tensed modal language $CANPLAN$ is valid in an information-based model for $CANPLAN$ iff $\Phi(\alpha, t, H) = T$ for all $t \in \Psi$ and all $H \in \Omega$. Note, for simplicity we have let names of agents A, B and names of groups of agents, $Group$, in the language, stand for agents and groups in the semantics. Thus $A, B \in Ag$ and $Group \subseteq Ag$.

Remarks on the Semantics:

$\Box_A \alpha$ says that α is informationally necessary at time t in the world H iff relative to the information I available to the agent A at time t in the world-situation H, α holds in all worlds K that are possible given the information I. The operator in $\Box_A \alpha$ is information based. It can be read as an information relative necessity operator when read as "it is necessary that α given the information available to agent A" or directly as an information operator when read as "agent A has the information that α". On both readings it is a time dependent operator. See [Werner 89a] for more details on tensed modal logics. What is possible or necessary depends on the information conditions existing for the agent A at the given time t in the world H.

$\rhd_A \alpha$ states that relative to the agent's plan state S_A given his information I_A, the event described by α will take place in all worlds allowed by A's plan state. The plan state insures the event will happen. Analogous to COCAN below we can also define a notion of COPLANS where an agent's plan achieves α given the plan state of other agents.

$\rhd_{Group} \alpha$ says that the interactions of the plan states of the group are such that the social event α will be generated by the activity of the group if it follows the group plan state S_{Group}.

$CAN_A \alpha$ says A CAN α at time t in the world H iff A has a strategy π where α holds in all possible futures K that are allowed by the strategy π and the information I at time t in world H.

$COCAN_A \alpha$ says A cocan α at time t in the world H iff A has a strategy that satisfies two conditions: (1.) The strategy must be compatible with the plans S_A^{Ag} of the other agents (first conjunct) (2.) The strategy must fit with what A knows about the other agent's plans S_A^{Ag} so that the strategy plus the plans of the other agents together bring about α.

For the two agent case, $COOPCAN_{Group} \alpha$ says that A can cooperate with B at time t in the world H to achieve α iff A and B have nonconflicting strategies π_A and δ_B that together with the information available at time t in the world H, insure the outcome α. To realize $COOPCAN_{Group}$ inter-agent communication may be necessary since there may be more than one pair of optimal cooperative strategies for achieving α (see [Werner 89b]).

The logic of CAN extends the logic of ability in [Brown 88], because, unlike Brown, we include multiple agents, strategies, time and partial information of state and plans in the semantics. For details see [Werner 90].

10 Tensed Modal Logics

The mixed tensed modal systems resulting from axioms that correlate both tenses and modal operators, are of special interest because they cannot be generated by simply combining standard modal and tense logics. For example, the following schemata of a tensed modal language is valid in every model for the language when the attribute of having nondiminishing information holds of the information ensemble.

Monotonic Information Axiom for P and $\Box$: $P\Box_A \alpha \rightarrow \Box_A P\alpha$

The axiom reads "If it was necessary that α then it is necessary that α was the case." Or "If agent A had the information that α then A has the information that α was the case". It holds only for the case where the information is nondiminishing [Werner 89a]. Analogous to temporally indexed modal axioms [Werner 88], the axioms of tensed modal logics can be interpreted as informational principles that give constraints on the information states of an agent. For example, the above tensed modal axiom for P and $\Box$ is a partial monotonicity constraint. Informationally, it asserts that if an agent has had the information that α in the past, then the agent will continue to have the information that he had the information that α. Note, this is a weaker information condition than complete monotonicity, i.e., no information loss. For the agent may no longer have the information that α, if $\neg\Box\alpha$ holds. Yet, the agent will still have the information that it was the case that α, $P\alpha$, since the axiom implies $\Box P\alpha$ still holds.

Perfect Information Axiom for P and $\Box$: $\alpha \rightarrow \Box_A \alpha$

Note, there are restrictions on α, in particular, that it contain no future tenses. This axiom only holds if there is perfect information about the state of the world. As an informational principle it expresses exactly that: If some fact α is true of the present or a past state of the world then the agent has the information that α holds. It puts no constraints on the agent's uncertainty about the future.

A Plan-Can Axiom for $\triangleright$ and CAN: $\triangleright_A \alpha \rightarrow \text{CAN}_A \alpha$

This axiom relates plan states to ability. An agent may be able to do α without having α result from his plan state. For the existence of a strategy does not mean that the agent will constrain his plan state to follow that strategy. If, however, an agent has α guaranteed by his plan state, then the agent must be able to achieve α.

11 Conclusion

In distributed artificial intelligence communication of state information and plan information are essential for reducing state and plan uncertainty. The reduction of state and plan uncertainty is a necessary condition for multi-agent cooperation. Furthermore, the formal modelling of state and plan uncertainty is important for a deeper understanding of communication, cooperation, coordination, as well as cooperation algorithms. In this paper we hope we have gone further in the direction of providing a logical foundation for work in planning and distributed artificial intelligence. In addition we have extended the concept of entropy to control entropy and applied fuzzy set theory to give an account of fuzzy plan states. Control entropy may provide a measure of the entropy of organizations in their dynamic activity. Fuzzy plan states formalize the notion of fuzzy control.

References

[Barwise & Perry 83] Barwise, J., and Perry, J., *Situations and Attitudes*, Bradford Books/MIT Press, 1983.

[Brown 88] Brown, M.A., "On the Logic of Ability", *JOURNAL OF PHILOSOPHICAL LOGIC*, 17, pp. 1-26, 1988.

[Khinchin 49] Khinchin, A.I., *MATHEMATICAL FOUNDATIONS OF STATISTICAL MECHANICS*, Dover Publ., New York, 1949.

[Mamdani 83] Mamdani, E.H., "Process Control Using Fuzzy Logic", Designing for Human Computer Communication, Academic Press, London, 1983.

[Shannon 48] Shannon, C.E., "The Mathematical Theory of Communication", Bell Syst, Techn. Journ., vol 27, 379-423; 623-656, 1948.

[Steel 91] Steel, S., "Knowledge Subgoals in Plans", *European Workshop on Planning*, Advanced Proceedings, Sankt Augustine, F.R.G., 1991.

[Werner 88] Werner, E., "The Modal Logic of Games", WISBER Report B48, University of Hamburg, Hamburg, Germany 1988.

[Werner 89a] Werner, E., "Tensed Modal Logic", WISBER Report B49, University of Hamburg, Hamburg, Germany, 1989a.

[Werner 89b] Werner, E., "Cooperating Agents: A Unified Theory of Communication and Social Structure", *Distributed Artificial Intelligence, Vol. 2*, M. Huhns & L. Gasser (eds.), Morgan Kaufmann and Pitman Publishers, London, pp. 3-36, 1989b.

[Werner 90] Werner, E., "What Can Agents Do Together? A Semantics of Cooperative Ability", *ECAI-90, Proceedings of the 9th European Conference on Artificial Intelligence*, Stockholm, Sweden, Pitman Publishers, pp. 694-701, 1990.

[Werner 91] Werner, E., "A Unified View of Information, Intention, and Ability", *Decentralized AI, Vol. II*, Y. Demazeau & J-P. Muller (eds.), Elsevier Science Publishers (North Holland), forthcoming, 1991.

Activity Coordination via Multiagent and Distributed Planning

Frank v. Martial
Gesellschaft für Mathematik und Datenverarbeitung (GMD)
Institut für Angewandte Informationstechnik
Schloss Birlinghoven
D-5205 Sankt Augustin 1

Multiagent planning is a relatively new (since 1980) and promising research topic, which has recently attracted many researchers. This paper gives an introduction to planning in multiagent domains. In a multiagent planning approach to cooperation and coordination, agents form a multiagent plan that specifies their future actions and interactions. Traditional planning approaches in AI assume that there is only one planner which plans its own actions. Therefore, the applicability of these planners is very restricted when dealing with problems in dynamic, multiagent worlds.

We will identify the planning paradigms in multiagent domains, namely multiagent and distributed planning, compare single-agent planning with multi-agent planning, and point out the relevance of communication with respect to plan coordination. The last part of the talk will introduce the author's approach to plan coordination. The two key factors are a taxonomy of relationships which may hold between the plans of different agents and a communication framework which is suited for autonomous agents to exchange their plans and negotiate about them.

In diesem Papier wird eine Übersicht zum verteilten Planen gegeben. Ein verteilter oder multiagenter Planungsansatz zur Kooperation und Koordination versucht, die zukünftigen Aktionen und Interaktionen der Agenten möglichst genau festzulegen. Traditionelle Planungsansätze gehen im Gegensatz zum verteiltem Planen davon aus, daß es nur einen Planer gibt, der einen Plan für genau einen Akteur erzeugt. Sie sind daher nicht geeignet für mehragentige und dynamische Welten. Dieser Artikel gibt eine Übersicht der Planungsparadigmen in verteilten Systemen, vergleicht traditionelle KI-Planungsansätze mit verteiltem Planen, zeigt die Bedeutung von Kommunikation für Koordination auf, und erläutert potentielle Anwendungsfelder für verteiltes Planen. Im letzten Teil wird ein aktueller Koordinationsansatz vorgestellt. In diesem Ansatz werden Beziehungen, die zwischen den Aktionen der Pläne von unabhängigen Planern existieren können, verwendet, um "Koordiniertheit" in verteilten Systemen zu definieren. Kommunikationsprotokolle sollen den planenden Agenten ermöglichen, ihre Pläne auszutauschen und eine Koordination ihrer Pläne auszuhandeln.

0   Introduction

S. Vere writes on multiagent planning: "Another immensely difficult topic is the generation of plans for multiple sentient agents that may have to communicate and negotiate to achieve and preserve mutual and conflicting goals" in [Shapiro & Eckroth 88].

In a multiagent planning approach to cooperation, agents form a multiagent plan that specifies their future actions and interactions [Durfee, Lesser & Corkhill 89]. Coordinating agents by multi-agent plans is different from other approaches in that one or more agents possess a plan that indicates exactly what actions and interactions each agent will take for the duration of an activity. This differs from approaches such as contracting, in which nodes typically make pairwise agreements about how they will coordinate and where there is no complete view of network coordination presented.

Problems addressed. What basic DAI (*Distributed Artificial Intelligence*) problems are addressed by multiagent planning?

- *Task allocation*. Multiagent planning is one way of allocating particular tasks to particular agents. Other approaches to allocate tasks embrace market mechanisms [Malone 87, 88] [Fox 81], organizational roles and voting.

- *Achieving coordination*. Multiagent planning is a medium to achieve better coordination by aligning behavior of agents towards common goals, with explicit division of labor. Techniques such as centralized planning for multiple agents, plan reconciliation, distributed planning, organizational analysis, and appropriate control transfers are ways of helping to align the activities of agents by assigning tasks.

Overview. Next, we will introduce the basic terminology. Then we will present a taxonomy of planning styles, which also covers single-agent planning. Chapter 3 will explain the plan coordination problem. In Chapter 4, potential application domains are surveyed. Related work and some research directions in multiagent planning are the topics of the subsequent chapters. In the last chapter, a novel approach for the coordination of distributed planners will be outlined.

1   What are Multiagent and Distributed Planning?

A *multiagent plan* is a plan which has been generated for multiple executing agents [Bond & Gasser 88]. *Multiagent planning* is the process of creating a multiagent plan. An important aspect of multiagent planning is whether planning is done by a single agent or by several agents. In *centralized multiagent planning* there is one agent which generates plans for multiple agents. In *decentralized (distributed) multiagent planning* also the planning activities are divided among the agents. In future, we will refer to the latter form of planning as *distributed planning*.

We would like to be a little bit more precise about what we mean by "planning activities" concerning *distributed* planning. We do not want to speak of distributed planning if the individual agents only contribute goals which then will be planned for by a single agent. It is also not sufficient if agents just deliver their individual plans which then will be synchronized or reconciled by a central agency having the role of an arbiter. Distributed planning includes always that the agents are actively involved in the process of reaching a reconciliation. That means, that also negotiation is an inherent component of distributed planning, and hence negotiation and communication also belong to what we mean by "planning activities" concerning distributed planning. As a summary, planning activities embrace both classical planning activities (formulating a set of steps to bring about a desired state of affairs or to reach a goal, action refinements, checking preconditions for actions, etc.) as well as negotiation and communication. Negotiation has the function of binding commitments among agents.

This may be summarized in the slogan: **distributed planning = multiagent planning + communication**.

In multiagent planning, one or more agents have information about each agent's activities and can recognize and prevent the duplication of effort. Another objective is to detect and avoid inconsistencies before they can occur. Interactions between the separate activities of the agents must be identified, and any conflicts should be identified and fixed before the plans are executed. A multiagent plan dictates exactly what actions each agent should take and when.

In distributed planning, a single plan is produced by the cooperation of several agents. Each agent produces a subplan, but there may be conflicts among subplans that need to be reconciled.

Mutual plan construction is not well understood. It is confounded by disparities in goals and intentions, as well as disparities in world knowledge. All the problems of multiagent planning exist along with the problem of inconsistent world views due to distribution.

2   Single-agent vs. Multi-agent Planning

A taxonomy of the different kinds of planning is shown in *figure 1*. It also includes *single-agent planning* which is only applicable in domains with a single agent which plans and executes its own actions in a usually static domain, i.e. is based on the "closed world assumption".

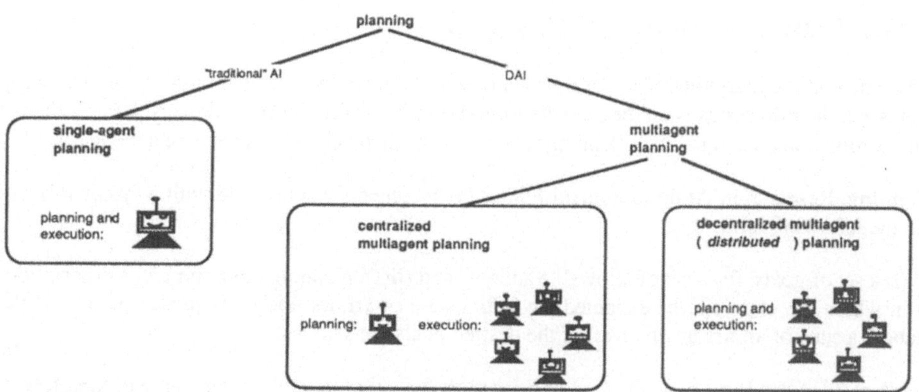

Figure 1: Planning categories

For the activities of several agents to be aligned using planning, interactions in the plans of different agents must be controlled. Plan interactions may involve incompatible states, incompatible order of steps, or competing resource requirements. A multiagent plan is built to avoid inconsistent or conflicting actions, and is typically used in agent networks to identify and plan around resource conflicts. Rather than risking incoherent and inconsistent decisions that agents might make using other approaches, multi-agent planning insists that agents plan out beforehand exactly how each will act and interact. Multiagent planning is one way of controlling these interactions.

The applicability of traditional single agent planners such as STRIPS [Fikes & Nilsson 71], NOAH [Sacerdoti 77], NONLIN [Tate 77], SIPE [Wilkins 84] is severely restricted in multiagent settings due to several reasons: (i) the world is assumed to be static and only affected by a single agent's actions; (ii) plans are constructed by one agent; (iii) tasks are usually carried out by one single agent; (iv) plans are concerned with prevention of conflicts, not with cooperation; (v) single-agent planners cannot reason about actions that the agent has no control over; (vi) there is no concept for concurrent activities; (vii) there is no cooperation and coordination between several agents; and (viii) communication does not occur.

Sometimes it is mistakenly understood that NOAH allows for concurrent and multiagent plans [Sacerdoti 75, 77]. In fact, NOAH simply allows for the representation of unordered actions during the intermediate stages of planning. This is not the same as representing concurrency: the final output of NOAH is always an ordered sequence of actions. Moreover, NOAH has no explicit representation for the actions of other agents (although this could conceivably be built in, as Corkhill has demonstrated [Corkhill 79]). Since NOAH cannot handle concurrency, general multiagent planning is clearly impossible.

Another problem which appears primarily in connection with, but is is not restricted to, single-agent planners is that plans are typically designed prior to, and distinct from, their execution. These plans have been constructed for a set of future conditions that are known in advance and are frozen. The implicit assumption is that the conditions for which a plan is being formed, usually called start state, will not change prior to execution. Even when it is assumed that the plans will be executed in single-agent environments, in which the only state changes are a result of the single agent's actions, it may be wrong to expect that the world stays fixed during an indefinitely long planning period. Even if the environment contains no other human or robot agents, nature often intrudes. As a consequence, these planners are only inadequately able to respond to changing environments, e.g. by replanning or plan adaption or interleaving planning and execution.

3 The Plan Coordination Problem

If we assume that the individual plans of the agents are given, i.e. the problem of *creating* individual plans is suppressed, then the focus is on the *coordination* of these existing individual plans. How is the problem of plan coordination related to other planning research in AI, namely planning and plan recognition?

AI Planning. Research in AI on (automatic) *planning* is generally concerned with ways of solving problems in the following form:

Given (i) a set of goals, (ii) a set of allowable actions, and (iii) a planning environment: a description of the world in which the plan is to be executed, an initial state of affairs. Find a sequence of actions that will bring about a state of affairs in which all of the desired goals are satisfied.

Problems of this form form were the first to be explored in automatic planning. We will therefore refer to them as *classical planning problems*. Classical AI planning can be described in a simplified form as: **planning**: $2^{goals} \longrightarrow 2^{actions}$.

Plan Recognition. Tightly related with the creation of plans is the recognition of plans [Kautz & Pednault 88]. A *plan recognition* problem consists of the following factors: (i) a set of allowable actions, (ii) a set of observed actions, and (iii) a plan recognition environment: descriptions of the world in which the observed actions were performed.

A solution of the plan recognition problem includes elements of the following: (i) a set of expected goals, (ii) a library of typical plans, and (iii) a preference ordering over the space of plans.

The most general goal of a plan recognition problem is to find an explanation of the observed actions in one or more plans in terms of one or more plans that can be attributed to an agent. In general only certain plans are acceptable explanations. Such a plan relates a typical pattern of actions to a goal that one may reasonably expect to arise in the current context. The process of inferring a plausible plan involves the use of heuristic assumptions and libraries of common plans. Most work on plan recognition has been empirical and experimental. The plan recognition in a simplified form is expressed as **plan recognition: $2^{actions}$ ——> 2^{goals}**.

Plan Coordination. Our concern is the problem of coordinating plans. The input for a plan coordination problem consists of several (partial) plans which have to be coordinated. In a plan coordination problem with distributed autonomous agents the actions belong to several planners and/or executors. Outcome of the coordination may be a synchronized set of actions. A simplified view of the coordination problem: **plan coordination: $2^{actions}$ ——> $2^{actions}$**.

The *plan coordination* problem is concerned with ways of solving problems with an *input* as follows: (i) a set of intended actions (= plans of autonomous agents); (ii) a description of the (state of the) world in which the plans are to be executed (the coordination environment); (iii) operations to modify actions. Output is a set of intended actions (= plans of autonomous agents) which is coordinated.

In order to coordinate, agents must be able to perform these principle operations: (i) communicate, i.e. send and receive messages, (ii) reason about plan interferences, (iii) develop solutions for coordination, (iv) modify plans.

4   Applications Areas

Potential application domains for plan coordination are populated by intelligent, autonomous agents. The agents may be both human beings or automated agents. There is an inherent distribution of agents, activities and resources. Some sort of cooperative problem solving is required.

Some application areas are, (see also [Durfee et al. 89]):

- *Distributed Interpretation.* Distributed interpretation applications require the integration and analysis of distributed data to generate a (potentially distributed) semantic model of the data. The most prominent artificial domain is the distributed sensor network, called DVMT [Lesser & Corkhill 83].

- *Distributed Planning and Control.* Distributed planning and control applications involve developing and coordinating the actions of a number of distributed effector agents to perform some desired task. Example application domains include distributed air-traffic control [Thorndyke et al. 81], cooperating robots, remotely piloted vehicles [Steeb et al. 81], distributed process control in manufacturing [Paranuk 85; Hynynen 88], and resource allocation control in a long-haul communication network [Adler et al. 89]. Usually, data is inherently distributed among agents, in this case because each has its own local planning database, capabilities and view of the world state.

- *Cooperating Expert Systems.* One means of scaling expert systems technology to more complex and encompassing problem domains is to develop cooperative interaction mechanisms that allow multiple experts systems to work together to solve a common problem. Illustrative situations include controlling an autonomous vehicle (with expert systems for system status, mission planning, navigation, situation assessment, and piloting) or negotiation among expert systems of two corporations to decide price and/or delivery time on a major purchase.

Computer-Supported Cooperative Work (CSCW). Coined by Irene Greif in 1984, the phrase "computer-supported cooperative work" was intended to delineate a new field of research focused on the role of the computer in group work [Greif 88]. Computer technology promises to provide people with more and better information for making decisions. However, unless the computers also assist people by filtering the information and focussing attention on relevant information, the amount of information can become overwhelming [Chang 87; Malone 88]. By building AI systems that have coordination knowledge we can remove some of the burden from people. Example domains where this is important include intelligent command and control systems and multiuser project coordination [Croft & Lefkowitz 87, 88; Nirenburg & Lesser 86; Sathi et al. 86] and distributed project planning [Sathi & Fox 89].

5 Related Work

We will only consider models with sophisticated intelligent, preferably autonomous, agents and no models where intelligent behavior is produced by the cooperation of relatively simple computational agents. In multiagent planning domains, it makes sense to differentiate between planning, executing and coordinating agents.

Very decisive is the differentiation between research in centralized multiagent and distributed planning. Work on *Centralized Multiagent Planning* includes [Cammarata et al. 83; Dean 86a, 86b; Georgeff 83, 84, 86; Katz & Rosenschein 89; Konolige & Nilsson 80; Lansky 87; Morgenstern 87; Pelavin 88; Rosenschein 82; Stuart 85, 88; Wilinsky 83]; work on *Distributed Planning* includes [Conry, Meyer & Lesser 86; Corkhill 79; Durfee 88; Durfee & Lesser 87; Grosz 90; Koo 88; Kuwabara & Lesser 89; Rosenschein 86; Rosenschein & Genesereth 85; Zlotkin & Rosenschein 89, 90].

Control distribution. The question of how control is distributed is tightly connected with how autonomous the agents are. The tendency in the work surveyed is to have autonomous and not dependent agents, which are centrally controlled. The controversy between control and independence is equivalent to the differentiation between multiagent and distributed planning.

Representation of actions and plans. Generating multiagent plans requires reasoning about how actions of different agents may interfere with one another, and thus requires explicit representations of parallel actions.

How actions and plans are represented is not only a problem in itself, but has a crucial impact on the whole coordination model. The representation of actions and plans is concerned with how actions are represented, what is a plan, and what is the state of the world.

We can differentiate between two general kinds of action representation leading to two different planning paradigms, the *state-based* and the *event-based planning paradigm*. The state-based paradigm has its origin in McCarthy's situation calculus [McCarthy & Hayes 69] and is exemplified in planning systems such as STRIPS [Fikes & Nilsson 71] and NOAH [Sacerdoti 77]. Corkhill [1979] uses NOAH type of plans. Planners using STRIPS type (state-based) of plans have serious difficulties to handle dynamic domains and simultaneous actions. This is mainly due to the so-called STRIPS assumption which handles the frame problem by assuming that an action only affects a small part of the world, leaving the rest of the world unchanged. In particular, it is not possible to capture what happens during the execution of an action.

Some researchers have approximated concurrent activity by using an interleaving approximation [Georgeff 83, 84; Pednault 87]. Other researchers have developed extensions of the STRIPS representation to deal with multiagent planning problems [Katz & Rosenschein 89; Konolige & Nilsson 80; Stuart 85]. Researchers supporting a state-based planning paradigm are [Georgeff 83, 84; Pednault 87; Zlotkin & Rosenschein 89, 90].

Several researchers have used an *event-oriented* domain description for multiagent planning [Lansky 87, Pelavin 88]. Also Hewitt's work on actor-based formalisms emphasizes an event based action model [Hewitt 77]. The event-based model is in contrast to the state-based approach, which is the primary object of most AI models. Typically, the world is viewed as a sequence of "states". For example, traditional planning systems maintain a description of world state as a set of atomic state formula. Change from one state to another is brought about by the occurrence of actions, i.e. domain actions or events are viewed as "state transformers". Within an event-based model, a notion of "state" is most naturally defined in terms of past activity: the state of the world at any point in time is merely a record of the events that have occurred and their interrelationships.

Time. Temporal information is crucial in multiagent domains and therefore should be taken care of in action and plan representations. Hence, an important aspect of a representation is whether and how time and temporal parameters are represented. In state-based planing models temporal aspects appear in the form of temporal precedence. In an approach which employs a PERT type representation of actions, e.g. [Dean 86a, 86b; Koo 88], absolute temporal values are given (for instance start and end time). Others use relative temporal expressions, e.g. by employing Allen's interval-based representation [Allen 84], to model time [Lansky 87, 88; Pelavin 88].

Resources. A notion of resources should be incorporated in every multiagent planning system. Often, resource requirements are an inherent part of tasks or plans. For many DAI researchers, resources mean the only concept for reasoning about how different activities interact. Regulating the use of resources is an important aspect —and often the only one considered— when working towards coherence and coordination. Not every approach has a concept for resources. But some explicitly handle resources and the resolution of conflicts between actions or agents competing for the same limited and sharable resources [Conry et al. 86; Dean 86; Kuwabara & Lesser 89; Martial 90a; Steeb et al. 81].

Point of synchronization. When are plans synchronized? Plan synchronization can be performed at several points. It can be done during problem decomposition [Corkhill 79]. It can be done during plan construction, by building smoothly interacting plans hierarchically [Corkhill 79], by aligning partial plans incrementally [Durfee & Lesser 87], or by reasoning about interactions and dependencies as a part of planning [Rosenschein 82]. It can also be done after plan construction [Georgeff 83]. The question of synchronizations points is tightly connected with the controversy of result formation in DAI systems, i.e. by synthesis or by decomposition.

6 Some Research Issues

In which areas of multiagent planning do we need more research? Issues for research in multiagent planning can be derived by looking at the deficiencies of existing approaches in this domain. A critique of existing coordination and multiagent planning approaches can be made from at least four standpoints: The crispness of the action and plan model (the representation of actions and plans), the variety of relations being considered, the flexibility in planning, and the way in which planning and negotiation are integrated. These points will be reflected in the following list.

Planning and communication. Centralized multiagent planning approaches do not consider aspects of communication and negotiation as part of the planning process. Although there has been done some work on centralized multiagent planning, there has been relatively little work involved in connecting the planning process with the process of communication and making commitments about actions and plans.

Not only conflicts as interactions. Often, resources are the only concept for reasoning about how different activities interact. When there is a harmful interaction between actions of different plans, then there is something that can be considered a resource for which the actions are contending. Coherence and coordination are often only defined via the regulation of resources. Multiagent planning has focussed and usually restricted itself on the issue of detecting and resolving conflicts among different agents plans. Although the requirements for resources and resolving conflicts pose an important concept of interaction, it is not the only one. We need not only consider remedies to handle conflicts but also measures to deal with situations in which beneficial effects (e.g., synergy) can be achieved by reconciling plans.

From theoretical models to practical systems. Theoretical models of cooperation allow to mathematically prove theories of what cooperating agents can and cannot do, and about how assumptions about their domains and characteristics affect their capabilities. However, formal models are usually far away from practical systems and provide only little help to bridge the gap between theories and implemented systems.

Dynamic domains. Still, multi-agent planning systems are poorly suited to dynamically changing domains, where agents cannot wait for complete information about potential interactions before they begin acting.

7 Plan Coordination via Relationship Resolution and Communication

Our approach for solving the problem of coordinating plans is based on two key factors: First, a taxonomy of relations ("multiagent plan relationships") which may hold between the plans of different agents [Martial 90b] and, second, a communication framework which is suited for autonomous agents to exchange their plans and to negotiate about how to resolve the relationships between their plans [Kreifelts & Martial 90].

The relationships between the actions of individual plans are divided into negative and positive ones. *Negative multiagent plan relationships* are all those relationships between plans, which may prevent one or both of the plans from being executed as intended. *Positive multiagent plan relationships* are all those relations between two plans from which some benefit can be derived, for one or both of the agents' plans, by combining them.

One type of negative multiagent plan relationship is a conflict of actions competing for limited resources. Plans are in a *resource driven negative relationship* if they require more from the same resource than is available at the requested time. A resource can be any object which is needed to perform a plan.

We differentiate between three types of *positive* relationships between preformed plans of agents, namely *equality*, *subsumption* and *favor*. Equality means that two agents intend to execute the same action, which then only needs to be executed by one of them. In case of a subsumption, the action of an individual plan implies the accomplishment of another individual plan's action. The favor relation can be used as a trigger to coordinate activities in situations, where one agent can contribute to another agent's plan by slightly modifying its plan, e.g. by incorporating an action [Martial 90c].

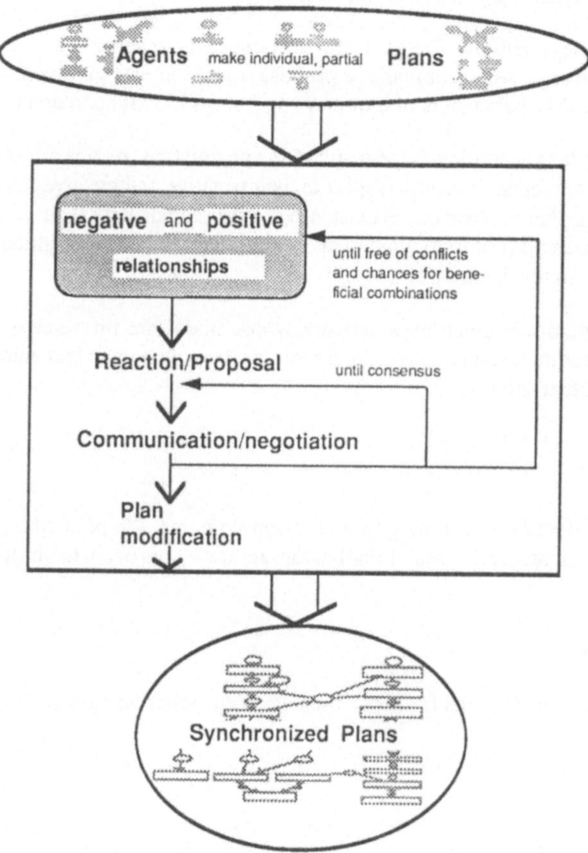

Figure 2: A relationship driven coordination process.

The scheme of coordinating the individual plans is illustrated in *figure 2*. This figure is a simplification of the actual coordination process, because it neglects the aspects of a dynamic environment (real time aspects), i.e. it does not reflect how coordination, planning and execution activities are interleaved. It gives a basic understanding of how planning, communication and coordination are coupled.

First, the agents develop their plans autonomously. Then, they transfer their individual plans to each other, a dedicated coordination agent or a blackboard which can be read by all agents. In order to reconcile these plans several tasks have to be executed:

- recognize and evaluate the possible relationships (negative or positive) between plans. Agents keep records of the actions which they are currently managing along with their relations to other actions and the state the respective negotiation has reached. The arrival of messages from ongoing negotiations calls for an update of the action list, a screening of this structure and an activation of one of the above phases, which in turn may eventually result in the dispatch of some new messages.

- work out solutions to deal with these relationships,

- initiate and perform negotiations. The goal of a negotiation is to achieve a commitment which is accepted by the participants. An agent makes a proposal for the agents involved. An agent can accept a proposal, reject it, modify parameters of it or may suggest a different approach to tackle a relationship.

The agents modify their plans according to the result of the negotiation. As a result of the coordination process the individual plans are reconciled with respect to their negative and positive relationships. This means for each agent to adapt its plan because of the existence of other agents with their plans. The result of coordination can also be seen as a set of individual plans being integrated into one global plan where the individual responsibilities are maintained.

The communication structure is given by a network whose nodes are interpreted as agents, and whose edges are interpreted as communication channels. Agents can be both human and automated and are considered as autonomous problem solvers.

8 Conclusions

This paper gave an introduction to planning in multiagent domains. We pointed out the potential and the specific problems of this research area. Finally, the author's approach to multi-agent planning was sketched.

Acknowledgements

I would like to thank Thomas Kreifelts for his comments on an earlier version of this paper.

References

[Adler et al. 89] M. R. Adler, A. B. Davis, R. Weihmeyer, R. W. Worrest. Conflict-resolution strategies for non-hierarchical distributed agents. In L. Gasser & M. N. Huhns (eds.) *Distributed Artificial Intelligence*, Vol. II, Pitman, London, pp. 139-161, 1989

[Allen 84] J. F. Allen. Towards a General Theory of Action and Time. *Artificial Intelligence 23*, pp. 123-154, 1984

[Bond & Gasser 88] A. H. Bond, L. G. Gasser (Eds.). *Readings in Distributed Artificial Intelligence*. Morgan Kaufmann Publishers, San Mateo California, 1988

[Cammarata et al. 83] S. Cammarata, D. McArthur, R. Steeb. Strategies of cooperation in distributed problem solving. *IJCAI-83*, pages 767-770, 1983

[Conry, Meyer and Lesser 86] S. E. Conry, R. A. Meyer, V. R. Lesser. Multistage negotiation in distributed planning. COINS Technical-Report 86-67, Amherst, MA, December 1986

[Conry, Meyer & Pope 89] S. E. Conry, R. A. Meyer, R. P. Pope. Mechanisms for assessing nonlocal impact of local decisions in distributed planning. In [Gasser & Huhns 89], pp. 245-258, 1989

[Corkhill 79] D. D. Corkhill. Hierarchical planning in a distributed environment. *IJCAI-79*, pp. 168-175, 1979

[Croft & Lefkowitz 88] W. B. Croft, L. S. Lefkowitz. Using a planner to support office work. Proc. *Conf. on Office Information Systems*, pp. 55-62, Palo Alto, Ca., ACM SIGOIS and IEEECS TC-OA, March 1988

[Dean 86a] T. L. Dean, *Temporal Imagery: An Approach to Reasoning about Time for Planning and Problem Solving*, PhD thesis, Yale University, 1986

[Dean 86b] T. L. Dean. Decision support for coordinated multi-agent planning. *ACM-SIGOIS*, pp. 81-91, 1986

[Demazeau & Müller 90] Y. Demazeau, J.P. Müller (Eds.). *Decentralized A.I*. North-Holland, Amsterdam, 1990

[Durfee 88] E.H. Durfee. *Coordination of distributed problem solvers*. 269 pages, Kluwer Academic Publishers, Boston, 1988

[Durfee & Lesser 87] E. H. Durfee, V. R. Lesser. Using partial global plans to coordinate distributed problem solvers. *IJCAI-87, pp. 875-883*, 1987

[Durfee et al. 89] E. H. Durfee, V. R. Lesser, D. D. Corkhill. Cooperative distributed problem solving. In Barr, Cohen & Feigenbaum (Eds.), *The Handbook of Artificial Intelligence Volume IV*, pp. 85-147, Addison-Wesley 1989

[Fikes & Nilsson 71] R.E. Fikes, N. Nilsson. STRIPS: a new approach to the application of theorem proving to problem solving. *Artificial Intelligence, 3(3-4), pp. 189-208*, 1971

[Fox 81] M.S. Fox. An organizational view of distributed systems. *IEEE Trans. on System Man, Cybernetics*, Vol. SMC-11, pp. 70-80, January 1981

[Gasser & Huhns 89] L. Gasser, M.N. Huhns (Eds.). *Distributed Artificial Intelligence*. Vol.2, Pitman, London, 1989

[Georgeff 83] M. Georgeff. Communication and interaction in multi-agent planning. *AAA-83, pp. 125-129*, 1983

[Georgeff 84] M. Georgeff. A theory of action for multi-agent planning. *AAAI-84, pp. 121-125*, 1984

[Georgeff 86] M. Georgeff. The representation of events in multiagent domains. *AAAI-86, pp. 70-75*, 1986

[Greif 88] I. Greif. *Computer-supported cooperative work: A book of readings*. Irene Greif (Ed.), Morgan Kaufmann, San Mateo, CA, 1988

[Grosz 90] B. F. Grosz. Collaborative planning in discourse. In *Proceedings of the ECAI-90*, pp.774-775, 1990

[Hewitt 77] C. Hewitt. Viewing control structures as pattern of passing messages. *Artificial Intelligence 8*, pp. 323-364, 1977

[Huhns 87] M. N. Huhns (ed.). *Distributed Artificial Intelligence*. 390 pages, Pitman, London 1987

[Hynynen 88] Juha Hynynen. *A framework for coordination in distributed production management*. 94 pages, Acta Polytechnica Scandinavica, Series No. 52, Helsinki 1988

[Katz & Rosenschein 89] M. Katz, J.S. Rosenschein. Plans for multiple agents. In L. Gasser & M. N. Huhns (eds.) *Distributed Artificial Intelligence*, Vol. II, Pitman, London 1989

[Kautz & Pednault 88] H. A. Kautz, E. P.D. Pednault. Planning and plan recognition. AT&T Technical Journal, Vol. 67, Issue 1, pp. 25-40, January February 1988

[Konolige & Nilsson 80] K. Konolige, N.J. Nilsson. Multiple-agent planning systems. *AAAI*-1980, pp. 138-142, 1980

[Koo 88] C. C. Koo, *A distributed model for performance systems: Synchronizing plans among intelligent agents via communication*, PhD thesis, Stanford University, Stanford, CA 1988

[Kreifelts & Martial 90] Th. Kreifelts, F. v. Martial. A negotiation framework for autonomous agents. Proceedings of the 2nd European *Workshop on Modelizing Autonomous Agents and Multi-Agent Worlds*, Paris, France, August 13-15, 1990, (to appear in [Demazeau & Müller 91] *Decentralized A.I. II* by Elsevier/North-Holland in 1991)

[Kuwabara & Lesser 89] K. Kuwabara, V.R. Lesser. Extended protocol for multistage negotiation. Proceedings of the *Ninth AAAI Workshop on Distributed Artificial Intelligence*, Orcas Island, M. Benda (ed.), pp. 129-161, October 1989

[Lansky 87] A. L. Lansky. A representation of parallel activity based on events, structure and causality. *Proceedings of the 1986 Workshop: Reasoning about Actions & Plans, Timberline Oregon*, 1987

[Lesser & Corkhill 83] V. R. Lesser, D. D. Corkhill. The distributed vehicle monitoring testbed: A tool for investigating distributed problem solving networks. *The AI Magazine*, pp. 15-33, Fall 1983

[Malone 87] T.W. Malone. Modeling coordination in organizations and markets. *Management Science*, 33(10):1317-1332, 1987

[Malone 88] T. Malone. What is coordination theory? *Proceedings of the Workshop on Distributed Artificial Intelligence*, 1988

[Martial 89] F. v. Martial. Multiagent Plan Relationships. Proceedings of the *Ninth AAAI Workshop on Distributed Artificial Intelligence*, Orcas Island, M. Benda (ed.), pp. 59-72, Sept. 1989

[Martial 90a] F. v. Martial. A conversation model for resolving conflicts among distributed office activities. In F. H. Lochovsky, R. B. Allen (Eds.), *COIS90- Conference on Office Information Systems*, MIT-Cambridge, ACM New York, April 1990, pp. 99-108

[Martial 90b] F. v. Martial. Interactions among Autonomous Planning Agents. In Y. Demazeau, J. P. Müller (eds.), *Decentralized Artificial Intelligence*, North-Holland, Amsterdam, July 1990, pp. 105-119

[Martial 90c] F. v. Martial. Coordination of plans in multiagent worlds by taking advantage of the favor relation. In M. Huhns (Ed.), Proc. of the *10th International Workshop on Distributed Artificial Intelligence*, AAAI, Chapter 21, Bandera, TX, Oct. 1990

[McCarthy & Hayes 69] J. McCarthy, P. Hayes. Some philosophical problems from the standpoint of artificial intelligence. In D. Michie & B. Meltzer (Eds.), *Machine Intelligence 4*, pp. 463-502, Edinburgh, Scotland, Edinburgh University Press, 1969

[Morgenstern 87] L. Morgenstern. Knowledge preconditions for actions and plans. *IJCAI-87, pp. 867-874*, 1987

[Nirenburg & Lesser 86] S. Nirenburg, V. Lesser. Providing intelligent assistance in distributed environments. ACM SIGOIS Providence, Rhode Island, pp. 104-112, 1986

[Paranuk 85] H. V. D. Paranuk. Manufacturing experience with the contract net. *Proceedings of the 1985 Distributed Artificial Intelligence Workshop*, pp. 67-91, December 1985

[Pelavin 88] R.N. Pelavin. *A formal approach to planning with concurrent actions and external events.* PhD thesis, TR 254, University of Rochester, 301 pages, New York, 1988

[Rosenschein 82] J. S. Rosenschein. Synchronization of multi-agent plans. *AAAI-82*, pp. 115-119, 1982

[Rosenschein 86] J. S. Rosenschein *Rational Interaction: Cooperation among Intelligent Agents.* PhD Thesis, Stanford University, 1986

[Sacerdoti 75] E. D. Sacerdoti. Planning in a hierarchy of abstraction spaces. *IJCAI-75*, 412, 1975

[Sacerdoti 77] E. D. Sacerdoti. *A structure for plans and behavior.* New York, Elsevier North-Holland, 1977

[Sathi & Fox 89] A. Sathi, M. Fox. Constraint-directed negotiation of Resource Reallocations. In L. Gasser & M. N. Huhns (eds.) *Distributed Artificial Intelligence,* Vol. II, Pitman, pp. 163-193, London 1989

[Sathi et al. 86] A. Sathi, T. E. Morton, S. Roth. Callisto: An intelligent project management system. *AI Magazine*, pp. 34-52, Winter 1986, also [Greif 88], pp. 269-310

[Shapiro & Eckroth 87] S. C. Shapiro, D. Eckroth (Eds.), *Encyclopedia of Artificial Intelligence*, Vol. 2, John Wiley & Sons Inc., New York, 1987

[Steeb et al. 1981] R. Steeb, S. Cammarata, F. A. Hayes-Roth, P. W. Thorndyke, R. B. Wesson. Distributed intelligence for air fleet control. R-2728-ARPA, The Rand Corporation, 1981, (an excerpt can be found in [Bond & Gasser 88], pp.90-101)

[Stuart 85] C. Stuart. An implementation of a multi-agent plan synchronizer. *IJCAI-85*, pp. 1031-1033, 1985

[Stuart 88] C. J. Stuart. Branching Regular Expressions and Multi-Agent Plans. in [Georgeff & Lansky 88], pp. 161-188 , 1988

[Tate 77] A. Tate. Generating Project Networks. Proc. *IJCAI*, Cambridge, USA, August 1977

[Thorndyke et al. 81] P. Thorndyke, D. McArthur, S. Cammarata. Autopilot: A distributed planner for air fleet control. Proc. 7th *Int. Joint Conf. Artificial Intelligence*, Vancouver, pp. 171-177, August 1981

[Wilkins 84] D.E. Wilkins. Domain-independent planning: Representation and plan generation. *Artificial Intelligence Vol. 22*, pp. 269-301, 1984

[Zlotkin & Rosenschein 89] G. Zlotkin, J. S. Rosenschein. Negotiation and Task Sharing among autonomous agents in cooperative domains. IJCAI-89, pp. 912-917, Detroit, August 1989

[Zlotkin & Rosenschein 90] G. Zlotkin, J. S. Rosenschein. Blocks, Lies and Postal Freight: The Nature of Deception in Negotiation. in M. Huhns (Ed.), *Proc. of the 10th International Workshop on Distributed Artificial Intelligence*, AAAI, Chapter 8, October 1990

A DEVELOPMENT AND SIMULATION ENVIRONMENT FOR COOPERATING KNOWLEDGE-BASED SYSTEMS

Kurt Sundermeyer
Daimler-Benz AG Research Institute Berlin
Alt-Moabit 91b
W-1000 Berlin 21 Germany
++30-39982-236
sun@b21.uucp

This is a progress report on an experimental tool (DASEDIS) within a project serving for establishing a methodology for multi-agent systems. The cognitive skills of each agent are realized as a knowledge-based system. The knowledge- based systems are imbedded in DASEDIS and are accessible by its development and simulation component. In the development component DASEDIS provides procedures for implementing the knowledge-base and the problem- solving and cooperation component with various control and communication strategies. In its simulation component DASEDIS allows for simulating the intentional, robotic, and communicative aspects of each agent.

This contribution addresses the motivation of our work, the conceptual framework of DASEDIS, the underlying general agent model and control structure for cooperative problem-solving, and a comparison with other test-bed like DAI tools.

1. Motivation and Goals

Research in Distributed Artificial Intelligence has yielded a plethora of concepts [Bond and Gasser 88]. Some of these have resulted from empirical approaches and some from theoretical investigations. The questions that arise from theoretical work give valuable insight on how far the research community is away from concepts which are both well-defined and practicable. The empirical approaches give hints, as to which concepts should be preferred.The State-of-the-Art can be characterized as a patchwork of ideas which either are very specific to applications (and thus are not transferable to other areas) or are developed on idealized toy worlds (and thus cannot be used for real-life problems). The situation is unsatisfactory as one is far off a systematic methodology for DAI systems which would be needed for a clean specification and a well-founded development of such systems.

The goal of our project COSY (COoperating SYstems) is to arrive at a systematics for the design of cooperating systems [Burmeister and Sundermeyer 90]. Our aim is to get from currently practiced handcrafted solutions to engineering methods. We pick up the loose ends in DAI research and investigate theoretical and empirical concepts in carefully directed experiments. These concepts are implemented, tested, and evaluated in order to find out control structures and communication strategies most appropriate for large classes of applications. Our experimental tool is DASEDIS, a "Development And Simulation Environment for Distributed Intelligent Systems".

Although we are primarily interested in cooperating knowledge-based systems we extend our considerations to scenarios with more general systems ("agents") interacting in some environment. Each agent has some degree of sophistication, autonomy and cooperativeness. Agents perceive their surrounding and act intentionally. To realize intentions an agent needs resources, which in general are limited and have to be shared. An agent eventually undertakes steps to realize intentions. The interaction among the agents consists of their mutual perception and of coordinating activities.

The architecture and functionality of DASEDIS derives, besides its tasks, from a modelling approach for these kinds of scenarios.The different skills of agents have counterparts in modules of DASEDIS.The cognitive skills of each agent are realized as a knowledge-based system, which are embedded in DASEDIS, whereas the intentional, robotic, and communicative aspects of each agent can be modeled in a simulation component.

In its development component DASEDIS provides procedures for implementing the knowledge-based systems, for inspecting the knowledge bases and for observing the problem-solving and cooperation component.

From its purpose, its architecture, its functionality, and its realization, DASEDIS has similarities with other tools. We decided to develop our own one, since as itself being part of the strived for methodology DASEDIS realizes a general agent model and control strategy. These are necessary in order to be able to implement already existing concepts and to compare and to refine them.

2. Modeling Agents

2.1 Multi-Agent Scenarios

We think of a DAI scenario as a set of *agents* which exist in an *environment* and which *interact* with each other and with the environment [Sundermeyer 90].

An agent perceives its *surrounding*, i.e. the environment and other agents, acts in accordance with its intentions and needs resources for performing perception or actions.

- As for *perception* we distinguish between whether more than one agent is explicitly involved (*receiving* messages from other agents) or not (*sensing* other agents and/or the environment).
- Whereas perception happens unintentionally and on a continuous basis, *actions* are intended and can actively be planned and executed by an agent to any desired moment.
  We differentiate *cognitive actions* from *effectoric actions*. Cognitive actions of an agent can not be directly perceived by other agents. They only become apparent by effectoric actions they may initiate.
  The effectoric actions are further divided into *sending* and *acting*.
  For our purpose it is convenient to talk of *behavior* as comprising both actions and perception.
- The role of *intentions* has recently been investigated in depth by several authors (e.g. [Cohen and Levesque 90]). In accordance with this work we distinguish long-term intentions, like superior goals, preferences, interests, responsibilities as *strategic intentions* from *tactical intentions* (short- and mid-term intentions, like subgoals, plans, and plan-steps). The difference can be seen in that tactical intentions are tied to actions.
- The technical term *resources* is used in a very broad sense and covers everything that is needed for executing perception or actions. Thus resources may be divided into sensing resources (physical sensors, the content of buffers, ...), sending and receiving resources (communication hardware, low-level protocols, bandwidth, message-queues, ...), acting resources (robot arms, time, space, energy, ...), and cognitive resources (knowledge and belief).

Intentions, behavior and resources are intimately tied together: Every intention is associated with the necessary resources for realizing it, every realized intention is an action, and every type of behavior needs and/or provides its typical resources.

The interaction among agents consists of their mutual perception and their coordination of activities: comparison of intentions (to identify goal conflicts and common interests), adjustment of resources (in case of resource conflicts and resource sharing) and synchronization of actions. By our broad usage of the term resources this lastly amounts to the exchange of resources among the agents and among an agent and the environment.

2.2 Agent Architecture

The features of agents being discussed in section 2.1 can be transformed almost uniquely into a modular system architecture with modules COGNITION, responsible for "cognitive actions", SENSORS, responsible for "sensing", ACTUATORS, responsible for "acting", COMMUNICATION, responsible for the connected pair of "receiving" and "sending", and INTENTION representing only strategic intentions, since moulding and revising tactical intentions is counted as cognitive actions.

The model of the DAI scenario is completed by a module ENVIRONMENT. The full architecture is shown in Fig.1.

The dataflow through the interface of the agent to the outside world and from COGNITION to the other agent modules largely depends on the application. On the other hand, the dataflow within COGNITION mainly depends on the system architecture employed. We decided to realize COGNITION as a knowledge-based system.

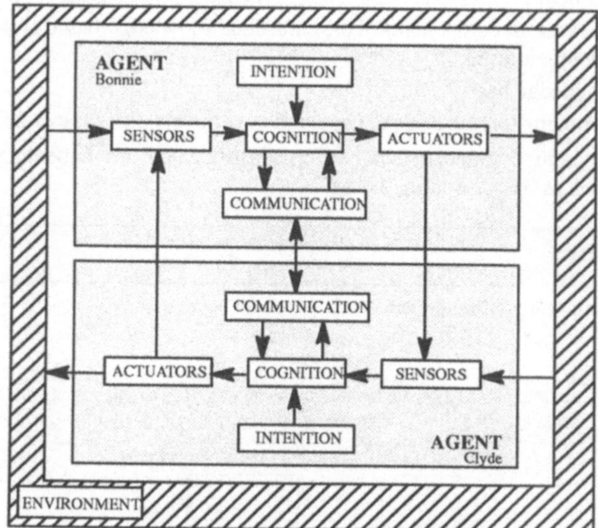

Fig.1: AGENTs and their Modules

Since our prime interest lies in modeling the cognitive skills of an agent, the module COGNITION is placed into the foreground. All other modules of the agent architecture are simulated to the extent that this is essential for an application.

3. DASEDIS

3.1 Architecture and Functionality

The previous considerations determine the architecture of DASEDIS, a "Development And Simulation Environment for Distributed Intelligent Systems".

DASEDIS consists of a simulation- and a development component, which operate under a common graphical interface, and of the embedded knowledge-based systems KBS_1 to KBS_n; see Fig.2.

There are both application independent parts (in the DASEDIS-frame) as well as application specific pieces in the DASEDIS-kernel.

Simulation Component

The simulation component contains models for INTENTION, SENSORS, ACTUATORS, COMMUNICATION, and ENVIRONMENT for each application.

The DASEDIS-frame contains generic simulation models. These are refined by concrete simulation models in the applications COx, COy .... Furthermore the frame provides constructs for handling the simulation time and for treating the concurrency of processes.

In the simulation component
– simulation models can be configured
– initial conditions for a simulation can be set
– a simulation can be started and interrupted
– a simulation can be visualized and internally traced
– it can be re-initialized, repeated and documented.

Development Component

The development component is completely contained in the DASEDIS-frame. It serves for the
– implementation of the various components of the embedded knowledge-based systems based on the tools of the software environment used
– inspection of the knowledge bases
– observation of the problem-solving and the cooperation components by traces and protocols.

Ultimately the development component shall offer constructs for implementing agents, control and communication strategies as basic building blocks.

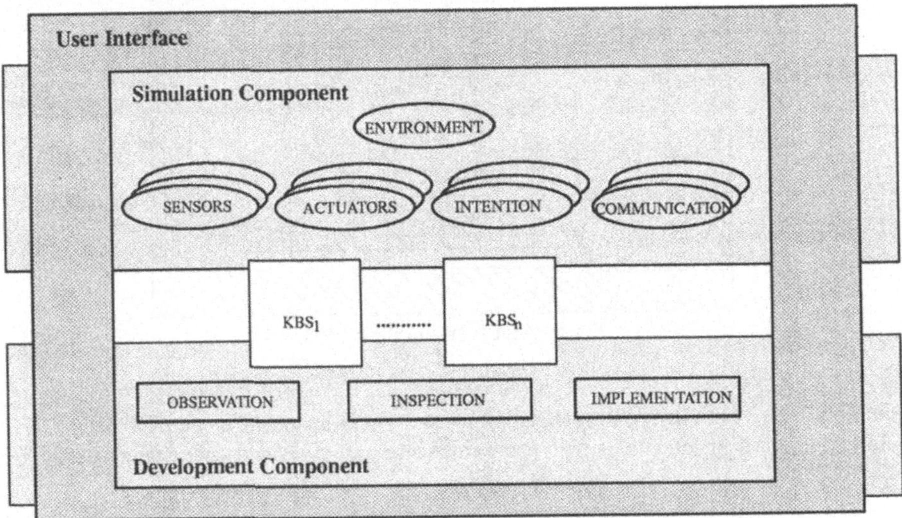

Fig.2: Knowledge-Based Systems in DASEDIS

User Interface

The part of the user interface belonging to the DASEDIS-frame provides functions for mounting the simulation and the development component and methods for visualization and animation. The functions and methods by graphical means (windows, menus, browsers).

Although the visualization and animation is largely application dependent there are some general classes and methods for simulated objects, graphic objects and animated objects (i.e. objects whose graphical form on the screen is changed by the simulation).

DASEDIS offers functions to proceed with working on an already implemented application, functions for demonstrating documented running examples, or functions to implement a new application.

Knowledge-Based Systems

As mentioned before, the cognitive skills of each agent, as being incorporated in the module COGNITION, are realized as a knowledge-based system.

In addition to the knowledge base and the problem-solving component (as they are standard for isolated knowledge-based systems) it contains a cooperation component.

- The problem-solving component PC performs those cognitive actions which an agent can perform without coordination with other agents, e.g. moulding and revising its tactical intentions, evaluating informations from the surrounding.
- The cooperation component CC is responsible for all those processes which arise during the interaction with other agents, such as negotiation processes, suitable selection of message types, resource allocation.

COGNITION has interfaces to the other modules as shown in Fig.3.

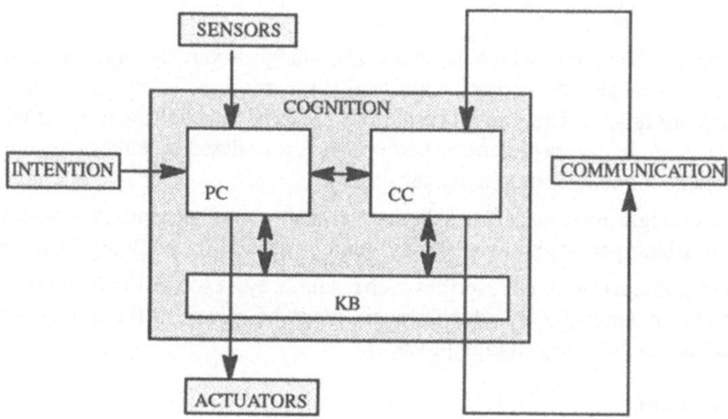

Fig.3: COGNITION and its Interfaces

According to our motivation and goals to make DASEDIS a general purpose and integrative tool, the internal structure of the knowledge-based systems is part of the DASEDIS-frame. This concerns the concepts for structuring the knowledge and for a general control strategy. The knowledge for each specific application (in the DASEDIS-kernel) can then appropriately be filled into the predefined form. Also the control structure may be adapted to the application in mind.

3.2. Cooperative Problem-Solving

The essential ideas behind the general control flow for problem solving and cooperation are the following; for details see [Burmeister and Sundermeyer 91].

- The basic distinction between unaware perception and intended actions discussed in section 2.1 is observed in treating those cognitive actions that analyze perception different from those that prepare actions. Only the latter are treated explicitly by the tuple <actions, intentions, resources>, since each agent aims to act in a perceived world according to its intentions and on behalf of available resources.
- Each agent has a repertoire of generic actions which it is aware of. Generic actions are partially ordered in the sense that some have recourse to others in form of execution procedures. At the top of this ordering are 'strategic' actions, which only make sense in specific world situations. At the bottom of the ordering are 'primitive' actions.
- The strategic intentions and the knowledge of the state of the world (world model) determine the chosen tactical intention of an agent.
- Committing to an adopted intention means to follow the partial ordering of the tactical intentions related to the corresponding type of behavior and adopting recursively intentions lower in the ordering.

- In order to successfully follow a tactical intention, that is to have a chance to realize it, the agent needs resources. If resources are not immediately at the agents disposal they possibly may be obtained from the environment or from other agents by negotiation.This amounts to intending further generic acting or sending processes with their necessary resources, etc. Negotiation steps are also considered as generic actions.

How these ideas are realized within the knowledge-based systems is described in the subsequent paragraphs.

Knowledge Base

As for structuring the knowledge we found the most natural and efficient way in a tree-like decomposition with a number of composite objects. The knowledge base KB is composed of parts 'self', 'others' and 'environment'. Each of these parts is divided into generic and actual knowledge, and these in turn into knowledge about behavior, intentions and resources (except for 'environment', which is solely described by resources), leaning on the agent model in section 2.1.

The main pieces of knowledge are

- Knowledge about generic behavior, which includes knowledge about its initial conditions and its execution. Knowledge about generic actions additionally incorporates knowledge about the tactical intention to which they are related. Their initial conditions are to be matched against the world model as part of the knowledge base. In contrast, generic perception is initialized by either message queues (for generic receiving) or sensor queues (for generic sensing).

- The knowledge about strategic intentions relates these to favorable strategic generic behavior. Knowledge about tactical intentions incorporates knowledge of resources needed for realizing these intentions.

- The (generic) knowledge about resources describes each resource by its source (self, others, environment), to which agent module it belongs and by which process it can be gained. If the source is not 'self' this process is formulated as kind of a negotiation protocol.

Problem-Solving Component

The task of the problem-solving component PC is the analysis of *sensing* and the preparation of *acting* together with the provision of its necessary resources.

The control flow within the problem-solving component is as follows (compare Fig.4).

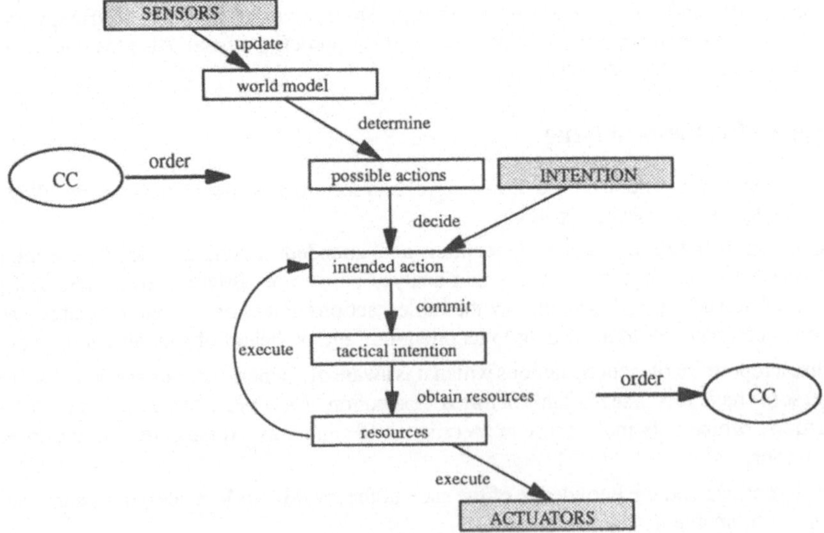

Fig.4: Control Structure for the Problem-Solving Component

0. The agent acts according to a default behavior, which directly derives from its strategic intentions. This behavior is performed as long as nothing else happens, if the performance of a generic action is interrupted or as long no new one has been chosen.

1. By analyzing sensor data the models for the environment and for the other agents within KB are updated.

2. Possible actions are determined from the set of generic actions by comparing the world model with the initial conditions of the generic actions.

3. If several possible actions exist, a decision for one of them is made by the strategic intentions.

4. The agent commits itself to perform the chosen action.

5. To realize the tactical intention its necessary resources are checked:

   If the necessary resources are immediately present, i.e. if they are at the agents disposal, the adjoined generic action can be executed according to the execution procedure; see step 6.

   If the necessary resources are not immediately available, the agent aims to get the resources from the environment or from other agents. The task to obtain resources from other agents is delegated to the cooperation component CC; see next paragraph.

   If the necessary resources cannot be made available a commitment to another generic action is to be made.

6. A generic action is executed by following an execution procedure. In general this leads again to a commitment to a tactical intention of an action lower in the partial order. The execution of 'primitive acting' directly happens by calling the interface function to ACTUATORS.

Cooperation Component

The tasks of the cooperation component CC are to obtain resources from and to provide resources to other agents. To fulfill these tasks CC negotiates (and for this communicates) with other agents, i.e. prepares sending activities for COMMUNICATION and analyses received messages from COMMUNICATION. According to our attitude of treating actions different from perception, 'sending' is described in terms of tactical intentions in contrast to 'receiving'.

Negotiation and communication follows protocols. As mentioned before, these protocols are represented as generic behavior.

CC is initiated by either an order from PC to obtain/ provide resources or by an incoming message from another agent asking for resources.

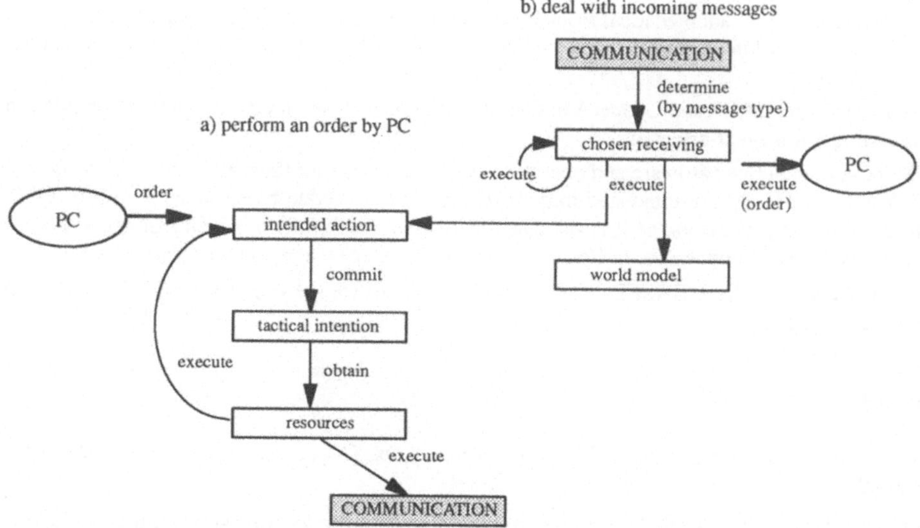

Fig.5: Control Structure of the Cooperation Component

a) If CC is initiated by PC (see Fig.5a) to obtain a certain resource, CC searches within the description of the resource in KB for a generic sending which must be executed to obtain the resource.

This generic sending is treated similar to generic acting within the problem-solving component, namely by committing to a tactical intention, by checking and obtaining necessary resources and by following an execution procedure, which eventually leads to a function that directly can be executed by COMMUNICATION.

b) Otherwise CC observes the message queue in order to handle incoming messages; see Fig.5b.

There is 'generic receiving' that deals with incoming messages. Protocols specify special receiving behavior for every message type they include. CC follows the respective execution procedure.

The execution of 'primitive receiving' can have different effects: The content of the received message can complete or change the world model, the received message can initiate (or follow) a negotiation as described in a) or it can determine an acting behavior to be prepared (and executed) by PC.

3.3 Comparison with Other Work

DASEDIS is in the tradition of general multi-agent testbeds with an underlying integrative framework, and not as much a tool for testing specific types of agents or a specific coordination technique. DASEDIS has similarities and dissimilarities with other testbeds:

— Like MACE [Gasser et.al.], ABE [Hayes-Roth et al. 88] and SOCIAL [Adler and Cottman 89] it contains language constructs for agents and suitable development tools.

— The method for implementing agents chosen in DASEDIS, using a class hierarchy like in object- oriented programming, has many similarities with the one in MACE or CooperA [Avouris et al. 89]. The classes and their attributes in DASEDIS carry the same information as the ones in these comparable implementations.They are, however, more systematically distinct and rooted in our general agent model.

— Although in principle also usable for blackboard systems, DASEDIS is from its outset in the spirit of the actor-model. Thus it is primarily meant to support message passing as communication paradigm. It also incorporates the notion of 'acquaintance' (as does MACE).

— The distinction of a problem-solving and a cooperation component, although neither easy nor obvious, has analogues in CNET, DVMT [Lesser and Corkill 88], and also in the work of other authors, e.g. [Evans and Anderson 89]. By some the cooperation and the communication component are not explicitly separated.

— Although our first application is drawn from traffic control (see next section), DASEDIS is designed to be much more general than for instance the DVMT, the ATC-testbed [McArthur et al. 82], or LCCPS [Lo and Findler 88]. Nevertheless we adopted ideas from these experimental testbeds. This especially concerns the cooperation strategies within the ATC-testbed, and the dynamic role distribution and incremental shallow planning in LCCPS.

— DASEDIS differs from MACE and CooperA in that its components (user interface functions, simulation etc.) themselves are not agent-oriented.

— DASEDIS does not integrate hardware and operation system concepts for the real distribution of agents, like ABE. We are at present not interested in distributing the knowledge-based systems in DASEDIS physically on different processors, as it is the case for SIMULACT [MacIntosh and Conry 87]. Also real-time aspects, being of importance in CoCo [Ishida 89], are at present not in the focus of our project.

— Comparable to SIMULACT the DASEDIS tool provides methods for the simulation and distribution of concurrently acting agents.

4. COroad

The example in this chapter refers to one of the applications COx, COy, ..., and especially concerns the DASEDIS-kernel.

Our first prototypical examples in COSY are drawn from the area of traffic securing and optimizing systems. This can be road bound or unbound two-dimensional traffic (cars or ships), or three-dimensional traffic (air planes or space vehicles). Work presently concentrates on road-bound traffic in the subproject COroad.

We started with a very simple scenario, in which two to ten agents (with possibly different performances and intentions) move on a highway. They change lanes and overtake, or they enter or leave convoys. Each agent has knowledge about parameters (for example velocities, vehicle type), relative position (distance, lane) and intentions of other agents.

Each agent decides with respect to the perceived world and with respect to its strategic intentions of whether it should drive with a certain speed, adopt the speed of another agent, overtake, or interrupt an overtaking maneuver. These correspond to strategic generic behavior *ride, follow, overtake, interrupt-overtaking*. The default generic behavior is *ride*, which is performed if no other agent is involved.

The vehicle model in ACTUATORS describes the rough geometry of the vehicle, its velocity, its acceleration/braking behavior. Different vehicle types are characterized by their maximal velocity and their power/weight ratio. The simulation functions are *drive, brake, accelerate, changelane*. Thus these are the primitive acting types. The driver model in INTENTION describes the attitudes and long term goals of a driver, such as driving cautiously, economically, fast. SENSORS "measure" the relative position of other vehicles. COMMUNICATION simulates the communication between vehicles. ENVIRONMENT describes the road in its topology, its qualities, as well as restrictions due to speed regulations and the like.

The knowledge base KB contains generic knowledge like the "driving school knowledge", models of other typical agents (ordinary cars, trucks etc.) and of the typical environment (two-lane, three-lane highway, merging lane, construction sites) as well as actual knowledge like parameters describing the environment, the current own data (velocity etc.), the actual problem solving state (concerning intentions, behavior, resources), as well as the state of other agents.

The DASEDIS user interface allows to input vehicle with their data and driver's strategic intentions. As output it shows the scenario in a graphical form (vehicle symbols moving on a road drawn on the visualization window) and parameters of selected vehicles.

5.   Conclusion and Outlook

The development and simulation environment DASEDIS serves two purposes:
- concepts for interacting knowledge-based systems are systematically developed and tested.
- approved and generally usable concepts become constructs in DASEDIS as modular parts in the sense of a tool box.

Thus DASEDIS is not ready. It is a growing tool, eventually taking shape as a prototypical development environment.

The functions and interfaces within the DASEDIS-frame and kernel for the different parts (user interface, simulation component, development component, knowledge-based systems), and between the frame and the kernel were specified completely and are partly implemented.

At present, COroad being the only application, functions for exchanging one scenario by another are only specified, but not realized in the implementation.

The general control structure, as described in section 3.2, was implemented. More refined control and communication procedures can ultimately be interactively selected and placed by the user as "prefabricated" cooperation strategies. DASEDIS will support centralized, decentralized, and hierarchical control. The control structures are in general mounted dynamically, but can also be static or dynamically- initialized. DASEDIS will support communication directed to a specific agent (to a group, to all agents), requested or unsolicited communication, and acknowledged or unconfirmed communication.

As basic message types we presently use INFORM (where a reaction of the receiving agent is not expected, or not important to the sender), QUERY (where the receiver is expected to send an answer), DEMAND (where an acting behavior of the receiver is expected).
Higher communication types, e.g. 'propose, deny, confirm, request, inform, answer, bid, agree', leaning on speech act theories, and richer dialogue structures, like the contract net protocol [Smith 79] or knowledge interchange protocols [Campbell and D'Iverno 90], are designated.

Our very first problems comprise only few agents, and we assume agents with the same skills and with comparable knowledge. The coupling is moderate. This will be extended towards societies of agents with differing sophistication, a larger number of agents and a tighter coupling.

We also want to incorporate theoretical ideas about the interplay of intention, knowledge and action, [Cohen and Levesque 90], and its relation to ability, organizations and roles [Werner 90].

Acknowledgements

I thank the members of the COSY group for their contributions to the conceptual framework and the implementation of DASEDIS, and especially Birgit Burmeister for her kind and critical reading of this article.

References

R.M.Adler, B.H.Cottman
"A Development Framework for Distributed Artificial Intelligence", Proc. 5th Conf. Artif. Intell. Applic. 1989, 115-121

N. M. Avouris, M. H. Van Liedekerke, L. Sommaruga
"Evaluating the CooperA Experiment: The Transition from an Expert System Module to a Distributed AI Testbed for Cooperating Experts", in M. Benda (ed.): "Proc. Ninth Workshop on Distributed Artificial Intelligence", 1989, pp. 351-366

A.H.Bond, L.Gasser (eds.)
"Readings in Distributed Artificial Intelligence", Morgan Kaufmann, 1988

B.Burmeister, K.Sundermeyer
"COSY: A Project for the Methodology of Multi-Agent Systems", Draft Proc. CKBS, Univ. Keele, Oct.90

B.Burmeister, K.Sundermeyer
"Cooperative Problem-Solving Guided by Perception and Intention", to be presented at MAAMAW-91.

J.A.Campbell, M.P.D'Iverno
"Knowledge Interchange Protocols", in: Y.Demazeau, J.P.Müller (ed.), Decentralized A.I. (Proc. MAAMAW-89), Elsevier/North-Holland, 1990, pp. 63-80

P.R.Cohen, H.J.Levesque
"Intention is Choice with Commitment" Artif. Intell. 42 (1990) 213-261

M. Evans, J. Anderson
"A Constraint-Based Architecture for Multi-Agent Problem Solving", in M. Benda (ed.): "Proc. Ninth Workshop on Distributed Artificial Intelligence", 1989, pp. 1-24

L.Gasser, C.Braganza, N.Herman
"MACE: A Flexible Testbed for Distributed AI Research", in M. N. Huhns (ed.): "Distributed Artificial Intelligence", Pitman & Morgan Kaufmann, 1987

F.A. Hayes-Roth, L.D.Erman, S.Fouse, J.S.Lask, J.Davidson
"ABE: A Cooperative Operation System and Development Environment", in [Bond and Gasser 88]

T. Ishida
"CoCo: A Multi-Agent System for Concurrent and Cooperative Operation Tasks", in M. Benda (ed.): "Proc. Ninth Workshop on Distributed Artificial Intelligence", 1989, pp. 197-213

V.R. Lesser, D.D.Corkill
"The Distributed Vehicle Monitoring Testbed: A Tool for Investigating Distributed Problem Solving Networks", in: R. Engelmore and T.Morgan (eds.), Blackboard Systems, Addison-Wesley, 1988

R.Lo and N.V.Findler
  "Empirical Studies on Distributed Planning for Air Traffic Control", TR-88-007, Computer Science Department, Arizona State Univ., 1988

D.J. MacIntosh. S.E.Conry
  "A Distributed Development Environment for Distributed Expert Systems", Proc. Conf. Expert Systems in Government, 1987, 72-79

D.McArthur, R.Steeb, S.Cammarata
  "A Framework for Distributed Problem Solving", Proc. AAAI-82, 181-184

R.Smith
  "A Framework for Distributed Problem Solving", UMI Research Press, 1979,1981

K.Sundermeyer
  "Modellierung von Szenarien Kooperierender Akteure", in: H.Marburger (ed.), German Workshop on Artificial Intelligence: GWAI-90, Springer, Berlin, 1990, pp.11-18

E. Werner
  "What Can Agents Do Together ? – A Semantics for Reasoning About Cooperative Ability", Proc. ECAI-90, 694-701

Produktionsplanung und -steuerung mit Verteilten Wissensbasierten Systemen

Mark Weigelt
Peter Mertens
Universität Erlangen/Nürnberg
Abteilung Wirtschaftsinformatik
Lange Gasse 20
8500 Nürnberg 1

Die hohe Komplexität der Planungsprobleme in der Werkstattfertigung führt bei Anwendung konventioneller Methoden entweder zu einer Vielzahl isolierter Teillösungen, die weit vom Gesamtoptimum entfernt liegen, oder aber zu extrem zeitaufwendigen Simultanlösungen, die insbesondere zur kurzfristigen Störungsbewältigung ungeeignet sind. Prinzipien der Verteilten Künstlichen Intelligenz könnten zur Überwindung dieser Schwierigkeiten beitragen. Der Referent gibt eine Bestandsaufnahme der verschiedenen Typen Verteilten Problemlösens bei der Werkstattsteuerung. Anschließend werden an der Universität Erlangen-Nürnberg im Rahmen des DFG-Sonderforschungsbereichs 182 (Multiprozessor- und Netzwerkkonfigurationen) entwickelte Prototypen vorgestellt. Dabei wird vorwiegend auf erste Konzeptionsmerkmale einer dezentralen Produktionssteuerung von teils kooperierenden/teils konkurrierenden Agenten und deren erhoffte Nutzeffekte eingegangen.

1 Motivation für den Einsatz Verteilter Wissensbasierter Systeme

Herkömmliche zentrale Produktionsplanungs- und -steuerungssysteme haben ihre Vorzüge und Nachteile. Deshalb wird nach wie vor in ganz unterschiedlichen Richtungen nach neuen und/oder ergänzenden Lösungen gesucht. Eine der Entwicklungsrichtungen bildet die dezentralisierte PPS. Dort sind die Ansätze mit sogenannten "teilintelligenten Agenten" (TIA) hervorzuheben. Unter TIA können kleine Informationsverarbeitungssysteme verstanden werden, die wissensbasierte Komponenten für eng umschriebene Aufgaben enthalten und beim Zusammenwirken mit anderen TIA Interessen für Einheiten eines Betriebes wahrnehmen.

Bei derartigen Ansätzen mit Verteilten Wissensbasierten Systemen besteht neben den allgemeinen Vorteilen der Dezentralisierung der Rechnerleistung, wie beispielsweise verminderter Störanfälligkeit gegenüber Ausfällen einzelner Komponenten, Entlastung zentraler Rechner, Vermeiden langer Informationswege, Rechnerleistungen am Ort des Datenanfalls usw., die Hoffnung auf eine erhöhte Flexibilität, verbunden mit einer besseren Auslastung der Ressourcen und damit auf eine höhere Effizienz des Gesamtsystems.

Die Mängel der gegenwärtigen PPS-Pakete sind vielfältig[1]. Abbildung 1/1 systematisiert die Kritikpunkte zum einen nach ihrer konzeptionellen Ursache, zum anderen nach der Art der Problemstellung, die der Kritik zugrundeliegt.

Auf betriebswirtschaftlich/qualitativer Ebene existieren durch eine adäquate Anpassung Verteilter Wissensbasierter Systeme an bestehende Organisationsstrukturen beachtliche Nutzenpotentiale. Idealerweise können so Problemlösungen im Dialog zwischen dem jeweiligen menschlichen Experten und der zugehörigen Systemkomponente erfolgen.

Abbildung 1/1	Klassifikation der Kritikpunkte an gegenwärtigen PPS-Konzeptionen

Art der Problemstellung \ Ursache	Mangelhafte Ausführung der Konzeptionen	Mangelnde Berücksichtigung in den Konzeptionen
Problem eher technisch/ quantitativ	● Bei Anwendung von OR-Verfahren werden wesentliche Restriktionen vernachlässigt	● Unterstützung der Werkstattsteuerung bleibt weitgehend ausgeklammert
	● Interpendenzen zwischen den einzelnen Planungsebenen werden kaum berücksichtigt	● Kurzfristige Umdispositionen werden unzureichend unterstützt
	● Aufgaben- und benutzerspezifische Arbeitsteilung zwischen Rechner und Benutzer ist unangemessen	● Beschaffungstermine von Rohstoffen werden nicht mit der Fertigungssteuerung abgestimmt
	● Einseitige Fixierung auf Minimierung der Durchlaufzeiten oder Maximierung der Kapazitätsauslastung	● Daten werden häufig nicht entscheidungsbezogen aufbereitet
Problem eher betriebswirtschaftlich/ qualitativ	● Terminierungsvarianten werden mit irrelevanten Kosten bewertet	● Rentabilität als betriebswirtschaftliches Oberziel geht nicht in die Bewertung ein

Die hohe Komplexität der eher technisch/quantitativen Problemstellungen, die häufig zur Mißachtung wesentlicher Restriktionen oder zur isolierten Betrachtung einzelner Teilbereiche geführt hat, legt ebenfalls einen Lösungsansatz mit Verteilten Systemen nahe. Bei Bedarf muß dann die lokale Sichtweise einzelner Experten (Mensch und/oder Rechner) mittels Kommunikation um entscheidungsrelevante globale Informationen erweitert werden.

Besonders auf die neueren, in bisherigen Konzeptionen wenig berücksichtigten Forderungen kann mit Verteilten Systemen eingegangen werden. Reizvoll erscheint dabei auch die Möglichkeit, Problemstellungen, die konfligierende Zielsetzungen beinhalten, mit konkurrierenden Problemlösern zu bearbeiten. Dies wird in Abschnitt 4.4 eingehender erläutert.

2 Stand der Forschung

Im Bereich der Produktionsplanung und -steuerung sind bisher nur einige wenige Systeme bekannt, bei denen umfassend Prinzipien des Verteilten Problemlösens angewandt werden[2]. Sie lassen sich grob in Konzeptionen unterteilen, deren grundlegendes Prinzip

- Konkurrenz oder
- Kooperation

zwischen den einzelnen Problemlösern ist.

Das vermutlich bekannteste Beispiel für ein System aus konkurrierenden Problemlösern stellt YAMS (Yet Another Manufacturing System) dar[3]. Es arbeitet nach dem Kontrakt-Netz-Modell[4]. Gegenstand der Verhandlungen sind Fertigungsaufträge, die top-down über die Hierarchiestufen der Fertigung bis auf Arbeitsgangebene zerlegt werden. Auf der jeweiligen Ebene werden die Vorgaben der übergeordneten Stufe in Einzelaktionen zerlegt und analog einem Ausschreibungsverfahren der öffentlichen Hand den Problemlösern der darunterliegenden Schicht bekannt gemacht. Diese arbeiten ihrerseits Angebote aus, die an den sogenannten Manager der darüberliegenden Schicht gemeldet werden. Der Manager wählt das für ihn günstigste aus und schließt mit dessen Anbieter einen Vertrag. Der Anbieter wird daraufhin selbst zum Manager und zerlegt seinerseits die ihm übertragene Aufgabe weiter. Der Prozeß stoppt, wenn das Problem in elementare Einzelaufgaben aufgesplittet ist.

Einen ähnlichen Ansatz, allerdings auf der Basis von kooperierenden Problemlösern, verfolgen Ow et al. mit CSS (Cooperative Scheduling System)[5]. Im Gegensatz zu YAMS gehen sie von keiner hierarchischen Fertigungsstruktur aus, sondern gruppieren sich ersetzende Maschinen jeweils zu einer Maschinengruppe, die von einem resource broker verwaltet wird. Ein sogenannter work-order manager (WOM) ist dafür zuständig, die in Arbeitsgänge zerlegten Fertigungsaufträge auf die Ressourcen zu verteilen. Sein Ziel ist, eine minimale Bearbeitungszeit und damit eine möglichst geringe Durchlaufzeit pro Auftrag zu erreichen, während die resource broker bestrebt sind, die Fertigungskosten und die Wartezeiten vor ihren Maschinen möglichst niedrig zu halten. Das Verhandlungsprotokoll orientiert sich ebenfalls am Kontrakt-Netz-Modell. Um den Fertigstellungstermin für einen potentiellen Fertigungsauftrag abschätzen zu können, versendet der WOM Aufforderungen zur Abgabe eines Angebots an diejenigen Broker, die für den Arbeitsgang in Frage kommen. Diese suchen innerhalb ihrer Auftragswarteschlange nach freien Kapazitäten (slots) und bieten dem WOM nun ihrerseits einen oder mehrere dieser slots an. Anschließend sucht sich der WOM den slot aus, der seinen Zielen am besten gerecht wird, und errechnet den potentiellen Endtermin. Dieser Prozeß wird gemäß dem Arbeitsplan des betrachteten Auftrags fortgesetzt, bis alle Arbeitsgänge eingeplant sind und der Endtermin des gesamten Auftrags feststeht.

Beim System CORTES[6] ist einer Gruppe von Ressourcen jeweils ein Modul zugeordnet, das die Aufgabe der Auftragseinplanung für diese Gruppe wahrnimmt. Auch hier verhalten sich die Problemlöser kooperativ. Negative Auswirkungen von Störungssituationen sollen durch eine adaptive Berücksichtigung von Sicherheitszeiten bei der Maschinenbelegungsplanung abgeschwächt werden.

Für die knapp erläuterten Systeme gilt aber ebenso wie für eine Reihe weiterer Ansätze[7], daß insbesondere die eher betriebswirtschaftlich/qualitativen Problemstellungen gemäß der in 1 aufgeführten Klassifikation vernachlässigt werden.

3 Stand der betrieblichen Praxis

In der betrieblichen Praxis ist die Entwicklung von dezentralen Leitstandsystemen zu beachten, die PPS-Systeme teilweise ergänzen, teilweise sogar vollständig ersetzen können. Umfangreiche Marktanalysen von DV-Beratungsgesellschaften belegen, daß in vielen Systemen eine hierarchische oder parallel gekoppelte Zusammenarbeit mehrerer Leitstände möglich ist[8]. Bisher werden aber die in einigen Fällen bereits wissensbasiert unterstützten Planungsoptimierungen lediglich isoliert für einzelne Fertigungsbereiche durchgeführt. Kooperationen über den reinen Datentransfer hinaus sind nicht vorgesehen. Von Verteilten Wissensbasierten Systemen kann man daher sicher noch nicht sprechen.

Forderungen nach

- sinnvoller Koordination der Teilpläne,
- transparenter Auflösung von Terminverletzungen oder

Anpassung der Eckdaten von Fertigungsaufträgen an den aktuellen Zustand der Fertigung

sind jedoch nur mit einer intelligenten Vernetzung mehrerer Leitstände zu erfüllen. Derartige Lösungsansätze einer überzeugenden Integration sind bis heute noch nicht bekannt[9]. Hier ist ein praxisbezogener Ansatzpunkt für weitere Forschungsaktivitäten zu sehen.

4 Eigene Vorarbeiten

4.1 Überblick

An der Abteilung Wirtschaftsinformatik der Universität Erlangen/Nürnberg wurde das Gedankengut des Verteilten Problemlösens bereits früh aufgegriffen und in Problemlösungen der Produktionsplanung und -steuerung eingebracht. Dabei sind im Rahmen des DFG-Sonderforschungsbereichs 182 die beiden Prototypen UMPADI und DUMDEX entstanden, die nach der unter 2 getroffenen Klassifikation den kooperierenden Systemen zuzurechnen sind. Die Weiterentwicklung DEPRODEX befindet sich in der Konzeptionsphase und beinhaltet vermehrt konkurrierende Problemlöser.

Um möglichst realitätsnahe und aussagekräftige Ergebnisse erzielen zu können, wurden den implementierten Prototypen Fertigungsausschnitte eines großen Nürnberger Fahrradherstellers zugrundegelegt.

4.2 UMPADI

UMPADI[10] (Expertensysteme zur Umdisposition, Parametereinstellung und Schwachstellendiagnose) ergänzt ein PPS-Paket auf unterschiedlichen Ebenen. Es besteht aus den drei unabhängig voneinander operierenden Teilsystemen UMMOD, PAMOD und DIPROMOD. Die Aufgabe von UMMOD liegt in der Unterstützung der kurzfristigen Umdisposition. Um jedoch bestehende Schwachstellen in der Fertigung, wie beispielsweise zu hohe Bestände, die DIPROMOD aus den Fertigungsdaten analysiert hat, nicht durch kumulierte Auswirkungen einzelner Maßnahmen zu verstärken, muß UMMOD mit den Nachbarsystemen PAMOD und DIPROMOD kooperieren. PAMOD fällt dabei die Aufgabe zu, mit Hilfe der von DIPROMOD übermittelten Daten die aktuelle Parametereinstellung des PPS-Pakets an die aktuelle Fertigungssituation anzupassen.

Das wesentlichste Ergebnis dieses Projektes besteht in der Erkenntnis, funktionale Interdependenzen innerhalb des PPS-Bereichs durch geeignete Kooperationen einzelner Teilmodule wirkungsvoll berücksichtigen zu können.

4.3 DUMDEX

DUMDEX[11] (Dezentrale Umdisposition durch Expertensysteme) ist auf der Ebene der Werkstattsteuerung innerhalb des Querschnittsprojekts HEDAS (Heterogene, durchgängige Anwendungssysteme) des Sonderforschungsbereichs 182 angesiedelt. Nach dem Prinzip des Turnpike Scheduling soll im Störungsfall eine vorgegebene Feinterminierung möglichst rasch mit möglichst geringen Grenzkosten wieder eingehalten werden.

Es existieren zwei verschiedene Typen von Problemlösern:

- Maschinenagenten und
- Auftragsmanager.

Jeder Maschine in der Fertigung ist grundsätzlich ein Maschinenagent zugeordnet. Eine Zusammenfassung mehrerer Maschinen unter einem Agenten bzw. die Einführung zusätzlicher Agenten pro Maschinengruppe ist denkbar, bringt jedoch konzeptionell keinen weiteren Erkenntnisgewinn. Darüber hinaus wird jedem Auftrag ein Problemlöser zugeordnet, der jedoch erst dann aktiv wird, wenn er von den Maschinenagenten eine entsprechende Nachricht erhält.

Um die Analyse in DUMDEX zu strukturieren, wurde ein achtstufiges Phasenschema entwickelt. Dem Grundsatz größtmöglicher Planungsruhe folgend, werden dabei Umdispositionen so lokal wie möglich und so global wie nötig analysiert. Dementsprechend steigt der mit einer Maßnahme verbundene Aufwand mit jedem Eintritt in eine neue Phase kontinuierlich an. In den Phasen 1 bis 4 sind die Maschinenagenten tätig (vgl. Maßnahmenübersicht in Abbildung 4.3/1), in den Phasen 5 bis 8 die Auftragsmanager (vgl. Abbildung 4.3/2).

Nach Eintritt einer Störung startet der Agent der betroffenen Maschine Phase 1. Hierbei muß zunächst festgestellt werden, ob und wie stark Arbeitsgänge in Verzug geraten sind. Ist ein Eingriff notwendig, so versucht der Maschinenagent innerhalb seines eigenen Arbeitsvorrates durch aufwandsneutrales Verschieben von Arbeitsgängen das Problem zu lösen. Gelingt dieses, wird er umdisponieren und die Durchführung anstoßen. Andernfalls müssen kapazitätserweiternde und damit aufwandswirksame Maßnahmen (Phase 2) ergriffen werden. Wird der Aufwand niedrig eingeschätzt, so führt der Agent die Maßnahme aus, wenn nicht, tritt der Problemlösungsprozeß in Phase 3.

Abbildung 4.3/1	Verfügbare Maßnahmen auf Ebene der Maschinenagenten		
		Verfügbare Maßnahmen des primär betroffenen Maschinenagenten	Verfügbare Maßnahmen der übrigen Maschinenagenten
Phase 1	Beurteilung von aufwandsneutralen Maßnahmen im eigenen Bereich	Nutzen von Freikapazität	———
Phase 2	Beurteilung von aufwandswirksamen Maßnahmen im eigenen Bereich	Überstunden, Verschieben von Wartungsarbeiten	———
Phase 3	Verhandlungen über aufwandsneutrale Maßnahmen auf Maschinenebene	Überstunden, Verschieben von Wartungsarbeiten	Nutzen von Freikapazität
Phase 4	Verhandlungen über aufwandswirksame Maßnahmen auf Maschinenebene	Überstunden, Verschieben von Wartungsarbeiten	Überstunden, Verschieben von Wartungsarbeiten, Splitten

Hier wird der betrachtete Lösungsraum auf alle Maschinen dieser Maschinengruppe ausgeweitet, die sich in der Regel gegenseitig ersetzen können. Dadurch eröffnen sich weitere Möglichkeiten, da jetzt jede dieser Maschinen prüft, ob sie den in Verzug geratenen Arbeitsgang ganz oder teilweise übernehmen kann. Voraussetzung ist, daß entweder im angefragten Zeitraum die Maschine ohnehin leersteht (Phase 3) oder aber durch Überstunden Kapazität geschaffen werden kann (Phase 4). Im ersten Fall ist die Angelegenheit erledigt, im zweiten muß wegen der damit verbundenen Zusatzkosten erneut überprüft werden, ob nicht Maßnahmen der Phase 5 die günstigere Alternative darstellen.

Durch diese Beurteilungsanfrage vollzieht sich, wie für den Fall, daß bisher noch überhaupt keine Lösung gefunden wurde, der Wechsel auf die Ebene der Auftragsmanager. Der für den Auftrag zuständige Manager untersucht zunächst, ob ein eventuell vorhandener Puffer (über alle Arbeitsgänge des Auftrages betrachtet) nutzbar ist, so daß der eingetretene Verzug aufgefangen werden kann. Ist eine einfache Verschiebung nicht möglich, versucht er diese in Zusammenarbeit mit anderen Auftragsmanagern im Zuge der Phase 6 zu realisieren. Scheitern diese aufwandsneutralen Lösungen, kann also kein anderer Auftragsmanager durch Umdisposition die benötigte Kapazität freimachen, so tritt der Analyseprozeß in Phase 7. Wie in Phase 5 bemüht sich der Auftragsmanager zunächst, Maßnahmen in seinem eigenen Verantwortungsbereich zu finden, die jetzt jedoch Aufwand verursachen. Schließlich werden in der achten und letzten Phase erneut die Möglichkeiten anderer Auftragsmanager in den Problemlösungsprozeß mit einbezogen.

Abbildung 4.3/2	Verfügbare Maßnahmen auf Ebene der Auftragsmanager		
		Verfügbare Maßnahmen des primär betroffenen Auftragsmanagers	Verfügbare Maßnahmen der übrigen Auftragsmanager
Phase 5	Beurteilung von aufwandsneutralen Maßnahmen im eigenen Bereich	Verschieben von Arbeitsgängen	——
Phase 6	Verhandlungen über aufwandsneutrale Maßnahmen auf Auftragsebene	Verschieben von Arbeitsgängen	Verschieben von Arbeitsgängen
Phase 7	Beurteilung aufwandswirksamer Maßnahmen im eigenen Bereich	Ausweichkapazität, Überlappen, Splitten	——
Phase 8	Verhandlungen über aufwandswirksame Maßnahmen auf Auftragsebene	Verschieben von Arbeitsgängen	Ausweichkapazität, Überlappen, Splitten

Ist es bis jetzt noch immer nicht gelungen, eine geeignete Maßnahme zur Bewältigung der Störung zu finden, so bleibt als letzter Ausweg, einen neuen Planungslauf des PPS-Systems anzustoßen oder aber, sofern Disponenten bisher noch nicht in den Prozeß involviert waren, einen menschlichen Entscheider zu informieren.

Die Kommunikation innerhalb des zweistufig-hierarchischen DUMDEX-Systems wird durch eine Blackboard-Architektur unterstützt: Auf Auftragsebene existiert ein gemeinsames Blackboard der Auftragsmanager, auf Maschinenebene ist jeder Maschinengruppe ein Blackboard zugeordnet.

Bei einer realen Einbindung in die Fertigung könnten die Auftragsmanager logisch verteilt, aber physisch zentralisiert auf einem Fertigungsleitrechner implementiert werden. Die logische und größtenteils auch physische Verteilung der Maschinenagenten würde auf verschiedene Zellenrechner erfolgen.

Die Erfahrungen mit dem implementierten Prototypen unterstreichen, daß sich der gewählte Ansatz insbesondere für häufiger auftretende Störungen geringeren Ausmaßes als sehr wirkungsvoll erweist. In diesem Fall kann das System Echtzeitanforderungen erfüllen und dem Disponenten unmittelbar nach Störungseintritt detaillierte Umdispositionen aufzeigen. Die Aufwandsbewertung der unterschiedlichen Maßnahmen mit fünf verschiedenen Kategorien erscheint der Urteilskraft eines Benutzers angemessen.

Aus diesen positiven Ergebnissen entwickelte sich als logische Konsequenz die Vorstellung, auch den wesentlich komplexeren Sachverhalt der Produktionssteuerung in allen Verknüpfungen zu angelagerten Funktionen mit einer Verteilten Konzeption abzubilden.

4.4 DEPRODEX

Mit DEPRODEX (**De**zentrale **Pro**duktionssteuerung **d**urch **Ex**pertensysteme) sollen die Möglichkeiten und Grenzen einer dezentralen Produktionssteuerung durch teils kooperierende/teils konkurrierende Agenten erforscht werden. Ziel ist eine effektive und transparente Unterstützung der Produktionssteuerung als Bindeglied zwischen der datentechnischen Planungs- und der realen Prozeßebene. Dabei sollen in hohem Maße Mensch/Maschine Interaktionen verwirklicht werden, um einerseits das Wissen möglichst vieler am Prozeß beteiligter Personen einzubeziehen und andererseits deren kooperative Zusammenarbeit zu unterstützen.

Abbildung 4.4/1 verdeutlicht den Bezugsrahmen sowie die einzelnen Systembausteine von DEPRODEX. Die Teilfunktionen und deren Zusammenwirken sollen im folgenden kurz erläutert werden. Voraussetzung der gegenwärtigen Konzeption ist eine vorhandene Grobterminierung.

Die Verteilung der Systemkomponenten orientiert sich an den Produktionsfaktoren: Maschinengruppenagenten sowie je ein Werkzeuglager- und ein Transportagent unterstützen die Betriebsmittelbelegung, ein Materiallageragent hilft bei der Materialwirtschaft und ein Personalagent erleichtert die Personaleinsatzplanung. Als koordinierende Instanzen existieren außerdem Auftragsagenten. Mit dieser Verteilung soll eine Anpassung der Informationsverarbeitung an die Organisationsstruktur der Fertigung erzielt werden.

Die dezentrale Maschinenbelegungsplanung der Maschinengruppenagenten bildet das Zentrum von DEPRODEX. Jeder dieser Agenten führt zunächst eine dezentrale Reihenfolgeoptimierung innerhalb der von der Planungsebene vorgegebenen Puffer für die Maschinen der zugeordneten Maschinengruppe durch. Anschließend tauscht er die veränderten Ecktermine mit den Problemlösern der vor- und nachgelagerten Fertigungsstufe aus. Nach dieser Rückkopplung beginnt eine neue Dispositionsrunde auf der Basis der aktuellen Puffer. Je mehr Zeit für weitere Planungsrunden zur Verfügung steht, desto komplexere Planveränderungen bzw. -verbesserungen sind möglich. Es handelt sich somit um eine rollierende, dynamische Terminierung.

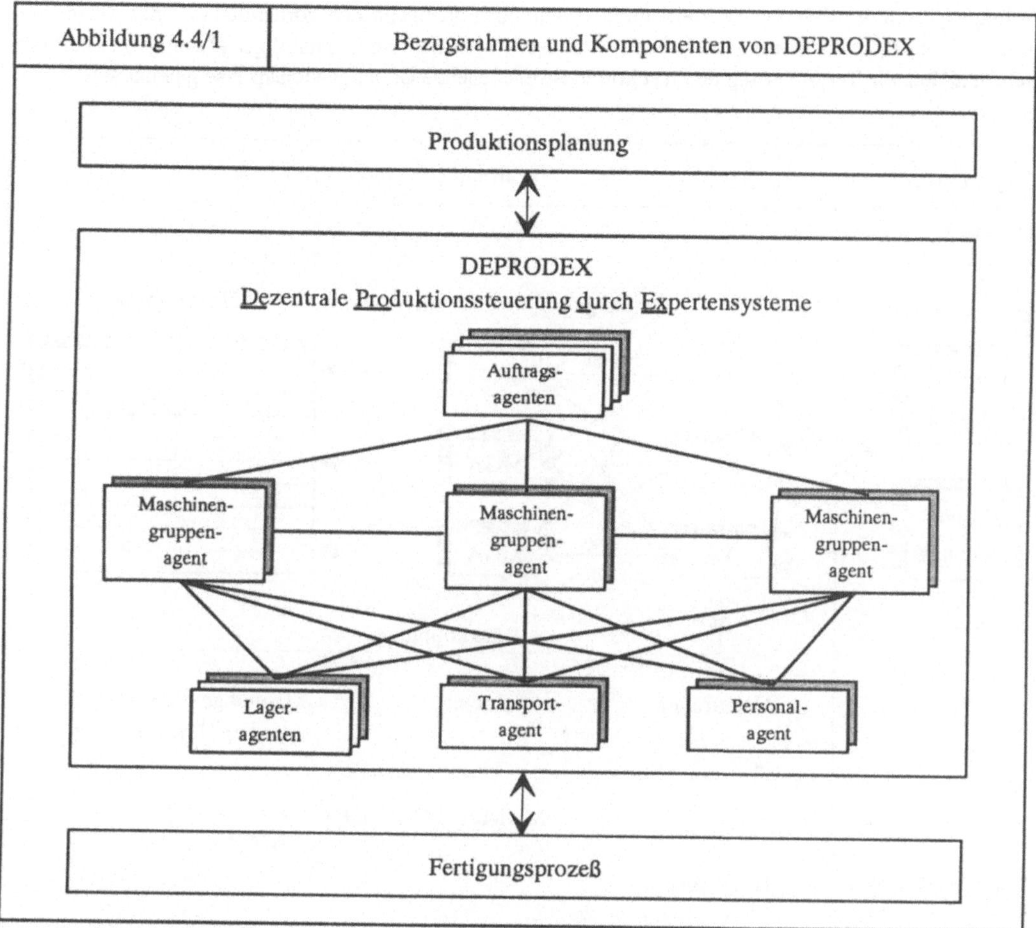

Welche und wieviele Maschinen jeweils einem Maschinengruppenagenten zugeordnet werden sollten, hängt in hohem Maße von der jeweils konkreten Fertigungsstruktur ab. In Zusammenhang mit der Entwicklung von Prototypen sollen verschiedene Alternativen verglichen werden, um zu klaren Aussagen zu gelangen.

Die Kriterien bzw. Weisungen, nach denen die Belegungsplanung durchgeführt werden soll, liefern die Auftragsagenten. Diese stehen im Gegensatz zu den kooperierenden Maschinengruppenagenten untereinander in Konkurrenz um den Einsatz der Produktionsfaktoren. Ihre Aufgabe besteht in der Rentabiltätsmaximierung der Fertigungsaufträge, um die Abstimmung zwischen den bisher häufig isoliert betrachteten Unternehmens- und Fertigungszielen zu verbessern. In Anlehnung an Mechanismen der freien Marktwirtschaft soll sich dadurch in einer Konfliktsituation jeweils der rentabelste aller Fertigungsaufträge durchsetzen.

Das Zusammenwirken zwischen Maschinengruppen- und Auftragsagenten zeigt Abbildung 4.4/2: Die Auftragsagenten werden als Nachfrager bezüglich der von den Maschinengruppenagenten angebotenen Kapazitäten begriffen. Die Weisungen der Auftragsagenten müssen "Preise" beinhalten, die dem jeweiligen Maschinengruppenagenten in Konfliktsituationen als Entscheidungsgrundlage dienen. Nach einer

Disposition, die gegebenenfalls eine Reihe der oben erläuterten Dispositionsrunden beinhaltet, können die Auftragsagenten das Ergebnis beurteilen und - wenn noch genügend Zeit vorhanden ist - mit neuen Weisungen erneut Planveränderungen einleiten. Auf diese Weise soll ein vollständiger Planungskreislauf entstehen, in dem die Terminierung durch schrittweise entstehende Gleichgewichtspreise gelenkt wird.

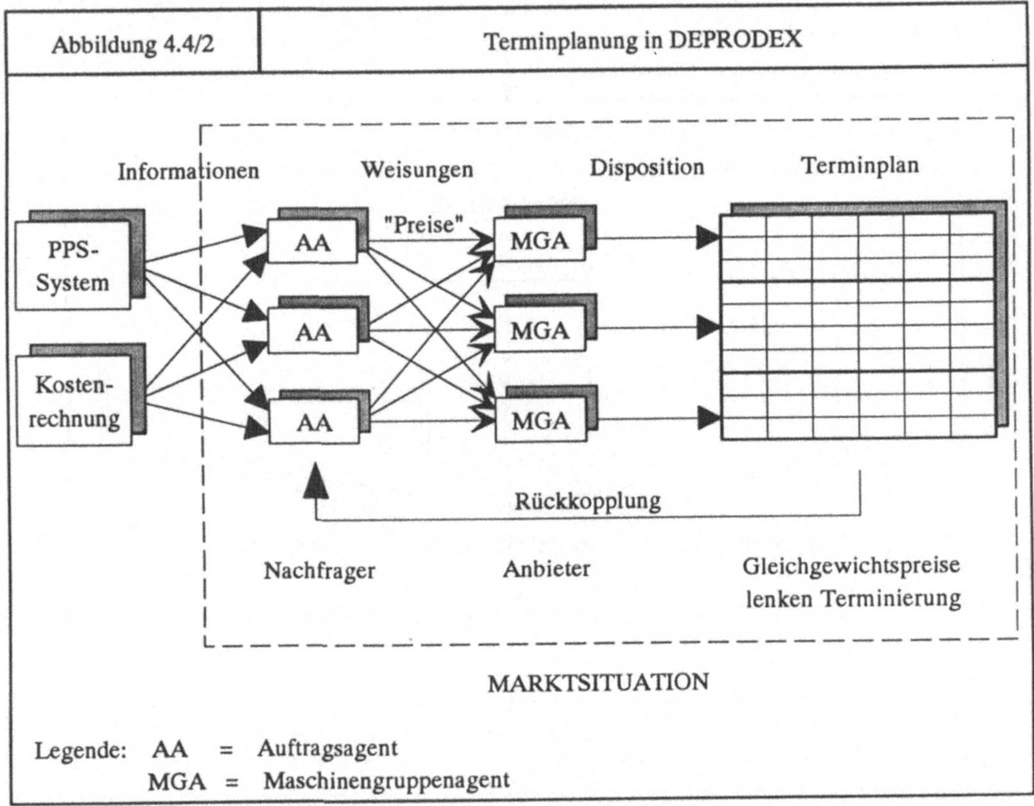

Die Auftragsagenten übernehmen in DEPRODEX folglich u. a. die Aufgabe der Bewertung verschiedener Terminierungsvarianten. Derzeit wird geprüft, inwieweit sich Gedanken aus theoretischen Ansätzen der Prozeßkostenrechnung oder der "Agency Theorie" auf diese Problemstellung übertragen lassen. Über einen Auftragsagenten können auch Eilaufträge kurzfristig eingeplant werden. Weiterhin überwacht und kontrolliert jeder Auftragsagent seinen Auftrag. Durch die Aufnahme von Kennlinien sollen dem sachverständigen Benutzer zusätzliche Informationen bereitgestellt werden. Gedacht ist an die Ermittlung der Auswirkungen verschiedener Zustandsgrößen der Fertigung (z. B. Kapazitätsauslastung oder Verteilung der eingelasteten Aufträge bezüglich der verschiedenen Produkte) auf die Durchlaufzeiten.

Die Lageragenten, der Transport- und der Personalagent sind ebenfalls in den Dispositionsprozeß involviert. Sie überprüfen, ob die jeweils vorgeschlagenen Maschinenbelegungen mit ihren eigenen Planungen in Einklang zu bringen sind. Diese Agenten übernehmen folglich die Konsistenzprüfung und bilden gegebenenfalls Restriktionen.

Der Werkzeuglageragent überprüft, ob in der aktuellen Fertigungssituation alle Werkzeuge verfügbar sind. Ist dies nicht der Fall, muß in Kooperation mit den betroffenen Maschinengruppenagenten eine Konfliktlösung erzielt werden.

Der Materiallageragent stellt die Verbindung zur Beschaffungsfunktion in der Unternehmung her. Einerseits ist er für die bedarfsgerechte Bereitstellung der Materialien verantwortlich. Andererseits können über ihn auch Anfragen durchgeführt werden, ob durch das spätere Einlasten einzelner Fertigungsaufträge eine Verringerung der Kapitalbindungskosten durch zeitsynchrone Materialbeschaffung möglich wird.

Der Transportagent ist für die Belegung der Transporteinrichtungen unter Einhaltung der vorgegebenen Randbedingungen durch die Maschinenbelegungspläne zuständig. Ausgehend von einer bereits spezifizierten zentralen Steuerungsstrategie, sollen in Zukunft auch Überlegungen in Richtung einer verteilten Lösung angestellt werden. Dabei wird jeder Transporteinrichtung jeweils ein Transportagent zugeordnet.

Der Personalagent soll einen Überblick über die aktuelle Aufteilung der Arbeitskräfte liefern und deren zukünftige Einplanung unterstützen. Auch die Beurteilung von Auswirkungen verschiedener Personalanpassungsmaßnahmen (z. B. Überstunden) soll auf diese Weise unterstützt werden.

Demnächst soll mit der stufenweisen Implementierung der verschiedenen Agenten innerhalb eines aus PC's und einer Workstation bestehenden Netzes begonnen werden. Die Leistungsfähigkeit des so entstehenden Prototypen von DEPRODEX soll anschließend durch komplexere Verhandlungs- und Kommunikationsmechanismen weiter verbessert werden. Zusammenfassend wird mit diesem Projekt die begründete Hoffnung verknüpft, zumindest bezüglich einiger der in 1 genannten Kritikpunkte Verbesserungen zu erzielen.

Literatur

[1]   vgl. u. a.: Adam, D., Ansätze zu einem integrierten Konzept der Fertigungssteuerung bei Werkstattfertigung, in: Adam, D. (Hrsg.), Neuere Entwicklungen in der Produktions- und Investitionspolitik, Wiesbaden 1987, S. 20; Huthmann, A., Trefz, B., Tjiok, C., Wissensbasierte Feinplanung in einem Fertigungsleitstand, in: Bullinger, H.-J. (Hrsg.), Expertensysteme in Produktion und Engineering, IAO-Forum am 25. April in Stuttgart, Berlin u. a. 1990, S. 309 ff.; Kurbel, K., Meynert, J., Flexibilität in der Fertigungssteuerung durch Einsatz eines elektronischen Leitstands, Zeitschrift für wirtschaftliche Fertigung 83 (1988), S. 581; Mertens, P., Industrielle Datenverarbeitung 1, Administrations- und Dispositionssysteme, 7. Aufl., Wiesbaden 1988, S. 131 ff.; Meyer, W., Expert Systems in Factory Management, Chichester 1990, S. 114; Scheer, A.-W., CIM, Der computergesteuerte Industriebetrieb, 4. Aufl., Berlin u. a. 1990, S. 24 ff.; Schröder, H., Entwicklungsstand und -tendenzen bei Produktionsplanungs- und -steuerungssystemen: eine kritische Bestandsaufnahme, Information Management 5 (1990) 4, S. 65; Zäpfel, G., Strategisches Produktions-Management, Berlin u. a. 1989, S. 190 ff.; Zäpfel, G., Dezentrale PPS-Systeme - Konzepte und theoretische Fundierung, in: Zäpfel, G. (Hrsg.), Neuere Konzepte der Produktionsplanung und -steuerung, Linz 1989, S. 47 f.

[2]   Mertens, P., Hildebrand, R. J. N., Kotschenreuther, W., Verteiltes Wissensbasiertes Problemlösen im Fertigungsbereich, Zeitschrift für Betriebswirtschaft 59 (1989), S. 839 ff.

[3]   Parunak, H. V. D., Manufacturing Experience with the Contract Net, in: Huhns, M. (Hrsg.), Distributed Artificial Intelligence, Vol 1, London 1987, S. 285 ff.; Parunak, H. V. D., Distributed Artificial Intelligence Systems, in: Kusiak, A. (Hrsg.), Artificial Intelligence, Implications for CIM, Berlin u. a. 1988, S. 225 ff.

[4]   Davis, R., Smith, R. G., Negotiation as a Metaphor for Distributed Problem Solving, Artificial Intelligence 20 (1983), S. 63 ff.; Smith, R. G., The Contract Net Protocol: High Level Communication and Control in a Distributed Problem Solver, IEEE Transactions on Computers 29 (1980), S. 1104 ff.

[5]   OW, P. S., Smith, S. F., Howie, R., A Cooperative Scheduling System, in: Oliff, M. D. (Hrsg.), Expert Systems and Intelligent Manufacturing, New York u.a. 1988, S. 43 ff.

[6]   Fox, M. S., Sycara, K. P., Overview of Cortes: A Constraint based Approach to Production Planning, Scheduling and Control, in: Goslar, M. D. (Hrsg.), Proceedings of the Fourth International Conference on Expert Systems in Production and Operations Management, Columbia, S.C. 1990, S. 1 ff.; Sycara, K. P., Roth, S., Sadeh, N., Fox, M. S., Distributing Production Control, ebenda, S. 80 ff.

[7]   vgl. z. B. Shaw, M. J., FMS Scheduling as Cooperative Problem Solving, Annals of Operation Research 17 (1989) 1, S. 323 ff.; O'Grady, P., Lee, K. H., An Intelligent Cell Control System for Automated Manufactoring, International Journal of Production Research 26 (1988) 5, S. 845 ff.

[8]   Hoff, H., Liebrand, T., Elektronische Leitstände - Auswahl und Einführung elektronischer Leitstände, eine Marktstudie, Fortschrittliche Betriebsführung und Industrial Engineering 39 (1990) 6, S. 280 ff.; O.V., Was bieten rechnerunterstützte Leitstände?, Zeitschrift für wirtschaftliche Fertigung 86 (1991), S. 62 ff.

[9]   von Lippe, J., Bringt die nächste Leitstand-Generation die Integration?, Zeitschrift für wirtschaftliche Fertigung 85 (1990), S. 619 f.; Poensgen, W., Produktionssteuerung mit feinem Planungsraster, Zeitschrift für wirtschaftliche Fertigung 85 (1990), S. 638 f.

[10]   Weber, E., Kotschenreuther, W., Mertens, P., Ein Verhandlungsmechanismus zwischen drei einfachen Wissensbasierten Systemen, Wirtschaftsinformatik 32 (1990), S. 59 ff.; Kotschenreuther, W., Ein Verhandlungsmechanismus zwischen verteilten Expertensystemen zur Unterstützung eines PPS-Pakets, in: Ostbayerisches Technologie Transfer Institut e.V. (Hrsg.), Tagungsband zum Fünften Regensburger KI-Anwenderforum, Regensburg 1990, S. 299 ff.

[11]   Kotschenreuther, W., Unterstützung der Störungsbewältigung in der Produktion durch Verteilte Wissensbasierte Systeme, Veröffentlichung in der Zeitschrift Wirtschaftsinformatik, Nürnberg 1991, in Vorbereitung.

Temporale Planung in Multiagentenumgebungen

Andreas Winklhofer, Gerhard Köstler

Bayerisches Forschungszentrum für wissensbasierte Systeme (FORWISS)
Orleansstr. 34, 8000 München 80
email: winklhof@forwiss.tu-muenchen.de

Zusammenfassung

In konventionellen Planungssystemen, die auf dem Situationskalkül basieren, ist Zeit nur implizit repräsentiert. Aktionen beschreiben dabei einen instantanen Übergang von einer Situation in eine Folgesituation. Pläne bestehen aus einer total oder partiell geordneten Menge von solchen zeitlich punktförmigen Aktionen. In dieser Arbeit wird ein Planungsalgorithmus vorgestellt, der auf einer expliziten Repräsentation der Zeit arbeitet. Ein Szenario ist hier die Darstellung bzw. Einschränkung eines zeitlichen Ablaufs. Die Repräsentation eines Szenarios erfolgt mit einer temporalen Logik, die ähnlich der Allenschen Zeitlogik aufgebaut ist, und beinhaltet sowohl qualitative als auch quantitative Information. Erweiterungen der temporalen Planungmethode ermöglichen es, jederzeit zusätzliche Informationen in die Planung mit einzubeziehen. Es werden Agenten modelliert, die diese Planungstechnik verwenden. Sie sind in der Lage, flexibel in mehreren Stufen der Planung auf Informationen ihrer Sensor- oder Kommunikationseinheit zu reagieren.

1. Einleitung:

Konventionelle Planer wie STRIPS [FN71] und NOAH [Sac74] stützen sich zur Modellierung von Aktionen und deren Auswirkungen auf den Situationskalkül [MH69]. Dieser Kalkül basiert auf Situationen und Aktionen. Eine Situation repräsentiert eine Momentaufnahme, einen Schnappschuß der Welt. Aktionen sind Funktionen, die eine gegebene Situation in eine Folgesituation abbilden, wobei die dabei auftretenden Änderungen durch die Aktionen beschrieben sind. Der zeitliche Ablauf ergibt sich in diesem Modell durch eine Abfolge von Situationen, also zeitlich punktförmigen Momentaufnahmen der Welt, die durch momentane Aktionsausführungen ineinander überführt werden.

Es ergeben sich dadurch einige Einschränkungen bezüglich der lösbaren Planungsprobleme. Es ist z.B. nicht möglich, eine Ausgangssituation mit der Aussage "erst ist die Ampel grün, später ist sie rot" darzustellen. Auch für die Zielbedingung gilt, daß in ihr nur Ziele beschrieben werden können, die in einer Momentaufnahme gleichzeitig gelten. In der Planung und an den Plänen macht sich die implizite Repräsentation der Zeit dadurch bemerkbar, daß Ausführungszeiten von Aktionen sich nicht überlappen können bzw. nicht gleichzeitig stattfinden können und meist eine exakte Reihenfolge geplant wird, in der wenig Spielraum für die Anpassung durch eine Ausführungskomponente besteht. Durch eine explizite Repräsentation der Zeit werden diese Nachteile vermieden.

Die Grundform unseres temporalen Planers ist vergleichbar mit Tsangs TLP [Tsa87b], wird jedoch dahingehend erweitert, daß er als Planungskomponente in autonomen Agenten eingesetzt werden kann. Der wesentliche Punkt ist dabei, daß während der Planung zusätzliche Information miteinbezogen wird, die von anderen Agenten oder einer Sensoreinheit geliefert wird. Mehrere Agenten, die sich aus Planungs-, Ausführungs- Sensor- und einer Kommunikationskomponente zusammensetzen, bilden eine Multiagentenumgebung. Letztere Komponente stellt die Kommunikation zu Agenten gleichen Aufbaus her. Einsatzmöglichkeiten eines solchen verteilten Systems sind beispielsweise in der Fertigungsplanung und -steuerung gegeben. Für diese Anwendungsbereiche hat eine Organisationsstruktur mit verteilten Agenten gegenüber einer hierarchischen Struktur den Vorteil, daß auf Störungen flexibel reagiert werden kann, da die Agenten autonom arbeiten.

2. Temporale Planung

Eine Situation, die durch mehrere Aktionen aus einer Anfangssituation entstanden ist, hat in der zustandbasierten Planung zwei Aspekte: Die Situation stellt erstens eine Vorhersage dessen dar, was die Aktionen aus der Anfangssituation erzeugen. Zweitens repräsentiert die Situation einen späteren Zeitpunkt oder momentanen Zustand als den, den die Ausgangssituation beschreibt. Bei der temporalen Planung werden nun durch Verwendung einer Zeitlogik zur Repräsentation einer Situation, die wir dann nicht mehr Situation nennen, sondern Szenario, die beiden Aspekte der Zeit getrennt und explizit dargestellt. Eine Aktion als Abbildung eines Szenarios in eine anderes stellt nicht mehr ein Fortschreiten der Zeit dar, sondern beschreibt Auswirkungen der Aktion auf den gesamten Zeitablauf. Ein Szenario ist nicht mehr, wie eine Situation, eine Momentaufnahme der Welt, sondern entspricht einer gedachten Weltgeschichte. Diese wird allerdings nicht exakt in allen Details und allen zeitlichen Abhängigkeiten im Szenario festgelegt, sondern das Szenario enthält nur Abhängigkeiten, die für die erfolgreiche Ausführung von geplanten Aktionen nötig sind, und solche, die im initialen Planungsszenario vorgegeben wurden. Szenarien können also durch zusätzlich erworbenes Wissen weiter eingeschränkt werden. In diesem Abschnitt werden die für das weitere Verständnis wichtigen Teile der temporalen Logik und Wissensrepräsentation vorgestellt. Danach werden der Planungsalgorithmus in seiner Grundform und seine Erweiterungen erläutert. Die vollständige Formalisierung der temporalen Logik, die ähnlich der Allenschen Zeitlogik [All84] aufgebaut ist, findet sich bei Köstler [Kös91].

2.1. Repräsentation der Zeit

Allens Grundrelationen zwischen Zeitintervallen

Allen [All83] stellt 13 qualitativ unterschiedliche Anordnungen zweier Intervalle in einer Dimension vor. Bild 1 zeigt diese 13 Grundrelationen zwischen Zeitintervallen. Eine Relation **R** zwischen zwei Intervallen kann aus der Disjunktion mehrerer Grundrelationen **r** bestehen (z.B. i_1 (**d s f**) i_2, d.h. i_1 ist während oder startet oder beendet i_2). Ein vollvermaschtes Netz aus n Zeitintervallen enthält dann $(n(n-1))/2$ relevante Relationen, da die zu $R = (r_1 .. r_n)$ inverse Relation $\bar{R} = (\bar{r}_1 .. \bar{r}_n)$ nur redundante Information darstellt und ein Intervall immer in der Relation **eq** zu sich selbst steht. Eine Transitivitätstabelle (z.B. in [Ric89]) enthält alle transitiven Verknüpfungen $trans(r_1, r_2)$ von je zwei Grundrelationen. Man spricht in einem Netz von *Pfadkonsistenz* oder *lokaler Konsistenz*, wenn für je drei Intervalle i_1, i_2 und i_3 gilt:

$$\forall (i_1, i_2, i_3): (i_1 \; R_1 \; i_2, i_2 \; R_2 \; i_3 \Rightarrow i_1 \; R_{trans} \; i_3) \quad mit: \quad R_{trans} = \bigvee_{r_1 \in R_1, r_2 \in R_2} trans(r_1, r_2)$$

Ein Zeitnetz ist global konsistent oder nur konsistent, wenn jede Grundrelation r aus einer Relation R in einer eindeutigen Belegung des Netzes mit Grundrelationen vorkommt und dieses eindeutig belegte Netz lokal konsistent ist.

2.2. Temporale Informationspakete

Temporale Informationspakete (TIP, *temporal information packages*) bestehen aus mehreren unterschiedlichen Informationsarten. Sie werden verwendet um Szenarien, Aktionen, Ziele und Kommunikationsinformation zu repräsentieren. Die drei Informationsarten in einem TIP sind:

- eine Menge von *PE-Formeln* (property-event-Formeln). Das sind entweder *Eigenschaften* (*properies*) oder *Ereignisse* (*events*), die mit den Prädikaten Holdsfor(Eigenschaft, Intervall) bzw. Occur(Agent, Ereignis, Intervall) Zeitintervallen bzw. auch einem Agenten zugeordnet werden. Eigenschaften und

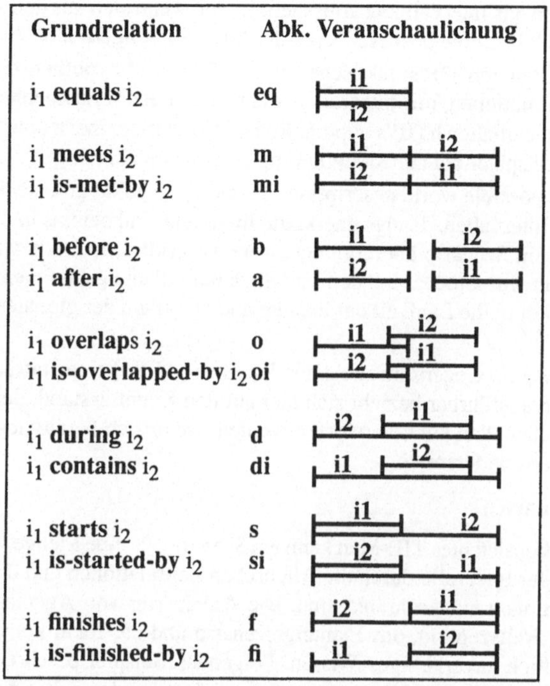

Grundrelation	Abk.	Veranschaulichung
i_1 **equals** i_2	eq	
i_1 **meets** i_2	m	
i_1 **is-met-by** i_2	mi	
i_1 **before** i_2	b	
i_1 **after** i_2	a	
i_1 **overlaps** i_2	o	
i_1 **is-overlapped-by** i_2	oi	
i_1 **during** i_2	d	
i_1 **contains** i_2	di	
i_1 **starts** i_2	s	
i_1 **is-started-by** i_2	si	
i_1 **finishes** i_2	f	
i_1 **is-finished-by** i_2	fi	

Bild 1: Die 13 Grundrelationen zwischen Intervallen.

Ereignisse sind Prädikate einer Logik, die durch die Technik der Reifikation zu eine temporalen Logik erweitert wurde. Dabei wurden die Eigenschaften und Ereignisse zu Termen der temporalen Logik.

- eine Menge von *Allenschen Zeitrelationen* (*temporal constraints*) zwischen Zeitintervallen
- eine Menge von *quantitativen Restriktionen* (*quantitative constraints*) der Form min(i) = Wert oder max(i) = Wert für die minimale bzw. maximale Dauer von Intervallen

Mit Beschränkungen bezeichnen wir sowohl die Zeitrelationen als auch die quantitativen Restriktionen. Eigenschaften spiegeln die statischen Aspekte der Welt wieder, während Ereignisse die Ausführung einer Aktion wiedergeben.

Das Prädikat **Holdsfor(p, i)** soll bedeuteten, daß die Eigenschaft p während des Intervalls i gilt und, daß i maximal ist. Es gilt also der *propositional constraint* [Tsa87a]:

$$(\forall (i_1, i_2)) : [\, (Holdsfor(p, i_1) \wedge Holdsfor(p, i_2)) \to i_1 \,(\text{b eq a})\, i_2]$$

Das Prädikat **Occur(a, e, i)** soll bedeuteten, daß der Agent a während des Intervalls i das Ereignis e (die Aktion) durchführt. Ist a unbekannt, so handelt es sich um ein Ereignis, das ohne Beteiligung eines Agenten von statten geht. Für Ereignisse nehmen wir an, daß ein und dieselbe Aktion in einem Zeitpunkt nicht doppelt stattfinden kann. Das schlägt sich auch in der Axiomatisierung der temporalen Logik nieder, aus der sich der Aktionssingular (*event singularity*) ableiten läßt.

$$(\forall (a_1, a_2))\,(\forall e)\,(\forall (i_1, i_2)) : [\, (Occur(a_1, e, i_1) \wedge Occur(a_2, e, i_2)) \to \neg (i_1 \,(\text{o oi d di s si f fi})\, i_2)]$$

Die für Intervallnetzwerke bestehenden Begriffe der Konsistenz erweitern wir auf TIP's. Ein TIP ist *lokal konsistent*, wenn das Intervallnetz lokal konsistent ist, der propositional constraint und die event singularity erfüllt sind und wenn gilt:

$$(\forall i) : (0 < min(i) \le max(i))$$
$$(\forall (i_1, i_2)) : (\,(min(i_1) \ge max(i_2)) \to \neg (i_1 \,(\text{s d f})\, i_2)\,)$$

Ein TIP ist *konsistent*, wenn das Intervallnetz konsistent ist und wenn sich aus den Zeitrelationen und quantitativen Restriktionen des TIP's eine positive Dauer der Intervalle folgern läßt.

Wir unterscheiden zwei Arten von TIP's: faktische TIP's (fTIP's) und hypothetische TIP's (hTIP's). fTIP's beinhalten gesicherte Informationen, mit Intervallen, die meist in der Vergangenheit liegen und nicht mehr revidierbar sind.[1] Dagegen enthalten hTIP's hypothetische Information, meist über den zukünftigen Ablauf. Diese Unterscheidung wird später bei der Modellierung der Agenten benötigt.

Im Unterschied zu Tsangs possible world descriptions [Tsa86] / [Tsa87a] unterscheiden wir nicht zwischen erklärten und unerklärten Intervallen. Tsangs unerklärte Intervalle sind bei uns in der Zielbeschreibung enthalten und werden erst in ein Szenario übernommen, wenn sie erklärt sind, d.h. wenn Aktionen existieren, mit denen die Ziele erreicht wurden. Das hat den Vorteil, daß im Planungslauf weniger Intervalle betrachtet werden müssen, was wiederum die Laufzeit der lokalen und vor allem der globalen Konsistenzalgorithmen verbessert.

Wie auch Tsang erhalten wir im Gegensatz zu Allen / Koomen [AK83] einen tatsächlich ausführbaren konsistenten Plan. Tatsächlich ausführbar bezieht sich hier auf den Kenntnisstand, der während des Planungsprozesses vorlag. Ein solcher Plan kann verworfen werden, wenn sich herausstellt, daß neue Information der Ausführung dieses Plans widerspricht.

Repräsentation von Szenarien

Ein *Szenario* ist ein lokal konsistentes TIP. Man kann ein Szenario als eine Menge von Intervallen auffassen, wobei die zeitliche Lage der Intervalle durch die Allenschen Zeitrelationen und ihre mögliche Dauer durch die quantitativen Restriktionen eingeschränkt sind. Die Architektur von Agenten wird drei verschiedene Szenarien enthalten: das Weltszenario, das Planungsszenario und das lokal konsistent geplante Szenario. Sie enthalten unterschiedlich zuverlässiges Wissen. Folgendes Beispiel beschreibt das initiale Planungsszenario einer Fahrsituation, für die ein Überholmanöver geplant werden soll. Es sind drei Fahrzeuge relevant: Ego soll überholen, er fährt hinter hugo, während lego in gewisser Entfernung entgegenkommt.

```
PE-Formeln:                          Zeitrelationen:
Holdsfor(hinter(ego,hugo),i1)        i1 (o s d f) i5        i2 (o s d f) i5
Holdsfor(rechts(ego),i2)             i3 (s d f eq) i5       i5 (m) i6
Holdsfor(links-frei,i3)              i1 (o oi s si d di f fi eq) i4
Holdsfor(zu-nahe(ego,hugo),i4)       quantitative Restriktionen[2]:
Holdsfor(überholen-möglich,i5)       Min(i5)=min1          Max(i5)=max1
Holdsfor(zu-nahe(ego,lego),i6)       Min(i1)=min2          Max(i4)=max2
                                     Min(i6)=min3
```

Repräsentation von Zielbeschreibungen

Eine *Zielbeschreibung* ist ein konsistentes TIP. Wir fordern hier Konsistenz und nicht lokale Konsistenz, um nicht Gefahr zu laufen, widersprüchliche Ziele zu fordern. Die eigentlichen Ziele sind die PE-Formeln der Zielbeschreibung, während die Beschränkungen die zeitlichen Abhängigkeiten zwischen den Zielen und dem initialen Planungsszenario oder nur zwischen den Zielen repräsentieren. Quantitative Restriktionen in Zielbeschreibungen dürfen sich nur auf Intervalle der Zielbeschreibung beziehen.

Folgende Zielbeschreibung impliziert, daß ego einen Überholvorgang planen soll, da die Eigenschaft gefordert wird, daß ego vor hugo ist.

```
PE-Formeln:                          Zeitrelationen:
Holdsfor(vor(ego,hugo),iz1)          i1 (b) iz1            i2 (b) iz2
Holdsfor(rechts(ego),iz2)            iz1 (s d f) i5        iz2 (s d f) i5
quantitative Restriktionen: hier keine
```

Repräsentation von Aktionen / Ereignissen

Die Beschreibung einer *Aktion* / eines *Ereignisses* besteht aus zwei in sich konsistenten TIP's, das Vorbe-

---

1. Die Beschränkungen von fTIP's lassen aber dennoch eine weitere Eingrenzung zu. Sie sind nur nicht mehr aufzuheben.
2. Die Werte für min1, max1, min2, max2, min3 werden aus den geometrischen Parametern der Situation und einem vorgegebenen Sicherheitsabstand berechnet.

dingungs- und das Effekt-TIP, die dadurch in Beziehung stehen, daß Beschränkungen des Effekt-TIP's auch Intervalle des Vorbedingungs-TIP's enthalten. Eine "delete list", wie sie von STRIPS [FN71] her bekannt ist, ist nicht nötig, da das Ungültig-werden einer PE-Formel dadurch ausgedrückt wird, daß eine Zeitrelation hinzukommt, die das Intervall beendet. Eine Aktionsbeschreibung enthält im Effekt-TIP immer auch eine Ereignisformel (Occur(agent, aktion, i)), die ausdrückt, daß diese Aktion während eines Intervalls i stattfindet. Beschränkungen von Aktionsbeschreibungen beziehen sich nur auf Intervalle der Vorbedingungs- und Effekt-TIP's. Die Beschreibung einer der drei Aktionen ausscheren, passieren und einscheren, die zur Planung eines Überholvorgangs nötig sind, lautet:

```
Aktion: einscheren
Vorbedingungen:
PE-Formeln:                                    Zeitrelationen: hier keine
Holdsfor(links(agent1),ie1)
Holdsfor(vor(agent1,agent2),ie3)
quantitative Restriktionen: hier keine
Effekte:
PE-Formeln:                                    Zeitrelationen:
Occur(agent1,einscheren(agent1,agent2),ie0)    ie0 (d f) ie3      ie0 (o) ie4
Holdsfor(rechts(agent1),ie4)                   ie0 (oi) ie1       ie0 (a mi) ie5
Holdsfor(zu_nahe(agent1,agent2),ie5)           ie1 (b) ie4        ie5 (s) ie3
quantitative Restriktionen[1]: min(ie0)=1, max(ie0)=2, min(ie5)=min4
```

Repräsentation von Plänen

Ein *Plan* ist ein konsistentes TIP, in dem nur Grundrelationen als Zeitrelationen zugelassen sind. Er beinhaltet alle Ziele sowie Ereignisse (Aktionen), die zum Erreichen der Ziele notwendig sind. Ein Plan muß konsistent und nicht nur lokal konsistent sein, da er tatsächlich ausführbar sein soll und dies durch im Plan enthaltene Inkonsistenzen unmöglich wäre [Tsa86]. Dadurch, daß die Zeitrelationen in einem Plan eindeutig sind, stehen die Anfangs- und Endpunkte der im Plan vorkommenden Intervalle in einer eindeutigen Anordnung, sie bilden also eine Zeitlinie.

Als Beispiel für einen Plan wird hier nun das Ergebnis der temporalen Planung für das Überholproblem angegeben. Es zeigt den Vorteil der temporalen Planung. Das Ergebnis (der Plan) stellt einen detaillierten Zeitplan (ähnlich einem Gant-Diagramm) für die Ausführung dar. Aktionen stehen darin in einer eindeutigen zeitlichen Relation zueinander und zum restlichen Ablauf. Quantitative Restriktionen beschränken ihre mögliche Dauer. Der Planungsvorgang wird später an diesem Beispiel erklärt.

```
Holdsfor(überholen-möglich,i5),        min(i5)=12,      max(i5)=19
--------------------------------------------------------------------------

Holdsfor(links-frei,i3),               min(i3)=9,       max(i3)=19
        ---------------------------------------------------

Holdsfor(hinter(ego,hugo),i1) ,        min(i1)=5,       max(i1)=5
        ---------------------------

Holdsfor(rechts(ego),i2),              min(i2)=0,       max(i2)=10
        ---------

Occur(ego,ausscheren(ego hugo),*i26),  min(*i26)=1,     max(*i26)=1
        -----------

Holdsfor(links(ego),*i61)              min(*i61)=8      max(*i61)=19
                -------------------------------

Occur(ego,passieren(ego,hugo),*i44),   min(*i44)=4,     max(*i44)=17
                -------------

Holdsfor(vor(ego,hugo),*i76)           min(*i76)=4      max(*i76)=13
                        ----------------------------------

Occur(ego,einscheren(ego,hugo),*i39),  min(*i39)=1,     max(*i39)=2
                        ------------------------

Holdsfor(rechts(ego),*i74)             min(*i74)=0      max(*i74)=10
                                --------
```

---

1. Der Wert für min4 ergibt sich aus der Berechnung eines Sicherheitsabstands.

Ein * im Intervalbezeichner kennzeichnet Intervalle, die vom Planer eingeführt wurden. Es wurden nur die wichtigsten vorkommenden Holdsfor-Formeln aufgenommen. Die Grundrelationen zwischen den Intervallen und die Zeitlinie lassen sich direkt am Diagramm ablesen, nicht jedoch die quantitativen Beschränkungen der Intervalle. Sie sind hinter den PE-Formeln angegeben.

2.3. Planungsalgorithmus

Wir stellen zunächst den Planungsalgorithmus in seiner Grundform vor. Hier existiert noch keine Möglichkeit, auf während der Planung zusätzlich erworbenes Wissen einzugehen oder es zu berücksichtigen. Später zeigen wir Erweiterungen, die uns dies ermöglichen.

Die temporale Planung findet in zwei Stufen statt (Bild 2). Auf der ersten, der lokal-konsistenten-Planung,

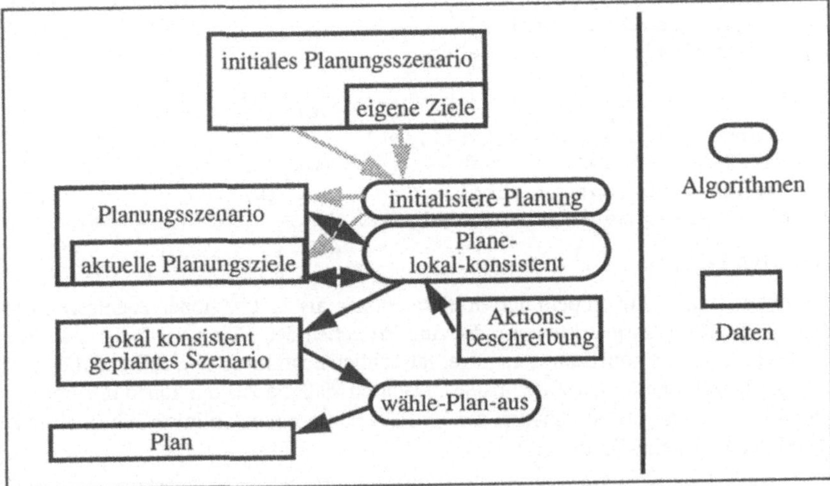

Bild 2: Der zweistufige temporale Planungsalgorithmus

wird mit einem nur lokal konsistenten Szenario gearbeitet. Das Ergebnis, ein lokal konsistent geplantes Szenario, kann man als nicht eindeutig festgelegten Plan auffassen, aus dem ein eindeutig festgelegter Plan gewonnen werden kann. Die lokale Konsistenz garantiert jedoch noch nicht die Existenz eines solchen global konsistenten Plans. Van Beek [vB89] zeigt aber, daß der Allensche Konsistenz-Algorithmus [All83] in typischen Planungsanwendungen die meisten Inkonsistenzen erkennt [vB89]. Die zweite Stufe, wähle-Plan-aus, gewinnt aus diesem lokal konsistent geplanten Szenario einen global konsistenten Plan.

Bei Planungsaufgaben ist der Verzweigungsgrad für Rückwärtssuche meist niedriger als für Vorwärtssuche, da die Szenariobeschreibung fast immer deutlich komplexer als die Zielbeschreibung ist. Der Planungsalgorithmus läuft deshalb, wie die meisten Planer, als Rückwärtssuche. Das heißt bei temporaler Planung nicht unbedingt, daß die als letztes auszuführende Aktion auch als erstes geplant wird.

2.3.1 Lokal konsistente Planung

Die Eingabe von Plane-lokal-konsistent sind die Zielbeschreibung und ein initiales Planungsszenario. Dieser Backtracking-Algorithmus terminiert, wenn alle Ziele, d. h. PE-Formeln der Zielbeschreibung erfüllt sind. Begonnen wird mit der Auswahl eines Ziels. Es sind zwei Fälle zu unterscheiden: Ein Ziel kann bereits ohne die Einplanung einer Aktion im Planungsszenario erfüllt sein. Im anderen Fall muß eine Aktion eingeplant werden, deren Effekte das Ziel erfüllen. Auf jeden Fall muß geprüft werden, ob die Beschränkungen der Zielbeschreibung, die sich auf das Intervall dieser Zielformel beziehen, im Planungsszenario eine Inkonsistenz erzeugen würden.

Die Arbeitsweise des lokal konsistent planenden Algorithmus wird am Überholbeispiel erklärt. Das initiale Planungsszenario läßt sich wie folgt graphisch darstellen; dabei können immer nur eindeutige Intervallrelationen veranschaulicht werden.

```
Holdsfor(überholen-möglich,i5)
```

```
Holdsfor(links-frei,i3)
```

```
Holdsfor(hinter(ego,hugo),i1)
```

```
Holdsfor(rechts(ego),i2)
```

```
Holdsfor(zu-nahe(ego,hugo),i4)
```

```
Holdsfor(zu-nahe(ego,lego),i6)
```

Die Zielbeschreibung des Beispiels ist:
```
Holdsfor(vor(ego,hugo),iz1),Holdsfor(rechts(ego),iz2),
i1 (b) iz1, i2 (b) iz2, iz1 (s d f) i5, iz2 (s d f) i5
```
Versucht der Algorithmus nun die PE-Zielformel `Holdsfor(rechts(ego),iz2)` durch Unifikation mit der des initialen Planungsszenarios `Holdsfor(rechts(ego),i2)` zu erfüllen, müssen die Beschränkungen (Zeitrelationen und quantitative Restriktionen) aus der Zielbeschreibung überprüft werden, die sich auf das Intervall `iz2` beziehen. Da für `iz2` keine quantitativen Restriktionen angegeben wurden, können sie auch nicht denen des Planungsszenarios widersprechen. Die Zeitrelationen `i2 (b) iz2`, `iz2 (s d f) i5`, die überprüft werden müssen, führen zu einer Inkonsistenz des Planungsszenarios: Da `i2` und `iz2` miteinander identifiziert wurden, muß `i2 (eq) iz2` gelten. Dies ist mit der Relation `i2 (b) iz2` unverträglich. Die oben vorgenommene Unifikation wird deshalb verworfen und das Ziel `Holdsfor(rechts(ego),iz2)` ist nur durch eine Aktionseinplanung zu erfüllen.

Eine mögliche Aktion ist *einscheren*, da diese `Holdsfor(rechts(agent1),ie4)` als einen Effekt hat (siehe Repräsentation von Aktionen). Dieser Effekt ist unifizierbar mit dem Ziel `Holdsfor(rechts(ego),iz2)`, wodurch `agent1` mit `ego`, und `iz2` mit `ie4` belegt wird. Alle Effekte von *einscheren* werden in das Planungsszenario hinzugenommen. Als nächstes werden die hinzugenommenen Beschränkungen der Effekte `ie0 (d f) ie3`, `ie0 (o) ie4`, `ie0 (oi) ie1`, `ie0 (a mi) ie5`, `ie1 (b) ie4`, `ie5 (s) ie3`, `min(ie0)=1`, `max(ie0)=2`, `min(ie5)=min4` und die Beschränkung `i2 (b) iz2` aus der Zielbeschreibung am Planungsszenario überprüft. Dies geschieht mit Hilfe des lokalen Konsistenzalgorithmus für Zeitnetze (siehe [All83]). Auch die Gültigkeit des propositional constraint und der event singularity wird sichergestellt. Ergibt sich im Planungsszenario eine Inkonsistenz, so würde die Aktionseinplanung verworfen. Im Beispiel ist das nicht der Fall und als neues Planungsszenario ergibt sich:
```
Holdsfor(überholen-möglich, i5)
```

```
Holdsfor(links-frei, i3)
```

```
Holdsfor(hinter(ego, hugo)
```

```
Holdsfor(rechts(ego),i2)
```

```
Holdsfor(links(ego),*i61)
```

```
Occur(ego,einscheren(ego,agent2),*i39)
```

```
Holdsfor(rechts(ego),*i74)
```

Die PE-Formeln `Holdsfor(zu-nahe(..,..),..)` wurden weggelassen. Da Plane-lokal-konsistent eine rückwärtsverkettete Suche durchführt, müssen nun die Vorbedingungen von *einscheren* zur Zielbeschreibung hinzugenommen werden. Die nun erfüllte PE-Zielformel `Holdsfor(rechts(agent1),iz2)` wurde in der neuen Zielbeschreibung gestrichen.

```
Holdsfor(vor(ego,hugo),iz1)          i1 (b)  iz1
Holdsfor(links(agent1),ie1)          iz1 (s d f) i5
Holdsfor(vor(ego, agent2),ie2)
```

Danach wird Plane-lokal-konsistent mit dem neuen Planungsszenario und der neuen Zielbeschreibung auf-
gerufen. Der Algorithmus versucht bevorzugt, ein Ziel ohne die Einplanung einer Aktion zu erfüllen. Bild 3
zeigt Plane-lokal-konsistent in pseudo-algorithmischer Form. Die Beachtung der Beschränkungen während

---

Plane-lokal-konsistent(*Zielbeschreibung*, *Planungsszenario*)

WENN *Zielbeschreibung* leer: **DANN** Ausgabe: *Planungsszenario*

SONST

Z = wähle-und-lösche-eine-PE-Formel(*Zielbeschreibung*)

Substmenge = alle Substitutionen, die Z mit einer Formel des *Planungszenarios* unifizieren

SOLANGE *Substmenge* <> leer:

    /* Erfüllung von Zielen ohne Aktionseinplanung */

    Subst = wähle-und-streiche-Element(*Substmenge*)

    wende *Subst* auf alle Beschränkungen der *Zielbeschreibung* an

    Beschr = Beschränkungen, die durch Anwendung von Substitutionen auf die
                    Zielbeschreibung überprüfbar geworden sind

    Neues-Planungsszenario = lokal-konsistent(*Planungsszenario* mit *Beschr*)

    WENN *Neues-Planungsszenario* lokal konsistent ist **DANN**

        Neue-Zielbeschreibung = *Zielbeschreibung* ohne *Beschr*

        Plane-lokal-konsistent(*Neue-Zielbeschreibung*, *Neues-Planungsszenario*)

Aktmenge = Menge der Aktionen, von denen ein Effekt mit Z unifizierbar ist

SOLANGE *Aktmenge* <> leer:

    /* Erfüllung von Zielen mit Aktionseinplanung */

    Aktion = wähle-und-streiche-Element(*Aktmenge*)

    Subst = Unifikation von Z mit einem Effekt(*Aktion*)

    wende *Subst* auf Vorbedingungen und Effekte von *Aktion* sowie die *Zielbeschreibung* an

    Neues-Planungsszenario = lokal-konsistent(*Planungsszenario* mit Effekten)

    WENN *Neues-Planungsszenario* lokal konsistent ist **DANN**

        Neue-Zielbeschreibung = *Zielbeschreibung* mit Vorbedingungen(*Aktion*)

        Plane-lokal-konsistent(*Neue-Zielbeschreibung*, *Neues-Planungsszenario*)

Bild 3: Grundform des temporalen Planungsalgorithmus

der Rückwärtssuche führt zum Abschneiden von Teilbäumen im Suchbaum. Durch die Verwendung von
domänenspezifischen Beschränkungen kann dies noch intensiver genutzt werden. Für das Beispiel wäre

$$Holdsfor\,(links\,(agent),i1)\,\wedge\,Holdsfor\,(rechts\,(agent),i2)\,\rightarrow\,i1\,(\text{b a m mi})\,i2$$

eine sinnvolle Beschränkung, die aussagt, daß kein Agent gleichzeitig links und rechts sein kann.

2.3.2 Auswahl eines Plans

Der Algorithmus wähle-Plan-aus gewinnt aus dem lokal konsistent geplanten Szenario einen Plan. Dies
erfolgt durch local propagation and backtracking [Güs89], das nach jeder Auswahl einer Belegung im Intervallnetz wieder lokale Konsistenz im Rest des Relationennetzes herstellt. Im Plan, der ja eindeutige Bele-
gungen der Zeitrelationen enthält, werden auch die Spannen der Intervalldauern mit einer Technik der
linearen Programmierung so weit wie möglich eingeschränkt. Ein Beispiel für einen Plan des Überholvorgangs wurde bereits bei der Repräsentation von Plänen angegeben. Da ein Plan eine eindeutige Belegung
des lokal konsistent geplanten Szenarios ist, läßt er sich graphisch veranschaulichen.

2.4. Erweiterung des Planungsalgorithmus

Die bisher beschriebene Planung geht davon aus, daß vor dem Aufruf alle relevanten Informationen bekannt und in der Eingabe enthalten sind. In der Realität läßt sich aber viel Wissen, das die Planung beeinflußt, erst während der Planung erschließen. Es ist daher sinnvoll, Information über Änderungen der Umwelt oder von anderen Agenten bereits während der Planung zu berücksichtigen. Dies geschieht bei uns auf zwei Stufen, die der Aufteilung der Planung in die Prozesse Plane-lokal-konsistent und wähle-Plan-aus entsprechen.

Kommunikationsinformation ist ein in sich konsistentes TIP bestehend aus (möglichst wenigen) PE-Formeln, Zeitrelationen und quantitativen Beschränkungen. Kommunikationsinformation ist deshalb immer konsistent, da vermieden werden soll, daß Inkonsistenzen weitergegeben werden. Zeitrelationen in Kommunikationsinformation können sich auch auf Intervalle von Szenarien beziehen, da ohne diesen Bezug eine zeitliche Einordnung der Information gar nicht möglich wäre. Diese Intervalle müssen dann sowohl dem Sender als auch dem Empfänger bekannt sein.

Plane-lokal-konsistent ist dafür zuständig, ein lokal konsistent geplantes Szenario zu erstellen. Bild 4 zeigt einen Ausschnitt eines Suchbaums, wie er sich durch den Backtracking-Algorithmus Plane-lokal-konsistent ergibt. Jeder Knoten steht für ein verändertes Planungsszenario. Zur Zeit der Bearbeitung von Knoten k erhält der Prozeß TIP's. Diese werden in das Planungsszenario integriert und deshalb auch im Unterbaum von k beachtet. Findet später ein Backtracking zum Vaterknoten von k statt, so werden die TIP's, die im Unterbaum eingegangen sind, zusammen mit den in k erhaltenen TIP's zurückgegeben und im Vaterknoten in das Planungsszenario eingefügt. So ist sichergestellt, daß ein gefundenes lokal konsistent geplantes Szenario alle bis zu seiner Fertigstellung angefallenen TIP's berücksichtigt.

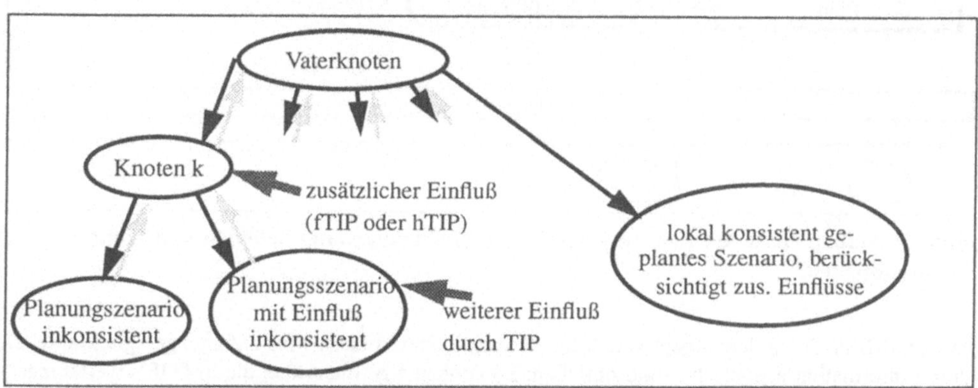

Bild 4: Ausschnitt eines Suchbaums des Prozesses Plane-lokal-konsistent. Während der Bearbeitung von Knoten k und in dessen Unterbaum wird zusätzliche Information in Form von TIP's verarbeitet und falls erforderlich zurückgegeben an den Vaterknoten.

Die zweite Einflußmöglichkeit besteht darin, TIP's in das lokal konsistent geplante Szenario aufzunehmen. Der Prozeß wähle-Plan-aus, der für die Generierung eines von der Ausführung angeforderten Plans zuständig ist, arbeitet also, wenn er einen neuen Plan auswählen soll, auf dem neuesten lokal konsistent geplanten Szenario.

3. Aufbau von Agenten mit einer temporalen Planung

Bild 5 zeigt den Aufbau eines Agenten mit der erweiterten temporalen Planung. Mehrere dieser Agenten stellen eine Multiagentenumgebung dar. Die wichtigste Datenstruktur der Agenten ist das Weltszenario. Es beinhaltet das faktische Wissen des Agenten über die Vergangenheit. Die Aktualisierung des Weltszenarios erfolgt durch fTIP's, die von der Sensoreinheit oder der inter-Agenten Kommunikation geliefert werden.

Bei kommunizierten TIP's ergibt sich das Problem, daß dem Sender bekannt sein muß, welche Intervalle der Empfänger kennt und welche er damit in Beschränkungen des TIP's verwenden kann. Dafür hält jeder Agent für jeden anderen eine Kommunikationsbasis. Sie beinhaltet eine Menge von Intervallen, für die

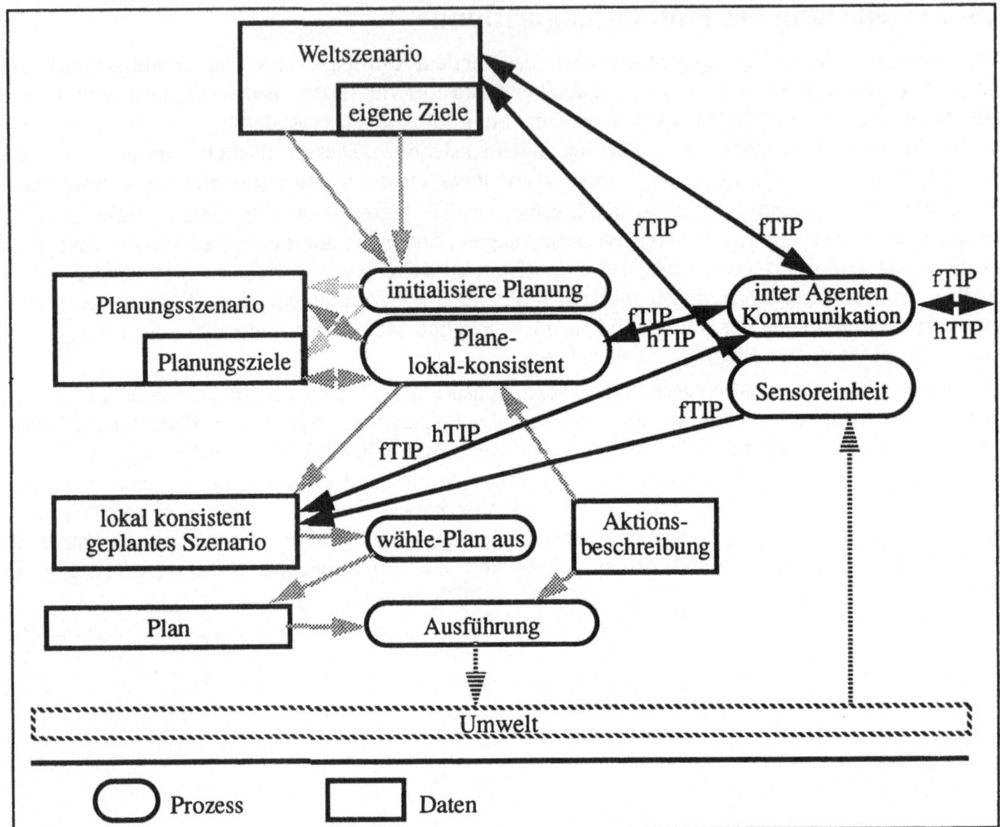

Bild 5: Aufbau eines Agenten. In einer Multiagentenumgebung befinden sich mehrere solcher Agenten.

bekannt ist, daß sie der andere Agent kennt. Die Kommunikationsbasis wird anfangs geeignet initialisiert und durch Informationsaustausch fortgeschrieben. So können z.B. Intervalle, die in fTIP's weitergegeben wurden, auf Empfänger- und Senderseite in der entsprechenden Kommunikationsbasis vermerkt werden.

Da der Agent selber hTIP's und fTIP's erhält und alle Agenten den gleichen Aufbau haben, muß er auch selbst Information aussenden können. Dies geschieht wiederum in Form von fTIP's und hTIP's, die die Kommunikationsbasis als Grundlage benutzen, indem ihre zeitlichen Relationen sich darauf beziehen können. Die ausgesandten fTIP's enthalten Information aus dem Weltszenario, denn nur dort liegt gesichertes Wissen vor. Ausgesandte hTIP's stammen aus dem lokal konsistent geplanten Szenario. Wir nehmen an, daß die Objekte der realen Welt von allen Agenten gleich benannt werden, so daß dadurch keine Mißverständnisse entstehen können.

Durch die Aktualisierung des Weltszenarios ergibt sich indirekt ein Zeitfortschritt, da das Weltszenario durch fTIP's von der Sensoreinheit oder von anderen Agenten mit neuen Intervallen angereichert wird oder durch die zusätzliche Information die Beschränkungen des Weltszenarios verschärft werden. Ein Gegenwartszeitpunkt läßt sich im Weltszenario nicht exakt bestimmen, da die Beschränkungen dafür unter Umständen nicht ausreichen.

Die vorgegebenen eigenen Ziele eines Agenten, die er von außen erhält, werden anhand des Weltszenarios geprüft und gestrichen, sobald sie erreicht sind.

Das Planungsszenario stellt einen hypothetischen Ablauf dar, auf dem der Prozeß Plane-lokal-konsistent arbeitet. Das Planungsszenario wird zu Beginn eines Planungslaufs mit dem aktuellen Weltszenario vorbesetzt, sowie die Planungsziele mit den eigenen Zielen. Sind alle Planungsziele im Planungsszenario erfüllt

(z. B. durch Aktionseinplanungen), so wird dieser Stand des Planungsszenarios als lokal konsistent geplantes Szenario ausgegeben. Wie das Weltszenario werden auch das Planungsszenario und das lokal konsistent geplante Szenario durch ankommende fTIP's aktualisiert. Zusätzlich werden aber auch hTIP's aus der inter-Agenten Kommunikation verwendet. Der Mechanismus dafür wurde bereits im vorherigen Abschnitt vorgestellt. Das lokal konsistent geplante Szenario kann man als nicht eindeutig festgelegten Plan auffassen, der durch fTIP's und hTIP's laufend eingeschränkt wird.

Die Ausführung fordert von wähle-Plan-aus einen Plan an. Sie sucht das erste Intervall i im Plan, dem ein Ereignis e (Aktion) zugeordnet ist, das vom Agenten a selbst ausgeführt werden soll (d. h. es gilt die Formel Occur(a,e,i)) und das nicht bereits im Weltszenario vorkommt. Der Zeitraum, im Plan, von dem wir sicher wissen, daß er in der Vergangenheit liegt, wird durch ein spezielles Intervall i_V repräsentiert. Dieses Intervall endet vor dem letzten Endpunkt von Intervallen, die sowohl im Plan als auch im Weltszenario vorkommen. Bevor die Ausführung das Ereignis startet, also der Agent die Aktion tätigt, werden folgende Tests durchgeführt.

1. Sollte nicht i_V (**m b**) i gelten, d. h. der Anfangspunkt von i sicher in der Vergangenheit liegen, wird der Plan verworfen und ein neuer angefordert.

2. Als nächstes überprüft die Ausführung, ob die Vorbedingungen des Ereignisses e im Weltszenario erfüllt sind. Dies geschieht dadurch, daß für die Intervalle $i_1, \ldots, i_n$, die für die Vorbedingung stehen, Intervalle $i_1', \ldots, i_n'$ im Weltszenario gesucht werden, denen entsprechende PE-Formel zugeordnet sind. Sollten einige Vorbedingungsintervalle keine Entsprechung im Weltszenario haben, so wird erneut zu Test 1 verzweigt. Dieser Zyklus wird, falls er sich nicht von selbst durch Fortschreibung des Weltszenarios auflöst, nach einer bestimmten Zeit abgebrochen und es wird ein neuer Plan angefordert.

3. Die temporalen Relationen zwischen den Intervallen $i_1, \ldots, i_n$ müssen Einschränkungen der entsprechenden Relationen der Intervalle $i_1', \ldots, i_n'$ sein.

4. Die Ausführung überprüft nun, ob die möglichen Zeitdauern, die das Weltszenario für Intervalle zuläßt, Einschränkungen der möglichen Dauern aus dem Plan sind. Überprüft werden jedoch nur Intervalle j, für die gilt j (**b m**) i. Da unter Umständen eine Vorbedingung im Weltszenario noch nicht genügend lang anhält, muß bei einem Scheitern dieses Tests der Plan noch nicht gleich verworfen werden, sondern es wird mit Test 1 fortgefahren. Auch hier wird ein sich eventuell ergebender Zyklus nach einer bestimmten Zeit abgebrochen und ein neuer Plan angefordert.

Sind alle Tests (1 - 4) erfolgreich, startet die Ausführung das Ereignis e und bearbeitet die nächste Aktion, die der Agent durchzuführen hat.

Fordert die Ausführung einen Plan an (weil sie entweder noch keinen erhalten hat oder der alte verworfen wurde), so geschieht dies durch einen Aufruf von wähle-Plan-aus. Wähle-Plan-aus erzeugt aus dem lokal konsistent geplanten Szenario einen global konsistenten Plan. Im lokal konsistent geplanten Szenario werden eventuell eintreffende fTIP's und hTIP's ständig miteinbezogen und wieder lokale Konsistenz hergestellt. Sollte kein lokal konsistent geplantes Szenario vorliegen oder sich herausstellen, daß es inkonsistent geworden ist, wird von Plane-lokal-konsistent eine neues angefordert. Plane-lokal-konsistent reagiert auf eine solche Anforderung mit einer Neuplanung auf der Basis des aktuellen Weltszenarios als initiales Planungsszenario und den aktuell gegebenen Zielen als Planungszielen. Wie im vorherigen Abschnitt erläutert, nimmt Plane-lokal-konsistent während der Abarbeitung des Suchbaums fTIP's und hTIP's auf.

Effekte von Aktionen werden über die Sensoreinheit in das Weltszenario aufgenommen. Da die Aktion aber in der Realität anders ablaufen kann, als im Plan vorhergesehen, können Diskrepanzen zwischen Weltszenario und Plan auftreten. Die Ausführung bemerkt dies, wenn es die Tests 1-4 für noch ausstehende Aktionen durchführt. Sie fordert dann einen neuen Plan an, der die unerwartete Entwicklung des Weltszenarios berücksichtigt. Es muß dabei aber selten ganz neu geplant werden, da fTIP's der Sensoreinheit ja auch in das lokal konsistent geplante Szenario aufgenommen werden und, falls sie dort die Konsistenz nicht zerstören, nur wähle-Plan aus mit der Selektion eines neuen Plans beauftragt wird.

4. Gegenwärtiger Stand und Ausblick

Die Grundform der temporalen Planung, wie sie in Abschnitt 2.3 vorgestellt wurde, wurde in Common Lisp implementiert. Die Erweiterung des temporalen Planers, der eine Berücksichtigung von Einflüssen während der Planung ermöglicht (siehe Abschnitt 2.4) und die Zerlegung seiner zwei Stufen in eigenständige Prozesse befindet sich gegenwärtig in der Implementierungsphase. Die Realisierung der Agenten und die Simulation der Welt wird in KEE, einer Expertensystemschale, erfolgen.

Ein zukünftiger Schwerpunkt der Forschung wird sein, die temporale Planungskomponente der Agenten durch Verwendung von Wissen in Form von allgemeinen und domänenabhängigen Heuristiken zu optimieren. Dies bezieht sich vor allem auf eine günstige Anordnung der zu bearbeitenden Ziele und die Auswahl der Ereignisse.

Domänenabhängiges Wissen und Erkenntnisse über die Ziele und Fähigkeiten anderer Agenten kann dazu eingesetzt werden, die inter-Agenten Kommunikation auf die wesentliche Information zu beschränken.

Ein interessantes Problem stellt auch die geeignete Aufteilung der Ziele auf die Agenten dar, die diese dann autonom bearbeiten. Ein denkbares Modell sind beispielsweise kooperativ konkurrierende Agenten, die sich um die Zuteilung von Zielen mit einem Angebot bewerben. Spezialisierte Agenten könnten dann aufgrund ihres besseren Angebots den Zuschlag erhalten.

Danksagung

Wir danken den Herren Prof. Dr. Paul Levi und Prof. Dr. Bernd Radig für ihre Anmerkungen.

5. Literatur

[AK83]   James F. Allen und Johannes A. Koomen. Planning using a temporal world model. In *Proc. of the 8th* International Joint Conference on Artificial Intelligence, S. 741-747, Karlsruhe, FRG, 1983.

[All83]   James F. Allen. Maintaining knowledge about temporal intervalls. *Communications of the ACM*, 26(11):832-843, 1983.

[All84]   James F. Allen. Towards a general theory of action and time. *Artificial Intelligence*, 23:123-154, 1984.

[FN71]   Richard E. Fikes und Nils J. Nilson. STRIPS: A new approach to the application of theorem proving to   problem solving. *Artificial Intelligence*, 2:189-205, 1971.

[Güs89]   Hans W. Güsgen. *CONSAT: A System for Constraint Satisfaction*. Morgan Kaufmann, San Mateo, CA, 1989.
           Forschungs- und Lehreinheit Informatik IX, 1991.

[Kös91]   Gerhard Köstler. *Untersuchung temporaler Planungsmethoden und die Implementierung eines Verfahrens am Beispiel eines Verkehrsagenten*. Diplomarbeit, TU München, Forschungs- und Lehreinheit Informatik IX, 1991.

[MH69]   John McCarthy und Patrick J. Hayes. Some philosophical problems from the standpoint of artificial   intelligence. In B. Meltzer und D. Miche (Hrsg.), *Machine Intelligence*, Bd. 4, S. 463-502. Elsevier, New York, 1969.

[Ric89]   Michael M. Richter. *Prinzipien der Künstlichen Intelligenz*. Teubner Verlag, Stuttgart, 1989.

[Sac74]   Earl D. Sacerdoti. Planning in a hierarchy of abstraction spaces. *Artificial Intelligence* 5: 115-135, 1974.

[Tsa86]   Edward P. K. Tsang. Plan generation in a temporal frame. In *Proc. of the 7th* European Conference on Artificial Intelligence, S. 479-493, Brighton, UK, 1986.

[Tsa87a]   Edward P. K. Tsang. *Planning in a Temporal Frame: A Partial World Description Approach*. Dissertation, Department of Computer Science, University of Essex, Colchester, UK, 1987.

[Tsa87b]   Edward P. K. Tsang. TLP - A temporal planner. In *Proc. of the 1987 AISB Conference*, S. 63-78, University of Edinburgh, 1987.

[vB89]   Peter van Beek. Approximation algorithms for temporal reasoning. In *Proc. of the 11th* International Joint Conference on Artificial Intelligence, S. 1291-1296, Detroit, MI, 1989.

Concepts and Implementation
of
Migrating Office Processes [1]

Bernhard Karbe, Norbert Ramsperger
IABG mbH
Dept. ITV
Einsteinstr. 20
D-8012 Ottobrunn

ProMInanD's migration system deals with office tasks consisting of steps to be carried out by persons playing office roles. This kind of cooperation is supported by migrating office processes which in ProMInanD are represented by Electronic Circulation Folders (ECF). Instantiations of task related types of ECF's migrate automatically through an office organization. The migration specification of an ECF describes the steps to be performed, their possible sequences and the roles which have to be played for their performance. However, in real life offices a strong need exists for deviations from predefined migration routes and for exception handling.

Migration specifications are complex frameworks of objects. They are recursively built up of different building blocks and can be modified due to office workers' dispositions such as referring back, refusal, delegation. During control of migration the specification has to be navigated through in different directions. In order to resolve the address of the office worker whose turn it is next, an extended slot mechanism is exploited. The resolution is performed as late as possible in order to take decisions based on the latest information. This information is described by means of an electronic organizational description which is kept in a relational database.

1   Introduction

Office work in detail is carried out by single office workers playing office roles [7]. Usually, it is part of encompassing activities which can often be understood as parts of a higher level activities the effective performance of which is an office organization's concern. To that end, the office organization is structured in an appropriate way and has laid down procedures for the different office tasks which, in general, have to be carried out by cooperating office workers who contribute to them the results of their work [1]. The procedures specify what has to be performed and by whom. Normally, the performer is given as an organizational unit or an office worker filling a post or having certain responsibilities. The stricter a procedure is specified the more formalized a task is. However, not only because office workers are human beings - having different working styles, being subject to different moods, making errors - but also because of the necessity of flexible reactions on changing or unforeseen circumstances, exception handling comes into being even for simple routine tasks.

A conventional tool for supporting the processing of office tasks is the ubiquitous circulation folder (CF). Its contents, consisting of arbitrary but task-related documents, is to be worked on by performers who are specified on the cover of the CF by other office workers at their discretion. An internal messenger service takes care of the transfer of closed CF's from an office worker's out-tray to the in-tray of the one who is

---

1)   This paper is an outcome of the Project ProMInanD - Extended Office Process Migration with Interactive Panel Displays. ProMInanD is supported in part by ESPRIT - European Strategic Programme for Research and Development in Information Technologies.

next . A clear distinction can be made between intrinsic work on the contents of an CF and its transfer through an organization. The CF is an approved and very flexible tool which, however, suffers from some drawbacks, in particular, from the slowness of the messenger service and, often, the problem of finding certain documents [10].

In the literature several promising approaches [6, 7, 8, 9, 11] are described for supporting office tasks. Among other things they attack or study different problems: shortcuts of work flow [6], user roles of office workers [7], consistency of related office procedures [7], and fully automated agents for steps to be carried out without an intervening office worker [8]. Modeling the work flow in [9, 11] is based on certain types of Petri-Nets which, however, complicate exception handling.

All these approaches do not achieve the flexibility of the CF the support of which has been one of ProMInanD's main goals. To that end, ProMInanD replaces the CF by the electronic circulation folder (ECF). ProMInanD is designed in such a way that all its concepts can be explained by showing the relationship between the conventional CF and its electronic counterpart. But the ECF offers more: Its migration through an office organization is automatic due to its specification. Nevertheless, it offers the same flexibility the office worker is used to from the CF. In addition, ProMInanD allows to locate ECF's which are currently circulating in the organization. An ECF consists of two main parts: its content, containing task specific documents to be worked on, and its procedure description. Both, the procedure description and the migration control are in this paper's main focus.

2   An Example

A simple formalized task is considered, the appeal of which is, on the one hand, that it is understood all over the world and, on the other hand, that it allows at the same time quite different aspects of the flow of office work to be demonstrated. The task is the so-called "Application for Vacation". It is assumed that this task is represented by an appropriate form which is forwarded through an organization as the contents of a CF. Ideally, it is performed according to the organizational procedure in the following way: an office worker applying for vacation starts this task in step APPLICATION by filling in the vacation form. In the step SIGNATURE the colleague entered as substitute confirms his taking over. Then, the head of department approves the application in step APPROVAL. The secretary will then enter the dates of the office worker's leave of absence into a vacation list during step UPDATE. Eventually, the applicant is informed of the application's success in the final step NOTIFICATION. There are some cases which have to be differentiated: if for some reason no substitute is entered the step SIGNATURE is to be skipped, if the application is not approved the step UPDATE is to be skipped, too, and if the vacation is of the type "special leave" a copy has to be sent to the personnel department for some FILING purposes.

In real life many reasons may occur for deviations from this ideal flow. These exceptions are considered in a representative way [2]:

- In order to get his manager involved the applicant may insert an additional step and forward the form and a note to his manager and ask him to continue normal processing.
- The applicant may decide to cancel the vacation at any time after having finished the step APPLICATION.
- The substitute selected by the applicant may refuse to take over. Thus, he sends the folder back possibly with a slip on it giving some explanation.
- The head of department may be on a business trip. Thus, the step APPROVAL should be performed by his substitute.
- The head of department may wonder whether the substitute can really take over. Thus, he may refer back explaining his doubts on a folder slip.

In the description of the organizational procedure of the task "Application for Vacation" and its possible deviations several notions of the organizational structure description are used. Two organizational units "department" are involved: the one in which the applicant is a member and the personnel department. Several "employees", "posts" and "functions" located on three different hierarchical levels are referred to: the applicant himself, his colleague, his manager, the head of the department, the secretary of the department, and the permanent substitute for the post "head of the department". An additional office worker is referred to implicitly by the organizational unit personnel department, namely one of those who are responsible for filing.

Thus, the performance of an office task is described as a whole not only by naming the documents to be worked on - here an appropriate application form - but also by means of structural and procedural notions.

3   Organizational Structure Description

Basic structural notions deal with the organizational structure itself. It is the backbone for any type of task allocation [3]. It is kept in the electronic organizational structure description which is realized as a set of tables of the global database of ProMInanD. The most elementary definitions concern the hierarchical structure of an organization, in particular:
- which office workers are employed, i.e. the employees,
- which posts are established,
- how are the posts grouped into organizational units,
- which post inside an organizational unit defines its manager,
- how is the hierarchy of organizational units, i.e. the relation "<unit1> is superior to <unit2>", and
- which employee fills which post.

Office workers involved in an ECF are addressed by their organizational function, their so-called office role. Roles are the basic items defining who has to carry out a certain portion of work. Superimposed on the hierarchical structure office roles are defined with their relation to posts and employees. Roles are grouped into organizational units like projects, task forces etc., each of them having one of the roles as manager role. For each post one corresponding role exists in order to unify addressing of organizational functions, e.g. the notion of "head of department". A single role may be assigned to one or more posts or to one or more employees. For example, a role "member of project" may be directly assigned to a person, whereas the role "member of the managing board" may be assigned to the posts of the two topmost levels. Then, an office worker is "member of the managing board" because he fills an appropriate post. Usually, several roles are assigned to one post or employee. Thus, the organizational structure description keeps information about:
- roles established in the organization,
- organizational units like projects, task forces etc. consisting only of roles,
- how are the roles grouped into organizational units,
- hierarchy relation between those organizational units,
- which roles inside an organizational unit defines its manager,
- actual assignments of roles to office workers and to posts, and
- actual assignments of posts to locations and workstations.

In addition, substitutions can be defined. Long term substitutions concern the fact that an office worker filling a post P1 may always be substituted by the office worker filling a post P2. Temporary substitutions are defined in terms that an office worker substitutes another in a certain role during a period of time. In a more sophisticated situation an office worker may have different substitutes for different roles, e.g. one as "head of department" and one as "member of the worker s' council". Data representing entities of the real office world like employees, roles, posts and organizational units have unique systemwide identifications. Roles can be addressed by procedure specifications through their identification. This suffice for central organizational functions. But in most cases organizational notions evitably go beyond these. They are represented by so-called office worker relations which exploit the electronic organizational structure description. How this can be done is exemplified by considering how to find the head of department of an office worker <ow>.:
- what is the post of <ow> ,
- what is the organizational unit of that post,
- along the hierarchy of organizational units go upward to the department level,
- what is the manager post of the organizational unit found,
- is this post actually assigned to an office worker, and, if not,
- is there a substitute post defined, and
- what is the identification of the corresponding role to that post.

The description of the organization is set apart from the algorithmic part of the ProMInanD. That makes it easy to respond to changes in the organization such as restructuring, changing temporary or permanent assignments, or introducing new office tasks.

4   Organizational Procedure Description

An organizational procedure description, called migration specification, is modelled by a complex framework of different types of objects. Besides offering a graphical interface, specification objects are produced by a generator which interprets a script written in Objective-C which is employed in ProMInanD. The specification objects produced are passivated and stored in files from which other programs may load and activate them. In the following, parts of scripts are referred to in order to give more details on migration specifications.

By means of building blocks, migration specifications define the sequencing of and the relations between the different parts of office tasks. Building blocks have attributes which model entities of the outside office world. These entities are called basic elements of migration specifications. In order to evaluate the current status of the modelled world a general specification and evaluation mechanism is used, called the slot mechanism. In the following bottom-up description, the most important elements of migration specifications are presented in terms of objects, classes and their relations.

4.1 Slot Mechanisms

The main problems with ECF's in general are that
- the time between specification of migration and its interpretation is unpredictable and arbitrarily long,
- organizations almost always change, and the changes may affect ECF's under migration.

In order to tackle these problems ProMInanD follows a twofold approach: on the one hand, keeping basic information in a global database, on the other hand, performing evaluations as late as possible by means of an extended slot mechanism which is heavily used in the following two areas: start of application-dependent programs and determination of office workers who have to perform steps.

A slot [5] is an instance variable of an object which either has a value or knows where to get its value from when it is needed. Values of slots are computed at the time they are needed. Then, an a-priori named message is sent to an already known receiver object in order to provide the requested value. A slot could be specified by:

[Slot receiver: anObject selector: aMethodDescriptor] ;

Asking for the slot's value causes the following message to be sent:

[anObject aMethodDescriptor] ;

4.1.1 Slots using Objects

In ProMInanD a slot is an object which returns its current value as response to the message with the descriptor "evaluate". A model of Kaye's slot is the ObjectSlot class of ProMInanD. Obvious extensions are that a parameter can be passed to the receiver, and that the receiver as well as the parameter of the message are, in turn, values of slots. In order to evaluate a slot's current value an ObjectSlot needs the following information:
- the object a message has to be sent to in the case of evaluation, called the receiver. The receiver may be evaluated dynamically by means of another slot being known to an ObjectSlot instance through an instance variable.
- the message descriptor which has to be sent in the case of evaluation, called the selector.
- the parameter, if any. It may also be evaluated dynamically by means of another slot.

In the case of evaluation an ObjectSlot produces a message of the type:

[receiver perform: selector with: parameter] ;

which means that a message with the descriptor *selector* and the parameter *parameter* is sent to the object *receiver*. The basic mechanism exploited is provided by Objective-C; it is the possiblility to perform an object's method of which the name is known only. That name is represented as a string and can, therefore, be communicated between different programs. The Objective-C message resolution mechanism, then, transforms the name to a function call at runtime.

A specialization of ObjectSlot is ClassSlot handling the case that not an instance but a class is the receiver of the message. A generalization is Slot which is only able to keep a value (see the examples below). Slot is an abstract superclass defining the methods needed for slots in general. Some of them are supposed to be overridden by more specialized subclasses.

4.1.2 Slots Using External Programs

The mechanism above is fine as long as the problems can be solved inside an object-oriented program. This mechanism does not suffice if, for example, the ECF needs to exploit information from the document's content. Then, an application-dependent so-called decision program has to be started which looks up that document. To that end, the concept of slots has been extended so that it becomes possible to start independent programs, and to obtain results from "standard out". This extension is modelled by the ProgramSlot class. In order to evaluate its current value a ProgramSlot needs a Program object which is able to compose a program call string. That string is forwarded to the operating system interface class System which returns the result of the program execution. In the case of evaluation a ProgramSlot sends the message:

```
[System evaluate: [program callString]] ;
```

4.1.3 Slots Using an External Data Base

Another extension is the possibility to run arbitrary queries on databases. This is necessary in order to evaluate relations between office workers using the global organizational structure description. Data base evaluations are modelled by the DBSlot class. Each instance knows the tables it has to deal with and the matching attributes. Sequences of queries are defined through slot nesting, i.e. by giving a slot another slot as a parameter. The intermediary result produced by a DBSlot object is stored in a temporary table (3). A temporary table has the same structure as the target table of a join (2). The description of the target table is taken from the database's definition table (1). Thus, a simple DBSlot may run the following queries:

```
(1)    select <columnName>, <columnType>, <columnAttributes>
           from <systemTable>
           where <tableName> = "<targetTable>" ;
(2)    create table <newTemporaryTable> (<description of targetTable>) ;
(3)    insert into <newTemporaryTable>:
           select <attribute list of targetTable> from <targetTable>
           where [ targetMatchAttribute ]
               in (select <sourceMatchAttribute> from <lastTemporaryTable>) ;
```

The <lastTemporaryTable> of the topmost DBSlot is either a temporary table filled from the result of another but non-DBSlot or it is a permanent table. The topmost DBSlot object also controls transaction begin and abort as well as otains the result from the last temporary table. The transaction abort is used in order to destroy the temporary tables after evaluation.

4.2   Basic Elements

Some basic elements model parts of the outside office world. The most important ones are given by the classes OfficeWorker, Machine, Document and Program. While OfficeWorker and Machine define who has to do something, objects of the classes Document and Program define what it is. In general, if an attribute of these object is specified explicitly by a constant string that string has to be an existing attribute value in the global data base.

4.2.1   Office Worker and Machine

The description of office workers by means of the OfficeWorker class contains two major constituents, an office role description and an employee description. Each of them is a pair of Slots, one for the evaluation of its systemwide unique identification, one for its systemwide name. If an identification is given the related name can be found easily. If an existing name is given one finds at least one identification for that name. For example, several employees with different identifications may exist having the name "Brown". The definition of an office worker may contain either the identification of a role or the name of the role. In addition, the employee may be defined either by his/her identification or name.

An example is the definition of the substitute: The substitute is addressed as person, i.e. the role name "person" is used as the specifying attribute. (Each employee known to the system can at least play the role "person".) The name of the substitute may be given by a certain field of the vacation form.

```
substitute = [OfficeWorker new];
[substitute employeeName: [ProgramSlot program: formLookupProgram]];
[substitute roleName: [Slot str:"person"] ];
```

In some cases, parts of the work can be performed by a server station automatically. Or, a certain resource is only available on certain hardware. Then one may specify which workstation or which workstation type has to be used using the Machine class. This is similar to the definition of office roles or employees.

4.2.2 Program and Document

ProMInanD makes a strict distinction between flow of work, being represented by an ECF, and the intrinsic work performed by office workers for instance. It is not at all interested in the specific structure, representation and handling of documents inside an ECF. Its only concern is the integration and presentation of them. The intrinsic work as well as all other application-specific operations are performed by concrete programs. In the example, at least one application-dependent program is necessary which supports filling, presentation and evaluation of vacation forms.

All documents needed for an ECF have to be described. Necessary for each document is at least the definition of its name, the name of the file containing its contents, and of its type. The possible document types are defined by the global data base. The name of the file containing the contents is specific to an ECF.

In the example only one document, the vacation form, is needed. It may have the document type "FORM":

```
form = [Document create: [String str:"vacForm"]];
[form documentType: [String str:"FORM"]];
```

The programs used are specified in an abstract way by their abstract program type. For each type of document known to the system at least two types of programs, a full editing program and a read only type program have to be available. All known types of programs are kept in the global data base. In an heterogeneous environment there may be functionally equivalent programs running on different platforms and having different names.

The global data base also contains information about which concrete programs, noted by their name and version, can be used if a certain type of program shall be applied to a certain type of document on a certain (type of) workstation. Thus, an ECF only needs to know which type of program to apply on which type of document. An abstract specification of a program contains its program type and, if more than one document is used, its primary document type. In addition, the collection of constant or variable paramaters have to be specified.

In the example a lookup program is used in order to find the name of the substitute. It shall be of the type "EXTRACT" while the application-specific field name for the substitute's name is "substitute_name". When starting that program it needs the path of the vacation form file.

```
formLookupProgram = [Program new];
[formLookupProgram abstractName: [String str:"EXTRACT"]];
[formLookupProgram addParam: [Slot str: "substitute_name"]];
[formLookupProgram addParam:
        [ObjectSlot receiver: form selector: "path" with: nil]];
```

4.3 Building Blocks of Migration Specification

The sequencing description concerning the different parts of migration specification is composed from building blocks. Building block objects contain information on their predecessor and their successor. The classes described in the following are subclasses of the BuildingBlock class. In the figure a graphical representation of the migration specification including its building blocks of the task "Application for Vacation", the "Vacation ECF", is presented.

4.3.1 Step

Roughly speaking, a step defines WHO (in terms of office workers or machines) has to do WHAT (in terms of programs and documents).

Beside the application-specific program which is used to perform a step and which is called a step program, an additional one may be specified which is invoked if the work on the step has to be undone. In general, complete undo is not possible. What, however, is possible is some kind of compensation [4]:

- **passive compensation** puts the documents back into the state they were in at the first start of the work on the step,
- **active compensation** invokes an application specific compensating program. ProMInanD provides a communication area for the step program and its peering compensating program. This can be used for, e.g., recording information on the activities performed by the step program on the basis of which the compensating program can execute inverse operations.

notification is performed in the remaining cases. It only informs the office worker about the ongoing compensation. Then, the office worker can react appropriately and might be able to compensate activities concerning the world outside ProMInanD.

The documents to be checkpointed in a step for later passive compensation have to be specified. However, the performance of a step may mark a border after which cancellation of an ECF is not possible any more. The office worker performing a step can be enabled to cancel the ECF at a later time, i.e. that step defines a possible aborter for the whole ECF.

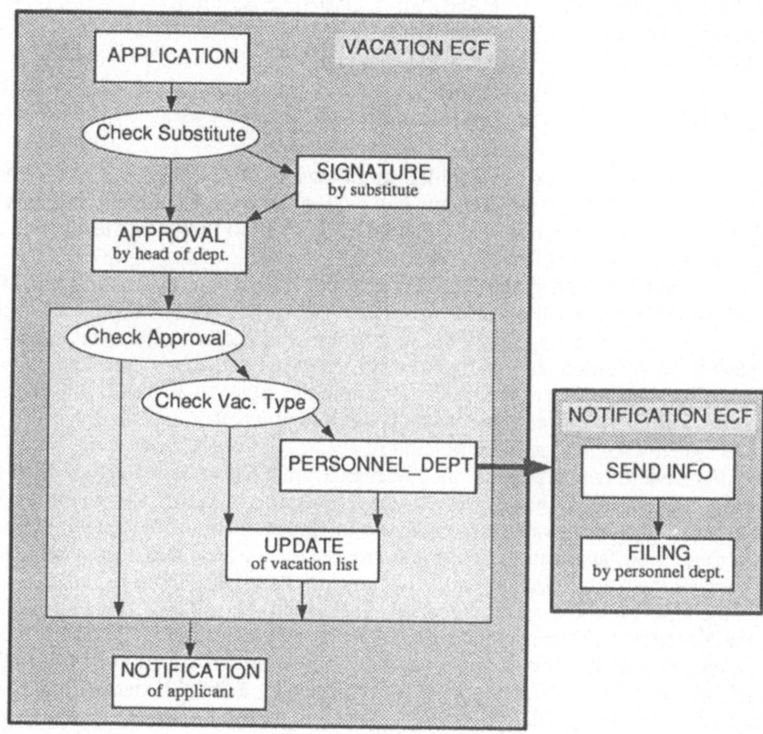

An Example Migration Specification

In the example, what has to be defined for the steps SIGNATURE, APPROVAL and NOTIFICATION is how the responsible office workers have to be determined. The office worker of the step APPLICATION is the initiator of the Vacation ECF and becomes known at the time of its instantiation. The step UPDATE is performed automatically at a server station where the vacation list is accessible.

As an example, the script for the step APPROVAL is shown. The assumption is that an appropriate step program with the name "approvalSTP" is already specified. The office worker is evaluated as follows:

- Take the identification of the office worker who has performed the step APPLICATION, given by the object with the name "initiatorStep".
- Ask the Organigram class for the role of the head of that department which contains the post of that office work.
- Use the unique identification of that role only.

```
id applicant, aHod, hodRole, hod, hodStep;
applicant  = [ObjectSlot  receiver:  [initiatorStep officeWorker]
                          selector:  "lastEmployeeId"
                          with:      nil];
aHod       = [ClassSlot    class:     "Organigram"
                          selector:  "headOfDepartment:"
                          with:      applicant];
```

```
hodRole    = [ObjectSlot   receiver:  aHod
                           selector:  "atKey:"
                           with:      [String str: STR_ROLE_ID]];
hod        = [[OfficeWorker new] roleId: hodRole];
hodStep    = [Step         create:    [String str: "Approval by Head of Department"]
                           ofID:      [String str: "Step3"]];
[hodStep officeWorker:      hod];
[hodStep stepProgram:       approvalSTP];
[hodStep kindOfCompens:     PASSIVE_COMPENSATION];
[hodStep addCheckedDoc:     form];
[hodStep definesAborter:    YES];
```

4.3.2 DECF Starter

Office tasks may ask for performance in parallel. In CF-based offices parallelism can easily be accomplished by putting a copy of the CF's documents into a CF of its own which then migrates independently through the organization. This straightforward approach is applied to ECF's and leads to dependent ECFs. Despite having a father a dependent ECF (DECF) is a normal ECF.

What has to be specified is which type of DECF it is and how it is initialized. Application dependent programs, so-called DECF initialization programs, have to be provided which produce appropriate documents for the DECF. For the control of migration some information defining the relation between the DECF and its father have to be specified, especially, whether the DECF has to be cancelled consequently if the father ECF is cancelled, and whether the DECF has to join the father ECF. These information all together are kept in a specific "DECF reference" object which also knows whether the DECF has been started or not, and if so, what its systemwide unique identification is.

If results of DECF's have to be merged into the father ECF what has to be defined is when the join should take place, whether the father ECF has to wait for the termination of the DECF, whether the father is able to accept the DECF's results in advance, and whether the father ECF will be able to progress even if the DECF is not on time. Also, application-dependent programs, so-called DECF join programs, have to be provided which merge in an appropriate way the documents of the DECF into its father.

In the example, the task "Application for Vacation" is split into two ECF's: one father ECF defining the main stream, the Vacation ECF itself, and a DECF being a Notification ECF. The DECF initialization program is a simple one which just copies the vacation form from the Vacation ECF into the Notification ECF. The initialization of the Notification ECF is performed by a "DECF starter" building block named PERSONNEL_DEPT which uses a DECF reference object. The Notification ECF is started automatically by the Vacation ECF after the step APPROVAL. It consists of two steps, one for the sending and one for the receiving office worker. The receiver is defined by an appropriate role inside the personnel department. By default, the sender is the one who has performed the step APPROVAL, i.e. the last interactive step inside the father ECF. The Notification ECF has to be cancelled consequently but, due to its simplicity, does not need to join the father ECF.

4.3.3 Alternative

An alternative comes into play if a selection is to be made between several further migration routes. Accordingly, it has several possible succeeding branches of which one represents the default route. The other ones are guarded by Condition objects. A condition knows what to check and how. The check is, in most cases, based on the result of an evaluation which is carried out by an application-dependent decision program interpreting the ECF's content. A branch is chosen if the corresponding condition hold. If no one holds the further migration goes along the default route.

In the example, depending on whether the decision program finds the surname of the substitute the next step is SIGNATURE, named "substituteStep", or APPROVAL. Thus, the Condition object will respond with true if the surname string found is (lexicographically) greater than blank. As an illustration, the script part of the alternative "Check Substitute" is shown:

```
id evalSubstitute, condition;
evalSubstitute   = [Alternative create: [String str: "Check if a substitute is filled in"]
                                 ofID:   [String str: "Step4"]];
```

```
[evalSubstitute decisionFunction: [ProgramSlot program: formLookupProgram]];
condition  = [[Condition new] setGreater: [String str: " "]];
```

4.3.4 Sub-Task

Special building blocks are sub-tasks which contain sub-tasks and other building blocks and, thus, allow the recursive structure of migration specifications. Often, complex ECF's and sub-tasks can be divided into sub-tasks in a natural way according to their relation to organizational units. Office workers of other sub-units do not need to know which steps are used to process a sub-task. Particulary, they do not need to know whether office worker driven deviations have taken place during the performance of the sub-task. Their view on the representation of the migration specification shows the sub-task with the steps hidden. In particular, the concept of sub-tasks eases the definition of migration specifications.

In the example there are no sub-tasks besides a basic one which is the task itself. However, in order to hide internals to the users one could think of making a sub-task, named "vacUpdate", from the UPDATE step, the DECF starter and their preceding alternatives. The advantage is that with respect to deviations sub-tasks behave like steps - they can be moved and skipped whereas alternatives cannot.

Sub-tasks are modelled by Fragment objects. A fragment knows of the first building block of a sequence of building blocks. Usually, this sequence is prepared first. As an example, the script part of sequencing specification for the whole task is shown:

```
id rootFragment;
[initiatorStep     append:        evalSubstitute];
[evalSubstitute addBranch:    substituteStep  if: condition];
[evalSubstitute defaultRoute: hodStep];
[substituteStep append:       hodStep];
[hodStep        append:        vacationUpdate];
[vacUpdate      append:        notifyApplicantStep];
rootFragment    = [Fragment   create:[String str: "Vacation Application Task"]
                              ofID:   [String str: "Frgmt1"] ];
[rootFragment  sequence: initiatorStep];
```

4.4   The Whole Procedure

A migration specification is modelled by a "migrating office process" (MOP) object. Besides status information an MOP object consists of two main parts, a representation of the ECF's root fragment and of its contents. Only the root fragment has to be specified explicitly. The contents of an ECF is divided into two folders, the work part folder and the appendix folder.

Making a root fragment known to an MOP object also initiates some assembling operations like linking to that office worker specification which represents the initiator of the ECF. All DECF references are connected to the whole ECF in order to support their later operation. The work part folder is composed from the documents used by any program referenced from any building block inside the root fragment. An empty appendix folder is prepared as well as an empty folder slip object [1].

As an example, the script part producing the whole migration specification is shown:

```
id mop;
mop = [MOP create: [String str: "Vacation Application"]
           ofID:    [String str: "vacApp1"] ];
[mop rootFragment: rootFragment];
```

Besides defining a migration specification, an appropriate directory for the new type of ECF has to be established containing not only the migration specification file but also blank versions of the documents referenced. The creation of these documents has to be done by application-specific tools, for example by a form generator. All together define an ECF schema from which instances are created by office workers by a simple selection of the ECF type at the user interface.

4.5   Dynamic Modification of Procedures

Support of exception handling has been a design goal from the beginning. In particular, it includes deviations from pre-specified procedures. Thus, office workers should be able to change migration specifications of ECF instances by appending new steps, starting DECF's, shifting building blocks, or skipping building blocks. (The last two deviations are possible only if the attributes of the building blocks concerned enable them.)

In order to show the power of the procedure description method developed in ProMInanD the following will demonstrate how to add a new step at an office worker's discretion. Two activities only are necessary:

- Make a copy of the current step including its program specification, but not its office worker description and insert the step after the current one into the migration specification. This can be formulated as:

```
new = [currentStep copy];
[new stepProgram: [[currentStep stepProgram] copy]];
[currentStep append: new];
```

- Ask the user for an office role the office worker has to play who shall work on the appended step, and forward this information to the new step.

By means of a graphical user interface and the information on the organizational structure in the global data base, the last activity can be supported in many ways.

5 Work Flow Control

Decisions on who has to perform the next step are made as late as possible in order to take into account all possible organizational changes which might have taken place since the ECF has been instantiated. Thus, a decision is to be made just before delivery. The decision can be divided into finding the next step of an ECF and resolving its receiver.

5.1 Migration Control

A significant status information of an ECF is its current step. If a new ECF is instantiated the current step reference is moved from the root fragment to the first step. If an ECF is forwarded the reference is moved from the current step to the next one. This navigation mechanism has to take into account the fragment structure.

Navigation can take place in forward as well as in backward direction [2]. Forward navigation along the sequence of building blocks is the normal case. Backward navigation takes place in "compensation" mode or in "navigation only" mode, whihc are caused by e.g. an office worker's "not me" or by e.g. "refer back" respectively. These modes define different contexts of navigation. Another contxt comes into being if a forward to the next step is performed the first time.

A forward navigation has to consider the context. The current context is passed to the successor building blocks of that building block a navigation has been started from, i.e. from the current step. The current context of a step is evaluated by exploiting the history of that step.

In the following only forward navigation is considered because, essentially, backward navigation does the same. The navigation mechanism is implemented by means of two recursive navigation methods of the building block protocol. One of them is used when the navigation starts at the current object. A forward navigation is initiated by:

```
forwardFrom: aContext { return [ self goForwardBecause: aContext ]; }
```

In principle, except steps all building blocks which are involved during navigation have to perform some specific work, e.g.: An alternative has to select the further route, an DECF starter has to start an DECF. Correspondingly, during backward navigation and in the case of compensation they compensate their work, i.e. alternatives reset their selection and DECF starter cancel DECF's they have started. Thus, each type of building block has a forward navigation function of its own:

```
forwardTo: aContext {
        if ( [ aContext isAsInitial ] )
              < do some specific actions >
        return [ self goForwardBecause: aContext ];
}
```

A fragment behaves differently as it navigates to its first building block:

```
forwardTo: aContext { return [ first forwardTo: aContext ]; }
```

A step terminates navigation by returning itself as the next step:

```
forwardTo: aContext { return self; }
```

If the last building block of a fragment, i.e. one without a successor, is reached during navigation the encompassing fragment can be closed. Therefore, building blocks need to know their encompassing fragment in order to be able to initiate navigation on the higher level of their encompassing fragment. Thus, the "forwardFrom:" method is not only applied to steps but also to fragments. The entire forward navigation mechanism is as follows:

```
goForwardBecause: aContext {
        if ( successor )
                return [ successor forwardTo: aContext ];
        else
                return [ encompassingFragment forwardFrom: aContext ];
}
```

It should be emphasized that the procedure description method together with the navigation mechanism provides the possibility to support the handling of all typical exceptions in office organizations.

5.2   Receiver Resolution

If the next step is found the performer of that step has to be evaluated. To that end, the office worker and his office role as well as the machine concerned is resolved by means of the slot mechanisms. As a result some systemwide unique identifications are available. In most cases, an ECF is requested to be forwarded to an office worker playing a certain role <rl>.

From the organizational description as well as from the information on substitutions the set of roles can be derived which an office worker is able to play at a certain point in time. He may enter and leave these roles at any time. ProMInanD knows which office workers are currently playing which roles. If one of them fits the ECF will be delivered to that office worker playing role <rl>. If more than one office worker fit the ECF is delivered to that one with the least current deliveries. Otherwise, the ECF will wait for the next office worker entering the requested role.

For example, when referring an ECF back to a previous office worker, the next office worker is not only specified by his/her office role, but also directly by his/her name or identification. If that office worker does not enter the system for too long ProMInanD tries to deliver the ECF to another office worker playing the same role. Only in the case, that the ECF is forwarded to an office worker personally, i.e. to its role "person", the ECF will wait unconditionally for that office worker.

6   Summary and Outlook

An outline has been given on how ProMInanD supports cooperative work on office tasks by means of ECF's which migrate automatically through an office organization to the office workers involved. ProMInanD relies on organizational procedure descriptions and - unlike other systems - heavily on an organizational structure description. Together with an extended slot mechanism it is, therefore, possible to resolve addresses of office workers to whom ECF's are to be delivered just before delivery. Also, this approach enables exception handling which is a must in office organizations. Thus, the flexibility of the conventional circulation folder has been achieved which the office worker is used to, but its drawbacks have been overcome.

The organizational structure description of the organization is set apart from the migration control algorithms. Specified and even instantiated ECF's are not affected by certain changes of the organization. Also remarkable seems to be the clear distinction between the control of work flow and the work itself. ProMInanD deals mainly with the control but allows to integrate arbitrary application programs supporting the intrinsic work.

Demonstrations at fairs and exhibitions have shown that ProMInanD meets the office workers' requirements and have led to a first pilot installation from which valuable feedback is expected. Further pilot installations are under discussion. Also, ProMInanD has become one central part of a further ESPRIT project on office automation.

Acknowledgments: Many thanks to Prof. Rudolf Bayer and his students of the Technical University Munich who have, well guided by Pavel Vogel, contributed with much work to the development and implementation of ProMInanD.

References

[1]   B.Karbe, N.Ramsperger, P.Weiss: Support of Cooperative Work by Electronic Circulation Folders, COIS90 - Conference on Office Information Systems, Cambridge, MA, April 1990

[2]   B.Karbe, N.Ramsperger: Influence of Exception Handling on the Support of Cooperative Office Work, IFIP WG8.4 Conference on Multi-User Interfaces and Applications, Heraklion, Crete, Greece, September 1990

[3]   B.Karbe, N.Ramsperger: Advanced Task Allocation in ProMInanD, HCI'91, Stuttgart, Sept. 1991

[4]   R.Erfle, P.Vogel: Backtracking Office Procedures, in preparation

[5]   A.R.Kaye, G.M.Karam: Cooperating Knowledge-Based Assistants for the Office, ACM TOOIS, v5n4, 1987

[6]   C.A.Ellis, M.Bernal: OfficeTalk-D - An Experimental Office Information System, First SIGOA Conference on Office Information Systems, 1982

[7]   W.B.Croft, L.S.Lefkowitz: Task Support in an Office System, ACM TOOIS v2n3, 19 84

[8]   L.Aiello, D.Nardi, M.Panti: Modeling the Office Structure: A First Step Towards the Office Expert System, Second SIGOA Conference on Office Information Systems, 1984

[9]   Th.Kreifelts: Coordination Procedures: A Model for Cooperative Office Processes, Kommunikation in verteilten Systemen - Anwendung und Betrieb, GI/NTG Fachtagung (ed. O.Spaniol), 1984

[10] H.Plank, N.Ramsperger, B.Schwindt: Analyses of Paper Work and Communication in the Ministry of Foreign Affairs, IABG Report B-SZ 1462, 1985 (in German)

[11] Th.Kreifelts, G.Woetzel: Distribution and Error Handling in an Office Procedure System, IFIP Conference on Office Systems - Methods and Tools, Pisa, 1986

Trademark: Objective-C is a registered trademark of The Stepstone Corporation.

Coordination of Distributed Work: From Office Procedures to Customizable Activities

Thomas Kreifelts

GMD

Institute for Applied Information Technology

Schloß Birlinghoven

D-5205 Sankt Augustin

All forms of organizational activity require some form of coordination, especially when the number of tasks and individuals involved is large. As computer networks and personal computers are becoming a common infrastructure in many organizations computer systems have evolved that support the coordination of distributed work using asynchronous communication (store-and-forward techniques, e-mail). Work in this area that has been carried out at GMD's Institute for Applied Information Technology will be presented: the office procedure system DOMINO is introduced along with the structured interaction paradigm on which it is based, related systems (meeting scheduler, organizational knowledge base) and practical experiences with DOMINO will be discussed, and an approach for a new generic coordination support tool ("Activity Assistant") will be presented that features user configuration of cooperation structures and flexible support.

1   Coordination of Distributed Work

The coordination of distributed work is concerned with the management of cooperative activity in organizations. Cooperative activities involve groups of people where each member of the group is carrying out part of the overall work; the nature of activities may vary from perfectly structured to unstructured. Coordination of distributed work is part of "Computer-Supported Cooperative Work (CSCW)", however, it has been a research subject long before the term CSCW was coined. Research started around the time when the technological basis for coordination via computer became available: computer networks and personal computing.

The computer infrastructure of today's organizations was hardly imaginable some fifteen years ago when the first prototype systems were built for cooperation support, for use by groups rather than by single users. While the first prototype systems focussed on the automation of organizational processes — the research area was then named "Office Automation" — the spectrum of cooperation support systems has opened up since then and nowadays includes systems like group calendars, conference room support systems, or joint editing systems for groups.

CSCW systems may be categorized according to the work situations or work modes they support: whether users are at the same place (*co-located*) or at different places (*distributed*), whether users use the system at the same time (*synchronous*) or at different times (*asynchronous*), whether the information exchange uses message passing (*direct*) or information sharing (*indirect*). Each of these work modes has its advantages and disadvantages and depends on the application context: with an asynchronous system, for example, users can work at any time they want, but they have no direct response to their actions by other users. Applying these categories, a conference room support system would belong to the co-located, synchronous, and indirect class. While not excluding these work modes, systems that support the coordination of distributed work tend to be at the other end: they use asynchronous (and direct) store-and-forward techniques for information exchange and allow their users to be geographically distributed.

The design task with coordination systems is (and has been) to build useful systems that address the problems people have with coordination of distributed work. In addition, the usefulness has to prove itself despite the fact that coordination is never at the focus of the work but rather considered overhead that has to be done in order to keep the organization running.

GMD's Institute for Applied Information Technology is doing research in the area of coordination systems for ten years now. Our work started with modelling structured cooperative office processes ("office procedures"); over the years several prototypes of the DOMINO office procedure system have been developed, the key ideas of the DOMINO design were generalized and also applied to meeting scheduling and plan coordination with autonomous agents. In the following, various aspects of office procedure coordination will be highlighted — modelling office procedures, performance of office procedures using asynchronous communication, "binding" office procedures to organizational structures —, the results and consequences of a practical experiment will be discussed, and our new approach to coordination systems will be presented: moving from pre-structured coordination patterns of office procedures to user configurable and modifiable coordination structures of cooperative activity of a more general nature.

2   Office procedures as Petri Nets

Office procedures are considered the most structured group activities, they are split up into individual tasks where a particular order of tasks is pre-defined and almost always adhered to. They account for a lot of organizational processes usually associated with a particular kind of form (purchase procedures, business trip procedures, etc.). An office procedure system is to relieve office workers from monitoring the performance of these repetitive activities. This includes notification of new tasks, routing results from one task to another, and providing status information on the whole procedure.

In order to enable a computer system to perform these coordination tasks there must be a precise way of describing the cooperation patterns. There are two assumptions we have made concerning the office procedures of our DOMINO system:

(a) Every office worker has a private working domain; cooperation takes place by exchanging messages between these working domains (rather than by working on common domains, i.e. by information sharing).

(b) Cooperation in an organizational setting concerning groups of people is organized by specifying the input/output relations of the elementary work steps that are carried out in the working domains of the office workers responsible.

DOMINO office procedures are specified in a specific, application oriented language named CoPlanS. A procedure description specifies which elementary steps ("actions") a procedure consists of, and what dependencies exist between these actions by denoting the data needed and produced during the execution of the actions ("forms"). The various actions of the procedure are assigned to "roles" responsible for their performance; at run-time, these roles are assigned to persons. Procedure specifications also have a graphical representation. We give an example of a simple purchase procedure in figure 1; actions are represented as boxes, and forms as circles, while role labels are attached to the action boxes. The information flow is indicated by arrows.

The DOMINO procedure descriptions are rather simple and straightforward, the class of office processes that can be described within the DOMINO model comprises concurrent as well as alternative courses of activity within the procedure. The underlying procedure model is based on Petri nets, i.e. DOMINO procedures have a mathematical foundation in Petri net theory that allows for consistency checks, e.g. the exclusion of possible deadlocks. This is used by the DOMINO office procedure compiler which checks procedure specifications for consistency and translates them into executable form. The system is meant to control a variety of office procedures at a time which may be of different types.

While it is quite easy to specify office procedures and to change these definitions, the rather rigid and complex process model does not allow for changes in the definition of running procedures which leads us to the next section concerned with the performance of office procedures.

3 Coordination as Formalized Conversation

Now that we have shown how office procedures can be defined, we are going to consider their performance. Again, we have made some assumptions guiding our design of the DOMINO system:

(a) The messages exchanged in a cooperative context (like the execution of an action in an office procedure) are regarded as "speech acts" of a conversation concerning a certain task in the sense of Winograd and Flores [1986].

(b) An autonomous agent is used to coordinate the performance of the steps of an office procedure via conversations for action.

(c) The specification of the input/output relations of the actions in an office procedure is regarded as an "ideal" procedure; exceptions from this procedure can be handled within the action conversations and by the mediating agent.

So, the main role of the DOMINO system lies in mediating and controlling the task related communication by notifying the participants about actions due, by providing them with the information needed, and by

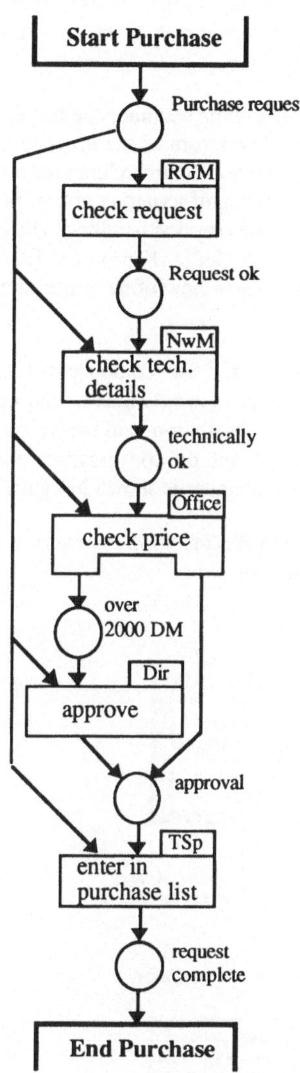

Roles

RGM: Research Group Manager
NwM: Network Manager
Dir: Director of Institute
TSp: Technical Support Person
Office: Pseudo-role for automated actions

Figure 1. A DOMINO office procedure

routing the results of such actions to the parties responsible. Thus, DOMINO coordinates the activity of a group of persons working on a common task. It is able to inform about the progress of task execution, and provides mechanisms for exception handling in office procedures like delegating an action, or setting back a procedure in case of complaints by participants.

The execution of an office procedure is started on request of a user who thus becomes the initiator of this procedure instance. The communication between the initiator, the other actors of the procedure and the DOMINO system employs message types which are important in the context of procedure processing. The message types "order", "completion", "confirmation" are used for the straightforward course of procedure. "Complaint", "forwarding", "cancellation" (and some more) are used for exception handling. The exchange of these messages follows conventions which are summarized in the CoPlanX protocol [Kreifelts & Woetzel 1987]. The use of this *conversation for action* ensures a consistent view of the procedure state by all participants.

The DOMINO system consists of an automated agent (called "mediator") and user components which communicate via electronic mail using the CoPlanX protocol. The mediator is installed as a fully automated pseudo-user in the mail network. It is responsible for the compilation, installation, and execution of office procedures. It consists of the procedure compiler, the procedure control, and the conversation monitor. All components are implemented in C under UNIX. The overall system architecture is shown in figure 2.

The user components for local user support in procedure processing are installed for every user of the system. They consist of an interface module and the conversation monitor.

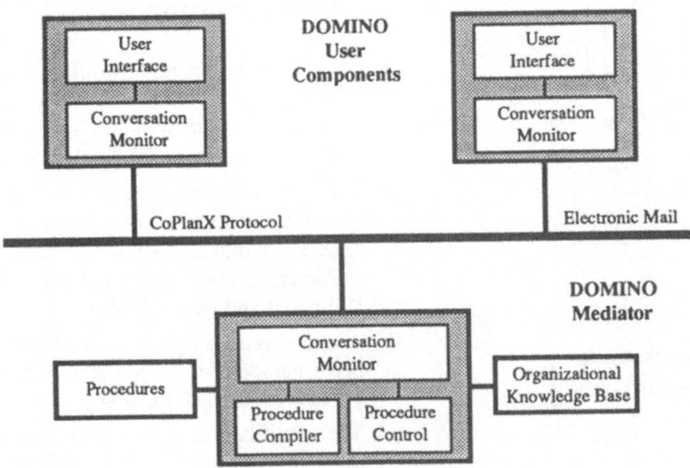

Figure 2. The DOMINO system architecture

The key idea of the DOMINO system architecture is splitting the coordination support into two types of agents: the user agent which is responsible for the support of an individual user, and the group agent or mediator which is responsible for providing a group service like office procedure coordination. These two types of agents use a formalized conversation (the CoPlanX protocol of semi-structured messages) for their communication concerning the performance of office procedures. The group agent mediates the communication between the group members involved in the office procedure, and ensures the execution of the office procedure according to its specification.

This architecture can be generalized into a concept for coordination systems that use the structured interaction paradigm: the conversational systems model [Kreifelts & Woetzel 1988]. This model has semi-structured messages, roles and conversation rules pertaining to the message exchange between the role-players, as well as the possibility of having fully-programmed mediators taking part in the conversations in order to provide certain group services. The conversational systems model has in fact been applied to meeting scheduling [Woitass 1990] and to plan coordination with autonomous agents [Kreifelts & v. Martial 1990]. In both applications, the conversation types employed were adapted to the necessary negotiations about dates for meetings and tasks in plans, respectively. However, the mediators in these cases operated following a fixed strategy, and could not — as the DOMINO mediator — be "programmed" with different office procedure specifications.

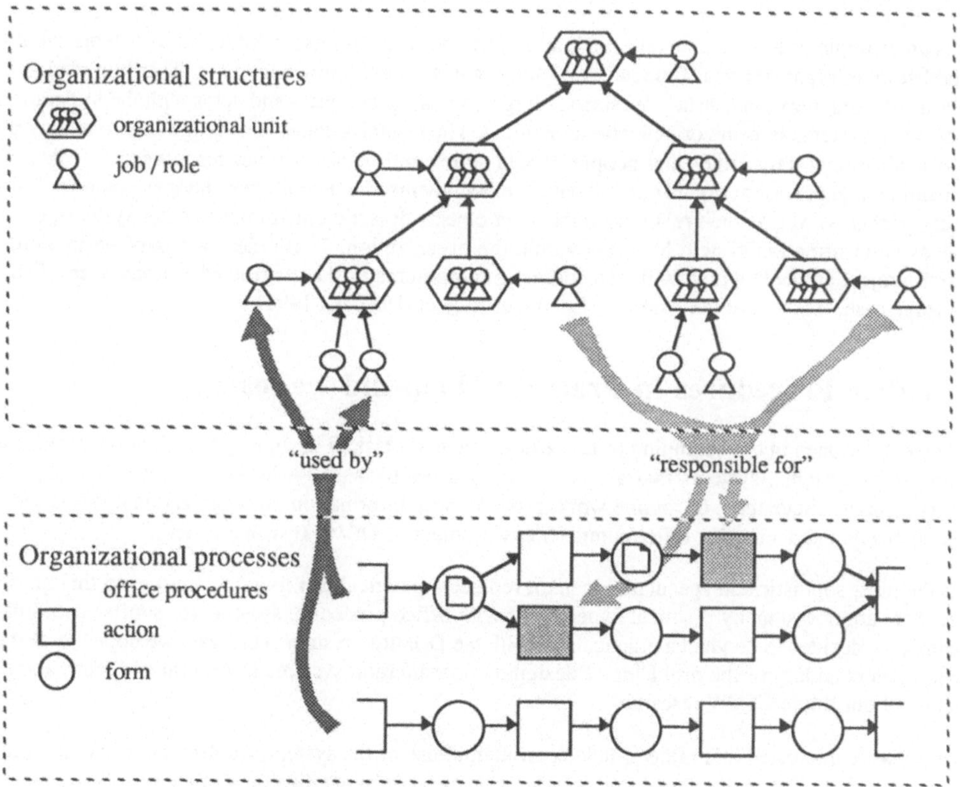

Figure 3. Use of organizational data in the DOMINO system

4 Mapping Roles to People: The Organizational Knowledge Base

We have not yet treated the assignment of the roles of an office procedure to real people. Of course, the originator of a procedure could simply assign certain (fixed) persons to the roles, and thus to the actions of an office procedure. But this is not what is usually required in administrative procedures: roles in an office procedure correspond to roles in the organization and may also depend on the actual data of the procedure at hand ("the supervisor of the initiator of the procedure", "the manager of the project to whose account the purchase is charged").

In order to gain this flexibility in role assignment, a specific role language was developed for DOMINO that has as elements organizational units, projects, jobs, people, and relations between these entities like "supervisor of" and set theoretical operators "and", "or", "but not", "else" (denoting a default if the preceding set is empty) [Kreifelts & Seuffert 1988]. Expressions in this language are used to specify roles in DOMINO procedures which are interpreted at run-time using a knowledge base containing the organizational structures of the enterprise where the office procedure is running (cf. the organizational knowledge base in figure 2 which is a prototype that has been implemented in Prolog).

This is an example of a more general principle: in order to be of full use, coordination systems should be embedded in an organizational framework — the organizational knowledge base. This knowledge base represents the organizational structures surrounding cooperative activities and helps with the integration of coordination systems into the organizational context. The organizational knowledge base contains more than organizational units, roles and people, it also stores and manages other resources and rules of an organization, e.g. persistent organizational data and documents, document types, budgets, responsibilities, or access rights, as well as their relations to the other objects. It is not only of use to other systems, but also serves as an information system for users within the organization. These ideas are pursued in a current research project at GMD which will also address the problems of the distributed maintenance of such a knowledge base. It is part of the Assisting Computer Project [Hoschka 1991].

5 Office Procedures in Practice: What did we learn?

As I have mentioned in the beginning of this article, the main task in designing coordination systems is to design useful systems: systems that are accepted by users because — in the case of office procedure support — they relieve them of routine work, provide more information on organizational processes, and integrate nicely with their other office computer environment. Is DOMINO such a system?

Even the most sophisticated speculation cannot replace a practical test to get an answer to this question. Since there are not so many practical experiences with office procedure systems (or similar coordination systems), we decided to conduct a practical test with the DOMINO system. This way, we hoped to also gain a better understanding of the problems of designing coordination systems in general and learn about the direction of our future CSCW research.

Since we were interested in a rather quick experimental use of the system, we decided to try it out in our own organization. This is usually not the best decision as far as generalizability of the results is concerned, but one is freed from additional overhead in preparing the implementation of the system. The DOMINO user interface was designed anew for the practical test of the system in an environment of personal computers (Apple Macintoshes) connected to some server machines running Unix (SUN's). The main characteristics of the user interface (cf. figure 4 for an example) are form-orientation and inclusion of informal and free format communication, i.e. note stickers and arbitrary enclosures.

The target group was our own institute comprising approximately 120 researchers. The candidates for DOMINO were clerical procedures (business trips, purchasing, vacations, etc.) The purchase procedure turned out to be the most suitable test application, it involves four steps of processing within the institute where the purchase request is processed in various ways (cf. figure 1 which gives the definition). The roles involved are the research group manager, the network manager, the director of the institute, and the technical support person. After these checks, the purchase form leaves the institute and is passed on to the administration department . The (electronic) DOMINO procedure ends at this point, the rest of the purchase procedure is carried out with paper forms (because of incompatible computer networks and systems it was impossible to also let the administration department participate in the experiment).

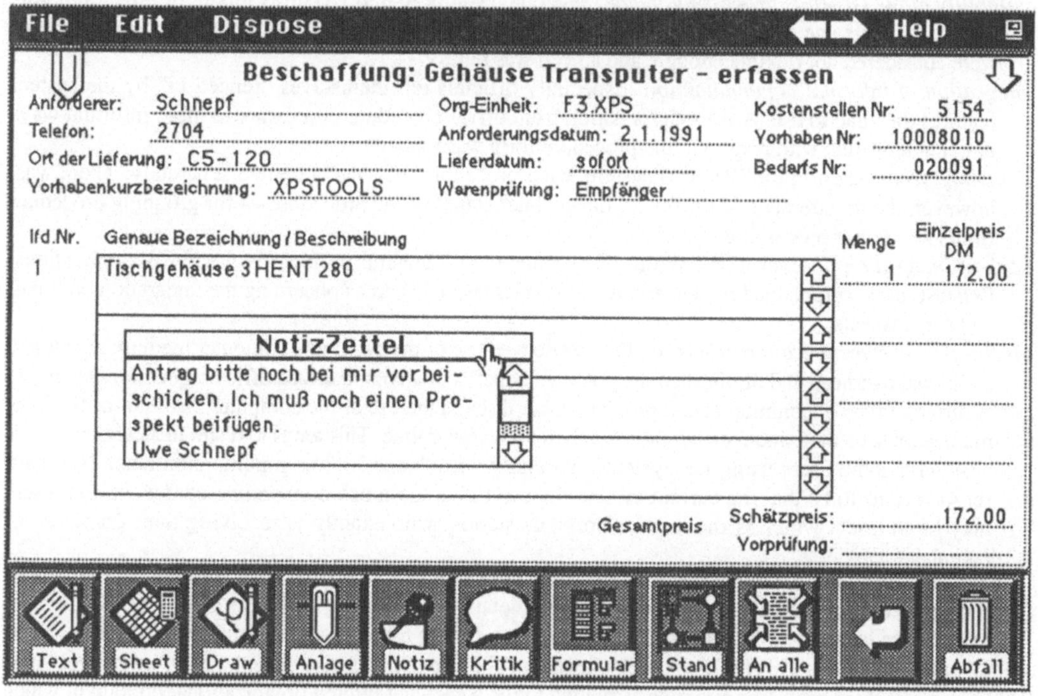

Figure 4. The DOMINO user interface

DOMINO was introduced for purchasing in our institute in October 1990, and has been in use since then. Because the majority of employees place orders very seldom or never at all, it was decided to have two to five "purchasers" per research group who act on behalf of others. This resulted in a user community of ca. 25 people. We did not intend a systematic evaluation since our experimental basis is too narrow, but rather operated with informal discussions and user meetings. But still, we think that the qualitative judgements we have derived from both positive and negative experiences during our current experiment are still quite valuable:

User interface. In general, the user interface was judged as easy to use and mainly self-explanatory. Sometimes missing local context was criticized.

Keeping track of purchases. The better trackability of purchases was appreciated: the person currently processing the purchase order can be looked up at any time by the people involved in the procedure.

Unified treatment of purchases. One of the main benefits of an office procedure system is the unified treatment of all purchases according to the rules laid down in the procedure definition. This also results in a more complete, consistent, and up-to-date budgeting. In the beginning this advantage was hampered by the occasional use of paper forms in parallel to DOMINO.

Suitability of the DOMINO procedure model. First, the DOMINO procedure model turned out to be too complex. For the task at hand — purchase procedure processing — a simple sequential procedure model would have been sufficient. Secondly, the strict input/output relations between the actions of a procedure do not allow the data produced in one action to be changed in a subsequent action. While this safeguards against unauthorized changing of procedure data, the mechanism is rather rigid in that it requests the procedure to be set back to the person who produced the data to be changed.

Suitability of the DOMINO processing model. The conversation-based DOMINO model of procedure processing offers some provisions for exception handling. However, this exception handling facilities were considered not flexible enough, and a need was felt for

Integration of informal communication. Especially officials felt themselves "fenced in" by the system features they had to use. A smooth transition from office procedure processing to more informal ways of communication with respect to the procedure form was missed.

Grouping procedures. In the DOMINO system, each procedure instance is treated separately. There was, however, the requirement — especially during later stages of the procedure — for grouping procedure forms for further processing.

Lack of integration of other tools. While this seems to be a general problem with CSCW applications, DOMINO users complained particularly about two issues in this area concerning the integration of e-mail and spreadsheets.

Media specific communication problems. The interleaved use of the paper and computer medium resulted in additional overhead and diminished the potential benefits of a computerized office procedure system.
A different type of communication problem arose through the use of the computer medium itself. Communication gets more indirect and more explicit at the same time. This tends to result in a certain uneasiness with some users using the system, especially with "negative" communication acts. The main reason seems to be that the current system does not give too much cooperative context so that users may be in doubt which is the next or previous station, who exactly is receiving their comment or complaint.

The experiences of this first experiment (for a more detailed account see [Kreifelts et al. 1991]) show that we have succeeded in building an easy-to-use procedure system for an office environment, which is able to demonstrate the potential benefits of such a system. The experiences also reveal a number of problems. While some of these problems might be attributed to the somewhat limited organizational domain in which DOMINO was used or the initial mixed mode of paper and electronic forms, some of these problems indicate weaknesses of the system:

- The DOMINO procedure and processing model with its pre-structured net of actions and its given exception handling facilities turned out to be too rigid or ineffective in some respects.

- Easy transition to more informal or simple ways of communication and cooperation was felt to be missing.

- The environment for working on office procedures was lacking tailorability, e.g. individual grouping of procedures, or integration of personal tools.

- The organizational or group context was not or not adequately represented.

Some of these weaknesses may be overcome within or around DOMINO, e.g. e-mail and simpler and more informal cooperation support tools (circulation folders and information requests with replies) will be integrated into the DOMINO environment and put to use in the same organizational environment. But the main lesson learned is that office procedure systems like DOMINO have to be complemented by coordination systems which offer flexible and tailorable support of the more informal day-to-day cooperative activities in organizations.

6 A New Approach: Flexible Coordination Support with Configurable Activities

Within GMD's Assisting Computer Project [Hoschka 1991] we have begun to develop a new approach for tools that help an individual office worker coordinate his activities with those of others, e.g. in the same working group or project — cooperation support is regarded an important property of future assisting computers. As a consequence of our DOMINO experience, we think that more flexible group support tools are needed which lend themselves easily to serve as a medium for groups as well as individuals to organize their work in areas which are not dominated by pre-structured procedures. Our current research aims at such tools for the coordination of distributed work which we have summarized under the name of *Activity Assistant.*[1]

The Activity Assistant is to address the following issues: flexibility and configurability, easy transition to and from informal communication, better overview of individual work and its group context. Consequently, our direction in CSCW research is: from pre-structured cooperation to unstructured or user configurable/ modifiable cooperation patterns, from processing of "official" procedures to coordination of day-to-day work in a rich environment allowing for different views on tasks and representing the group context more explicitly, and from a coordination model governed to a large extent by the formalized conversation paradigm to a coordination model where there is still structured interaction but also non-formalized communication, conferencing, and some simple ways of information sharing. While not excluding synchronous techniques from our conceptual considerations, the Activity Assistant will be based mainly on asynchronous store-and-forward technology.

The application domain of the Activity Assistant will be cooperative work extending over a period of time, in small to medium-sized teams spatially distributed. Typical examples are the preparation of a workshop, the preparation of a project review, the collaborative creation of a report, or the development of a software system prototype. The Activity Assistant is to help organize such activities by supporting the planning as well as the performance, also under the condition of frequently changing goals and work assignments. The main functions of the Activity Assistant consist of:

- offering a better and more consistent overview of complex cooperative activities,
- documenting and monitoring progress of cooperative work,
- allowing for dynamic changes in cooperative work plans during performance,
- allowing access to, and communication of, necessary background material (documents, notes, comments, etc.), and
- offering individual and group related time management.

The Activity Assistant is not meant as a comprehensive coordination system ("the corporate activity management system") but rather as a *medium for the (self-) organization of work in teams.*

Coordination in the Activity Assistant is centered around the action-oriented aspects of cooperation and is based on a task-oriented coordination model [Kreifelts et al. 1991]. In modelling a cooperative activity, the tasks to be carried out by the individual group members are the central point of interest:

- What tasks have to be carried out?

---

[1] This research is partly funded by the Commission of the European Communities in the ESPRIT project EuroCoOp (project no. 5303).

- Who will be responsible for the performance of a task?
- What is the deadline for a task?
- Which resources are needed to carry out a task?
- Which dependencies exist between tasks?

An activity basically consists of a set of tasks, the activity in turn forms the context for the execution of its tasks. A task is described by a number of attributes such as intended results, required resources, and completion dates. Tasks may be assigned to actors responsible for their execution, otherwise they remain in the responsibility of the originator of the activity. Within an activity, tasks may depend on each other resulting in a dependency network of actions which constitutes a certain execution order of tasks. In order to allow for information sharing and informal exchanges within an activity, each activity has an information base and a conference associated.

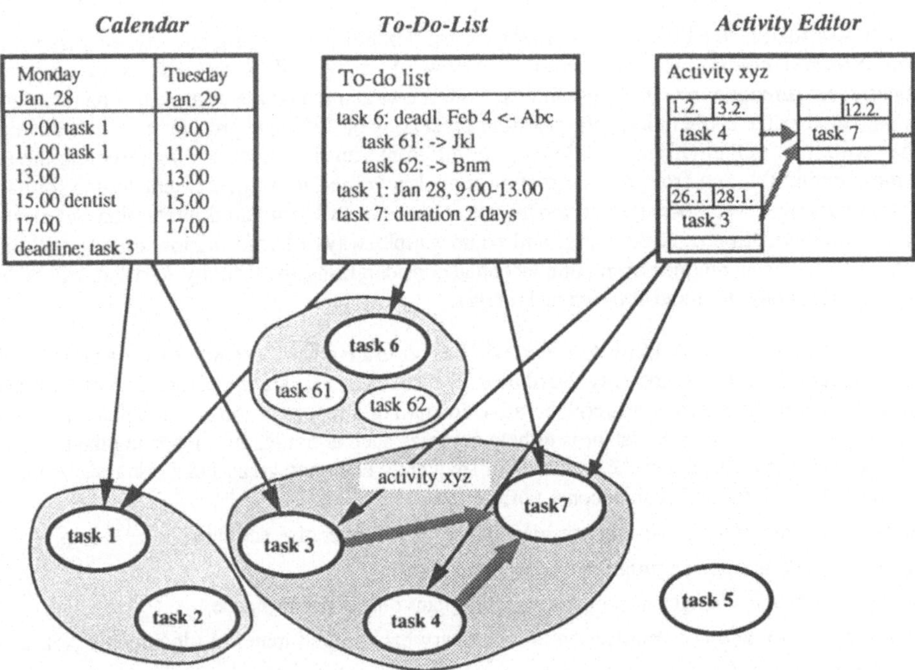

Figure 5. Different views of activities in the Activity Assistant

An activity that has been defined by its originator is executed via communication with the prospective actors that have been asked to do the tasks. This task related communication is governed by simple conversation types depending on the nature of the task (action, negotiation, inquiry). The respective conversation type is an attribute of the task, and also allows for informal communication related to the task (questions, answers, comments). Activity monitoring and task execution are managed by an activity monitor which is part of the Activity Assistant. On both sides — activity originator and task actor — the activity monitor keeps track of the formalized task conversation, reminds of deadlines, helps in monitoring complex activities, and supplies the context for task and activity execution. As a rule, this context will usually be different on the two sides because the actor may embed a delegated task into an activity of his own. Tasks may be negotiated between originator and actor, activity definitions may also be modified, refined, or gradually completed during execution. All this is managed by the activity monitor.

As we have learned from the DOMINO experience, the integration of activity coordination into the local environment (computer or other) is very important. Activity coordination is not an end in itself but rather a facility to help users in getting their work done. Therefore, the coordination tools should be closely embedded into the local working environment.

The central notion of the user environment for activity coordination will be the task. A task is closely related to the resources it employs, in particular documents, and to the communication objects it uses for coordination, i.e. the conversations. Tasks can be found at various places, and in different representations. For example, a template for a report that has to be produced is a document and an e-mail message arrived is a communication object, but both may represent a task (in some sense) to the user. So, the goal of a user-friendly environment is to provide extensive possibilities of interchange between the various representations of tasks and to widely integrate the notion of resource and communication into the task management environment.

Tasks may appear in the many contexts, e.g. as items in to-do lists, as deadlines or occupied time in calendars, as items in mail lists (along with e-mails, faxes, etc.), attached to documents, or as "boxes" in the activity editor. As tasks occur in various contexts, they are viewed differently by the user, the underlying task and activity objects, however, remain the same (see figure 5). The different contexts are managed by respective tools (to-do tool, calendar tool, etc.), consistency across different contexts is managed by the activity monitor. If tasks (or other objects like appointments, messages) are "opened", they are viewed in detail by specialized tools (e.g. task tool, or e-mail tool). So, while a task may be viewed differently in various contexts, its representation in detail remains the same.

In closing, we would like to point out the novel aspects of coordination support in the Activity Assistant:

Integration of planning and execution: Both phases of distributed work management — specification and performance — are supported in an integrated way (in contrast, existing project management systems are single-user applications for the project manager).

Flexibility/Configurability: Personal and group related work plans can always be adapted to changes in the current situation; this includes replanning, incomplete specifications, gradual refinement of abstract plans, negotiation and delegation of tasks.

Integration of different forms of coordination support: The structured interaction paradigm is the basis for task negotiation and execution, however, this is complemented by other ways of collaboration within the context surrounding a task: information sharing using the activity information base, and informal exchanges using the activity conference.

Usability in a variety of situations: The Activity Assistant may be used across a variety of situations ranging from individual planning and scheduling to the coarse planning and coordination of larger projects. This also facilitates its implementation in an organization.

Above, we have presented some of GMD's research activities in the area of CSCW. We have highlighted problems in designing and implementing systems for the coordination of distributed work with examples from our own history, especially with the office procedure DOMINO.We have discussed practical experiences with the DOMINO system, and have motivated our new direction of research striving for more flexible forms of coordination support that can be customized by its users. Finally, we have sketched a new approach for distributed work management which is part of the Assisting Computer Project of GMD.

References

Hoschka, P. (1991) "Assisting Computer – A new generation of support systems," in this volume.

Kreifelts, Th. and Woetzel, G. (1987) "Distribution and exception handling in an office procedure system," in G. Bracchi, D. Tsichritzis (eds.) *Office Systems: Methods and Tools*, Proc. IFIP WG 8.4 Work. Conf. on Methods and Tools for Office Systems, (Pisa, Italy, Oct. 22 - 24, 1986), North-Holland, Amsterdam, 1987, pp. 197-208.

Kreifelts, Th. and Seuffert, P. (1988) "Addressing in an office procedure system," in R. Speth (Hrsg.) *Message Handling Systems, State of the Art and Future Directions*, Proc. IFIP WG 6.5 Work Conf. on Message Handling Systems (München, April 27-29, 1987), North-Holland, Amsterdam, 1988, pp. 117-127.

Kreifelts, Th. and Woetzel, G. (1988) "Conversational systems: A conceptual model for off-line group support systems," in *Information Technology Towards 2000*, Proc. Australian Comp. Conf. '88 (Sydney, Sept. 21-23, 1988), Austr. Comp. Soc., Sydney, 1988, S. 71–88.

Kreifelts, Th. and v. Martial, F. (1990) "A negotiation framework for autonomous agents," in *MAAMAW-90*: Proc. 2nd European Workshop on Modelizing Autonomous Agents and Multi Agent Worlds (Paris, Aug. 13-15, 1990), pp.167-182.

Kreifelts, Th., Pankoke-Babatz, U, and Victor, F. (1991) "A model for the coordination of cooperative activities," in K. Gorling, C. Sattler (ed.) *International Workshop on CSCW*, (Berlin, April 9 - 11, 1991), Informatik, Informationen Reporte Berlin 7 (1991) 4, Inst. für Informatik und Rechentechnik, Berlin, 1991, pp. 85-100.

Kreifelts, Th., Hinrichs, E., Klein, K.-H., Seuffert, P. and Woetzel, G. (1991) "Experiences with the DOMINO office procedure system," to appear in Proc. ECSCW '91 (Amsterdam, Sept. 27-29, 1991).

Woitass, M. (1990) "Coordination of intelligent office agents – Applied to meeting scheduling" in S. Gibbs, A. A. Verrijn-Stuart (eds.) *Multi-User Interfaces and Applications*, Proc. IFIP WG 8.4 Conf. on Multi-User Interf. and Appl., (Heraklion, Crete, Sept. 24-26, 1990), North-Holland, Amsterdam, 1990,p. 371-387.

Winograd, T. and Flores, F. (1986) *Understanding Computers and Cognition: A New Foundation for Design*, Ablex, Norwood NJ, 1986.

Cooperation Structures in Multi-Agent Systems

Hans Haugeneder
Siemens AG, ZFE IS INF 2
DFKI Saarbrücken
Otto-Hahn-Ring 6
8000 München 83

Donald Steiner
Siemens AG, ZFE IS INF 2
DFKI Kaiserslautern
Postfach 2080
6750 Kaiserslautern

We propose a multi-agent environment (MECCA) for supporting cooperation between humans and machine systems in weakly structured task domains. The two basic ingredients of this environment are the generalised structure of an individual agent and the representation of a variety of available cooperation strategies and their use by the agents. After a characterisation of the targeted application domains, the global architecture and the integration of cooperation structures within this framework will be discussed.

1   Introduction

The work presented here is being performed by Project KIK[1], the aim of which is to integrate Distributed Artificial Intelligence (DAI) approaches with modern telecommunication and network technology in order to use the synergetic potential of these two areas to create the basis for a new class of applications with high degrees of distribution and cooperation.

More specifically we will concentrate on the logical aspects of distribution which are the focus of the TEAMWARE subproject (Problem Solving in a Distributed Man-Machine Team) ([10]) of KIK.[2] The impact of our approach to supporting cooperation on the network and communication level will be only briefly discussed; it is presented in more detail in [5].

Typical application scenarios which we want to support with our multi-agent environment are, among others:

- **Cooperative Knowledge Acquisition** (for linguistic knowledge sources)([11]),

- **Distributed Resource Scheduling**

- **Order Handling** (of complex technical devices)

---

[1]KIK stands for the German K̲ünstliche I̲ntelligenz (Artificial Intelligence) und K̲ommunikationstechnologie (Communications Technology) a collaborative effort between Siemens AG and the German Center for Artificial Intelligence (DFKI)

[2]This work has been partially supported by the Commission of the European Communities under the ESPRIT II programme in the form of the IMAGINE project (Project 5362).

- **Air Traffic Control** (sector management)

- **Telecommunication Network Management**[3]

These scenarios, although varying in specifics, can be characterized by the following fundamental features (cf. [19]):

Heterogeneity A team[4] may have members with a wide variety of problem solving behavior, ranging from simple components like printers and sensors via complex software such as knowledge based systems to humans, which have drastically varying individual functionalities and cooperative capabilities.

Distribution Collaboration among the members of a team has to take into account distribution along the following dimensions:

Space The team members work at different places.

Time The team members work during different, possibly non-overlapping intervals of time in synchronous and asynchronous manners.

Competence In general the competence with respect to the overall task is spread across the whole team; certain subdomains of the overall competence, however, may be totally localized within a subset of the team (so called competence ensembles).

Responsibility The responsibility for various aspects of the problem solving process is distributed over different members or subsets of members of the team.

Dynamism The cooperation roles of individual team members and the cooperative links among them are not predetermined on the basis of a rigid organizational structure or a specific limited work procedure embedded in the organisation; rather, they are adopted dynamically during the work process, depending on the technical competence of the collaborators and on the structure of the collaborative task.[5]

Redundancy The competence of the team members in a given cooperation structure may be overlapping, competing and even contradictory. This allows for the possibility of error detection and alternate solutions which in turn leads to increased requirements concerning the modeling of the overall cooperation process.

Stability The team is able to withstand the (partial) loss of communication or of individual members to a certain degree, even if it may not function as smoothly or as efficiently.

In order to cover the logical aspects of distribution and cooperation in the described applications, we strive to integrate the approaches of several fields[6] that address the problems of cooperation and distribution under quite different, complementary viewpoints. These are:

1. the multi-agent approaches developed in the field of DAI (cf. [7]) which offer a flexible cooperation paradigm for distributed, locally limited (i.e. restricted with respect to the overall problem to be solved) problem solvers.

---

[3]The latter two application areas are under investigation in the IMAGINE project.

[4]In this section we use the non-technical notions of "team" and "member of a team" instead of the more formal concept of "agent" which is introduced in section 2.

[5]This does not exclude the use of organisationally determined work procedures (as described in section 3.2) for suitable subtasks.

[6]Our view of this integration is not a symmetric one, rather we emphasize the DAI approaches.

2. the cooperation and work procedure models for human interaction (cf. [9]) developed in the field of Computer-Supported Cooperative Work (CSCW).

3. the approaches under investigation in Human-Computer Cooperative Work (HCCW) (cf. [8]).

Thus, our aim is to develop an extended[7] multi-agent framework MECCA (Multi-Agent Environment for Constructing Cooperative Applications). This framework will be used as the underlying architecture for constructing applications in multi-person/machine cooperation tasks.

We believe that such (D)AI based approaches for group work will have great impact, a view which is also expressed in [2]:

> "At present, AI techniques for group work are still at their infancy. These techniques, however have the potential to dramatically alter the way we choose to organize our work. For instance, imagine a future in which you work at a workstation connected to many other on a corporate network. Vast amounts of knowledge are stored on-line. Your workstation contains most of the letters, reports, calendars, business cards, drawings and other papers that clutter your office today. It also *knows* what tasks you are working on..."

2 The Multi-Agent Environment MECCA

2.1 The Environment

The MECCA Environment as a whole consists of the following two parts:

The Agent Formalism which provides the representational means for the specification of the single agents and their interaction

The Development Environment which provides facilities to implement an application by specifying agents and debugging their behavior

The agent formalism comprises the agent model[8] and the agent interaction language. The agent model defines a single agent's internal structure and the various types of knowledge that an agent has to be provided with, whereas the agent interaction language defines a protocol which is used by the agents to perform the fundamental, domain-independent communicative and cooperative interactions. This language's major two expressive means is a set of performative operators (like *POST, WANT, CAN, ASK, COMMIT*, etc.) and a component for specifying propositional content.

The development environment consists of an (agent) editor, debugger and inspector, all of which allow their functionality to be applied on the conceptual level defined by the agent formalism. Thus, they provide means for editing agents and their components, introducing new, more specialized agents and to debug the interaction between the various agents (or groups of agents) and monitor their state changes.

2.2 The Agent Model

An agent as the central computational entity of MECCA can be decomposed into the following three components: the functional, task-solving component, the *agent body*, the cooperative superstrate, the *agent head*, and the communication functionality, the *agent communicator*. The roles of these components are as follows:

---

[7]i.e. incorporating suitable functionality for both human-human and human-machine cooperation
[8]to be specified in section 2.2

Agent Body This component constitutes the agent's internal problem-solving expertise; that part of its overall functionality which the agent is able to perform without any cooperative embedding. Thus, it provides the agent's *basic functionality*, which is per se completely independent of any particular multi-agent system and may participate in several systems. Only by supplying the body with additional functionality (i.e. the appropriate head and communicator) is it upgraded to an agent. This is primarily manifested by its ability to follow the general rules of the specific multi-agent application by communicating and cooperating with other agents.

The functionality provided by the agent body can be of any complexity;[9] in practice it is determined by the functional needs of a specific application. Thus, pre-existing hardware or software components can be used as a body of an agent. This allows for reusability and duplication of bodies of machine agents.

Agent Head The head of an agent allows the agent to participate in the cooperation process underlying the overall problem solving process, i.e. it enables the agent to contribute its basic functionality in a sensible way. For machine agents, it is generally a software system with several components. For human agents it will be comprised of the human's own knowledge and suitable interfaces to the system.

In order for an agent to contribute to the overall problem solving process in a goal directed fashion it must have access to knowledge of different types:[10]

- **Autoepistemic Knowledge** about its own basic functionality,
- **Communication Knowledge** about inter-agent communication facilities,[11]
- **Global Task Knowledge** about the task hierarchy and the global problem state (goal tree),
- **Activity Knowledge** about the current task(s) it is trying to achieve,
- **Group Knowledge** about functionalities and capabilities of other agents (acquaintances), and
- **Cooperation Structure Knowledge**[12]

These types of an agent's knowledge are partly determined upon startup of the system (i.e. spawning of the corresponding agent) or are acquired dynamically, by transfer between agents in the course of the problem solving process.

In order to interact with other agents in the problem solving process an agent uses this knowledge by means of suitable inference mechanisms (classifying, deductive planning etc.) to perform three types of basic activities:

1. Perform its basic functionality on an identified (sub)problem,
2. Cooperate with another agent or an agent ensemble to solve a problem, to which the contribution of its basic functionality is necessary, or
3. Refusal or delegation of an demanded performance (due to different reasons[13]).

---

[9]This supports the requirement for high heterogeneity as specified in section 1.

[10]The different types of knowledge are not assumed to be fully specified, they may well be incomplete (group knowledge for example) and partly contradictory to the corresponding knowledge of another agent (global task knowledge for example); it is important, however, that the availability of this type of knowledge (especially the cooperation relevant knowledge such as group knowledge and cooperative structure) is central for constituting a non-trivial level of "agenthood".

[11]This type of knowledge is essential, if the system is implemented on a physically distributed platform.

[12]The latter two types constitute the cooperative knowledge which is specified in more detailed in section 4.2.

[13]such as unsatisfactory basic functionality, resource limitation, exclusive commitment to other activities etc.

Thus, the agent head can be seen as a mediator between the agent's basic functionality (which constitutes the agent body) and the overall problem solving context.

Agent Communicator In order to communicate with other agents, an agent needs to have access to appropriate telecommunication channels and network information about other agents, such as their various addresses, features of the transmission channels (like speed, availability, costs etc.). That portion of the agent which implements this communication functionality is called the *agent communicator*. The communicator of an agent processes a message from the head, finds out which address to deliver it to and how to send the message. It also receives messages from other agents and determines the way to deliver them to the head for further processing. Thus, the communicator represents the interface from the agent to the cooperative context in which it is participating.

The role and requirements of the communicator may seem straightforward at first glance, but it may become quite complex, since there are many times when one form of communication will be appropriate, other times where it wouldn't be. Additionally, agents may be available at a variety of addresses on the same type of communication link. It is the role of the communicator to provide the agent with the most suitable type of communication according to the agent's needs and global features of the entire network environment.[14]

3   Cooperation Structures

In addition to providing MECCA with the basic agent architecture, agents must know how to cooperate with each other in order to solve problems effectively. This yields the incorporation of a variety of cooperation strategies, and a basis for building more strategies in MECCA.

3.1   Cooperation Structures in DAI

We refer to a *cooperation strategy* as a particular type or principle of cooperation where the roles and activities of the agents are described as well as the process of cooperation. A number of cooperation strategies have been defined in DAI, and there may be one or more cooperation strategies which can be used most effectively to achieve a goal. Some of the major cooperation strategies proposed in DAI are:

Master Slave one agent has complete control over another, and can command it to carry out tasks.

Contract Net (cf. [16]) a *contractor agent* contracts the solution of a goal to one or more agents by requesting *bids* for execution of the goal. These bids are evaluated according to specified criteria (e.g. cost or reliability) and the winning bidder gets the contract. This is also often referred to as a market style cooperation.

Blackboard (as originally introduced in the HEARSAY system (cf. [6])) agents share goals and their solutions. Goals are posted to the blackboard, which is continually monitored by other agents. Upon solving a posted goal, an agent posts the solution to the blackboard, to be used by other agents.

---

[14]There is a wide variety of forms of communication agents can use: electronic mail, telephone (between human agents and machine agents with voice language interpretation capabilities), video conference (between human agents and machine agents with appropriate interfaces), telnet for low bandwidth real-time communication, ethernet (for slightly faster real-time communication), high performance LANs like FDDI or WANs like B-ISDN (for high quality communication facilities), etc.

We refer to a *cooperation structure* as a the instantiation, or implementation, of a particular cooperation strategy which arises from specifying exactly which agents are to have which roles, which links are established, when and how the cooperation process is to be carried out and so on. Thus, where a typical strategy would be "contract net", a cooperation structure would be a specific contract net as realised by Agent A being the contractor, Agents B, C, and D, the bidders, G_0, the active goal. A variety of factors need to be specified when instantiating a given cooperation strategy. For example, "contract-net" may have required arguments, *contractor* and *active goal* and optional arguments *bidders, bulletin boards* etc.[15]

Thus, an agent will be able to select the cooperation strategy best suited for accomplishing a goal, and will invoke this strategy. The corresponding structure will be automatically set up by MECCA and all participating agents informed. The agents, also knowledgeable about the cooperation strategy, will know what roles they are expected to play, and what is required of them.

The cooperation structures will be highly dynamic, involving a number of different strategies, not only being based on a pre-determined organizational structure, as is the case in many office-oriented CSCW applications. They additionally reflect the structure of the overall task, corresponding subtasks and the current state of the cooperation process as well as the degree of collaborative freedom. The latter describes the relative autonomy of an agent, which is essential in the case where human agents are part of the cooperation process, or where the task to be performed does not presuppose a rigid structure of actions.

A *cooperation world* (*c-world* for short) is the totality of agents, their communication links, and cooperation structures to carry out a top level goal (unique to a c-world). A particular c-world may be highly fluid, with new links and new agents being created, modified, and deleted. We will generally refer to the top-level goal of a specific c-world as G_0. Note that the same agent may be in different c-worlds, albeit with different roles. The following table shows some of the agents which participate in different c-worlds.

CONFERENCE	COMPANY
Chairperson	Project Leader
Attendees	Project Members
Conference Database	Appointment Management System

Table 1: C-Worlds With Their Agents

Most of our future discussion will be restricted to agents in one c-world; we have developed further mechanisms (cf. [18]) to support participation of a single agent in several c-worlds.

3.2 Cooperation in CSCW

Today's CSCW approaches to modeling cooperation lack a clear *CSCW-specific* theoretical foundation; they also tend to be overgeneralisations of the developers' idiosyncratic experience in their own research settings.[16] Thus, these approaches draw their theoretical framework from various disciplines such as anthropology, social theory, ecology, speech act theory, discourse analysis, action psychology and others, mostly in a rather metaphorical fashion.[17] This theoretical indeterminacy or vagueness has led to the phenomenon that existing CSCW systems materialize cooperative concepts in a very

---

[15]Some of these arguments will be required for all cooperation strategies, specific cooperation strategies will probably require further arguments.

[16]See [1] for an in-depth discussion of these points.

[17]A more comprehensive overview of the state of the art in CSCW can be found in [8, 34 –53].

application specific, mostly ad hoc way. Furthermore, essential chunks of the knowledge for modeling cooperative processes are available only implicitly or in a hard-wired fashion with the specific cooperative needs of the application in mind.

Aside from these general shortcomings with respect to the explicitness and extensibility of the underlying cooperative concepts, CSCW applications concentrate on modeling two fundamental types of cooperation which are located at the extreme points along the dimension of structuredness of the cooperative processes to be supported. These are:

(Extremely) Fixed Cooperation Structures (FCS) This type of cooperation is characterized by the traditional bureaucratic model of cooperation, in which a task is performed by a number of people (or organisations) according to a typically quite limited set of explicitly specified work procedures. The underlying organisational structure with its responsibilities and its flow of information determines the cooperation regime adopted to activate and control the necessary subactivities in order to perform a specific task.

(Totally) Loose Cooperation Structures (LCS) This type of cooperation occurs in highly creative and/or unstructured domains like document production with shared editors. Here no fixed procedures govern the cooperation between the participating members, rather there are rudimentary control and interaction facilities like clicking the mouse in a shared editor which enable the partners to take the initiative with a cooperative intention of any type.[18]

These two extreme types of cooperation correlate with two fundamental classes of CSCW systems, which exhibit the following two underlying metaphors:[19]

The Communication Medium Metaphor (CMM) This metaphor considers the computer as a communication medium channeling communication within the borders given by specific certain behavioral (i.e. social and linguistic) rules.

The Shared Material Metaphor (SMM) Here the computer is seen as materializing a shared object (or a shared set of objects) of the work process as the shared workspace in a multi-user editor or a blackboard-like device in idea generation scenarios.

Of these two types, CMM applications mainly exhibit FCS type cooperation, whereas SMM applications correlate with LCS type cooperation as shown in Table 2.

	CMM	SMM
Cooperative Freedom	low-none (FCS)	very high (LCS)
Cooperative Explicitness	strict	none
HCC Support	no	no
Theoret. Found.	partly (adapted)	no

Table 2: Modeling of Cooperation in CSCW

A final point to be made is the observation that CSCW does not address the problem of human-computer cooperation in a sense that assumes humans and machines to be entities that actively take part in a cooperative process. This is no surprise since CSCW is not inherently aiming towards modeling artificial (in the sense of non-human) computational entities exhibiting cooperative behavior.

---

[18]It is important here to be aware of the fact that this type of action does not exhibit any specific cooperative "semantics".

[19]The classification used here is based on the one proposed by Lyytinen ([12]); this proposal classifies, among other dimensions, the cooperative view that is taken with respect to the role of the computer.

Table 2 gives a synopsis of the discussion so far.[20] In summary, it can be interpreted along the following lines: CSCW provides support for very specific forms of cooperation among humans, but does neither take into account human-computer cooperation nor model the fundamental concepts underlying cooperation processes explicitly. Both types of cooperation have their place in human-computer cooperation especially in the human-human cooperation fraction of it; thus CSCW can well contribute to certain aspects of a generic model of human-computer cooperation.

3.3 Cooperation in HCCW

Humans are different from machine agents in that they often do not require special hardware or software support to participate in cooperative activities. This is especially the case when humans are cooperating in a "face-to-face" mode. However, when humans cooperate with other machine agents, or less accessible humans, they need to have an appropriate interface to the c-world. Humans actually have a lot of cooperation knowledge, but some of it may lie in a computer program. It may at times, be hard to distinguish between the human heads and their agent's bodies. However, the computer program representing the human, may act as an aide, keeping him up to date on what his current role in the cooperation structure is, and may advise him of a variety of ways to cooperate.

As an example, a call for papers for a conference as described in Table 3 is very similar to a contract net, where the paper chairman is the contractor and authors submitting papers the bidders. The paper chairman sends out a request for bids, the call for papers, with active goal "form technical program." The authors send in their bids in the form of extended abstracts which are then reviewed by the paper chairman. (How the paper chairman accomplishes this is immaterial - he may even use another cooperation strategy to distribute the bids to reviewers to get their comments.) The authors of accepted bids are then notified, and requested to accomplish their goals, of writing the papers for the proceedings. In this scenario, the conference itself would form the c-world, and the call for papers a particular structure of the contract net cooperation strategy.

DAI	HH
Contract Net	CS_2:Call for Papers
active goal	$CS_1 \rightarrow$ Papers for Conference
contractor	Paper Chair
request-for-bids	Call for Papers
bidders	Authors
bid	Extended Abstracts
Selection	Review $\rightarrow CS_3$
Acceptance	Acceptance
Solution	Final Papers $\rightarrow CS_1$

Table 3: Call for Papers Modeled as Contract Net

Here CS_i represents a cooperation structure and "$\rightarrow CS_i$" and "$CS_i \rightarrow$" indicate branching to CS_i and from CS_i, respectively. The exact form of the cooperation structures CS_1 and CS_3 is immaterial for the the call for papers cooperation structure (CS_2). Thus, for example, the review might be well performed as a master-slave cooperation. This entire process has been initiated by CS_1, representing the global conference organisation cooperation structure, and when the goal has been accomplished, the process reports achievement back to CS_1.

---

[20]Although this table is oversimplifying we feel it expresses the addressed issues in an adequate way. In particular, this synopsis is intended to be a description of today's CSCW approaches to cooperation from the point of view of modeling human-computer cooperation, not a criticism with respect to CSCW's successes or failures.

4 Support of Cooperation

4.1 Generic Activities

In order to characterize cooperation in a manner that aids multi-agent system design, we identify a taxonomy of activities (cf. [18]) which we term *generic activities* that are independent of the domain of cooperation. Generic activities may be related in various ways to each other. They may be composed of other generic activities (giving rise to a taxonomy). In addition these activities may be temporally and causally related. For example, selecting an agent for role assignment is followed by requesting the agent to perform the role, and then generation of an expectation for a reply that is caused by the request. We briefly describe some of the generic activities and their inter-relations below. At the top of our taxonomy there are four kinds of activities:

Initialization results in the establishment of a goal for an agent, or a group of agents. This may involve a considerable amount of communication and sharing of beliefs as can be seen in, for example, a group of agents debating whether they should accept a new project.

Planning involves the exploration of alternative ways of achieving a goal, selecting preferences between these alternatives, establishing commitments for planned activities, allocating resources for the activity, etc. It is clear that planning is required, not only for handling the complexity of the environment, but also since the activities of the agents have to be coordinated.

Execution is the performance of the activities in the plan, while monitoring the execution involves the detection of discrepancies between effects of an action and an agent's expectations.

Evaluation is the problem solving that underlies all the activities of agents, whether explicit or implicit. Evaluation of the results of an action may indicate potential problems with current plans, and can initialize new goals for an agent or a group.

In cooperative environments, any generic activity may be delegated to other agents or performed by negotiation. For example, an agent may select another for a role by a bidding mechanism. In the generic activity framework, it is the exploration of alternatives for the selection of an agent, and negotiation that results in establishing preferences for the role assignment.

Generic activity structures yield a set of protocols, similar to language/action structures [21], which allow for the common understanding and representation of the problem solving tasks and facilitate communication during the cooperative process. Such protocols have been used in distributed AI for coordinating task allocation [15]. This work explores their applicability for supporting goal-based human cooperation.

Thus, the culmination of the planning process will result in one or more cooperation structures in a c-world. This forms the basis for human agents to cooperate in a dynamic fashion with each other and machines and carry out their individual tasks. This basis is extended by providing an individual agent with cooperation knowledge and agents with a cooperation language, concepts which are now discussed in more detail.

4.2 Cooperative Knowledge

In order for an individual agent to participate in different cooperative structures, its head, as described in Section 2.2, must have a certain amount of knowledge about the relevant aspects of cooperation. We call this *cooperative knowledge*; it is formed of the following components:

- globally available cooperation strategies, which it can use to solve goals and from which it can choose to implement new cooperation structures.

- current cooperation structures it is involved in.

- its own cooperation role(s) in a specific cooperation structure (e.g. the role of a bidder in a contract-net structure)

- other agents' cooperation role(s) in specific cooperation structure (this may not be all agents in the c-world)

- other agent's potential cooperative roles (d-agents, s-agents)[21]

Thus, MECCA will support a wide variety of possible cooperation strategies to which agents will have access in the planning activity such as master-slave, blackboards, contract nets, democratic leadership and others. Each agent's head will know about these strategies and the applications to which they are most suited. During a planning phase, an agent will be able to analyze the current task and propose the appropriate cooperation strategy to other agents. Our formalism will allow for updating a head with new strategies as they are developed in the DAI community.

4.3   Cooperation Language

In order for several agents to cooperate effectively, they must be able to communicate with each other, using a common language, about the cooperation process at hand, including the planning and execution steps. For example, some of the more relevant operators of this language would be:

POST This operator is used by an agent to post a goal, solution or message to any of a number of bulletin boards, which are viewed on a regular basis by other agents. This would be used, for example, in posting a request-for-bids in a contract net scenario.

WANT This operator is used to express an unsolved goal, for which an agent needs a solution. It may have additional arguments expressing the required time and costs within which the solution needs to be achieved. This can be used in the request-for-bids message in the contract net scenario.

CAN An agent may inform another agent that it can actually accomplish a goal, within a certain time, with certain costs etc. If it is a reply to a previous "WANT" message, the arguments may default to the required values.

COMMIT This operator can be used to see if an agent could commit to a certain cooperation role (such as being the slave in a master-slave relation), or to performing a certain task in a cooperative process. The agent would be bound to perform the task, with certain penalties if it were to not participate.

This set provides a suggestion of the possible cooperative operators to be supported by the MECCA environment.

5   Conclusion and Outlook

The multi-agent environment MECCA was decribed with focus on the agent model and the role of cooperative knowledge. The agent architecture presented provides the capability for different sub-systems to participate in cooperative problem solving process in a flexible way. Thereby the explicit

---

[21]D-agents (delegation agents) are agents which delegate the basic functionality to be performed to another agent, s-agents (substitution agents) delegate their overall functionality in a c-world to another agent, i.e. they are completely substituted by it.

representation of cooperative knowledge is of central importance for providing effective support for human-computer cooperation in the scenarios of the type decribed. The work described is still in its conceptual phase with only minor implementation studies on the way. So the proof of the usefulness of the model proposed has to wait for its use in a comprehensive prototypical application.

References

[1] L.J. Bannon and K. Schmidt. CSCW: Four Characters in Search of a Context. In *Proceedings of the First European Conference on Computer Suported Cooperative Work*, London, 1989.

[2] K. Crowston and T. Malone. Intelligent Software Agents. *BYTE*, 267 – 274, December 1988.

[3] R. Davis and R.G. Smith. Negotation as Metaphor for Distributed Problem Solving. *Artificial Intelligence*, 20, 63 – 109, 1983.

[4] Keith S. Decker, Edmund H. Durfee, and Victor R. Lesser. Evaluating Research in Cooperative Distributed Problem Solving. In L. Gasser and M. N. Huhns, editors, *Distributed Artificial Intelligence, Volume II*, 487–519. Pitman/Morgan Kaufmann, London, 1989.

[5] C. Dietel, et al. KIK Projektbeschreibung (Version 2). Technical Report, Siemens AG/DFKI, 1990.

[6] D.L. Erman, et al. The HEARSAY-II Speech Understanding System: Integrating Knowledge to Resolve Uncertainty. *ACM Computing Survey*, 12, 213 – 253, 1980.

[7] L. Gasser, C. Braganza and N. Herman. Implementing Distributed AI Systems Using MACE. In Alan H. Bond et al. editors *Readings in Distributed Artificial Intelligence*, 445 – 450. San Mateo/Ca, 1988.

[8] Paul de Greef et al. Analysis of Human Computer Cooperative Work. IMAGINE Technical Report, August 1991.

[9] I. Greif. *Computer Supported Cooperative Work: A Book of Readings*. Morgan Kaufmann, 1988.

[10] H. Haugeneder, D. Scheidhauer, and D. Steiner. TEAMWARE: Computergestützte Lösung komplexer Aufgaben im distribuierten Mensch-Maschine Team. Technical Report, Siemens AG, 1989.

[11] H. Haugeneder and D. Steiner. Towards a Distributed Multi-Person Lexical Environment. In B. Rieger and B. Schaeder, editors, *Lexikon und Lexikographie*, 255 –264. Hildesheim, 1990.

[12] K. Lyytinen. Computer Supported Cooperative Work Issues and Challenges; a Structural Analysis. Technical Report, University of Jyvaskyla, Finland, 1990.

[13] P. Nii. Blackboard Systems: The Blackboard Model of Problem Solving. *AI Magazine*, 7(3), 38 – 53, 1986.

[14] Jeffrey S. Rosenschein and John S. Breese. Communication-Free Interactions Among Rational Agents: A Probabilistic Approach. In L. Gasser and M. N. Huhns, editors, *Distributed Artificial Intelligence, Volume II*, 99–118. Pitman/Morgan Kaufmann, London, 1989.

[15] Arvind Sathi and Mark S. Fox. Constraint-Directed Negotiation of Resource Reallocations. In L. Gasser and M. N. Huhns, editors, *Distributed Artificial Intelligence, Volume II*, 163–194. Pitman/Morgan Kaufmann, London, 1989.

[16] R.G. Smith. The Contract Net Protocol: High Level Communication and Control in a Distributed Problem Solver. *IEEE Trans. on Computers*, 29, 1104 – 1113, 1980.

[17] R.G. Smith and R. Davis. Frameworks for Cooperation in Distributed Problem Solving. *IEEE Trans. on Systems, Man and Cybernetics*, 11(1), 61 – 70, 1981.

[18] D. Steiner, D. Mahling, and H. Haugeneder. Human Computer Cooperative Work. In *Proc. of the 10th International Workshop on Distributed Artificial Intelligence*, MCC Technical Report ACT-AI-355-90, Austin/TX, 1990.

[19] D. Steiner, D. Mahling, and H. Haugeneder. Collaboration of Knowledge Bases via Knowledge Based Coordination. In *Proc. of International Working Conference on Cooperating Knowledge Based Coordination*, Keele, 1991.

[20] E. Werner. Toward a Theory of Communication and Cooperation for Multi-Agent Planning. In *Proceedings of the 2nd Conference on Theoretical Aspects of Reasoning*, 1988.

[21] T. Winograd and F. Flores. *Understanding Computers and Cognition*. Ablex, 1986.

[22] T. Winograd. A Language/Action Perspective on the Design of Cooperative Work. *Human Computer Interaction*, 3, 3 – 30, 1988.

Knowledge-Based Cooperative Publication System

Christoph Hüser
Erich J. Neuhold
GMD-IPSI Integrated Publication and Information Systems Institute
Dolivostrasse 15, D-6100 Darmstadt, West Germany
e-mail:{hueser, neuhold}@darmstadt.gmd.dbp.de

The publishing process can be characterized as preparation, production, and communication of documents. During this process the involved parties like authors, editors, designers, animators, reprographers produce a variety of interim multimedia products. Documents, video clips, layout specifications etc. are stored, manipulated, communicated, discussed and annotated.

At GMD-IPSI we are building an integrated Publication Development Environment (PDE) based on an assistant model to provide users with homogeneous access to their tools. The PDE reflects a ßtructured-documentäpproach to publishing in which classes of documents, such as newspaper, lexicon, technical documentation, are described by generic models.

Documents are characterized as structures containing content and separate associated orthogonal styles that specify aspects of presentation, navigation, and interaction for the production of electronic publications. This separation facilitates the identification of dedicated roles of the involved contributors, the planning and specification of their tasks and the required cooperation between them. Rule-based design tools are built for the generic production of electronic publications and for the specification of the above roles.

This paper describes the design of the PDE and reports on experiences gained from the implementation of an application.

Der Publikationsprozeß kann als Aufbereitung, Produktion und Kommunikation von Dokumenten charakterisiert werden. Die verschiedenen Partner wie Autoren, Redakteure, Designer, Animateure und Reprographen produzieren beim Publizieren eine Reihe von multimedialen Zwischenprodukten. Dokumente, Video-Clips, Layoutspezifikationen usw. werden gespeichert, manipuliert, kommuniziert, diskutiert und annotiert.

Im GMD-IPSI wird eine integrierte Publikationsentwicklungsumgebung (PDE) realisiert. Das PDE beruht auf einem Assistenz-Modell, das den Anwendern homogenen Zugriff auf ihre Werkzeuge ermöglicht und basiert auf dem Ansatz des Publizierens von strukturierten Dokumenten, in dem die Dokumentklassen (z.B. Zeitung, Lexikon, technische Dokumentation) durch generische Modelle beschrieben werden.

Dokumente werden dabei als Strukturen mit Inhalt charakterisiert, denen durch separat assoziierte orthogonale Styles die Aspekte der Präsentation, Navigation und Interaktion für elektronische Publikationen aufgeprägt werden. Diese Trennung von Inhalt und Style ermöglicht die Identifikation dedizierter Rollen der am Publikationsprozess Beteiligten, der Planung und Spezifikation ihrer Aufgaben, und der benötigten Kooperation zwischen ihnen. Für die generische Produktion elektronischer Dokumente und die Spezifikation der identifizierten Rollen werden regel-basierte Design Tools entwickelt. Dieser Artikel beschreibt das Design des PDE und berichtet über Erfahrungen bei der Implementierung einer Anwendung.

1   Introduction

In conventional publications authors provide contents and specialists such as book designers, desk editors, and typographers add value to the authors work cooperatively to produce a final product. Traditionally, this is done with distinct tools and methods which do not support close collaboration between the partners involved. Todays widely spread tools, that are based on the paradigm of Desktop Publishing have not brought the expected benefits of reusability or cost-cutting even where they provide rich functionality. These systems have to be used in isolation and thus are not effectively integrated into the work environment. As single user systems they cannot support cooperative work. Moreover, authors usually lack the knowledge necessary for high quality production, e.g. professional layout expertise. As a consequence these systems overload the authors with details of style and presentation specification, distracting them from focussing on the contents.

Todays competitive pressures in the publication process result in a new level of requirements. The publication process must be faster, the quality has to be improved, and new media providing innovative forms of presentation and distribution have to be integrated. Electronic publication, especially in the form of hypermedia documents, suggests qualitatively new possibilities for communicating knowledge. Advanced communications will enable efficient access to large databases storing multimedia documents, which may consist of combinations of text, audio signals, still images and moving images of various definitions.

But creating content and adding value for electronic publication also demands qualitatively enhanced support for authors, publishers and users. It is the strength of electronic documents that they can be used in many different ways. They can be presented as linear documents or as hypertext, they can be multimedia, dynamic, or contain active components. They also can be used and reused by publishers to produce related products like individualized versions. Readers can embed the documents in their own personal information systems enabling enhancement and personal annotation. Thus, the traditional division between producing documents and storing data for personal use are beginning to disappear.

As an answer to these requirements we propose an integrated publication development environment (PDE), that can be used by the different specialists, e.g. authors, editors, layout designers, typesetters, to jointly produce and distribute a publication. Central to this environment is a publishing model separating the Publication Design and Planning from the Publication Preparation and Production. This publishing model reflects a ßtructured documentäpproach to publishing in which classes of document are described by generic models so that effective support tools can exploit the control, modularity, and flexibility afforded by an object-oriented approach. Applying structured documents allows to specify document styles for the different types of publications. Implementing this model with a layered document application architecture leads to an environment providing support for cooperative work for the generic production of hypermedia publications. Furthermore the environment offers version management for the handling and exchange of interim documents.

PDE is being developed by the department PaVE (Publication and Visualization Environment) of IPSI. An individualized science news magazine has been developed in this environment as a prototypical hypermedia application - an information system with dynamic content - to test the architecture and the involved concepts. Furthermore in cooperation with partners of the RACE project 1075 Telepublishing tools are being developed to demonstrate the production and distribution of an individualized electronic newspaper (IEN) using advanced high bandwidth communication systems.

This paper describes the design of the integrated publication development environment (PDE) and reports on experiences gained from the implementation of the individualized electronic newspaper application. The paper is organized as follows: after characterizing the design issues (section 2) we suggest the publishing process model (section 3) followed by the layered document architecture model (section 4). The paper closes with the presentation of IEN, a sample application (section 5).

2 Design Issues in an Integrated PDE

The document interchange format plays a central role in any integrated publication environment. It represents the means to communicate both final products to readers and unfinished documents between tools and people involved in the preparation and production processes.

In the publishers world a family of document standards are used for electronic publishing. The basic standard is the Standard Generalized Markup Language (SGML) [3]. SGML itself is not a document interchange format but a tool to define application based document interchange formats. These formats are called document type definitions (DTD). A DTD contains a content structure specification for a class of documents. It guides the content acquisition and structuring of the document content. A basic feature is the definition of elements to specify the content structure. In the object-oriented domain an element declaration is an object class description. The attribute declarations of an element define properties of the object. The content model of the element declaration defines the allowed sub elements. Beginning by the root element declaration in the DTD the content models of all element declarations specify the logical structure of a document and correspond to a con! text free grammar. The logical st

However, SGML cannot be used for a description of the presentation or the use the information (except implicitly by understood conventions of structuring documents). Just as rules for page layout must be given to a formatter, for hypermedia publications user-dependent ßemanticsfor presentation and use (whether in editing, producing or consuming) have to be added.

The Document Style Semantics and Specification Language (DSSSL) [4] is a companion standard of SGML. It defines syntax and semantics of a language for the specification of document processing which conforms to SGML. The semantics of DSSSL include a document architecture for the definition of typographic presentation styles and other document processing specifications. DSSSL provides a conceptual process model. The first of the DSSSL processes is the General Language Transformation Process (GLTP) which is used to transform an SGML source document instance into another hierarchically structured instance conforming to SGML or other standards such as ODA [2]. The second one is the Semantic-Specific Process for e.g. formatting. The model can be used for other types of processes such as document assembly or data base load and extract.

DSSSL allows the separation between logical and layout structures and also permits a rationalized automated publication preparation. It eases reusability (e.g. several layout structures for a document class) and encourages the development of and experimentation with functionalities well suited for consuming electronic publications.

To model hypermedia documents using SGML a special SGML application has been defined: the Hypermedia/Time-based Structuring Language (HyTime) [5]. It may be seen as a basic model and language for the representation of hyperdocuments. HyTime is intended to be used in platform-independent information interchange of hypermedia applications. Beside many other features this model enables the exchange of structured hypertext and structured multimedia documents.

The interchange of documents between the tools in the publication process will at the least enable a loose coupling between the various publication tasks. The tools may internally work with different structural and semantic models. This is quite sufficient for the set of dedicated functionality contained in individual tools.

For the network communication facilities and for the window systems standards such as X11 or NeWS are well established. They enable open system interfaces based on layered architectures separating the use of services from implementation aspects. Our idea is to transfer this concept to electronic publishing. In our integrated PDE we utilize the benefits of SGML and its companion standards combined within a layered system architecture. This approach fulfills the following goals:

1. The application independent architecture incorporates a high level object oriented document access interface and thus prepares the PDE for rapid prototyping and for the adoption of tools as well as the integration of existing tools.

2. The integrated concept for the management of structured documents frees tools from dealing with questions of storage management. It also enables data sharing which again provides the basis for cooperative work.

3. The support of hypertext and multimedia functionality transcends the limitations of the traditional structured document approach and allows nonlinear document presentations.

4. The separate management of content, structure and semantic of document objects enables the reuse of document parts for different purposes. Styles for the organization and management of the collaboration between the involved parties are of special importance. One particular application of the style concept is the creation of dynamic documents.

5. The separation of the document access model from the storage concepts allows us to employ different storage techniques such as file systems, relational databases or object-oriented database systems without affecting the application tools. However the management of large amount of structured documents requires adequate tools for their organization and access. Database systems play a crucial role within such an environment. It turned out that conventional database systems cannot provide sufficient functionality to support the needs of applications in the publication field. We propose to use object oriented database systems if possible.

6. The document access model contains a query language. This language also serves as the basic concept for the location of objects for a general transformation language to be used to realize views on documents. First of all adequate views are needed to support different roles (e.g. authoring, editing, producing, consuming) and the corresponding activities. Secondly, when considering for example, formatted documents as specials views on the document, it will be used to support the formatting of documents. Thirdly the transformation language enables the flexible reuse of content and explicit structure.

7. The management of the many interim products arising in the publishing process has to be supported by a powerful versioning concept [13]. Different versions and variants of documents under development have to be maintained for future exploration or discussions of alternatives.

8. Although we focus on an overall integrated system we do not expect to install such an environment at all the sites of the involved partners. As a consequence the system is a truly distributed computing environment. For example, a reporter and a camera man may be recording life and a journalist together with a video cutter may be integrating these recordings into a report at the same time, each using only the functionality of the system needed for this task. A journalist may write a life report on his laptop using only the hypertext writing aspects of PDE. However, the importing and exporting of document parts including their versions is an important requirement such an activity.

3 Process Model of the PDE

Our approach is to base the publication environment on a methodology that can support an efficient, organized publication process. In order to control the publication process in its complexity we propose the publishing model shown in Figure 1. The results of the Design and Planning phase guide and support the publication preparation and leads towards automatic production of the final publications. We will explain each subphase in detail.

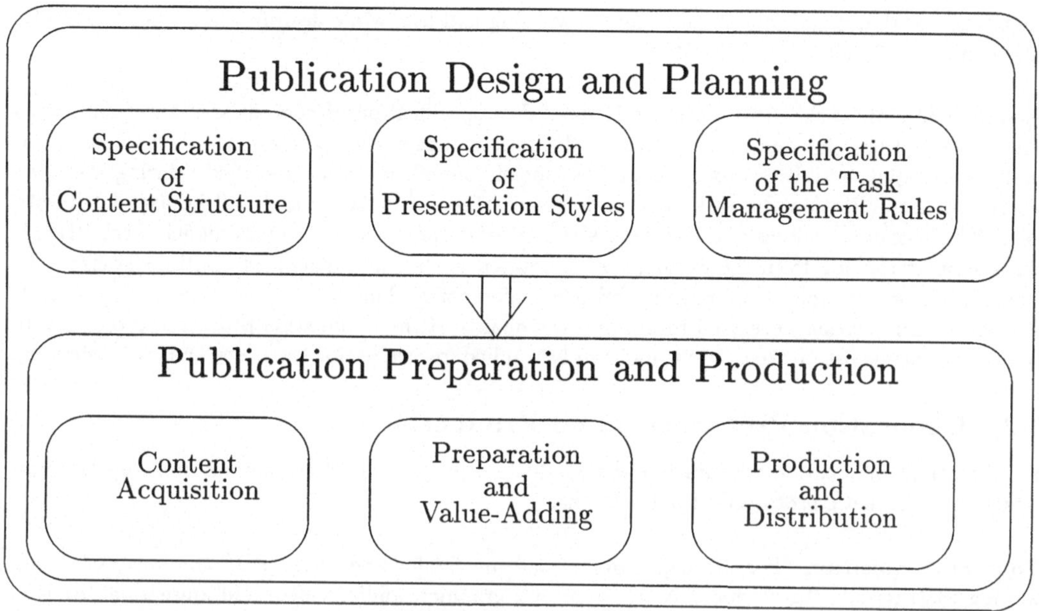

Abbildung 1: Process Model of the PDE

3.1 Publication Design and Planning

In our model documents are characterized as structures with content and associated orthogonal styles
that can specify aspects of layout, interaction, versioning and browsing semantics. This separation
facilitates the identification of dedicated roles, the planning and specification of their tasks, and the
needed cooperation for individual publications.

Specification of Content Structure The content structure specification of a hypermedia document is a long cooperative process. SGML provides a rich language for modelling content structures
as nested elements with attributes. To enhance control in the publication process through syntactic
checking, it appears advisable to model the structure in depth. This also provides more possibilities
for reusing the material. On the other hand, the more deeply modelled the structure, the more
is required from the contributors. It is necessary to specify role-specific content structures. This
suggests that various granularities should be used for various tasks, with a careful choice of when to
use interactive refinement.

For the IEN the journalist needs a well-defined structure of the individual article during content
acquisition. An editor-in-chief will focus both on the structure of a section and of the article in order
to specify the current content of the sections and their relative priority for an edition.

Specification of Styles The way of viewing and using an electronic publication is not fixed by
conventions. The structure of hyperdocuments involves complex nets. To overcome the resulting
complexity in handling, tools are required for the design and management of how various types
of electronic publications are to be created and read. The PDE provides for the definition of role-
specific views and uses. For example, the granularity with which the document should be manipulable
for a certain task might be described by associating task-specific editing styles with the DTD. To
generate different presentations needed for the individualized newspaper several layout structures and
processes can be specified. Using such concepts of layout, browsing, retrieval, and transformation in
our approach to publishing the specifications are independent of particular system tools. This has

the advantage that equal functionality for the viewing and use, while desirable, does not have to be fully supported by all tools of the PDE.

Specification of Task Management Rules The specification of content structures and styles builds the platform for the specification of the task management. For every task a requirement analysis for input, activities, resources and output of content has to be specified. During the development of a publication the task concept is given a finer granularity and will be associated with roles. The necessary collaboration support is provided by the document access model of the PDE. It offers support ranging from the exchange of annotated documents, enhanced multimedia electronic mailing, to closely coupled joint editing and tele-conferencing. The task concept defines the life cycle of a certain publication, it is used to improve the quality of the publication process and product, to facilitate multiple use of the content, and can be applied for evaluation purposes and cost reduction.

3.2   Publication Preparation and Production

For the actual publication preparation and production process the PDE offers a multi-media infrastructure for realistic prototypical publications.

Content Acquisition For the acquisition of multimedia documents the PDE contains various authoring tools for structured documents, hypertext, graphics, audio, video, and animation. At IPSI the department WIBAS develops a content acquisition tool called SEPIA (Structured Elicitation and Processing of ideas for Authoring) [10]. It is a knowledge-based authoring tool for hypertext environments developed on the basis of cognitive models of authoring. For the acquisition of paper documents, scanner and software for optical character recognition are used. The department PISA tackles the problems of document structure recognition. Importing content into the PDE plays a central role within the publication process. Documents and text files in various formats are transformed into SGML document instances. Various image conversions are supported. The automatization of import is definitely required to handle news from the network and other sources timely and inexpensively.

Preparation and Value-Adding This phase involves markup and restructuring of documents followed by the integration of separate content portions into a semi-final form. Interim versions between editors and authors get exchanged, consistency checks and previewing of the final product as well as fine-tuning has to be performed. To automate specific tasks, such as link generation according to the specified browsing styles, we develop generic tools. Nevertheless, a large amount of work has to be invested to prepare the publication for the desired look and use. Intelligent tool to support this process are currently under development. They are based on concepts derived from information retrieval and layout oriented human computer interfaces. The verification and editing of links is crucial for the quality of a hypermedia publication. Today it must be done iteratively on the final product.

For different publications the tools have to offer different functionality. The Editor's Workbench, developed within the Race Project, is an example for an adaptable tool supporting a variety of specialist tasks. It will be described further down.

Production and Distribution The final output of a PDE application can be a print and/or electronic publication. Various output formats, such as color postscript and hypertext stacks, are supported. Devices for print publications include a raster image processor for laser image setters allowing for high-resolution output of formatted material.

The final electronic products are delivered as a set of hypermedia stacks for a number of systems, such as HyperCard or HyperNeWS. HyTime will be applied as standardized exchange format between

<table>
<tr><td>Application Layer</td></tr>
</table>

Document Application Interface Layer

Navigation	Object-Oriented Mechanisms
Manipulation	for Style Associations
Retrieval	with Document Content e.g.:
Transformation	Layout Browsing
	Interaction Editing

Object-Oriented Storage Layer
Pool Management for Structured Documents

Abbildung 2: Layered Architecture of the PDE

systems. The distribution of electronic publications is possible via network communication systems, floppy or optical disks.

4 Layered Architecture of the PDE

The aim of using a layered architectural approach (Figure 2) is to produce a stable effective kernel system for the publication designer and for the editor, providing multi-user support, style design tools, and version management. In order to provide sensible and efficient access to the stored structured documents, we needed a specialized document access system that provides efficient support for our object-oriented approach. Applications build upon the system have access to components of structured documents in the object-oriented storage layer through the document application interface layer. The layer are described in the following.

4.1 Object-Oriented Storage Layer

The storage layer supports the management of pools of structured documents. It conforms to a subset of the basic SGML Document Standard. The actual implementation supports the management of elements with their attributes and entities. A pool is an organizational unit that provides all information for document access and holds a collection of document type definitions (DTDs) and document instances that conform with one of the document type definitions stored in the pool. Different pools may contain different collections of document type definitions. The usage of several pools in one application is possible and recommend for document management purpose. For example, for IEN a wide variety of document structures needs to be supported.

The pool of articles stores these publication constituents: different kinds of articles (report, news, comment), references to images, advertisements, background information for topics discussed in the newspaper (e.g. original material, such as complete scripts of interviews, scientific reports or magazine articles), and explanation information (glossaries, lexicons for different purposes). The pool approach provides an entry to a well-linked hyperdocument base including materials at different depth of knowledge (e.g. lexicon and encyclopedia). The pool has to integrate and store these data that are provided by the different contributors via the communication network and has to deliver them for many kinds of readers via different delivery systems.

The pool is managed as a directed graph structure starting with the pool object. The DBMS provides a data definition language to specify the conceptional schema and some of the details regarding the implementation of the conceptual schema by the physical schema (performance enhancements like predefined joins etc.). A data dictionary is an extension of the database schema. In our model the DTD will be used as a document dictionary and may be seen as part of the schema of the database. A similar approach based on context-free grammars was presented in [6].

The storage layer manages the document instances as well as their DTDs. DTDs themselves are kept as structured documents that must conform to a master DTD designed by GMD that describes all legal document type definitions. They can be stored, manipulated (especially edited), and retrieved as any other kind of document.

4.2 Document Access Interface Layer for Structured Documents

The object-oriented document access interface (DAI) provides the management mechanisms for the pool, but also the functionality to develop applications with different usage of document structures and different levels of access:

- Navigation and retrieval methods for consumer applications such as e.g. newspaper reading tools, lexicon browsers or retrieval interfaces that generate different views of the selected contents.

- Manipulation methods for structure or hypertext editors, contents or layout composer discussed later in the paper.

- Versioning and link mechanisms to be used in a versioned document editor without disrupting the primary document structure.

- Support for document structure transformation on the basis of a transformation language interpreter that will be used by the hypertext layout composer, which is discussed in section 4.4.

The interface assures SGML conformity of all documents. Therefore the content check for SGML elements is integrated in the DAI.

The query language corresponds to the association specification for the source instance of the General Language Transformation Process of DSSSL. It is path oriented and works in conjunction with the object management functions. Accessing a document instance by an application is done with respect to the syntactical structure. For example, to select all elements that conform to the element Chapter within a document instance the expression "CHAPTER"will have to be specified. For access purposes path terms may be used that locate one or more elements in the tree via element names e.g. "BOOK/CHAPTER/SECTIONänd properties e.g. "CHAPTER [LANGUAGE = 'ENGLISH']". Retrieval operations may use three of global contexts:

- Query on one document instance in the pool such as a lexicon to find an entry.

- Query on all instances of a DTD. For example, to compose a newspaper part, all articles of a day for the section science and technology have to be selected.

- Query on all instances or DTDs in the pool according to the declarations in the master DTD. This is useful to find text parts which e.g. contain the word SGML.

SGML specifies various conventions for the declaration of attributes and their usage. For example, the attribute value declaration ID is used for the definition of an unique identifier of the object. The attribute value declaration IDREF is an ID reference value to a unique identifier of another object. In HyTime this is called "Locations addressed by name". This provides also for direct access to an element without knowing the actual tree structure. It allows the use of links to support semantic or context sensitive interrelationships between elements in a document or between all documents in the pool, if a unique name space over all elements in the pool is guaranteed.

The DAI supports an extensible interface through the development of new object classes (e.g. multi-media objects) or the integration of a hypertext system e.g. such as HyperNeWS [11]. It

```
<!ENTITY % objects      "Button, EditText, Slider,
                         PullDown, ColorSel, Canvas">
<!ENTITY % false        "0">
<!ENTITY % true         "1">
<!ENTITY % PC   "#PCDATA">


<!--                                                      -->
<!-- CONTENT MODEL of HyperNeWS specification             -->
<!--                                                      -->


<!--          ELEMENT          CONTENT                    -->
<!ELEMENT HNdoc   - -    (Stack*, CrInfo?)*     -- Document   -->
<!ELEMENT Stack   - -    (BackGr | CardObj)* -- StackObject   -->
<!ELEMENT BackGr  - -    (Card, CardObj)* -- BackGroundObject -->
<!ELEMENT Card    - -    (CardObj)*    -- Card of Stack       -->
<!ELEMENT CardObj - -    (%objects;)   -- Objects             -->
<!ELEMENT (%objects;)- -    EMPTY       -- Object on a Card    -->


<!--CREATION-INFORMATION-->
<!ELEMENT CrInfo- -(date?, creator?)>
<!--creation information includes date of entrys creation
 and its creators (= first contributors) name/initials;     -->
<!ELEMENT creator - - (((initials)?|(name&firstnam*)),project?)>
<!ELEMENT (initials|name|firstnam|project)   - -(%PC;)>
<!ELEMENT date     - -(%PC;)>
....
...
```

Abbildung 3: Element Declaration Part of the HyperNeWS DTD

is a user interface development tool based on OpenWindows, a window server system developed by Sun Microsystems. HyperNeWS is a vehicle for the implementation of knowledge-based and hypertext systems. HyperNeWS will be used by tools to realize hypertext functionalities, for example the traversal of links between articles via buttons, the implementation of sophisticated browsing tools, path traversals, etc. The development of HyperNeWS has been influenced by the concepts of HyperCard (stacks, cards, script language).

The instantiation and management of objects is bound by the element declaration of the used DTD. This concept is also used in a similar way by HyTime and other SGML application specifications. The hierarchical object structure of HyperNeWS is modelled in a special DTD. In Figure 3 a part of the HyperNeWS DTD is presented:

On the one hand a HyperNeWS document instance may be created and edited in the structure editor like any normal document. Stacks, cards, buttons, scripts and their attributes will be changeable. On the other hand the document instance can be directly connected via an object-oriented interface to HyperNews. In this mode every object in the document will become an HyperNeWS object. In reverse order the HyperNeWS stacks will be converted into document instances. This enables the flexible use of the interactive modelling benefits of HyperNeWS for the design of the user interface and the integration into the publishing process using the DAI. Using the transformation language, developed for the hypertext layout composer, the content of documents e.g. newspaper articles may be mapped into the HyperNews document. The effect is the direct representation of the content in the user interface..

4.3   Storage Model

The underlying database management system is strongly separated from the internal document model. The storage organization is fully independent of the stored content. We use an object based approach. The storage model does not make a difference between composite objects, atoms or links like in other approaches such as the Dexter Hypertext Reference Model [1] or HyperBase [9], developed at our institute. Rather the element declarations defining the semantics of the objects also determine how the objects have to be stored. The actual implementation of the storage layer uses the relational database management system Sybase.

4.4   Application Layer

The application layer of the integrated PDE is based on an assistant model described in [7]. The architecture of the PDE is defined by three basic types of components: assistants, agents and tools. Each user of the publication environment owns a personalized assistant. The assistant reflects the user's knowledge about his/her specific role in the publication process. The users tasks are performed by accessing specific tools. Agents offer direct access to non-local tools, originally available only through the assistants of other users.

The Editor's Workbench, being developed in the Race Project, is a basic component of the role-specific assistants. It is implemented using the Andrew Toolkit [8] and is a powerful integrated object-oriented environment for the development of complex multimedia applications.

5   A Sample Application: Individualized Electronic Newspaper (IEN)

The IEN is intended as an innovative product in the publishing industry. The main idea is to support individualization of the newspaper content as well as its look and use. An issue of the IEN will be compiled according the interests a reader has stated in an individual profile, and can be delivered as paper product on a printer or as electronic product on-screen as hypermedia version. As a prerequisite, the information contained in the newspaper has to be stored in a flexible reusable form. Thus, the preparation of the information involves new database storage techniques for structured documents, tools to classify and link the information, tools to prepare multilingual newspapers, and support for management of versions of articles. In order to build the IEN application pilot the following tools are being developed:

- Editor's Workbench, Translator's Workbench, Versioned Document Editor

- Content Composer, Layout Composer, Hypertext Layout Composer

- Structured Document Base

The Structured Document Base represents the implementation of the PDE layered architecture and includes parsers for the content acquisition. For the specification of the readers' profiles and the selection of the individualized newspaper issue special reader interfaces are provided. In the following, the important steps in the IEN publication process will be explained.

5.1   Design and Planning of the IEN

In the Race project the partners contributed a number of preliminary studies investigating IEN requirements from the readers' and contributors' standpoint. For the publication process various content structures and presentation styles have been specified, including:

- article input DTD (for content acquisition)

- newspaper content DTD (for content composition)

- newspaper layout DTD (for layout and typographic processing)

- image DTD (for image acquisition)

Hypertext Layout Composition needs a specification of the layout transformation rules for Hyper-NeWS stack generation. It includes rules for the mapping of the newspaper content onto HyperNeWS objects and a set of layout design rules for the newspaper cards. Special interaction semantics (e.g. scripts for buttons) are also required for browsing through articles. The association of links to text objects enhances the usability. User- and/or editor-defined layout and interaction rules drive the individual look and useöf the newspaper issue.

5.2   Content Acquisition

Content acquisition comprises the following activities:

- Converting non-SGML document formats into the specified SGML article structure using a recognition style-driven document preprocessor.

- Assuring SGML conformance and database load of articles using the Amsterdam Parser System [12], which was adapted and integrated into the PDE.

5.3   Preparation and Value-Adding

The pool of articles contains a set of independent articles that need to be prepared to guarantee automatic composition of individualized newspaper issues. The following steps have to be performed:

- Editing content using the Editor's Workbench A preview mode is also integrated to test the allowed article presentation according to the valid layout styles for the hypertext composition.

- Guiding the translation of structured documents using the Translator's Workbench, an extension of the Editor's Workbench.

- Management of versioned documents and interchange of interim products with the Versioned Document Editor, which is also based on the Editor's Workbench.

5.4   Production and Distribution

The production of the IEN is divided into two steps. The first one is the selection of the information components from the pool according to individual user profiles and selections with the content composer and the creation of an individual newspaper instance according to the contributors' requirements, e.g. rules for advertisements. The second one is the production of the final output of a newspaper using one of the alternatives:

- Producing final output of the IEN for printing via the layout composer. Formatting articles, images and advertisements according to newspaper layout rules into the final output. This output is represented by a postscript file which can be send to the reader via electronic mail.

- Composing a hypertext layout via transforming the constructed newspaper document instance into a newspaper layout instance to perform formatting. The formatted newspaper layout instance will then be transformed into the resulting HyperNeWS document instance. With the described HyperNeWS interface the newspaper stacks are automatically created. The HyperNeWS SGML document or the HyperNeWS stacks can both be used for the distribution of the product.

6   Acknowledgement

The PDE is the work of all the members of the PaVE department of GMD-IPSI. Special thanks are given to the former manager Roberto Minio, and the scientific and technical contributors to the described project.

Literatur

[1] F. Halasz and M. Schwartz. The Dexter Hypertext Reference Model. In *Presented at the NIST Hypertext Standardization Workshop*, Gaithersburg, MD, January 16-18 1990.

[2] ISO/DIS 8613. *Information Processing - Text and Office Systems - Office Document Architecture (ODA) and Interchange Format*, 1986.

[3] ISO/DIS 8879. *Information Processing - Text and Office Systems - Standard Generalized Markup Language (SGML)*, 1986.

[4] ISO/IEC CD 10179. *Information Technology - Text and Office Systems - Document Style Semantic and Specification Language (DSSSL)*, May 1991.

[5] ISO/IEC CD 10744. *Information Technology - Hypermedia/Time-based Structuirng Language (HyTime)*, April 1991.

[6] P. Kilpeläinen, G. Lindén, H. Mannila, and E. Nikunen. A structured document database system. In R. Furuta, editor, *Proceedings of the International Conference on Electronic Publishing, Document Manipulation and Typography* , September 1990.

[7] P. Muth, T. C. Rakow, W. Klas, and E. J. Neuhold. A Transaction Model for an Open Publication Environment. *IEEE Data Engineering, Special Issue on Transaction Models for Advanced Applications, to be published*, 1991.

[8] A. J. Palay, W. J. Hansen, M. L. Kazar, M. S. und Maria G. Wadlow, T. P. Neundorffer, Z. Stern, M. Bader, and T. Peter. The Andrew Toolkit- An Overview. Technical report, Carnegie Mellon University, Information Technology Center, Pittsburgh, PA 15213.

[9] H. Schütt and N. Streitz. HyperBase: A Hypermedia Engine Based on a Relational Database Management System. In A. Rizk, N.Streitz, and J. Andre, editors, *Proceedings of the European Conference on Hypertext (ECHT-90): Hypertext: Concepts, Systems, and Applications*, pages 95–108, Versailles, France, Cambridge Series on Electronic Publishing, November 27-30 1990.

[10] N. A. Streitz, J. Hannemann, and M. Thüring. From Ideas and Arguments to Hyperdocuments: Travelling Through Activity Spaces. In *Proceedings of the ACM-Conference HYPERTEXT'89, Special Issue of SIGCHI Bulletin*, pages 343–364, Pittsburgh, Pennsylvania, November 1989.

[11] The Turing Institute, 36 North Hanover Street, Glasgow G1 2AD, United Kingdom. *HyperNeWS1.4*.

[12] Vrije Universitei Amsterdam. *The Amsterdam SGML Parser*.

[13] A. Weber. Publishing Tools Need Both: State-Oriented and Task-Oriented Version Support. In *Accepted for the: Fifteenth Annual International Computer Software and Applications Conference 1991*, Tokyo, Japan, September 1991.

The Document Preparation System REGENT: Concepts and Functionality

Dimitris Karagiannis

FAW - Research Institute for Applied Knowledge Processing

P.O.Box 2060

D-7900 Ulm/Germany

email: karagian@faw.uni-ulm.de

The REport GENeration Tool is a software environment suitable for constructing report structures as well as planning, executing and monitoring the tasks needed to produce the specified report. In this paper we describe the design of REGENT and the techniques suggested for its implementation. It employs three major parts which enable the development of a system architecture to be shared in a distributed environment. First, structuring, planning, executing and monitoring facilities run cooperatively, based on a common knowledge bases consisting of meta knowledge on the common modeling facilities and on the respective application-specific knowledge. Second, a requirement-specific object-oriented model is developed in order to manage and maintain an application specific functionality. Third, a cooperative communication approach depending on the distributed environment is suggested for supporting negotiation and interaction between different types of users, as well as for performing internal subsystem communication which is based on the blackboard architecture. In addition to describing the main advantages of the developed approach, the functionality of the REGENT demonstrator is shown, based on the scenario of the prototypic application "FAW Annual Report".

1 Introduction

Motivation

The OSSY project — Organization Support Systems — [7] has been established in order to support cooperative office work via knowledge-based technology. This technology should facilitate the integration of the fundamental approaches, task-, communication-, and document handling, forming the basis of existing office systems [24].

To achieve the project's objective, we have started developing a methodology which allows the integration of various approaches in order to design tools for office information systems. An important aspect for the suggested development of an office tool is the possibility of integrating an appropriate organizational model which exists and can be used. In the following we describe the design and the development of the office information tool REGENT based on the following requirements:

- to use the knowledge-based tools for

  a) decoupling the knowledge-based tasks from the conventional ones, i.e., no more recoding

  b) generating "autonomous" application models, i.e., no more utilization of intermediate logical models

- to design a multiagent system architecture, i.e., no more individual views

- to build tools for realistic application environments, i. e., no more prototypic islands

Techniques from traditional office automation are combined with new database technology and AI approaches for knowledge-based office information systems in accordance with the philosophy of Flexible Office Systems [28]. The concept of the chosen modeling approach and its realization is primarily based on the object-oriented paradigm [19], [26].

The Application Domain

The main objective of the REGENT system is to support the structuring process, the cooperative writing process and the maintenance and updating of large organizational reports, i.e., annual reports of diverse companies or biannual environmental reports, etc. In the present stage of the project we are concentrating on knowledge acquisition and formalization of the FAW Annual Report and its production.
The goal of the project work was to develop a tool which can be used for report generation, if the reports possess certain characteristics. During the analysis phase, the generalization of the results will receive special emphasis. Therefore, it is expected that the tool can be used as a platform from which more specific application-customized tools can be easily derived. Whenever appropriate, we will utilize knowledge-based methods and techniques to provide support for the tasks of cooperative document preparation.
Most cooperative report-writing activities take place in offices. The system must be integrated in a target environment that is primarily made up of some preexisting information system and general office communication software. Consequently, there is a definite need to interface well with the IS to facilitate the collection, the preparation and the adaption of data and partial documents. The REGENT system is therefore divided into two main subsystems, the knowledge-based part REGENT-K and the data-based part REGENT-D. The report structuring process will take place in the subsystem REGENT-K, the link to the "external" world will be achieved by the REGENT-D subsystem. REGENT-C integrates the two components.
The report preparation application consists basically of the following phases:

(1) Generation of a description of the report structure, based on a formal specification language

(2) Generation of the plan necessary to produce the report

(3) Execution, controlling and monitoring of the tasks

(4) Specification and printing of a report version

Besides group and organizational communication and coordination techniques, the successful application depends on an advanced report model. In order to handle electronic documents we need a formal representation of documents and their structures. Two norms exist for the structural aspects of documents concerning — although not exclusively — their logical structure.
The model we will describe in this paper has to reflect the requirements, which result out of two objectives. The report model has to be used for a (semi-) automatic report structuring process and must facilitate in a wider sense the job and database management activities. For the latter category we have to consider, e.g., task assignment, production schedule, monitoring, writing tasks executed in parallel or sequentially, the necessity to store the parts of the report in a database as well as format compatibility of the text editors.

2 Concepts

We are facing the problem of how AI techniques can be used efficiently in office applications and which types of solutions have been proposed. New developments in databases are leading to better database management systems which support features such as objects, inheritance, rules and inference procedures [5]. In addition, we use research results on communication in cooperative systems and promising approaches concerning performance enhancements for office workers [1], [2]. The approach is illustrated throughout with examples from an office environment.

Office work can be compared to production work. Producing an engine with a fully automated production-line does not mean that we also need the production-line for maintaining and running it. The concepts needed for these tasks — like the oil-, water-, gasoline concept — can be deduced from the construction process. Some guidelines, e.g. how the electrical circuit has to be maintained, can also be deduced. We regard

- the production of an engine as analogous to the preparation of a report, and

- the guidelines and concepts applied to maintain the engine as analogous to the concepts for selecting, updating and supporting different report versions.

We used REGENT in place of the production-line quoted in the example above and a requirement specific database model based on the object-oriented paradigm for the running process [16]. Such a model will be necessary to run and maintain the report preparation process without having to use the expert system shell in every workstation, personal computer or mainframe which participates in the realized application. We consider that the production process provides different useful solutions which can be mapped onto the developed system architecture.

2.1   The Document Model

After analyzing various reports, e.g. enterprise-, status-, annual- and environmental reports and taking into consideration several specific reports such as technical documentations and user manuals, we regard the described conceptual document model as suitable for efficient automatic report generation.

Each document is classified by a logical and a conceptual structure. The logical structure determines which "standard-norm" level, e.g. SGML [11], ODA/ODIF [18], [12] can or should be used for a document. The conceptual structure expresses the semantic aspects for a document depending on the activated application. All reports belong to a class "document" which has some predefined structural units (slots). Reports can be structured semi-automatically by reusing predefined report-specific concepts. The process which recursively combines these items is called structuring process. The planning and executing methods deduce their tasks from the general and terminal topic concept using a reasoning process. The ontological structure of the document model seems as follows:

```
document value_class {report, ...}
class: report
logical_structure value_class terminal_topic
conceptual_structure part_of topic
topic is_a {general, terminal}
terminal_topic value_class {graphic, text-entities, images, ...}
general_topic value_class {basic-entities}
. . .
inferencing: reusability aspects
structuring: <method>
. . .
inferencing: reasoning aspects
planning: <method>
monitoring: <method>
```

2.2   The System Architecture

The described tool is developed in order to support activities being necessary for preparing a report.
It provides as well a technically sophisticated layout design using existing word-processing software.
The architecture is realized under consideration of three basic aspects:

- integration of the most adequate technologies for the suggested application requirements

- support of a sophisticated communication between the different tool users

- improvement of office work in the given soft- and hardware environment

The REGENT system supports these requirements by three different components. Within the framework of the project, appropriate concepts for a *knowledge-based part* named REGENT-K, an *object-
oriented database part* REGENT-D as well as for a *cooperative communication part* named REGENT-C
have been developed. Their functionality can be briefly described as follows:

- REGENT-K:

    - generates a report structure
    - delivers structured messages to the persons involved
    - configures a realization plan based on the report structure
    - coordinates, executes, monitors the processing of tasks
    - supports an application knowledge base

- REGENT-D:

    - supports the involved agents
    - retrieves stored report pieces
    - interprets a specified report, and
    - uses the created conceptual scheme

- REGENT-C:

    - supports the user communication
    - manages the intersystem connections
    - activates the needed network facilities

2.3   Hardware and Network Environment

The REGENT architecture is designed within a given hard- and software environment which is determined by previously existing organizational and operational demands. Due to integrational aspects
and economic reasons this pre-existing configuration has to be used for the REGENT system; therefore, the inherent hardware and software restrictions and options have to be considered during the
development of the REGENT architecture. Naturally, this approach does not always offer a "comfortable" development process from a software engineer's point of view, but unrealistic "island solutions"
for real problems are avoided.
The configuration consists of three different system types:

- Mainframe:
    In our case, the machine is an IBM 9370 running under VM/SP. It supplies the database and
    communications services.

- Workstation:
  The REGENT environment includes several workstations (Motorola 68030 - 68881) under UNIX System BSD 4.2. These systems offer the high performance and versatility necessary for using knowledge-based tools and AI programming languages. The actual prototype implementation is realized using the Knowledge Engineering Environment KEE.

- Personal Systems:
  These Intel-80386-based systems under MS-DOS and OS/2 are used as the user front-end for the REGENT system. Major functionalities of the system are located on these nodes as well as tools for managing authorized information.

These different processing nodes are interconnected via LAN. We employ different LAN architectures within the workstation environment (Ethernet) and the personal systems (Token Ring), but rely upon TCP/IP as system-wide homogeneous networking protocol with the mainframe providing the necessary routing services between the two other components. Thus it is also possible to utilize the networking security and external communication features (X.25, SDLC-Links) of the mainframe.

3   Development Issues

Certainly, the actual preparation of the reports is connected with regulations and office procedures. Regulations are used to represent the constraints that are relevant for the report. This is especially important for designing and maintaining reports. Procedures have the purpose of keeping track of which (partial) reports or texts are needed before starting a specific task, or, conversely, which texts are produced or consumed by the activated task.

Flexible Task Management (FTM)

The FTM component realizes the exchange of data, procedure activation and message interpretation between the REGENT-K and the other system components based on the Virtual Office System (VOS) approach [8]. With this approach we are able to implement a software system for the integration of knowledge-based systems (KBS) into a distributed and heterogeneous office environment by simulating the functionality of existing office systems primarily with predefined UNIX processes. In our case, the KBS is the REGENT-K, and the office information system is primarily formed by REGENT-D and REGENT-C.

Issues concerning the domain and structuring knowledge and its representation regarding the report generation and structuring process and the underlying document architecture are of special interest and we will deal with them in the following.

3.1   REGENT-K

With this component, the report structure can be directly generated from guidelines, rules and constraints. It also supports the coupling with the needed database conceptual scheme and partly manages the internal interconnections. The example — the rule annotations needed by the FAW annual report — is represented in the following form:

- Give an enterprise goal concerning the annual report.

- Define the available resources.

Report Structuring

The virtual report structure is given by the predefined guidelines. These are applied after the knowledge acquisition process and will be represented to the system in form of production rules. For this reason, the REGENT specification language is under development. From the given guidelines and the system knowledge the structuring component deduces a desired report structure.

The first step of the structuring process is to generate and present a stereotype report structure. Depending on the chosen report class and on the actual knowledge available in the knowledge bases, the system will select the relevant topics. The structured report will be presented as a traditional outline or as a tree-structure of the topics on a graphical display. During the second step some modifications on the generated structure are allowed. The organizer can delete topics, create new ones, or rearrange some of them. During this restructuring process he can be supported by an extended system as to which operations are allowed in order to handle an incompleteness and inconsistency of the report knowledge [17].

It is assumed that the structuring phase is completed before any other report preparation activities are started. An important presumption of our approach is that the application is set up by a knowledge engineer, while the user can only make use of the system knowledge and its functionality. Since we develop a tool, the domain-specific knowledge depends on the special report to be prepared using the system. It cannot be part of the system from the very beginning. More details about the specification and functionality of the structuring process are given in [29].

Task Planning

Task planning is a process based on the structuring results and the actual state of the knowledge base. The task decomposition for operation analysis can be interpreted in terms of predefined or generated activities. The task planning process consists of two different parts: the *selection* and the *configuration*.

Selection: This component interprets the structuring results and identifies the needed predefined activities or — if they are missing — generates new ones.

Configuration: The configuration process schedules sequentially or parallelly the chosen actions and composes them to a "plan-fragment" which can be processed by the executing component. An exact description about the formal model, syntax and specific report planning aspects is given in [32].

Task Execution and Monitoring

This component controls the execution of the tasks. Several subcomponents are used for executing a plan created by the planning component. The execution control expects partially instantiated plans as input. To these plans, supplementary information for the monitoring and coordination process will be added. According to the plan language semantics and the available knowledge, an action from the plans is chosen and passed on — in form of an "interaction object" — to the Flexible Task Management (FTM) component. As mentioned before this component is responsible for converting interaction objects into FTM procedures, considering communication with the external systems. The task can be interpreted in terms of predefined FTM procedures by decomposing them.

The execution and monitoring component interprets and manages external messages about status and results of executed tasks. In case of contradictions, a replanning process is started. This process provides an alternative plan taking into account the current status of the knowledge base.

Knowledge, Rules and Objects

An office system is based on a model of an organization and an office environment. An adequate conceptualization of this domain knowledge plays a dominant role according to [25]. Slightly diverging from [14], the REGENT knowledge bases contain

- meta knowledge:
  For the knowledge-based representation, knowledge about the structure of enterprises, possible communication structures and classification schemata for documents are used. Also, common-sense knowledge about concepts and relations must be considered, which is especially relevant

for heuristic problem-solving or the treatment of temporal and causal dependencies in task generation.

and

- knowledge about

    - organizational knowledge about departments and positions within them, projects, events
    - knowledge about individual staff members
    - knowledge about non-human resources such as office technologies at the office layer of REGENT or documents or standard forms and databases
    - knowledge about office procedures and tasks
    - knowledge about goals and perspectives of the enterprise itself

Instead of implicitly using this knowledge in structuring the knowledge base, it is represented explicitly in the knowledge management system, giving the possibility to use it in different applications and to deduce further information. A very simple example for the use of this conceptual knowledge is the description of relations in terms of transitivity, reflexivity and symmetry. By explicitly representing theses concepts, a simple and general deduction about a relation can be drawn by knowing that it is an equivalence relation.

The domain knowledge contains descriptional and procedural aspects. The representation of the descriptional aspects is based on the object-oriented views of the office world. The procedural aspects are represented in form of rules and methods which are also implemented using object-oriented programming techniques.

3.2 REGENT-D

Realistic or large-scale applications often involve more than one software systems, like expert systems or databases, but also conventional programs. Therefore the requirement for an "integrated methodology" to facilitate communication and support information transparency for the user is obvious. Unfortunately, the principles underlying the construction of existing databases and knowledge bases are fundamentally different, thus making such transparency a major source of inefficiency, hard to design and expensive to implement.

Designing a DBMS for supporting office applications does not only mean storing and retrieving data, but also supporting structured document management, multimedia object modeling and at least storing large amounts of hypertext documents. Under these conditions the REGENT-D conceptual model has been developed using the RSOM (Requirement-Specific Object-Oriented Model) methodology as described in [13]. The model's objective is to get an "integrated interface" realized by object-oriented techniques. It reflects the entire information of the considered application for a specific functionality, such as maintenance, updating, selection and specification. Approaches in this category are described in [4], [9] and [22]. RSOM supports three different kinds of requests:

a) those produced by the knowledge-based part,

b) those set up by the users, and

c) those activated after a change in the database entry.

3.3 REGENT-C

The cooperative communication approach consists of the following kinds of interaction:

a) user – system interaction
   designed by the user interface

b) user – user interaction
   designed by the negotiation process

c) system – system interaction
   designed by the communication facilities

a) User Interfaces

Depending on the support intentions of the REGENT system, we need a proper model for user interaction [3]. We distinguish three user groups of the REGENT system: *organizer*, e.g. an executive assistant, *producer*, e.g. an office worker, *selector*, e.g. a visitor. Concerning the system functionality these users may be classified into two groups: production and consumption. Organizer and producer belong to the production group, while the selector belongs to the consumption group.

The organizer mostly interacts directly with the REGENT-K subsystem. He is responsible for coordination on the management level of the report preparation activities within a given organization. He fulfills an editorial role and his activity can be viewed as a preplanning activity with respect to the report structuring process. This is because certain writing tasks can be deduced — depending on the topics to be covered by the report. Since the reports we consider are created by teams of authors, their work is brought together, coordinated and standardized by the organizer. It is clear that the organization's structure is essential with respect to authority, direction and control.

The producer manipulates the report pieces which are available in REGENT-D. He is responsible for writing and modifying report parts. Working on a PC, he starts the system by activating REGENT-C and identifying himself as "Producer" (as opposed to "Selector"; the DB contains a classification system managing the different access rights different users have).

The selector also interacts only with the REGENT-D, using the available REGENT-C interface facilities. He can choose either the standard version of a report, or he can configure his own version according to organizational, semantical, or application-specific information. The call results in opening a form which presents the list of contents of the standard report version. Furthermore, the selection process can be invoked on predefined topics.

b) Negotiation: A Cooperative Action

One of the most important aspects concerning office applications is that of "negotiation". Here we classify the negotiation process according to various characteristics. Regardless, whether the persons (agents) involved in the negotiation belong to the same organisation or not, the results depend on the actual situation and the strategical goal of the enterprise.

Existing negotiation approaches define different process stages and given suggestions and solutions for any kind of applications. Defining the following stages of a negotiation process, I think we can find a correspondence to the real situation and assume the conditions which should be valid for processing them. The following negotiation stages are valid, whether the participants (agents) belong to the same organisation or not:

Stage:	Condition:
Constitute	The participants agree to discuss a common topic.
Agree	The participants discuss factual questions, exchange objective arguments and find alternative solutions. The result can e.g. be "compromise", "majority".
Harmonize	The participants agree on objective, social and human level.
Discontinue	The participants have achieved a point of discussion in which a "break" is necessary.
Disperse	There exists no way to reach a "positive" solution.

A promised technique which we suggest is the mediator [31]. The basic idea behind this is to use an "emotionless independant instance" (EII). Emotionless regarding the participants' reactions, and independent concerning the negotiation results. We will try to develop and realize an EII using different approaches. In our application it can be, e.g., a piece of software which supports the organizer with different office workers to coordinate a succesful annual report, meeting the predefined deadline. A description of the approach which is pursued at FAW, named "goal-directed multiagent model for negotiation support" can be found in [27]. Negation as a cooperative action is supported by the existing knowledge bases and will be realized with KB techniques.

c) Communication Facilities

In the previous user interface section we defined how the user-system interaction should be realized. Here we describe how REGENT supports the internal communication. The system interaction facilities are classified according to which component they are needed or used by:

- requirements specific o-o model,

- user interface model, and

- interconnection model.

This interconnection model supports various interfacing types,

- *blackboard approach*:
  entries for automatic update of the knowledge base

- *message-passing approach*:
  the specified user query includes a receiver / sender

- *coupling approach*:
  user predefined functionality for data exchange

An evaluation and overview of the blackboard technology can be found in [20]. The coupling solution guarantees data exchange using a predefined functionality [6]. Reviews concerning the problem of coupling and the types of solutions that have been proposed are described in [21], [10], [15], [30] and [23].

4 Remarks

In this paper, we presented the REGENT system based on a three component architecture. In the first prototype it was assumed that the system could exploit a good organizational structure, and a functional networking environment like it exists at FAW. Among the desired prerequisites for a cooperative document preparation application in an industrial environment are: *computer supported organisational structure* and *facilities for the integration of existing information resources.*
These requirements must be met during the further implementation of the REGENT prototype. The proposed system is at an evaluation stage and this prototype is under further development.

5 Acknowledgements

I would like to thank the Office Automation group at FAW, and especially the OSSY project members, who realized the first prototype. My thanks go also to Eugen Maier for his helpful collaboration on this paper.

References

[1] Bertino E., Negri M., Pelagatti G., Sbattella L., Integration of Heterogeneous Database Integration through an Object-Oriented Interface, Information Systems, Vol. 14, No. 5, 1989

[2] Baecker, R. M., W. A. S. Burton (eds.), Readings in Human-Computer Interaction: A Multidisciplinary Approach, Morgan Kaufmann Publishers, Inc., California, USA, 1987

[3] Balzert H., Software-Ergonomie und Software-Engineering, Berlin - New York 1987

[4] Cacace F., Ceri S., Crespi-Reghizzi S., Tanca L., Zicari R., Integrating Object-Oriented Data Modelling with a Rule-Based Programming Paradigm, in: proc. of the int. conf. Management of Data, ACM SIGMOD 90, pp. 225-236, May 23-25, Atlantic City, NJ, 1990

[5] Dittrich K. R., Objektorientierte Datenbanksysteme, Informatik-Spektrum, pp. 215 - 220, Springer-Verlag

[6] Engelmore R., T. Morgan (eds.), Blackboard Systems, Addison-Wesley Publishing Company, Wokingham, England, 1988

[7] Faidt K., Grünberger H., Heller H., Hinkelmann K., Karagiannis D., Salzmann W., Schebiella S., Organizations Support System. Interner Bericht (in German language), FAW, Ulm, 1990

[8] Faidt K., Karagiannis D., Knowledge-Based Applications in Office Information Systems: An Integration Approach. in Proc. of the Int. Conference on Data Base and Expert Systems Application, DEXA'90, Springer Verlag, 1990

[9] Huhns M. N. (ed.), Distributed Artificial Intelligence, Pitman, London, England and Morgan Kaufmann Publishers, Inc., Los Altos, California, USA, 1987

[10] Risch T., Reboh R., Hart P., Duda R., A Functional Approach to Integrating Database and Expert Systems, Comm. of the ACM, Vol. 31, No 12, 1988

[11] Information Processing - Standard Generalized Mark-up Language (SGML), International Organization for Standardization, Geneva / Switzerland, 1986

[12] Information Processing - Office Document Architecture (ODA) and Interchange Format, International Organization for Standardization, Geneva / Switzerland, 1989

[13] Karagiannis D., Database Requirements and Conceptual Modelling in Office Automation, Workshop on Current Research Trends in Computer Science, Institute of Computer Science FORTH, Crete, Greece, July 26-30, 1990

[14] Kaye A. K., Karam G. M., Cooperating Knowledge-Based Assistants for the Office, ACM Transactions on Office Information Systems, Vol. 5, No. 4, 1987

[15] Kerschberg L., Proceedings From the Second International Conference on Expert Database Systems, The Benjamin / Cummings Publishing Company, Inc., 1986

[16] Kim W., Lochovsky F. (eds.), Object-Oriented Concepts, Databases, and Applications, acm press, Addison-Wesley Publishing Company, Reading, MA, USA, 1989

[17] Kowalewski L. D., Nichtmonotonie im prototypischen Dokumenten-Konfigurationssystem KOKON, KI 4/89, Oldenbourg-Verlag, 1989

[18] Krönert G., Genormte Austauschformate fr Dokumente, Informatik-Spektrum, No. 11, pp. 71 - 84, Springer-Verlag, 1988

[19] Lieberman H., A Preview of Act 1, AI Memo 625, MIT Artificial Intelligence Laboratory, Cambridge / MA, U.S.A., June 1981

[20] Nii P. H., Blackboard Systems: The Blackboard Model of Problem-Solving and the Evolution of Blackboard Architectures, The AI Magazine, Summer, 1986, pp. 38-53

[21] Risius J., Schütze P., Schweppe H., Kopplung relationaler Datenbanksysteme mit Prolog: Das PROMOX-System, Preprint B89-1, FU Berlin, 1989

[22] Sinz E. J., Datenmodellierung betrieblicher Probleme und ihre Unterstützung durch ein wissensbasiertes Entwicklungssystem, Habilitationsschrift, Regensburg, 1987

[23] Sciore L., Warren D. S., Towards an Integrated Database-Prolog System, in: [15]

[24] Tsichritzis D. C. (ed.), Office Automation, Springer Verlag. Berlin, Germany, 1985

[25] Wimmer K., An Approach to the Representation of Offices, Bundeswehrhochschule München, Dissertation, 1989

[26] Weinreb D., Moon, D., Flavors: Message Passing in the Lisp Machine, AI Memo 602, MIT Artificial Intelligence Laboratory, Cambridge / MA, U.S.A., November 1980

[27] Binbasioglu M., Karagiannis D., Radermacher F.J., A Goal-Directed Multiagent Model for Negotiation Support, FAW Technical Report, FAW-Bericht, Ulm, 1990

[28] Karagiannis D., Flexible Bürosysteme (FBS) – Architektur und Einsatzmöglichkeiten, in S. Fuhrmann and T. Pietsch, editors, Praktische Anwendungen moderner Bürotechnologien, Band 12, Erich Schmitt Verlag, 1989.

[29] Schebiella S., REGENT: The Structuring Component, FAW-Bericht, Ulm, 1990

[30] Karagiannis D. (ed.), Information Systems and Artificial Intelligence: Integration Aspects, Lecture Notes in Computer Science No. 474, Springer-Verlag, 1991

[31] Jarke M., Knowledge Sharing and Negotiation Support in Multiperson DSS, in: Decision Support Systems 1 (1986) 2, pp. 93–102, North-Holland.

[32] Hinkelmann K., Karagiannis D., Context-Sensitive Office Tasks: A Generative Approach, in: Decision Support Systems, in preparation.

ConceptTalk :
Kooperationsunterstützung in Softwareumgebungen[1]

Carlos Maltzahn
Universität Passau
Postfach 2540
D-8390 Passau

Thomas Rose
Dept. of Computer Science
University of Toronto
Toronto, Canada

Die meisten CAD-Umgebungen betonen die Unterstützung einzelner Arbeitsplätze und helfen nur sekundär bei deren Kooperation. Wir schlagen einen umgekehrten Ansatz vor: Entwürfe entstehen im Rahmen von interagierenden Sharing-Prozessen, die den gemeinsamen Zugang aller Beteiligten zu Konzepten, Aufgaben und Ergebnissen strukturieren. Dieser Ansatz und seine Konsequenzen werden am Beispiel des Software Engineering dargestellt. Auf der Basis einer Formalisierung dieser Prozesse steuert der ConceptTalk-Prototyp eine verteilte Softwareumgebung und spezielle Kommunikationswerkzeuge über das Wissensbanksystem ConceptBase. Erfahrungen mit ConceptTalk unterstützen ein neues Paradigma, das ein Informationssystem als Medium für komplexe Kommunikation betrachtet.

1 Einleitung

In der Industrie ist es heute Standard, daß selbst komplexe und innovative Entwicklungsprojekte in streng begrenzter Zeit durchgeführt werden müssen. Hieraus ergibt sich die Tendenz, solche Projekte mit vielen Mitarbeitern auszustatten, um Zeit einzusparen. Mit der Zahl der Mitarbeiter wächst der Aufwand, der nötig ist, um die Aufgaben optimal auf die Entwickler zu verteilen und die Ergebnisse dieser Verteilung zu einem Ganzen zusammenzufügen. Die Aufgaben sind i.a. zu komplex, als daß eine Aufteilung unmittelbar ersichtlich ist, und so stark vernetzt, daß sie nicht unkontrolliert getrennt gelöst werden können. Es sind Konzepte der *Kooperation* zur Verteilung von Aufgaben und die Integration von Arbeitsergebnissen gefordert.

Heutige Software-Entwicklungsumgebungen [14] konzentrieren sich auf das Produkt. Aus dieser Perspektive sind Software-Systeme komplexe Entwurfsobjekte, die in Komponenten strukturiert sind und durch die Modifikation der Komponenten entwickelt und gewartet werden. Softwaredatenbanken [2], [5] und Projektdatenbanken [13] modellieren die Struktur von Software-Systemen und verwalten Komponentenversionen. Die Strukturierung und Konfiguration von Systemen bildet eine notwendige Plattform für kooperative Projekte, weil sie den Zugriff zu einer großen Menge von Teilentwürfen organisiert und komplexe Zusammensetzungen mehrerer Systemvarianten verwaltet. Transaktionskonzepte regeln den Zugriff auf bestehende Entwürfe, die in einer gemeinsamen Datenbasis verwaltet werden. Ein Transaktionskonzept kann durch ein Datenbankverwaltungssystem oder durch Operationen auf Arbeitsbereiche innerhalb einer Entwicklungsumgebung gegeben sein [10]. Unabhängig davon sollen

---

[1] Diese Arbeit wird z.T. von der Deutschen Forschungsgemeinschaft im Schwerpunktprogramm "Objektbanken für Experten" (Ja-445/1-2) gefördert.

Transaktionskonzepte den Mehrbenutzerbetrieb möglichst *unsichtbar* erscheinen lassen, da dadurch der Zugriff auf die Datenbasis einfach und vor allem sicher ist. Aufgrund der damit einhergehenden technischen Synchronisationsmechanismen müssen sich jedoch eng kooperierende Entwickler bei der Bearbeitung des gleichen Entwurfs abwechseln. Zusätzliche Koordination ist erforderlich, um Interaktionen der Entwickler wieder *sichtbar* zu machen. Es gilt, Wege zu finden, die diesen Umweg überflüssig machen, ohne die Sicherheit von Entwurfsobjektbeständen zu gefährden.

Produktorientierte Software-Entwicklungsumgebungen reichen jedoch nicht aus, um Teilentwürfe auf kooperative Weise aufeinander abzustimmen.Mitarbeiter und Kooperation sind als unabdingbare Bestandteile von Entwicklungsumgebungen zu berücksichtigen. Unstrukturierte Sichtbarkeit von Interaktionen führt allerdings zur Informationsüberladung der Mitarbeiter. Der Versuch, die Sichtbarkeit durch ein technisches System zu strukturieren, bedeutet aber eine mechanische Strukturierung der Gruppenkommunikation. Sind die gewachsenen Kooperationsbeziehungen der Gruppe zur mechanischen Kooperationsunterstützung inkompatibel, so führt dies zu Abwehrreaktionen der Mitarbeiter [8]. Um dies zu verhindern ist Kooperation auch als soziale Aktivität zu studieren und durch verträgliche Konzepte zu unterstützen: Z.B. werden in der Gruppe Strategien besprochen, Vereinbarungen getroffen, Meldungen gemacht und Ergebnisse begutachtet.

Wir bezeichnen diese Vorgänge als *Kooperationsprozesse*. Die Ereignisse eines solchen Prozesses sind Operationen, die allen Beteiligten in irgendeiner Weise kommuniziert werden. Dies kann durch Nachrichten geschehen, aber auch durch Manipulationen auf einem Objekt, welches allen Beteiligten sichtbar ist. In dieser Arbeit stellen wir ein System vor, das Kooperationsprozesse in Entwurfsverwaltungssysteme integriert. Ausgehend von einer Analyse der Anforderungen in Kapitel 2 skizzieren wir in Kapitel 3 unser Konzept sogenannter *Sharing-Prozesse* zur Steuerung und Dokumentation entwurfsbezogener Kooperation. Dieses Modell ist formal in der Wissensrepräsentationssprache Telos beschrieben. Dies ermöglicht es zum einen, die Bezüge der Kooperationsprozesse zu den von einer kommerziellen Softwareumgebung geleisteten Objektverwaltungsaufgaben herzustellen; zum anderen strukturiert und dokumentiert das Prozeßmodell den Nachrichtenaustausch zwischen den Entwicklern in asynchroner (Mail = elektronische Post) oder synchroner (Talk = Realzeitkonferenz) Gruppenarbeit. Diese konzeptbasierte Integration von Objektverwaltungs- und Kommunikationsaufgaben motiviert auch den Namen des von uns entwickelten Prototypsystems, *ConceptTalk*. Die prototypische Realisierung durch ConceptTalk wird in Kapitel 4 vorgestellt, während das abschließende Kapitel 5 über einige Erfahrungen und Schlußfolgerungen berichtet.

2 Kooperationsunterstützung in Entwicklungsprozessen

Es ist nützlich, sich als Metapher ein Software-Entwicklungsbüro vorzustellen, in dem sich Mitarbeiter regelmäßig treffen und besprechen, was als nächstes zu tun ist. Dabei kristallieren sich Aufgaben heraus, die entweder sofort gelöst werden oder - bei umfangreicheren Projekten - an einzelne Personen oder kleinen Gruppen delegiert werden. In den Konferenzen werden auch Ergebnisse vorgeführt und begutachtet, Verbesserungsvorschläge gemacht oder Testabläufe vereinbart. Nachteilig ist, daß erstens die Entwurfsobjekte nicht direkt zur Verfügung stehen, zweitens nur durch individuell hastig notierte Stichwörter dokumentiert wird und drittens jeder Teilnehmer physisch zugegen sein muß. Ist letzteres nicht der Fall, wird die fehlende Dokumentation der Konferenz noch schwerwiegender. Eine auf vernetzten Workstations simulierte Konferenz würde diese Nachteile alle beheben: Entwurfsobjekte können eingeblendet, sogar manipuliert werden, Ereignisse in einer Konferenz können vom System protokolliert werden, und die Konferenzteilnehmer können physisch über die ganze Welt verteilt sein. In großen Organisationen können mehrere Konferenzen gleichzeitig stattfinden, in denen die jeweiligen Teilnehmer gleiche Entwurfsobjekte sehen, aber unterschiedlich manipulieren. Oder es werden in verschiedenen Konferenzen ähnliche Aufgaben identifiziert und unabsichtlich an unterschiedliche Personen delegiert.

Durch die Einführung von vernetzten Systemen verbreitete sich der Einsatz elektronischer Postsysteme insbesondere für Organisationsaufgaben [17]. Mit der der Fähigkeit, schnell und einfach eine Nachricht an beliebig viele Adressaten zu senden, entstand aber auch eine Überladung der Empfänger mit größtenteils unwichtiger Post. Grund dafür ist, daß elektronische Post als Kontextinformation i.a. nur den Absender und ein informelles, kurzes "Betrifft" aufweist. Dabei ist der wahre Kontext der Nachrichten ein komplexes und sich ständig wandelndes Netz aus sozialen Erwartungen der Kommunikationspartner und Objekten, die Gegenstand der Kommunikation sind. Es bietet sich daher die Integration von Medium und Programmierumgebung zu einer Umgebung zur kooperativen Programmentwicklung an. An ein solches Kooperationsunterstützungssystem werden folgende Forderungen gestellt (vgl. z.T. auch [7]):

Projektstrukturierung. Eine wesentliche Voraussetzung für eine effiziente Kommunikation ist der einfache Zugang zu der *objektiven Gruppenrealität*, welche die Geschichte der Ideen und Aufgaben und ihre Zuordnung zu dem Gegenstandsbereich des Projekts, z.B. eine Hierarchie von Software-Objekten, beinhaltet. Das Kooperationsunterstützungssystem zeigt diese Struktur und deren Zuordnungen an, und gibt dem Benutzer Gelegenheit neue Ideen oder potentielle Aufgaben hinzuzufügen.

Verwaltung von Projektergebnissen. Die in Kooperationsprozessen definierten Aufgaben werden in Teilprojekten ausgeführt. Jedem Teilprojekt ist ein Arbeitsbereich zugeordnet, der die betreffenden Software-Objekte verwaltet. Die Ergebnisse des Teilprojekts werden in den übergeordneten Arbeitsbereich integriert, wobei Transfer-Mechanismen die Software-Objekte zwischen Arbeitsbereichen übertragen und Konflikte erkennen können. Diese Konflikte sind kooperativ mit Hilfe des Mediums zu beheben.

Projekt-Planung. In innovativen Projekten kann diese Funktionalität keine sehr zentrale Rolle mehr spielen, da für die Planung eine Spezifikation der Produkte notwendig, jedoch bei innovativen Projekten unmöglich ist. Neuerdings lassen sich allerdings Planungsverfahren angeben, die relativ robust gegen Veränderungen der Pläne sind (vgl. etwa [16]).

Protokollierung der Aufgabenausführung. Jede Aufgabe ist in einen Kooperationsprozeß eingebettet, der sich in eine Definitionsphase, eine Realisierungsphase und eine Inspektionsphase untergliedern läßt. Bestimmte Ereignisse, i.e. Interaktionen mit speziellen Kommunikationswerkzeugen, führen zu Phasenübergängen, die den Status einer Aufgabe bzgl. einer Kooperation verändern. Eine Aufgabenausführung ist beendet, wenn die Aufgabe fertiggestellt oder die Ausführung abgebrochen wurde.

Vermittlung von Problemen und Problemlösungen. Die Durchführung innovativer Projekte ist vom Wesen her explorativ. Es lassen sich nur recht grobe Pläne aufstellen, da der Projektalltag durch das Auftreten unerwarteter Probleme geprägt ist. Entscheidend für den Erfolg ist es daher, daß bei neuen Problemen schnell einschlägige Experten unter den Projektmitarbeitern gefunden werden. Die Suche nach diesen richtet sich nach zwei Qualitätsmerkmalen: (1) Grad der Kenntnisse in der speziellen Domäne des Problems und (2) zur Verfügung stehende Zeit. Ein Kooperationsunterstützungssystem kann die fachliche Qualifikation eines Agenten anhand der im Rahmen eines bestimmten Teilprojektes *erfolgreich erfüllten Aufgaben* abschätzen. Für die Abschätzung der Verfügbarkeit kann die *Zuständigkeit* eines Agenten herangezogen werden. Diese besteht aus einer Aufzählung der in der Realisierungsphase befindlichen Aufgaben, für die sich das Kooperationsmitglied verpflichtet hat (vergl. hierzu [4]).

Sichtbarkeit von Ereignissen. Wir unterscheiden zwischen *gleichzeitiger* und *nicht-gleichzeitiger* Sichtbarkeit von Ereignissen eines Kooperationsprozesses. Gleichzeitige Sichtbarkeit ist bei gemeinsamen Real-Zeit-Sichten auf Objekte gegeben, wie sie durch elektronische Konferenzen realisiert werden. Für nicht-gleichzeitige Sichtbarkeit von Ereignissen bietet das Kooperationsunterstützungssystem einen Notifikationsdienst an, den jedes Kooperationsmitglied in Anspruch nehmen kann. Es können prinzipiell alle Vorgänge notifiziert werden, die durch das Kooperationsunterstützungssystem protokolliert werden.

Durchsetzung spezieller Richtlinien. In den nächsten Abschnitten stellen wir *protokollgesteuerte* Aufgabenausführungen und Ergebnisverwaltungen vor und zeigen, wie diese beiden Prozesse gekoppelt werden können. Die Steuerprotokolle und im besonderen Maße die Kopplungen sind dazu geeignet, die gruppenspezifischen Richtlinien zu repräsentieren und deren Befolgung zu kontrollieren. Dies funktioniert allerdings nur, wenn sich das Kooperationsunterstützungssystem für die Befolgung der Richtlinien "bedankt", indem es jedem kooperativen Mitarbeiter die genannten Dienstleistungen zur Verfügung stellt, und diese Dienstleistungen dem Mitarbeiter als nützlich erscheinen. Nur dadurch ist sichergestellt, daß das Kooperationsunterstützungssystem von den Gruppenmitgliedern akzeptiert und umfassend verwendet wird.

3 Sharing-Prozesse

Sharing-Prozesse modellieren den kooperativen Umgang mit *Ideen, Aufgaben* und *Ergebnissen*. Ziel ist es, aus typischen Situationen die Sichtbarkeit bzw. die Zugriffsrechte für Entwurfsobjekte herzuleiten, die im Zusammenhang mit den Aufgaben auftreten. I.a. sollen kompliziert zu realisierende Zugriffskonstellationen durch natürlich erscheinende Kooperationsereignisse automatisiert und gesteuert werden.

Zunächst definieren wir allgemein einen Prozeß als eine Klasse von Objekten, (1) welche durch Strukturelemente strukturiert sind, (2) deren Zustand durch Strukturelemente ausgedrückt wird und welchen (3) Ereignisse zugeordnet werden können, die jeweils eins der Strukturelemente ausführen. Konkrete Prozesse bilden Instanzen dieser Klasse, konkrete Ereignisse sind Instanzen der Klasse *Ereignis* usw. In dem Kontext einer Kooperation werden Ereignisse durch *Agenten* hervorgerufen. Agenten können sowohl Personen als auch aktive technische Ressourcen sein. Ferner können Ereignisse installierte Notifikationsdienste auslösen. In der folgenden Abbildung ist diese Definition als semantisches Netz entsprechend den Konventionen der Wissensrepräsentationssprache Telos [11] dargestellt[2].

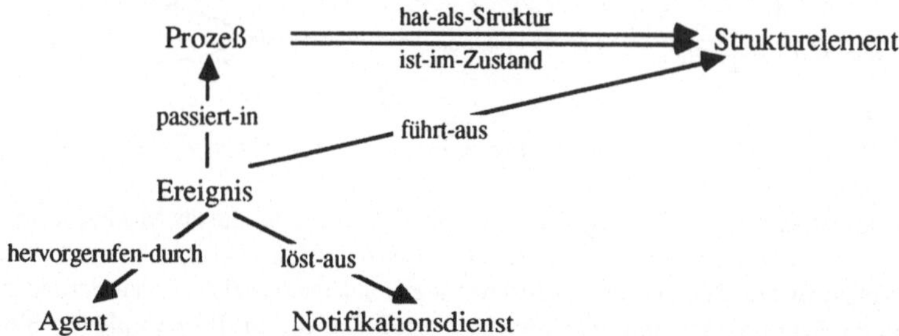

Sharing-Prozesse finden im Rahmen von Projekten statt. Ein Projekt ist ein Kooperationsprozeß, der als partiell geordnete Aufgabenmenge definiert ist. Ereignisse in einem Projekt sind Aufgabenausführungen. Der Zustand eines Projekts wird durch die Menge der ausgeführten Aufgaben repräsentiert. Eine Aufgabenausführung kann einem Projekt zugeordnet werden, wenn alle vorgeordneten Aufgaben in dem Projektzustand enthalten sind.

In Projekten werden Aufgaben definiert, koordiniert und Ergebnisse integriert. Die Ergebnisse der Aufgaben sind meist über eine Hierarchie von *Arbeitsbereichen* verteilt; der oberste Arbeitsbereich enthält die bereits projektweit integrierten Ergebnisse; jede Ebene darunter enthält Teilintegrationen, die als Zwischenergebnisse von Teilprojekten angesehen werden können. Aufgrund dieser konzeptuellen

---

[2] Da eine genaue Kenntnis der Sprache Telos für das Verständnis des Folgenden nicht erforderlich ist, beschränken wir uns auf die Feststellung, daß alle hier angegebenen Modelle mit einer durch Strukturen, Deduktionsregeln und Integritätsbedingungen festgelegten formalen Semantik ausgestattet sind.

Ähnlichkeit modellieren wir Arbeitsbereiche als hierarchisch geordnete Projektprozesse, die Sichten auf Entwurfsobjekte besitzen und einer Gruppe von Agenten zugänglich sind.*Die Sichten werden durch Ergebnis-Sharing und der Zugang durch Aufgaben-Sharing definiert* (s.u.).

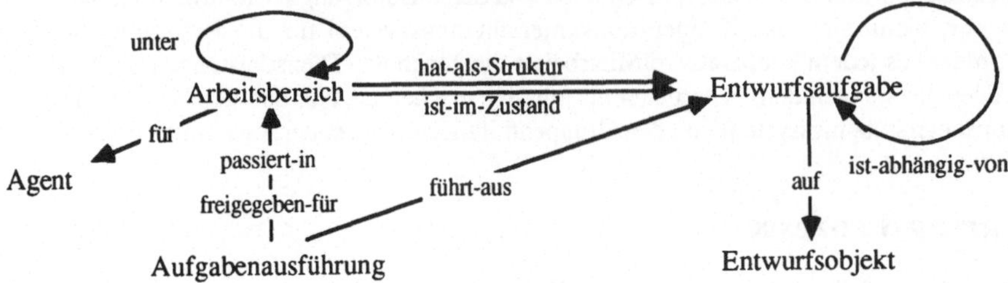

Für die Modellierung der Struktur von Sharing-Prozessen haben wir nach mehreren Experimenten nicht-deterministische endliche Automaten gewählt. Ereignisse von Sharing-Prozessen sind linear geordnet und führen Kanten des endlichen Automaten aus, i.e. stellen Zustandsübergänge dar. Der Zustand des Sharing-Prozesses ist der Zustand des endlichen Automaten, der nach dem letztem Zustandsübergang erreicht worden ist. Ein Prozeßautomat hat einen Startzustand und mehrere Zielzustände. Kanten können durch beliebige Objektklassen markiert werden. Ein Ereignis kann einem Sharing-Prozeß zugeordnet werden, wenn vom aktuellem Zustand eine Kante ausgeht, deren Markierung eine Klasse des Ereignisses ist.

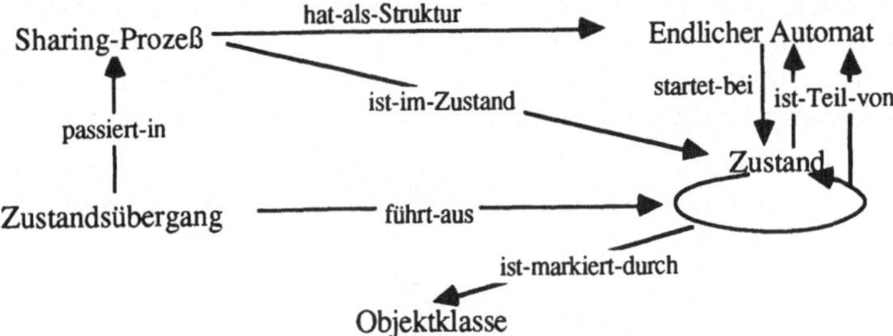

Wenn wir die Ablaufstruktur von Sharing-Prozessen modellieren und dieses Modell in irgendeiner Weise operationalisieren, erzeugen wir ein *technisches Protokoll*, welches kooperative Abläufe einschränkt. Demgegenüber stehen *soziale Protokolle*, die Teil der sozialen Eigenschaften kooperierender Menschen sind und von Gruppe zu Gruppe variieren. Technische Protokolle, die in die komplexen Kommunikations-gewohnheiten von Menschen eingreifen, werden schnell zu restriktiv. Werden dagegen zu schwach strukturierte Protokolle verwendet, ist die Aussagekraft eines Prozeßzustandes gering.

3.1 Aufgaben-Sharing

Aufgaben-Sharing beschreibt den kooperativen Umgang mit Aufgaben. In einer *Orientierungsphase* diskutieren die Agenten ein Problem und identifizieren ggf. eine Menge von Aufgaben. Das Aufgaben-Sharing spaltet sich nun in *Unterprozesse*, die den Aufgaben zugeordnet sind. Die Gruppe kann in verschiedene Arbeitsstrukturen organisiert sein [3]. Eine *integrative Arbeitsstruktur* arbeitet über realzeitliche Kommunikation. Eine *delegative Arbeitsstruktur* liegt vor, wenn eine Aufgabe einem Mitarbeiter oder einer Teilgruppe zugeordnet wird. Die Zuordnung einer Aufgabe kann durch eine Vielzahl sozialer Protokolle geschehen, wie z.B. Befehl, Angebot, Versprechen oder Bereiterklärung.

Wir abstrahieren von diesen Protokollen, indem wir ein Ereignis namens *Vereinbarung* definieren, welches einen Phasenübergang von der Definitionsphase zur *Realisierungsphase* repräsentiert. In dieser Phase wird die Aufgabe in einem untergeordneten Arbeitsbereich bearbeitet. Im Rahmen der Realisierungsphase können weitere Aufgaben-Sharings stattfinden. Zu einem bestimmten Termin sollen Ergebnisse präsentiert werden. Ein *Aufruf zur Vorführung* löst dann die *Inspektionsphase* aus, in der die Teilnehmer des Aufgaben-Sharing die Ergebnisse überprüfen. In der Praxis werden solche Ergebnisse auch als Beta-Versionen bezeichnet, die an die Agenten verteilt werden, welche die Aufgabendefinition beeinflußt haben. Oft werden Fehler und Entwurfsschwächen entdeckt und kritisiert. Die Vermittlung dieser Erkenntnisse wird durch ein Ereignis namens *Kritik* zusammengefaßt, welches wieder die Realisierungsphase einleitet. Ruft jedoch die Lösung der Aufgabe die Zustimmung aller Beteiligten hervor, so werden die Ergebnisse *bestätigt* und der betreffende Unterprozeß ist *fertig*. Die zuständigen Agenten bekommen die Aufgabe als *erfolgreich gelöst* zugeordnet. Das Aufgaben-Sharing wird beendet, wenn alle Unterprozesse fertig sind.

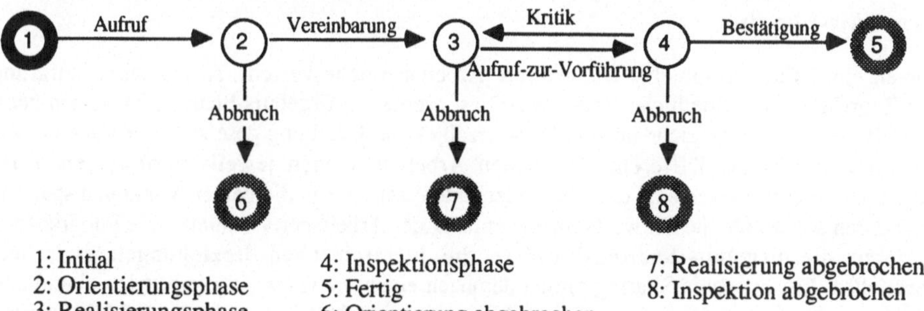

Die folgende Abbildung zeigt die spezielle Form der Sharing-Prozeßstruktur, die durch das obige Protokoll kontrolliert wird.

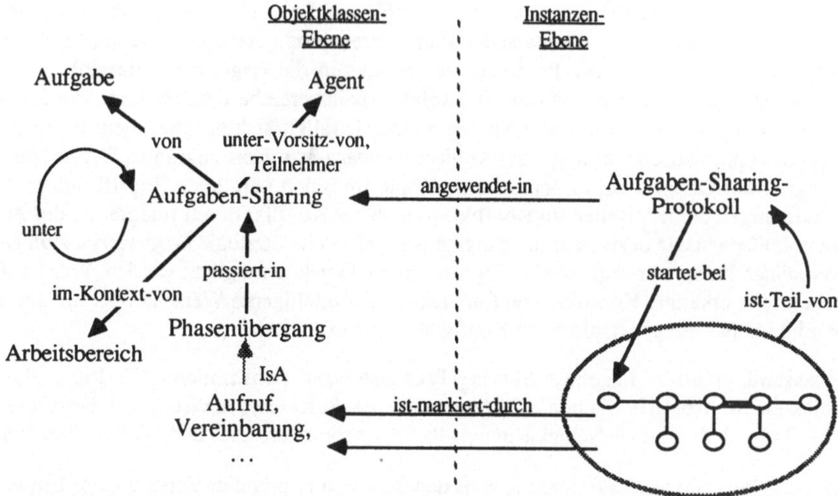

Wird ein Unterprozeß eines Aufgaben-Sharing beendet, so gilt die Aufgabe als ausgeführt. Aufgaben-ausführungen sind aber Ereignisse eines Projektes, so daß Unterprozesse des Aufgaben-Sharing auch als Ereignis modelliert werden können. Projekte erhalten durch die verschiedenen Phasen von Aufgabenausführungen einen weit differenzierteren Status, als es durch den oben definierten Projektzustand als Menge von ausgeführten Aufgaben möglich ist. Der Projektverlauf wird direkt durch den Ablauf der Aufgaben-Sharing-Prozesse dokumentiert.

Diese Modellierung von Aufgabenausführungen ermöglicht ferner eine Kontrolle über den Status von Unterprozessen des Aufgaben-Sharing: Aufgaben sind bzgl. der Projektstruktur untereinander vergleichbar, wenn die Ausführung einer Aufgabe die Ausführung der anderen voraussetzt, d.h. auf den Ergebnissen der Ausführung aufbaut. Ist die vorgeordnete Aufgabe nicht in dem Projektzustand enthalten, so sind in dem Arbeitsbereich, der das Projekt repräsentiert (s.o.), noch nicht die vorausgesetzten Entwurfsobjekte bzw. Entwurfsobjektversionen enthalten. Es wäre wenig sinnvoll, eine Aufgabe auf veralteten oder falschen Entwurfsobjekten auszuführen. Wir bezeichnen daher einen Unterprozeß als *freigegeben*, wenn die vorgeordneten Aufgaben alle ausgeführt worden sind.

3.2 Ergebnis-Sharing

Sind Kopien eines Entwurfsobjekts auf mehrere Arbeitsbereiche verteilt, so entstehen aufgrund von parallelen Zugriffen unterschiedliche Versionen. Diese werden in Ergebnis-Sharing-Prozessen verwaltet, indem jeweils zwei Arbeitsbereiche und ein Entwurfsobjekt in Beziehung gesetzt werden und der Zustand des Ergebnis-Sharings die Differenz der in den Arbeitsbereichen jeweils verfügbaren Versionen repräsentiert. Diese Differenzen sind dann besonders interessant, wenn die beiden Versionen später wieder gemischt werden sollen. Da die Entwurfsobjekte entlang der Arbeitsbereichshierarchie integriert werden, repräsentieren die Ergebnis-Sharing-Prozesse die hierarchischen Beziehungen zwischen den Arbeitsbereichen. Ein Ergebnis-Sharing ordnet demnach einen *privaten* Arbeitsbereich einem anderen, *öffentlichen* unter. Aufgrund der strengen Hierarchisierung von Arbeitsbereichen (keine Multi-Hierarchien) ist das Ergebnis-Sharing durch die Angabe eines Entwurfsobjekts und eines privaten Arbeitsbereiches eindeutig bestimmt. Die Existenz eines Ergebnis-Sharings repräsentiert somit die Verfügbarkeit eines Objekts in einem Arbeitsbereich.

Die Ereignisse eines Ergebnis-Sharings stellen Zugriffe auf Entwurfsobjekte dar und repräsentieren Operationen, die die Entwurfsobjekte zwischen den referenzierten Arbeitsbereichen transferieren. Die Prozesstruktur der Ergebnis-Sharing-Prozesse versetzt uns in die Lage, die Zulässigkeit von solchen *Arbeitsbereichoperationen* über die Differenz zweier Arbeitsbereiche darzustellen. Die Struktur eines Ergebnis-Sharings repräsentiert somit die Strategie einer Parallelitätskontrolle. Dem unten vorgestellte Protokoll liegt das optimistische Strategie des *Kopieren-Ändern-Mischens* zugrunde. Dieses Verfahren läßt parallelen Zugriff auf Objekte zu, in dem es eine Kopie für jeden parallelen Zugriff anlegt. Stehen die parallelen Änderungen beim Mischen im Konflikt, so muß der Konflikt durch Integration der Änderungen gelöst werden. Im Gegensatz dazu steht die gängige pessimistische Strategie *Reservieren-Ablegen*, welche Konflikte *vermeidet*, indem nur sequentielle Zugriffe auf ein Objekt ermöglicht werden. Wenn aufgrund der Parallelitätskontrolle erkannte Konflikte von Entwicklern auf intelligente Weise kooperativ gelöst werden, so ist das Produkt höher integriert, als wenn Konflikte vermieden werden [3].

Zusammenfassend erfüllen Ergebnis-Sharing-Prozesse vier Funktionen: (1) *Verfügbarkeit* von Entwurfsobjekten in Arbeitsbereichen, (2) *hierarchische Beziehung* zwischen Arbeitsbereichen, (3) *hierarchische Ordnung* der Entwurfsobjekte innerhalb eines Arbeitsbereiches und (4) *Parallelitätskontrolle*.

Zustände des Ergebnis-Sharing definieren jeweils den Status einer privaten Version eines Entwurfsobjekts gegenüber einer öffentlichen Version des gleichen Objekts. Ausgehend von einem Startzustand wird ein Ergebnis-Sharing erzeugt, wenn in einem Arbeitsbereich ein Objekt hinzugefügt wird. Dieses steht zunächst nur in diesem Arbeitsbereich zur Verfügung. Weil wir die Verfügbarkeit von Objekten in privaten Arbeitsbereichen beschreiben, heißt der Zustand *Nur Privat*. Das Objekt kann in diesem Zustand ohne

Auswirkung auf das Ergebnis-Sharing beliebig oft geändert werden. Wird es in dem privaten Arbeitsbereich wieder gelöscht, endet das Ergebnis-Sharing. Wird es dagegen in den öffentlichen Arbeitsbereich *integriert*, oder wird aus dem öffentlichen Arbeitsbereich eine Objektversion *kopiert*, so sind in beiden Arbeitsbereichen die Versionen *Identisch*. Erneutes integrieren oder *aktualisieren* ändert an diesem Zustand des Ergebnis-Sharings nicht. Wird dagegen das Entwurfsobjekt *privat geändert*, so tritt der Zustand *Privat geändert* ein. Eine Aktualisierungsoperation hat in diesem Zustand keine Auswirkungen auf die Version, da sonst die privaten Änderungen zerstört würden. Wird die private Version jetzt mit der öffentlichen integriert, so sind die Versionen wieder identisch, da einfach die öffentliche durch die private Version ersetzt wird.

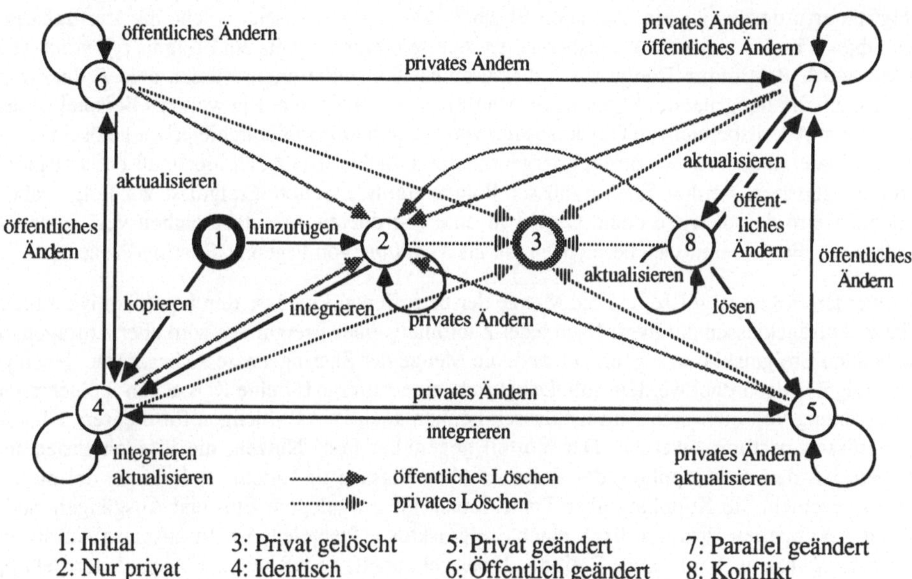

1: Initial   3: Privat gelöscht   5: Privat geändert   7: Parallel geändert
2: Nur privat   4: Identisch   6: Öffentlich geändert   8: Konflikt

Wird schließlich in dem Zustand *Privat* geändert und die öffentliche Version des Entwurfsobjekts *öffentlich geändert*, so sind beide Versionen *Parallel geändert*. Dieser Zustand tritt auch dann ein, wenn das Entwurfsobjekt zuerst *öffentlich geändert* und erst dann *privat geändert* wird. Ist ein Objekt nur *Öffentlich geändert*, so kann die private Version aktualisiert werden, sodaß wieder beide Versionen identisch sind. Sind die Versionen parallel geändert, führt der Versuch, die private Version zu aktualisieren zu einem *Konflikt*, da die privaten Änderungen nicht zerstört werden sollen. Stattdessen wird die öffentliche Version unter einem anderen Namen in den privaten Arbeitsbereich kopiert. Dadurch wird die Verfügbarkeit der öffentlichen Version nicht gestört. In dem privaten Arbeitsbereich wird der Konflikt durch geeignete Werkzeuge vom Entwickler *gelöst*. Trat in der Zwischenzeit keine weitere Änderung der öffentlichen Version auf, erreicht das Ergebnis-Sharing durch die Konfliktlösung den Zustand *Privat geändert*. Die private Version kann dann wieder mit der öffentlichen integriert werden. Aus jedem Zustand eines Ergebnis-Sharings kann ein Entwurfsobjekt entweder privat oder öffentlich gelöscht werden (außer *Nur privat*: Objekt kann nur privat gelöscht werden). Wird es privat gelöscht, endet damit das Ergebnis-Sharing. Wird es öffentlich gelöscht, so geht das Ergebnis-Sharing in den Zustand *Nur privat* über.

3.3 Kopplung von Ergebnis-Sharing-Prozessen

Ein Ergebnis-Sharing, das sich auf einen öffentlichen und einen privaten Arbeitsbereich bezieht, definiert nur die Verfügbarkeit eines Objekts in dem privaten Arbeitsbereich. Die Verfügbarkeit des Objekts in dem öffentlichen Arbeitsbereich wird durch einen weiteren Ergebnis-Sharing-Prozeß repräsentiert, der sich auf diesen Arbeitsbereich als privaten Arbeitsbereich bezieht. Für den "öffentlichsten" Arbeitsbereich, d.h. den Arbeitsbereich des Gesamtprojekts, wird die Verfügbarkeit durch Ergebnis-Sharing-Prozessen repräsentiert, die sich auf keinen öffentlichen Arbeitsbereich beziehen und infolgedessen nur den Zustand *Nur privat* annehmen können. Angenommen, einem öffentlichen Arbeitsbereich sind mehrere private Arbeitsbereiche untergeordnet: Wird nun in dem öffentlichen Arbeitsbereich ein Objekt geändert, so ist das zunächst eine Arbeitsbereichoperation, welche dem Ergebnis-Sharing zugeordnet wird, das die Verfügbarkeit des Objekts in dem öffentlichen Arbeitsbereich definiert.

Die Integrität erfordert es jedoch, daß allen Ergebnis-Sharing-Prozessen, welche die Verfügbarkeit des gleichen Objekts in den privaten Arbeitsbereichen repräsentieren, jeweils ein Ereignis *öffentlich geändert* zugeordnet wird. Bestimmte Ereignisse in bestimmten Konstellationen müssen also *Folgeereignisse* hervorrufen, um die Integrität der Ergebnis-Sharing-Prozesse zu wahren. Ein weiteres Beispiel ist der Fall, in dem in einem Arbeitsbereich ein Objekt aus der verfügbaren Objekthierarchie privat gelöscht wird. Dies stellt eine private Änderung des direkt übergeordneten Objekts dar. Auch hier muß das entsprechende Folgeereignis generiert werden. Ebenso müssen Folgeereignisse weitere Ereignisse zur Folge haben, hier genau dann, wenn das übergeordnete Objekt in untergeordneten Arbeitsbereichen verfügbar ist. Das Hervorrufen von Folgeereignissen bezeichnen wir als *Kopplung* von Ergebnis-Sharing-Prozessen.

In Telos werden Folgeereignisse und die Menge der betroffenen Prozesse durch prädikative Ableitungs-regeln bzw. Anfrageklassen definiert: Nach jeder Zuordnung eines Ereignisses wird über Anfragen, die der entsprechenden Ereignisklasse zugeordnet sind, die Menge der Sharing-Prozesse bestimmt, denen jeweils ein Folgeereignis zugeordnet werdern soll. Dabei steht eine Anfrage für eine Klasse von Folgeereignissen. Durch Zuordnung von mehreren Anfrageklassen können auch Prozeß-mengen für mehrere Klassen von Folgeereignissen bestimmt werden. Der Vorteil gegenüber Petri-Netzen, die ja auch Prozeßmengen beschreiben, ist, daß die Kopplung der Prozesse über Klassen und nicht Individuen definiert ist. In Petrinetzen geschieht die Kopplung über Transitionen mit festgelegten Ein- und Ausgängen, sodaß die Anzahl der gekoppelten Prozesse bzgl. einer Ereignisklasse festgelegt ist. In unserem Ansatz werden dagegen *Prozeßklassen* bzgl. einer Ereignisklasse gekoppelt, sodaß wir die Anzahl der gekoppelten Prozesse nicht festzulegen brauchen.

3.4 Kopplung von Aufgaben-Sharing und Ergebnis-Sharing

Je besser die Kommunikation funktioniert, desto *leichter* sind koordinierende Maßnahmen zu vermitteln. Je besser die Kollaboration funktioniert, desto *weniger* muß koordiniert werden. Aufgaben-Sharing unterstützt Kommunikation, und Ergebnis-Sharing unterstützt Kollaboration. Koordination wird darüberhinaus unterstützt, wenn Aufgaben- und Ergebnis-Sharing *formal* gekoppelt werden. In der Tat legen einige Ereignisse des Aufgaben-Sharings Folgeereignisse des Ergebnis-Sharings nahe.

Tritt ein Unterprozeß eines Aufgaben-Sharings in die Realisierungsphase, so müssen den Agenten die notwendigen Objekte in ihren Arbeitsbereich zur Verfügung stehen. Da die Ergebnisse wieder in den Arbeitsbereich des Aufgaben-Sharings integriert werden sollen, ist es sinnvoll, den neuen Arbeitsbereich direkt unterzuordnen. Werden also im Rahmen des Aufgaben-Sharings Aufgaben *vereinbart*, so sind die betreffenden Entwurfsobjekte in einen privaten Arbeitsbereich zu *kopieren*. Das Aufgaben-Sharing definiert dabei, welche Agenten Zugang zu dem Arbeitsbereich haben, während das Ergebnis-Sharing die Verfügbarkeit von Entwurfsobjekten repräsentiert. Eine bedeutende Erleichterung der Koordination kann es sein, wenn bei der *Integration* eines Entwurfsobjekts der *Aufruf zur Vorführung* automatisiert wird. Dies setzt allerdings voraus, daß eine Integration in ein Aufgaben-Sharing eingebettet ist, d.h. daß ein Beitrag vereinbart ist. Spontane Beiträge können über die Kopplung erkannt werden. Ob sie verhindert werden sollen oder aber sogar erwünscht sind, ist von der jeweiligen Organisation zu entscheiden.

Obige Beispiele stellen nur einige der möglichen Kopplungen von Sharing-Prozessen dar. Sie zeigen die Möglichkeiten, die in der formalen Kopplung liegen. Jede Kopplung beschreibt aber wieder ein technisches Protokoll, das in den Arbeitsablauf und in die Arbeitsgewohnheiten einer Gruppe eingreift. Es ist somit jeweils zu entscheiden, wo formale Kopplungen förderlich und wo sie ungünstig sind.

4 ConceptTalk

Die genannten Modelle des Sharing bleiben theoretische Spielerei, wenn sie nicht in reale Systeme umgesetzt und praktisch erprobt werden. Im Entwurf von ConceptTalk wird auch daher bewußt das Ziel der Wiederverwendung kommerzieller Softwaretools und deren Integration durch ein wissensbasiertes System verfolgt. Die Idee ist, bestehende Werkzeuge zur Unterstützung der Kommunikation, Kollaboration und Koordination zu verwenden. Zum einen ermöglicht dies die Nutzung existierender Objektverwaltungs-systeme und -techniken. Zum anderen ist die Integration eine "sanfte" Erweiterung, welche zusätzliche Kooperationshilfen bereitstellt, ohne ärgerlich in gewohnte Arbeitsabläufe einzugreifen.

ConceptTalk ist in C implementiert und integriert das Unix-Werkzeug *mail* und das Wissensbanksystem *ConceptBase* [9] in die verteilte Entwicklungsumgebung *NSE* (Network Software Environment) der Fa. SUN [1]. Die Kommunikation über *mail* und die Kollaboration über NSE wird über die von ConceptBase verwalteten Telos-Modelle koordiniert. Das Aufgaben-Sharing in ConceptTalk nutzt das in [18] vorgeschlagene Protokoll in leicht modifizierter Form. Aufgrund der nicht realzeitlichen Kommunikation wird in diesem Protokoll nach jedem jeweils zulässigen Nachrichtentyp ein Zustand definiert. Die Nachrichtentypen und ihre zustandsabhängige Zulässigkeit ist aus Erkenntnissen der Sprechakttheorie [15] abgeleitet. In dem Protokoll lassen sich die Orientierungs-, Realisierungs- und Inspektionsphase identifizieren. Ein Vorteil der Modellierung in einer erweiterbaren Wissens-repräsentationssprache wie Telos liegt darin, daß sich derartige Beziehungen zwischen Protokollen durch Generalisierungshierarchien ausdrücken lassen und damit den Entwicklern stets die Möglichkeit gegeben ist, auf weniger restriktive Protokolle auszuweichen oder gar die Protokolle dynamisch anzupassen, ohne daß völlig die Kontrolle verlorengeht.

Die Benutzeroberfläche von ConceptTalk ergänzt die sprachsenitiven und graphischen Werkzeuge von ConceptBase um eine einfache Kommandoschnittstelle, die es uns erlaubte, Sharing-Prozesse rasch zu operationalisieren und in unixbasierten Software-Entwicklungsgruppen zu erproben.

confer ist ein erweitertes *mail*, welches die jeweils zulässigen typisierten Nachrichten zur Verfügung stellt und den Nachrichtenaustausch in Form von Aufgaben-Sharing-Prozessen protokolliert. Die Berechnung der jeweils zulässigen Nachrichtentypen und die Verwaltung der protokollierten Prozesse geschieht in ConceptBase. Zusätzlich kann noch angezeigt werden, welche gesendeten Nachrichten vom Empfänger noch nicht gelesen wurden und welche neuen, noch nicht gelesenen Nachrichten, eingetroffen sind.

```
Syntax: confer start
               next on <message>
               send <type> to <agent>
                           on <message>
               new
               pending
```
liefert alle initialen Nachrichtentypen
liefert alle erlaubten Nachrichtentypen
sendet eine Nachricht mit initialen Typ
antwortet auf Nachricht mit bestimmten Typ
liefert alle neu eingetroffenen Nachrichten
liefert gesendete Nachrichten, die noch warten

Mit **note** kann jeder Mitarbeiter eigene Notifikationsdienste einrichten, welche einen individuellen Prozeß oder eine Klasse von Prozessen auf bestimmte Ereignisse hin "beobachten" und diese bei ihrem Eintritt über *mail* mitteilen. Die zu notifizierenden Ereignisse werden entweder über eine Ereignisklasse oder über ein Strukturelement, z.B. eine Kante eines endlichen Automaten, spezifiert. Die zur Verfügung stehenden Prozeßklassen und die bereits eingerichteten Notifikationsdienste können angezeigt werden.

```
Syntax: note classlist                          liefert alle Prozeßklassen
        list                                    liefert alle eingerichteten Dienste
        new of <class> at <eventclass>          Dienst für Prozeß- und Ereignisklasse
                     to <structure element>     " für Prozeßklasse und Strukturelem.
              on <process> at <eventclass>      " für best. Prozeß und Ereignisklasse
                     to <structure element>     " für best. Prozeß und Strukturelem.
```

Mit dem Werkzeug **pose** werden Arbeitsbereiche als Projektprozesse strukturiert, indem - u.U. kausal voneinander abhängige - Probleme oder potentielle Aufgaben spezifiziert und Arbeitsbereichen auf konzeptueller Ebene zugeordnet werden. Dokumente von Aufgaben, die eine Problembeschreibung beinhalten, werden in einem gesonderten Systemverzeichnis verwahrt und können editiert werden.

```
Syntax: pose schedule < <schedule file name>   Eingabe eines Projektplans
        list <workspace>                        Ausgabe der Struktur eines Projekts
        edit <task>                             Spezifizieren einer Aufgabe
```

Das Ergebnis-Sharing ist in ConceptTalk durch NSE-Befehle implementiert, die Arbeitsbereichsoperationen implementieren. In ConceptTalk arbeiten diese Befehle nicht autonom, sondern werden in ConceptBase auf ihre Zulässigkeit hin kontrolliert - insbesondere aufgrund eventueller Kopplung mit dem Aufgaben-Sharing. Bei **acquire**, dem *Kopieren* von Entwurfsobjekten, wird zuerst überprüft, ob das betreffende Entwurfsobjekt oder dessen Unterobjekte in parallelen Arbeitsbereichen verfügbar sind. Wenn dies der Fall ist, listet ein vordefinierter Notifikationsdienst die parallelen Arbeitsbereiche mit deren Besitzern auf und fordert den Benutzer auf, die Operation zu bestätigen oder abzubrechen. Durch Kopplung mit Aufgaben-Sharing-Prozessen können zusätzliche Maßnahmen festgelegt werden, wenn z.B. keine Vereinbarung zwischen dem Besitzer des öffentlichen Arbeitsbereichs und dem des privaten existiert.

resync *aktualisiert* Entwurfsobjekte. Objekte, die nur öffentlich geändert worden sind, werden durch die öffentlichen Versionen ersetzt. Objekte, die nur privat geändert worden sind, werden nicht aktualisiert. Bei Objekten dagegen, die parallel geändert worden sind, gelangen die betreffenden Ergebnis-Sharing-Prozesse in einen Konfliktzustand. Diese Konflikte müssen über **resolve** gelöst werden. **resolve** ruft jeweils objektklassenspezifische Werkzeuge auf, die die interaktive Auflösung von Konflikten unterstützen. Ergebnis ist eine Version, die die beiden konfligierenden Versionen integriert.

Mit **reconcile** werden Entwurfsobjekte in den übergeordneten Arbeitsbereich *integriert*. Dazu wird zunächst versucht, die privaten Objekte zu aktualisieren. Entstehen keine Konflikte, so werden die Entwurfsobjekte anschliessend in den übergeordneten Arbeitsbereich zurückgespielt. Konflikte führen zu einem Abbruch von **reconcile** und müssen über **resolve** gelöst werden, bevor sie durch einen weiteren **reconcile**-Aufruf integriert werden können. Eine in ConceptTalk realisierte Kopplung zwischen Ergebnis-Sharing und Aufgaben-Sharing besteht beim Integrieren beispielsweise darin, zunächst zu überprüfen, ob Aufgaben-Sharing-Prozesse zwischen den Besitzern der beiden Arbeitsbereiche existieren und ob sie sich in der *Realisierungsphase* von Aufgaben befinden, die sich auf die zu integrierenden Entwurfsobjekte beziehen. Ist dies nicht der Fall, so wird der Benutzer aufgefordert, dem Besitzer des übergeordneten Arbeitsbereiches die Integration über ein Aufgaben-Sharing anzubieten, und **reconcile** wird abgebrochen.

5   Erfahrungen und Schlußfolgerungen

Wir haben einerseits gezeigt, daß die Objektverwaltung einen überraschend starken Einfluß auf die Kooperation von Entwicklern hat. Viele Probleme der Informationsüberladung durch Nachrichten sind auf das Fehlen kooperativer Kontexte zurückzuführen. Andererseits hat die Ansammlung von Einbenutzer-Anwendungen und die Unsichtbarkeit des Mehrbenutzerbetriebs in datenbankorientierten Entwicklungsumgebungen zur Isolation von Entwicklern geführt, die durch verstärkte Koordinationsmaßnahmen wieder ausgeglichen werden muß. Nach unserer Auffassung ist es für die Unterstützung von innovativen Entwicklungsprojekten unerläßlich, Kooperation nicht als Menge von Individuen zu sehen, die nach Plan arbeiten, sondern als eine Menge von Gruppen, die **gemeinsam** etwas produzieren.

Im Vergleich zur Kooperationsunterstützung im Datenbank-Bereich ist ein Sharing-Prozeß ein Konzept für die Sichtbarkeit von Operationen auf Objekten [6], welches nicht die Sichteinschränkungen traditioneller Transaktionen aufweist. Ferner gibt es nicht nur eine Konfliktvermeidung durch exklusive Rechte, sondern in erster Linie eine Konflikterkennung und -auflösung. Die Verlagerung des Gewichts auf Konflikterkennung ist sinnvoll, weil die Integration von Teilbeiträgen zu einem Ganzen eine Tätigkeit darstellt, die von intelligenten Entwicklern durchgeführt wird, und die Auflösung von Konflikten ein wesentlicher Bestandteil dieser Tätigkeit ist [12].

Erfahrungen mit ConceptTalk haben gezeigt, daß Sharing-Prozesse nützliche Konzepte darstellen, um diese Art von Kooperation zu unterstützen. Für den nächsten Prototypen wird an einer Präsentationsebene gearbeitet, die eine benutzerfreundliche Realzeitkonferenz-Schicht über die Sharing-Prozeßverwaltung legt. Das Entwurfsprinzip dieser Schicht ist, daß jede Session mit ConceptTalk grundsätzlich eine realzeitliche Konferenz mit variabler Teilnehmerzahl ist, der Einbenutzerbetrieb ist ein Spezialfall. Eine wichtige Eigenschaft ist die (bereits ansatzweise realisierte) Multimedia-Fähigkeit dieser Konferenzen.

[1]   E.W. Adams, M. Honda, T.C. Miller (1989). Object Management in a CASE Environment. *Proc. 11th Intl. Conf. Software Eng.*, Pittsburgh, Pa, 154-163

[2]   N. Belkhatir, J. Estublier (1987). Software Management Constraints and Action Triggering in the ADELE Program Database. *Proc. 1st Europ. Conf. Software Eng.*, Straßburg, 47-58

[3]   S.Bendifallah, W.Scacchi (1989). Work Structures and Shifts: An Empirical Analysis of Software Specification Teamwork. *Proc. 11th Intl. Conf. Software Eng.*, Pittsburgh, Pa, 260-270

[4]   F.DeCindio, et al (1986). Chaos as Coordination Technology. *Proc. CSCW-86*, Austin, Tx, 325-342

[5]   K. Dittrich, W. Gotthard, P.C. Lockemann (1986). DAMOKLES - A Database System for Software Engineering Environments, *Proc. Intl. Workshop Advanced Programming Environments*, Trondheim, Norway

[6]   M.Dowson, B.Nejmeh (1989). Nested Transactions and Visibility Domains. *Proc. ACM SIGMOD Workshop Software CAD Databases*, Napa, Ca, 36-38

[7]   L.Gilham et al (1987). Knowledge-Based Software Project Management. Report KES.U.87.3, Kestrel Institute, Palo Alto, Ca

[8]   E.Hildebrandt, R.Seltz (1989). Wandel betrieblicher Sozialverfassung durch systemische Kontrolle? Die Einführung computergestützter Produktionsplanungs- und -steuerungssysteme im bundesdeutschen Maschinenbau. *edition sigma*, Berlin

[9]   M.Jarke, Ed. (1991). ConceptBase V3.0 User Manual. Bericht MIP-9106, Uni Passau

[10]   G. Kaiser (1991). Concurrency Control in Advanced Database Applications, *ACM Computing Surveys* (to appear).

[11]   J.Mylopoulos, A.Borgida, M.Jarke, M.Koubarakis (1990). Telos: a language for representing knowledge about information systems. *ACM Trans. Information Systems 8*, 4, 327-363

[12]   B.Mack-Crane, A.Pal (1989). Conflict Management in a Source Version Management System. *Proc. 2nd Int. Workshop Software Config. Mgmt.*, Princeton, NJ, 149-151

[13]   M. H. Penedo (1986). Prototyping a Project Master Data Base for Software Engineering Environments, *ACM SIGPLAN Notices 22*, 1, 1-11

[14]   D. Perry, G. Kaiser (1991). Models of Software Developement Environments. *IEEE Trans. Software Eng. 17*, 3, 283-295

[15]   J.R.Searle (1969). *Speech Acts*. Cambridge University Press

[16]   R.Srikanth, M.Jarke (1989). The Design of Knowledge-Based Systems for Managing Ill-Structured Software Projects. *Decision Support Systems 5*, 4, 425-447

[17]   M.Sumner (1986). A Workstation Case Study. *Datamation*, Feb. 15, 71-79

[18]   T. Winograd (1988). A Language / Action Perspective on the Design of Cooperative Work, *Human-Computer Interaction 3*, 1, 3-30.

Parallelen zwischen den Komponenten des natürlichsprachlichen Interfaces NLI-AIDOS und dem zugrundeliegenden Informationsrecherchesystem

Hellfried Böttger, Hermann Helbig, Frank Ficker, Frank Zänker
SRS Software- und Systemhaus Dresden GmbH
8012 Dresden, PSF 412

Abstract: The natural language access to information retrieval systems is a modern AI-based approach to knowledge extraction from factual data bases. It can be considered as a comfortable supplement or as an alternative to more traditional methods, for instance menu-driven dialogue or the use of formal query languages for data banks. From the technical point of view the natural language communication with the computer is realized by means of a natural language interface. The aim of the paper consists in the elucidation of correspondences between the components of a natural language interface and the associated methods of language oriented AI-research on the one side and traditional data base management or information retrieval systems on the other side.

1 Einleitung

Die Hinwendung zu multimedialen Informationssystemen, die unterschiedliche Informationsarten (wie Bildinformationen, Datenbankinformationen traditionellen Typs oder natürlichsprachige Informationen) miteinander vereinen, hat auch das Interesse an natürlichsprachiger Kommunikation mit Informationsrecherchesystemen wieder verstärkt. Insbesondere für einen "naiven" oder gelegentlichen Nutzer, der keine Kenntnisse oder Erfahrungen im Umgang mit der Rechentechnik besitzt, ist die natürliche Sprache ein geeignetes Kommunikationsmittel für die Interaktion mit dem Rechner. Der Dialog zwischen einem solchen Nutzer und einem Informationsrecherchesystem (abgekürzt: IRS) wird im allgemeinen über eine besondere Programmschnittstelle, ein natürlichsprachliches Interface (NLI) realisiert. Ein Prototyp für ein NLI ist das in [1] beschriebene NLI-AIDOS, das eine natürlichsprachige Kommunikation mit dem IRS AIDOS [2] ermöglicht.
Gegenstand der vorliegenden Arbeit ist es, die Korrespondenzen zwischen den verschiedenen Komponenten des Teilsystems zur natürlichsprachlichen Verarbeitung (dem eigentlichen NLI) und dem Zielsystem (dem IRS AIDOS) aufzuzeigen. Die Herausarbeitung dieser Zusammenhänge ist wichtig, weil sie einerseits die transformationellen Beziehungen und den Übergang zwischen den Teilsystemen erhellen und andererseits die Beziehungen zwischen den Wissensbeständen beider Komponenten herstellen. Damit werden auf theoretischer Ebene die Begriffe und Konzeptionen der einen Seite für die andere fruchtbar gemacht, während auf der Realisierungsebene konkrete Hinweise für eine gemeinsame Nutzung von Programmbausteinen oder Wissensbestandteilen gegeben werden.
Die wichtigsten der in den folgenden Abschnitten diskutierten Parallelen sind in Bild 1 im Überblick dargestellt. Sie betreffen

sowohl Datenstrukturen bzw. sprachliche Schnittstellen (ovale Umrahmung) als auch Programmbausteine (rechteckige Umrahmung). Die linke Bildseite repräsentiert Methoden und Verfahren, die stark von der sprachorientierten KI-Forschung beeinflußt sind, während auf der rechten Seite traditionelle Datenbanktechniken überwiegen.

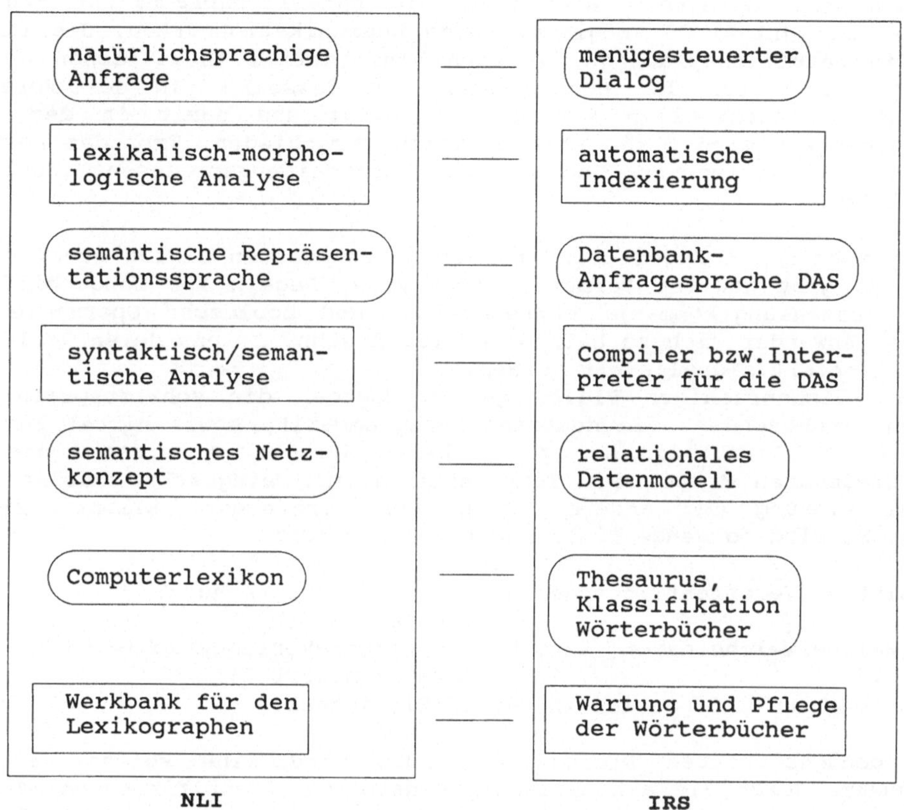

Bild 1. Korrespondenzen zwischen natürlichsprachlicher Verar-beitung und traditioneller Informationsrecherche

Die in diesem Schema angegebenen Komponenten stellen kein Blockdiagramm der beiden Subsysteme oder gar des Gesamtsystems dar. Es werden viel-mehr die Aspekte gegenübergestellt, die wir in der Arbeit diskutieren wollen. Dabei wird in den konkreten Beispielen immer auf das System NLI-AIDOS bzw. das IRS AIDOS Bezug genommen. In dem betrachteten Anwen-dungsfall einer Literaturdatenbank wird jedes Dokument durch eine Rela-tion (Tabelle) mit folgenden Attributen beschrieben: KLASSIFI - Rubrik in der zugrundeliegenden Dezimalklassifikation, DESKR - Deskriptor, VERF - Verfasser/Autor, VERL - Verlag, TITEL - Titel des Dokuments, STANDORT - Standort in einer Bibliothek, JAHR - Erscheinungsjahr.

2. Oberflächenstrukturen und Dialogverhalten

Das Zielsystem AIDOS dient vorwiegend zum Speichern und Wiederauffinden bibliographischer oder faktographischer Datenbestände. Für das Mainframe-System von AIDOS [2] steht eine formale Abfragesprache (DAS) zur Verfügung, während das Retrieval mit der Mikrorechner-Variante von AIDOS [3] menügesteuert erfolgt (vgl. Abschn. 3). Der Zugang zu beiden Systemen ist alternativ auch über die natürlichsprachliche Schnittstelle, das NLI-AIDOS, möglich. Beide Kommunikationsarten, die formale wie die natürlichsprachige, leisten hinsichtlich thematischen Umfangs und Resultats für den Nutzer letztlich dasselbe. In der Form, im sprachlich-konzeptuellen Niveau, im Ablauf und damit in der Oberflächengestalt sind beide aber deutlich verschieden. Trotzdem bestehen auf den verschiedenen Ebenen des Verarbeitungsprozesses deutliche Parallelen.

Die syntaktischen Regeln sind beim menügesteuerten Dialog gewollt einfach: Es gibt gewisse Formate, Datentypen, Regeln für Mengenbildungen (z.B. Aufzählungskommas), Wertebereiche und boolesche Operatoren, an die der Anwender sich zu halten hat (s. Abschn. 3) und deren Verletzungen ihm sofort signalisiert werden.
Im natürlichsprachigen Dialog gelten dagegen die schriftsprachlichen Normen, insbesondere die deutsche Satzgrammatik, sowie Mittel zur Wiedergabe von Strukturen der gesprochenen Sprache. Außerdem können die verschiedensten Mittel zur Textkonstituierung eingesetzt werden (Pronominalisierung und andere Formen von Koreferenz, Elliptifizierung usw.). So sind folgende Dialogsequenzen möglich:

N: "Gibt es Veröffentlichungen über XPS im Umweltschutz?"
S: "..."   (Systemantwort 1)
N: "{Welche/welche davon} sind beim Springer-Verlag erschienen?"
S: "..."   (Systemantwort 2)
N: "Welche aus 2 finde ich in der TU-Bibliothek?"

Beim menügesteuerten Dialog mit AIDOS wird eine solche textuelle Bezugnahme durch die automatische Vergabe von Identifikatoren (Zeilennummern) für die Ergebnisse von vorangegangenen Suchanfragen und deren Wiederverwendung in Ausdrücken ermöglicht. Es gibt auch regelhaft verkürzte Dialoge der Art:

N: "Gibt es Bücher zum Umweltschutz aus dem Springer-Verlag?"
S: "Ja, ..."
N: "Welche/Wieviele/Von wem ?"

Ellipsenerzeugung und -rekonstruktion sind oft verwendete Mittel im natürlichsprachigen Dialog. Kommunikative Kohärenz wird u.a. durch syntaktische Parallelität und Weitergeltung realisierter Satzstrukturen erreicht. Im menügesteuerten Dialog gibt es keine unmittelbare Entsprechung dazu, aber durch expliziten Bezug auf vorhergehende Antworten sind ähnliche Dialogphänomene nachbildbar wie in elliptischen oder textreferentiellen Konstruktionen der natürlichen Sprache. (Bild 2).

<table>
<tr><td>

Gibt es Veröffentlichungen über
Expertensysteme im Umweltschutz?

Welche davon stammen von
Springer?

Stehen diese in der
TU-Bibliothek?

</td><td>

```
1 KLASSIFI = K.12.4
2 DESKR = EXPERTENSYSTEM
3 DESKR = UMWELTSCHUTZ
4 (1 ODER (2 UND 3))
IN 4
  1 VERL = SPRINGER?
  2 VERF = SPRINGER?
  3 STANDORT = SPRINGER?
  4 (1 ODER (2 ODER 3))
5 START
6 STANDORT = TU-BIBLIOTHEK
7 (5 UND 6)
```

</td></tr>
</table>

Bild 2. Natürlichsprachiger und formalsprachiger Dialog

Das Problem der Homonyme und der syntaktisch wie semantisch mehrdeutigen Strukturen tritt nur beim NLI auf; ihre (gegebenenfalls interaktive) Behebung macht einen wesentlichen Teil der Arbeit des Sprachprozessors aus. Im Falle rein formaler Anfragen geht man stets von eindeutigen Zeichenfolgen und Strukturen aus (das wird ja gerade oft als Argument gegen die Verwendung der natürlichen Sprache im Mensch-Maschine Dialog vorgebracht). Der pragmatische Aspekt, d.h. die Deutung und Bewertung von Sprachäußerungen im Kontext, findet in natürlichsprachlichen KI-Systemen mit Modellen der Dialogsituation, mit Partnermodellen, mit Unterscheidungen zwischen Wissen, Glauben und Sagen (Beliefsystems), durch den Umgang mit vagen Ausdrücken und vagem Wissen usw. seinen Ausdruck (vgl. [4]). Das NLI-AIDOS in seiner bisher implementierten Fassung ist demgegenüber für die Anwendung in einem festen, vorgeplanten Kontext vorbereitet. In menügesteuerten Dialogsystemen ist der pragmatische Aspekt implizit in das Design, in die Architektur des Gesamtsystems eingegangen. Ein zu diesem Kreis gehörender Gesichtspunkt, nämlich die Fokussierung des Dialogs und eine damit u.U. verbundene Einengung der thematisierten, in Rede stehenden Objekte findet bei den DB-Systemen mit dem "stepwise refinement" seine Entsprechung.

3. Semantische Repräsentationssprache und Datenbankanfragesprache

Der Bedeutungsgehalt einer natürlichsprachigen Anfrage wird im NLI durch eine semantische Tiefenstruktur repräsentiert, die an das Wissensrepräsentationsparadigma der semantischen Netze angelehnt ist. Demgegenüber sind Datenbankanfragesprachen vorwiegend am relationalen Datenmodell orientiert. Eine Gegenüberstellung der dem semantischen Netzmodell und dem relationalen Datenmodell zugrundeliegenden theoretischen Konzepte findet sich im Abschnitt 5. Die etwas vereinfachte linearisierte Darstellungsform der Tiefenstruktur von Fragen im NLI-AIDOS und die Struktur der Ausdrücke der Datenbankanfragesprache von AIDOS (abgekürzt: DAS) sind im Bild 3 syntaktisch beschrieben.

```
<TS-Struktur          ::= [<Frageklasse> <Referenzteil> <Fokus>
                          (<T-Spezifikation>) ]
<T-Spezifikation> ::= <R-Term> | ~ <R-Term> |
                          (<T-Spezifikation> UND <T-Spezifikation>)|
                          (<T-Spezifikation> ODER <T-Spezifikation>)
<R-Term>              ::= (<Relation> <Argument>*)
```

```
<DAS-Ausdruck>        ::= [SEARCH O = <Name der Objektklasse>
                                  (<D-Spezifikation>)
                              DISPLAY ATTR = (<Attribut>*) ]
<D-Spezifikation> ::= <V-Term> | ~ <V-Term> |
                          (<D-Spezifikation> UND <D-Spezifikation>)|
                          (<D-Spezifikation> ODER <D-Spezifikation>)
<V-Term>              ::= (<Attribut> <Vergleichsoperator> <Wert>)
```

Bild 3. Gegenüberstellung von Bedeutungsstrukturen natürlichsprachiger
Anfragen und Ausdrücken der DAS

Bei Benutzung einer Datenbankanfragesprache teilt der Nutzer von AIDOS
dem System seine Intention entweder als geschlossenen Ausdruck der DAS
(Bild 3) oder aufgelöst als Termfolge, sogenannte Dialogform der DAS,
mit (Bild 2). Die Dialogform der DAS unterscheidet direkte Suchanweisungen und sequentielle Suchanweisungen. Eine direkte Suchanweisung ist
ein V-Term oder eine Konjunktion oder Disjunktion von Zeilennummern,
die die Ergebnismengen vorangegangener Suchanweisungen bezeichnen. Eine
sequentielle Suchanweisung ist ein Block aus direkten Suchanweisungen,
den eine Anweisungszeile START abschließt. Die vorangestellte Zeile
IN <Zeilennummer> verknüpft das Ergebnis für den Block konjunktiv mit
dem Ergebnis einer durch die Zeilennummer bezeichneten vorangegangenen
Suchanweisung.

Die Syntax der TS-Strukturen und die der DAS-Ausdrücke besitzen bestimmte Gemeinsamkeiten. Die stärksten Analogien bestehen im logischen
Aufbau der Spezifikationsteile, weil sich in den verschiedensten
Bedeutungsdarstellungen wenigstens die logischen Junktoren wiederfinden
müssen. Außerdem haben sich für die elementaren Spezifikationen (R-
Terme und V-Terme) einfache relationale Tripel für viele Anwendungen
als ausreichend erwiesen. Quantisierungen spielen demgegenüber in den
für ein IRS typischen Diskursbereichen eine untergeordente Rolle. Sie
werden teilweise durch implizite Konventionen (Suche auf jeden Fall
nach allen relevanten Nachweisen!) ersetzt.
In der inneren Struktur der elementaren Spezifikationen unterscheiden
sich die beiden Darstellungen. Während in den R-Termen als Relationen
linguistische Universalien auftreten, wie sie zum Aufbau semantischer
Netze verwendet werden ([5], Kap.3.4), kommen in den V-Termen nur einfache Vergleichsoperatoren (wie =, <, > usw.) vor. Auch die Attribute
und Werte der V-Terme lassen sich nicht direkt mit den Relationen bzw.
Argumenten der R-Terme vergleichen. Sie müssen aus letzteren durch
spezielle Mechanismen erschlossen werden (s. Abschn. 5).
Als Beispiel sollen die TS-Struktur und der entsprechende geschlossene
DAS-Ausdruck für eine etwas komplexere Anfrage wiedergegeben werden,

die etwa die Information der ersten beiden Sätze aus Bild 2 enthält:
"Welche aktuellen Veröffentlichungen über Expertensysteme im Umweltschutz, die vom Springer-Verlag herausgegeben wurden, kennst Du?".

```
TS-Struktur:    [ ERG NIL (SUB ? VEROEFFENTLICHUNG)
                ((THM ? G01) UND (SUB G01 EXPERTENSYSTEM) UND
                (ZWECK G01 G02) UND (SUB G02 UMWELTSCHUTZ) UND
                (SUBA G03 HERAUSGEBEN) UND (OBJ G03 ?) UND
                (PROP ? AKTUELL) UND (AGT G03 SPRINGER-VERLAG))]

DAS-Ausdruck:   [SEARCH O = LITERATUR
                (((KLASSIFI = K12.4) ODER
                 ((DESKR = EXPERTENSYSTEM) UND
                 (DESKR = UMWELTSCHUTZ))) UND
                 ((JAHR > 1989) UND (VERL = SPRINGER-VERLAG)))
                DISPLAY ATTR = (VERF, TITEL)]
```

Bild 4. Tiefenstruktur und DAS-Ausdruck für Beispielanfrage

Als Frageklassen für Datenbankanfragen kommen vor allem Ergänzungsfragen (Typ: ERG), Entscheidungsfragen (Typ: ENT) und Zählfragen
(Typ: COUNT) vor (zur Frageklassifizierung vgl. [5], Kap. 9.3.1). Sogenannte Essayfragen: "Was ist ein Expertensystem?", "Wie arbeitet ein
Expertensystem?" können i.a. über den üblichen Datenbankinhalten nicht
beantwortet werden. Typisch für Ergänzungsfragen ("Welche XYZ ...?",
"Wer ...?" usw.) und Zählfragen ("Wieviele XYZ ...?") ist das Vorhandensein eines Fragefokus, der dasjenige Objekt bezeichnet, das erfragt
wird. Dies geschieht durch Angabe einer besonderen Fragevariablen '?'
und deren Unterordnung unter einen Oberbegriff. Bei Entscheidungsfragen
ist der Fragefokus leer.
Die vom NLI automatisch erschlossene Frageklasse besitzt in Abhängigkeit vom jeweiligen Typ eine unterschiedliche Entsprechung im
DAS-Ausdruck: Ergänzungsfragen geben Anlaß zur Generierung eines
SEARCH-Teils (Spezifikation des Inhalts der Frage) und eines DISPLAY-
Teils (Spezifikation dessen, was auszugeben ist). Entscheidungsfragen
liefern nur einen SEARCH-Teil, während COUNT-Fragen zunächst wie Ergänzungsfragen behandelt werden, an deren Beantwortung sich u.U. ein Zähl-
vorgang anschließt. Eine Zählung ist nur dann überflüssig, wenn sich
der Fragefokus auf ein Attribut mit numerischen Werten richtet. In man-
chen Systemen, wie AIDOS, wird die Zählung der gefundenen relevanten
Nachweise automatisch angestoßen, in anderen Systemen ist das explizit
zu spezifizieren (so sieht SQL ausdrücklich eine COUNT-Konstruktion
vor, die bei diesem Fragetyp vom NLI konstruiert werden müßte).
Der Fragefokus bestimmt bei Ergänzungs- und Zählfragen insbesondere die
Form des DISPLAY-Ausdrucks der DAS (s. Bild 3). Zu diesem Zweck muß im
Wissensbestand des NLI vermerkt sein, durch welche Attribute der Datenbank der dem Frage-Fokus übergeordnete Begriff hinreichend charakterisiert wird (im Falle des Begriffs VEROEFFENTLICHUNG z.B. könnte das
VERF und TITEL sein). Die im SEARCH-Teil der DAS anzuführende Objektklasse O (das ist die Tabelle, in der zu suchen ist), muß aus dem Fragefokus automatisch erschlossen werden.

Als Relationen werden in der TS-Struktur semantische Tiefenbeziehungen eingesetzt, wie sie typisch für die Konstruktion semantischer Netze sind. Im einzelnen bedeuten: SUB - Unterordnungsbeziehung, THM - thematisch-inhaltliche Charakterisierung einer Information/eines geistigen Konzepts, ZWECK - Zweck eines Objekts/einer Handlung, SUBA - Unterordnung von Handlungen, OBJ - Objekt einer Handlung, AGT - Handlungsträger, PROP - Eigenschaftszuordnung.

4. Sprachverarbeitungsprozesse

4.1 Lexikalisch-morphologische Analyse und automatisches Indexieren

Semantische Bedeutungsstrukturen von Fragen entstehen aus der natürlichsprachigen Anfrage an ein IRS als Ergebnis der computerlinguistischen Verarbeitung in einem NLI. Dieser Prozeß umfaßt die Etappen: lexikalisch-morphologische Analyse, syntaktische und semantische Analyse. Anschließend wird die erhaltene Bedeutungsstruktur in die Datenbankanfragesprache übersetzt (Abschn. 5). Das NLI ersetzt also gewissermaßen die Prozesse, die bei der Formulierung formalsprachiger Anfragen im Kopf des Nutzers vor sich gehen.
In AIDOS werden Verfahren für die lexikalisch-morphologische Analyse beim automatischen Indexieren eingegebener Texte eingesetzt. Zur Realisierung des automatischen Indexierens in Dokumentenrecherchesystemen gibt es verschieden aufwendige, damit aber auch unterschiedlich leistungsfähige Verfahren.
Die Analyse- und Linguistik-orientierten Vorgehensweisen (vgl. [6]) erfordern eine erhebliche intellektuelle Vorarbeit (Wörterbücher, Grammatiken). Sie stehen den Sprachverarbeitungsverfahren der KI und Computerlinguistik am nächsten. Diese Verfahren bedienen sich linguistischer Algorithmen zur Lemmatisierung und zur Analyse von Wortgruppen und stützen sich auf große Computerlexika. Ein solches Lexikon enthält im morphologisch relevanten Teil Angaben über: Wortklassenzugehörigkeit, Flexionsverhalten, Angaben über abweichende Wortstämme, Partizip- bzw. Zeitformenbildung (bei Verben), Geschlecht (bei Nomen) usw. Als gemeinsame Ressourcen können Morpheminventare, Funktions- und Banalwortlisten sowie algorithmische Komponenten der Morphemzerlegung für beide Aufgabenbereiche (Indexierungsverfahren in AIDOS und morphologische Analyse im NLI) genutzt werden.

4.2 Syntaktisch-semantische Analyse

Wie bei der Verarbeitung von anderen Programmiersprachen auch schließt sich sowohl bei der Verarbeitung der natürlichsprachigen Eingabe ins NLI wie bei der Interpretation von Eingaben mit der Menüsprache in AIDOS ein Prozeß der syntaktisch-semantischen Analyse an.
Die syntaktische Analyse der formalsprachigen Nutzereingaben bietet bei AIDOS keine Probleme, da der Eingabetext schon durch die Zeilenstruktur klar gegliedert ist und keine syntaktischen Mehrdeutigkeiten auftreten.
Die Semantik einer Suchanweisung ist ein Suchauftrag nach den Nachweisen, die vom Suchterm beschrieben werden bzw. für diesen Suchterm relevant sind. Die Deutung eines V-Terms hängt davon ab, ob er in einer direkten oder einer sequentiellem Suchanweisung auftritt: Bei einer di-

rekten Suchanweisung wird mittels invertierter Dateien die Menge der relevanten Nachweise direkt zugegriffen; bei einer sequentiellen Suchanweisung wird der Merkmalswert für das im Suchterm spezifizierte Attribut in jedem einzelnen Nachweis der Bezugsmenge gesucht. Eine Leistung des NLI-AIDOS besteht darin, die Unterscheidung zwischen direkter und sequentieller Suche automatisch durchzuführen.
Entsprechend den Besonderheiten der natürlichen Sprache wird im NLI-AIDOS für die Erzeugung der Bedeutungsstrukturen ein computerlinguistischer Apparat eingesetzt, der von den Grundtypen traditioneller Grammatikformalismen abweicht und auch keine unmittelbare Entsprechung in den Sprachverarbeitungsprozessen des IRS besitzt. Dieses Verfahren ist in [6] erstmals beschrieben. Es kann am ehesten mit den in der Computerlinguistik bekannten "Wort- bzw. Wortklassenexperten" [8] verglichen werden.

5. Beziehungen zwischen semantischen Netzen und dem relationalen Datenmodell

Der Spezifikationsteil einer TS-Struktur ist einer Graphenstruktur äquivalent, die die allgemeinen Charakteristika eines semantischen Netzes erfüllt - d.h., es handelt sich um einen gerichteten, kantenmarkierten Graphen, dessen Knoten begriffliche Entitäten repräsentieren; die Kanten bestimmen die Zugehörigkeit des verbundenen Knotenpaares zu der durch die Kantenmarkierung bezeichneten Relation. Die Inhaltsworte einer natürlichsprachigen Aussage treten als Endknoten im semantischen Netz auf, während die inneren Knoten die Bedeutung komplexerer sprachlicher Konstrukte (wie z.B. Teilphrasen) repräsentieren.
Die angegebene Spezifikation des Beispielsatzes: "Gibt es aktuelle Veröffentlichungen über Expertensysteme im Umweltschutz, die vom Springer-Verlag herausgegeben wurden?" kann man als semantisches Netz wie folgt veranschaulichen (Bild 5):

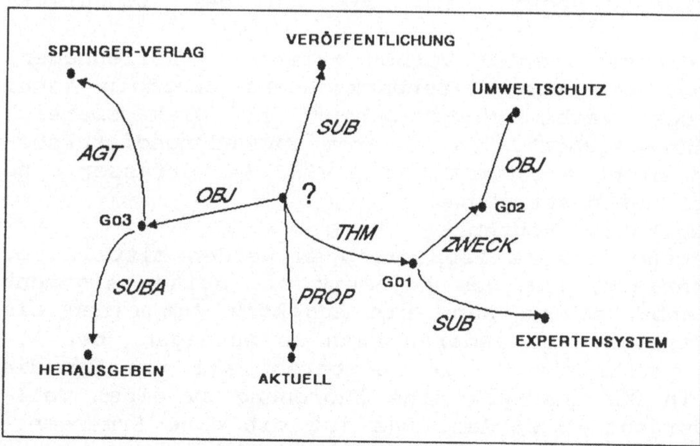

Bild 5. Netzdarstellung einer Anfrage

Der Formalismus der semantischen Netze verfügt über wesentlich reichere Ausdrucksmittel für Sachverhalte und Anfragen als eine relationale Datenbankmodellierung. Ein genereller Vergleich der Beziehungen zwischen semantischen Netzen und dem Coddschen Relationenmodell findet sich in [9]. Wir betrachten hier aber nur die Mittel zur Beschreibung solcher Diskursbereiche, für die das relationale Datenbankmodell adäquat ist, und für Anfragen, die nicht über die Ausdrucksmittel der DAS hinausreichen.

Zur Herstellung der Beziehungen zwischen semantischer Netzdarstellung und dem Relationenmodell lassen sich in der Graphenrepräsentation der TS-Strukturen Teilgraphen herausheben, die in einer prädikatenlogischen Deutung von bestimmten prädikativen Konzepten getragen werden. Folgende Typen solcher Konzepte sind für die Transformation in dem Anwendungsbeispiel relevant:

a) Direkte semantische Relationen

Es gibt eine kleine Menge von Tiefenrelationen, die direkte Beziehungen zwischen Entitäten des Diskursbereichs herstellen und in der natürlichen Sprache vorwiegend durch grammatische Mittel, wie Artikelgebrauch, Präpositionalphrasen, Genitivkonstruktionen u.a. ausgedrückt werden. In der TS-Struktur des Beispielsatzes sind das die Relationen SUB, THM und ZWECK. Im Datenbankmodell werden sie durch ein Attribut oder mehrere verfeinernde Attribute dargestellt. Im Beispieldiskursbereich "Literatur" gilt: Wenn der Anfangsknoten einer ZWECK-Kante ein Element der Objektklasse bezeichnet, dann ist der Endknoten (die ganze daran hängende Teilstruktur) als Wert der Attribute "Deskriptor" und "Klassifikation" zu interpretieren.

b) Verb-getragene prädikative Konzepte

Handlungsverben oder Vorgangsverben (im Beispielsatz "herausgeben") als Träger eines prädikativen Konzepts in der Oberfläche werden in der TS-Struktur zum Endknoten einer SUBA-markierten Kante, deren Anfangsknoten (im Beispiel G03) die Proposition repräsentiert. Die anderen aus dem Propositionsknoten auslaufenden Kanten binden die Aktanten des Verbs. Die semantischen Relationen dafür sind die in der Linguistik gebräuchlichen Tiefenkasus.

Für die Kasus diskursbereichsrelevanter Verben existieren Rollennamen, denen man Attribute eines konkreten Datenbankschemas zuordnen kann. z.B. ist der Agent des Verbs "herausgeben" im Diskursbereich "Literatur" i.a. ein "Herausgeber". In unserem Anwendungsdiskursbereich, wo dieses Attribut nicht existiert, sind VERF (= Verfasser) und VERL (= Verlag) die zugeordneten Attribute.

c) Adjektiv-getragene prädikative Konzepte

Von einem Adjektiv getragene atomare Propositionen werden mittels der TS-Relation PROP repräsentiert, die das Adjektiv mit seinem Argument verknüpft. In einem Datenbankschema kann ein Adjektiv zum einen als Wert eines Attributs auftreten, zum anderen kann es Aussagen über Attribut-Wert-Ausprägungen qualifizieren. Im letzteren Fall muß für die Übersetzung TS-Struktur in DAS-Ausdruck eine Zuordnung zu einem vollständigen DAS-Ausdruck vorgegeben werden. Das ist oft eine Ermessensfrage, wie man an dem gewählten Diskursbereich erkennt. Dort ist es z.B. sinnvoll, dem Begriff "aktuell" im Zusammenhang mit "aktueller Veröffentlichung" den DAS-Suchterm (JAHR >1989) zuzuordnen.

6. Computerlexikon und Datenmodell

Ein wesentlicher Teil der für den Anwendungsbereich typischen Terminologie ist in den verschiedenen Datenstrukturen des IRS enthalten. Deshalb können diese Informationen für das Computerlexikon des NLI nutzbar gemacht werden (Bild 6).
Der rechnergestütze Aufbau des Lexikons wird durch ein Programmsystem, die "Werkbank des Lexikographen" [1], realisiert, das die computerlinguistisch verwertbaren Inhalte aus den Wissensbeständen des IRS automatisch extrahiert. Die grammatischen und semantischen Informationen, die nicht in der Datenbank stehen, werden von der Werkbank in einem nutzerfreundlichen Dialog abgefragt.

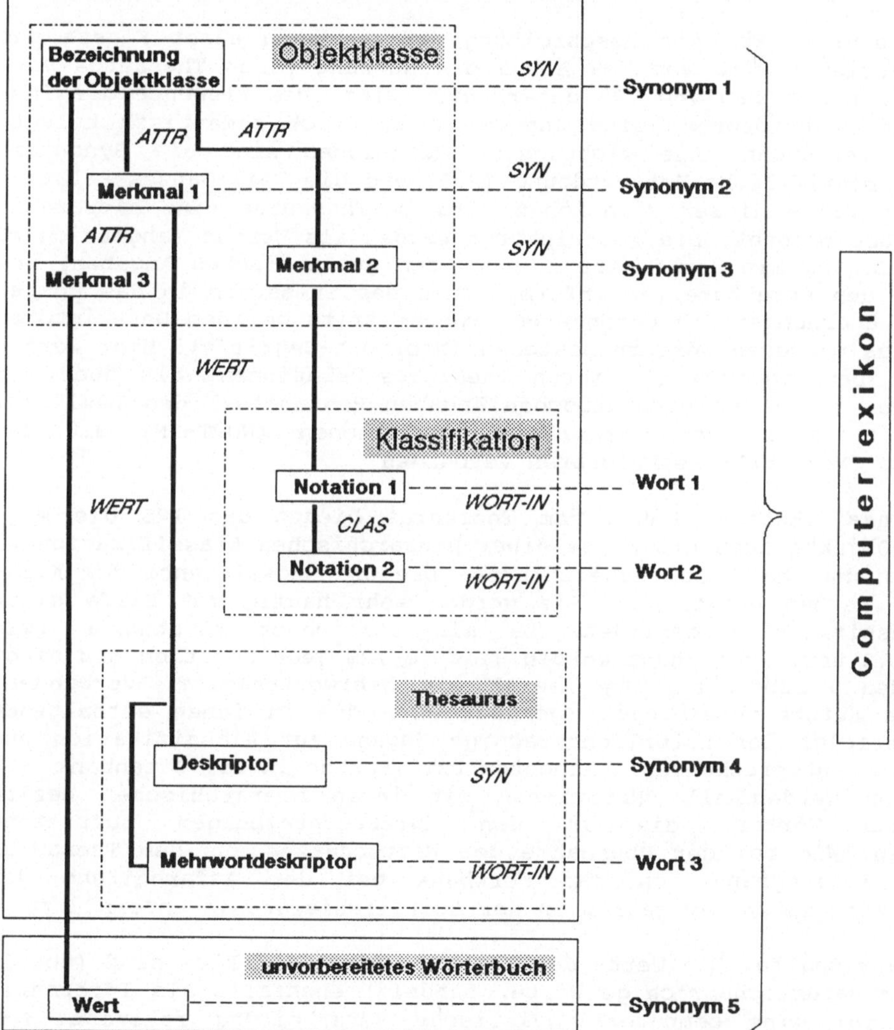

Bild 6. Aus der Datenbank für das Computerlexikon extrahierbare Inhalte

Vergleicht man die Anforderungen an das Computerlexikon für ein NLI mit den Wissensbeständen eines IRS, dann lassen sich folgende Strukturen des IRS für die Lexikonerstellung nutzen:
1. Die Objektklassenbeschreibung. Im IRS AIDOS wird das Datenmodell durch eine anwendungsspezifische, aber sonst feststehende Objektklassenbeschreibung festgelegt. Jedes Objekt entspricht einer Relation (im Sinne des Relationenmodells) und ist durch einen eindeutigen Namen sowie eine Menge von Attributen/Merkmalen gekennzeichnet. Die semantischen Relationen zwischen Objektklassennamen und den Merkmalsnamen werden automatisch aus der Objektklassenbeschreibung erzeugt und ins Lexikon übernommen (Synonyme für Abkürzungen müssen vom Lexikographen vergeben werden).

2. Der Thesaurus. Für die Beschreibung von Objekten einer Klasse und für das Retrieval wird vom IRS AIDOS die Nutzung eines Thesaurus vorgesehen, dessen Aufbau vom IRS unterstützt wird. Die Elemente des Thesaurus, die Deskriptoren, sind untereinander durch semantisch belegte Relationen verbunden. Die wichtigsten Relationen sind die Synonymie (SYN), die begriffliche Unterordnung (SUB) und die Teil-Ganzes-Relation (PARS). Mit Hilfe dieser Relationen wird im Thesaurus eine hierarchische Struktur erzeugt. Die Deskriptoren werden als Wörter (angereichert um die im Dialog mit der Werkbank ergänzten grammatischen Angaben) zusammen mit den strukturellen Informationen des Thesaurus in das Computerlexikon übernommen.Ein besonderes Problem tritt bei den Deskriptoren auf, die aus mehreren Wörtern bestehen (Mehrwort-Begriffe). Hier werden sowohl die Deskriptoren mit ihren Thesaurus-Relationen, als auch die Einzelwörter mit ihren grammatischen Angaben Bestandteil des Lexikons. Diese Wörter sind über lexikalische Relationen (WORT-IN) mit den zugehörigen (Mehrwort-)Deskriptoren verbunden.

3. Die Klassifikation. Neben dem Thesaurus bietet das IRS die Möglichkeit, Objekte auch mit Hilfe einer hierarchischen Klassifikation zu beschreiben und damit zu recherchieren. Die Ordnungselemente der Klassifikation heißen Notationen. Sie werden sehr häufig mit Hilfe einer Dezimalklassifikation gebildet. Da als Bezeichner Kunstnamen (wie K.1.1, K.1.2 usw.) verwendet werden, ist im IRS jede Notation mit einer erläuternden Kurzbeschreibung (meist ein Mehrwortbegriff) verbunden. Über diese Kurzbeschreibungen (genauer über die in ihnen enthaltenen Wörter), erfolgt der natürlichsprachige Zugang zur Klassifikation und damit zu den entsprechenden Dokumenten bzw. Fakten in der Datenbank.
Ins Lexikon werden alle Notationen mit ihren hierarchischen Beziehungen und Wörter, die in den Kurzbeschreibungen auftreten, eingetragen. Wie bei der Übernahme des Wortschatzes aus dem Thesaurus wird der Lexikograph von der Werkbank bei der Aufarbeitung der Klassifikation durch Navigation in der Begriffshierarchie unterstützt.

4. Datenbankinhalte. Die Werte der Merkmale eines Objektes sind (soweit es sich um natürlichsprachige Wörter handelt) ebenfalls als Informationsquelle für eine computerlinguistische Verarbeitung relevant. Man denke hier nur an die große Zahl von Eigennamen (von Produkten, Autoren, Verlagen usw.), die niemals für ein Computerlexikon vorbereitet werden können (unvorbereiteter Wortschatz). Wenn aber in einer Litera-

turdatenbank z.B. bekannt ist, daß NILSSON der Name eines Autors ist (in unserem Anwendungsfall z.B. Wert des Merkmals VERF), dann läßt sich daraus automatisch auf eine Reihe linguistisch bedeutungsvoller Informationen für dieses Lexem schließen: "artikelloser Gebrauch des Wortes", "kein Plural", "handlungsfähig", "belebt" usw.

Auf diese Weise läßt sich also unter Ausnutzung der Korrespondenz zwischen dem Wissensbestand des IRS und dem Computerlexikon der Aufbau des Lexikons rechentechnisch unterstützen.

7. Schlußbemerkungen

Die automatische Verarbeitung natürlicher Sprache, die im Grenzgebiet von Computerlinguistik und Künstlicher Intelligenz angesiedelt ist, hat eine Reihe von Methoden und Verfahren hervorgebracht, die bereits für die Verbesserung der Leistungsfähigkeit von Informationsrecherchesystemen wirksam geworden sind. Die Bereitstellung natürlichsprachlicher Interfaces ist in dieses Spektrum einzuordnen. Durch den Vergleich von Methoden und Verfahren der KI bzw. der Computerlinguistik mit denen traditioneller Datenbanksysteme wird ein Beitrag zur Verschmelzung dieser Informationstechnologien und zur Verbesserung der entsprechenden Systeme geleistet. Dieser Prozess ist noch nicht beendet und sollte auch andere wissensbasierte Systeme, wie Expertensysteme und Frage-Antwort-Systeme einbeziehen.

8. Literatur

[1] Helbig, H. et al.: The natural language interface NLI-AIDOS, J.New Generation Computer Systems., 3(3),221-246,1990
[2] Naumann, P.: Informacionno-poiskovaja sistema AIDOS/VS, MZNTI, Moskau 1986
[3] Wenzel, R.-D.: AIDOS/M im DCP, Informatik 36(5),167-170,1989
[4] Kobsa, A.; Wahlster, W. (Hrsg.): Special issue on user modelling. Computational Linguistics 14(3),1988
[5] Helbig, H.: Künstliche Intelligenz und automatische Wissensverarbeitung, Verlag Technik, Berlin 1991
[6] Schwarz, Ch.; Thurmair, G. (Hrsg.): Informationslinguistische Texterschließung, Georg Olms Verlag, Hildesheim 1986
[7] Helbig, H.: Syntactic-semantic analysis of natural language by a new word-class controlled functional analysis. Computers and Artificial Intelligence, Bratislava 5(1),53-59,1986
[8] Eimermacher, M.: Wortorientiertes Parsen. Dissertation D83, TU Berlin (W) 1988
[9] Böttger, H., Helbig, H.: Vergleich zwischen relationalem Datenmodell und semantischen Netzen, VEB Robotron ZFT, Forschungsbericht, März 1980.

Assisting Computer – A New Generation of Support Systems

Peter Hoschka

GMD

Institut für Angewandte Informationstechnik
Schloß Birlinghoven
5205 Sankt Augustin

Providing support systems with more knowledge about tasks, users and the system itself should enable computers to better support their users. The key principle is that computers should assist and not automate. Three factors distinguish Assisting Computers (AC) from previous systems:

– Assistance properties: AC´s should be able to interpret imprecise instructions on the basis of current and previous contexts, they should be adaptable to their user´s individual needs and personal style, and they should be able to explain their behavior and functionality when desired.

– Domain competence: AC´s should possess knowledge about selected application domains, including problem solving knowledge in the domain; they should be able to assess their competence.

– Support of cooperation: AC´s should support not only the work of individuals, but also work within teams and organizations.

These are the goals of the "Assisting Computer" project of the German National Research Center for Computer Science (GMD). The paper outlines this project and illustrates its state, especially in the field of providing systems with assistance properties.

1 Introduction

Research on the "Assisting Computer" – AC for short – is concentrating on looking for new ways of dividing labor between human and computer. The systems being developed are to take on more tasks than existing ones do, especially those that seem tedious or difficult for humans. On the other hand, it is an explicit goal *not* to automate tasks completely. The basic paradigm is rather that of assistance. Many application fields of computers are characterized by the fact that either their complexity or the sheer number of problems to be addressed is so great that any attempt to develop an automaton with complete problem-solving competence must fail. What is called for instead is a set of calibrated tools that the user can combine, adapt and employ as he sees fit. Exhaustive coverage and treatment of a problem is precisely *not* the goal of assisting computers.

The assistance metaphor not only expresses the primary guideline of the project, but also the goal of devising systems whose behavior is characterized by assistance properties. There are many charcteristics that make up effective assistance. A human assistant, for instance, is naturally expected to be competent in his domain of expertise, know his limitations, be able to process vague instructions, adjust to a client and learn from him, and be able to explain his own behavior and suggestions. Assistance in communication and cooperation is a central function of the assistant in a secretary office. The more domain knowledge an assistant has, and the more he knows his client, the more aptly will he be able to offer such services.

The assisting computer concept does not entail building a duplicate of the human assistant. But we want to try to produce in a computer system some of the properties necessary and useful to assistance functionality – with no claims to cognitive adequacy. So, if computer systems are to offer assistant capabilities, they must be supplied with domain knowledge and knowledge about the user. And there is an additional requirement for computer systems: they need knowledge about themselves, that is, about their own functioning. Only if a system can observe its own behavior, and reflect on it, will it be able to correctly evaluate its own competence and explain its behavior.

The most important assistant properties, for whose realization in computer systems we are currently laying the groundwork, are compiled in the following (Fig.1).

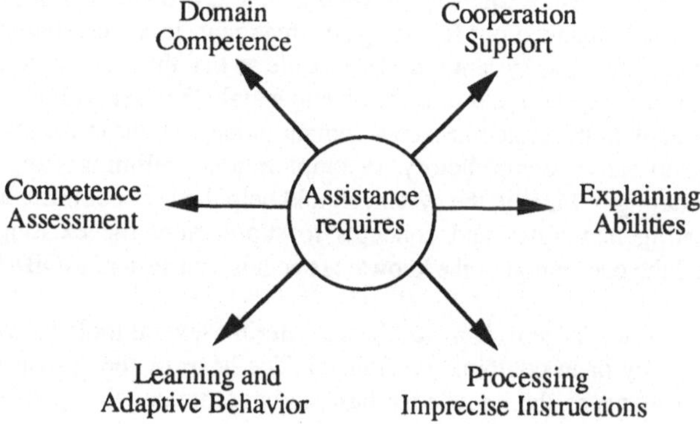

Figure 1: Fundamental Assistance Properties

- Domain Competence: Assisting computers could be equipped with domain knowledge in certain areas of importance to their users; they should be able to support problem-solving processes in these areas.
- Competence Assessment: Within their domain, assisting computers should be able to assess their own competence and its limitations. The user should be able to engage in a dialogue with the system to find out which problems it can solve, which not, and why not.
- Learning and Adaptive Behavior: Assisting computers should be able to adapt both behavior and functionality to a user´s individual needs and personal style. The system should learn from the user by monitoring and analyzing his work.
- Processing Imprecise Instructions: The assisting computer should be able to interpret incomplete, vague, ambiguous, even contradictory instructions on the basis of knowledge about the user and the current task.
- Explaining Abilities: The systems should be able to explain and give reasons for each of its actions, conclusions and suggestions – in terms the user can understand.
- Cooperation Support: Assisting computers are not only to support the isolated work of individuals, but also work in teams and organizations. They should help coordinate tasks treated in a distributed manner and provide the organizational knowledge required for cooperation and coordination.

The following sections describe the concepts and methods we are using in our endeavors to equip systems with the assistance properties discussed above, and the results attained so far.

2 Domain competence

Supplying systems with domain knowledge is the goal of conventional expert systems. A number of examples that deviate somewhat from the usual expert system scenario are to show how assisting computers can incorporate some of the knowledge that must, at present, be supplied by the user. We are currently working on three examples:

- An assistant for knowledge acquisition that supports the development of a knowledge base.
- A statistics interpreter that helps analyze and interpret statistical data.
- A graphics designer that assists the design of business and presentation graphics.

2.1 Assistant for knowledge acquisition

A system to support the acquisition of knowledge cannot be limited to offering the user some formalisms for the representation of knowledge. Acquiring knowledge in a new domain is, however, not a straightforward task that can be easily planned out for computer treatment. It is a creative process with frequent mental leaps and many iterations. The system must be flexible so that the user can work in his own manner and is not forced to adapt to the system´s. It must be able to supply the user with the consequences of new knowledge that the user adds to the system. Since a domain model is built in the course of work with the system, it must be able to accept contradictory, incomplete and preliminary inputs. We call this the paradigm of "sloppy modeling"[1]. Finally, the system should help the user complete and rectify the model, for instance by suggesting new rules and concepts to supplement the existing knowledge. These requirements have guided the conception of the knowledge acquisition system MOBAL.[2]

MOBAL (model based learning system) is a workbench offering several tools for knowledge acquisition that can be used individually or in combination (Fig. 2). The heart of the system is the Coordinator & Inference Engine, which manages the knowledge base and coordinates the system´s various functions. MOBAL uses facts and rules to represent a domain model. Existing facts and rules can be modified at any time; the inference engine makes sure that entries relying on the changed ones are modified as well. If entries are incomplete or erroneous, they do not have to be corrected immediately. The system maintains an agenda of such "open ends", and the user can address himself to these at any time he sees fit. Even contradictory entries can be processed; the system recognizes contradictions and offers a special tool, the Knowledge Revision Tool, with the help of which a contradiction can be analyzed and resolved.

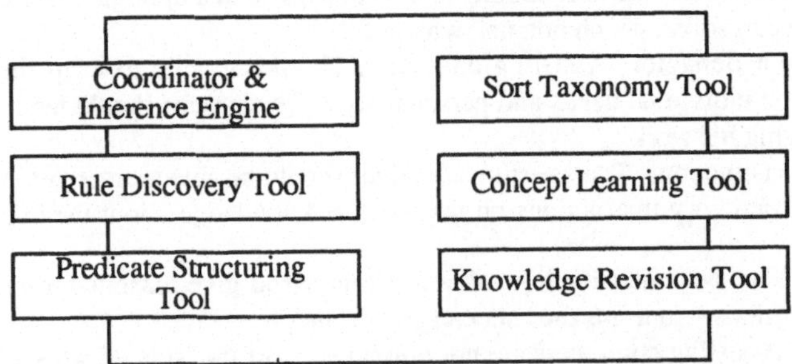

Figure 2: Tools in the knowledge acquisition system MOBAL

---

1 K. Morik. Sloppy Modeling. In K. Morik (ed.). Knowledge Representation and Organisation in Machine Learning. Springer Verlag, Berlin, 1989, p. 107-134

2 MOBAL is part of the MLT (Machine Learnig Toolbox) research project, partially funded by the Comission of the European Communities under ESPRIT project number P 2154.

The other tools that comprise MOBAL serve the purpose of supporting the user with various machine learning techniques. They produce suggestions that can help resolve incompleteness, improve knowledge base structure or recognize and point out regularities in the facts. The user can use these suggestions or decide to make similar (or other) entries. The Sort Taxonomy Tool allows declaration of the types of arguments the predicates of the knowledge base use. It can construct a taxonomy of concepts on the basis of the argument types that actually appear in the facts of the knowledge base. The Rule Discovery Tool can point out regularities in the facts entered into the system. The Predicate Structuring Tool produces an abstract overview of the complete rule set. In this, it points out the global structure of the knowledge base. The user can, however, also specify the structure beforehand; the learning algorithms then abide by this by considering only such rules that instantiate the connections specified in the structure. The Concept Learning Tool, finally, supports the user in discovering useful concepts and integrating them into the representation language. All machine learning techniques in MOBAL play the role of an assistant to the user. Modeling is understood as a cooperative and balanced process between human and computer.[3]

A first version of MOBAL is currently being evaluated in several applications. The most advanced of these are a medical application (in a greek hospital) and a technical application in the area of diagnosis for satellites (British Aerospace).

2.2 Statistics interpreter

A second example of an assistance system with domain competence is the statistics interpreter EXPLORA. It is meant to discover interesting findings in statistical data and aide the user in interpreting them. EXPLORA has knowledge about the domain background and about methods for the analysis of statistical data. To this end, the objects, relations and queries used in the statistical analysis of a data set must be represented in the system. From these, EXPLORA constructs a proposition space for these data and searches it for interesting findings. In traditional statistics packages, the user himself must specify each hypothesis individually. In EXPLORA, this is different: knowledge-based and systematic processing of the proposition search space allows the system to discover results that might have been overlooked in traditional analysis. The statistics interpreter usually has to cover a very large search space of potential findings. However, this space can be pruned substantially with the help of redundancy filters and generalization methods. This assures that only the "strongest" findings are presented to the user and he is not flooded with redundant statements. For instance, if the system discovers that it is raining all over Germany, then it need not mention that it is also raining in Bonn and Berlin – unless the downpour is especially strong there. Fig. 3 shows the functional model of the system.

EXPLORA accepts propositions of arbitrary type which are useful to formulate knowledge about data and incorporates them in a "discovery system". In other words, the system is not limited to specific types of hypotheses (as, for instance, rule learners are). It also supports the user in navigating through the space of potentially interesting findings by being able to refine, specialize, condense and generalize propositions. The user can drag individual findings into an "outliner" and add comments and pointers. The outline of a report can thus be developed in parallel with data analysis. A prototype of EXPLORA has been implemented and is currently being tried out by several large companies who are using it to evaluate poll data for marketing research.[4]

---

[3] K. Morik. Balanced Cooperative Modeling. Proc. International Workshop on Multistrategy Learning (Harpers Ferry, West Virginia, November 1991), in press. This paper contains more details on the MOBAL system.

[4] An overview of EXPLORA can be found in: P. Hoschka, W. Klösgen. A Support System for Interpreting Statistical Data. In G. Piatetsky-Shapiro/W. Frawler (eds). Knowledge Discovery in Data Bases, MIT-Press, in press

223

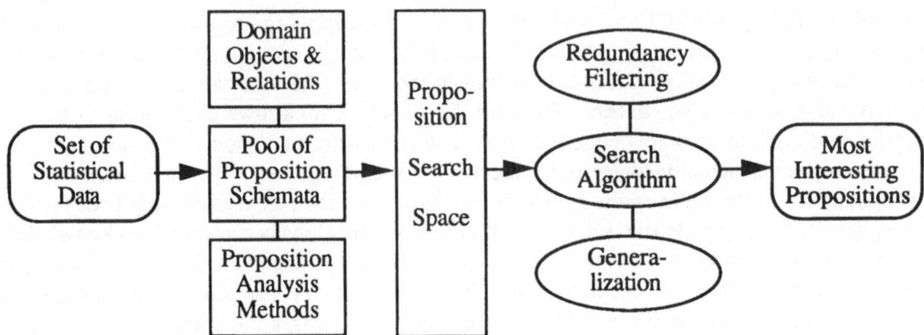

Figure 3: Functional Model of the EXPLORA Statistics Interpreter

2.3 Graphics Designer

A further example in which we attempt to incorporate domain knowledge in a computer system is the graphics designer. Today´s graphics packages allow anyone to produce graphics easily and comfortably. Current systems do not, however, offer any assistance where aesthetic beautification or the choice of suitable graphical means of expression is concerned. It is here that the graphics designer aims to provide assistance.[5]

In creating graphics, certain rules of design that govern expressiveness must be observed. These rules state, for instance, which diagram type is suited for time series, and which for rank orders, or which colors make for a good background and which for a good foreground. The layman is usually unfamiliar with such rules and, as a study has shown, at times they elude even professionals. In the graphics designer project, such rules are developed in cooperation with a professional designer. This is a first step towards an expert system for graphics design. In order to codify graphical knowledge, we require a language adequate to the description of the interesting aspects of a picture. To this end, the object-oriented graphic language EPICT was developed.[6] It not only supports the standard graphic elements and attributes, but also allows the definition of relations between elements and attributes of arbitrary parts of a graphic. Current work involves the application of machine learning methods in order to extract concepts from existing graphics, so that the language can be adapted dynamically to a given context.

In the fine calibration of a picture, graphical elements must be aligned to each other and spread out evenly across the available space. The more precisely a graphic can be printed out on a laser printer, the more conspicuous discrepancies in layout and slight inaccuracies in size and position become. The graphics designer can describe typical errors in graphics in a "situation language" which we have developed, and automatically find these errors. A knowledge-based criticism module decides which corrections are to be made in which order, and plans out the individual steps in such a way as to ensure that later corrections do not revert previous ones.

Rules of design often do not have absolute validity; different rules must be weighed against each other. Rules about favorable font sizes, for instance, may well be in conflict with rules governing the distribution of available space. Conflict situations such as these cannot be handled in traditional expert systems. They

---

[5] The graphics designer is developed within the project TASSO (Technical Assisting System for Processing Inexact Knowledge) partly supported by the German Federal Ministery for Research and Technology under grant number ITW 8900 A7.

[6] E. Rome, K. Wittur, D. Bolz. EPICT – Eine erweiterbare Grafik-Beschrcibungssprache. TASSO-Report Nr. 4, GMD, Sankt Augustin, 1990

require methods of non-monotonic reasoning. To this end, the graphics designer uses the EXCEPT system, which can assign rules priorities and exceptions and handle them in rescindable inferences.[7] The graphics designer´s main components have been implemented as prototypes, with a narrow focus towards business and presentation graphics. Current work involves extensions in the direction of a more general scenario.[8]

The graphics designer, statistics interpreter and knowledge aquisition assistant are examples of systems with domain competence. They do, however, contain already elements of other assistance properties. The knowledge acquisition system, for instance, is able to learn from the user and identify and manage imprecise instructions. The graphics designer already is a typical example of processing imprecise instructions: the user develops his graphic to a certain point and then passes on this raw version to the system, which takes over the details of producing an aesthetically pleasing end product. The following section is concerned with a further assistance property closely related to domain competence: evaluation of system competence and recognition of its limits.

3   Competence Assessment

According to the basic paradigm of assisting computers, we do not try to build systems with exhaustive and perfect competence. But if systems are not perfect, they should be able to assess their own competence.[9] Competence assessment means judging the potential ability of a system to solve a particular problem. More specifically, competent behavior means:[10]

- Before jumping into the solution process, a competent system checks whether it understands the problem, which might be incomplete or ambiguous.
- It does not try to tackle problems that are unsolvable in principle, for instance if the problem statement is in itself contradictory.
- Nor does it try to solve problems surpassing its capabilities and resources. If necessary, it is able to negotiate the problem statement.
- A competent system is able to detect and remove redundancies and can therefore reduce complexity.
- It monitors its progress and changes focus by adapting strategies or redistributing resources in case progress is behind expectations.
- Finally, it evaluates its solutions in retrospect, so as to store its problem solving experience. Later, when confronted with a similar case, decisions can be made based on this experience.

Competence assessment requires stepping back and viewing the system from the outside in order to detect its malfunctions. Hence, competence assessment may be regarded as reflective behavior – the inspection of the system by itself.[11] In order to represent the system itself, a reflective system has a meta-level architecture, i.e. the part of the object system that is reasoned about is represented in a more abstract model at the meta-level (the self-representation). Reflective modules inspect, observe and possibly correct their "object" system from a higher, meta-level (Fig. 4). They do not operate on the actual implementation of the

---

[7]   U. Junker. EXCEPT: A Rule-Based System for Multiple Contexts, Inconsistencies, and Exceptions. Arbeitspapiere der GMD 371, Sankt Augustin, 1989

[8]   K. Kansy. Leitbeispiel Graphikdesigner. TASSO-Report Nr. 14, GMD, Sankt Augustin, 1990

[9]   The research reported here was carried out in the course of the REFLECT project. This project is partially funded by the ESPRIT Basic Research Programme of the Commission of the European Communities as project number 3178.

[10]   A. Voß, W. Karbach, U. Drouven, D. Lorek. Competence Assessment in Configuration Tasks. AI Communications 3(3), 1990, 107-114

[11]   M. Reinders et al. A Conceptual Modeling Framework for Knowledge-level Reflection. Submitted to AI Communications.

object system but use an abstract, knowledge level model of the underlying system, thus being generic and applicable to a broader class of object systems.

Competence assessment is regarded as a diagnosis and repair task consisting of the basic inference steps shown in figure 4. According to this scheme, we have built several modules for the class of assignment and constraint satisfaction problem solvers.[12] They can recognize overspecified and overcomplex problems, cope with redundancies and contradictions, decompose complex problems, schedule problem solving steps with respect to time limitations, and switch to a propose-and-revise strategy in case constraint satisfaction fails. The time management module, for instance, analyzes the time already spent and compares it to the time available, interprets its findings possibly as a malfunction "overcomplexity", proposes how to continue the problem solving process and applies this repair by modifying the flow of control of the given object system.

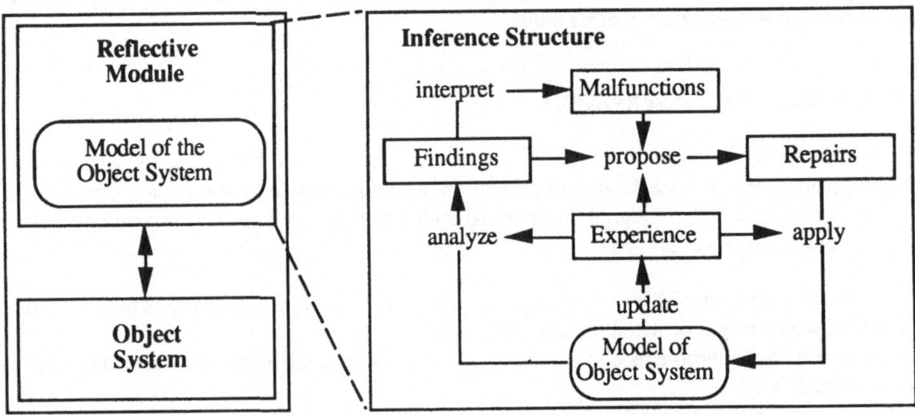

Figure 4: A conceptual framework for reflection. The object system is causally connected to its model in the reflective module. Competence assessment is regarded as a diagnosis and repair task.

4 Adaptivity and Adaptability

An important requirement for assisting systems is the ability to adapt to users´ individual styles and tasks.[13] Two forms of adaptation should be distinguished here: one which occurs on the user´s initiative (adaptability), and the other initiated by the system itself (adaptivity or better: auto-adaptation). While the call for adaptability is uncontroversial in principle, there are differing positions on auto-adaptation of systems. Our own research[14] has shown that in practice there are only few starting points for auto-adaptive services. Those that have been implemented (adaptation of parameter defaults, control of dialog queries, offering abbreviated commands) are based only on the evaluation of simple frequencies in user behavior. We are currently experimenting with learning algorithms for artificial neural nets that, through training, learn, identify and generalize individual user action sequences (the example application is processing electronic mail).

12 A. Voß, W. Karbach, U. Drouven, B. Bartsch-Spörl, B. Bredeweg. Reflection and competent problem solving. In: Th. Christaller (ed). GWAI-91, Proc. 15th German Workshop on Artificial Intelligence. Springer Verlag, Berlin, 1991

13 The research about adaptivity and adaptability of systems is carried out within the SAGA project, which is partially funded by the German Federal Ministery for Research and Technology under number 01HK5370.

14 R. Oppermann. Ansätze zur individualisierten Systemnutzung durch manuell und automatisch anpaßbare Software. In M. Frese et. al. (eds). Software für die Arbeit von morgen. Springer Verlag, Berlin, 1991, 81-92

System adaptivity is especially desirable in the offering of help when the user is having difficulties. Help facilities should be adjusted according to the current dialogue situation and the individual user. We have developed such a context-sensitive help system for the spreadsheet program EXCEL™. The HYPLAN system consists of two modules, a plan-recognition program and an interactive multimedia help environment.[15] The plan recognition unit gets a continuous input protocol listing the commands entered by the EXCEL user. Guided by a knowledge base of hierarchical action nets, dynamic state models of the user´s probable goals are instantiated and incrementally extended as new protocol data comes in. Confirmed goals, and ones activated as hypotheses, are marked on "blackboards". When the user calls for help, the system selects a context-specific help offering based on the goals currently marked on the blackboards. The offerings themselves are realized as voice commented illustrations and animated scenes (Fig. 5).

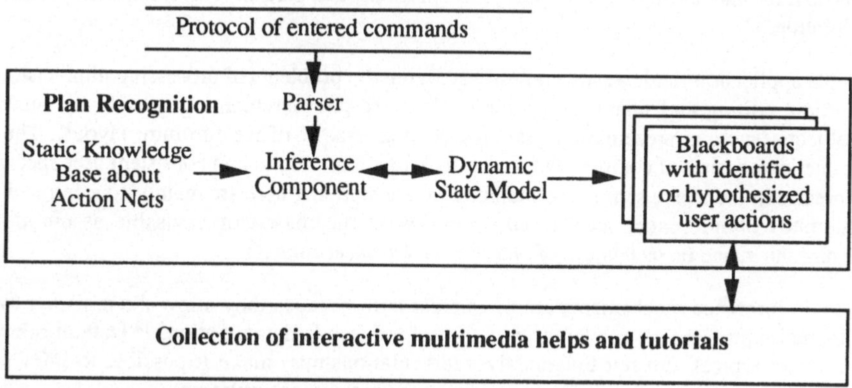

Figure 5: Architecture of the adaptive help system HYPLAN

A central idea of this help system is that the goals and work situations represented internally were collected empirically, by watching users work with EXCEL. By this concentration on notoriously problematic situations, it was possible to significantly reduce the number of recognizable goals and corresponding help offerings. The system is nevertheless able to offer specific help for frequently arising problems. HYPLAN does not yet have a component that allows the tailoring of support to individual users.

Our empirical studies have shown that the possibilites of system adaptation on the user´s initiative are by far not used as intensively as the system designers intended.[16] From this we conclude that the proper exploitation of adaptability requires special support by the system. We are currently looking into the possiblities of using an auto-adaptive component to point out to the user the adaptability capabilities of a system. In any case, dialog editors and macro editors are necessary so that the user can modify the surface of the system. Exploration possibilities are useful in this context as well. To this end, we have devised some new ways of exploring a system (the example application again being EXCEL). In critical situations, the user can "freeze" the state of his work (document and system states) and give it a name. With the help of these names, he can navigate through his dialogue history. He can also record a dialog and augment it with spoken comments. In this way the user can compile his own "videotheque" of commented sample solutions to his individual assignments.

---

[15] G. Grunst, R. Oppermann, C. Thomas. Intelligente Benutzerschnittstellen. Kontext-sensitive Hilfen und Adaptivität. In: R. Katzsch (ed.). Benutzerschnittstelle. HMD Nr. 160. Forkel-Verlag, Wiesbaden, in press

[16] C. Karger, R. Oppermann. Empirische Nutzungsuntersuchung adaptierbarer Schnittstelleneigenschaften. In D. Ackermann, E. Ulich (eds.). Software-Ergonomie 91. Benutzerorientierte Software-Entwicklung. Teubner Verlag, Stuttgart, 1991, 272-280

5   Processing Imprecise Instructions

Assistance systems should be able to perform meaningful actions even if the instructions or the available information are imprecise and the action to be executed is not definitely given. In this context, imprecision means:
- The available information can be incomplete, so that decisions must be based on plausible additional assumptions (defaults), which may have to be revised later.
- The available information can be vague or ambiguous, e.g. because certain relationships are true only with some probability, or because terms used in an instruction have no precise meaning (draw a triangle *near* the rectangle).
- The available information can be contradictory, which means that parts of it must be faded out and left out of consideration.

As an example application field, we are currently studying the problems of processing imprecision during the construction, editing and search of graphics. The user can incrementally specify the attributes of graphical objects (such as presentation graphics or diagrams of office furniture layout). The central assistance function consists of completing and /or making more precise and consistent user specifications that are imprecise in the above sense. The methods we are studying here are mainly concentrated on non-classical methods of inference, such as *non-monotonic* (i.e. based on revisable assumptions) and *associative* reasoning, and on techniques of *planning under uncertainty*.[17]

Non-monotonic inference mechanisms are of interest here because they allow the assisting system to complete imprecise problem specifications with the help of standard assumptions.[18] Default rules (that is, rules that express typical, but not universally valid relationships) make it possible to infer plausible conclusions, which can lead to meaningful decisions in the case of incompleteness.

The EXCEPT system[19] developed in the course of this project provides a powerful, logic-oriented language for knowledge representation and can process default rules like those discussed above. In addition, the defaults can be assigned priorities in order to avoid ambiguities. Inconsistent information is handled by producing multiple contexts, each of which is consistent in itself and incorporates as much of the available information as possible. Maintaining multiple contexts also makes it possible to work with several alternative completions of a partial problem specification and offer the user a choice between them. EXCEPT was used successfully in the implementation of the graphics designer (see Section 2.3).

Associative reasoning techniques based on neural networks are being used – in a memory-based approach – for the storage and retrieval of known problem specifications and solutions. The solution of a current problem is supported by looking at similar, already solved problems. These are re-activated in a content-driven, associative manner. To realize this, analog surface information can be connected with qualitatively formulated properties of objects. Reactivation is attained on the basis of incompletely specified "sketches", which are produced with the help of the graphical system itself. To this end, auto-associative mechanisms are used, realized as local spreading activation, or based on matrix storage and weight sets learned through back propagation.[20]

---

17 The research reported here is carried out in the project TASSO (Technical Assisting System for Processing Inexact Knowledge) partially funded by the German Federal Ministery for Research and Technology under number ITW 8900 A7.

18 G. Brewka. Nonmonotonic Reasoning – Logical Foundations for Commonsense Reasoning. Cambridge University Press, Cambridge, 1990

19 U. Junker. EXCEPT: A Rule-Based System for Multiple Contexts, Inconsistencies, and Exceptions. Arbeitspapiere der GMD 371, Sankt Augustin, 1989

20 P. Henne. Ein experimentelles Assoziativspeicher-Modell. TASSO Report Nr. 12, GMD, Sankt Augustin, 1991

Finally, research on planning under uncertainty is motivated by the special role this can play in the construction of graphics. The design and beautification of semi-standardized graphics like business presentations can be viewed as a configuration task. In this context, existing AI techniques for planning and configuration must be extended to allow imprecision in the planning model, the planning operators and the goals.[21]

6 Explanation Abilities

If assisting systems process imprecise instructions, make suggestions for system adaptation and offer domain competence for solving problems, then these properties inevitably give rise to a further requirement: the systems must be able to explain their own behavior and suggestions – in terms the user can understand. Assisting systems have no chance of being accepted as black boxes. It is a well-known phenomenon in existing expert systems that their explanation components actually explain very little. They are usually limited to confronting the user with a more or less flexible presentation protocolling the problem solving steps executed. Explanation ability in the assisting computer sense, on the other hand, not only entails making a system more transparent, but also implementing pedagogical competence so that the user´s understanding of a problem can be estimated and improved in the course of dialogue. Consequently, a system must have tutorial faculties, and not be limited to simply showing the formal structures of a knowledge based system.

As a first step towards better explanations, we are currently working on improving knowledge representation methods so as to make them more suited to explanation purposes. We are examining the possibilities of using conceptual models that represent knowledge in several levels of abstraction (as, for instance, the KADS model does) to determine the focus and level of detail for an explanation to be produced. Further improvements are expected from the generation of natural language explanations. Coherent and concisely formulated texts using rhetorical means such as ellipses and anaphora should replace stereotypical trace protocols.[22]

7 Support of Cooperation

Every form of activity in organizations requires cooperation among its members: work in organizations is distributed and has to be coordinated. Assisting computers should therefore not only support the isolated work of the individual. They should also help him coordinate his activities with those of others – for instance in his project team, or some other organizational group – and provide access to the necessary knowledge about the organization. These functions of assisting computers are realized in two components:

– the activity assistant[23], which provides coordination support for each user, and
– the organizational knowledge base, which contains knowledge about members and structure of the organization and offers all users access to this.

Both components are currently under development; first prototypes are planned for 1992.

---

[21] J. Hertzberg. Revising Planning Goals: On Concept and Implementation. TASSO-Report Nr. 3, GMD, Sankt Augustin, 1990

[22] Research on natural language explanation components is partially funded by Northrhine-Westphalia´s joint research programme "Applications of Artificial Intelligence" (Project DIAMOD).

[23] Work on the activity assistant is partially funded by the Commission of the European Communities in the ESPRIT project EuroCoOp (grant number 5303).

7.1 The Activity Assistant

The activity assistant is meant to help organize asyncronous and decentralized work in teams on tasks that are to be handled in a distrubuted manner within an organization. The assistant supports planning and execution of cooperative tasks, especially taking into consideration frequent changes in task goals and work load distribution. Experience with existing cooperation support systems has shown that special emphasis must be put on offering users the ability to tailor a system to their own needs.[24]

The main functions of the activity assistant consist of
– offering a better and more consistent overview of complex distributed group work,
– documenting progress in the task at hand,
– allowing dynamic changes in procedure planning while they are being executed,
– allowing access to and communication of necessary background information and messages,
– offering individual and group related date planning.

The projected scenario for the activity assistant is support of work in smaller groups (5 to 10 people), with a planning horizon of several weeks or months. It is not meant to be an exhaustive management system for large units or projects, but rather a medium for the (self-) organization of work in teams.

The activity assistant is based on an activity model which provides for tasks that can be combined to form activities.[25] Tasks have a number of attributes, such as intended goals, required resources and completion dates, and can be assigned to responsible actors. Coordination within an activity is realized by exchanging semi-structured messsages according to the structured interaction paradigm ("Conversation model").

Novel aspects of cooperation support in the activity assistant are:
– Integration of planning and execution of distributed activities (in contrast, existing project management systems are single-user applications for the project manager).
– Flexibility ("more order without the constraints"): personal and group-related planning can be adapted to the current situation; replanning, incomplete planning, gradual refinement of abstract plans; negotiation of work distribution and delegation.
– Integration of diverse types of computer support for group work: the underlying principle of the activity assistant is support of asyncronous group work according to the structured interaction paradigm. Beyond this, however, other forms of support are also offered: information sharing (commonly accessible information base of task results and other background information pertaining to the execution of activities), informal communication and integration of syncronous forms of cooperation.
– Reusability with rich structure: from individual work planning to coarse planning and coordination of projects. Use of the assistant is bound only to minimal organizational requirements; it can function in a group even if neighboring groups employ other or no coordination aides.

7.2 The Organizational Knowledge Base

Cooperation in organzations is bounded to organizational conditions. Consequently, information about organizational structures and regulations plays an important role. The organizational knowledge base compiles such information and provides access to it. It contains objects of the organization, such as employees, organizational roles, organizational units, projects, forms and document types, and the

---

24 Th. Kreifelts. Coordination of Distributed Work: From Office Procedures to Customizable Activities. In this volume
25 Th. Kreifelts, U. Pankoke-Babatz, F. Victor. A model for the coordination of cooperative activities. In K. Gorling, C. Sattler (eds.) International Workshop on CSCW, (Berlin, April 9-11, 1991), Informatik Berlin 7 (1991) 4, Institut für Informatik und Rechentechnik der AdW, Berlin, 1991, S. 85-100

relationships between these objects, describing how they form regulations, such as responsability, subordination and access restriction.

The organizational knowledge base is an important prerequisite for the use of cooperation support systems such as the activity assistant, in that it manages, interprets and provides the information on objects, structures and regulations of an organization in a distributed manner. In this way it builds up the connection between an activity and the organizational environment in which it takes place. The information is not only useful for the computer based cooperation systems, but equally important for the human users. Equipped with an adequate user interface, the organizational knowledge base represents an information system in its own right. Implementation of the organizational knowledge base is grounded in application and extension of the X.500 directory concepts for distributed maintenance of object data.[26] [27]

8   Tools and Implementation

The projects that comprise the research on assisting computers aim at a number of subgoals under the roof of the overall ambition. In the current first phase of our efforts, work is focussed on the subgoals. Nevertheless, we wished to lay the ground for later integration of results from the very beginning. We have therefore defined a common development base for all projects: the UNIX operating system, C++ and LISP (with CLOS) programming languages, X-Windows and OSF/Motif graphical interface.

The individual components´ user interfaces are to be designed according to uniform guidelines. To support this goal on the software engineering side, we have developed our own tool, GINA (Generic Interactive Application).[28] GINA is an object-oriented, generic application framework built ontop of the interface toolkit OSF/Motif. A first version of GINA is available for Common Lisp and is presently being tested in several projects. This version includes an interface builder, which allows the development of an interface through direct graphical manipulation. A C++ version is currently under development.

babylon, a further toolbox system developed by our institute, is a mature development environment for expert systems in use at over 70 installations around the world. It offers formalisms for object-oriented, rule-based and constraint-based knowledge representation, and also interfaces to other systems, such as databases.[29] babylon is available for various platforms. It is a well suited tool for our expert system developments in the AC project.

Work on the assisting computer concept began in 1989. First results, which are reported in this paper, show that we have come closer to our goals and been able to demonstrate, at least in exemplary fashion, some of the striven for assistance properties. New methodological approaches have been found for a number of problems.[30] But on the whole, we are still in the initial phase of reaching the goals we have set. The AC project is a long-term undertaking with a planning horizon that reaches to the year 2000. Its goals are challenging and require many more years of concentrated research.

---

[26] W. Prinz, P. Penelli. Relevance of the X.500 Directory to CSCW Applications. In J. Bowers, S. Burford (eds). Studies in Computer Supported Cooperative Work. North-Holland, Amsterdam, 1991, 267-283

[27] An overview of our work in CSCW can be found in: Th. Kreifelts, H. Santo (eds.). Group Support Systems. Springer Verlag, Berlin, in press

[28] M. Spenke, C. Beilken. An Overview of GINA – The Generic Interactive Application. In D. Duce et al. (eds.). User Interface Management and Design. Proc. Workshop on UIMS and Environments (Lissabon, 4.-6.6.91) Springer Verlag, Berlin, 1991, 273-293

[29] Th. Christaller, F. di Primio, A. Voß (eds). Die KI-Werkbank Babylon. Addison-Wesley, Bonn, 1989

[30] This paper reports only on a selection of results. A complete list of publications to date in the Assisting Computer project can be requested from GMD, Institute for Applied Information Technology (F3), Sankt Augustin.

Hypertext and Structured Object Representation: A Unifying View

Hermann Kaindl

Siemens AG Österreich
Programm- und Systementwicklung

Gudrunstraße 11
A—1100 Vienna / Austria

Mikael Snaprud*

Technische Universität Wien
Inst. für Maschinen- und
Prozeßautomatisierung

Gußhausstraße 27–29
A—1040 Vienna / Austria

This paper addresses combining hypertext with knowledge representation as used in knowledge-based systems. Hypertext imposes explicit structure on text, whereas certain knowledge representation formalisms of AI are designed for structuring knowledge. We propose a way of tight integration of hypertext and structured object representation, using (AI) frames for the basic representation of hypertext nodes. Moreover, we propose to allow for the additional option of explicit representation of structure using partitions of hypertext nodes, which are realized as slots. In order to make the text more dynamic, our approach facilitates some aspects of object-oriented programming using message passing from the text in the browser.

The proposed tight integration is useful for design tasks, in particular for building knowledge-based systems. According to our experience, hypertext provides a useful intermediary representation of knowledge. Based on a level of basic hypertext functionality, we propose several features useful for supporting knowledge acquisition. As an example of our results of using this method of knowledge acquisition, we illustrate the strategic knowledge in our domain of application. In addition, the tight integration supports important aspects of software engineering and the user interface. Moreover, we discuss several advantages from a hypertext point of view. In particular, the partitions of hypertext nodes can be useful for selective inheritance of text. In summary, both AI and hypertext will benefit from such a tight integration.

1   Introduction

The basic theme of *hypertext* is the explicit structuring of *text*. There is as yet no agreement whether this is sufficient for "idea processing". However, certain fields of application are promising, for instance authoring. (E.g., the production of this paper was supported by an authoring tool based on hypertext [17].)

Independently, formalisms for structuring *knowledge* have been developed in AI, such as *frames* [23] and *semantic networks* [27]. We will subsume these approaches for knowledge representation by the notion *structured object representation* [26]. While we believe in the importance of questions of what these representation schemes exactly mean in a formal sense (see for instance [14]), we focus in this paper on integration with an informal way of representing "knowledge".

Meaningful text represents knowledge for humans, whether this text is formal or informal. However, knowledge represented as informal text is in general not operational for a machine. Significant advances in NLU may change this in the future. At today's state of the art, however, too narrow concepts of "knowledge" are prevalent in computer science (see also [9]).

There is a striking similarity of hypertext and semantic networks due to the common elements of *nodes* and *links*. Both approaches are characterized by explicit relations between chunks of knowledge

---

*The author's work is partially supported by the Austrian *Fonds zur Förderung der wissenschaftlichen Forschung* (Project No. P7857-TEC).

(represented formally or informally). In addition, also the links represent important knowledge themselves. "Typed" links even emphasize this. Hence we can support the view that in hypertext this amounts to a "semi-formal" representation of knowledge.

Moreover, we propose to allow for the additional option of explicit representation of structure "inside" of hypertext nodes. While ordinary paragraphs can serve this purpose as they do in conventional linear text, our *partitions* are explicitly represented and support machine processing. *Frames* allow for such a representation via *slots*, much as they do for representing the internal structure of nodes in a semantic network.

First, we present a review of previous work. Then, we propose a way of tight integration between hypertext and structured object representation. Thereafter, we show its usefulness for knowledge acquisition, (software) design and maintenance of knowledge-based systems. Moreover, this integration may also improve the user interface of such systems. Then we point to advantages from the hypertext point of view. Finally, we conclude that both hypertext and AI will benefit from a tight integration as proposed here.

2 Previous Work

Often the relationship between hypertext and semantic networks has been noted (see e.g. [4]). Most of the more concrete work on AI and hypertext dealt with the support of knowledge acquisition, since hypertext appears to provide a useful means of human-computer interaction for this purpose. Some approaches are based on existing hypertext tools such as *Notecards* [9] or *HyperCard* [28]. A reason for using hypertext before writing for instance rules is to avoid deciding for a *tool* before knowledge acquisition [29]. While this issue is less important when using a hybrid tool, still the decision for a *formalism* before knowledge acquisition is to be avoided [34]. Unfortunately, the phenomenon of premature structuring is also known in hypertext itself.

In our opinion, it is more promising to integrate hypertext in a frame-based environment (see also [6] and [13]). Again, an important reason is the support of knowledge acquisition, for instance by a hypertext system implemented in *Smalltalk* [15]. Another goal is the representation of manager's mental models in order to support their decision making [3]. While in this approach nodes are represented by *Smalltalk* frames, this is not the case in all implementations [19]. Here frames are only used for higher level structuring in the sense of composition of nodes, which can be easily done in our system, too.

In addition, there are approaches of loosely combining a hypertext system with a knowledge-based system or environment (for instance *HyperCard* and CLIPS [30]). *HyperCard* has also been combined with BABYLON and moreover with the knowledge acquisition tool KSS0 into one environment named *Hyper-KSE* [22]. Hypertext is used here for explanations, which is the primary goal of the approach described in [8] and [7]. The "code inspection tutor" reported in [32] uses AI for simulation and utilizes hypertext descriptions about the software to be inspected for training purposes.

There are also interesting software engineering aspects of a combination. One is the support for traditional software engineering (see [10] and [2]). Moreover, we argue that the development and maintenance of knowledge-based systems themselves can benefit as well, especially when the knowledge bases become large. Therefore, *Cyc's* [21] very large knowledge base would probably be easier to handle and read if the original (natural language) text of the encyclopedia and the notes on the additional knowledge incorporated would be *within* the knowledge base.

3 Proposed Way of Tight Integration

We have implemented our approach by use of a hybrid tool (KEE), which is based on structured object representation as the central paradigm. In a strict sense, however, only *frame-based representation* is necessary for implementing the key features of this approach. Since the term "frame" is also often used in the context of hypertext, we note that it is meant in this paper in the sense of [23] and [14]. Our representation of hypertext is based on such frames, much the same way as other (formal) knowledge representation paradigms are often based on it, i.e. rules, methods, active values, etc.

As a more distinctive feature, we allow for explicit *partitioning* of the hypertext nodes, which is implemented using slots. The records implementing the modules in the *Document Examiner* [33] are similarly composed of so-called fields. While these are mainly used to represent standard information like name or version number to be used by the editor and by other supporting software, our emphasis lies on partitioning the textual content by the user.

3.1   A dual view of the overall representation

First of all, we think that an epistemological view of the approach may be useful. Fig. 1 shows an example knowledge base which is organized as a "hypertext space". It is divided into two disjoint "halfspaces". One contains pure hypertext nodes, the other "associated" objects. The example is the prototypical implementation of hypertext itself. So, the latter represent the operational knowledge of this implementation, while the former document it.

The graphic only shows the hierarchical links in the inheritance lattice. Of course, there are also other links between nodes containing text, and the objects containing machine interpretable representations may be related as necessary. The latter represent relationships *between* the two halfspaces. From the hypertext view, these are just special "typed" links. All nodes are either in one or in the other halfspace, more precisely, they are defined to be. In order to allow for convenient navigation—especially between the two halfspaces—we use a kind of bi-directional links. The explicitly given link in the text of node F points *from F to* the referenced node T. Its inverse points from T to F, and it is maintained automatically. Moreover, we also allow for links *into* nodes. Our feature of explicit partitioning of hypertext nodes supports this, and in effect these links point to *slots*.

This is the view of hypertext, the *dual* one is that of a semantic network. The former emphasizes nodes containing text, which includes "special" nodes with formal knowledge representation. The latter view focuses on objects with certain relationships, of which links between text are just a special case.

3.2   Basic representation of hypertext nodes

The basic element in our approach is an (AI) frame. While this is not completely novel (see [19], [15] and [3]), none of the descriptions in the literature is very explicit (with the exception of [6], where a different approach than ours is described). Moreover, while frames are used for higher level structuring in the approach presented in [19], the hypertext nodes are *not* represented as frames there.

In our approach, a hypertext node is represented as an (AI) frame. Text is stored in a slot, which is originally inherited from HT.NODES. This text contains links to other nodes (in the hypertext view). These are represented in the same way as any reference to another frame in the basic system (KEE). However, the links are indirectly stored within the frame, i.e. the real reference is stored in a specific slot, and only this is referred to from the text. The main reasons for chosing this internal representation are related to the maintenance of the objects and their names, in particular to renaming and deletion.

The *partitions* of a hypertext node are also realized using slots. This approach is especially useful for our current main goal, using hypertext as intermediary representation in the process of knowledge acquisition for a frame-based system.

Although it would be easy to provide each frame in the system with a slot for representing text (via inheritance), we decided not to have such text in the frames containing formal knowledge representation. It is only possible to have hypertext links with such frames. The main reason is that we want to have a clear separation between the two halfspaces. Generally, such a representation using frames offers all the possibilities to easily implement more sophisticated hypertext concepts, for instance composite nodes.

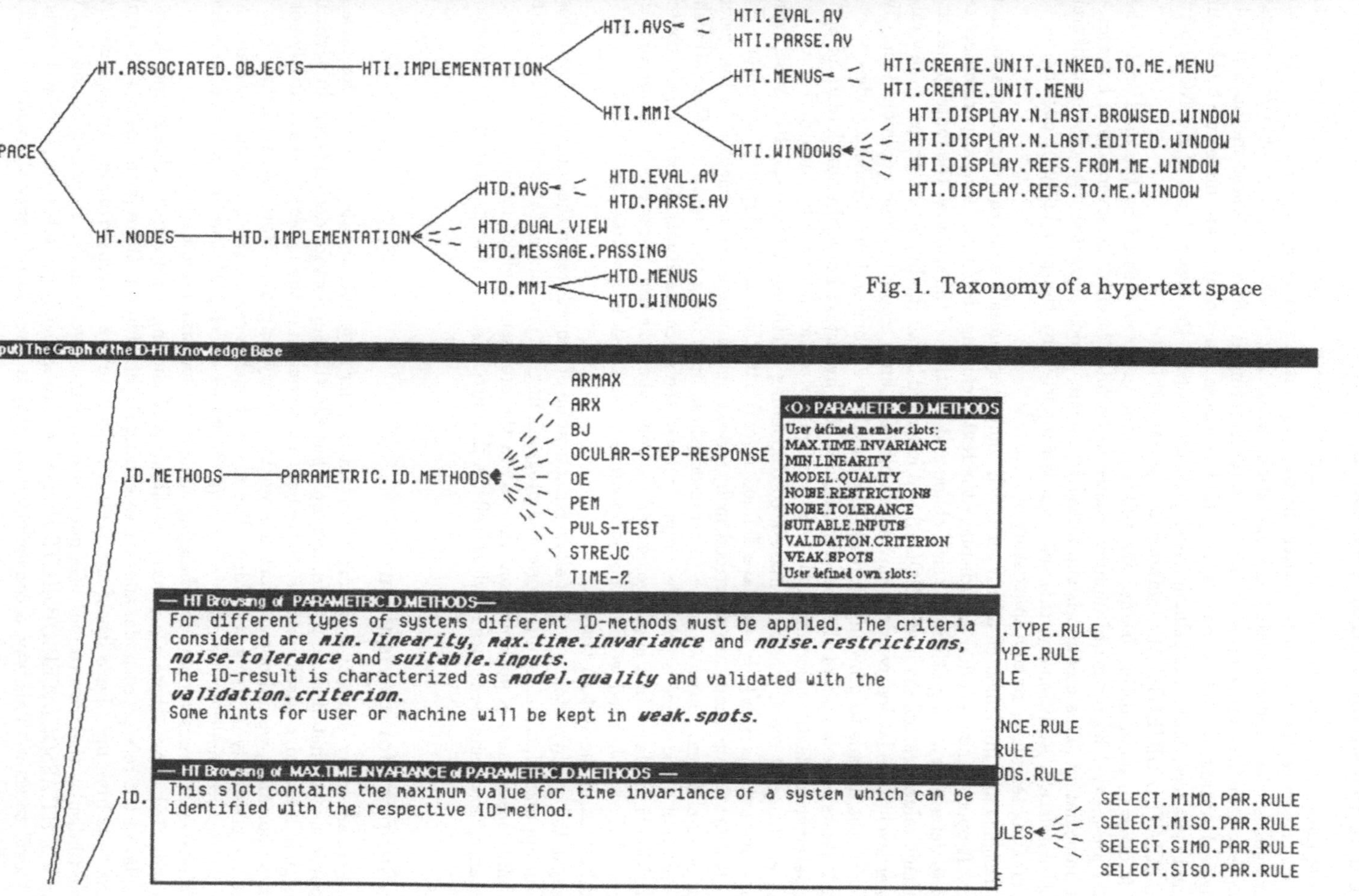

Fig. 1. Taxonomy of a hypertext space

Fig. 2. Example of node partitioning

3.3 Basic operations on hypertext nodes

One of the most important issues for selecting and evaluating a representation is its use. In particular, our chosen representation facilitates the basic operations for entering, editing and browsing hypertext nodes. We implemented these operations according to the paradigm of *object-oriented programming*, attaching procedures to the frame representing HT.SPACE. These methods (e.g. for browsing and editing) as well as data specifying the mouse functionality are inherited by the subclasses and instances. Since the behavior is slightly different for the descendants of HT.NODES and HT.ASSOCIATED.OBJECTS, the methods are specialized there.

If references to non-existing frames are added by the user (as checked by the used tool), then *templates* are created by means of dummy frames to be filled later. The inverse link, however, is entered immediately. This creation is supported by menus, which allow the user to select different kinds of templates. Additionally, this selection is supported by the possibility of clicking on the lattice, creating templates related to existing objects.

We designed and implemented a browser which completely hides the internal representation from the user. It opens a new window and displays the text including the links. Several parameters can be used to determine among others the size, shape and location of the window, the fonts (type, size) etc. Default values are defined in HT.NODES and inherited by all the hypertext nodes. A new value at a lower level in the lattice overrides such a default. The links are highlighted and mouse-sensitive, and clicking them leads to browsing, editing, or even other actions on the referenced node.

Fig. 2 shows an example of the use of partitions of a hypertext node. In our domain of application, parametric identification methods can be characterized for instance by their maximum time invariance. Hence, it seems useful to make a corresponding partition of the respective node, which describes this aspect. Similarly, we have defined several partitions as displayed in a window. The actual identification methods are described in hypertext nodes which are connected to the generic description as children. Since we chose to represent these links using the "instance-of" relationship of the used tool, inheritance is possible, in particular of the given partitions. Currently, the content of a partition is displayed in a newly generated window, when the user clicks on the mouse-sensitive area around the emphasized words. Another possibility we consider is a treatment analogous to the expand buttons of the system *Guide*.

Many of today's hypertext systems allow for activation of procedures in the course of traversing a link. Our approach facilitates object-oriented programming by procedural attachment to hypertext nodes. *Message passing* is possible from the text in the browser, in effect making it "active text". For instance, text could be returned which reflects the current status of some part of the knowledge base.

3.4 Support for navigation

While there are many issues of designing hypertext in order to facilitate *navigation* (see for instance [24]), our focus was first of all on providing simple but effective support for design tasks, in particular the design of knowledge-based systems. Since here active search in the hypertext was initially not of primary importance, we did not support this yet by a query language. However, we found it useful to have the possibility of string searching. The scope of such a search can be specified within parts of the hierarchy of nodes or by other criteria (for instance chosing all the nodes linked to a given one). Moreover, there is support for changing strings and locating node names.

As indicated above, there are several possibilities of clicking a reference. One simply leads to the display of the referenced node, another to editing it. In addition, there is the option to display only the "refs from me", i.e. a list of the explicit links from the referenced node. Analogously, it is possible to display the "refs to me" of a node, utilizing the inverse links. Browsing of nodes in the halfspace of HT.ASSOCIATED.OBJECTS always leads to a display of "refs to me" since there is no other "text" to show. This way, a convenient possibility is given to reference the nodes describing such an object.

Two *history lists* keep track of browsed and edited nodes, respectively. They allow for the usual operation of *backtrack*, as well as the more advanced operation called *backjump* in the hypertext information system HIS [16] (in analogy to the procedure with this name proposed by Gaschnig [11] for *constraint satisfaction*, and as used e.g. in [35].) The latter operation allows to jump back directly to any node on the currently visited path in hyperspace. Both these lists can be used for editing, browsing, and displaying the "refs to me" and the "refs from me" of the stored entries.

While we unfortunately have different interfaces for editing and browsing, we can mix these actions arbitrarily. E.g., it is immediately possible to edit a node referenced from the browser, and even the currently browsed node. (Several hypertext systems today have different programs for these operations, which poses certain restrictions on their use.) We think that this freedom of use is important for supporting *design* activities.

4 Usefulness for Knowledge-Based Systems

Such marked design phases like that in conventional software engineering may neither be useful nor necessary in the process of building a knowledge-based (expert) system. However, the immediate representation of just acquired knowledge in a fully formalized way sometimes leads to epistemologically bad representations. Hence, whenever it is not completely clear how to represent something appropriately, structured text may first of all serve as a means for "semi-formal" representation. Once having represented this chunk of knowledge formally, it is immediately connected to the text in our approach. This process leads then directly to a useful documentation of the knowledge bases. Although not every detail of this documentation will be of interest to the user of the resulting knowledge-based system, selected parts of it may be directly used for explanations.

4.1 Knowledge acquisition

Major part of the existing literature on AI and hypertext deals with the support of knowledge acquisition (see [9], [34], [15], [29] and [22]). In fact, it looks very appealing to have the possibility to represent the knowledge informally first, since the experts provide it also in such a form. This way the very difficult process of modeling can be done more consciously, based on the explicit representation as hypertext. Still, much work remains to find appropriate methods for actually doing it right.

We propose to use a tight integration of hypertext with frame-based representation for supporting knowledge acquisition. The semi-formal way of knowledge representation in hypertext may serve as a mediating representation to be used for coping with the representation mismatch, which has been identified as a major issue of knowledge acquisition by Gruber [12]. This way, experts can become more independent of knowledge engineers, since they can represent their knowledge informally first as linear text and formalize it step by step introducing hypertext links and slots of text. Only then, together with a knowledge engineer, this knowledge is made operational for the machine. We have experimented with this approach in the domain of modeling and *identification* of systems.

Similar to a "rhetoric" for authoring hypertext as intended for readers [20], rules for designers using hypertext will have to be formulated. In the system gIBIS [5] special links are used for supporting cooperative work. We have experimented with *special nodes* for use in knowledge acquisition, such as WHY, HOW, TO.DO, DIARY, etc. In this respect, we make heavy use of the "refs to me". For instance, the TO.DO node serves as an "agenda". We can write the reference to this node into some of the hypertext nodes. Clicking TO.DO for the "refs to me" lists all these nodes. Analogous treatment of WHY leads to the functionality of "question cards" in [15]. However, our implementation appears to be better due to the use of the inverse links.

Also inheritance can be useful in such a context. For instance, newly created nodes in a certain part of the hierarchy can immediately inherit a reference to TO.DO in their text slot. In effect, we have created a level of knowledge acquisition functionality above the basic hypertext functionality.

Now let us briefly sketch how we are actually *doing* knowledge acquisition in this environment. First, we create and edit hypertext nodes, describing the concepts to be represented and the issues involved. Simultaneously the system helps to create templates for not yet existing objects, which can be either hypertext nodes or nodes in the halfspace of HT.ASSOCIATED.OBJECTS. Then these templates are filled with informal text or knowledge represented in some formal language, respectively. Meanwhile some related idea may have come to mind which is immediately described in a hypertext node, etc.

From this procedure many useful ideas and partially also their formal representation should arise. However, they still may be unordered or only slightly ordered. Hence, there should be a phase of ordering the concepts and their realization, which may lead to a *taxonomy*.

Taxonomies play a major role in object-oriented programming and for structuring knowledge bases. Hierarchies in general are considered a backbone of hypertext in order to facilitate navigation. Organizing a hypertext "knowledge base" around a taxonomy of the stored concepts has proven useful in HIS [16]. Hence, we think that in an integrated environment hierarchical structuring is at least as useful. While it is possible to define special types of hierarchical links for hypertext nodes, we chose to directly use the *subclass/superclass* and *instance* relationships as supported by the used tool for this purpose. This way the built-in mechanism for inheritance can be used for free.

When the internal structure of a concept is becoming more and more clear, it can be conveniently represented first using partitions of the corresponding hypertext node, which are implemented by slots. When the concrete formal representation is to be done, this structure can be transferred to the corresponding frames in the other halfspace (supported by the system). This leads to templates of slots, which are filled then with operational knowledge. Hence, also the internal structure of objects can be transferred to the "operational" halfspace.

An example of our results of using this method of knowledge acquisition is illustrated in Fig. 3. It shows the data flow and control flow of *system identification*. This version of the so-called identification loop is more elaborated than any such representation we found in the corresponding literature. In particular, we emphasize the explicit distinction between control flow and data flow using typed links in our hypertext representation. According to our knowledge acquisition methodology we developed it by first identifying steps (shown in boxes) and data/knowledge units (shown in circles), and representing them using hypertext nodes. Then they were described using informal text which originates partially from books and partially from our own considerations and discussions with an expert. Relations between these nodes were represented explicitly by use of typed hypertext links, and the internal structure of the textual descriptions was represented by partitions. The external and the internal structure were mapped then to the operational halfspace.

The resulting frames and slots can be viewed as a declarative representation of *strategic* (control) knowledge. A rather simple interpreter uses it for driving the identification task. Uniformly, the frames representing a step have slots containing rule classes to by activated and messages to be passed. The interpreter just initiates these in the given order, taking into account also some given conditions.

An interesting point is that on the global level there are several options to return to a previous step. (Hence, this can be viewed as an *indeterministic algorithm*.) In this domain it is a delicate problem to determine the step to return to. However, the following meta-principle representing *abstract control knowledge* can help. Whenever some subsequent step does not achieve satisfying results, it must propose some change in the current assumptions of the overall procedure. Since each step has some input associated with it, the step to return to is identified as the nearest preceding one whose input data are affected by this change.

Based on the central philosophy of tightly integrating hypertext and knowledge-based systems, we can approach a powerful methodology for knowledge acquisition. The enhancements of special nodes and links for this purpose can be seen as steps towards an advanced KA tool.

4.2 Support for (software) engineering the knowledge-based system

Hypertext also has high potential to support software engineering (see [1] and [10]). For the approach of additionally using AI methods, the notion HAISE was coined in [2]. Since knowledge-based systems are typically software, the question is whether and how these approaches can also support the development of such systems.

In fact, the process of knowledge acquisition sketched above adds a flavor of top-down design to the more usual bottom-up procedure of building knowledge-based systems. However, it is *not* in accordance with the pure cascade model of traditional software design. We believe that there should be a balance between top-down and bottom-up processing, depending on the degree of prior understanding of the domain concepts. Most of the advantages of using hypertext for developing

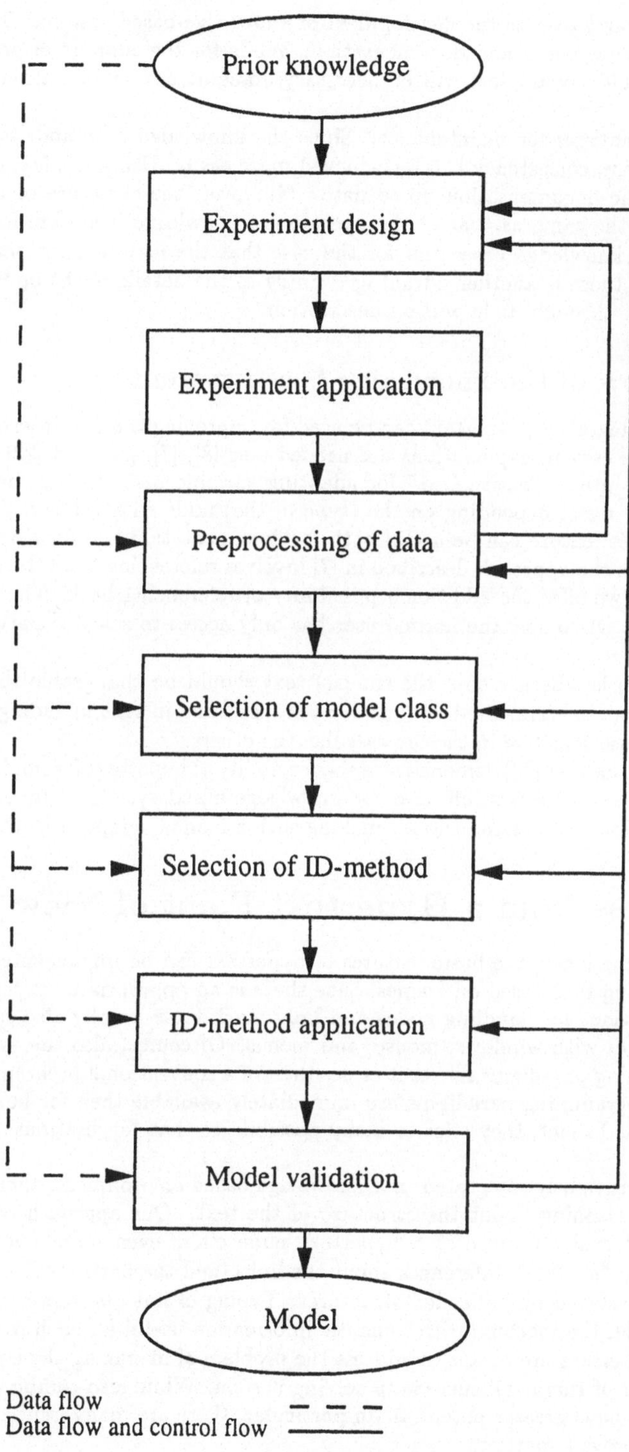

Fig. 3. Control and data flow of system identification

traditional software carry over to the development of knowledge-based systems. These are primarily related to project management and documentation. While for the support of project management in our environment additional effort will be necessary, integrated documentation is gained more or less for free.

This implies advantages for maintenance. Since the knowledge base and its documentation is available in *one* system, consistency can be achieved more easily. Using the feature of "active text" also helps keeping the documentation up to date. Moreover, the structure of the documentation can be more or less the same as that of the operational knowledge base (see for instance Fig. 1). Especially for larger knowledge bases and for the case that the maintenance personnel is different from the developers, there is another advantage. Entry to the details of the operational knowledge representation can be through its hypertext description.

4.3   User's view of the knowledge-based system

Also without tight integration, hypertext can be used for improving the user interface of a knowledge-based system in case certain explanations are needed (see [8], [7], [30] and [22]). In addition, our tight integration can utilize "active text" for adapting variable parts to the current situation. Its behavior can also be made depending on the (type of the) node where it is activated from, and it can be inherited. This feature can be useful both for documentation and for help text.

While for instance the approach described in [7] involves referencing from the (formal) knowledge base into hypertext, we offer the additional possibility of referencing back. The bi-directional links support this feature. Of course, the normal user has only access to selected parts of the knowledge base.

An open question is whether only the (linear) text should be changeable this way, or also the links. For instance, we experimented with active text resulting in text including links. These links are immediately mouse-sensitive in the browser like the others.

The *Document Examiner* [33] demonstrates the feasibility of hypertext for implementing electronic manuals. So this should be possible also for knowledge-based systems. In particular, the tight integration offers additional possibilities for making such a manual adaptive to the current situation.

5   Usefulness from a Hypertext Point of View

According to our experience, the basic features of hypertext can be implemented conveniently in a knowledge engineering tool based on frames, once there is an appropriate concept available. While this may appear obvious for handling nodes and links, such tools usually also support building advanced user interfaces with windows, mouse, and menus. Of course, also the availability of several advanced programming paradigms makes it easier than in a conventional programming environment. Moreover, these programming paradigms are immediately available then for building advanced hypertext applications. In fact, they offer so many possibilities that "stylisations" may be useful (see [18]).

Once hypertext is tightly integrated in a knowledge-based environment, there is great potential for actively doing reasoning about the structure of the text. Our approach of explicit partitions representing the internal structure of a hypertext node offers even more possibilites. Since the inference engines are "for free", inferences about the links (and the partitions) can be made, instead of passively being enslaved by pre-coded structures. Typing of links becomes even more important here, since it provides the machine with semantic information useful for such reasoning.

Both AI and hypertext are means to address the problem of managing the complexity of modern society [25]. Neither of them will succeed in solving it soon. While also combinations probably will not, they appear to have greater potential. In particular, there are many issues where AI reasoning capabilities can improve hypertext.

Still, navigation is a central issue in hypertext. One possibility to address it is given by including an AI monitoring system which supports the navigation for novices [25]. This can be seen as a method for providing flexible *guided tours*. Other desirable capabilities of hypertext systems potentially providable by use of AI technology are sketched in [31]. For instance, simple deductive inference can conclude a grandparent relation from parent relations. Much more difficult are the issues of identifying missing information or of keeping consistency when new facts are entered. Unless there is an excellent NLU machinery involved or formal descriptions of a node's contents are added, only the information of the links (and partitions) can be used for these tasks. Inductive reasoning may be useful for generalizations based upon what already exists. This may lead to changes of the hypertext structure and should probably be supervised by a human "oracle".

While the realization of such capabilities will be difficult also within a knowledge engineering environment, it will be easier than by conventional means. In particular, we believe that a tight integration like the one proposed in this paper will be useful. Our "active text" leading to message passing from the text appears to provide an adequate entry to the advanced capabilities of AI systems.

Our approach of explicit partitioning of nodes allows for utilizing inheritance of text in new ways. In specifiying which partitions are to be inherited, a clean method exists for controlling this process.

6 Conclusion

In this paper we addressed the issue of combining hypertext with structured object representation for use in knowledge-based systems. Also more general design tasks can be supported this way. The basic features of hypertext can be implemented conveniently in a frame-based environment, using our concept of tight integration. Of course, for a full-fledged hypertext tool more effort has to be spent. Nevertheless, the availability of several programming paradigms facilitates such an implementation. It is also of great help that there is usually strong support for graphics in such environments.

In general, the more structure is explicitly represented, the more can be automatically reasoned about. Partitioning of hypertext nodes is a possibility for representing the *internal* structure.

Primarily, based on a level of basic hypertext functionality support for knowledge acquisition suggests itself. According to our experience, however, it is very important to efficiently manipulate nodes for this purpose. For this reason, our focus related to human-computer interaction was on providing menus and clicking options to achieve this goal. Moreover, the machine itself must be reponsible for keeping links and their inverse consistent. From the way of doing knowledge acquisition we propose, documentation results as a "side effect". For keeping it consistent we utilise "active text". If the link structure is changed this way, in effect *dynamic* hypertext arises. All this is also useful for end user support.

While it is cheaper and faster to combine existing tools for hypertext and knowledge engineering, only such a tight integration as the one we proposed can take full advantage of both worlds. Inversely, *both* hypertext and AI will benefit from this integration.

References

[1] J. Bigelow. Hypertext and CASE. *IEEE Software*, 23–27, March 1988.

[2] P. Carando. Shadow: Fusing hypertext with AI. *IEEE Expert*, 4(4):65–78, 1989.

[3] D. A. Carlson and S. Ram. HyperIntelligence: The next frontier. *Communications of the ACM*, 33(3):311–321, March 1990.

[4] G. H. Collier. Thoth-II: Hypertext with explicit semantics. In *Proceedings of Hypertext '87*, pages 269–289, ACM, Chapel Hill, NC, November 1987.

[5] J. Conklin and M. L. Begeman. gIBIS: A hypertext tool for exploratory policy discussion. *ACM Transactions on Office Information Systems*, 6(4):303–331, October 1988.

[6] R. Fikes. Integrating hypertext and frame-based domain models. In *Proceedings of the AAAI-88 Workshop on AI and Hypertext: Issues and Directions*, AAAI, 1988.

[7] G. Fischer, A. C. Lemke, and R. McCall. Towards a system architecture supporting contextualized learning. In *Proceedings of the Eighth National Conference on Artificial Intelligence*, pages 420–425, AAAI, AAAI Press/The MIT Press, Boston, MA, July/August 1990.

[8] G. Fischer, R. McCall, and A. Morch. JANUS: Integrating hypertext with a knowledge-based design environment. In *Proceedings of Hypertext'89*, pages 105–117, ACM, Pittsburgh, PA, November 1989.

[9] B. R. Gaines and M. Sharp. A knowledge acquisition extension to NoteCards. In *Proceedings of the First European Workshop on Knowledge Acquisition for Knowledge-Based Systems*, Reading, MA, September 1987.

[10] P. K. Garg and W. Scacchi. ISHYS: Designing an intelligent software hypertext system. *IEEE Expert*, 4(3):52–63, 1989.

[11] J. Gaschnig. *Performance measurement and analysis of certain search algorithms*. PhD thesis, Carnegie-Mellon University, Pittsburgh, PA, 1979. Available as Tech. Rept. CMU-CS-79-124.

[12] T. R. Gruber. Automated knowledge acquisition for strategic knowledge. *Machine Learning*, 4:293–336, 1989.

[13] F. G. Halasz. Reflections on NoteCards: Seven issues for the next generation of hypermedia systems. *Communications of the ACM*, 31(7):836–852, 1988.

[14] P. J. Hayes. The logic of frames. In D. Metzing, editor, *Frame Conceptions and Text Understanding*, pages 46–61, de Gruyter, 1979.

[15] M. Hofmann, U. Schreiweis, and H. Langendörfer. An integrated approach of knowledge acquisition by the hypertext system CONCORDE. In *Proceedings of the European Conference on Hypertext (ECHT-90)—Hypertext: Concepts, Systems, and Applications*, pages 166–179, Paris, 1990.

[16] H. Kaindl and H. G. Ziegeler. HIS—An information system about hypertext on hypertext. 1991. Submitted for publication.

[17] H. Kaindl and H. G. Ziegeler. HyperAuthor—An authoring tool based on hypertext. In H. Maurer, editor, *Proceedings of Hypertext/Hypermedia'91*, pages 156–163, Graz, Austria, May 1991.

[18] H. Kaindl and H. G. Ziegeler. Reasoning types and AI programming paradigms. In *Proceedings of the Third International Conference on Software Engineering and Knowledge Engineering*, Skokie, IL, June 1991. To appear.

[19] T.-T. Koh, P. L. Loo, and T.-S. Chua. On the design of a frame-based hypermedia system. In R. McAleese and C. Green, editors, *Hypertext: State of the Art*, chapter 17, pages 154–165, Intellect, Oxford, England, 1990.

[20] G. P. Landow. The rhetoric of hypertext: Some rules for authors. *Journal of Computing in Higher Education*, 1(1):39–64, Spring 1989.

[21] D. B. Lenat, R. V. Guha, K. Pittman, D. Pratt, and M. Shepherd. Cyc: Toward programs with common sense. *Communications of the ACM*, 33(8):30–49, August 1990.

[22] M. Linster and B. Gaines. *Supporting Acquisition and Interpretation of Knowledge in a Hypermedia Environment*. Arbeitspapiere der GMD 455, Subreihe Künstliche Intelligenz 6, Gesellschaft für Mathematik und Datenverarbeitung, St. Augustin, Germany, July 1990.

[23] M. Minsky. A framework for representing knowledge. In P. Winston, editor, *The Psychology of Computer Vision*, pages 211–277, McGraw-Hill, New York, 1975.

[24] J. Nielsen. The art of navigating through hypertext. *Communications of the ACM*, 33(3):296–310, 1990.

[25] J. Nielsen. *Hypertext and Hypermedia*. Academic Press, San Diego, CA, 1990.

[26] N. Nilsson. *Principles of Artificial Intelligence*. Tioga, Palo Alto, CA, 1980.

[27] M. R. Quillian. Semantic memory. In M. Minsky, editor, *Semantic Information Processing*, chapter 4, pages 216–270, The MIT Press, Cambridge, MA, 1968.

[28] J. A. Rantanen. Hypermedia in knowledge acquisition and specification of user interface for KBS: An approach and a case study. *Knowledge Acquisition*, 2:259–278, 1990.

[29] D. Rochowiak. A tool for the management of document driven knowledge acquisition. In *Proceedings of the AAAI-90 Workshop on Knowledge Acquisition: Practical Tools and Techniques*, AAAI, Boston, MA, July 1990.

[30] D. Rochowiak, B. Ragsdell, and L. Wurzelbacher. An integrated hypertext and rule based system for explanation. In *Proceedings of the Expert Systems'89*, pages 345–352, 1989.

[31] B. Shneiderman and G. Kearsley. *Hypertext Hands-On! An Introduction to a New Way of Organizing and Accessing Information.* Addison-Wesley, 1989.

[32] S. M. Stevens. Intelligent interactive video simulation of a code inspection. *Communications of the ACM*, 31(7):832–843, July 1989.

[33] J. H. Walker. Document Examiner: Delivery interface for hypertext documents. In *Proceedings of Hypertext'87*, pages 307–323, ACM, Chapel Hill, NC, November 1987.

[34] T. L. Wells. Hypertext as a means for knowledge acquisition. *SIGART Newsletter*, (108):136–138, April 1989.

[35] H. G. Ziegeler and H. Kaindl. A cyclic pattern resulting from a constraint satisfaction search. In *Proceedings of the Seventh IEEE Conference on Artificial Intelligence Applications (CAIA-91)*, pages 373–344, IEEE, Miami Beach, FL, February 1991. An earlier version has been presented at the *AAAI-90 Workshop on Constraint Directed Reasoning*, Boston, MA, July 1990.

Constraint-basierte Verarbeitung graphischen Wissens *

Winfried Graf und Wolfgang Maaß
Deutsches Forschungszentrum für Künstliche Intelligenz (DFKI)
Stuhlsatzenhausweg 3
W-6600 Saarbrücken 11
e-mail: graf@dfki.uni-sb.de

Zusammenfassung

Bei der Entwicklung neuerer intelligenter Benutzerschnittstellen, die wie im Beispiel des multimodalen Präsentationssystems WIP natürliche Sprache und Graphik kombinieren, spielt insbesondere die wissensbasierte Gestaltung des Layouts multimodaler Dokumente eine wichtige Rolle. Am Beispiel des Layout-Managers in WIP soll gezeigt werden, wie aufgrund der von einem Präsentationsplaner spezifizierten semantischen und pragmatischen Relationen, die von den media-spezifischen Generatoren erzeugten Graphik- und Textfragmente in einem Dokument automatisch arrangiert werden können. Dabei wird das Layoutproblem als Constraint-Satisfaction-Problem behandelt. Es wird hier gezeigt, wie der Constraint-Ansatz sowohl zur Repräsentation von graphischem Wissen, als auch zur Berechnung der Plazierung der Layoutobjekte auf einem Design-Grid verwendet werden kann. So werden semantische Kohärenzrelationen wie etwa *'sequence'* oder *'contrast'* durch entsprechende Design-Constraints reflektiert, die perzeptuelle Kriterien (Alignierung, Gruppierung, Symmetrie, etc.) spezifizieren. Zur Realisierung wird in WIP ein mehrschichtiger inkrementeller Constraint-Solver mit lokaler Propagierung verwendet, der es erlaubt, Constraints dynamisch zu generieren.

1 Einleitung

Das Design bildet den zentralen Punkt bei vielen komplexen menschlichen Tätigkeiten, wie z.B. auch der Gestaltung des Layouts von multimodalen Präsentationen. Dabei wollen wir in dieser Arbeit unter dem Design von Dokumenten die Bestimmung einer adäquaten äußeren Form verstehen, die gewünschten ästhetischen Charakteristika genügt und darüberhinaus gewisse funktionale Anforderungen erfüllt.

Psychologische Untersuchungen haben gezeigt, daß eine klare und logische Gestaltung der Form einer Präsentation ihre *Effizienz* und *Expressivität*, d.h. Lesbarkeit, Verständlichkeit und Glaubwürdigkeit, erheblich fördern. Auf der Graphikseite unterscheiden wir nach [33] *funktionales* vs. *künstlerisches* Layout. Wir wollen uns bei den nachfolgenden Betrachtungen ausschließlich auf das beim Entwurf von Dokumenten relevante funktionale Layout konzentrieren. Hier steht insbesondere die Übermittlung des Inhalts im Vordergrund, während beim künstlerischen Layout im wesentlichen die äußere Form der Darstellung dominiert. Ein gutes funktionales Layout zeichnet sich dabei vor allem durch seinen transparenten, sachlichen, funktionalen und ästhetischen Charakter aus (vgl. [8]).

Der menschliche Designer steht heute unter dem ständigen Druck der Erhöhung der Produktivität durch immer innovativere und effizientere Produkte und erhofft sich deshalb durch den Einsatz von neuen wissensbasierten Techniken eine Entlastung. Die meisten der bisherigen Systeme zur Automatisierung des graphischen Designs bezogen sich jedoch im wesentlichen auf die Unterstützung

---

*Die vorliegende Arbeit entstand im Rahmen des vom BMFT unter dem Förderkennzeichen ITW 8901 8 geförderten Projektes WIP (Wissensbasierte Informationspräsentation)

von Routine-Designaufgaben, für die bereits eine Vielzahl von Designheuristiken bekannt war und die somit eine effektive Kontrolle des Designraums ermöglichten. In letzter Zeit rückten dann Systeme zum konzeptionellen Design stärker in den Vordergrund. Die überwiegende Mehrheit dieser Systeme versteht dabei Design als Kombinatorikproblem in einem diskreten Suchraum (vgl. auch [29]).

Wir wollen im weiteren das als Such- oder Optimierungsproblem vorliegende Layoutproblem als Constraint-Satisfaction-Problem (*CSP*) formulieren und mittels Konsistenztechniken lösen. Dabei werden wir zeigen, daß sich hier Constraint-Formalismen sehr gut sowohl zur deklarativen Wissensrepräsentation als auch als Berechnungsmodell und effiziente Kontrollstrategie eignen. Dieser modellbasierte Ansatz ermöglicht es, sich im Gegensatz zu bisherigen regel-basierten Ansätzen, durch die Einbeziehung von strukturellem Wissen über den Layoutprozeß, auf einige wenige Heuristiken in Form von kompiliertem Wissen zu beschränken. Dadurch kann graphisches Wissen unabhängig von domänespezifischen Designstrategien verarbeitet werden. Wir werden insbesondere zeigen, wie sich semantische Zusammenhänge in multimodalen Dokumenten in graphische *Gestaltprinzipien* (vgl. z.B. [3]) geeignet abbilden lassen.

Im Bereich der intelligenten Benutzerschnittstellen besteht derzeit, bedingt durch die wachsende Komplexität der von wissensbasierten Anwendungssystemen zu übermittelnden Information, ein zunehmender Bedarf an Werkzeugen zur flexiblen und effizienten Informationspräsentation, deren Layout in Abhängigkeit des Benutzers und der Situation variiert. Ziel dieser Arbeit ist es, am Beispiel des für das multimodale Präsentationssystem WIP (vgl. [38, 39]) entwickelten Layout-Managers, einen neuen constraint-basierten Formalismus zur Verarbeitung von designrelevantem graphischen Wissen vorzustellen.

2 Stand der Forschung

Das Problem der Bestimmung eines ästhetisch optimalen Layouts eines multimodalen Dokumentes unter vorgegebenen Randbedingungen, wie etwa Platzrestriktionen, Ausgabemedium, Benutzer, etc. ist NP-vollständig (vgl. [5]).

Bisherige Arbeiten im Bereich der graphischen Benutzerschnittstellen bezogen sich in erster Linie auf die Entwicklung von interaktiven 3D-Graphikeditoren. Hierbei wurde dem Benutzer eine Fülle an Graphiktechniken angeboten, die es ihm erlauben sollte, das Design effizienter als mit konventionellen Methoden zu gestalten. Da der Benutzer jedoch in der Regel nicht über das Wissen eines erfahrenen Graphik-Designers verfügt, konnte er die Möglichkeiten solcher Systeme nur schwer ausschöpfen. Außerdem standen ihm zumeist nur sehr rudimentäre Mittel zur Layoutunterstützung zur Verfügung.

In späteren Ansätzen wurde dann eine regel-basierte Unterstützung des Benutzers verfolgt. Da diese Systeme jedoch nur die zu präsentierende Information betrachten, nicht aber das Benutzerspektrum, die Präsentationssituation oder Zeitaspekte, untersuchen aktuelle Ansätze die automatische Planung des Inhalts und der Form von graphischen Präsentationen (vgl. insb. die Systeme *VIEW* [14], *APT* [21] und *APEX/IBIS* [10, 32]). Ein erster Ansatz zum automatischen Layout von Bildschirmpräsentationen ist das von Feiner entwickelte System *GRIDS* [11]. Hier wird jedoch die Generierung der Form unabhängig von der Planung des Inhalts behandelt.

Neben rein graphischen Präsentationen erfährt das automatische Design von multimodalen Präsentationen in jüngster Zeit zunehmende Aufmerksamkeit innerhalb der KI-Forschung, da in vielen Situationen eine einfache und effiziente Informationspräsentation nur durch eine Kombination verschiedener Kommunikationsmodi, wie z.B. Text, Graphik, Animation und Gestik, möglich ist. In vielen Anwendungen sind häufig sehr heterogene Arten von Information, wie z.B. räumliche Lokationen, kausale und zeitliche Beziehungen, Intentionen, konditionale Aktionen oder disjunktive Alternativen, zu übermitteln (vgl. [4]). Hierbei spielt dann insbesondere die koordinierte Generierung solcher multimodaler Präsentationen eine wichtige Rolle, die eine parallele Verwendung der verschiedenen Modi unter Ausnutzung ihrer individuellen Stärken erlaubt. Konkurrierende Ansätze bilden derzeit die Systeme *COMET* [12], *FN/ANDD* [25, 24], *SAGE* [31] und *WIP* [38, 39] sowie die Arbeiten von Hovy et al. am ISI [2].

Die Automatisierung des geometrischen Layouts zählt zu den frühesten Anwendungsfeldern für constraint-basierte Sprachen und Systeme (vgl. [18]). Eine Pionierarbeit auf diesem Gebiet stellt das von Sutherland 1963 am MIT entwicklete System *Sketchpad* [35] dar. Basierend auf diesem Ansatz folgten weitere Arbeiten von Borning et al. im Rahmen des *ThingLab*-Projektes bei Xerox PARC (vgl. [6]). Constraint-basierte Ansätze zum geometrischen Layout liegen auch den Systemen *Magritte* [15], *Juno* [30] und *IDEAL* [37] zugrunde.

3 Architektur des Layout Manager

Bei der automatischen Generierung multimodaler Präsenationen unterscheiden wir zwischen der Planung des Inhalts und der Wahl der verschiedenen Modi sowie der Bestimmung der äußeren Form des Dokumentes. Eine zentrale Komponente in der hierarchisch organisierten Kaskadenarchitektur von WIP (**Wissensbasierte Informationspräsentation**) nimmt somit neben einem Präsentationsplaner (vgl. [1]) der Layout-Manager (vgl. [16, 19]) ein.

Während der Präsentationsplaner die Selektion der zu präsentierenden Inhalte und die Wahl der Modi vornimmt, besteht die wesentliche Aufgabe des Layout-Managers darin, aufgrund der vom Präsentationsplaner spezifizierten semantischen und pragmatischen Relationen, die von den mediaspezifischen Generatoren erzeugten Text- und Graphikfragmente auf einem Dokument zu arrangieren, d.h. es sind Größe und Position der einzelnen Boxen zu bestimmen.

Der Layoutprozeß wird auf zwei unterschiedlichen Detaillierungsebenen durchgeführt. Zunächst wird ein Groblayout auf der Basis von Defaultannahmen bestimmt. Zur Plazierung der instanziierten Layoutobjekte im Dokumentraum verwenden wir dann das aus dem Bereich Graphik-Design bekannte Konzept des typographischen Rasters (*Grid*, vgl. [28]). Dieses garantiert ein effizientes (d.h. uniformes, kohärentes und konsistentes) Design funktionellen Layouts.

Die Architektur des Layout-Manager in WIP (s. Abb. 1) umfaßt neben der im folgenden beschriebenen Plazierungskomponente (vgl. auch [19]) eine regel-basierte Komponente zur Gridgenerierung (vgl. [20]), eine automatische Typographie-Komponente sowie ein Modul zum automatischen Rendering des multimodalen Dokumentes.

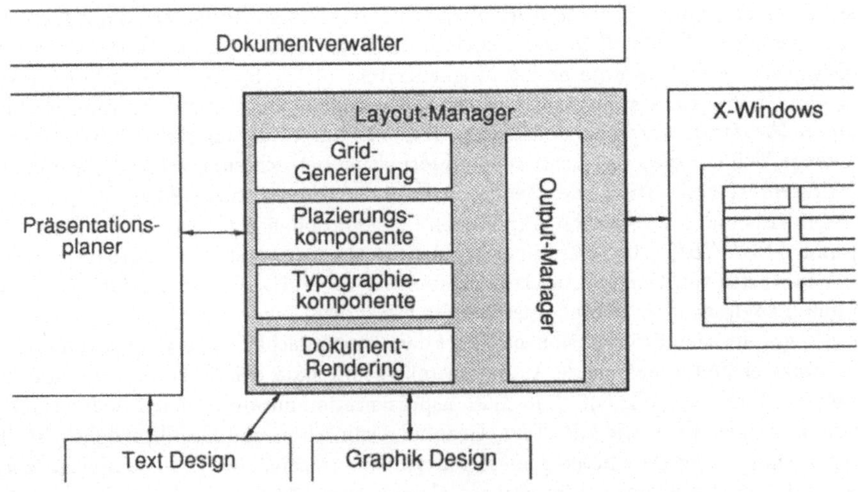

Abbildung 1: Architektur von WIP's Layout-Manager

Im Gegensatz zu anderen Ansätzen (vgl. [12]), in dem die Layoutkomponente erst nach Abschluß des Generierungsprozesses die von den media-spezifischen Generatoren erzeugten Text- und

Graphikelemente geeignet arrangiert, interagiert in WIP der Layout-Manager mit dem Präsentationsplaner schon vor der eigentlichen Generierungsphase. Somit können mögliche Layoutbetrachtungen schon zu einer frühen Phase in den Planungsprozeß einfließen und auch die einzelnen mediaspezifischen Generatoren entsprechend beschränken. So ist es dem Layout-Manager schon zu diesem Zeitpunkt der Planung möglich, aufgrund der vom Präsentationsplaner spezifizierten semantisch-pragmatischen Relationen und der Modiwahl, ein Groblayout zu bestimmen. Als mögliche Auswirkungen graphischer Constraints (z.B. Platzrestriktionen) auf Inhaltsplanung und Modeselektion kommen u.a. eine Revision des Inhalts (Inhaltsreduktion, Mitteilung zusätzlicher Information) und eine Umstrukturierung des Dokumentes in Betracht (vgl. auch [38]).

4 Repräsentation von graphischem Wissen

Ein zentrales Problem beim automatischen Layout-Design ist die Repräsentation des designrelevanten Wissens über die ästhetische, funktionale und strukturelle Gestaltung eines Dokumentes (vgl. auch [17]). Das hier aus dem Bereich Graphik-Design vorliegende Wissen bezieht sich auf perzeptuelle Kriterien zur Anordnung der Layoutobjekte, wie z.B. horizontale vs. vertikale Ordnung, Alignierung, Gruppierung, Symmetrie oder Ähnlichkeit (vgl. u.a. [3, 28, 8, 33]).

Dieses Wissen liegt jedoch größtenteils in Form von Heuristiken und Intuitionen vor und ist daher häufig unstrukturiert und unformalisiert. Darüberhinaus haben empirische psychologische Studien gezeigt, daß es eine sehr hohe Variabilität in den für eine Präsentation verwendeten Layoutmustern bei der Anordnung von Text-Bild-Kombinationen gibt (vgl. [40]). D.h. zur Modellierung des Layout-Prozesses ist neben domänespezifischem Wissen auch *Common-Sense-Wissen* zu repräsentieren.

Die zentrale Idee des hier vorgestellten Ansatzes, besteht in einer möglichst natürlichen Kodierung der perzeptuellen Merkmale durch die Einbeziehung von strukturellem Wissen. Ein Teil des für die Bestimmung des Layouts relevanten Designwissens (z.B. zur Beschreibung von Topologie und Geometrie) läßt sich dabei mittels Constraint-Netzen (vgl. [22, 27]) deklarativ beschreiben. Constraints repräsentieren hierbei sehr heterogene Beziehungen zwischen den einzelnen Layoutobjekten.

Zur Beschreibung der verschiedenen graphischen Wissensarten unterscheiden wir numerische und symbolische Constraints, die *semantische* bzw. *pragmatische* und *topologische* bzw. *geometrische* sowie *temporäre* Relationen (bei animierten Darstellungen) spezifizieren. Sie eignen sich insbesondere auch zur Repräsentation lokaler Randbedingungen, wie von außen vorgegebene Formatrestriktionen, Randbereiche, Abstände, Überlappungsfreiheit etc.

Die Struktur eines multimodalen Dokuments wird im wesentlichen durch funktionale Abhängigkeiten zwischen den einzelnen Dokumentteilen, also Bildern, Texten oder Bild-Textkombinationen, die ihrerseits wieder Aktionen repräsentieren können, bestimmt. Die inhaltlichen Beziehungen zwischen Bildern und Texten werden vom Präsentationsplaner in Form von sog. *'rhetorischen Relationen'*, basierend auf der von Mann und Thompson vorgeschlagenen *RST-Theorie* (vgl. [23]) zum Aufbau von Texten, spezifiziert. Solche RST-Relationen sind z.B. *'sequence'*, *'contrast'*, *'elaboration'*, *'organization'*, *'motivation'*, etc. Für einige dieser semantisch-pragmatischen Kohärenzrelationen sind geeignete Designheuristiken bekannt, die sie in Form graphischer Constraints adäquat reflektieren (vgl. auch [17, 19]).

Über diese rein inhaltliche Klassifizierung der Constraints hinaus ergibt sich eine Priorisierung dieser nach deren Einfluß auf die Gesamtpräsentation, in *obligatorische* Constraints, deren Erfülltsein für die Verständlichkeit des Dokumentes unabdingbar ist (z.B. Überlappungsfreiheit), *optionale* Constraints, die über eine Präferenzskala geordnet sind und ästhetisch wünschenswerte Objektkonstellationen spezifizieren (z.B. optimale Distanz zwischen zwei Boxen) und *Default-Constraints*. Letztere repräsentieren a priori Annahmen über Dokumenttypen, die solange gelten, bis sie von neuen stärkeren Constraints überschrieben werden. Durch die Einführung einer Präferenzskala über dem Constraint-Netz wird somit eine Hierarchisierung der Constraints möglich. Das hier verwendete Constraint-Verfahren orientiert sich an einem von Borning et al. (vgl. [7]) vorgeschlagenen Ansatz zur Hierarchisierung von Constraints.

Ein typisches Beispiel für die Benutzung einer Constraint-Hierarchie im geometrischen Layout ist das Problem der Bestimmung des Leerraums zwischen zwei kontrastierenden Graphiken. Die entsprechenden Designkriterien lassen sich durch folgende zwei Constraints repräsentieren:

- Ein obligatorisches Constraint spezifiziert, daß der Abstand zwischen den beiden Graphikboxen > 0 sein muß.

- Eine Disjunktion von zwei optionalen Constraints gibt an, daß die Boxen bevorzugt horizontal und ansonsten vertikal zu alignieren sind.

Neben Constraints, die statische Designheuristiken repräsentieren, müssen dynamische Constraints *on the fly* aus den vom Präsentationsplaner spezifizierten inhaltlichen Relationen kompiliert werden. Zu den dynamisch zu generierenden Constraints zählen auch solche, die sich auf Relationen zwischen einer a priori nicht bekannten Anzahl von Objekten beziehen (vgl. z.B. *'sequence'*).

Da bei Syntheseaufgaben, wie z.B. Konfigurationsaufgaben, viele Constraints nur lokalen Einfluß haben, wird die für die Lösung relevante Variablenmenge und damit das Constraint-Netz bzw. die Constraint-Hierarchie häufig dynamisch in Abhängigkeit des Problemlösungsprozesses verändert (vgl. auch [26]). Wir verwenden deshalb einen inkrementellen Constraint-Propagierungsalgorithmus, der es erlaubt Constraints zur Laufzeit hinzuzufügen bzw. zu löschen (vgl. Kap. 5).

Der vorgestellte Constraint-Formalismus erlaubt die Aggregierung von primitiven Constraints (wie z.B. *'beside'*) zu zusammengesetzten Constraints (sog. *Compound-Constraints*). Ein Beispiel für ein Compound-Constraint ist die Repräsentation des graphischen Constraints für die Relation *'contrast'*, deren Rumpf zwei verschiedene Designalternativen zur sequentiellen Alignierung enthält (vgl. Abb. 2). Abb. 3 zeigt zur Illustration die entsprechende Netzwerkdarstellung dieser Definition.

```
Name :        'CONTRAST
Methods : (   ((BESIDE ?1 ?4 ?5 )
              (EQUAL ?2 ?6))
              ((UNDER ?2 ?3 ?6)
              (EQUAL ?1 ?5)) )
```

Abbildung 2: Repräsentation des Compound-Constraints *CONSTRAST*

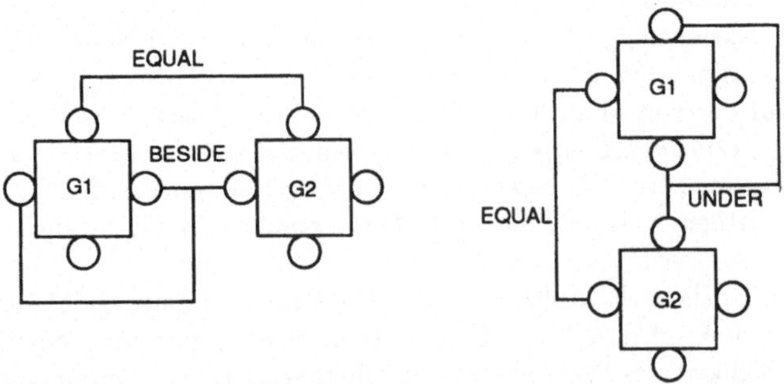

Abbildung 3: Netzwerkdarstellung der Definition aus Abb. 3

5 Ein mehrschichtiger Constraint-Solver zur Verarbeitung graphischen Wissens

Die Planung des Layoutprozesses läuft in zwei Phasen auf drei unterschiedlich detaillierten Ebenen ab. In der ersten Phase wird ein Groblayout für die vom Planer spezifizierten uninstanziierten Text- und Graphikboxen bestimmt. Dabei benutzt die Layout-Komponente Defaultannahmen u.a. über Designstrategien zum Arrangement der Layoutobjekte im zweidimensionalen Dokumentraum.

Nach Abschluß der Generierungsprozesse werden die bisher leeren Boxen mit den von den mediaspezifischen Generatoren erzeugten aktuellen Graphiken bzw. Texten instanziiert. Daraufhin kann die zweite Phase das Feinlayout planen, wobei den Text- und Graphikelementen reale Koordinaten im Layoutraum zugewiesen werden.

Das funktionale Layout des Dokumentes wird durch ein Grid unterstützt, was aus den geometrischen Grunddaten der Objekte, den Generierungsparametern und dem dokumentspezifischen Wissen dynamisch bestimmt wird (vgl. [20]). Die Layoutobjekte werden entsprechend dem Grid so auf der zweidimensionalen Plazierungsebene angeordnet, daß ein Objekt eine ganzzahlige Menge von Rasterfeldern überdeckt.

Die für die Layouterstellung relevanten Beziehungen lassen sich in lokale und globale Beziehungen unterteilen. Lokale Beziehungen sind inhaltliche Relationen zwischen Layoutobjekten, die vom Planer vorgegeben werden. Sie fassen Objekte teilweise verschiedener Modalität zu größeren Einheiten zusammen. Globale Beziehungen sind Abbildungen geometrischer Relationen, die Einheiten zueinander plazieren. Diese können vom Planer explizit vorgegeben werden oder werden mittels einer Heuristik geeignet zu der jeweiligen Einheit ausgewählt. Neben inhaltlichen Daten, wie etwa der Typ eines Objektes, sind die geometrischen Ausmaße bei der Plazierung von grundlegender Bedeutung. Hierzu wird ein Objekt durch den kleinsten ihn umschließenden Rahmen modelliert.

Eine zentrale Idee dieses Ansatzes ist die Unterteilung des Plazierungsprozesses in die Bestimmung der lokalen Topologie und der hieraus folgenden expliziten Berechnung der geometrischen Plazierung im Grid. Diese Aufgabe wird von zwei dedizierten inkrementellen Constraint-Solvern übernommen, die in einem hierarchischen Modell organisiert sind und über Constraint-Hierarchien bzw. nach dem Domänen-Konzept arbeiten (s. Abb. 4).

Um ein effizientes Verhalten eines solchen mehrschichtigen Constraint-Systems, zu garantieren, ist eine geeignete Ansteuerung der verschiedenen Kontrollmechanismen erforderlich. Das geschieht auf der obersten Ebene des Solver-Modells, die Metawissen in Form von Designheuristiken über die Abarbeitung der vom Präsentationsplaner spezifizierten Dokumentrepräsentation enthält und so den Evaluierungsprozeß steuert. Dieses Metawissen ist zum Teil deklarativ über Default-Constraints als auch durch Regeln repräsentiert.

5.1 Verarbeitung lokaler Beziehungen

Da das Layout durch eine klare Aufteilung geprägt wird, die z.B. Zusammenhänge und Gegensätze in der zu präsentierenden Information reflektiert, wird dies in der Designstrategie durch die Bildung lokaler Einheiten berücksichtigt. Lokale Beziehungen ergeben sich aus den vom Planer vorgegebenen semantisch-pragmatischen Relationen zwischen den Objekten und betreffen die relative Lage der Objekte untereinander. Die entsprechenden Layout-Constraints repräsentieren topologische Anordnungsmöglichkeiten, die durch die Relationen impliziert werden (s. Kap. 4).

Durch die feste Vorgabe der Beziehungen zwischen den Layoutobjekten, bietet sich ein Constraint-Solver an, der nach der *Value-Inference*-Technik arbeitet und feste Werte durch das Constraint-Netz propagiert (vgl. auch [35, 34, 6]). Damit werden die Objekte relativ zum Koordinatenursprung positioniert und erst später durch die Anwendung globaler Beziehungen an explizite Koordinaten gebunden.

Da man insbesondere bei der Generierung multimodaler Präsentationen wie z.B. in WIP Constraints häufig nach ihrer Stärke gewichten will, haben wir einen speziellen Constraint-Solver, ähnlich

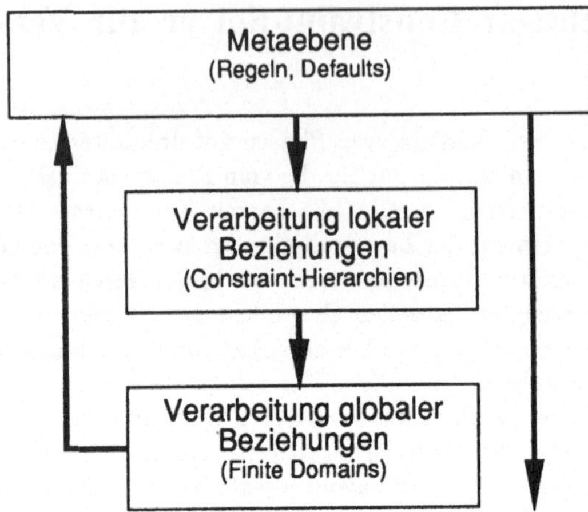

Abbildung 4: Modell des mehrschichtigen Constraint-Solvers

dem von Freeman-Benson et al. entwickelten *DeltaBlue*-Algorithmus (vgl. [13]) verwendet, der die Bearbeitung von Constraint-Hierarchien unterstützt.

Die *Inkrementalität* dieses Solvers erlaubt es, zur Laufzeit Änderungen am Constraint-Netz vorzunehmen, ohne das gesamte Netz neuzuberechnen, d.h. es können dynamisch Constraints hinzufügt bzw. gelöscht werden. Aus allen zulässigen Lösungen zu einer Constraint-Hierarchie berechnet der inkrementelle Constraint-Solver unter Verwendung eines schnellen lokalen Propagierungsalgorithmus mittels des sog. *local-predicate-better* Komparators (vgl. [13]) die beste Lösung.

Da die hier verwendete Constraint-Sprache über die Möglichkeit zur Definition von Compound-Constraints verfügt, lassen sich durch die Angabe von alternativen Basis-Constraints verschiedene graphische Darstellungsformen für die lokalen Beziehungen ausdrücken, wobei der Constraint-Solver entscheidet, in welcher Reihenfolge die einzelnen Basis-Constraints evaluiert werden. Können die Constraints einer Designstrategie nicht erfüllt werden, so wird durch *Backtracking* eine andere ausgewählt.

5.2 Verarbeitung globaler Beziehungen

Im Gegensatz zu den lokalen Beziehungen sind die globalen Beziehungen schwächerer Natur. Sie verbinden Einheiten von lokal zusammenhängenden Objekten entsprechend der vorliegenden Dokumentstruktur und arrangieren diese nach dokumentspezifischen Designheuristiken relativ zu anderen Einheiten im Layoutraum. Durch die Verwendung eines Design-Grids erhalten wir eine zusätzliche Einschränkung des Layoutraums. Diese läßt sich ebenfalls über Constraints repräsentieren, wobei dann die Grid-Koordinaten endliche Wertebereiche (*Finite-Domains*) für die Variablen beschreiben.

Ähnlich dem Repräsentationsformalismus lokaler Beziehungen können wir Constraint-Netze verwenden, um globale Beziehungen zu repräsentieren. Da für jede Einheit, nach Einbettung in das bestehende Constraint-Netz, im allgemeinen nur eine endliche Anzahl von möglichen Plazierungsflächen zur Auswahl steht, verwenden wir einen speziellen Constraint-Ansatz, der auf endlichen, diskretwertigen Intervallen von natürlichen Zahlen arbeitet.

Die Ideen bei der Entwicklung des Constraint-Solvers zur Behandlung von Finite-Domains gehen auf die Arbeit von Van Hentenryck (vgl. [36]) im Rahmen des *CHIP*-Projektes zum *Constraint Logic Programming* am ECRC zurück. Der Propagierungsalgorithmus benutzt hier ähnlich der *Label-Inference*-Technik (vgl. [22, 9]) Constraints zur Einschränkung der Wertemengen. Als effizienten Inferenzmechanismus verwenden wir zur *a priori* Einschränkung des Suchraumes eine Prozedur ähnlich dem *Forward-Checking* in CHIP (vgl. [36]). Dadurch wird frühzeitig eine Nichterfüllbarkeit der

Relationenmenge erkannt, so daß von der Kontrollebene die nächste Alternative ausgewählt werden kann. Der Constraint-Solver arbeitet inkrementell, d.h. bei Einführung neuer Constraints wird nur ein Teil des Netzes neu berechnet.

Constraints repräsentieren hier zumeist arithmetische Ausdrücke, die durch Basis-Constraints ausgedrückt werden. Abb. 5 zeigt die entsprechende Constraint-Definition zur Repräsentation der Designstrategie für die globale Beziehung *RightOf.*

```
(DefFDConstraint   'RightOf
 '((             ((FDADD (FDMIN ?1) ?4)              ;;; dx2-min
                  (FDMAXRIGHT MIN ?8 ?2))            ;;; dx2-max
                 ((FDMIN ?2)                         ;;; dy2-min
                  (FDDIFF(FDMAX ?2)(FDDIFF ?7 ?3)))) ;;; dy2-max
                (((FDMIN ?1)                         ;;; dx1-min
                  (FDDIFF (FDMAX ?5) ?4))            ;;; dx1-max
                 ((FDMIN ?2)                         ;;; dy1-min
                  (FDDIFF (FDMAX ?6)(FDDIFF ?3 ?7))))))  ;;; dy1-max
```

Abbildung 5: Constraint-Definition für RightOf

Durch die Angabe von neuen unteren und oberen Grenzen für die Einheiten werden die Wertebereiche der Constraint-Variablen weiter restringiert, bis diese nur noch aus einem Element bestehen. Um in der Plazierung möglichst flexibel zu sein, erhalten globale Beziehungen die maximale Plazierungsfreiheit in X- und Y-Richtung ohne dadurch ein Constraint zu verletzen. Enthält ein Intervall nur noch einen Wert, so ist die Einheit in dieser Variablen festgelegt. Trifft dies sowohl für die X- als auch für die Y-Richtung zu, so vermerkt ein internes *Gridgedächtnis* die Belegung und blockiert den entsprechenden Teil der Plazierungsfläche. Auf diese Weise wird eine global-konsistente Plazierung garantiert, in der sich keine Einheiten überlappen können (vgl. Abb. 6).

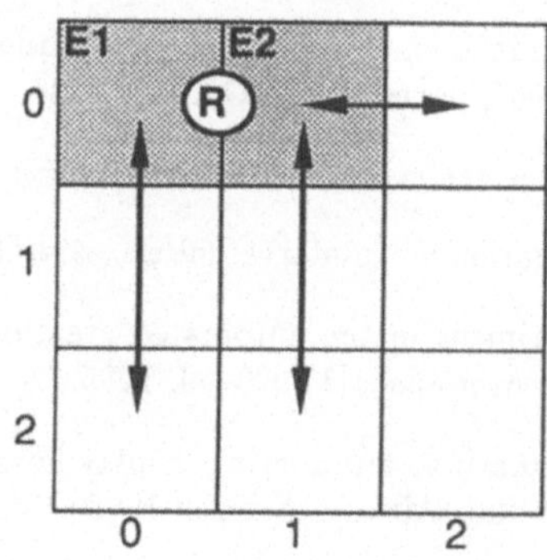

Abbildung 6: Illustration der globalen Beziehung RightOf E1 E2

6 Resümee

Die automatische Layoutgestaltung zählt zur großen Menge diskreter Kombinatorikprobleme, die als NP-vollständig nachgewiesen sind. In der vorliegenden Arbeit wurde gezeigt, daß sich das Layoutproblem als CSP auffassen läßt und durch die Verwendung von Such- und Konsistenztechniken zur Beschränkung des Layoutraums effektiv lösbar ist. Das Ziel dieser Arbeit bestand darin, am

Beispiel des Layout-Managers in WIP, Möglichkeiten zur Repräsentation und Verarbeitung von designrelevantem graphischen Wissen bei der automatischen Generierung des Layouts von multimodalen Präsentationen aufzuzeigen. Es wurde dazu ein neues hierarchisches Verarbeitungsmodell, bestehend aus zwei speziellen inkrementellen Constraint-Solvern, zur Bearbeitung von Constraint-Hierarchien bzw. Finite-Domains, die von einer Metaebene aus regel-basiert angesteuert werden, vorgestellt. Die Effizienz dieses Constraint-Verfahrens zeigt sich in ersten Performanzanalysen, diese ergaben für das Layout einer Dokumentseite Laufzeiten unter 5 Sekunden. Ein Prototyp des Layout-Managers (vgl. [20]) wurde auf Apple MacIvory in Common Lisp/CLOS implementiert und in WIP integriert.

Literatur

[1] E. André and T. Rist. Synthesizing illustrated documents: A plan-based approach. In *Proceedings of InfoJapan '90, Vol. 2*, pages 163–170, Tokyo, 1990. Also DFKI Research Report RR-91-06.

[2] Y. Arens, E. Hovy, and M. Vossers. Descrying the knowledge underlying the processing of multimedia instruction manuals. Submitted to Cognitive Science '91, 1991.

[3] R. Arnheim, editor. *Visual Thinking*. Faber and Faber, London, 1969.

[4] N. Badler and B. Webber. Task communication through natural language and graphics: A workshop report. Dept. of Computer and Information Science, University of Pennsylvania, June 1990.

[5] R. Beach. *Setting Tables and Illustrations with Style*. PhD thesis, Dept. of Computer Science, University of Waterloo, Ontario, 1985.

[6] A. Borning. The programming language aspects of ThingLab, a constraint-oriented simulation laboratory. *ACM Transactions on Programming Languages and Systems*, 3(4):353–387, October 1981.

[7] A. Borning, R. Duisberg, B. Freeman-Benson, A. Kramer, and M. Woolf. Constraint hierarchies. In *Proceedings of OOPSLA '87*, pages 48–60, October 1987.

[8] G. Braun, editor. *Grundlagen der visuellen Kommunikation*. Bruckmann, München, 1987.

[9] E. Davis. Constraint propagation with interval labels. *Artificial Intelligence*, 32:281–331, 1987.

[10] S. Feiner. APEX: An experiment in the automated creation of pictorial explanations. *IEEE Computer Graphics and Applications*, 5(11):29–39, 1985.

[11] S. Feiner. A grid-based approach to automating display layout. In *Proceedings of the Graphics Interface '88*, pages 192–197, Los Altos, CA, June 1988. Morgan Kaufmann.

[12] S. Feiner and K. McKeown. Coordinating text and graphics in explanation generation. In *Proceedings of the 8th National Conference of the American Association for Artificial Intelligence*, pages 442–449, Boston, MA, July 1990.

[13] B. Freeman-Benson, J. Maloney, and A. Borning. An incremental constraint solver. *Communications of the ACM*, 33(1):54–63, 1990.

[14] M. Friedell. Automatic synthesis of graphical object descriptions. *Computer Graphics*, 18(3):53–62, 1984.

[15] J. Gosling. *Algebraic Constraints*. PhD thesis, Dept. of Computer Science, Carnegie Mellon University, 1983.

[16] W. Graf. Spezielle Aspekte des automatischen Layout-Designs bei der koordinierten Generierung von multimodalen Dokumenten. GI-Workshop 'Multimediale elektronische Dokumente', Heidelberg, November 1990.

[17] W. Graf. Constraint-based processing of design knowledge. In *Proceedings of the AAAI-91 Workshop on Intelligent Multimedia Interfaces*, Anaheim, CA, July 1991.

[18] W. Leler, editor. *Constraint Programming Languages: Their Specification and Generation*. Addison-Wesley, Reading, MA, 1988.

[19] W. Maaß. Constraint-basierte Repräsentation von graphischem Wissen am Beispiel des Layout-Managers in WIP. Master's thesis, Dept. of Computer Science, University of Saarbrücken, 1991. forthcoming.

[20] W. Maaß, T. Schiffmann, and D. Soetopo. LAYLAB: Ein System zur automatischen Plazierung in multimodalen Dokumenten. Fortgeschrittenenpraktikum 'Wissensbasierte Graphikgenerierung', Dept. of Computer Science, University of Saarbrücken, 1991.

[21] J. Mackinlay. *Automatic Design of Graphical Presentations*. PhD thesis, Dept. of Computer Science, Stanford University, Stanford, CA, 1985.

[22] A. Mackworth. Consistency in networks of relations. *Artificial Intelligence*, 8(1):99–118, 1977.

[23] W. Mann and S. Thompson. Rhetorical structure theory: Towards a functional theory of text organization. *TEXT*, 8(3), 1988.

[24] J. Marks. The competence of an automated graphic designer. In *Proceedings of the 1991 Long Island Conference on Artificial Intelligence and Computer Graphics, NYIT*, pages 53–61, New York, March 1991.

[25] J. Marks and E. Reiter. Avoiding unwanted c onversational implicatures in text and graphics. In *Proceedings of the 8th National Conference of the American Association for Artificial Intelligence*, pages 450–456, Boston, MA, July 1990.

[26] S. Mittal and B. Falkenhainer. Dynamic constraint satisfaction problems. In *Proceedings of the 8th National Conference of the American Association for Artificial Intelligence*, pages 25–32, Boston, MA, July 1990.

[27] U. Montanari. Networks of constraints: Fundamental properties and applications to picture processing. *Information Science*, 7(2):95–132, 1974.

[28] J. Müller-Brockmann, editor. *Grid Systems in Graphic Design*. Verlag Arthur Niggli, Niederteufen, Switzerland, 1981.

[29] D. Navinchandra, editor. *Exploration and Innovation in Design*. Springer-Verlag, Berlin, Germany, 1991.

[30] G. Nelson. Juno, a constraint-based graphics system. *Proceedings of the SIGGRAPH '85*, 19(3):235–243, 1985.

[31] S. Roth, J. Mattis, and X. Mesnard. Graphics and natural language as components of automatic explanation. In J. Sullivan and S. Tyler, editors, *Architectures for Intelligent Interfaces: Elements and Prototypes*. Addison-Wesley, Reading, MA, 1990.

[32] D. Seligmann and S. Feiner. Specifying composite illustrations with communicative goals. In *Proceedings of the UIST '89 (ACM SIGGRAPH Symp. on User Interface Software and Technology*, pages 1–9, Williamsburg, VA, November 1988.

[33] A. Stankowski and K. Duschek, editors. *Visuelle Kommunikation*. Dietrich Reimer, Berlin, 1989.

[34] G. Sussman and G. Steele. Constraints – a language for expressing almost-hierachical descriptions. *Artificial Intelligence*, 14(1):1–39, 1980.

[35] I. Sutherland. Sktechpad: A man-machine graphical communication system. In *IFIPS Proceedings of the Spring Joint Computer Conference*, pages 329–345, 1963.

[36] P. van Hentenryck, editor. *Constraint Satisfaction in Logic Programming*. MIT Press, Cambridge, MA, 1989.

[37] C. van Wyk. A high-level language for specifying pictures. *ACM Transactions on Graphics*, 1(2):163–182, 1982.

[38] W. Wahlster, E. André, S. Bandyopadhyay, W. Graf, and T. Rist. WIP: The coordinated generation of multimodal presentations from a common representation. In A. Ortony, J. Slack, and O. Stock, editors, *A.I. and Cognitive Science Perspectives on Communication*. Springer-Verlag, Berlin, Germany, 1991. Also DFKI Research Report RR-91-08.

[39] W. Wahlster, E. André, W. Graf, and T. Rist. Designing illustrated texts: How language production is influenced by graphics generation. In *Proceedings of the 5th Conference of the European Chapter of the Association for Computational Linguistics*, pages 8–14, Berlin, Germany, April 1991. Also DFKI Research Report RR-91-05.

[40] D. Willows and H. Houghton, editors. *The Psychology of Illustration, Vol. 1, 2*. Springer-Verlag, Berlin, Germany, 1987.

Techniken der Wissensrepräsentation zur Repräsentation des Gegenständlichen

Roman Cunis
Universität Hamburg
Labor für Künstliche Intelligenz
Bodenstedtstr. 16
2000 Hamburg 50

Unter den vielfältigen Wissensrepräsentationsaufgaben der KI besitzt die Wissensrepräsentation von konkreten Gegenständen und Vorgängen eine besondere Bedeutung. Zahlreiche KI-Anwendungen beruhen auf einer computer-internen Modellierung des Gegenständlichen, insbesondere modellgestützte Verfahren zur Situationserfassung, u.a. Die heute zur Verfügung stehenden Werkzeuge zur Wissensrepräsentation bieten hierfür nur begrenzt Unterstützung. Der Beitrag zeigt anhand von verschiedenen Projekten des KI-Labors der Universität Hamburg, welche Anforderungen ein fortgeschrittenes Werkzeug zur Wissensrepräsentation bei der Beschreibung von Gegenständen und Vorgängen im technischen Bereich befriedigen muß. Es werden verschiedene Erweiterungen konventioneller objektorientierter Techniken vorgestellt, insbesondere im Hinblick auf die Repräsentation zeitlicher Aspekte, funktionaler Zusammenhänge sowie quantitativer und qualitativer Informationen.

1 Einleitung

Dieser Beitrag befaßt sich mit technischen, ingenieursmäßigen Anwendungen der KI und speziell mit dem dafür unentbehrlichen Werkzeug zur Wissensrepräsentation. In Anbetracht der fundamentalen Bedeutung der Wissensrepräsentation für die von der KI entwickelten wissensbasierten Systemarchitekturen wäre es eigentlich zu erwarten, daß man hier auf fundierte Methoden und erprobtes Werkzeug zurückgreifen kann. Dies ist jedoch noch nicht in dem Maße der Fall, wie es für eine Ingenieursdisziplin anzustreben ist. Probleme gibt es im ganzen Spektrum von den Wissensinhalten hin zu den Repräsentationsformalismen. Bekannte Problembereiche sind z.B. die Verwaltung zeitveränderlicher Daten, die Organisation großer Wissensbasen, die Repräsentation unscharf gefaßter Alltagskonzepte, der Aufbau von Erfahrungswissen, die Modifikation von Wissensbasen, aber auch Probleme handwerklicher Art, z.B. mit Werkzeugen zur Wissensrepräsentation.

Neben den vielfältigen grundlegend-theoretischen Forschungsarbeiten, die zu diesem Thema zur Zeit in aller Welt durchgeführt werden, scheint es uns wichtig, daß Wissensrepräsentation auch von Anwendungsproblemen ausgehend systematisch vorangebracht wird. Anwendungsprobleme bringen es mit sich, daß die Untersuchungen an konkreten Problemen orientiert werden und das Diktat der Allgemeingültigkeit in sinnvoller Weise eingeschränkt werden kann. Ergebnisse, die für einen wohl abgegrenzten Anwendungsbereich gelten, bringen trotz ihrer möglichen Beschränktheit bereits den Vorteil der Wiederverwendbarkeit, schaffen die Basis für generische Wissensbasen und geben Orientierung für die Entwicklung dedizierter Werkzeuge.

Ein Leitthema des KI-Labors der Universität Hamburg ist die gegenständliche Modellierung technischer Systeme und die Entwicklung des dafür erforderlichen Werkzeugs zur Wissensrepräsentation. Die Bedeutung technischer Systeme für ingenieursmäßige KI-Anwendungen braucht nicht hervorgehoben zu werden — die klassischen Aufgabenstellungen der Technischen Diagnose und Konfigurierung sind bekannte Beispiele. Die besondere Akzentsetzung betrifft das Gegenständliche. Wir gehen davon aus, daß ein Zugang zur Wissensrepräsentation, der vom Sichtbaren, Handgreiflichen herkommt, zu einer soliden Theorie und zu einem breit (aber nicht notwendigerweise universell) verwendbaren Werkzeug führen kann.

Die gegenständliche Repräsentation technischer Systeme führt mit großer Zwangsläufigkeit auf einen objektorientierten Formalismus, der jedem Realweltobjekt ein eigenes Schema (einen Frame) zuordnet und Wissen nur insofern außerhalb dieser Objektbeschreibungen ansiedelt, als es den Zusammenhang zwischen Objekten betrifft. Abstraktionen kommen auf natürliche Weise durch die Repräsentation von Objektklassen hinzu, also in Gestalt von generischen Beschreibungen. Im Gegensatz zu allgemeinen physikalischen Objekten lassen sich technische Objekte meist mit wohldefinierten Eigenschaften beschreiben (dazu sind sie entworfen) und erlauben deshalb auch eher eine rechnerinterne Verhaltenssimulation als ein beliebiger Realweltausschnitt. Technische Systeme sind in dieser Hinsicht Schrittmacher für eine der großen Perspektiven der KI: durch rechnerinterne Modellierung der Realwelt zu Aussagen zu gelangen, die uns bei der Problemlösung in der Realwelt unterstützen.

Im nächsten Abschnitt werden Projekterfahrungen des KI-Labors angesprochen und Anforderungen aufgezeigt, die sich daraus für die Repräsentation technischer Systeme ergeben. Der Hauptteil des Beitrags beschäftigt sich mit Repräsentationstechniken, die das KI-Labor in diesem Zusammenhang entwickelt bzw. konzipiert hat.

2 Anforderungen an die Modellierung — Erfahrungen des Hamburger KI-Labors

Das KI-Labor der Universität Hamburg [11] ist in verschiedenen Kooperationen mit der Industrie auf Themen gestoßen, in denen die Modellierung eines technischen Systems zum Kern des Problems gehörte.

Eine klassische Anwendung ist die modellgestützte Diagnose, die vom KI-Labor im Kontext der Schiffsleittechnik untersucht wurde. Als konkretes Beispiel wurde ein Ballastwasser-System betrachtet, bei dem es auf die Diagnose von Fehlern (etwa Ventilschäden) aufgrund von Meßwerten über das dynamische Verhalten bei Füllvorgängen ankommt. Ein wesentlicher Bestandteil der modellgestützten Diagnose ist das rechnerinterne Modell des zu diagnostizierenden Systems. In diesem Fall war das dynamische Verhalten des Ballastwasser-Systems zu simulieren, um Fehlerhypothesen mit dem beobachteten Verhalten abgleichen zu können. Eines der Ergebnisse dieses Projekts waren Anforderungen an eine Komponentenrepräsentation [2], die insgesamt bisher durch kein existierendes Werkzeug erfüllt werden können, z.B. multiple Granularität der Repräsentation, qualitative und quantitative Verhaltensbeschreibungen, Fehlerverhalten als Alternativen zu korrektem Verhalten, Speicherung zeitveränderliche Eigenschaften und Komponierbarkeit (interaktiver Aufbau einer Verbindungsstruktur).

Eine ähnliche Aufgabe wurde für einen Hersteller von Transportfahrzeugen bearbeitet. Dabei ging es um die Fehlerdiagnose eines elektromechanischen Lenksystems, die durch einen modellbasierten Ansatz zu leisten war. Hier ergaben sich ähnliche Anforderungen an die komponentenorientierte Modellierung, aber auch interessante Hinweise auf den Bedarf einer Visualisierung. Zur Wissensrepräsentation gehört auch eine benutzerfreundliche Darstellung, die im Falle von zeitlich veränderlichen Werten besondere Anforderungen an entsprechende graphische Grundfunktionen stellt.

Zur Fehlerdiagnose an einem Flexiblen Fertigungssystem (FFS) wurde ein fallbasierter Ansatz entwickelt [5], der auf einer Unterstützung der Fehlersuche durch Vergleich mit protokollierten Fehlerfällen basiert. Hier wird der Bedarf an einer gegenständlichen, nichtinterpretierenden Beschreibung von Vorgängen besonders deutlich, denn ein Fallvergleich muß im wesentlichen aufgrund von Beobachtungen erfolgen. Tiefergehende Interpretationen des Gesehenen liegen i.A. noch nicht vor, wenn das Diagnosesystem zur Unterstützung herangezogen wird. Dennoch wird vom Diagnosesystem auch erwartet, daß es grundlegende Wirkungszusammenhänge kennt. Die im wesentlichen gegenständliche Repräsentation eines komplexen Systems muß also eine qualitative Verhaltensbeschreibung in Form von Wirkungsketten umfassen können.

Eines der ersten Projekte des KI-Labors hatte das Ziel, mögliche KI-Anwendungen in der Deutschen Airbus Industrie zu ermitteln. Dies Projekt ist insofern besonders interessant, als es einen Einblick in den Bedarf von „modellgestützten" Ansätzen in einem umfangreichen, hochtechnisierten Fertigungsbetrieb erlaubt. Die Studie [9] identifizierte ca. 60 mögliche KI-Anwendungen verschiedenster Art, von denen etwa ein Viertel auf die rechnerinterne Modellierung eines technischen Systems angewiesen war.

Aus dieser Studie resultierte u.a. ein Projekt, das die Entwicklung eines Expertensystems zum Kabinenlayout von Flugzeugen zum Ziel hat. Es zeigte sich dabei, daß räumliches Layout ein Problem ist, welches besondere räumliche Repräsentations- und Verarbeitungsverfahren erfordert, um effektive Lösungen erreichen zu können. Die Entwicklung derartiger Verfahren ist auf der Agenda des KI-Labors, kann aber noch nicht Gegenstand dieses Beitrags sein.

Bei diesem Konfigurierungsproblem konnte das KI-Labor auf das Werkzeug PLAKON zurückgreifen, das im Verbundprojekt TEX-K unter Mitwirkung der Univ. Hamburg entwickelt wurde. PLAKON ist ein Expertensystemkern für Planungs- und Konfigurierungsaufgaben in technischen Domänen. Ein zentrales Merkmal ist auch bei PLAKON eine Trennung des Anwendungswissens in ein Domänenmodell und davon unabhängiges Kontrollwissen, mit dessen Hilfe sich PLAKONs Problemlöseprozeß an dem Domänenmodell orientiert [4].

3 Ein einheitliches Konzept für technische Modellierung

Das Interesse am Expertensystem-Einsatz für verschiedene Aufgaben in ein und derselben Anwendungsdomäne — Fehlerdiagnose, Variantenkonfiguration, Dokumentationserstellung, um nur einige zu nennen — erfordert neue Herangehensweisen an die Repräsentation der Anwendungsdomäne: Lösungen, bei denen Wissen über die Vorgehensweise mit Wissen über die Domänenstruktur vermischt wird, sind ungeeignet. Sie müssen durch Ansätze ersetzt werden, bei denen sich ein aufgabenspezifischer Problemlöser an einem zentralen Domänenmodell orientiert. In diesem Modell werden Objekte und Abhängigkeiten einer Domäne *konzeptuell*, d.h. *generisch*, beschrieben. Es ist Aufgabe des Problemlösers, diese konzeptuellen Beschreibungen für seine Zwecke geeignet zu interpretieren.

Welche Anforderungen muß ein solches Domänenmodell erfüllen? Aus der Sicht des Anwenders sind die wesentlichen Forderungen

- hohe Ausdrucksfähigkeit,
- gute Strukturierbarkeit,
- gute Wartbarkeit und damit verbunden
- Unterstützung der Wissensakquisition,
- vielseitige Verwendbarkeit.

Technisch gesehen bedeutet das:

- Klassifikation von Objekten,
- Beschreibung von Objekten der Domäne und ihren Eigenschaften,
- Beschreibung der *Zerlegung* von Objekten in Teile bzw. Komponenten,
- Formulierung *lokaler* Einschränkungen auf Eigenschaftswerte.
- Formulierung *globaler* Abhängigkeiten zwischen mehreren Eigenschaften eines oder mehrerer Objekte.

Es ist leicht zu sehen, daß die hinreichend bekannte *semantische Modellbildung* unter Verwendung von Konzepten (oder Klassen), die in einer *Begriffshierarchie* (auch bekannt als konzeptuelle Hierarchie, *Is-a*-Hierarchie oder Taxonomie) angeordnet sind, die allgemeineren Anforderungen erfüllt. Die

```
(ist! (ein Leiter)
      (eine E-Komponente
            (I-ein (ein Strom))
            (U-ein (eine Spannung))
            (I-aus (ein Strom))
            (U-aus (eine Spannung)))))

(ist! (ein Widerstandselement)
      (ein Leiter
            (R (ein Widerstand)))))
```

Abbildung 1: *Beispiel für eine Konzeptdefinition*

Mechanismen der Vererbung unterstützen die Wissensakquisition und ermöglichen eine frühzeitige Konsistenzüberprüfung. Für PLAKON wurde unter den genannten Rahmenbedingungen die Begriffsmodellierungssprache BHIBS entwickelt [4], die sich im wesentlichen an Ideen aus KL-ONE [3] und OMEGA [1] orientiert. Auch wenn BHIBS ursprünglich auf die Anforderungen eines Konstruktionssystems ausgerichtet wurde, so stellte sich doch das gefundene Domänenmodell in nachfolgenden Diskussionen über Expertensysteme für andere Aufgabenstellungen in ebenfalls technischen Domänen als in seinen wesentlichen Zügen vielseitig verwendbar heraus.

Abschnitt 3.1 enthält eine Kurzbeschreibung von BHIBS, Abschnitt 3.2 schildert das darauf aufbauende — und ebenfalls ursprünglich für PLAKON konzipierte — dreistufige Constraint-Modell, das zur Repräsentation und Operationalisierung globaler Abhängigkeiten eingesetzt werden soll. In den nachfolgenden Abschnitten wird gezeigt, wie spezielle Modellierungsanforderungen aus der Simulation technischer Modelle mit den Mitteln von BHIBS und den Constraints erfüllt werden können bzw. welche Erweiterungen dazu notwendig sind.

3.1 Begriffshierarchie

Mit BHIBS wird eine Begriffshierarchie aufgebaut, in der alle Objekte der Anwendungsdomäne und die Abhängigkeiten zwischen ihnen konzeptuell beschrieben werden. Diese Konzepte bilden eine taxonomische (*is-a-*)Hierarchie, die dazu dient, Objekte zu typisieren, Klassen und Spezialisierungen (Unterklassen) von Objekten zu beschreiben und deren Eigenschaften festzulegen. Eigenschaften werden innerhalb der Hierarchie vererbt.

Konzepte werden durch einen Bezug zu einem übergeordneten Konzept und durch eine Menge von Eigenschaften oder Parametern beschrieben, die das Konzept charakterisieren (und für die Konstruktion relevant sind). *Objektdeskriptoren* beschreiben die zulässigen Wertemengen für Eigenschaften. Zusätzliche Angaben an den Eigenschaften können genutzt werden, um z.B. Defaults oder Werte-Berechnungsfunktionen vorzugeben. Objektdeskriptoren können Anzahlmengen, Zahlintervalle, Prädikate oder wiederum Konzepte von anderen Objekten sein. Semantisch repräsentieren sie *einen* Wert, für den nur bekannt ist, daß er in der angegebenen Menge enthalten ist. Spezialisierende Konzepte dürfen vorhandene Slot-Beschreibungen nur einschränken, nicht aber überschreiben, und zusätzliche Eigenschaften einführen. Für ein einfaches Beispiel siehe Abbildung 1.

Die so entstehende taxonomische Hierarchie stellt also eine *strenge Spezialisierungshierarchie* dar. Dies ermöglicht die Überprüfung der Konsistenz neudefinierter Konzepte mit bereits vorhandenen hinsichtlich ihrer Eigenschaften und der Einordnung in die Hierarchie. Diese Überprüfung kann jederzeit im Verlaufe des Wissensakquisitionsprozesses durchgeführt werden und unterstützt diesen daher in einem wesentlichen Punkt. Die Definition der Begriffshierarchie als Baum schließt Mehrfachvererbung explizit aus. BHIBS stellt stattdessen *Sichten* bereit, um der Mehrfachvererbung vergleichbare Ausdrucksmöglichkeiten zu schaffen. Diese werden in Abschnitt 3.4 beschrieben.

```
(mass! (ein Strom) A (mA 1/1000 A))
(mass! (ein Widerstand) Ohm (mOhm 1/1000 Ohm) (kOhm 1000 Ohm))
```

Abbildung 2: *Maßeinheitendefinition*

In technischen Domänen stellt die Möglichkeit zur Verwendung von *Maßeinheiten* bzw. *dimensionierten Zahlen* bei der Beschreibung technischer Parameter eine große Erleichterung dar. Aus diesem Grunde wurden Maßeinheiten in den Beschreibungsformalismus von BHIBS integriert. Nach den in Abbildung 2 gegebenen Definitionen sind nicht nur die Angaben 6A und 6000mA äquivalent, bei der Berechnung von Widerstand aus dem Verhältnis von Spannung(sdifferenz) zu Strom entstehen (automatisch korrekt skaliert) Werte mit den richtigen Einheiten. Dimensionierte Zahlen tragen ihre Größenzugehörigkeit in sich, d.h. eine Konsistenzprüfung kann unabhängig vom Wissen über den Eintragungsort einer Zahl erfolgen.

Über diese taxonomische Hierarchie wird eine *kompositionelle Hierarchie* gelegt, die die Zerlegung von Konstruktionsobjekten in Komponenten beschreibt. Sie wird durch die *has-parts-* (bzw. *part-of-*) Beziehung aufgebaut. In den Konzept-Frames wird die *has-parts*-Relation durch mengenwertige Slots dargestellt, die Verweise auf die Konzepte der Teilkomponenten enthalten (s. Beispiel in Abbildung. 7). Um mehrfaches Vorkommen von Komponenten eines Typs in einem Aggregat ausdrücken zu können, kann mit dem entsprechenden Konzept eine Anzahlangabe assoziiert werden.

Die kompositionelle Hierarchie gibt ein gutes Beispiel für die unterschiedliche Interpretation eines Domänenmodells durch einen Problemlöser: Das Konfigurationssystem von PLAKON nutzt die Zerlegungsinformation zur schrittweisen Instantiierung der Gesamtkonfiguration z.B. in einem Top-Down-Vorgehen. Ein Simulations- und Diagnosesystem kann dieselbe Information auswerten, um auf einer tiefere Detaillierungsstufe zu genaueren Analyseergebnissen für eine Komponente zu kommen.

3.2 Constraints

Constraints („Beschränkungen") dienen zur Repräsentation und Auswertung der in einer Domäne bestehenden Abhängigkeiten zwischen Modellobjekten. Sie können sich auf einzelne Objekteigenschaften oder auf die Existenz von Objekten beziehen.

Im allgemeinen beschreiben Constraints über eine Constraint-Relation Abhängigkeiten zwischen einer Menge von Constraint-Variablen. Die Constraint-Relation definiert dabei die Art der Abhängigkeit. Werden bestimmte Variablen eines Constraints mit Werten belegt, so sorgt es dafür, daß für die übrigen Anschlüsse Werte entsprechend der Constraint-Relation generiert werden. Werden dagegen von vornherein alle Anschlüsse mit Werten belegt, so kann das Constraint feststellen, ob die Anschlußbelegung in Bezug auf die Constraint-Relation konsistent ist [14, 8].

Die darin enthaltene *Multidirektionalität* von Constraints macht ihren großen Vorteil gegenüber funktionalen oder regelhaften Abhängigkeitsbeschreibungen aus, die typischerweise unidirektional ausgedrückt werden. In Konfigurationsaufgaben können Constraints zur Wahrung von Nebenbedingungen und globalen Randbedingungen genauso eingesetzt werden, wie zur Ableitung neuer Parameterwerte aus bekannten — wobei im Modell nicht vorgegeben ist, in welcher Reihenfolge Werte bekannt werden müssen. Bei der Simulation dienen Constraints beispielsweise dazu, Werten von als Eingängen deklarierten Komponentenparametern zu als Ausgängen deklarierten zu propagieren. Gleichzeitig können sie bei einem anschließenden Diagnoseschritt zur Postulierung von Eingangswerten aus beobachteten Ausgangswerten genutzt werden.

Wir schlagen ein dreistufiges Constraint-Modell vor, daß in PLAKON bereits erfolgreich verwendet wird [15, 4]. Auf der obersten Stufe stehen die sogenannten *Constraint-Klassen*. Sie stellen domänenunabhängige Spezifikationen von Abhängigkeitsbeziehungen zur Verfügung (z.B. Adder, Multiplier). Aufbauend auf den Constraint-Klassen können auf der zweiten Stufe sogenannte *konzeptuelle Constraints* definiert werden, die die in der betrachteten Domäne bestehenden Abhängigkeiten

```
(constrain ((#?W (ein Widerstandselement)))
    (adder (#?W U-ein) ?spannungsdifferenz (#?W U-aus))
    (multiplier (#?W I-ein) (#?W R) (#?W ?spannungsdifferenz))
    (equal (#?W I-ein) (#?W I-aus)))
```

Abbildung 3: *Beispiel für ein konzeptuelles Constraint*

Für jeden Stromkreis muß es eine Sicherung geben.

```
(constrain ((#?SK (ein Stromkreis)))
    (exist (eine Sicherung (part-of #?SK))))
```

Abbildung 4: *Beispiel für ein existenzforderndes Constraint*

beschreiben. Sie stellen eine Zuordnung von Objekten bestimmter Konzepte und ihren Parametern zu Constraint-Klassen dar. Abbildung 3 zeigt ein Beispiel.

Für alle Objekte einer konkreten Modellausprägung werden die zugehörigen konzeptuellen Constraints instantiiert und an die Slots dieser Objektinstanzen gebunden. Dadurch, daß mit jedem Instanzenslot mehrere Constraint-Variablen verbunden sein können, entsteht eine Vernetzung der instantiierten Constraints zu einem *Constraint-Netz*. Dieses Netz bildet die dritte Stufe im verwendeten Constraint-Modell und spiegelt die Menge der Abhängigkeiten innerhalb der Modellausprägung wider. Bei Konfigurationsproblemen aber auch bei der interaktiven Entwicklung eines konkreten Simulationsmodells wächst das Constraint-Netz dynamisch mit der Erzeugung neuer Objekte (s. Abbildung. 5).

Außer Abhängigkeiten zwischen Eigenschaften von Objekten gibt es noch eine weitere, häufige Art von Einschränkungen, die die Existenz von Objekten fordern oder verbieten. Um diese Art von Constraints repräsentieren und evaluieren zu können, sind zwei spezielle Constraint-Klassen **Exist** und **Not-Exist** eingeführt worden. Abbildung 4 zeigt dazu ein einfaches Beispiel. Diese Art von Constraints sind wiederum ganz wesentlich bei Konfigurationsaufgaben, können aber auch zur Konsistenzüberprüfung von Modellausprägungen für die Simulation verwendet werden.

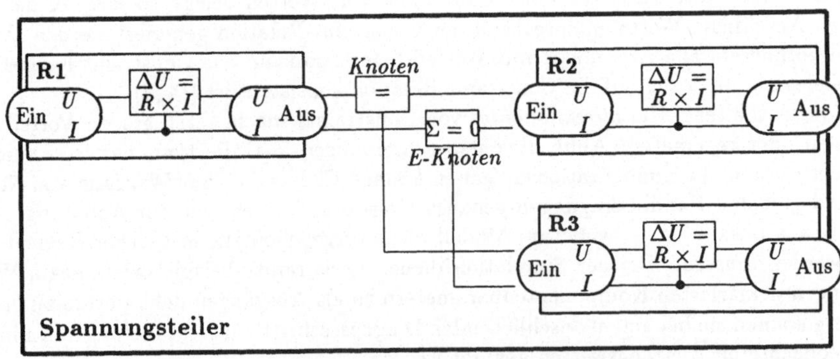

Abbildung 5: Constraint-Netz für einen Spannungsteiler

```
(ist! (ein Widerstandselement)
      (ein Leiter
           (Status {OK FEHLERHAFT})
           (Eingang (ein E-Port))
           (Ausgang (ein E-Port))
           (R (ein Widerstand))))

(ist! (ein E-Port)
      (ein Port
           (I (ein Strom))
           (U (eine Spannung))))

(constrain ((#?W (ein Widerstandselement)))
    (in-case (equal (#?W Status) OK)
        (adder (#?W Eingang U) ?spannungsdifferenz (#?W Ausgang U))
        (multiplier (#?W Eingang I) (#?W R) ?spannungsdifferenz) ...))
```

Abbildung 6: *Beispiel für eine Komponentendefinition mit Ports*

3.3 Modelle für Simulation und Diagnose

Im Bereich modellbasierter Simulation und Diagnose hat sich eine Modellierungsweise durchgesetzt, bei der zwischen *Komponenten, Anschlüssen* (*Ports, Terminals*) und *Verbindungen* (*nodes, conduits*) unterschieden wird [13, 6]. Dabei sind Komponenten und ihre Verbindungen die Objekte des Modells. Als Ports werden wesentliche Bestandteile einer Komponente ausgezeichnet, über die die Komponente via Verbindungen mit anderen Komponenten verknüpft werden kann. Da eine Verbindung zwischen zwei oder mehr Komponenten oft mehrere E/A-Variablen betrifft (bei elektrischen Komponenten z.B. immer Strom und Spannung gemeinsam), macht es Sinn, Ports selbst wieder als strukturierte Objekte aufzufassen. Verbindungen garantieren im einfachen Falle die Identität von miteinander verbundenen Port-Variablen. Im Falle einer elektrischen Verknüpfung mehrerer Komponenten können sie aber auch genutzt werden, um beispielsweise die Gültigkeit des Kirchhoffschen Gesetzes an jedem Knotenpunkt einer Schaltung zu überwachen (s. Abb. 8).

Diese Konzepte — im übertragenen wie im technischen Sinne — können leicht mit BHIBS und dem beschriebenen Constraint-Modell integriert werden. Abbildung 6 zeigt das Widerstand-Beispiel aus Abbildung 1 in entsprechend geänderter Form. Bei den konzeptuellen Constraints muß die Syntax zur Angabe eines Konzept-Slots als Constraint-Variable um eine Notation zur Angabe von Zugriffspfaden erweitert werden (im Beispiel, um eine Variable innerhalb eines Port-Objektes in einem Ausgangs-Slot der Komponente zu referenzieren).

Das Verhalten einer Komponente wird in Form von Constraints zwischen ihren Ports und internen Variablen (oder Parametern, d.h. im Verlaufe der Simulation unveränderlichen Werten wie z.B. der Stärke "R" eines Widerstands) ausgedrückt. Zur Angabe von Verhalten gehört in einem Diagnosekontext auch mögliches Fehlverhalten einer Komponente. Die Gültigkeit der verhaltensdefinierenden Constraints kann daher vom Zutreffen bestimmter Bedingungen, d.h. vom Erfülltsein anderer Constraints, abhängig gemacht werden: im einfachsten Falle von der Belegung einer speziellen Zustandsvariablen „Status" mit einem der Werte OK oder FEHLERHAFT, wie in Abbildung 6 gezeigt.

Die *Verbindungsstruktur* zwischen mehreren Komponenten wird ebenfalls konzeptuell beschrieben. Typischerweise betrifft eine derartige Beschreibung Aggregate und ihre Subkomponenten. Durch die konzeptuelle Vorgabe wird sichergestellt, daß für mehrfache Instantiierungen eines Aggregat-Konzeptes identische Verbindungsstrukturen erzeugt werden. Verbindungsstrukturen werden aufgebaut durch Objekte vom Typ „Knoten", deren Vorhandensein durch entsprechende existenzfordernde Constraints vorgeschrieben wird. Abbildung 7 zeigt ein stark vereinfachtes Beispiel eines Spannungs-

```
(ist! (ein Spannungsteiler)
      (eine E-Komponente
            (has-parts (:set (:some (ein Widerstandselement) 3))) ))


(constrain ((#?SPT (ein Spannungsteiler))
             (#?R1 (ein Widerstandselement (part-of #?SPT)))
             (#?R2 (ein Widerstandselement (part-of #?SPT)))
             (#?R3 (ein Widerstandselement (part-of #?SPT))))
     (connect (#?R1 Ausgang) (#?R2 Eingang) (#?R3 Eingang)
          using (ein E-Knoten)))
gleichbedeutend mit:
(constrain ((#?SPT (ein Spannungsteiler)) ...)
     (exist (ein E-Knoten
                 (verbindet (:set (#?R1 Ausgang) (#?R2 Eingang) (#?R3 Eingang))))))))
```

Abbildung 7: *Beispiel für eine Verbindungsstruktur*


```
(ist! (ein E-Knoten)
      (ein Knoten
            (verbindung (:set (:some (eine E-Komponente) 1 inf)))))


(constrain ((#?EK (ein E-Knoten))
             (#?P :all (ein E-Port (verbunden-durch #?EK)))
     (sum 0A (#?P I))
     (all-equal (#?P U))))
```

Abbildung 8: *Konsistenzerhaltende Constraints an Knoten*

teilers mit drei Widerständen und deren Verbindungsstruktur. Die dort verwendete connect-Syntax entspricht der —etwas umständlicheren— exist-Syntax (s. 3.2) wie in der Abbildung gezeigt. Abbildung 8 zeigt die Vereinbarung des Kirchhoffschen Gesetzes für den speziellen Knotentyp „E-Knoten" mit den Mitteln des dreistufigen Constraint-Modells. Die gezeigten Vereinbarungen resultieren in einem Constraint-Netz wie in Abb. 5.

3.4   Sichten und Abstraktionen

BHIBS erlaubt es, für Objekte unterschiedliche *Sichten* zu definieren. Sichten bieten die Möglichkeit, Objekte der Begriffshierarchie unter unterschiedlichen Gesichtspunkten zu betrachten (z.B. für Geräte elektrische und thermische Aspekte, siehe auch [12]). Innerhalb einer Sicht können wiederum Aufteilungen nach Sichten vorgenommen werden, d.h. Sichten können selbst hierarchisch organisiert sein.

Die Spezialisierung eines Objektes bzw. eines Konzeptes kann in jeder Sicht (mit Einschränkungen) unabhängig geschehen. Dies bedeutet insbesondere, daß unter dem Konzept, auf dem die Sichten definiert sind, für jede Sicht eine separate Taxonomie definiert wird. Ein Konzept wird *sichtenübergreifend* genannt, wenn es seine Eigenschaften aus mehreren Sichten ererbt, d.h. es hat dann in jeder Sicht ein eigenes Oberkonzept. Instanzen sind immer sichtenübergreifend und erben demgemäß ihre Eigenschaften aus all ihren Sichten.

Es ist leicht zu sehen, daß das geschilderte Sichten-Konzept letztlich dasselbe leistet, wie eine taxonomische Hierarchie mit *Mehrfachvererbung*. Gegenüber dieser haben Sichten jedoch den Vorteil, daß die „Vererbungslinie" für einzelne Eigenschaften eindeutig ist. Dadurch können der Zugriff auf

```
(ist! (ein Widerstandselement)
      (ein Leiter
            /quantitativ   (I-ein (ein Strom)) ... (R (ein Widerstand))
            /qualitativ    (I-ein {+ 0 -})     ... (R {+ 0 -}))))

(constrain ((#?W (ein Widerstandselement)))
      (number-to-sign (#?W I-ein/quantitativ) (#?W I-ein/qualitativ))
      ...)
```

Abbildung 9: *Konzeptdefinition mit Sichten*


```
(ist! (ein JK-Flipflop)
      (eine Komponente
            /funkt   (J (ein Bit-Port))
                     (K (ein Bit-Port))
                     (Q (ein Bit-Port))
                     (not-Q (ein Bit-Port))
                     (Takt (ein Bit-Port))
            /funkt/log   (takt-aufgetreten {true false})
            /funkt/el    (Stromversorgung (ein E-Port))
            /funkt/strukt  (has-parts (:set (:some (ein 3And-Gate) 2)
                                            (:some (ein Nor-Gate) 2)))
            /therm   (Oberflaeche (ein Waerme-Port)) ))
```

Abbildung 10: *Sichten: ein ausführliches Beispiel*

einzelne Attribute optimiert und Konflikte durch Ererbung derselben Eigenschaft auf verschiedenen Pfaden vermieden werden. Darüberhinaus erfolgt eine klare Zuordnung einzelner Attribute zu einer Sicht. Dadurch können „logisch gleiche" Slots in jeder Sicht unterschiedlich beschrieben werden (z.B. Variablen mit alternativ quantitativer oder qualitativer Wertebelegung) oder vermittels Constraints (z.B. zur Transformation von quantitativ nach qualitativ) unterschiedlich interpretiert werden. Siehe dazu das um Sichten erweiterte Beispiel der Widerstandsdefinition in Abbildung 9.

Gesichtspunkte, nach denen eine Aufteilung des Modellwissens in Sichten sinnvoll sein kann, gibt es viele: In der Konfiguration kann eine Komponente beispielsweise nach funktionalen und physikalischen Gesichtspunkten unterschiedlich zerlegt werden. In der Simulation und Diagnose können verschiedene Verhaltensaspekte einer Komponente (z.B. elektrisch vs. thermisch), verschiedene Interpretationsweisen des gleichen Verhaltens (z.B. logisch vs. elektrisch bei logischen Schaltelementen), verschiedene Abstraktionsebenen (qualitativ vs. quantitativ, vereinfacht vs. ausführlich) und/oder verschiedene Detaillierungsstufen (unstrukturiert vs. strukturiert, d.h. unter Betrachtung einer Zerlegung in Komponenten) die Grundlage für eine Aufteilung in Sichten bilden.

Abbildung 10 zeigt ein ausführliches Beispiel für die Modellierung eines JK-Flipflops mit den Sichten „logisch" (/log), „elektrisch" (/el), „strukturiert" (/strukt) und „thermisch" (/therm). Hieran zeigt sich gut der Vorteil einer hierarchischen Organisation von Sichten: Während die Port-Struktur für das logische und elektrische Verhalten, sowie bei einer Zerlegung nach funktionalen Gesichtspunkten („strukturierte" Sicht) übereinstimmt — und darum unter der übergeordneten Sicht „funktional" (/funkt) zusammengefaßt wird —, sind unter thermischen Aspekten völlig andere Variablen und Verhaltensweisen relevant. Durch diese Art der Modellierung ist es möglich, die funktionale Verbindungsstruktur des Flipflops zu anderen Komponenten und nach innen hin zu seinen Subkomponenten unabhängig von der betrachteten Sicht zu spezifizieren. Das Beispiel in Abbildung 10 zeigt weiter-

```
(ist! (ein Bit-Port)
      (ein Port
           /log  (Bit {0 1})
           /el   (I (ein Strom))
                 (U [0V 5V])))

(constrain ((#?BP (ein Bit-Port)))
     (table ((#?BP Bit/log) (#?BP U/el))
            (      0           [0V 1V]   )
            (      1           [4V 5V]   )))
```

Abbildung 11: *Port-Definition mit Sichten und Transformations-Constraint*

hin, daß innerhalb einzelner Sichten auch zusätzliche Ports vereinbart werden können (im Beispiel die Stromversorgung unter der Sicht /el).

Der Zusammenhang zwischen Eigenschaften in verschiedenen Sichten (bzw. verschiedenen Sichten auf eine Eigenschaft) wird durch Transformations-Constraints ausgedrückt. Ein Beispiel dafür zeigt der „Bit-Port", der ebenfalls nach logischen und elektrischen Aspekten unterschiedlich betrachtet werden muß. Dies erfolgt am Konzept „Bit-Port" durch entsprechende Sichten und ein Transformations-Constraint wie in Abbildung 11 gezeigt.

3.5 Modellierung von zeitlichem Verhalten

Modellierung zeitlicher Phänomene ist ein Themenkomplex für sich, dem gerecht zu werden in dem zur Verfügung stehenden Raum kaum möglich ist. Wir wollen daher an dieser Stelle lediglich darstellen, wie zeitlich ausgedehntes Verhalten konzeptuell mit den Mitteln der Begriffshierarchie und der Constraints beschrieben werden kann.

Wir gehen davon aus, daß zeitlich veränderliche Eigenschaften von Objekten dadurch repräsentiert werden, daß die entsprechenden Slots statt eines einzelnen Wertes eine *Historie* der Eigenschaft enthalten, d.h. eine Liste von Werten mit assoziierter Zeitinformation. Welcher Art diese Zeitinformation ist (z.B. Gültigkeitsintervalle) und welche Zeitpunkte oder -räume mit einzelnen Werten verbunden werden, muß von Fall zu Fall entschieden werden. Passend dazu muß darüberhinaus eine „Zeit-Maschine" (*Time Box*) bereitgestellt werden, die Zeitinformation geeignet verrechnet. (Im Zusammenhang mit Gültigkeitsintervallen könnte hier z.B. ein Konzept wie der *Extended Episode Propagator* [7] Verwendung finden.)

Als konzeptuelle Beschreibungen von Ereignissen dienen *Ereignismodelle*. Sie sind besonders geeignet, wenn z.B. aus beobachteten Fakten (z.B. Sensordaten) auf das Auftreten bestimmter Ereignisse geschlossen werden soll oder wenn ein Plan als eine Menge von zeitlich (partiell) geordneten Ereignissen erstellt werden soll.

Eine einfache Form von Ereignismodellen besteht darin, Constraints, die ja bereits Zusammenhänge zwischen Werten verschiedener Eigenschaften ausdrücken, die Möglichkeit zu geben, auch Zusammenhänge zwischen Werten zu verschiedenen Zeitpunkten zu beschreiben. Ein Beispiel dafür gibt Abbildung 12, in der ein konzeptuelles Constraint das Modell für ein Ereignis „ansteigende Takt-Flanke" an einem Flipflop verkörpert: Es vergleicht den Wert am Takt-Eingang des Flipflops zu verschiedenen Zeiten (bezogen auf ein globalen „aktuellen Zeitpunkt" t_0) und vermerkt ein Eintreten des Ereignisses in einer (symbolischen) Zustandsvariablen (s. Abb. 10). Dieser Ansatz ist ausreichend, wenn z.B. Constraints genutzt werden sollen, um in einer Simulation Werte über den Verlauf der Zeit zu propagieren.

Alternativ können Ereignismodelle auch als Konzepte einer Begriffshierarchie beschrieben werden. Konkrete Ereignisse, Instanzen dieser Konzepte, sind dann Objekte der Domäne. Sie entsprechen Aggregaten, deren Zerlegung in Teile (d.h. Teilereignisse) zusätzlich mit einer zeitlichen Ausdehnung assoziiert wird. Der Vorteil dieser Art von Ereignismodellierung liegt darin, daß die Klassifikati-

```
(constrain ((#?FF (ein JK-Flipflop)))
   (table ((#?FF Takt :before t0) (#?FF Takt :after t0) (#?FF takt-aufgetreten :at t0))
      (       0                       0                      false                 )
      (       0                       1                      true                  )
      (       1                       0                      false                 )
      (       1                       1                      false                 ) ))
```

Abbildung 12: *Konzeptuelles Constraint mit Zeitzugriff*

```
(ist! (ein Takt-0-Ereignis)
      (ein Prim-Ereignis
           (t (ein Zeitpunkt))
           (betrifft (ein JK-Flipflop (Takt 0)))
           (dauer [10msec inf.sec])))

(ist! (eine Ansteigende-Takt-Flanke)
      (ein Komplexes-Ereignis
           (betrifft (ein JK-Flipflop))
           (has-parts (:sequence (ein Takt-0-Ereignis)
                                 (ein Takt-1-Ereignis)))))
```

Abbildung 13: *Beispiel für Ereignismodelle*

onseigenschaften von BHIBS genutzt werden können, um Taxonomien von Ereignissen aufzubauen, konsistent zu halten und auch — beispielsweise für eine schrittweise verfeinernde Analyse von Sensordaten — auszunutzen. Ein vereinfachtes Beispiel für das Ereignis „Ansteigende-Takt-Flanke" an einem Flipflop zeigt Abbildung 13. (Darin wird zwischen zwei Arten von Ereignismodellen unterschieden: Primitive Ereignismodelle beschreiben einen bestimmten Zustand eines Objektes, charakterisiert durch eine bestimmte Wertekonstellation an dessen Variablen zu einem Zeitpunkt oder in einem Zeitraum. Komplexe Ereignisse werden durch eine Zerlegung in Teilereignisse ausgedrückt.) Für einen vergleichbaren Ansatz in der Szenenanalyse siehe [10], für den Einsatz von Ereignissen als Objekte zum Planen mit PLAKON siehe [16].

4 Zusammenfassung

Der Beitrag geht von der These aus, daß die Modellierung gegenständlicher technischer Systeme eine sinnvolle Orientierung für die Entwicklung von Wissensrepräsentationswerkzeugen ist. Dies wurde anhand einiger Projekte des KI-Labors der Universität Hamburg illustriert, die wichtige Anforderungen an ein Werkzeug zur ingenieursmäßigen Wissensrepräsentation erkennen lassen. Der Hauptteil des Beitrags stellte Lösungsmöglichkeiten zu verschiedenen Aspekten der Wissensrepräsentation vor. Insbesondere wurden die vielseitige Rolle eines Constraint-Systems und Verwendungsmöglichkeiten für Sichten dargestellt. Ein Werkzeug mit den beschriebenen Eigenschaften entsteht gegenwärtig am KI-Labor.

Literatur

[1] Attardi, G., Corradini, A., DeCecco, M., Simi, M.: *The Omega Primer*. In: Technical Report ESP/85/8, Delphi SpA, Italien, 1985.

[2] Bäcker, A., Kockskämper, S., Neumann, B., Reetmeyer, H., Nicklas, G.: *Modellbasierte Diagnose in der Schiffsleittechnik*. In: VDI-Berichte Nr. 855, S. 243–252, VDI, 1990.

[3] Brachman, R.J., Schmolze, J.G.: *Overview of KL-ONE*. In: Cognitive Science 9, S. 171–215, 1985.

[4] Cunis, R., Günter, A., Strecker, H. (Hrsg.): *Das PLAKON-Buch*. Informatik Fachberichte Nr. 266, Springer, 1991.

[5] Cunis, R., Neumann, B., Jaschinski, J.: *Fallbasierte Diagnoseunterstützung für ein flexibles Fertigungssystem — Ergebnisse einer Vorstudie*. LKI-Bericht LKI-M-2/91, Labor für Künstliche Intelligenz, Univ. Hamburg, 1991.

[6] DeKleer, J., Brown, J.S.: *A Qualitative Physics Based on Confluences*. In: Artificial Intelligence 24 (1–3), 1984.

[7] Guckenbiehl, Th.: *Formalizing and Using Persistence*. In: Proc. IJCAI '91, Sidney, 1991.

[8] Güsgen, H.-W.: *CONSAT—A System for Constraint Satisfaction*. Dissertation, GMD, St. Augustin, 1987.

[9] Jaschinski, J., Wittgen, P., Neumann, B.: *Einsatzmöglichkeiten von Methoden der Künstlichen Intelligenz bei der Deutschen Airbus*. LKI-Bericht LKI-M-1/89, Labor für Künstliche Intelligenz, Univ. Hamburg, 1989.

[10] Neumann, B.: *Natural Language Description of Time-Varying Scenes*. In: D.L. Waltz (Ed.), Semantic Structures, Lawrence Erlbaum Associates, Hove and London, 1989.

[11] Neumann, B.: *Das KI-Labor der Universität Hamburg — Ziele und erste Erfahrungen*. In: Proc. Wissensbasierte Systeme '89, Informatik Fachberichte Nr. 227, Springer, 1989.

[12] Struß, P.: *Multiple Representation of Structure and Function*. In: J. Gero (ed.), Expert Systems in Computer-Aided Design, Amsterdam, 1987.

[13] Struß, P.: *Qualtitative Reasoning*. In: Proc. KIFS-89, S. 224–257, Springer, 1989.

[14] Sussman, G.J., Steele, G.L.: *CONSTRAINTS — A Language for Expressing Almost Hierarchical Descriptions*. In: Artificial Intelligence 14(1), 1980.

[15] Syska, I., Cunis, R., Günter, A., Bode, H., Peters, H.: *Solving Construction Tasks with a Cooperating Constraint System*. In: Proc. of Expert Systems '88, S. 199–299, Brighton, 1988.

[16] Vietze, Th.: *Planen mit Ereignismodellen*. Diplomarbeit, Universität Hamburg, 1991.

Integrated Plan Generation and Recognition
- A Logic-Based Approach -

M. Bauer, S. Biundo, D. Dengler, M. Hecking, J. Koehler, G. Merziger*

Abstract

The work we present in this paper is settled within the field of intelligent help systems. Intelligent help systems aim at supporting users of application systems by the achievements of qualified experts. In order to provide such qualified support our approach is based on the integration of plan generation and plan recognition components. Plan recognition in this context serves to identify the users goals and so forms the basis for an active user support. The planning component dynamically generates plans which are proposed for the user to reach her goal. We introduce a logic-based approach where plan generation and plan recognition is done on a common logical basis and both components work in some kind of cross-talk.

1 Introduction

Intelligent help systems aim at supporting users of application systems by the achievements of qualified experts, e.g., cf. [NWWng], [HKN+88]. This support can be considerably improved if help systems are provided with plan recognition and plan generation components. In this context *Plan recognition* serves to identify the users goals and thus forms the basis for providing active help (cf. [Fin83], [DGH87]). *Plan generation* is an essential prerequisite for supporting the user with plans to reach his goals (cf. [Lur88], [Bre90], [Heg91]).

Whereas previous approaches were working with separated plan recognition and plan generation components it is our aim to realize some kind of *cross-talk* between both: Plan recognition and plan generation components work in integrated mutual cooperation. We distinguish between three different kinds of cross-talk which will be introduced in section 2.

Plan recognition as well as planning will be done in a deductive way and will be based on a common logical formalism. A brief sketch of the underlying logic will be given in section 3. Finally, sections 4 and 5 show by means of short examples how plan recognition, plan generation and *plan reuse* can be realized in an appropriate deductive framework based on this logic.

2 Architecture and Cross-Talk Modes

We intend to implement a system called PHI[1] (see figure 1) that constitutes the kernel of an active intelligent help system. An *Application Interface* provides as input observed actions and goals. On the other hand, it receives recognized, generated, and optimal plans.

Plan recognition and plan generation use a common knowledge base containing planning knowledge and state information as well as user and domain specific knowledge.

One main point of interest in our research concentrates on realizing the *cross-talk* between plan recognition and plan generation. This cross-talk in particular presupposes a common logical representation formalism for all kinds of knowledge. We distinguish between three different cross-talk modes:

---

*Deutsches Forschungszentrum für Künstliche Intelligenz GmbH, Stuhlsatzenhausweg 3, W-6600 Saarbrücken 11, e-mail: <last name>@dfki.uni-sb.de

[1]The PHI project is supported by the BMFT (Bonn) under Grant ITW 9000 8.

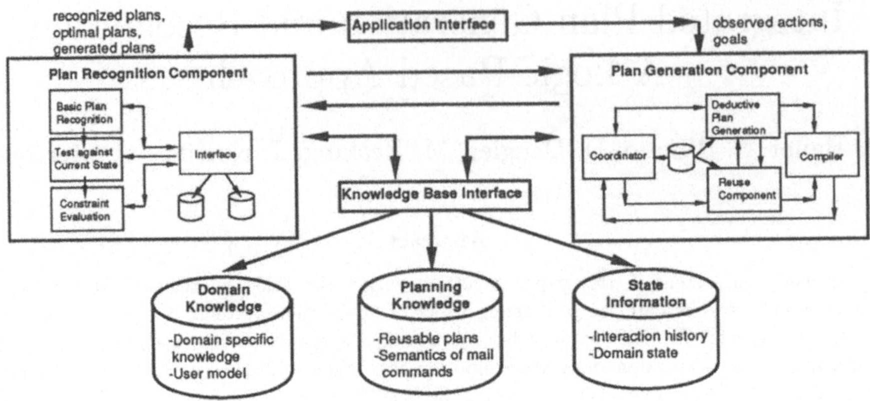

Figure 1: The PHI Architecture

- **First cross-talk mode**
  The plan recognizer works with plans produced by the plan generator. The basis for generation consists of already *observed actions* and *standard assumptions* about goals, that typically occur in the domain considered. The user-specific characteristics as designated in the *user model* also play a role in the generation process. If a set of hypothetical plans has been produced by the plan generator, it is made available to the plan recognizer. If the new observed actions cannot be mapped on the hypothetical plans or standard assumptions change, the plan generator is activated again and the plan recognizer is supplied with a set of hypotheses that covers the increased number of observed actions. The plan recognition process is successfully completed when a plan has been found which connects the observed actions in such a way that they lead to one of the assumed goals.

- **Second cross-talk mode**
  The main topics in this mode are the *identification of suboptimal plans* and the *generation of optimal plans*. The plan recognizer employs given domain-specific suboptimal plans which typically show up. If after a few observed actions a suboptimal plan is assumed by the plan recognizer, these actions and the goal corresponding to the plan are given to the plan generator. The plan generator then produces one or more optimal plans for this goal and provides them to the application system.

- **Third cross-talk mode**
  The third mode is an example for the application of our approach to plan monitoring. For a given goal, the plan generator creates a plan, which is passed to the user. If the user does not execute the plan as expected, the plan recognizer determines the goal pursued with the changed plan. The plan monitoring component then analyses both existing goals in order to determine inconsistency, subsumption or compatibility of the goals.

3 Formalization of the Application Domain

Since our work is settled within the context of intelligent help systems where users have to be supported in applying software, the planning domain of our system has to be based on some kind of command language. As a first example domain we therefore use a subset of the operating system

UNIX, namely the UNIX mail system, which is of manageable size and additionally provides a great variety in building and recognizing plans.

The deductive plan recognition and plan generation formalisms are based on a many-sorted modal temporal logic (cf. [RP86], [Krö87], [Hal89]). Besides the temporal operators $\bigcirc(next)$, $\Diamond$ (*sometimes*), $\square$ (*always*), and ; (chop), *assignments* and *control structures* are provided following imperative programming languages . The idea behind using those programming language constructs is that plans and in particular *abstract* plans which subsume a variety of concrete ones can in general be viewed as programs (cf. [MW86], [Bib86]).

The mail commands (e.g. *read, delete, quit*) are axiomatized as basic actions in the following form:

$$precondition \wedge EX(command) \rightarrow \bigcirc effect.$$

The *read*-command, for example, is defined according to its effect of changing the flag of a current mail object:

$$\forall x : mail\_object$$
$$[\neg flag(x) = \text{``}d\text{''} \wedge EX(read(x)) \rightarrow \bigcirc flag(x) = \text{``}r\text{''}\,],$$

where $EX(c)$ means: "Execution of command c".

The control structures are the following:

- ; (chop operator)
  The formula $\phi; \psi$ means that ϕ holds *before* ψ thus denoting the sequential composition of both subformulas.

- if ... then ... else (conditional)
  The formula if ϕ then ψ_1 else ψ_2 stands for $[\phi \rightarrow \psi_1] \wedge [\neg\phi \rightarrow \psi_2]$.

- while ... do ... od (while - loop)
  The while-operator is axiomatized according to
  $$[\text{while } \phi \text{ do } \psi \text{ od}; \alpha] \leftrightarrow [\text{if } \phi \text{ then } \psi; [\text{while } \phi \text{ do } \psi \text{ od}; \alpha] \text{ else } \alpha].$$

Certain formulas of our temporal logic are viewed as *plans*. Those *plan formulas* are

- all formulas $EX(c)$, where c is a term of type *command_name*;

- assignments of form $a := t$, where a is a *local variable* and t is a term;

- all formulas $\phi; \psi$ where ϕ and ψ are plan formulas;

- all formulas if ϕ then ψ_1 else ψ_2, where ψ_1 and ψ_2 are plan formulas and ϕ is a formula not containing any temporal operator or basic plan formula;

- all formulas while ϕ do ψ od ; α, where ψ and α are plan formulas and ϕ is a formula not containing any temporal operator or basic plan formula;

- all formulas $\Diamond \phi$, where ϕ is a plan formula;

- all formulas $\phi \vee \psi$ where ϕ and ψ are plan formulas.

4 Plan Recognition

The plan recognition component differs in two aspects from the systems mentioned in e.g.[FLS85], [SC85], [Hec87], [HKN+88]: It works deductively and communicates with a plan generation component in different cross-talk modes (cf. figure 1). It will work incrementally and non-monotonically (first approaches are described in [Hec91] and [Mer91]).

During the recognition process, which is described below in more detail, the following functionality must be realized:

Basic Plan Recognition: Identify those plans which contain the observed action.

Test against Current State: Test whether the observed action fits into the time structure.

Constraint Evaluation: Test whether all constraints are fulfilled.

Recognized plans, plan hypotheses, and the recognition history are stored in the knowledge base to be used later.

The plan recognition process is an

iterative process for selecting plan hypotheses which account for the observed actions.

Before describing the plan recognition procedure, we first consider some properties of its input: the plan hypotheses and the observed actions.

In general, the plan hypotheses are no concrete action sequences, but contain several degrees of abstraction:

1. The commands may not be completely instantiated, i.e., they contain formal parameters instead of an actual argument.

2. The temporal structure of the plan hypotheses may be ambiguous. They may contain subformulas like $\Diamond EX(a)$ which means "execute command a *sometimes* within the duration of the plan hypothesis currently considered."

3. Nondeterministic choices like $EX(a) \vee EX(b)$ can appear which mean "execute command a *or* command b".

4. Besides actual domain commands, a plan hypothesis may also contain *abstract commands* like *readmails* (cf. example below).

Observed single actions are described by formulas like $EX(a)$, whereas action sequences are expressed by $EX(a_1); EX(a_2); ...; EX(a_n)$.

At the beginning of the process a set of possible plan hypotheses Δ_0 is provided by the plan generation component. Together with the observed action $EX(Command_1)$ the plan recognizer determines in the next state the set of hypotheses Δ_1 so that every member of Δ_1 contains the observed action, or more formally:

$$\Delta_0 \cup \{EX(Command_1)\} \vdash_{PR} \Delta_1$$

($\vdash_{PR}$ means that plan recognition specific deductions are used). If a sequence of observations $EX(Command_1), ..., EX(Command_n)$ must be processed, the recognition process can be abstractly described as follows ($\bigcirc^i$ means that the command is executed in the i-th state):

$$\Delta_0 \cup \{EX(Command_1)\} \vdash_{PR} \Delta_1$$
$$\vdots$$
$$\Delta_i \cup \{\bigcirc^i EX(Command_{i+1})\} \vdash_{PR} \Delta_{i+1}$$
$$\vdots$$

During this iterative process:

- completely recognized plans can be deleted from Δ_i, and

- if no hypothesis can explain the observed actions, an adapted set Δ_0 of generated possible hypotheses must be delivered by the generation component.

Assume that until now an action sequence $\Phi = EX(a_1); ...; EX(a_{n-1})$ was observed and that each of the plan hypotheses in $\Delta_{n-1} = \{P_1, P_2, ..., P_m\}$ could explain those observations. Let a_n be the next observed action. Then the plan recognition procedure works as follows: It selects those hypotheses for which the formula $\Phi; EX(a_n)$ constitutes a valid starting sequence of actions. For each such P_i this means:

(a) The formula $\Phi' = EX(a_1); ...; EX(a_n)$ contains the same actions as P_i wherever the hypothesis demands these actions to be executed at a certain time and a parameter binding compatible to the one demanded in P_i.

(b) There is a suitable concrete domain command in Φ' wherever the plan hypothesis contains an abstract command.

(c) For every nondeterministic choice in P_i, Φ' contains exactly one of the alternative actions.

(d) Φ' induces a temporal structure compatible with the initial part of P_i.

The process taking place at each step of the recognition process can be described for each plan hypothesis $P \in \Delta_i$ as follows: Let $EX(Command_i)$ be the formula describing the last observed action. Then the plan recognizer tries to derive a new hypothesis P' which will become a member of Δ_{i+1}:

$$P \wedge \bigcirc^i EX(Command_i) \vdash_{PR} P'$$

where P and P' are related in the following way: There is a way to split P into an initial segment $Init_P$, a terminating segment $Rest_P$ and a segment Mid_P of commands describing just that part of P currently considered. Informally, $Init_P$ is that part of the hypothesis already recognized. It exactly corresponds to the sequence of observed actions of former recognition steps, whereas $Rest_P$ is that part which will be considered in the next step if the current recognition step is successful, i.e., if Mid_P and $EX(Command_i)$ fulfill the requirements (a) – (d) listed above. Thus we have

$$P = Init_P; Mid_P; Rest_P$$

$$P' = Init_P; EX(command_i); Rest_{P'}$$

where $Rest_{P'}$ results from $Rest_P$ by substituting formal parameters bound in the last step. If $Rest_{P'}$ becomes empty, the plan corresponding to this hypothesis was successfully recognized.

The potential of the plan recognition capabilities with a temporal logic described abstractly above is explained through an example. The following *plans* are used as hypotheses:

$$\forall arg1 : mbox, arg2 : integer \ [EX(Plan1(arg1, arg2)) \leftrightarrow$$
$$EX(folder(arg1));$$
$$\Diamond EX(showmails());$$
$$\Diamond EX(readmails(arg2));$$
$$EX(d(arg2));$$
$$EX(folder(['\#'])) \vee EX(quit())]$$

$$\forall arg1 : mbox, arg2 : integer \ [EX(Plan2(arg1, arg2)) \leftrightarrow$$
$$EX(folder(arg1));$$
$$\Diamond EX(showmails());$$
$$\Diamond EX(readmails(arg2));$$
$$EX(quit())]$$

The definition of the *abstractions between commands* is expressed by:

$$EX(f(['*'])) \;\to\; EX(showmails())$$
$$EX(h([])) \;\to\; EX(showmails())$$

$$\forall x : integer.EX(read(x)) \;\to\; EX(readmails(x))$$
$$\forall x : integer.EX(next(x)) \;\to\; EX(readmails(x))$$
$$\vdots$$

The following sequence of commands is observed:

$$EX(folder([UnansweredMails]))$$
$$EX(h([]))$$
$$EX(read([7]))$$
$$EX(d([7]))$$
$$EX(folder(['\#']))$$

Assume that the initial set Δ_0 of plan hypotheses contains *Plan1* and *Plan2*. The first observation $EX(folder([UnansweredMails]))$ fulfills the constraint (a) for both hypotheses, (b) – (d) need not be considered. Thus, after the first step we have:

$$\Delta_1 \;=\; \{Plan1^1, Plan2^1\}$$
$$Init_{Plan1^1} \;=\; Init_{Plan2^1} \;=\; EX(folder([UnansweredMails]))$$
$$Mid_{Plan1^1} \;=\; Mid_{Plan2^1} \;=\; \Diamond\, EX(showmails())$$
$$Rest_{Plan1^1} \;=\; \Diamond\, EX(readmails(arg2))\,;...;\, EX(folder(['\#'])) \vee EX(quit())$$
$$Rest_{Plan2^1} \;=\; \Diamond\, EX(readmails(arg2))\,;...;\, EX(folder(['\#']))\,;\, EX(quit())$$

The description of the second observed command is $\bigcirc EX(h([\,]))$. None of the hypotheses in Δ_1 contains a concrete action in its *Mid* part, but the abstract command *showmails*. The command abstraction axioms tell us that $h([\,])$ is a suitable instance for this command, so that (b) holds for $Plan1^1$ and $Plan2^1$. While (c) plays no role, we see that the temporal structure of $\bigcirc EX(h([\,]))$ is compatible with those of Mid_{Plan1^1} and Mid_{Plan2^1}, and (d) holds.[2] Thus

$$\Delta_2 \;=\; \{Plan1^2, Plan2^2\}$$
$$Init_{Plan1^2} \;=\; Init_{Plan2^2} \;=\; EX(folder([UnansweredMails]));\, EX(h([\,]))$$
$$Mid_{Plan1^2} \;=\; Mid_{Plan2^2} \;=\; \Diamond\, EX(readmails(arg2))$$
$$Rest_{Plan1^2} \;=\; EX(d([arg2]));\, EX(folder(['\#'])) \vee EX(quit())$$
$$Rest_{Plan2^2} \;=\; EX(quit())$$

Having skipped one step where $\bigcirc^2 EX(read([7]))$ was observed, we get $\bigcirc^3 EX(d([7]))$. $Plan2^3$ is no longer a valid hypothesis because (a) is not fulfilled. So we get

$$\Delta_4 \;=\; \{Plan1^4\}$$
$$Init_{Plan1^4} \;=\; EX(folder([UnansweredMails]));\, EX(h([\,]));\, EX(read([7]));\, EX(d([7]))$$
$$Mid_{Plan1^4} \;=\; EX(folder(['\#'])) \vee EX(quit())$$
$$Rest_{Plan1^4} \;=\; \emptyset$$

---

[2] If it is allowed to do some action *sometimes*, it is feasible to execute it in the *next* state.

In the final step, the observation of $\bigcirc^4 EX(folder(['\#']))$ leads to a successful recognition of the first hypothesis because $Rest_{Plan1}5$ contains no more actions. Thus,

$$\Delta_5 \;=\; EX(folder([UnansweredMails])); EX(h([\,])); EX(read([7]));$$
$$EX(d([7])); EX(folder(['\#']))$$

is a concrete instance of our initial hypothesis *Plan1* and the recognition process succeeds.

5 Plan Generation

The plan generation facility consists of four different modules and a local knowledge base. The *deductive planner* takes formal logic plan specifications as its input and automatically generates abstract plans from them. These plans are represented by plan formulas as described in section 3. The generation of plans is guided by strategies and heuristics which have succesfully been developed for a deductive program synthesis system [Biu88]. To produce concrete and executable plans, the abstract ones are forwarded to a *compiler* module which incrementally generates sequences of basic operations. These sequences constitute the output of the plan generation facility in the second cross-talk mode. The *coordinator* module (see figure 1) analyzes user inputs, actions, and goals and activates the planner to completely generate a new plan or it activates the *reuse component*. This module enables the system to reuse previously generated plans and implements *planning from second principles*.

Subsequently, we focus on the deductive planner and its integrated reuse facility as the main parts of the plan generation system and explain how the generation and reuse of plans proceeds.

5.1 Deductive Planning

The deductive plan generator starts from a formal plan specification given as a formula of modal temporal logic. This *specification formula* contains as a subformula an atom of the form $EX(z)$, where z is an existentially quantified variable of type command-name.

Generating a plan from such a specification means to first replace the variable z by an appropriate *skolem term*, e.g., $plan(x)$ and then produce an axiom $\forall x(EX(plan(x)) \leftrightarrow \phi)$, where ϕ is a modal *plan formula* as described in section 3. It additionally must have the property that replacing $EX(z)$ by ϕ in the specification formula makes this formula true, i.e., the plan ϕ to be generated has to satisfy its specification. To achieve this, the plan formula ϕ is derived from the specification formula using special plan generation rules. These rules are partly borrowed from a set of transformation rules initially developed for the deductive synthesis of programs in [Biu91] and adapted to the solution of planning problems in [Biu90].

To give an idea of how deductive planning works in this context we give a short example. Suppose we want to generate a plan for reaching the goal: *"Read and delete all mails from sender otto"*. This plan specification is represented by the following specification formula:

$$\forall m : mbox \; \exists z : command\_name$$
$$[EX(z) \rightarrow \forall x : mail\_object \quad [member(x,m) \wedge sender(x) = \text{``otto''} \wedge \neg flag(x) = \text{``d''}$$
$$\rightarrow \Diamond\,[flag(x) = \text{``r''} \wedge \Diamond\, flag(x) = \text{``d''}\,]\,]\,]$$

Skolemization of this formula replaces z by the term $plan(m)$, where $plan$ is supposed to be a new function symbol, and yields the formula

$$\forall m : mbox \ [EX(plan(m))$$
$$\rightarrow \forall x : mail\_object \quad [member(x, m) \wedge sender(x) = \text{``}otto\text{''} \wedge \neg flag(x) = \text{``}d\text{''}$$
$$\rightarrow \Diamond \, [flag(x) = \text{``}r\text{''} \wedge \Diamond \, flag(x) = \text{``}d\text{''} \,]] \,]$$

In order to obtain an axiom $\forall m : mbox \ (EX(plan(m)) \leftrightarrow \phi)$ defining the specified plan two tasks have to be performed. The first one is deriving a subplan $plan'(x)$ which for *any* of the specified mail objects reaches the subgoals of reading and deleting it. The second task is to find an appropriate control structure (in our case a *while* loop) which guarantees that $plan'(x)$ will be carried out for *each* of the described mail objects.

We will start with the first task and show how this part of the final plan can be derived using a widely extended version of the so-called *implication rule* (cf. [Biu91]) together with the following axioms which are supposed to be available in our knowledge base:

Ax1: $\bigcirc \phi \rightarrow \Diamond \, \phi$

Ax2: $\bigcirc(\phi \wedge \psi) \leftrightarrow (\bigcirc \phi \wedge \bigcirc \psi)$

Ax3: $\bigcirc \Diamond \, \phi \leftrightarrow \Diamond \, \bigcirc \phi$

Ax4: $\forall x : mail\_object$
$$[\neg flag(x) = \text{``}d\text{''} \wedge EX(read(x)) \rightarrow \bigcirc flag(x) = \text{``}r\text{''} \,]$$

Ax5: $\forall x : mail\_object$
$$[\neg flag(x) = \text{``}d\text{''} \wedge EX(delete(x)) \rightarrow \bigcirc flag(x) = \text{``}d\text{''} \,]$$

Ax4 and Ax5 describe the *read* and *delete* actions, respectively.

Let C, L, M, and $K_i (1 \leq i \leq n)$ be formulas. The implication rule then reads:

IMPL:
$$\frac{C \rightarrow (\sigma L \wedge M)}{C \rightarrow (\sigma K_1 \wedge M), \ldots, C \rightarrow (\sigma K_n \wedge M)}$$

provided there exists an axiom $(K_1 \wedge \ldots \wedge K_n) \rightarrow L$ in the knowledge base. According to the underlying modal logic the following rule derived from IMPL will also be used:

NEXT_IMPL:
$$\frac{C \rightarrow (\bigcirc \sigma L \wedge M)}{C \rightarrow (\bigcirc \sigma K_1 \wedge M), \ldots, C \rightarrow (\bigcirc \sigma K_n \wedge M)}$$

The implication rule is used to replace a (sub)goal in the plan specification by new subgoals which are sufficient for it.

In order to derive a plan formula for our subplan $plan'(x)$ from its specification

$$\forall x : mail\_object \ [EX(plan'(x))$$
$$\rightarrow [\neg flag(x) = \text{``}d\text{''} \rightarrow \Diamond \, [(flag(x) = \text{``}r\text{''} \wedge \Diamond \, flag(x) = \text{``}d\text{''} \,)] \,] \,]$$

we start with

$$[\neg flag(x) = \text{``}d\text{''} \rightarrow \Diamond \, [flag(x) = \text{``}r\text{''} \wedge \Diamond \, flag(x) = \text{``}d\text{''} \,]]$$

and apply the implication rule together with axiom Ax1, i.e., we replace the conclusion by

$$\bigcirc [\, flag(x) = \text{``}r\text{''} \wedge \Diamond \, flag(x) = \text{``}d\text{''} \,] \text{ obtaining}$$

$$[\neg flag(x) = \text{``}d\text{''} \rightarrow \bigcirc [\, flag(x) = \text{``}r\text{''} \wedge \Diamond \, flag(x) = \text{``}d\text{''} \,]]$$

as a new formula.

According to Ax2 this formula can be equivalently transformed into

$$[\neg flag(x) = \text{``}d\text{''} \rightarrow \bigcirc flag(x) = \text{``}r\text{''} \wedge \bigcirc \Diamond \, flag(x) = \text{``}d\text{''} \,].$$

Now the implication rule together with axiom Ax4 is applied in order to replace the subgoal

$$\bigcirc flag(x) = \text{``}r\text{''} \quad \text{by the plan formula } EX(read(x)).$$

We obtain two new formulas:

$$\phi_1 : \neg flag(x) = \text{``}d\text{''} \rightarrow EX(read(x)) \wedge \bigcirc \Diamond\, flag(x) = \text{``}d\text{''}$$

and

$$\phi_2 : \neg flag(x) = \text{``}d\text{''} \rightarrow \neg flag(x) = \text{``}d\text{''} \wedge \bigcirc \Diamond\, flag(x) = \text{``}d\text{''} \ .$$

The formula ϕ_1 is now transformed in order to even obtain a plan formula for the second subgoal $\bigcirc \Diamond\, flag(x) = \text{``}d\text{''}$.
First of all ϕ_1 can, according to Ax3, be replaced by:

$$\neg flag(x) = \text{``}d\text{''} \rightarrow EX(read(x)) \wedge \Diamond \bigcirc flag(x) = \text{``}d\text{''}$$

Now the implication rule is applied with Ax1 to get

$$\neg flag(x) = \text{``}d\text{''} \rightarrow EX(read(x)) \wedge \bigcirc \bigcirc flag(x) = \text{``}d\text{''}$$

and finally applying that rule with Ax5 yields:

$$\neg flag(x) = \text{``}d\text{''} \rightarrow EX(read(x)) \wedge \bigcirc EX(delete(x)) \ .$$

Applying rule NEXT_IMPL in a final step we again obtain two new formulas:

$$\phi_3 : \neg flag(x) = \text{``}d\text{''} \rightarrow EX(read(x)) \wedge \bigcirc EX(delete(x))$$

and

$$\phi_4 : \neg flag(x) = \text{``}d\text{''} \rightarrow EX(read(x)) \wedge \bigcirc \neg flag(x) = \text{``}d\text{''} \ .$$

From ϕ_3 the following plan formula can be derived:

$$\phi_3 : \neg flag(x) = \text{``}d\text{''} \rightarrow EX(read(x)); \ EX(delete(x)).$$

Hence, we obtain

$$\forall x : mail\_object \quad [EX(plan'(x)) \leftrightarrow [\neg flag(x) = \text{``}d\text{''} \rightarrow EX(read(x)); EX(delete(x))]\,]$$

as a defining axiom for the specified plan $plan'(x)$.
The formulas ϕ_2 and ϕ_4 which also have been derived during the generation process describe two properties of the new plan:

$$\forall x : mail\_object[EX(plan'(x)) \rightarrow \ [\neg flag(x) = \text{``}d\text{''}$$
$$\rightarrow [\neg flag(x) = \text{``}d\text{''} \wedge \bigcirc \Diamond\, flag(x) = \text{``}d\text{''} \ ]$$

and

$$\forall x : mail\_object[EX(plan'(x)) \rightarrow \ [\neg flag(x) = \text{``}d\text{''}$$
$$\rightarrow [EX(read(x)) \wedge \bigcirc \neg flag(x) = \text{``}d\text{''}]]$$

They represent so-called *verification formulas* that have to be proved in order to guarantee that the generated plan indeed satisfies its specification. This proof can be easily done using the definition of $plan'(x)$ above and an axiom asserting the *read-* and *delete-*flags to be different.
Selecting the appropriate axioms and rules is essential for the plan generation process to succeed. Additionally, this selection in particular influences the degree of abstraction the generated plan has. If, for example, we had decided to use instead of axioms Ax4 and Ax5 the *weaker* versions Ax4' and Ax5' with

Ax4': $\forall x : mail\_object$
$$[\neg flag(x) = \text{``}d\text{''} \wedge EX(read(x)) \rightarrow \Diamond\, flag(x) = \text{``}r\text{''}\,]$$

Ax5': $\forall x : mail\_object$
$$[\neg flag(x) = \text{``}d\text{''} \wedge EX(delete(x)) \rightarrow \Diamond flag(x) = \text{``}d\text{''}],$$

then the generated plan definition would have read:

$$\forall x : mail\_object[EX(plan'(x)) \leftrightarrow \ [\neg flag(x) = \text{``}d\text{''} \rightarrow$$
$$\Diamond EX(read(x)) ; \Diamond EX(delete(x))] \,]$$

To finally end up with the plan generation process starting from our initial specification of *plan*:

$$\forall m : mbox \ \ [EX(plan(m)) \rightarrow$$
$$\forall x : mail\_object \ \ [member(x,m) \wedge sender(x) = \text{``}otto\text{''} \wedge \neg flag(x) = \text{``}d\text{''}$$
$$\rightarrow \Diamond [flag(x) = \text{``}r\text{''} \wedge \Diamond flag(x) = \text{``}d\text{''}] \,] \,]$$

we have to introduce a while-loop in order to work through the list of all mail objects from sender "otto" and carry out the generated subplan $plan'(x)$ for each of its elements.
Finally we obtain the following plan definition:

$$\forall m : mbox \ [EX(plan(m)) \leftrightarrow \ [a := from(sender, \text{``}otto\text{''}, m);$$
$$while \ \neg Empty(a) \ do$$
$$b := first(a); \ EX(plan'(b)); \ a := tail(a) \ od] \,]$$

5.2 Plan Reuse

A plan as generated in section 5.1 represents problem solving knowledge that was used by the planning system to achieve a given goal state from a particular initial state. Therefore, we develop a reuse mechanism that enables the planner to save generated plans for a later reuse and thus extend the problem solving knowledge. The planning knowledge can now be applied to find out whether a problem can be solved by adapting an already existing plan. The architecture of the *reuse component* is based on a 4-phase model (cf. [Köh91]) describing the reuse process:

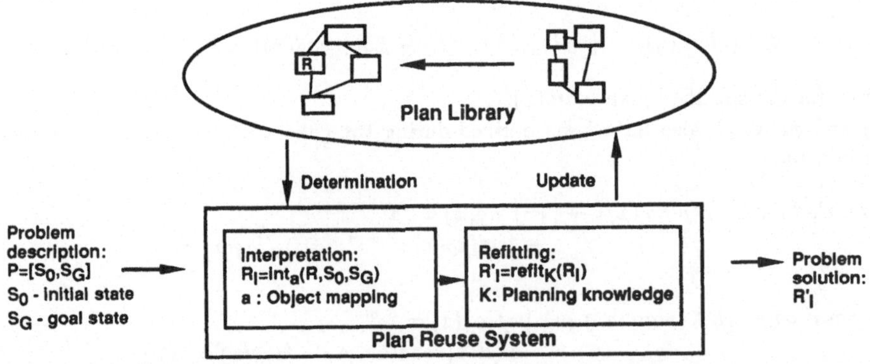

Figure 2: A 4-Phase Model of Plan Reuse

To explain how the reuse process works we reuse the plan that was generated in the preceding example to solve the new planning task: *"Read all mails from otto, save them in the folder with the sender's name, and then delete the mails"*. It is represented by the following specification formula:

$$\langle P : \rangle \ \ \forall m, n : \ mbox \ \exists z : command\_name$$
$$[EX(z) \ \rightarrow \forall x : mail\_object$$
$$[member(x,m) \wedge sender(x) = \text{``}otto\text{''} \wedge \neg flag(x) = \text{``}d\text{''} \wedge \ folder(n) = \text{``}otto\text{''}$$
$$\rightarrow \Diamond [flag(x) = \text{``}r\text{''} \wedge \Diamond [flag(x) = \text{``}\star\text{''} \wedge member(x,n) \wedge \Diamond flag(x) = \text{``}d\text{''}] \,] \,] \,]$$

5.2.1 Determination of a Reuseable Plan Entry

To solve the planning problem, a stored plan entry from the plan library is determined. We presuppose that the plan library does not contain (user-)predefined plan entries, but is built up using information provided by the deductive plan generation component, e.g., the generalized specification formula, the generalized plan schema, the verification formulas for the plan. The determination process mainly concentrates on a syntactical comparison of the current specification formula P with the generalized specification formulas R occurring in the various plan entries. In our example the determination process chooses the following generalized plan specification R from the plan library as a hypothesis on which a solution for P can be based upon:

$$\langle R :\rangle \quad \forall u : mbox \quad \forall s : sender \quad \exists v : command\_name$$
$$[EX(v) \rightarrow \quad \forall w : mail\_object$$
$$[member(w, u) \land sender(w) = s \land \neg flag(w) = \text{``}d\text{''}$$
$$\rightarrow \Diamond [flag(w) = \text{``}r\text{''} \land \Diamond flag(w) = \text{``}d\text{''} \,]\,]\,]$$

5.2.2 Interpretation of the Plan Entry in the Current Planning Situation

Now R has to be interpreted in the current planning situation by matching the two formulas. The main problem here is to find the correct mapping a of objects in P to the variables in R to generate a correct instantiation of R. Obviously, an optimal solution can be obtained by applying the substitution $\{v \leftarrow z, u \leftarrow m, w \leftarrow x, s \leftarrow otto\}$ to R leading to its instantiation:

$$\langle R_I :\rangle \quad \forall m : mbox \quad \exists z : command\_name$$
$$[EX(z) \rightarrow \forall x : mail\_object$$
$$[member(x, m) \land sender(x) = \text{``}otto\text{''} \land \neg flag(x) = \text{``}d\text{''}$$
$$\rightarrow \Diamond [flag(x) = \text{``}r\text{''} \land \Diamond flag(x) = \text{``}d\text{''} \,]\,]\,]$$

5.2.3 Refitting of the Interpreted Plan Entry

By completing the instantiation phase in our example we obtain a fully instantiated plan specification R_I which we can now compare with the current plan specification P to evaluate whether we already obtained a solution. In general, we will be confronted with the problem that the plan specifications differ in the description of the initial or the goal state, thus requiring a refitting of the plan corresponding to R_I. In our example a number of formulas in P have no corresponding formula in R_I, meaning that the plan we want to choose for reuse will only partially solve the current goal. Thus, we obtain a formula R_I' which contains the generated plan $plan'(x)$, but also an open subgoal for which the planner has to be activated again:

$$\langle R_I' :\rangle \quad \forall m, n : mbox \quad \exists z : command\_name$$
$$[EX(z) \rightarrow \forall x : mail\_object$$
$$[member(x, m) \land sender(x) = \text{``}otto\text{''} \land \neg flag(x) = \text{``}d\text{''} \land folder(n) = \text{``}otto\text{''}$$
$$\rightarrow EX(read(x)); \Diamond flag(x) = \text{``} \star \text{''} \land member(x, n); EX(delete(x))]\,]$$

This specification describes that the plan to be reused has to be modified in such a way, that an additional condition has to hold in the initial state and that an additional action has to be included.

5.2.4 Updating the Plan Library

The reuse process finishes with the update of the plan library. The decision whether a plan is "worth" storing in the plan library depends on its similarity to already stored plans. A new plan entry is built up from the specification formula for the plan, the plan itself, the verification conditions for the plan, and the transformation rules used in the generation process. Furthermore, an abstraction process (cf. section 4) will be applied leading to the storage of abstract plan entries.

References

[Bib86]   W. Bibel. A deductive solution for plan generation. *New Generation Computing*, 4:115–132, 1986.

[Biu88]   S. Biundo. Automated synthesis of recursive algorithms as a theorem proving tool. In *Proceedings of the 8th European Conference on Artificial Intelligence, München*, pages 553–558, 1988.

[Biu90]   S. Biundo. Plan generation using a method of deductive program synthesis. Research Report RR-90-09, German Research Center for Artificial Intelligence Inc., 1990.

[Biu91]   S. Biundo. *Automatische Synthese rekursiver Algorithmen als Beweisverfahren*. Informatik Fachberichte. Springer, Berlin, 1991. forthcoming.

[Bre90]   J. Breuker. *EUROHELP Developing Intelligent Help Systems*. EC, Kopenhagen, 1990.

[DGH87]   D. Dengler, M. Gutmann, and G. Hector. Der Planerkenner REPLIX. Memo No. 16, Dept. of Computer Science, University of Saarbrücken, W.Germany, 1987.

[Fin83]   T. W. Finin. Providing help and advice in task oriented systems. In *Proceedings of the 8th International Joint Conference on Artificial Intelligence*, pages 176–178, 1983.

[FLS85]   G. Fischer, A. Lemke, and T. Schwab. Knowledge-based help systems. In *Proceedings of Human Factors in Computing Systems (CHI'85)*, pages 161–167, 1985.

[Hal89]   R. W. S. Hale. Programming in temporal logic. Technical Report 173, Computer Laboratory, University of Cambridge, England, 1989.

[Hec87]   M. Hecking. How to Use Plan Recognition to Improve the Abilities of the Intelligent Help System SINIX Consultant. In *Proceedings of the Second IFIP Conference on Human-Computer Interaction, held at the University of Stuttgart, Federal Republic of Germany, 1-4 September, 1987*, pages 657–662, 1987.

[Hec91]   M. Hecking. *Eine logische Behandlung der verteilten und mehrstufigen Planerkennung*. PhD thesis, University of Saarbrücken, 1991. forthcoming.

[Heg91]   S.J. Hegner. Plan realization for complex command interactions in the unix help domain. In P. Norwig, W. Wahlster, and R. Wilensky, editors, *Intelligent Help Systems for UNIX - Case Studies in Artificial Intelligence*. Springer, 1991.

[HKN+88]   M. Hecking, C. Kemke, E. Nessen, D. Dengler, M. Gutmann, and G. Hector. The SINIX Consultant - A Progress Report. Memo No. 28, Dept. of Computer Science, University of Saarbrücken, W.Germany, 1988.

[Köh91]   J. Köhler. Approaches to the reuse of plan schemata in planning formalisms. Technical Memo TM-91-01, German Research Center for Artificial Intelligence Inc., 1991.

[Krö87]   F. Kröger. *Temporal Logic of Programs*. Springer, Heidelberg, 1987.

[Lur88]   M. Luria. Knowledge intensive planning. Technical Report UCB/CSD 88/433, Computer Science Division, University of California, Berkeley, 1988.

[Mer91]   G. Merziger. Approaches to abduction - an overview. Technical memo, German Research Center for Artificial Intelligence Inc., 1991. forthcoming.

[MW86]   Z. Manna and R. Waldinger. How to clear a block: Plan formation in situational logic. In *Proceedings of the 8th International Conference on Automated Deduction*, pages 622–640, 1986.

[NWWng]   P. Norwig, W. Wahlster, and R. Wilensky. *Intelligent Help Systems for UNIX - Case Studies in Artificial Intelligence*. Springer, Heidelberg, 1991 (forthcoming).

[RP86]   R. Rosner and A. Pnueli. A choppy logic. In *Symposium on Logic in Computer Science*, Cambridge, Massachusetts, 1986.

[SC85]   M. Sullivan and P. R. Cohen. An endorsement-based plan recognition program. In *Proceedings of the 9th International Joint Conference on Artificial Intelligence*, pages 475–479, 1985.

Knowledge Representation in Kernel Lisp[1]

María Victoria Cengarle   Heiner Brand
Luis Mandel   Klaus Däßler
Martin Wirsing   Thekla Schneider

Bayerisches Forschungszentrum für   Siemens-Nixdorf AG
Wissensbasierte Systeme (FORWISS)   8TM SD 211
Universität Passau   Bereich Datentechnik
Postfach 2540   Otto-Hahn-Ring 6
W-8390 Passau   W-8000 München 83

Abstract

In this paper several examples for knowledge representation in DKLISP are presented. DKLISP
is a kernel LISP-language, which combines essential features from functional, procedural and
object-oriented programming. It is not a new LISP dialect. Its intended target is to be as
compatible as possible with the ANSI COMMON-LISP (ACL) Draft and the EULISP Definition.
We envision our planned industrial LISP to be a scientific-technological language with features
for software engineering, class-oriented programming and knowledge processing.

1 Introduction

LISP is the language most widely used for knowledge representation and for artificial intelligence.
Today it is in the process of standardization, where COMMON-LISP and EULISPare the two main
candidates. They differ in several aspects such as: two name space vs. one name space, evaluation
of the function symbol in an invocation, binding, etc. The most used is COMMON-LISP, but up to
now it is not available for small computers. Therefore, our goal was to develop a small kernel, easily
extendible (or transformable) into COMMON-LISP and EULISP, which could be seen as a "turbo
LISP."

In this paper we present the programming language "DIN-LISP kernel" (or DKLISP) and its
class system called "GAUß." DKLISP was proposed to the DIN community as a first approach to
the DIN-LISP definition. The goal of DKLISP is to be a subset as compatible as possible with the
ANSI COMMON-LISP (ACL) Draft and the EULISP Definition. The general characteristics of GAUß
are the single inheritance and the unification of the concepts of class, type and structure. In what
follows, type and class are to be understood as the same concept. Each type is a class and each
structure is also a class: in GAUß a new class is a type. A class is defined as a collection or record

---

[1]This work is part of the FORWISS project ESCL between the Universität Passau and the Siemens-Nixdorf AG.

of slots, each of which is to be filled with information. Slots can be typed or not; classes can be defined in terms of themselves (recursively).

The kernel includes the basic control abstractions of a LISP language in an orthogonal way. Derived constructs which are easily implementable by means of others were, in general, left out. Object abstraction is divided into two parts: classes and packages. The class concept supports the structuring of data with a simple but powerful data refinement concept, that is, single inheritance. In order to have a compact presentation, the concepts of type, class and record are unified. As in any general purpose language, the basic data structures of DKLISP comprise the usual predefined structures. The kernel must be reasonably small, efficient and easily implementable.

We present DKLISP with several examples which compose a computer game. In it, a robot is placed on a surface possibly containing obstacles. The robot's task is to reach a target position, avoiding the obstacles in its way. Additionally, the robot has an initial amount of "power" which is partly consumed by each movement. There are two kinds of obstacles: edible and movable obstacles. The movable obstacles can only be shifted from one position to another; by performing such an action, the robot loses a bit more power. On the other hand, the robot can gain power if it eats an edible object. If the robot has exhausted all its power, then it cannot move any more and the game ends with failure. The game ends with success if the robot reaches its target position. These examples cover great part of the features of DKLISP.

In section §2 we show how classes can be created and which are the possibilities for the slots' description, whereas in section §3 the procedure is described for the refinement of classes. In section §4 we present different methods for the same generic function. In section §5 the package system is sketched, and in section §6 we give examples of functions in DKLISP. Finally, in section §7 we give some comments to the whole work and give a sketch of our next work on DKLISP.

2 Classes and Slots

Classes are defined in terms of previously defined and built-in classes. The system starts with a (finite) number of predefined classes, and the user may dynamically add new ones. At any time a class has a finite number of superclasses. Because of single inheritance, there is exactly one class, called the *direct superclass*, in terms of which a new one is defined. The new class is called a *direct subclass* of the previously existing one. The *superclass* (resp. *subclass*) relation is the reflexive-transitive closure of the *direct superclass* (resp. *direct subclass*) relation. Both the subclass and superclass relations are antisymmetric and thus define a partial order over the set of classes. The most general class in this hierarchy, the only one with no superclass, is the `object` class.

Let us take as an example the class of all the points in the real plane. For their description, we only need a structure with two fields, the abscissa and the ordinate of a point. This class is not defined in terms of a previous one, so we create it as subclass of `object`.

```
(defclass point (object)
    ((x-coord
        initarg     x-coord
        initform    0
        typed-slot  'integer
        reader      x-coord
        writer      set-x)
```

```
(y-coord
   initarg    y-coord
   initform   0
   typed-slot 'integer
   reader     y-coord
   writer     set-y)
)  )
```

Here we stated that each coordinate must be of type `integer` with default value specified by the `initform` option; any attempt to assign non-`integer` values to these slots will lead to an error signaling. The `reader` and `writer` give a name to the functions of inspection and modification, respectively. The `initarg` parameter specifies the name of the slot for creation.

Let us now enlarge our example. We want to write a program which guides the movements of a robot through a space possibly containing obstacles. In a first approach, obstacles are simply defined as records with two attributes: name and weight.

```
(defclass obstacle (object)
    ((obstacle-name              ;;; the name of the obstacle
        initarg    obstacle-name
        reader     obstacle-name)
     (obstacle-weight            ;;; its weight in kg
        initarg    obstacle-weight
        typed-slot 'real
        reader     obstacle-weight)
)  )
```

The language allows the definition of global symbols, which may hold variable or constant values. In this way, we can represent the surface upon which the robot walks as a matrix global to the package. This matrix will hold elements of type `obstacle`; for the case there is no obstacle in a matrix position, we define a "null obstacle."

```
(defconstant *dim-x* 8)

(defconstant *dim-y* 8)

(defconstant *null-obstacle*
          (make-instance 'obstacle
                         'obstacle-name nil
                         'obstacle-weight 0)
)

(deflocal matrix-space
          (make-array (list *dim-x* *dim-y*)
                      initial-element *null-obstacle*
)        )
```

The matrix may contain elements of type `obstacle` and each one of its positions is initialized with `*null-obstacle*`. We may assume there is a process which puts obstacles in this space.

3   Inheritance

The data structure of a class is inherited by all its subclasses. This means that an instance of a subclass will contain values for all the slots defined in the subclass, as well as for all the slots defined in its superclass.

When a class is created, it is always created in terms of an existing one, which, as mentioned above, is called its superclass. The same is valid for all the built-in classes except for `object`, which is the most general class in the subclass sense. The new class inherits all the slots of its superclass. If new slots are added, they all must have different names. That is, name collision is forbidden.

We can think the obstacles blocking the path of our robot as edible or movable. This leads to the creation of two subclasses of `obstacle` for describing these two possibilities.

```
(defclass edible-obstacle (obstacle)
    ((obstacle-flavour          ;;; its flavour
        initarg obstacle-flavour
        reader  obstacle-flavour)
)   )

(defclass movable-obstacle (obstacle)
    ((obstacle-color            ;;; its color
        initarg obstacle-color
        reader  obstacle-color)
)   )
```

In this way, if we have a local variable `my-obstacle` which holds an instance of the class `edible--obstacle`, then one can ask for the value of the `obstacle-flavour` slot of `my-obstacle` can be asked for the value of the `obstacle-flavour` slot, as well as for the value of the `obstacle-weight` slot, but it cannot be asked for a `obstacle-color`.

We have chosen the approach of *state space* for representing the path of the robot. A state will be the point at which the robot is located and the remaining power the robot has for doing its task.

```
(defclass state (point)
    ((power-value
        initarg  power-value
        initform 0
        reader   power-value
        writer   set-power)
)   )
```

The initial and the final states can be represented as

```
(deflocal *start-state*
        (make-instance 'state 'x-coord 0
                              'y-coord 0
                              'power-value 15))

(deflocal *end-state*
        (make-instance 'state 'x-coord 5
                              'y-coord 7))
```

where the value for the `power-value` in the `*end-state*` is left unspecified since it is uninteresting for our purposes.

4   Generic Functions and Methods

A method is a function defined for a tuple of typed parameters, which are instances of specific classes. An untyped parameter is understood as being typed with the most general object class (w.r.t. the subclass relation). Methods are not attached to a particular class as in the message passing model. Different methods with the same name can be defined, if they have the same number of parameters. Then, according to the generic function model, all methods with the same name are collected in one generic function. There is no explicit creation of generic functions; the user only defines and redefines methods. A generic function can be seen as a standard LISP function, whose behavior is determined by the class of its arguments. Given a tuple of parameters, the generic function decides –by use of a decision process– which is the method that will effectively compute a result. If a method is applicable to an instance of a class, then it is also applicable to any instance of the class' subclasses.

All methods with identical names must have the same arity. Two methods are different if the tuples of parameters they accept belong to different cartesian products of classes. Otherwise, if two methods have the same domain, the most recently defined method destroys the previous definition for that domain.

For storing the path of the robot, we will use a stack. The advantage of that representation is its appropriateness for implementing backtracking. The backtracking algorithm will not be included in the present paper because of space and simplicity reasons. For a complete implementation of this game, see [Cengarle & Mandel 91]. A stack will have a slot which contains all the values pushed to it, represented as a list, which defaults to `nil` (the empty stack). Methods associated with the stack class are (as usual) one for adding a new element to a stack, one for reading the last element inserted into a stack, one for removing from a stack its last element, and one for testing emptiness of a stack.

```
(defclass generic-stack-class (object)
   ((stack
        initarg    stack
        initform   nil
        reader     stack
        writer     set-stack)
)   )

(defmethod stack-push ((s generic-stack-class) x)
   (set-stack s (cons x (stack s)))
)

(defmethod stack-top ((s generic-stack-class))
   (if (null (stack s))
       (print "Empty Stack")
       (car (stack s))
)   )
```

```
(defmethod stack-pop ((s generic-stack-class))
    (if (null (stack s))
        (print "Empty Stack")
        (progn (set-stack s (cdr (stack s))) s)
)   )

(defmethod stack-is-empty ((s generic-stack-class))
    (null (stack s))
)
```

As a subclass of the class `generic-stack-class` of general stacks we will have the class `typed--stack-class` for stacks which can additionally contain only elements of a particular type. For the instances of `typed-stack-class` the method `stack-push` must be refined.

```
(defclass typed-stack-class (generic-stack-class)
    ((type-of-stack
         initarg   type-of-stack
         reader    type-of-stack)
)   )

(defmethod stack-push ((s typed-stack-class) x)
    (if (subclassp (class-of x) (type-of-stack s))
        (call-next-method)
        (print "Invalid Value")
)   )
```

When a generic function is invoked with particular actual parameters, all the applicable methods are searched and ordered by means of the lexicographic extension of the subclass relation w.r.t. the tuples built by their domains. Because of single inheritance, this ordering is total, and its first method is the so-called *effective method*, which is selected to be applied to the actual parameters. The invocation of the "next method" (`call-next-method` in method `stack-push`, for instance) refers to the immediately greater method in the ordering of applicable methods, which will be passed the actual parameters. For a formal definition of this method invocation protocol, see [Gauß 91].

5   Packages

Programming in the large is achieved by a simple package system. One can encapsulate function definitions, symbols, etc. In order to avoid name collision the qualifier mode is given. A package can import some or all exported definitions of another package. It may change the binding of an imported symbol if this was not forbidden by the export declaration.

Packages are provided for encapsulating and hiding code. A package is an entity with a definition part or interface and an implementation part. In the interface the relation of the package with the external world is stated by declaring what it needs and what it offers from/to other packages. In the implementation part at least the exported features must be defined.

The packages are flat, i.e., they cannot be nested. If a package M_2 imports definitions from a package M_1, the definiton part of M_1 must be prepared for execution before the definition part of M_2. Thus, the packages form a directed acyclic graph, where there is an arc from a package M_1 to a package M_2 iff M_2 imports definitions from M_1.

For the robot program, it will be useful to separate the definitions for creating and manipulating stacks from the definitions of classes and functions particular to the robot movement. In this way, other users that may find interest in using our `stack` will not have to care about `obstacle`'s and `point`'s. For that, we can write

```
(defpackage stack
            (export generic-class-stack typed-class-stack
                    stack-push stack-top stack-pop stack-is-empty)
)
```

and before and after the text defining `generic-class-stack`, push, pop, etc., we should then write (`in-package stack`) and (`end-package stack`), respectively.

6 Functional Programming Style

In this section we present the algorithm for manipulating the data and guiding the robot from its start position to its target one. The general idea of the algorithm is –given any position of the robot– to generate all the surrounding positions, to filter out those positions which do not fit in the matrix space, and finally to select as next position the one minimizing an heuristic function. With each movement, the robot loses power; it also loses power if it shifts a movable obstacle. On the contrary, it can increment its power by eating an edible obstacle. This algorithm may be implemented as follows.

```
(defun inference-engine ()
   (let ((way (make-instance 'typed-stack-class 'type-of-stack 'state)))
      (do ((actual-state *start-state* (advance-state actual-state)))
          (;; end test:
           (or (equal-point actual-state *end-state*)
               (= (power-value actual-state) 0))
           ;; return value:
           (progn
              (if (equal-point actual-state *end-state*)
                  (stack-push way actual-state)
                  (print "No More Power!"))
              (dump way)
          ))
          ;; do body:
          (stack-push way actual-state)
   )  )  )
```

The heuristic function may be a combination of functions. So, for example, we may calculate the minimum of the sum of the euclidean distance and the function which calculates the loss of power.

```
(deflocal *heuristics* '(euclides loss-of-power))

(defun euclides (point)
    (sqrt (+ (sqr (- (x-coord point) (x-coord *end-state*)))
             (sqr (- (y-coord point) (y-coord *end-state*)))
)  )    )
```

```lisp
(defun loss-of-power (point)
    (let* ((obstacle-in-point (aref *matrix-space*
                                    (x-coord point)
                                    (y-coord point)))
           (weight-in-point (weight obstacle-in-point)))
       (case (class-name (class-of obstacle-in-point))
             ('edible-obstacle (- weight-in-point))
             ('movable-obstacle weight-in-point)
             ('obstacle 0)
) ) )
```

But we can have even more criteria, which can be added dynamically afterwards using a function
add-heuristic. Or we can remove some of the heuristics using delete-heuristic. Performing
such changes the behavior of the robot is altered. Then we may define the following.

```lisp
(defun add-heuristic (fname)
    (if (functionp fname)
        (setq *heuristics* (adjoin fname *heuristics*))
        (print "Not a Function")
) )

(defun delete-heuristic (fname)
    (setq *heuristics* (delete fname *heuristics*))
)
```

Let us now show how to use these heuristic functions. As we said before, given an actual position,
the next will be calculated by selecting the most promising one amongst a set (represented by a
list) of points around the actual one (omitting those which do not fit inside the matrix). This can
be done in the following way.

```lisp
(defun advance-state (actual-state)
    (let ((next-state (select (filter (generate actual-state)))))
         (update-matrix actual-state next-state)
         next-state
) )

;;; "generate" and "filter" are obvious.
;;; "update-matrix" removes an eated edible-object, and
;;; changes the position of a shifted movable-object.

(defun select (point-list)
    (nth (cdr (min-position (sel point-list))) point-list)
)

(defun sel (point-list *heuristics*)
    (if (null (cdr *heuristics*))
        (mapcar (car *heuristics*) point-list)
        (mapcar + (mapcar (car *heuristics*) point-list)
                  (sel point-list (cdr *heuristics*))
) ) )
```

`minimum` is a function which returns a pair (`value` . `position`), where `value` is the minimum heuristic value of the points in the `point-list` (the valid surrounding points) and `position` is the position of its inverse image in the list `point-list`.

The remaining functions, which complete this example, can be found in [Cengarle & Mandel 91].

7   Concluding Remarks

In the preceding sections we have presented a short introduction to DKLISP and to its class system GAUß. Although DKLISP is a kernel language, we hope to have shown by the examples that DKLISP is powerful enough for supporting functional programming, programming in the large with a simple package system, and structuring of data with a compact, simple, object-oriented class system.

Now we are working on the implementation of DKLISP. DKLISPis also being enlarged with a second layer of new features which allow, for instance, multiple inheritance in the class system and the definition of metaclasses. Also, more forms are added which facilitate the programming. The implementation of these new features will not necessarily be written in terms of the kernel.

References

[Cengarle & Mandel 91]   María Victoria Cengarle, Luis Mandel. *Peti: a Game in DKLisp*. FOR-WISS Passau Intern Report FR I-Passau-1991-004 (June 1991).

[DKLisp 91]   Heiner Brand, María Victoria Cengarle, Klaus Däßler, Luis Mandel, Thekla Schneider, Martin Wirsing. *An Approach to the DIN Kernel Lisp Definition*. Version 0.1 (unpublished).

[EuLisp 90]   Julian Padget, Greg Nuyens. *The EuLisp Definition*. Version 0.69 and posteriors (unpublished).

[Feel 90]   Concurrent Research Group, School of Mathematical Sciences, University of Bath, United Kingdom. *Feel: An implementation of EuLisp*. Version 0.38 (unpublished).

[Franz 84]   Franz Inc. *COMMON LISP: The Reference*. Addison-Wesley (1988).

[Gauß 91]   Heiner Brand, María Victoria Cengarle, Klaus Däßler, Luis Mandel, Thekla Schneider, Martin Wirsing. *Gauß: The DIN Lisp Object System* Version 0.1 (unpublished).

[Keene 89]   Sonya Keene. *Object-Oriented Programming in COMMON LISP*. Addison-Wesley (1989).

[Lang & Pearlmutter 86]   Kevin Lang, Barak Pearlmutter. "Oaklisp: An Object-Oriented Scheme with First Class Types." *Proceedings of the ACM Conference on Object-Oriented Systems, Languages, and Applications (OOPSLA) '86* (Special Issue of SIGPLAN Notices, November 1986), pp 30–37.

[Steele 90]   Guy Lewis Steele Jr. *COMMON LISP: The Language*. Digital Press, 2nd. edition (1990).

Belief Revision, Diagnosis and Repair

Wolfgang Nejdl

Technical University of Vienna, Paniglgasse 16

A-1040 Vienna, Austria

e-mail: nejdl@vexpert.dbai.tuwien.ac.at

Abstract

Models play a prominent role in reasoning about physical systems. Two problems in this context are constructing an initial model and revising a model depending on new data. Belief revision is a way to formalize the second process. This paper discusses the principles of belief revision and their application to reasoning in model-based systems for diagnosis and repair.

We define diagnosis and repair in model-based reasoning systems as belief revision operators. Starting from the definition of diagnosis used in current model-based reasoning systems, we first show the properties of such a diagnosis revision operator.

As the concept of diagnosis is not able to formalize important aspects of the complete diagnosis and repair process, we then describe the concept of a repair revision operator and show how to combine these two operators to define a diagnosis and repair process. This process extends diagnosis by taking the repair purpose into account and allows the integration of both knowledge and actions into our mental model of the world.

1 Introduction

In this paper we will discuss the diagnosis and repair process in model-based systems viewed as the reasoning process of a diagnostic agent. This agent uses a mental model of the system to be diagnosed and repaired. Diagnosis and repair are shown to be two different tasks whose effects on this mental model are implemented by two different *belief revision operators*. We show how these operators are tightly integrated during the diagnosis and repair process and which other problem solving aspects have to be considered.

In the following we will use logical formulas to represent the actual world and the mental models of this world. The general principles discussed in this paper are nevertheless valid in other representations as well. For example, [2] use a representation based on temporal logic.

We will first describe a small circuit which we will use as working example throughout the paper. In Section 2 we discuss the concepts necessary for the diagnosis task: actual, possible and plausible worlds and the integration of additional knowledge into our set of beliefs during the diagnosis phase. In Section 3 we discuss the integration of (repair) actions and the concept of a system/repair purpose. Finally, in Section 4 we give an algorithm scheme for the general diagnosis and repair process and close with a small example using the concepts developed in this paper.

1.1 Working Example

We will use a primitive circuit as running example, which consists of three multipliers and two adders as depicted in Figure 1.

This system satisfies a set of integrity constraints (valid in each situation) describing the behavior of the components and the structure of the specific device. In our examples we will use the following set of integrity constraints, assuming defect components may act in an arbitrary way:

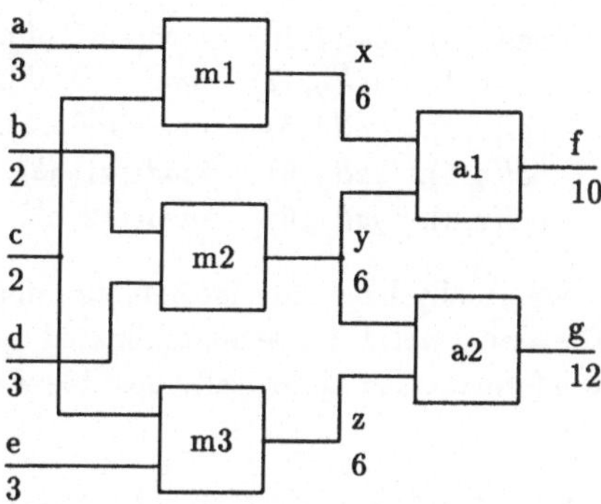

Figure 1: Circuit: $m1, m2, m3$ are multipliers, $a1, a2$ are adders

$type(M,multiplier) \wedge\ mode(M,ok) \wedge\ val(in1(M),V1) \wedge\ val(in2(M),V2) \wedge\ val(out(M),V3)$
$\rightarrow V3 = V1 \times V2.$

$type(A,adder) \wedge\ mode(A,ok) \wedge\ val(in1(A),V1) \wedge\ val(in2(A),V2) \wedge\ val(out(A),V3)$
$\rightarrow V3 = V1 + V2.$

$val(P,V1) \wedge val(P,V2)$
$\rightarrow V1 = V2.$

$conn(P1,P2) \wedge\ val(P1,V1) \wedge\ val(P2,V2) \rightarrow V1 = V2.$

$type(C,\_) \rightarrow mode(C,ok) \vee mode(C,ab).$

Additionally, we have facts describing the type and connections of the five components $m1, m2, m3, a1, a2$.

2 Diagnosis

2.1 Actual and Possible Worlds

Why do we need diagnosis at all? The answer is simple: Because we do not know the actual state of the system. Viewed in this light diagnosis is simply a problem solving process to find a mental model corresponding as much as possible to the actual state of the system. During an iterative process we refine our model using additional observations until we are reasonably sure that it represents the actual system.

So the first concept we have to define is that of the *actual world*.

Definition 1 (Actual World) The *actual world* is a set of logical formulas representing the actual state of the world. We will denote this set by *AW*.

Assuming that the integrity constraints described in the last section are valid in each situation, we can represent the actual world by these integrity constraints plus the following set of facts:

$$val(a,3). \quad val(f,10). \quad mode(m1,ok).$$
$$val(b,2). \quad val(g,12). \quad mode(m2,ok).$$
$$val(c,2). \quad val(x,6). \quad mode(m3,ok).$$
$$val(d,3). \quad val(y,6). \quad mode(a1,ab).$$
$$val(e,3). \quad val(z,6). \quad mode(a2,ok).$$

The problem now is that we usually have only incomplete information, usually consisting of a subset of the observations. The actual world can be approximated by a set of *logically possible worlds* which extend the incomplete information in all logically possible ways consistent with the integrity constraints.

Definition 2 (Logically Possible World) A *logically possible world* is an approximation consistent with what is known about the actual world. It consists of a set of logical formulas. We will denote the set of all logically possible worlds by LW.

As we are interested mainly in component states we will use the set of defect components as a key uniquely identifying a world, i.e. each possible combination represents a different world. Disjunctions of other values (if the exact value is unknown) do not split a world into several different ones. Note, that our notion of a world is more general than that of a logical model.

Let us assume, that we have measured the values for $a - e$ so far. According to the set of integrity constraints all combinations of state assignments (ok or ab) to the five components are consistent with these observations. The set of possible worlds consists of 32 worlds, starting with the world in which all components work correctly (w_1) to the world where all components are defect (w_{32}). These worlds correspond to all consistent diagnosis candidates from [1].

w_1 is represented by the following facts:

$$val(a,3). \quad val(f,12). \quad mode(m1,ok).$$
$$val(b,2). \quad val(g,12). \quad mode(m2,ok).$$
$$val(c,2). \quad val(x,6). \quad mode(m3,ok).$$
$$val(d,3). \quad val(y,6). \quad mode(a1,ok).$$
$$val(e,3). \quad val(z,6). \quad mode(a2,ok).$$

w_{32} is represented by the following facts:

$$val(a,3). \quad mode(m1,ab).$$
$$val(b,2). \quad mode(m2,ab).$$
$$val(c,2). \quad mode(m3,ab).$$
$$val(d,3). \quad mode(a1,ab).$$
$$val(e,3). \quad mode(a2,ab).$$

In w_{32} no values (not even disjunctions) can be predicted for x, y, z, f, g as our integrity constraints do include neither fault models nor domain axioms.

2.2 Monotonic Integration of Knowledge

Integrating additional knowledge (observations) makes some of these worlds inconsistent and allows us to make more predictions in other worlds. This revision of our mental model in terms of LW is strictly monotonic, i.e. worlds can only be removed, not added. All inferences drawn in a specific situation remain valid after we add facts representing additional knowledge.

This revision can be formalized by a *monotonic belief revision operator* $\circ_m$, which integrates new knowledge A into our mental model LW computing a new mental model LW'.

$$LW \circ_m A = LW'$$

As this operator is monotonic, we have

$$LW' \subseteq LW$$

Obviously, we also have

$$AW \in LW$$

If we use failure probabilities to assign probabilities to the different worlds, they have to be renormalized each time some worlds get inconsistent. Otherwise, probabilities have not effect.

What happens if we have a complete set of measurements? Let us assume, that all values of $a - e, x - z$ and f, g in our circuit are known already. 16 of 32 of our previous worlds (the ones, which assume $a1$ to be correct) get inconsistent, leaving a set of possible worlds of 16. Assuming we are not able to check the components directly, we are stuck with 16 possible worlds. It does not seem plausible that we really reason with the whole set of possible worlds. The concept of logically possible world is therefore not able to represent our reasoning process.

2.3   Plausible Worlds

What is still missing from the concept of a logically possible world is some kind of preference or plausibility relation, which represents the fact, that we usually take only the most plausible worlds into account. This is especially true when we reason about choosing additional measurement points or evaluate repair actions, which we will discuss in a later section of this paper.

This is addressed by the concept of *plausible world*. The set of plausible worlds is a subset of the set of logically possible worlds and represents the worlds we reason with during the diagnosis process.

Definition 3 (Plausible World) A *plausible world* is a logically possible world which is "plausible" enough to be included in the reasoning process. We denote the set of plausible worlds by PW, which is a subset of the set of logically possible worlds ($PW \subseteq LW$).

Contrary to logically possible worlds we do not necessarily have $AW \in PW$, i.e. the actual world may not be included in the set of plausible worlds.

If we use the minimality criterion defined in [7] and [1] only the worlds corresponding to the minimal diagnoses in a set-theoretic sense are included in the set of plausible worlds. In our example (given a complete set of measurements), the only remaining plausible world is the one corresponding to the diagnosis [$a1$] (only component $a1$ is faulty), which correctly represents the actual world.

$$
\begin{array}{lll}
val(a,3). & val(f,10). & mode(m1,ok). \\
val(b,2). & val(g,12). & mode(m2,ok). \\
val(c,2). & val(x,6). & mode(m3,ok). \\
val(d,3). & val(y,6). & mode(a1,ab). \\
val(e,3). & val(z,6). & mode(a2,ok).
\end{array}
$$

Which world to include into the set of plausible worlds may be determined by a number of ways. While we will not discuss any specific possibility in detail, we will define the general principle of plausibility based on a preference relation.

Definition 4 (Plausibility and Preference) Given a preference relation $\leq$ between worlds, a world w_i is at least as preferable as w_j, iff $w_i \leq w_j$.

The preference relation is a partial pre-order, i.e. it has the following properties:

- reflexivity: $w_i \leq w_i$
- transitivity: $w_i \leq w_j \wedge w_j \leq w_k \rightarrow w_i \leq w_k$

Another interesting property is modularity which is defined by

$$(w_i \leq w_j) \wedge (w_j \leq w_i) \wedge (w_k < w_i) \rightarrow (w_k < w_j)$$

where $(a < b) \equiv (a \leq b) \wedge (b \not\leq a)$.

Basically this means, that the preference relation orders the worlds into layers of equally plausible worlds. Minimal cardinality (minimal number of defect components in a diagnosis) leads to a modular preference relation (diagnoses with the same cardinality are in the same plausibility layer), but set-theoretic minimality as defined in [7] does not.

2.4 Nonmonotonic Integration of Knowledge

To integrate additional knowledge into the set of plausible worlds, let us formalize the integration of additional knowledge into PW by a *belief revision operator for knowledge* denoted by $\circ_k$.

$$PW \circ_k A = PW'$$

Integrating additional knowledge into PW is no longer monotonic. Although inconsistent worlds are deleted from PW as before, new plausible worlds may be included into PW' in the process of integrating additional knowledge.

Now it is interesting to determine in which cases conclusions valid in the old set of beliefs PW are still valid in the new belief set PW'. This is desirable as the set of plausible worlds serves as a focus to make the reasoning process both more efficient and more understandable which can be done more easily if inferences are as monotonic as possible.

We will discuss this issue using the concept of *conditional implication*. Let us denote a world where a formula A is true by the term A-world. Then the conditional implication $A \Rightarrow B$ is true, iff B is true in all most plausible A-worlds. That is, given an initial set of worlds and a proposition A, we compute the most plausible revision such that A is true in each revised world and check if B is true in these worlds, too. We do this starting from the world included in the set of plausible worlds, PW:

$$PW \models A \Rightarrow B$$

Using the concept of PW' which results from the revision of PW with A, i.e. $PW' = PW \circ_k A$, the formula above is equivalent to

$$PW' \models B$$

That is, conditional implication can be useful in determining which conclusions are valid, if we revise the initial belief base PW by a logical formula A. Its semantics (like that of our belief revision operator $\circ_k$) is tied to the preference ordering of worlds which determines the notion of plausibility needed in its evaluation (for a more detailed elaboration see [6]).

As mentioned above, a high degree of monotonicity is preferable. In the general case, conditional implication does not satisfy the axiom of monotonic logic, *strengthening antecedents*, i.e. the following formula is not an axiom:

$$(A \Rightarrow C) \rightarrow (A \wedge B \Rightarrow C)$$

This is easy to see, if we consider the case, where in all most plausible A-worlds (denoted by PW) B is false. We have to compute a set of completely new $A \wedge B$-worlds (corresponding to PW'), where we know nothing about C at all.

However, we may guarantee monotonicity in case at least some plausible A-worlds also include B, i.e.

$$(A \Rightarrow C) \wedge \neg (A \Rightarrow \neg B) \rightarrow (A \wedge B \Rightarrow C)$$

This implies that

$$PW' \subseteq PW \text{ iff } (PW \wedge A) \text{ is consistent,}$$

if we neglect the possibility, that the observations are inconsistent with the integrity constraints (which would lead to $PW' = \emptyset$).

This axiom is valid if the preference relation is modular. It leads to a diagnosis process focusing on a set of plausible worlds which only adds new worlds if none of the worlds in the current set is consistent with the additional assumptions.

2.5 Example

Let us consider our running example and take as initial measurements $a - e$ and f. Additionally, we will use the cardinality of diagnoses as a preference relation (i.e. worlds with less faulty components are preferred to worlds with more faulty components). The initial set of plausible worlds PW consists of the worlds representing the single fault diagnoses $[m1], [m2]$ and $[a1]$.

The set of conditional implications implied by PW includes the following:

$$
\begin{aligned}
val(out(m1), 6) &\Rightarrow mode(m1, ok) \\
val(out(m2), 6) &\Rightarrow mode(m2, ok) \\
val(out(a2), 12) &\Rightarrow mode(m2, ok)
\end{aligned}
$$

As our preference relation is modular, these implications stay valid after additional observations and therefore can be used to explain why certain measurement points are suggested (e.g. "If I knew the value of x and it were 6, then I would consider $m1$ to be ok."),

Integration of additional measurements results in a monotonic reduction of PW, except when measurements are taken which are inconsistent with all three plausible worlds (i.e. $val(out(m3), 4)$) (in which case also the conditional implications have to be re-evaluated). The integration of the additional observation g, $val(out(a2), 12)$, for example reduces PW' to the two worlds corresponding to $[m1]$ and $[a1]$.

What happens if we use the principle of minimal diagnosis as defined in [7], where a diagnosis is minimal, if its set of faulty components is not a superset of another diagnosis? In this case, PW' consists not only of the two worlds corresponding to $[m1]$ and $[a1]$, but also of the worlds corresponding to the two double fault diagnoses $[m2, m3]$ and $[m2, a2]$. As a result the third conditional implication (a correct value at g implies the correctness of $m2$) is not valid, although it would be expected given that our set of hypotheses before measuring g consisted of the three single fault worlds $[m1], [m2], [a1]$ which implied this prediction.

2.6 Summary: Diagnosis

To summarize our concept of diagnosis, we can describe the diagnosis process as follows:

- We do not know each detail of the actual world, therefore we have to approximate it by a set of plausible worlds.

- The relative plausibility of a world is determined by an absolute preference relation between all worlds.

- It is not necessary that the actual world is one of the plausible worlds (for example if we do not have enough knowledge). Therefore nonmonotonic jumps are inevitable, which make our previous conclusions invalid.

- To minimize nonmonotonicity (which allows us to focus the diagnosis process and explain it to a human expert) the preference relation should be modular.

- Diagnosis is the process of revising our beliefs (which are represented by the set of plausible worlds) in response to additional knowledge about the actual world.

The diagnosis process so far is a two-step process:

1. Find the most plausible diagnosis.

2. Do the appropriate repair actions.

3 Repair

3.1 Motivation

Although almost all current (model-based) diagnosis systems can be described by using the belief revision operator and diagnosis process as defined above, many concepts are missing if we want to describe a *diagnosis and repair process* in general. Such a process does not consist of just adding new knowledge until we know exactly which components are faulty, although this is an important subtask. Rather, the diagnosis and repair process is oriented towards a goal, namely that of restoring all or part of the functionality of the system. Knowledge-gathering operations are often interleaved with change-recording operations (for example repair actions).

We will first describe how to integrate (repair) actions into our mental models (belief sets) and then how the concept of a purpose is used to describe the goal of the repair purpose.

3.2 Integration of Actions

If we want to perform some actions (to change or repair something in the actual world) we have to represent these actions in our mental model. The main difference of integrating actions compared with integrating new knowledge is that actions change the actual world while additional knowledge helps us to identify the actual world but does not change it.

The semantics of a *belief revision operator for action* is therefore different to our previous revision operator. The belief revision operator for knowledge o_k treats the set of plausible worlds PW as a whole. Those worlds which are consistent with the new information (PW') are considered to be possible representatives of the actual world.

The belief revision operator for action o_a treats the worlds in PW separately. Given the fact, that each of them might represent the actual world and that an action A changes the actual world, we have to reflect the change caused by this action in each of these worlds. Each world is transformed separately into a new world (or several ones, if the action has several plausible outcomes or exceptions) and all of these new worlds together form the new set of plausible worlds PW'. An axiom which is therefore valid for this (local) revision operator but not for the (global) one used for knowledge is the following one (see also [4]):

$$(w_i \vee w_j) \, o_a A = (w_i \, o_a A) \vee (w_j \, o_a A)$$

The results of an action are computed for each world separately. Usually a theory of causality will help to compute these results (such as the one described in [3]).[1]

If we use probabilities, the probability of a transformed world is transferred to the resulting ones according to the probabilities of the possible outcomes of the action.

---

[1] A more elaborate formalization of a general semantics of different belief revision operators for revision and update is described in [5].

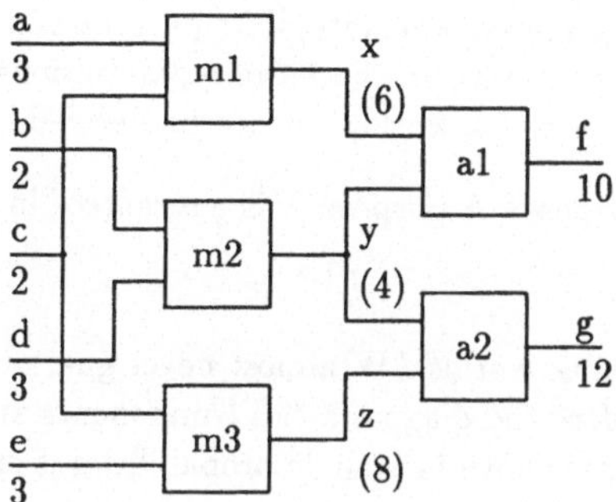

Figure 2: Diagnosis: $[m2, m3]$

3.3 Example

Let us analyze a typical repair action (component replacement) on our running example. We will use the causal theory framework discussed in [3] minimizing unexplained changes. The indices 0 and 1 will distinguish between facts previous or after the repair action.

Example 1 Consider the circuit depicted in Figure 2 and the world, where the multipliers $m2$ and $m3$ are faulty. $a - g$ have been measured. Our causal theory states, that an output can change either if one of the inputs changes, or if the mode of a component is changed.

Besides other facts, the world represented by the diagnosis $[m2, m3]$ includes $val(in1(a2), 4)_0$, $val(in2(a2), 8)_0$ and $val(out(a2), 12)_0$ for state 0. We (successfully) repair $m2$ producing $mode(m2, ok)$ and the new system state 1. Without further measurements we can deduce $val(in1(a2), 6)_1$, a change which is explained by the causal theory.

We then have to choose between consistent models differing in the following facts:

Model 1: $val(out(a2), 12)_1$, $val(in2(a2), 6)_1$, where the change in the second value is not explained by the causal theory.

Model 2: $val(out(a2), 14)_1$, $val(in2(a2), 8)_1$, where all changes are explained by the causal theory. This model is therefore the preferred one.

Note, that this specific repair action does not have any effect on the worlds represented by $[m1]$ or $[a1]$.

During a diagnosis and repair process a set of actions will be available which will be used to change the state of the world (including component replacements, changes of input values or any other possible actions). In this context we will call these actions *repair actions*.

3.4 Repair Purpose

Repair actions are used to change the state of the world to (re-)establish a certain functionality of the device. This functionality will be called *purpose* of the device. This purpose will usually be context dependent, and will be more stringent for a final production check than for a quick and dirty repair. In our logical framework we have:

Definition 5 (Purpose) The *purpose* of a system is expressed by a logical formula $\mathcal{T}$ which represents the correct function of the device and/or the functionality which has to be guaranteed after the repair process.

A system is *repairable* in a given system state, if its purpose can be guaranteed after applying an appropriate sequence of actions included in the set of repair actions.

The purpose can be guaranteed in a world, if it can be derived in this world. In general we have:

Definition 6 (Guaranteed Purpose) A purpose T is *guaranteed* in a set of plausible worlds PW, iff

$$PW \models T$$

The set of all logically possible worlds LW almost never guarantees the purpose, especially if we use no fault models and therefore the diagnosis "all components are faulty" represents a consistent world. Generalizing the concepts above to include probabilities is straightforward and is done in [2].

3.5 Summary: Repair

The main concepts used for repair can be summarized as follows:

- The repair process is oriented towards establishing a specific functionality of a device described by the system or repair purpose.

- A set of actions is available to achieve this goal, i.e. to change the world such that the purpose is guaranteed.

- The integration of actions is done locally for each world while integration of knowledge is done globally for a set of worlds.

- The set of plausible worlds serves as a focus of attention and computation (which is even more important in the repair phase than in the diagnosis phase). Worlds outside this focus are not considered and therefore not evaluated.

4   Diagnosis and Repair

4.1 Diagnosis and Repair Process

We have now discussed the main concepts necessary to describe the whole *diagnosis and repair process* which interleaves knowledge-adding operations (observations) with change-recording operations (actions).

Algorithm Scheme 1 The diagnosis and repair process can be defined as follows:

1. Start with an initial set of plausible worlds PW approximating the actual world.
2. Assume an initial purpose T representing the desired functionality of the system after the repair process.
3. *If* the purpose T is guaranteed by the current PW, *then* stop.
4. Generate a set (or a schedule) of possible repair operations including observations and actions and evaluate their utility.
5. Choose the next operations from the repair set (or schedule) and execute them. This will change PW to PW' and possibly T to T'.
6. *go to 3*

Let us remark, that this process also includes a planning phase in Item 4, which we did not discuss in this paper. Nevertheless, plan generation and utility evaluation are still topics for further research, although they may be easier to solve in our diagnosis/repair context than in the general case.

4.2 Example

Let us close with a final example including the concepts discussed in this paper. Take again our circuit example and assume we already know the inputs $a - e$, as well as $f = 10$. *PW* consists the three single fault diagnosis worlds $[a1], [m1], [m2]$.

As repair actions we may exchange adders (we do not have any spare multipliers) as well as change inputs. The repair purpose which has to be achieved is $f = 12 \wedge g = 12$, i.e. not necessarily a correctly functioning circuit, only the correct outputs have to be present. (We simply want the correct output values, no matter how they are achieved.)

We next measure $g = 12$, which decreases *PW* to $[a1]$ and $[m1]$. Both worlds imply $y = 6$. An additional measurement $x = 6$ narrows *PW* down to one world $([a1])$. We now can employ a repair action, which exchanges the component $a1$ (represented by $mode(a1, ok)$). This changes the world $[a1]$ to $[\,]$ which is the only one included in *PW*.

To test the success of the repair, we measure f again and still get $f = 10$. Assuming that exchanging components is always successful, we conclude that we have exchanged a correctly functioning component. Taking the previous measurements into account, the new set of possible worlds consists of the two double fault worlds, $[m2, m3]$ and $[m2, a2]$. Both worlds imply $y = 4$. After changing the input a to 4, both imply $f = 12$, guaranteeing the first part of our purpose. As nothing of our repair actions has influenced the value of g, it is still 12, satisfying the second part of our purpose.

Therefore we are finished, even though two components are still faulty and we do not even know exactly which. Depending on the ultimate use of the circuit, a second repair cycle may be necessary later to restore the full functionality of the device.

5 Summary and Future Work

We have shown how to define the diagnosis and repair process using concepts from belief revision. We have discussed the necessary notions of plausible worlds, the integration of new knowledge and actions into a set of beliefs and the concept of a system/repair purpose. The resulting diagnosis and repair purpose is more general than current (model-based) diagnosis systems and more appropriately models the goals of a diagnostic agent.

One of the main points to address in future work is the generation of diagnosis and repair schedules and their evaluation.

Acknowledgements

This paper is based on previous work which was done together with Gerhard Friedrich and Georg Gottlob. As usual this does not imply complete agreement. The research has been supported in part by the Christian Doppler Laboratory for Expert Systems.

References

[1] J. de Kleer and B. C. Williams. Diagnosing multiple faults. *Artificial Intelligence*, 32:97–130, 1987.

[2] G. Friedrich, G. Gottlob, and W. Nejdl. Formalizing the repair process. Technical report, Technical University of Vienna, Apr. 1991. Submitted for publication.

[3] H. Geffner. Causal theories for nonmonotonic reasoning. In *Proceedings of the National Conference on Artificial Intelligence (AAAI)*, pages 524–530, Boston, Aug. 1990. Morgan Kaufmann Publishers, Inc.

[4] G. Grahne. Updates and counterfactuals. In *Proceedings of the International Conference on Principles of Knowledge Representation and Reasoning*, pages 269–276, Cambridge, MA, Apr. 1991. Morgan Kaufmann Publishers, Inc.

[5] H. Katsuno and A. O. Mendelzon. On the difference between updateing a knoweldge base and revising it. In *Proceedings of the International Conference on Principles of Knowledge Representation and Reasoning*, Cambridge, Apr. 1991.

[6] W. Nejdl. The P-Systems: A systematic classification of logics of nonmonotonicity. In *Proceedings of the National Conference on Artificial Intelligence (AAAI)*, Anaheim, CA, July 1991. To appear.

[7] R. Reiter. A theory of diagnosis from first principles. *Artificial Intelligence*, 32:57–95, 1987.

Fehlerdiagnose an technischen Geräten mit dynamischem Verhalten

Klaus Nökel

Siemens AG, ZFE IS INF 21, Otto-Hahn-Ring 6, 8000 München 83[1]

Bislang setzen Expertensysteme für technische Fehlerdiagnose meist voraus, daß das zu diagnostizierende Gerät ohne explizite Repräsentation des zeitlichen Verhaltens modelliert werden kann. Wir zeigen, daß sowohl assoziative als auch modellbasierte Ansätze vom Grundsatz her auch zur Diagnose an Geräten mit dynamischem Verhalten geeignet sind. Jedoch sind in beiden Fällen Erweiterungen der Repräsentationsmittel und der Inferenzmechanismen erforderlich. Dabei spielen qualitative Modellierungs- und Schlußweisen eine wesentliche Rolle, da der Modellierungsaufwand durch eine ergebnisorientierte Wahl des Detaillierungsgrades begrenzt werden soll. Einige ausgewählte Erweiterungen assoziativer und modellbasierter Diagnoseansätze, die Ergebnisse anwendungsorientierter Forschung im Sonderforschungsbereich 314 "Wissensbasierte Systeme" sind, werden näher vorgestellt.

1. Einführung

1.1. Technische Diagnose

Seit jeher zählen Diagnoseaufgaben zu den populärsten Anwendungsklassen für Expertensysteme. Viele grundlegende KI-Techniken, wie Regeln und Theorien für die Behandlung von unsicherem oder unscharfem Wissen, gehen auf Anforderungen aus der Diagnose zurück. Obwohl die ersten Expertensysteme (z.B. MYCIN [1], ABEL [2]) Aufgaben aus dem medizinischen Bereich lösten, erkannte man bald, daß sich die Techniken auch auf die Fehlerdiagnose an technischen Geräten übertragen ließen.

Trotz dieser prinzipiellen Einsicht unterscheiden sich technische und medizinische Diagnose dennoch in grundlegenden Punkten, die weitreichende Konsequenzen bis in die Repräsentation des diagnostischen Wissens und die Schlußfolgerungsmechanismen besitzen. Da technische Geräte[2] im Gegensatz zu Menschen von Ingenieuren hergestellt werden, hat man – zumindest im Prinzip – vollständige Information über ihren Aufbau und ihre Funktionsweise. Diese Information legt zusammen mit Wirtschaftlichkeitsüberlegungen (lohnt eine feinere Diagnose, wenn ohnehin das komplette Modul ausgetauscht wird?) die Diagnosestrategie fest.

Auf der Basis dieser Beobachtungen sind in der Vergangenheit viele Diagnose-Expertsysteme entwickelt worden, die jedoch auf einer vergleichsweise kleinen Zahl grundlegender Ansätze aufbauen. Die beiden populärsten sind assoziative/heuristische Diagnose (vgl. [3], [4]) bzw. modellbasierte Diagnose ([5], [6]). Ein Vergleich dieser allgemeinen Ansätze mit konkreten Implementierungen zeigt, daß allerdings häufig Zusatzannahmen getroffen werden, um das Diagnoseproblem zu vereinfachen und rascher zu praktisch verwertbaren Ergebnissen zu kommen. So werden oft solche Anwendungsbereiche ausgewählt, in denen das Diagnosewissen von besonders einfacher Form ist oder nur wenige technische Wirkprinzipien eine Rolle spielen. Nach den so erzielten Anfangserfolgen gilt es jetzt, die selbstauferlegten Einschränkungen genauer zu prüfen und durch eine geeignete Erweiterung der Diagnosetechniken möglichst zu überwinden.

---

[1] Die dargestellten Arbeiten wurden am FB Informatik der Universität Kaiserslautern durchgeführt.

[2] Überall im Text werden "Gerät" und "System" synonym für das technische Objekt der Diagnose benutzt. Die diagnostizierende Software wird dagegen stets als "Expertensystem" oder "Diagnosesystem" bezeichnet.

1.2. Statische vs. Dynamische Systeme

Die überwiegende Zahl technischer Diagnosesysteme beschränkt sich beispielsweise auf sogenannte *statische Systeme*, d.h. Geräte, bei denen das zeitliche Verhalten "keine wesentliche" Rolle spielt. Wie [7] herausstellt, gibt es vom Prinzip her überhaupt keine statischen Systeme, da Energie sich nie verzögerungsfrei übertragen läßt und daher der Output eines Systems zu einem Zeitpunkt nicht nur von den gleichzeitig anliegenden Inputs, sondern stets auch von der Vorgeschichte abhängt. Allerdings ist dieser Verzögerungseffekt in vielen Geräten vernachlässigbar kurz, so daß man für praktische Zwecke von einer zeitlich konstanten Relation zwischen Inputs und Outputs ausgehen kann. Entsprechend lassen sich für sie Näherungsmodelle angeben, die ohne explizite Bezugnahme auf die Zeit auskommen. Auch diese Systeme nennen wir noch im weiteren Sinne statisch. Typische Beispiele hierfür sind alle rein kombinatorischen Schaltungen, die nicht zuletzt aus diesem Grund zu den beliebtesten Anwendungsgebieten für technische Diagnosesysteme zählen (Bild 1 links).

A	B	A $\wedge$ B
0	0	0
0	1	0
1	0	0
1	1	1

J(t)	K(t)	Q(t+1)	~Q(t+1)
0	0	Q(t)	~Q(t)
0	1	0	1
1	0	1	0
1	1	~Q(t)	Q(t)

Bild 1: Die Input-Output-Relation des Und-Gatters ist zeitunabhängig, während die des J-K-Flipflops von der Vorgeschichte abhängt

Bei anderen Systemen kann die zeitliche Komponente des Verhaltens jedoch nicht ohne weiteres ignoriert werden, weil ihre Input-Output-Relation nicht zeitunabhängig ist. Meist sind dies Geräte mit Rückkopplungsschleifen, die ihnen eine Art "Gedächtnis" verleihen, die wir den *inneren Zustand* des Systems nennen. Wenn dieser innere Zustand nicht direkt beobachtbar ist, macht sich sein Einfluß nur durch (scheinbar) zeitlich entkoppelte Änderungen zwischen Inputs und Outputs bemerkbar. Beispiele für dynamische Systeme finden sich ebenfalls schon im Bereich einfacher elektronischer Schaltungen, etwa bei einem Flip-Flop (Bild 1 rechts).

In Grenzfällen hängt die Brauchbarkeit eines statischen Näherungsmodells für ein im Grunde dynamisches System auch von den Fehlern ab, die man diagnostizieren will. Bereits in [18] wird gezeigt, daß auch in kombinatorischen Schaltungen Fehler auftreten (vgl. Bild 2), die sich mit den üblichen statischen Modellen für die logischen Operationen nicht, wohl aber mit dynamischen Modellen unter Berücksichtigung von Gatterlaufzeiten nachweisen lassen.

Statische Systeme bilden in unserer Sprechweise einen Sonderfall dynamischer Systeme, bei dem es genau einen inneren Zustand gibt, in dem sich das System befinden kann. Sie sind deshalb so attraktiv für die Diagnose, weil sich die Ursache eines Fehlers notwendigerweise im gleichen (weil einzigen) inneren Zustand des Systems nachweisen lassen muß, in dem er entdeckt wurde. Bei der Planung der Diagnosestrategie können daher Überlegungen, welche Zustandsübergänge seit der Beobachtung des Fehlers aufgetreten

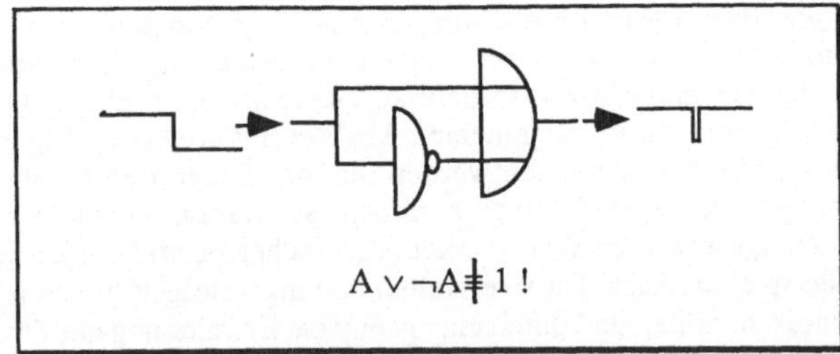

Bild 2: Durch Gatterlaufzeiten bedingt entspricht das Verhalten realer Schaltungen nicht immer der logischen Schaltfunktion

sein können oder ob die Untersuchung selbst Auswirkungen auf diesen Zustand hat, außer acht gelassen werden. Weiterhin kommt es nicht auf die Reihenfolge der Messungen statt, da ja alle im gleichen Kontext erfolgen.

Bei dynamischen Systemen ist die Situation zumindest potentiell komplizierter: Analog zum zeitlich variablen Normalverhalten manifestieren sich auch die Fehler im allgemeinen durch Symptome, die sich über einen Zeitraum hinweg erstrecken. Nach der Länge dieses Zeitraums können wir unterscheiden:

- *kurzfristige Symptome*: Symptome, deren kurze Dauer einen Nachweis durch diskrete Messungen der Signalform nicht zuläßt. Diese Symptome (z.B. Vibrationen) werden üblicherweise nur in Form ihrer zeitlichen Abstraktionen (z.B. Frequenz) behandelt.

- *mittelfristige Symptome*: Ihre Dauer ist von einer Größenordnung, in der der Verlauf durch Einzelbeobachtungen nachgewiesen bzw. widerlegt werden kann.

- *langfristige Symptome*: Ihre Dauer liegt über der Länge einer Diagnose-Sitzung (z.B. Werkzeugverschleiß). Für ihre Behandlung bietet sich zeitliche Abstraktion durch Anwendung statistischer Verfahren an (z.B. Zeitreihenanalyse).

Nicht alle Fehlverhalten dynamischer Systeme müssen also auch mit explizitem Einbezug der Zeitdimension behandelt werden. Zwischen kurz- und langfristigen Symptomen existiert aber eine Bandbreite von Symptomen, die zweckmäßig als sich über die Zeit entwickelndes (Fehl-) Verhalten repräsentiert und nachgewiesen werden. Ihre Einordnung auf einer absoluten Zeitskala, nicht jedoch ihre Existenz, hängt naturgemäß von den zur Verfügung stehenden Beobachtungsmöglichkeiten ab. Um ihren Charakter zu verdeutlichen, sprechen wir von *zeitlich verteilten Symptomen*.

1.3. Zeitlich verteilte Symptome (ZVS)

Charakteristisch für Geräte mit ZVS ist die Beobachtung, daß ein Schnappschuß der Inputs und Outputs zu einem einzelnen Zeitpunkt im allgemeinen nicht ausreicht, um über das Vorhandensein eines ZVS entscheiden zu können. Ein ZVS kann punktuell durchaus mit dem Normalverhalten (oder einem anderen ZVS) übereinstimmen; erst eine spezifische Abfolge von Meßwerten unterscheidet es von anderen Verhaltensweisen. Im allgemeinen Fall erfordert der Nachweis eines ZVS ein Experiment, das aus folgenden Teilen besteht:

1) Das System wird durch bestimmte Aktionen in einen definierten Ausgangszustand gebracht bzw. der gegenwärtige innere Zustand des Systems ist bekannt.

2) Durch Beeinflussung der Inputs wird das System durch eine vorgeplante Abfolge innerer Zustände geführt.

3) Für eine Menge beobachtbarer Outputs wird vorhergesagt, wie sich ihre Werte über die Dauer des Experiments bei An- bzw. Abwesenheit des ZVS entwickeln.

4) Die Werte dieser Outputs werden zu verschiedenen, vorgeplanten Zeitpunkten gemessen, um die Übereinstimmung mit den in 3) vorhergesagten Werten zu überprüfen.

Ein bekanntes Beispiel für diese Vorgehensweise findet sich in der Kfz-Diagnose. Wird etwa vermutet, daß ein Zylinder des Motors nicht arbeitet, so besteht eine Diagnosestrategie darin, den Motor leerlaufen zu lassen und der Reihe nach von jedem Zylinder das Zündkabel abzuziehen. Genau dann, wenn dies zu einem Abfall der Drehzahl führt, arbeitet der Zylinder. Wichtig ist die Feststellung, daß die Aktionen (Entfernen der Zündkabel) und die Beobachtungen der Drehzahl in einer ganz bestimmten Reihenfolge ausgeführt werden, und daß sich Aktionen und Beobachtungen sinnvoll nur als Einheit planen lassen.

Offenkundig erfordern Planung und Durchführung eines solchen Experiments einen bedeutend höheren Aufwand als der Nachweis eines statischen Symptoms. Spielen ZVS unter diesen Umständen überhaupt eine praktische Rolle? Die Antwort hierauf hängt in jedem Einzelfall von mehreren Faktoren ab: im Falle von Systemen mit langsam veränderlichen inneren Zuständen reichen isolierte statische Beobachtungen in der Regel aus. In anderen Fällen sind die potentiell nützlichen, direkten Messungen aber in praxi undurchführbar (z.B. weil sie destruktiv sind), so daß die gleiche Information stattdessen aus mehreren Beobachtungen leichter zugänglicher Quellen abgeleitet werden muß. Zwischen beiden Extrema existiert ein weites Spektrum, in denen ZVS ihre Berechtigung haben, weil statische Messungen zwar nicht unmöglich, aber doch teurer, unpraktischer etc. sind.

2. Erweiterung assoziativ/heuristischer Diagnose für ZVS

2.1. Ausgangssituation

Assoziative bzw. heuristische Diagnose (Bild 3) bildet die Grundlage für die überwiegende Anzahl existierender medizinischer und technischer Diagnose-Expertensysteme. Hierbei wird das Expertenwissen in einer Menge von Assoziationen (meist Regeln, daher: Regelbasis) codiert, die jeweils einen Zusammenhang zwischen einem beobachteten Symptom und einer möglichen Diagnose herstellen. Jede Assoziation besteht aus einem Bedingungsteil, der ein Symptom beschreibt, bei dessen Beobachtung die Regel anwendbar ist, und einem Konsequenzteil, in dem der Verdacht auf eine bestimmte Diagnose erhöht (bei bestätigenden Symptomen) bzw. verringert (bei ausschließenden Symptomen) wird.

Der Diagnose-Algorithmus wertet zunächst die Konsequenzteile der auf die Anfangsbeobachtungen passenden Assoziationen aus, um zu (i.d.R. mehreren) Diagnosehypothesen zu gelangen. Danach werden (u.U. durch Analyse der Regelbasis) potentiell nützliche neue Beobachtungen angefordert, durchgeführt und schließlich durch erneute Anwendung von Assoziationen die Hypothesenmenge verändert, bis im Idealfall schließlich nur eine Diagnose übrig bleibt. Grundlegend ist offenbar die Operation "passende Regeln anwenden", die sich – wie in Bild 4 gezeigt – in zwei Teilschritte zerlegen läßt.

Erst nachdem eine Übereinstimmung zwischen dem Bedingungsteil einer Assoziation und den

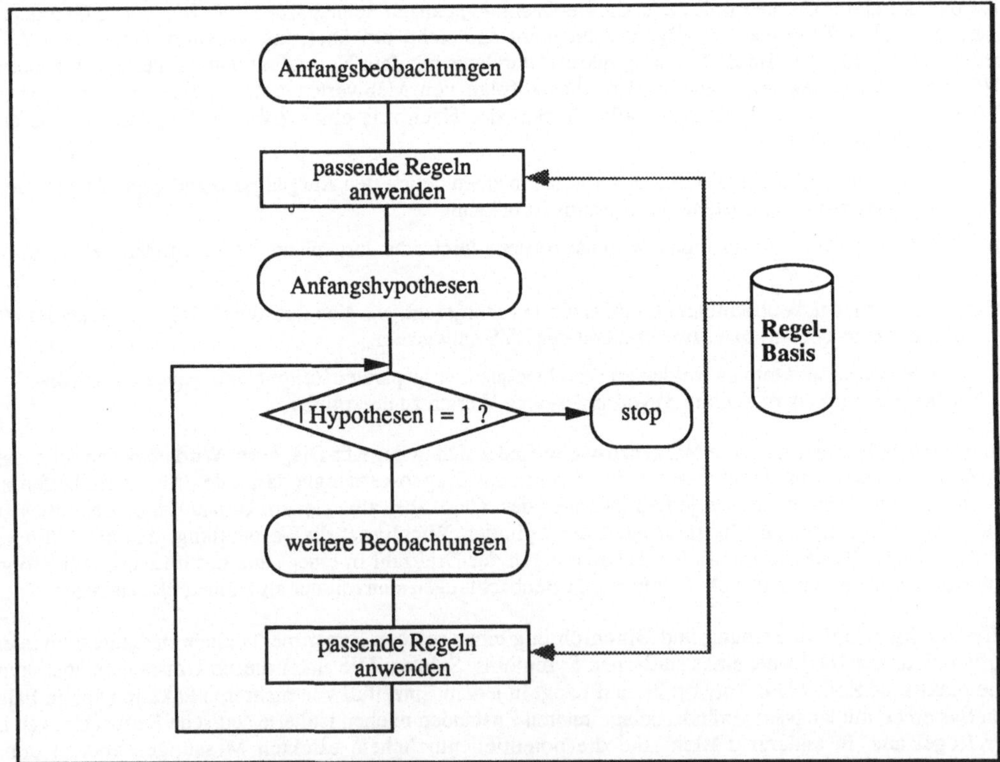

Bild 3: Assoziativ/heuristischer Diagnose-Algorithmus
(sehr stark vereinfacht, ausführlichere Darstellungen finden sich u.a. in [3] und [4])

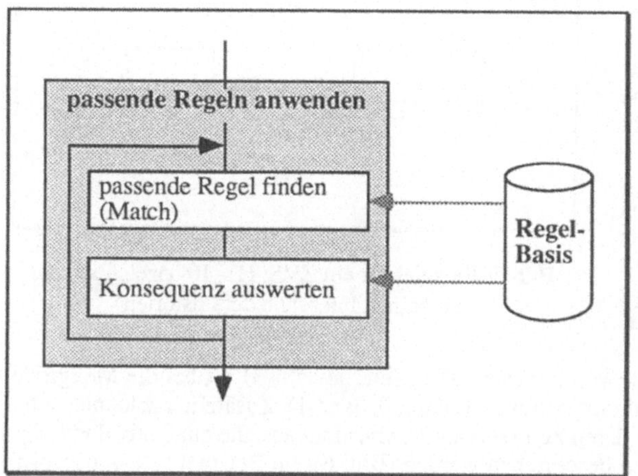

Bild 4: Verfeinerung der Operation "Passende Regeln anwenden"

Beobachtungen festgestellt worden ist (*Match*), darf der Konsequenzteil ausgewertet werden.

Zwei Folgerungen lassen sich aus dieser Darstellung ziehen:

- An keiner Stelle setzt der assoziative Diagnose-Algorithmus voraus, daß die verarbeiteten Symptome statisch sein müssen. Vielmehr ist ihre Komplexität ausschließlich durch die Struktur der Beobachtungen und die Ausdrucksmächtigkeit der Bedingungsteile in den Assoziationen bestimmt.

- Eine Erweiterung der Ausdrucksmächtigkeit ist durch relativ lokale Änderungen im Diagnose-Algorithmus zu erreichen: betroffen ist nur die Match-Operation.

2.2. Herkömmliche Behandlung von ZVS

Auch wenn der Algorithmus an sich universell ist, so erlauben doch die wenigsten Implementationen zeitliche Elemente in den Bedingungsteilen. Am verbreitetsten ist die Methode, ZVS zu spezifizieren, in dem man eine Folge von Messungen zu a priori festgelegten, absoluten Zeitpunkten vorschreibt. Beispielsweise könnte das ZVS "Puls an Port P" durch

$$(*) \quad \mathrm{Wert}(P, t_0) = 0 \textbf{ and } \mathrm{Wert}(P, t_0+1 \text{ ms}) = 1 \textbf{ and } \mathrm{Wert}(P, t_0+2 \text{ ms}) = 0$$

beschrieben werden. In extremen Formen (z.B. ALVEN [9]) ähnelt die Spezifikationssprache einer rudimentären Programmiersprache, in der für jedes Symptom ein maßgeschneidertes Meßprogramm geschrieben wird. Diese Beschreibungsform bietet sich immer dann an, wenn das Symptom auch in der Denkweise des Experten durch das Meßverfahren bestimmt ist. Sie besitzt aber in anderen Situationen gravierende Nachteile:

- Bei komplizierteren Symptomverläufen ist nicht immer unmittelbar einsichtig, welche Beobachtungen für den Nachweis hinreichend sind, so daß der Spezifikationsprozeß fehleranfällig ist.

- Mit Messungen an festen Zeitpunkten lassen sich qualitativ definierte ZVS (z.B. "Puls unbestimmter Länge an Port P") nur mangelhaft beschreiben.

- Assoziationen wie (*) können keinen Gebrauch von Beobachtungen an anderen als den geforderten Zeitpunkten machen.

2.3. Temporales Matchen

Um diesen Problemen Rechnung zu tragen, haben wir im Rahmen des MOLTKE-Projekts[3] die Ausdrucksmächtigkeit der Assoziationen auf andere Weise erweitert.[4] Wir illustrieren die Erweiterung anhand eines ZVS aus der Leitanwendung von MOLTKE, der Diagnose eines CNC-Bearbeitungszentrums.

---

[3] Models, Learning and Temporal Knowledge in an Expert System for Technical Diagnosis. Gefördert durch die DFG im Sonderforschungsbereich 314 "Wissensbasierte Systeme". In [16] stellen die beteiligten Forscher ihre Ergebnisse im Zusammenhang dar.

[4] Eine ausführlichere und formale Darstellung findet sich in [17].

Für die Diagnose einer bestimmten Fehlfunktion am Antrieb der Maschine ist es charakteristisch, wenn zwei Statusmelder den in Bild 5 gezeigten zeitlichen Verlauf aufweisen; wesentlich sind dabei lediglich die relativen Lagen der Flanken zueinander, nicht ihre absoluten Zeitpunkte.

In MOLTKE wird ein solches ZVS nicht durch ein Meßverfahren, sondern durch seinen Signalverlauf beschrieben. Wie jedes ZVS besteht auch das Beispiel aus einer Menge von *Meßgrößen* (hier IN29 und IN30), die bestimmte Werteverläufe – *Historien* –

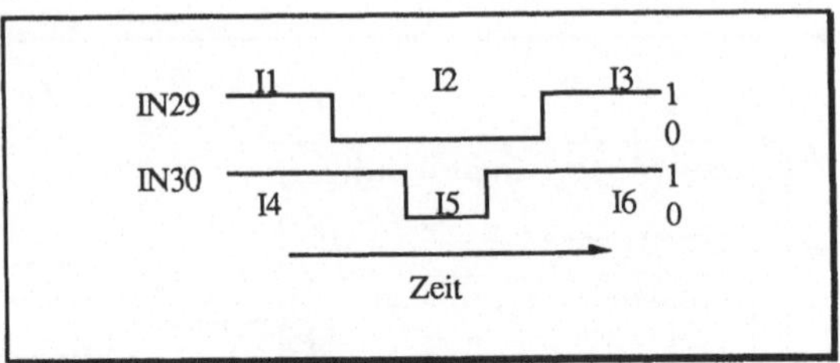

Bild 5: Beispiel für ein ZVS; I1 – I6 bezeichnen die einzelnen Intervalle der Historien

zeigen. Jede Historie besteht aus einer Kette von Zeitintervallen (hier jeweils 3), wobei die Meßgröße in jedem Intervall einen bestimmten Wert annimmt (anfangs 1, dann 0, dann 1). Zusätzlich zeichnet sich das ZVS durch die Lage der Historien (genauer: deren Zeitintervalle) zueinander aus, die qualitativ durch die 13 von Allen [10] definierten Lagebeziehungen beschrieben werden (Bild 6). Im Beispiel ist etwa gefordert, daß sich das erste und das letzte Intervall der Historie von IN30 mit dem mittleren Intervall von IN29 überlappen, was den Allen-Relationen "I4 overlaps I2" und "I2 overlaps I6" entspricht.

Relation	Symbol	Beispiel
A before B	A < B	
B after A	B > A	
A meets B	A m B	
B met by A	B mi A	
A overlaps B	A o B	
B overlapped by A	B oi A	
A during B	A d B	
B contains A	B di A	
A starts B	A s B	
B started by A	B si A	
A finishes B	A f B	
B finished by A	B fi A	
A equals B	A = B	

Bild 6: Die 13 möglichen qualitativen Allen-Relationen zwischen (Zeit-) Intervallen

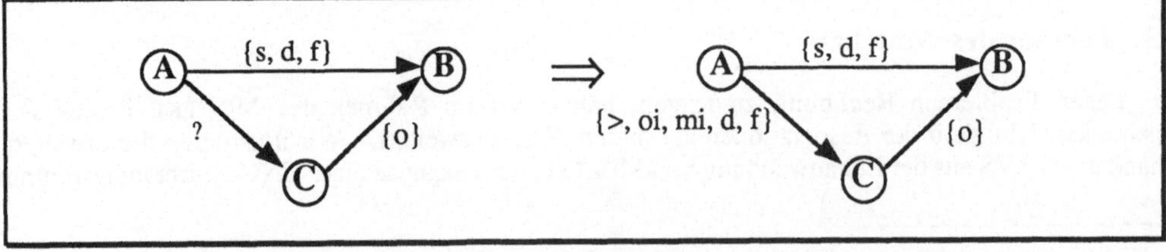

Bild 7: Durch Komposition der Lagebeziehungen zwischen A und B bzw. C und B kann die Relation zwischen A und C erschlossen werden

Um so spezifizierte ZVS im Diagnose-Algorithmus benutzen zu können, muß neben der Spezifikationssprache auch die Match-Operation, die ein Vorkommen des Symptoms erkennt, entsprechend erweitert werden. In MOLTKE wurde hierzu ein Algorithmus für das temporale Matchen implementiert, der auf der Basis einer ZVS-Beschreibung eine Folge von Messungen inkrementell plant, durchführt und auswertet. Dieser Algorithmus benutzt sowohl für die Planung der Beobachtungen als auch für die Entscheidung, ob die letzte Beobachtung mit einem Match verträglich ist, den qualitativen Kalkül auf den Allen-Relationen. Jede Einzelmessung steuert dazu Information über die noch möglichen Lagen der Zeitintervalle bei, die die Information aus den vorangegangenen Messungen ähnlich wie in Bild 7 gezeigt weiter einschränkt. Ein Vorkommen des ZVS gilt als nachgewiesen, wenn nur noch die in der Spezifikation vorgegebene Konstellationen mit den Beobachtungen verträglich sind.

Durch die inkrementelle Arbeitsweise garantiert der temporale Match-Algorithmus eine effiziente Entscheidung über das Vorliegen eines ZVS. Außerdem sind Planung und Bewertung von Messungen derart voneinander entkoppelt, daß auch das Ergebnis einer anderen als der angeforderten Messung in den aktuellen Zustand des Match-Versuchs einbezogen und in die nächste Planung einbezogen werden kann.

3. Erweiterung modellbasierter Diagnose für ZVS

3.1. Ausgangssituation

In der technischen Diagnose, in der Struktur und Verhalten des zu diagnostizierenden Geräts i.d.R. bekannt sind, ist eine Strategie, die sich ausschließlich auf von Experten geäußerte Assoziationen stützt, aus verschiedenen Gründen wenig attraktiv:

- *Vollständigkeit:* Bei assoziativ/heuristischen Diagnosesystemen läßt sich ausgesprochen schwierig beurteilen, welcher Prozentsatz der potentiellen Fehler des Geräts vom Diagnosesystem erkannt werden kann. Wird das Diagnosesystem mit Fehlern konfrontiert, die bei seiner Entwicklung nicht antizipiert wurden, so ist die Reaktion im allgemeinen nicht vorhersehbar.

- *Mehrfachfehler:* Selbst wenn alle möglichen Einzelfehler eines Systems bekannt sind, gestatten die für jeden Fehler getrennt aufgestellten Assoziationen keine Vorhersage über die Symptome mehrerer gleichzeitig auftretender Fehler (z.B. bei Folgefehlern). Hierfür wären spezielle Assoziationen für jede mögliche Kombination von Einzelfehlern erforderlich; dies verbietet sich jedoch wegen der kombinatorischen Explosion.

- *Erklärbarkeit:* So ausgefeilt Erklärungskomponenten assoziativer Diagnosesysteme auch sein mögen, die kleinste Einheit jeder Erklärung ist notwendigerweise die einzelne vom Experten geäußerte Assoziation (bzw. ihre verbale Begründung). Da Expertenwissen subjektiv gefärbt sein kann, ist eine solche Erklärung einer auf allgemein akzeptierten physikalischen Grundprinzipien beruhenden stets an Glaubwürdigkeit unterlegen.

Modellbasierte Diagnose versucht, alle diese Kritikpunkte zu überwinden, indem Beobachtungen nicht mit subjektiven Assoziationen, sondern mit dem simulierten Verhalten des diagnostizierten Geräts verglichen werden. Simuliert wird ein *Modell* der Maschine, das auf Basis objektiv nachvollziehbarer physikalisch-technischer Wirkprinzipien (*first principles*) konstruiert wird.

Bild 8 zeigt die grundsätzliche Vorgehensweise modellbasierter Diagnose. Die anfänglichen Beobachtungen werden mit dem simulierten Verhalten der intakten Maschine verglichen, um Kandidaten (Fehlerhypothesen) für die Diagnose zu generieren. Jedem Kandidaten wird eine a priori-Wahrscheinlichkeit zugeordnet. Sofern mehr als ein Kandidat existiert, werden die möglichen weiteren Meßpunkte hinsichtlich ihres erwarteten Informationsgewinns bewertet. Die aussichtsreichste Beobachtung wird durchgeführt und der gemessene Wert mit den jeweiligen unter den einzelnen Fehlerhypothesen vorhergesagten Verhalten verglichen. Nur unter den Kandidaten, deren simulierte Verhalten nicht im Widerspruch zum beobachteten Wert stehen, wird im nächsten Zyklus weitergesucht. Um die Wahrscheinlichkeitsmasse der wegfallenden Kandidaten auszugleichen, werden die Wahrscheinlichkeiten der übrigbleibenden Kandidaten entsprechend erhöht.

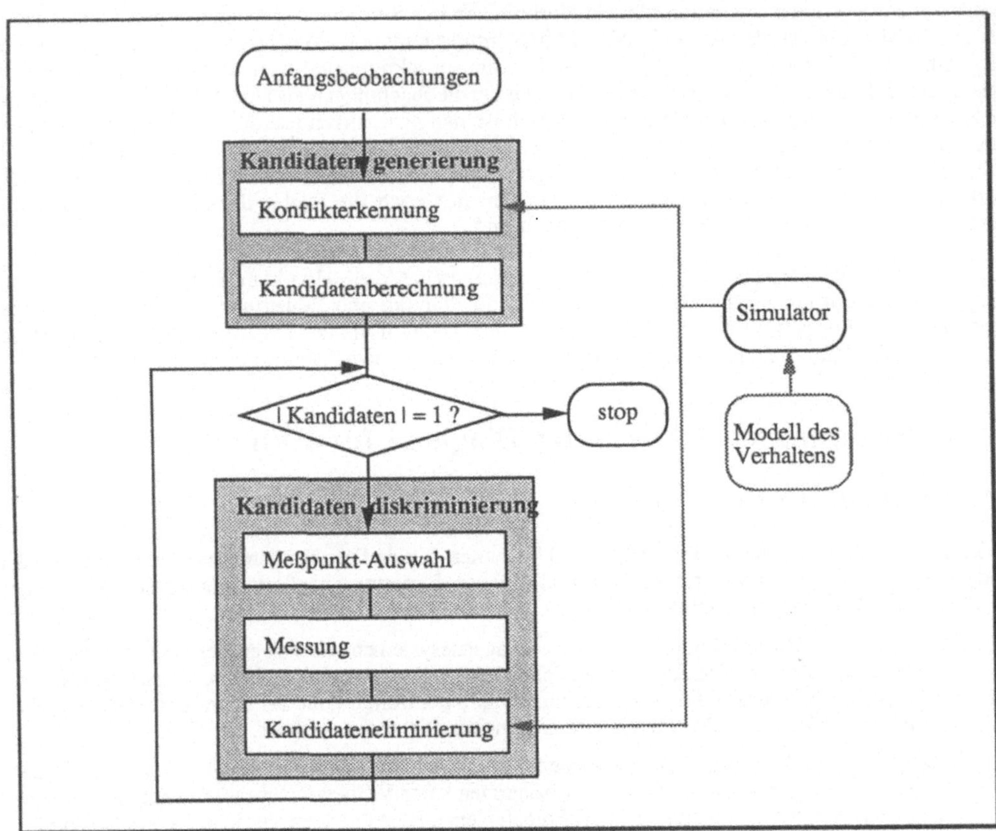

Bild 8: Modellbasierte Diagnose

3.2. Herkömmliche Behandlung von ZVS

Wie der assoziativ/heuristische ist auch der modellbasierte Diagnosealgorithmus so allgemein formuliert, daß er durch geeignete Interpretation der Begriffe "Modell", "Meßpunkt", "Beobachtung" und "vorhergesagtes Verhalten" sowohl auf statische als auch auf dynamische Geräte und Symptome angewendet werden kann. Dennoch nutzen die bekanntesten Implementationen, GDE [5], GDE+ [6] und SHERLOCK [11], in den publizierten Beispielen bislang stets nur statische Modelle.

Meist gelingt dies, indem rückgekoppelte (und damit eigentlich dynamische) Teilsysteme als black box betrachtet werden, die als atomare Komponente mit ihrem resultierenden, nach außen sichtbaren Gesamtverhalten ins Modell eingehen. Als Preis für diesen Ausweg ist eine Diagnose innerhalb des eingekapselten Teilsystems allerdings nicht mehr möglich.

Die Grenzen der Einkapselungs-Technik zeigen sich naturgemäß genau dort, wo eine solche weitergehende Diagnose erwünscht ist. Wir betrachten hierzu das Beispiel einer Thyristorbrückengleichrichterschaltung aus [8]. Diese Schaltung verwendet eine Anordnung aus mehreren Thyristoren, Halbleiter-Bauelementen mit einem nicht direkt beobachtbaren inneren Zustand, um eine Drehspannungsquelle gleichzurichten. Die genaue Funktionsweise ist an dieser Stelle unwesentlich, wichtig sind dagegen die Feststellungen, daß

a)   bei einer Fehlfunktion der verantwortliche Thyristor identifiziert werden soll,

b)   die gelieferte Gleichspannung zu jedem Zeitpunkt vom Zustand aller Thyristoren abhängt und

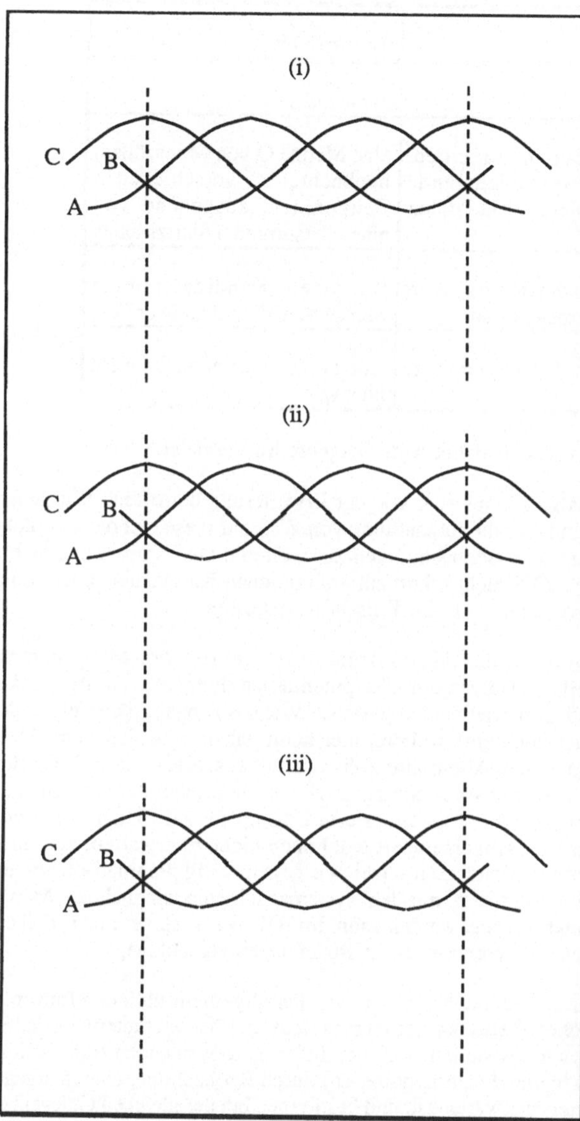

Bild 9: Laststromverläufe bei (i) normaler Funktionsweise der Thyristoren, (ii) bei blockierendem Thyristor T1, (iii) bei blockierendem T6 (aus [8])

c) die Symptome unterschiedlicher Fehler bis auf Phasenverschiebung identisch sind (vgl. Bild 9).

Während Feststellung a) verbietet, die gesamte Schaltung mit allen Thyristoren einzukapseln, verhindern b) und c) gemeinsam, daß der fehlerhafte Thyristor allein aufgrund statischer Beobachtungen ermittelt werden kann.

3.3. Einbettung von temporalem Matchen in modellbasierte Diagnose[5]

Die Aufgabe läßt sich nur lösen, wenn dynamische Modelle und ZVS zugelassen werden; Bild 10 zeigt, welche Veränderungen sich dadurch ergeben. Der wichtigste Unterschied besteht darin, daß das Systemmodell dynamisch ist. Folglich besteht die Aufgabe der Verhaltensvorhersage nicht mehr ausschließlich darin, durch Propagierung über die räumliche Struktur des Systems die Werte einiger Meßgrößen aus den Werten anderer *im gleichen Systemzustand* zu erschließen; vielmehr wird zusätzlich das zeitliche Verhalten über eine *Folge von Zuständen* simuliert. Daher kann man auch nicht mehr von dem (einzelnen) Wert sprechen, den eine Fehlerhypothese für eine Meßgröße voraussagt; im dynamischen Fall erhält man für jede Meßgröße und jeden Ausgangszustand eine Historie von Werten. Da sich die Bedeutung einer Historie u.U. erst durch ihre zeitliche Lage zu den Historien anderer Meßgrößen ergibt, verallgemeinern wir den Begriff des Meßpunkts auf eine Menge von Meßgrößen und das vorhergesagte und das beobachtete Verhalten entsprechend.

Im Schaltungsbeispiel bestünde ein denkbarer verallgemeinerter Meßpunkt aus den drei Phasen der Drehstromquelle und dem resultierenden Laststrom. Die dafür und für verschiedene Kandidaten von einem willkürlichen, gemeinsamen Ausgangszustand aus vorhergesagten Verhalten[6] zeigt Bild 9. Ähnlich wie zuvor im Fall der Bedingungsteile von Assoziationen besteht nun die Aufgabe, durch geschickt geplante Beobachtungen zu entscheiden, welche dieser vorhergesagten Verhalten mit der Realität verträglich sind.

---

[5] Auch hierzu enthält [17] eine ausführlichere Darstellung.
[6] Genaugenommen handelt es sich jeweils um endliche Anfangsstücke von in die Zukunft unendlichen Verhalten.

Begriff	statisch	dynamisch
Modelltyp	statisch	dynamisch
Meßpunkt	eine Meßgröße q zu einem Zeitpunkt (Systemzustände ändern sich nie und sind daher irrelevant)	eine Menge Q von Meßgrößen, beobachtet zu verschiedenen Zeitpunkten, ausgehend von einem bestimmten Startzustand
vorhersagtes Verhalten	für jeden Kandidaten ein Wert aus der Wertemenge zu q	für jeden Kandidaten eine Menge von Verhalten über Q
Meßergebnisse	ein Wert aus der Wertemenge zu q	eine Folge von Beobachtungen über Q

Bild 10: Statische und dynamische modellbasierte Diagnose im Vergleich

Welche Teile des modellbasierten Diagnosealgorithmus sind von der Erweiterung betroffen? Wir gehen davon aus, daß aufgrund des erhöhten Aufwands für die Behandlung von ZVS auf diese erst dann zurückgegriffen wird, wenn — wie im Beispiel — statische Beobachtungen zur weiteren Diskriminierung nichts mehr beitragen können. Insbesondere werden ZVS nicht schon zur anfänglichen Kandidatengenerierung eingesetzt. Dagegen sind in der Kandidatendiskriminierung alle Teilschritte betroffen.

Interessanterweise erweist sich dabei die Bewertung und Auswahl eines verallgemeinerten Meßpunkts als das härteste Problem, und zwar deshalb, weil das Universum aller potentiellen dynamischen Meßpunkte verglichen mit der Menge der potentiellen statischen Meßpunkte riesig ist. Wie das Eingangsbeispiel aus der Kfz-Diagnose zeigt, eröffnen Aktionen sogar noch eine weitere, hier noch gar nicht weiter betrachtete Dimension für die "Konstruktion" von Meßpunkten. Allein ihre Zahl schließt aus, alle verallgemeinerten Meßpunkte aufzuzählen, ihre erwarteten Informationsgewinne zu berechnen und dann den attraktivsten auszuwählen. Eine zuverlässige, formal abgesicherte, modellbasierte Lösung für die Generierung von Meßpunkten existiert bisher nicht und ist in aller Allgemeinheit wohl auch nicht zu erwarten; auf einen möglichen Ansatz gehen wir am Schluß kurz ein. Stattdessen setzen wir gegenwärtig pragmatisch voraus, daß im Anwendungsgebiet heuristisches Wissen existiert, mit dem systematisch eine handhabbare Menge vielversprechender verallgemeinerter Meßpunkte erzeugt werden kann. Im Beispiel ist zu vermuten, daß ein solches Orakel auch die simultane Beobachtung der vorkommenden Spannungen vorschlüge.

Für die Bewertung der vom Orakel gelieferten Meßpunkte haben wir den allgemein üblichen Entropie-Ansatz aus [5] auf Historien anstelle einfacher Werte bei vorhergesagtem und beobachtetem Verhalten verallgemeinert. Auf diese Weise können wir feststellen, welcher Informationszuwachs (d.h. welche zusätzliche Differenzierung zwischen den aktuellen Fehlerhypothesen) durch Beobachtung eines vorgegebenen verallgemeinerten Meßpunktes im Mittel zu erwarten ist, und bestimmen bei der gleichen Gelegenheit durch Vergleich der für die einzelnen Kandidaten vorhergesagten Verhalten auch eine Folge von Beobachtungen für die einzelnen Meßgrößen des Meßpunktes, mit denen sich die Verhalten am zweckmäßigsten trennen lassen. Da die einzelnen Verhalten vom Simulator im selben Format bereitgestellt werden, das oben für die Bedingungsteile von Assoziationen benutzt wurde, können wir dazu wiederum den temporalen Match-Algorithmus verwenden.

Derselbe Algorithmus dient auch dazu, bei der konkreten Beobachtung des verallgemeinerten Meßpunkts die einzelnen Meßwerte mit den vorhergesagten Verhalten zu vergleichen, um frühzeitig Differenzen aufzudecken.

Nach Abschluß der Einzelbeobachtungen werden schließlich die unverträglichen Fehlerhypothesen aus der Kandidatenmenge entfernt und für die restlichen Kandidaten die Wahrscheinlichkeiten neu berechnet.

Bild 11 zeigt den erweiterten Algorithmus für die Kandidatendiskriminierung im Überblick.

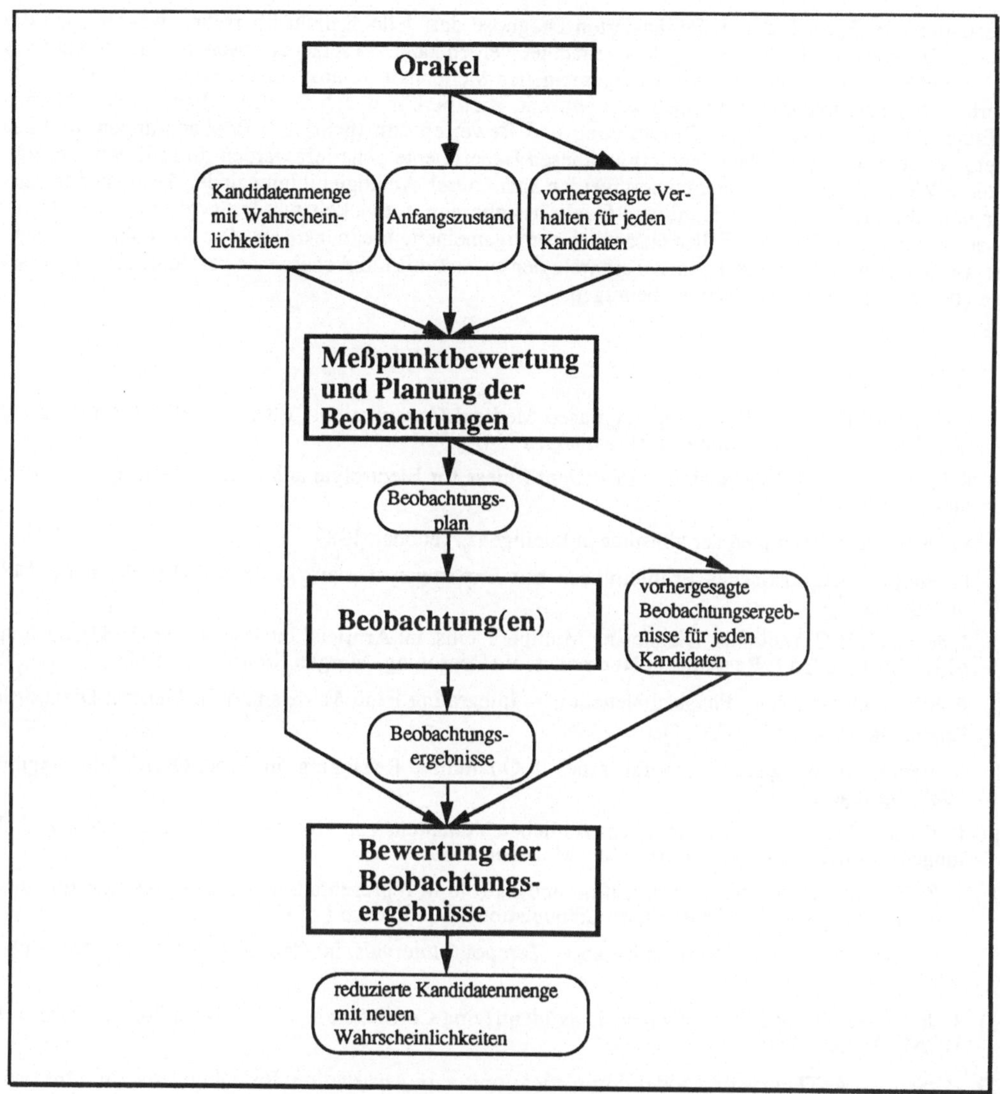

Bild 11: Für ZVS erweiterte Kandidatendiskriminierung

4. Zusammenfassung und Ausblick

Wie die vorangehende Diskussion zeigt, eignen sich sowohl assoziativ/heuristische als auch modellbasierte Diagnose für die Fehlersuche in beliebigen Systemen, werden jedoch bislang fast ausschließlich auf statische bzw. statisch modellierte Systeme angewendet. Ein Grund dafür ist sicherlich der erhöhte Aufwand für die Bearbeitung von ZVS, der im Einzelfall gegen die verbesserte Leistungsfähigkeit des Diagnosesystems abgewogen werden muß. Stellt sich dabei heraus, daß auf die explizite Berücksichtigung des dynamischen Systemverhaltens nicht verzichtet werden kann, so bieten die dargestellten Techniken dafür eine Grundlage. Neuere Arbeiten zur Verwendung multipler Modelle [12] ermöglichen zudem, erst dann auf ZVS auszuweichen, wenn das Potential statischer Symptome und Beobachtungen erschöpft ist.

Insbesondere im Bereich der modellbasierten Diagnose darf jedoch nicht übersehen werden, daß die Gesamtaufgabe noch keineswegs als gelöst betrachtet werden kann. So setzt der erweiterte Algorithmus aus Bild 11 ein Orakel für die potentiellen verallgemeinerten Meßpunkte voraus; von der Kreativität, ausgefeilte Experimente zu ersinnen, ist man noch weit entfernt. Hier berühren sich die Fehlerdiagnose im üblichen KI-Sinne, d.h. das Vorschlagen, Durchführen und Bewerten von (paasiven) Beobachtungen, und das Testen, bei dem für vorgegebene Fehlerhypothesen Experimente generiert werden. In [13] wird gezeigt, daß diese Wechselbeziehung konkretisiert werden kann: durch Analogiebildung zu den Testgenerierungsstrategien, die im Bereich der Hardware-Qualitätssicherung entwickelt wurden (vgl. z.B. [14], [15]), können zumindest in einfachen Fällen tatsächlich verallgemeinerte Meßpunkte aus dem Systemmodell abgeleitet werden. Auf diese Weise können Teststrategien in Zukunft möglicherweise vermehrt zur Verbesserungen technischer Diagnoseverfahren beitragen.

5. Literatur

[1] E.H. Shortliffe: MYCIN: Computer-Based Medical Consultations, Elsevier, 1976 (basierend auf Shortliffes Dissertation, Stanford University, 1974)

[2] R.S. Patil: Causal Representation of Patient Illness for Electrolyte and Acid-Base Diagnosis, PhD thesis, MIT, 1981

[3] M.M. Richter: Prinzipien der künstlichen Intelligenz, Teubner, 1989

[4] F. Puppe: Diagnostisches Problemlösen mit Expertensystemen, Informatik-Fachberichte 148, Springer, 1987

[5] J. de Kleer, B.C. Williams: Diagnosing Multiple Faults, in: Artificial Intelligence **32** (1987), auch in: M.L. Ginsberg (ed.): Readings in Nonmonotonic Reasoning, Morgan Kaufmann, 1987

[6] P. Struss, O. Dressler: "Physical Negation" – Integrating Fault Models into the General Diagnostic Engine, in: Proc. 11th IJCAI, Detroit, 1989

[7] R. Leitch, M. Wiegand: Temporal Issues in Qualitative Reasoning, in: Proc. ÖGAI-Jahrestagung 1989, Springer, 1989

[8] R. Decker: Qualitative Simulation des zeitlichen Verhaltens von Thyristorbrückengleichrichterschaltungen, Technical Report, Siemens AG, München 1989

[9] J. K. Tsotsos: Knowledge organization and its role in representation and interpretation for time-varying data: the ALVEN system, in: Computational Intelligence **1** (1985)

[10] J. F. Allen: Maintaining Knowledge about Temporal Intervals, in: Comm. ACM **26**(11), November 1983

[11] J. de Kleer, B.C. Williams: Diagnosis as Identifying Consistent Modes of Behavior, in: Proc. 11th IJCAI, Detroit, 1989

[12] P. Struss: A Theory of Model Simplifications and Abstraction for Diagnosis, in: Proc. 5th International Workshop on Qualitative Reasoning, Austin, 1991

[13] H. Lamberti: Modellbasierte Generierung zeitlich verteilter Tests zur technischen Diagnose, Diplomarbeit, Universität Kaiserslautern, 1990

[14] M.H. Shirley: Generating Circuit Tests by Exploiting Designed Behavior, PhD thesis, MIT AI Lab TR 1099, 1988

[15] J.P. Roth, W.G. Bouricius, P.R.Schneider: Programmed Algorithms to Compute Tests to Detect and Distinguish Between Failures in Logic Circuits, in: IEEE Transactions on Electronic Computers, vol. EC-16, no. **5**, 1967

[16] M.M. Richter (Hrsg.): Das MOLTKE-Buch, erscheint als Informatik-Fachbericht, Springer-Verlag, 1991

[17] K. Nökel: Temporally Distributed Symptoms in Technical Diagnosis, Dissertation, Universität Kaiserslautern, 1990, erscheint als Lecture Note in Artificial Intelligence, Springer-Verlag, 1991

[18] R. Decker: Zeitliches Schließen in Constraint-Systemen, Siemens AG, Report INF2 ARM-4-87, München, 1987

Qualitative Modeling of Time in Technical Applications

Jürgen Dorn

Christian Doppler Labor für Expertensysteme

Technische Universität Wien

Paniglgasse 16

A-1040 Wien

A characteristic of many technical processes is the impossibility to foresee their behavior in the future. Propositions about the duration of individual processes are often not quantifiable. Therefore qualitative modeling is the only way to reason about the process and the capabilities to control it. Nevertheless, it is also necessary to reason about quantities to synchronize a program with the application. As an example to demonstrate these techniques an expert system is taken that schedules heats in a steelmaking plant for high-grade steels.

1 Introduction

The domain of scheduling production processes can be seen as prototypical for applications of AI. Although there is a well established theory based on quantitative methods, it is applicated only in few real production processes. Qualitative methods that rely on symbolic computation are an approach to overcome problems with quantitative methods. Nevertheless, a combination of both is necessary [1].

The roots of the scheduling theory are found in operations research, and first theoretical works were published in the fifties [2]. Mathematical-analytical methods prevail. They are exact, describe the problem with few concepts and therefore they are applicable in a wide range of problems. They are universally valid for many applications, because only an abstract resource is regarded instead of a machine with all its characteristics.

If real plants shall be modeled, limits of computability are reached. One reason is the amount of different resources and operations with characteristics which are important for the scheduling process, and the diversity of goal functions. Efficient algorithms with one or two goal functions are easy to find, but in real plants more than these are desired. Common aims in manufacturing that lead to complex algorithms are maximal throughput, due dates, minimizing of costs and stocks, and maximal use of machines. Sometimes also goal functions are desired that are not quantifiable like ecological goals.

These functions can be expressed by qualitative constraints and heuristics are used to reduce the complexity by applying more "intelligent" search techniques. One of these is the least-commitment strategy that postpones unnecessary decisions to avoid backtracking and with this complexity. The propagation techniques for qualitative time as described here are in accordance with this search technique.

The second disadvantage of traditional OR methods is the impossibility to express uncertain knowledge. Often the duration of operations are unknown and only an approximate value can be given. If a set of operations is scheduled and a due date is exceeded only minimally, the system should reason that this time may be made up by speeding up some operations.

2 Requirements in the Domain of Scheduling Production Processes

If common requirements for scheduling applications exist, it seems meaningful to develop a general scheduling tool to capture these requirements in a framework. We try to work out which kind of features should be supported by such a tool and demonstrate this by means of an example from an steelmaking plant for high-grade steels. One of the most important techniques will be temporal reasoning. Therefore the used knowledge representation technique should support the representation of time adequately. In AI several approaches to represent and process time were developed. It will be seen that different techniques are appropriate for the scheduling application and that every approach has advantages.

Producing high-grade steels is a very specialized production process that relays on high experience and therefore we can easyly differentiate between domain knowledge and common sense knowledge for scheduling. If a knowledge representation model is dedicated to scheduling applications, it should support the common sense knowledge with automatic reasoning and the domain specific knowledge should be easy to represent and to modify.

The described application is situated at Böhler company in Kapfenberg (Styria). An expert system was developed for this problem without using the proposed qualitative representation of time [3], [4].

2.1 Scheduling

Scheduling of factory processes involves the simultaneous consideration of jobs to be performed and of resources which they require. Usually a *job* is identified with a deliverable product which has to meet a certain quality. Associated with each job is some formal specification of the product to be produced. In our case jobs are heats in the steelmaking plant. A specification prescribes chemical ingredients of the heat and the sizes of the ingots, billets, and slabs to cast.

Resources are typically those tools, units, materials, and personnel which are provided by the factory to be used or consumed in the production process. Associated with each resource is some formal specification of its characteristics and capabilities. Here, these are characteristics of the electric arc furnace, the horizontal continuous caster, and capacities of the teeming bay.

In a *job shop* a scheduler considers the two specifications and generates a set of operations for each job which produces the desired result together with a set of explicit ordering constraints on the operations and a set of resource requirements for the operations. In contrast, in our application the operations for the several jobs are fixed. For every steel quality there exists already a sequence of operations. These plans are called *process plans*.

When a number of jobs are to be executed together, the composition of their resource requirements implies additional ordering constraints which prohibit simultaneous demands on nonsharable resources. A scheduler must consider both the explicit ordering constraints imposed by the sequences of operations and the implicit ordering constraints derived from the availabilities of the resources. The scheduler must also take into account due dates. Moreover, chemical residuals in the electric arc furnace that influence the quality of steel result in important constraints for the sequence of jobs.

The task of scheduling jobs and resources in a steelmaking plant is difficult for at least two reasons. First, there is combinatorial complexity since the set of jobs can be accomplished in a number of different ways, and secondly, there is an uncertainty in the execution of the jobs.

2.2 The Steelmaking Plant

The production of Böhler company is order-oriented which means that almost no products are stored intentionally. Although a "just-in-time"-production is desired, delivery dates can often not be guaranteed. The situation before using the expert system was that about 15% of the appointments could not be met. This is due to the amount of different qualities and constraints in the technical process.

Böhler company is divided into several plants. Plants like rolling mills and forges order products of a certain quality and size from the steelmaking plant. These orders are co-ordinated to jobs, and a list of jobs for the following week is worked out. The task of the expert system is now to find a possible sequence of these jobs with violating as few constraints as possible.

The steelmaking plant consists of five electric arc furnaces, two ladle furnaces, three ladle-refining equipments with several units to enable chemical reactions, casting cranes, moulds, slots for moulds in a teeming bay, and a horizontal continuous casting unit.

First steel and scrap iron is melted in an electric arc furnace. This operation takes between two and five hours. The duration varies with steel qualities depending on the heat's ingredients and due to external reasons. The molten steel is emptied into ladles and a heat treatment is performed in a ladle furnace, the duration is about the same as in the electric arc furnace. After this, special treatments may be performed in one of the two vacuum oxygen decarburation units (VOD) or in the vacuum decarburation unit (VD).

The next step may be the processinf of the steel in a horizontal continuous caster to form slabs and billets or it may be casted into moulds to form ingots. In the latter case a place in the teeming bay is required where ingots can solidificate in the moulds. The solidification process may take up to 24 hours depending on the size of the ingots. A team of workers is needed to set up and strip off the moulds. The effort for casting many small ingots is greater than that required for a few large ingots. About 70% of the jobs are casted into ingots despite the higher costs of this process when compared to the continuous caster process.

2.3. Constraints and Strategies

During the construction of a schedule several constraints have to be considered. The human expert – the engineer in the plant – has no pretension to generate an optimal schedule, because the uncertainty in the execution of his schedule would break the optimality. Moreover, he can not consider every detail.

The problem in scheduling is that residuals of one heat in the electric arc furnace may pollute the next heat. As a general rule it can be said that 3% of a chemical element in a heat remains in the electric arc furnace. And 3% of the difference of the elements in two following heats will be assimilated by the second heat. This rule is effective for 42 chemical elements, but usually only 8 main elements are considered. This general rule has some exceptions that have to be handled separately. Furthermore, it is important not to waste expensive elements. If one job demands a high percentage of an expensive element like cobalt the subsequent job should use as much of the residual as possible.

For some qualities it is necessary that the steel is still hot after casting for subsequent treatments like forging. There will be an appointment between the steelmaking plant and the subsequent plant and the schedule must take care of these due dates. The average number of jobs with due dates in the past was about 10%. For some jobs no appointments are made, although their subsequent treatment should be done immediately after casting. These jobs must not be scheduled at the end of the week, because the subsequent plants are not working. Some jobs with difficult treatments should be performed during day shifts, because an engineer should supervise these jobs. The varying job durations which depend on the steel quality must also be considered in the scheduling process.

Further constraints for the scheduling process are restrictions on and among the units. The duration of the solidification of big ingots (50 t) is about one day, and only one can be produced per day, because there exists only one place for such an ingot in the teeming bay. If a heat should be casted in many small ingots the burden for the workers is larger than for few big ingots, because the handling of every mould takes approximately the same time. As a heuristic, the engineers recommend to schedule only three jobs with small ingots in a sequence. Jobs with the same steel quality that should be processed on the continuous caster with the same size should be scheduled in a sequence. This sequence of jobs is called a *serial casting*, and it is important that as few delays occur as possible between the subsequent jobs. Due to bad experience with delays the engineers schedule all jobs in a period of two or three days for the continuous caster on the same furnace. If an amount of a steel quality is ordered that does not make a full heat, it can be coupled with another heat of compatible quality forming a *double-* or *triple-casting*. This means that only a part of the heat is emptied in the ladle. Durations of treatments in the refinement and casting process will be shorter for this job, because the heat is smaller. This must be observed in the scheduling process.

An important aspect and problem we have just mentioned is the uncertainty in the application. For a heat often a certain amount of scrap iron is used for economical and technical reasons. The scrap iron is classified in regard of its ingredients, but the ingredients are only known approximately. For a given job scrap iron is chosen that contains already some desired elements. Whether an actual heat fulfils its requirements is uncertain. Perhaps some additional treatments have to be performed after the scrap is melted in the furnace. So the duration of a job varies independent. Moreover, the duration of the melting process in the electric arc furnace varies depending on interruptions of the power supply.

The scheduling problem is too complex to use any uninformed search strategy. The expert system just as the engineers applies heuristic strategies to reduce the complexity. Due to continuous changes in the steel market and the production policy these strategies have to be changed too and sometimes even new ones have to be developed. This problem was the principal reason to develop an expert system instead of a traditional software system.

One strategy in planning is to minimize stocks in the production process and to produce just in time. As a consequence, the amount of work on each machine will be reduced and slack times between operations will be needed. These slack times must be scheduled due to uncertainties in the production. Another strategy is the balanced load of the workers in the teeming bay. The expert system therefore tries to distribute jobs with large and small amount of work uniformly over the week.

3 Representation of Time

In standard predicate calculus and other formalisms for knowledge representation the validity of propositions is projected on the values „true" or „false". A proposition is either true or false. We have shown in [5] and [6] that for technical processes this is not adequate, because permanent changes occur and the truth of propositions is limited to time periods. Therefore *temporal logic* in which the validity of a proposition is restricted to a *temporal interval* is proposed. The following proposition states that between 9 and 11.45 pm the heat 3 is melted in furnace 1:

$$\text{melts(furnace 1, heat 3) @ } \langle 9.00 - 11.45 \rangle$$

The representation of several propositions that hold at different periods can be formulated independently. A *temporal* or *causal dependency* between two propositions can be represented explicitly and a dedicated treatment of time is possible, because the temporal expressions have a defined syntax and semantic. In [7] 13 possible temporal relations between two intervals were defined. These *interval relations* can be used to represent a technical process qualitatively.

Several approaches to process an interval-based representation were developed for knowledge-based systems. They differ in expressiveness and in the quality of the applied technique of consistency checking and computing new knowledge. The applied technique influences the complexity of three aspects: the time for finding a relation between propositions, the storage that is needed for all relations and the time for consistency checking. We do not discuss the pros and cons of these approaches here.

3.1 Time Quantities

Quantitative time is mostly used to synchronize an application with its environment. So the steelmaking plant must be synchronized with subsequent plants like the forge. Some orders must be delivered hot and the forge must know in advance when such an order is delivered to prepare its machinery. Thus every week engineers of the different plants meet and make appointments for the next week. It is expected that those dates will be hold within a granularity of two hours. So an important concept for the representation of time is a range of allowed time units. It should be possible to represent that a given job is finished between one and three o'clock.

Also the durations of operations in the plant are uncertain. Nevertheless, the melting can be constrained to a range between two and five hours. Applying additional knowledge about the ingredients and the situation of the power supply, the range can be constrained further. Here it seems promising to have a computational model that allows to strengthen constraints step by step.

In a production process not only appointments with clients need to be synchronized, but also with the workers in the plant. Changes of shifts, week-ends, and public holidays must be represented temporally. The engineer that plans the weekly schedule endeavors to schedule technical risky and difficult operations into the day shift when he will be present. Of course he wants to be able to specify this also in an expert system. In an interval-based representation we could define the intervals "monday" and "production-of-heat". By means of interval relations we can constrain that the heat shall be performed sometime during the interval "monday" without scheduling the heat in an exact time.

To allow computing and reasoning between the different time expressions a smallest common time unit must be defined. In our application this granulation interval is a quarter of an hour. Addition, subtraction, and ordering relations are needed to conclude new knowledge. For scheduling applications usually there is no need for a representation of continuous time as in physical processes.

3.2 Process Plans

The plans that describe the operations of one job or heat and their temporal inter-relations are called process plans [8]. They describe the production technique with all its constraints on resources and time. It makes no sense to restrict the production process too strongly, because this could result in situations where no schedule will be found. So in a process plan attributes should be constrained qualitatively.

The temporal relations and the durations of the different operations are needed to compute, when a given order with a due date must be initiated. From the process plan a shortest and longest duration for the whole plan should be deducible. Which one of the two times is used for scheduling, is dependent of the scheduling strategy. The following figure illustrates a simple process plan in the application. During the first interval the heat is in the electric arc furnace, during the second in the ladle furnace, during the third in the vacuum treatment, and in the last interval in the caster.

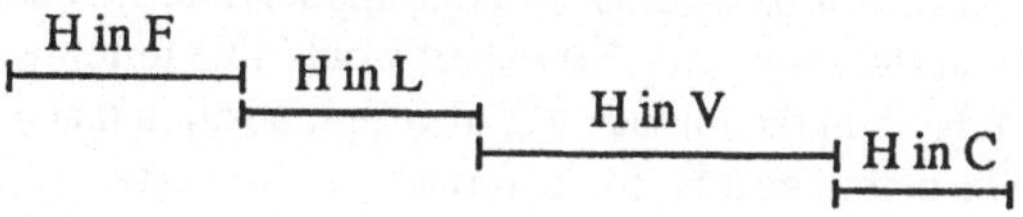

Figure 1: Simple Process Plan

In this figure no uncertainties are shown. Graphically these uncertainties are difficult to represent, but they can be represented easily by sets of possible granulation intervals. We have just mentioned that for "just-in-time" production slack times are needed. We can describe them by intervals whose duration is in a range between zero and a certain limit of time units. The following representation also includes slack times.

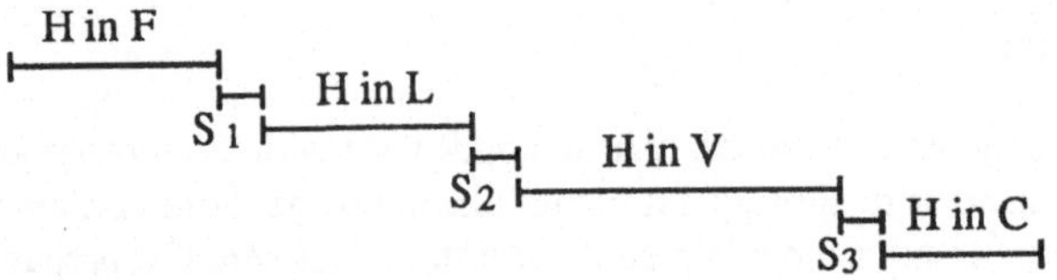

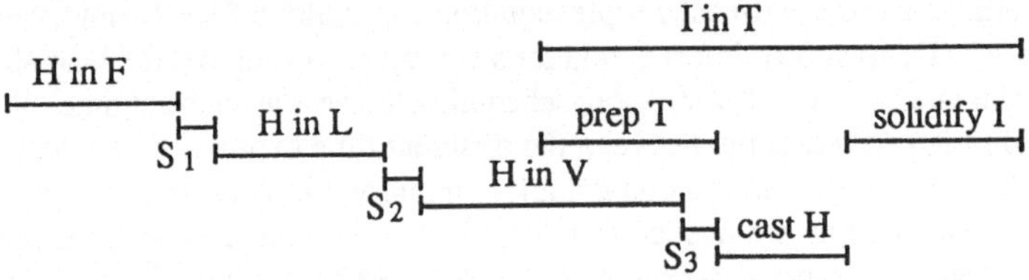

Figure 2: Process Plan with Slack Times

Jobs in the steelmaking plant are specified by their quality and by their forms and sizes. We can generate groups of specifications that have common process plans. Process plans of different groups differ in used units and durations. A process plan can be seen as prototypical for a number of similar jobs. In such a prototypical description no absolute times may occur. Therefore the temporal relation between operations must be described by a qualitative constraint. It must be defined that the melting in the furnace occurs <u>before</u> the heat treatment in the ladle furnace. For simple process plans the notation of sequences would suffice, but the following example shows that also overlapping intervals occur.

If a heat is casted into ingots, moulds must be prepared in the teeming bay and after casting the ingots must solidificate for a certain time. The preparation will take place during the vacuum treatment.

Figure 3: Process Plan with Simultaneous Intervals

In the application a lot of such process plans exist. They differ in used units, treatments, and durations. It can not be the task of a scheduling system to determine these plans. In our case they are given by the engineers. It would be of great support for them if they could describe these plans with simple representation techniques. One representation for such process plans are *scripts* [5]. In scripts the involved objects and agents of a complex activity are represented explicitly and implicit conclusions are taken from this representation. Using scripts it will be easy to adapt an expert system to changes in the production process.

3.3 Resources, Products, and Capacities

One implicit conclusion in scripts concerns the involved objects. One typical kind of object in scheduling is a resource. This resource can be a furnace in our application. It is common sense that no two heats may be in the furnace at the same time. No expert would like to represent this explicitly. If the proposition exists that a heat H_1 is in the furnace and also a proposition that a heat H_2 is in the furnace, it follows that heat H_1 must be before heat H_2 in the furnace or vice versa.

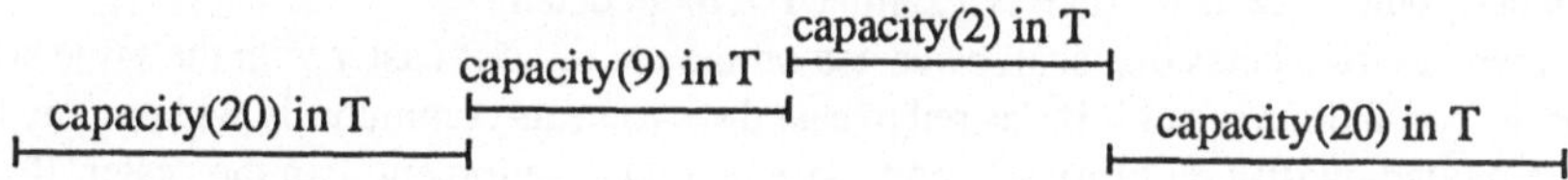

Figure 4: General Temporal Constraint on Resources

Another important fact is that one heat can not be at the same time in two different units. In our application a special case exists – the double or triple castings. These are products that will be divided during their production. In this case a product can be in two units at the same time. Therefore it should be possible to represent two different kinds of products – separable and inseparable products. For inseparable products the given temporal constraint should be deduced automatically.

Figure 5: Inseparable Products

The mentioned units are a special kind of resource. Single machines like furnaces or the caster are explicitly named. Other resources like places in the teeming bay, ladles, or raw material are given by specifications of amount. If many places exist in a stock, each place should not be represented explicitly. Sometimes the amount is also given by continuous quantities. This should be represented by functional propositions that hold over an interval. In the following figure the capacity of the teeming bay is represented. The integer signifies the number of free places.

Figure 6: Representation of Capacities

3.4 Schedules

To find a schedule for a set of orders, a set of process plans are combined and the temporal constraints between them must be considered. In each process plan there will be temporal constraints, constraints on delivery dates, constraints due to chemical restrictions, and constraints posted due to common resources. This shall be illustated by an example.

Heat H_1 is produced on the same units as heat H_2 with one exception. Heat H_1 is casted into ingots and heat H_2 is casted on the continuous caster. Heat H_2 has a due date and H_1 should be produced immediatly before H_2 due to chemical constraints. For heat H_1 the longest duration for each operation must be considered and therefore slack times must be scheduled for H_2 before the heat treatment in the ladle furnace (L) and before the vacuum treatment in the refinement unit (V).

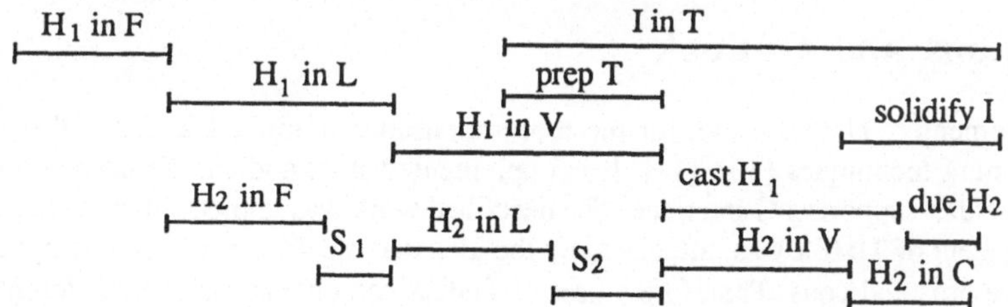

Figure 7: Schedule

For H_2 the shortest durations of each operations should be considered and duration of the subsequent slack time should be longer than the difference between shortest and longest duration of the operation.

3.5 Reactivity

The main problem of today's scheduling systems is that no control of the production process is integrated. Usually no complete knowledge about the environment exists during planning. This incompleteness has many reasons that can not be eliminated. Therefore a kind of feedback about the actual execution is needed to adapt the schedule. This closed loop is not only demanded in scheduling, but also in overall modern manufacturing management [9].

The reaction on an unexpected event in the production process can be planned in different ways. The brute force solution that is often used initiates new planning. The old schedule is not considered anymore. From its concept this approach is very simple and easy to implement. In large applications such a replanning can not be performed very often, because a lot of other decisions are based on the schedule that must be changed, too. In our application the steelmaking plant gives a complete schedule to its clients in order to allow them a co-ordination of their tasks. This schedule should be changed as few as possible.

The better approach uses the old plan and tries to change only necessary features of the schedule. In many cases a shifting of single jobs or groups of them will be sufficient. If an operation needs more time than expected, then this will be the usual solution. The subsequent jobs are shifted. This technique has some limitations. There can be a due date that can not be shifted or a problem with two jobs that conflict with each other. The latter shall be examined in more detail.

Suppose there are two heats that shall be casted on the continuous caster with the same size. For the operation of the continuous caster it is desired to cast the two heats continuously without any break. The two heats are melted on different furnaces and share no other equipment than the caster. If now a prolongation occurs during the treatment of the first heat, the casting time must be shifted. This will collide with the casting time of the second heat. If the prolongation is large enough and the treatment of the first heat may be finished earlier than expected, the sequence of the two casting intervals could be changed. Usually, this will not be possible. The operations of the second heat must be shifted, too. Now it must be decided which operations should be prolonged artificially. Ranges of durations from intervals support this reasoning. The following picture illustrates this situation.

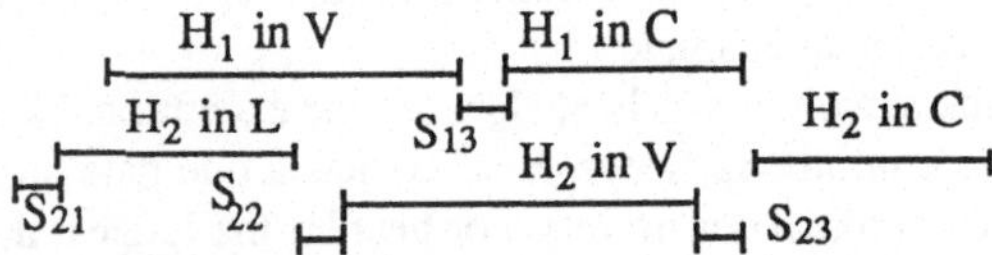

Figure 8: Example for Reactivity

4 Conclusions and Outlook

We have implemented TIMEX a tool for the representation of temporal intervals that incorporates different reasoning techniques [10], [11]. It is implemented in C and can be used from any expert system language that supports a C-interface. The described work was implemented in QuintusProlog.

The development of TIMEX was influenced by the idea that the different known temporal reasoning techniques have pros and cons. Therefore a user of TIMEX can choose between different representational features and reasoning techniques. An application is described by one or more graphs whose points are intervals and whose edges are temporal relations. For every graph different representation and reasoning capabilities may be chosen. Scheduling for example may now be done hierarchically with separate graphs for every layer of abstraction. Therefore it is also necessary that one interval may exist in more than one graph.

One possibility is to compute the transitive closure of a graph by means of a table. This technique called *interval algebra* was first described by Allen [7]. The advantage of this approach is its expressiveness, which allows to represent that two intervals are disjoint, i.e. they are not overlapping. We have seen that this is a usual statement in scheduling. Its disadvantage is the complexity for guaranteeing consistency. Local consistency may be achieved in cubic time and by quadratic space requirements. The alternative approach is the *time point algebra* [12]. By relating endpoints of intervals we get ordered sets with four elements that describe the temporal relation of two intervals. If the $\{<, >\}$-disjunction between time points is excluded, we achieve a model that needs only cubic time for global consistency. Its disadvantage is that some relations like the disjoint-relation can not be expressed anymore.

A user can decide whether intervals have quantitative attributes. Begin, end, and duration then may be restricted by a time bound which is a range of possible granulation intervals. A granulation interval is the smallest possible interval. So an interval is an implicit specification of a set of intervals. The attributes of an interval are constrained against each other and from two attributes the range of the third can be restricted automatically. These quantitative constraints may have consequences on interval relations and attributes of other intervals which are computed, too. The computation of the transitive closure is not as expensive as for the qualitative constraints. At most linear time for modifications of one attribute is needed.

Most algorithms for temporal reasoning use complete graphs. Therefore quadratic space is required. Reference intervals were suggested by Allen as an improvement. This approach can not be automated, because a user must decide which intervals shall be reference intervals. As a consequence, Koomen [13] has introduced reference intervals with a restricted expressiveness. A further approach to structure graphs and with that to improve time and space requirements are sequence graphs [14].

In the actual implementation of TIMEX it is not possible to choose reference intervals, because we believe that in technical applications the hierarchies of reference intervals would not be very large. Therefore no significant advantage will be gained by applying this technique.

Actually TIMEX is used for two applications. After completion of these projects it is intended to revise TIMEX and to add some known techniques for interval propagation. Probably, then also reference intervals will be available. A further extension could be a component to represent intervals and relations graphically. An important improvement for interactive and cooperative scheduling will be non-monotonic reasoning. It should be possible to retract relations from a graph with all consequenses that the insertion of this relation has had.

We have seen that for scheduling beside of temporal knowledge, knowledge about capacities is important. A scheduling tool should therefore contain further reasoning capabilities. Now it is intended to develope a script-based tool that is based on reasoning about time and capacities.

Acknowledgements

The author would like to thank Mr. Alexander Bek, Mrs Alexandra Eder, and Mr. Wolfgang Slany for contributions to this work and for reading of several drafts.

References

[1] Andrew Kusiak. "Expert Systems for Planning and Scheduling Manufacturing Systems". *European Journal on Operations Research*, Vol. 34, pp. 113 – 130, 1988.

[2] R. W. Conway, W. L. Maxwell, L. W. Miller. *"The Theory of Scheduling"*. Addison Wesley, 1967.

[3] Dorothea Czedik, Jürgen Dorn, Alexandra Eder. "Scheduling in a Steelmaking Plant". *Proceedings of the International Workshop on Expert Systems in Engineering – Principles and Applications*, Vienna, pp 253 – 254, 1990.

[4] Jürgen Dorn, Reza Shams. "An Expert System for Scheduling in a Steelmaking Plant". *Proceedings of the World Congress on Expert Systems*, Orlando Fla, Pergamon Press, 1991.

[5] Jürgen Dorn. *"Wissensbasierte Echtzeitplanung"*. Vieweg Verlag, 1989.

[6] Jürgen Dorn. "Learning and Performing Hard Real-Time Skills". *Proceedings of the IFIP TC5 Working Conference on Dependability of Artificial Intelligence Systems*, Vienna, 1991.

[7] James F. Allen. "Maintaining Knowledge about Temporal Intervals". *Communications of the ACM*, Vol. 26, No 11, 1983, pp 823 – 843.

[8] Tien-Chien Chang. *"Expert Process Planning for Production"*. Addison Wesley, 1990.

[9] Roger Kerr. *"Knowledge-Based Manufacturing Management"*. Addison Wesley, 1991.

[10] Jürgen Dorn. "TIMEX – A Tool for Interval-Based Representation for Technical Applications". *Proceedings of the 2nd Conference on Tools for Artificial Intelligence*, Washington, DC, 1990, IEEE Press, pp 501 – 506.

[11] Alexander Bek. "Implementierung eines Zeitintervallkalküls" Diplomarbeit, TU Wien, 1991.

[12] Marc Vilain, Henry Kautz, Peter van Beek. "Constraint Propagation Algorithms for Temporal Reasoning". *Readings in Qualitative Reasoning about Physical Systems*, Daniel S. Weld, Johan de Kleer, Morgan Kaufmann, pp 373 – 381, 1990.

[13] Johannes A. G. M. Koomen. "Localizing Temporal Constraint Propagation". *Proceedings of the 1st International Conference on Principles of Knowledge Representation and Reasoning*, Toronto, pp 198 – 202, 1989.

[14] Jürgen Dorn. "Propagation of Intervals in Sequence Graphs". *Technical Report CD-TR 90-9*, Christian Doppler Laboratory for Expert System, TU Vienna, 1990.

Knowledge-based Systems -
The Second Generation Sets to Work

Peter Struss

Siemens AG

Otto-Hahn-Ring 6

8000 München 83

Second generation knowledge-based systems have reached a stage where they start proving their superiority over traditional expert systems not only in theory but also in applications. Starting from requirements in the domain of DPNet, a diagnosis system for fault localization in high voltage power transmission networks, we outline the foundations of model-based diagnosis. An extension of the theory is presented that allows the system to simplify the model-based reasoning process based on working hypotheses, thus reducing its complexity without sacrificing completeness. Particular emphasis is given to the use of multiple models which turns out to be crucial for a trade-off between completeness of the model-based approach and efficiency requirements when dealing with simple standard cases.

1 Introduction

After more than twenty years of research and development, expert systems deployed in real applications are still fairly limited both in their number and scope of competence. In the domain of applications in engineering, this is mainly due to limitations inherent in the technology of the first generation. This technology is basically organized around the paradigm of capturing experiential knowledge in its favorite representation formalism, rules. To go beyond the exploration of purely empirical associations, work on foundations for a second generation of knowledge-based systems had to provide representations and reasoning mechanisms reflecting nature and structure of principled knowledge in engineering. In particular, it had to develop formalisms for creating "deep" models of the technical systems that were to be designed, diagnosed, or simulated by a computer system.

Diagnosis is probably the most prominent domain of expert systems applications, and can be used to discuss distinctions between the two generations. Traditional knowledge-based diagnosis systems are crucially based on establishing more or less direct links between symptoms that can be observed and faults (or deseases) that have been known to cause the symptoms (with a certain probability) (Fig. 1).

In this approach, reasoning goes from symptoms to faults, and obviously this approach heavily depends on the completeness of knowledge about all three elements: the symptoms, the faults, and the associations between them. The resulting restriction of the system to what has been encountered and widely experienced before, are prohibitive for most industrial applications; handling newly designed systems and new kinds of failures are a must. An even more significant impediment to industrial applications of this technology lies in the fact that each diagnostic system dedicated to a particular type of device has to be developed individually, even though the engineering knowledge required may be essentially the same for a much broader class of devices. Intolerably high costs in development and maintenance of such systems are a consequence.In contrast, second generation diagnosis systems aim at

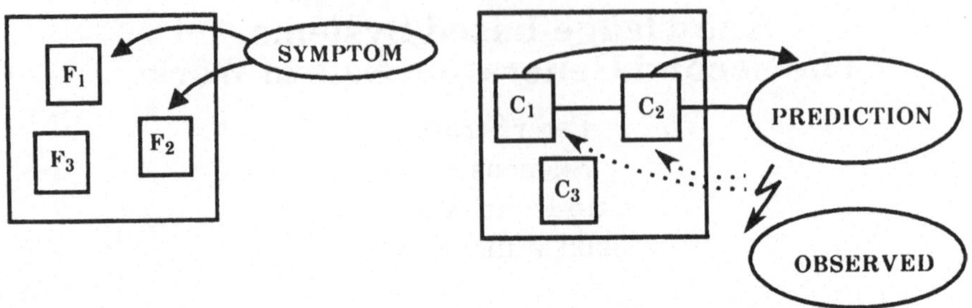

Figure 1 First Generation:
Linking Symptoms to Faults

Figure 2 Second Generation: Model-based
Prediction of Observable Behavior

getting closer to the diagnostic skills of engineers, including
- handling of unknown symptoms,
- detecting new kinds of faults,
- diagnosing unexperienced devices (as long as they are composed of known components and principles),
- generating causal, or "deep", explanations, and
- generating diagnostic systems for particular devices based on their structural description only, given a body of principled knowledge about the domain ("component library").

Obviously, this is a goal much more ambitious than what can be covered by traditional expert systems. In order to achieve it, model-based diagnosis uses the following principle: based on knowledge about the structure of a device and the behavior of its constituents ("components"), predictions about the behavior of the entire device are made, given some observations (e.g. input-output values). If an inconsistency is detected, its origins are traced back to the constituents involved in the prediction. They form **diagnosis candidates** which are then discriminated through further testing and probing (Fig. 2). As opposed to first generation systems, this approach is not dependent on a priori knowledge about possible faults, and is applicable to new compositions of known constituents.

This new quality requires the development of
- general representations of scientific and engineering knowledge (instead of purely empirical associations),
- general diagnostic algorithms (independent of the particular device and domain).

Although being far from claiming the ultimate solution to these problems, research in model-based reasoning has now reached a stage where it starts proving its superiority over the first generation in applications rather than merely dealing with toy systems.

In this paper, we start by presenting problems in the domain of failure localization in high voltage power transmission networks to which we successfully applied the technology of model-based reasoning. The example prompts, in particular for the use of different, alternative models of components, some of which are based on simplifying assumptions which may be wrong in particular cases. In section 3, we discuss some basic issues in model-based reasoning, and outline the principles of consistency-based diagnosis in section 4. Next, we present an extension to this approach that allows the system to control the model-based reasoning process based on simplifying working hypotheses without loosing its completeness. This forms the basis for the use of simplified and approximate models (section 6) and, hence, for solving problems set by the network diagnosis application (section 7).

2 An Example - Fault Localization in Power Transmission Networks

2.1 The Problem

In this section, we briefly introduce an application domain we are currently working on: high voltage power transmission networks ([Beschta et al. 90]). As of this writing, a prototype, called DPNet, has been completed, which successfully solves all problems taken from a collection of about 20 cases (real data from a regional network in Germany) using a model-based approach. Current work focuses on elaborating the models.

What is the problem to be tackled? The purpose of a power transmission network is connecting a number of sinks (potentially transformers to a lower voltage level) to operating sources (also possibly transformers). This has to be done in a way that guarantees energy transmission also in cases of local faults, and, hence, such networks tend to be highly redundant. Their elements are, besides transformers and connections to sources, basically lines and so-called bus-bars acting as nodes. Fig. 3 shows a section of a 220/110kV network. Another element of the network is formed by the **protection system**. Its task is to detect

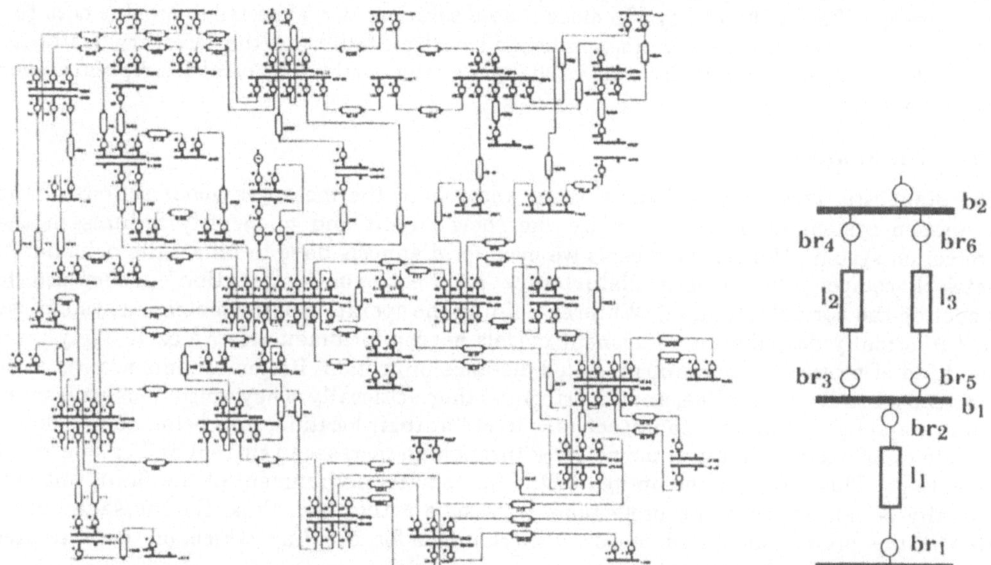

<table>
<tr><td>Figure 3 Power Transmission Network</td><td>Figure 4 A Portion of the Network</td></tr>
</table>

disturbances (short circuits) and respond to them by automatically isolating the affected substructure from the rest of the network by opening switches. Partially conflicting with the goal of optimal protection of the equipment against damage, a guiding principle is to restrict the detached portion to what is really necessary to isolate the fault. Before we describe the technology developed for this purpose, we conclude the description of the problem to be solved by the diagnostic system. The protection system is decentralized and consists of a number of devices which observe local conditions (basically voltage and current), detect anomalies, and, if certain conditions are met, automatically change the network topology by opening switches at their location (so-called breakers). Such activities (alarms and automatic interventions) are reported to a control center. Because a local disturbance (short circuit) immediately affects the overall network, the operator is confronted with a burst of messages; hundreds of them being transmitted within a few seconds is normal. From this message burst, the operator has to infer the type and location of the fault, assess whether the automatic reaction of the protection system is adequate, and, if necessary, undertake suitable actions for network reconfiguration. Typically, the time limit for this task is 30 to 60s.

Characteristics of the problem that demand for support by a computer system are:
- **Information overload**, as pointed out above.
- **Incomplete information** is the dual feature. Missing information can be due to old

equipment used in the protection system (which is simply not designed to report interventions), transmission errors, or receipt of the message after the analysis has started.
- **Multiple faults** can occur, although rarely in the form of simultaneous short circuits, but rather because the protection system itself can be malfunctioning.
These problem characteristics combine with requirements upon the utilization of a diagnostic system:
- **Adaptability** to different network **topologies**, not only for being applicable to different networks; even for a particular network, the topology is frequently changed with the goal of equal distribution of load.
- **Adaptability** to new **technology** introduced for part of the network equipment.

Together, these features suggest not only a knowledge-based approach to failure localization, but more specifically the utility of a model-based solution. It is expected to provide both the robustness required to deal with unexpected and multiple faults and the necessary flexibility due to the possibility of local, declarative changes applied to the structural description and/or the component library.

2.2 The Models

The diagnostic task in this domain is an analysis of the messages about actions of the protection system in order to localize the short circuit and to identify failures in the protection system. Hence, the models we need for diagnosis have to reflect the behavior of network components under a **disturbance of the normal operation** (as opposed to modeling the normal situation). While explaining the operation of the protection system, we will informally describe the component models needed for diagnosis. We exclusively treat one kind of protection mechanism, called distance protection. Its components are installed between a bus-bar and a line, and (in principle) they act locally. They continuously measure voltage and (direction and magnitude of) current at their location, thus being able to detect the effects of a short-circuit in the network through an increase in current and/or a decrease in voltage. This effect is not limited to the immediate environment of the fault, but acts globally (what causes many protections to become active and, thus, the message burst). Hence, the protection system needs a mechanism for deciding which of the activated protections actually have to intervene.
The goal is to detach the smallest substructure necessary to isolate the fault. For instance, line l_1 in Fig. 4 is protected by breakers br_1 and br_2, and a fault on bus-bar b_1 is isolated by br_1, br_4 and br_6 (this illustrates that distance protections are oriented towards the attached line). To achieve this, each protection determines the distance to the fault location by measuring the impedance at its location. Only if this distance corresponds to the length of the connected line (and energy flows towards it), the protection sends a tripping command to a breaker which disconnects the line. Accordingly, a model for the breaker (including the protection) could simply express that it is opened exactly when the fault is on the connected line or the bus-bar behind this line:

$$\text{STATUS} = \text{OPEN} \Leftrightarrow \text{FAULT-DISTANCE} = (1, 2)$$

where the distance is an abstract one, measured in terms of the number of components to be passed, and $(1, 2)$ denotes a disjunction of values 1 and 2.
The task is then to propagate the distance through the network and find the component with $\text{FAULT-DISTANCE} = 0$. The model for correct lines and bus-bars for this purpose, besides diminishing the distance by 1, simply has to state

$$\text{FAULT-DISTANCE} = 0$$

We will refer to this model as M_{NAIVE}, because, although it works amazingly well for many standard cases even with incomplete information, it is based on a number of assumptions which restrict its applicability. In particular, it fails if a protection does not work properly. For instance, br_2 might not intervene although there is a short circuit on l_1. The protection

system covers such cases, being more sophisticated than we indicated so far. Actually, the protection distinguishes 4 distance levels, which roughly correspond to
- almost the entire length of the directly connected line (for br_1 this is l_1),
- the rest of this line, the adjacent bus-bar, and part of the lines beyond it (end of l_1, b_1, and partly l_2 and l_3),
- the remaining parts of the latter lines with the bus-bars they are connected to and, potentially, part of further lines (rest of l_2 and l_3, b_2 and lines beyond it),
- everything beyond these three levels.

The intervention time is determined to be 0.05s, 0.4s, 0.9s, or 3.0s, dependent on the actual level. Thus, if br_2 fails, and, hence, energy flow towards the short circuit continues, br_4 and br_6 should finally intervene (on level 2 or 3, i. e. after 0.4s or 0.9s). A refined breaker model has to reflect the various levels, and could look like
$$STATUS = OPEN \land LEVEL = 1 \Leftrightarrow FAULT\text{-}DISTANCE = (1)$$
$$STATUS = OPEN \land LEVEL = 2 \Leftrightarrow FAULT\text{-}DISTANCE = (1, 2, 3) \text{ etc.}$$

With this model, M_{LEVEL}, but without explicit information about the actual levels, a diagnosis (l_2, br_2) could be obtained from the information $STATUS = OPEN$ for br_1, br_4, br_6, whereas M_{NAIVE} offers a fault on b_1 as the only solution (It must be noted that information about the level, at which the protection intervened, is not always part of the messages).

However, even the improved model may fail in some situations. A short circuit does not necessarily imply almost zero resistance; high-resistance faults may occur, for instance, if a broken line touches ground with low conductance. In this case, impedance measured by the protection is higher than for a "standard" short circuit, suggesting a longer distance to the fault. Still, the respective protection would intervene, though at a higher level, and diagnosis based on M_{LEVEL} might be mislead. We can mend this by propagating impedance rather than the abstract fault distance. Note that by introducing this more powerful model, $M_{IMPEDANCE}$, we consider new kinds of faults.

An even more sophisticated model, M_{TIME}, is possible if we abandon the static view of the preceding ones and consider changes over time. Information about the intervention time or temporal order of interventions can be helpful for discriminating between possible diagnoses (although reliable temporal information is available not in all cases).

And yet there are further aspects not covered by the models we described so far, for instance the impact of several lines on the impedance and, hence, on the estimate of the distance. Other implicit assumptions underlie all models outlined before. A fundamental assumption is that there is only one short circuit present, or, at least, if there are several, they are distant and not interacting. Without this assumption, FAULT-DISTANCE can be ambiguous. Furthermore, faults are assumed to be persistent. Still, this not the end of possible elaborations of the model.
The point we want to make here is that, even if we are able to develop a detailed model, that accounts for all aspects mentioned and that covers all possible situations we might encounter in diagnosis, we would **not want to use this complex universal model at all times**, because we do not have to. The majority of problems can be solved using the simplified versions of the model, and it would be unnecessarily complex or even infeasible if all the details would be included (Note that a more detailed model may not only increase the cost of inferences but also potentially require more variables to be measured which may be impossible or expensive to obtain). We would rather want a diagnostic system to mimic a human expert whose skills include choosing the right level of detail and simplifying the problem in an appropriate way. This requires representing the various chunks of the model separately, enabling the diagnostic system to focus on the relevant parts, and combining the results obtained from the use of different models. Thise problem is addressed in [Struss 91a,b]. Before we outline the proposed solution, we discuss some fundamentals of model-based reasoning and, in particular, of consistency-based diagnosis.

3 Model-based Reasoning

Models are a representation of our knowledge about the real-world behavior of real-world systems or processes that can be used in order to derive a more complete description of an actual behavior given some partial information.

We take the view that
- a system is composed of some behavioral constituents (such as components or processes),
- the system's behavior is established by the behaviors of its constituents,
- the behavior of some constituent can be specified by a tuple of local variables.

We assume that a constituent has a number of distinct possible *behavioral modes*, due to its different physical conditions. A correct (unbroken) wire in a circuit exhibits a particular behavioral mode, and a (permanently) broken wire has another one. A behavioral mode can be described by a relation R, the set of tuples of values for local variables that are physically possible in this mode.

For principled reasons, our knowledge about the behavioral modes of a constituent is limited:
- globally: we may be unable to enumerate the set of behavioral modes, because we cannot anticipate all possible physical conditions of a constituent (in particular, the faults)
- locally: we may be unable to exactly describe the relation characterizing a particular behavioral mode, for instance, due to incomplete knowledge about the physical principles.

Even if we consider the second restriction irrelevant for the application we have in mind (i. e. we pretend to be able to explicitly and precisely associate a behavioral mode with some relation, R) it is, again for fundamental reasons, **impossible to positively verify a particular behavioral mode** to be present. Firstly, in most cases, R is infinite, and, hence, we cannot exhaustively check the space of possible tuples. Secondly, even if we (in the finite case) detected in experiments all tuples of R and none outside R, we can still not guarantee that future observations will not include a tuple out of R's complement which would consequently invalidate the respective behavioral mode.

This is what we are normally capable of: **falsifying the presence of a behavioral mode** based on an observation or an inference that is definitly inconsistent with this mode. For this purpose, we are not required to have an explicitly given precise relation for this mode. We only have to use a relation that is **guaranteed to include** the unknown ideal relation.

Positively identifying the presence of a particular behavioral mode can only be done by ruling out all other modes. But in order to do so, we have to enumerate and model all other modes, which was stated above to be, in principle, impossible.

To summarize:
- We can **rule out** the presence of behavioral modes based on assumptions of the **quality of the single models** (i. e. ignoring the local restrictions of modeling).
- We can **positively identify** a behavioral mode if we additionally assume we have **complete knowledge** about the **set of modes** (i. e. ignoring the global restrictions of modeling).

The first issue formulates the principle of consistency-based diagnosis and suggests that it is the natural approach to model-based diagnosis. The second issue explains why "pure" consistency-based systems never infer the innocence of a constituent, and shows that, if other approaches do so, this is based on some global assumption about the possible behavioral modes, either explicitly or implicitly.

4 Consistency-based Diagnosis

The consistency-based approach is oriented towards an assignment of behavioral modes (correct or faulty) to the constituents (components) of the artifact that is consistent with the observations (OBS) and the system description (SD), which contains models of the system's constituents and a representation of its structure. A diagnosis is defined to be a set of faulty components, $\Delta \subseteq COMPS$ such that

$$SD \cup OBS \cup \bigcup_{C \in \Delta} FAULTY(C) \cup \bigcup_{C \in COMPS \setminus \Delta} CORRECT(C)$$

is consistent. Finding possible diagnoses is strongly driven by exploiting known *conflicts*. A conflict is a set of mode assignments, $\cup mode_{k_i}(C_i)$, to a number of components, $C_1, ..., C_n \in COMPS$, that leads to an inconsistency with $SD \cup OBS$:

$$SD \cup OBS \cup \cup mode_{k_i}(C_i) \vdash \perp,$$

which is detected mainly through the derivation of contradictory values of one parameter. The General Diagnostic Engine (GDE, [de Kleer-Williams 87]) is the archetype of systems built upon this principle.

The main focus of work in this area and the subject where considerable progress has been achieved concerns the problem: *Determine diagnostic candidates given the system description, SD, and the set of observations, OBS*. Formal, sound solutions to this problem have been achieved; however, because of several presumptions and simplifications, they constitute but one element of a theory of diagnosis and do not provide a sufficient foundation for building diagnostic systems that handle real problems effectively and efficiently. This purpose requires progress towards a theory of diagnosis that treats diagnosis as a controlled and focused process of acting and non-monotonic reasoning including the use of multiple and simplified models. Hence, rather than facing the task of characterizing the space of possible diagnoses **given the conflicts**, we try to tackle the problem of **how to obtain conflicts**, or, more general, information about the consistency of mode assignments, in a controlled and focused manner. In particular, we want to exploit simplifications and to structure the model appropriately. In ([Struss 89]), we proposed DP as a step in this direction. It has the advantage of generalizing existing formalisms and systems in a very coherent way which even supports an implementation of the generic framework by existing systems, such as GDE$^+$ ([Struss-Dressler 89]).

5 DP - Diagnosis as a Process

5.1 The Basic Idea

The basic idea is very simple. So far, in systems like GDE, Sherlock, or GDE$^+$, and papers like [Reiter 87] and [de Kleer et al. 90], the elements of the diagnostic theories were the system description, SD, the observations, OBS, and the possible mode assignments to the elements of COMPS, in the simplest case the choice between CORRECT (or normal) and FAULTY (or abnormal). However, in the present diagnostic systems, a number of assumptions are implicitly used, such as assumptions about the correctness of the observations independence and non-intermittency of faults, completeness of knowledge about possible faults, and the system structure being unchanged. They are all reasonable for many cases, and they help to make diagnosis more efficient or work at all in these cases. But they limit the applicability of the system in other cases. The problem is that they are present only in an implicit, hardwired form, and, hence, cannot be subject to reasoning and be retracted.

Consequently, DP introduces another element to the theory: the *set of diagnostic hypotheses*, DHYP, which represent working hypotheses that guide and focus the problem solving process unless they are recognized to be inadequate and dropped. This includes simplifying assumptions and, when working with multiple models, modeling assumptions. A diagnosis is now defined as the union of a set of faulty components, Δ_{COMPS} , **and a set of retracted diagnostic hypotheses**, Δ_{DHYP} , such that

$$SD \cup OBS \cup DHYP\backslash\Delta_{DHYP} \cup \neg\Delta_{DHYP} \cup \bigcup_{C \in \Delta_{COMPS}} FAULTY(C) \cup \bigcup_{C \in COMPS\backslash\Delta_{COMPS}} CORRECT(C)$$

is consistent, where $\neg\Delta_{DHYP} := \{\neg dhyp \mid dhyp \in \Delta_{DHYP}\}$. In other words, we search for a mode assignment to constituents that is consistent with SD $\cup$ OBS **under certain assumptions.**

We want to emphasize that, on the one hand, existing consistency-based systems can be regarded as instances of DP. On the other hand, it is easy to realize that assigning TRUE or FALSE to diagnostic hypotheses can be viewed as an analogy to mode assignments to constituents. This provides us with the basis for the implementation of DP, since we can apply an existing diagnostic engine, in our case GDE^+, to debug the diagnostic hypotheses as well as the device.

5.2 An Example for Reasoning with Diagnostic Assumptions

GDE^+ exploits the extended ATMS ([Dressler 88,90]) to generate diagnostic candidates. Here, we can only give a brief sketch of the technical details. We assume the system has detected a minimal conflict involving the constituents, A, B, and C:

(5.1) $\{CORRECT(A), CORRECT(B), CORRECT(C)\}$.

Hence, {A}, {B}, and {C} are the minimal candidates for diagnosis, provided there are no further conflicts. If there are, any valid candidate has to intersect each conflict. In addition, GDE^+ uses models of possible faults for prediction and concludes that a constituent works correctly, if none of its possible faults can be present:

(5.2) $\neg FAULTY_1(C) \wedge ... \wedge \neg FAULTY_n(C) \Rightarrow CORRECT(C).$

In order to illustrate the effect, assume the correct models of A and B together are inconsistent with all fault models, $FAULTY_i(C)$, of C, given SD and OBS:

(5.3) $\forall i\ CORRECT(A) \wedge CORRECT(B) \wedge FAULTY_i(C) \Rightarrow \perp,$

Based on (5.2), GDE^+ concludes

(5.4) $CORRECT(A) \wedge CORRECT(B) \Rightarrow CORRECT(C)$

and reduces (5.1) to give the minimal conflict

(5.5) $\{CORRECT(A), CORRECT(B)\},$

and, hence, the minimal candidates {A} and {B} only. In GDE^+, C will never again be considered as a possible single fault, although the derivation of this result is based on an assumption which might be questioned: (5.2) postulates completeness of C's fault models; there are no failures other than the ones described in the model. We already pointed out in [Struss-Dressler 89] how this problem can be handled, and we will continue with the example in order to illustrate the features of DP. In this framework, the solution is to make the hidden completeness assumption in (5.2) explicit and include it in the dependency recording mechanism of the ATMS. (5.2) is replaced by

(5.2') $\neg FAULTY_1(C) \wedge ... \wedge \neg FAULTY_n(C) \wedge FMC(C) \Rightarrow CORRECT(C)$,

where $FMC(C) \in DHYP$ denotes the assumption that no unspecified fault occurs. With this change, (5.3) results in

(5.4') $CORRECT(A) \wedge CORRECT(B) \wedge FMC(C) \Rightarrow CORRECT(C),$

and in adding another conflict,

(5.5') $\{CORRECT(A), CORRECT(B), FMC(C)\},$

instead of replacing (5.1). What candidates are constructed from conflicts (5.1) and (5.5') depends on DP's *focus of suspicion* which specifies which (types of) assumption sets are currently considered as interesting candidates. For instance, as long as the diagnostic problem solver does not consider unknown faults, sets with FMC assumptions are excluded from the focus of suspicion, and DP generates the minimal candidates {A} and {B} thus reproducing what followed from the **implicit** completeness assumption in (5.2). If the focus of suspicion is extended to cover also FMC assumptions, we obtain the minimal candidates {A}, {B}, and {C, FMC(C)}; besides A and B, C is considered as a possible single fault again, but only if FMC(C) is retracted, i.e. when failing in an unknown mode. The example should convey an intuition of how DP supports reasoning with simplified and approximate models and modeling assumptions.

6 Diagnosis with Multiple Models - The Theory

From a theoretical point of view, the best way to model a device is to construct and use "exact" and detailed models only. However, besides the fundamental objection that our knowledge may not suffice, reasoning with the most detailed models is often too expensive and in many cases unnecessary, as we argued before. This is why we want to split the model and maintain models at different levels of abstraction and simplification. Sometimes, working with a weaker model is much less expensive, but still effective. This motivates:

Definition (View)
　　A model M' is a view of another model, M if
　　　　$M \Rightarrow M'$.

In other words, M' is a necessary condition for M to hold.

In [Struss 91a], a theory of representational transformations is developed that provides a characterization of classes of transformations that turn models into weaker versions that are still valid. In particular, a model, M', obtained as the image of an **abstraction** (e.g. qualitative abstraction) of a model, M, establishes a view of M.

As illustrated by the example in section 2, we sometimes modify models in a way that makes them simpler (e.g. by assuming all breakers intervene at level 1), but inappropriate for particular situations. Using the simplification nevertheless, is based on the **assumption** that the potential deviations from the real behavior mode do not occur in the case we are looking at. In the DP system such diagnostic assumptions can be included in the set DHYP.

Definition (Simplification)
　　M' is a simplification of M, if
　　　　$\exists \{dhyp_i\} \subseteq DHYP \quad M_1 \wedge \bigwedge_i dhyp_i \Rightarrow M'$.

In [Struss 91b], more basic relations are introduced in order to structure the model set. Thus we turn a simple list of behavioral modes into a graph which contains models as nodes and labelled arcs defined by the model relations. The model graph is used to guide the selection and instantiation of models (and also their deactivation) in the course of the diagnostic process, as will be illustrated in section 7. Basically, we start at the leaves; views and simplifications are to be used first in order to save costs in prediction. We climb up in the model graph if there is evidence that a revision of modeling assumptions and/or a refinement of models is required. The system description, SD, is no longer fixed for the entire diagnostic process, but may change.

SD can (and for practical purposes has to) be decomposed into different knowledge sources. In a first step, we can identify that SD comprises (at least) knowledge about the **domains** of the variables used to define models, the **constituents** in the application domain (the *library*), and the **structure** of the device to be diagnosed. Furthermore, the library contains the **model graphs** for the constituents, i.e. inferences such as

$M_1 \wedge dhyp \Rightarrow M_1'$,

and the set of **model definitions** for the explicit models, M-DEF. We assume that, at each stage of the diagnostic process, SD is given by

$$SD = SD_{CORE} \cup M\text{-}DEF_{ACT},$$

where the set of active models, $M\text{-}DEF_{ACT} \subseteq M\text{-}DEF$, normally contains only a small subset of model definitions at a time (Again, we refer to [Struss 91b] for a more detailed description of SD's content).

Organizing the use of constituent models in the diagnostic process according to the principle stated above is based on a monotonicity property whose ultimate foundation is captured by the following theorems.

Theorem

Let M, and M' be models of one constituent C, and M-DEF(M) and M-DEF(M') be the respective model definitions.

if Δ is a diagnosis for

      $OBS \cup SD_{CORE} \cup M\text{-}DEF_{ACT} \cup \{M\text{-}DEF(M)\}$

and   M'(C) is a view of M(C),

then Δ is a diagnosis for

      $OBS \cup SD_{CORE} \cup M\text{-}DEF_{ACT} \cup \{M\text{-}DEF(M')\}$.

Basically, this theorem says that when working with a view of a model, we do not miss a diagnosis we would obtain when using the original model; or, stated differently, that switching to this more powerful model is really a step of refinement. This provides the ultimate justification for applying models, which are gained by (qualitative) abstraction or which model only particular physical aspects, in order to cut down the space of possible diagnoses before further investigation with more fine-grained, but also more costly models.

Of course, when using simplified models, this kind of monotonicity will be restricted, as indicated by the following theorem.

Theorem

Let M, and M' be models of one constituent C, and M-DEF(M) and M-DEF(M') be the respective model definitions.

if Δ is a diagnosis for

      $OBS \cup SD_{CORE} \cup M\text{-}DEF_{ACT} \cup \{M\text{-}DEF(M)\}$,

and   M'(C) is a simplification of M(C): $M \wedge dhyp \Rightarrow M'$,

then Δ is a diagnosis for

      $OBS \cup SD_{CORE} \cup M\text{-}DEF_{ACT} \cup \{M\text{-}DEF(M')\}$,

or $dhyp \in \Delta$.

This theorem formulates what is in accordance with our intuition, namely that by using a simplified model, the system will infer all diagnoses that can be obtained from the original model and do not contain the retraction of the underlying simplifying assumption. Part of the diagnosis space that is based on $\neg dhyp$ may be invisible; however, it can be regained in DP, since the diagnostic assumptions are made explicit and kept in dependencies.

7   Back to the Example

We illustrate this process by returning to the initial example. Fig. 5 shows a possible model graph for components of the power transmission network. σ-arcs correspond to simplifications, v-arcs are views, and choices (disjunctions of models) are marked with "c". The graph indicates, for instance, that under simplifications $\sigma_1, \sigma_2, \sigma_3$, the model M_{LEVEL} is a valid model for the correct behavior, and we have to consider M^F_{SHORT} as the only possible fault. Graph nodes with bold labels are the (ideal) behavioral modes which are checked by views and/or simplifications.

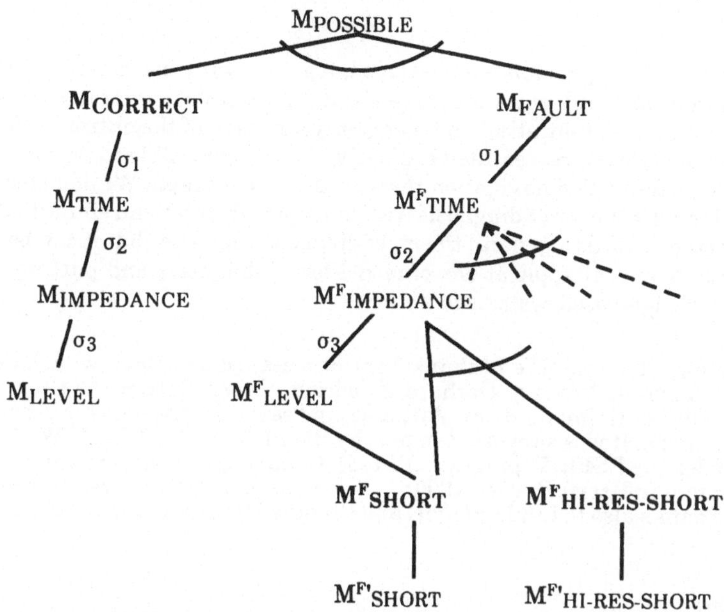

Figure 5 A model graph for network components

These ideal behavioral modes define the places where assumptions are introduced (namely that the respective mode is the actual one) which are then recorded by the ATMS and propagated via view and simplification links. Only simplification links add further assumptions representing the respective simplification conditions. For instance, M_{LEVEL} might be labelled by the assumption set $\{M_{CORRECT}, \sigma_1, \sigma_2, \sigma_3\}$. This allows us to use ATMS-based focusing techniques as described in [Dressler-Farquhar 90] for letting simplification assumptions guide the focus for prediction.

Imagine, we start diagnosis by activating the correct modes only while maintaining all simplifying assumptions:

$\text{M-DEF}_{ACT1} = \{\text{M-DEF}(M_{LEVEL})\}$.

Let us further assume that predictions based on the model $L1_{LEVEL}$ for some line, L1, are inconsistent with the observations, i.e. $\{L1_{CORRECT}, \sigma_1, \sigma_2, \sigma_3\}$ is a conflict, then, under a focus of suspicion that does not contain diagnoses involving any of $\sigma_1, \sigma_2, \sigma_3$ (the diagnostic hypotheses currently taken for granted), $\Delta = \{L1_{CORRECT}\}$ is the only diagnosis, and L1 is considered faulty.

If now fault models are activated by the system, while still maintaining the simplifications $\sigma_1, \sigma_2, \sigma_3$, we have

$\text{M-DEF}_{ACT2} = \{\text{M-DEF}(M_{LEVEL}), \text{M-DEF}(M^{F'}_{SHORT})\}$.

Let us assume that the fault model, $L1F'_{SHORT}$, also contradicts the observations. This invalidates $L1F_{SHORT}$ and also $L1F_{LEVEL}$. Under the simplifying assumptions $\sigma_1, \sigma_2, \sigma_3$, now both $L1_{CORRECT}$ and $L1_{FAULTY}$ are refuted, and so is $L1_{POSSIBLE}$, which is considered to be a fact. This inconsistency triggers **a change in the focus of suspicion**, since it can only be resolved by retracting simplifying assumptions, in our case (at least) σ_3. Allowing the respective modeling assumption to occur in diagnoses extends the space of diagnoses again and activates new models:

$\text{M-DEF}_{ACT3} = \{\text{M-DEF}(M_{IMPEDANCE}), \text{M-DEF}(M^{F'}_{SHORT}), \text{M-DEF}(M^{F'}_{HI-RES-SHORT})\}$.

If $L1F'_{HI-RES-SHORT}$ is also inconsistent with the observations while the correct model, $L1_{IMPEDANCE}$, is not, L1 is considered correct, under the simplifying assumptions σ_1, σ_2.

8 Summary

The concepts for structuring models we developed, together with the capabilities of the DP framework enables us to chunk our knowledge about a system's behavior in such a way that we can obtain results by instantiating and using only a portion of the entire model. Because modeling assumptions can be represented explicitly, the system is able to reason about them and has a basis for a controlled navigation through the model graph. We demonstrated that progress in developing a theory of diagnosis with multiple, abstract and simplified models is not only a major step towards a general theory of diagnosis, but also that it can be crucial for expanding the range of real applications of model-based diagnosis and putting the second generation of knowledge-based systems to work.

Acknowledgements I would like to thank Toni Beschta, Danny Bobrow, Johan de Kleer, Oskar Dressler, Hartmut Freitag, Gerhard Friedrich, Georg Gottlob, Walter Hamscher, Wolfgang Nejdl, Olivier Raiman, Brian Williams, and several reviewers for discussions and comments on this work. It was supported in part by BMFT (ITW 8506 E4, ITW 9001 A9) and by the C.E.C. under the ESPRIT program (P5143). Collaboration with Stefano Cermignani and Giorgio Tornielli in Esprit Project ARTIST helped us to better understand the domain of power systems. Thanks also to Linda Pfefferl and Claudia Urbach for technical assistance.

References

[Beschta et al. 90]
Beschta, A., Dressler, O., Freitag, H., and Struss, P., *A Model-based Approach to Fault Localization in Power Delivery Networks*, Siemens Technical Report INF 2 ARM-15-D-90, 1990 (In German)

[de Kleer et al. 90]
de Kleer, J., Mackworth, A., and Reiter, R., *Characterizing Diagnoses*. In: Proceedings of the AAAI 90

[de Kleer-Williams 87]
de Kleer, J., and Williams, B. C., *Diagnosing Multiple Faults*. In: Artificial Intelligence, 32(1):97-130, April 1987

[Dressler 88]
Dressler, O., *An Extended Basic ATMS*. In: Proceedings of the Second Workshop on Non-Monotonic Reasoning, Springer 1988

[Dressler 90]
Dressler, O., *Computing Diagnoses as Coherent Assumption Sets*. In: G. Gottlob, W. Nejdl (eds), Expert Systems in Engineering, Heidelberg, 1990

[Dressler-Farquhar 90]
Dressler, O. , Farquhar, A., *Putting the Problem Solver Back in the Driver's Seat: Contextual Control of the ATMS*. In: J.P.Martins (ed.). Proceedings of the ECAI 90 Truth Maintenance Workshop

[Reiter 87]
Reiter, R., *A Theory of Diagnosis from First Principles*. Artificial Intelligence 32(1):57-96, April 1987

[Struss 89]
Struss, P., *Diagnosis as a Process*. First International Workshop on Model-Based Diagnosis, Paris, 1989

[Struss 91a]
Struss, P., *A Theory of Model Simplification and Abstraction for Diagnosis*. 5th International Workshop on Qualitative Reasoning, Austin, Texas, 1991

[Struss 91b]
Struss, P., *What's in SD? - Towards a Theory of Model-based Diagnosis*. Working Paper, Munich, 1991

[Struss-Dressler 89]
Struss, P., Dressler, O., *"Physical Negation" - Integrating Fault Models into the General Diagnostic Engine*, Proceedings IJCAI-89

Qualitative Modellierung Kinematischer Systeme

Boi Faltings, Emmanuel Baechler
Laboratoire d'Intelligence Artificielle
Ecole Polytechnique Fédérale de Lausanne (EPFL)
MA-Ecublens
1015 Lausanne, Schweiz

Jedes physikalische System besteht aus Objekten mit räumlicher Ausdehnung, und oft spielt die kinematische Wechselwirkung rigider Objekte eine wichtige Rolle. System-analyse oder auch qualitatives Schließen können erst angewandt werden, nachdem zuvor das System in konkreten Parametern formalisiert worden ist. Dieser Artikel stellt Verfahren zur qualitativen Modellierung kinematischer Systeme mit komplexen irregulären Formen vor. Wir betrachten insbesondere zwei repräsentative Beispiele: die Analyse von elementaren Mechanismen, und die Programmierung von Robotern.

1 Kinematische Wechselwirkung

Die Aufgabe der *Kinematik* ist es, die durch Berührungen von Körpern vermittelten Bewegungen und Kräfte zu beschreiben. Kinematik ist grundlegend etwa für das Verständnis von Mechanismen oder die Planung von Robotern, und spielt eine Rolle im Verhalten fast aller physikalischen Systeme. Als Beispiel betrachte man die in Abbildung 1 dargestellte Ratsche, ein Mechanismus, welcher die Rotation des Rades in der einen Richtung erlaubt, sie aber in der anderen blockiert. Die Blockierung wird im in Abbildung 1 a) dargestellten Zustand erreicht.

Die *Simulation* der Kinematik ist eine Vorbedingung für jegliche Analyse des Verhaltens eines solchen Apparates. Aufgrund der Tatsache, daß die Kinematik nur durch *Ungleichungen* bestimmt ist, ist eine numerische Simulation mit traditionellen Methoden ([NIK88]) unzweckmäßig. Die in diesem Artikel vorgestellten Verfahren zur *qualitativen* Simulation erlauben hingegen eine adequate Beschreibung des Verhaltens.

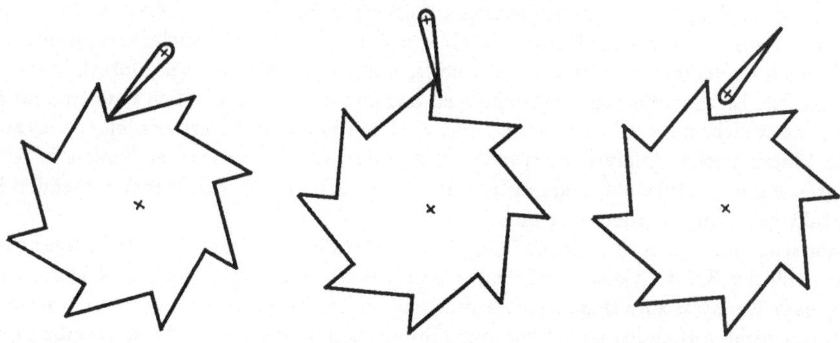

Abbildung 1: *Eine Ratsche, und einige ihrer typischen Zustände (siehe Text).*

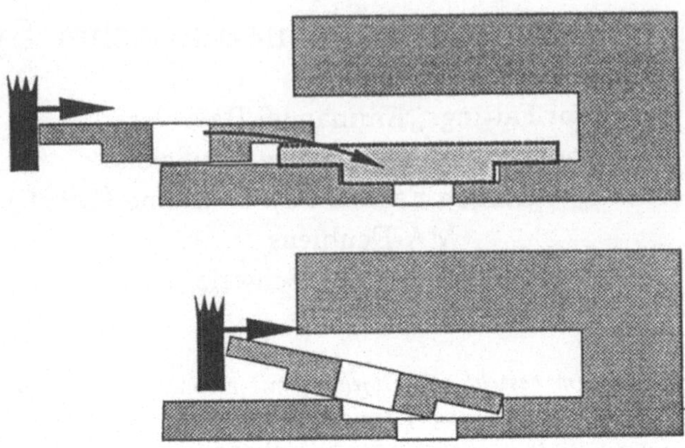

Abbildung 2: *Das Einsetzen einer Mutter in einen begrenzten Raum durch einen Roboter ist ein Problem, welches nur unter Ausnützung der kinematischen Zusammenhänge gelöst werden kann. Es muss zum Beispiel die Verkantung der Mutter vermieden werden (unterer Teil der Abbildung).*

Ein weiteres wichtiges Anwendungsgebiet für qualitative Kinematik ist die Programmierung von Robotern. Insbesondere beim Zusammensetzen von Geräten, wie in Abbildung 2, müssen oft die kinematischen Wechselwirkungen zwischen den bewegten Teilen ausgenützt werden. Im Beispiel der Abbildung 2 kann die Mutter nicht während der ganzen Bewegung vom Roboter geführt werden, sondern muß unter dem Einfluß der Umgebung in ihre endgültige Position hineingeschoben werden. Hierbei zeigt eine kinematische Analyse die Möglichkeit des Verkantens (Abbildung 2 unten) auf, die im Plan vermieden werden sollte. Bei der Roboterplanung sind (wenn überhaupt) nur sehr ungenaue Messungen der Positionen der Objekte bekannt ([LTM90]), so daß die kinematische Analyse notwendigerweise *qualitativ* sein muß.

2   Kinematische Simulation

Durch Modellierung eines Mechanismus in Form eines Gleichungssystems kann sein Verhalten numerisch simuliert werden, ein Verfahren, welches zum Beispiel bei Gestängen Anwendung findet. Jedoch lassen sich Mechanismen wie die Ratsche (Abbildung 1) nicht durch Gleichungen, sondern nur durch *Ungleichungen* modellieren: es ist nur die Überlappung von Teilen ausgeschlossen, deren Loslösung jedoch erlaubt. Ein System von Ungleichungen hat nur in Ausnahmefallen eine eindeutige Lösung, und kann somit nicht mit traditionellen numerischen Methoden simuliert werden. Es ist zum Beispiel aufgrund kinematischer Analyse nicht möglich zu entscheiden, welcher der beiden in Abbildung 1 c) gezeigten Fälle als Folge auf Zustand b) auftritt: je nach der auf den Hebel wirkenden Kraft kann der Kontakt gebrochen werden oder nicht.

Numerische Simulation von allgemeinen Mechanismen ist nur unter Berücksichtigung ihrer *Dynamik*, das heißt der Kräfte, Geschwindigkeiten und Beschleunigungen, möglich. Hierzu benötigt man jedoch genaue Kenntnis zum Beispiel der auftretenden Trägheitsmomente und Reibungskoeffizienten, welche meist nicht vorhanden ist. Numerische Simulation wird daher in Maschinenbau und Robotik nur selten verwendet.

Ein weiteres Problem ist die Tatsache, daß die kinematischen Ungleichungen mit der Bewegung des Mechanismusses wechseln. Zum Beispiel sind die auf Abbildung 1 a) anwendbaren Bedingungen sehr verschieden von denen für die in b) gezeigte Position. Man benötigt daher zur Analyse zunächst ein Modell, welches die verschiedenen möglichen Kombinationen und Übergänge explizit darstellt. Im Falle von Mechanismen mag es noch möglich sein, diese von Hand aufzustellen, im Falle der Roboterplanung macht dies hingegen die automatische Planung fragwürdig.

Beide Probleme, die Mehrdeutigkeit wie auch die Modellierung, lassen sich durch ein qualitatives kinematisches Modell lösen. Ein solches qualitatives Modell kann in Form eines *Platzvokabulars* ([FAL90a, FAL86], eine vereinfachter Form findet sich auch in [JOS88]) aufgestellt werden und weist die folgenden Eigenschaften auf:

- Die durch die Unterbestimmtheit des Systems hervorgerufenen Mehrdeutigkeiten können im qualitativen Modell ohne weiteres dargestellt werden. Es ist gezeigt worden ([NIE88a]), daß Platzvokabulare eine hinreichende Grundlage für die qualitative Simulation von Mechanismen wie zum Beispiel Uhrwerken darstellen. Eine solche qualitative Simulation ist die einzige allgemeine Analyse rein kinematischen Verhaltens, die heute bekannt ist.

- indem die verschiedenen möglichen Kombinationen von Kontakten im Platzvokabular explizit dargestellt sind, können auf dieser Grundlage weitergehende Analysen durchgeführt werden. Insbesondere läßt sich Wissen über *Technologie* anwenden, zum Beispiel die von bestimmten Materialien erzeugte Reibungshitze oder die maximal möglichen Kontaktkräfte.

In diesem Artikel definieren wir Platzvokabulare in einer allgemeineren Form als in [FAL90a] und zeigen ihre Anwendbarkeit auf die oben gezeigten Probleme. Wir gehen weiterhin auf die Berechnung von Platzvokabularen und deren Nutzen in der mechanischen Problemlösung ein. Wir beschränken uns hierbei auf zwei-dimensionale Objekte. Die beschriebenen Methoden sind bis jetzt nur für Polygone implementiert, lassen sich jedoch ohne große Schwierigkeiten auf allgemeine Formen generalisieren.

2.1 Qualitative Analyse Kinematischer Wechselwirkungen

Bis heute befaßt sich die qualitative Physik ausschließlich mit der Analyse von durch skalare Größen dargestellten Systemen, wobei die Werte der Größen durch *qualitative Werte*, meist Intervalle, dargestellt werden. Die ein-dimensionale Struktur der reellen Zahlen bedingt hierbei starke topologische Einschränkungen, welche Axiome für eine qualitative Algebra liefern.

Für multidimensionale Systeme gelten wesentlich schwächere topologische Bedingungen, und dieser herkömmliche Ansatz läßt sich daher nicht auf mehrdimensionale Größen wie etwa die Position eines Objekts im Raum anwenden. Wir stellen die Position durch Vektoren aus drei Komponenten $(x, y$ und θ, die Orientierung) dar, von denen jede Komponente einen qualitativen Wert annehmen kann (Abbildung 3).

Die Euklidischen x- und y-Koordinatenaxen sind raumfest, während die Orientierungen der einzelnen Objekte werden durch Winkel θ beschrieben sind, welche die Rotation um einen heuristisch ausgewählten Schwerpunkt ausdrücken. Im Falle einer Ratsche ist es zum Beispiel nützlich, die Schwerpunkte in die Rotationszentren zu legen, wie dieses in der Abbildung 3 gezeigt ist.

In der Kinematik geht es vor allem um Änderungen der Positionen, und das gezeigte Koordinatensystem eignet sich besonders für Schlüsse über die Änderungen der Koordinaten. Die qualitative Position der Objekte wird besser durch die vorliegenden Kontakte dargestellt; wir werden später hierauf zurückkommen.

Die einzelnen Komponenten werden qualitativ durch ihr Vorzeichen dargestellt: +, 0 oder -. Hierbei bezeichnet die Notation [x] den qualitativen Wert einer Größe x, also ihr Vorzeichen, und $[\delta x]$ die qualitative Richtung ihrer Änderung. Mithilfe einer qualitativen Algebra (siehe z.B. [FAL89]) kann mit qualitativen Werten gerechnet werden. Zum Beispiel ergibt die Addition von + und + wiederum +, die Addition von + und - aber den mehrdeutigen Wert +, 0, -, da ja die absoluten Werte der Größen nicht bekannt sind.

Jeder Kontaktpunkt zwischen zwei Objekten definiert eine kinematische Ungleichung, die qualitativ wie in Abbildung 3 gezeigt dargestellt werden kann. Hierbei bedeuten die hohlen Operationszeichen die Addition oder Subtraktion von qualitativen Werten, wobei die Ungleichung alle diejenigen Kombinationen von qualitativen Werten zuläßt, für die zumindest einer der möglichen qualitativen Werte der Summe die Ungleichung nicht verletzt. Der Kontakt bewirkt, daß die Objekte sich nur in

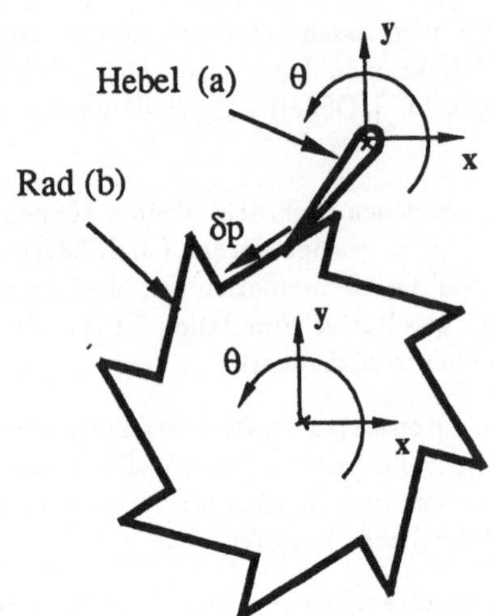

Kinematische Ungleichung:

$$\textbf{+}\ [\delta(x_a\text{-}x_b)] \ \square\ [\delta(y_a\text{-}y_b)] \ \textbf{+}\ [\delta\theta_a] \ \textbf{+}\ [\delta\theta_b] \leq 0$$

Bewegungsrichtung des Kontaktpunktes :

$$[\delta p] = \square\ [\delta(x_a\text{-}x_b)] \ \square\ [\delta(y_a\text{-}y_b)] \ \textbf{+}\ [\delta\theta_a] \ \square\ [\delta\theta_b]$$

Abbildung 3: *Die Position eines Objektes ist durch drei Parameter gegeben. Jeder Kontakt definiert eine Ungleichung mit 4 Parametern: die Änderungen der relativen Position der Schwerpunkte, sowie die Drehungen. Folgezustände können aus der Bewegung der Kontaktstelle hergeleitet werden.*

den diesen Wertekombinationen entsprechenden Richtungen bewegen können. Die Ungleichung kann auch als Inferenzregel formuliert werden ([NIE88b, FAL90a]).

Man beachte, daß die qualitativen Ungleichungen unabhängig von der genauen Konfiguration gültig sind. Die Menage alle Konfigurationen, in denen sowohl dieselben Ungleichungen als auch dieselben Kontaktpunkte existieren, definiert einen qualitativen Zustand, den wir *Platz* nennen. Die qualitativen Ungleichungen können in gewissen wohldefinierten Konfigurationen wechseln; diese grenzen dann verschiedene Plätze voneinander ab.

Die qualitativen Ungleichungen können mit Grundregeln der Newton'schen Dynamik kombiniert werden und erlauben es dann, das Verhalten selbst recht komplizierter Mechanismen wie Uhrwerke zu simulieren ([NIE88a]). Zum Beispiel lassen sich aufgrund der in Abbildung 3 gezeigte Ungleichung unter Zuhilfenahme der Tatsache, daß beide Teile um feste Zentren rotieren:

$$[\delta x_a] = 0 \quad ; \quad [\delta y_a] = 0$$
$$[\delta x_b] = 0 \quad ; \quad [\delta y_b] = 0$$

die folgenden Schlüsse ziehen:

$$[\delta\theta_a] = + \quad \Rightarrow \quad [\delta\theta_b] = -$$
$$[\delta\theta_a] = 0 \quad \Rightarrow \quad [\delta\theta_b] = \{0, -\}$$
$$[\delta\theta_a] = - \quad \Rightarrow \quad [\delta\theta_b] = \{+, 0, -\}$$

welche wiederum folgende Tatsachen ausdrücken:

- bei Drehung des Rades im Uhrzeigersinn dreht sich der Hebel im Gegenuhrzeigersinn.

- bei stillstehendem Rad kann sich der Hebel entweder auch stillstehen, oder im Gegenuhrzeigersinn drehend vom Rad abheben.

- bei Drehung des Rades im Gegenuhrzeigersinn sind alle Bewegungsrichtungen des Hebels möglich.

Dieses sind genau die normalerweise vom menschlichen Betrachter gemachten Vorhersagen über das Verhalten.

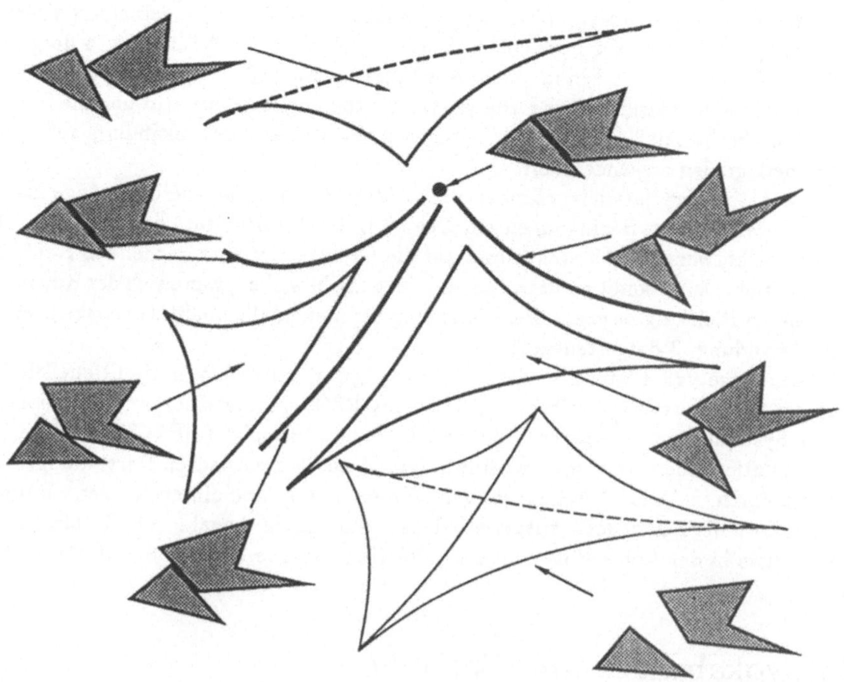

Abbildung 4: *Die topologische Struktur eines (Teils eines) Platzvokabulars für zwei Polygone. Je nach Anzahl der vorhandenen Kontaktpunkte in einem Platz haben die Objekte eine verschiedene Anzahl von Freiheitsgraden, und somit die Plätze verschiedene Dimensionalität, von Punkten (keine Freiheitsgrade) über Kanten (ein Freiheitsgrad) und Flächen (zwei Freiheitsgrade) bis zu Räumen (drei Freiheitsgrade). Für jeden Platz ist eine Beispielkonfiguration gezeigt. Man beachte, daß sich die hier gezeigte Struktur allein aus der Analyse des null-dimensionalen Platzes herleiten lässt.*

Wenn gleichzeitig mehrere Kontaktpunkte vorhanden sind, kann die Situation durch ein System von mehreren Ungleichungen modelliert werden. Dabei ergeben sich in gewissen Fällen überflüssige Lösungen, die sich aus der qualitativen Repräsentation erklären ([STR88]). Im Falle der Kinematik lassen sich allerdings durch Verwendung mehrerer Koordinatensysteme zusätzliche Bedingungen gewinnen, welche genauere Schlüsse zulassen.

2.2 Platzvokabulare als Darstellung des Raums

Für das Verhalten eines Mechanismusses spielt die Abfolge der qualitativen Zustände eine wichtige Rolle. Alle möglichen Abfolgen sind im Platzvokabular durch einen *Graphen* aus Plätzen und Übergängen dargestellt. Ein Platz ist bestimmt durch

- eine bestimmten Kombination von Kontakten, und

- die dadurch bestimmten qualitativen Ungleichungen. Wenn diese für eine bestimmte Kombination von Kontakten nicht eindeutig sind, existieren mehrere Versionen des Platzes.

Je nach Anzahl der Kontaktpunkte haben die Objekte eine variable Anzahl von Freiheitsgraden und somit die entsprechenden Plätze eine variable Anzahl von Dimensionen. Die möglichen Übergänge von einem Platz zu anderen sind durch Verbindungen im Platzvokabular explizit dargestellt. Hierbei finden Übergänge aus Gründen der Kontinuität immer zwischen Plätzen statt, die sich um genau eine Dimension unterscheiden. Eine solche Struktur, eine Art verallgemeinerter Graph, wird in der Mathematik als *Zellkomplex* bezeichnet. Ein Beispiel ist in der Abbildung 4 dargestellt. Die einzelnen Plätze können als Regionen in einem Konfigurationsraum (configuration space) verstanden werden. Jedoch sind für die kinematische Analyse nur die topologische Struktur und die Inferenzregeln von Belang. Man beachte, daß sich die topologische Struktur eines Platzvokabulars auf Systeme mit beliebigen Freiheitsgraden anwenden läßt.

Für eine qualitative Simulation ist es nicht nur wichtig zu wissen, welche Übergänge möglich sind, sondern auch, unter welchen Bedingungen ein Übergang tatsächlich statt finden kann. Übergänge werden dann erreicht, wenn der Kontaktpunkt auf die Grenzen der entsprechenden Kante fällt. Die Bewegung der Objekte kann somit nur dann einen Übergang bewirken, wenn sich der Kontaktpunkt in der entsprechenden Richtung bewegt. Diese Richtung kann ebenfalls qualitativ ausgedrückt werden, wie es in der Abbildung 3 dargestellt ist.

Auf der Grundlage von Platzvokabularen ist es möglich, mithilfe von traditionellen Methoden des qualitativen Schließens (zum Beispiel [DKB84, FOR84]) Simulationen und Envisionments von mechanischen Systemen zu berechnen. So berichtet zum Beispiel ([FAL87, NIE88a]) von der qualitative Simulation einer mechanischen Uhr aufgrund aus geometrischen Darstellungen berechneten Platzvokabularen. Auch Bewegungen von Objekten im (zweidimensionalen) Raum können qualitativ simuliert werden, jedoch tritt hierbei eine sehr große Anzahl von Zuständen auf. Für Anwendungen etwa in der Robotik ist es besser, die kinematische Analyse direkt in die Planung zu integrieren.

3 Platzvokabulare und Formen

Für die Analyse von bestimmten Systemen ist es wichtig, das Platzvokabular effizient aus geometrischen Objektbeschreibungen berechnen zu können. Darüberhinaus ist bei Konstruktionsproblemen besonders die Beziehung zwischen Form und Verhalten von Interesse, die in der Berechnung des Platzvokabulars aus der Objektgeometrie explizit wird. Es ist daher nützlich, das Platzvokabular auf weitgehend symbolische Art aus der Geometrie abzuleiten ([FAL87, FAL88]). Die Grundlage für die Berechnung von Platzvokabularen ist deren Herleitung aus den Eigenschaften *bestimmter* Konfigurationen. Die Anordnung dieser Konfigurationen und ihrer benachbarten Plätze ist durch eine separat berechnete *Topologie* gegeben. Diese beruht auf einer Repräsentation der Objekte als *Flächen*, während die geometrische Analyse auf ausschlißlich auf den Kanten der Objekte aufbaut.

3.1 Berechnung der Lokalen Struktur

Wie in Abbildung 4 gezeigt, besteht ein Platzvokabular aus Plätzen verschiedener Dimensionalität, von denen jeder einer bestimmten Kombination von Kontaktpunkten entspricht. Dabei existieren jedoch nur diejenigen Plätze, für die auch wirklich eine legale (nicht überlappende) Position der Objekte möglich ist. Diese Bedingung läßt sich direkt nur für die null-dimensionalen Plätze verifizieren, die ja einer einzigen bestimmten Konfiguration entsprechen. Die Existenz von mehrdimensionalen Plätzen kann aber aus der Struktur des Platzvokabulars hergeleitet werden, da sie immer einem null-dimensionalen Platz benachbart sind.

Der erste Schritt in der Berechnung des Platzvokabulars ist somit die Berechnung der Menge der null-dimensionalen Plätze. Wie in der Abbildung 4 gezeigt, ist ein null-dimensionaler Platz immer Nachbar einer Reihe von höherdimensionalen Plätzen (in Abbildung 4 ein-, zwei- und dreidimensional). Diese benachbarten Plätze und ihre Eigenschaften sind direkt aus der Analyse des null-dimensionalen Platzes bestimmbar. Weiterhin schließt es die Definition des Platzvokabulars aus, daß ein Platz in sich selber endet. Alle Platze der Dimension n sind somit von Plätzen der Dimension n-1 begrenzt, und lassen sich letztendlich auf Plätze der Dimension 0 zurückführen. Die Analyse der null-dimensionalen Plätze ist somit hinreichend, um alle Plätze des gesamten Platzvokabulars zu finden..

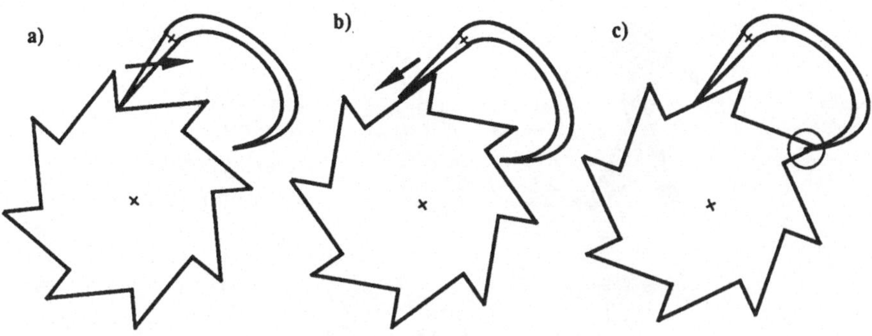

Abbildung 5: *Der durch Konfigurationen zwischen a) und b) gebildete Platz wird durch die in c) gezeigte Überlappung zweigeteilt.*

Null-dimensionale Plätze sind dadurch ausgezeichnet, daß die Anzahl der Kontaktpunkte gleich der Anzahl Freiheitsgrade des Systems ist. Hierbei werden jedoch gewisse Kontaktpunkte doppelt gezählt: der Kontakt zwischen zwei Ecken, sowie ein Kontakt an einer Stelle, an der sich die Inferenzregeln ändern (siehe [FAL90a]). Die Gesamtheit der legalen null-dimensionalen Plätze kann durch Suche generiert werden, die sich jedoch auf einen gewünschten Teilbereich (zum Beispiel die Nachbarschaft der momentanen Position) beschränken kann. Die Konfigurationen werden für Polygone durch direkte Berechnung generiert; für generellen Formen müssen sie numerisch approximiert werden.

Die in der Nachbarschaft eines null-dimensionalen Platzes gefundenen höherdimensionalen Plätze können durch die in ihnen vorliegenden Kontaktpunkte identifiziert werden. Jedoch ist diese Identifizierung nicht notwendigerweise eindeutig. Ein Platz kann nämlich durch eine anderweitige Überschneidung unterbrochen werden (Abbildung 5), wobei mehrere Versionen mit gleicher Identifikation entstehen. Dieser Fall ist besonders für Plätze ohne irgendeinen Kontakt wichtig: man kann nämlich nicht ohne weiteres feststellen, ob zwei Positionen eines Objektes im Raum zu derselben topologischen Region zählen, d.h. kontinuierlich und ohne Überlappungen ineinander überführbar sind. Zum korrekten Zusammenbau der lokalen Information in den das Platzvokabular beschreibenden Graphen ist die Kenntnis der Topologie der globalen Struktur notwendig.

3.2 Globale Struktur

Die Berechnung von Kontakten und daraus hervorgehenden Plätzen stützt sich auf die Betrachtung der Beziehungen zwischen *Kanten*. Das Platzvokabular ist jedoch nichts anderes als die Grenzfläche zwischen legalen und illegalen Objektkonfigurationen. Den Raum der illegalen Objektkonfigurationen kann man auch aus Betrachtung der möglichen Überlappungen der Objekt*flächen* gewinnen. Aufgrund einer flächenbasierten Objektrepräsentation kann eine Repräsentation der möglichen Topologien des Platzvokabulars direkt bestimmt werden ([FBP89]).

Hierzu wird die Oberfläche der Objekte aufgeteilt in konvexe *Stücke* und *Hohlräume*. Jedes Paar von Stücken auf verschiedenen Objekten erzeugt eine Region von Objektkonfigurationen, in welchen die Stücke sich überlappen (Abbildung 6). Wir nennen eine solche Region ein *Hindernis*. Man beachte, daß sich jeder Pfad von Konfigurationen in einem Hindernis auf einen einzigen Punkt zusammenziehen läßt und somit das Hindernis eine einfach zusammenhängende Region ist. Da jede Überlappung mindestens ein Paar von Stücken beinhaltet, deckt die Gesamtheit der Hindernisse den gesamten illegalen Raum ab.

Im Gegensatz zu Hindernissen stehen die *Blasen*, welche *möglich* Regionen von legalen Konfigura-

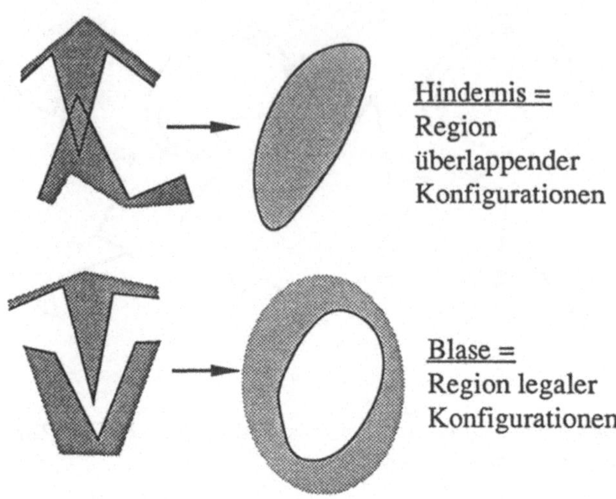

Abbildung 6: *Die Herleitung von Hindernissen und Blasen.*

tionen darstellen. Wie in Abbildung 6 gezeigt, werden sie durch Paare von Stücken und Hohlräumen erzeugt; intuitiv entsprechen sie den Konfigurationen, in welchen das Stück in den Hohlraum fällt.

Genauer läßt sich die Bedeutung von Hindernissen und Blasen aufgrund der folgenden Konstruktion verstehen. Wir betrachten die kinematische Wechselwirkung zweier Objekte A und B. Eine erste Approximation der Topologie ist die durch die Wechselwirkung ihrer konvexen Hüllen erzeugte einfach zusammenhängende Region, ein Hindernis. Durch Herausschneiden der Hohlräume aus den konvexen Hüllen werden zusätzliche Freiräume erzeugt, die durch Blasen dargestellt werden. Jede Blase ist wiederum eine einfach zusammenhängende Region, die das umgebende Hindernis in mehrere Teile teilen kann. Daher zerfallen bei der Hinzufügung der Hohlräume die Stücke und somit auch die Hindernisse in mehrere Teile. Man beachte, daß jede Blase nur eine *potentielle* Region legaler Konfigurationen darstellt.

Die Topologie des Raumes ist gegeben durch die Anordnung der Hindernisse und Blasen. Diese ist zunächst gegeben durch die Nachbarschaft der Stücke und Hohlräume in den Objekten selber. Sie wird modifiziert durch Überlappungen der Hindernisse. Diese entstehen sowohl lokal, d.h. zwischen benachbarten Hindernissen, wie auch global, durch das gleichzeitige Auftreten von Kontakten zwischen verschiedenen Teilen der Objekte. Jede Überlappung von Hindernissen teilt dazwischenliegende Blasen in mehrere Teile.

Lokale Überlappungen werden durch direkte Berechnung gefunden. Globale Überlappungen treten in der Topologie genau dann auf, wenn auf beiden Objekten ein Paar von Stücken mit gleicher Distanz voneinander existiert. Nach Hinzufügen der durch Überlappungen bedingten Modifikationen entsteht ein Graph, der die möglichen Topologien des Platzvokabulars wiedergibt. In diesem Graphen sind zwar alle Regionen durch Hindernisse oder Blasen dargestellt, jedoch entspricht nicht unbedingt jede Blase einer Region legaler Konfigurationen. Diese Zweideutigkeit wird erst durch die Kombination mit der geometrischen Analyse behoben.

Man beachte, daß jedes topologische Hindernis geometrisch von den Kontakten zwischen den Kanten der erzeugenden Stücke begrenzt ist. Somit kann jeder mögliche Kontakt einem Hindernis zugeordnet werden. Eine an ein Hindernis angrenzende Blase existiert genau dann, wenn auch die entsprechenden Kontakte ohne Überlappung möglich sind. Somit definieren die geometrischen Kriterien die genaue Form der Topologie. Auf der anderen Seite ist in dem durch schrittweises

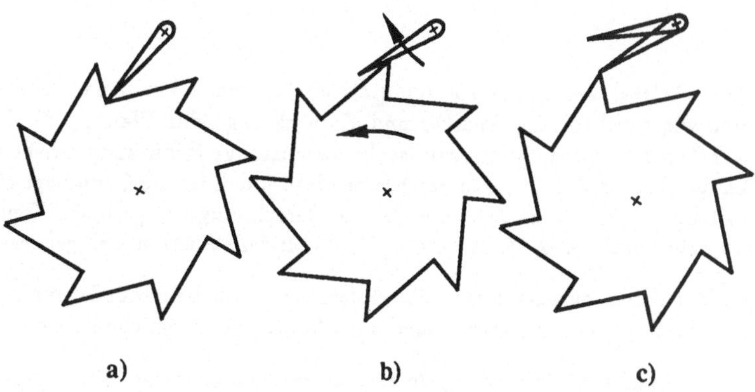

a)   b)   c)

Abbildung 7: *Drei Versionen einer Ratsche. Die Linke funktioniert normal, die Mittlere beeinflusst das Rad überhaupt nicht, und die Rechte blockiert das Rad dauernd.*

Hinzufügen der Hindernisüberlappungen erzeugten Graph jede potentiell einfach zusammenhängende Region durch eine Blase repräsentiert. Dies hat zur Folge, daß sich mehrfach zusammenhängende oder gar geteilte Plätze immer in der Nachbarschaft zu einer entsprechenden Struktur von Blasen befinden und daher aus der Darstellung der Topologie ablesbar sind. Die Verwendung der Topologie löst somit die beim inkrementalen Aufbau von Platzvokabularen auftretenden Probleme der Identifikation.

Die Benützung einer separat berechneten Topologie bietet zwei wichtige Vorteile gegenüber rein geometrischen Berechnungen. Zum einen ist die Berechnung der Topologie *robust* gegenüber numerischen Fehlern und erlaubt es, solche auch in der geometrischen Analyse zu erkennen. Zum anderen ermöglicht sie es, nur die gerade benötigten Teile des Platzvokabulars zu berechnen. Da die Berechnung der Topologie sehr schnell ist, wächst die Komplexität einer qualitativen Simulation des Verhaltens dann etwa proportional zu der Komplexität des generierten Verhaltens. Dieses ist eine wesentliche Verbesserung im Vergleich zu bekannten, auf Konfigurationsräumen basierenden Methoden, deren Komplexität unabhängig von der Größe der Lösung ist, jedoch stark von der Anzahl und Komplexität der vorhandenen Objekte abhängt.

3.3 Schließen über Form und Verhalten

Zur Lösung räumlicher Probleme, insbesondere zum Entwurf von Mechanismen, müssen Schlüsse gezogen werden über die Art, in der Veränderungen in Form oder Dimensionen von Objekten deren kinematisches Verhalten beeinflussen. Zum Beispiel will man den Einfluss einer Veränderung der Distanz zwischen den Rotationszentren einer Ratsche auf deren Verhalten vorraussagen (Abbildung 7).

Die Darstellung der Funktionen durch Platzvokabulare ([FAL91]) unterscheidet die qualitativ verschiedenen Versionen der Ratsche ([FAL88]). Weiterhin können das Vorhandensein und die Eigenschaften der einzelnen Plätze aufgrund der symbolischen Berechnung direkt auf Einzelheiten der Objektformen zurückgeführt werden.

Die Beziehung zwischen Objektform und Verhalten kann im Bezug auf Veränderungen der Form analysiert werden und erlaubt es, gezielt gewisse Verhaltensweisen zu erzeugen. Zum Beispiel kann in der Version von Abbildung 7 durch Verlängerung des Hebels die Ratschenfunktion wiederhergestellt werden, und diese Veränderung kann durch Analyse der Herleitung des Platzvokabulars erzeugt werden. Auf diese Art lassen sich durch qualitative Analyse auch Konstruktionsprobleme automatisch lösen ([FAL90b]).

4 Schluß

Wir haben in diesem Artikel Methoden zur qualitativen kinematischen Analyse vorgestellt, mit denen sich Probleme wie mechanische Analyse und Entwicklung oder Planung für Roboter lösen lassen. Ein wichtiger Aspekt unserer Methoden ist die gleichzeitige Benützung zweier verschiedener Objektmodelle. Ein die *Kanten* der Objekte beschreibendes Modell ist die Grundlage für die geometrische Analyse des lokalen Verhaltens, während für die Berechnung der globalen Topologie ein auf den Flächen der Objekte beruhendes Modell dient. Beide Modelle stützen sich gegenseitig:

- Die Topologie ist effizient zu berechnen, fehlertolerant und für beliebige Formen gültig, enthält jedoch unwirkliche Regionen und gibt keinerlei Auskunft über mögliche kinematische Schlüsse.

- Die lokale Analyse definiert Inferenzregeln und unterscheidet in der Topologie wirkliche von unwirklichen Regionen, ist jedoch zur Berechnung des vollständigen Platzvokabulars zu ineffizient und fehleranfällig.

Die Verbindung beider Methoden erlaubt wesentlich verbesserte Algorithmen für kinematische Analyse. Durch Verwendung einer separat berechneten Topologie sind die Algorithmen fast vollständig tolerant gegenüber Rundungsfehlern bei der Berechnung. Weiterhin müssen nur die Teile des Platzvokabulars berechnet werden, die auch wirklich gebraucht werden, was eine wesentliche Effizienzsteigerung mit sich bringt. Schließlich erlaubt die Methode im Prinzip auch eine Analyse auf der Basis von Bildern der Objekte, welche dann beliebige Formen haben können.

Auf dem Gebiet der qualitativen Kinematik sind weiterhin die Arbeiten von Joscowicz ([JOS88]) zu erwähnen, dessen *Region Diagram* im wesentlichen von Platzvokabularen abstammt, sich jedoch auf qualitative Gleichungen beschränkt. Da diese Theorie nie implementiert wurde, ist nicht klar, wieweit diese Vereinfachung gültig ist. Andrew Gelsey ([GEMD90]) beschreibt ein Programm, welches das Verhalten von Mechanismen durch eine Reihe von numerischen Simulationen erforscht und hieraus eine qualitative Beschreibung ableitet. Durch die numerische Berechnung kann dieses Programm präzisere Analysen liefern als die rein qualitative Analyse mit Platzvokabularen. Es kann jedoch nur Mechanismen analysieren, deren Bestandteile in einer vorgegebenen Bibliothek von Modellen vorhanden sind.

Es bleibt noch viel Arbeit zu tun, bis die Theorie des Platzvokabulars auf wirkliche Probleme angewandt werden kann. Wichtig ist die Generalisierung auf drei Dimensionen, die wir wegen der damit verbundenen komplizierten Grafik bis jetzt noch nicht erforscht haben. Ein weiteres interessantes Gebiet ist die Entwicklung von Methoden zur Berechnung des Verhaltens von Objekten mit beliebigen Formen. Wir erforschen momentan die Anwendung der Degree-of-Freedom Analysis ([KRA90]) zur Synthese der zu analysierenden Konfigurationen.

Literaturhinweise

[DKB84] J. DeKleer, J.S. Brown: "A Qualitative Physics based on Confluences," *Artificial Intelligence* 24, 1984

[FAL86] Boi Faltings: "A Theory of Qualitative Kinematics in Mechanisms," University of Illinois Technical Report UIUCDCS-R-86-1274, May 1986

[FAL87] Boi Faltings: "Qualitative Kinematics in Mechanisms,"Ph. D. Thesis, University of Illinois, 1987

[FAL88] Boi Faltings: "A Symbolic Approach to Qualitative Kinematics," *Proceedings of the 3rd International Conference on 5th Generation Computer Systems*, Tokyo, 1988

[FAL89] Boi Faltings: "Wissensrepräsentation und qualitatives Schließen," *Informationstechnik* 31(2), 1989

[FBP89]   **Boi Faltings, Emmanuel Baechler, Jeff Primus**: "Reasoning about Kinematic Topology," *Proceedings of the IJCAI 89*, Detroit, 1989

[FAL90a]   **Boi Faltings**: "Qualitative Kinematics in Mechanisms," *Artificial Intelligence* **44** (1), June 1990

[FAL90b]   **Boi Faltings**: "Qualitative Kinematics and Intelligent CAD," in: H. Yoshikawa, T. Holden (eds.): *Intelligent CAD, II*, North Holland, 1990

[FAL91]   **Boi Faltings**: "Qualitative Models in Conceptual Design: A Case Study," *Proceedings of the 1st International Conference on Artificial Intelligence in Design*, Edinburgh, 1991

[FOR84]   **Ken Forbus**: "Qualitative Process Theory," *Artificial Intelligence* **24**, 1984

[GEMD90]   **Andrew Gelsey, Drew McDermott**: "Spatial Reasoning About Mechanisms," in Su-shing Chen (ed.): *Advances in Spatial Reasoning*, Ablex Publishing Co., 1990

[JOS88]   **Leo Joscowicz**: "Reasoning about Shape and Kinematic Function in Mechanical Devices," Ph. D. Thesis, New York University, 1988

[KRA90]   **Glenn Kramer**: "Solving Geometric Constraint Systems," *Proceedings of the 9th National Conference on Artificial Intelligence*, Boston, 1990

[LTM90]   **Tomás Lozano-Pérez, Matthew Mason, Russel Taylor**: "Automatic Synthesis of Fine-Motion Strategies for Robots," in Patrick Winston, Sarah Shellard (eds).: *Artificial Intelligence at MIT - Expanding Frontiers*, MIT Press, 1990

[NIE88a]   **Paul Nielsen**: "A Qualitative Approach to Rigid Body Mechanics," Ph. D. Thesis, University of Illinois, 1988

[NIE88b]   **Paul Nielsen**: "A Qualitative Approach to Mechanical Constraint," *Proceedings of the 7th National Conference on Artificial Inteligence*, St.-Paul, 1988

[NIK88]   **Parviz E. Nikravesch**: "Computer-aided Analysis of Mechanical Systems," Prentice Hall, 1988

[STR88]   **Peter Struss**: "Mathematical Aspects of Qualitative Reasoning," *Intenational Journal for Artificial Intelligence in Engineering*, 1988

Model-Based Analogue Circuit Diagnosis with CLP($\Re$)

Igor Mozetič
Austrian Research Institute for Artificial Intelligence
Schottengasse 3, A-1010 Vienna, Austria

Christian Holzbaur
Austrian Research Institute for Artificial Intelligence, and
Department of Medical Cybernetics and Artificial Intelligence
University of Vienna
Freyung 6, A-1010 Vienna, Austria

Franc Novak
Jozef Stefan Institute
Jamova 39, 61000 Ljubljana, Slovenia

Marina Santo-Zarnik
Iskra HIPOT
Šentjernej, Slovenia

Abstract

Model-based diagnosis is the activity of locating malfunctioning components of a system solely on the basis of its structure and behavior. Diagnostic systems usually rely on qualitative models and reason by local constraint propagation methods. However, there is a large class of applications where ATMS-like systems or pure logic programs are unpractical since they are unable to solve simultaneous equations. In particular, modeling real-valued system parameters with tolerances requires some degree of numerical processing, and feedback loops in general cannot be resolved by local constraint propagation methods. Examples of such systems are analogue circuits, e.g., amplifiers or filters. In the paper we describe the role of Constraint Logic Programs over the domain of reals (CLP($\Re$)) in representing both, qualitative and numerical models. CLP($\Re$) is a logic programming system extended with a solver for systems of linear equations and inequalities over real-valued variables.

1 Introduction

Different Computer Aided Engineering tools are available for electronic circuit and systems design. CAE solutions to the *digital* design problem can be regarded as mature, while *analogue* design still lacks sufficient support even in the early design phases. In digital design, schematic capturing process and simulation with timing analysis are tightly coupled to fault simulation and test vector generation. Once a designer has verified the logic scheme of a circuit and has completed logic simulation, a full description of a defect-free version of the circuit together with an initial set of test vectors are available. Fault simulation uses the description and systematically inserts defects (i.e., simulates faults) to check if the given set of test vectors can detect the difference between the operation of the defect-free and the simulated faulty circuit. Usually, the initial set of test vectors has to be upgraded to reach the desirable fault coverage, typically close to 100%.

A similar approach in analogue design would face serious difficulties due to the fact that fault modeling is still a controversial issue (Ohletz 1991). Besides catastrophic (hard) faults which could be to some extend related to the popular digital *stuck-at* fault model, the class of deviation (soft) faults, due to the parameters deviating from the nominal values, must be considered (Duhamel & Rault 1979, Bandler & Salama 1985). As regards fault simulation, in the worst case a complete transient simulation must be performed for each fault. Fault simulation time for a given range of deviation faults may quickly reach unacceptable limits (Ohletz 1991). Hence, fault simulation is relatively uncommon for analogue circuits (Duhamel & Rault 1979).

This situation seems ideal for the application of an AI technique called model-based diagnosis (e.g., Genesereth 1984, Davis 1984, de Kleer & Williams 1987, Reiter 1987). In model-based approach one starts with a model of a real-world system which explicitly represents just the structure and normal behavior of the system components. When the system's actual behavior is different from the expected behavior, the diagnostic problem arises. The model is then used to identify faulty components and their internal states which account for the observed behavior.

However, the applicability of model-based techniques is largely limited to academic problems. In our view one of the major obstacles which prevented a wider application to real-world problems is that models are usually restricted to qualitative (non-numeric) descriptions, and to an ATMS-like local constraint propagation methods. General Diagnostic Engine (GDE, de Kleer & Williams 1987), for example, is unable to solve simultaneous equations, which makes it unpractical for a large class of applications.

In the paper we describe the role of Constraint Logic Programs over the domain of $\Re$eals (CLP($\Re$), Jaffar *et al.* 1986, Cohen 1990) in representing and diagnosing a larger class of models. CLP($\Re$) is a logic programming system extended with a solver for systems of linear equations and inequalities. It is well suited to model real-valued system parameters with tolerances and feedback loops which in general cannot be resolved by local constraint propagation methods.

In section 2 we give a brief overview of the CLP($\Re$) system. In section 3 we show how models of analogue circuits (operating under the AC conditions) can be concisely specified in CLP($\Re$). The main advantage of our approach, in contrast to standard simulation packages, is that the same model can be used for both, simulation and diagnosis. In section 4 we concentrate on diagnosis of soft faults due to a single parameter value (e.g., a resistor or a capacitor) out of tolerances. The manufacturing technology of a specific device under consideration makes internal probing difficult and undesirable. Preliminary results indicate that CLP($\Re$) has a potential to become a basis for software tools used in the design and testing of analogue circuits.

2   The CLP($\Re$) system

The Constraint Logic Programming scheme (Jaffar *et al.* 1986) provides a general framework from which extensions of Prolog can be derived. The unification mechanism, as used in Prolog, is replaced by a more general operation — constraint satisfaction over specific domains (Cohen 1990). An instance of the scheme, CLP($\Re$), extends Prolog with interpreted arithmetic functions and a solver for systems of linear equations and inequalities over the domain of $\Re$eals.

We illustrate the CLP($\Re$) language by specifying addition and multiplication of complex numbers.

A complex number $Z = Re+j*Im$ is represented by a pair $c(Re,Im)$.

   add(c(Re1,Im1), c(Re2,Im2), c(Re1+Re2, Im1+Im2)).

   *mult(c(Re1,Im1), c(Re2,Im2), c(Re1*Re2−Im1*Im2, Re1*Im2+Im1*Re2)).*

The above program allows for queries involving not only addition and multiplication, but subtraction and division of two complex numbers as well. For example:

   ← *mult(c(1,2), c(3,4), Z).*
   Z = c(−5,10)

   ← *mult(X, c(3,4), c(−5,10)).*
   X = c(1,2)

Answering the second query actually requires to solve the following system of equations:

   *3*Re1 − 4*Im1 = −5,*
   *4*Re1 + 3*Im1 = 10.*

which yields the solution *Re1=1, Im1=2*.

In our implementation of CLP($\Re$) linear equations are kept in *solved form*. Variables appearing in the equations are split into two disjoint sets: *dependent* variables and *independent* variables. Dependent variables are expressed through terms containing independent variables. When a new equation is to be combined with a system of equations in solved form, all its dependent variables are replaced by their definitions which results in an expression over independent variables. An independent variable is selected then, and the expression is solved for it. After the resulting definition has been back-substituted into the equation system, the isolated variable can be added as a new dependent variable, and the equation system is in solved form again. Inequalities are expressed in terms of independent variables.

The satisfiability of a system of linear inequalities is decided by a version of the Shostak's 'Loop Residue' algorithm (Shostak 1981, Kraemer 1989). Each inequality is represented as an edge in the inequality graph G. The algorithm only deals with loops in G. For each loop, the residual inequality of the loop is computed and entered as a new edge into G. The loop residue computation is iterated until no more loops can be created, or one of these new edges is determined to correspond to an unsatisfiable inequality. Each loop residue computation essentially eliminates one variable — therefore an unsatisfiable inequality will eventually result in a ground inequality $k < 0$, where k is a positive constant. The basic algorithm was extended to strict and nonstrict inequalities.

The ability to solve systems of linear inequalities enables simple computation with intervals. Each interval is implemented as a conjunction of two inequalities which associate an upper and a lower bound with a variable. Having the graph G to encode the set of inequalities is particularly useful when one is interested in implied inequalities, i.e., in current upper and lower bounds of a variable. Asking for implied inequalities is nothing but the residual inequality computation along a path in G. In many cases one is interested in a relation between a specific variable and zero, i.e., in interval bounds for the variable. The algorithm computes the set of all paths from the variable to zero, which is a distinguished node in G. Among many possible paths the one yielding the tightest bound is selected.

In order to account for tolerances in model parameters we allow constants in linear expressions to be specified by a pair $i(Min, Max)$ which denotes a lower and an upper bound. Take the following specification of the behavior of a resistor:

   *resistor(R, V1, V2, I) ← V1−V2 = R*I.*

Now consider two resistors in a series, with voltages of 12.5 and 10 Volts applied at the ends (an example from McKeon & Wakeling 1990). Both resistances are within the range $i(1000, 2000)$ Ω.

The question is: What is the voltage range at the node between the two resistors? The query returns the following set of constraints:

$\leftarrow$ *resistor(i(1000,2000), 12.5, V, I), resistor(i(1000,2000), V, 10, I).*

$12.5 \geq 1000*I + V,$
$2000*I + V \geq 12.5,$
$V \geq 10 + 1000*I,$
$10 + 2000*I \geq V,$
$I > 0$

from which the interval bounds for the voltage $11.6667 \geq V,\ V \geq 10.8333$ are deduced. In contrast to our, symbolic approach, McKeon & Wakeling use an iterative, numeric approach to compute the interval bounds.

Our implementation of CLP($\Re$) is preferred over existing versions (Heintze *et al.* 1987a, Jaffar 1990) since it allows for the simultaneous use of solvers for different domains in a consistent framework. This suits well the computational demands that arise in the context of hierarchical abstractions (Mozetic & Holzbaur 1991a). The numerical level of the model can be formulated with CLP($\Re$) for example, and successive abstractions thereof typically utilize constraint propagation over finite domains. The implementation of the specialized solvers is based on user-definable extended unification. As the solvers are written in Prolog, they can easily be customized to specific demands. The choice of Prolog as an implementation language for the equation solver for CLP($\Re$) led to a reduction in code size by an order of magnitude.

Beside the principal (software engineering) issues that motivated our implementation of CLP($\Re$), the availability and the quality of Sicstus Prolog (Carlsson & Widen 1990) somehow aposteriori justified the selection of Prolog as an implementation language. Sicstus Prolog has a compiler which can produce native machine code and a garbage collector. The basic mechanisms provided for the implementation of *freeze/2* and *dif/2* are very useful for the implementation of extended unification, the basis of our approach.

Our first CLP($\Re$) implementation was based on the C-Prolog interpreter (Holzbaur 1990). For the performance comparison against the C implementations of CLP($\Re$) this was disadvantageous, as the unification extensions, i.e., the CLP($\Re$) solver, were interpreted only. However, given the Sicstus compiler, the performance of our current Prolog CLP($\Re$) implementation is somewhere in-between the IBM (Jaffar 1990) and the Monash (Heintze *et al.* 1987a) implementations. A further improvement of our version of CLP($\Re$), which did not require any extra effort from our side, accrues from the increased numerical precision in floating point operations in Sicstus (double precision). Since Sicstus also provides infinite precision integer arithmetics, the implementation of CLP($\mathcal{Q}$) ($\mathcal{Q}$ = rationals) is easy and reasonably efficient.

3 Modeling analogue circuits

Model-based reasoning about a system requires an explicit representation (a model) of the system's components and their interconnections. Reasoning is typically based on theorem proving if a model is represented by first-order logic (Genesereth 1984, Reiter 1987), or on constraint propagation coupled with an ATMS (de Kleer & Williams 1987). Dague *et al.* (1990) use an ATMS-like system, augmented with the ability to compute with intervals, but unable to solve simultaneous equations, for the diagnosis of analogue circuits.

We represent models by logic programs, by CLP($\mathcal{B}$) ($\mathcal{B}$ = booleans) (Mozetic & Holzbaur 1991b), or by CLP($\Re$), depending on the domain of application. The first application of CLP($\Re$) to the analysis of analogue circuits was reported by (Heintze *et al.* 1987b).

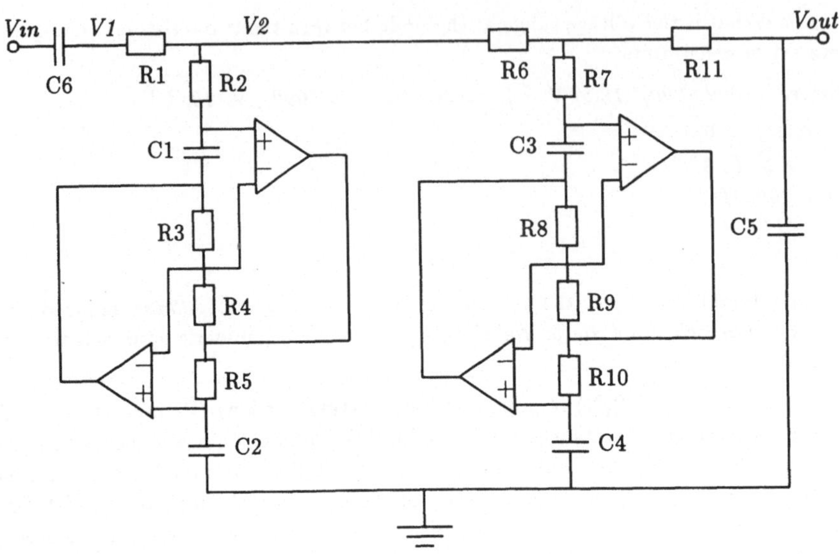

Figure 1: A low pass filter consisting of two structurally equivalent stages, and additional resistor *R11* and capacitors *C5* and *C6*.

Definition. A *model* of a system is a triple $\langle SD,\ COMPS,\ OBS \rangle$ where

1. *SD*, the system description, is a logic program with a distinguished top-level binary predicate *m(COMPS, OBS)* which relates states of the system components to observations.

2. *COMPS*, states of the system components, is an n-tuple $\langle S_1, \ldots, S_n \rangle$ where n is the number of components, and variables S_i denote states (e.g., normal or abnormal) of components.

3. *OBS*, observations, is an m-tuple $\langle P_1, \ldots, P_i, In_{i+1}, \ldots, In_j, Out_{j+1}, \ldots, Out_m \rangle$ where P are the model parameters, and *In* and *Out* denote inputs and outputs of the model, respectively.

In a logic program, n-tuples are represented by terms of arity n. Variables start with capitals and are implicitly universally quantified in front of a clause, and constants start with lower-case letters. In *SD* we refer to a distinguished constant *ok* to denote that the state S_i of the component i is normal.

We illustrate design and modeling of analogue circuits on a filter example. Using Micro-cap III (Spectrum), a standard electronic circuit simulation package, an active 5th order low pass RC filter has been designed (Figure 1). The filter is actually composed of two FDNR stages realized in thick film hybrid technology connected on a printed circuit board. In order to simplify the example, we concentrate on a single filter stage and ignore parameter tolerances. In what follows we also omit the operational amplifier model which was taken from the Micro-cap III manual and instantiated with the data provided by the manufacturer.

SD of the filter stage model (Figure 1) consists of the following CLP($\Re$) program. *COMPS* is a seven-tuple *comps(R1,...,R5,C1,C2)*, where R_i and C_i denote states of resistors and capacitors, respectively — we assume that the amplifiers do not fail. *OBS* is a triple *obs(F,V1,V2)*, where F is a given frequency, and *V1*, *V2* are input and output voltages of the stage, respectively.

```
stage( comps(R1,R2,R3,R4,R5,C1,C2), obs(F,V1,V2) )  ←
    W = 2*3.14159*F,  Vgnd = c(0,0),
    resistor( R1, 5513, V1, V2, Ir1 ), Ir1 = Ir2,
    resistor( R2, 727, V2, V3, Ir2 ),
    add( Ic1, Ia1, Ir2 ),
    capacitor( C1, 10.0e-9, W, V3, V4, Ic1 ),
    add( Ic1, Io2, Ir3 ),
    resistor( R3, 10000, V4, V5, Ir3 ),
    add( Ir4, Ib, Ir3 ), add( Ib1, Ib2, Ib ),
    resistor( R4, 10000, V5, V6, Ir4 ),
    add( Ir4, Io1, Ir5 ),
    resistor( R5, 5693, V6, V7, Ir5 ),
    add( Ic2, Ia2, Ir5 ),
    capacitor( C2, 10.0e-9, W, V7, Vgnd, Ic2 ),
    amplifier( W, V3, V5, V6, Ia1, Ib1, Io1 ),
    amplifier( W, V7, V5, V4, Ia2, Ib2, Io2 ).
```

The model relates states of resistors and capacitors to the frequency and measurable voltages. Since the filter operates under the AC conditions, all the voltages and currents are represented by complex numbers. Literals in the body of the clause represent model components which enforce local constraints between voltages and currents (e.g., Ohm's law). In nodes, Kirchoff's current law is enforced by the *add/3* predicate. Shared variables represent connections between the components and enforce global constraints, e.g., Kirchoff's law for voltages.

In addition to the structure of the model, behavior of its components must be defined. Normal behavior of a component specifies a relation between voltages and currents when the component is in a state *ok* (e.g., for a capacitor, $V1 - V2 = -\frac{i}{\omega C} * I$):

```
resistor( ok, R, V1, V2, I )  ←
    add( DV, V2, V1 ),
    mult( c(R,0), I, DV ).

capacitor( ok, C, W, V1, V2, I )  ←
    add( DV, V2, V1 ),
    mult( c(0,W*C), DV, I ).
```

For analogue components, it is relatively easy to specify the behavior in the case of hard faults (e.g., open or shorted). However, there is an infinite number of soft faults in between, due to the possible shifts in parameter values. In order to capture them all, no constraints between voltages and currents should be imposed by the fault model, i.e., a *weak* fault model must be used:

```
resistor( ab(R), _, V1, V2, I )  ←
    add( DV, V2, V1 ),
    mult( c(R,_), I, DV ).

capacitor( ab(C), _, W, V1, V2, I )  ←
    add( DV, V2, V1 ),
    mult( c(_,W*C), DV, I ).
```

We denote an abnormal state of a component by a term *ab(X)* instead of a constant *ab*. The idea is that a faulty resistor exhibits some unknown resistance R, and a faulty capacitor some unknown capacitance C which can be computed from voltages and currents. This can help in estimating relative likelihood of an individual component beeing faulty during diagnosis, as described in the next section.

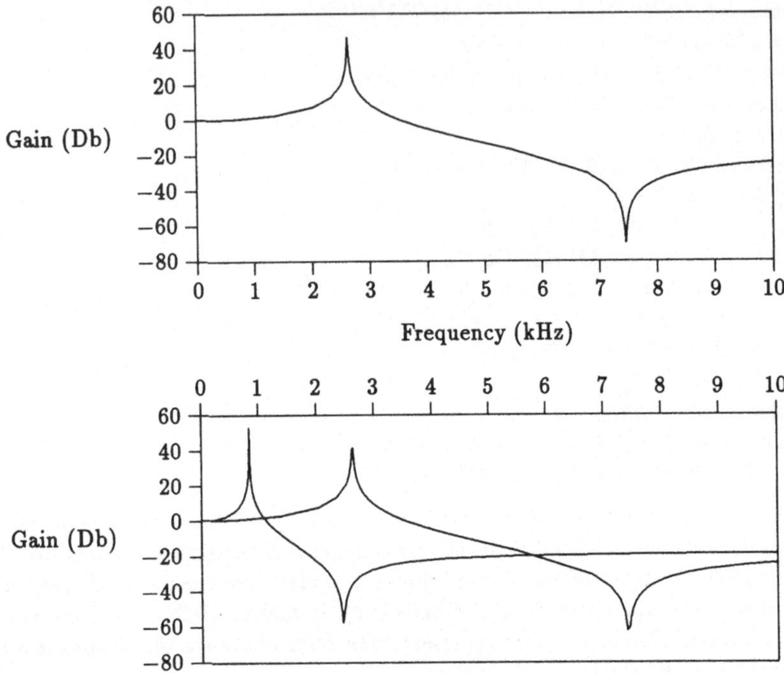

Figure 2: The gain-frequency graph of a normal filter stage (top), and two examples of faults (bottom). Pole and zero shifted to the left are due to a wrong capacitor ($C1 = 100$ nF instead of 10 nF), and cut off peaks are due to a resistor out of tolerances ($R5 = 5760$ Ω instead of 5693 Ω).

4   Analogue diagnosis

Assume that the design of the filter stage has been proven to meet the desired specification and that a prototype series has been manufactured. The gain-frequency characteristics of the designed stage is depicted in Figure 2 (top). The graph was obtained by simulating the CLP($\Re$) model, and results closely match the simulation results of the Micro-cap III package. However, it should be noted that in practice the simulation results might be quite different from reality, and that construction of good simulation models of analogue circuits cannot be taken for granted. Nevertheless, we will assume that for our purposes the simulation model does match the reality.

During the fabrication process, thick film resistors $R1$, $R2$, $R3$, and $R4$ are adjusted to nominal values within the expected tolerances. Resistor $R5$ is used for active laser trimming to compensate for variations in other components values. In the process of adjusting $R5$, possible hard faults are detected, hence only deviation faults in $R1$, $R2$, $R3$, $R4$ and $C1$, $C2$ may pass undetected. The filter stage is set to a chosen pole frequency by adjusting $R5$. Now, let us assume that due to a drift or possible failures in laser trimming process, the resistor $R5$ has achieved a value that deviates from the correct one. Let faulty $R5$ value be 5760 Ω instead of the correct 5693 Ω; assume also that other components have correct nominal values (Figure 2, bottom).

Analogue testing can be regarded as a process of checking whether a given product operates within acceptable margins for critical parameters (GO, NO-GO test). If a specification is not met we try to localize faults. Fault location is motivated either by the cost of rejecting and the possibility of repairing a board containing discrete analogue components, or by identification of a possible cause in order to prevent malfunctioning of the subsequent series of products. In our particular case, imprecise laser trimming process may cause malfunctioning of the whole series of products. Hence, it is neccessary to locate possible faults in the very first few manufactured stages.

The stage production process makes internal probing difficult and potentially destructive, therefore we rather avoid it. Instead, measurements are taken under different testing conditions, and a consistent hypothesis which explains most of the differences between the expected and measured values is sought after. For diagnosis one can use a standard simulation package. Based on the expert knowledge, a value is assigned to a suspected component, the circuit operation is simulated, and results are compared to the measured values. The process is repeated until the simulated values are close to the measured ones.

On the other hand, we can use the same CLP($\Re$) model for both, simulation and diagnosis. The simulation proceeds under the assumption that all model components are ok. For a given frequency F, an input voltage $V1$ is applied to the model, and the amplitude $Vmax$ and $Phase$ delay of the output voltage $V2$ are computed:

$$simulate(\ F,\ Vmax,\ Phase\ )\ \leftarrow$$
$$V1 = c(1,0),$$
$$stage(\ comps(ok,ok,ok,ok,ok,ok,ok),\ obs(F,V1,V2)\ ),$$
$$polar\_coord(\ V2,\ Vmax,\ Phase\ ).$$

Suppose that we measured $Vmax$ and $Phase$ delay at 7400 and 2800 Hz. The simulation yields the following predicted values which differ from the measured ones:

$\leftarrow\ simulate(\ 7400,\ Vmax,\ Phase\ ).$ % Measured $Vmax = 0.00054$, $Phase = -145$
$Vmax = 0.00440081$, $Phase = -3.75498$

$\leftarrow\ simulate(\ 2800,\ Vmax,\ Phase\ ).$ % Measured $Vmax = 6.27$, $Phase = -180$
$Vmax = 4.8306$, $Phase = -179.894$

For diagnosis, the same model is used just the other way around. Input and output voltages, $V1$ and $V2$, are given and we are asking for the states of the model components (presumably some will be abnormal) such that the consistency between the input and output is restored. This effectively means that some local constraints, governing the behavior of abnormal model components, are suspended. Here we also make a single fault assumption, i.e., all but one component are ok:

$$diagnose(\ F,\ Vmax,\ Phase,\ Diag\ )\ \leftarrow$$
$$V1 = c(1,0),$$
$$complex\_coord(\ Vmax,\ Phase,\ V2\ ),$$
$$single\_fault(\ Diag\ ),$$
$$stage(\ Diag,\ obs(F,V1,V2)\ ).$$

For the first measurement, we get the following seven alternative diagnoses:

$\leftarrow\ diagnose(\ 7400,\ 0.00054,\ -145,\ comps(R1,R2,R3,R4,R5,C1,C2)\ ).$

$R1 = ab(-46503.5)$, $R2=ok$, $R3=ok$, $R4=ok$, $R5=ok$, $C1=ok$, $C2=ok$;
$R2 = ab(700.32)$, $R1=ok$, $R3=ok$, $R4=ok$, $R5=ok$, $C1=ok$, $C2=ok$;
$R3 = ab(9647.06)$, $R1=ok$, $R2=ok$, $R4=ok$, $R5=ok$, $C1=ok$, $C2=ok$;
$R4 = ab(10365.8)$, $R1=ok$, $R2=ok$, $R3=ok$, $R5=ok$, $C1=ok$, $C2=ok$;
$R5 = ab(5759.79)$, $R1=ok$, $R2=ok$, $R3=ok$, $R4=ok$, $C1=ok$, $C2=ok$;
$C1 = ab(9.6334e-09)$, $R1=ok$, $R2=ok$, $R3=ok$, $R4=ok$, $R5=ok$, $C2=ok$;
$C2 = ab(9.65935e-09)$, $R1=ok$, $R2=ok$, $R3=ok$, $R4=ok$, $R5=ok$, $C1=ok$

A diagnosis consists of an assignment of states ok or $ab(X)$ to all the components. In addition, for an abnormal component, its predicted value X (resistance or capacitance) is computed. The measured output voltage can be accounted for only if the faulty resistor or capacitor actually assumes the predicted value. From the above diagnoses we can immediately rule out $R1$ as a candidate of beeing faulty, since a resistor cannot have negative resistance. In order to decide between the remaining

Faulty component	Relative standard deviation (%)	Predicted (mean) value (Ω, nF)	Nominal value (Ω, nF)
R5	0.002	5760	5693
C2	0.003	9.66	10
R4	0.085	10360	10000
R3	0.086	9653	10000
C1	0.19	9.65	10
R2	18	620	727
R1	180	-20600	5513

Table 1: Relative ordering of components in decreasing likelihood of faults after two measurements.

alternatives we take another measurement.

The seconds measurement yields the following diagnoses:

$\leftarrow$ *diagnose(2800, 6.27, -180, comps(R1,R2,R3,R4,R5,C1,C2)).*

R1 = ab(5296.07), R2=ok, R3=ok, R4=ok, R5=ok, C1=ok, C2=ok ;
R2 = ab(539.949), R1=ok, R3=ok, R4=ok, R5=ok, C1=ok, C2=ok ;
R3 = ab(9658.83), R1=ok, R2=ok, R4=ok, R5=ok, C1=ok, C2=ok ;
R4 = ab(10353.3), R1=ok, R2=ok, R3=ok, R5=ok, C1=ok, C2=ok ;
R5 = ab(5759.62), R1=ok, R2=ok, R3=ok, R4=ok, C1=ok, C2=ok ;
C1 = ab(9.65867e-09), R1=ok, R2=ok, R3=ok, R4=ok, R5=ok, C2=ok ;
C2 = ab(9.65894e-09), R1=ok, R2=ok, R3=ok, R4=ok, R5=ok, C1=ok

Now we make an assumption that faults are non-intermittent. A faulty component assumes some value different than nominal, but this value does not change during testing. This means that predicted values should remain stable across several measurements. Consequently, we can rule out $R2$ as a possible diagnosis since its predicted values considerably vary.

Due to the imprecision of measurements, even the predicted value of the component known to be faulty slightly varies. We assume the standard Gaussian distribution of predicted values of individual components, and calculate the mean and standard deviation across several measurements. Table 1 gives a list of faulty components, ranked by the relative standard deviation of their predicted values. $R5$ seems the most probable cause of malfunctioning, but additional test measurements have to be taken to single it out. $R2$ and $R1$ can already be eliminated as possible causes with a high degree of confidence.

In general, predicted values of faulty components are not constants but intervals. We have to take into account the accuracy of measurements and tolerances of fault-free components which leads to internal voltages and currents beeing within some interval ranges. Their tightest bounds can be extracted only at the end of the model simulation, and from them the predicted interval values of faulty components can be computed. This increases the computational demands of the CLP($\Re$) model interpreter, but the basic diagnostic strategy remains the same.

5 Conclusion

In the paper we outlined first experiences with the use of CLP($\Re$) for analogue circuits testing. For a non-trivial circuit we re-created simulation results as produced by a dedicated simulation package. The advantage of CLP($\Re$) is that it is a general purpose programming language, and that it tightly integrates numeric and symbolic computation. Models of circuits can be specified concisely, and used for both, simulation and diagnosis.

For a designer of analogue circuits, closing the gap between the simulation model and the reality is important. More realistic models may require more sophisticated numerical processing that current implementations of CLP($\Re$), restricted to linear systems, provide. However, our implementation of CLP($\Re$) makes extensions easier, and allows for the integration of several specialized solvers within the same framework. We envision CLP($\Re$) as a potential basis for software tools which support rapid model specification, experimentation in the design process, and testing during the early manufacturing phases.

Acknowledgements

The first two authors are supported by the Austrian Federal Ministry of Science and Research. They wish to thank Robert Trappl for making some of this work possible. The last two authors acknowledge the support of the Slovene Research Council.

References

Bandler, J.W., Salama, A.E. (1985). Fault diagnosis of analog circuits. *Proc. IEEE 73 (8)*, pp. 1279-1826.

Carlsson, M., Widen, J. (1990). Sicstus Prolog user's manual, SICS/R-88/88007C, Swedish Institute of Computer Science, Kista, Sweden.

Cohen, J. (1990). Constraint logic programming languages. *Communications of the ACM 33 (7)*, pp. 52-68.

Dague, P., Deves, P., Luciani, P., Taillibert, P. (1990). Analog systems diagnosis. *Proc. 9th ECAI*, pp. 173-178, Stockholm.

Davis, R. (1984). Diagnostic reasoning based on structure and behaviour. *Artificial Intelligence 24*, pp. 347-410.

de Kleer, J., Williams, B.C. (1987). Diagnosing multiple faults. *Artificial Intelligence 32*, pp. 97-130.

Duhamel, P., Rault, J.C. (1979). Automatic test generation techniques for analog circuits and systems: a review. *IEEE Trans. on Circuits and Systems CAS-26 (7)*, pp. 411-440.

Genesereth, M.R. (1984). The use of design descriptions in automated diagnosis. *Artificial Intelligence 24*, pp. 411-436.

Heintze, N., Jaffar, J., Michaylov, S., Stuckey, P., Yap, R. (1987a). The CLP($\Re$) programmer's manual. Dept. of Computer Science, Monash University, Australia.

Heintze, N., Michaylov, S., Stuckey, P. (1987b). CLP($\Re$) and some electrical engineering problems. *Proc. 4th Intl. Conference on Logic Programming*, pp. 675-703, Melbourne, Australia, The MIT Press.

Holzbaur, C. (1990). Specification of constraint based inference mechanisms through extended unification. Ph.D. Thesis, Vienna University of Technology, Austria.

Jaffar, J. (1990). CLP($\Re$) version 1.0 reference manual. IBM Research Division, T.J. Watson Research Center, Yorktown Heights, NY.

Jaffar, J., Lassez, J.-L., Mahler, J. (1986). A logic programming language scheme. In D. de Groot, G. Linstrom (eds.), *Logic Programming: Functions, Relations, and Equations*, Prentice-Hall, Englewood Cliffs, NJ.

Kraemer, F.-J. (1989). A decision procedure for Presburger arithmetic with functions and equality. SEKI working paper SWP-89-4, FB Informatik, University of Kaiserslautern, Germany.

McKeon A., Wakeling, A. (1990). Model-based analogue circuit fault diagnosis. *Proc. TEST'90*, pp. 1-14, London.

Mozetic, I., Holzbaur, C. (1991a). Integrating qualitative and numerical models within Constraint Logic Programming. Proc. *1991 Intl. Logic Programming Symposium, ILPS-91*, San Diego, MIT Press.

Mozetic, I., Holzbaur, C. (1991b). Controlling the complexity in model-based diagnosis. Report TR-91-3, Austrian Research Institute for Artificial Intelligence, Vienna, Austria.

Ohletz, M.J. (1991). Hybrid built-in self test for mixed analogue/digital integrated circuits. *Proc. 2nd European Test Conf. TEST'91*, pp. 307-316, Munich.

Reiter, R. (1987). A theory of diagnosis from first principles. *Artificial Intelligence 32*, pp. 57-95.

Shostak, R. (1981). Deciding linear inequalities by computing loop residues. *Journal of the ACM 28 (4)*, pp. 769-779.

Spectrum. Micro-cap III electronic circuit analysis program instruction manual. Spectrum Software, 1021 S. Wolfe Road, Sunnyvale, CA 94086.

Natural Language Processing:
An Overview

Henry S. Thompson
Human Communication Research Centre
Department of Artificial Intelligence
Centre for Cognitive Science

University of Edinburgh
SCOTLAND

0. Introduction

This paper is a lightly edited version of the slides for a talk of the same title. It provides a brief introduction to the subject matter of natural language processing, its relationship with artificial intelligence and its methodology. It includes slightly more detailed discussion of a pair of examples of exemplary natural language processing problems—speech recognition and machine translation.

1. Natural Language Processing and Artificial Intelligence

1.1. Artificial Intelligence Defined

Artificial Intelligence is the effective computational deployment of knowledge. The knowledge may be explicit, e.g. a grammar of German, or tacit, e.g. ones knowledge of how to tie ones shoelaces.

1.2. Applying Artificial Intelligence

There are two related tasks in any application of artificial intelligence:

1)   Represent the knowledge in a computationally tractable form;

2)   Design and implement algorithms which effectively employ that knowledge so represented to achieve the desired processing.

1.3. Natural Language Processing Using the Artificial Intelligence Methodology

Natural language processing is a natural candidate for the artificial intelligence methodology. Many natural language processing tasks can be viewed as transforming one sort of representation (letters, sounds, words, syntactic structures, meanings) into another, using the artificial intelligence methodology at each step.

2. The Overall Structure of Natural Language Processing

Many different tasks fall under the general heading of natural language processing.

It helps to distinguish three dimensions—modality (text or speech), direction (input or output) and aspect (accident, form or content). Figure 1 below indicates how these dimensions categorise particular application types.

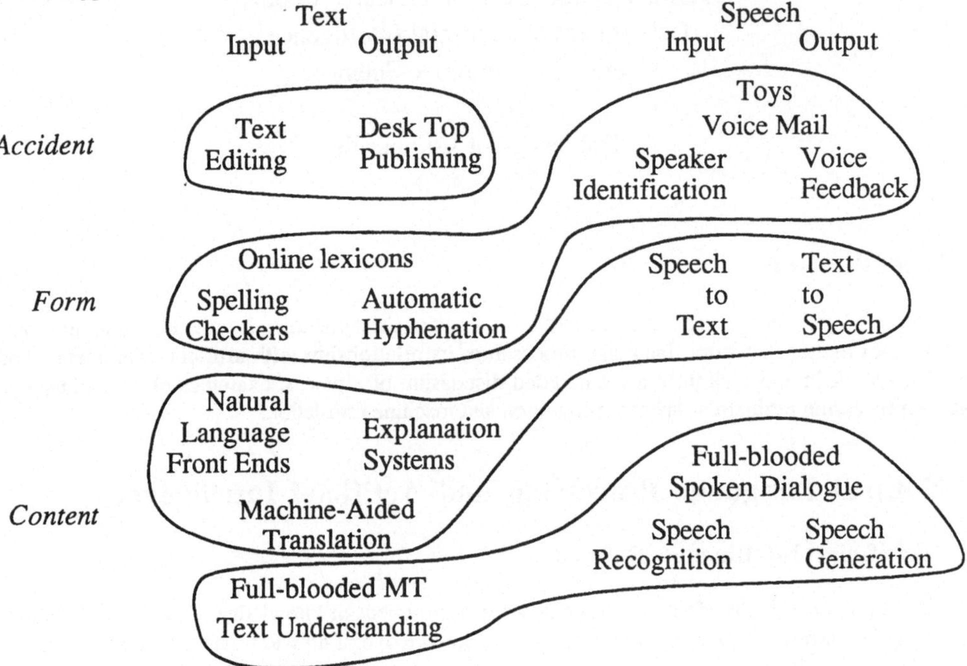

Figure 1. A categorisation of natural language processing applications

The groupings indicate rough equivalence of status, both technological and commercial.

The inclusion of the row labelled *accident* is contentious. By accident I mean to identify systems which deal only incidentally with language, or rather, deal with linguistic objects but without any appeal to their linguistic nature.

Arguably natural language processing proper only includes the form and content rows of the diagram.

3. State of the Natural Language Processing Market and Technology

As we go down the groups outlined in Figure 1, the current market size shrinks. It is interesting to note that speech lags behind text at each step.

3.1. Large-scale Existing Market

- The first group, accident-oriented text processing, represents a multi-billion dollar market world-wide, but as remarked above, is not really a part of the language industry.

3.2. Niche Market Technologies

- The second group, accident-oriented speech systems and form-oriented text systems, comprises those components which are based on relatively stable technology, and have a significant, although not terribly large, market presence.

These are essentially niche-market systems, which will never in themselves sustain the dramatic market growth we are looking for in the language industry.

3.3. Near Market Technologies.

- The third group, form-oriented speech systems and restricted content-oriented text systems, is the most interesting, being those components which, in one form or another, are to be found in research and development laboratories, but not, with a few small exceptions, in the marketplace as yet.

This is where the market growth of the industry will need to occur if it is to achieve its potential.

3.4. The Distant Future.

- The presence in the diagram of the fourth group, systems requiring robust understanding, is somewhat deceptive, as the point about it is that it does not exist, nor can we expect any substantial progress in these areas for the foreseeable future, pending a full solution to the knowledge representation problem.

4. Schematic natural language processing System Architecture

Almost all natural language processing systems of any complexity are organised in a pipeline, as illustrated below in Figure 2. Note that the units at the module interfaces differ only in the upper half as between speech processing and text processing—with the partial exception of intonation, which is rarely treated in current systems in any case, the balance of processing at more abstract levels of analysis is common to the two media.

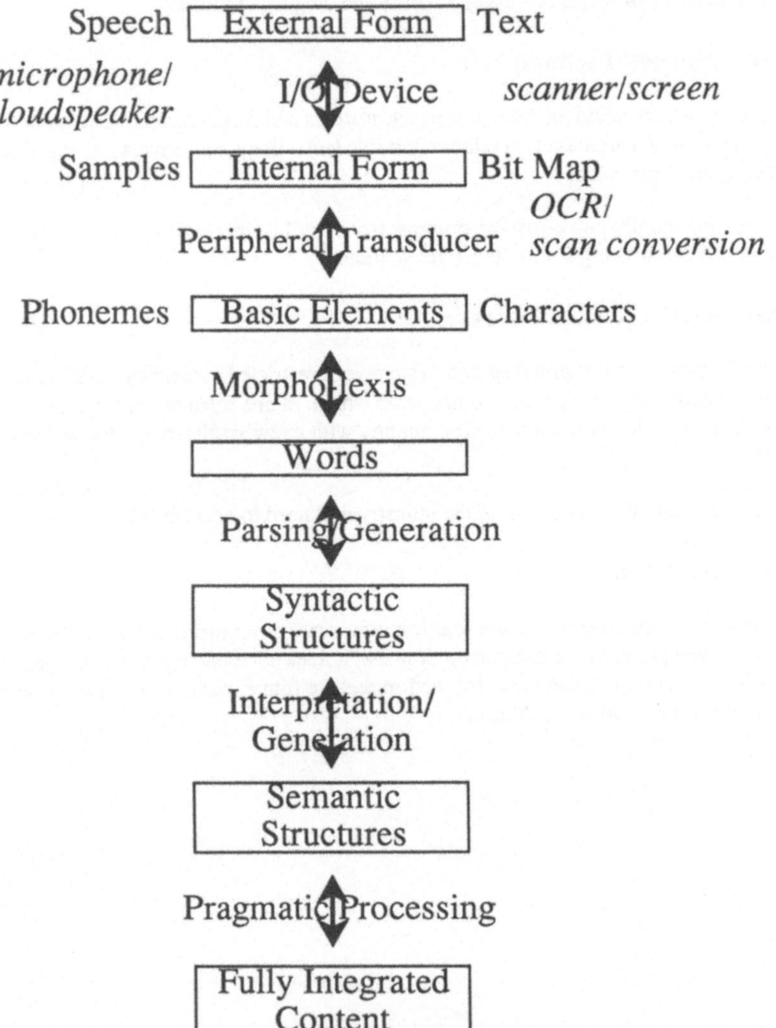

**Figure 2. Schematic diagram of paradigmatic natural language processing
system architecture**

5. Two Fundamental Problems for natural language processing

There are two principal sources of difficulty in virtually all natural language processing applications:

- Ambiguity—The transformation from one representation to another is often one-to-many.

- Ellipsis—At all levels, a lot is left out and must be supplied from context.

5.1. Solving the Problems

Each step in the system, as shown in Figure 2 above, uses knowledge (the artificial intelligence methodology) to reduce ambiguity and fill in gaps.

Each step needs different knowledge: phonetic, orthographic, lexical, morphological, grammatical, semantical, pragmatic, common-sensical.

The last appears to be crucial, for both people and machines. In the analysis direction, we can think of it as a filter, removing the final ambiguities by insisting that the proposed interpretation make good sense in the current application context.

5.2. A Bigger Problem

Unfortunately, applying the artificial intelligence methodology (represent and compute) to provide a common-sense filter cannot yet be accomplished in the general case. The technology of knowledge representation and mechanical reasoning is not as yet up to the task of representing and deploying general purpose knowledge.

5.3. The Fundamental Limitation

Another way of looking at the common sense filter is that it demands true understanding for its implementation. In consequence, we observe that

Fully Automatic High Quality Unrestricted

Continuous Speech Recognition
or
Machine Translation
or
Scene Analysis

. . .

crucially involves *understanding* and is therefore out of reach for the time being.

5.4. Two possible responses:

1)   Give up Unrestricted;

2)   Give up Fully Automatic.

We'll look at Speech Recognition as an example of (1), and Machine Translation as an example of (2).

6. Speech Recognition

6.1. What Makes Speech Recognition Hard—Real Problems

Some problems in speech recognition are intrinsic to the application:

- The signal is lousy—noisy, sloppy, lazy

- There are no reliable cues to the division of the signal into words

6.1.1. The Signal is Lousy

The acoustic signal from which speech recognition must proceed is less than ideal for this purpose in a number of ways. In almost all circumstances, it is contaminated with noise. Furthermore, speakers are less than completely articulate and careful in their speech—they depend on the highly sophisticated capabilities of human listeners to fill in the gaps and make up for the imperfections. For example, in a normal conversational pronunciation of the word *potato*, the vowel in the initial syllable, the 'o', will frequently be so weakly articulated that it lasts no more than 15 or 20 milliseconds, barely time for more than one pulse of the vocal cords. It may even be absent altogether. Human listeners are well used to compensating for such sloppiness, but computer systems which depend in part on detailed analysis of the frequency distributions of the energy spectrum to identify vowels have great difficulties.

6.1.2. Word Boundaries are Not Marked

Not only do we imagine much in the way of sound that we think we hear but which is actually missing, as discussed in the previous section, but our subjective impression of what we hear is incorrect in another way. When listening to speech, a human listener hears it as a sequence of discrete words, subjectively separated by silence. But in fact no such silence is present in the normal flow of speech. A plot of the acoustic energy produced during the utterance of a sentence will reveal if anything negative correlation between silence and the boundaries between words.

In other words there is no 'space' in the phonetic alphabet—neither silence nor anything else is correlated well with word boundaries. What human listeners find easy, namely dividing up the continuous speech stream into words, machines find very difficult.

6.2. What Makes Speech Recognition Hard—Technology Problems

In addition to fundamental problems, there are also a number of weaknesses in existing technology for speech recognition:

- Sound-to-symbol mapping is imperfectly realised—context and individual differences have profound and complex effects

- "Does this make sense" filter cannot be done yet, and available approximations all are flawed

6.2.1. Sound-to-symbol mapping

We don't have complete theories about what aspects of context and what properties of the speaker determine the acoustic properties of (the sound which corresponds to) an individual phoneme.Our systems only imperfectly embody such incomplete theories as we do have.

6.2.2. Common Sense Filter

Set against the uncertainties arising from real problems and front weaknesses, we have the filters of lexis and syntax. But as we've seen, for people and machines, that isn't always enough.

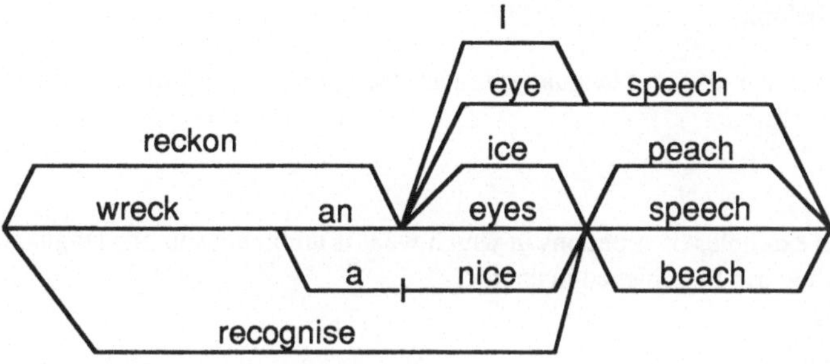

Figure 3. Sample word lattice

Of all the 22 paths through this lattice, two are syntactically consistent with the prologue "People can easily ...". But only one makes sense in context.

7. State of the Art in Speech Recognition

Presently there are two basic routes to robust working systems with high performance:

Template-based systems for small vocabulary, isolated word input;

HMM-based systems using context-sensitive 'phoneme' models for either large vocabulary discrete input, or heavily constrained small vocabulary continuous input.

7.1. HMM-based Systems for Speech Recognition

Two alternative ways around the common-sense problem, both abandoning the Unrestricted goal:

- Dissolve by discrete utterance style input, in which short silences are used to demarcate words;

- Solve, for limited domains, by mandating a grammar and/or using domain constraints. Current technology depends heavily on statistical `language models' to accomplish this.

7.2. Near to Medium Term Prospects for Speech Recognition

More of the same. Breakthroughs in the knowledge representation problem are not obviously imminent. There will be quantitative improvements (what counts as a sufficiently limited domain, etc.), but no qualitative leaps.

The major challenge will be to move to a more principled appeal to domain knowledge to implement the restricted common-sense filter.

8. Machine Translation

8.1. What Makes Machine Translation Hard—Real Problems

- Ambiguity, as mentioned before;

- Ellipsis, in particular the fact that different languages require the expression of different aspects
of message content.

8.1.1. Ambiguity

Both grammar and lexis provide examples of situations in which what is ambiguous in one language must
be disambiguated before translation can be achieved in another

English: red apples and grapes
French: pommes rouges et raisins
    or

    pommes et raisins rouges

Note that in this case the opportunity exists for a translation which preserves the ambiguity, namely *raisins
et pommes rouges*, but especially as the languages involved are less and less close to one another, this is
rarely possible.

French: porter une robe
English: wear a dress
    or

    carry a dress

8.1.2. Ellipsis

We also find that in many cases something left implicit in one language must be made explicit in another:

English: hand bag
French: sack de main
    or

    sack a main

French: Il est parti
English: He left
    or

    He has left

8.2. What Makes Machine Translation Hard—Technology Problems

- Format translation;

- Lack of symmetry between analysis and synthesis;

- Tension between interlingua-based approaches and transfer-based approaches:

9. State of the Art in Machine Translation

9.1. Interlingua-based approach

Systems based on what is called an *interlingua* attempt to analyse the source all the way to a language-independent representation of text content, and then generate the corresponding target language text from that.

Outside very restricted domains, where the knowledge representation problem is not overwhelming, this approach has largely been abandoned.

A notable exception is Philips's Roseta system, which has a very liberal interpretation of what constitutes an interlingua.

9.2. Transfer-based approach

Such systems attempt to analyse the source only as far as some sort of language-specific semantic structure, and then rely on a language-pair-specific transfer mapping to produce the corresponding structure for generation in the target language.

The basic difficulty here, aside from the still serious problems of ambiguity and ellipsis, is the number of transfer modules required—72 just for the EEC as of 1991, for example.

9.3. Translator's Assistant/Post Editing

Most machine translation systems today actually function as machine-*aided* translation systems, in the system is viewed as an augmentation to the translator, not a replacement. The machine does what it can, producing a more or less rough translation, and the translator, who must be fluent in both source and target languages, cleans it up to the extent required for the particular application. Such systems are available, and definitely increase translator efficiency.

9.4. Multi-lingual Document Creation

An alternative, more exciting, approach, is to view the system's role as that of helping an author create a document in a language s/he doesn't speak. Here rather than cleaning up the output translation, the user is expected to disambiguate and fill in missing bits in dialogue with the system in the source language.

For example, in translating the ambiguous example above, *red apples and grapes*, the system would query the author. "Do you mean the grapes are red as well, or just the apples? "

10. Conclusions

There is a great wealth of basic technology available for natural language processing. Practical applications which make effective use of this technology, however, need to be very carefully chosen so that the demands they make on the technology can be satisfied. Exaggerating the capabilities of the systems we can build today is not in anybodies interests—real progress has been made, real systems of real value can be built, but there is a long way to go before we will have systems which can interact robustly in unconstrained natural language.

Incremental Syntax Generation with Tree Adjoining Grammars

Karin Harbusch, Wolfgang Finkler, Anne Schauder
Deutsches Forschungszentrum für Künstliche Intelligenz
Stuhlsatzenhausweg 3
6600 Saarbrücken 11, FRG

Phone: (+49 681) 302 5271/5269/5255
Fax: (+49 681) 302 4261
E-Mail: harbusch/finkler/schauder@dfki.uni-sb.de

With the increasing capacity of AI systems the design of human–computer interfaces has become a favorite research topic in AI. In this paper we focus on aspects of the output of a computer. The architecture of a sentence generation component – embedded in the WIP system – is described. The main emphasis is laid on the motivation for the incremental style of processing and the encoding of adequate linguistic units as rules of a Lexicalized Tree Adjoining Grammar with Unification.

1 Introduction

The acceptance of an AI system directly depends on its user interface facilities. For the next generation of user interfaces it is no longer acceptable to use a restricted input mode (e.g., an inflexible sequence of prompts of the system and required user input) or inadequate canned text as output (e.g., "Rule 31 was chosen because of precondition 2.").

An AI system with user interface should be capable to play the role of the producer as well as the role of the consument in conversational situations. Therefore it must be able to analyze user input and to present new information in an adequate way. To be adequate human–computer dialogue must share the properties of human–human dialogue. This means for the generation of ouput that e.g., size and granularity of the presented information should depend on the communicative context (novices must be informed in a more detailed manner than skilled persons).

The central topic of this paper is the generation of natural language output. Since natural language analysis and generation share a lot of properties, they could be seen as two directions of the same process. In order to motivate the extra research on natural language generation we have to differentiate between the two topics. One example for such a difference is given by the used search spaces: During analysis all syntactic and semantic ambiguities of an input sentence (e.g., "Time flies like an arrow.") must be resolved in order to find the intended meaning. Generation means to choose between an infinite number of utterances which are possible but more or less adequate in a situation ("Would you please close the window?", "Shut the window!", "It is cold here.", "I already had three influenzas this year.", ...).

Our generation component is embedded in the WIP[1] system whose architecture is presented

---

[1] WIP is the acronym for "**W**issensbasierte **I**nformationspräsentation" which means knowledge–based presentation of information. The WIP project is supported by the German Ministry of Research and Technology under grant ITW8901 8.

in Section 2. The decision for an incremental processing mode is essential for the architecture of the generation component as well as for the determination of size and shape of processed linguistic units. We motivate this processing mode with psycholinguistical and computational arguments in Section 3. In Section 4 we argue that the formalism of Lexicalized LD/LP–Tree Adjoining Grammars with Unification is well suited for the representation of the knowledge used during verbalization (grammar and lexicon). The overall architecture of our sentence generation module is explained in Section 5. It is a system of concurrently and cooperatively working objects which manage the composition and linearization of the linguistic units.

2   The WIP System

The aim of the WIP project (see, e.g., [Wahlster et al. 91]) is to contribute in basic research in the field of 'Intelligent User Interfaces'. With increases in the amount and sophistication of information that must be communicated to the user of a complex technical system, new ways to present that information flexibly and efficiently become necessary. Since in many situations information is presented efficiently only through particular combinations of communication modes (e.g., graphics and text), the automatic generation of multimodal presentations is an important task of such a system. One basic principle of the WIP system is that the various constituents of a multimodal presentation should be generated dynamically from a common representation, i.e. no predefined pictures or texts are used. This is the presupposition for flexibility (e.g., change of perspective) and interrelationship in the different modes of output (e.g., the use of cross–modal references).

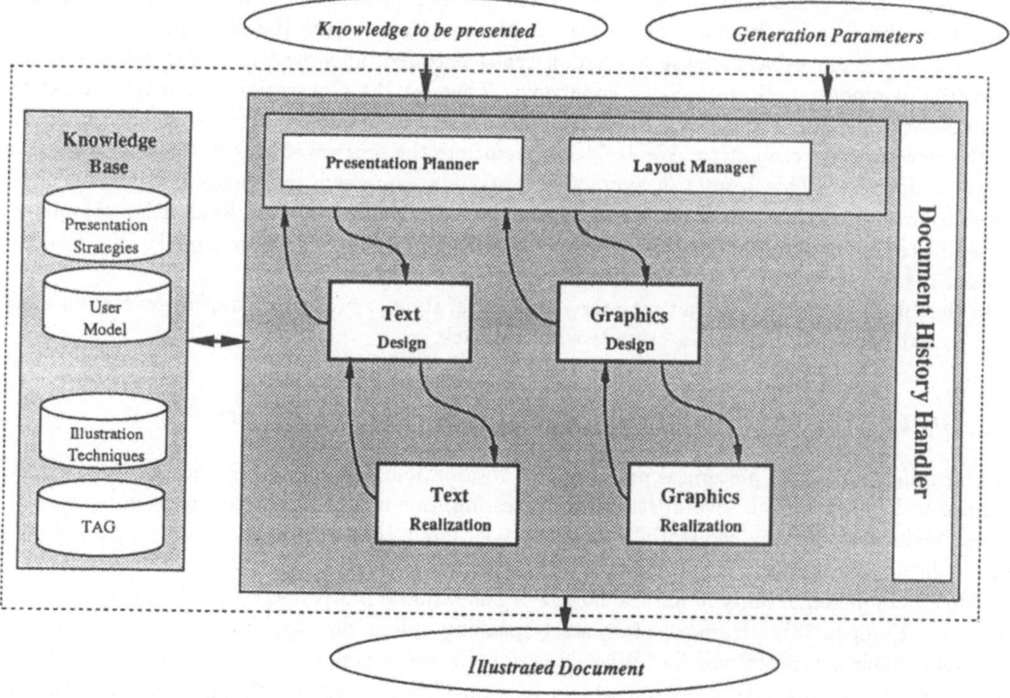

Figure 1: The Architecture of the WIP System

The *Presentation Planner* (see Figure 1) is the component that is responsible for the selection of contents. Furthermore, it decides which parts of the presentation shall be realized as text and which as graphics. The input for the planner consists of the knowledge to be presented together with some information about the communicative context in form of so–called *Generation Parameters*. A second control instance of the system is the *Layout Manager*. It uses semantic and pragmatic relations specified by the planner to arrange the graphical and textual fragments produced by the two mode–specific generators (see W. Graf and W. Maaß in this volume for detailed information about the Layout Manager). The two generator components are divided into a design and a realization part. They produce textual and graphical parts of output without direct communication. References and influences between the two generators are nevertheless required for multimodal output: The *Document History Handler* as a central blackboard is the shared medium for communication between the different components. Here the need for a common representation for all components becomes obvious again. In the following we focus on the text generation part of WIP.

The Text Design component receives as input from the Presentation Planner exactly that piece of knowledge, which was chosen to be presented as text. Furthermore the Presentation Planner defines an adequate set of parameters for the Text Design component which consists partially of the parameters that are given as input to the Presentation Planner itself. The other parameters are specific to text not to graphics and are set dynamically by the Presentation Planner or the Layout Manager (e.g., "sentence mode: noun phrase" for the generation of titles, "short utterance" to have some text fitted into a given graphical box, ...). The Text Design component determines in which order the given input elements shall be realized in the text. The structure of a text is worked out at several levels. This comprises for example the partition of a paragraph into sentences, the assignment of a perspective or the use of anaphora to obtain a coherent text. Therefore, this component is comparable with the so–called "Micro–planner", a part of the What–to–Say component – where the Presentation Planner can be seen as "Macro–planner" (cf. [Levelt 89]).

The resulting preverbal message is grammatically encoded, linearized and inflected in the Text Realization component (How–to–Say component). Thereby, the Generation Parameters direct the choice of syntactic structures. One difficulty is to define the boundary between the What–to–Say and the How–to–Say component. We decided to associate the process of lexical choice with the Text Design component. This results in syntactic constraints expressed as valency information of the chosen lemmas which could lead to conflicts during verbalization in the Text Realization component. To be able to report these problems to the Text Design component we propose a model with feedback between the two modules.

In the following section we motivate the incremental style of processing during generation which is supported by such a model of a cascade with feedback.

3   Incremental Natural Language Generation

Incrementality stands for piecemeal processing of information. For the text generation task which is assumed to be executed on several stages of processing, this means an interconnection between the stages: Instead of working sequentially on the whole input the components work on partial input and produce parts of output for the next stage as soon as possible.

The idea of incrementality in natural language generation is motivated by psycholinguistic studies (see, e.g., [Kempen 78]). Humans often start speaking before they know exactly what the whole contents of their utterance will be. When describing a scene where a big man and a smaller man are visible and the big man does something, it is possible to focus on this man without knowing how to describe his activity. Thereby incremental processing is possible because the disambiguating modifier "big" can be added to the noun "man" without regarding the actions of the two persons. This observation can be interpreted as follows: The time that passes during the articulation of the first parts of the utterance can be used to process further parts of information which shall be realized in the utterance (e.g., that the action can be described as "laughing"). Special kinds of human speech errors and empirical results of other psycholinguistical experiments give evidence for this interpretation.

Advantages of incrementality in human language generation are that less information must be kept in mind, that pauses between parts of the utterance become shorter and consequentially that the danger of being interrupted by the dialogue partner decreases. Most important for AI generation systems are the first two facts.

From a computational point of view the main advantage of an incremental approach is the improvement of efficiency. A reduction of response time enhances the user's acceptance of an information system. Different components of the text generation system (see Section 5) can start working as soon as they obtain their first partial input. They should produce their output in a piecemeal fashion, too. Therefore, efficiency is gained by *parallelism* in the cascade of text generating components. On the contrary, a strictly sequential mode of operation would force them to work one after the other; their processing times would have to be added up.

There is a need for *incremental presentation* in WIP, especially, if knowledge to be presented is not completely available when the processing in the WIP system starts. A scenario can be imagined where information is continuously supplied by the application system (e.g., data obtained from measuring instruments) and where such information must be simultaneously presented in a condensed form to assist human decision–makers. In addition, an *online presentation mode* that aims to instantaneously illustrate the development of the document on a screen can be more appropriate for users even in situations where all information to be presented is available before the system starts. The advantage is that the user receives the reaction of the system earlier, i.e. before the output is completed.

For the transfer of an incremental approach to a computational model basically two questions must be examined: Firstly, how can an incremental and parallel mode between the components of the system (here, e.g., Presentation Planner, Text Design, ...) be realized, and secondly, can this kind of processing be furthermore enhanced by parallelism inside the components (e.g., parallel processing of parts of a sentence in the Text Realization component)?

Our answer to the first question is the previously mentioned model of a cascade for the architecture of the WIP system. "Coarse grained" parallelism between the text generator, the graphics generator and the planning component is possible.

In this paper, we will try to answer the second question with regard to the Text Realization component. A simultaneous activity on existing parts of the syntactic structure would support the incremental processing of such parts (cf. [Finkler & Neumann 89]). A discussion about the degree of parallelism possible inside a component ends up in a discussion about the degree of independence that can be observed between the computed parts. On the other hand, this question has some influence on the determination of the size of entities the sentence generator should work with.

Our ideas to solve these problems are presented in the next two sections. We will translate the incremental mode of processing into a parallel model of cooperating objects which deal with entities from our knowledge base: structures of a Lexicalized LD/LP–Tree Adjoining Grammar with Unification.

4 The Grammar of the Text Realization Component

The task of our generator consists in finding a syntactic realization for the preverbal message which has been given as input. The additional information contained in the parameter settings has likewise to be integrated. Therefore we must have a look at the structure of syntactic knowledge and find a good representation for it.

We refine the problem stepwise. First an adequate formalism for the representation of syntactic knowledge is presented (Tree Adjoining Grammars with some extensions). Then the appropriateness of the TAG extension 'Lexicalized LD/LP-UTAG' for grammatical encoding is evaluated.

4.1 Lexicalized LD/LP–TAGs with Unification

Tree Adjoining Grammars

In 1975, the formalism of Tree Adjoining Grammars (TAGs) was introduced (see [Joshi et al. 75]). Since then, a wide variety of properties – formal properties as well as linguistically relevant ones – were studied (see, e.g., [Joshi 85] for a good overview).

A Tree Adjoining Grammar is a tree generation system. It consists of two different sets of trees, *initial* and *auxiliary trees*, which together form the set of *elementary trees*. Intuitively the set of initial trees can be seen as context–free derivation trees. The start symbol of the grammar is the root node, all inner nodes are nonterminals and all leaves are terminals (e.g., tree α in Figure 2). Auxiliary trees (e.g., tree β in Figure 2) can be combined with initial (or already modified initial) trees by replacing an inner node of the latter. This combination operation is called *adjoining* or *adjunction*. The result of an adjoining must again have the form of a derivation tree (e.g., the rightmost tree in Figure 2). This demand restricts the structure of auxiliary trees: In order to replace a node labelled X, the root node of the auxiliary tree must also be labelled with X and one of its leaves, called the *foot node*, serves as the new root for the former subtree below the adjoining node. Another restriction for auxiliary trees is the requirement, that such a tree must derive at least one terminal. This disallows the repetition of arbitrary many adjunctions without growth in the terminal string.

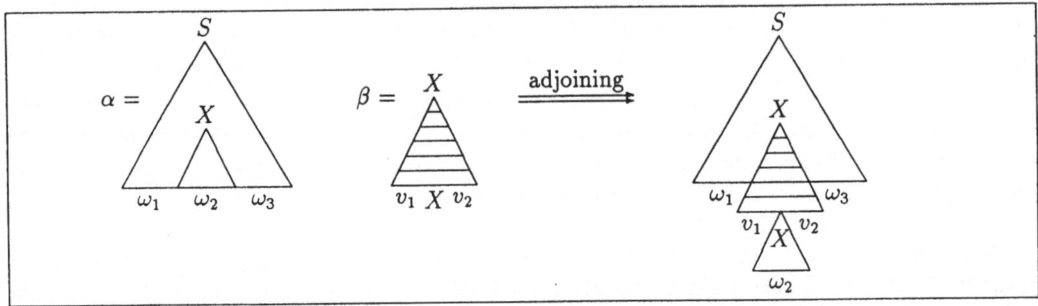

Figure 2: Elementary Trees and the Adjoining Operation in a TAG

The most obvious property of TAG trees which arises from the close relation with context–free derivation trees is the easy way to write and understand syntactic rules. The advantage over CFGs (context–free grammars) is that related facts can be described inside one rule (see, e.g., [Kroch & Joshi 85]). TAGs are more powerful than CFGs, they are mildly context–sensitive (cf. [Weir 88]). In the linguistic community, it is discussed controversially, how powerful a linguistic formalism should be (see, e.g., [Pullum 84]). Our decision for the TAG formalism is oriented at the thesis that natural language can be described very well by a mildly context-sensitive formalism.

One disadvantage of the TAG formalism is the redundancy of subtrees as a consequence of the relatively large size of the structures. One attempt to weaken this disadvantage is the introduction of a second combination operation – *substitution* – into the TAG formalism. This operation allows non-terminal leaves of elementary trees to be substituted by *substitution trees*. A substitution tree looks like an initial tree but the root node may be labelled with any nonterminal symbol. Substitution does not increase the power of the formalism because it can be eliminated by context–free preprocessing. Substitution nodes always mark places of obligatory expansions of a tree. A derivation tree is not completed until all substitutions have taken place.

The extensions of the TAG formalism that are described in the following are primarily linguistically motivated.

TAGs with Unification

Tree Adjoining Grammars – same as the CFGs – lack the necessary structures to express and compute complex attributes in the linguistic application domain, e.g., agreement. The encoding of such attributes (like person, number and case for nouns) in the category name (e.g., NP1plnom) leads to combinatory explosion of the grammar. In the framework of CFGs, this disadvantage is removed by combining the CFG with feature structures thereby defining a Unification Grammar (see [Shieber 86] for an introduction to Unification Grammar). This technique can also be applied to the TAG formalism. The formal definition is given in [Buschauer et al. 89] and in [Harbusch 90].

TAGs with Unification (UTAGs) allow each node of a tree to be associated with a list of specification rules. Such a rule consists either of a pair of two paths or of a path and a value. A path consists of a number uniquely referring to a node of an elementary tree followed by some feature names, e.g., ((0 pers) (01 pers)) means that the value of feature *person* must be shared by node 0 and node 01. If the second part of a rule is an atomic value then the rule specifies a 'definition'. All rules associated with nodes of a TAG tree are unified if there exists no contradiction between them, e.g., ((01 pers) 3) unified with ((001 pers) 2) and ((01 pers) (001 pers)) fails. The specification rules of a node are often represented as DAG (directed acyclic graph), where common prefixes are only represented once and different sons of a common prefix become brothers.

The trees in Figure 3 describe an example UTAG which allows the propagation of some syntactic information (here just the value of the feature *person*) from the lexical item "Mann" upwards. For

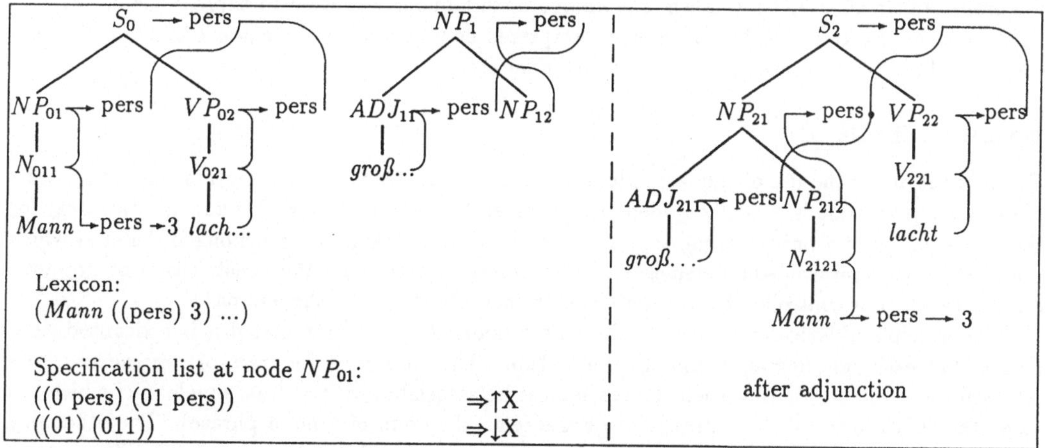

Figure 3: Trees of a TAG with Unification

reasons of simplification the determiner which is obligatory for the represented german sentence is left out. The example illustrates that information specified in DAGs at nodes can be propagated upwards as well as downwards in the tree. Thus there may be links (points of unification) between the DAGs all over the elementary tree, graphically represented as arcs in Figure 3. The question is how to manage these links during adjunction. If a node becomes an adjoining node it is replaced by an auxiliary tree. Thereby existing links from this node into the tree have to be cut and newly connected with parts of the auxiliary tree in order to fit in this tree correctly.

More formally spoken, we divide the specification lists of the adjoining node X into the three sets $\uparrow X$, $\downarrow X$ and oX, stressing the different partner nodes mentioned in the rule: $\uparrow X$ is the set of all specifications which relate X to its father or brothers in the tree, $\downarrow X$ is the set of all specifications which relate X to its sons, oX is the set of value definitions for X. During the adjoining with unification at a node X, first this node is replaced by the auxiliary tree. All links of X upwards and downwards in the tree are cut-off. Then the DAG of the root node of the auxiliary tree is unified with $\uparrow X$ and the DAG of the foot node is unified with $\downarrow X$ (see the links in the resulting tree in Figure 3). The value definitions of oX are reintroduced at positions in the auxiliary tree, which are computed by a specific inheritance examination (see [Buschauer et al. 89]), to avoid unexpected unification failures. It becomes clear that TAGs can be naturally combined with the extending unification to form a representation for specific linguistic terms.

LD/LP-TAGs

Another disadvantage of the TAG formalism as well as for context–free grammars is that both formalisms cannot handle the problem of free word order efficiently. Each constellation of leaves has to be expressed by an individual tree. For CFGs this disadvantage was eliminated by defining two sets: *Immediate Dominance Rules (ID–rules)* contain information about the sons of a node without specifying their ordering (e.g., (NP $\rightarrow$ DET, ADJ, N), which specifies the constituents of a noun phrase as determiner, adjective and noun, corresponds to the context–free rules which result from the permutation of the three constituents on the right side). *Linear Precedence rules (LP–rules)* restrict the set of permutations (e.g., DET $<$ ADJ produces only the context–free rules NP $\rightarrow$ DET ADJ N, NP $\rightarrow$ DET N ADJ and NP $\rightarrow$ N DET ADJ). This idea can be used for TAGs as well but with a slight modification. For CFGs the LP–rules are defined globally on the base of the nonterminals of the grammar. In the TAG formalism the unique node numbers are used to express the constraints on the elementary trees locally: Trees are interpreted as mobiles. In the name *LD/LP–UTAG* LD stands for Local Dominance (trees as domains of locality).

Lexicalized TAGs

The motivation for the use of the last extension of the formalism is the assumption that the process of syntactic generation is lexically guided (see [Kempen & Hoenkamp 87]): The adequate strategy for the verbalization of a preverbal message seems to be lexicalization, i.e. the choice of lemmas which are suitable to represent some elements of the message followed by the construction of syntactic structures which is controlled by syntactic constraints introduced by the lemmas.

The principle of lexical guidance can best be supported by the grammar if it is lexicalized, that means that each rule has an anchor in the lexicon. The constraint for trees of *Lexicalized TAGs* (cf. [Schabes et al. 88]) is that each structure must be associated with at least one lemma which has to be the lexical head of the represented phrase (e.g., the noun of a noun phrase). The other way round, each input lemma from the Text Design component can directly be associated with a tree of the Lexicalized TAG.

4.2   Adequacy of the Formalism for Incremental Generation

The extended domain of locality within the basic TAG formalism (in contrast to CFGs) allows to express many linguistic phenomena by single trees. This property remains valid in all of the presented extensions of the formalism. TAGs with Unification allow a detailed declarative description of all kinds of syntactic phenomena (e.g., the formulation of agreement between subject and predicate of a sentence). However, it must be mentioned that the use of unification results in a formalism which is no longer context–sensitive and probably too powerful for the representation of natural language. The LD/LP-extension that divides the grammar rules into a set of mobiles and a set of order restricting constraints allows a more compact description of syntactic structures and their possible linearizations. Finally lexicalization demands that TAG trees contain at least (and for practical purpose often just) their lexical head as a leaf so that the focus lies on the description of all obligatory parts required for this lexical entry, i.e. the subcategorization frame.

The adequacy of Lexicalized LD/LP-UTAGs for sentence generation in the WIP system must be examined with respect to the incremental mode of processing and the incorporation of the generation parameters.

The consequence of incremental processing through the components of the text generator is that the input to the Text Realization component – the lemmas – are given step by step, as soon as the corresponding concepts are chosen by the Presentation Planner and the lexical choice inside the Text Design component is done. To gain best efficiency these input elements should be processed by the Realizer as soon as possible. This presupposes that with each given input lemma a syntactic rule (a TAG tree) can be chosen at once. The lexicalization property of our formalism allows such a one to one correspondence between lexical items and syntactic structures whose respective heads they are. Remember the example of the conceptual addition of a modifier to a noun in Section 3. As soon as the noun "man" is given to the Text Realization component it can be mapped to a substitution tree with root *NP* and sole son *N*. This tree describes the complete phrase opened by the noun at this moment. The modifier "big" can be mapped to an auxiliary tree with leaf *ADJ* and root and foot node *NP* because it modifies a noun phrase.

With the given example it should be intuitively clear that each lemma can be associated with an appropriate lexicalized structure. The combination of these structures depends on the defined relations between the lemmas (which are also given as input) and can be handled by applying the grammar internal operations adjoining and substitution. In our example the auxiliary tree representing the modifier can be adjoined into the NP node of the substitution tree.

Notice, that a given lexical item can be associated with a whole set of alternative syntactic representations instead of exactly one lexicalized tree. Another possible realization of the modifier "big" could be a relative clause with the verb "to be" ("which is big"). A specific choice on such sets of rules is possible by using the given parameter settings, so the size of knowledge base entities seems adequate again.

5 The Architecture of the Syntax Generation Component

The integration of the syntax generation component into the WIP system imposes some specific requirements upon its architecture. They are described in the next section as well as some more general software engineering demands. The effects of an incremental processing mode on the architecture are shown in Section 5.2.

5.1 Requirements and Design Criteria for our Generator

To produce interrelated multimodal output – the overall task of the WIP system – its two mode specific generators must influence each other. They must be able to communicate. For this purpose the Document History Handler serves as a shared medium. One example for *crossmodal references* between the different modes is the generation of "middle knob" versus "left knob" for the same object in the knowledge representation according to its different graphical realizations, where the same knob can be seen either between two other knobs or – with another perspective in an enlargement of a part of the picture – as the leftmost of two knobs (cf. [Wahlster et al. 91]).

Another relation to surrounding components of the WIP system is indicated by the *feedback* arrow from the Text Realization component back to the Text Design component shown in the architecture in Figure 1. The syntax generator must be able to signal back a fail during its processing which can lead to revision processes in higher components.

By means of the incoming parameter settings the WIP system should be able to trigger the production of different utterances. This results in a *flexible* output medium which can be used to produce appropriate presentations for different users and which can be easily expanded by further parameter values, e.g., new categories of users.

The use of the WIP system in its online presentation mode where illustrated documents are shown on the screen – in contrast to the production of a whole document in batch mode – demands that the response time of the system should be acceptable for the user. The response time can be shortened and better *efficiency* can be gained by *incremental processing* which itself can be supported by parallelism (see Section 3). This demands of the generator to process its input in a piecemeal fashion and to be able to integrate later specified input into already produced partial processing results.

In the following we describe some more general aspects which are important for the architecture of our generator.

By identifying different processes within the overall task of natural language generation they can be treated in distinct modules of the system (see Figure 4) leading to a *modular design*. They differ with respect to the used knowledge and/or methods. This separation makes it easier to test and exchange single components. Examples for tasks which can be isolated are the inflection of lexemes, linearization or the selection of grammar trees.

A strict separation of knowledge sources and operations, i.e. a declarative formulation of the knowledge sources, supports the transparency of the descriptions and the *extendability* and *adaptability* of the system. For the grammar and the lexica this is very common. In addition to that there are further knowledge sources (see, e.g., the Meta–Rule box described in Section 5.2), which are declaratively specified. Another advantage of this technique is that the operations can be developed without a detailed consideration of the actual content of the knowledge sources.

Of course, the produced utterances should obey the grammar rules of the target language, resulting in *grammatically correct* surface sentences.

5.2   The Individual Components

The individual components of the generator and their relations are shown in Figure 4.

The left side of the architecture shows the connections of the generator to other components of the WIP system. In the following they are shortly described together with the modules of the syntax generator (on the right side of the picture) which use them. For more details see [Harbusch et al. 91].

The goal of the utterance contains content words and their functional relations. It is passed stepwise to the *Interface* which selects the corresponding elementary trees for the lemmas. This selection varies according to the setting of the parameters. For example, the parameters which concern resources like space and execution time of the utterance can lead to the selection of "less expensive" trees (e.g., if a modifier of a noun shall be verbalized, an adjective phrase is preferred to a relative clause). Combinations of parameters must be explicitly controlled because they can contradict or strengthen each other. The selection relative to the parameter setting is done by declarative rules in the left Meta–Rule box.

An object in a *distributed parallel model* is created for each input element in order to process the chosen tree set. Trees in a lexicalized TAG have an adequate size which allows the objects to manage exactly the local syntactic and semantic information of the incoming concepts. The task of verbalization is distributed among several active objects which try to work as independent as possible. This introduces "fine–grained" parallelism into our generator in addition to the "coarse–grained" parallelism resulting from the cascaded architecture of the text generator as a whole.

In the *Phrase Formulator* the objects attempt to combine their locally represented trees with those of other objects according to the specified conceptual information using the TAG operations

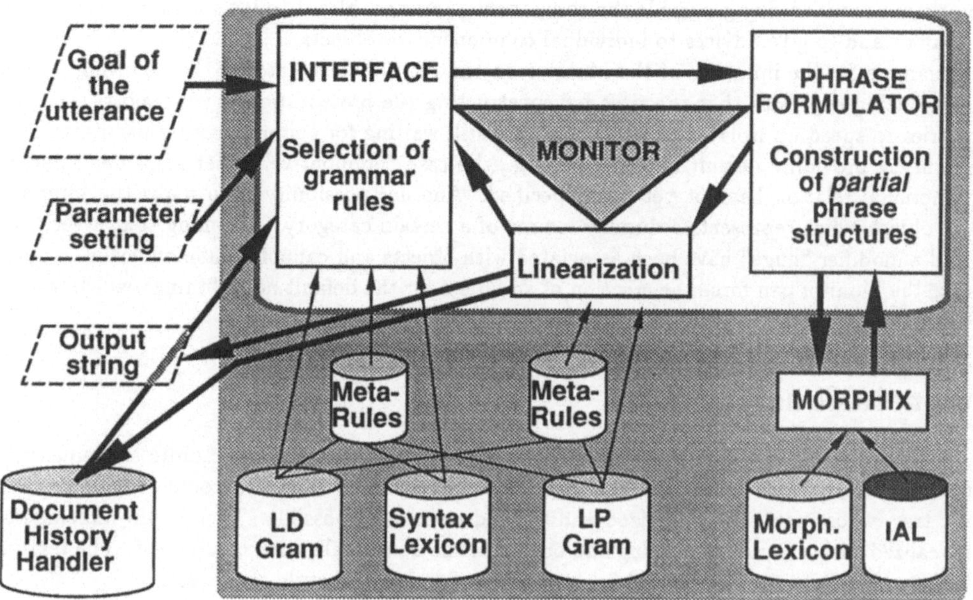

Figure 4: The Architecture of the Syntax Generator

substitution and adjunction. According to the separation of the grammar into an LD- and an LP–part the combination operations are performed without regarding linear precedence constraints.

Since a distributed parallel model is used and the objects have to communicate and exchange data during these attempts, it follows that the overall task of verbalization cannot optimally be parallelized. Optimal parallelism would mean that the objects could run totally independent of each other. However, partial phrase structures can be simultaneously assembled at different nodes. To avoid inconsistency the following restriction is imposed on the objects: They must not participate in more than one communication at a time. Each object controls an own history of its represented structures which is expanded after a successful communication. This history will be used if a combination of structures must be retracted (e.g., in the case of syntactic dead–ends which are likely to occur during incremental generation).

The fact that objects represent sets of trees enables the objects to create several alternative partial structures as paraphrases at the same time. The decision between the alternatives must be made when an object hands over some structure to the Linearization component.

The inflection of the lemmas according to morphosyntactic information which has been collected in the DAGs is performed by the package MORPHIX (see [Finkler & Neumann 88]).

The *Linearization* component tests whether a partial phrase can be uttered next – i.e. according to the text already uttered and the associated LP–rules. In that case, the surface string is sent to the output window. In the case that incoming partial structures cannot be integrated to the existing linearized structure, the Linearization component informs the Interface component to choose new phrase structures for the embedded lemmas. The second Meta–Rule box contains rules which direct the new selection.

Interface, Phrase Formulator and Linearization component seem to work sequentially. But with the central control instance – the *Monitor* component – an integrated system has been constructed. Since the Monitor is attached to each of the three components it can identify all transitions of data between them as well as changes inside the components. This enables it to have a global view of the states of affair and to give advices to individual components or objects.

One example for the influence of the Monitor on the Phrase Formulator is the following: If the parameter setting expresses that the time for constructing the presentation is very short, then the monitor tries to speed up isolated objects which are still waiting for communication partners. This can be done by providing default information, e.g., the case "nominative" is set for a noun phrase whose functional relation has not yet been specified. Another possibility is to make the Interface create an object which represents a dummy lemma of a certain category. Assuming that a verb "to burn" and a modifier "huge" have been associated with objects and cannot combine because a noun is missing, the Monitor can force the creation of an object for the default noun "thing" which results in the alarming utterance: "A huge thing burns."

6 Conclusions

Lexicalized LD/LP-TAGs with Unification provide a set of adequate linguistic units as elementary structures. The trees can be chosen and processed incrementally and are combined to a whole syntactic tree, whose parts are linearized and uttered as soon as possible. Thereby an incremental mode is realized within input, processing and output of the Text Realization component. The textual output of an AI system can be speeded up by using an incremental style of processing.

We have implemented a first prototype (see [Schauder 90]) separated from other components of the WIP system. The input is simulated and there is just one fixed combination of parameters (target language German, no time or space restrictions, free style). All central components of the generator – Interface, Phrase Formulator, Linearization component and Monitor – are basically implemented, but with restricted features. A grammar is prototypically realized which covers a small part of German. The inflection component MORPHIX is embedded as a complete module.

Our experience with the prototype is very promising. The separation of generation tasks into the presented components has shown to be an adequate solution. The definition of active objects in a distributed parallel model has turned out to be realizable and will be used more intensively within the system.

Acknowledgements

We would like to thank Tilman Becker and Christoph Kilger for their valuable suggestions.

References

[Buschauer et al. 89] B. Buschauer, P. Poller, A. Schauder, K. Harbusch: *Parsing natürlicher Sprache: Tree Adjoining Grammars mit Unifikation*, "AI-Laboratory" Memo in press, Department of Computer Science, University of the Saarland, Saarbrücken, 1989

[Finkler & Neumann 88] W. Finkler, G. Neumann: *MORPHIX: A Fast Realization of a Classification-Based Approach to Morphology*, Proceedings of the fourth ÖGAI, Wiener Workshop Wissensbasierte Sprachverarbeitung, Wien, 1988

[Finkler & Neumann 89] W. Finkler, G. Neumann: *POPEL–HOW: A Distributed Parallel Model for Incremental Natural Language Production with Feedback*, Proceedings of the 11th IJCAI, Detroit, 1989

[Harbusch 90] K. Harbusch: *Constraining Tree Adjoining Grammars by Unification*, Proceedings of the 13th International Conference on Computational Linguistics (COLING'90), Helsinki, 1990

[Harbusch et al. 91] K. Harbusch, W. Finkler, A. Schauder, T. Becker, B. Buschauer, P. Poller: *Generation with Tree Adjoining Grammar in the WIP project*, forthcoming, German Research Center for Artificial Intelligence, Saarbrücken, 1991

[Joshi et al. 75] A. Joshi, L. Levy, M. Takahashi: *Tree Adjunct Grammars*, Journal of the Computer and Systems Science, Volume 10, No 1, 136-163, 1975

[Joshi 85] A. Joshi: *An Introduction to Tree Adjoining Grammars*, Technical Report MS-CIS-86-64, LINC-LAB-31, Department of Computer and Information Science, University of Pennsylvania, Philadelphia, Pennsylvania, 1985

[Kempen 78] G. Kempen: Sentence construction by a psychologically plausible formulator, in R. Campbell, P. Smith (eds.): *Recent advances in the psychology of language*, Plenum Press, New York, 1978

[Kempen & Hoenkamp 87] G. Kempen, E. Hoenkamp: *An incremental procedural grammar for sentence formulation*, Cognitive Science, Volume 11, 201-258, 1987

[Kroch & Joshi 85] A. Kroch, A. Joshi: *Linguistic Relevance of Tree Adjoining Grammars*, Technical Report MS-CIS-85-16, Department of Computer and Information Science, University of Pennsylvania, Philadelphia, Pennsylvania, 1985

[Levelt 89] W. Levelt: *Speaking: From Intention to Articulation*, The MIT Press, Cambridge, Massachusetts, 1989

[Pullum 84] G. Pullum: *On two Recent Attempts to show that English is not a CFL*, Computational Linguistics, Volume 10, No 4, 1984

[Schabes et al. 88] Y. Schabes, A. Abeillé, A. Joshi: *Parsing Strategies with Lexicalized Grammars: Application to Tree Adjoining Grammar*, Proceedings of the 12th International Conference on Computational Linguistics (COLING'88), Budapest, 1988

[Schauder 90] A. Schauder: *Inkrementelle syntaktische Generierung natürlicher Sprache mit Tree Adjoining Grammars*, Master's Thesis, Department of Computer Science, University of the Saarland, Saarbrücken, 1990

[Shieber 86] S. Shieber: *An Introduction to Unification-based Approaches to Grammar*, CSLI Lecture Notes, No. 4, Stanford University, Stanford, California, 1986

[Wahlster et al. 91] W. Wahlster, E. André, W. Graf, T. Rist: *Designing Illustrated Texts: How Language Production is influenced by Graphics Generation*, Fifth Conference of the European Chapter of the ACL, Berlin, 1991

[Weir 88] D. Weir: *Characterizing mildly context-sensitive grammar formalisms*, PhD Thesis, Department of Computer and Information Science, University of Pennsylvania, Philadelphia, Pennsylvania, 1988

Linking Typed Feature Formalisms and Terminological Knowledge Representation Languages in Natural Language Front-Ends

Rolf Backofen, Harald Trost, Hans Uszkoreit
Deutsches Forschungszentrum für Künstliche Intelligenz (DFKI)
Stuhlsatzenhausweg 3
6600 Saarbrücken 11
e-mail: backofen@dfki.uni-sb.de

Abstract

In this paper we describe an interface between typed feature formalisms and terminological languages like KL-ONE. The definition of such an interface is motivated by the needs of natural language front-ends to AI-systems where information must be transmitted from the front-end to the back-end system and vice versa.

We show how some minor extensions to the feature formalism allow for a syntactic description of individual concepts in terms of typed feature structures. Namely, we propose to include intervals and a special kind of sets. Partial consistency checks can be made on these concept descriptions during the unification of feature terms. Type checking on these special types involves calling the classifier of the terminological language. The final consistency check is performed only when transferring these concept descriptions into structures of the A-Box of the terminological language.

1 Introduction

Typed feature formalisms[1] are currently the most successful means for representing linguistic knowledge. There is even a tendency to extend their use to linguistic levels like semantics (e.g. in HPSG [PS87]) and phonology (e.g. [Col90]) and [Wie90]) which were traditionally described in different notations.

A number of terminological languages like KL-ONE[2] have been implemented during the last few years. They are theoretically well-understood and are widely used for the representation of world and domain knowledge in various types of AI-systems.

For natural language front-ends which are used in dialog situations, a continous communication with the back-end system (e.g. a planning component) is required. Consequently, there is a need to transmit pieces of information between these two components. Since each component encodes information in its own representation language it must be possible to exchange information between these two languages.

One can think of two different approaches for managing this communication process. The first one is to create a unique formalism to represent both kinds of knowledge. But this seems not to be very promising because the resulting formalism becomes to powerful to allow for efficient processing. Moreover, the modularity of the different knowledge bases would not be preserved, i.e. the natural

---

[1] for an overview see, e.g., [Shi86] or [Smo88]
[2] for an overview see, e.g., [NS90]

language front end would impose too strict requirements on the representation formalism the back-end system makes use of.

Therefore we opt for the second strategy, namely linking both formalisms via a syntactic translation. To tyhis end we encode concept descriptions in a special subtype of feature structures which entails the concept type, the set of role-value-maps, and role descriptions. Such a role description will contain the information associated to one role, for example the number restriction and the value restriction. Furthermore we have to provide for the ability to invoke the KL-ONE realizer on the translation of such structures.

We have organized the paper in such a way that we start by giving a syntax and a semantics for both feature formalism and terminological language. We then discuss the differences between the two formalisms. We sketch the workings of our interface which in turn motivates some minor extensions to the feature formalism. These extensions are discussed in some detail. At this point we are in the situation to describe how concept descriptions from the terminological language can be represented in terms of typed feature structures in this extended formalism. Finally we show how a partial consistency check on these concept descriptions can be performed during unification.

2 Typed Feature Logic

Typed feature formalisms as they are used in todays language processing systems have evolved from directed acyclic graphs (e.g., the PATR system [Kar86]). To allow for a more adequate description of linguistic data that formalism was extended in several ways. One very important extension was to allow for the use of disjunction. Another extension was the integration of types or sorts into the formalism. Many other extensions have been proposed and implemented in various systems. In the following we will define a core feature formalism which is provided with all the features which are important with regard to the interface definition.

2.1 Syntax

For the basic definition of feature terms we assume a *signature* Σ, which consists of a set of *variables* $\mathcal{V}$ (written $x, y, \ldots$), *features* $\mathcal{F}$ (written $f, g, \ldots$) and *atoms* $\mathcal{A}$ (written $a, b, \ldots$). Additionally, the language allows for the use of type symbols $A, B, C, \ldots \in \mathcal{T}$. On $\mathcal{T}$ a partial order $\preceq$ is defined with $\top \in \mathcal{T}$ as the greatest and $\bot \in \mathcal{T}$ as the least element (usually called *top* and *bottom*, respectively). The operator $\prec$ induces a lower semilattice on $\mathcal{T}$ (that means for every $A, B \in \mathcal{T}$ the greatest lower bound $GLB(A, B)$ is in $\mathcal{T}$). All these sets are pairwise disjoint.

Although feature terms can be seen as data objects with some internal structure, it is formally handier to describe them as complex constraints built out of primitive ones using conjunction and disjunction. The set of all *feature terms* is then given by the following context-free production rules:

$$
\begin{array}{rcll}
s, t & \longrightarrow & A & \text{a sort} \\
 & | & x & \text{a variable} \\
 & | & a & \text{an atom} \\
 & | & f : x & \text{selection} \\
 & | & \neg x & \text{negated coreference} \\
 & | & s \sqcap t & \text{conjunction} \\
 & | & s \sqcup t & \text{disjunction}
\end{array}
$$

2.2 Semantics

There is a set theoretic semantics for feature terms, which is defined in terms of interpretations (see e.g. [Smo88]. An interpretation $\mathcal{I} = (D^{\mathcal{I}}, \cdot^{\mathcal{I}})$ consists of a *domain* $D^{\mathcal{I}}$ and an interpretation function such that the following conditions are satisfied:

1. $\top^{\mathcal{I}} = D^{\mathcal{I}}$ and $\perp^{\mathcal{I}} = \emptyset$

2. for all sorts $A, B : GLB(A, B)^{\mathcal{I}} = A^{\mathcal{I}} \cap B^{\mathcal{I}}$

3. every feature f is map to a function $f^{\mathcal{I}} : D^{\mathcal{I}} \mapsto D^{\mathcal{I}}$

4. for every feature f and every atom $a : a \notin \mathbf{ran}(f^{\mathcal{I}})$

For assigning a meaning to an expression containing variables, it is necessary to introdoce *variable assignment*. An assignment α is a function $\alpha : \mathcal{V} \mapsto D^{\mathcal{I}}$ and maps every variable of $\mathcal{V}$ to an element of the interpretation domain. The *denotation* of a feature term s under a valuation α in $\mathcal{I}$ is a subset of $D^{\mathcal{I}}$, which is defined inductively as:

1. $[\![x]\!]_{\alpha}^{\mathcal{I}} := \{\alpha(x)\}$ for a variable x,

2. $[\![a]\!]_{\alpha}^{\mathcal{I}} := \{a^{\mathcal{I}}\}$ for an atom a,

3. $[\![f : t]\!]_{\alpha}^{\mathcal{I}} := \{d \in D^{\mathcal{I}} \mid f^{\mathcal{I}}(d) \in [\![t]\!]_{\alpha}^{\mathcal{I}}\}$

The denotation $[\![s]\!]^{\mathcal{I}}$ of s in $\mathcal{I}$ is defined as

$$\bigcup_{\alpha \text{ valuation on } \mathcal{I}} [\![s]\!]_{\alpha}^{\mathcal{I}}$$

A feature term s is *consistent*, if there is an interpretation $\mathcal{I}$ with $[\![s]\!]^{\mathcal{I}} \neq \emptyset$.

2.3 Subsumtion and unification

Computationally, the two main operations are *subsumtion* and *unification*. A feature term s is said to be subsumed by a feature term t (abrev. $s \sqsubseteq t$) iff in every interpretation $\mathcal{I}$ the denotation of s is a subset of $[\![t]\!]^{\mathcal{I}}$. The relation $\sqsubseteq$ induces a lower semilattice that can be viewed as the extension of the type hierachy to the set of feature terms.

The most commonly used operation is unification. Unification takes two different terms as arguments and decides whether the conjunction of both terms is consistent. This consistency check is performed by rewriting the conjunction into a so-called *solved normal form*. This form is also the result of the unification operation. If during rewriting a clash occurs, the conjunction is inconsistent and unification fails. For details on rewriting rules see e.g. [Smo88] or [Smo89]

3 Terminological languages

Knowledge representation systems of the KL-ONE family make a distinction between terminological and assertional knowledge. The first one is stored in the so-called *T-Box* and describes the world (or domain) knowledge. The latter one is gathered in the so-called *A-Box* and describes the actual state of the world (or domain).

Although there exist many different systems with different syntax, one can define an abstract KL-ONE system, the properties of which are shared by most of the existing systems. The terminological formalism consists of a concept description language in order to define concepts and relations between concepts. The relations are called roles and are always binary. Main parts of the following abstract definition are taken from [Hol90].

3.1 Syntax and semantics of our terminological language

We assume two disjoint alphabets of symbols, called *concepts* (written A, B) and *roles* (denoted by R, S). There are two special concept symbols $\top$ and $\bot$. Then *concept descriptions* (written C, D) are defined by the following production rules:

$$
\begin{array}{lll}
C, D \longmapsto & A & \text{atomic concept} \\
\mid & C \sqcap D & \text{conjunction} \\
\mid & \forall R.C & \text{value restriction} \\
\mid & (\geq n\ R) \mid (\leq n\ R) & \text{number restrictions, } n \in \mathbb{N}
\end{array}
$$

An interpretation $\mathcal{I} = (D^{\mathcal{I}}, \mathcal{I}[\cdot])$ of a concept description consists of a set $D^{\mathcal{I}}$ (the domain of $\mathcal{I}$) and an interpretation function $\mathcal{I}[\cdot]$ such that the following holds:

1. For every concept description C and for every role R: $\mathcal{I}[C] \subseteq D^{\mathcal{I}}$ and $\mathcal{I}[R] \subseteq D^{\mathcal{I}} \times D^{\mathcal{I}}$.

2. $\mathcal{I}[\bot]$ is the empty set and $\mathcal{I}[\top]$ the whole domain.

3. The conjunction $\sqcap$ is interpreted as set intersection.

4. The following equations are satisfied:

$$
\begin{array}{rcl}
\mathcal{I}[\forall R.C] &=& \{a \in D^{\mathcal{I}} \mid \forall (a, b) \in \mathcal{I}[R] : b \in \mathcal{I}[C]\} \\
\mathcal{I}[(\geq n\ R)] &=& \{a \in D^{\mathcal{I}} \mid |\{b \in D^{\mathcal{I}} \mid (a, b) \in \mathcal{I}[R]\}| \geq n\} \\
\mathcal{I}[(\leq n\ R)] &=& \{a \in D^{\mathcal{I}} \mid |\{b \in D^{\mathcal{I}} \mid (a, b) \in \mathcal{I}[R]\}| \leq n\}
\end{array}
$$

Consistency and subsumtion of concept descriptions are defined as in the feature logic formalism. With the notion of concept description we can now define the T-Box and the A-Box. The T-Box consists of a finite set of concept definitions. Each definition has either the form $A \doteq C$ or $A \sqsubseteq C$, where A is a concept and C is a description. An interpretation $\mathcal{I}$ is a model of a terminolgy (T-Box) iff every definition holds in $\mathcal{I}$. This is equivalent to the following conditions:

$$
\begin{array}{l}
\mathcal{I}[A] \subseteq \mathcal{I}[C] \text{ for every } A \sqsubseteq C \in \text{T-Box} \\
\mathcal{I}[A] = \mathcal{I}[C] \text{ for every } A \doteq C \in \text{T-Box.}
\end{array}
$$

Now let's turn to the assertional part (the A-Box). As previously mentioned, the A-Box describes the actual state of the world. This is done in terms of individuation, that means introducing individual objects. The A-Box contains a finite sets of propositions about these individuals. Each proposition states either that one individual is of some sort or that two individuals are connect by a role. The syntax for those propositions is given by

$$
\begin{array}{ll}
a : A & \text{(sort subsumtion)} \\
(a, b) : R & \text{(role instantiation)}
\end{array}
$$

where a, b are individuals.

Formally, individuals are treated as constants and the interpetation function is extended to these constants. The notion of model is also extended to the A-Box in a straightforward way.

Supplementary, some systems contain another kind of constraints in the terminological formalism, namely *role value maps*. With role value maps one can enforce the equivalence of two sets of elements. Each set is obtained by successively following a chain of roles starting from the same element.

3.2 Computational services

There are two kinds of operations which are usually available in terminological formalisms, namely *classifier* and *realizer*. Classifying a T-Box means to calculate the subsumtion hierarchy of concepts. With the realizer one determines for a given individual the least concept the individual is subsumed by[3].

---

[3]For a precise description of these features see [Hol90].

4 Differences between the two formalisms

Although feature logic formalisms and terminological languages have a similar semantics there are significant differences. The most important of these differences are:

- Feature formalisms use functional roles while terminological languages allow for relational roles, where the cardinality of the filler set may be restricted by an integer interval called number restriction.

- To express the fact that certain roles must have an identical filler feature formalisms use the notion of coreference (there is also current research on integrating negated coreference). Most terminological languages employ the somewhat broader concept of role value maps where a number of operators besides equality may be used.

- Terminological languages distinguish between conceptual and assertional level (i.e. concept vs. instance) while feature formalisms do not make this distinction.

- Typed feature formalisms usually support general disjunction (and sometimes negation) while only a very limited notion of disjunction is available in terminological languages (at least at the level of terminological description).

In conclusion, one may say that terminological languages tend to be more expressive than typed feature formalisms. But for most tasks in natural language processing the expressiveness of typed feature formalisms is adequate.

5 Linking the two formalisms via a syntactic translation

As mentioned, we want to encode concept descriptions within feature structures, which can be translated into the KL-ONE system whenever necessary (these objects are called *syntactic concept descriptions*). The semantics of such an object will be the set of all instances in the KL-ONE systems, which satisfies the translation of the syntactic description. During unification we want to do partial consistency check. A full consistency check is done by evaluating the translation of the description within the KL-ONE system.

To this end we need to extend the expressive power of the feature logic by numeric intervals for encoding the number restriction and some sort of set values for describing filler sets. The extension should be easily integrable whithin an existing unification formalism. Although both extensions can be integrated independently they will influence each other in our context. This has some effects on the way such constraints are evaluated. Although one can think of a combine constraint, which partially describes the filler set *and* the lower and upper bound of its cardinality, we didn't choose this alternative. One reason for us to keep both distinct is that we do want to keep the extension of the feature logic as simple as possible. Another reason is that these constraints can be used for other purposes too (e.g. one could use the intervals to encode position features).

5.1 Extensions to feature logic for coping with concept descriptions

5.1.1 Intervals

The first extension are numeric intervals. The syntax of such intervals is given by

$$[i..j] \quad \text{with } i \in \mathbb{N}_0, j \in \mathbb{N} \cup \{\infty\} \text{ and } i < j$$

The semantics of the interval constraint is just the set of all (natural) numbers in the range of the interval.

The rewriting rules for intervals have the following form:

$$(R1) \quad [i_1..j_1] \sqcap [i_2..j_2] \longrightarrow [\max(i_1, i_2), .., \min(j_1, j_2)]$$

$$(R2) \quad [i..j] \sqcap a \longrightarrow a$$

$$(R3) \quad [i..j] \sqcap f\!:\!s(\text{resp. } \sqcap A\,) \longrightarrow \perp.$$

This means that no features are defined on intervals and that they are not element of some type.

5.1.2 Set values

The second extension are set values which are necessary for the description of sets of possible fillers. One can distinguish different ways to treat the cardinality of set values. Cardinality can be restricted in two different ways: via abstraction or via enumeration. Abstraction means to use an additional constraint restricting the cardinality of the set value (e.g. the cardinality is between n and m, $n < m$). But this seems to make no sense in our context. Let $s_1, \ldots, s_n$ be some description of the elements of the set value. As the cardinality is only restricted by abstraction and not by enumeration, there could be additional elements not mentioned yet. Moreover, because feature terms are only partial descriptions, some of the s_i could denote the same element (the set may even shrink to a single element in extreme cases). Consequently, such a kind of set value is too vague in order to be useful.

For enumeration there are two different possibilities. Let again $s_1, \ldots, s_n$ be some description of the elements of the set value. In the first case every element of the interpretation of the set value must fit into some description of s_i. Again some s_i could collapse. Therefore n is only an upper bound for the cardinality (for an example of such set values see [PM89]). But in terminological languages filler sets may have no upper bound (i.e. the upper bound equals ∞). Such a situation cannot be modeled with this approach.

Therefore we have decided for a second possibility. Here $s_1, \ldots, s_n$ are an an enumeration of *distinct* elements of the set value. As a result n defines the lower bound for the cardinality of the set value. This means, that the unique name assumption has to be applied to $s_1, \ldots, s_n$.

Now let's turn to the definition of these set values. Set values can appear at every point within feature structures. The syntax is given by

$$s, t \quad \longrightarrow \quad \ldots$$
$$\mid \quad \{s_1, \ldots, s_n\} \quad \text{sets}$$

where $s_1, \ldots, s_n$ are feature terms.

For the set values we have the following semantics:

$$[\![\{s_1, \ldots, s_n\}]\!]_\alpha^I := \{m \in 2^{D^I} \mid \exists d_1..d_n : \bigwedge_{i \neq j} d_i \neq d_j \ \wedge \ \forall i : [d_i \in [\![s_i]\!]_\alpha^I \wedge d_i \in m]\} \tag{1}$$

The first condition in (1) is exactly the before-mentioned unique name assumption for the objects w.r.t the set-value[4]. With this condition one ensures that set values will never shrink.

Our sets are lower bound by enumeration and one could not give an upper bound for the set value by enumeration at the same time[5]. Therefore the semantics of a set value is the set of all possibly extensions of $\{[\![s_1]\!]_\alpha^I, \ldots, [\![s_n]\!]_\alpha^I\}$ (c.f. the second condition in (1)).

Given this semantics for set values, the conjunction of two set values (unification) describes all sets which at least contain all the elements of both set values. Because these elements are only partially described some of the elements of each set value could collapse.

This leads to the following extensions of the rewriting rules:

---

[4]We think that it in the framework of linguistic processing a unique name assumption in general makes no sense. Such an assumption would state that in every interpretation the denotation consist of a singleton set. Although one can think of introducing such an assumption for some elements of the set value, this could not be applied to all members of set values, because then no elements of different set values could ever collapse.

[5]This would lead to sets with fixed arity. Besides the fact that this is not suitable for describing set values such set values would not describe real sets anymore. Such set values would best be interpreted as fixed arity terms.

$(R4)$ $x \sqcap t\langle\{\ldots, x \sqcap t, \ldots\}\rangle \longrightarrow \bot$ Here $t\langle s\rangle$ denotes a pure conjunctive term which has s as an subterm.

$(R5)$ $\{\ldots, x, \ldots, x \ldots\} \longrightarrow \bot$

$(R6)$ $\{z_1, \ldots, z_l, s_1 \ldots, s_n\} \sqcap \{z_1', \ldots, z_l', t_1 \ldots, t_m\} \longrightarrow$

$$\bigsqcup_{k=1}^{\min(n,m)} \quad \bigsqcup_{\substack{I \subseteq \{1,\ldots,n\} \\ J \subseteq \{1,\ldots,m\} \\ |I| = |J| = k}} \quad \bigsqcup_{\phi \in I^J} \{ (z_1 \sqcap z_1'), \ldots, (z_l \sqcap z_l'), (s_{i_1} \sqcap t_{\phi(j_1)}), \ldots, (s_{i_k} \sqcap t_{\phi(j_k)}), x_{i_{k+1}}, y_{j_{k+1}}, \ldots, x_{i_n}, y_{j_m} \}$$

where $(z_1, z_1'), \ldots, (z_l, z_l')$ is the set of element pairs which share the same variable, $i_1, \ldots, i_k$ resp. $j_1 \ldots, j_k$ some arbitrary but fixed enumeration of I resp. J and $i_{k+1}, \ldots, i_n$ resp. $j_{k+1} \ldots, j_m$ an enumeration of the remaining elements.

Here are some comments on this set of rules. Rule R4 guarantees that there are no cycles envoling set values. This guarantees that the given set rewrite rules will always terminate[6]. Rule R5 is the before-mentioned unique name assumtion. Instead of introducing this rule we could have stated this assumtion using negated coreferences.

Now let us turn to R6, the most complex rule. Applying R6 during every unification is neither intended nor would the resulting algorithm be tractable. In this rule the value of k is the number of elements that have to be identified in order to get a set value with lower bound $n + m - k$. The problem that occurs during unification of set values is that one has different descriptions for the elements of the generated set value. In the regular case many of them will be identified during further linguistic processing. This enlarges the set of common elements $z_1 \ldots z_l$ which will in turn make it easier to apply this rule. Therefore we delay evaluation of rule R6.

Moreover, applying this rule would not be necessary if there where no restriction on the cardinality of the set. But in our application this is the case, because the cardinality of the filler set is constrained by the number restriction. For checking the consistency it suffices to identify as many elements as necessary to satisfy the number restriction.

5.2 Encoding of concept description

For the encoding of concept descriptions we use a special class of feature terms, which have some given structure[7]. All such special feature terms are typed by a KL-ONE concept. The features which are defined on such terms correspond to role names of the KL-ONE concepts and have again some distinguished structure. We will call a subclass of feature terms *role descriptions*. Role descriptions consist of three different feature-value pairs. The first entry contains a numeric interval for the number restriction, the second stores the value restriction. The last entry contains a set value for the description of the filler set, whose members are again syntactic concept descriptions.

The encoding of the concept descriptions is organized such that the unification of two syntactic concept descriptions results in a syntactic concept description the translation of which is equivalent to the conjunction of the translation of the input structures. Furthermore, unification does some partial consistency check:

1. combining the concept types (by calling the classifier in order to find the glb of both types)

2. unifying role descriptions of roles shared by both input structures. Within this process the type of the value restriction is calculated (see 1) and the conjunction of the number restrictions is determined by interval intersection.

---

[6]We assume that allowing cycles involving set values would lead to undecidability (because of the simliarity of coreference and role value-maps of length 1)

[7]Such structural information could be stated using type definitions and closed types

A full consistency check is made transferring such structures to the KL-ONE System. As we have shown, it is sensible to delay the unification of set values until such a full consistency check.

Now let's turn to the translation of such syntactic concept descriptions. A straight-forward semantics for the translation is to assign a fixed KL-ONE instance to each syntactic concept description. But the notion of an underspecified KL-ONE instance does not fit to the notion of underspecification used in feature logics. A KL-ONE instance is underspecified in the sense, that it denotes one specific object the properties of which are only partially known. Underspecification in feature logic on the other hand means that a description denotes the set of all objects satisfying the description. Different descriptions can be satisfied by the same object, whereas different instances can never be equal.

This leads to an interpretation of concept descriptions as the set of all instances in the terminological language, which satisfies the translation of the description. But, as mentioned, only a partial consistency check is made during unification, which means that the set is possibly empty. There are two ways to check whether there exists some element satisfying the translation of a description. The first one is to classify the translated description within the T-Box of the KR-system. But we assume that it is not useful to change the terminology during processing. Therefore we use the second approch via Skolemisation, namely to create a new instance satisfying the description.

For the translation of a syntactic concept description we have to translate the syntactic concept descriptions that are contained in the set values of the filler entries. To do this we have perform the delayed set value unifications for this entry. As mentioned in the discussion of rule R6, we have to identify only as many elements such that the resulting filler set fits into the number restriction.

6 Conclusion

In work on natural language front-ends there is the problem of exchanging information with the back-end system. A prerequisite for such an exchange is that the respective knowledge bases of front-end and back-end are compatible with each other.

In this paper we have described a method for the linking of typed feature formalisms and terminological languages. The basic idea is to describe structures from the terminological language syntactically in the feature formalism. Such a syntactic description is possible with only minor extensions to the feature formalism. Furthermore, we can perform a partial consistency check on these structures during unification which helps in reducing spurious ambiguities at an early stage of processing.

Such a method of linking the two formalisms via an explicit interface is preferable to creating a unique more powerful formalism for two reasons. First, the expressiveness of terminological languages is not necessary at most stages of linguistic processing. Second, the interface approach leads to a more modular systems architecture because the back-end system may keep its own distinct formalism.

References

[Col90] J. Coleman. Unifikation phonology. In H. Karlgren, editor, *COLING-90*, volume 3, pages 79–84. Helsinki, 1990.

[Hol90] Bernhard Hollunder. Hybrid inferences in KL-ONE-based knowledge representation systems. Research Report RR-90-06, Deutsches Forschungszentrum für künstliche Intelligenz, Saarbrücken, May 1990.

[Kar86] Lauri Karttunen. D-PATR: a development environment for unification-based grammars. In *Proceedings of the COLING'86*, volume 1, pages 74–80. Budapest, 1986.

[NS90]   Bernhard Nebel and Gert Smolka. Representation and reasoning with attributive descriptions. In K.H. Blæsius, U. Hedtstueck, and C.R. Rollinger, editors, *Sorts and Types in Artificial Intelligence*. Springer, Berlin, 1990.

[PM89]   Carl J. Pollard and M. Drew Moshier. Unifying partial descriptions of sets. In P. Hansen, editor, *Information, Language and Cognition*, volume 1 of *Vancouver Studies in Cognitive Sience*. University of British Columbia Press, Vancouver, 1989.

[PS87]   Carl Pollard and Ivan A. Sag. *Information-Based Syntax and Semantics. Vol. 1: Fundamentals*, volume 13 of *CSLI Lecture Notes*. Chicago Univ. Press, Chicago, 1987.

[Rou88] William Rounds. Set values for unification-based grammar formalisms and logic programming. Report CLSI-88-129, CSLI, Stanford (CA), June 1988.

[Shi86] Stuart M. Shieber. *An Introduction to Unification-Based Approaches to Grammar*, volume 4 of *CSLI Lecture Notes*. Stanford University, Stanford (CA), 1986.

[Smo88] Gert Smolka. A feature logic with subsorts. LILOG-Report 33, IBM Deutschland GmbH, Stuttgart, May 1988.

[Smo89] Gert Smolka. Feature constraint logics for unification grammars. LILOG-Report 93, IBM Deutschland GmbH, Stuttgart, November 1989.

[Wie90] R. Wiese. Towards an unifikation-based phonology. In H. Karlgren, editor, *COLING-90*, volume 3, pages 283–286. Helsinki, 1990.

On the Form of Lexical Entries and their Use in the Construction of Discourse Representation Structures[*]

Hans Kamp and Antje Roßdeutscher
Universität Stuttgart
Institut für Maschinelle Sprachverarbeitung
Keplerstr. 17
D-7000 Stuttgart 1

1. Introduction

The central task of natural language semantics is to articulate how meaning is determined by form. From a computational perspective this task divides into two. On the one hand a computationally viable semantics should describe the formal aspects of interpretation: it should describe how the meaning of a natural language expression or text can be culled from its recognizable form - in other words, how a recognizer of form, that is, a (syntactic) parser, can be paired with an algorithm which converts the structures that the parser computes into specifications of content. On the other hand, the theory should account for language generation, i.e., for the conversion of content specifications into actual sentences or texts. Here we only consider the problem of interpretation.

Traditionally the problem of how form determines meaning is regarded as capable of factorization into two separate problems, a lexical and a structural problem. The lexical problem is that of determining the meaning of what is recognizable by its form as a particular word or lexical item. One way of solving this type of problem in daily life is to look up the given word in a lexicon or dictionary - indeed, this is what most dictionaries are designed for. The second problem is that of determining how the meanings of the individual words of which a complex expression (such as in particular a sentence or text) is made up jointly produce the meaning of the expression (the sentence, text, or whatever) as a whole.

Syntactic structure is essential to the second problem. For it is primarily the way in which the words occurring in a complex fit together syntactically which determines how their meanings combine into the meaning of the entire expression. For long formal semantics of natural language was almost exclusively concerned with this second problem—i.e., with analyzing how the syntax of a complex expression determines its meaning as composed from the words contained in it. The analysis of the meanings of individual words was left to the lexicographers and lexical theorists, while formal semantics itself made do with very general assumptions about what sorts of things the meanings of lexical items are. This method can go a surprisingly long way towards providing insight into the form-meaning relation of complex expressions. Nevertheless it is evident that the semantic description of an individual sentence or text which differentiates it from others with parallel syntactic structure, but built from different words, will have to supply more than a purely schematic account of the particular lexical items the sentence or text contains. A semantics able to provide this kind of differentiation must combine the insights of formal semantics with those of a theoretically informed lexicography.

[*]The research reported in this paper is being supported by the DFG in the context of Sonderforschungsbereich 340. We thank Nicholas Asher, Franz Beil and many other colleagues in the IMS for suggestions, criticism and other forms of valuable assistance.

The very project of computational semantics - that of associating specifications of content, or semantic representations, with syntactic structures - derives its point from the conviction (which goes back at least as far as Frege) that syntactic structure tends to conceal semantic and logical structure. In particular, accounting for the logical relations between different sentences or texts in terms of their syntactic structure directly tends to be very awkward and can as a rule be accomplished much more perspicuously using derived structures, usually referred to as semantic representations or logical forms. There is also another, arguably more compelling reason why syntactic structures cannot serve as representations of meaning. According to generally accepted views of syntax the unit of syntactic representation is simply the sequence consisting of the unrelated syntactic structures of the sentences which compose it. In contrast, the unit of semantic analysis is not the individual sentence but the coherent discourse or text: the meaning of a coherent text usually resides partly in certain connections between the sentences of which it consists, and thus transcends the meanings which those sentences can be recognized as having on their own. A sequence of unrelated syntactic structures is unable to capture those connections.

The approach towards semantics on which the present paper is based was developed with the specific aim of accounting for the intersentential connections between sentences that distinguish coherent texts from mere concatenations of sentences. This approach - Discourse Representation Theory, or DRT for short - analyzes how the meaning of the i-th sentence s_i of a text $s_1,\ldots,s_n$ is determined by the syntactic structure of s_i together with the context K_{i-1}, which in turn is determined, partly or wholly, by the meanings of the preceding sentences $s_1,\ldots,s_{i-1}$. In fact, the ways in which s_i is semantically connected with the antecedent part of the text often make it impossible for its meaning to be represented in isolation, and the only possibility of capturing it lies in showing how the meaning representation K is updated through incorporation of the information which s_i contributes. Thus we arrive at the following text interpretation schema:

$$K_0 \rightarrow K_1 \rightarrow K_2 \ldots K_{n-1} \rightarrow K_n$$

$$s1 \quad s2 \quad s3 \ldots sn$$

K_n captures the meaning of the entire text $s_1, \ldots, s_n$. The representations K_i are called *Discourse Representation Structures* or *DRS*s.

Let us look at an example to see how this might work in some detail. Consider the following three sentence "text":

(1) Der Tourist erkrankte an Typhus. Nach drei Wochen war er wieder gesund. Ein Arzt aus Izmir hat ihn geheilt.

(The tourist came down with typhoid. After three weeks he was well again. A doctor from Izmir has cured him.)

We will assume for simplicity that the starting representation K is empty. So the first sentence is to be interpreted and represented free of context. The processing of the sentence (in fact this is true for the great majority of sentences; it is true in particular for the two remaining sentences of (1)) consists in introducing representatives - so-called *discourse referents* - for the arguments of the verb. On the one hand these are inserted into the argument positions of the verb; on the other hand they act as arguments to conditions which express the descriptive information contained in the argument phrases themselves. A quite distinct assumption that is crucial to the representation of (1) concerns the referential arguments of verbs: we assume that the verb of a sentence has, in addition to the arguments expressed by actual argument phrases, also, as an implicit argument, an event (or state of affairs, as the case may be); this is an event of the type defined by the verb together with its other argument(s). The verb's tense determines, sometimes in cooperation with temporal adverbs, prepositional phrases or subordinate clauses, where this event or state of affairs is located in time, relative to the utterance time of the represented discourse or text and/or with respect to other times or events that are already present in the representation. Thus the first sentence of (1) is analyzed as saying "There exists an event before the utterance time n (n stands for "now") which is an event of the tourist coming down with typhoid". In the notation customary for DRSs this analysis is represented as follows:

(2)

```
┌─────────────────────────────────┐
│           n  e  y  z            │
├─────────────────────────────────┤
│  der Tourist(y)   Typhus(z)     │
│  e < n   e:  y erkranken an z   │
└─────────────────────────────────┘
```

(The condition "e: y erkranken an z" expresses that e is an event consisting of y coming down with z.)

Similarly the second sentence is analyzed as saying that there is a state of affairs s before n which is located three weeks after the event e and which consists in the tourist being healthy. Note that in order to arrive at this analysis the second sentence has to be related to the (DRS of the) first sentence in several ways. First, a connection must be made between the pronoun *er* and the tourist mentioned in the first sentence, or—this is how anaphora is viewed in DRT—between *er* and the discourse referent y that represents the tourist in (2). Second, the prepositional phrase *nach drei Wochen* has to be interpreted as denoting a time three weeks after event e. (There is also a third connection, which has to do with the adverb *wieder*. We will ignore this connection for now, but will come back to it below.) The update of (2) with this new information is as in (3):

(3)

```
┌──────────────────────────────────────────────┐
│              n  e  y  z  s  u                │
├──────────────────────────────────────────────┤
│  der Tourist(y)  Typhus(z)  u = y           │
│       e < n  e: y erkranken an z            │
│  s < n  |[e,s]|_weeks = 3  s: u gesund sein │
└──────────────────────────────────────────────┘
```

("$|[e,s]|_{weeks} = 3$" expresses the fact that the temporal distance between e and s measured in weeks is equal to 3.)

The effect of updating (3) with the information contained in the third sentence is given in (4):

(4)

```
┌──────────────────────────────────────────────────┐
│         n  e  y  z  s  u  e/  x  v  w           │
├──────────────────────────────────────────────────┤
│  der Tourist(y)   Typhus(z)   u = y   v = y     │
│           Izmir(w)   Arzt aus w(x)              │
│       e < n     e: y erkranken an z             │
│  s < n   |[e,s]|_weeks = 3   s: u gesund sein   │
│       e/ < n   e/ < s   e/: x heilen v          │
└──────────────────────────────────────────────────┘
```

It should be noted that the total meaning which (4) represents cannot be analyzed as a conjunction of three propositions expressed by the three sentences of (1). To see this, one has to know that a DRS is to be read as an assertion to the effect that there exist entities corresponding to its discourse referents (displayed in the top line) which satisfy all the conditions that are specified for those dicourse referents in the lines below. Thus (4) means that there was a time before the utterance time n at which the given tourist came down with typhoid and a later time at which he was healthy again and that there was a doctor from Izmir who cured the tourist. In other words, (4) amounts to an existentially quantified conjunction with conjuncts coming from the different sentences of (1). It is a fact well-known from symbolic logic that such an existential formula is normally not equivalent to a conjunction of formulas that correspond to the individual conjuncts.

DRSs such as (2) - (4) suffer from a fundamental deficiency. In fact, this is generally true of DRSs as they have been constructed until recently (see for instance Kamp (1981), Kamp and Reyle (1991)).

The deficiency is this: the DRS-conditions "e: y erkranken an z", "s: u gesund sein" or "Arzt(x)" of (4) are treated as unanalyzed predicates, unrelated to any lexicon or lexical theory to account for the specifics of their meanings or the semantical and logical relations between them. DRSs of this kind reflect the perspective of formal semantics as sketched above, and are deficient for the reason given there. It was to remedy this lacuna that the work we will outline in the next two sections has been undertaken.

2. The syntax and semantics of lexical entries

The lexical entries which we will discuss concern a small number of related words, such as *heilen, gesunden, gesund, erkranken*. Some of these are found in our sample discourse (1). According to the analysis we will offer all these words relate to a central concept which we will denote as HEILEN. This concept is expressed directly in an intransitive sentence such as (5):

(5) Der Fuß heilte.

Our lexicon has an entry for this intransitive use of the verb *heilen* which looks as follows:

$$(6) \qquad \text{heil-en} \qquad \{\langle \theta 1, f1 \rangle\}$$
$$\text{Theme1}$$
$$\text{HEILEN} \qquad \text{SEL RESTR:}$$
$$(e, y_{th1}, z_{th2}) \qquad \text{bodily part}$$

Heilen can also be used transitively. In fact, it has several transitive uses which our approach must distinguish. One of them is exemplified by the sentence

(7) Ein Arzt aus Izmir hat den Touristen vom Typhus geheilt.
(A physician from Izmir has cured the tourist of typhoid.)

The lexical entry corresponding to (7) is given in (8)

$$(8) \qquad \text{heil-en} \qquad \{d\langle \theta 1, f1 \rangle \qquad \langle \theta 2, f2 \rangle\} \qquad \text{von+DAT}$$
$$\text{Agent} \qquad \text{Theme1} \qquad \text{Theme2}$$
$$\text{CAUS(HEILEN)} \quad \text{SEL RESTR:} \quad \text{SEL RESTR:} \quad \text{SEL RESTR:}$$
$$(ec, x_{ag}, y_{th1}, z_{th2}) \quad \text{capable of} \qquad \text{organism} \qquad \text{ailment}$$
$$\text{intention} \qquad \text{or bodily part} \quad \text{or disease}$$
$$\text{to cure}$$

Like the vast majority of entries in the lexicon we are developing, (6) and (8) consist of a syntactic component (the top tier) and a conceptual one (the bottom tier). The conceptual component is often shared, in part or in whole, with several other entries. It is this component which contains the information that should flow into the DRSs which represent sentences or texts containing the lexical items in question. The syntactic component of an entry is specific to that entry and serves to identify it as corresponding to particular uses of the particular words. The introduction of lexical information into the DRS involves replacing a lexical item occurring in some minimal DRS condition—such as e.g. the condition "e*l*: x heilen v" from (4)—by the conceptual component of the relevant lexical entry, while substituting discourse referents for some or all of the argument symbols occurring in that component. For instance the DRS for (7) will not contain the word *heilen*, but rather the conceptual structure the verb expresses and so will look like this:

(9)

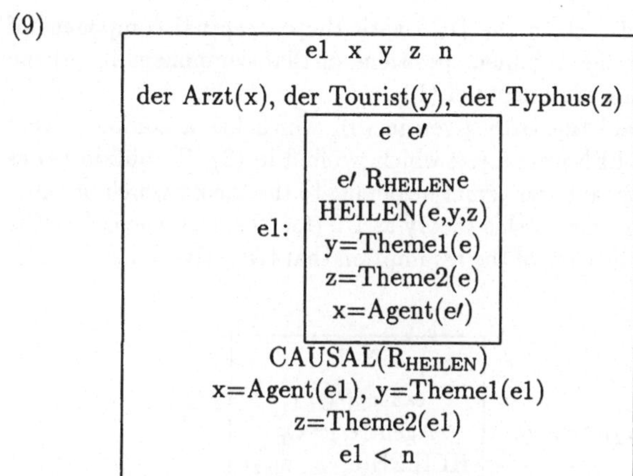

Let us have a closer look at how (9) is obtained. In section 1 we implied that DRSs are constructed from syntactic structures. More specifically, we assume that these syntactic structures are the ones postulated in Frey and Tappe (1991). (The theory which postulates these structures - an interpretation of X-bar-Theory for German - is being developed in a project which, like our own, belongs to a larger research effort - the SFB 340: Sprachtheoretische Grundlagen für die Computerlinguistik, located at the Universities of Stuttgart and Tübingen.) According to the theory of Frey and Tappe the syntactic structure of (7) has the following form:

(10)

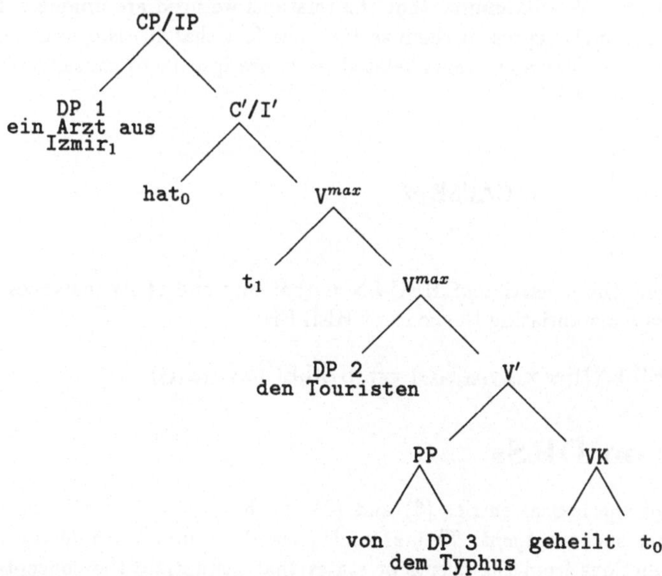

In syntactic trees of this sort the arguments of the verb are readily identified by their positions: They are those phrases whose base positions are subordinate to the maximal projection (the Vmax node) of the verb. In order to replace the verb *heilen* by the corresponding conceptual component in the DRS built from (10), the parser, which has already constructed (10), must match the verb arguments of (10) with those of a suitable lexical entry for this verb. In the present instance the parser will select (8) as the correct entry, because it can recognize the arguments specified by that entry as matching those found in (10). (We omit the details) The match enables the DRS construction procedure to replace the lexical verb in the DRS with the conceptual component of (8) while substituting for the symbols filling the argument positions of that component in (8) the discourse referents that represent the matching arguments of (10).

In the present case this does not yet yield the DRS given in (9), which has a complex event structure in lieu of the condition CAUS(HEILEN)(e1, x,y,z) which we find in (8). To obtain (9) as specified, the construction procedure must appeal to an *axiom* belonging to the theory which provides the logical foundation for the lexicon; we will refer to this theory as LT (for "Lexical Theory"). The axiom in question spells out the principal implication of the assumption that transitive *heilen* denotes the causative of the concept HEILEN:

$$(11) \qquad (\mathrm{CAUS(HEILEN))(ec,}x_{ag},y_{th1},z_{th2}) \iff \mathrm{ec}: \boxed{\begin{array}{c} e' \quad e \\[4pt] e' \ \mathrm{R_{HEILEN}} \ e \\ \mathrm{Agent}(e') = x_{ag} \\ \mathrm{HEILEN}(e,y_{th1},z_{th2}) \end{array}} \\ \mathrm{CAUSAL(R_{HEILEN})}$$

This axiom expresses the notion that the subject of *heilen* as it is used in (7) does something —i.e. is involved in some event e'— which causes an event e instantiating the concept HEILEN (as we find it for instance in (6)) and that the other two arguments of the verb are the two participants of e. However, transitive *heilen*, like its English counterpart *cure*, involves more than just causing someone to get better. Lexicalized causatives – i.e. causative concepts that are expressed by a single verb rather than by the compound "cause + intransitive verb" – involve not just any causal relation, but one of a special "direct" and/or "intended" kind. It has proved extremely difficult to articulate what distinguishes the causal relations which are implied by lexicalized causatives from causal relations in general. We will assume that the relations we need are uniquely determined by the concepts C and accordingly represent them as R_C. The fact that R_C is causal, i.e. satisfies the predicate CAUSAL, implies that any events related by it are ipso facto causally related. This is expressed by another axiom of LT:

$$(12) \qquad \boxed{\begin{array}{l} e1 \quad e2 \\[4pt] \mathrm{CAUSAL(R)} \\ e1 \ \mathrm{R} \ e2 \end{array}} \implies e1 \ \mathrm{CAUSE} \ e2$$

A further fact about the causative of HEILEN is that any one of its instances ec entails the occurrence of a process e instantiating the concept HEILEN:

$$(13) \qquad (\mathrm{CAUS(HEILEN))(ec,}x_{ag},y_{th1},z_{th2}) \implies \mathrm{HEILEN}(e,y_{th1},z_{th2})$$

3. Inferences on DRSs

There is one aspect of the lexical entries (6) and (8) which we have not yet explained. This is the use of specifications such as *Agent*, *Theme1* and *Theme2*. These terms denote *thematic roles*. Thematic roles are functions from the events or states that instantiate the concepts expressed by verbs to certain participants of those events or states. These functions turn out to be useful in capturing certain generalizations over clusters of concepts. For instance, the concept HEILEN is one of a number of process concepts C all of which involve a participant that has a particular property RES(C) once the process is completed which it did not have when the process started. For the case of HEILEN this implication is captured by the following pair of axioms:

(14)

$$\boxed{\begin{array}{c} e \\ \hline \text{HEILEN}(e) \end{array}} \Rightarrow \boxed{\begin{array}{c} s1 \\ \hline s1{:}\neg\ (\text{RES}(\text{HEILEN}))(\text{Theme1}(e))) \\ s1)(e \end{array}}$$

$$\boxed{\begin{array}{c} e \\ \hline \text{HEILEN}(e) \end{array}} \Rightarrow \boxed{\begin{array}{c} s2 \\ \hline s2{:}\ (\text{RES}(\text{HEILEN}))(\text{Theme1}(e))) \\ e)(s2 \end{array}}$$

("s1)(e" is to be read as "s1 abuts e".)

Another feature of HEILEN is that its two themes—the patient and the ailment—are "separated" at the time the process is complete. In this respect HEILEN resembles a number of other lexicalized concepts, among them concepts of cleaning, where the separation between Theme1, the thing cleaned, and Theme2, that of which the thing is cleaned, admits of a more literal interpretation. For concepts C belonging to this class we denote the associated relation as SEP(C). The relation between C and SEP(C) can also be captured in the form of a pair of axioms of LT. We only give the special instances for the case where C is HEILEN

(15)

$$\boxed{\begin{array}{c} e \\ \hline \text{HEILEN}(e) \end{array}} \Rightarrow \boxed{\begin{array}{c} s1 \\ \hline s1{:}\ \neg\ (\text{SEP}(\text{HEILEN}))\ (\text{Theme1}(e),\text{Theme2}(e)) \\ s1)(e \end{array}}$$

$$\boxed{\begin{array}{c} e \\ \hline \text{HEILEN}(e) \end{array}} \Rightarrow \boxed{\begin{array}{c} s2 \\ \hline s2{:}\ (\text{SEP}(\text{HEILEN}))\ (\text{Theme1}(e),\text{Theme2}(e)) \\ e)(s2 \end{array}}$$

(As (15) shows, the language of LT must be able to represent polyadic as well as monadic predicates)

To conclude, we will illustrate how DRSs can be used, in combination with the lexicon, to verify certain inferential relations between sentences and texts. As an example consider our original text (1):

(1) Der Tourist erkrankte an Typhus. Nach drei Wochen war er wieder gesund. Ein Arzt aus Izmir hat ihn geheilt.

Intuitively (1) entails

(16) Der Tourist gesundete vom Typhus.

(17) Der Arzt hat den Touristen vom Typhus geheilt.

In order to verify the implication to (16) we need lexical entries for some of the other words occurring in (1). First the entry for *erkranken*.

(18)   erkrank-en $\{\langle \theta 1, f1\rangle\ \}$ an+DAT
                              Theme1   Theme2
      (ANT(HEILEN))   SEL RESTR: SEL RESTR:
         (e, y_{th1}, z_{th2}) organism   disease

Erkranken is the antonym of the verb *gesunden*, which instantiates the concept HEILEN(e, y, z), as illustrated by (16). This relation of antynomy is one which we find between many pairs of lexical items. In case those lexical items denote processes, the relation has the - obvious - logical properties given in

(19) If C is a process concept such that s: RES(C)(theme$_i$(e)),
      then ANT(C) is a process concept such that s: ¬RES(C)(theme$_i$(e))

Since *gesunden* directly expresses the concept HEILEN, its antonym *erkranken* expresses the concept ANT(HEILEN). Instantiating (19) to this concept gives:

(20)

e (ANT(HEILEN))(e)	⇒	s1 s1: (RES(HEILEN))(Theme1(e))) s1)(e
e (ANT(HEILEN))(e)	⇒	s2 s2: ¬(RES(HEILEN))(Theme1(e))) e)(s2

A second set of implications involving ANT(HEILEN) derives from the separation axioms (15) for HEILEN. Since ANT(HEILEN) is the reverse of HEILEN, its result state is one in which the two themes, patient and ailment, are no longer "separate":

(21)

e (ANT(HEILEN))(e)	⇒	s1 s1: (SEP(HEILEN)) (Theme1(e),Theme2(e)) s1)(e
e (ANT(HEILEN))(e)	⇒	s2 s2: ¬(SEP(HEILEN)) (Theme1(e),Theme2(e)) e)(s2

With the help of (18) we can construct a representation for the first sentence of (1). To extend this DRS to a representation of the second sentence we also need an entry for the adjective *gesund*. As *gesund* denotes the state which results from a process of HEILEN (though it need not necessarily arise in this way), its entry can be represented in the following form:

(22)   gesund   {Θ}

(RES(HEILEN))   Theme1
       (y_{th1})   SEL RESTR
                     organism or
                     bodily part

To process the second sentence of (1) we need to know something about the word *wieder*. All that is needed in the present context is this: When *wieder* is part of a clause describing a state of affairs s, it entails that a state s/ answering to the same description obtained at some earlier time t_1 and that at some intermediate time t_2 a state s// obtained which did not answer the description. In the present case the entailment is that our tourist mentioned in the first sentence, y1, had been healthy at some time in the past and that since then he had been ill. These implications are supported by the DRS for the first sentence of (1) (which acts as context for the interpretation of the second sentence). For this DRS entails, via the implications given in (20), that y1 was healthy before he caught typhoid and then was not healthy once he had caught it. In the light of what has been said it should now be clear how the second sentence can be processed. As the third sentence presents no further problems, we give the DRS for the entire three sentence text, without showing the intermediate stages:

(23)

> el, yl, zl, s2, y2, **z2**, t, **e/**, **z/**, **e//**, **z//**, e3, x3, y3, **z3**, n
>
> der Tourist(yl), Typhus(zl)
> (ANT(HEILEN))(el,yl,zl)
> yl = Theme(el), zl = Theme2(el)
> el < n
> (WIEDER(RES(HEILEN)))(s2,y2,**z2**)
> yl = y2 = Themel(s2)
> zl = **z2** = Theme2(s2)
> (ANT(HEILEN))(**e/**, y2, **z/**)
> y2 = Themel(**e/**), zl = **z/** = Theme2(**e/**)
> HEILEN(**e//**, y2,**z//**)
> y2 = Themel(**e//**), zl = **z//** = Theme2(**e//**)
> $\|[el,s]\|_{weeks} = 3$
> el = **e/** < **e//**)(s2 < n
> Arzt(x3)
>
> e3:
> > **e°**, **e°/**
> >
> > **e°/**R_{Heilen}**e°**
> > HEILEN(**e°**,y3,**z3**)
> > y3 = Themel(**e°**), **z3** = Theme2(**e°**)
> > x3 = Agent(**e°/**)
>
> CAUSAL(R_{Heilen})
> x3 = Agent(e3), yl = y3 = Themel(e3)
> zl = **z2** = **z3** = Theme2(e3)
> el = **e/** < **e//** = **e°**)(s2 < n

(The boldface discourse referents are ones that belong to the concepts but are not explicitly mentioned in the sentences. See Kamp and Rodeutscher (1991) for details.)

Note that (23) supports the inference that between the time of the completion of the process el described by the first sentence and the state s2 described in the second yl changed from a state of non-health into one of health. Moreover, (21) tells us that the first of these two states is one in which yl is ill with typhoid. On the assumption of the existence of such a change, i. e., of the existence of a process that leads from the first state to the second, a discourse referent **e//** with the appropriate conditions has been added to the DRS. The thus expanded DRS contains a smaller DRS, representing the sentence (16), as a part.

(16) Der Tourist gesundete vom Typhus.

The inference to (17) involves a further step, in which **e//** is identified with **e°**, the process that is part of the event of the doctor curing the patient. It should be noted that this last identification doesn't strictly follow—it would in principle have been possible for yl to have suffered simultaneously from another disease and for the doctor to have cured him of that one, while he overcame the typhoid on his own account. For lack of space we cannot go into the nature of such default inferences here.

References

[Frey,Werner / Tappe, Thilo (1991)] "Zur Interpretation der X-bar-Theorie und zur Syntax des Mittelfeldes. Grundlagen eines GB-Fragments" AIMS-Reports, Stuttgart to appear.

[Kamp, Hans (1981)] "A Theory of Truth and Semantic Representation", in: Jeroen Groenendijk, Theo M. V. Janssen and Martin Stokhof (eds.), *Formal Methods in the Study of Language*, Vol.I, Mathematisch Centrum, Amsterdam, reprinted in J. Groenendijk, T. Janssen and M. Stokhof (eds.), (1984), *Truth, Interpretation and Information*, Foris, Dordrecht, pp. 1–41.

[Kamp, Hans / Reyle, Uwe (1991)] *From Logic to discourse*. Vol.I, to appear: Kluwer, Dordrecht 1991

[Kamp, Hans/ Roßdeutscher, Antje (1991)] "Remarks on Lexical Structure and DRS-Construction", AIMS-Reports, Stuttgart 1991

Sachverhaltsbeschreibungen, Verbsememe und Textkohärenz

Jürgen Kunze
Zentralinstitut für Sprachwissenschaft
Prenzlauer Promenade 149-152
0-1100 Berlin

Jedes System zur Textanalyse oder -generierung muß auf Regeln für die thematische Progression in Texten basieren - dies in Verbindung mit der funktionalen Satzperspektive - damit die Kohärenz des Textes in ausreichendem Maße gesichert ist. Es zeigt sich, daß Verbsememe, die auf der Ebene der Sachverhalte (Ereignisse, Zustände, ...) gleichvertig sind, eine unterschiedliche Eignung für die Konstituierung thematischer Strukturen aufweisen. Diese Unterschiede finden ihre Erklärung durch den Begriff "semantische Emphase". Er ermöglicht die Einführung von Verbfeldstrukturen, in denen jeder Position genau definierte Eigenschaften der genannten Art zugeordnet sind. Das gesamte Modell besteht aus zwei Ebenen, den semantischen Grundformen und den Sememrepräsentationen. Letztere drücken unterschiedliche Perspektiven auf die invarianten Sachverhalte aus, die durch erstere gegeben sind.

1   Die Problemstellung

Die Vielzahl sprachlicher Formen, die zum Augdruck eines einfachen Sachverhalts zur Verfügung stehen, mag auf den ersten Blick als Luxus, wenigstens doch als Redundanz erscheinen. Der anscheinende Luxus verwandelt sich in ein Inventar differenzierter und aufeinander bezogener Mittel, wenn es um den Ausdruck komplexer Sachverhalte, also letztlich um Texte geht. Nunmehr ist die Auswahl unter den vielen Ausdrucksformen auf relativ wenige beschränkt. Es entsteht ein Geflecht von Determinanten, die sich wechselseitig bedingen und erfüllen. Dies beginnt mit den Mechanismen, nach denen ein Komplexer Sachverhalt, der eine netzartige Struktur aufweist, als linear angeordnete Sequenz einfacher Sachverhalte ausformuliert wird. Hierüber gibt es detaillierte Einsichten, die zeigen, daß dafür recht enge Grenzen bestehen (LEVELT 1989, speziell S. 138 ff.). Es setzt sich fort mit der Gruppierung der Einheiten in komplexe Sätze, Absätze usw.

Die einmal festgelegte lineare Anordnung der einfachen Sachverhalte hat erhebliche Konsequenzen für ihre sprachliche Form. Dies kann man leicht feststellen, indem man in einem Text ein derartiges Segment außblendet und sachverhaltsäquivalente Ausdrücke einsetzt, so daß das Ganze ein Text bleibt.

Weitere Beschränkungen ergeben sich z.B. aus Wertungen, beabsichtigten Effekten stilistischer Art und Vorgaben "von außen" (etwa bei Übersetzungen).

Im folgenden wird aus diesem texttheoretischen Kosmos ein einziges Teilproblemchen behandelt: Im Sinne der eben genannten Substitutionsprobe steht nur die Äquivalenz des Prädikats in einem clause bei konstanter lexikalischer Belegung aller Aktanten zur Diskussion. Mit anderen Worten: Es soll nur erlaubt sein, das Verb selber oder/und seine Formmerkmale sowie die morpho-syntaktischen Merkmale seiner Aktanten zu verändern, alle übrigen Konstituenten (also freie Angaben usw.) sind ohnehin tabu. Die Frage lautet dann: Welche derartigen Veränderungen sind bei Invarianz des ausgedrückten Sachverhalts möglich, damit die Determinanten des umgebenden Textes jeweils in gleicher Weise erfüllt sind. Statt der Substitution kann man natürlich auch den von den Anwendungen her viel interessanteren Rahmen der Generierung wählen. Für die folgenden Betrachtungen ist dies unerheblich.

2 Einige Beobachtungen

Das oben genannte Geflecht reduziere ich für das folgende auf Sequenzen von jeweils zwei Sätzen, d.h. ich abstrahiere in den Beispielen von denjenigen Bedingungen, die aus weiter voran stehenden Sätzen herrühren können. Es lassen sich u.a. drei Fälle unterscheiden:

a) Sachverhaltsäquivalente Konversen oder Ableitungen weisen eine unterschiedliche Eignung zur Konstituierung einer bestimmten Satzperspektive auf.

> (1a) Der Chef war auf Annas Geburtstag.
> (1x) Er hat sie mit einer Vase beschenkt.
> (1y) Er hat ihr eine Vase geschenkt.
> (1z) ?Er hat eine Vase an sie verschenkt.
> (2b) Der Chef hat neulich eine Vase gekauft.
> (2x) ?Er hat Anna damit/mit ihr beschenkt.
> (2y) Er hat sie Anna geschenkt.
> (2z) Er hat sie an Anna verschenkt.
> (3a) In dieser Region gibt es viel Erdöl.
> (3x) Es wird dort zu Benzin verarbeitet.
> (3y) ?Aus ihm wird dort Benzin hergestellt.
> (4b) Diese Region exportiert viel Benzin.
> (4x) ?Erdöl wird dort zu ihm verarbeitet.
> (4y) Es wird dort aus Erdöl hergestellt.

Ich umgehe hier eine genauere Einstufung der Akzeptabilität, es kommt nur darauf an, daß die mit "?" markierten Sätze schlechter abschneiden als die übrigen Konkurrenten innerhalb einer Gruppe. Umordnungen machen die fraglichen Sätze meist auch nicht besser.

b) Das Genus verbi hat den gleichen Einfluß auf die Eignung.

> (5a) Der Chef war auf Annas Geburtstag.
> (5x) Er hat ihr eine Vase geschenkt.
> (5y) ?Von ihm wurde ihr eine Vase geschenkt.
> (6b) Anna hat eine wundervolle Kristallvase.
> (6x) ?Ein Freund hat sie ihr geschenkt.
> (6y) Sie ist ihr von einem Freund geschenkt worden.

c) Bei Verben, die ohne Veränderung der Bedeutung mehrere Aktantifizierungen gestatten, hängen diese Aktantifizierungen ebenfalls mit der Eignung zusammen.

> (7a) Für diese Technologie benötigt man einen neuen Prozessor.
> (7x) Er soll aus billigen Bauelementen zusammengesetzt verden.
> (7y) ?Billige Bauelemente sollen zu ihm zusammengesetzt werden.
> (8b) Karl hat einige billige Bauelemente besorgt.
> (8x) ?Aus ihnen soll ein neuer Prozessor zusammengesetzt werden.
> (8y) Sie sollen zu einem neuen Prozessor zusammengesetzt werden.

Man beachte, daß mit gleichen Buchstaben x, y oder z markierte Sätze einer Gruppe bis auf die Pronominalisierung immer die gleiche syntaktische Struktur besitzen. Das Pronomen kann man jederzeit vermeiden, d.h. durch eine volle NP ersetzen, indem man z.B. sein Antezedens weiter nach vorn verlagert. Die Akzeptabilitätsunterschiede bleiben, wenn die volle NP als kontextuell gebunden erscheint (also etwa das Merkmal +definit hat).

Diese Beispielsammlung, die vielleicht etwas schematisch wirkt, läßt sich einerseits wesentlich erweitern und andererseits auch durch existierende Texte untermauern, wenngleich man die genannten Erscheinungen nur selten unter den hier suggerierten Laborbedingungen vorfindet. Auch hinsichtlich der Vorerwähnung oder kontextuellen Bindung eines Arguments muß der Horizont noch erweitert werden: Argumente können auch (mehr indirekt) durch Frames oder Situationen eingeführt sein Ist von einer Hochzeit die Rede, so sind die Braut, der Bräutigam, der Standesbeamte/Pfarrer usw. kontextuell präsent, ohne daß sie erwähnt sind.

Cum grano salis läßt sich jedoch festhalten, daß kontextuell gebundene Argumente (d.h. Topic-Kandidaten) eher als reine Kasus aktantifiziert werden, "neue" Argumente dagegen eher als Präpositionsphrasen. Von dieser oberflächlichen Charakterisierung sind allerdings einige Abstriche zu machen, und sie ist auch nicht die Behauptung, die ich ansteuere.

Die skizzierten Befunde lassen sich auch so einordnen, daß nicht in jedem Fall ein reibungsloser Übergang zwischen Grundverben und Ableitungen oder Aktiv und Passiv möglich ist. Die Beispiele unter b) relativieren somit den bedeutungserhaltenden Charakter der Aktiv-Passiv-Transformation. Ähnliches gilt auch für die *be*-Konversen: Die öfter herbeizitierte holistische Komponente der *be*-Verben (s. auch EROMS 1980) liegt in (lx, 2x) nicht vor (und ich bezweifle sie generell: ein beschriebenes Blatt ist nicht vollgeschrieben). Was die *be*-Konverse (im Regelfall) bewirkt, ist ein Wechsel der Perspektive, wie er sogleich behandelt wird.

3 Der Erklärungshintergrund

Wenn man die Sachverhaltsäquivalenz der jeweiligen Verben unterstellt, so bleibt die Frage, wie die deutlichen Akzeptabilitätsunterschiede zu erklären sind und wo ihre Ursache angesiedelt ist. Sie muß von einer Ebene stammen, die die ontologische Ebene überlagert und Perspektiven und Sachverhalte erzeugt. Für

> (9) *Hans kauft ein Auto von Karl.*
> (10) *Karl verkauft ein Auto an Hans.*

besteht die unterschiedliche Perspektive darin, daß bei *kaufen* der Erwerb der Ware, bei *verkaufen* ihre Veräußerung in den Vordergrund rückt, wenngleich das eine ohne das andere nicht möglich ist. Von zwei simultanen Vorgängen erscheint der eine wesentlicher als der andere. Damit korreliert die Tatsache, daß Argumente, die nur in dem "unwesentlichen" Vorgang auftreten, auf der Oberfläche fehlen, ja sogar referentiell unbestimmt sein können: In

> (11) *Karl will sein Auto verkaufen/verschenken/... .*

braucht nicht bekannt zu sein, wer der neue Besitzer sein wird, das entsprechende Argument tritt daher natürlicherweise als ein fakultativer Aktant an die Oberfläche. Dasselbe gilt auch bei Aktiv vs. Passiv: Im Passiv tritt die kausierende Handlung des AGENS in den Hintergrund, auf der Oberfläche verwandelt es sich vom obligatorischen Subjekt in eine fakultative Präpositionalphrase. In

> (12) *Karls Auto ist gestohlen worden.*

besteht auf der Sachverhaltsebene das Problem meistens darin, daß das AGENS referentiell nicht bekannt ist. Der Satz

> (13) *Jemand hat Karls Auto gestohlen.*

wirkt demgegenüber etwas redundant oder tautologisch.

Die skizzierte Perspektive auf Sachverhalte, die bestimmte Teilsachverhalte in den Vordergrund rückt, läßt sich durch Befragungen ziemlich eindeutig dingfest machen, d.h. sie ist offenbar ein wesentliches Merkmal für die Verwendung von Verben. Daneben gibt es weitere deutliche Oberflächenindikatoren, die man aus dem folgenden Musterbeispiel sehen kann, das keineswegs ein Einzelfall ist:

(14) x_N tauscht v_A gegen u aus.
(15) x_N setzt u_A für v ein.

- u und v belegen alternativ die syntaktischen Positionen "obligatorischer Akkusativ" und "fakultative Präpositionalphrase";
- die Präpositionen sind antonym;
- die Verbzusätze sind antonym.

Diese Verteilung ist aus einer Repräsentation des invarianten Sachverhalts, d.h. aus der semantischen Grundform, eindeutig ableitbar, wenn man zu den Sememrepräsentationen (s. 4) übergeht. Die semantische Grundform der Besitzwechselverben liefert bei einfacher Aktantifizierung (pro Argument gibt es genau einen Aktanten) u.a. folgendes Schema:

(16) q_N nimmt u_A $^*p_D$/von p an,
(17) q_N nimmt u_A p_D/*von p ab.
(18) p_N schickt u_A q_D/*an q zu .
(19) p_N schickt u_A $^*q_D$/an q ab.

Dieses Mal wechseln p und q entsprechende syntaktische Positionen, die Präpositionen und die Verbzusätze sind jeweils wieder antonym. Selbstverständlich gibt es auch Besitzwechselverben ohne Präfix oder Verbzusatz, die sich passend einordnen. Die Präfixe/Verbzusätze erzeugen normalerweise eine Perspektive, sind dafür aber nicht notwendig. *schenken* hat eben die Perspektive, die zu (18) gehört.

4 Grundformen und Sememrepräsentationen

Für die in (14), (15) vorkommenden Verben zeige ich nun, wie die behandelten Erscheinungen formal dargestellt werden können. Als gemeinsame semantische Grundformen der beiden Verben nehme ich folgenden Ausdruck an:

(20) CAUSE(ACT(x),ET(BEC(P(q,u)),BEC(NOT(P(q,v)))))

Dabei ist P ein geeignetes Lokalisierungsprädikat (PLACE-d in KUNZE 1991, 5. G3 f.), dessen Besonderheiten hier nicht weiter interessieren, zumal ich das etwas kompliziertere Problem der Aktantifizierung von q ausklammere. Die Proposition (20) geht durch Instantiierungsregeln in folgende Sachverhaltsbeschreibung über (dies ist die "Interpretation" von (20)):

(21) Eine Handlung von ref(x) kausiert, daß

- ref(u) zu einenl Platz gelangt, der sich an/auf/in ref(q) befindet, und
- ref(v) diesen Platz verläßt.

ET ist die konjunktive Verknüpfung von zwei Propositionen, die simultan gelten.
Aus (20) ergeben sich folgende mögliche Rollen in der Reihenfolge des Vorkommens (das ich als das rollendefinierende Vorkommen für die genannte Rolle des betreffenden Arguments bezeichne):,

x: < AGENS,ACT >
Eine Handlung von ref(x) kausiert etwas.

q: < GOAL,P >
Etwas gelangt zu einem Platz, der zu ref(q) in einem Verhältnis steht, das durch P repräsentiert ist.

u: < TO-OBJ,P >
ref(u) gelangt zu einem Platz, der in einem durch P repräsentierten Verhältnis zu etwas anderem steht.

q: < SOURCE,P >
Etwas verläßt einen Platz, der zu ref(q) in einem Verhältnis steht, das durch P repräsentiert ist.

v: < FROM-OBJ,P >
ref(v) verläßt einen Platz, der in einem durch P repräsentierten Verhältnis zu etwas anderem steht.

(zu den Instantiierungsregeln und Rollendefinitionen vgl. KUNZE 1991, S. 50 ff., 78 ff.).

Sememrepräsentationen entstehen aus Grundformen durch eine Verteilung von semantischen Emphasen und eine Auswahl aktueller Rollen aus den möglichen. Wie ich hier nicht weiter ausführen kann, gibt es für (20) genau vier Emphaseverteilungen (bei Verwendung naheliegender Abkürzungen, $U = P(q,u)$, $V = P(q,v)$):

(22) $C(\underline{A},\mathrm{ET}(B(\underline{U}),B(N(V))))$: Aktiv von *einsetzen*
(23) $C(A,\mathrm{ET}(B(\underline{U}),B(N(V))))$: Passiv von *einsetzen*
(24) $C(\underline{A},\mathrm{ET}(B(U),B(N(\underline{V}))))$: Aktiv von *austauschen*
(25) $C(A,\mathrm{ET}(B(U),B(N(\underline{V}))))$: Passiv von *austauschen*

Die Teilpropositionen mit Emphase (unterstrichen) sind diejenigen, die im oben erklärten Sinne im Vordergrund stehen. Es kommt bei der Verteilung nur auf diejenigen Teilpropositionen an, die rollendefinierende Vorkommen als direkte Argumentstellen haben (in (20) sind dies genau ACT(x),P(q,u),P(q,v)). Die Emphase vererbt sich bottom-up.

Der Mechanismus der Auswahl aktueller Rollen läuft bei (20) leer, da für die betrachteten Argumente x, u und v nur eine mögliche Rolle zur Verfügung steht.

Eine Rolle trägt eine Emphase genau dann, wenn ihr rollendefinierendes Vorkommen direkte Argumentstelle einer Teilproposition mit Emphase ist. Diese Definition ordnet in (22) - (25) jeder Rolle genau ein Merkmal +Emph. oder -Emph. zu. Für die morpho-syntaktischen Merkmale der Aktanten gelten folgende Regeln, die nur Spezialfälle allgemeinerer Regeln sind:

< AGENS,ACT >
+Emph.: Nom.
-Emph.: von + Dat.
< TO-OBJ,P >
+Emph.: Nom. oder Akk.
-Emph.: gegen + Akk.
< FROM-OBJ,P >
+Emph.: Nom. oder Akk.
-Emph.: für + Akk.

Dabei gelte die Nebenbedingung, daß Nom. mindestens einmal vergeben werden muß und jeder reine Kasus höchstens einmal vergeben werden darf.

Die Verteilungen (22 - 25) gehen dann über in folgende:

(26) x: AGENS,+E: N; u: TO-OBJ,+E: A; v: FROM-OBJ, -E: für X_N V u_A (*für* v)

(27) x: AGENS,-E: von; u: TO-OBJ,+E: N; v: FROM-OBJ ,-E: für u_N V (*von* x) (*für* v)

(28) x: AGENS,+E: N; u: TO-OBJ,-E: gegen; v: FROM-OBJ,+E: A x_N V v_A (*gegen* u)

(29) x: AGENS,-E: von; u: TO-OBJ,-E: gegen; f: FROM-OBJ,+E: N v_N V (*von* x) (*gegen* u)

Zur Frage, wie die Eigenschaft "obligatorisch/fakultativ" der Aktanten abzuleiten ist, verweise ich auf KUNZE 1991, S. 122 ff. Ich habe dies in (26 - 29) einfach durch Klammern angedeutet.

Damit ist anhand zweier Varben der Zusammenhang zwischen Sachverhaltsperspektive (dargestellt durch semantische Emphasen und Rollenauswahl) und den Oberflächenmustern expliziert. Mit dem gleichen Instrumentarium lassen sich auch alle anderen Beispiele und ferner ganze Verbfelder behandeln. Dabei kommen die beschriebenen Regularitäten um so mehr zur Geltung, je größer das Verbfeld ist. Auf der anderen Seite gibt es unter den Verben viele semantische Einzelkinder (meist solche mit Präpositionalobjekten, wo die Präposition zwar bedeutungsleer aber unsystematisch ist), die sich einer entsprechenden Behandlung widersetzen.

Es sei noch vermerkt, daß es zahlreiche Fälle gibt, wo Aktanten mit Emphase als (obligatorische) Präpositionalphrase erscheinen und umgekehrt nicht jeder reine Kasus eine Emphase trägt. Beispiele sind Richtungsbestimmungen einerseits und der dativus commodi andererseits. Worauf es bei den in 3 und 4 behandelten Fällen vor allem ankommt, ist das Merkmal +-Emph. und nicht die Oberflächenform.

Als Fälle, bei denen neben einer Veränderung der Emphase auch verschiedene Rollenauswahlen zur Etablierung einer Perspektive beitragen, nenne ich *geben* vs. *erhalten* (dasselbe Argument als AGENS vs. SOURCE) und bestimmte *be*-Ableitungen wie *bauen* vs. *bebauen*.

5 Einige Anknüpfungspunkte zur Wissensrepräsentation

Ein erster Gesichtspunkt, der das Verhältnis zur Wissensrepräsentation betrifft, ergibt sich aus den in 4 genannten Instantiierungsregeln. Diese führen die Grundformen in netzartige Strukturen über, wobei schon für eine einigermaßen komplizierte Grundform wie etwa die von *kaufen* (mit vier Argumenten) ein echtes Netz (d.h. keine baumartige Struktur) entsteht. Der Vorteil kommt jedoch erst dann deutlich zur Geltung, wenn
- mehrere Grundformen miteinander verknüpft werden, d.h. wenn z.B. ein komplexer Satz repräsentiert werden soll,
- die Argumente der Grundformen durch netzartige Strukturen ersetzt werden.

Beide Anforderungen können durch Prädikat-Argument-Strukturen wie (20) im Grunde gar nicht erfüllt werden. Insbesondere bereiten referentielle "Querverbindungen", die Integration taxonomischer Hyperstrukturen und (partielle) Argumentidentifikationen bei diesen Strukturen die bekannten Probleme, während man in Netzen damit formal wesentlich besser umgehen kann.

Der in diesem Beitrag nicht behandelte rekursive Definitionsmechanismus für die Rollen, die sich in einer Grundform für ihre Argumente ergeben, stellt den Übergang zu den Netzen jedoch auf eine genau definierte Basis: Die Rollen (natürlich ohne die Emphasemerkmale, die ja in den Grundformen gerade nicht existieren) sind die ableitbaren (und nicht nur gemutmaßten) Labels für bestimmte Kanten des Netzes und stehen in unmittelbarem Zusammenhang mit dem repräsentierten Sachverhalt.

Kehrt man die Blickrichtung um, d.h. geht man vom Netz zum Satz, so entstehen gleich mehrere grundsätzliche Probleme: Zunächst die Dekomposition eines großen Netzes, d.h. seine Portionierung in solche Teile, die als Rohmaterial für die Generierung von clauses taugen und als Repräsentationen einfacher Sachverhalte im eingangs erklärten Sinne anzusehen sind. Dies ist eng verbunden mit den (an den Kanten) auftretenden Labels, womit man unmittelbar zu der Frage kommt, wie man ihre sprachliche Ausformulierbarkeit garantieren kann. Eine notwendige Bedingung dafür ist, daß die Rollenlabels überhaupt in geeignete Aktanten umsetzbar sind, sofern man sie bei der Dekomposition so miteinander kombinieren kann, daß sie in vorhandene Kasusrahmen passen. Diese Bedingung wäre dann als hinreichend erfüllt anzusehen, wenn sich das Rolleninventar als vollständiges System von Primitiva nachweisen ließe. Dies ist meiner Meinung nach genau die Stelle, wo durch empirische und theoretische Untersuchungen eine mögliche Lücke zwischen formalisierter Wissensrepräsentation und natürlichsprachlicher Semantik zu schließen ist. Immerhin bieten die (verbunabhängigen) Umsetzungsregeln für Rollen nach dem Muster von (26 - 29) einen Ansatzpunkt für eine indirekte Überprüfung. Sie vereinfachen die Problemstellung insofern, als man die Kombinatorik der Aktanten ignorieren kann. Andererseits bleibt dann die Frage, was ein mögliches Verb (in einer Sprache oder allgemein) ist.

6   Literatur

EROMS 1980: H.-W. Eroms, Be-Verb und Präpositionalphrase. Heidelberg.
KUNZE 1991: J. Kunze, Kasusrelationen und semantische Emphase. Studia grammatica XXXII, Akademie Verlag, Berlin.
LEVELT 1989: W.J.M. Levelt, Speaking. From Intention to Articulation. The MIT Press, Cambridge (Mass.), London (UK).

Portability of Natural Language Systems

Peter Bosch
Institute for Knowledge–Based Systems
Scientific Centre
IBM Deutschland GmbH
Postfach 80 08 80
7000 Stuttgart 80

One major problem for the processing of human language on the computer is that the general public as well as industrial management and funding agencies do not fully understand the current limitations of natural language processing (NLP). This tends to result in frustrations for the researchers as well as for everybody else. The non–specialist is often lead to generalize too quickly from smart demonstrations and easily overestimates current technology. I don't mean to suggest that anybody intentionally misleads or deceives anybody else. The fact of the matter rather is that the functioning of natural language is a good deal more complicated than is generally appreciated.

In this paper I want to make a small contribution to help the non–specialist, including colleagues from neighbouring disciplines, to understand where we stand in the machine processing of natural language, and what will and what will not be possible in the coming period.

0   What's the problem ?

Learning a language means to learn the grammar and the vocabulary – this at least is the common sense theory of learning foreign languages. And probably most people would come up with a theory very much like this one at first blush.

Now if this theory is true, what then is the problem in building natural language systems on the computer? And why do computational linguists and AI researchers claim that a natural language system they have built, say, for hotel reservation is useless for other applications, such as making airline reservations ? If the language is the same, then, one ought to think, at least the linguistic modules of the system should be the same. – This paper will try to explain some of the reasons why this view is wrong.

We shall start by looking at computer programs that process natural language on a very superficial level, word processors, and we shall discuss some the current inadequacies of these systems as well as the deeper reasons for these inadequacies. Then we shall look at the LILOG text understanding system as an example of an advanced research system and shall particularly look at its limitations in order to see where the problems of natural language systems lie and what progress can be expected in the coming years.

1   What there is

1.1   Non–linguistic devices

There is a good variety of very good reasons for the automatic processing of human language – written as well as spoken – and everybody is at least familiar with the blessings of word processing.

But what happens in word processing ? Not very much that has anything to do with language. The whole spiel is about how to arrange characters on a page and the big advantage over the good old typewriter is only that we can re–arrange, cut and paste, correct mistakes, and all this with no scissors, glue or correction fluid. But in an ordinary word processor there is no more linguistics than in a typewriter.

The next step up is often called electronic publishing or desk–top publishing; but also here, language plays no role. The point is rather that while ordinary word processing replaces the typewriter, electronic publishing attempts to replace the composer or type setting machine. In either case, the device does not care whether you type in words of a language or arrange them in the form of sentences or whether you just type in some gibberish – but this is no different for the typewriter.

1.2   Words

The first step where language enters the scene is when a word processor has a capability for hyphenation or spelling correction. For spelling correction the thing must be able to distinguish words from non–words and inform the typist about what it thinks are non–words, and, possibly, about what words it knows that look similar and hence may be the words that the typist intended to type but misspelled or mistyped. The spelling correction device needs at least a word list of the relevant language to do this job and an algorithm that tells it something about likely spelling or typing errors. Similarly, a hyphenation device may just use a word list where for each word the potential hyphenation points are marked.

Eventually, however, just a word list won't do. Because a word comes in many shapes. In the extreme case, these shapes have no part of their spelling in common: the English word *go* not only turns up as *goes* or *gone* but also as *went*. So what the spelling dictionary needs is either a morphological algorithm that derives at least the regular forms of a word from its root or a list of each and every possible word form of the language, and not just the few irregular cases. The latter may mean, when we consider highly inflected languages, like French or German, rather than English, that the word list will become four or five times as long. – So here we have, for purely technical reasons, a good case for the introduction of some linguistics, in this case, morphology. A morphology component can keep the word list small and hence save memory and, more importantly, will make the program easier and cheaper to maintain.

Another reason for the introduction of some linguistics is that word lists can never be complete. There are many words that everyone understands but that cannot be found in a dictionary. I do not mean four–letter words, which we could well do without, but words that people make up as they go along, by ordinary rules for word formation that everyone masters who masters the language. New words may be formed by morphological derivation: we may add prefixes, such as *de–*, *re–*, *anti–* etc. to familiar verbs or nouns, or suffixes like *–ize*, *–arize*, *–ization*, *–arization*, *–ify*, *–ification*, etc. New words formed in this way are understood with no difficulty and usually pass unnoticed. Another way of forming new words is by composition of already familiar words. In many languages, German is a particularly notorious case, such compound words are written with no blanks or hyphens, all in one word.

Compounding and morphological derivation are ordinary forms of linguistic creativity, i.e. they form part of the ordinary use of language. But neither compounds nor morphologically derived words car. satisfacto–

rily be handled by most spelling correction programs, because they are based on word list. What is required, in addition to the word list is proper linguistic knowledge: morphology as well as the regularities of compound formation, plus, as we shall see below, semantics.

1.3   Grammar

But there are more problems, still in the fairly simple area of spelling correction. Spelling correction devices are fundamentally dictionary based. This means, first of all that the name *spelling correction* arouses the wrong expectations. For what the devices do is only to check for each individual string that occurs between two blanks whether it corresponds to a word in the word list, or, if there is a morphology component, if the string is a regular derivation from a word that is in the dictionary. But this means that spelling mistakes are not recognized whenever the incorrectness of a string only follows from the context. Typical cases in English are words like *its* and *it's* or *their* and *there*, which are frequently mixed up. But only syntactic analysis can tell us which is which and which is right in a particular place in a sentence.

A further problem in spelling that cannot be dealt with on the basis of a dictionary (with or without morphology) is the problem of whether to write an expression as one or two words or with a hyphen. The mere fact that two words occur singly in a dictionary does not imply that there is not also a word that consists of the concatenation of the two strings (*in* and *deed* happen to occur singly in the dictionary, but there is also a word *indeed*). Another problem of the same sort is capitalization: one and the same word form may occur in the language capitalized or non–capitalized and only the syntactic context, or worse, the meaning, will tell us which is at stake.

It is clear from these observations that there is quite a way to go until we will reach a stage in automatic spelling correction that approaches a stage at which we could honestly speak of "spelling correction" or even "automatic proof reading". And it is also clear that a good deal of linguistics is required in order to get closer to this goal: syntax, morphology, and, eventually, semantics.

2   Why not be happy with what there is ?

2.1   Taking the user serious

Why should one proceed this direction and add more linguistic knowledge to word processors rather than just be happy with what there is ? The major reason to be dissatisfied with what there is is that there is too much of a difference between the user's expectations and what current programs can do. When I write a French text and ask a Frenchman to correct the spelling, I expect at least that he gets rid of mistakes of the type just mentioned, for this is what we ordinarily mean by "correcting the spelling". But when I run the spelling correction program on my word processor, I have to be aware that it does a good deal less: that the device does not detect or correct mistakes on the basis of any form of linguistic understanding but merely uses a bunch of tricks. Hence, in order to appreciate what exactly the program does, the user must learn to understand the program.

We find ourselves back in the familiar situation which we would rather like to get away from: the user has to adjust to the machine, has to first understand the machine, rather than having machines that are adjusted to the user and fit in with the user's expectations.

That the problem is real is quickly appreciated when we look at customer complaints about spelling correction devices. In one case a large factory complained that a whole set of technical terms they (and nobody else) use for some of their products were not in their word processor's dictionary. "These are perfectly ordinary everyday words", they said and were dissatisfied that the spelling correction device kept marking them as spelling mistakes. In another case, a customer complained that their spelling correction program not only kept marking such "perfectly ordinary everyday words" wrong, but also suggested "silly" corrections. An example the customer gave was the name of the then Prime Minister of the GDR, *de Maizière*, which the program preferred to correct as *Malzbier* [brown ale]. In another case in the German word for liability insurance *Haftpflichtversicherung* the typist had missed out an *e* and got proposals for correction that included *Haftpflichtversdichtung* and *Haftpflichtverschwörung* ["liability versified poetry" and "liability conspiracy" respectively].

Of course such proposals, which result already from the inclusion of a facility that treats compound words, can only be prevented with the addition of a semantic module that recognizes that the proposed compounds are just regular nonsense. – But how should the user know ? Cases of this kind were regularly passed on to my department when we had the responsibility for the word lists included in some of IBM's word processors.

The point is that we have to take the user seriously: either educate him to understand how the systems work, or build systems that do not need this understanding because they process language in a way sufficiently similar to the human being, i.e. systems that propose corrections on the basis of at least a superficial form of linguistic understanding. The only option we have, in the long run, is the latter. A user can perhaps be brought to accept that particular technical jobs just have to be done with the help of an awkward tool that never quite does what it should do, and the user may even blame his own incompetence in such cases. But this does not work for things everybody is an expert on: the use of ordinary language.

2.2 Taking human language serious

A more general point is that computer programs are tools tailored for particular tasks and applications. A program will work fine within the boundaries of what the designers of the program, at the design stage, considered part of the application and it will work less satisfactorily when it is used for borderline cases. For many conventional or standardized applications, there is no problem in designing the program so that it fits exactly the user's conception of the application. The user will not expect anything of the device that is beyond its capabilities, because the designers knew in advance what the user would expect. In some, surely less ideal, cases, the user accepts that a certain amount of training is required to use a program comfortably and understand its capabilities.

But human language is not limited to conventionalized or standard uses but is a tool of nearly universal capabilities. It does not care what you speak about nor how much you know about what are talking about. You can use the same English language to inquire about the train schedule, to write a love poem, or to give somebody instructions for the repair of a diesel engine. There is a little difference in the vocabulary, but this seems about all; it is still English.

Now why can computational linguists not just model exactly this linguistic knowledge that allows us to inquire about train schedules as well as write love poems and give instructions about diesel engines ? Why can we not have an English language module that does for the computer precisely what our knowledge of a language does for us ? In other words: why can we not have a fully portable English language engine than can be connected to whatever program you please: say a database, to allow us to query the database or add information to it, or to another language engine, say one for German, to give us automatic translation between the two languages, or to some complicated technical system in order to control the relevant processes by the word of our mouth rather than by some silly Fortran or Pascal program that nobody understands ?

Before we proceed and try to answer this question, I would like to present to you a computer system that understands German text and try to show, by discussing the limitations of this system, what can and what can currently not be done in this line of business.

3 Full text understanding

3.1 Goals of the LILOG project

The LILOG project was set by IBM Germany in 1985 in order to investigate the possibilities of semantic information processing for natural language, in particular for German. The initial goal was not to develop a product, but rather to do research and develop new technologies for natural language processing and for knowledge–based systems more generally. The idea of the project was to jump in at the deep end and accept the challenge of the most complex and most difficult task in natural language processing: full text understanding. But why start with the most difficult task, rather than continue, say, in improving spelling correction devices ?

In text understanding we meet many, if not all, of the problems that occur also in simpler tasks of natural language processing, and, what is more, we can investigate these tasks in their mutual interaction. The crucial point, of course, is that in text understanding the two traditionally distinct disciplines of linguistics and logic (hence LI–LOG), or, more specifically, computational linguistics and artificial intelligence, have to be brought to together in order to achieve interesting results.

The research task of the LILOG project then has been to investigate text understanding and to implement a system on the computer that actually understands written text, German text in this case. – But how can we judge whether a computer has understood a text or has even read it ? Well, the same way a teacher checks whether a student has read and understood a text: by asking questions about the contents. Hence the system that had to be built not only had to be able to read and understand texts, but also to understand questions about the texts and answer them.

3.2 What the LILOG system does

The current version of the LILOG system, LEU/2, reads texts from tourist guides about the City of Düsseldorf like the following:

> *Im Palais Nesselrode ist das Hetjensmuseum, das 1909 eröffnet wurde, untergebracht. Es befindet sich an der Ecke Schulstraße und Hafenstraße. Die Keramiksammlung umfaßt zehntausend Objekte. Der Eintritt der Ausstellung, die von 10 Uhr bis 17 Uhr geöffnet ist, beträgt 2 DM.*

> *[The Hetjens Museum, which was opened in 1909, is housed in Palais Nesselrode. It is located at the corner of Schulstrasse and Hafenstrasse. The ceramics collection contains ten thousand items. The admission for the exhibition, which is open from 10 a.m. til 5 p.m., is DM 2.]*

When this text is processed a representation of its content is stored in the system's text knowledge base, or, in a little more detail: first each word in the text is looked up in the system's dictionary and the morphological, grammatical, and semantic information is handed on to the parser, which produces a linguistic analysis for the first sentence. Then a number of semantic operations are performed on the sentence, linking the contents of the sentence to information in the knowledge base of the system, and finally a translation of the sentence into a logical knowledge representation language (L_{LILOG}) is produced and put into the text memory. The following sentences are processed in a similar fashion, except that here the semantic analysis takes into account the contents of the preceding sentences.

The importance of this latter point is seen when we want the system to answer questions like for instance the following:

> *Wann hat das Hetjensmuseum geöffnet ?*
> *[When is the Hetjens Museum opened ?]*

The answer of the system,

> *Von 10 Uhr bis 17 Uhr.*
> *[From 10 a.m. til 5 p.m.]*

is evident to anyone who has read the text, but how does the system arrive at this answer ? Explicitly the text only gives the opening times of an exhibition. So the system must figure out that the exhibition is the exhibition of the ceramics collection, that the ceramics collection is presumably part of the museum and that, whenever the exhibition is opened, presumably the museum will be open too – a fairly complex task of resolving anaphorically definite NPs, which relies on fairly sophisticated knowledge representation and reasoning. In particular, we need common sense knowledge (e.g. that museums tend to have collections and exhibitions) and the knowledge of the various sentences of the text must be integrated – otherwise the exhibition would have nothing to do with the ceramics collection and the museum, and there would be no way of answering the above question.

Also in a dialogue with the user the system must keep track of what was just said before. Otherwise a question like

> *Ist es um 14 Uhr geöffnet ?*
> *[Is it open at 2 p.m.?]*

following the above question, would make no sense. The *es* [it] would not be related to the museum. Similarly questions like

> *Wieviel kostet der Eintritt ?*
> *[How much is the admission?]*

require an appropriate preceding discourse, because only then *the admission* can be interpreted in the intended fashion as *the admission for the Hetjens Museum.*

The LILOG text understanding system does a good many other things, like tell the user how to get from A to B in Düsseldorf, in words as well as with the help of a map, find its way round words it doesn't know, and it has very interesting capabilities in reasoning, ordinary logical reasoning as well as reasoning in an analogue fashion with mental images. But here we want to stick to the more strictly linguistic capabilities and the knowledge that is required for them.

3.3   What the LILOG system cannot do

At a demonstrations of the LILOG system at a technology show we were approached by an officer of the Inland Revenue with the proposal that we might apply the system to the German laws and regulations for income tax. The idea being that once all these texts have been understood by the system, it would be quite easy to ask questions like *Can someone who is self–employed deduct the expenses for their camping van from their income tax?* – Perhaps the system would initiate a dialogue with the user in order to clarify all the relevant details, but eventually it should tell the user whether and under what conditions the intended tax deduction is possible.

The application is certainly attractive and one of the longer term goals of text understanding systems of course is that they should be able to understand in principle any old text, even the law. But at present there are two important obstacles that make it inconceivable to consider such an application.

One is that understanding a text not only requires knowledge of the language, but also a conceptual model of the subject matter of the text. This is why most people do not understand the tax laws and need professional help (and not from linguists), despite their good knowledge of German. In fact, the situation is worse, particularly in law: there is not only no assurance that the law is consistent, but we know that jurisdiction interprets the law in the sense of deciding cases that are not clearly decided by what it says in the text of the law.

But even if the application was not to legal texts, but to a subject matter that is simpler in the sense that we can be reasonably sure that there is a consistent model, there would still be difficulties. In the first instance in actually building the relevant conceptual model, i.e. in carrying out the knowledge engineering for that domain. This is not as task with any principled obstacles, at least for many applications it is not, but the challenge is in the amount of work. – If we know that the technical documentation for a jumbo jet, printed out on paper, is heavier than the plane could carry, then we get a good idea of what it means to represent a complex domain of technical knowledge. But whenever natural language enters the scene, a good deal of common sense knowledge is required as well. Now, nobody knows anything about how large the common sense knowledge of an average person is, but what we do know, is that it is probably less consistent that a complex legal text. In sum: as long as research into natural language systems is a matter of pure research, it is very unlikely that anybody will fund the amount of work that is required just on the knowledge engineering side for either complex technical application or generic, i.e. application-independent, natural language systems that require full common sense knowledge.

3.4　The problems of ambiguity and polysemy

The other obstacle is the linguistic one. Already when we want to apply the LILOG system to much smaller and less complicated domains than the one just sketched, we run into difficulties, in particular with word meaning.

Consider, for instance, the meaning of *Eintritt* [admission], as it is relevant for the current application. What does the system know about the semantics of this word ? It basically knows just one type of context, the one in which *Eintritt* means *admission fee* and it knows that museums as well as other art institutions charge for admission. Now suppose we were to tell the system that someone "was not granted admission to" a particular museum. Then the first problem is that the construction *to grant admission to* will not be understood. For two reasons: one is that the verb *to grant* has a very large number of senses and this particular one is not included in the current linguistic module. The　other reason is that the sense of *admission* that is required, is not in the dictionary. As far as the LEU/2 system is concerned, *Eintritt*, or *admission*, is a certain amount of money you pay to be allowed into a museum. – Clearly, these two senses are only the tip of the iceberg and there are many more.

The way natural language systems start with the problem of word senses is probably also how we, as human beings, once started with most words: we learnt them in one particular context and gradually we found more applications in other contexts so that eventually we came to develop a representation of the meaning of words that more or less covers the regular uses the word has in our language. There is, however, no assurance, that we will not hit upon a use of the word that is actually new to us. And it is this situation where the LILOG system, as well as any current natural language system, differs from the human being: the system has no capabilities for relaxing the conditions the meaning of a word imposes, or slightly modifying them, to cover a newly encountered variant.

This means that the only option we have for natural language systems, at the moment, is to actually explicitly code each and every known sense of a word. The reason that we don't do this is not only that no–one would be prepared to fund this gigantic activity or that we were genuinely lazy. A more important reason is that we could currently not cope with the resulting ambiguity in processing. The more word senses we have in a system the more ambiguity we create. Each time an ambiguous word is encountered in a text, the ambiguity must be resolved, and since ambiguity resolution is not a matter of single words but a matter of a word in a context, we first get a combinatorial explosion of ambiguity (each ambiguous words combines, in principle, in each of its senses with each sense of each other word).

The pragmatic approach that is taken for all current natural language systems to cope with the problem of combinatorial explosion of lexical ambiguity or polysemy is to keep the systems relatively dum: the fewer word senses the system knows, the less of a problem it has with the explosion of ambiguity. (It seems that Nature takes a similar approach with children: they discover more word senses as their capability to handle them in language processing increases.) – Now, plainly, when we restrict a natural language system to a small and reasonably limited application, its limited knowledge of word senses yields no problems at all and has the additional advantage that also the knowledge engineering for the application remains manageable.

A consequence from these considerations is that in the near future there is no realistic option for large generic natural language systems, i.e. application–independent systems. This is no news to the specialist, but it is a priori not easy to understand for the non–specialist. The non–specialist is not usually aware of the considerable dependence of linguistic understanding on non–linguistic knowledge of the relevant subject matter, even though also he is aware of extreme cases: in order to understand the German tax regulations, mere knowledge of German is plainly insufficient. But also in less specialized areas the dependence on knowledge is just the same, the only difference being that there we are concerned with common sense or everyday knowledge that is generally and naturally available to anyone and that we acquire as we grow up, simultaneous with the acquisition or our mother tongue. The non–specialist is also not usually aware of the considerable number of relevant differences in the specification of word senses as they are required whenever explicit representation of meaning is necessary, as in computer systems. To someone who masters a language, the differences between various word senses are normally unnoticeable, just as a fluent speaker of a language is entirely unaware of any rules of grammar.

3.5   The way ahead

Let me illustrate the case of the almost uncontrollable number of word senses, with an example: the colour adjective *red*. When we look up this word in a dictionary, we only get a very rough impression of what is at stake, and will not appreciate the full scope of the problem. But consider the following uses of *red*:

> *red tomato*
> *red apple*
> *red hair*
> *red wine*
> *red grapefruit*
> *red indian*
> *red nose*

We are here not concerned with an ambiguity of the kind we find with words like *bank*, where there is a straightforward choice between either the financial institution and the bank of a river. There is good reason for the suspicion that there are not just the seven variants of the concept of redness that we find in the examples, but that this list can be extended ad libitum. And the equivocation we observe is definitely an equivocation that is relevant for language understanding, for the inferences our system must draw, and is not just a matter of shades of meaning one might just as well ignore. If the adjective *red* were to make the same contribution to the inferences of the system in all these cases, the conditions for calling a tomato, an apple, hair, wine, etc. *red* should be the same, which they are not, and one would surely want to avoid the system's conclusion that tomato, hair, grapefruit, etc. are all of the same colour. When a tomato is called red, you may infer that it is ripe – not an appropriate conclusion for either the Indian or the nose. We may also infer that it is red all over (perhaps with the exception of a couple of green leaves) – and this conclusion is not appropriate for the red apple: apples may be called red even when they are partly white or yellow. And the red grapefruit, of course is yellow all over, only the pulp is sort of pink. So not only are not all these *red* objects of the same colour, but there are quite different ways in which the qualification *red* applies to them.

What we find here, perhaps more clearly than in many other cases, is an obvious interaction between the senses of a word and our knowledge of the world: someone who doesn't know about red grapefruits, for instance, will never be able to predict what *red* means in application to grapefruits.

But how do we get ambiguity and polysemy under control ? – The approach required is in fact the same we saw at the beginning of this paper for spelling correction devices. There we saw that we get nowhere as long as we attempt to just list all the word forms of a language and build our device on this basis. Similarly, the mere listing of word senses is a hopeless and, as the example of *red* shows, never–ending exercise. What is required rather is a way of generating new senses from ones already known (a semantic "morphology", if you want to keep up the analogy to the spelling correction problem). And this is by no means a hopeless task. But it is a task that spans the handling of world knowledge and its conceptualization as well as traditional linguistic semantic research, approaches from cognitive psychology and more recent work from machine learning. Another side of the problem, as we saw above, is the handling of combinatorial explosion of ambiguity. Thus it is not enough to have just any old mechanism that generates all possible senses of a given word, but we want this mechanisms to generate, at the right time in linguistic processing, exactly those senses that are required at that point in processing, ideally only one word sense: a great challenge for the interaction of linguistic and logical modules in a natural language system.

But a good amount of work will be required until we are anywhere near this goal. – The orientation I have sketched comes from an argument about the research problems that lie behind actual deficiencies in available products. But this does not imply that this is an orientation that leaves out applications. The research work ahead can, I believe, only successfully be carried out when intermediate results are regularly tested in application work. However, the guiding principles have to come from a good understanding of the research situation.

This way of tackling current problems in natural language processing and working towards increasingly less application–dependent systems is in fact suitable for industrial as well as academic research environments. Next to the longer–term research topics of a more basic orientation, small applications can be developed in which intermediate results are used to demonstrate the practical usefulness and actual progress of the more basic research. The only serious danger in this situation is that overdrawn expectations based on insufficient understanding of the problems that lie at the roots of natural language systems will make us too impatient and go in for a purely application driven research, with no perspective for the general problems.

Unification Grammars: A Unifying Approach

Roland Seiffert
IBM Deutschland GmbH
Institut für Wissensbasierte Systeme
P.O. Box 80 08 80
W-7000 Stuttgart 80
Germany

Abstract

Unification-based grammar formalisms have recently received great interest in computational linguistics, because they allow for a very high-level, declarative description of grammatical relations over linguistic objects. Feature structures are used to encode all kinds of information about any given linguistic object, e.g., certain syntactic properties or semantic content. Grammar rules define the relation between surface strings of a language and the information associated with it. Special purpose theorem provers – parsers and generators – operate on these grammar rules to compute this relation in either direction, from a string to a feature structure or vice versa.

Recent formalisms, like the STUF formalism developed and used within the LILOG project at IBM Germany, go even one step further: surface strings are made an integral part of informational structures and general relations can be defined on them. There is no longer a special notion of 'grammar rule' relating surface strings to feature structures. Consequently, there is also no parser or generator. A very general inference mechanism evaluates the relational specification when given an input structure representing, e.g., a string. Aspects of controlling the inference process thus become a crucial research topic.

Work on the STUF formalism revealed a lot of interesting similarities between some of the most active research areas in AI: computational linguistics, constraint logic programming, functional programming, and knowledge representation systems.

1   Introduction

Unification-based grammar formalisms have recently received great interest in computational linguistics because they allow for a very high-level, declarative and modular description of grammatical relations over linguistic objects. Feature structures are used to encode various kinds of information about any given linguistic object, e.g., certain syntactic properties or semantic content. Lexical entries and grammar rules define the relation between surface strings of a language and the information associated with it. Special purpose theorem provers – parsers and generators – operate on these grammars to compute this relation in either direction, from a string to a feature structure, or vice versa.

When we speak about "unification grammars" we should carefully distinguish between *unification-based theories of grammar* and *unification-based grammar formalisms*. Theories like Lexical-Functional Grammar (LFG, [KB82]), Categorial Unification Grammar (CUG, [Usz86]), or Head-Driven Phrase Structure Grammar (HPSG, [PS87]) employ features structures to represent *linguistic objects*, and the actual form and content of these structures depends on the underlying linguistic theory. Most grammars also state a number of additional principles, which include universal principles that are deemed to hold for any natural language, as well as language-dependent principles, for instance concerning word order. These principles are either stated on a meta level, like, e.g., completeness and coherence in Lexical-Functional Grammar, or directly on the level of feature structures using implications, e.g., the Head-Feature Principle in Head-Driven Phrase Structure Grammar.

Formalisms like Functional Unification Grammar (FUG, [Kay79]), PATR-II ([SUP+83]), or STUF ([DR91], [DS91]) are theory-neutral. They use feature structures as their central *data structure*, and they impose no restrictions on the actual use of these structures. These formalisms have the status of very high-level programming languages that are especially well-suited to encode linguistic theories. They provide the means to represent linguistic objects using feature structures, and to encode additional theory-specific principles. For instance, the Head-Feature Principle applies to all "phrasal signs" and is represented by the specification that a phrasal sign via the unification mechanism inherits all properties provided by the principle.

This article describes ideas that have been integrated in the $\underline{S}tuttgart\ \underline{T}ype\ \underline{U}nification\ \underline{F}ormalism$ *(STUF)* which is being developed in the LILOG project of IBM Germany. STUF is a real formalism and is not committed to any particular linguistic theory. The grammar for German that is developed using STUF now follows the HPSG approach, but previous versions of the formalism have also been successfully applied to CUG.

2   The Traditional Approach

Early unification-based grammar formalisms were designed as a generalization of context-free grammars. They use grammar rules with a context-free skeleton and additional constraints, which are usually feature structures[1]. The symbols used in the grammar rules bear no real meaning, they are simply used as labels to identify which part of the rule refers to which part of the associated feature structure. The basic idea is to replace atomic nonterminal symbols with complex feature structures, i.e., the second rule shown in Figure 1 actually stands for [cat]: vp --> [cat]: v1, ([cat]: np & [agr, case]: dat). We now interpret rules analogously to context-free rules: To obtain a constituent [cat]: vp spanning a string $\alpha_0 = \alpha_1 \bullet \alpha_2$, we have to find a constituent [cat]: v1 spanning α_1 and a constituent ([cat]: np & [agr, case]: dat) spanning α_2. The essential difference to context-free rules is that *feature structure unification* is employed to match the nonterminals instead of literal identity. For instance, ([cat]: np & [agr, case]: dat) in rule 2 of Figure 1 unifies with the nonterminal [cat: np] & [agr]: ([case]: dat & [person]: third & [number]: sg) associated with the lexical entry **sokrates**, and therefore this rule would be applicable here. A formal definition of *derivation* in unification grammars is provided, e.g., in [Sei91b].

```
vp --> v0 --                     schlaeft :=
    [vp, cat]: vp &                  [cat: v0].
    [v0, cat]: v0.               vertraut :=
vp --> v1, np --                     [cat: v1].
    [vp, cat]: vp &              liebt :=
    [v1, cat]: v1 &                  [cat: v2].
    [np, cat]: np &              gibt :=
    [np, agr, case]: dat.            [cat: v3].
vp --> v2, np --                 sokrates :=
    [vp, cat]: vp &                  [cat: np] &
  · [v1, cat]: v2 &                  [agr]: ( [case]: dat &
    [np, cat]: np &                           [person]: third &
    [np, agr, case]: akk.                     [number]: sg
vp --> v3, np1, np2 --                     ).
```

---

[1]One might count Definite Clause Grammars also as unification grammars. In this case the constraints are first-order terms attached to nonterminal symbols.

```
[vp, cat]: vp &
[v3, cat]: v3 &
[np1, cat]: np &
[np1, agr, case]: dat &
[np2, cat]: np &
[np2, agr, case]: akk.
```

Figure 1: Simple unification grammar

The use of unification within a derivation step in general leads to Turing power of unification grammars. This is due to the fact that the various nonterminals in one rule can share parts of their information. A very simple grammar for the wellknown context-sensitive language $L = \{a^n b^n c^n\}$ is shown in [Sei91a].

When we look at the evolution of linguistic theories that follow the unification-based approach over the last years, we discover that more and more information is encoded in feature structures, whereas grammar rules tend to degenerate to very simple combination schemata. The most radical approach is CUG, where all syntactic information is encoded in the feature structures associated with a lexical entry, and there are only two or four general purpose combination schemata. We want to motivate this trend by discussing the example of a verb phrase syntax shown in Figure 1. The various rules account for different verb classes, e.g., intransitive verbs (v0), transitive verbs (v1, v2) .... There are of course a lot more possible verb classes, which would lead to many more rules. Intuitively, the verb itself demands a certain number of arguments with specific requirements, and we would like to specify this information where it belongs, namely in the lexical entry for the verb. But there we only specified a verb class and the "meaning" of this verb class is given in the grammar rules. Figure 2 shows a possible solution: We provide a *subcategorization list* for every verb that contains all its arguments in the correct order and all restrictions on them. Now, we only need two grammar rules to account for all possible verb phrases. The first rule handles the case of an empty subcategorization list, i.e., all required arguments have been found. The second rule combines one argument with an incomplete verb phrase that expects this argument as the first element of its subcategorization list. The feature structure on the lefthand side of the rule is another incomplete verb phrase that expects exactly the rest of the specified arguments.

```
vp --> x --
  [vp, cat]: vp &
  [x, cat]: v &
  [x, subcat]: nil.
x --> h, c --
  [x, cat] = [h, cat] &
  [h, subcat, first] = [c] &
  [x, subcat] = [h, subcat, rest].

schlaeft :=
  [cat: v] &
  [subcat: nil].
vertraut :=
  [cat: v] &
  [subcat, first]: ( [cat]: np &
                     [agr, case]: dat ) &
  [subcat, rest]: nil.
liebt :=
  [cat: v] &
  [subcat, first]: ( [cat]: np &
                     [agr, case]: akk ) &
  [subcat, rest]: nil.
```

```
gibt :=
   [cat: v] &
   [subcat, first]: ( [cat]: np &
                      [agr, case]: dat ) &
   [subcat, rest, first]: ( [cat]: np &
                            [agr, case]: akk ) &
   [subcat, rest, rest]: nil.
```

Figure 2: Lexicalization of subcategorization information

When we take the idea of lexicalization of linguistic information seriously, we soon run into problems that you might have already noticed. The structures associated with lexical entries get very complex. In Figure 2 the structure are already quite complicated, although they only specify a very small part of the information we need in a real grammar. Also, we arrive at a highly redundant representation since large parts of the structures for different entries are identical, and we have to guarantee the consistency of our modelling throughout the whole grammar. Unification formalisms came up with a solution to these problems very early by introducing a *template mechanism*. Templates are very similar to *macros* in conventional programming languages. They abbreviate larger structures that can be imbedded at any point by simply referring to the name of the template. Figure 3 shows the use of templates to encode the same lexicon as that of Figure 2. When we use a template name it is simply replaced by the feature structure provided in the template definition, and this structure is then unified with the rest of the particular structure. Templates allow for a modular and nonredundant representation of information in a grammar, and since unification is employed to merge the information coming from different sources we are also able to structure our grammar in a hierarchical way with built-in multiple inheritance. For instance, in Figure 3 the lexical entries for verbs only specify a verb class, which is really a template. The definition of 'V1' then states that the verbs in this particular class inherit all properties from the general verb description 'V' and this is specialized by adding the subcategorization information 'SUBCAT'(cons('NP'(dat),nil)), i.e., the verb expects exactly one argument which is a dative NP. Note that it is very convenient to use templates with additional parameters that are substituted with the actual values before the template is expanded[2].

```
schlaeft := 'V0'.                        liebt    := 'V2'.
vertraut := 'V1'.                        gibt     := 'V3'.


'V0' :=                                  'V' :=
   'V' & 'SUBCAT'(nil).                     [cat]: v.
'V1' :=                                  'SUBCAT'(Subcat) :=
   'V' & 'SUBCAT'(cons('NP'(dat),nil)).     [subcat]: Subcat.
'V2' :=                                  'NP'(Case) :=
   'V' & 'SUBCAT'(cons('NP'(acc),nil)).     [cat]: np &
'V3' :=                                      [agr, case]: Case.
   'V' & 'SUBCAT'(cons('NP'(dat),       cons(First,Rest) :=
              cons('NP'(acc),nil))).        [first]: First &
                                            [rest]:  Rest.
```

Figure 3: Lexical entries using templates

Feature structures are a very simple data structure for representing linguistic information, and it turns out that in many cases they have reached their limits now. For instance, consider the problem that we have to encode lexical entries for a word like **go**. Looking only at the agreement properties of this word, we'll notice that it could be either plural, first person singular, or second person singular—in other words, everything else but third person singular. Using simple feature structures, we would

---

[2] *Parametrized templates* are available in the STUF formalism, but not, e.g., in PATR-II

have to specify one complete lexical entry for each of the possibilities. What we would like to do instead is to specify only one structure that is *disjunctive* with respect to the agreement properties, or to use a *negative* specification. For instance, this could look like the following example:

```
go :=                                    go :=
    ... [agr]: { [number]: pl                ... [agr]: not ( [number]: sg &
                ; ( [number]: sg &                            [person]: third
                  { [person]: first                         )
                  ; [person]: second       ...
                  }
                )
              }
    ...
```

Figure 4: Feature descriptions using disjunction and negation

This idea has been carefully studied during the last years[3] and from this the notion of *feature descriptions* or *feature terms* emerged. The basic idea is to allow for a richer language for feature descriptions containing, e.g., disjunctions and negations. These descriptions are then semantically interpreted as a specification of a (possibly infinite) *set of feature structures*. Unification of two feature description means now to compute a representation of a feature description for the intersection of the sets denoted by the original descriptions. Unification fails, if this result denotes the empty set. Good algorithms must avoid to explicitly construct these sets and research in this area is still very active.

3 The Principle-Based Approach

We could summarize the traditional approach of unification-based grammars as follows: Feature structures are employed to encode the informational contents of any linguistic object, and grammar rules define the relation between surface strings of a language and the associated information. The principle-based approach goes one step further: Strings are made an integral part of linguistic objects with arbitrary relations – principles – defined between them. Obviously, this includes the very special relation definable through grammar rules. But the flexibility gained by this generalization is tremendous. For instance, languages like German or Dutch are very complicated with respect to word order phenomena, and it seems that the simple concatenation operation on the string level being imposed by grammar rules is too weak to describe the phenomena adequately. [Rea89] proposes a solution that makes use of various operations defined on the string level depending on the other information being present in the structure of linguistic objects. These operations can be easily defined as relations within the grammar if strings are available at the descriptive level.

Also, we are no longer restricted to a one-dimensional set of rules which enumerates all possible local trees, but rather may have a whole hierarchy of rules, expressed through a hierarchy of principles, including, e.g., principles that hold on any local tree no matter which rule is used to build it. This approach is exactly the one taken in HPSG ([PS87]), which is a typical representative of a linguistic theory following the principle-based approach. In HPSG a grammar defines all possible *signs* of a language, i.e., all linguistic objects that are either an instance of a lexical sign or one of the grammar rules, and that satisfy all principles. Principles are in essence generalizations which hold over sets of rules. All principles formulated for HPSG are local in the sense that only one local tree, i.e., a mother category with its immediate daughter categories, is regarded at once. They never talk about head or complement of some daughter category, or of any part of its structure. Also, lexical signs

---

[3]There are quite a lot of publications on that particular topic. To name only a few of them, see [Ait84], [DE89], [DE90], [Kas87], [KR86], [Sei88], [Smo88].

never make direct use of the notion of constituency. These considerations lead us to propose that principles and rules should be formalized as relations of three arguments: mother, head daughter, and a list of complement daughters. Figure 5 shows part of an HPSG grammar written in STUF, including principles and rules.

Note, that we employ a functional notation to define relations in STUF. This reflects directly the way we want to describe linguistic objects. The purpose of this grammar is to build a representation of a sign providing, e.g., its phonology[4]. We start by defining that a `sign` is either a `phrasal_sign` or a `lexical_sign`. Then a `phrasal_sign` is a structure built from a head daughter and a list of complement daughters that obeys all `principles` and at least one `rule`. Principles include universal principles and language-dependent principles. For instance, consider the definition of the `subcat_principle`. We assume that in a phrase there always exists a head that imposes certain requirements on its complements, e.g., the verb in a verb phrase specifies all its possible arguments. The subcategorization principle simply says: If in any phrasal sign we have a head that subcategorizes for a list of arguments and we have found a number a arguments now, then the phrasal sign needs to find the rest of the arguments later to become a complete sign. STUF allows that the principle uses other relational dependencies (`append`) within its definition, even on argument positions, which leads to very elegant and concise descriptions.

```
% a 'sign' can be either phrasal or lexical
sign ==> phrasal_sign.
sign ==> lexical_sign.

% a phrasal sign has to obey all principles and at least one rule
phrasal_sign ==>
    principles(HeadDtr, ComplementDtrs) &
    rule(HeadDtr, ComplementDtrs).

% principles relate a head (a sign) to its complements (a list of signs)
principles(HeadDtr & sign, ComplementDtrs & signs) ==>
    universal_principles(HeadDtr, ComplementDtrs) &
    german_principles(HeadDtr, ComplementDtrs).

% universal principles
universal_principles(HeadDtr, ComplementDtrs) ==>
    subcat_principle(HeadDtr, ComplementDtrs) &
    head_feature_principle(HeadDtr).

% language specific principles
german_principles(HeadDtr, ComplementDtrs) ==>
    constituent_order_principle(HeadDtr, ComplementDtrs).

% the subcategorization principle:
% if a head subcategorizes for a list of complements (append(S1,S2))
% and some of these complements are found (S2)
% then the remaining complements have to be found later (S1)
subcat_principle([syn, loc, subcat]:append(S1,S2), S2) ==>
    [syn, loc, subcat]: S1.

% the head-feature principle:
% the values of all 'head-features' (as opposed to local features)
% of the head daughter are passed to the mother constituent as its
% head-features
```

---

[4]This corresponds to the analysis of an input string using a traditional unification-grammar.

416

```
head_feature_principle([syn, loc, head]: X) ==>
   [syn, loc, head] : X.


% constituent order principle:
% orders the head daughter and its complements according
% to language-specific constraints and returns the
% phonology of the ordered list
constituent_order_principle(HeadDtr, ComplementDtrs) ==>
   [phon]: collect_phon(order_constituents([first]: HeadDtr &
                                           [rest]:  ComplementDtrs)).


% grammar rules (or what is left of them)
% RULE 1: combine a non-lexical head with exactly one complement
%         (usually the subject) and return a saturated sign,
%         i.e. a sign with an empty subcat list
rule([syn, loc, lex]: minus, [first]:X & [rest]:nil) ==>
   [syn, loc, subcat]: nil.
% RULE 2: combine a lexical head with all its complements, but one
%         and return a non-lexical sign which subcategorizes
%         for the missing complement
%         (non-inverted phrase)
rule([syn, loc]: ( [head, inv]: minus &
                   [lex]: plus ),          X) ==>
   [syn, loc, subcat]: ( [first]: Y &
                         [rest]: nil ).
% RULE 3: combine a lexical head with all its complements
%         and return a saturated sign
%         (inverted phrase)
rule([syn, loc]: ( [head, inv]: plus &
                   [lex]: plus ),          X) ==>
   [syn, loc, subcat]: nil.


% a list of signs
signs ==> nil.
signs ==>
   cons &
   [first]: sign &
   [rest]:  signs.
```

Figure 5: HPSG-style grammar written in STUF

We want to stress that our functional notation does not imply any consequences for the procedural interpretation of STUF. The whole formalism is still totally declarative. "Functions" are not at all directional. They can be used to compute a result structure provided with all the arguments, or to obtain the arguments providing the result, or even an arbitrary mixture with partial structures for both result and arguments. Consider the definition of append shown in Figure 6.

```
append(nil,Y) ==> Y.
append(cons & [first]: X & [rest]: Xs, Y) ==>
   [first]: X &
   [rest]: append(Xs,Y).
```

Figure 6: Definition of append

Figure 7 shows a possible situation in STUF[5]: The value of append is known, and the arguments are only partially instantiated. This structure actually stands for a disjunction of three different feature structures shown in the same figure below.

---

[5]We have abbreviated the occurring lists in an obvious way.

```
[f]: ( X & <a.Xs> ) &
[g]: Y &
[h]: ( append(X,Y) & <a,b,c> )

[f]: <a> &        [f]: <a,b> &      [f]: <a,b,c> &
[g]: <b,c> &      [g]: <c> &        [g]: <> &
[h]: <a,b,c>      [h]: <a,b,c>      [h]: <a,b,c>
```

Figure 7: **append** is a relation

4 STUF Seen as a Constraint Logic Programming Language

In this section we will present some of the basic ideas underlying our current STUF implementation. First, recall that STUF specifications employ a quasi-functional notation to define relations. We can make these relations explicit by systematically introducing an additional argument for all relations. Figure 9 shows a translation function *trans* that converts a given definition $r(\vec{s}) := t$ into a new, equivalent definition of the form $r(X, \vec{X}) \leftarrow t'$, where t' is a formula built of conjunctions and disjunctions of *basic constraints* (Figure 8). We call the first three forms *primitive constraints*. They are just the feature constraints needed to describe ordinary feature structures with subsorts (see [Smo88]).

$$f(X) = Y, \text{ where } f \text{ is a feature, } X \text{ and } Y \text{ are variables}$$
$$X \in A, \text{ where } A \text{ is a sort, } X \text{ is a variable}$$
$$X = Y, \text{ where } X \text{ and } Y \text{ are variables}$$
$$r(X_0, \ldots, X_n), \text{ where } r \text{ is a (defined) } n\text{-ary relation; } X_0, \ldots, X_n \text{ is}$$
$$\text{usually written as } \vec{X}$$

Figure 8: The basic constraints

$$\text{trans}(r(\vec{s}) := t) \Rightarrow r(X, \vec{X}) \leftarrow \text{trans}(X,t) \wedge \text{trans}(X_i, s_i), \text{ for all } X_i$$
$$\text{in } \vec{X} \text{ and corresponding } s_i \text{ in } \vec{s}, \text{ and } X \text{ and all}$$
$$X_i \text{ are new variables}$$

$$\text{trans}(X, f : t) \Rightarrow f(X) = Y \wedge \text{trans}(Y,t), \text{ where } Y \text{ is a new variable}$$
$$\text{trans}(X, A) \Rightarrow X \in A$$
$$\text{trans}(X, Y) \Rightarrow X = Y$$
$$\text{trans}(X, t_1 \& t_2) \Rightarrow \text{trans}(X,t_1) \wedge \text{trans}(X,t_2)$$
$$\text{trans}(X, t_1 ; t_2) \Rightarrow \text{trans}(X,t_1) \vee \text{trans}(X,t_2)$$
$$\text{trans}(X, r(\vec{t})) \Rightarrow r(X, \vec{X}) \wedge \text{trans}(X_i, t_i), \text{ for all } X_i \text{ in } \vec{X} \text{ and corresponding } t_i \text{ in } \vec{t}, \text{ and all } X_i \text{ are new variables}$$

Figure 9: The translation function *trans*

As an example consider the definition for **append** shown in Figure 6. The function *trans* applied to all definitions in this example yields[6]:

$$append(Y, X, Y) \leftarrow$$
$$X \in nil.$$
$$append(Z, X, Y) \leftarrow$$
$$Z \in cons \land first(Z) = X1 \land rest(Z) = Zs\land$$
$$X \in cons \land first(X) = X1 \land rest(X) = Xs\land$$
$$append(Zs, Xs, Y).$$

Each of the definitions resulting from *trans* can be easily transformed into an equivalent set of *normal form clauses*. The normal form is defined as

$$r_0(\vec{X_0}) \leftarrow \phi \land r_1(\vec{X_1}) \land \ldots \land r_n(\vec{X_n})$$

ϕ is a formula containing arbitrary conjunctions and disjunctions of primitive constraints. If our system contains only definitions in normal form – definite clauses – then this fits nicely into the refined Constraint Logic Programming scheme described in [HS88]. In fact, our definite relations correspond exactly to the relational extensions of simple feature logic as described in [Smo88] for which efficient constraint solvers exist. This immediately gives us an operational semantics for solving the relational constraints, which is a generalization of SLD-resolution. In this approach we can resolve in a sequence of goals $r_0(\vec{X}) \land Rel Atoms \land \phi_0$ with the above clause by replacing ϕ_0 by a solved form of $\phi_0 \land \phi \land \vec{X} = \vec{X_0}$, if that exists. This constraint solving step corresponds to the term unification of a goal and the head of a clause in conventional logic programming. Our implementation of STUF is based on this SLD-resolution scheme and thanks to [HS88] we know that this approach is sound and complete.

Another observation is that a very common optimization technique from conventional logic programming can be integrated into our framework: Some of the (non-relational) constraints of ϕ are associated with the head of a definite clause (ϕ_{Head}) and others with the body (ϕ_{Body}), i.e., $\phi = \phi_{Head} \land \phi_{Body}$.

$$r_0(\vec{X_0}) \leftarrow \phi_{Head} \land \phi_{Body} \land r_1(\vec{X_1}) \land \ldots \land r_n(\vec{X_n})$$

ϕ_{Head} should be very simple but impose very strong constraints. Then it can be used to efficiently cut down the search space significantly. When selecting a clause, we first unify with ϕ_{Head} and if this fails, we reject the clause immediately. Typical constraints in ϕ_{Head} are sort restrictions on the variables occurring in the head of the clause.

On our way moving from traditional unification-based grammar formalisms to the principle-based approach we have not only abandoned "grammar rules" but also the corresponding algorithms for analysis and generation of sentences. A parser or a generator can be easily specified within the formalism, for instance by supplying the following rules:

```
parse(Phon) ==>
   sign & [phon]: Phon.
generate(Semantics) ==>
   generate1([semantics]: Semantics).
generate1(sign & [phon]: Phon)  ==>
   Phon.
```

---

[6]Equations between simple variables are already eliminated through variable substitution

With these definitions and a grammar a very general inference procedure is, e.g., able to compute a complete sign associated with the string **Hans liebt Maria** by simply proving the goal **parse(<hans, liebt, maria>)** and returning the righthand side of **parse**. But how can this be achieved efficiently? We have shown that STUF can be viewed as a CLP language, and that a variant of SLD-resolution is a correct and complete calculus for this logic. Of course, to obtain efficient proofs we have to select the single resolution steps in the right order. Strategies and heuristics to guide the proof procedure become a most important research topic. Currently, we are investigating two ideas that we want to combine in one implementation. First, we want to adopt techniques from logic programming to detect deterministic subgoals wherever possible and prefer them, and also to detect sources of possible combinatoric explosion and delay those goals. Second, we have great experience in conventional parsing techniques for unification grammars and we want to make those results available for guiding our new, more general proof procedure.

5 Related Research in Other Areas

Work on the STUF formalism revealed a lot of interesting similarities between some of the most active research areas in AI: computational linguistics, constraint logic programming, functional programming, and knowledge representation systems.

In the previous section we have already shown in some detail how STUF can be understood and implemented as a *constraint logic programming* language. The simplicity, clarity and elegance of this approach made it possible to implement a first version of STUF within surprisingly short time. Now we attempt to integrate results of CLP research into our work to yield a more efficient system.

Research in the area of *functional programming languages* is often concerned with extensions like non-deterministic functions, function inversion, or logical variables. For instance, [Red85] proposes a language that makes available these features and studies *narrowing* as an operational semantics. Narrowing an expression is applying to it the minimum substitution such that the resulting expression is reducible and then reducing[7] it. Narrowing not only subsumes reduction, but also SLD-resolution for Horn logic. [DP85] adds logical variables and conditions to an applicative language and provides a semantics in terms of *conditional narrowing*. The basic form of a conditional rule in their system is **l :- p -> r.** where **l** and **r** are *terms* and **p** is a *predicate*. Basically, such a rule says: "you may *rewrite* a term **l** to a term **r** if the condition **p** is met." This is further extended by using logical variables within the terms and the predicate. Unification is used to select applicable rules for a given term instead of literal matching. The TFS system[8] described in [EZ90] looks like a variant of this approach where the first-order terms have been replaced by feature terms. The current TFS implementation is based on a conditional rewriting algorithm using feature term unification to match structures.

Interestingly enough, the TFS implementation was *not* derived from [DP85], but follows mainly [Ait84] who describes a *Knowledge Base Language (KBL)* using only recursively defined feature terms and an interpreter for KBL. Ait-Kaci also describes some relations of KBL to functional and logical programming languages. Later, the language LIFE[9] was developed ([AP91]) as an attempt to integrate into one programming language the three orthogonal programming paradigms: logic, functional, and object-oriented programming.

[NS89] surveys terminological representation languages – which can be regarded as offsprings of KL-ONE ([BS85]) – and feature-based unification grammars pointing out the similarities and differences between these two families of attributive description formalisms.

---

[7]Functional programs have conventionally been used with the operational semantics of *reduction*.

[8]TFS is being developed with the same applications in mind as STUF: principle-based grammars for natural languages.

[9]LIFE – Logic, Inheritance, Functions, Equations

6 Conclusion

We view the STUF formalism as a "unifying approach" to unification-based grammar formalisms in at least two ways: First, the possibility to define general relations over feature structures increases the descriptive power of the formalism in a very useful way for linguists. It allows to express linguistic generalization not only through the restrictive template mechanism but much more generally. For instance, principles as known from HPSG can be directly represented using recursive definitions of signs, relying on unification to inherit all information from the principles including also word order information on the string level. Old-fashioned grammar rules are no longer needed. Also extensions of feature descriptions like *functional uncertainty* in LFG are simply a special subclass of recursively defined feature structures. Second, our view of the formalism makes it possible to relate our research to many other very active areas in AI research as has been pointed out above. This enables us to adopt their solutions in our implementation of STUF. Currently, we are investigating techniques used in constraint logic programming. This includes strategies and heuristics to control the proof procedure, for instance by detecting deterministic subgoals or delaying certain subgoals that would lead to a combinatorial explosion of the search space, as well as efficient constraint solving algorithms. On the other hand we want to profit from previous experiences in the development of parsing algorithms and apply these techniques to devise especially well-suited proof procedures for STUF. We hope that the integration of results from so many different areas has a considerable synergy effect and leads to a very powerful grammar formalism for computational linguistics that can nevertheless be efficiently processed.

References

[Ait84] H. Ait-Kaci. *A Lattice Theoretic Approach to Computation Based on a Calculus of Partially Ordered Type Structures*. PhD thesis, University of Pennsylvania, 1984.

[AP91] H. Ait-Kaci, A. Podelski. *Is there a Meaning to LIFE?*. Draft of a paper submitted to ICLP '91.

[BS85] R. J. Brachman, J. G. Schmolze. *An Overview of the* KL-ONE *Knowledge Representation System*. In: *Cognitive Science*, 9(2):171-216, April 1985.

[Car90] B. Carpenter. *Typed Feature Structures: Inheritance, (In)equality and Extensionality*. In: *Proceedings of the Workshop on Inheritance in Natural Language Processing*, Tilburg University, The Netherlands, 1990.

[DE89] J. Dörre, A. Eisele. *Determining Consistency of Feature Terms with Distributed Disjunctions*. In: D. Metzing (ed.): *GWAI-89, 13th German Workshop on Artificial Intelligence*. Informatik-Fachberichte 216, Springer-Verlag, Berlin, Heidelberg, 1989.

[DE90] J. Dörre, A. Eisele. *Feature Logic with Disjunctive Unification*. In: *Proceedings of the 13th International Conference on Computational Linguistics*, Helsinki, 1990.

[DE91] J. Dörre, A. Eisele. *A Comprehensive Unification-Based Grammar Formalism*. Deliverable R3.1.B, DYANA — ESPRIT Basic Research Action BR3175, 1991. to appear.

[DP85] N. Dershowitz, D. A. Plaisted. *Logic Programming cum Applicative Programming* Symposium on Logic Programming, IEEE, Boston, 1985.

[DR90] J. Dörre, W. C. Rounds. *On Subsumption and Semi-Unification in Feature Algebras*. In *Proceedings of the 5th Annual Symposium on Logic in Computer Science*, pages 300-310, Philadelphia, PA., 1990.

[DR91] J. Dörre, I. Raasch. *The Stuttgart Type Unification Formalism - User Manual*. IWBS Report 168, IBM Deutschland GmbH, Institute for Knowledge Based Systems, 1991.

[DS91] J. Dörre, R. Seiffert. *Sorted Feature Terms and Relational Dependencies*. IWBS Report 153, IBM Deutschland GmbH, Institute for Knowledge Based Systems, 1991.

[EZ90] M. Emele, R. Zajac. *Typed Unification Grammars*. In: *Proceedings of the 13th International Conference on Computational Linguistics*, Helsinki, Finland, 1990.

[HS88] M. Höhfeld, G. Smolka. *Definite Relations Over Constraint Languages.* LILOG Report 53, IWBS, IBM Deutschland, Postfach 80 08 80, 7000 Stuttgart 80, W. Germany, October 1988. To appear in the Journal of Logic Programming.

[KB82] R. M. Kaplan, J. Bresnan. *Lexical-Fuctional Grammar: A Formal System for Grammatical Representation.* In: J. Bresnan (ed.): *The Mental Representaion of Grammatical Relations*, MIT Press, Cambridge, Mass., 1982.

[Kas87] R. T. Kasper. *Feature Structures: A Logical Theory with Application to Language Analysis.* PhD thesis, University of Michigan, 1987.

[Kay79] M. Kay. *Functional Grammar.* In: *Proceedings of the Fifth Annual Meeting of the Berkeley Linguistic Society*, Berkeley, Cal., 1979.

[Kni89] K. Knight. *Unification: A Multidisciplinary Survey.* In: *ACM Computing Surveys*, Vol. 21, No. 1. pages 93–124, March 1989.

[KR86] R. T. Kasper, W. C. Rounds. *A Logical Semantics for Feature Structures.* In *Proceedings of the 24th Annual Meeting of the ACL, Columbia University*, pages 257–265, New York, N.Y., 1986.

[NS89] B. Nebel, G. Smolka. *Representation and Reasoning with Attributive Descriptions.* IWBS Report 81, IBM Deutschland GmbH, Stuttgart, Germany, 1989.

[PS87] C. Pollard, I. A. Sag. *Information-Based Syntax and Semantics.* CSLI Lecture Notes 13. Center for the Study of Language and Information, Stanford University, 1987.

[Rea89] M. Reape. *A Logical Treatment of Semi-Free Word Order and Bounded Discontinuous Constituency.* In: *Proceedings of the 4th Conference of the European Chapter of the Association for Computational Linguistics*, pages 103–110, Manchester, England, 1989.

[Red85] U. S. Reddy. *Narrowing as the Operational Semantics of Functional Languages.* Symposium on Logic Programming, IEEE, Boston, 1985.

[Sei88] R. Seiffert. *Operationen in erweiterten Typenunifikationsformalismen.* LILOG-Report 46, IBM Deutschland GmbH, Stuttgart, 1988.

[Sei91a] R. Seiffert. *Chart-Parsing of STUF Grammars.* To appear in: O. Herzog, C.-R. Rollinger (eds.): *Text Understanding in LILOG: Integrating Computational Linguistics and Artificial Intelligence*, Springer-Verlag, Berlin, Heidelberg, 1991.

[Sei91b] R. Seiffert. *Unification-ID/LP Grammars: Formalization and Parsing.* To appear in: O. Herzog, C.-R. Rollinger (eds.): *Text Understanding in LILOG: Integrating Computational Linguistics and Artificial Intelligence*, Springer-Verlag, Berlin, Heidelberg, 1991.

[She89] M. J. Shensa. *A Computational Structure for the Propositional Calculus.* In: *Proceedings of the 11th International Joint Conference on Artificial Intelligence*, Detroit, Michigan, USA, 1989.

[Smo88] G. Smolka. *A Feature Logic with Subsorts.* LILOG Report 33, IWBS, IBM Deutschland, Postfach 80 08 80, 7000 Stuttgart 80, W. Germany, May 1988. To appear in the Journal of Automated Reasoning.

[Smo89] G. Smolka. *Feature Constraint Logics for Unification Grammars.* IWBS Report 93, IWBS, IBM Deutschland, Postfach 80 08 80, 7000 Stuttgart 80, W. Germany, November 1989. To appear in the Proceedings of the Workshop on Unification Formalisms—Syntax, Semantics and Implementation, Titisee, The MIT Press, 1990.

[SUP+83] S. M. Shieber, H. Uszkoreit, F. C. N. Pereira, J. J. Robinson, M. Tyson. *The Formalism and Implementation of PATR-II.* In: *Research on Interactive Acquisition and Use of Knowledge*, Artificial Intelligence Center, SRI International, Menlo Park, Cal., 1983.

[Usz86] H. Uszkoreit. *Categorial Unification Grammars.* In: *Proceedings of the 11th International Conference on Computational Linguistics*, Bonn, 1986.

Integration
unterschiedlicher lexikalischer Ressourcen

Wilfried Hötker   Siegfried Kanngießer
Petra Ludewig
Fachbereich Sprach- und Literaturwissenschaft
Arbeitsbereich Computerlinguistik
und Künstliche Intelligenz
Postfach 44 69
4500 Osnabrück

Der hier vorgestellte Ansatz zur Integration lexikalischer Ressourcen soll zur Überwindung des 'lexical acquisition bottleneck' beitragen und unterliegt dem Paradigma der 'reusability of lexical resources'. Die Widersprüchlichkeit zwischen einem stabilen, kompakten und neutralen Lexikon einerseits und spezifischen, an konkrete Bedürfnisse angepaßten Lexika andererseits stellt ein den theorieübergreifenden und multifunktionalen lexikalischen Datenbanken bzw. Wissensbasen (LDBs/LKBs) inhärentes aber in den meisten Ansätzen vernachlässigtes Problem dar. In dem vorliegenden Beitrag soll diese Diskrepanz mit Hilfe eines um lokale reversible Konverter erweiterten Wissenspaketmechanismus überbrückt werden. Durch eine Korrelationsanalyse werden lexikalische Informationen unterschiedlicher Herkunft auf Ableitbarkeit untersucht. Die Informationen eines LKB-Eintrages werden - in Abhängigkeit ihrer Ableitbarkeit - auf die verschiedenen Wissenspakete verteilt. Die Wissenspaketstruktur gibt die Sichtbarkeits- und Konsistenzbedingungen der in der LKB abgelegten Daten wieder. Lokale reversible Konverter vermitteln zwischen den in einer direkten Nachfolgebeziehung stehenden Wissenspaketen, indem sie Ableitungsmechanismen und Transformationen bzgl. der Darstellungsweise spezifizieren. Lexikonimport und -export stellen vor diesem Hintergrund zwei Perspektiven auf ein und denselben von unten nach oben propagierten Umstrukturierungsprozeß dar, der mit einer iterativen Approximation einer neutralen Repräsentation lexikalischer Daten einhergeht.

1   Einführung

Die Entwicklung auf dem Gebiet der Computerlinguistik (CL) und der sprachorientierten Künstlichen Intelligenz (KI) macht es dringend erforderlich, sich Gedanken zur computergestützten Integration lexikalischer Daten unterschiedlicher Herkunft zu machen. Zur Zeit stehen dabei folgende Typen lexikalischer Ressourcen für eine maschinelle Weiterverarbeitung zur Verfügung:

- für das Setzen von Büchern konzipierte maschinenlesbare Versionen herkömmlicher Wörterbücher (MRDs),

- mehr oder weniger benutzerspezifische lexikalische Datenbanken (LDBs), insbesondere solche, die die Informationen konventioneller Wörterbücher in strukturierter, leicht vorverarbeiteter Form enthalten und gleichermaßen für Menschen und Systeme konzipiert sind,

- spezifische Lexika, die auf die speziellen Bedürfnisse konkreter natürlichsprachlicher Systeme zugeschnitten sind, sogenannte computational linguistics dictionaries (CLDs).

Bestrebungen, lexikalisches Wissen verschiedenen Ursprungs zu sammeln und in einheitlicher Form wieder zur Verfügung zu stellen, sind nicht neu. Schon seit etwa Anfang der 80er Jahre steht die Idee im Raum, neutrale, theorie- und anwendungsunabhängige lexikalische Datenbanken bzw. Wissensbasen (LDBs/LKBs) in Form multifunktionaler Objekte [5] zu entwickeln[1]. Diese neutralen und anwendungsunabhängigen LDBs bzw. LKBs sollen den Bedürfnissen so unterschiedlicher Benutzer wie sprachverarbeitende Systeme, Lexikographen, Linguisten (insbesondere Lexikologen) und Wörterbuchbenutzer im traditionellen Sinne nachkommen. Zu diesem Zweck wird versucht, maschinelle Methoden bereitzustellen, mit denen das in bereits vorhandenen lexikalischen Ressourcen enthaltene Wissen herausgefiltert und in ein geeignetes Format gebracht werden kann. Dieser Ansatz beruht auf dem Paradigma der sogenannten 'reusability of lexical resources' [3], das sich im wesentlichen aus zwei Postulaten zusammensetzt,

- der Wiederverwertbarkeit theorie- bzw. anwendungsabhängiger Lexika, wie sie durch MRDs und CLDs gegeben sind und

- der Konstruierbarkeit einer theorie- und anwendungsübergreifenden LDB bzw. LKB.

Dabei erinnert der erste Aspekt an einen mit dem Recycling bereits benutzter Materialien vergleichbaren Vorgang. Beim zweiten Aspekt wird die Konstruktion eines neutralen Lexikons in Form eines multifunktionalen Objektes als unabdingbar erachtet, auf das unterschiedliche Benutzer zugreifen können. Zentrales Problem einer entsprechenden LKB ist die Diskrepanz zwischen einem stabilen, kompakten und 'neutralen' Lexikon und spezifischen, an konkrete theoretische Ansätze und Anwendungsgebiete angepaßten Lexika. Hinzu kommt, daß derzeit noch keine universelle Lexikontheorie vorliegt, die eine Grundlage für eine wirklich neutrale Repräsentation lexikalischer Daten schaffen könnte, wenn eine solche Theorie denn überhaupt denkbar ist.

Der hohe Zeit- und Kostenaufwand für die Erstellung anwendungsrelevanter Lexika macht es aber dringend erforderlich, auf bestehende lexikalische Ressourcen zurückzugreifen. Dazu müssen die Beziehungen zwischen lexikalischen Informationen unterschiedlicher Herkunft aufgedeckt und geeignet repräsentiert werden. Der in diesem Papier vorgestellte Ansatz sieht hierfür Korrelationsanalysen und einen um lokale Konverter erweiterten Wissenspaketmechanismus vor.

2 Architekturentwurf einer LKB

Der im weiteren verfolgte Ansatz weist folgende Gemeinsamkeiten mit der von van der Eijk und van der Wouden [6] dargestellten modularen Lexikonarchitektur auf:

- die Verwendung reversibler Konverter

- die Idee, daß sich ein neutrales Lexikon über eine Art 'bottom-up Konstruktion' im Sinne der 'polytheoricity' [4] iterativ approximieren läßt.

Die LKB wird nicht wie in [1] ausschließlich als Behälter für lexikalische Informationen aufgefaßt. Zur Steigerung ihrer Effizienz und ihrer Akzeptanz müssen die in der LKB abgelegten Daten in Abhängigkeit ihrer Ableitbarkeit strukturiert werden. Außerdem ist ein Konversionsmechanismus erforderlich, der zwischen den so strukturierten lexikalischen Informationen vermittelt.

Die Repräsentation der Einträge in der LKB soll in einem allgemeinen Formalismus erfolgen (vgl. Aschnitt 4), in dem die lexikalischen Informationen durch Attribut(Feature)-Wert-Paare dargestellt

---

[1] Die Begriffe LDB und LKB werden zum Teil synonym verwendet, sind aber dahingehend zu unterscheiden, daß sich LDBs eher auf sprachliches Wissen im engeren Sinne beschränken, wohingegen LKBs zusätzlich auch stärker außersprachliches Wissen umfassen.

werden. Eine Menge von Attribut-Wert-Paar bezeichnen wir im folgenden als Featureterm, wobei die Werte von Features wieder beliebig komplexe Featureterme sein dürfen.

Was die Strukturierung der lexikalischen Daten betrifft, wird vorgeschlagen, die Beziehungen zwischen spezifischeren und stärker generalisierten Informationen über einen den Wissenspaketen (WPs) [8,14,15,16] ähnlichen Mechanismus zu repräsentieren. Die Strukturierung der lexikalischen Informationen erfolgt dabei insbesondere nach folgenden Prinzipien:

- Lexikalische Informationen, aus denen sich andere lexikalische Informationen ableiten lassen, sind in hierarchisch höher gelegenen WPs lokalisiert (principle of packing knowledge elements).

- Konkurrierende Varianten lexikalischer Informationen werden über parallele WPs verteilt, d.h. beide WPs stehen in einer hierarchischen Nachfolgerbeziehung zum gleichen WP (principle of competitive knowledge).

- Lexikalische Informationen von WPs, die in einer hierarchischen Vorgänger-/Nachfolgerbeziehung zueinander stehen, insbesondere die innerhalb eines WPs, müssen konsistent sein (principle of local consistency).

- Neben lexikalischen Informationen, die direkt einem Wissenspaket zugeordnet sind, sind aus diesem WP heraus, unter Berücksichtigung der Konversionsspezifikationen, auch die lexikalischen Informationen der ihm hierarchisch übergeordneten WPs sichtbar, d.h., daß auf diese lexikalischen Informationen zugegriffen werden kann (principle of eligibility of knowledge elements).

Diesen Prinzipien folgend gilt es, die zu einem Lemma zur Verfügung stehenden Informationen so über die wissenspaketartige Struktur zu verteilen, daß diejenigen Featureterme, aus denen sich lexikalische Informationen anderer in die LKB integrierter Ressourcen ableiten lassen, höher lokalisiert sind. Wegen der prinzipiellen Unvollständigkeit lexikalischer Informationen weisen dabei die Einträge in den WPs bezüglich gewisser Wörter Lücken auf.

Anders als in [8,14,15,16] können Mutter- und Tochter-WP in der um (lokale) Konverter erweiterten Wissenspaketstrukturierung dadurch voneinander abweichen, daß das von einem Mutter-WP ererbte Wissen aus dem Tochter-WP heraus anders repräsentiert erscheint. Unter Umständen werden sogar bestimmte Differenzierungen ignoriert (Informationsverdünnung). Beispielsweise könnten die Feature-Wert-Paare 'pos:adj' und 'pos:adv' in einem untergeordneten WP als Feature-Wert-Paar 'wortart:A' erscheinen.

Die lokalen Konverter, die für solche, nicht über den allgemeinen Formalismus der LKB hinausgehenden Überführungen von Repräsentationen verantwortlich sind, bilden einen integralen Bestandteil der LKB. Sie vermitteln zwischen den in einer direkten Nachfolgebeziehung zueinander stehenden Wissenspaketen und operieren nicht auf vollständigen Lexikoneinträgen, sondern nur auf Auszügen derselben. Die einem WP zugeordneten Konversionsspezifikationen geben darüber Auskunft, wie bestimmte seiner Featureterme mit denen in unmittelbar hierarchisch übergeordneten WPs zusammenhängen und in welche Richtung eine Konversion erfolgen darf. Da sie reversibel sind, können die ursprünglich für den LKB-Ausbau konzipierten Konverter auch zur Konstruktion benutzerspezifischer Repräsentationen verwendet werden bzw. die zunächst für die Generierung benutzerspezifischer Darstellungen entworfenen Konverter für LKB-Erweiterungen genutzt werden.

Über die lokalen Konverter hinaus werden bei der hier vorgeschlagenen LKB-Konzeption noch globale Konverter benötigt, die zwischen dem für die gesamte LKB zugrundegelegten Formalismus und den Repräsentationsformalismen der benutzerspezifischen Views, z.B. PATR-II, vermitteln. Sie führen sozusagen aus der LKB heraus bzw. in sie hinein und müssen deshalb invertierbar sein. Eine Abstimmung mit den anderen Nutzern der LKB und die Einstellung auf einen anderen Repräsentationsformalismus ist durch die Invertierbarkeit der globalen Konverter nicht erforderlich. Erweiterungen und Änderungen bezüglich lexikalischer Informationen können auf der Ebene der Views stattfinden. Sie wirken, sofern die geänderten Informationen nicht korrelierbar sind, nur auf den einzelnen Nutzer. Diese globalen Konverter bilden keinen Bestandteil der LKB. Die Aufgabe der LKB kann lediglich darin bestehen, dem Nutzer Softwarewerkzeuge zur Erstellung der globalen Konverter zur Verfügung zu stellen.

Um eine wie oben dargestellte Strukturierung lexikalischer Informationen unterschiedlicher Herkunft vornehmen zu können und eine Nutzung der wissenspaketartig strukturierten Datenbestände erst möglich zu machen, wird spezielle Software benötigt. Diese Software stellt einen weiteren unabkömmlichen Bestandteil einer nach dem hier vorgestellten Ansatz aufgebauten LKB dar.

Es handelt sich dabei insbesondere um:

- Software zum Aufdecken von Korrelationen

- Software zum Aufdecken von Inkonsistenzen

- Tools zur Generierung von reversiblen Konvertern,

- Software zur Erzeugung und Wartung der Wissenspaketstruktur.

Der Einsatz dieser Programme soll durch einen LKB-Manager gesteuert werden. In Abb.1 ist die Architektur einer nach dem hier vorgestellten Ansatz konzipierten LKB zu sehen.

3 Dynamik in der Wissenspaketstruktur

Die Wissenspaketstruktur liegt nicht ein für allemal fest. Ihre Dynamik kann sowohl aus der Perspektive des LKB-Aufbaus (Lexikonimport) als auch aus der Perspektive der LKB-Nutzung (Lexikonexport) betrachtet werden. Die Integration bereits vorhandener Lexika und die Anpassung an neue Benutzerprofile führen in der Regel zu Veränderungen in der Wissenspaketstruktur. In beiden Fällen wird der Strukturwandel von unten ausgelöst und nach oben propagiert. Die Umstrukturierung der Wissensbestände erfolgt durch einen bottom-up-Prozeß, bei dem lexikalische Daten generalisiert und entsprechend in hierarchiehöhere WPs transferiert werden.

3.1 Lexikonimport

Der 'Anfangszustand' der LKB zeichnet sich dadurch aus, daß die zu diesem Zeitpunkt vorliegenden WPs parallel angeordnet sind und genau den zu integrierenden lexikalischen Ressourcen entsprechen. Dabei stehen die WPs in keinerlei Beziehung zueinander. Gemeinsam ist nur ein einheitlicher Datenbankmechanismus.

Es darf jedoch angenommen werden, daß zumindest ein Teil der aus den verschiedenen Quellen stammenden lexikalischen Informationen redundant ist oder zueinander in Beziehung gesetzt werden kann. Durch das Aufdecken von Korrelationen wird nun ein Wandel in der Wissenspaketstruktur ausgelöst. Den WPs, aus denen Informationen miteinander korrelierbar sind, werden gemeinsame 'Mutter-WPs' zugeordnet, in die die korrelierbaren Informationen überführt werden. Dabei gehen die Bestrebungen dahin, die lexikalischen Informationen in generalisierter Form und möglichst weit oben in der WP-Hierarchie anzusiedeln, so daß sie von vielen WPs aus sichtbar und verwertbar sind. Der durchgeführte Strukturwandel hat keinerlei Auswirkungen auf das konzeptuelle Schema der Views.

Voraussetzung für die Integration eines weiteren Lexikons ist, daß die Einträge mittels globaler Konverter auf das allgemeine Datenformat der LKB gebracht worden sind. Die Einträge werden nun einem neuen WP zugewiesen, das noch keine Verbindungen zu den übrigen WPs aufweist und entsprechend isoliert ist (siehe obere Baumstruktur in Abbildung 2).

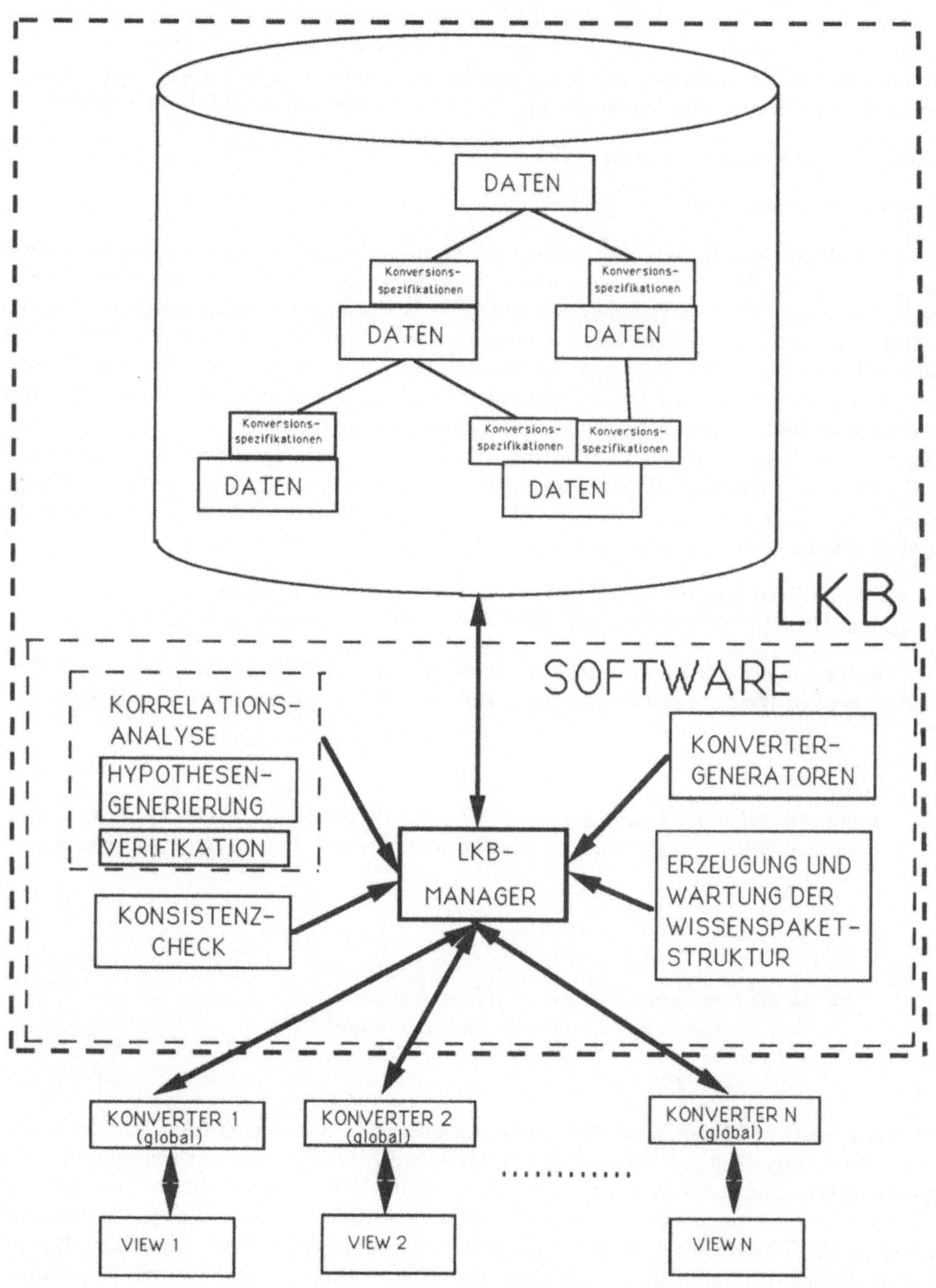

Abbildung 1: Architekturentwurf einer LKB

In einem weiteren Schritt werden dann diejenigen Featureterme des zu integrierenden WPs, bei denen Beziehungen zu bereits vorher in der LKB abgespeicherten Daten aufgedeckt werden können, aus dem neu hinzugekommenen WP herausgefiltert und in generalisierter Form in entsprechende hierarchiehöhere WPs transferiert. Das Aufdecken der Beziehungen zu bereits vorher abgespeicherten Daten wird als Korrelationsanalyse bezeichnet. Die Korrelationsanalyse wird dabei aufgeteilt in

- eine *Hypothesengenerierungsphase* und

- eine *Verifikationsphase.*

Sofern keine Hypothesen für eine Korrelierbarkeit bereits vorhandener, auf die Wissenspakete verteilter Daten mit den Daten des zu integrierenden Lexikons vorliegen, ist die Anzahl der auf Korrelierbarkeit zu untersuchenden Featureterme sehr groß. Deshalb gilt es, durch geeignete Heuristiken Hypothesen für die auf Korrelierbarkeit zu untersuchenden Featureterme aufzustellen. Beim Aufstellen dieser Heuristiken werden Verfahren des Maschinellen Lernens eine entscheidende Rolle spielen. Allerdings wird man am Anfang auf sehr einfache Heuristiken zurückgreifen können, um Hypothesen für die auf Korrelierbarkeit zu untersuchenden Featureterme aufzustellen.

An dieser Stelle soll eine einfache Heuristik zur Generierung von Hypothesen vorgestellt werden. Es soll untersucht werden, ob Hypothesen auf Korrelierbarkeit zwischen Feature fi_0 aus WP_{k_0} mit Wert x (fi_0:x) und Feature fj_0 aus dem neu zu integrierenden Wissenspaket WP_{l_0} mit Wert y (fj_0:y) aufgestellt werden können. Hier könnte man nach folgender Heuristik vorgehen:

Wähle n Wörter aus, die sowohl in WP_k als auch in WP_l vorkommen. Die Anzahl n der ausgewählten Wörter soll klein gegenüber der Anzahl der Wörter aus $WP_k \cap WP_l$ sein.

- *$\exists i \exists j$, so daß $\forall$ der n ausgewählten Wörter aus $WP_k \cap WP_l$ gilt: Feature fj aus WP_l hat den Wert y, wenn Feature fi aus WP_k den Wert x hat, dann stelle die Hypothese*

  $fi{:}x \Rightarrow fj{:}y$

  auf.

- *$\exists i \exists j$, so daß $\forall$ der n ausgewählten Wörter aus $WP_k \cap WP_l$ gilt: Feature fi aus WP_k hat den Wert x, wenn Feature fj aus WP_l den Wert y hat, dann stelle die Hypothese*

  $fj{:}y \Rightarrow fi{:}x$

  auf.

'$\Rightarrow$' ist als Implikation zwischen 2 WPs aufzufassen,
d. h. Prämisse und Konklusion sind unterschiedlichen
WPs zugeordnet

Die Qualität der Hypothesen hängt dabei sicherlich entscheidend von der Größe n und der Repräsentativität der n ausgewählten Wörter ab. Mit Hilfe der in der Hypothesengenerierungsphase erzeugten Hypothesen kann nun in der Verifikationsphase die eigentliche Korrelationsanalyse beginnen. In dieser Phase gilt es, die zuvor erzeugten Hypothesen zu bestätigen oder zu widerlegen, indem man die Analyse auf die Schnittmenge der in WP_{k_0} und WP_{l_0} vorkommenden Wörter ausdehnt. Betrachten wir exemplarisch den Fall, daß sich die Hypothese fj_0:y $\Rightarrow$ fi_0:x bestätigt und die Hypothese fi_0:x $\Rightarrow$ fj_0:y widerlegt wird. Dann werden diejenigen lexikalischen Informationen des zu integrierenden WP_{l_0}, die die Prämisse erfüllen, und die daraus ableitbaren Informationen aus WP_{k_0} in generalisierter Form in ein beiden übergeordnetes Wissenspaket transferiert. Dieser Vorgang kann eine Einführung neuer WPs erforderlich machen, um den neuen Sichtbarkeitsanforderungen Rechnung zu tragen (siehe Abb.2).

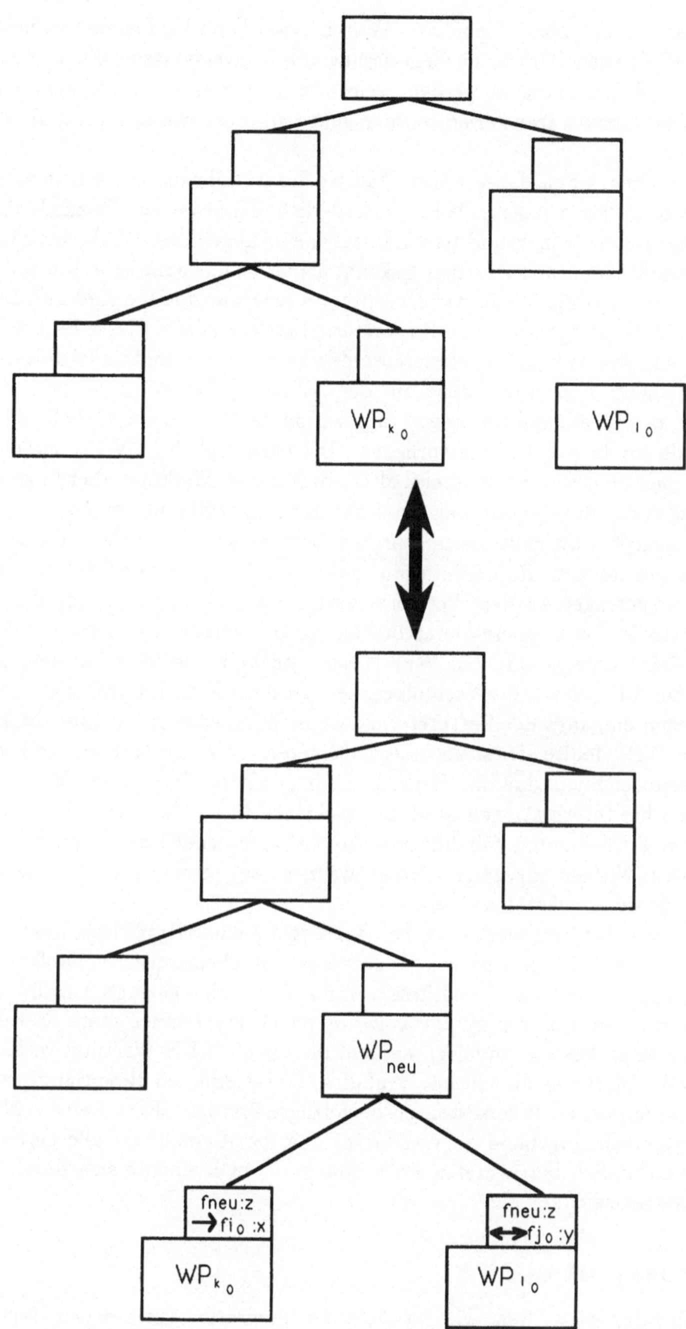

Abbildung 2: Änderung der Wissenspaketstruktur durch die Einfügung eines neuen WPs, in dem sich die aus WP$_{k_0}$ und WP$_{l_0}$ generalisierten Daten befinden

Der Datentransfer in ein hierarchiehöheres Wissenspaket kann Umbenennungen der Features und deren Werte zur Folge haben. Durch die Generierung von Konversionsspezifikationen (lokale Konverter) muß den WPs bekannt gemacht werden, welche lexikalischen Informationen wie in ein (direkt) übergeordnetes Wissenspaket transferiert worden sind und in welche Richtung die Konversion erfolgen darf.

Angenommen, in dem oben dargestellten Fall ist die Einführung eines neuen, WP_{k_0} und WP_{l_0} direkt übergeordneten Wissenspaketes WP_{neu} erforderlich, dann werden die aus WP_{k_0} und WP_{l_0} herauszufilternden Featureterme f_{i_0}:x und f_{j_0}:y z.B. auf fneu:z abgebildet. WP_{l_0} wird durch Einführung der Konversionsspezifikation fneu:z ↔ f_{j_0}:y bekannt gemacht, daß sämtliche Informationen zum Featureterm f_{j_0}:y aus dem in WP_{neu} kodierten Featureterm fneu:z abzuleiten sind und daß bei später hinzukommenden Lexikoneinträgen, die den Featureterm f_{j_0}:y enthalten, dieser Featureterm in das hierarchiehöhere Wissenpaket WP_{neu} transferiert werden kann. Zuvor sollte allerdings jeweils überprüft werden, ob diesbezüglich auch Konsistenz mit dem Wissenspaket WP_{k_0} besteht, da die Hypothese f_{j_0}:y $\Rightarrow$ f_{i_0}:x keine ein für allemal bewiesene Implikation darstellt, sondern lediglich zu diesem Zeitpunkt gute Gründe für ihre Annahme vorliegen. Bei nachträglich in WP_{k_0} aufgenommenen Lexikoneinträgen, die den Featureterm f_{i_0}:x enthalten, darf dieses Merkmal allerdings nicht transferiert werden. Dies wird durch die Generierung der Konversionsspezifikation fneu:z $\rightarrow$ f_{i_0}:x dokumentiert.

Durch einen solchen Umstrukturierungsprozeß kann gleichermaßen zur Redundanzbeseitigung, zum Gewinn einer generelleren Repräsentation sowie zur Schließung von Lücken aus der Perspektive bestimmter WPs beigetragen werden. Letzteres kommt dadurch zustande, daß durch die Integration eines weiteren Lexikons Daten in ein hierarchiehöheres WP gelangen können, die dann auch aus den übrigen, diesem Paket untergeordneten WPs heraus zugänglich werden. In dem oben behandelten Fall würden z.B. für WP_{k_0} und seine Nachfolgepakete auch die Featureterme fneu:z derjenigen Wörter zugänglich, zu denen eingangs der Featureterm f_{j_0}:y in WP_{l_0} kodiert war, für die aber eine entsprechende Angabe in WP_{k_0} fehlte. Diese gewissermaßen ererbten Informationen sind so, z.B. durch eine Indexierung, zu kennzeichnen, daß ihre Herkunft rekonstruierbar bleibt. Die Rekonstruierbarkeit des Ursprungs lexikalischer Informationen ist in zweierlei Hinsicht von Interesse. Zum einen wird dadurch die Möglichkeit zur Zurücknahme fälschlicherweise angenommener Korrelationen gewährleistet, zum anderen kann jedem Nutzer angezeigt werden, wenn er auf maschinell erschlossene Informationen zugreift und woraus sie abgeleitet wurden.

Bislang wurde nur die Vorgehensweise bei Bestätigung einer Hypothese beschrieben. Allerdings kann man sich auch bei Widerlegung von Hypothesen Vorgehensweisen vorstellen, die eine Korrelation noch ermöglichen. Wird eine Hypothese z.B. nur durch eine geringe Anzahl von Featuretermen widerlegt (wobei man spezifizieren muß, was gering bedeutet), können diese Featureterme noch einmal zur Kontrolle einer Person vorgelegt werden, die für die LKB-Wartung verantwortlich ist oder diese Einträge in die LKB eingebracht hat. Auf diese Weise kann zur Beseitigung von Codierungsfehlern und damit verbundenen Inkonsistenzen beigetragen werden. Eine weitere Möglichkeit besteht darin, die Hypothese dahingehend zu verfeinern, daß die Ausnahmen alle gerade eine bestimmte Subklasse der ursprünglich betrachteten Fälle bilden, deren Elemente sich durch Gemeinsamkeiten weiterer Merkmale auszeichnen.

3.2 Lexikonexport

Als Nächstes soll skizziert werden, wie man sich die Integration eines neuen Benutzers in dem hier verfolgten Ansatz vorstellen kann. Es soll dabei besonders auf den mit der Anpassung an neue Benutzerprofile verbundenen möglichen Wandel in der Wissenspaketstruktur eingegangen werden.

Die genaue Spezifikation der jeweils benötigten Daten und ihrer Darstellung stellt eine notwendige Voraussetzung für die Erzeugung eines auf konkrete Interessen zugeschnittenen Lexikons dar. Sie kann im Grunde genommen auf zweifache Weise erfolgen.

Der Benutzer erhält einen mit Beispielen angereicherten Überblick über die in der LKB bereits abgelegten lexikalischen Merkmale und beschreibt dann mit Hilfe der Konversionssprache, wie die von ihm gewünschten Features mit den in der LKB bereits gespeicherten Merkmalen zusammenhängen. Der Nachteil dieser Vorgehensweise besteht darin, daß der LKB-Kunde die ihm angezeigten LKB-Einträge interpretieren und die Konversionssprache beherrschen muß.

Die zweite Möglichkeit besteht darin, dem Benutzer Wörter vorzuschlagen, für die er die von ihm gewünschten Lexikoneinträge (im allgemeinen Datenformat der LKB) zu formulieren hat. Die Auswahl der Wörter soll von der LKB nach folgenden Kriterien erfolgen:

1. Die zu diesen Wörtern in der LKB abgespeicherten Features sollen ein möglichst breites Spektrum der überhaupt vorhandenen Features in der LKB abdecken.

2. Das Spektrum möglicher Werte von Features soll hinreichend gut durch die Auswahl der Wörter abgedeckt werden.

Die vom Benutzer zu den Wörtern entworfenen Lexikoneinträge werden einem neuen WP zugeordnet, das noch keine Verbindungen zu den anderen WPs aufweist. Wie bei der Integration eines bereits vorhandenen Lexikons (siehe Abschnitt 3.1) werden dann die in diesem Wissenspaket befindlichen Featureterme für die Generierung von Hypothesen bezüglich der Korrelierbarkeit herangezogen. Im Gegensatz zur Integration bereits vorhandener lexikalischer Ressourcen ist hier allerdings der Eingriff des Benutzers zur Bestätigung oder Verwerfung einer Hypothese erforderlich.

4 Datenbankmodell und Repräsentationsformalismus

Die Frage, welches Datenbankmodell sich am besten für die Speicherung lexikalischer Daten eignet, ist derzeit noch weitgehend ungeklärt. Die wohl ausschlaggebenden Gründe für den Einsatz des relationalen Datenmodells liegen im wesentlichen

- in der geringen Fehleranfälligkeit und Ausgereiftheit entsprechender Produkte,

- in der Tatsache, daß eine Mehrbenutzerumgebung, in der mehrere Personen zur gleichen Zeit Daten modifizieren und abfragen können, vorhanden ist und

- darin, daß eine Übertragung der Daten in andere Systemumgebungen wegen der Verbreitung des relationalen Datenbankmodells leichter möglich ist.

Neben anderen Forschungsgruppen (vgl. [2]) halten wir den relationalen Ansatz für die Speicherung lexikalischer Informationen nur für bedingt geeignet, da

- die Struktur von Lexikoneinträgen (insbesondere von traditionellen Wörterbüchern) zu komplex und variabel ist, um in Tabellen mit in der Regel fest vorgegebenen Größen repräsentiert werden zu können, und

- der vorliegende LKB-Entwurf regelhaft repräsentierte Konverter vorsieht, die die Möglichkeit des deduktiven Schließens erforderlich machen.

Aus diesem Grund soll versucht werden, dem hier vorgestellten Ansatz ein effizientes, deduktives Datenmodell zugrundezulegen. Entsprechende Datenbanksysteme sind allerdings zur Zeit kaum auf dem Markt verfügbar, sondern liegen fast ausschließlich als Prototypen vor.

Im Rahmen des LILOG-Projektes (Linguistische und logische Methoden für das maschinelle Verstehen des Deutschen) konnten erste Erfahrungen mit der deduktiven Datenbank des Trierer LILOG-Teilprojektes gesammelt werden. Mit der LILOG-DB [10,11] liegt eine wissenschaftlich ausgereifte, auf die Verwaltung großer Wissensbasen, insbesondere LKBs, zugeschnittene deduktive Datenbank vor.

Bei der Auswahl des Repräsentationsformalismus ist folgendes zu beachten:

1. Er muß so liberal sein, daß alle potentiellen Nutzer der LKB ihre Informationen repräsentieren können.

2. Der Formalismus sollte die Abbildung auf unterschiedliche Views unterstützen.

3. Das ausgewählte Datenbanksystem muß mit diesem Formalismus verträglich sein.

Wir halten den Stuttgarter Typen-Unifikationsformalismus STUF [12,13], der im Kontext des LILOG-Projektes entwickelt wurde, für einen Formalismus, der den drei aufgeführten Anforderungen weitestgehend gerecht wird. Die Datenbank des Trierer LILOG-Teilprojektes ist auf diesen Formalismus zugeschnitten.

5 Ausblick

Daß die für eine weiterreichende Integration von MRDs und deren semantische Angaben benötigten Konverter mehr als simples 'pattern matching' leisten müssen, liegt wohl auf der Hand: sie erfordert schließlich eine Analyse quasi-natürlichsprachlicher Lexikoneinträge. Eine erste Idee, wie dieses Problem angegangen werden könnte, ergibt sich aus den in [7,9] angestellten Überlegungen.

Dort werden vier interagierende Strategien zur inkrementellen Wortschatzerweiterung in textverstehenden Systemen erörtert: kontextuelles Erschließen, der Einsatz von Wortbildungsregeln, interaktive Benutzereingaben und Zugriffe auf externe Lexika. Aus der Perspektive der oben vorgestellten LKB-Konzeption bedeutet die letzte Alternative, daß einem textverstehenden System zwei unterschiedliche Views auf die LKB zur Verfügung gestellt werden.

Die erste Sicht enthält formale Repräsentationen. Sie übernimmt die Funktion des systeminternen Lexikons und wird demzufolge standardmäßig in Anspruch genommen.

Die zweite Sicht umfaßt Daten, wie sie in einem konventionellen Wörterbuch enthalten sind, allerdings in leicht vorstrukturierter Form. Sie wird in Anspruch genommen, wenn das System in dem zu verarbeitenden Text auf unbekannte Wörter stößt, genauer auf Wörter, zu denen keine Einträge in dem internen Lexikon, sprich in der ersten View, vorliegen. In diesen Fällen wird der über die zweite View bereitgestellte Lexikoneintrag - insbesondere die in ihm enthaltene Definition - geparst und daraus, soweit möglich, eine Repräsentation im Format der ersten View abgeleitet, was natürlich auch einen Informationsgewinn für die LKB bedeutet.

Der dabei zum Einsatz kommende Parser hat Zugriff auf das dem textverstehenden System über die erste View zur Verfügung stehende lexikalische Wissen und kann demzufolge als ein wissensbasierter Konverter aufgefaßt werden. Seine Leistungsfähigkeit wird überdies noch dadurch gesteigert, daß die verschiedenen Strategien zum Erschließen unbekannter Wörter auch aus der Analyse der quasi-natürlichsprachlichen Lexikoneinträge heraus initiiert werden können.

Literatur

[1] Robert A. Amsler. Lexical Knowledge Bases. In Proceedings of the 10th International Conference on Computational Linguistics (COLING-64), Standfort, 1984.

[2] B. Bläser, M. Wermke. Projekt "Elektronische Wörterbücher/Lexika": Abschlußbericht der Definitionsphase. IWBS Report 145, IBM Stuttgart, 1990.

[3] Branimir K. Boguraev, Ted Briscoe (eds.). Computational Lexicography for Natural Language Processing. London/New York (Longman), 1989.

[4] J. Calder. Polytheoretic Lexicons and Reusable Dictionaries. University of Edinburgh, 1988.

[5] Nicoletta Calzolari. Computer-Aided Lexicography: Dictionaries and Word Data Bases. In Isvan Batori, Winfried Lenders Wolfgang Putschke (eds.). Computational Linguistics, de Gruyter, Berlin, 1989.

[6] Pim van der Eijk, Ton van der Wouden. A Modular Lexicon Architecture for NLP. In Uri Zernik (eds.). Proceedings of the First International Lexical Acquisition Workshop, Detroit, Michigan, 1989.

[7] Helmar Gust, Petra Ludewig. Zielgerichtete Wortschatzerweiterungen in natürlichsprachlichen Systemen. In D. Metzing(eds.). Proceedings of the 13th German Workshop on Artificial Intelligence (GWAI-89), Informatik-Fachberichte 216, Springer-Verlag, Berlin, 1989.

[8] Helmar Gust. Strukturiertes Wissen als Grundlage für Sprachverstehensprozesse. In LDV-Forum 4(2): 9-14, 1986.

[9] Petra Ludewig. Incremental Vocabulary Extensions in Text Understanding Systems. Erscheint in Otthein Herzog, Claus-Rainer Rollinger (eds.). Text Understanding in LILOG: Integrating Computational Linguistics and Artificial Intelligence, Springer-Verlag, Berlin.

[10] Thomas Ludwig. A Brief Overlook of LILOG-DB. IWBS Report 102, IBM Stuttgart, 1989.

[11] Stefan Benzschawel, Erich Gehlen, Michael Ley, Thomas Ludwig, Albert Maier, Bernd Walter. LILOG-DB: Database Support for Knowledge Based Systems. Erscheint in Otthein Herzog, Claus-Rainer Rollinger (eds.). Text Understanding in LILOG: Integrating Computational Linguistics and Artificial Intelligence, Springer-Verlag, Berlin.

[12] Roland Seiffert, Jochen Dörre. Sorted Feature Terms and Relational Dependencies. IWBS Report 153, IBM Stuttgart, 1991.

[13] Roland Seiffert, Jochen Dörre. A Formalism for Natural Language -STUF. Erscheint in Otthein Herzog, Claus-Rainer Rollinger (eds.). Text Understanding in LILOG: Integrating Computational Linguistics and Artificial Intelligence, Springer-Verlag, Berlin.

[14] Ipke Wachsmuth. On Structuring Domain-Specific Knowledge. LILOG-Report 12, IBM Stuttgart, 1987.

[15] Ipke Wachsmuth. Zur intelligenten Organisation von Wissensbeständen in künstlichen Systemen. IWBS Report 91, IBM Stuttgart, 1989.

[16] Ipke Wachsmuth, Barbara Gängler. Knowledge Packets and Knowledge Packet Structure. Erscheint in Otthein Herzog, Claus-Rainer Rollinger (eds.). Text Understanding in LILOG: Integrating Computational Linguistics and Artificial Intelligence, Springer-Verlag, Berlin.

Methods for the Intentional Description of Image Sequences[*]

Markus Tetzlaff

SFB 314, FB 14 – Informatik IV, Universität des Saarlandes
D–6600 Saarbrücken 11
E-Mail: tetzlaff@cs.uni-sb.de

Gudula Retz-Schmidt

Arbeitsbereich KOGS, FB Informatik, Universität Hamburg
D–2000 Hamburg 50
E-Mail: retz@informatik.uni-hamburg.de

Abstract

The system REPLAI-II extends the range of capabilities of natural language systems describing real-world image sequences. The systems developed so far in this field merely extract spatio-temporal information from image sequences and verbalize it in natural language. Such a system is, for instance, the system SOCCER, which describes extracts of soccer games in German ([AHR88], [HSA+89]). REPLAI-II extends this description generation by recognizing and verbalizing intentional entities such as intentions, interactions and the causes of plan failures. Intentions are central to all goal-directed behaviour and are realized by carrying out plans. Interactions typically occur in domains containing multiple agents. We distinguish cooperative and antagonistic interactions between the plans of multiple agents. In addition, REPLAI-II tries to recognize plan failures and to determine their causes. The recognized entities are verbalized in natural language (German).

Zusammenfassung

Das System REPLAI-II soll die Möglichkeiten der natürlichsprachlichen Beschreibung von Szenenfolgen erweitern. Die bisher in diesem Bereich entwickelten Systeme extrahieren aus Realwelt-Bildfolgen nur raum-zeitliche Informationen und geben sie in natürlicher Sprache aus. Ein solches System ist beispielsweise SOCCER, das Ausschnitte aus Fußballspielen in deutscher Sprache kommentiert ([AHR88], [HSA+89]). REPLAI-II erweitert die Beschreibung, indem es intentionale Entitäten - wie Intentionen, Interaktionen und Ursachen für das Scheitern von Plänen - erkennt und verbalisiert. Intentionen sind für jedes zielgerichtete Handeln von zentraler Bedeutung und werden durch die Ausführung von Plänen verwirklicht. Interaktionen treten typischerweise in Domänen mit mehreren Agenten auf. Dabei unterscheiden wir kooperative und antagonistische Interaktionen zwischen den Plänen verschiedener Agenten. Weiterhin versucht REPLAI-II das Scheitern von Plänen zu erkennen und die Ursachen hierfür zu bestimmen. Die erkannten Entitäten werden in deutscher Sprache verbalisiert.

The system REPLAI-II extends the range of capabilities of natural language systems describing real-world image sequences. The systems developed so far in this field merely extract spatio-temporal

---

[*]The work reported in this article was partially supported by the Special Collaborative Program on Artificial Intelligence and Knowledge-Based Systems (SFB 314) of the German Science Foundation (DFG), project N2: VITRA.

information from image sequences and verbalize it in natural language. Such a system is, for instance, the system SOCCER, which describes extracts of soccer games in German ([AHR88], [HSA+89]). REPLAI-II extends this description generation by recognizing and verbalizing intentional entities such as intentions, interactions and the causes of plan failures. Intentions are central to all goal-directed behaviour and are realized by carrying out plans. Interactions typically occur in domains containing multiple agents. We distinguish cooperative and antagonistic interactions between the plans of multiple agents. In addition, REPLAI-II tries to recognize plan failures and to determine their causes. REPLAI-II interprets — as does SOCCER — time-varying scenes. The interpretation process is incremental, i.e., incoming scene information is being processed immediately. Interpretation thus not have to wait until the whole scene is terminated. Although REPLAI-II works in a specific domain, the used methods are domain independent.

A more detailed description of REPLAI-II can be found in [RS91].

1   The Architecture of REPLAI-II

SOCCER receives for each instance of time the spatial coordinates of all dynamic objects (players and ball) from the vision system ACTIONS and extracts from them events and spatial relations between the objects ([Nag88], [HSA+89]). Using an interface (*observations* in figure 1), REPLAI-II can access these data. A focusing process bounds the following plan recognition to some interesting agents with the help of domain-specific heuristics. To these agents, the plan recognizer attributes intentions using a plan library.

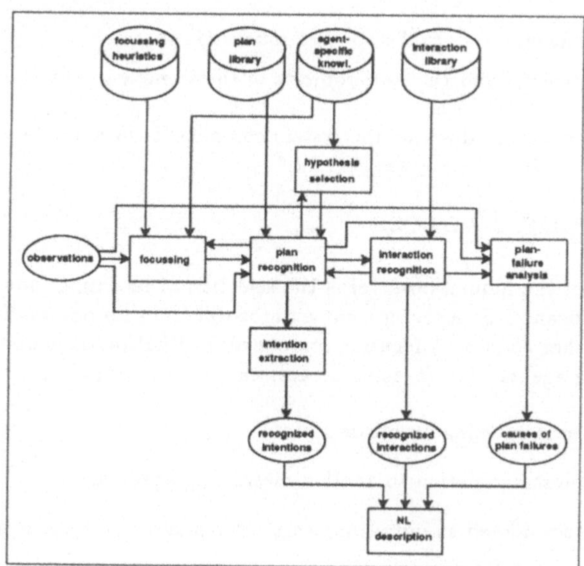

Figure 1: The architecture of REPLAI-II.

A further component uses the recognized plans to examine the interactions of the plans of multiple agents (*interaction recognition*). The necessary knowledge is represented in a separate library (*interaction library*). The failures of plans and interactions are recognized and analyzed by a failures-detection component obtaining all necessary information from the SOCCER interface. If a failing is observed, an attempt is made to find the causes. These causes are — just as the recognized intentions and interactions — verbalized in natural language (*NL-description* in figure 1).

2 Knowledge Used in REPLAI-II

Domain-specific knowledge is of great importance in REPLAI-II. Therefore, static and dynamic knowledge is used. The static knowledge consists of:

- knowledge about the structure of plans of single agents (*plan library*) and interactions between multiple agents (*interaction library*)

- agent-specific knowledge such as name, team membership, etc.

- heuristics determining which players are interesting at this instance of time (*focusing heuristics*).

Moreover, REPLAI-II needs dynamic knowledge about the scene. Therefore, at each instance of time it receives the following information:

- Events

    - actions of the agents, e.g. *(Laufen Spieler1)*
    - dynamic properties of the agents as *(Ballbesitz Spieler2)*.

- Spatial relations

    - between the agents; e.g. *(nahe Spieler3 Spieler4)*
    - between the agents and the static objects of the scene; e.g. *(in Spieler 5 Strafraum)*.

In the following sections we will describe the system components in more detail.

3 The Focusing Process

An important ability of the human observer is the selection of incoming information depending on its importance or significance. So a soccer commentator will focus his observations to the player with the ball and to a few other players. A focusing component in REPLAI-II bounds the plan recognition to the most interesting agents. The focusing process chooses all agents

- that participate in interesting events or

- that have an interesting relation to another interesting agent or

- that are a priori considered as interesting (e.g., star players in the soccer domain).

Interesting events are, for example, *Ballbesitz* or *Balltransfer*, an interesting relation is *nahe*.

4 The Plan Hierarchy

The plan hierarchy contains knowledge about the structure of plans and their hierarchical order. For representation, a tree like structure is used, which leaves are elementary events [1]. We distinguish two kinds of hierarchical relations between a node A and its children: *specialization* and *decomposition*. In the case of decomposition, temporal order is additionally specified. In addition to forward directed temporal edges, backward directed and reflexive temporal edges are allowed. By means of this, not only simple forward directed sequences, but also loops can be realized. A decomposition using only forward directed temporal edges is called *sequence*.

We call a subtree of the plan hierarchy *plan* if the relation between the subtree and its children is a decomposition relation. An example is the plan *Einzelangriff* in figure 2. According to this definition, plans can be parts of superordinate plans. Plans not being parts of other plans are called *top-most plans*. The backward directed and the reflexive temporal edges are optional.

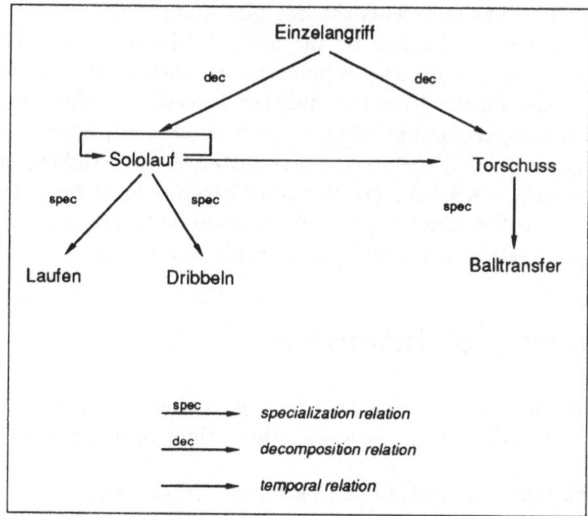

Figure 2: An extract of the plan hierarchy.

The plans are complemented by information in the nodes. For instance, the *Balltransfer* in figure 2 is a shot at the goal only if it is directed towards the opponent's goal. This *precondition* is an important part of the plan and hence represented in the node *Balltransfer*. Moreover, the effect intended with the action is related to each action in a plan. This *intended state* is, just as the preconditions, important information belonging to the plan node. Thus, after the *Balltransfer* in figure 2 the ball should be in the opponent's goal.

These conditions — preconditions and intended states — are events or relations that are recognized by SOCCER, e.g., *(Balltransfer Spieler6 Gegnertor)* and *(in Ball Gegnertor)*. Moreover, like static properties further conditions — such as team membership — can be tested. All these conditions can be composed to more complex terms using the logical connectives AND, OR and NOT. Usually, the terms contain variables. So *((nahe Spieler7 (? x)) (eigene_Mannschaft (! x)))* is an example of the conjunction of two conditions and for the use of variables. The term yields all partners of player7 being near him.

---

[1] For us, *elementary events* are events not decomposable into smaller units.

5   The Plan Recognition

First let us introduce some terms. An *instantiated plan* (*plan instance*) is a copy of the plan (the subtree that describes the plan) added by the information which leaf (*plan step*), a concrete agent has attained and with the variable binding that resulted by matching the preconditions.

The task of the plan recognition is to attribute to every newly focused agent such plan instances (*plan hypotheses*) and to update them later on, i.e., to trace the found plans.

In this way, we have to distinguish two cases: for newly focused agents, the recognition process starts from the root of the plan hierarchy and top-down searches all leaves, that match events in which the agent currently participates. But the search is restricted to paths whose nodes satisfy the preconditions. For every successfully matched event, a plan instance is created containing the plan step and the variable bindings. However, we inspect only top-most plans. All plans now instantiated are stored with a link to the agent carrying out the plan.

On the other hand — if for the agent plans are already instantiated - the system examines for every plan instance the node that represents the last plan step:
First, it tests whether the event described by the node is still going on. If so, the plan instance remains unchanged. In the other case, the system checks whether the intended state of the node is satisfied. If not, the event did not have the intended success, i.e., the plan has failed. This fact is signaled to the system component that analyzes plan failures. If, however, the intended state is achieved, the plan recognizer tries to update the plan instances by matching successor nodes. If this is successful, a new plan step is reached. On the other hand, it must be tested whether the end of the plan is reached. If that is the case the plan has successfully terminated. Otherwise the plan has failed and the plan-failure-analysis component is informed of this fact.

6   The Extraction of Intentions

As *intention* of an agent, we regard every short-term goal that the agent pursues and of which he thinks he is able to achieve. REPLAI-II recognizes three kinds of intentions:

- *state-directed* intentions, e.g., intentions to achieve a certain state

- *action-directed* intentions, e.g., intentions to perform a certain action

- *supergoals*, i.e., the superordinated goals of plans.

The state-directed intentions are derived from the intented state of the current plan step. The supergoal of a plan is represented by the root of the subtree that represents the plan. In principle, the action-directed intentions are all successive plan steps, so all successor nodes of the current node. However, we inspect only the direct successors.[2] In spite of this restriction, we will often have a great number of possible successive actions. In figure 2 this would be for *Dribbeln* the set {*Laufen, Dribbeln, Balltransfer*}. Preferring forward directed temporal edges, we can reduce this set to {*Balltransfer*}, which contains the most interesting successive action. Further heuristics will be necessary to select only the most interesting action-directed intentions.

All recognized intentions are verbalized by the NL-description component.

---

[2]So we do not take interest in what the agent will do as next but one.

7   The Interaction Library

Knowledge about possible interactions between multiple agents in typical situations is represented in the domain-specific interaction library. The interaction library contains *interaction schemata*, which each represent aggregations of plans and interactions of multiple agents typically occurring jointly in a situation. The interaction schemata are graphs whose nodes represent plans and whose arcs represent interactions between plans of agents. Interactions can either be *cooperative* or *antagonistic*.

Both cooperative and antagonistic interactions can be either *simultaneous* or *successive*. Thus, four kinds of interactive relations between plans (cf. figure 3) exist. We distinguish *sequential* and *parallel* interaction schemata, depending on whether sequential relations do or do not occur. The example in figure 3 is a parallel interaction schema since it does not contain any sequential relations.

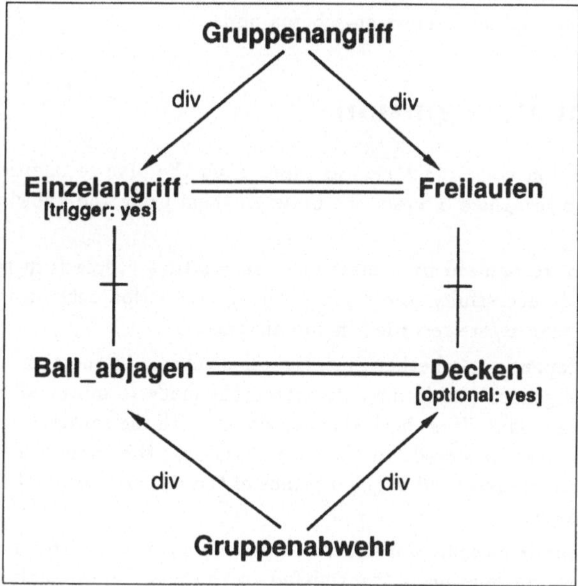

Figure 3: Interaction schema and collective actions.

Interactions in our approach are construed as two-place relations between plans and thus can only exist between two plans in each case. That does not mean, however, that interactions between more than two agents are not considered. This is possible because a plan in an interactive relation with another plan can at the same time be carried out by more than one agent (e.g., *Freilaufen*). Depending on certain additional constraints (e.g., team membership), many or even all of them can be found to be interacting with the agent(s) of the other plan. This way, groups carrying out the same plan can be dealt with.

Several cooperative plans can sometimes be part of the same *collective action*, which can often be referred to by a natural language expression (e.g. "offside trap", "counter"). The individual plans are in a kind of decomposition relation to the collective action. The interaction schema depicted in figure 3 contains two collective actions.

For each interaction schema, a *trigger plan* is defined. In the recognition process, an interaction schema is instantiated when its trigger plan matches one of the observed plans. The trigger plan has to be specified in each interaction schema. In the soccer domain, it is usually a plan of the player who has the ball. In figure 3, the trigger plan is *Einzelangriff*.

Furthermore we distinguish *compulsory* and *optional* plans in interaction schemata. That allows the recognition of only partially instantiated interaction schemata if at least the compulsory plans are instantiated. The compulsory plans constitute a prototypical subset of the interaction schema. They have to be specified for each interaction schema. The trigger plan is always compulsory. In figure 3, all plans are compulsory.

Generally a plan in an interaction schema must be carried out by at least one agent. Those agents found by the plan-recognition component to be carrying out the plan will be recorded in the instance of the interaction schema. So to speak, the agents in the interaction-schema nodes are *existentially quantified*. In some cases, however, it may be necessary to *universally quantify* them in order to find all agents who satisfy certain conditions (e.g., offside trap requires that all opponent players in a certain area run away from their own goal). This universal quantification is also possible and has to be specified in the corresponding interaction-schema node.

8 Interaction Recognition

The interaction-recognition component gets as input from the plan-recognition component the observed plans in order to recognize interactions between them using the knowledge in the interaction library.

Plan interactions are recognized by a matching process that proceeds in the following way: If a trigger plan is matched successfully, the corresponding interaction schema is instantiated and the agent(s) of the trigger plan is/are recorded in the instance.

Further processing depends on whether the interaction schema in question is parallel or sequential. In the case of a parallel schema, an immediate attempt is made to match all remaining plans of the schema with the observed plans. It is checked in agreement with the constraints on the agents whether the missing plans have been observed. In the case of success, the current nodes of the schema and the corresponding agents are recorded in the instance of the schema. Sequential interaction schemata are matched incrementally.

An interaction schema is *recognized* if all its compulsory plans have been matched successfully. In that case, the following information is transmitted to the plan-failure-analysis and NL-description components:

- the name of the interaction schema

- the extent of the instantiation (completely or partially)

- the names of the involved agents with the corresponding plans and interactions.

If all division-successors of a collective action have been matched successfully, the corresponding collective action is transmitted to the NL-description component.

The *bottom-up* recognition process from focusing via plan recognition to interaction recognition can yield the result that interaction schemata that — on the basis of the information provided by SOCCER — are recognizable cannot be recognized because some of the required agents are not focused. Conversely, interaction schemata can be erroneously recognized if — on the basis of the focused agents — it is falsely assumed that all agents carrying out a plan and satisfying certain conditions have been found in the case of universal quantification over agents. The former problem is not yet dealt with by REPLAI-II.

In order to remedy the matter mentioned in the latter case, a *top-down* recognition process initiated by the interaction-recognition component is necessary. That is realized in the following way: If a plan with universal quantification over agents occurs in an interaction schema, the interaction-recognition component triggers the plan-recognition component to recognize the plan in question. The plan-recognition component decomposes the plan into its actions according to the information in the plan hierarchy. The heuristics of the focusing component are temporarily modified in that the actions derived by the plan-recognition component are used as focusing criteria. A new focusing process is started with these new criteria. This way, the focus is expanded and the bottom-up recognition process is started anew for the newly focused agents.

9 Recognizing and Analyzing Plan Failures

As described in the section about the plan recognition, there are two events indicating the failure of plans:

- The intended state of the current plan step is not satisfied.

- No successive action can be found although the current node is not the terminal node of the sequence.

During the plan recognition REPLAI-II tests whether one of the two cases occurs and examines the potential causes below:

- The failure results from the agent's insufficient knowledge about the current situation. Normally, the agents can only overview a part of the scene. The system that has complete information about the scene, simulates this limitation by determining all objects in the visual field (*subjective view*) of the current agent. If a plan failure occurs, it checks whether the evaluation of the preconditions under this subjective view differs from the (objective) evaluation of the system. In this case, the system attributes the plan failure to the agent's unsufficient knowledge about the situation.

- There are antagonistic plans of opposing agents. The system inspects the plan schemata to find plans antagonistic to the plan of the current agent. If such a plan is instantiated, REPLAI-II supposes this as the cause of failure.

- Some plans need cooperative plans of partners. If there no such a plan is instantiated, the system assumes the missing of the cooperative plan as the cause of the failure.

- It is possible that an agent stops the execution of his plan if he notices that the conditions have changed (in his subjective view).

- As a final cause, REPLAI-II presumes the insufficient execution of an action if its intended state is not reached and none of the other causes have been found; for example, a shot that missed the goal.

There is a principle limitation of the current version of REPLAI-II: it can not recognize whether a plan was appropriate to achieve a certain goal. That is the case because of the assumption that the system itself as well as all agents has the same planning knowledge (i.e., plan hierarchy).

10   Natural Language Description

REPLAI-II has the ability to verbalize recognized intentions in natural language. Using sentence patterns, the diverse kinds of intentions and their relations are described. For verbalizing state-directed intentions the following patterns are used:

> "... damit <agent> <patient> <object> <predicator>."
> "... um <patient> <object> <predicator>."

Here *<predicator>* is the verbal description of the state the agent wants to achieve. The other terms tag the nominal phrases with their semantic relation (deep case relation or case role).[3] Thus, *<agent>* represents the agent performing the act. The deep case relations are noted for every plan in the plan hierarchy. The morphological transformation is performed by the NL-component. E.g., it generates the following sentence:

> "... damit Müller den Ball bekommt."[4]

For phrasing the action-directed intentions we use the following pattern:

> "<agent> will <patient> <object> <predicator>."

Here *<predicator>* is the verbal description of the intended action, the other terms as above. So the system can produce sentences of the following type:

> "Müller will Maier den Ball zuspielen."

Finally, for the verbalization of the supergoal we make use of the following pattern:

> "<agent> <predicator> <patient>",

whereas the predicator is the verbal phrase that describes the supergoal. An example:

> "Müller führt einen Einzelangriff durch."

In the current state of implementation, the natural language description is limited to the description of intentions.

11   Conclusions and Future Work

At present, the system REPLAI-II accomplishes — using plan recognition methods — the recognition of intentions in time-varying scenes and their natural language description. Moreover, plan failures and their causes are recognized. A further component examines the interactions between the plans of multiple agents.

An important task of future work is the natural language description of the interactions, the recognized plan failures and their causes. Since we will have a large amount of extracted information further methods must be developed to decide which part of the information in a certain instance of time has priority to be verbalized. In most cases, it is not appropriate to verbalize for all agents at each time all kinds of intentions, interactions and causes of plan failures. For adequate NL-description of time-varying scenes intelligent information extraction, selection and compression has to be performed.

---

[3]See the conception of the *case grammar*, e.g. in [GW81].

[4]Normally, verbs such as *sein, bleiben*, etc., must be used. However, to avoid monotonous phrasing, we also allow verbs describing the aiming towards a state, as, e.g., *gelangen, werden* or *bekommen*.

References

[AHR88]   E. André, G. Herzog, and T. Rist. On the Simultaneous Interpretation of Real World Image Sequences and their Natural Language Description: The System SOCCER. In *Proc. of the 8th European Conference on Artificial Intelligence*, pages 449–454, Munich, West Germany, 1988.

[GW81]   T. Göller and K. H. Wagner. Kasusgrammatik und Fremdsprachendidaktik: Bestandsaufnahme. In G. Radden and R. Dirven, editors, *Kasusgrammatik und Fremdsprachendidaktik*, pages 27–37. WVT Wissenschaftlicher Verlag Trier, Trier, 1981.

[HSA+89]   G. Herzog, C.-K. Sung, E. André, W. Enkelmann, H.-H. Nagel, T. Rist, and W. Wahlster. Incremental Natural Language Description of Dynamic Imagery. In C. Freksa and W. Brauer, editors, *Wissensbasierte Systeme. 3. Internationaler GI-Kongreß*, pages 153–162, Berlin, 1989. Springer.

[Nag88]   H.-H. Nagel. From Image Sequences Towards Conceptual Descriptions. *Image and Vision Computing*, 6(2):59–74, 1988.

[RS91]   G. Retz-Schmidt. Recognizing Intentions, Interactions, and Causes of Plan Failures. *User Modeling and User-Adapted Interaction*, 1, 1991.

Vector Quantization Algorithm for Time Series Prediction and Visuo-Motor Control of Robots

Stan Berkovitch, Philippe Dalger, Ted Hesselroth,
Thomas Martinetz, Benoît Noël, Jörg Walter
and Klaus Schulten
Beckman-Institute and Department of Physics
University of Illinois
Urbana,IL 61801, USA

We describe a new algorithm for vector quantization and control. The algorithm, in addition to generating a discrete representation of input data by means of Voronoï polyhedra, also generates a tesselation associated with these polyhedra. The tesselation corresponds to a graph which connects neighbouring Voronoï polyhedra and, hence, reflects neighborhood relationships of the embedding space of the data. The algorithm can be extended to approximate through 'training' arbitrary functions defined on the data points. The tesselation allows one to speed up the 'training' through cooperative learning involving nearest, next-nearest, etc. Voronoï polyhedra, reducing the range of cooperation progressively during training. The algorithm produces a table look-up program, assigning optimally tables to inputs and generating rapidly optimal table entries. The entries can be complex data structures, e.g., combinations of scalars, vectors, and tensors. The use of the algorithm has been demonstrated for time series prediction, surpassing existing algorithms, and for visuo-motor control of an industrial robot, e.g., for precise end effector position control. We will attempt to demonstrate by the time of the lecture also an application of the algorithm for visuo-motor control of a pneumatically driven robot arm, a Bridgestone 'RUBBERTUATOR'. This light-weight robot, capable of compliant motion, can be operated in contact with humans. The presented algorithm can acquire the complex response characteristics of this arm through training and, thereby, allows accurate and swift control of pneumatic robot motion.

The Control Problem Addressed

In our lecture we want to introduce a novel algorithm for time series prediction and control tasks. We want to provide an overview of the key aspects of this algorithm. For this purpose we describe the algorithm in the context of a particular control problem, namely visuo-motor control of a pneumatically driven robot arm.

The algorithm we seek, in its simplest ramification, should move the end-effector of a multi-jointed robot arm to specified positions $\mathbf{v}$ in the robots 3-dimensional, finite work space V, i.e., $\mathbf{v} \in V$. In its simplest form, the N angles $\theta_1, \theta_2, \ldots \theta_N$ at the robots N joints need to be specified such as to achieve the desired position $\mathbf{v}$ of the arms end, i.e., one needs to learn the vector valued function $\mathbf{v}(\vec{\theta})$, where $\vec{\theta}$ represents the N-dimensional column vector $(\theta_1, \theta_2, \ldots, \theta_N)^T$. In case of $N = 3$ the functional dependence represented by $\mathbf{v}(\vec{\theta})$ is unique (actually, for wide intervals from which values for $\theta_j, j = 1, 2, \ldots, N$ can be taken, the function can assume two or more discrete branches), for $N > 3$ a continuum of possibilities exists to realize end effector positions $\mathbf{v}$. In the latter case one wants to select $\vec{\theta}$ such that certain conditions are met, e.g., that the arm reaches around obstacles. The issues involved are discussed at length in [1].

Why a Learning Scheme is Needed

The control problem just stated can be solved by means of conventional robot algorithms. The situation becomes more difficult, and more interesting from our perspective, in case that the control signals actually employed do not specify directly the joint angles. An example is a novel robot arm design which moves arm joints pneumatically through pairs of tubes: inflating and deflating the tubes leads to forces along the tubes which, hence, can move the joints according to the same agonist-antagonist principle realized in the familiar muscle–joint systems of vertebrates. The advantage of such systems is that the motion of joint j is controlled by two pressure variables, the average pressure $\bar{p}_j$ in the two tubes and the pressure difference Δp_j between the two tubes. Pressure difference drives the joints, average pressure controls the force with which the motion is executed. This latter feature allows operation at low average pressures and, thereby, allows one to carry out compliant motion of the arm. This makes such robots suitable for operation in fragile environments, in particular, allows direct contact with human operators. The price to be paid for this advantage is that the response of the arm to signals $(\bar{p}_1, \bar{p}_2, \ldots, \bar{p}_N)^T$ and $(\Delta p_1, \Delta p_2, \ldots, \Delta p_N)^T$ cannot be described by 'a priori' known mathematical equations, but rather must be acquired heuristically. One expects that the response characteristsics change during the life time of an arm through wear, after replacements of parts and, in particular, are subject to hysteretic effects.

The RUBBERTUATOR – A Pneumatically Driven Robot

To master the control of a pneumatically driven robot arm is a worthwhile challenge in two respects. First, the mentioned robot, presently built by Bridgestone under the brand name 'RUBBERTUA-TOR', through its light weight, its relatively low price and its capacity for compliant motion and direct robot–human contact, might constitute a new robot generation for which control programs need to be furnished; presently, the robot is controlled through a feed-back cycle involving joint angle sensors, the control being slow and relatively imprecise. Second, the close analogy between the joint motions of the RUBBERTUATOR and biological vertebrates opens the possibility that through mastering this robot system we may gain understanding on animal motion, a subject matter which from a theoretical perspective is still ill understood.

How can one obtain information on the response characteristics of the robot arm. We have suggested earlier (see [1] and references quoted therein) to employ a pair of stereo cameras. We have demonstrated in conjunction with an industrial robot (PUMA 560, see [2]) that the signals from the two camera backplanes can be employed for the purpose, i.e., a robot–camera–computer system learns, in fact, to control the arm solely on account of camera images.

Employing a Linear Feedback Loop

At this point a rather straight forward concept of utmost practical importance needs to be introduced, the linearly controlled feed-back loop. The idea is that rather than to learn directly the precise relationship between joint angles (or other control signals) and end effector positions one learns such relationship only approximately and only for a coarse set $\{\mathbf{v_s}, \mathbf{s} \in A\}$ of end effector position, i.e., one learns a set of joint angles $\vec{\theta}_\mathbf{s}, \mathbf{s} \in A$ for some set A (to be specified later) such that

$$\mathbf{v_s} = \mathbf{v}(\theta_\mathbf{s}) \tag{1}$$

and assigns the remaining control to linear feed-back loops which are based on the expansion

$$\mathbf{v}^{(n)} = \mathbf{v}^{(n-1)} + \mathbf{v}\left(\mathbf{A_s}\left(\mathbf{v}_{\text{target}} - \mathbf{v}^{(n-1)}\right)\right) \tag{2}$$

where $\mathbf{A_s}$ is the Jacobian tensor $\partial\vec{\theta}/\partial\mathbf{v}$ evaluated at the locations $\theta_\mathbf{s}, \mathbf{s} \in A$. This expansion attempts to move the end effector to the target location $\mathbf{v}_{\text{target}}$ by linearly correcting the joint angles on account of the remaining deviation $\mathbf{v}_{\text{target}} - \mathbf{v}^{(n-1)}$. Repeated application of (2) starting with $\mathbf{v}^{(0)} = \mathbf{v}(\theta_\mathbf{s})$ leads to a series of end effector positions $\mathbf{v}^{(1)}, \mathbf{v}^{(2)}, \ldots$ which approaches $\mathbf{v}_{\text{target}}$ for suitable $\mathbf{A_s}$.

Schemes for acquiring θ_s and $\mathbf{A_s}$ have been presented in [1] and their capacity for real applications has been demonstrated in [2,3]. Rather than learning θ_s, $\mathbf{s} \in A$ on a very fine mesh A one can learn θ_s and $\mathbf{A_s}$ on a coarse mesh. For the control of the end effector position of a PUMA 560 through stereo cameras a few hundred mesh points suffice [2,3]. Further control, e.g., grasping motions, require submeshes, which (using a corresponding principle) can be limited to significantly less than hundred mesh points [4]. Obviously, the mesh points must be judiciously chosen, a subject matter which constitutes another important aspect of the algorithm.

Vector Quantization Scheme

In fact, the choice of mesh points is the most cardinal part of the proposed algorithm as we like to explain now. This part of the algorithms entails two aspects, the aspect of a vector quantization algorithm and the aspect of a graph matching algorithm. We like to explain these two aspects now.

The control algorithm suggested here actually generates, in a training period, a table look-up program. Our discussion above has been mainly concerned with the generation of the table entries. The following discussion is concerned with the assignement of table entries to control tasks. In case of end effector control the tasks can be designated simply by the target positions v_{target}. However, the algorithm can be applied to more general tasks.

The essential property which we require for the task space V is the existence of a distance metric, i.e., for all $\mathbf{u}, \mathbf{v} \in V$ exists a real, positive, etc. distance $d(\mathbf{u}, \mathbf{v})$ such that a *small* $d(\mathbf{u}, \mathbf{v})$ (in most cases) implies that the tasks $\mathbf{u}$ and $\mathbf{v}$ are *similar*, a *large* $d(\mathbf{u}, \mathbf{v})$ implies that the tasks are *dissimilar*. The algorithm determines now a set $\{\mathbf{v_s}, \mathbf{s} \in A\}$ of points $\mathbf{v_s} \in V$ which assign table entries, labelled by $\mathbf{s} \in A$ to tasks. This assignment works as follows. The table entry, labelled $\mathbf{s}$, is connected with the Voronoï polyhedron

$$Vor_1(\mathbf{s}) = \{\mathbf{v} \in V \mid \forall \mathbf{r} \in A, \mathbf{r} \neq \mathbf{s}, d(\mathbf{v_s}, \mathbf{v}) \leq d(\mathbf{v_r}, \mathbf{v})\} \tag{3}$$

The Voronoï polyhedra provide a complete partition of the task space V, i.e., $V = \cup_{\mathbf{s} \in A} Vor_1(\mathbf{s})$. Hence, any $\mathbf{v} \in V$ can be assigned to a table entry $\mathbf{s}(\mathbf{v})$, specified through the label $\mathbf{s}$ of the Voronoï polyhedron to which $\mathbf{v}$ belongs. (The fact, that a $\mathbf{v}$ may belong to several Voronoï polyhedra is not a nuisance, but rather a great benefit, as we will see shortly.) The question arises how the 'centers' $\mathbf{v_s}$ of the Voronoï polyhedra should be chosen. A suitable criterion is to choose the centers according to the distribution of tasks $P(\mathbf{v})$ encountered in a training episode, i.e., to select more centers in regions of V where $P(\mathbf{v})$ is large and *vice versa*. A possible criterion would be to assign $\{\mathbf{v_s}, \mathbf{s} \in A\}$ such that

$$E(\{\mathbf{v_s}, \mathbf{s} \in A\}) = \int d\mathbf{v} P(\mathbf{v}) d(\mathbf{v}, v_{\mathbf{s}(\mathbf{v})}) \tag{4}$$

assumes a minimum. Such criteria are well-known in the theory of vector quantization algorithms (for a more detailed discussion and references see [1]). We will explain below how the minimization of (4) is achieved. Details can be also found in [5].

Learning a Neighborhood Graph

So far the algorithm assigning table entries to tasks has been of a rather conventional vector quantization type. A crucial new feature of the algorithm is that a graph is being developed, the nodes of which are the elements of A, the edges being defined below. This graph can be exploited to enhance training results and training speeds. In fact, without exploiting such graph structures many control problems cannot be learned (see [1,2,3]). Also the gain in training speed can be very considerable (see [1,2,3]). The assignement of edges can be achieved in principle (a practical algorithm is presented in [5]) as follows. One considers so-called second order Voronoï polyhedra defined through

$$Vor_2(\mathbf{r}, \mathbf{s}) = \{\mathbf{v} \in V \mid \forall \mathbf{t} \in A, \mathbf{t} \notin \{\mathbf{r}, \mathbf{s}\}, d(\mathbf{v}, \mathbf{v_r}) \leq d(\mathbf{v}, \mathbf{v_t}) \wedge \mathbf{v_s}) \leq d(\mathbf{v}, \mathbf{v_t})\} \tag{5}$$

One assigns now edges between all pairs of nodes $(\mathbf{r}, \mathbf{s})$ the associated second order Voronoï polyhedra (5) of which are not empty. One obtains, thereby, a graph which reflects the neighborhood relationships of the first order Voronoï polyhedra (4).

Unfortunately, actual algorithms [5] can achieve assignements of edges only if the volume of the second order Voronoï diagrams is large enough, a condition which is not necessarily met in Euclidean tasks spaces of dimension three or larger. However, the algorithm presented in [5] usually captures a large fraction of neighborhood relationships through edge assignement.

A particularly straightforward interpretation of the graph described above can be given in case of a two-dimensional Euclidean space. In this case the Voronoï polyhedra are actually polygons and the structure of edges are the dual of these polygons, called the Delaunay tesselation.

We like to comment finally on the reason why the graph structure described can improve the generation of table entries for control tasks. The reason is that the edges of the graph structure connect those tables which are closest with respect to the metric of the task space. The edges provide a hierarchy of nearest neighbors, next nearest neighbors (connected through at least two edges), etc. During training one can asume then that tables, which are neighboring, have to learn similar entries. One can exploit this by incorporating a cooperative learning scheme involving nearest, next-nearest, etc. Voronoï polyhedra, reducing the range of cooperation progressively to achieve asymptotically an optimal resolution of table content.

Summary

The algorithm described above in the context of a control problem, has the important feature that it employs a nodes $\mathbf{v_s}$, $\mathbf{s} \in A$ together with a self-generated graph (edges between nodes). Previous algorithm (the extended Kohonen algorithm, see [1]) employed a lattice of nodes (which also corresponds to a node–edge, i.e., graph, structure) which was fixed 'a priori'. The new algorithm 'learns' the topology (neighborhood relationships) of the task space and, hence, does not require that the topology of the task space is known before hand and it can deal with complex topologies, like those of disjoint task spaces of mixed dimensionalities.

The algorithm can also be used in a somewhat simpler context of time series prediction. In this case the input data, corresponding to the tasks in the aforementioned example, are time series $y(t_1), y(t_2), \ldots, y(t_n)$ of a function $y(t)$, and the algorithm is asked to 'predict' the function value $y(t_{n+1}), t_{n+1} > t_1, t_2, \ldots t_n$. The problem, in principle, corresponds to learning to approximate the function $Y = y(t_{n+1})$ for vector-valued arguments $Y_r = (y(t_1), y(t_2), \ldots, y(t_n))^T$. We have developed a suitable learning rule for this purpose and applied it succesfully to a function $y(t)$ described by the Mackey-Glass equation [6]. This application will be presented in our lecture, in particularly, it will be demonstrated that the algorithm compares very favourably with existing algorithms, e.g., those of Moody and Darken and of Lapedes and Farber.

The algorithm is described in detail in [5], the original report, as well as in [2-4, 6-7].

References

[1] *Neuronale Netze: Eine Einführung in die Neuroinformatik selbstorganisierender Abbildungen*, H. Ritter, Th. Martinetz, and K. Schulten (2nd enlarged edition, Addison-Wesley, Bonn, 1990)
Neural Computation and Self-Organizing Maps: An Introduction, H. Ritter, Th. Martinetz, and K. Schulten (revised, English edition, Addison-Wesley, New York, 1991)
[2] Industrial Robot Learns Visuo-Motor Coordination by Means of 'Neural Gas' Network, J.A.Walter, Th.M.Martinetz, and K.Schulten, *Proceedings of the International Conference on Artificial Neural Networks, Helsinki, 1991)*
[3] Neural Network with Hebbian-like Adaptation Rules Learning Control of a PUMA Robot, Th.Martinetz and K.Schulten, (submitted to NIPS-91)
[4] Hierarchical Neural Net for Learning Control of a Robot's Arm and Gripper, Th.Martinetz and K.Schulten, *IJCNN International Joint Conference on Neural Networks, San Diego, California, July 1990*, pp. II–747 to II–752 (The Institute of Electrical and Electronics Engineers, New York, 1990)

[5] A 'Neural Gas' Network Learns Topologies, Th.Martinetz and K.Schulten, *Proceedings of the International Conference on Artificial Neural Networks, Helsinki, 1991)*

[6] S. Berkovitch, Th, Martinetz and K. Schulten, application to time series prediction, manuscript in preparation

[7] Ph. Dalger, B. Noël, Th. Martinetz and K. Schulten, mathematical analysis of Delaunay tesselation on the basis of 1st and 2nd order Voronoï polygons in case of 2-dimensional task spaces, manuscript in preparation

Neural network music composition
and the induction of multiscale temporal structure

Michael C. Mozer
Department of Computer Science and
Institute of Cognitive Science
University of Colorado
Boulder, CO 80309-0430
USA

Algorithmic music composition involves the use of rules to generate melodies. One simple but interesting technique is to select notes sequentially according to a transition table that specifies the probability of the next note as a function of the previous context. We describe an extension of this transition table approach using a recurrent connectionist network called CONCERT. CONCERT is trained on a set of melodies written in a certain style and then is able to compose new melodies in the same style. A central ingredient of CONCERT is the incorporation of psychologically-grounded representations of pitch, duration, and harmony. CONCERT was tested on sets of examples artificially generated according to simple rules and was shown to learn the underlying structure, even where other approaches failed. In larger experiments, CONCERT was trained on sets of J. S. Bach pieces, traditional European folk melodies, and waltzes, and was then allowed to compose novel melodies. Although the compositions are surprisingly pleasant, CONCERT has difficulty capturing the global structure of a composition. We describe an improved algorithm that is better able to induce temporal structure at multiple scales.

1   Introduction

In creating music, composers bring to bear a wealth of knowledge about musical conventions. If we hope to build automatic music composition systems that can mimic the abilities of human composers, it will be necessary to incorporate knowledge about musical conventions into the systems. However, this knowledge is difficult to express: even human composers are unaware of many of the constraints under which they operate.

In this paper, we describe a connectionist network that composes melodies. The network is called CONCERT, an acronym for <u>con</u>nectionist <u>c</u>omposer of <u>er</u>udite <u>t</u>unes. Musical knowledge is incorporated into CONCERT via two routes. First, CONCERT is trained on a set of sample melodies from which it extracts rules of note and phrase progressions. Second, we have built representations of pitch, duration, and harmony into CONCERT that are based on psychological studies of human perception. These representations, and an associated theory of generalization proposed by Shepard (1987), provide CONCERT with a basis for judging the similarity among notes, for selecting a response, and for restricting the set of alternatives that can be considered at any time.

2 Transition table approaches to composition

We begin by describing a traditional approach to algorithmic music composition using Markov *transition tables*. This simple but interesting technique involves selecting notes sequentially according to a table that specifies the probability of the next note as a function of the current note (Dodge & Jerse, 1985). The tables may be hand-constructed according to certain criteria or they may be set up to embody a particular musical style. In the latter case, statistics are collected over a set of examples (hereafter, the *training set*) and the table entries are defined to be the transition probabilities in these examples.

In melodies of any complexity, musical structure cannot be fully described by pairwise statistics. To capture additional structure, the transition table can be generalized from a two-dimensional array to n dimensions. In the n-dimensional table, often referred to as a table of order $n - 1$, the probability of the next note is indicated as a function of the previous $n - 1$ notes. Unfortunately, extending the transition table in this manner gives rise to two problems. First, the size of the table explodes exponentially with the amount of context and rapidly becomes unmanageable. Second, a table representing the high-order structure masks whatever low-order structure is present.

Kohonen (1989) has proposed a scheme by which only the *relevant* high-order structure is represented. The scheme is symbolic algorithm that, given a training set of examples, produces a collection of rules—a context-sensitive grammar—sufficient for reproducing most or all of the structure inherent in the set. However, because the algorithm attempts to produce deterministic rules—rules that always apply in a given context —the algorithm will not discover regularities unless they are absolute; it is not equipped to deal with statistical properties of the data. Both Kohonen's musical grammar and the transition table approach suffer from the further drawback that a symbolic representation of notes does not facilitate generalization. For instance, invariance under transposition is not directly representable. In addition, other similarities are not encoded, for example, the congruity of octaves.

Connectionist learning algorithms offer the potential of overcoming the various limitations of transition table approaches and Kohonen musical grammars. Connectionist algorithms are able to discover relevant structure and statistical regularities in sequences (e.g., Elman, 1990; Mozer, 1989), and to consider varying amounts of context, noncontiguous context, and combinations of low-order and high-order regularities. Connectionist approaches also promise better generalization through the use of distributed representations. In a local representation, where each note is represented by a discrete symbol, the sort of statistical contingencies that can be discovered are among notes. However, in a distributed representation, where each note is represented by a set of continuous feature values, the sort of contingencies that can be discovered are among *features*. To the extent that two notes share features, featural regularities discovered for one note may transfer to the other note.

3 The CONCERT architecture

CONCERT is a recurrent network architecture of the sort studied by Elman (1990). A melody is presented to it, one note at a time, and its task at each point in time is to predict the next note in the melody.[1] Using a training procedure described below, CONCERT's connection strengths are adjusted so that it can perform this task correctly for a set of training examples. Each example consists of a sequence of notes, each note being characterized by a pitch and a duration. The current note in the sequence is represented in the input layer of CONCERT, and the prediction of the next note is represented in the output layer. As Figure 1 indicates, the next note is encoded in two different ways: The next-note-distributed (or *NND*) layer contains CONCERT's internal representation of the note, while the next-note-local (or *NNL*) layer contains one unit for each alternative. For now, it should suffice to say that the representation of a note in the NND layer, as well as in the input

---

[1]In ongoing work, we have trained CONCERT on melodies with a harmonic accompaniment (chord progressions), but this extension will not be described here.

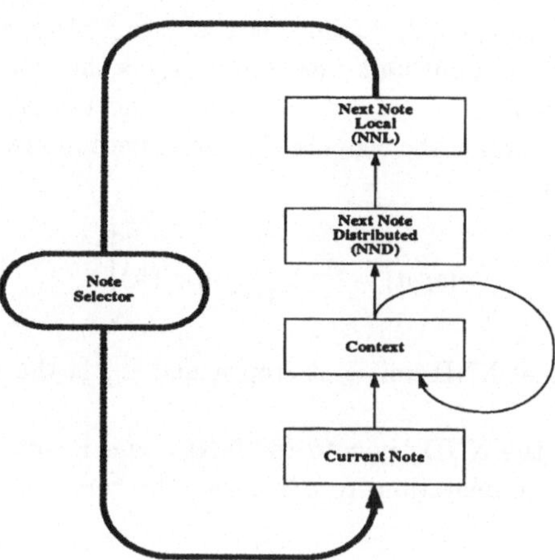

Figure 1: The CONCERT architecture. Rectangles indicate a layer of units, directed lines indicate full conectivity from one layer to another. The selection process is external to CONCERT and is used to choose among the alternatives proposed by the network during composition.

layer, is distributed, i.e., a note is indicated by a *pattern* of activity across the units. Because such patterns of activity can be quite difficult to interpret, the NNL layer provides an alternative, explicit representation of the possibilities.

The context layer represents the the temporal context in which a prediction is made. When a new note is presented in the input layer, the current context activity pattern is integrated with the new note to form a new context representation. Although CONCERT could readily be wired up to behave as a k-th order transition table, the architecture is far more general. The training procedure attempts to determine which aspects of the input sequence are relevant for making future predictions and retain only this task-relevant information in the context layer. This contrasts with Todd's (1989) seminal work on connectionist composition in which the recurrent context connections are prewired and fixed, which makes the nature of the information Todd's model retains independent of the examples on which it is trained.

Once CONCERT has been trained, it can be run in *composition mode* to create new pieces. This involves first seeding CONCERT with a short sequence of notes, perhaps the initial notes of one of the training examples. From this point on, the output of CONCERT can be fed back to the input, allowing CONCERT to continue generating notes without further external input. Generally, the output of CONCERT does not specify a single note with absolute certainty; instead, the output is a probability distribution over the set of candidates. It is thus necessary to select a particular note in accordance with this distribution. This is the role of the selection process depicted in Figure 1.

3.1 Activation rules and training procedure

The activation rule for the context units is

$$c_i(n) = \tanh\left[\sum_j w_{ij}x_j(n) + \sum_j v_{ij}c_j(n-1)\right],$$

where $c_i(n)$ is the activity of context unit i following processing of input note n (which we refer to as *step n*), $x_j(n)$ is the activity of input unit j at step n, w_{ij} is the connection strength from unit j of the input to unit i of the context layer, and v_{ij} is the connection strength from unit j to unit i Within the context layer, and tanh is the sigmoid-shaped hyperbolic tangent function. Units in the NND layer follow a similar rule:

$$nnd_i(n) = \tanh\left[\sum_j u_{ij} c_j(n)\right],$$

where $nnd_i(n)$ is the activity of NND unit i at step n and u_{ij} is the strength of connection from context unit j to NND unit i.

The transformation from the NND layer to the NNL layer is achieved by first computing the distance between the NND representation, $\mathbf{nnd}(n)$, and the target (distributed) representation of each pitch i, ρ_i:

$$d_i = |\mathbf{nnd}(n) - \rho_i|,$$

where $|\cdot|$ denotes the L2 vector norm. This distance is an indication of how well the NND representation matches a particular pitch. The activation of the NNL unit corresponding to pitch i, nnl_i, increases inversely with the distance:

$$nnl_i(n) = e^{-d_i} / \sum_j e^{-d_j}.$$

This normalized exponential transform (proposed by Bridle, 1990, and Rumelhart, in press) produces an activity pattern over the NNL units in which each unit has activity in the range (0,1) and the activity of all units sums to 1. Consequently, the NNL activity pattern can be interpreted as a probability distribution—in this case, the probability that the next note has a particular pitch.

CONCERT is trained using the back propagation unfolding-through-time procedure (Rumelhart, Hinton, & Williams, 1986) using the log likelihood error measure

$$E = -\sum_{p,n} \log nnl_{tgt}(n, p),$$

where p is an index over pieces in the training set and n an index over notes within a piece; tgt is the target pitch for note n of piece p.

3.2   Pitch representation

Having described CONCERT's architecture and training procedure, we turn to the representation of pitch. To accommodate a variety of music, CONCERT needs the ability to represent a range of about four octaves. Using standard musical notation, these pitches are labeled as follows: C1, D1, ..., B1, C2, D2, ..., B2, C3, ..., C5, where C1 is the lowest pitch and C5 the highest. Sharps are denoted by a #, e.g., F#3. The range C1-C5 spans 49 pitches.

One might argue that the choice of a pitch representation is not critical because back propagation can, in principle, discover an alternative representation well suited to the task. In practice, however, researchers have found that the choice of external representation is a critical determinant of the network's ultimate performance (e.g., Denker et al., 1987; Mozer, 1987). Quite simply, the more task-appropriate information that is built into the network, the easier the job the learning algorithm has. Because we are asking the network to make predictions about melodies that *people* have composed or to generate melodies that *people* perceive as pleasant, we have furnished CONCERT with a psychologically-motivated representation of pitch. By this, we mean that notes that people judge to be similar have similar representations in the network, indicating that the representation in the head matches the representation in the network.

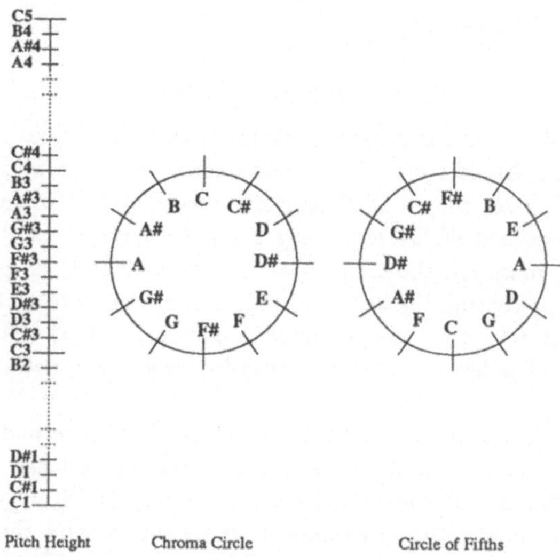

Figure 2: Pitch representation proposed by Shepard (1982)

Shepard (1982) has studied the similarity of pitches by asking people to judge the perceived similarity of pairs of pitches. He has proposed a theory of generalization (Shepard, 1987) in which the similarity of two items is exponentially related to their distance in an internal or "psychological" representational space. (This is the primary justification for the NNL layer computing an exponential function of distance.) Based on psychophysical experiments, he has proposed a five-dimensional space for the representation of pitch, depicted in Figure 2.

In this space, each pitch specifies a point along the *pitch height* (or *PH*) dimension, an (x, y) coordinate on the *chromatic circle* (or *CC*), and an (x, y) coordinate on the *circle of fifths* (or *CF*). we will refer to this representation as PHCCCF, after its three components. The pitch height component specifies the logarithm of the frequency of a pitch; this logarithmic transform places tonal half-steps at equal spacing from one another along the pitch height axis. In the chromatic circle, neighboring pitches are a tonal half-step apart. In the circle of fifths, the perfect fifth of a pitch is the next pitch immediately counterclockwise. Figure 2 shows the relative magnitude of the various components to scale. The proximity of two pitches in the five-dimensional PHCCCF space can be determined simply by computing the Euclidean distance between their representations.

A straightforward scheme for translating the PHCCCF representation into an activity pattern over a set of connectionist units is to use five units, one for pitch height and two pairs to encode the (x, y) coordinates of the pitch on the two circles. Due to several problems, we have represented each circle over a set of 6 binary-valued units that preserves the essential distance relationships among tones on the circles (Mozer, 1990). The PHCCCF representation thus consists of 13 units altogether. Rests (silence) are assigned a code that distinguish them from all pitches. The end of a piece is coded by several rests.

4 Simulation experiments

4.1 Learning the structure of diatonic scales

In this simulation, we trained CONCERT on a set of diatonic scales in various keys over a one octave range, e.g., D1 E1 F#1 G1 A1 B1 C#2 D2. Thirty-seven such scales can be made using pitches in the C1-C5 range. The training set consisted of 28 scales—roughly 75% of the corpus—selected at random, and the test set consisted of the remaining 9. In 10 replications of the simulation using 20 context units, CONCERT mastered the training set in approximately 55 passes. Generalization performance was tested by presenting the scales in the test set one note at a time and examining CONCERT's prediction. Of the 63 notes to be predicted in the test set, CONCERT achieved remarkable performance: 98.4% correct. The few errors were caused by transposing notes one full octave or one tonal half step.

To compare CONCERT with a transition table approach, we built a second-order transition table from the training set data and measured its performance on the test set. The transition table prediction (i.e., the note with highest probability) was correct only 26.6% of the time. The transition table is somewhat of a straw man in this environment: A transition table that is based on absolute pitches is simply unable to generalize correctly. Even if the transition table encoded relative pitches, a third-order table would be required to master the environment. Kohonen's musical grammar faces the same difficulties as a transition table.

A version of CONCERT was tested using a local pitch representation in the input and NND layers instead of the PHCCCF representation. The local representation had 49 pitch units, one per tone. Although the NND and NNL layers may seem somewhat redundant with a local pitch representation, the architecture was not changed to avoid confounding the comparison between representations with other possible factors. Testing the network in the manner described above, generalization performance with the local representation and 20 context units was only 54.4%. Experiments with smaller and larger numbers of context units resulted in still poorer performance. Thus, CONCERT clearly benefits from its psychologically-grounded representation of pitch.

4.2 Learning interspersed random walk sequences

The sequences in this simulation were generated by interspersing the elements of two simple random walk sequences. Each interspersed sequence had the following form: $a_1, b_1, a_2, b_2, \ldots a_5, b_5$, where a_1 and b_1 are randomly selected pitches, a_{i+1} is one step up or down from a_i on the C major scale, and likewise for b_{i+1} and b_i. Each sequence consisted of ten notes. CONCERT, with 25 context units, was trained on 50 passes through a set of 200 examples and was then tested on an additional 100. Because it is impossible to predict the second note in the interspersed sequences (b_1) from the first (a_1), this prediction was ignored for the purpose of evaluating CONCERT's performance. CONCERT achieved a performance of 94.8% correct. About half the errors were ones in which CONCERT transposed a correct prediction by an octave. Excluding these errors, performance improved to 95.5% correct.

To capture the structure in this environment, a transition table approach would need to consider at least the previous two notes. However, such a transition table is not likely to generalize well because, if it is to be assured of predicting a note at step n correctly, it must observe the note at step $n - 2$ in the context of *every possible* note at step $n - 1$. We constructed a second-order transition table from CONCERT's training set. Using a testing criterion analogous to that used to evaluate CONCERT, the transition table achieved a performance level on the test set of only 67.1% correct. Kohonen's musical grammar would face the same difficulty as the transition table in this environment.

Figure 3: A sample composition produced by CONCERT

4.3   Generating new melodies in the style of Bach

In a final experiment, we trained CONCERT on the melody line of a set of ten simple minuets and marches by J. S. Bach. The pieces had several voices, but the melody generally appeared in the treble voice. Importantly, to naive listeners the extracted melodies sounded pleasant and coherent without the accompaniment.

In the training data, each piece was terminated with a rest marker (the only rests in the pieces). This allowed CONCERT to learn not only the notes within a piece but also when the end of the piece was reached. Further, each major piece was transposed to the key of C major and each minor piece to the key of A minor. This was done to facilitate learning because the pitch representation does not take into account the notion of musical key; a more sophisticated pitch representation might avoid the necessity of this step.

In this simulation, each note was represented by a duration as well as a pitch. The duration representation consisted of five units and was analogous the PHCCCF representation for pitch (see Mozer, 1990, for details). It allowed for the representation of sixteenth, eighth, quarter, and half notes, as well as triplets. Also included in this simulation were two additional input units. One indicated whether the piece was in a major versus minor key, the other indicated whether the piece was in 3/4 meter versus 2/4 or 4/4. These inputs were fixed for a given piece.

Learning the examples involves predicting a total of 1,260 notes altogether, no small feat. CONCERT was trained with 40 hidden units for 3000 passes through the training set. The learning rate was gradually lowered from .0004 to .0002. By the completion of training, CONCERT could correctly predict about 95% of the pitches and 95% of the durations correctly. New pieces can be created by presenting a few notes to start and then running CONCERT in composition mode. One example of a composition produced by CONCERT is shown in Figure 3. The primary deficiency of CONCERT's compositions is that they are lacking in global coherence.

5   Capturing higher-order musical organization

The compositions produced by CONCERT are acceptable, but they tend to wander without direction, modulating haphazardly from major to minor keys, flip-flopping from the style of a march to that of a waltz. The problem is that CONCERT has mastered the rules of composition for notes within a phrase, but not rules operating at a more global level—rules for how phrases are connected.

To discover structural regularities within a phrase, only temporally local contingencies need to be examined. To discover regularities at a more global level, CONCERT may need to examine the relationships among many dozens of notes over a potentially long interval of time. For example, consider a simple phrase structure, AABA. A and B each represent a musical phrase of, say, 20 notes; the piece is thus composed of two repetitions of phrase A, followed by phrase B, followed by a final repetition of A. To predict the third repetition of individual notes in A correctly, it is necessary to remember notes that occurred 40 steps back. Moreover, the intervening information is irrelevant.

In principle, the context layer, with a sufficient number of units and a sufficient amount of training, should be capable of holding on to as much history as is relevant for the task. In practice, however, we have found that back propagation is not sufficiently powerful to discover arbitrary contingencies, in particular those which span long temporal intervals and which involve extremely high order statistics. One focus of the present work is on the problem of learning hierarchical or multiscale temporal structure. This difficult problem has been identified and studied by several other researchers, including Miyata and Burr (1990), Rohwer (1990), and Schmidhuber (1991). The implications of such work carry far beyond music composition to a variety of problems in temporal pattern recognition.

The basic idea behind our work involves building a *reduced description* (Hinton, 1988) of the sequence that makes global aspects more explicit or more readily detectable. In the case of the AABA structure, this might involve taking the sequence of notes composing A and redescribing them simply as "A." Based on this reduced description, recognizing the phrase structure AABA would involve little more than recognizing the sequence AABA. By constructing the reduced description, the problem of detecting global structure has been turned into the simpler problem of detecting local structure.

The challenge of this approach is to devise an appropriate reduced description. We've experimented with a scheme that constructs a reduced description that is a bird's eye view of the musical piece, sacrificing a representation of individual notes for the overall contour of the piece. Imagine playing back a song on a tape recorder at double the regular speed. The notes are to some extent blended together and indistinguishable. However, events at a coarser time scale become more explicit, such as a general ascending trend in pitch or a repeated progression of notes. Figure 4 illustrates the idea. The curve in the top graph, depicting a sequence of individual pitches, has been smoothed and compressed to produce the bottom graph. Mathematically, "smoothed and compressed" means that the waveform has been low-pass filtered and sampled at a lower rate. The result is a waveform in which the alternating upwards and downwards flow is unmistakable.

Multiple views of the sequence are realized in CONCERT using context units that operate with different *time constants*:

$$c_i(n) = \tau_i c_i(n-1) + (1 - \tau_i) \tanh[net_i(n)], \tag{1}$$

where $c_i(n)$ is the activity of context unit i at note n, $net_i(n)$ is the net input to unit i at note n, including activity both from the input layer and the recurrent connections, and τ_i is a time constant associated with each unit that has the range $(0, 1)$ and determines the responsiveness of the unit—the rate at which its activity changes. With $\tau_i = 0$, the activation rule reduces to the standard one and the unit can sharply change its response based on a new input. With large τ_i, the unit is sluggish, holding on to much of its previous value and thereby averaging the response to the net input over time. At the extreme of $\tau_i = 1$, the second term drops out and the unit's activity becomes fixed. Thus, large τ_i smooth out the response of a context unit over time. This is one property of the waveform in Figure 4a relative to the waveform in Figure 4b.

The other property, the compactness of the waveform, is also achieved by a large τ_i, although somewhat indirectly. The key benefit of the compact waveform in Figure 4 is that it allows a longer period of time to be viewed in a single glance, thereby explicating contingencies occurring during this interval during learning. The context unit activation rule (Equation 1) permits this. To see why this is the case, consider the relation between the error derivative with respect to the context units at step n, $\partial E/\partial c(n)$, and the error back propagated to the previous step, $n-1$. One contribution

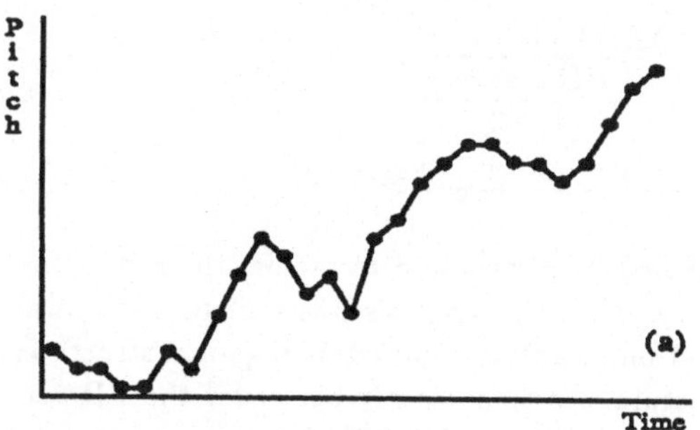
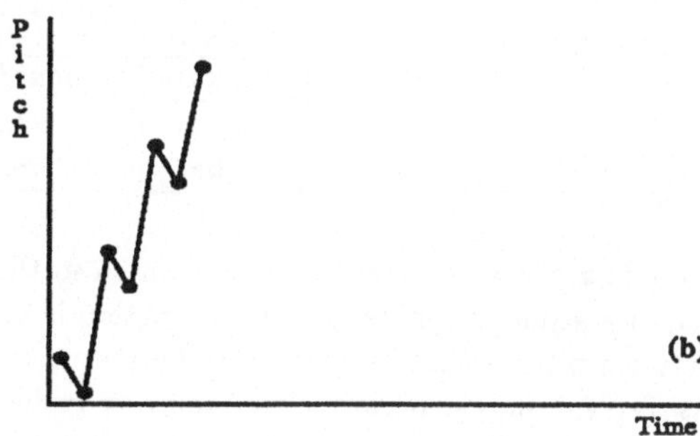

Figure 4: (a) A sequence of individual notes. The vertical axis indicates the pitch, the horizontal axis time. Each point corresponds to a particular note. (b) A smoothed, compact view of the sequence.

to $\partial E/\partial c_i(n-1)$, from the first term in Equation 1, is

$$\frac{\partial E}{\partial c_i(n)}\frac{\partial}{\partial c_i(n-1)}\left[\tau_i c_i(n-1)\right] = \tau_i\frac{\partial E}{\partial c_i(n)}.$$

This means that when τ_i is large, most of the error signal in context unit i at note n is carried back to note $n-1$. Thus, the back propagated error signal can make contact with points further back in time, facilitating the learning of more global structure in the input sequence.

6   Learning AABA phrase patterns

A simple simulation illustrates the benefits of temporal reduced descriptions. The melodies in this simulation were formed by generating two random walk phrases, call them A and B, and concatenating the phrases in an AABA pattern. The A and B phrases consisted of five-note ascending chromatic scales, the first pitch selected at random. The complete melody then consisted of 21 elements—four phrases of five notes followed by a rest marker—an example of which is:

    F#2 G2 G#2 A2 A#2 F#2 G2 G#2 A2 A#2 C4 C#4 D4 D#4 E4 F#2 G2 G#2 A2 A#2 REST.

Two versions of CONCERT were tested, each with 35 context units. In the *standard* version, all 35 units had $\tau = 0$; in the *reduced description* or *RD* version, 30 had $\tau = 0$ and 5 had $\tau = 0.8$. The training set consisted of 200 examples and the test set another 100 examples. Ten replications of each simulation were run for 300 passes through the training set.

Because of the way that the sequences are organized, certain pitches can be predicted based on local structure whereas other pitches require a more global memory of the sequence. In particular, the second through fifth pitches within a phrase can be predicted based on knowledge of the immediately

Table 1: Performance on AABA phrases

structure	standard version	RD version
local	97.3%	96.7%
global	58.4%	75.6%

preceding pitch. To predict the first pitch in the repeated A phrases and to predict the rest at the end of a sequence, more global information is necessary. Thus, the analysis was split to distinguish between pitches that required only local structure and pitches that required more global structure. As Table 1 shows, performance requiring global structure was significantly better for the RD version ($F(1,9)=179.8$, $p < .001$), but there was only a marginally reliable difference for performance involving local structure ($F(1,9)=3.82$, $p=.08$). The global structure can be further broken down to prediction of the end of the sequence and prediction of the first pitch of the repeated A phrases. In both cases, the performance improvement for the RD version was significant: 88.0% versus 52.9% for the end of sequence ($F(1,9)=220$, $p < .001$); 69.4% versus 61.2% for the first pitch ($F(1,9)=77.6$, $p < .001$).

Experiments with different values of τ in the range .7–.95 yielded qualitatively similar results, as did experiments in which the A and B phrases were formed by random walks in the key of C major.

7 Discussion

Initial results from CONCERT are encouraging. CONCERT is able to learn musical structure of varying complexity, from random walk sequences to Bach pieces containing nearly 200 notes. We presented several examples of structure that CONCERT can learn but that cannot be captured by a simple transition table or by Kohonen's musical grammar.

CONCERT's main weakness, which we have begun to address, is its inability to master temporal structure at more global time scales. This is a general weakness with back propagation in recurrent networks. The notion of hidden units that operate with different time constants is one component of a solution, but is not the complete answer. We are currently extending the approach in several directions. First, we are examining a special case of the general architecture shown in Figure 1 in which the context layer is split into two successive layers and the RD units lie in the upper layer. Second, we are testing a training procedure in which slower time scale units are fed an error signal only on trials where the faster scale units are unable to master the task. Third, we are using back propagation to train the time constants directly. And finally, we are using the RD units to learn aspects of the harmonic accompaniment, which by nature changes more slowly in time.

8 Acknowledgements

This research was supported by NSF Presidential Young Investigator award IRI-9058450, grant 90-21 from the James S. McDonnell Foundation, and DEC external research grant 1250. Thanks to Paul Smolensky for helpful comments regarding this work, and to Hal Eden and Darren Hardy for technical assistance.

References

[1] Bridle, J. (1990). Training stochastic model recognition algorithms as networks can lead to maximum mutual information estimation of parameters. In D. S. Touretzky (Ed.), *Advances in neural information processing systems 2* (pp. 211–217). San Mateo, CA: Morgan Kaufmann.

[2] Dodge, C., & Jerse, T. A. (1985). *Computer music: Synthesis, composition, and performance.* New York: Shirmer Books.

[3] Elman, J. L. (1990). Finding structure in time. *Cognitive Science, 14*, 179–212.

[4] Hinton, G. E. (1988). Representing part-whole hierarchies in connectionist networks. *Proceedings of the Eighth Annual Conference of the Cognitive Science Society* (pp. 48–54). Hillsdale, NJ: Erlbaum.

[5] Kohonen, T. (1989). A self-learning musical grammar, or "Associative memory of the second kind." *Proceedings of the 1989 International Joint Conference on Neural Networks*, 1–5.

[6] Miyata, Y., & Burr, D. (1990). Hierarchical recurrent networks for learning musical structure. Unpublished manuscript.

[7] Mozer, M. C. (1987). RAMBOT: A connectionist expert system that learns by example. In M. Caudill & C. Butler (Eds.), *Proceedings fo the IEEE First Annual International Conference on Neural Networks* (pp. 693–700). San Diego, CA: IEEE Publishing Services.

[8] Mozer, M. C. (1989). A focused back-propagation algorithm for temporal pattern recognition. *Complex Systems, 3*, 349–381.

[9] Mozer, M. C. (1990). *Connectionist music composition based on melodic, stylistic, and psychophysical constraints* (Tech Report CU–CS–495–90). Boulder, CO: University of Colorado, Department of Computer Science.

[10] Rohwer, R. (1990). The 'moving targets' training algorithm. In D. S. Touretzky (Ed.), *Advances in neural information processing systems 2* (pp. 558–565). San Mateo, CA: Morgan Kaufmann.

[11] Rumelhart, D. E., Hinton, G. E., & Williams, R. J. (1986). Learning internal representations by error propagation. In D. E. Rumelhart & J. L. McClelland (Eds.), *Parallel distributed processing: Explorations in the microstructure of cognition. Volume I: Foundations* (pp. 318–362). Cambridge, MA: MIT Press/Bradford Books.

[12] Rumelhart, D. E. (in press). Connectionist processing and learning as statistical inference. In Y. Chauvin & D. E. Rumelhart (Eds.), *Backpropagation: Theory, architectures, and applications.* Hillsdale, NJ: Erlbaum.

[13] Schmidhuber, J. (1991). *Neural sequence chunkers* (Report FKI–148–91). Munich, Germany: Technische Universität München, Institut für Informatik.

[14] Shepard, R. N. (1982). Geometrical approximations to the structure of musical pitch. *Psychological Review, 89*, 305–333.

[15] Shepard, R. N. (1987). Toward a universal law of generalization for psychological science. *Science, 237*, 1317–1323.

[16] Todd, P. M. (1989). A connectionist approach to algorithmic composition. *Computer Music Journal, 13*, 27–43.

Building Faster Connectionist Systems With Bumptrees

Stephen M. Omohundro
International Computer Science Institute
1947 Center Street, Suite 600
Berkeley, California 94704

This paper describes "bumptrees", a new approach to improving the computational efficiency of a wide variety of connectionist algorithms. We describe the use of these structures for representing, learning, and evaluating smooth mappings, smooth constraints, classification regions, and probability densities. We present an empirical comparison of a bumptree approach to more traditional connectionist approaches for learning the mapping between the kinematic and visual representations of the state of a 3 joint robot arm. Simple networks based on backpropagation with sigmoidal units are unable to perform the task at all. Radial basis function networks perform the task but by using bumptrees, the learning rate is hundreds of times faster at reasonable error levels and the retrieval time is over fifty times faster with 10,000 samples. Bumptrees are a natural generalization of oct-trees, k-d trees, balltrees and boxtrees and are useful in a variety of circumstances. We describe both the underlying ideas and extensions to constraint and classification learning that are under current investigation.

1 Introduction

Connectionist models are currently being employed with great success in a wide variety of domains. Much of the current interest in connectionist systems is due to their unique combination of representing information using real values, of being well-suited to learning, and providing a naturally parallel computational framework. Real-valued representations are capable of expressing "fuzzy", "soft", or "evidential" information. It also makes connectionist systems ideal for use in geometric or physical situations. They form a natural bridge between the primarily geometric nature of sensory input and the physical world and the more symbolic nature of higher level reasoning processes. In this paper we will focus primarily on the representation, learning, and evaluation of geometric information.

Despite the many advantages of connectionist systems, they often do far more computational work than is required for computing the results that they produce. This is particularly obvious in networks with localized representations. In the standard approach, the activity of every unit in a connectionist system is evaluated on every time step without regard to its contribution to the current output. This has the advantage that every network update looks exactly the same, but can lead to a lot of unneccessary work. For example, the computation going on in the neurons of a person's legs is not useful while that person is engaged in solving a mathematics problem. In biological systems, much of the hardware is not sharable between tasks and so no great advantage would accrue if we were able to determine that certain neurons need not perform their computation in certain time steps. Most engineered systems, on the other hand, can timeshare computational hardware and idle processesors may be used for other useful work. This is certainly true for serial machines, where avoiding the simulation of units directly reduces the time for simulation. It is also true for parallel machines in which individual processors simulate more than one "virtual" connectionist unit.

For the past several years we have been developing a variety of algorithms which are connectionist in spirit but which try to avoid performing unneeded computations. Like connectionist systems, information is represented in a real-valued evidential way and the structures are organized around learning. The computational paradigm no long follows a fixed network structure in choosing which computations to perform, however. These algorithms can be many orders of magnitude faster than corresponding connectionist approaches both in learning time and in evaluation time. This has often meant the difference between our being able run a simulation on a workstation or not. Many of these algorithms parallelize, though we will not discuss this issue here. In geometric domains this work uses concepts from computational geometry to identify which parts of a representation are relevant to the part of a space that the current input lies in. During learning, only those parts of the representation which are relevant to the training data are updated. During evaluation, only the relevant portions of the knowledge base are retrieved.

These approaches typically work by introducing a new structure on top of the knowledge base which is used to facilitate access. Often this structure has a hierarchical form and some kind of branch and bound is used to prune away unneccessary work. The structures described in this paper have this character and are a natural generalization of several previous structures.

2 What is a Bumptree?

A bumptree is a new geometric data structure which is useful for efficiently learning, representing, and evaluating geometric relationships in a variety of contexts. They are a natural generalization of several hierarchical geometric data structures including oct-trees, k-d trees, balltrees and boxtrees. They are useful for many geometric learning tasks including approximating functions, constraint surfaces, classification regions, and probability densities from samples. In the function approximation case, the approach is related to radial basis function neural networks, but supports faster construction, faster access, and more flexible modification. We provide empirical data comparing bumptrees with radial basis functions in section 3.

A bumptree is used to provide efficient access to a collection of functions on a Euclidean space of interest. It is a complete binary tree in which a leaf corresponds to each function of interest. There are also functions associated with each internal node and the defining constraint is that each interior node's function must be everwhere larger than each of the functions associated with the leaves beneath it. In many cases the leaf functions will be peaked in localized regions, which is the origin of the name. A simple kind of bump function is spherically symmetric about a center and vanishes outside of a specified ball. Figure 1 shows the structure of a two-dimensional bumptree in this setting.

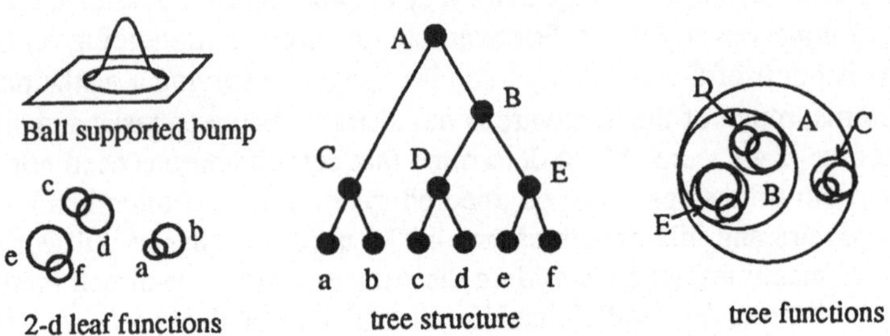

Figure 1: A two-dimensional bumptree.

A particularly important special case of bumptrees is used to access collections of Gaussian functions on multi-dimensional spaces. Such collections are used, for example, in representing smooth probability distribution functions as a Gaussian mixture and arises in many adaptive kernel estimation schemes. It is convenient to represent the quadratic exponents of the Gaussians in the tree rather than the Gaussians themselves. The simplest approach is to use quadratic functions for the internal nodes as well as the leaves as shown in Figure 2, though other classes of internal node functions can sometimes provide faster access

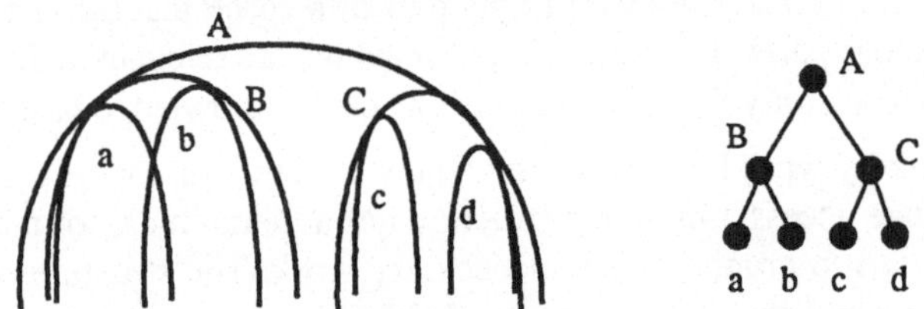

Figure 2: A bumptree for holding Gaussians.

Many of the other hierarchical geometric data structures may be seen as special cases of bumptrees by choosing appropriate internal node functions as shown in Figure 3. Regions may be represented by functions which take the value 1 inside the region and which vanish outside of it. The function shown in Figure 3D is aligned along a coordinate axis and is constant on one side of a specified value and decreases quadratically on the other side. It is represented by specifying the coordinate which is cut, the cut location, the constant value (0 in some situations), and the coefficient of quadratic decrease. Such a function may be evaluated extremely efficiently on a data point and so is useful for fast pruning operations. Such evaluations are effectively what is used in [7] to implement fast nearest neighbor computation. The bumptree structure generalizes this kind of query to allow for different scales for different points and directions. The empirical results presented in the next section are based on bumptrees with this kind of internal node function.

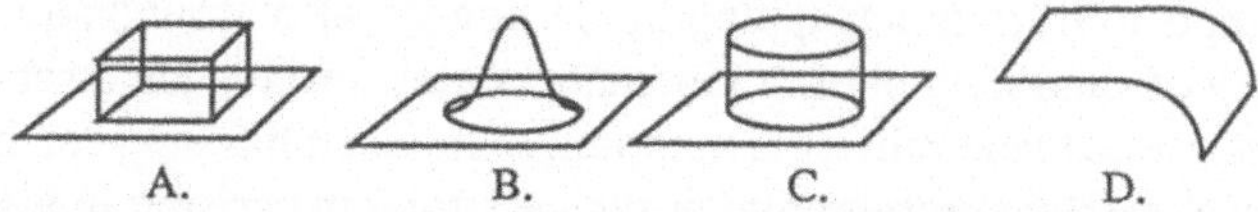

Figure 3: Internal bump functions for A) oct-trees, kd-trees, boxtrees [4], B) and C) for balltrees [5], and D) for Sproull's higher performance kd-tree [7].

There are several approaches to choosing a tree structure to build over given leaf data. Each of the algorithms studied for balltree construction in [5] may be applied to the more general task of bumptree construction. The fastest approach is analogous to the basic k-d tree construction technique [2] and is top down and recursively splits the functions into two sets of almost the same size. This is what is used in the simulations described in the next section. The slowest but most effective approach builds the tree bottom up, greedily deciding on the best pair of functions to join under a single parent node. Intermediate in speed and quality are incremental approaches which allow one to dynamically insert and delete leaf functions. These intermediate quality algorithms are used in the implementation of the bottom up algorithm to build a structure to efficiently support the queries needed during construction.

Bumptrees may be used to efficiently support many important queries. The simplest kind of query presents a point in the space and asks for all leaf functions which have a value at that point which is larger than a specified value. The bumptree allows a search from the root to prune any subtrees whose root function is smaller than the specified value at the point. More interesting queries are based on branch and bound and generalize the nearest neighbor queries that k-d trees support. A typical example in the case of a collection of Gaussians is to request all Gaussians in the set whose value at a specified point is within a specified factor (say .001) of the Gaussian whose value is largest at that point. The search proceeds down the most promising branches first, continually maintains the largest value found at any point, and prunes away subtrees which are not within the given factor of the current largest function value.

3 The Robot Mapping Learning Task

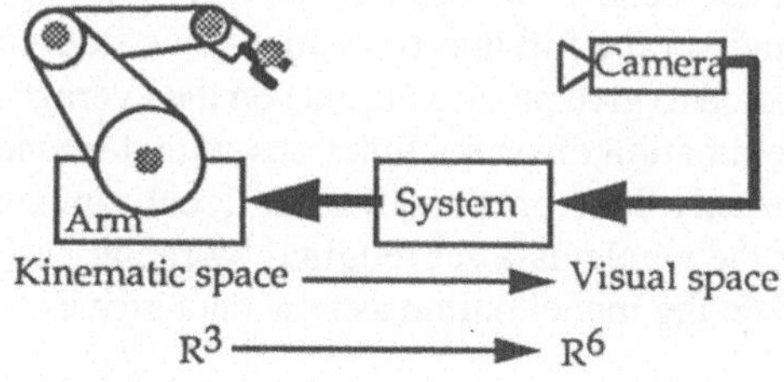

Figure 4: Robot arm mapping task.

Figure 4 shows the setup which defines the mapping learning task we used to study the effectiveness of the balltree data structure. This setup was investigated extensively by Mel in [3] and involves a camera looking at a robot arm. The kinematic state of the arm is defined by three angle control coordinates and the visual state by six visual coordinates of highlighted spots on the arm. The mapping from kinematic to visual space is a nonlinear map from three dimensions to six. The system attempts to learn this mapping by flailing the arm around and observing the visual state for a variety of randomly chosen kinematic states. From such a set of random input/output pairs, the system must generalize the mapping to inputs it has not seen before. This mapping task was chosen as fairly representative of typical problems arising in vision and robotics.

The radial basis function approach to mapping learning is to represent a function as a linear combination of functions which are spherically symmetric around chosen centers

$f(x) = \sum_i w_i g_i (x - x_i)$. In the simplest form, which we use here, the basis functions are centered

on the input points. More recent variations have fewer basis functions than sample points and choose centers by clustering. The timing results given here would be in terms of the number of basis functions rather than the number of sample points for a variation of this type. Many forms for the basis functions themselves have been suggested. In our study both Gaussian and linearly increasing functions gave similar results. The coefficients of the radial basis functions are chosen so that the sum forms a least squares best fit to the data. Such fits require a time proportional to the cube of the number of parameters in general. The experiments reported here were done using the singular value decomposition to compute the best fit coefficients.

The approach to mapping learning based on bumptrees builds local models of the mapping in each region of the space using data associated with only the training samples which are nearest that region. These local models are combined in a convex way according to "influence" functions which are associated with each model. Each influence function is peaked in the region for which it is most salient. The bumptree structure organizes the local models so that only the few models which have a great influence on a query sample need to be evaluated. If the influence functions vanish outside of a compact region, then the tree is used to prune the branches which have no influence. If a model's influence merely dies off with distance, then the branch and bound technique is used to determine contributions that are greater than a specified error bound.

If a set of bump functions sum to one at each point in a region of interest, they are called a "partition of unity". We form influence bumps by dividing a set of smooth bumps (either Gaussians or smooth bumps that vanish outside a sphere) by their sum to form an easily computed partiton of unity. Our local models are affine functions determined by a least squares fit to local samples. When these are combined according to the partition of unity, the value at each point is a convex combination of the local model values. The error of the full model is therefore bounded by the errors of the local models and yet the full approximation is as smooth as the local bump functions. These results may be used to give precise bounds on the average number of samples needed to achieve a given approximation error for functions with a bounded second derivative. In this approach, linear fits are only done on a small set of local samples, avoiding the computationally expensive fits over the whole data set required by radial basis functions. This locality also allows us to easily update the model online as new data arrives.

If $b_i(x)$ are bump functions such as Gaussians, then $n_i(x) = \dfrac{b_i(x)}{\sum_j b_j(x)}$ forms a partition of unity.

If $m_i(x)$ are the local affine models, then the final smoothly interpolated approximating function is $f(x) = \sum_i n_i(x) m_i(x)$. The influence bumps are centered on the sample points with a width determined by the sample density. The affine model associated with each influence bump is determined by a weighted least squares fit of the sample points nearest the bump center in which the weight decreases with distance.

Because it performs a global fit, for a given number of samples points, the radial basis function approach achieves a smaller error than the approach based on bumptrees. In terms of construction time to achieve a given error, however, bumptrees are the clear winner.Figure 5 shows how the mean square error for the robot arm mapping task decreases as a function of the time to construct the mapping.

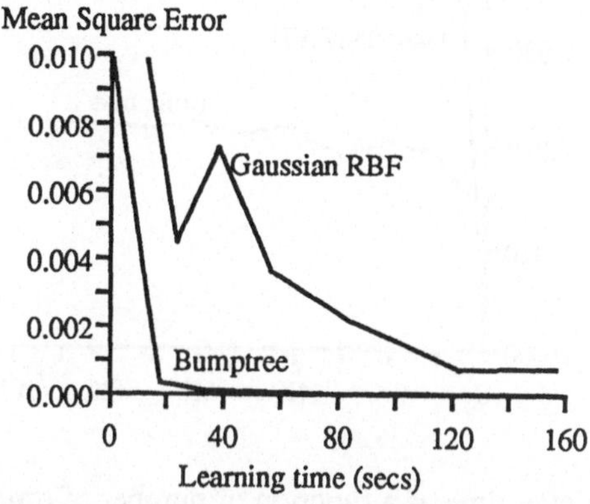

Figure 5: Mean square error as a function of learning time.

Perhaps even more important for applications than learning time is retrieval time. Retrieval using radial basis functions requires that the value of each basis function be computed on each query input and that these results be combined according to the best fit weight matrix. This time increases linearly as a function of the number of basis functions in the representation. In the bumptree approach, only those influence bumps and affine models which are not pruned away by the bumptree retrieval need perform any computation on an input. Figure 6 shows the retrieval time as a function of number of training samples for the robot mapping task. The retrieval time for radial basis functions crosses that for balltrees at about 100 samples and increases linearly off the graph. The balltree algorithm has a retrieval time which empirically grows very slowly and doesn't require much more time even when 10,000 samples are represented.

While not shown here, the representation may be improved in both size and generalization capacity by a best first merging technique. The idea is to consider merging two local models and their influence bumps into a single model. The pair which increases the error the least is merged first and the process is repeated until no pair is left whose meger wouldn't exceed an error criterion. This algorithm does a good job of discovering and representing linear parts of a map with a single model and putting many higher resolution models in areas with strong nonlinearities.

4 Extensions to Other Tasks

The bumptree structure is useful for implementing efficient versions of a variety of other geometric learning tasks [6]. Perhaps the most fundamental such task is density estimation which attempts to model a probability distribution on a space on the basis of samples drawn from that distribution. One powerful technique is adaptive kernel estimation [1]. The estimated distribution is represented as a Gaussian mixture in which a spherically symmetric Gaussian is centered on each data point and the widths are chosen according to the local density of samples. A best-first merging technique may often be used to produce mixtures consisting of many fewer non-symmetric Gaussians. A bumptree may be used to find and organize such Gaussians. Possible internal node functions include both quadratics and the faster to evaluate functions shown in Figure 3D.

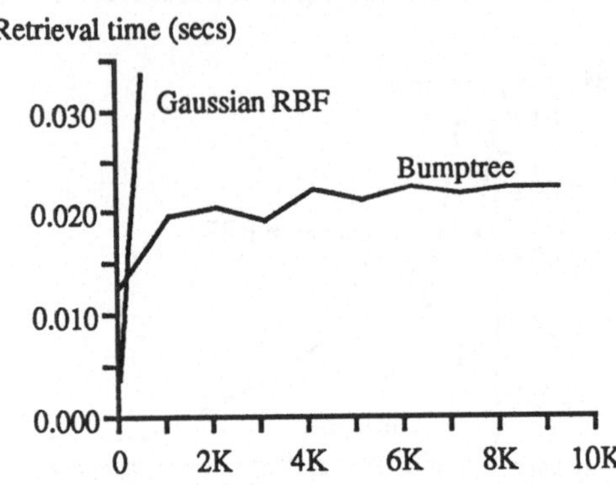

Figure 6: Retrieval time as a function of number of training samples.

It is possible to efficiently perform many operations on probability densities represented in this way. The most basic query is to return the density at a given location. The bumptree may be used with branch and bound to achieve retrieval in logarithmic expected time. It is also possible to quickly find marginal probabilities by integrating along certain dimensions. The tree is used to quickly identify the Gaussian which contribute. Conditional distributions may also be represented in this form and bumptrees may be used to compose two such distributions.

Above we discussed mapping learning and evaluation. In many situations there are not the natural input and output variables required for a mapping. If a probability distribution is peaked on a lower dimensional surface, it may be thought of as a constraint. Networks of constraints which may be imposed in any order among variables are natural for describing many problems. Bumptrees open up several possibilities for efficiently representing and propagating smooth constraints on continuous variables. The most basic query is to specify known external constraints on certain variables and allow the network to further impose whatever constraints it can. Multi-dimensional product Gaussians can be used to represent joint ranges in a set of variables. The operation of imposing a constraint surface may be thought of as multiplying an external constraint Gaussian by the function representing the constraint distribution. Because the product of two Gaussians is a Gaussian, this operation always produces Gaussian mixtures and bumptrees may be used to facilitate the operation.

A representation of constraints which is more like that used above for mappings constructs surfaces from local affine patches weighted by influence functions. We have developed a local analog of principle components analysis which builds up surfaces from random samples drawn from them. As with the mapping structures, a best-first merging operation may be used to discover affine structure in a constraint surface.

Finally, bumptrees may be used to enhance the performance of classifiers. One approach is to directly implement Bayes classifiers using the adaptive kernel density estimator described above for each class's distribution function. A separate bumptree may be used for each class or with a more sophisticated branch and bound, a single tree may be used for the whole set of classes.

In summary, bumptrees are a natural generalization of several hierarchical geometric access structures and may be used to enhance the performance of many neural network like algorithms. While we compared radial basis functions against a different mapping learning technique, bumptrees may be used to boost the retrieval performance of radial basis functions directly when the basis functions decay away from their centers. Many other neural network approaches in which much of the network does not perform useful work for every query are also susceptible to sometimes dramatic speedups through the use of this kind of access structure.

References

[1]   L. Devroye and L. Gyorfi. (1985) *Nonparametric Density Estimation: The L1 View*, New York: Wiley.

[2]   J. H. Friedman, J. L. Bentley and R. A. Finkel. (1977) An algorithm for finding best matches in logarithmic expected time. *ACM Trans. Math. Software* 3:209-226.

[3]   B. Mel. (1990) *Connectionist Robot Motion Planning, A Neurally-Inspired Approach to Visually-Guided Reaching*, San Diego, CA: Academic Press.

[4]   S. M. Omohundro. (1987) Efficient algorithms with neural network behavior. *Complex Systems* 1:273-347.

[5]   S. M. Omohundro. (1989) Five balltree construction algorithms. *International Computer Science Institute Technical Report* TR-89-063.

[6]   S. M. Omohundro. (1990) Geometric learning algorithms. *Physica D* 42:307-321.

[7]   R. F. Sproull. (1990) Refinements to Nearest-Neighbor Searching in k-d Trees. *Sutherland, Sproull and Associates Technical Report* SSAPP #184c, *to appear in Algorithmica.*

Algorithmisches Lernen auf der Basis empirischer Daten

Hans Ulrich Simon
Universität Dortmund
Fachbereich Informatik
Lehrstuhl II
Postfach 500500
4600 Dortmund 50
simon@nereus.informatik.uni-dortmund.de

26. Juni 1991

Es ist eine grundlegende menschliche Fähigkeit, empirische Erfahrungen in Hypothesen über die Wirklichkeit zu transformieren. Die resultierende Hypothese, gleichgültig ob sie bewußt oder unbewußt vorliegt, repräsentiert das in den Daten angereicherte Wissen in einer kompakteren und verallgemeinerten Form. Der andauernde Prozeß, Hypothesen und empirische Erfahrungen in Einklang zu bringen, ist eine Form des Lernens. Während das menschliche Lernen uns scheinbar mühelos befähigt, sprachliche oder visuelle Begriffe zu erwerben und komplexe motorische Aktionen auszuführen, widersteht es dennoch weitgehend allen Versuchen, es in eine algorithmische Form zu bringen und auf Maschinen zu übertragen.
Wir wollen in unserem Beitrag ein Lernmodell (das von L. Valiant 1984 entwickelte 'pac–learning') vorstellen und auf neuere Arbeiten am Fachbereich Informatik der Universität Dortmund eingehen. Im Rahmen dieses Modelles werden Begriffe wie 'effiziente und erfolgreiche Lernalgorithmen' in einer präzisen Weise gebraucht. Es wird dadurch möglich, mit Methoden der Statistik konkrete Aussagen über die erforderliche Größe empirischer Datenbestände zu machen, um zu zuverlässigen Hypothesen zu gelangen. Wir werden die grundsätzliche Vorgehensweise auf das Lernen mit neuronalen Netzen übertragen und an konkreten Netzarchitekturen veranschaulichen.

1 Approximation und Effizienz beim Lernen

Lernen ist ein vielfältiger Begriff. Es wäre übertriebener Ehrgeiz, alle Spielarten des Lernens in einem einzigen formalen Modell erfassen zu wollen. Wir werden uns in diesem Beitrag auf Klassifikationsaufgaben und das Lernen durch Beispiele beschränken. Eine typische Aufgabe dieser Art könnte folgendemaßen aussehen:

Ein Fahrschüler (evt. ein autonomes Fahrzeug) soll das Konzept 'Bremsen erforderlich' lernen. In der Trainingsphase erhält er eine (mehr oder weniger zufällige) Auswahl von Verkehrssituationen (also positive und negative Beispiele für das zu lernende Konzept) und jeweils ein zusätzliches Bit an Information (Bremsen oder Nicht–Bremsen). Nach dem Training soll er eigenständig entscheiden. Sofern diese Entscheidungen deterministisch sind, dürfen wir annehmen, daß er sich dabei nach einer Hypothese für das Konzept 'Bremsen erforderlich' richtet. Ein sinnvolles Gütekriterium für die Hypothese ist ihre erwartete Fehlerrate. Es gibt zwei gute Gründe anzunehmen, daß das Konzept nicht perfekt gelernt worden ist:

1. Die Trainingssituationen decken die relevanten Verkehrssituationen nur teilweise ab.

2. Mit einer kleinen Wahrscheinlichkeit war das Training sogar unrepräsentativ für das zu lernende Konzept.

Es ist daher vernünftig, der entwickelten Hypothese eine kleine Fehlerrate ϵ und den Stichproben eine kleine Inadäquatheit δ (beides Wahrscheinlichkeiten $0 < \epsilon, \delta \leq 1$) zuzugestehen. Es ist jedoch wünschenswert, diese Parameter beliebig klein einstellen zu können (Aspekt der Approximation), was im allgemeinen die Dauer des Trainings und den Aufwand zur Berechnung der Hypothese erhöhen wird. Der Mehraufwand sollte dabei nur in einer kontrollierten Weise ansteigen (Aspekt der Effizienz). Diese Aspekte der Approximation und Effizienz bilden die Grundlage für das im folgenden kurz geschilderte Lernmodell von Valiant (ausführlichere Beschreibung des Modells in [22]).

Definition des Lernmodelles von Valiant

Eine Klassifikationsaufgabe ist gegeben durch eine *Konzeptklasse C*, eine *Beispielklasse X* und eine *Hypothesenklasse H*. Jedes Konzept $c \in C$ repräsentiert eine Teilmenge von X, bestehend aus den *positiven Beispielen* für c. Die Beispiele außerhalb dieser Teilmenge heißen *negative Beispiele* für c. Die Ausgangssituation für einen konkreten Lernvorgang wird hergestellt, wenn ein (dem Lerner zunächst unbekanntes) Konzept $c \in C$ fixiert wird. Wir nennen dann c das *Zielkonzept*. Erfahrungen über c werden nur durch positive oder negative Beispiele gewonnen. Wir nehmen dabei an, daß die Beispiele unabhängig voneinander gemäß einer unbekannten (aber im Laufe des Lernvorgangs zeitlich stabilen) Wahrscheinlichkeitsverteilung D generiert werden. Eine Kollektion aus m solchen Beispielen (alle markiert mit ihrer korrekten $(+, -)$-Klassifikation) heißt eine *Stichprobe* der Größe m für c. Ein *Hypothesenfinder* ist ein Algorithmus A, der eine Stichprobe für c in eine Hypothese $h \in H$ transformiert. Wir nennen h ϵ-genau für c $(0 < \epsilon \leq 1)$, wenn die Wahrscheinlichkeit für eine Fehlklassifikation durch ϵ beschränkt ist, d.h., wenn

$$D(c \Delta h) = D((c \setminus h) \cup (h \setminus c)) \leq \epsilon.$$

Wir nennen C durch H *pac–lernbar*[1], wenn ein Hypothesenfinder A und eine Funktion $m(\epsilon, \delta)$ existieren, so daß folgendes gilt:
Für alle Konzepte c, Verteilungen D, $0 < \epsilon, \delta \leq 1$ und $m = m(\epsilon, \delta)$ ist die Wahrscheinlichkeit, daß A auf einer Stichprobe der Größe m für c eine ϵ-genaue Hypothese h für c produziert, mindestens $1 - \delta$. Aus Effizienzgründen verlangen wir zusätzlich, daß $m(\epsilon, \delta)$ polynomiell in $1/\epsilon, 1/\delta$ und die Laufzeit von A polynomiell in m beschränkt ist.

Obwohl die präzise Handhabung dieser Definition eine gewisse Einübung erfordert, zeigt ein kurzer Vergleich mit den vorangegangenen eher intuitiven Ausführungen, daß im wesentlichen die im Fahrschülerbeispiel entwickelten Ideen formalisiert worden sind. Die Stärken dieses Lernmodells liegen darin, daß eine klare Konzeption zugrunde liegt und somit Lernalgorithmen analysiert und miteinander verglichen werden können. Der enge Zusammenhang zur Komplexitätstheorie und zur theoretischen Statistik hat sich dabei als außerordentlich fruchtbar erwiesen. In der Anfangsphase wurde das Modell am intensivsten an aussagenlogischen und geometrischen Konzeptklassen erprobt (eine gute Übersicht bieten die Tagungsbände des seit 1988 jährlich stattfindenden 'Workshop on Computational Learning Theory'; Verlag Morgan–Kaufmann). In jüngster Zeit mehren sich die Versuche, die Grundkonzeption auf das Lernen mit neuronalen Netzwerken zu übertragen und mit neuen Varianten vermeintlichen und tatsächlichen Schwächen des Modells zu begegnen. In den folgenden beiden Abschnitten gehen wir auf diese Versuche, und insbesondere auf die in der Forschungsgruppe Dortmund gewonnenen Erfahrungen, näher ein.

---

[1]pac ist ein Kürzel für 'probably approximately correct'

2 Lernalgorithmen und neuronale Netze

Eine Konzeptklasse C liegt bei einer praktischen Lernaufgabe oft nicht in einem formalen Sinne vor. Das Konzept 'Bremsen erforderlich' ist zum Beispiel ein semantisches Konzept, das durch einen kompetenten Fahrlehrer repräsentiert werden kann. Eine äquivalente syntaktische und somit maschinenverarbeitbare Beschreibung ist oft unbekannt. Darüberhinaus kann das Konzept in dem Sinne probabilistisch sein, daß das gleiche Beispiel manchmal als positiv und manchmal als negativ gewertet wird (nicht klar definierte Grenzfälle). Die Definition der pac–Lernbarkeit muß dann entsprechend modifiziert werden:

Die positiven Beispiele eines Konzeptes c entsprechen einer Menge c_+ zusammen mit einer statistischen Verteilung D_+, die negativen einer (zu c_+ nicht notwendig disjunkten) Teilmenge c_- zusammen mit einer statistischen Verteilung D_-. Die minimale Fehlerrate $opt(c)$ kann dann größer als 0 sein. Der Parameter ϵ variiert zwischen $opt(C)$ und 1. Das Wachstum des getriebenen Aufwandes wird in Abhängigkeit von $1/(\epsilon - opt(C))$ gemessen.

Die Existenz von informellen oder probabilistischen Konzepten verhindert jedoch keineswegs die Herstellung einer Stichprobe aus $(+, -)$–markierten positiven und negativen Beispielen, die als Eingabe für den Hypothesenfinder A dient.

Die Hypothesenklasse H muß (im Gegensatz zu C) formal definiert werden, da sie den Suchraum des Algorithmus A darstellt. Was ist nun eine glückliche Wahl von H? Wenn H zu arm an Hypothesen ist, dann ist eine hohe Fehlerrate unumgänglich, da gegebenenfalls gar keine scharfe Darstellung des Konzeptes existiert. H kann den Lernerfolg auch umgekehrt durch einen zu großen Reichtum an Hypothesen sabotieren. Dies entspricht einer gängigen Erfahrung in der Mustererkennung, die letztendlich darauf beruht, daß soviele empirisch gleichwertige, real aber stark unterschiedliche, Hypothesen existieren, daß keine sinnvolle Generalisierung aus den empirischen Daten ablesbar ist. Die Hypothesenklasse darf also weder zu speziell noch zu allgemein gewählt werden. Ihre konkrete Festlegung beeinflußt den Lernerfolg in einer sensiblen Weise.

Ist die Hypothesenklasse H erst einmal fixiert, so hängt die Aufgabe des Hypothesenfinders mit dem kombinatorischen Optimierungsproblem zusammen, die Hypothese $h \in H$ mit der kleinsten empirischen Fehlerrate zu finden. Dieses Optimierungsproblem ist meistens zu hart, um effizient gelöst zu werden. Es hat sich jedoch gezeigt, daß bei geeigneter Wahl der Stichprobengröße Annäherungen an das Optimum ausreichen, um pac–Lernbarkeit zu garantieren (s. [23, 19, 13, 15]).

Wir wollen im folgenden skizzieren, was diese allgemeinen Vorbemerkungen für neuronales Lernen besagen:
Die Wahl der Hypothesenklasse entspricht der Festlegung einer Netzarchitektur. Der Hypothesenfinder entspricht einem Algorithmus, der die frei wählbaren Netzparameter an die empirischen Daten adjustiert. Eine Hypothese entspricht dann einer konkreten Architektur mit konkreten Werten für die Netzparameter. Die Abschnitte 2.1 und 2.2 sind diesen Entsprechungen gewidmet. Der Abschnitt 2.3 beschreibt, wie wir uns das Zusammenspiel einer Voradjustierung des Netzes und einer inkrementellen Verbesserung vorstellen. Wir beschränken uns von jetzt an auf die Beispielklasse $X = R^d$ (d-dimensionale reelle Merkmalsvektoren) und auf 'feedforward'–Netze aus sogenannten 'Mac-Culloch-Pitts'–Neuronen, die eine boolesche lineare Schwellenfunktion

$$f(x_1, \ldots, x_d) = \begin{cases} 1 & \text{falls } \sum_{i=1}^{d} w_i x_i \geq t \\ 0 & \text{sonst} \end{cases}$$

für einen Gewichtsvektor $\bar{w} \in R^d$ und einen Schwellenwert $t \in R$ realisieren. Die positiven (bzw. negativen) Beispiele zu einem solchen Netz sind die reellen Merkmalsvektoren, die auf die Netzausgabe 1 (bzw. 0) abgebildet werden.

2.1 Hypothesenklassen und neuronale Netzarchitekturen

Es ist nützlich, für einfache neuronale Netzarchitekturen NNA eine geometrische Intuition zu besitzen. Besteht NNA1 aus einem einzigen Neuron, so formen die positiven Beispiele einen (abgeschlossenen) linearen Halbraum im R^d (s. Fig.1). Besteht NNA2 aus einem 'hidden layer' mit n 'hidden–units' und einem Ausgabeneuron, daß ein logisches–Und realisiert, so formen die positiven Beispiele ein konvexes d–dimensionales Polyeder mit n Seiten (s. Fig.2). Wenn die Merkmalsvektoren $\bar{x} = (x_1, \ldots, x_d)$ boolesch sind ($\bar{x} \in \{0,1\}^d$), so sind Monome über den x_i mit jeweils einem Neuron realisierbar (nämlich durch die Abfrage: ist die Summe der k beteiligten Variablen mindestens k ?). Besteht NNA3 aus einem 'hidden layer' zur Berechnung einer Kollektion von (booleschen) Monomen und einem Ausgabeneuron, so entspricht dies algebraischen Halbräumen im R^d. Fig. 3 zeigt ein Beispielnetz, das auf booleschen Eingaben x_1, x_2 die Paritätsfunktion $x_1 \oplus x_2$ (Addition modulo 2) realisiert.

Die Wahl der Architektur sollte von dem Prinzip bestimmt sein: die einfachste Architektur, die die minimale Fehlerrate $\text{opt}(C)$ (approximativ) erreicht, ist die beste. NNA1 ist offensichtlich genau dann ausreichend, wenn die positiven und negativen Beispiele der Konzepte linear optimal separiert werden können. Es ist bekannt (s. [8]), daß dieser Fall zum Beispiel dann eintritt, wenn die statistischen Verteilungen D_+ auf den positiven und D_- auf den negativen Beispielen

1. Normalverteilungen mit den gleichen Kovarianzmatrizen oder

2. Verteilungen auf booleschen Vektoren mit statistisch unabhängigen Einzelmerkmalen

sind. Bei der Klassifikation von $k > 2$ Objekttypen hätte man auch k Beispieltypen (statt 2 wie bisher). Wenn nun diese Objekttypen paarweise linear separabel sind, so wird jeder einzelne Typ durch ein Polyeder mit $k - 1$ Seiten repräsentiert. Dies legt die Architektur NNA2 nahe. Die Architektur NNA3 weist einen interessanten Zusammenhang zu booleschen Entscheidungsbäumen auf. Boolesche Entscheidungsbäume sind binäre Bäume, deren innere Knoten binäre Abfragen und deren Blätter Klassifikationsentscheidungen repräsentieren. Ein Merkmalsvektor wird gemäß seiner Abfrageergebnisse 'top–down' durch den Baum geroutet bis er ein Blatt erreicht und entsprechend klassifiziert wird. Die Darstellungskomplexität solcher Bäume T wird durch einen numerischen Parameter angezeigt: ihren Rang $r(T)$ (den wir hier nicht formal definieren wollen). In [21] wurde gezeigt, daß zu jedem booleschen Entscheidungsbaum vom Rang r ein äquivalentes Polynom (genauer: der davon induzierte algebraische Halbraum) vom Grade r existiert. Dies legt dann die Architektur NNA3 nahe. NNA3 ist ebenfalls dann ausreichend (s. [3]), wenn D_+ und D_- Verteilungen boolescher Vektoren sind, die eine Chow–Expansion kleiner Ordnung k besitzen, d.h., wenn sowohl bei positiven wie bei negativen Beispielen $\bar{x}$ die Ausprägung des i–ten booleschen Merkmales x_i statistisch nur von den vorangegangenen k booleschen Merkmalen $x_{i-1}, \ldots, x_{i-k}$ abhängt (eine genauere Behandlung der Chow–Expansionen befindet sich in [8]). Voraussetzungen dieser Art sind bei der Mustererkennung bei zeitlichen Prozeßen (sprechen, schreiben) oder räumlichen Anordnungen (Bildern, Schrift) üblich, sofern man glaubt, daß der zeitlich oder räumlich lokale Kontext besonders viel zur Erklärung von Einzelmerkmalen beiträgt. In [3] ist weiterhin eine relativ einfache Architektur NNA4 entwickelt worden (mit NNA1 und NNA3 als Unterarchitekturen), die für statistische Verteilungen geeignet ist, die durch Bahadur–Lazarsfeld–Expansionen einer kleinen Ordnung gegeben sind (zur Definition dieser Expansion s. [8]).

Die statistischen Verteilungen, die in der Praxis vorkommen, sind in der Regel weder Normalverteilungen noch Expansionen kleiner Ordnung. Das Prinzip, aus der vorliegenden statistischen Verteilung eine passende und möglichst einfache Architektur abzuleiten, erscheint uns dennoch als sehr aussichtsreich. Die hierzu bislang entwickelten Methoden besitzen einen starken 'ad hoc'–Charakter und müssen systematisiert werden.

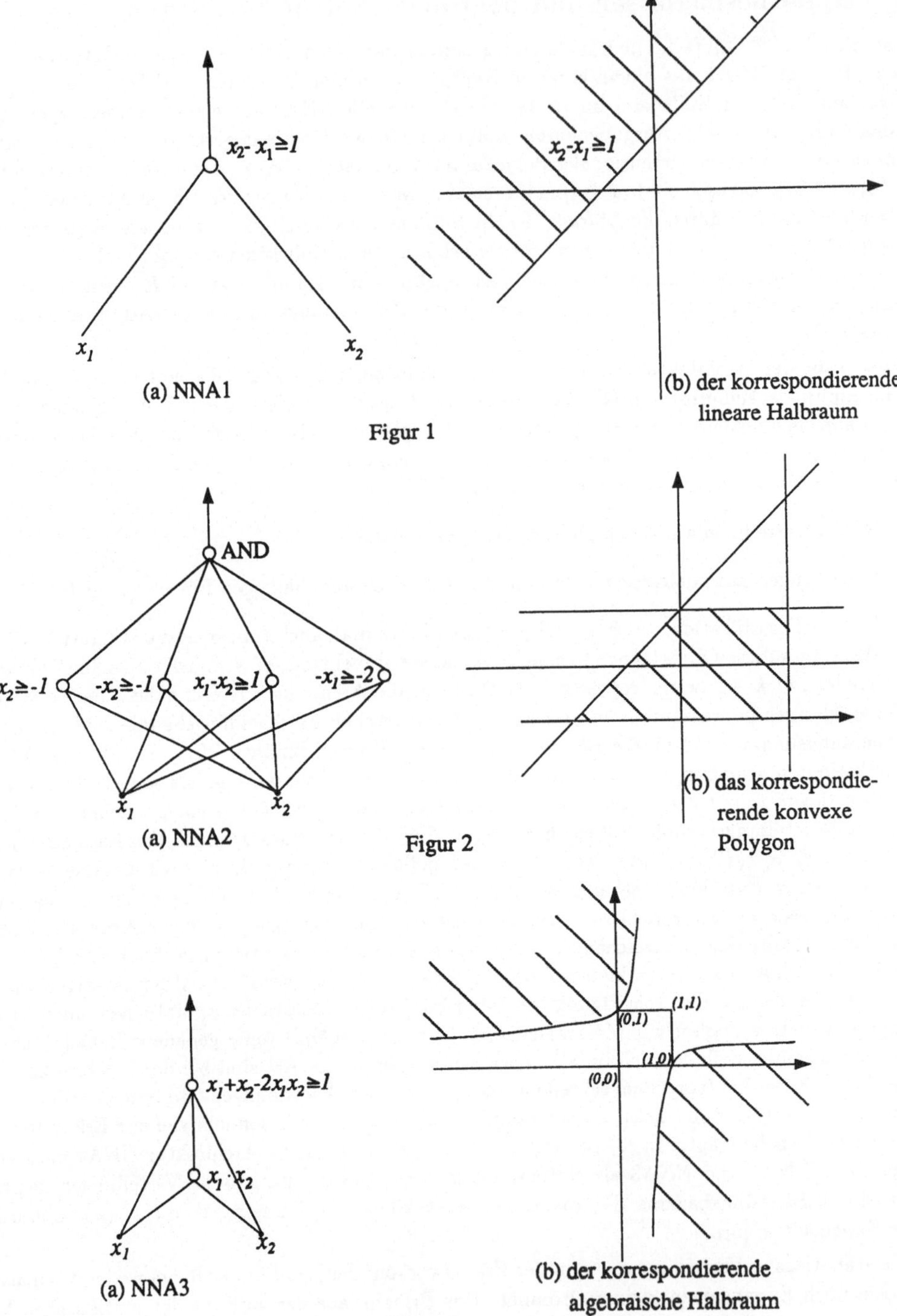

Figur 1

Figur 2

Figur 3

2.2 Hypothesenfinder und Adjustieren der Netzparameter

Welches algorithmische Problem steckt hinter einer optimalen Adjustierung der Netzparameter an die empirischen Daten? Wir wollen dieser Frage erst einmal für die oben beschriebenen Beispielarchitekturen NNA nachgehen und sprechen in diesem Zusammenhang von dem *Ladeproblem* LP(NNA).

LP(NNA1) Gegeben positive und negative Vektoren im R^d, finde eine Hyperebene, so daß möglichst wenige Vektoren im 'falschen' Halbraum liegen (nachdem ein Halbraum als 'positiv' und der andere als 'negativ' deklariert wurde).

Mit einer Dualisierungstechnik aus der kombinatorischen Geometrie (s. [9]) können die Rollen von Vektoren und Hyperebenen derart vertauscht werden, daß eine äquivalente Problemstellung die folgende ist:

Suche einen Vektor, der für möglicht wenige Hyperebenen auf der falschen Seite liegt (also möglichst wenig vorgegebene lineare Bedingungen verletzt).

Falls eine fehlerfreie Lösung möglich ist (perfekte lineare Separabilität), resultiert das Problem, einen Punkt in einem (durch lineare Bedingungen) vorgegebenen Polyeder zu konstruieren. Dies ist mit Algorithmen zur linearen Programmierung (Simplex– oder Ellipsoidalgorithmus) lösbar. Im allgemeinen Fall jedoch ist LP(NNA1) ein NP–hartes Problem[2] (s. [14]). Wir vermuten, daß bereits das Auffinden sehr grober Annäherungen an das Optimum von LP(NNA1) ein NP–hartes Problem darstellt. Eine einigermaßen brauchbare Heuristik für den allgemeinen Fall scheint das 'Perceptron' von Rosenblatt (s. [20, 8]) zu sein.

LP(NNA2) Gegeben positive und negative Vektoren im R^d, finde ein Polyeder mit n Seiten, daß möglichst selten die Regel verletzt, positive, aber keine negativen, Vektoren zu enthalten.

Selbst im fehlerfreien Spezialfall (Algorithmus darf versagen, falls keine fehlerfreie Lösung existiert), resultiert bereits für $n = 2$ ein NP–hartes Problem (s. [18, 6]). Das verwandte Problem, ein fehlerfreies Polyeder mit möglichst wenig Seiten zu konstruieren, enthält zudem Graphenfärbung als Teilproblem (das läßt für Kenner der 'Graphenfärbungsszene' auch für approximative Lösungen nichts Gutes erwarten).

LP(NNA3) Gegeben positive und negative Vektoren im R^d, finde eine algebraische Hyperfläche, gegeben durch ein Polynom vom Grade k, so daß möglichst wenige Vektoren im 'falschen Halbraum' liegen.

Für $k = 1$ ist dieses Problem identisch mit LP(NNA1). Mit einer einfachen Substitutionstechnik läßt sich einsehen, daß es auch nicht schwerer als LP(NNA1) ist: kreiere für jedes der $O(d^k)$ möglichen Monome eine Extravariable und bette so das Problem in einen höherdimensionalen Raum ein. Die algebraischen Hyperflächen werden durch diese Substitution gleichsam zu linearen Hyperflächen 'geradegestreckt'. Im höherdimensionalen Raum gelten die für LP(NNA1) geschilderten Verhältnisse.

Was (außer bitterer Verzweiflung oder Ladehemmung) bleibt dem Menschen angesichts dieser NP–harten Ladeprobleme noch übrig? Der angenehmere Teil unserer Botschaft lautet: wenn wir die konkreten Gegebenheiten der vorliegenden statistischen Verteilungen ausnutzen, können wir das kombinatorische Problem umgehen und direkt auf statistisch brauchbare Hypothesen zusteuern. Wenn zum Beispiel die NNA1–Architektur auf der Grundlage statistisch unabhängiger boolescher Einzelmerkmale gewählt wurde, so kann mit hoher statistischer Zuverlässigkeit eine separierende Hyperebene (und somit eine Adjustierung von NNA1) mit fast–minimaler statistischer Fehlerrate in Polynomialzeit gefunden werden (s. [11]).[3] Analoge Bemerkungen gelten für die auf Paarvergleichen aufbauende NNA2–Architektur, die Chow–Expansion und die NNA3–Architektur sowie die Bahadur–Lazarsfeld–Expansion und die NNA4–Architektur (s. [11, 3]).

---

[2]Dies impliziert vermutlich, daß keine effiziente Lösung existiert; genauere Definition von 'NP–hart' in [12].

[3]Dieser Ansatz ist insofern interessant, als daß die entwickelten Hypothesen auf einigen Stichproben empirisch sehr viel schwächer sein können als die empirischen Optima.

2.3 Voradjustierung und inkrementelles Lernen

Die bislang von uns eingenommene Grundposition entspricht nicht dem allgemeinen Grundverständnis des sogenannten neueren Konnektionismus. Ein häufig gebrauchtes Argument ist zum Beispiel, daß die besondere Stärke neuronaler Netze gerade darin liegt, daß die Lernaufgabe unscharf definiert und die Stichprobe fehlerhaft sein darf. Die Adjustierung der Netzparameter wird meist 'on–line' mit inkrementellen Lernregeln (wie bei 'Backpropagation' oder Boltzmann–Netzen) vorgenommen. Diese Lernregeln 'treiben' die Netzparameter in ein 'lokales empirisches Optimum'. Auf der Ebene der Plausibilität und der experimentellen Absicherung wird dann versucht darzulegen, daß man einem 'globalen statistischen Optimum' nahe gekommen sei. Dies führt bei guter Intuition der 'Netzdesigner' in Einzelfällen durchaus zu brauchbaren Ergebnissen. Die von uns dargelegte Sichtweise ist in folgenden Punkten unterschiedlich:

1. Wir versuchen durchaus eine analytische Beschreibung der Lernaufgabe herzustellen (pac–Lernmodell, klar definierte statistische Gütekriterien für Lernalgorithmen; aus den empirischen Daten abgeleitete analytische Grundannahmen über die statistische Verteilung der Merkmalsvektoren).

2. Wir schauen die Stichprobe in ihrer Gesamtheit an und entwerfen 'off–line' eine innerhalb unseres Modelles möglichst gute Hypothese.

Beide Grundpositionen haben ihre Sonnen– und Schattenseiten. Unsere hat den Vorzug, eine genaue Begrifflichkeit herzustellen, die empirischen Daten in aller (durchschaubaren) Konsequenz auszuschlachten und in Einzelfällen beweisbar zumindest fast-optimale Lernergebnisse zu erzielen. Es hat jedoch den Nachteil, daß die analytischen Grundannahmen in der Tat verletzt sein können und daß die 'off–line' Berechnung der Hypothese für Echtzeitanwendungen zu schwerfällig ist.[4] Es liegt daher auf der Hand beide Grundpositionen zu einem Gesamtkonzept zu vereinen:

1. Mit einem relativ hohen Aufwand an statistischer Modellierung der Lernaufgabe, Festlegung der Netzarchitektur und Voradjustierung der Netzparameter bringen wir (gewissermaßen in einem einmaligen Kraftakt) das neuronale Netz auf ein der Lernaufgabe angemessenes gutes Ausgangsniveau.

2. Mit inkrementellen Lernregeln versorgen wir das Netz mit der Flexibilität die bei unscharfen und zeitlich variierenden Konzepten erforderlich ist.

Sinkt die Performanz des Netzes unter ein kritisches Niveau, wird diese Vorgehensweise gegebenenfalls iteriert. Dieses Gesamtkonzept birgt die Chance, flexibles Operieren in Echtzeit mit sorgfältiger Analyse der Leistungsstärke neuronaler Netze zu verknüpfen.

3 Modelle neuronalen Lernens

Im Abschnitt 2 haben wir diskutiert, ob und wie sich pac–Lernbarkeit auf neuronalen Netzen realisieren läßt. Es hat sich dabei als sinnvoll herausgestellt, das in Abschnitt 1 dargestellte Lernmodell von Valiant von Fall zu Fall zu variieren. Wir wollen daher in diesem Abschnitt die Diskussion über ein adäquates Lernmodell für neuronale Netze wieder aufnehmen.

Für neuronales Lernen ist es zweckmäßig, den ursprünglichen Konzeptbegriff in zwei Richtungen auszudehnen: zum einen in Richtung 'probabilistische Konzepte' (mit nicht klar definierbaren Grenzfällen); zum anderen in Richtung 'Lernen von Funktionen' (zum Beispiel das Lernen der Transformation von sensorischer in motorische Information). Beide Erweiterungen können im Einklang

---

[4]Es ist ein offenes Forschungsproblem, ob die von uns entworfenen fast–optimalen 'off–line' Hypothesenfinder auch 'on–line' zu realisieren sind.

mit der 'Philosophie' des pac–Lernbegriffes durchgeführt werden. Der interessierte Leser sei hier auf die Arbeiten [13] und [15] verwiesen.

Neben diesen Modifikationen 'im Geiste des pac–Lernens' gibt es auch solche, die auf potentielle Kritikpunkte verweisen. Eine objektive Schwäche besteht zum Beispiel darin, daß Resultate der Nichtlernbarkeit sich in diesem Modell manchmal auch dann herleiten lassen, wenn erfolgreiche Heuristiken in einem praktisch bedeutsamen Sinne realisierbar sind. Bei nicht–Lernbarkeitsresultaten unterscheidet man den Fall einer zu hohen Informationskomplexität (zu große Stichproben) von dem Fall einer zu hohen Berechnungskomplexität (zu große Laufzeit des Hypothesenfinders). Die Informationskomplexität stellt für neuronales Lernen keine grundsätzliche Schwierigkeit dar (s. dazu [5]). Sie kann zudem durch einen kombinatorischen Parameter, die sogenannte Vapnik–Chervonenkis–Dimension der Konzeptklasse C bzw. Hypothesenklasse H sehr gut charakterisiert werden (s. [7, 10, 13]). Das ernstere Hindernis zum neuronalen Lernen ist die hohe Berechnungskomplexität. Es gibt im wesentlichen zwei Vorschläge, wie das Modell zu ändern ist, um die Berechnungen des Hypothesenfinders substantiell zu beschleunigen:

1. verteilungsabhängige Resultate,

2. mächtigere Lernmethoden.

Das Modell von Valiant besitzt die Eigenschaft der Verteilungsunabhängigkeit. Gemeint ist die Forderung an den Hypothesenfinder, mit beliebigen statistischen Verteilungen D (bzw. D_+, D_-) zurechtkommen zu müssen. Wir haben in Abschnitt 2.2 angedeutet, wie bei stärkeren Voraussetzungen an die Verteilungen positive Resultate erzielt werden können. Die Idee der 'mächtigeren Lernmethoden' beruht auf der Überzeugung, daß auch das menschliche Lernen sich nicht ausschließlich über die Präsentation zufälliger Beispiele vollzieht. Es stellt sich somit die Frage, welche anderen Lernprotokolle in einen algorithmischen Lernprozeß eingespeist werden können. Wir wollen diesen Punkt hier nicht weiter ausführen und verweisen auf die Arbeiten [1, 2, 16, 17, 4]. Das Auffinden geeigneter Modellvarianten für die spezifischen Bedürfnisse neuronalen Lernens ist weiterhin Gegenstand aktueller Forschung.

Literatur

[1] D. Angluin. Learning regular sets from queries and counterexamples. *Information and Control*, 75:87–106, 1987.

[2] D. Angluin. Queries and concept learning. *Machine Learning*, 2:319–342, 1988.

[3] S. Annulova, J. Cuellar, K. U. Höffgen, and H. U. Simon. Probably almost optimal neural classifiers. In preparation.

[4] E. B. Baum. Polynomial time algorithms for learning neural nets. In M. A. Fulk and J. Case, editors, *Proceedings of the 3rd Annual Workshop on Computational Learning Theory*, pages 258–273, San Mateo, California, Aug. 1990. Morgan Kaufmann.

[5] E. B. Baum and D. Haussler. What size net gives valid generalization? *Neural Computation1*, 1:151–160, 1989.

[6] A. Blum and R. L. Rivest. Training a 3–node neural network is NP–complete. In *Proceedings of the 1st Annual Workshop on Computational Learning Theory*, pages 9–18, San Mateo, California, Aug. 1988.

[7] A. Blumer, A. Ehrenfeucht, D. Haussler, and M. K. Warmuth. Learnability and the Vapnik–Chervonenkis dimension. *Journal of the Association on Computing Machinery*, 36(4):929–965, Oct. 1989.

[8] R. O. Duda and P. E. Hart. *Pattern Classification and Scene Analysis.* Wiley–Interscience. John Wiley & Sons, New York, 1973.

[9] H. Edelsbrunner. *Algorithms in Combinatorial Geometry*, volume 10 of *EATCS Monographs on Theoretical Computer Science.* Springer Verlag, Berlin, 1987.

[10] A. Ehrenfeucht, D. Haussler, M. Kearns, and L. Valiant. A general lower bound on the number of examples needed for learning. *Information and Computation*, 82(3):247–261, Sept. 1989.

[11] P. Fischer, S. Pölt, and H. U. Simon. Probably almost bayes decisions. In *Proceedings of the 4th Annual Workshop on Computational Learning Theory*, San Mateo, California, Aug. 1991. To appear.

[12] M. R. Garey and D. S. Johnson. *Computers and Intractability: A Guide to the Theory of NP–Completeness.* Freeman, San Francisco, 1979.

[13] D. Haussler. Generalizing the pac model: Sample size bounds from metric–dimension based uniform convergence results. In *Proceedings of the 30'th Annual Symposium on the Foundations of Computer Science*, pages 40–46, Los Alamitos, CA, Oct. 1989. IEEE Computer Society, Computer Society Press.

[14] K. U. Höffgen and H. U. Simon. Computationally hard consistency problems. In preparation.

[15] M. J. Kearns and R. E. Schapire. Efficient distribution–free learning of probabilistic concepts. In *Proceedings of the 31'th Annual Symposium on the Foundations of Computer Science*, pages 382–392, Los Alamitos, CA, Oct. 1990. IEEE Computer Society, Computer Society Press.

[16] W. Maass and G. Turán. On the complexity of learning from counterexamples. In *Proceedings of the 30th Symposium on Foundations of Computer Science*, pages 262–267. IEEE Computer Society, Oct. 1989.

[17] W. Maass and G. Turán. On the complexity of learning from counterexamples and membership queries. In *Proceedings of the 31st Symposium on Foundations of Computer Science*, pages 203–211. IEEE Computer Society, Oct. 1990.

[18] N. Megiddo. On the complexity of polyhedral separability. *Discrete Combinatorial Geometry*, 3:325–337, 1988.

[19] D. Pollard. *Convergence of Stochastic Processes.* Springer Verlag, 1984.

[20] F. Rosenblatt. *Principles and Neurodynamics: Perceptrons and the Theory of Brain Mechanisms.* Spartan Books, Washington, D.C., 1962.

[21] H. U. Simon. On the number of examples and stages needed for learning decision trees. In M. A. Fulk and J. Case, editors, *Proc. of the 3rd Annual Workshop on Computational Learning Theory*, pages 303–314, Palo Alto, California, Aug. 1990. Morgan Kaufmann. Also to appear in IPL.

[22] L. G. Valiant. A theory of the learnable. *Communications of the ACM*, 27(11):1134–1142, Nov. 1984.

[23] V. N. Vapnik. *Estimation of Dependencies Based on Empirical Data.* Springer Verlag, 1982.

Theory and Practice of Neural Networks

Georg Dorffner, Erich Prem, Claudia Ulbricht, Herbert Wiklicky
Austrian Research Institute for Artificial Intelligence
Schottengasse 3
A-1010 Wien

When attempting to apply neural networks to real-world problems one is confronted with a major problem – there is no general theory about which network model to choose and how to optimally set all parameters. The large number of publications on neural networks is in strong contrast to a lack of means for comparison between, and appraisal of different systems found in literature. Furthermore, most existing applications focus on simple associative multi-layer architectures that are not suitable for many aspects of real-world problems, such as time-dependencies between inputs.

This paper reports about research being done at the Austrian Research Institute for Artificial Intelligence as part of the ESPRIT-II project NEUFODI ("Neural Networks for Forecasting and Diagnosis Application").[1] It aims at narrowing the gap between neural networks' apparent successes and their lack of theory. In one part of the project a unified description formalism is being developed. It is designed as a tool for directly comparing different models with each other, and to put them into perspective. Another part of the project deals with the development and analysis of network architectures for processing time sequences. Mainly applications in the domains of diagnosis and forecasting are considered.

1 Introduction

For the last years neural networks as a tool for practical applications have gained attention with an enormous rate. Today they are being used or considered in an extremely wide-spread variety of fields, ranging from medical diagnosis to banking. In many cases, quick success almost seems guaranteed. As a result, a few well-known and published network types, such as feedforward-networks with back-propagation, have been accepted as "universal" tools for reaching solutions, in many cases without serious analysis whether the approach is sufficient or even reasonable for the specific application.

This development has lead to an obvious discrepancy: Despite all the apparent successes in applying neural networks and the wide-spread interest in this new engineering tool, there hardly seems to exist any thorough theory about, or classification of neural network models. Many authors have tried to comparatively describe network paradigms (e.g. [10]), but there is hardly any unique formalism to put most existing networks in perspective. As a result, an engineer interested in applying neural networks is almost forced to use one of the above mentioned well-published models, not knowing whether this is appropriate or whether there exists a much better network solution.

Engineers wishing to use neural networks are faced with yet another problem. Most existing networks assume that the problem can be reduced to a mapping from an input to an output pattern

---

[1]Neufodi is sponsored by the EC commission and the Austrian Federal Ministry of Science and Research as ESPRIT-II project No. 5433 and is conducted in cooperation with the Babbage Institute for Knowledge and Information Technology (Belgium); Lyonnaise des Eaux Dumez (France); Elorduy, Sancho y CIA, S.A.; Laboratories de Ensayos e Investigaciones Industriales (both Spain); and Kobenhavens Telefon Aktieselskab (Denmark).

in one or several steps. Applications that deal with sequential data usually do not fall in this category. Of course, many neural models can be found in literature that can exhibit sequential behaviour (see below), but from an engineering point of view again a unified theory is missing.

The project described in this paper is aimed toward closing these gaps between theory and practice of neural networks. Among others it focusses on two major goals:

(a) to develop a close-to-unified framework for describing and classifying neural networks with respect to their paramaters, as a first step to analysing them with respect to their power and applicability to real-world problems.

(b) to develop, test and compare several architectures for dealing with sequential input data.

This project is entitled Neufodi – "Neural Networks for Forecasting and Diagnosis Applications" – and is part of the ESPRIT-II initiative. It focusses on two of the most widely found application types, diagnosis and forecasting.

The following sections describe in more detail the two aforementioned goals of Neufodi and how they are being approached.

2 A General Unified Neural Theory

One objective of this project is to develop a *"unified framework for neural networks"*. This should be achieved by developing an abstract model for neural networks first, and later formalizing this in combination with practical applications and experiences.

From now on we will refer to this conceptual framework as the **General Unified Neural (Network) Theory** or **GUNT**. In this section we try to give a sketch of such a theory or framework.

2.1 The Aims of GUNT

First we have to make clear why such a theory is needed. We think that the following minimal requirements should be fulfilled by the framework we are going to develop:

- It shall be possible to describe **most** (as many as possible) existing neural network architectures and paradigms in a unique, unambigous and efficient way.

- Such a description should cover **most** aspects of neural models. Different points of view shall be coverable by that theory.

- The proposed framework should be suitable both as a tool for theoretical analysis **and** software development.

- It should include some heuristics and a framework for benchmarking (simulation) to prove its relevance for future research and development activities.

In some way, this minimal set of requirements is a compromise, since we have decided not to place emphasis on either the analysis or synthesis of neural networks. In developing such a theory we have to consider not only models already existing, but also possible variations and new ideas. This is certainly a difficult task and may require some broader approach to the whole problem.

2.2 Elements of GUNT

In its final form the proposed framework should contain the following:

- **A description language** for neural networks. Such a language should in principle be a formal one, enriched perhaps with some graphical elements.

- **A glossary** to specify a sound and usable terminology. The used terms should be described by refering to our conceptual framework.

- Some **theoretical results, heuristics** and a **benchmarking framework**.

- **A catalogue of the neural paradigms** consisting of the most well-published network types found in literature.

2.3 Hypothesis of Three Entities

One of the strongest possible structures we can give to the model is based on system-theoretical considerations. It is well defined and allows a clear separation of the overall topic into different sub-topics which can then be investigated by separate partners of the Neufodi project. On the other hand it is general enough so that it does not imply any restrictions with which we could come into conflict during the evolution and development of more detailed concepts.

We propose a three-fold separation of the formalism leading to the following three sub-systems or entities (EIOC):

- the **environment** in which the neural network operates.

- the **I/O-Component** (including pre- and postprocessing).

- the **core**, i.e. the neural network itself.

The novelty of this approach – as compared to other attempts of description or unification – is the emphasis on all three entities. Most of those other attempts mainly focus on the core and are therefore incomplete. In other words, by not explaining how the network interacts with the environment, and how it receives input and teaching data, one leaves out important components of a network model. Consider feed-forward networks using backpropagation. Besides defining the network architecture and the update and learning laws it is vital that one specifies the order in which input-target pairs are presented and how the environment decides when to start and stop learning, in order to fully understand what the network is doing. Such a specification much too often is left out of a network description.

2.4 Levels of Concretization

Another way to give a structure to our framework is to distinguish between several levels of concretization (LOC). This structure is also very important because we have seen that some misunderstandings in the discussion about neural networks actually come from confusing the different levels. Additionally, such a distinction is important from a practical point of view. It is neither a priori clear nor obvious that we should use the same formalism for all levels.

What we mean by different **levels of concretization** is simply different levels of abstraction in which a smaller or greater number of parameters or structure elements are fixed. For example, in a theory of the core of neural networks we could find at least the following levels.

0. The **State** of a neural network (e.g. initial state).

1. The actual (implemented) **network** (e.g. a certain XOR-network).

2. A concrete **architecture** (e.g. a 4-2-4 feed forward network).

3. An abstract **paradigm** (e.g. Back-Propagation).

4. A general **theory** of the core (e.g. GUNT).

A similar scheme can be set up for the other basic entities. In a theory of the environment component of a neural network the following levels might be distingushed:

0. A concrete **pattern** for a neural network (e.g. a pixel grid).

1. The **collection** of patterns actually realized (e.g. a time sequence).

2. A concrete **application** (e.g. consumption forecasting).

3. An abstract **environment model** (e.g. Markov chains).

4. A general **theory** of the environment (e.g. GUNT).

Additional criteria may be needed to arrive at a finer structure. For example one might argue that in the case of a theory for the core of neural networks one should have an additonal conceptual level between *paradigms* and *architectures*. Such a level would correspond, for example, to the concept of *feed forward networks using back propagation*. This model clearly is more concrete than just a back propagation architecture but less concrete than a 4-2-4 network. On the other hand one might also argue that there is no principle difference between architectures and implementation and therefore we should not distinguish between these two levels.

We see that it is not a trivial issue to establish certain clearly defined and separated levels of concretization. It is, however, apparent that there are such levels and that there is a method to pass from one to another. Getting from one level to another means making a concept more concrete by "filling in" some parameters. This mechanism can also be reversed by taking a concept from one level and leaving out certain details, thus for example abstracting from concrete architectures to abstract paradigms.

This identification of levels constitutes another clear difference to most known approaches (like, for example, PYGMALION) which concentrated for the most part on the description or definition of a concrete implementation of a neural network.

2.5   Different Views on Neural Networks

One can look at a neural model or theory from different **points of view**. which, in principle, belong to specific well established fields of science.

For example, one might ask how one could parallelize a certain paradigm on a concrete hardware platform; this is clearly a problem for computer scientists. Or one could ask what kind of associations or mappings can be performed by a neural network; here probably mathematicans could provide assistance if they had a model for neural networks which is suitable for their discipline in terminolgy and structure.

Our project has neither the aim nor the resources to cover all fields of science. We can only try to prepare a mechanism which makes it possible to get (restricted) models for neural networks which incorporate aspects relevant for a certain special field of science. Therefore to cover the different aspects of Neural Networks we could use the following approach:

- Develop an **abstract model** for neural networks.
- Formulate a description language for the **full theory**.
- Define transitions to **special theories** like graph theory, automata theory, logic, control theory, optimization
- Investigate the properties of these transitions.

As we see it, Neufodi has to cover only the first two issues. The remaining ones are not being investigated during our project but should be kept in mind. We think such an approach could establish a fruitful basis on which to develop a sound theoretical analysis of neural networks by incorporating other fields of science into the investigations.

2.6   A Theory of the Core

At the Austrian Research Institute for Artificial Intelligence mainly the conceptual model of the neural network *core* is being developed. The fundamental approach to this could be described as follows:

480

The basic structure elements of the **core** *of a neural network are*

- **systems** *or* **modules** *which are interacting*
- *through* **interfaces** *between them.*

These **elements** *of a neural network core are attributed with*

- **data structures** *and*
- **algorithms**

and they are organized on different **hierarchical levels**.

Note that the Hierarchical Levels are not identical with the Levels of Concretization as discussed above. This might become clearer in the next subsection.

Such an endeavour of designing a concept of the core could be interpreted as an attempt to find a precise definition of a neural network. However, in our context we are more interested in a conceptual *construction* than in a clear-cut *definition* of the notion "neural network". We are not looking for a criterion to exclude certain models as not being a neural network. Instead, we try to find the elementary constituents which we can use to build a neural network. The problem with such a bottom-up approach is that we might get a wider class of entities than what is usually called a "neural network". We do not think that this has important consequences.

2.6.1 Different Hierarchical Levels

To explain the difference between the above mentioned hierarchical levels and the levels of concretization discussed in the previous section, we give an example of what we understand by the *architectural hierarchicy* in the context of the core of neural networks.

Such an architectural hierarchicy could be realized in the follwing way. The terms used here are only preliminary and might change in a final and sound framework.

Level 0 — Atomic Level:

- units (processing elements, ...) – links (weights, ...)

Level 1:

- layer – inter-layer connections

...

Highest Level:

- core and environment – I/O-component

Unfortunately this **architectural hierarchy** is, although distinct, actually *not* totally independent of the **abstraction hierarchy**. One could, for example, think of a level of concretization where the topology of the neural network core is defined in terms of layers (e.g. a three layer network). A more concrete level would then be established by specifying the types of the Units used in the different layers (e.g. a three layer back propagation network). Thus, by specifying the architectural hierarchy some implications for the abstraction hierarchy are imposed. Such a interdependence has its consequences on the development of a GUNT.

2.6.2 Construction of Neural Entities

Concerning the problem of describing, respectively defining, an actual neural model (i.e. network, paradigm etc.) we can observe the following: Finding an appropriate formalism to describe the attributes of the basic elements, i.e. data structures and algorithms, should not be too complicated. There are a lot of conventional (programming) languages around which allow a precise and effective specification of data structures and algorithms.

We need a description language and a theory which is capable of dealing with the hierarchical constructions we mentioned above. We need a language by which we can describe how to build up the topology of a Neural Network core. Among the operations for constructing an appropriate topology or architecture which we will investigate are:

Aggregation of low level entities (systems or modules and interfaces) to get higher level entities.

Connection of systems or modules through interfaces (i.e. creation of interfaces).

Disconnection of systems or modules (i.e. destruction of interfaces).

Creation and initalization of entities.

Destruction of entities.

All these operations have to by analysed and efficient ways for describing them have to be found.

3   A Realized Formalism

During the first project phase a rudimentary formalism fulfilling the criteria described in the previous section has been developed [9]. Several well-known neural network models have been successfully defined in this formalism, so as to permit efficient comparisons between them. It is still incomplete and has its shortcomings, but it serves as a testbed for the ideas presented above during future research.

Basically, the formalism provides an object-oriented view of neural network paradigms. It is not supported by the main component of connectionist models, namely the connections. These parts of neural networks are not easy to describe within a scheme of objects because links connect the objects but are not part of them. This is why we decided to dissect network topology into interfaces between objects. The relation between contained and containing objects is defined by terms such as "feedforward" or "id" which express the *nature of connectivity* between the objects.

An object in the formalism consists of the following elements:

- Object type

- Algorithms (mostly update and learning)

- Contained objects and parameters for the algorithms

- Interface description to contained objects

The following is a part of a typical framework description, namely a *Perceptron Unit*.

```
Object     U                              (* Perceptron Unit *)
Contents   [W]                            (* Weights in this Unit *)
Paramt.    delta:REAL;
in         L-id->[W]                      (* Interface to the weights*)
out        [W]-1->L                       (* Interface to the layer*)
up         in;
           >L := threshold(sum[W]-);
lrn        in;
           delta := >L - threshold(sum([W]-));
           [W]- := delta;
```

Besides parameters needed to store values, this description specifies two interfaces between an instance of a layer (L) and an array of instances of weights ([W]). These interfaces can be referenced in the algorithms specifying update and learning. The involved entities such as "unit" and "layer" are ordered in a strict hierarchy with "environment" being on top.

3.1 Some Experiences Gained

The design of such a unified framework made it necessary to clarify certain notions of connectionist terminology. Most important was the definition of *paradigm*. We decided that a *paradigm* in our framework is a rudimentary (i.e. incomplete) description of an environment object, whereas the description of a neural network must not have any unspecified parts.

This distinction between paradigm and network is most important, because it tells the difference between selecting the right paradigm for a given task and filling in the missing values in a paradigm description. This last process means the design of a concrete network out of a given paradigm. Note that this process of concretization can be continued to the realization level of the network, i.e. to the running net.

The research on this framework also revealed that no description tool for neural network can be found in which for all cases similar paradigms (with respect to topology or behavior) lead to similar descriptions. This is mainly due to the fact that descriptions must contain algorithms, which are basically permitted to be equivalent to Turing-machines.

4 Open Problems

The rough ideas presented above cannot constitute the whole framework to be developed. A lot of problems are still to be solved before it indeed might be called a General Unified Neural Theory. Some of those problems are:

- Control structures — events

- Concurrency and parallelism — real time aspects

- Development of a sound and usable terminology

- Investigation on the relation between

    - structural hierarchy

    - levels of concretization

    - variational inheritance

By **Variational Inheritance** we understand another hierarchy distinct but, unfortunately, again not independent from the two others. This hierarchy is closely related to practical software-engineering problems. Its nature may become most obvious in an object-oriented description formalism using some inheritance mechanism. With this Variational Hierarchy we try to capture the observation, that some types of elements used in a neural network (the core) can be interpreted just as *variations* of others.

For example, a unit in the context of *Frequency Sensitive Competitive Learning* (see [1]) is more or less just the same as a unit in plain *Competitive Learning*, except that it has an additional data structure, the `frequency` parameter, or `conscience`, and procedures related to this data structure. Note that it makes a difference whether some attribute or concept is not specified or whether it is just not existent. Thus, the transition between these two types of units does not correspond to a change of the level of concretization. A *"frequency sensitive unit"* is not just a more specified concept than a *"competitive unit"*, it is a **variation** of the former. A similar relation might be established between unit types which are atributed in a similar way, except that one might use an integer and the other one a real activation value.

The formalism briefly introduced in the previous section can account for such a variational inheritance due to its object-oriented nature. However, much work will have to be done to fully address this and the other aforementioned aspects.

5 Dealing with Sequences

Another large part of the project attempts to cope with the fact that many applications cannot be reduced to a single mapping from one input set to an output. Instead, many real-world problems – especially forecasting problems, but also recognition tasks such as in speech – involve interdependencies within sequences of inputs. A large amount of literature on neural networks for processing sequential input exists, but little consensus as to which approach is appropriate for which problem. Therefore, in this part of the project extensive research is being conducted to explicitly compare different sequential networks with respect to certain criteria based on real-world applications.

5.1 Paradigms

In the introductory phase of the project the literature has been collected and roughly classified according to the network architecture. The following table gives an overview of this classification:

1. Feedforward Networks

    (a) Windowing Approaches
    For example, TRACE ([7])

    (b) Time Delay Approaches
    For example, time delay neural networks ([4]) or finite impulse response networks ([12])

    (c) Other Approaches
    For example, higher order correlation networks ([13]) or heterosynaptic modulation networks ([2]

2. Recurrent Networks

    (a) Feedback from Net to Net
    For example, feed forward networks with global feedback ([8])

    (b) Single Feedback from Layer to Layer
    For example, the state network ([5]) or the context network ([3])

    (c) Multiple Feedback Connections

        i. networks with bidirectional feedforward connections
        ii. Fully Recurrent Networks
        For example, RTRL Networks ([11])
        iii. Networks with Competitive Layers
        For example, the sequence detector model ([6])
        iv. Kohonen's Self-Organizing Maps

This classification of methods for handling input sequences dealt as a basis for splitting up the task among the partners. These methods are ordered according to the type of network architecture used, because it is most reasonable to have each partner work on another type of network architecture.

The two main groups are feedforward networks employing windows or time delays and recurrent networks. The latter group employs feedback. No input values are stored or delayed but output values reenter the network. This way information of previous time steps is fed back to the network. Several approaches, as for example the state network by Jordan [5] and the context network by Elman [3], are based on a single feedback of one layer in a feedforward network. Other network architectures contain multiple feedback connections enabling the reentry of past information.

5.2 Criteria

From each category of models typical network models will be investigated by each Neufodi partner. They will be evaluated with respect to criteria such as the following.

- Input

  - Maximum Length and Order of a Sequence Processed
  - Maximum Number of Sequences Distinguished
  - Ability to Handle Sequences Without Margins
  - Ability to Profit from Redundant Information
  - Ability to Identify a Sequence from Partial Input
  - Tolerance Toward Missing or Superfluous Parts, Errors

- Output

  - Ability to Classify Sequences
  - Ability to Forecast the Next Sequence Element
  - Ability to Complete Partial Sequences

At the Austrian Research Institute for Artificial Intelligence networks with multiple feedback between competitive layers or Kohonen maps will be dealt with. These networks can be considered as learning the sequencing of localizable states (those winning in the competition). They appear especially suited for forecasting sequences but could have problems with some types of error tolerance. Special extensions to learning seem to be necessary (such as the one described in [6]) to cope with higher-order sequences.

It is expected that this comparative evaluation will lead to insights as to which sequential paradigm to use for a given application. To approach this goal, data from real-world applications, quasi-real-world sequences, as well as some "artificial" sequences will be used for testing.

6 Conclusion

In this paper two major endeavours within the ESPRIT-II project Neufodi have been outlined – namely the design of a unified description framework for neural networks, and the research on network models processing input sequences – especially the part that is being done at the Austrian Research Institute for Artificial Intelligence. Both endeavours lie between basic and application-oriented research and are aimed toward bridging the gap between theory and practice. More specifically, they are aimed toward providing some theory for neural networks and their application to real-world problems where it has been badly needed. These goals are very ambitious, too ambitious to be solved fully satisfactorily. However, the results already achieved are promising enough to ensure the value of future research in this project.

References

[1] Ahalt S.C., Chen P., Krishnamurthy A.K.: Performance Analysis of Two Image Vector Quantization Techniques, in *Proceedings of the International Joint Conference on Neural Networks*, I-169 - I-175, 1989.

[2] Dehaene S., Changeux J., Nadal J.: Neural networks that learn temporal sequences by selection, *Proc. Natl. Acad. Sci USA*, Vol.84, pp. 2727-2731, 1987.

[3] Elman J.L.: Finding Structure in Time, *Cognitive Science*, 1990.

[4] Hataoka N., Waibel A.H.: Speaker-Independent Phoneme Recognition on TIMIT Database Using Integrated Time-Delay Neural Networks (TDNNs), in *International Joint Conference on Neural Networks*, San Diego, IEEE, Volume I, pp. 57-62, 1990.

[5] Jordan M.I.: Attractor dynamics and parallelism in a connectionist sequential machine, in *Proceedings of the Eight Annual Conference of the Cognitive Science Society*, Erlbaum, Hillsdale, NJ, pp. 531- 546, 1986.

[6] Mannes C., Dorffner G.: Self-Organizing Detectors of Spatio-Temporal Patterns, in Kindermann J., Linden A. (eds.): *Distributed Adaptive Neural Information Systems*, Oldenbourg, Muenchen/Wien, pp. 89-102, 1990.

[7] McClelland J.L., Elman J.L.: Interactive Processes in Speech Perception: The TRACE Model, in Rumelhart D.E., McClelland J.L. (eds.): *Parallel Distributed Processing, Vol 1*, MIT Press, Cambridge, MA, 1986.

[8] Norrod F.E., O'Neill M.D., Gat E.: Feedback-Induced Sequentiality in Neural Networks, in Caudill M., Butler C.(eds.), *IEEE First International Conference On Neural Networks*, San Diego, IEEE, 1987.

[9] Prem E.: *A Description Framework for Solving the "Theory Problem" in Connectionism*, Master's Thesis at the Dept.of Medical Cybernetics and Artificial Intelligence, University of Vienna, 1991.

[10] Simpson P.K.: *Artificial Neural Systems*, Pergamon Press, 1990.

[11] Smith A.W., Zipser D.: Encoding Sequential Structure: Experience with the Real-Time Recurrent Learning Algorithm, in *IEEE International Conference On Neural Networks*, Washington D.C., IEEE, Volume I, pp. 645-648, 1989.

[12] Wan E.A.: Temporal Backpropagation: An Efficient Algorithm for Finite Impulse Response Neural Networks, in Touretzky D.S., et al.(eds.), *Connectionist Models*, Morgan Kaufmann Publishers, San Mateo, CA, pp. 131-137, 1990.

[13] Wolf L.: Recurrent Nets for the Storage of Cyclic Sequences, in Kosko B.(ed.), *IEEE International Conference On Neural Networks*, San Diego, IEEE, Volume I, pp. 53-60, 1988.

Neuronale Netze in der Automatisierungstechnik

T. Waschulzik*, D. Böller, D. Butz*, H. Geiger, H. Walter[+]

Kratzer Automatisierung GmbH, Maxfeldhof 5–6, 8044 Unterschleißheim

[+] Volkswagen AG, 3180 Wolfsburg 1

Die Firma Kratzer Automatisierung München setzt seit längerem in der Automatisierungstechnik neuronale Netze ein. Die zugrundeliegende Philosophie wird vorgestellt, Methodik und Technik werden erläutert. Im Speziellen gehen wir auf die Anwendung neuronaler Netze in der Regelungstechnik ein, wo ein multivariabler Regler in vollautomatischen KFZ–Prüfständen das Gaspedal und die Kupplung bedienen soll. Dieses als "konnektionistischer Fahrer" bezeichnete System wurde für die Volkswagen AG erstellt. Das Netzwerk hat die Aufgabe, Stellwerte für das "Nachfahren" von vorgegebenen Geschwindigkeitsprofilen auszugeben und lernt selbständig an Hand von Trainingskurven die prinzipiellen Zusammenhänge der Regelungsaufgabe. Es werden Tests mit unterschiedlichen Geschwindigkeitsprofilen und Motoren präsentiert. Im Anschluß daran gehen wir auf Erfahrungen mit neuronalen Netzen ein, die wir in anderen Anwendungsgebieten gesammelt haben.

1 Einleitung

Künstliche neuronale Netze (ANNs) breiten sich immer weiter in Forschung und Industrie aus. Praktisch jede große Firma hat mindestens einen Mitarbeiter damit beauftragt, im Rahmen von "zukunftssichernden Maßnahmen", "Innovationsstudien" oder ähnlichen Programmen Informationen über ANNs und deren Verwendbarkeit in der Praxis zu sammeln. In fast allen Fachzeitschriften, auch in den typischen Zeitschriften der Maschinenbauer und Automatisierungstechniker, sind immer wieder Artikel über Grundlagen, Anwendungen und Zukunftsperspektiven von ANNs zu lesen.

Trotz dieses ungebrochenen Aufwärtstrends (auch manifestiert in Form von stetig zunehmenden nationalen und internationalen Fördermaßnahmen) sind aber die Anwendungen von ANNs im großen Stil national und international noch dünn gesäht.

So scheint beim Verkauf der zahlreich angebotenen Hard– und Softwaresysteme für die Erstellung und Beurteilung von neuronalen Netzen ein relativer Sättigungsgrad erreicht worden zu sein: Ein starkes Wachstum des Marktes ist erst wieder zu erwarten, wenn der momentanen Phase des Kennenlernens eine Anwendungsphase in größerem Stil folgt.

Woran liegt es, daß diese Anwendungsphase noch auf sich warten läßt?

○ Das Henne–Ei–Problem

Es gibt eine konservative Haltung vieler (auch großer) Industriebetriebe gegenüber neuen Technologien. Die Firmen würden diese neue Technik sofort einführen, wenn sie diese bereits irgendwo im praktischen Einsatz besichtigen könnten; der erste praktische Einsatz ist aber solange nicht möglich, solange keiner der möglichen Interessenten die Erstanwendung zu riskieren bereit ist. Aus diesem Grund sind pilotartige Projekte, wie die hier präsentierten, von besonderer innovativer Bedeutung.

* Teilweise gefördert durch das Bundesministerium für Forschung und Technologie 413–5839–ITR 8800 E3

◯ ANNs als Problem – ANNs als Lösung

Es wird noch zu wenig berücksichtigt, daß es zwei grundsätzlich verschiedene Sichtweisen von ANNs gibt: ANNs als höchst interessantes Problem, also als Aufgabenstelllung an sich, oder ANNs als Lösung, wobei vorhandenen Aufgaben mit ANNs gelöst werden sollen.

Die Untersuchung eines bestimmten Netzwerktyps x "am Beispiel von Problem y" ist vom Ansatz her etwas grundsätzlich anderes als die Bearbeitung der Problemstellung y "unter Verwendung des neuronalen Netzes vom Typ x".

◯ Vielschichtiger Begriffsinhalt

Der Begriff "neuronale Netze" ist zu vielschichtig, als daß man ein geschlossenes Bild der Fähigkeiten und Grenzen erstellen könnte.

Wenn die Evaluationsabteilung einer Firma "die" neuronalen Netze daraufhin prüft, ob damit ein bestimmtes Problem gelöst werden kann, kann man ganz sicher ein ANN finden, mit dem dieses Problem nicht gelöst werden kann, woraus dann vom Praktiker oft vorschnell der Schluß gezogen wird, daß "die" ANNs eben doch nicht praktisch verwendbar sind (wobei die oft in der Presse überzogen dargestellten Ansprüche von ANNs sehr hinderlich sind). Unserer Meinung nach sind es aber gerade die populärsten Netzwerktypen, die in dieser Hinsicht die größten Defizite aufweisen. Andere Ansätze, die gerade hier in Deutschland seit längerem systematisch untersucht werden, gehen häufig weit über die bekannten Limitationen beispielsweise von mit Backpropagation trainierten Multi–Layer–Perceptrons hinaus; diese Ansätze sind aber zu wenig bekannt und werden zu wenig durch entsprechende kommerzielle Interessen, im Sinne der z.B. in den USA so weite verbreiteten Universitäts–spin–offs, unterstützt.

Es stellt sich daher die Frage, warum in einigen Industriezweigen das Interesse an ANNs erwacht ist. Dies liegt unserer Erfahrung nach daran, daß die möglichen Vorteile der Anwendung von ANNs gerade auf den Gebieten liegen, die für die zukünftige Automatisierung der Betriebe die größten "Stolpersteine" darstellen.

Die neuartigen Aufgaben, mit denen die Ingenieure gegenwärtig konfrontiert werden, können grob in zwei Hauptgruppen aufgeteilt werden, nämlich a) immer größere Annäherung an die physikalische Realität einerseits und b) immer einfachere (und damit kostengünstigere) Bedienbarkeit durch einen immer größer werdenden Anteil von nicht speziell ausgebildeten Anwendern andererseits.

a) Die Annäherung an die physikalische Realität ist meistens gleichbedeutend mit der Berücksichtigung von zusätzlichen Meßwerten, die als zusätzliche Variable in den verwendeten physikalischen Modellen die Verfeinerung der Modelle, vor allem aber die Berücksichtigung von Störgrößen erlaubt.

Als typisches Beispiel sei hier die optische Mustererkennung genannt, die ja theoretisch als gelöst betrachtet werden kann, bei deren praktischem Einsatz aber der Hauptteil des Realisierungsaufwands in einer Berücksichtigung der möglichen Störeinflüsse liegt.

Die explizite Aufnahme von zusätzlichen Variablen in ein algorithmisch formuliertes Verfahren erfordert die exakte Kenntnis der gegenseitigen Abhängigkeiten aller Variablen untereinander, wobei die Einführung eines zusätzlichen Wertes u.U. eine Neuerstellung der gesamten Modelltheorie erforderlich macht. Gerade bei Störgrößen ist diese Kenntnis zwar oft "intuitiv" beim erfahrenen Anwender vorhanden, läßt sich aber schwer oder gar nicht in einen Formalismus umsetzen. Für diese Umsetzung ist es notwendig, auch "unscharfe" Sachverhalte und qualitative statt quantitative Zusammenhänge zu berücksichtigen.

b) Die flexible Anpassung von vorhandenen Hard– und Softwarelösungen an neue Aufgaben sowie die Benutzung solcher Systeme in breitem Rahmen erfordert eine weit über den bisherigen Stand hinausgehende Kommunikation zwischen Mensch und Maschine. Gegenwärtig muß sich der Mensch der Maschine anpassen, wobei diese Anpassung nicht nur das Erlernen einer neuen "Sprache" (Programmiersprache, Datenbankabfragesprachen etc.) sondern darüber hinaus auch noch eine Einschränkung des menschlichen Denkens auf Denkmuster der Maschine bedeutet. Diese Einschränkung widerspricht aber gerade dem oben dargelegten Gedanken, daß implizite, unscharfe Aussagen in nicht formaler Weise als Basis für die Vorgehensweise der Maschine dienen sollte.

Es zeigt sich hier ein deutlicher Zusammenhang zwischen den beiden angesprochenen Punkten, die im wesentlichen darauf hinauslaufen, daß die Maschine die Umwelt aus der Sicht des Menschen (eigentlich besser: aus der Sicht des auf diese Umwelt spezialisierten biologischen Systems) sehen sollte.

Da die konnektionistischen Systeme oder neuronalen Netze ja ursprünglich gerade mit dem Anspruch angetreten waren, das menschliche Denken auf die Rechner zu übertragen (ein Anspruch, den allerdings auch die symbolischen Ansätze für sich reklamieren), wird hier allgemein eine Chance gesehen, diese Aufgaben unter praxisrelevanten Randbedingungen lösen zu können.

2 Vorteile von ANNs bei der Lösung der gestellten Aufgaben

Die erhofften und/oder bereits nachgewiesenen Vorteile der ANNs sind bereits so allgemein bekannt, daß sie hier nur stichpunktartig angerissen werden sollen. Es sind dies (unter anderem):

- Durch die Assoziativität sowohl bei der Speicherung als auch der Verarbeitung von Information kann unscharfes Wissen gut dargestellt werden.

- Die Selbstorganisationsfähigkeit vermeidet den Flaschenhals der formalen Festlegung von funktionalen Abhängigkeiten etc., da dadurch ANNs in der Lage sind, solche Abhängigkeiten auch dann zu finden, wenn sie dem Konstrukteur des Netzes nicht vorher bekannt waren. Eine "Algorithmisierung" des Problems ist nicht notwendig.

- Spezielle Lösungsstrategien des Menschen – z.B. bei der Mustererkennung – können kopiert werden, ohne formal beschrieben werden zu müssen.

- Die programmtechnische Implementierung eines neuronalen Netzes kann weitgehend problemunabhängig "off-line" erfolgen, die Anpassung an eine bestimmte Aufgabe geschieht dann vor Ort ohne Mitwirkung eines externen Spezialisten wie *knowledge engineer* etc.

3 Vorteile unseres speziellen Ansatzes

Die von uns verwendeten Netze stellen Eigenentwicklungen dar, die auf dem Ansatz der stark strukturierten, nicht formalen ANNs beruhen, wobei soweit praktikabel biologisch motivierte Erweiterungen des Modells mit vorgesehen wurden. Für die unten aufgeführten Applikationen haben wir ratenkodierte Neurone verwendet. Eine formale Beschreibung unseres Ansatzes nach [1] ist in [2] angegeben.

Es soll im folgenden auf einige Besonderheiten genauer eingegangen werden:

- Verteilte oder topologische Kodierung

  Bei "sensornahen" Aufgabenstellungen müssen sehr häufig numerische Werte mit relativ großer Genauigkeit verarbeitet werden. Die konventionelle Art der Repräsentation numerischer Information durch die (reellwertige) Aktivität einzelner Neurone ist hier für viele Probleme nicht adäquat.

Die bereits in früheren Arbeiten vorgeschlagene verteilte oder auch topologische Kodierung [3] [4] bietet bei nur leicht erhöhtem Aufwand gravierende Vorteile in der Anwendung. So kann eine große Klasse von nichtlinearen Abhängigkeiten bereits in einem einschichtigen Netzwerk dargestellt werden.

Klassifikationsverfahren in einem numerischen Merkmalsraum können ebenfalls ohne *hidden layer* nichtlineare Entscheidungsflächen erzeugen, mit denen auch z.B. XOR–Probleme gelöst werden können.

Die numerische Genauigkeit für die Darstellung der Zahlenwerte läßt sich durch Anpassung der Neuronenanzahl pro Wert auf einen beliebigen Wert bei gleichem Dynamikbereich der Aktivtätsvariablen der Einzelneurone steigern – also sparsam in der Rechenzeit [13]. Da der numerische Wert einer Variablen durch die topologische Anordnung von Neuronen gegeben ist, können die Aktivitäten der Neurone dazu benutzt werden, um zusätzlich noch Information, z.B. über die Zuverlässigkeit eines Zahlenwerts, zu kodieren.

Der vielleicht größte Vorteil dieser Darstellung besteht unserer Meinung nach aber darin, daß auf diese Weise der Begriff des assoziativen Speichers auf die Speicherung von reellwertigen Vektoren unter Berücksichtigung der numerischen Ähnlichkeit ausgedehnt werden kann.

Als typische Anwendung dafür sei ein Speicher für Prozeßzustände genannt. Ein solcher Speicher soll einen Zustand, der nur durch einen Satz von physikalischen Variablen definiert ist, so ablegen, daß *ähnliche* Zustände wiedererkannt werden können. Da mit der klassischen Physik beschreibbare Vorgänge in der Regel keine Unstetigkeitsstellen besitzen kann als Abstand zweier solcher Zustände der Vektorabstand benutzt werden.

Im Gegensatz zur Kodierung solcher Zustände durch die Aktivität jeweils eines Neurons pro Variable kann bei der topologischen Kodierung ein sehr brauchbarer assoziativer Speicher für solche Zustände realisiert werden. Anwendungen dafür siehe unten.

◯ Kombination mehrer, modifizierter Lernverfahren

Wir verwenden in unseren Modellen eine Kombination aus mehreren, für unsere Zwecke modifizierte Lernverfahren. Soweit möglich, wird eine modifizierte Deltaregel [17] angewandt, bei der die Schrittweite, also die betragsmäßige Änderung der Kopplungskoeffizienten pro Lernschritt variabel als Funktion des Kopplungskoeffizienten selbst sowie der prä– und postsynaptischen Aktivität bestimmt wird. Damit kann eine gute Konvergenz unter lokaler Berücksichtigung von Dynamikbegrenzungen der Koeffizienten erreicht werden. [18] [7] [8] [19]

Die nach Singer [5] modifizierte Hebbsche Regel wird für *unsupervised learning* sowie für das Lernen in assoziativen Speichern verwendet. Auch hier wird die Schrittweite dynamisch geändert.

In vielen Fällen wird eine Zufallskomponente mit eingebaut, die ein den Boltzmann–Maschinen nachempfundenes Lernverhalten ermöglicht. Diese Vorgehensweise ist speziell geeignet für den Aufbau eines Merkmalsraums, in dem vorgegebene Muster unter Minimierung der Besetzungsdichte repräsentiert und gespeichert werden können. [6] [10] [2]

◯ Strukturierung der Netzwerkverschaltungen

Von ausschlaggebender Bedeutung ist auch die starke, nur durch Anpassung an die zu lösende Aufgabe gegebene Strukturierung der Netzwerkverschaltungen. Die Aufgabe der formalen Analysierbarkeit zugunsten einer optimalen Problemorientiertheit ermöglicht erst die Anpassung an komplexe Umgebungsbedingungen sowie die Integration von vorhandenem Vorwissen in das Netzwerk. [8] [9] [10]

Um dies in für den Anwender transparenter Weise zu realisieren, verwenden wir eine eigens dafür entwickelte symbolische Netzwerkbeschreibungssprache, mit deren Hilfe auch komplexe Verbindungsstrukturen definiert und realisiert werden können. Zusätzlich ergibt sich die Möglichkeit, den in der konventionellen Softwaretechnik bewährten modularen Aufbau eines Gesamtsystems zu übernehmen. Teilnetze können einzeln erstellt, trainiert und getestet und schrittweise integriert werden. [8] [12] [15]

4 Die verwendete Methodik

Für die Bearbeitung einer Aufgabenstellung erfolgt zunächst eine Zergliederung in Teilaufgaben. Es wird dann bestimmt, mit welchen Hilfsmitteln (z.B. konventionell oder mit ANN's) die Teilaufgaben bearbeitet werden. Wenn eine konventionelle Komponente eine Teilaufgabe adäquat bearbeiten kann, ist die konventionelle Realisierung zu wählen.

Für die Realisierung der konnektionistischen Komponenten folgt nun eine genaue Analyse der zu bearbeitenden Informationen. Daraus ergibt sich die am besten geeignete Repräsentation der Informationen. Für numerische Informationen z.B. ist dies die oben erwähnte topologische Kodierung. Oft ist es auch sinnvoll, dem Netzwerk die gleiche Information in unterschiedlichen Repräsentationsformen anzubieten. Das Netzwerk kann sich dann selbst die für die Aufgabenstellung am besten geeignete Repräsentation auswählen (siehe dazu [4] [13] [14]).

Die konnektionistische Komponente wird dann, soweit es möglich und sinnvoll ist, in verschiedene Module unterteilt. Die Schnittstellen werden durch die Ein- und Ausgabeneurone der Module festgelegt. Anschließend werden die verdeckten Neurone und die Verbindungsstrukturen in und zwischen den Modulen definiert. Dabei können mehrere Entwickler parallel an unterschiedlichen Netzwerkmodulen arbeiten. Die Module werden nun einzeln implementiert und auf ihre Funktion getestet. Schrittweise werden die verschiedenen Module integriert. Dabei werden die Komponenten soweit wie möglich in einer vortrainierten Form verwendet. Bei dem integrativen Training wird die Funktion der einzelnen Module aufeinander abgestimmt.

Bei massiv rückgekoppelten Systemen sind der Modularisierung gewisse Grenzen gesetzt, da für bestimmte Netzwerkstrukturen das vollständige Netzwerk zum Training zu Verfügung stehen muß. In diesem Fall kann man sich jedoch normalerweise Hilfskonstruktionen schaffen, die zumindest eine starke Vereinfachung der Netzwerkstruktur ermöglichen.

Der hier beschriebene Vorgang ist ein Entwicklungszyklus, bei dem bestimmte Entwicklungsschritte häufiger durchlaufen werden. Dieses Vorgehen ist aus dem Bereich der konventionellen Softwareentwicklung sehr gut bekannt. Auch bei den neuronalen Netzen ist es wichtig, Fehler in der Konzeption möglichst frühzeitig zu erkennen, um Kosten zu sparen.

Nach dem Test der neuronalen Komponenten gegen die Spezifikation, wird die Integration der konnektionistischen und konventionellen Komponenten durchgeführt, soweit dies für die Testphase noch nicht notwendig gewesen war.

Ein zentraler Punkt ist die richtige Auswahl der Test- und Trainingsdaten. Es ist hier ein Umdenkprozeß notwendig, da für die Stichprobenauswahl nicht nur die "typischen", sondern vor allem auch die Problemfälle die größte Rolle spielen. Während man dies bei Klassifikationaufgaben noch intuitiv nachvollziehen kann, scheint die absichtliche Auswahl möglichst gestörter, problematischer Fälle als Trainingsbeispiel z.B. für einen selbstlernenden Regler eher unvernünftig. Andererseits steckt hinter der gezielten Auswahl der Stichproben im Normalfall so viel aufgabenspezifisches Wissen, daß diese Auswahl am besten durch den Endanwender selbst durchgeführt wird.

Für ein Vorgehen in der oben beschriebenen Form ist es notwendig, auf der technischen Seite die notwendigen Voraussetzungen zu haben. Wir verwenden dazu die aus NETUSE [8] [15] hervorgegangenen NEUROtools: NETdesign, NETmonitor, NETmerge, NETrun und NETset.

Die Eigenschaften der Neurone und die Netzwerkstruktur werden mit der zu NETdesign gehörenden Netzwerkbeschreibungssprache beschrieben. Der zugehörige Compiler übersetzt diese Beschreibung in die Netzwerkdatenstruktur. Es ist wichtig, daß man für komplexe Netzwerke diese Beschreibung in mehrere unabhängige Module zerlegen und damit effizient warten und erweitern kann. Auf diesem Weg ist es uns auch möglich, eine Bibliothek (NETset) von ausgetesteten Teilnetzwerken aufzubauen, die flexibel kombiniert werden können.

Mit Hilfe von NETmonitor wird die Netzwerkstruktur analysiert und das Verhalten des Netzwerks in der Trainings- und Testphase beobachtet. Bei der Entwicklung haben wir beachtet, daß die in diesen Phasen anfallenden großen Datenmengen einfach und schnell behandelt werden können. Es ist aus Effizienzgründen notwendig, daß man komplexe Trainings- und Testabläufe automatisieren und entsprechend auch automatisch protokollieren kann.

Für die Kombination von bereits vortrainierten Netzwerken wird NETmerge verwendet. Dieses Werkzeug ist die entscheidende Voraussetzung für eine weitgehende Modularisierung und Parallelisierung des Entwicklungsvorganges.

Nach Abschluß der Testphase wird das neuronale Netz durch das Softwarepaket NETrun bearbeitet, das eine Schnittstelle in Form einer geschlossenen Datenstruktur zur Verfügung stellt. Auf diesem Weg sind neuronale Komponenten sehr einfach in bestehende Systeme zu integrieren. Andere Möglichkeiten der Integration von neuronalen Komponenten in andere Systeme wurden bereits in [15] beschrieben.

Es hat sich in der Praxis gezeigt, daß es notwendig ist, ein sehr breites Spektrum an unterschiedlichen Rechenleistungen zur Verfügung zu stellen. Für Aufgaben mit geringen Datenraten genügen oft Universalsysteme, wir setzen Syteme z.B. unter VAX/VMS und SCO/Unix ein. Für Aufgabenstellungen mit hohen Datenraten (z.B. visuelle Objekterkennung s.u.) verwenden wir auch Transputer–Systeme. Für noch größere Datenraten sind aufgrund der verwendeten Algorithmen auch sehr schnelle Realisierungen in Form von Spezialchips denkbar.

5   Applikationen

Es werden nun einige konkrete Anwendungen von neuronalen Netzen vorgestellt. Dabei wird ein neuronaler Regler, der sog. *konnektionistische Fahrer*, genauer besprochen. Anschließend werden weitere Anwendungen aus dem Bereich der Analyse großer Datenmengen, der visuellen Objekterkennung und der assoziativen Sprachverarbeitung behandelt.

5. 1.   Der *konnektionistische Fahrer*

Der *konnektionistische Fahrer* wurde von der Firma Kratzer Automatisierung München für die Volkswagen AG Wolfsburg, Abteilung Versuchsautomatisierung, im Frühjahr 1991 realisiert [16] .

5. 1. 1.   Aufgabenstellung

Für den Einsatz auf KFZ–Prüfständen sollte ein Regler realisiert werden, der vorgegebene Geschwindigkeitsprofile mit geringen Abweichungen *nachfahren* kann. Dabei ist gefordert, daß der Regler parallel Kupplung und Gaspedal bedient. Eine weitere Anforderung an das System war, daß der Regler auch noch einfach nach weiteren Kriterien z.B. dem Benzinverbrauch und dem Schadstoffausstoß optimiert werden kann.

Bei dem mit einem neuronalen Netz erstellten System entfällt die Aufnahme der Motoren–Kennfelder und der Regler kann sich bei Langzeitversuchen (sog. Dauerlaufversuchen) automatisch an die dynamischen Veränderungen der Eigenschaften von Prüfling und Prüfstand während eines Prüflaufs anpassen. Wie groß diese Unterschiede in diesem Bereich sind, kann man sich an Hand der Bedienung einer Kupplung und des Ansprechverhaltens eines Motors bei einem neuen Kfz und bei einem 20.000 oder 100.000 km gefahrenen Modell verdeutlichen.

5. 1. 2. Warum ein neuronaler Regler

Es wurde zuerst geprüft, ob das Problem nicht durch konventionelle Verfahren gelöst werden könnte. Dabei hat es sich gezeigt, daß die bekannten Regler für diese Aufgabenstellung nicht ohne die vorhergehende Bestimmung der Motoren–Kennfelder eingesetzt und unter den gegebenen Randbedingungen auch nicht für weitere Kriterien (s.o.) optimiert werden können.

Es war also notwendig, einen alternativen Lösungsweg zu suchen. Auf Grund der positiven Erfahrungen mit neuronalen Netzen in anderen industriellen Anwendungen wurde ein neuronales Netzwerk als "konnektionistischer Fahrer" entwickelt und implementiert.

5. 1. 3. Realisierung

Für die Realisierung diente das von VW beigestellte Softwarepaket MOTOR/MOVIE als Fahrzeugsimulator; zum Entwerfen, Bearbeiten und Beobachten der verwendeten Netzwerke wurden die oben beschriebenen NEUROtools verwendet.

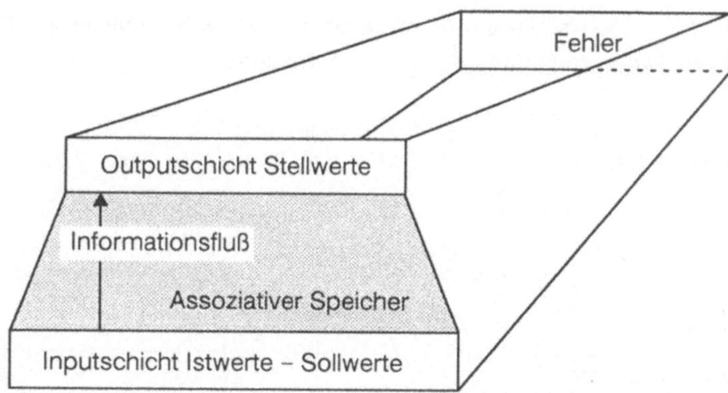

Bild 1 : Prinzipdarstellung des verwendeten Netzwerkes mit Informationsfluß

Das Netzwerk besteht aus einer Inputschicht für die Repräsentation des aktuellen Prozeßzustandes, einer Outputschicht für die Repräsentation der Stellgrößen und für den vom Netzwerk prognostizierten Fehler in der aktuellen Situation. Für das Lernen der Verbindungen wird eine modifizierte Delta-Regel [16] verwendet, die auch als *forced–learning* [17], [2] bezeichnet wird. Die Verbindungsstärken wurden vor Beginn des Trainings mit Zufallszahlen initialisiert.

Auf Grund der aktuellen Ist– und Sollwerte bestimmt das Netzwerk die Stellwerte und den aktuellen Fehler. Daraus werden die neuen Stellwerte bestimmt und anschließend an den Prozeß ausgegeben.

5. 1. 4. Ergebnisse

Bei den Versuchen mit dem oben dargestellten Netzwerk wurden sehr zufriedenstellende Ergebnisse erzielt, von denen die wichtigsten dargestellt werden sollen. Zunächst wurde ein Netzwerk auf ein bestimmtes Geschwindigkeitsprofil trainiert. Die Verbesserung der Regelung von dem ungeübten "Fahrschüler-Netz" (1. Durchlauf), dem "Kavaliersstart-Netzwerk" (2. und 3. Durchlauf) und dem "geübten konnektionistischen Fahrer" (50. Durchlauf) ist offensichtlich:

1. Durchlauf
MW: 3.18 km/h, max. Abw.: 12.94 km/h

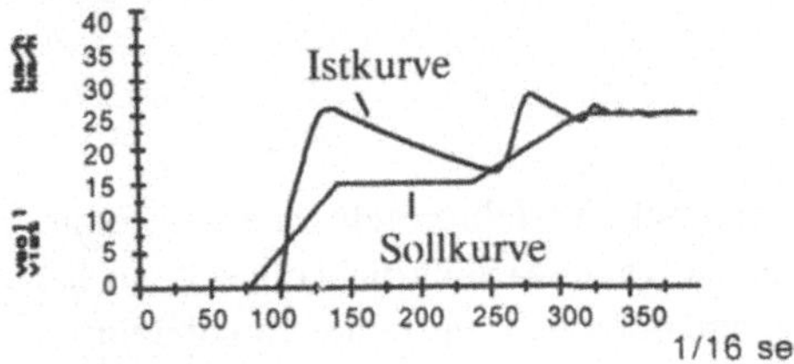

2. Durchlauf
MW: 0.55 km/h, max. Abw.: 8.58 km/h

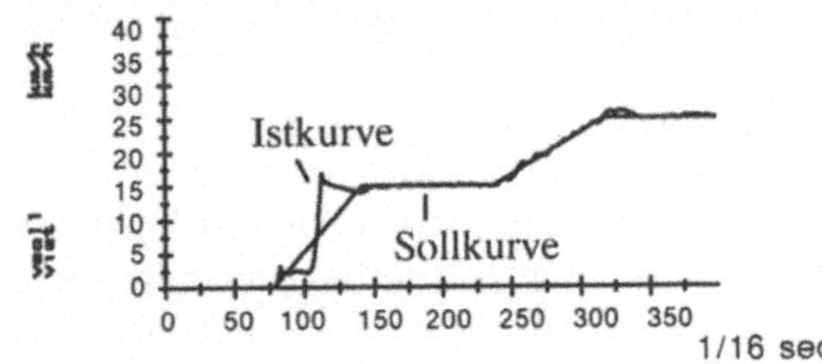

3. Durchlauf
MW: 0.35 km/h, max. Abw.: 6.52 km/h

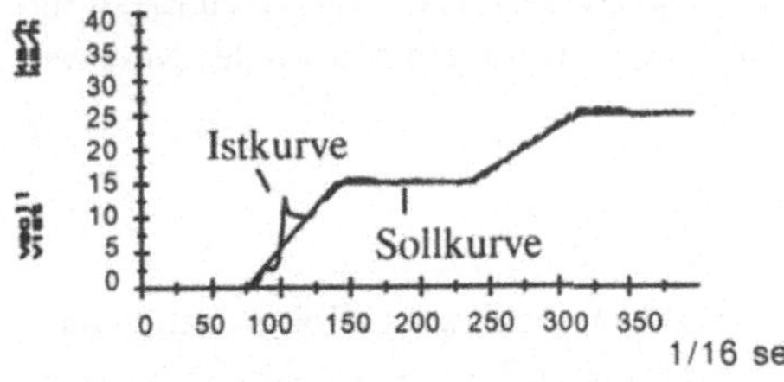

50. Durchlauf
MW: 0.28 km/h, max. Abw.: 1.90 km/h

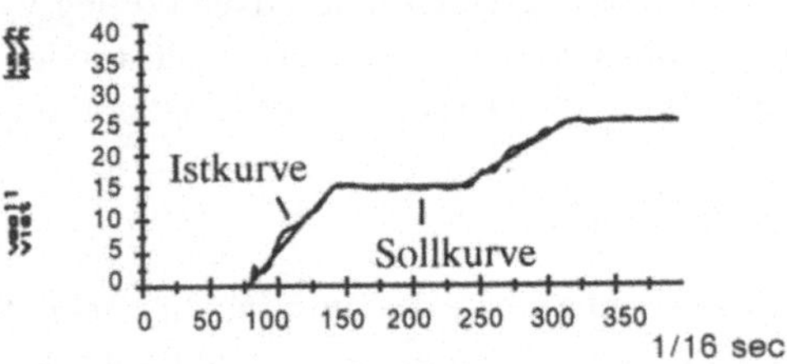

Bild 2: 1., 2., 3. und 50. Durchlauf

Als nächste Aufgabe wurde dem so trainierten Netzwerk ein neues Geschwindigkeitsprofil vorgegeben. Der *konnektionistische Fahrer* zeigt nun folgendes Fahrverhalten:

Ohne zusätzliches Lernen
MW: 1.00 km/h, max. Abw.: 5.56 km/h

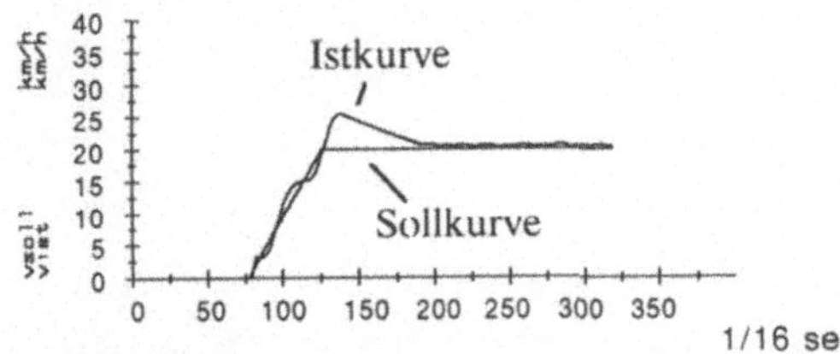

2. Durchlauf
MW: 0.62 km/h, max. Abw.: 3.38 km/h

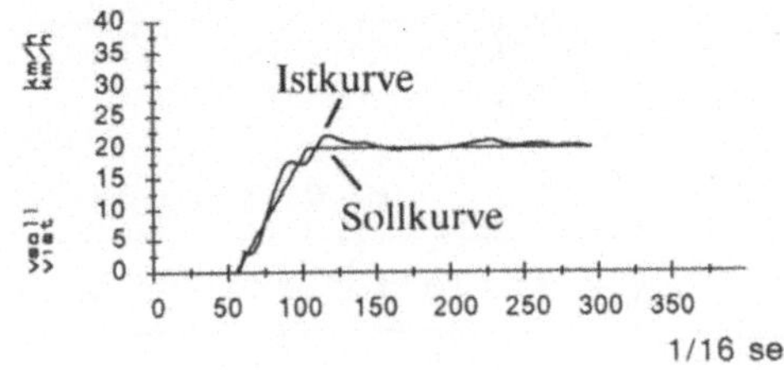

5. Durchlauf
MW: 0.35 km/h, max. Abw.: 1.73 km/h

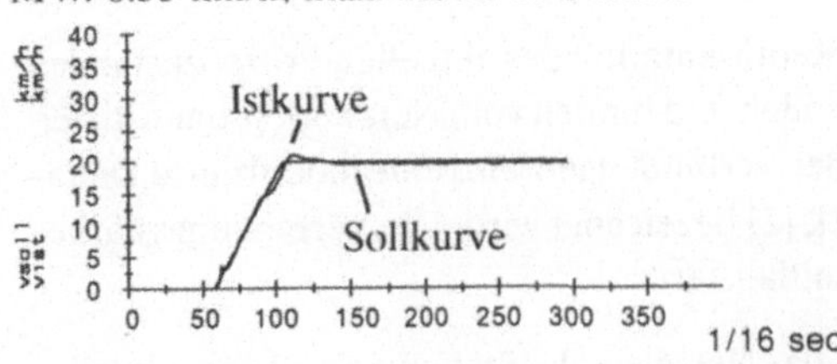

Bild 3: anderes Geschwindigkeitsprofil, 1., 2. und 5. Durchlauf

Der *konnektionistische Fahrer* zeigt in seinem Verhalten zunächst eine Überspezialisierung, da er bisher nur an einem einzigen Geschwindigkeitsprofil trainiert worden war. Dieser Effekt war jedoch nach dem 5. Durchlauf ausgeglichen.

Das so trainierte Netzwerk wurde nun auch für die Regelung eines anderen Motortyps verwendet. Dieser neue Motor hatte eine wesentlich höhere Leistung und ein vollkommen anderes Kennfeld als der ursprüngliche Trainingsmotor.

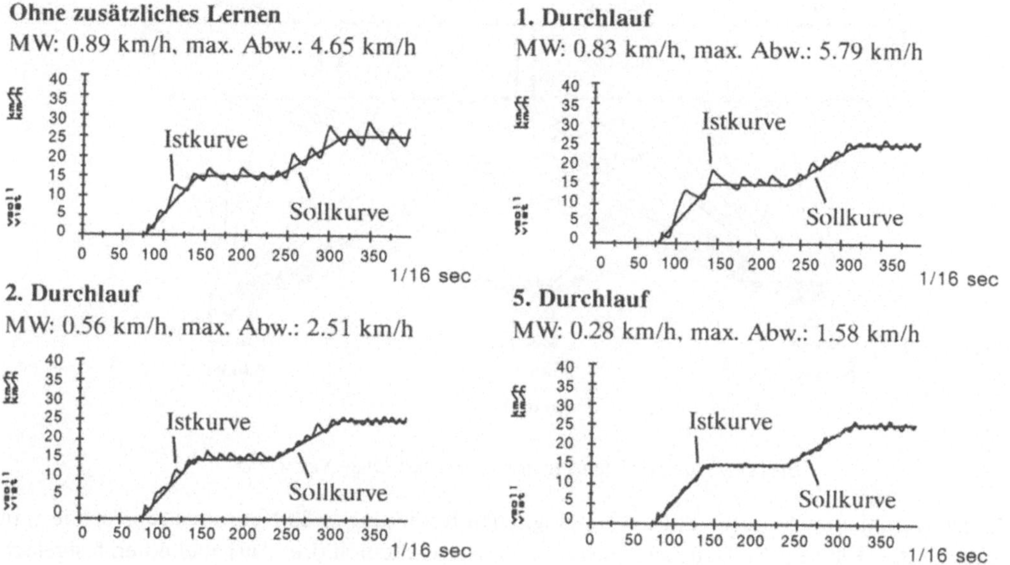

Bild 4: Übertragung auf einen anderen Motor

Der *konnektionistische Fahrer* hat sich auch in diesem Fall bereits nach dem 5. Anfahrvorgang auf die veränderten Randbedingungen angepaßt.

5. 1. 5. Ausblick

Der *konnektionistische Fahrer* soll in der nächsten Stufe um die Bedienung der Bremse und der Schaltung erweitert werden. Ferner sollen sekundäre Optimierungen wie z.B. die Verringerung des Schadstoffausstoßes und des Benzinverbrauchs realisiert werden. In der dritten Stufe ist dann der Einsatz des *konnektionistischen Fahrers* auf einem echten Prüfstand geplant.

5. 2. Analyse großer Datenmengen

Bei vielen technischen Aufgabenstellungen müssen Objekte oder Ereignisse, die durch bestimmte Datensätze repräsentiert sind, in verschiedene Klassen, z.B. gut oder schlecht, eingeteilt werden. Mit neuronalen Netzwerken kann man auf Grund von Trainingsdaten Merkmale bestimmen, welche für die Klassifikation geeignet sind.

Wir haben dies u.a. mit Daten aus dem Bereich der Botanik getestet (IRIS–Daten [21]), die auch als Test für Klassifikatoren verwendet werden [21] [22]. Es handelt sich dabei um 150 Datensätze mit jeweils 4 Zahlenwerten. Jeder Datensatz gehört zu einer von drei Klassen. Wir haben die ersten 25 Datensätze jeder Klasse zum Trainieren des Systems verwendet.

Nach ca. 30 Minuten CPU–Zeit auf einem PC–System (386/20 MHz) hatte das Netzwerk diese 75 Datensätze gelernt, d.h. es konnte alle 75 Datensätze den 3 Klassen korrekt zuordnen. Von den restlichen 75 Datensätzen, die man dem System noch nicht angeboten hatte, ordnete das System 69 Datensätze in die richtige Klasse ein. Die Klassifikation eines Datensatzes benötigt auf dem oben erwähnten System deutlich weniger als 0.1 Sekunden.

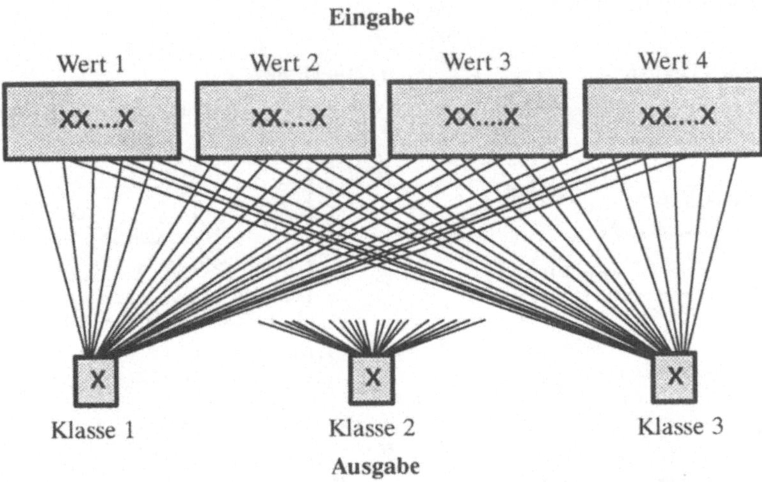

Bild 5: Prinzipdarstellung des Klassifikations–Netzwerks

Jeder der 4 Zahlenwerte wurde mit der topologischen Kodierung in 20 Neuronen repräsentiert. In welche der drei Klassen der Datensatz einzuordnen ist, wird durch drei Ausgabeknoten festgelegt, wobei jeder Ausgabeknoten die Zugehörigkeit des aktuellen Datensatzes zu einer Klasse kodiert. Jeder Ausgabeknoten ist mit allen Eingabeknoten verbunden, es werden keine verdeckten Knoten verwendet. Das Netzwerk hat also 83 Knoten und 240 Verbindungen. Dieses einfache Netzwerk liefert ein Ergebnis, das besser ist als alle anderen uns bekannten Lösungen.

Wir konnten inzwischen auch komplexere Netzwerke im Rahmen einer Projektstudie erfolgreich auf praktische Klassifikationsprobleme mit höherer Dimensionalität aus dem Bereich der Automatisierungstechnik anwenden. Dabei wurden Datenmengen von 400 MB untersucht. Nach Beendigung der Trainingsphase kann man die Struktur des Netzwerks analysieren und bestimmen, auf welchen Kriterien die Klassifikation des Netzwerks basiert.

Auf diesem Weg kann man ein neuronales Netz auch nach kausalen Zusammenhängen für bestimmte Ereignisse suchen lassen.

5. 3. Visuelle Objekterkennung

Die visuelle Objekterkennung wird in der Praxis für die Klassifikation von Massengütern eingesetzt.

Ein Massenfluß von 60.000 Objekten pro Stunde kann mit 4 Transputern (T800) in Echtzeit bearbeitet werden. Vorteile gegenüber konventionellen Systemen ergeben sich bei den Wartungskosten und bei der Umstellung auf andere zu beurteilende Objekte. Das Training von 4 neu zu klassifizierenden Objekten dauert 5 Minuten. Dabei wird mit einer Auflösung von 128 x 256 Bildpunkten pro Bild gearbeitet. Bei entsprechenden Training kann das Netzwerk auch so trainiert werden, daß es bestimmte

Translationen von Objekten toleriert. Die extreme Toleranz des Systems gegen veränderte Beleuchtungsverhältnisse und Veränderungen des Hintergrundes war überraschend gut.

5. 4. Assoziative Sprachverarbeitung

In diesem Bereich entwickeln wir ein assoziatives Dialogsystem, welches es einem Benutzer erlaubt, ohne Kenntnis einer formalen Abfragesprache Datenbankabfragen durchzuführen.

Ein Anwendungsbeispiel dazu sehen wir im Prüffeld:
Auf einem Prüfstandsrechner will der Bediener Informationen über durchgeführte Versuche abfragen, die in einer Datenbank abgespeichert sind. Maskenbäume können dem Bediener in diesem Fall nicht die notwendige Flexibilität bieten oder sind schwer zu bedienen. Man will dem Bediener aber auch nicht zumuten, formale Datenbankabfragesprachen, z.B. SQL lernen zu müssen. Durch ein natürlichsprachliches Benutzerinterface, das in eine Maskensoftware integriert werden kann, soll der Benutzer seine Abfrage in natürlicher Sprache formulieren und über die Tastatur eingeben können. [21] [11]

Als erste Stufe dieses Projektes haben wir unter anderem einen sehr schnellen fehlertoleranten assoziativen Zugriff auf Wörter NEUROfind realisiert. Es kann damit z.B. auf eine Menge von 2000 Wörtern bei Verwendung eines PC-Systems mit Antwortszeiten unter 1 Sekunde voll assoziativ zugegriffen werden. Dabei sind Tippfehler, Auslassungen und Vertauschungen in einem sehr hohen Grad zulässig. Dies ist ein willkommenes Hilfsmittel beim Zugriff auf Lieferanten- oder Kundendateien, das auch das Doppelnamenproblem Meier–Schmid oder Schmitt–Mayr zuverlässig löst. Weitere Informationen hierzu findet man in [7], [19], [20] und [21].

Literatur

[1] D.E.Rumelhart, J.L.McClelland (Hrsg.). Parallel Distributed Processing, Vol. 1, MIT Press, Cambridge London, 8/1988.

[2] T. Waschulzik, H. Geiger. Theorie und Anwendung Strukturierter Konnektionistischer Systeme. In: G. Dorffner (Hrsg.). Konnektionismus in Artificial Intelligence und Kognitionsforschung, 6. Österreichische Artificial-Intelligence-Tagung (KONNAI), Proceedings, Springer-Verlag, Berlin, 1990.

[3] D.H. Ballard. Interpolation Coding, Biological Cybernetics, 57, 389–402, 1987.

[4] H. Geiger. Storing and Processing Information in Connectionist Systems. In: R. Eckmiller (Hrsg.). Advanced Neural Computers, International Symposium on neural networks for Sensory and Motor Systems (NSMS 1990), Proceedings, Elsevier Science Publishers, Amsterdam, 1990.

[5] J.P. Rauschecker, W. Singer. The effects of early visual experience on the cat's visual cortex and their possible explanation by Hebb synapses, J. Physiol. (Lond.), 310, S. 215–239, 1981.

[6] D. Böller. Realisierung eines Hierarchischen Neuronalen Netzwerks zur assoziativen Erkennung von Objekten in natürlicher Umgebung, Diplomarbeit TU München, 1988.

[7] R. Kahler. Untersuchungen zur Anwendung selbstorganisierender, assoziativer Netzwerke für Zugriffe auf Datenbanken, Diplomarbeit TU München, 1986.

[8] T. Waschulzik, Optische Mustererkennung in neuronalen Architekturen, Diplomarbeit TU München, 1988.

[9] A. Nischwitz, Objekterkennung und Kamerasteuerung mit neuronalen Netzwerken, Diplomarbeit TU München, 1989.

[10] M. Arnoldi, Mustererkennung mit Hilfe selbstorganisierender adaptiver Mechanismen, Diplomarbeit TU München, 1989.

[11] K. Eder, Satzerkennung mit konnektionistischen Methoden, Diplomarbeit TU München, 1990.

[12] T. Waschulzik, H. Geiger, M. Arnoldi, D. Böller, A. Nischwitz, W. Brauer. New Concepts for Information Processing in Connectionistic Systems. In: R. Eckmiller, G. Hartmann, G. Hauske (Hrsg.). Parallel Processing in Neural Systems and Computers. A selection of papers of the International Conference on Parallel Processing in Neural Systems and Computers (ICNC), Düsseldorf 19 to 21 March 1990, Elsevier Science Publishers, Amsterdam, 1990.

[13] M. Kinder, Repräsentation mehrdimensionaler funktionaler Abhängigkeiten in neuronalen Netzen, Diplomarbeit TU München, 1990.

[14] M. Eldracher, Klassifikation großer Datenmengen anhand dynamisch extrahierter relevanter Merkmale mit neuronalen Netzen, Diplomarbeit TU München, 1990.

[15] T. Waschulzik, H. Geiger. Eine Entwicklungsmethodik für strukturierte konnektionistische Systeme. In: G. Dorffner (Hrsg.). Konnektionismus in Artificial Intelligence und Kognitionsforschung, 6. Österreichische Artificial–Intelligence–Tagung (KONNAI), Proceedings, Springer-Verlag, Berlin, 1990.

[16] D. Böller, H.Geiger. KS/Fahr, Studie, Kratzer Automatisierung München, 1991.

[17] B. Widrow, M.E.Hoff. Adaptive Switching Circuits, Western Electronic Show and Convention, Convention Record IV, S. 96–104, 1960.

[18] H. Frohn, H. Geiger, W. Singer, A Self–Organizing Neural Network Sharing Features of the Mammalian Visual System, *Biol. Cybernetics* (55), S. 333–343, 1987.

[19] T. Krempl. Automatische Transkription mit Hilfe selbstorganisierender Netzwerke, Diplomarbeit TU München, 1986.

[20] N. Zeßel. Sprachverarbeitung mit konnektionistischen Netzen, Diplomarbeit TU München, 1989.

[21] R. Deffner, H. Geiger. Associative Word Recognition with Connectionist Architectures. In: R. Fugmann (Hrsg.). Tools for Knowledge Organization and the Human Interface, Proceedings of the 1st International ISKO–Conference, Darmstadt, 14–17 August 1990, Frankfurt/Main, Indeks–Verlag, 1990.

[22] R.A. Fisher. The Use of Multiple Measurements in Taxonomic Problems. In: Annals of Eugenics Vol. VII, Pt. II, S. 179–188, 1936.

[23] J.E. Mezzich. An Evaluation of Quantitative Taxonomic Methods; Ph.D. dissertation, Ohio State University, 1975.

Neural Network Approaches for Sensory-Motor-Coordination

Sensormotorische Koordination mit Neuronalen Netzen

Helge Ritter, Technische Fakultät

Holk Cruse, Fakultät für Biologie

Universität Bielefeld

Abstract: Sensor-based coordination of movements is a central task for artificial robots and biological organisms as well. While traditional algorithms have largely relied on rather detailed models of the kinematics and dynamics of this process, neural networks offer the possibility to replace a significant amount of modeling by adaptation and learning. Moreover, principles of movement coordination observed in biological organisms can be used to construct networks exploiting these principles for the control of artificial devices. In this contribution, we will report on some work that adresses both issues and that is part of a larger, interdisciplinary research effort aiming at the construction of a neural-network controlled robot system.

Die sensorbasierte Steuerung von Bewegungen bildet eine zentrale Aufgabe für Roboter und biologische Organismen gleichermaßen. Während traditionelle Algorithmen in erster Linie auf vergleichsweise detaillierten Modellen der Kinematik und der Dynamik des Bewegungsvorgangs beruhen, bieten Neuronale Netze die Möglichkeit, einen erheblichen Teil dieser Modellierung durch Adaptation und Lernen zu ersetzen. Darüberhinaus können in der Natur beobachtete Bewegungskoordinationsmechanismen als Grundlage für das Design von Netzwerken zur Steuerung künstlicher Systeme dienen. In diesem Beitrag soll über Arbeiten berichtet werden, die beide Gesichtspunkte zum Gegenstand haben, und die Bestandteil eines größeren, interdisziplinären Forschungsprojekts sind, das die Realisierung eines durch Neuronale Netzwerke gesteuerten Robotersystems verfolgt.

1. Introduction

Carrying out skillful movements is a difficult task. This statement is not supported by our everyday experience; owing to the superb performance of the motor systems in our brain we can appreciate the involved complexities only when trying to program artificial robots ourselves (see, e.g. Brady 1989).

Programming robots can be viewed as a problem of knowledge acquisition. Much of the required knowledge concerns laws that can coordinate the movements of multiple joints, taking into account a complex context provided by a variety of sensory signals of tactile or visual origin (Hildreth and Hollerbach 1985). This points out an important difference to the knowledge acquisition problem faced by traditional knowledge based systems: in robotics, a major part of the relevant knowledge concerns inherently continuous quantities, such as sensor signals and joint torques. A second difference may at first glance seem extremely favorable: since the analysis of movements and of mechanical interactions can be based on the firm foundations of classical physics, one might hope that the problem of knowledge acquisition can to a large extent be bypassed by a mathematical analysis of the intended operations, something that usually cannot even be attempted in many other domains of interest. However, while extremely powerful in principle, such analytic approach is severely limited in practice. Most situations of interest are simply too complicated to be amenable to analysis at affordable costs. Imagine typical everyday tasks such as opening a button, walking over a pile of stones, picking a candy from a box, or manipulating spaghetti with a fork. Developing an analytical description for each of these tasks constitutes a daunting problem, yet many of the tasks we would like to delegate to robots are precisely of this type. One should note that the difficulty of these tasks is not rooted in issues of planning or sophisticated reasoning. Instead, the main source of their difficulty is the need to coordinate a large number of different mechanical degrees of freedom according to very complex sensory feedback signals from vision and from tactile and force sensors (Brooks 1990).

In view of the practical limitations of the analytical approach we must develop methods to complement it. Here, we advocate two additional sources of knowledge: the first is to develop good methods for robot learning. Since we all are experts at carrying out movements, good robot learning algorithms will greatly facilitate robot programming. However, we should not attempt to start with a "tabula rasa". To maximally exploit the potential of learning, we should try to identify generic types of movement patterns and control strategies that then need only be refined by learning. Biology offers a rich reservoir of such information. Natural motor systems employ a variety of different movement coordination and reflex patterns that have been optimized over millions of years (see, e.g. Cruse 1990). Analysing these patterns and their underlying laws of coordination can provide an extremely valuable basis for technological approaches.

For research on learning algorithms and on biological motor control strategies a most natural framework seems to be provided by neural networks (see , e.g., Rumelhart and McClelland 1985, Grossberg and Kuperstein 1986, Hertz et al. 1991, Ritter et al. 1991). Besides their obvious relations to both learning and biology, these systems have a couple of additional attractive features: they are well suited to represent both continuous and discrete, symbolic quantities; they offer simple mechanisms to achieve noise resistance; they can be taylored to work with imprecise inputs and they are inherently parallel. These are compelling reasons to investigate neural network-based strategies for movement coordination and robot programming (Brüwer und Cruse 1990, Martinetz et al.1989, Kawato 1987, Ritter et al. 1991). As concrete examples, this contribution reports on work that is focused on two important domains: the generation and control of hand and of walking movements. Both domains adress the important issue of multi-limb coordination under sensory feedback, but at different levels and with different aspects in the foreground. In the case of hand movements, the focus is primarily on the use of visual feedback signals to control the grasping process and it is chiefly the complex kinematics of the interaction between hand and object that must be controlled. In the case of the walking movements, the focus is on how to control multiple limbs in a synchronized fashion to achieve various gaits and to take the properties of the ground into account. Here, kinematics alone is no longer sufficient, and dynamic aspects also need to be considered.

Both projects are part of a larger, interdisciplinary research effort and are "bracketed" by cooperating research projects studying on the biological side the neural basis of vision in anurans, such as toads and frogs, and by a project dedicated to the development of an articulated robot hand on the technological side. The aim of this larger, joint effort is to evaluate the potential of neural networks for the realization of biologically inspired robot control strategies and to demonstrate their feasability by an actual implementation in an important practical domain.

2. Motor Learning and the Problem of Dimensionality

One major obstacle in the control of complex movements, such as grasp movements, seems to be the high dimensionality of the configuration space involved. Leaving aside any complexities arising from different object shapes, a human hand has of the order of 16 degrees of freedom. If we attribute to each degree of freedom the moderate number of five different independent positions, we arrive at 5^{16} or more than 10^{11} different hand configurations. Of these, we can at best only explore a tiny fraction during our human lifetime of considerably less than 10^{10} seconds. In fact, a considerable range of different hand postures can be generated even with "convex combinations"

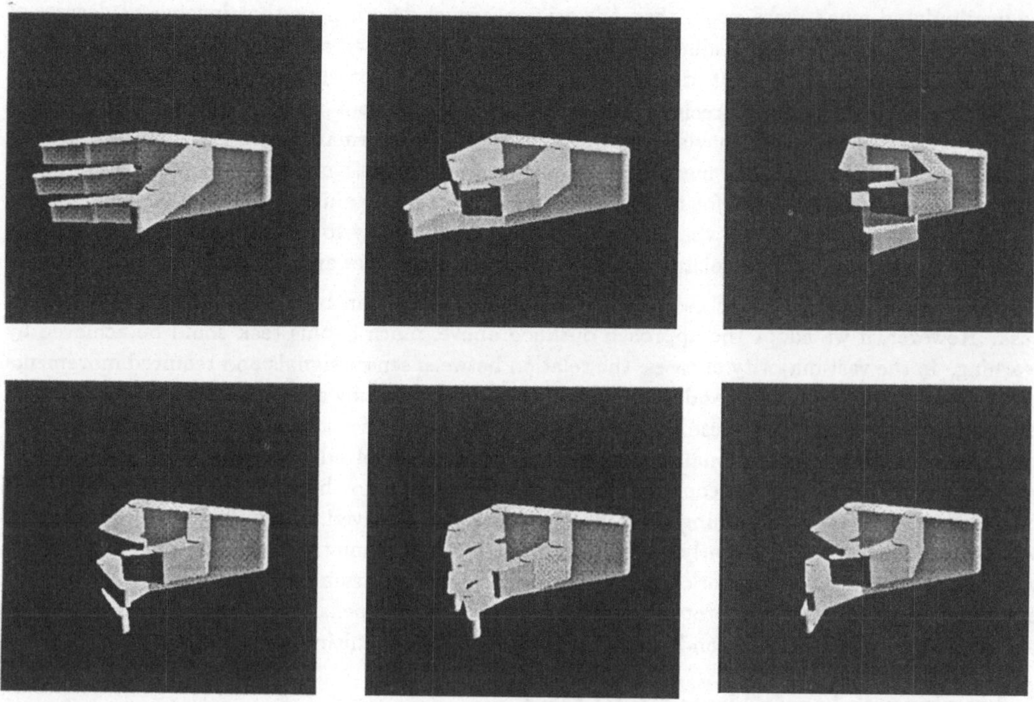

Fig.1a-f Top row (a-c): three "basis postures" used to parametrize configurations of a 12-jointed robot hand. Bottom row (d-f): some examples of further configurations obtained by linear combination of the three postures shown in Figs. (a-c).

of only three different hand postures. Figs.1a-f show a few examples for a simulated robot hand of 12 degrees of freedom: the first three images (Fig.1a-c) show a stretched hand, a "precision grip" and a fist, which may be used as a rather versatile set of "basis postures" from which many further configurations, such as those shown in Figs.1d-f, can be derived by linear combination. Any such combination involves only three coefficients (in our case, convex combinations were used, i.e. the coefficients were further constrained to sum to unity, so that only two degrees of freedom were involved), thus projecting the vast configuration space of 12 degrees of freedom of the full hand to a much more manageable space of three or even two dimensions. Of course, certain configurations cannot be realized in this way. However, for many tasks a sufficiently similar posture may be found among the linear combinations, and for the remaining actually occuring cases a special configuration may be easily stored, which then may serve as a "center" for a whole new submanifold of postures obtained by admixture of the previous three basis hand postures.

Similarly, actually occurring sensor signals range only over a tiny subset of the full set of their combinatorially possible combinations. Often, this subset can be well described by a fairly restriced number of "prototypes", so that the overlaps of the actual sensor readings with these prototypes provide sufficiently accurate information to e.g. make feedback adjustments to an ongoing movement. Below, we shall demonstrate the feasability of this approach for the task of reconstructing the 3d-posture of the hand shown in Fig.1 from 2d-pixel images.

In this way, we can both encode sensory input and motor output quantities for a robot, using only low-dimensional, approximate descriptions. These approximate descriptions can then be manipulated much more easily than the original, exact descriptions that involve all degrees of freedom that are potentially available. The price to pay is a limited accuracy; however, most of our movement skills are not a result of a particularly high degree of precision of our motor capabilities. For instance, our targetting precision for a reaching task without visual feedback is only in the percent range. However, with visual and tactile feedback information available, we are able to adapt our movements in very many ways to achieve an impressive range of sophisticated goals. This provides strong evidence for the view that precision and planning is of secondary importance for flexible movement control; what really counts is the capability to exploit a rich sensory context to shape an only coarsely pre-planned movement continuously towards its goal.

To explicitly program the use of such context, however, can be a very difficult and tedious task. However, if we adopt the approach outlined above, much of this task could be achieved by learning. In the vast majority of cases, the relation between sensor signals and required movements can be expected to be smooth and, therefore, can be represented by a continuous mapping between the quantities representing these data. Usually, a major obstacle for the determination of such mappings is the high dimensionality of the spaces that are involved. Working in low-dimensional representation spaces we can construct good approximations to these mappings on the basis of only a limited number of training examples. This can be achieved efficiently by neural networks which lend themselves excellently as flexible "function approximators". In the next section, we will describe a particular network type, which in addition to learning a smooth mapping, also can optimize the choice of the prototypes used to obtain a low-dimensional description of the input and output data, respectively, and which is therefore a very promising candidate for our approach.

3. Learning with Locally Linear Neural Maps

In this section, we want to illustrate the concepts of the previous section with some concrete simulation results. These concern the task of extracting the three-dimensional configuration of a simulated robot hand from perspective pixel images. The traditional approach would require a sequence of at least several processing steps, such as filtering, edge-detection, segmentation, part identification and finally fitting of a model of the hand shape to the segmented parts thus obtained (see, e.g. Horn 1986). In the neural network approach, only some limited form of preprocessing is necessary. The network can then learn from a set of examples to extract the correct hand postures directly from the preprocessed image data.

We use a network with a single internal layer of units, labelled by an index r. Each unit receives the same input, which was chosen as a 9-dimensional vector $\mathbf{x}$. This vector is obtained from a (computer-generated) image of the hand, such as Fig.1., by some rudimentary preprocessing (Fig.2). Fig.2a shows a typical input image. Applying a 3×3-Laplace mask and clipping any negative values, we obtain an image in which mainly edge-information is preserved. A subsequent logarithmic transformation compresses the dynamic range of the intensity values so obtained. The resulting image (shown in Fig.2b) is convolved with 9 Gaussians located at the lattice positions indicated in Fig.2c (to better depict the locations of the Gaussians in Fig.2c, the displayed widths are only 20% of the widths actually used), and the resulting 9 real values are used as the components x_i of the 9-dimensional input vector $\mathbf{x}$. The task of the network is to learn a mapping from these 9-dimensional representation vectors $\mathbf{x}$ to the "mixture coefficients" $\mathbf{y} = (y_1, y_2, y_3)$ that determine the contribution of each posture prototype to the hand configuration shown in the original image. Weighting the joint angles of the 3 basis hand postures with these coefficients then yields the hand posture that is "perceived by the network".

The network itself consisted of $N = 20$ units. Each unit r implements a locally valid linear mapping, specified by an output weight vector $\mathbf{w}_r^{(out)} \in I\!\!R^3$ and a 3×9-matrix $\mathbf{A}_r$. In addition,

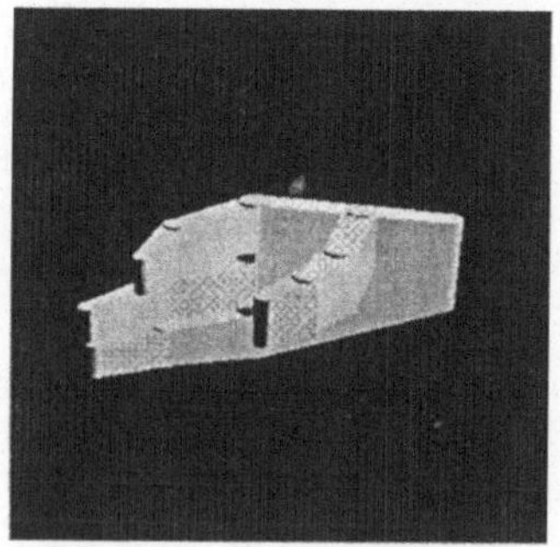 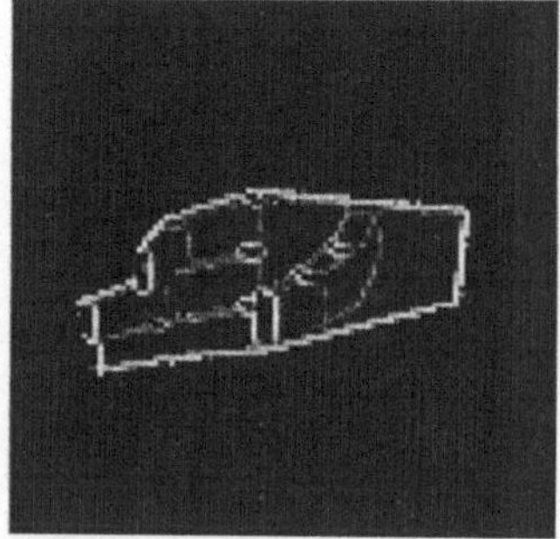 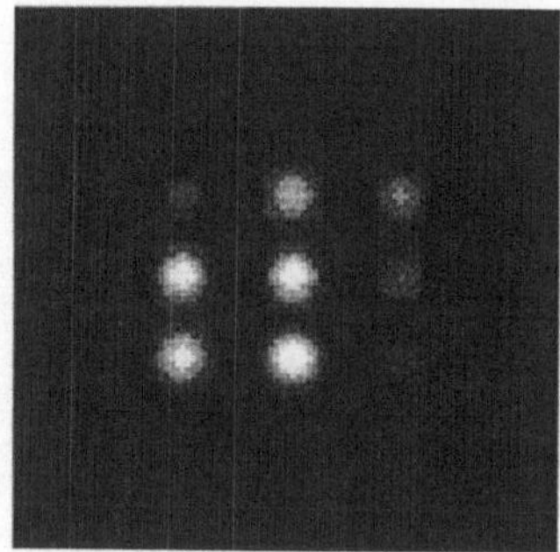

Fig.2 Preprocessing sequence to obtain input vector from pixel image. Left (a): input image, center (b): edge-image obtained after Laplace filtering and logarithmic intensity transformation, right (c): arrangement of Gaussian kernels used to derive 9-dimensional input vector.

each unit carries an input weight vector $\mathbf{w}_r^{(in)} \in \mathbb{R}^9$. The output $\mathbf{y}_r$ of a unit is given by

$$\mathbf{y}_r = \mathbf{w}_r^{(out)} + \mathbf{A}_r(\mathbf{x} - \mathbf{w}_r^{(in)}). \tag{1}$$

This represents a linear mapping with Jacobian $\mathbf{A}_r$, passing through the point $(\mathbf{x}, \mathbf{y}) = (\mathbf{w}_r^{(in)}, \mathbf{w}_r^{(out)})$. Which of these mappings is used to obtain the output $\mathbf{y}^{(net)}$ of the network is determined by the distances $d_r = \|\mathbf{x} - \mathbf{w}_r^{(in)}\|$. In the simplest case, the unit s for which $d_s = \min_r d_r$ is used ("winner-take-all"-network); usually a somewhat better accurracy can be obtained if a weighted superposition of the contributions of several units is used, e.g. according to

$$\mathbf{y}^{(net)} = \sum_r \mathbf{y}_r f_r, \tag{2}$$

$$f_r = Z^{-1} \exp(-d_r^2/\sigma_r^2), \tag{3}$$

$$Z = \sum_r \exp(-d_r^2/\sigma_r^2), \tag{4}$$

where σ_r is a measure of the radius of the "receptive field" of unit r and may be set, e.g., to $\min_s \|\mathbf{w}_r^{(in)} - \mathbf{w}_s^{(in)}\|$ (Saha and Keeler 1990). The ansatz (2)-(4) for fixed vectors $\mathbf{y}_r$ is also known as generalized radial basis function-approach ("GRBF", see, e.g. Girosi and Poggio 1990) and related to self-organizing maps (Kohonen 1984), which impose some additional structure by generalizing the weights associated with each unit among some subset of "topological neighbors". Note, however, that in contrast to the conventional GRBF-ansatz in our case the vectors $\mathbf{y}_r$ are not constant but instead are linear functions of the input vectors $\mathbf{x}$ that are given by (1). Due to either the winner-take-all rule (which emerges as the special limiting case $\sigma_r \to 0^+$) or as a result of the exponentials, each of these linear maps contributes only in the vicinity of the respective center $\mathbf{w}_r^{(in)}$. The whole, usually highly non-linear mapping is, therefore, represented as a weighted superposition of many locally valid linear maps instead of as a superposition of a corresponding number of fixed output values. This provides a significantly higher accuracy (Martinetz 1990, Ritter et al.1991).

Training of the network can proceed in a supervised manner, using a training set of correct input-output pairs $(\mathbf{x}^{(\alpha)}, \mathbf{y}^{(\alpha)})$, $(\alpha) = 1, 2 \ldots M$. Both, input and output weights may be adjusted

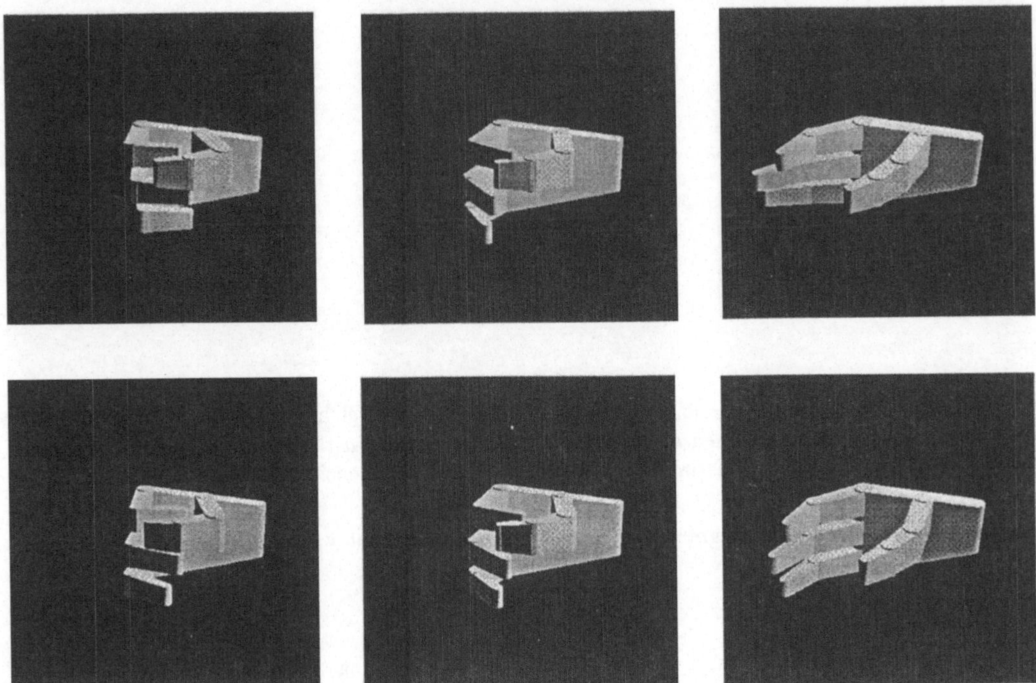

Fig.3 Performance of the network on some hand postures. Top row: input images. Bottom row: Corresponding images of the 3d-postures reconstructed by the network on the basis of the 9-d-input vectors obtained by the preprocessing steps outlined in Fig.2.

according to simple error-correction-type rules, i.e. no backpropagation is necessary:

$$\Delta\mathbf{w}_r^{(in)} = \epsilon_1(\mathbf{x}^{(\alpha)} - \mathbf{w}_r^{(in)})f_r, \tag{5}$$

$$\Delta\mathbf{w}_r^{(out)} = \epsilon_2(\mathbf{y}^{(net)} - \mathbf{w}_r^{(out)})f_r, \tag{6}$$

$$\Delta\mathbf{A}_r = \epsilon_3(\mathbf{y}^{(net)} - \mathbf{y}^{(\alpha)})(\mathbf{x}^{(\alpha)} - \mathbf{w}_r^{(in)})^T f_r/d_r^2, \tag{7}$$

where the $\epsilon_i > 0$ are learning step size parameters (a more detailed discussion of these learning rules in the context of self-organizing maps can be found, e.g. in Ritter et al. 1991).

Figs. 3a-c provide some impression of the performance of the network after training ($N = 20$ units, several repeated learning cycles through a data base of $M = 2000$ learning samples). Each picture in the top row shows an input image (not taken from the training set), while the corresponding picture below shows the hand posture as reconstructed by the network. As can be seen, these reconstructions are not entirely accurate; however, they provide a very good account of the correct hand posture. During training, some moderate variation of the viewpoint (rotations and translations) was introduced for each new example. As a result, the network can also correctly identify moderately rotated or translated versions of a posture, providing a useful degree of insensitivity against imprecise centering or moderate changes of the view-direction of the scene.

The present level of performance has been achieved without any sophisticated optimizations. There is still ample room for improvements: better preprocessing schemes can be devised to improve invariance, mechanisms for focusing attention to a subfield of the image may make particularly precise extraction of local posture information possible and several subnetworks may cooperate in a parallel or hierarchical fashion to assemble partial posture information into more global representations. Future research will adress these and related issues to explore the potential of neural approaches to sensory-motor control in the important domain of controlling visually guided grasp movements.

4. Movement Coordination in Biological Systems

Observation of the leg movements of a walking animal in the field shows that the legs are well coordinated in a specific gait. This spatio-temporal movement pattern of the legs seems to be quite fixed and its details only vary with walking speed. The pattern is in fact extremely stable with respect to disturbances which may result from an unpredictable environment as for example uneven surfaces. In some cases the underlying control system even copes with the problem of the loss of a leg. How is a system organized which is responsible for the coordination of leg movement? This is another example where an algorithmic solution is possible but requires much more time for computation if reactions to all sorts of disturbances are to be taken into account.

Biological experiments have been performed with six-legged insects or 8-legged crustaceans. On the basis of these experiments we know that this coordination is not achieved by means of a central controller. Rather, each leg has its separate sensory-neural unit which controls the movement of the leg. Each unit can be influenced by neighbouring units by way of specific signals enabling coordination of the movement of the different legs (for a review, see Cruse 1990). The coordination pattern can be regarded as an emergent property resulting from the local couplings between the units. Whereas for the stick insect six types of coordinating signals have been found, the crayfish seems to be much more simply organized as only three types of influences are sufficient to describe its behaviour. To give an example, Fig. 4 schematically presents those two types which act between ipsilateral legs, i.e., between neighbouring legs of the same side of the body. The two traces represent the movement of the legs. These consist of two parts, the power stroke (downward deflection) and the return stroke (upward deflection). During the power stroke the leg is moved to the rear and supports the body; during the return stroke the leg is swung back to the initial position to start the next power stroke. In Fig. 4 one leg is plotted in different phase situations relative to the other leg. These phases might have been produced by disturbances of the normal walk. One coordinating mechanism is only rostrally oriented, i.e, acts only from the posterior (rear) to the anterior (front) leg. This is illustrated in Fig. 4A: as long as the posterior leg performs a power stroke, the anterior leg has to perform or continue a return stroke. In addition, the velocity of the movement during the return stroke is also decreased to some extent. Thus the return stroke can be prolonged so that normal coordination is regained in the next step. The horizontally striped bar indicates the time during which this influence is active. The intensity of the influence is roughly indicated by the thickness of the bar. The second influence, illustrated in Fig. 4B, is caudally directed: when the anterior leg is near the end of its power stroke or at the beginning of its return stroke, an influence with increasing intensity has the effect of ending the return stroke and starting the power stroke of the posterior leg, thus shortening the return stroke of the latter. Again normal coordination is regained within one step. To couple contralateral legs, i.e., legs of opposite sides of the body, the crayfish uses a mechanism that closely resembles the ipsilateral, caudally directed influence. In contrast to ipsilateral influences, the contralateral ones act in both directions between the two legs.

The normal gait of the animal results from the fact that the units of all neighbouring legs are coupled by these local rules, as described above. Since, therefore, this system is found to be of an inherently parallel nature, it is well suited to be simulated by means of a neural network.

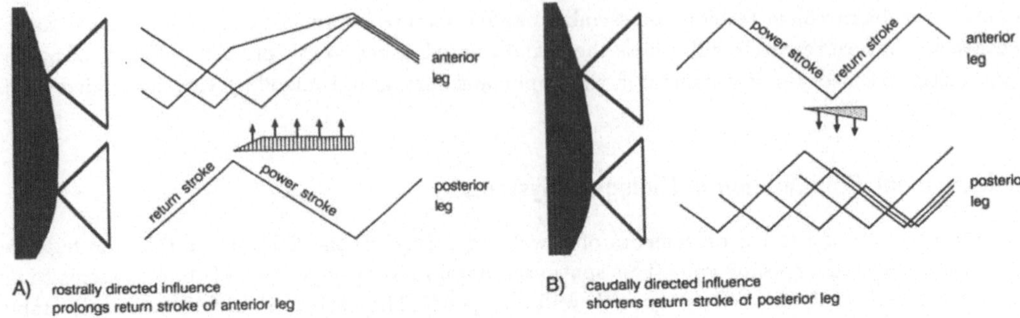

Fig.4 Coordination between the ipsilateral legs of a crayfish. The upper traces show the anterior leg. Abscissa is time, ordinate is position of the leg tip in a body fixed coordinate system. Each schema is drawn as if only one of the two coordinating mechanisms existed. In each case the influencing leg is drawn only once. For the influenced leg several traces are presented to show the effect of the coordinating mechanism. The duration and intensity of the influences are roughly indicated by the length and thickness of the wedges, respectively. (A) The rostrally directed influence is active during the power stroke of the posterior leg. It prolongs the return stroke of the anterior leg and can also decreases the speed of the limb movement. (B) The caudally directed excitatory influence is active at the end of the power stroke and the beginning of the return stroke of the anterior eg. It "excites" the start of a power stroke in the controlled, posterior leg.

The sensory-neural units, which have been described as controlling the movement of a leg, do themselves not correspond to single neurons but represent a more complicated system. For the sake of clarity we will simplify the system and consider only one property of the leg namely the performing of more or less rhythmic forward-backward movements, the alternating return and power strokes. This unit can then be considered as a simple oscillator. The oscillator includes sensory feedback because the transition from power to return stroke and vice versa is influenced not only by signals from the other legs, but also by sensory signals from its own leg. Thus each oscillator consists of several neurons. Our first aim is to build a network which consists of coupled neuronal oscillators. The whole system should produce a properly coordinated leg pattern which can compensate for external disturbances as fast as the animals can. To begin with we plan to utilize our knowledge obtained from biological experiments as much as possible for the structure of the network. Improvement by means of learning algorithms should only be used if the behaviour of this model shows deficiences.

As mentioned, the simplified model will only solve the problem of producing coordination between the legs. The question of how the different joints of the individual leg are coordinated to produce an appropriate leg movement during the power or the return stroke was not considered. This problem is particularly interesting when the leg becomes redundant, i.e., when it has more degrees of freedom than necessary for the task at hand. We investigated this question using as an example the control of the human arm and found that the behaviour could be explained by assuming the application of four rules (Cruse and Brüwer 1987). These are, first, an equal contribution of all joints to the movement (this corresponds to the well-known pseudo-inverse control); second, the minimization of the static costs by means of a cost function applied to each joint; third, the minimization of the inertial forces acting at the tip of the end effector by following a straight line in the workspace; and forth, by avoiding movements which are strongly non-monotonic in the joint space (this probably decreases dynamic costs).

These rules can be described by an algorithmic approach but the above-mentioned advantages of neural network systems ask for a simulation by means of these principles. Using a simple 3-layer feedforward network we successfully simulated one example of these rules (no. 2) (Brüwer and Cruse 1990). However, control of the actual leg or arm requires the use of sensory information. Therefore a network containing feedback channels is appropriate and will therefore be investigated in our project. This system, controlling a multilimbed leg, will then be implemented in the above-mentioned oscillator.

One particular problem remains to be solved in relation to the movement during power stroke. Walking on uneven surfaces means that the body-to-ground distance has to be adapted individually for each leg. For this case, too, information is available from biology: in the stick insect the vertical distance of each leg ("height") is subject to a proportional position controller (Cruse 1976). As the rearward movement component is subject to velocity control two different feedback systems control the same final elements. Thus we have a case of shared control which has to be solved by the network. As these controllers contain dynamic properties, the network has to cope with time derivatives and properties of temporal filters. In this case we also start designing the network by introducing as much a priori knowledge as possible; but later the question of how to learn dynamical properties will also be approached.

As mentioned, we are studying the network which controls the movement of a multilimbed leg. This "leg" can, of course, also be an arm or a robot manipulator. In this context it is of interest to know how the path of the end effector is planned. This is particularly interesting if the workspace contains obstacles. On the basis of experiments with human subjects we are currently investigating the strategies of human beings and plan to implement these strategies in a neural network model for path planning. These models could then be used to control the movement of a robot manipulator or to plan the path of a freely moving autonomous robot.

5.Conclusion

One of the aims of the research reported in the previous sections is to circumvent the knowledge acquisition bottleneck currently burdening the design and the construction of more intelligent and flexible robots. Neural networks seem to offer a framework that is particularly promising for approaching this goal. Several reasons can be given in support of this expectation: first, neural networks are well suited to implement learning algorithms, particularly in the sensory-motor domain, where continuous and noisy signals need to be processed, and where traditional, symbol-oriented approaches and purely analytical methods encounter great difficulties. The results reported in Section 3. provide a concrete example, showing that a visual recognition task, which, if to be achieved by conventional image processing techniques, would require a fairly sophisticated multi-stage system capable of identifying a complex object of variable shape, can be achieved by a rather small neural network on the basis of a modest number of training examples. By systematically exploring which kinds of input representations and network architectures are particularly useful for specific types of tasks, we may expect to gradually gain the capability to build larger and significantly more competent systems, for which a large portion of knowledge acquisition may boil down to the presentation of examples. An important role on this way will be played by biology: by taking information gained from biological organisms seriously into account for the design of artificial neural systems, we may be able to develop technological approaches that would be extremely hard — or, maybe even impossible — to arrive at by theorizing alone. From this point of view, neural network models emerge as a natural tool to efficiently integrate knowledge from basic biological research with existing approaches. The work reported in Sec.4 provides a concrete example of this second way of approach. Here, control strategies for the coordination of complex multi-limb movements that are robust against a wide range of disturbances are adopted from nature and implemented in artificial networks that then make these strategies usable for robust and yet computationally affordable real time control of artificial walking machines.

Acknowledgement

This work has been supported by the Bundesministerium für Forschung und Technologie (grant numbers ITN 9104A0 and ITN 9104B2). Any responsibility for the content of this publication is with the authors.

References

Arbib M.A., Amari S.I. (1985) Sensori-Motor Transformations in the Brain. J. theor. Biol. 112:123-155

Brady M. (1990) Robotics Science. MIT-Press

Brooks R. (1990) Elephants Don't Play Chess. Robotics and Autonomous Systems 6:3-15.

Brüwer M., Cruse H. (1990) A network model for the control of the movement of a redundant manipulator. Biol. Cybern. 62:549-555.

Cruse H. (1976) The control of body position in the stick insect (Cavansius morosus) when walking over unveven surfaces. Biol. Cybern. 24:25-33.

Cruse H. (1990) What mechanisms coordinate leg movement in walking arthropods?. Trends in Neurosciences 13:15-21

Cruse H., Brüwer M. (1987) The human arm as a redundant manipulator: The control of path and joint angles. Biol. Cybern. 57:137-144.

Girosi F. , Poggio T.(1990) Biol.Cybernetics 63:169-176.

Grossberg S., Kuperstein M. (1986) Neural Dynamics of Adaptive Sensory-Motor Control. North Holland, Amsterdam.

Hertz J., Krogh A., Palmer R.G. (1991) Introduction to the Theory of Neural Computation. Addison-Wesley, Redwood City

Hildreth E.C., Hollerbach J.M. (1985) The Computational Approach to Vision and Motor Control. AI-Memo 846, Massachusets Inst. of Technology.

Horn (1986) Robot Vision. McGraw-Hill, New York

Kawato M, Furukawa K, Suzuki R (1987) A Hierarchical Neural-Network Model for Control and Learning of Voluntary Movement. Biol Cybern 57:169-185

Kohonen T. (1984) Self-Organization and Associative Memory. Springer Series in Information Sciences 8, Heidelberg.

Kuperstein M. (1987) Adaptive Visual-Motor Coordination in Multijoint Robots using Parallel Architecture. Proc IEEE Int Conf Automat Robotics 1595-1602, Raleigh NC

Martinetz T., Ritter H., Schulten K. (1990) Three-dimensional Neural Net for Learning Visuo-motor-Coordination of a Robot Arm. IEEE-Transactions on Neural Networks, Vol.1, No.1, pp 131-136

Ritter H., Martinetz T., Schulten K. (1991) Neuronale Netze. Addison-Wesley Bonn, 2. erw. Auflage

Rumelhart D.E., McClelland J.L. (1984) Parallel Distributed Processing, Cambridge Massachusets: MIT-Press

Saha A., Keeler J.D. (1990) Algorithms for Better Representation and Faster Learning in Radial Basis Function Networks. In: Advances in Neural Information Processing Systems 2 (D.S. Touretzky ed.) 482-489 (Morgan Kaufman, San Mateo).

Wissensverarbeitung in neuronaler Architektur

G.Palm*, U. Rückert[+], A.Ultsch[+]

*Universität Düsseldorf	[+]Universität Dortmund
Moorenstr. 5	Postfach 500 500
D-4000 Düsseldorf 1	4600 Dortmund 50

Im Rahmen eines vom BMFT geförderten Verbundprojektes "Wissensverarbeitung in neuronaler Architektur" wird die Integration konnektionistischer Modelle mit symbolischer Wissensverarbeitung erforscht. Die anvisierten Bereiche für eine Integration sind: probabilistisches Schließen, die Einbeziehung nichtsymbolischer Wissensquellen (Daten aus physikalischen Prozessen; Meßdaten), eine Überführung gelernten Wissens in symbolische Form (maschinelles Lernen, Regelextraktion) und Information Retrieval.

1. Integration von neuronalen Netzen und K.I.-Systemen

In den letzten Jahren hat die Untersuchung und technische Umsetzung der Informationsverarbeitungs-eigenschaften neuronaler Netze einen enormen Aufschwung erlebt. Neuronale Netze sind für den Biologen Netze von Nervenzellen im Zentralnervensystem der Tiere, die diesen ihr erstaunlich komplexes und dabei zugleich flexibles, anpassungsfähiges Verhalten ermöglichen. Für den Informatiker sind neuronale Netze informationsverarbeitende Systeme aus einer großen Anzahl gleichartiger, relativ einfacher Operatoren, die erst durch ihre Zusammenschaltung zu interessanten, komplexen Gesamtoperationen fähig werden. Diese Operatoren können als Software oder als Hardware implementiert werden. Als Software bieten sie durch ihre Einfachheit und auch durch ihre lokale Adaptivität (vgl. [Palm 82]) die interessante Möglichkeit, neuartige Programmierstile zu entwickeln [Ultsch 91]. Als Hardware bieten sie zusätzlich den Vorteil der Parallelität. Die Organisation eines Verarbeitungsprozesses in neuronaler Hardware er-möglicht Parallelverarbeitung, d.h. gleichzeitiges Arbeiten sämtlicher Operatoren im Netzwerk, und damit eine weit höhere Verarbeitungsgeschwindigkeit [Ramacher/Rückert 90].

Bisher waren neuronale Netze als technische Systeme in relativ 'datennahen' Bereichen der Informa-tionsverarbeitung erfolgreich, also etwa im Bereich der Mustererkennung. Diese Bereiche entsprechen den peripheren Bereichen des menschlichen Nervensystems, etwa der Retina oder der Cochlea, in denen man auch in der Hirnforschung noch relativ leicht den Zusammenhang zwischen den biophysikalischen Eigenschaften einzelner Neurone und der dort wahrscheinlich stattfindenden Informationsverarbeitung herstellen kann.

Auf der anderen Seite, d.h. bei relativ abstrakten Leistungen des menschlichen Gehirns, wie etwa dem Aufstellen und Beweisen mathematischer Sätze, ist eine solche Beziehung zu den Eigenschaften einzel-ner Neurone nicht mehr so direkt herzustellen, und es ist in der Tat fraglich, ob solche Fähigkeiten über-haupt innerhalb des Gehirns genauer lokalisierbar sind, oder ob sie nicht eher als Gesamtleistung fast des ganzen Gehirns verstanden werden müssen. Gerade in diesem Bereich ist das regelbasierte, funk-tionsorientierte Vorgehen der modernen K.I.-Systeme relativ erfolgreich gewesen. Der erfolgreiche Ein-satz von Expertensystemen in den verschiedensten Gebieten wie Diagnose, Konstruktion und Planung zeugt von der Nützlichkeit einer symbolischen Wissensverarbeitung. Gespeichertes Wissen in symbolischer Repräsentation hat den Vorteil, daß es kommunizierbar ist, also schriftlich oder mündlich weitergegeben oder auch erklärt werden kann. Symbolische Wissensverarbeitung ist jedoch problematisch, wenn es um die Verarbeitung von Daten aus wirklichen physikalischen Prozessen geht. Solche Daten liegen oft in der Form von Meßwerten vor, die weit von einer symbolischen Repräsentation entfernt sind [Becks et al. 90].

Konnektionistische Systeme, beziehungsweise neuronale Netze können einen möglichen Brückenschlag zwischen den Rohdaten auf subsymbolischer Ebene und ihrer Verarbeitung in symbolischen Systemen darstellen. Hierzu werden die Rohdaten untersucht und in Gruppen (Cluster) klassifiziert. Die mit neuronalen Netzen gemachten Erfahrungen im Bereich der Clusteranalyse sind durchaus ermutigend. Die Interpretation der vorgenommenen Clusterungen kann zwar durch den Computer unterstützt werden [Ultsch/Siemon 90], liegt aber letztlich beim Anwender. Ein Ziel unserer Arbeit wird es sein, hier Methoden zu entwickeln, die eine Rückführung des im Netz implizit vorhandenen Wissens in eine explizite Regeldarstellung erlauben.

Eine weitere Motivation für den Einsatz neuronaler Netze liegt darin, daß die Erfassung von Eingabedaten verbessert werden kann, da neuronale Netze ohne weiteres mit einer großen Menge von Eingabedaten umgehen, die auch direkt von Sensoren abgeleitet werden können. Sie erlauben nicht nur das Finden und Erkennen von Regelmäßigkeiten in den Eingabedaten [Ultsch/Siemon 89] sondern bieten darüber hinaus noch eine Reihe anderer Vorteile, die klassische Verfahren nicht zeigen: (1) sie sind sehr robust gegenüber "verrauschten" Eingabedaten; (2) das Verfahren eignet sich hervorragend zur Parallelisierung [Siemon/ Ultsch 90, Ernoult 88]; (3) es kann für die Analyse und Einordnung neuer Daten benutzt werden und es hat (4) sehr gute prognostische Eigenschaften. Für Kohonen-Netze wurde dies exemplarisch gezeigt [Ultsch/Siemon 89, Marks/Goser 88].

Weiterhin können auch wirklich alle Inputs (gleichzeitig) Auswirkungen auf den Gesamtprozeß haben. Dies war bei den bisherigen, auf symbolischer Repräsentationsebene arbeitenden Expertensystemen nicht von vornherein gewährleistet. Hinzu kommt, daß eine große Anzahl von Eingabedaten auch die Verarbeitungsgeschwindigkeit dieser Systeme drastisch reduzierte.

Gerade im Bereich der wissensbasierten Verarbeitung ergeben sich jedoch noch weitere Probleme. Wissen in einem Expertensystem beruht auf einer Konzeptualisierung der realen Außenwelt [Genesereth /Nilsson 87] und somit auf einer Vergröberung. Auf der anderen Seite muß man damit rechnen, daß auch die Eingabedaten nicht immer exakt sind. Daher sind in Expertensystemen probabilistische oder vage Schlußfolgerungen letztlich unvermeidlich. Häufig finden sich daher in wirklichen Expertensystemen "ad-hoc"-Realisierungen von Evidenzverrechnungsfunktionen, die oft implementiert wurden, ohne daß ein klar definiertes Evidenzkalkül zugrunde lag. Allgemein kann man sagen, daß die bisher bekannten Kalküle im Bereich des probabilistischen Schließens bei genauer Betrachtung keine zufriedenstellenden Ergebnisse liefern [Puppe 88]. Eine Alternative zu den eingesetzten Kalkülen des unsicheren Schließens bietet der Einsatz von neuronalen Netzen. Es liegt daher nahe, aus "konventionellen" Expertensystemen und neuronalen Netzen hybride Architekturen zu entwickeln, bei denen der Bereich des probabilistischen Schließens durch die neuronalen Netze übernommen wird. Für solche Systeme gibt es bisher allerdings nur erste Ansätze.

Für den Bereich der Prognose (also Zuordnung von neuen Daten zu bestehenden Clustern; Ergänzung von fehlenden oder falschen Daten) gibt es bereits Ansätze zur Kopplung von regelbasierten Systemen mit neuronalen Netzen und dem Abruf des darin enthaltenen Wissens [Ultsch(Hrsg) 90, Marks/Goser 87]. Die Umwandlung von implizitem Wissen in Regeln wurde allerdings noch nicht geleistet. Erste Ansätze auf dem Gebiet der Classifier-Systeme und zugehörigen genetischen Lern-/Suchverfahren sind vorhanden [Forrest 85, Antonisse/ Keller 87]. Allerdings liegen hier noch keine Ergebnisse vor. Hinzu kommt, daß die dort gewählten Anwendungen sehr direkte Entsprechungen haben, so daß fast eine 1:1-Abbildung möglich ist.

Die beiden Zugänge zu den Informationsverarbeitungsleistungen des Gehirns, nämlich die an der neuronalen Struktur orientierte Neuroinformatik, die sozusagen 'von unten', d.h. von der physikalischen Basis der Neurone und Synapsen ausgeht, und die an der kognitiven Funktion orientierte Künstliche Intelligenz, die sozusagen 'von oben', d.h. von den kognitiven Leistungen des Menschen ausgeht, sind also nicht nur im Ansatz komplementär zueinander, sondern sie können sich auch in ihrer technischen Leistungsfähigkeit ideal ergänzen.

Wenn man sich nun mit der Integration von neuronalen Netzen und K.I.-Systemen in ein 'hybrides' Gesamtsystem befassen will, so muß man nicht nur viele Probleme der Definition von Schnittstellen und der Anpassung von Programmierumgebungen lösen, sondern es ist vor allem auch ein tiefgehendes gegenseitiges Verständnis dieser beiden so verschiedenen Denkansätze und Programmierstile zu erreichen. Die theoretischen Grundlagen für eine Integration neuronaler Netze mit symbolischer Wissensverarbeitung im besonderen für die Bereiche probabilistisches Schließen, Einbeziehung nichtsymbolischer Wissensquellen (Daten aus physikalischen Prozessen) und Wissensakquisition (maschinelles Lernen), sollen erarbeitet und in einem Prototyp praktisch erprobt werden. Konkretes Gesamtziel unseres Verbundvorhabens ist also die theoretische Untersuchung und die praktische Konzeption und Implementation eines hybriden Wissensverarbeitungssystems (siehe Abbildung), welches neuronale Netze und klassische K.I.-Komponenten vereinigt.

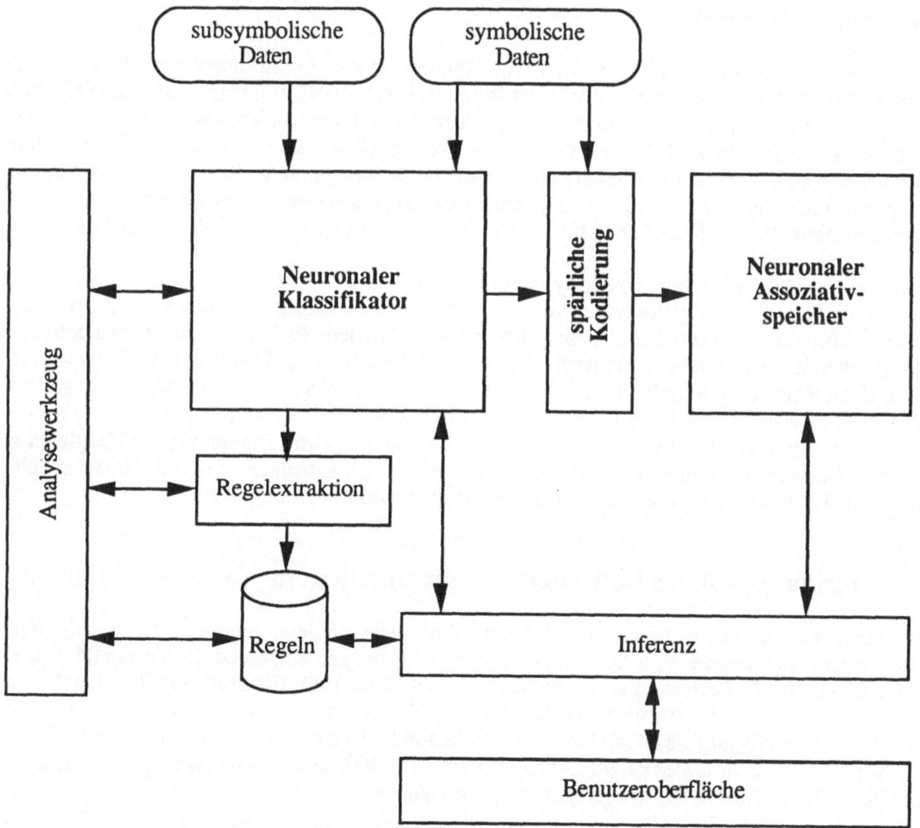

Abb. 1: Hybrides Wissensverarbeitungssystem

2. Übersicht über die Teilbereiche

Im Zentrum unseres Verbundvorhabens steht die Entwicklung eines hybriden Wissensverarbeitungs-systems (siehe Abbildung 1), in dem überwiegend neuronal organisierte Komponenten mit einer klassisch regelbasierten Inferenzkomponente integriert sind. Die Entwicklung eines solchen Systems erscheint uns besonders unter drei Aspekten interessant:

1) Konkrete Realisation eines prototypischen Systems; konkrete Lösung der dabei zu erwartenden Schnittstellenprobleme.

2) Theoretische Untersuchung der Einsatzmöglichkeiten neuronaler Netze in den verschiedenen Teilsystemen.

3) Möglichkeiten einer parallelen Hardware-Implementation von neuronalen Netzwerklösungen für zwei zentrale Teilsysteme (Assoziativspeicher und neuronaler Klassifikator).

Im Einzelnen wollen wir uns mit den folgenden Arbeitsbereichen näher beschäftigen.

2.1 Neuronale Inferenz

Logische Inferenz ist algorithmisch betrachtet eine Verkettung von Abbildungen zwischen Symbol-sequenzen. Dabei wird im allgemeinen jeweils der Wenn-Teil einer Folgerung auf den Dann-Teil abgebildet. Ein Assoziativspeicher (im Modus der Hetero-Assoziation) dient gerade zur Speicherung derartiger Zuordnungen, wobei zusätzlich eine Fehlertoleranz bezüglich der Eingaben besteht. Unser Teilziel besteht darin, eine Softwareschnittstelle herzustellen, die diese Verwendung eines neuronalen Assoziativspeichers zur fehlertoleranten Inferenz ermöglicht. Dies wäre eine direkte softwaretechnische Verbindung zwischen Methoden der Künstlichen Intelligenz und der neuronalen Netze [Ultsch/Panda 91].

Angestrebt ist ferner die Entwicklung einer hybriden Inferenzkomponente für ein Expertensystem, deren unsicheres Schließen auf den Eigenschaften von neuronalen Netzen beruht. Die theoretische Grundlage dieser Inferenzkomponente soll dabei klar ausgearbeitet sein, d.h. dem System soll eine genau definierte Semantik gegeben werden. Ein Forschungsziel dieser Arbeit besteht in der Untersuchung, inwieweit die Ergebnisse klassischer Kalküle (z.B. Bayes, Dempster-Shafer, Fuzzy Set) mit den Entscheidungen von neuronalen Netzen korrelieren. Darüberhinaus muß untersucht werden, wie das neuronale Netz Ungenauigkeiten in den Eingabedaten verarbeiten kann, und wie sich die Ergebnisse im Vergleich zu "klassischen" Auswertungsmethoden verhalten, bei der den Eingabedaten gewisse Unsicherheitsfaktoren (meist als Wahrscheinlichkeiten interpretiert) zugewiesen werden.

2.2 Verwendung subsymbolischer Wissensquellen in Expertensystemen

Von verschiedenen Autoren wurden in den letzten Jahren verschiedene neuronale Netze mit Hebb-artigen Lernregeln als Instrument zur Datenanalyse vorgeschlagen und eingesetzt ([Kohonen 84, Oja 82, Oja 89, Aertsen et al 86, Aertsen et al 87, Palm 90, Ultsch(Hrsg.) 90, Ultsch/Panda 91, Ultsch et al. 91a], sowie viele anwendungsorientierte Artikel in Konferenzbänden der letzten Jahre, wie [Eckmiller/von der Malsburg 88, Anderson 88]). Insbesondere kann man solche Netze zur Clusteranalyse ([Kohonen 84, Ultsch/Siemon 90 , Aertsen/Bonhoeffer 87]) und zur Hauptkomponentenanalyse ([Oja 82, Oja89, Baldi/Hornik 89, Krogh/Hertz 90]) verwenden.

Wir wollen die Effizienz verschiedener vorgeschlagener Netzwerktypen im Hinblick auf die Datenanalyse vergleichen. Hierzu müssen zunächst geeignete Vergleichsmaßstäbe gefunden werden, was gerade im Bereich der Clusteranalyse ein eigenes Forschungsziel darstellt. Es geht hier nicht nur um den rechnerischen Aufwand zur Clusterbildung, sondern zum Beispiel auch um die Form der Darstellung der entstandenen bzw. gefundenen Cluster, d.h. um möglichst strukturerhaltende Projektionen oder Abbildungen in niedrigdimensionale Darstellungsräume - möglichst sogar in 2-dimensionale Bilder (vgl. [Biswas et al 81, Sammon 69, Terekhina 71, Zahn 71]).

Die Leistungsfähigkeit verschiedener Ansätze wird in Computersimulationen an Beispielproblemen untersucht und verglichen. Darüberhinaus sollten die Eigenschaften verschiedener Netzwerkmodelle möglichst auch mathematisch analysiert werden, so daß man zu einem theoretisch fundierten Vergleich kommen kann, wobei natürlich auch gut untersuchte konventionelle Clusteranalyseverfahren (siehe z.B. [Anderberg 73, Fukunaga 72, Jain/Dubes 88], oder auch [McQueen 67, Gordon 81, Sneath/Sokal 73]) zum Vergleich herangezogen werden.

Ziel dieser Untersuchungen ist die Entwicklung einer neuronalen Klassifikationskomponente, die in der Lage ist, strukturelle Eigenschaften einer Datenmenge zu erkennen (Explorative Data Analysis (EDA)) und für die Inferenzkomponente verfügbar zu machen. Die Einbeziehung von nicht-symbolischem Wissen soll durch eine Vorverarbeitung der Daten durch neuronale Netze geleistet werden (z.B. Kohonen-Netze, Back-Propagation-Netze). Ob und wieweit diese Methoden den klassischen Methoden der EDA [Deichsel/Trampisch 85] überlegen sind, ist Gegenstand der Untersuchung. Die Mächtigkeit der verschiedenen Ansätze soll theoretisch untersucht und durch praktische Anwendungen verifiziert werden.

2.3 Überführung gelernten Wissens in symbolische Form (maschinelles Lernen, Regelextraktion).

Die Überführung nicht-symbolischen Wissens in symbolische Form ist bis jetzt für den Bereich der Classifier-Systeme in Verbindung mit genetischen Algorithmen [Antonisse/Keller 87], sowie für regelbasierte Systeme mit Hilfe von Kohonen Netzen [Ultsch 91], vorgeschlagen wurde. Ob dies für andere Formen von gelerntem Wissen auch möglich sein wird, und wenn ja, in welcher Form, soll untersucht werden. Die praktische Bedeutung dieser Frage ist offensichtlich und muß an Hand der ausgewählten praktischen Fälle überprüft werden.

In eigenen Vorarbeiten hat sich gezeigt, daß konnektionistische Modelle in der Lage sind, Meßwerte zu klassifizieren und Regelhaftigkeiten zu erkennen [Marks/Goser 88] [Ultsch/Siemon 90]. Wir werden Methoden entwickeln, diese Regelhaftigkeiten aus den Netzen zu extrahieren und sie als symbolische Regeln einem Expertensystem zur Verfügung zu stellen. Die dabei entwickelten Methoden und Werkzeuge sollen an Hand von konkreten Aufgaben aus der Praxis verifiziert und auf ihre Tauglichkeit hin untersucht werden.

Als ein Endergebnis dieses Projektes streben wir eine hybride Inferenzkomponente eines Expertensystems an, deren unsicheres Schließen auf den Eigenschaften von neuronalen Netzen beruht. Die theoretische Grundlage dieser Inferenzkomponente soll dabei klar ausgearbeitet sein, damit dem System eine klare Semantik gegeben werden kann. Damit soll verhindert werden, daß die Berechnungsergebnisse als "zufällig entstanden" interpretiert werden, wie neuronalen Netzen aufgrund fehlender theoretischer Fundierung von Seiten der Kritiker oft vorgeworfen wird.

2.4 Entwicklung von Methoden und Werkzeugen zur Analyse unüberwachter Lernverfahren

Wie sich in unseren Vorarbeiten gezeigt hat, ist die graphische Aufbereitung und Animation ein wesentliches Hilfsmittel sowohl zum Verständnis der in neuronalen Netzen ablaufenden Prozesse und Algorithmen, als auch bei der Beurteilung der Ergebnisse [Siemon/Ultsch 90]. Die vorhandene Hard- und Software erlaubte es bisher jedoch nur, statische Untersuchungen an größeren neuronalen Netzen mit großem Rechen- und Zeitaufwand vorzunehmen. Dabei hat sich jedoch gezeigt, daß die wichtigen dynamischen Aspekte des Verhaltens neuronaler Netze sich mit geeigneten Methoden, z.B. mit der U-Matrix-Methode [Ultsch/Siemon 90], in einer graphischen Darstellung gut beobachten lassen. Wir erwarten auch, daß sich aus der Beobachtungsmöglichkeit wichtige Rückschlüsse auf die Theorie neuronaler Netze ergeben.

2.5 Spezifikation von Hardwareanforderungen zur Implementation neuronaler Netze

Die für unser Vorhaben interessanten neuronalen Netzwerkmodelle sollen hinsichtlich der geforderten Rechenoperationen und -genauigkeit sowie der Parallelisierbarkeit qualitativ und quantitativ miteinander verglichen werden. Diese Kriterien, zu denen es bisher nur sehr wenige theoretische Betrachtungen gibt, beeinflussen im wesentlichen die Ausgestaltung einer in Betracht kommenden Hardwarerealisierung [Goser et al 89]. Es gilt zu untersuchen, inwieweit sich die verwendeten Modelle bezüglich dieser Kriterien schematisieren lassen. Damit kann eine einheitliche Hardware-Systemarchitektur zur schnellen Implementation vieler, wenn nicht sogar aller vorgeschlagenen Methoden gefunden werden. Diese Architektur sollte dann insbesondere unter zwei Gesichtspunkten ausgearbeitet werden:

1) einfache Skalierbarkeit des Gesamtsystems auf größere Problemdimensionen,

2) funktionelle Beschreibung eines geeigneten elementaren Hardwarebausteins (VLSI) zum Aufbau des Systems.

Die generelle Eignung der entwickelten Architekturkonzepte wird durch eine funktionale Simulation mit einem Architektursimulator nachgewiesen.

2.6 Aufbau eines Testsystems

Die erarbeitete Spezifikation von Hardwareanforderungen soll mit einfachen Mitteln an einem Prototypen erprobt werden. Mit Hilfe von programmierbaren Logik-Bausteinen und/oder modernen RISC-Prozessoren wird ein entsprechendes Testsystem aufgebaut, mit dem Simulationserfahrungen gesammelt werden kann. Ferner kann man die Funktionstüchtigkeit und Anwendbarkeit des Gesamtsystems in Hinblick auf Anwendungen nachweisen. Die Erfahrungen mit dem Prototypen bezüglich dessen Leistungsfähigkeit (gemessen an praktischen und theoretischen Aufgabenstellungen) werden letztlich zur Spezifikation von speziellen VLSI-Bausteinen führen, die einen optimalen Einsatz der entwickelten Lösungen ermöglichen. Diese Bausteine sollen bis zum fertigen Layout entwickelt und simuliert werden, so daß deren Eigenschaften sowie der Herstellungsaufwand hinreichend genau eingeschätzt werden können. Die Fertigung selbst ist aber nicht in unserem Vorhaben vorgesehen.

Diese Arbeiten bauen auf unseren bisherigen Arbeiten zur Implementation eines parallelen assoziativen Netzwerkrechners mit binären Modellneuronen [Erb/Palm 88] [Rückert et al 90] und anwendungsspezifischen integrierten Schaltungen zur parallelen Emulation von neuronalen Netzen auf [Goser et al 89, Rückert 90]. Ein Prototyp paralleler Hardware der mit 64 Kilobit Synapsen pro Neuron ausgestattet ist, wird derzeit bei Prof. Palm in Düsseldorf entwickelt. Dieses System kann mit bis zu Speicherkarten mit je 256 Neuronen bestückt werden. Dafür wurde ein Betriebssystem entworfen, welches mittels des Konzepts virtueller Netze die Grundlage für komplexe Netztopologien und Mehrbenutzerbetrieb bietet.

2.7 Entwurf spärlicher Kodierungen

Die Untersuchungen zur Daten-Strukturanalyse mit neuronalen Netzen unterstützen auf der anderen Seite auch den Entwurf ähnlichkeitserhaltender Kodierungen für Assoziativspeicher. So führt eine Clusteranalyse in natürliche Weise zu einer (u.U. sogar hierarchisch strukturierten) Klassifikation von Mustern in Klassen von jeweils untereinander ähnlichen. Die Zugehörigkeit zu einer dieser Klassen kann als ein Merkmal des Musters aufgefaßt werden. Auf diese Weise wird ein Muster in ähnlichkeitserhaltender Weise in einen spärlichen Merkmalsvektor überführt. Wir haben damit also eine Methode vor uns, die unsere bisherigen Überlegungen zum Entwurf spärlicher, ähnlichkeitserhaltender Kodierungen (vgl. [Palm 87, 88]) ergänzt.

Die Theorie der spärlichen Kodierung beinhaltet unter anderem die für den Einsatz eines assoziativen Speichers wesentliche Frage, inwiefern "Ähnlichkeiten" zwischen zu kodierenden Objekten in einem binären spärlichen Kode repräsentiert werden können. Daraus ergeben sich in natürlicher Weise zwei Fragestellungen:

1. Existieren ähnlichkeitserhaltende Kodes?

2. Wenn ja, welche von diesen Kodes kommen für einen Einsatz in einem assoziativen Speicher in Frage?

Insbesondere arbeiten wir an einer Theorie und Entwurfsstrategieen für spärliche ähnlichkeitserhaltende Kodierungen von möglichst beliebigen endlichen metrischen Räumen. Auch die Untersuchung hierarchisch aufgebauter assoziativer Speichersysteme soll im Rahmen dieses Projektes weitergeführt werden. Diese theoretischen Arbeiten können bei der Konzeption hybrider Systeme mit verschiedenen neuronalen und klassisch/symbolverarbeitenden Komponenten äußerst wichtig werden.

2.8 Assoziatives Information-Retrieval

Information-Retrieval ist die Extraktion von spezifischen Informationen aus einer großen Anzahl von (unformatiert) gespeicherten Informationseinheiten [Ultsch 87]. In diesem Projekt sollen unter anderem die folgenden Teilsysteme aufgebaut werden: neuronaler Klassifikator, spärliche Kodierung und Assoziativspeicher. Diese Teilsysteme sollen zusammen als ein assoziatives Information-Retrieval System verwendet werden.

In einer konkreten Anwendung wird von der Gruppe Palm eine spärliche Kodierung von Sprachdaten (gesprochene Wörter oder Silben) und von geschriebenen Textstücken (symbolische Beschreibungen der Sprachdaten) entworfen und implementiert werden. Hierzu soll eine spärliche Kodierung subsymbolischer Daten (etwa mittels Clusteranalyse) mit einer spärlichen Kodierung symbolischer Information (etwa von alphanumerischen Zeichenfolgen, vgl. [Bentz et al 89]) kombiniert werden. Die in der Gruppe Palm bereits weitgehend fertiggestellte Hardware-Implementation eines großen Assoziativspeichers soll dann zur Speicherung großer Mengen solcher kombinierter Merkmalsvektoren verwendet werden. Dieser Speicher bildet somit das Kernstück eines neuartigen assoziativen Information-Retrieval Systems, das komplexe Datenstrukturen mit subsymbolischen und symbolischen Anteilen verarbeiten kann. Ähnliche Arbeiten werden in der Gruppe Goser/Rückert durchgeführt. Auf der Basis des o.g. Assoziativspeichers in neuronaler Architektur wird hier ein (objektorientiertes) Information-Retrieval System für den VLSI Schaltungsentwurf entwickelt.

3. Nutzungsmöglichkeiten / Anwendungen

Konkrete Nutzungsmöglichkeiten für den neuronalen Assoziativspeicher liegen schon jetzt auf der Hand und sind bereits in anderen Verbundvorhaben gegeben. Ebenso wird das assoziative Information-Retrieval System auf direkte Anwendbarkeit zugeschnitten sein (siehe 2.8).

Ein Anwendungsbereich, in dem in der Gruppe Palm bereits eine große Menge von Daten mit nichttrivialer und schwer erfassbarer Struktur vorliegt, in dem subsymbolische und symbolische Aspekte der Daten stark miteinander verwoben sind, und in dem jetzt noch weit größere Datenmengen erhoben werden sollen, ist die Analyse gesprochener Sprache. Anhand von Spektrogrammen gesprochener Wörter könnte die Performanz verschiedener Methoden zur Datenanalyse getestet und verglichen werden.

Prototypische Anwendungsfälle, die in der Gruppe Ultsch bearbeitet werden sollen, sind Probleme aus der medizinischen Diagnostik (z.B. Pulsdruckmessung), aus der Qualitätssicherung (Maschinenbau), der Prozeßsteuerung und aus dem Umweltbereich (z.B. Abschätzung der Wasserqualität) dienen. Diesen Anwendungsbeispielen gemeinsam ist die Anforderung, sowohl (Experten-) Wissen wie auch Rohdaten aus einem physikalischen Prozeß verarbeiten zu können. Die Anwendungen werden in Zusammenarbeit mit anderen Fachbereichen verschiedener Universitäten und Anwendern aus den Umweltämtern benachbarter Großstädte entwickelt.

Die Entwicklung von paralleler Hardware zur schnellen Implementation neuronaler Netze ist sicherlich zumindest für den Forschungsbereich interessant. Es ist allerdings festzuhalten, daß wir in diesem Teilprojekt nicht eine Fertigung der zu entwickelnden Hardware beabsichtigen, sondern in der Gruppe Goser/Rückert einen durchdachten Chip-Entwurf im Rahmen eines getesteten Gesamtsystems produzieren wollen.

4. Zusammenfassung

Das hier skizzierte Verbundvorhaben *"Wissensverarbeitung in neuronaler Architektur"* zielt auf die Entwicklung eines Wissensverarbeitungssystems in dem Methoden aus dem Bereich der Künstlichen Intelligenz und der Neuroinformatik integriert sind. Es soll u.a. die Verwendung von neuronalen Netzen für die symbolische Wissensverarbeitung erforscht und geeignete Methoden zur Kopplung von neuronalen Netzen mit einer Inferenzkomponente (Expertensystem) entwickelt werden. Weitere Ziele sind die Realisierung von Werkzeugen zur Analyse des Verhaltens der verwendeten neuronale Netze und die Rückführung nicht-symbolischen Wissens aus neuronalen Netzen in eine symbolische Form.

Die theoretischen Grundlagen für eine Integration konnektionistischer Modelle mit symbolischer Wissensverarbeitung im besonderen für die Bereiche probabilistisches Schließen, Einbeziehung nicht-symbolischer Wissensquellen (Daten aus physikalischen Prozessen) und Wissensakquisition (maschinelles Lernen), sollen erarbeitet und in einem Prototyp praktisch erprobt werden.

Literatur

[Aertsen et al 86]   Aertsen, A; Gerstein, G; Johannesma, P: From neuron to assembly: neuronal organization and stimulus representation. In: Palm, G; Aertsen, A (eds.): Brain Theory: pp. 7-24. Springer, Berlin 1986

[Aertsen et al 87]   Aertsen, A; Bonhoeffer, T; Krueger, J: Coherent activity in neuronal populations: analyis and interpretation. In: Caianiello, E.R. (ed.): Physics of cognitive processes. World Scientific Publishing, Singapore 1987

[Anderberg 73]   Anderberg, M.R: Cluster analysis for applications. Academic Press, New York 1973

[Anderson 88]   Anderson, D.Z. (ed.): Neural information processing systems. Am. Inst. Phys., New York 1988

[Antonisse/Keller 87] Antonisse, H.J., Keller, K.S.: Genetic Operators for High-Level Knowledge Representation, Proc 2nd Intern. Conf. on Genetic Algor., 1987, pp.69-76

[Baldi/Hornik 89]   Baldi, P; Hornik, K: Neural networks and principal component analysis: learning from examples without local minima. Neural Networks 2: 53-58, 1989

[Becks et al. 90]   Becks, K.H, Cremers, A.B., Hemker, A., Ultsch, A.: Parallel Process Interfaces to Knowledge Systems, Proc. ICNC, Düsseldorf 1990, pp 465 - 470.

[Bentz et al 89]   Bentz, H.J; Hagstroem, M; Palm, G: Information storage and effective data retrieval in sparse matrices. Neural Networks 2: 289-293, 1989

[Biswas et al 81]   Biswas, G; Jain, A.K; Dubes, RC: Evaluation of projection algorithms. IEEE Trans. Pattern Anal. Machine Intell. PAMI-3: 701-708, 1981

[Deichsel/Trampisch 85]   Deichsel, G, Trampisch, H.J.: Clusteranalyse und Diskriminanzanalyse G.Fischer Verlag, Stuttgart, 1985

[Eckmiller/v.d. Malsburg 88] Eckmiller, R; v.d. Malsburg, C: Neural computers. Springer-Verlag, Berlin 1988

[Erb/Palm 1988]   Erb, M; Palm, G.: Lernen und Informations- speicherung in neuronalen Netzen. In: Digitale Speicher, ITG-Fachbericht 102, (W. Hilberg, ed.) VDE-Verlag GmbH, Berlin, Offenbach, 1988

[Ernoult 88]   Ernoult, C.: Performance of Backpropagation on a Parallel Transputer-Based Machine Proc. Neuro-Nimes 88,Nimes, France, pp.311-324

[Forrest 85]   Forrest, S.: Implementing Semantic Network Structures Using the Classifier System Proc. Int. GA Conf, pp.24-44, 1985

[Fukunaga 72]   Fukunaga, K: Introduction to statistical pattern recognition. Academic Press, New York 1972

[Genesereth/Nilsson 87] Genesereth, M, Nilsson N.: Logical Foundations of Artificial Intelligence, Morgan Kaufmann 1987

[Gordon 81]   Gordon, A.D: Classification. Chapman & Hall Ltd., London 1981

[Goser et al 89]   Goser, K., U. Hilleringmann, Rückert, U., K. Schumacher: "VLSI Technologies for Artificial Neural Networks", IEEE-Micro, Dec. 1989, pp. 28-44.

[Jain/Dubes 88]   Jain, A.K; Dubes, R.C: Algorithms for clustering data. Prentice Hall, Englewood Cliffs, New Jersey, 1988

[Kohonen 84]   Kohonen, T: Self-organization and associative memory. Springer Series in Information Sciences 8, Heidelberg 1984

[Krogh/Hertz 90]   Krogh, A; Hertz, J.A: Hebbian learning of principal components. In: Eckmiller, R; Hartmann, G; Hauske, G (eds.): Parallel processing in neural systems and computers. Elsevier Science Publishers B.V., North-Holland 1990

[Marks/Goser 87] Marks, K.M., Goser, K.F.: AI Concepts for VLSI Process Modelling and Monitoring Proc. Comp. Euro. 87, pp. 474-477, IEEE, 1987

[Marks/Goser 88] Marks, K.M., Goser, K.F.: Analysis of VLSI Process Data Based on Self-organizing Feature Maps Proc. Neuro-Nimes 88,Nimes, France, pp. 337-348

[McQueen 67]   McQueen, J: Some methods for classification and analysis of multivariate observations. Proc. 5th Berkeley Symp. Math. Stat. Prob. 281, 1967

[Oja 82]   Oja, E: A simplifies neuron model as a principal component analyser. J. Math. Biol. 15: 267-273, 1982

[Oja 89]   Oja, E: Neural netwoks: principal components, and subspaces. Int. J. Neural Systems 1: 61-68, 1989

[Palm 82]   Palm, G.: Neural Assemblies. An Alternative Approach to Artificial Intelligence. Springer-Verlag, Berlin, Heidelberg, New York, 1982

[Palm 87]   Palm, G.: Computing with Neural Networks. Science 235, 1227-1228, 1987

[Palm 88]   Palm, G.: Assoziatives Gedächtnis und Gehirntheorie. Spektrum der Wissenschaft, 54-64, Juni 1988

[Palm 90]   Palm, G.: Local Rules for Synaptic Modification in Neural Networks. In: Computational Neuroscience (E.L. Schwartz ed.). MIT-Press, Cambridge, London, 1990

[Puppe 88]   Puppe, F.: Einführung in Expertensysteme, Springer Berlin 1988

[Ramacher/Rückert 90] Ramacher,U; Rückert, U. (eds.) : "VLSI Design of Neural Networks", Kluwer Academic, 1990.

[Rückert et al 90] Rückert, U., Ch. Kleerbaum, Goser, K.: "Digital VLSI Implementation of an Associative Memory based on Neural Networks", Proceedings of the International Workshop on VLSI for Artificial Intelligence and Neural Networks, September 5-7, 1990, Oxford University.

[Rückert 90]   Rückert, U. : "VLSI Implementation of an Associative Memory based on Distributed Storage of Information", Proceedings of the ERASIP Workshop on Neural Networks, Portugal 1990, Springer Verlag, Lecture Notes in Computer Science, 1990, pp. 267-276.

[Sammon 69]   Sammon, J.W. jr.: A nonlinear mapping for data structure analysis. IEEE Trans. Computers C-18: 401-409, 1969

[Siemon/Ultsch 90] Siemon H.P., Ultsch A.: Kohonen Networks on Transputers: Implementation and Animation Accepted paper INNC 1990.

[Sneath/Sokal 73] Sneath, P.H.A; Sokal, R.R: Numerical taxonomy. W.H. Freedman and Company Publishers, San Francisco 1973

[Terekhina 71]   Terekhina, A.Y: Methods of multidimensional data scaling and visualization (survey). Avtom. Telemekh. 7: 80-94, 1971

[Ultsch 87]   Ultsch, A.: Control for Knowledge based Information Retrieval, Verlag der Fachferine, Zürich 1987.

[Ultsch 91]   Ultsch, A.: Konnektionistische Modelle und ihre Integration mit wissensbasierten Systemen, Habilitationsschrift, Univ.Dortmund, 1991.

[Ultsch(Hrsg.) 90] Ultsch, A. (Hrsg.): Kopplung deklarativer und konnektionistischer Wissensrepräsentation, Forschungsbericht Nr. 352, Institut für Informatik, Universität Dortmund, April 1990

[Ultsch et al 91] Ultsch A., et al.: Optimizing Logical Proofs with Connectionist Networcs, Intl. Conf. Artificial Neural Networks, Helsinki , Juni 1991

518

[Ultsch et al. 91a] Ultsch, A., Halmans, G., Mantyk, R.: CONCAT: A Connectionist Knowledge Ackquisition Tool, Proc. IEEE International Conference on System Sciences, January 9-11, Hawaii, 1991, pp 507 - 513.

[Ultsch/Siemon 89] Ultsch, A., Siemon, H.P.: Exploratory Data Analysis: Using Kohonen Net-works on Transputers Forschungsbericht Nr. 329, Universität Dortmund 1989.

[Ultsch/Siemon 90] Ultsch, A., Siemon, H.P.: Kohonen's Self Organizing Feature Maps for Exploratory Data Analysis, Proc. Intern. Neural Networks, Kluwer Academic Press, Paris, 1990, pp 305 - 308

[Utsch/Panda 91] Ultsch, A., Panda, PG.: Die Kopplung konnektionistischer Modelle mit wissensbasierten Systemen, Tagungsband Expertenystemtage Dortmund, Februar 1991.

[Zahn 71] Zahn, C.T: Graph-theoretical methods for detecting and describing Gestalt clusters. IEEE Trans. Computers C-20: 68-86, 1971

Bilderkennung mit dynamischen Neuronennetzen [*]

C. von der Malsburg   R. P. Würtz   J. C. Vorbrüggen

Institut für Neuroinformatik
Ruhr-Universität Bochum
D-4630 Bochum

Es wird ein Objekterkennungssystem beschrieben, um damit die Fähigkeiten der Dynamic Link Architecture zu illustrieren. Bei dieser handelt es sich um ein neues System für neuronales Rechnen. Objekte werden durch dünne Graphen repräsentiert. Die Knoten der Graphen werden mit lokalen Leistungsspektren (Morlet Jets) etikettiert, die Kanten mit Abstandsvektoren. Objekte werden durch Graphenvergleich erkannt. Die Ähnlichkeit zwischen Objektgraphen und Bildgraphen wird durch einen Diffusionsprozeß in der Bildebene optimiert, wobei gleichzeitig die einzelnen Jet-Ähnlichkeiten maximiert und die metrische Graphenverzerrung minimiert werden. Wir haben das System auf einem Transputernetzwerk implementiert, um seine Parallelisierbarkeit zu demonstrieren. Es ist sehr erfolgreich im Erkennen von menschlichen Gesichtern anhand von frei aufgenommenen Kamerabildern.

1   Einleitung

Die Aufgabe, ein bekanntes Gesicht in einer belebten Straße wiederzuerkennen, fällt einem Menschen sehr leicht. Versucht man, diese Leistung auf einem mit Videokamera ausgestatteten Computer zu simulieren, zeigt sich, wie schwierig sie in Wirklichkeit ist. Ein verwandtes Problem von hoher industrieller Bedeutung ist das Erkennen von Werkstücken unabhängig von ihrer räumlichen Lage und Beleuchtung. Beide Aufgaben sind Beispiele für invariante Objekterkennung.

Seit der Entwicklung von leistungsfähigen Computern wird daran gearbeitet, Objekterkennungssysteme zu implementieren. Neuerdings werden hohe Erwartungen in Verfahren gesetzt, die unter dem Namen „Neuronale Netzwerke" zusammengefaßt werden. Unter den derzeit erfolgreichsten sind mehrschichtige Strukturen von Einheiten, die verschiedene Grade von Aktivität besitzen und damit die Aktivitäten von anderen, mit ihnen verbundenen, kontrollieren. Information wird in den Stärken der einzelnen Verbindungen durch einen Lernalgorithmus (z.B. „Backpropagation of errors") gespeichert. Nach der (langen) Lernphase sind diese Netzwerke in der Lage, diese Information mit einem relativ hohen Grad von Flexibilität zu verwenden.

Die Verwendbarkeit dieser Art von Netzwerken für Bildverarbeitung und Objekterkennung erscheint durch folgendes Problem eingeschränkt. Visuelle Information muß auf verschiedenen Komplexitätsebenen verarbeitet werden. Auf der niedrigsten Ebene sind z.B. Helligkeitsgradienten auszuwerten, auf einer höheren Grundformen wie Geraden, Kreise, Ellipsen usw. Es folgen Objekte wie Gesichter, Telefone, Bücher, Bäume. Solche Objekte kombinieren sich zu Szenen, und genaugenommen zeigt jedes Grauwertbild eine solche Szene.

---

[*]Diese Arbeiten wurden vom BMFT (ITR-8800-H1), der AFOSR (88-0274), und dem Stimulus Programm der EG (BRAIN) gefördert. Der Text wurde in leicht abgewandelter Form als Abschlußbericht für den BMFT veröffentlicht.

Es ist klar, daß beim Übergang von jeder Stufe zur nächsten ungeheure Kombinationsmöglichkeiten bestehen, so daß es undenkbar scheint, für jedes Objekt und erst recht für jede Szene ein Neuron bereitzustellen, das für das Vorhandensein dieses Objekts im Bild kodiert (Kombinatorische Explosion). Ein möglicher Ausweg besteht darin, daß nicht einzelne Neuronen, sondern das Zusammenwirken eines ganzen Ensembles ein Objekt beschreibt. In diesem Fall muß allerdings darüber nachgedacht werden, wie diese Ensembles eigentlich ihre Zusammengehörigkeit bzw. ihre gegenwärtige Trennung zum Ausdruck bringen können (binding problem). In dem einfachen Bild, wo es nur Aktivitäten und Verbindungsstärken gibt, ist das nicht möglich.

Um diesen Mangel zu beheben, wurde von C. von der Malsburg vorgeschlagen, nicht nur Aktivitäten und Verbindungsstärken der Neuronen sondern auch die feine Zeitstruktur der sich ausbreitenden Signale für die Informationsverarbeitung nutzbar zu machen [11]. Für Netzwerke, die dies tun, wurde der Begriff „Dynamic Link Architecture" geprägt. Es wäre z.B. denkbar, daß verschiedene Neuronenensembles auf verschiedenen „Trägerfrequenzen" kommunizieren und sich somit nicht stören. Auch übereinstimmende Phasen der Aktivitätsmuster kommen für eine solche Kommunikation in Frage. Neuerdings gibt es experimentelle Indizien, daß solche synchronen Ensembles im visuellen Cortex tatsächlich Informationen höherer Ordnung kodieren [5]. Wie solche Systeme Objekterkennung betreiben können, ist in [12,1] beschrieben.

Um solche Prinzipien technisch nutzen zu können, muß Hardware gebaut werden, in die deren Eigenschaften direkt eingebaut sind. Dies ist in der Entwicklungsphase natürlich nicht möglich, daher müssen die zu untersuchenden Systeme auf Digitalrechnern simuliert werden, was wegen der hohen Dimensionalität der sie beschreibenden Differentialgleichungen sehr aufwendig ist.

Um dennoch die Fähigkeit zur invarianten Objekterkennung zu demonstrieren, haben wir das System soweit vereinfacht, daß die Neuronen zu Ecken, die (zeitlich kodierte) Zusammengehörigkeit zu Kanten in einem Graphen werden. Damit läßt sich das Problem in einen Vergleich von Graphen umformulieren und in dieser Form lösen. Die Einzelheiten werden im folgenden beschrieben. Selbst in dieser vereinfachten Form ist das Verfahren jedoch noch so rechenaufwendig, daß wir einen leistungsfähigen Parallelrechner (Transputersystem) zu seiner Lösung eingesetzt haben.

2 Unser Erkennungssystem

Um die Möglichkeiten, die die Dynamic Link Architecture bietet, an einem realistischen Problem zu demonstrieren, haben wir Grauwertbilder als Eingabedaten gewählt, die mit einer Videokamera aufgenommen wurden. Das System ist nicht auf eine bestimmte Objektklasse beschränkt, aber wir benutzen es, um menschliche Gesichter anhand von Portraitaufnahmen wiederzuerkennen. Aus der einleitenden Beschreibung der Architektur ist klar geworden, daß eine Implementierung im Stil eines neuronalen Netzwerkes mit zeitlich kodierten Bindungen eine sehr große Rechenleistung erfordern würde. Aus diesem Grund haben wir diese Bindungen nicht simuliert sondern durch Kanten eines Graphen ersetzt. Die Ablaufsteuerung erfolgt in der konventionellen Form eines sequentiellen Programmes.

2.1 Eckenbewertung

Die Ecken unseres Graphen sind einfach Punkte in der zweidimensionalen Bildebene. Sie werden mit Vektoren von 40 positiven reellen Zahlen bewertet. Die Bildinformation ist in diesen Vektoren verschlüsselt.

Ein Grauwertgebirge und seine Fouriertransformation kann man als zwei extreme Möglichkeiten betrachten, ein Bild darzustellen. Im ersten Fall wird das Bild durch eine Familie von δ-Funktionen analysiert, im zweiten durch komplexwertige Exponentialfunktionen. Das Grauwertgebirge ist sicherlich keine gute Basis für Objekterkennung, da schon sehr kleine Änderungen in der Position die

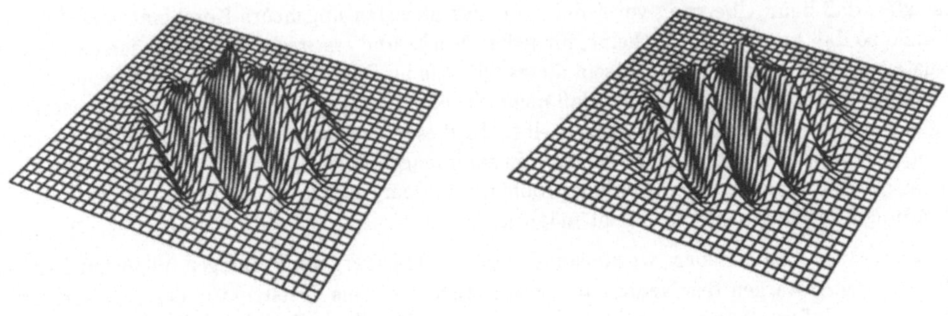

Abbildung 1: Zweidimensionale Wavelets. Die linke Seite zeigt den Realteil (Cosinusphase) für $|\vec{k}| = 0.72$, $\phi = 45°$, die rechte den Imaginärteil (Sinusphase). Alle Kerne sehen genau gleich aus, bis auf Ausdehnung und Richtung. Ein Quadrätchen steht für 4 × 4 Bildpunkte.

Grauwerte der einzelnen Bildpunkte sehr stark verändern. Auch das hochfrequente Rauschen der Videokamera stört sie merklich.

Die Fouriertransformation des Bildes kann in natürlicher Weise zu Invarianz gegen Positionsänderungen führen. Der Absolutbetrag der (komplexwertigen) Transformation enthält keinerlei Informationen über die Position mehr, er stellt eine translationsinvariante Bildbeschreibung dar. Überraschenderweise bietet er sogar eine brauchbare Darstellung in dem Sinne, daß die Bildinformation (bis auf absolute Position und Drehung um 180°) daraus zurückgewonnen werden kann [6]. Es ist jedoch unklar, ob man auf analoge Weise Bildbeschreibungen mit mehr Invarianzen erhalten kann. Ein großer Nachteil der Bildbeschreibung durch die Fouriertransformation besteht darin, daß alle Werte durch alle Grauwerte beeinflußt werden, d.h. bei einer Änderung in einem kleinen Bildausschnitt ändern sie sich alle.

Es ist also wünschenswert, einen Kompromiß zwischen den beiden Extremen zu haben, d.h. eine Familie von Funktionen, die sowohl im Orts- als auch im Frequenzbereich lokalisiert und geeignet sind, Signale oder Bilder zu analysieren. In den vergangenen Jahren ist ein relativ großer Forschungsaufwand getrieben worden, solche Familien zu finden und ihre Eigenschaften zu verstehen. Die Definition einer solchen „Wavelet-Familie" fordert, daß all ihre Mitglieder aus einer einzelnen Funktion (*analyzing wavelet*) durch Translation, Skalierung und Rotation entstehen. Die zweite Forderung ist, daß das Integral des analysierenden (und damit aller) Wavelets verschwindet (*Zulässigkeit*). S. Mallat [9] beschrieb eine Waveletfamilie, die eine Orthonormalbasis des $\mathcal{L}^2(\mathbf{R}^2)$ bildet, und fand eine sehr elegante und effiziente Art, die zugehörige Transformation numerisch zu berechnen.

Eine solche Orthonormalbasis hat den Vorteil, daß weder Bildinformation verlorengeht noch Redundanz eingeführt wird und somit das Bild immer praktisch exakt aus seiner Transformation rekonstruiert werden kann. Andererseits ist Orthogonalität zusammen mit Lokalisierung in Orts- und Frequenzraum eine sehr starke Forderung, die leider zur Folge hat, daß diese Wavelets für unsere Zwecke zu unflexibel sind. Wir haben gefunden, daß eine sog. *stetige Wavelettransformation* sehr viel besser geeignet ist. Sie unterscheidet sich von einer orthogonalen insofern, daß die Gruppe, die die Familie erzeugt, kontinuierlich ist. R. Murenzi [10] hat gezeigt, daß die die Gruppe $IG(2)$ der Translationen, Dilatationen und Rotationen in der Bildebene geeignet ist. Natürlich muß sich auch die Computerimplementierung einer „stetigen" Transformation auf eine endliche Zahl von Punkten beschränken.

Die Möglichkeit gleichzeitiger Lokalisierung in Orts- und Frequenzraum ist durch eine Ungleichung beschränkt, die in der Physik unter dem Namen „Heisenbergsche Unschärferelation" bekannt ist. Um wenigstens das Optimum zu erreichen, das diese Ungleichung zuläßt, muß man als analysierendes Wavelet einen Fourierkern (komplexe Exponentialfunktion) wählen, der mit einer Gaußglocke moduliert ist [4]. Nach dem Entdecker dieser Tatsache heißen solche Funktionen *Gaborfunktionen*. Wendet man darauf die Gruppe $IG(2)$ an, erhält man eine Waveletfamilie, die unter dem Namen *Morlet Wavelets* bekannt ist:

$$\psi_{\vec{k}}(\vec{x}) := n_{k,\sigma} \exp\left(-\frac{\vec{k}^2\vec{x}^2}{2\sigma^2}\right) \exp\left(i\vec{k}\vec{x}\right) \tag{1}$$

In dieser Form erfüllen die Wavelets die Zulässigkeitsbedingung nicht ganz exakt, aber die Abweichung ist für hinreichend großes σ vernachlässigbar. Die zugehörige stetige Wavelettransformation $\mathcal{W}$ des Bildes I ist nun definiert als das Skalarprodukt mit dieser Familie:

$$(\mathcal{W}I)\left(\vec{k},\vec{x_0}\right) := \left\langle \psi_{\vec{k}}(\vec{x}-\vec{x_0}),\, I(\vec{x}) \right\rangle = \int \overline{\psi_{\vec{k}}(\vec{x}-\vec{x_0})}\, I(\vec{x})\, d^2x\ . \tag{2}$$

Zur effizienten numerischen Berechnung kann Gleichung (2) als Faltungsprodukt geschrieben werden:

$$(\mathcal{W}I)\left(\vec{k},\vec{x_0}\right) = \psi_{\vec{k}}(\vec{x}) * I(\vec{x}) = \mathcal{F}^{-1}\left(\mathcal{F}\psi_{\vec{k}} \cdot \mathcal{F}I\right) \tag{3}$$

Die Fouriertransformierte $\mathcal{F}\psi_{\vec{k}}$ der Morletkerne ist einfach eine Gaußglocke, die in der charakteristischen Frequenz $\vec{k}$ zentriert ist (s. (4)). Sie ist reellwertig, wodurch die Faltung mit einem Kern sich auf zwei reelle Multiplikationen pro Bildpunkt gefolgt von einer inversen schnellen Fouriertransformation (FFT) reduziert. Die Vorwärts-FFT der Bilddaten muß nur einmal durchgeführt werden und hat somit auf die Rechenzeit der Gesamttransformation nur geringen Einfluß.

$$\left(\mathcal{F}\psi_{\vec{k}}\right)(\vec{\omega}) = m_{k,\sigma} \exp\left(-\frac{\sigma^2\left(\vec{\omega}-\vec{k}\right)^2}{2k^2}\right) \tag{4}$$

Die Formel (4) kann auch dahingehend interpretiert werden, daß die Wavelets einen Satz von Bandpaßfiltern bilden. Wenn sie den Frequenzraum dicht genug überdecken, kann man erwarten, daß eine exakte Rekonstruktion des Bildes aus der Transformation möglich ist.

Die Wahl der Normierungsfaktoren in (1) ist von großer Bedeutung. Gewöhnlich wird gefordert, daß das Quadratintegral (Energie) in jedem Kern gleich ist. Wir haben statt dessen die Vorfaktoren in (4) $m_{k,\sigma} = 1$ gewählt (die $n_{k,\sigma}$ ergeben sich daraus). Dies bedeutet, daß die Energie eines Kerns proportional zu $|\vec{k}^2|$ ist. Nach einer Arbeit von D. Field [3] nimmt in „natürlichen Bildern" die Energie pro Frequenzband wie $1/|\vec{k}^2|$ ab. Unsere Bilder zeigen ein ähnliches Verhalten [8]. Mit dieser Normierung tragen nun alle Frequenzbänder ungefähr gleich viel Energie zur Transformation bei, eine Eigenschaft, die sich als wichtig für die Erkennung herausgestellt hat.

Wir haben nun an jedem Bildpunkt x_0 eine Funktion von $\vec{k}$, die die Grauwertverteilung in der Umgebung des Punktes beschreibt. In [2] wurde demonstriert, daß die Grauwertverteilung mit annehmbarer Qualität aus dieser Funktion zurückgewonnen werden kann.

Um aus der Wavelettransformation eine geeignete Eckenbewertung für unsere Graphen zu erhalten, mußten wir noch folgendes Problem lösen: Morlet Wavelets reagieren sehr stark auf scharfe Kanten im Bild, die senkrecht zu ihrem Wellenvektor $\vec{k}$ liegen. An einer solchen Kante oszillieren aber Real- und Imaginärteil mit der charakteristischen Frequenz, anstatt ein glattes Maximum anzunehmen, das man in einem ähnlichen Bild leicht wiederfinden könnte. Aus diesem Grund wählten wir statt der Transformationswerte selber ihre Absolutbeträge, die das gewünschte Verhalten zeigen. Die entstehenden Vektoren nennen wir *Jets*:

$$\mathcal{J}I\left(\vec{k},\vec{x_0}\right) := |\mathcal{W}I|\ . \tag{5}$$

Mit diesen Jets werden die Ecken mit Koordinaten $\vec{x}_0$ unserer Graphen bewertet. Leider sind sie keine lineare Funktion des Bildes mehr, was ihre theoretische Behandlung erschwert.

 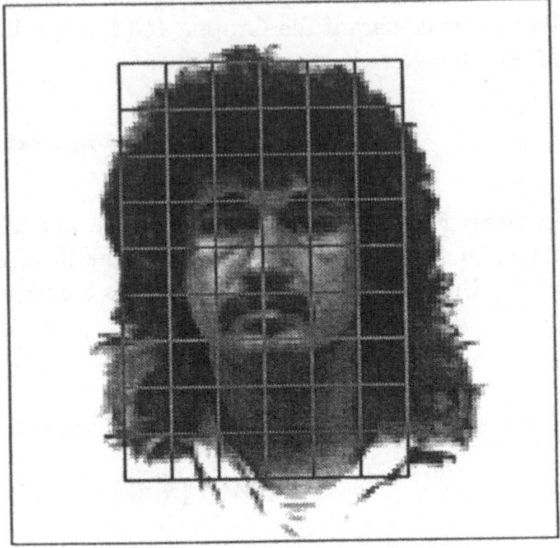

Abbildung 2: *Rechts*: Beispiel eines gespeicherten Objekts, dargestellt durch ein Rechteckgitter. Die Ecken sind mit Jets bewertet. Unter dem Graphen liegt das zugehörige Grauwertbild. *Links*: Dieses Bild wurde dem System angeboten. Der Graphenvergleich wurde mit einem unverzerrten Duplikat des Rechteckgitters initialisiert, das zunächst durch eine Reihe von „globalen Bewegungen" auf dem Gesicht zentriert wurde. Danach wurden die Ecken des Graphen mit einem Diffusionsverfahren ausgelenkt, um besser passende Jets zu finden. Der abgebildete Graph ist der nach Konvergenz resultierende mit $C_{total} = -57.7$ (das mögliche Optimum ist -70.0)

Bei der Implementierung der Erkennung wählten wir folgende Parameter: Für σ hat sich ein Wert von 2π als optimal herausgestellt. Der Frequenzraum wird in Polarkoordinaten diskretisiert:

$$\vec{k} = (k, \phi); \quad \phi \in \left\{ \frac{\mu\pi}{8} \mid \mu = 0, 1, \ldots, 7 \right\}, \quad k \in \left\{ \pi\sqrt{2}^{-\mu} \mid \mu = 2, 3, \ldots, 6 \right\}. \tag{6}$$

Die oben beschriebenen Vorverarbeitungsschritte führen dazu, daß die Vergleichsfunktion für Eckenbewertungen sehr einfach sein kann. Wir ignorieren die Tatsache, daß die Jets Funktionen auf dem zweidimensionalen Frequenzraum sind und betrachten sie einfach als Vektoren in einem Euklidischen Raum, dessen Dimension durch die Diskretisierung vorgegeben ist. Als Vergleichsfunktion der Eckenbewertungen benutzen wir den Cosinus des Winkels zwischen solchen Vektoren (mit einem negativen Vorzeichen, um zu erreichen, daß sie für gleiche Vektoren minimal ist).

$$S_v\left(\mathcal{J}^I, \mathcal{J}^O\right) := -\frac{\mathcal{J}^I \cdot \mathcal{J}^O}{\|\mathcal{J}^I\| \, \|\mathcal{J}^O\|}. \tag{7}$$

2.2 Kantenbewertung

Die oben beschriebenen Eckenbewertungen reichen schon aus, um ein Bild zu beschreiben. Benützt man jedoch keine zusätzliche Information, so kann der Graphenvergleich zu einem Problem hoher Komplexität werden, weil zuviele Kombinationen von Punkten ausprobiert werden müssen. Aus diesem Grund bewerten wir die Kanten unserer Graphen mit einem geometrischen Maß. Dadurch wird erreicht, daß zwischen zwei ähnlichen Graphen durchaus lokale Verzerrungen vorkommen können, aber keine beliebigen Permutationen von Punkten. Bei einer geplanten Erweiterung des Systems auf

Szenenerkennung wird sich diese geometrische Einschränkung ändern müssen, da dann die räumliche Konstellation der Einzelobjekte durchaus verschieden sein kann.

Es hat sich als brauchbar erwiesen, die Kanten $(i,j) \in E$ mit dem Abstandsvektor der beiden Punkte zu bewerten, die sie verbinden:

$$\vec{\Delta}_{(i,j)} := \vec{x_j} - \vec{x_i} \tag{8}$$

Die Vergleichsfunktion für diese Bewertung ist wie folgt:

$$S_e\left(\vec{\Delta}^I, \vec{\Delta}^O\right) := \left(\vec{\Delta}^I - \vec{\Delta}^O\right)^2 \tag{9}$$

2.3 Graphenvergleich

Die oben beschriebenen Vergleichsfunktionen für Ecken- bzw. Kantenbewertungen werden über den ganzen Graphen addiert und dann linear zu einer Kostenfunktion kombiniert, die den Unterschied zwischen dem gespeicherten Objekt und dem Bildgraphen beschreibt.

$$C_{total} := \lambda C_{top} + C_{jet} = \lambda \sum_{(i,j)\in E} S_e\left(\vec{\Delta}^I_{(i,j)}, \vec{\Delta}^O_{(i,j)}\right) + \sum_{i\in V} S_v\left(J^I_i, J^O_i\right) \tag{10}$$

Der Vorfaktor λ dient dazu, die geometrische Randbedingung mehr oder weniger stark zu erzwingen. Er kann sich während des Erkennungsprozesses dynamisch ändern, was wir benötigen werden, um die translationsinvariante Erkennung stark zu beschleunigen.

2.4 Graphendynamik

Die Kostenfunktion C_{total} kann als Funktion auf der Menge aller möglichen Bildgraphen für ein angebotenes Bild betrachtet werden. Ihr Infimum ist dann ein Maß für die Abweichung des gespeicherten Objektgraphen von dem präsentierten Bild. Dieses Infimum kann mit einer geeigneten Optimierungsverfahren näherungsweise berechnet werden.

Wir betreiben diese Optimierung folgendermaßen. Die Objektgraphen sind quadratische Gitter mit 7×10 Punkten, die horizontal und vertikal einen Abstand von 11 Bildpunkten haben. Die bearbeiteten Bilder sind 128×128 Bildpunkte groß.

Zunächst wird der Objektgraph unverzerrt an eine geeignete Stelle der Bildebene kopiert und seine Ecken mit den dort vorgefundenen Jets bewertet. Für dieses Paar von Objekt- und Bildgraphen wird C_{total} berechnet. Danach wird ein zufällig ausgewählter Punkt des Bildgraphen um einen ebenfalls zufälligen Vektor ausgelenkt. Für den so veränderten Graphen wird der Wert von C_{total} neu berechnet. Ist er kleiner als der vorhergehende, wird der neue Punkt beibehalten, andernfalls der alte. Dieses Verfahren wird bis zur Erfüllung eines Konvergenzkriteriums wiederholt. Es besteht darin, daß eine bestimmte Anzahl von Auslenkungsversuchen nicht zu einer Verbesserung geführt hat. Wenn man diese Höchstzahl mit 100 festlegt, ergibt sich ein guter Kompromiß zwischen Zuverlässigkeit und Geschwindigkeit. Ein Beispiel für einen resultierenden Graphen zeigt Abbildung 2.

Das eben beschriebene Verfahren ist ein Spezialfall von „Simulated Annealing". Da sich unsere Kostenfunktion in der Nähe des Optimums als glatt herausgestellt hat, reicht es hin, nur Punkte zu akzeptieren, die wirklich zu einer Verbesserung führen (Temperatur null). In anderen Fällen müssen auch Verschlechterungen mit einer gewissen Wahrscheinlichkeit akzeptiert werden, was natürlich zu höheren Rechenzeiten führt.

Das Funktionieren dieses Verfahrens hängt allerdings sehr stark von einer geeigneten Auswahl des Anfangsgraphen ab. Ist dieser nicht auf dem Objekt positioniert, so müßte das Verfahren den Graphen über eine große Strecke bewegen. Dabei würde es mit hoher Wahrscheinlichkeit in einem lokalen Minimum hängenbleiben, da immer nur ein Punkt geändert werden kann und dies in der Regel den

Beitrag des Geometrieterms verschlechtert. Daher führen wir vor dem oben beschriebenen Verfahren ein ganz ähnliches zur Initialisierung durch. Statt einzelne Punkte zu bewegen, wird ein Auslenkungsvektor gewürfelt und dann der ganze Graph um diesen Betrag verschoben. Danach wird C_{total} erneut berechnet und die Verschiebung beibehalten, falls eine Verbesserung eingetreten ist. Wenn der Hintergrund des Bildes einigermaßen gleichmäßig ist, funktioniert diese Initialisierung hervorragend. Die zugrundeliegenden „Kostenoberflächen" sind sehr glatt und haben ein einziges tiefes Minimum. Für Einzelheiten s. [8].

2.5 Signifikanz einer Erkennung

Der oben beschriebene Algorithmus wird nun auf sämtliche gespeicherten Objekte angewandt und liefert nach Erfüllung des Abbruchkriteriums für jedes einen Wert von C_{total}. Das Objekt mit dem niedrigsten Wert gilt als das erkannte.

Es muß aber noch die Möglichkeit bestehen, auch dieses als nicht erkannt abzulehnen, z.B. in dem Fall, daß die zu vergleichende Person noch nicht als Objekt gespeichert ist. Dies muß aus der Verteilung der Folge der C_{total} abgelesen werden, da der Algorithmus keine anderen Meßgrößen zurückgibt. Im Idealfall muß der beste Wert sehr weit von allen anderen entfernt sein. Es sind verschiedene Möglichkeiten denkbar, diese Forderung zu formalisieren — es hat sich gezeigt, daß es bereits genügt, einen Mindestabstand des besten zum zweitbesten zu fordern [8].

3 Implementierung auf einem Transputernetzwerk

Um die hohe Rechenleistung aufzubringen, die notwendig ist, um den beschriebenen Erkennungsalgorithmus in akzeptabler Zeit durchzuführen, verwenden wir ein System von T800 Transputern. Diese Mikroprozessoren enthalten eine Ganzzahl- und eine Gleitkommaeinheit, vier serielle Verbindungsmöglichkeiten (transputer links), 4 KB schnellem Speicher und einer flexiblen Speicherverwaltung auf einem Chip. Der Instruktionssatz ist auf das sog. CSP-Modell für parallele Datenverarbeitung ausgerichtet (Communicating Sequential Processes, vgl. [7]). Unsere derzeitige Hardwarekonfiguration enthält 22 T800-Prozessoren mit externem Speicher zwischen einem und vier Megabyte. Für Bildaufnahme und Graphikausgabe sorgt eine spezielle Transputerkarte.

Alle Programme wurden in OCCAM unter dem MULTITOOL Entwicklungssystem entwickelt. Dies bietet zwar keine sehr komfortable Programmierumgebung, aber hohe Rechenleistungen lassen sich relativ leicht erreichen.

3.1 Parallelisierung auf einer Prozessorfarm

Ein einfaches und doch für viele Anwendungen sehr effektives Konzept für Parallelverarbeitung auf einem MIMD-Rechner ist das der Prozessorfarm. Seine Anwendung setzt voraus, daß das Problem in eine Anzahl von unabhängigen Teilproblemen zerlegt werden kann. In einem solchen System werden die Teilaufgaben von einem *Verwalter*-Prozeß an eine Anzahl von *Arbeiter*-Prozessen verteilt, die Berechnungen durchführen und die Ergebnisse an den *Verwalter*-Prozeß zurücksenden. Dieser stellt auch sicher, daß die Verarbeitung erst dann wieder aufgenommen wird, wenn alle Resultate eingesammelt sind. Da alle für unser System benötigten rechenintensiven Teile (vgl. u.) diese Bedingung erfüllen, haben wir ein allgemein verwendbares Farmsystem implementiert, dessen Struktur in Abbildung 3 dargestellt ist.

Die Rechenleistung einer Prozessorfarm hängt jedoch stark von einem ausgewogenen Verhältnis zwischen Berechnungen und Kommunikation ab, da alle Daten den Engpaß des *Verwalter*-Prozessors passieren müssen. Daher ist eine grobkörnige Parallelisierung (relativ wenige Aufgaben pro Arbeiter)

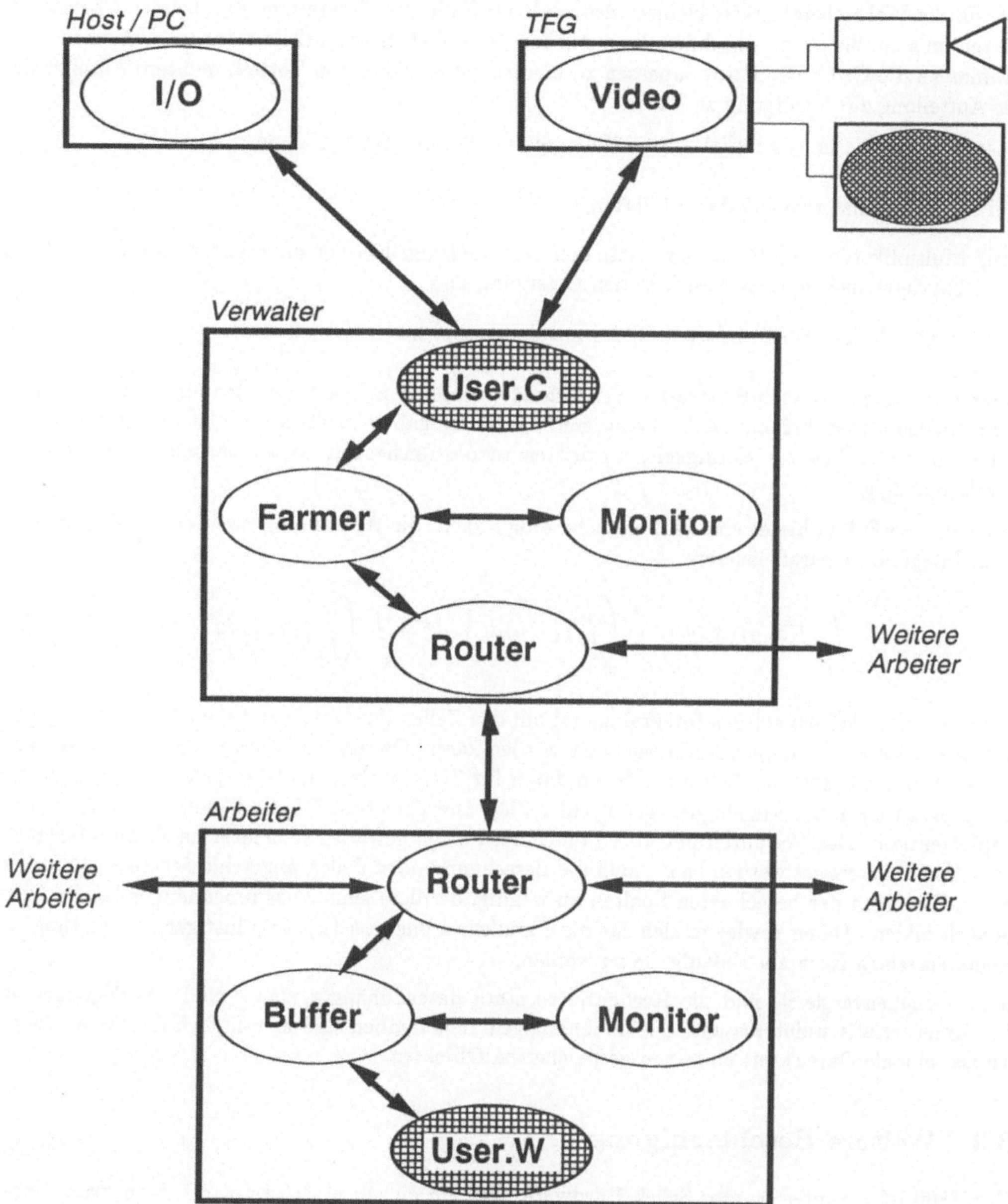

Abbildung 3: Die Struktur der Prozessorfarm. Jeder Kasten steht für einen Prozessor, jede Ellipse für einen Prozeß. Die Pfeile bedeuten OCCAM Kanäle, über die die Prozesse kommunizieren. Es gibt einen *Verwalter*-Prozessor und eine beliebige Zahl von *Arbeiter*-Prozessoren. Der Programmierer braucht nur die beiden Prozesse in den karierten Ellipsen zu schreiben, die übrigen bilden das Farmsystem. Der *Monitor*-Prozeß gestattet eine bequeme Auswertung der Lastverteilung im Netzwerk. Die *Router*-Prozesse unterstützen jede baumförmige Verbindungsstruktur zwischen den *Arbeiter*-Prozessoren. Der *TFG* (Transputer Frame Grabber) bildet die Schnittstelle zu Videokamera und Graphikausgabe.

wünschenswert. Andererseits ist für eine optimale Lastverteilung eine feinkörnige Zerlegung günstiger, da die Wahrscheinlichkeit kleiner wird, daß am Ende des Programms die meisten Prozessoren warten müssen, bis einige von ihnen die restlichen Teilaufgaben abgearbeitet haben. Um einen Algorithmus an die Größe der Farm anpassen zu können, ist es daher von Vorteil, mehrere Körnigkeiten der Aufteilung zur Verfügung zu haben.

Unser System hat im wesentlichen drei Teile, die die Parallelisierung lohnen:

(i) Fouriertransformation der Bilddaten,

(ii) Multiplikation des Ergebnisses mit den verschiedenen Kernen im Frequenzraum gefolgt von Fouriertransformation zurück in den Ortsraum, und

(iii) Vergleich des transformierten Bildes mit den gespeicherten Objekten.

Diese drei Fälle sind auch illustrative Beispiele für verschiedene Anwendungen einer Prozessorfarm, denn in den ersten beiden Fällen benötigen alle Teilaufgaben in etwa die gleichen Rechenzeiten, haben aber verschiedene Körnigkeit, im dritten ist die Rechenzeit stark von den Daten und vom Zufall abhängig.

Der Satz von Fubini bietet eine sehr einfache Möglichkeit, die Berechnung zwei- oder mehrdimensionaler Integrale zu parallelisieren:

$$\int\limits_{X \times Y} f(x,y)\,dxdy = \int\limits_{X} \left(\int\limits_{Y} f(x,y)\,dy \right)\,dx = \int\limits_{Y} \left(\int\limits_{X} f(x,y)\,dx \right)\,dy\,. \tag{11}$$

Dies bedeutet, daß ein solches Integral zuerst auf den Zeilen der Daten und danach auf den Spalten des Ergebnisses oder umgekehrt ausgeführt werden kann. Da die Zeilen bzw. Spalten voneinander unabhängig sind, sind sie natürliche Kandidaten für Teilaufgaben, und bei jeder vernünftigen Genauigkeit ist auch ihre Anzahl groß genug (hier 128). Die VorwärtsFFT der Daten ist auf diese Weise implementiert. Das Verfahren hat aber immer noch einen gewissen sequentiellen Anteil: Bevor die erste Spalte gerechnet werden kann, muß die Berechnung *aller* Zeilen abgeschlossen sein. Außerdem ist das Einfügen der berechneten Spalten aufwendig, da diese keine zusammenhängenden Speicherbereich bilden. Daher erwies es sich für die Parallelisierung von (ii) als günstiger, die Faltung mit einem einzelnen Kern als Teilaufgabe zu wählen.

Beim Graphenvergleich sind die Rechenzeiten stark datenabhängig, daher sind Überlegungen zur Körnigkeit relativ uninteressant. Die unabhängigen Teilaufgaben sind hier einfach die Vergleiche des Bildes (globale Daten) mit einzelnen gespeicherten Objekten.

3.2 Weitere Beschleunigung

Der T800 ist ein interessantes Stück Hardware, weil ein einzelner Prozessor schon mehrere Untereinheiten enthält, die parallel arbeiten können. Neben der üblichen Ganzzahleinheit sind dies die sehr effiziente Gleitkommaeinheit und die vier Kommunikationslinks. Die *Router*-Prozesse der Farmsoftware (s. Abbildung 3) sind daraufhin optimiert, daß sie versuchen, die Links mit Datentransfer beschäftigt zu halten, während der Prozessor Rechenarbeit erledigt. Da die verfügbaren Compiler diese Möglichkeiten nicht nutzen, wurden einige zentrale Routinen in Maschinensprache implementiert, die sich sehr elegant in OCCAM-Programmtext einbinden läßt.

Transputer haben einen MOVE-Befehl, der zusammenhängende Speicherbereiche mit hoher Geschwindigkeit kopiert, und der vom Compiler auch genutzt wird. In vielen Fällen sind die in Frage kommenden Speicherbereiche aber nicht zusammenhängend, wie z. B. beim oben erwähnten Einfügen der Spalten in ein zweidimensionales Feld. Hier kann man den MOVE2D-Befehl des T800 ausnützen, der eigentlich für Graphikanwendungen gedacht, aber für allgemeine mehrdimensionale Felder benutzt werden kann. Ganz besonders wichtig ist dies in unserem Falle, wenn die zweidimensionalen Faltungsergebnisse zu dem vierdimensionalen Feld der Wavelettransformation zusammengebaut werden. Da diese Operationen notwendigerweise auf dem Verwalter stattfinden, der ohnehin den wichtigsten Engpaß des ganzen Systems darstellt, konnte durch diese Optimierungen eine deutlich höhere Prozessorzahl effektiv genutzt werden. Eine genauere Diskussion dieser Optimierungsmöglichkeiten findet sich in [13].

4   Diskussion

Nachdem das oben beschriebene System implementiert und die Parameter geeignet gewählt waren, war die Erkennungsleistung gemessen an der grundsätzlichen Einfachheit des Algorithmus erstaunlich erfolgreich. Zu Beginn bauten wir unsere Datenbank sukzessive mit Bildern von Besuchern des Instituts auf, was zu einer ziemlich breiten Verteilung von Objektgröße und Beleuchtung in der Datenbank führte. Dies hatte zur Folge, daß einige falsche Erkennungen vom Signifikanzkriterium akzeptiert wurden. Im einzelnen wurde in 76 von 98 Versuchen die richtige Person erkannt, davon wurden 64 Erkennungen als signifikant akzeptiert. Von den 22 fehlgeschlagenen Erkennungsversuchen wurden 19 als nicht signifikant zurückgewiesen. Es gab jedoch auch drei „falsch postitive" Läufe. In einer später durchgeführten Untersuchung, wo die Datenbank sorgfältiger normiert war, konnte gezeigt werden, daß solche Fälle ausgeschlossen werden können, ohne allzuviele korrekte Erkennungen zurückzuweisen [8].

Es ist klar, daß das oben beschriebene System nur einen unreifen Vorläufer eines leistungsfähigen Objekterkennungssystems darstellen kann. Die gravierendsten Lücken sind das Fehlen der Trennung des zu erkennenden Objekts von einem strukturierten Hintergrund sowie Invarianz gegen geometrische Transformationen und Beleuchtungseffekte. Weiter ist die Rechenzeit einer Erkennung proportional der Anzahl der gespeicherten Objekte, was durch geschickte Organisation der Datenbank sicherlich stark zu verbessern wäre. An all diesen Problemen wird gegenwärtig in unserer Abteilung gearbeitet.

Danksagung: Ein großer Teil der hier beschriebenen Arbeiten wurde im Max-Planck-Institut für Hirnforschung in Frankfurt am Main durchgeführt. Wir danken Herrn Prof. Singer für die vorzüglichen Arbeitsbedingungen. Weiter danken wir Joachim Buhmann, Martin Lades, Peter König und Rainer Schmitz für ihre Beiträge.

Literatur

[1] J. Buhmann, J. Lange, C. v. d. Malsburg, J. C. Vorbrüggen, and R. P. Würtz. Object recognition in the dynamic link architecture — parallel implementation on a transputer network. In B. Kosko, editor, *Neural Networks: A Dynamical Systems Approach to Machine Intelligence.* Prentice Hall, New York, 1990. In print.

[2] Joachim Buhmann, Jörg Lange, and Christoph von der Malsburg. Distortion invariant object recognition by matching hierarchically labeled graphs. In *IJCNN International Joint Conference on Neural Networks, Washington,* pages I 155–159. IEEE, 1989.

[3] D.J. Field. Relations between the statistics of natural images and the response properties of cortical cells. *J. Opt. Soc. Am.* **A**, 4(12):2379–2394, 1987.

[4] D. Gabor. Theory of communication. *J. Inst. Elec. Eng. (London)*, 93:429–457, 1946.

[5] Charles M. Gray, Peter König, Andreas K. Engel, and Wolf Singer. Oscillatory responses in cat visual cortex exhibit intercolumnar synchronization which reflects global stimulus properties. *Nature*, 338:334–337, 1989.

[6] M.H. Hayes. The reconstruction of a multidimensional sequence from the phase or magnitude of its fourier transform. *IEEE Transactions*, ASSP-30(2), 1982.

[7] C.A.R. Hoare. *Communicating Sequential Processes*. Prentice Hall International, Hemel Hempstead, 1989.

[8] Martin Lades, Jan C. Vorbrüggen, Joachim Buhmann, Jörg Lange, Christoph v.d. Malsburg, Rolf P. Würtz, and Wolfgang Konen. Distortion invariant object recognition in the dynamic link architecture. *IEEE Transactions on Computers*, 1991. Submitted.

[9] Stephane Mallat. *Multiresolution Representations and Wavelets*. PhD thesis, University of Pennsylvania, Philadelphia, PA 19104-6389, 1988.

[10] R. Murenzi. Wavelet transforms associated to the n-dimensional euclidean group with dilations: Signals in more than one dimension. In *Wavelets, Time-Frequency Methods and Phase Space*, pages 239–246. Springer, Berlin, Heidelberg, New York, 1989.

[11] Christoph von der Malsburg. The correlation theory of brain function. Technical report, Max-Planck-Institute for Biophysical Chemistry, Postfach 2841, Göttingen, FRG, 1981.

[12] Christoph von der Malsburg. Pattern recognition by labeled graph matching. *Neural Networks*, 1:141–148, 1988.

[13] J. C. Vorbrüggen. Parallelverarbeitung in Hardware: Optimierung numerischer Routinen auf dem T800. In *Transputer-Anwender-Treffen 1990*, 1991.

Das BMFT–Verbundvorhaben SENROB: *
Forschungsintegration von Neuroinformatik, Künstlicher Intelligenz, Mikroelektronik und Industrieforschung zur Steuerung sensorisch geführter Roboter

Rolf Eckmiller
Heinrich–Heine–Universität Düsseldorf
Abteilung Biokybernetik, Institut für Physikal. Biologie
Universitätsstr. 1
4000 Düsseldorf 1

Im Rahmen des zweiten BMFT–Programmes zur Förderung der Neuroinformatik hat sich ein Konsortium gebildet, welches die wesentlichen sensorischen, motorischen und handlungsplanenden Komponenten für den optimalen Einsatz eines 6–achsigen Gelenkarmroboters für Montage oder Lastentransportaufgaben unter industriellen Bedingungen durch Integration von Lösungsansätzen der Neuroinformatik und der Künstlichen Intelligenz entwickeln will.

Die Aufgabenteilung im Konsortium ist wie folgt festgelegt:

A)Entwicklung von neuronalen Netz–Modulen zur Bahnplanung und Steuerung (Eckmiller/Düsseldorf)

B)Ankopplung wissensbasierter Montageplanung an sensorische neuronale Module einerseits und motorische neuronale Module andererseits (Freund/Dortmund)

C)Entwicklung von neuronalen Netz–Modulen zur visuellen Exploration des Greifraumes (Hartmann/Paderborn)

D)Entwicklung von neuronaler Netz–Hardware für den Echtzeit–Betrieb (Hosticka/Duisburg)

E)Anwendung neuronaler Netze für die Robotersteuerung beim dynamischen Lastentransport unter industriellen Bedingungen (Opitz/Ettlingen)

Ziel des Vorhabens ist einerseits die Demonstration des Einsatzes eines Gelenkarmroboters für Montageaufgaben mit gemischter wissensbasierter und neuronaler Netz–Technologie und andererseits Grundlagenforschung in den Bereichen lernfähiger Computersysteme und diverser Schnittstellen (u.a. zwischen wissensbasierten und neuronalen Netz–Modulen sowie zwischen diesen Modulen und der Netz–Hardware).

1 Gesamtziel von SENROB

Auf der Basis eines kommerziell verfügbaren 6–achsigen Industrieroboters (Manutec r2, Fa. Siemens) soll ein lernfähiges sensomotorisches System entwickelt werden, das sich an neurobiologischen Prinzipien orientiert. Die Lernfähigkeit durch Verwendung adaptiver neuronaler Netz–Module soll sich insbesondere auf folgende Funktionen beziehen:

---

*gefördert vom Bundesminister für Forschung und Technologie, ITN 9105

- inverse Kinematik, also die Zuordnung der zu jedem Zeitpunkt erforderlichen Gelenkwinkel zu den jeweiligen Elementen einer 3–dimensionalen Wunschtrajektorie,

- inverse Dynamik, also die Erzeugung von Drehmoment–Zeitfunktionen unter Berücksichtigung der Dynamik des Roboters auch unter dynamischen Lastverhältnissen,

- Wissen über den Greifraum und seine Objekte, also das Wissen über die Aktions–Umgebung des Roboters,

- das visuelle System soll gelernte Objekte wiedererkennen und Informationen über Eigenschaften und Lage der Objekte bereitstellen zum Zwecke der Ausführung einfacher Montagearbeiten.

Ein wichtiges Ziel besteht in der Kombination eines KI–Systems als handlungsplanender Komponente mit neuronal implementierten sensorischen und motorischen Modulen. Gegenwärtig sind klassische KI–Systeme neuronalen Ansätzen bei der expliziten Repräsentation von Symbolen für Objekte, Eigenschaften und Handlungen überlegen.

Ferner gehört zu den mittelfristigen SENROB–Zielen die Echtzeitfähigkeit des Systems, die durch Entwicklung und Einsatz spezieller neuronaler Netz–Hardware in VLSI–Technolgie angestrebt wird.

2 Stand der Wissenschaft und Vorarbeiten der Verbundpartner

Die für eine erfolgreiche Durchführung des SENROB–Projektes relevanten Voraussetzungen seitens der fünf Verbundpartner sind im folgenden kurz aufgeführt:

A (Neuronale Netze zur Bewegungs–Steuerung): In der Abteilung Biokybernetik der Heinrich–Heine–Universität Düsseldorf (Eckmiller) sind besondere Vorkenntnisse in den Bereichen: Hirnforschung, neuronale Netz–Hardware mit Puls–codierten Neuronen und Entwicklung neuronaler Netze zur Bahnplanung und inversen Kinematik eines redundanten Planar–Roboters vorhanden,

B (KI–Systeme zur Handlungsplanung): Am Institut für Roboterforschung der Universität Dortmund (Freund) sind besondere Vorkenntnisse in den Bereichen: Robotik incl. Kollisionsvermeidung, KI–Systeme für Handlungsplanung und Wissensbasierte Diagnose vorhanden.

C (Neuronale Netze zur visuellen Greifraum–Exploration): Am Fachbereich Elektrotechnik der Universität Paderborn (Hartmann) sind besondere Vorkenntnisse in den Bereichen: konventionelle Mustererkennung, Prozessoren zur Mustererkennung und Entwicklung neuronaler Netze zur Bilderkennung vorhanden;

D (Neuronale Netz–Hardware): Am Fraunhofer Institut für Mikroelektronische Schaltungen und Systeme in Duisburg (Hosticka) sind besondere Vorkenntnisse in den Bereichen: Integrierte Schaltungen (analog und digital) in CMOS–Technologie, Bild– und Spracherkennung mit neuronaler Netz–Hardware und Entwicklung puls–codierter neuronaler Netz–Hardware als VLSI–Chips vorhanden,

E (Neuronale Netze für dynamischen Transport): Bei der Pietzsch–Gruppe in Ettlingen (Opitz) sind besondere Vorkenntnisse in den Bereichen: Sensorik und Regelung von Antrieben, Simulation von neuronalen Netzen zur Fahrzeugsteuerung und Einsatz von Sensorsystemen für diverse Anwendungen vorhanden.

Aus der Liste ergibt sich eine natürliche Arbeitsteilung und enge Zusammenarbeit der beteiligten Verbundpartner im SENROB–Projekt. Alle Partner werden seit Jahren in verschiedenen nationalen und internationalen Forschungs–Programmen in den relevanten Bereichen durch Drittmittel unterstützt.

Einzelheiten des SENROB–Vorhabens werden in Zukunft durch die Veröffentlichung von wissenschaftlichen Ergebnissen verfügbar werden. Die Vorarbeiten der Verbundpartner sind in der Literarturliste durch einige Veröffentlichungen angedeutet.

Literatur

[1] Eckmiller R.: Neural computers for motor control. In: Advanced Neural Computers (Eckmiller, ed.), Elsevier, Amsterdam, 1990, pp.357–364.

[2] Freund, E.: The structure of decoupled non–linear systems. Int. J. Control $\underline{21}$,1975, pp.443–450.

[3] Hartmann, G.: The closed loop antagonistic network (CLAN). In: Advanced Neural Computers (Eckmiller, ed.), Elsevier, Amsterdam, 1990, pp. 279–285.

[4] Opitz, R. Das Lernfahrzeug, Neural Network Applications for Autonomous Mobile Robots, In: Advanced Neural Computers (Eckmiller ed.), Elsevier, Amsterdam, 1990, pp.373–379.

[5] Richert, P., Hess, G., Hosticka, B., Kesper, M., Schwarz, M.: Distributed processing hardware for realization of artificial neural networks, In: Parallel Processing in Neural Systems and Computers (Eckmiller, Hartmann, Hauske, eds.), Elsevier, Amsterdam, 1990, pp.311–314.

NEURAL CONTROL WITHIN THE BMFT–PROJECT NERES

B. Schürmann[1], G. Hirzinger[2], D. Hernández[3], H.U. Simon[4], H. Hackbarth[5]

[1]Siemens AG München,
[2]DLR Oberpfaffenhoffen,
[3]TU München,
[4]Universität Dortmund,
[5]SEL Stuttgart

Abstract

Whereas the identification and control of linear systems is well understood, this does not apply in general to nonlinear systems. Here, neural nets open up new paths for the treatment of multidimensional nonlinear systems as well as the possibility of adaptive readjustments to changes of the environment and of the system parameters. The advantages of neural control are of particular value for robotics. On the subsymbolic level, the goal is a symbiosis between sensorics and actuatorics and neural signal processing and control. However, we do intend to use traditional AI-techniques in cases where a robust knowledge representation is required which goes beyond the subsymbolic level, e.g. for space representation. In many applications, the problem is to extract significant control parameters from visual sensor data in a robust and efficient manner. For this task, neural nets are suited particularly well. Mathematical models for machine learning as well as unifying dynamical concepts will be utilized to achieve quantitative, generalizable results with respect to the efficiency of neural nets, by taking into account the real world requirements for control tasks with respect to performance, reliability and fault tolerance. Speech is of special significance for the dialogue with autonomous systems. Since neural nets have lead to encouraging results in speech processing, corresponding techniques will also be applied in robotics.

1 Introduction

Artificial neural nets are adaptive, massively parallel and robust tools for processing incomplete, noisy, distributed and sometimes even contradictory information. They are receiving growing attention in science and technology, with promising prototypical applications. The expectations are that the neural network research is on the right track to capture relevant and efficient principles in biological, physical and information-technical systems. It has initiated a thrust of interdisciplinary worldwide research activities whose range and methodical substance are as yet unsatisfactorily clarified. The long-term contributions of neural nets to information processing may be demonstrated most convincingly by solving those problems for which there are no satisfactory solutions otherwise. In the area of autonomous systems, the majority of solutions based on methods from AI- and adaptive systems theory are not convincing to date, mainly because of lacking real-time cabability, complicated handling and missing robustness. In contrast, neural solutions are expected to be flexible, user-friendly, fault-tolerant, and capable of using the massive parallelism for real-time applications.

The main goal of the NERES-project is to help raising neural solutions to the level of a 'proven technology'. The economic and political significance of the project results from the expected need for intelligent sensor-controlled robots in assembly, materials treatment and efficient process control in environmental engineering. The emphasis of our work is on basic aspects of neural learning, on control and on speech recognition.

The current lack of quantitative, generalizable statements concerning the efficiency of neural nets is equally unsatisfying, on a theoretical as well as on a practical level. It is necessary and possible, for feedforward neural networks to make use of mathematical models for machine learning, as well as to investigate the dynamics of recurrent networks within a unifying concept. Further research-oriented work aims at investigating the interaction of symbolic and subsymbolic techniques as well as to develop self-refering and subgoal-generating learning strategies. These investigations are to be performed by taking into account the real world requirements of the application domain with respect to performance, reliability and fault tolerance.

The aim of our work in the area of control is to study aspects of process- and robot control as well as object recognition with neural nets. Whereas the identification and control of linear systems is well understood, this does not apply in general to nonlinear systems [34]. Here, neural nets open up new paths for the treatment of multidimensional nonlinear systems as well as the possibility of adaptive readjustments to changes of the environment and of the system parameters.

The advantages of neural control may be of particular value for robotics in industry. On the subsymbolic level the goal is a symbiosis between sensorics and actuatorics and neural signal processing and control. However, we do intend to use traditional AI-techniques in cases where a robust knowledge representation is required which goes beyond the subsymbolic level, e.g. for space representation. In many applications, the problem is to extract significant control parameters from visual sensor data in a robust and efficient manner. For this task, neural nets are suited particularly well. Speech is of special significance for the dialogue with autonomous systems. Since neural nets have lead to encouraging results in speech processing, corresponding techniques will also be applied in robotics.

In the subsequent sections, the topics outlined in the introduction are discussed in more detail and first results obtained within the NERES- project are presented.

2   Topics of Basic Research

2.1   The Complexity of Neural Learning

The question of how to implement knowledge acquisition or other kinds of learning behaviour on neural networks has found much interest during the last decades. Although a large and promising variety of heuristic learning rules and network architectures has been proposed (an overview is presented in [19]), there is still a considerable lack of theoretical insights into the following questions:

- Which criterions are adequate for a performance evaluation of neural nets?

- Which analytical tools will help to perform this evaluation?

- What does 'generalization' exactly mean, and how can it be achieved?

- How many training examples are needed for a given learning task and a given architecture?

In the part of the project, devoted to the complexity of neural learning, we will put these questions into a clear and mathematically sound framework. Our approach is based on the ideas of L. Valiant (see [44]) concerning learning algorithms. Its basic ingredients are the concepts of 'approximation' and 'efficiency' which we are going to decribe briefly.

'Approximation' indicates that the results of a learning procedure are never perfect. There are two good reasons for that:

- The empirical data give only a partial insight into the underlying phenomenon.

- There is a small probability that the empirical data are even unrepresentative (in this case, a learning procedure cannot be expected to produce a successful generalization).

According to Valiant's model, a successful learning procedure performs approximation with an arbitrary and user–adjustable precision: The probabilities of getting a misleading set of data or of producing an inaccurate hypothesis can be made as small as we like.

The notion of 'efficiency' has also a twofold meaning:

- The number of training examples should be reasonably bounded in terms of the parameters which control the precision of the approximation.

- The running time of the procedure which computes a generalizing hypothesis from the empirical data should be reasonably bounded in terms of the total description length of the data.

The concepts of approximation and efficiency are therefore related in the sense that the amount of empirical data or computational resources will grow, if we put harder restrictions on the desired precision of the approximation. We assume, however, that this growth is reasonably bounded (say, for instance, by a polynomial). The so–called model of pac–learning has emerged from these ideas (pac is an acronym for 'probably almost correct'). Since the foundation of the model (in [44]), there have been many research activities, mainly concerning the learning of boolean or geometric concepts (an overview and additional references are obtained from [24, 7] or from the proceedings of the annual workshop on Computational Learning Theory published by Morgan&Kaufmann).

The research projects in Dortmund and at Siemens have the following aims:

- We want to adjust the pac–learning model to the specific requirements of neural learning.

- We want to apply the model to the specific learning tasks of our project partners.

- We want to weaken the model whenever it appears to be overrestrictive, i.e., whenever it produces negative results for learning tasks which are tractable in a practical sense.

Let us illustrate these aims for classification problems as particular learning tasks. For instance, the objective might be the recognition of objects in a visual scene. We assume that a feature extractor has already produced feature vectors which can be forwarded to a neural classifier. The empirical data base is then a random collection of feature vectors together with the appropriate classifications. A learning algorithm must transform these data into a neural net with appropriately adjusted weights and thresholds. The crucial questions are the following:

- How must we choose parameters like number of training examples, network architecture, weights, thresholds and appropriate updating rules such that everything fits into the strong requirements of pac–learning?

- The number of available training examples is usually bounded by practical constraints. Which (hopefully small) expected error rate is then feasible?

Valiant's model is distribution–independent, i.e., its theorems are valid for arbitrary statistical distributions of the feature vectors. This prevents us from imposing artificial assumptions on an unknown or weird distribution. The assumption of distribution–independence is, however, overrestrictive, if successful learning algorithms are heavily based on special features of the distribution at hand. In our research project, we will investigate how distribution–dependent knowledge can be incorporated into neural network design. First trials in this direction lead to a quite promising combination of Bayesian decision theory, pac–learning and neural network design. We show in [13] and [2] how almost optimal neural classificators are obtained for certain classes of distributions on binary feature vectors (Chow–expansions and Bahadur–Lazarsfeld–expansions of bounded order). The readers interested in neural learning within Valiant's model will gain deeper insights and additional references from [6, 17, 5, 4, 25, 43].

2.2 Reducing Complexity in Neural Networks

A central problem in neural network learning is to determine a network of appropriate size and configuration for a particular problem. If the network chosen is too small or has an inappropriate topology, then it will be unable to extract the relevant structure from the training-data. If the network chosen is too large and/or complex there will be a tendency for the network to fit not only the structural but also the stochastic (noise) elements in the data. A well established method for determining network architectures is to start with a large net then successively reduce the complexity of the network until a good compromise is reached between fit on the training data and generalization ability (measured for example by cross validation). Two predominant methods have established themselves to achieve this goal. The first consists of removing 'redundant' nodes and connections based on some measure of saliency, usually determined by an estimate of the effect the removal will have on the measure of fit, (see e.g. [29], [33], [23]). The second method consists of adding a further term to the cost or error function which penalizes complexity in the network measured by number and/or size of the weights in the network, (see e.g. [22], [16]). Most existing methods display deficiencies in either their performance or in their theoretic foundations. Currently we are investigating at Siemens a number of test variables for removing and/or replacing weights in oversized networks derived from statistical hypothesis testing variables and suitable for use both alone and in conjunction with penalty terms in the error function. Further, more refined measures of complexity than those suggested in the literature are being investigated, on the one hand to provide better measures of the complexity of a given network or class of networks, and on the other hand, to enhance the performance and stability of penalty term methods (see [10]).

2.3 Incorporating *A Priori* Knowledge in Networks of Locally-Tuned Units

In process control, it is necessary to approximate a high-dimensional nonlinear relation between input and output data. A typical example is the neural modeling of a process or its inverse. Training data are often sparse and difficult to obtain, so it is useful to take advantage of any form of *a priori* knowledge about the problem at hand. We are currently developing network architectures and training rules that allow minimal network sizes and the incorporation of *a priori* knowledge presented in either the form of fuzzy rules or mathematical formulas. The building blocks of our architecture are radial basis functions which are units with localized receptive fields [35], [32]. Since with increasing input dimensionality it becomes less feasible to cover the whole space with units of only local relevance we include in our network architecture normalization terms resulting in an essentially 'space-filling' architecture. In the research project at Siemens, we achieved a theoretical framework for this normalization and can show that by recasting the problem of approximation in Bayes decision theory, such a network can produce the optimal output function [21]. This theoretical framework also makes it possible to incorporate a *priori* knowledge and results in a network solution that approximates the training data in regions where these are available but relies on *a priori* knowledge in regions where the network has not seen any data, thus avoiding unpredictable behaviour.

2.4 Recurrent and Feedforward Multi-Layer Perceptrons in Comparison

Recurrent multi layer perceptrons will play a significant role in neural control. Hitherto, little is known about their learning speed. As we have shown in the part of the project at Siemens [42], contrary to common belief, they may learn faster than corresponding feedforward networks. The main results of [42] are briefly summarized in this section. For an exemplary application, we compare the generalization abilities of 3-layer perceptrons for recurrent and feedforward backpropagation (RBP and FBP, respectively) as a function of the number of learning epochs and the steepness of the neurons' threshold function. It is found that for an appropriate choice of the steepness, learning is considerably faster with recurrent than with feedforward backpropagation. As a theoretical framework for our investigations, a unified description of neural algorithms is employed [36]. This unified description can be applied to an arbitrarily structured system. For applications, we have to choose a specific net architecture and topology. Here, we settle for a 3-layer network architecture (input, hidden, output) with feedback connections between the output and hidden, and between the hidden and input layers, respectively. To guarantee stability of the dynamics, we choose the weights to be symmetric. There are no connections within layers. Without feedbackward connections, the net reduces to the conventional 3-layer feedforward perceptron.

As objective function we employ the usual quadratic error function and carry out performance comparisons for the example of handwritten character recognition. We use the *'United States Postal Service Office of Advance Technology Handwritten ZIP Code Database (1987)'*. The net acts as a classifier, with a 16×16 pixel array input layer, a hidden layer with 50 neurons, and an output layer with 10 neurons. The choice of the number of hidden neurons is entirely heuristic at this stage; a method for constructing a minimal network is outlined at the end of this section. We use only 10% of the data as training set. This saves run time and is sufficient for the exploratory nature of this investigation.

The generalization abilities (number of recognized patterns / number of patterns presented in the recall phase, subject to the condition that the patterns have not been presented in the training phase), are discussed in dependence of the learning epochs for sigmoidal threshold functions. It is seen that for RBP the number of epochs needed to reach a given reasonable performance depends sensitively on the steepness of the threshold function(cf. also [20]). For steep functions merely 2 epochs are needed, whereas for flat functions about a factor of ten more epochs are required. In contrast, FBP shows little sensitivity to the steepness, and, most importantly, always requiring an order of magnitude more training epochs to reach the degree of performance achieved with RBP after only 2 epochs. Therefore, even though a single learning epoch for RBP requires about a factor of 3 more time, the total learning time for a given generalization ability is only about one third of that for FBP.

Finally, we outline a method for constructing a minimal network. As a starting point we use the idea of 'optimal brain damage' introduced for feedforward backpropagation [29]. It consists of a Taylor expansion of the objective function E with respect to the weights around its global minimum obtained for an oversized net. Only diagonal terms up to second order are kept, putting those weights equal to zero which change E around its minimum least. The net is repeatedly retrained and retested. We generalize the approach [29] to recurrent nets. Its usefulness is currently being tested for various applications.

2.5 Novel Algorithms for Networks with Time-Varying Inputs and Outputs

In this section, novel algorithms relevant for neural control are listed and briefly explained. They have been developed at the TU München and partially at Siemens.

2.5.1 New Algorithms for Supervised Learning 1

Essentially two training methods can be found in the literature for time–dependent recurrent neural networks (n non-input nodes): *Real–time recurrent learning* (RTRL) being computationally expensive ($O(n^4)$ operations per time step) but making real–time learning feasible, and *backpropagation–through–time* (BTT) being computationally very efficient ($O(n^2)$) but requiring the storage of complete time–sequences and not supporting real–time learning.

Combining both methods, a new algorithm has been derived which has improved real–time capabilities compared with BTT, an average time complexity of $O(n^3)$ and fixed storage requirements like RTRL [41]. Further, calculus–of–variations techniques have been introduced for the construction of BTT–algorithms for arbitrary neural networks and performance indices. In order to reduce the high storage requirements, new BTT–implementations have been suggested [31].

2.5.2 New Algorithms for Supervised Learning 2: A learning Algorithm for Fast-Weight Short Term Memory

A learning algorithm has been derived for a sequence-processing system consisting of two *feed-forward* nets using *fast weights* (instead of recurrent connections as employed by previous approaches) [37]: The first net learns to produce context dependent weight *changes* for the second net whose weights may vary very quickly. The method offers a potential for STM storage efficiency: A simple weight (instead of a full-fledged unit) may be sufficient for storing short term information. Experiments with unknown time delays have shown how the system can be used for adaptive temporary variable binding, thus providing an alternative to oscillator-based 'phase-lock binding'.

2.5.3 Learning to Devide and Conquer 1 - Supervised Learning: History Compression for Adaptive Sequence Chunking

Previous 'neural' learning algorithms for sequence processing have severe drawbacks when it comes to *long* time lags. This investigation first introduces a simple principle for reducing the descriptions of event sequences without loss of information [39]. A consequence of this principle is that only unexpected inputs deserve attention. This consequence leads to the first neural systems for recursively composing sequences. The focus is on a recurrent 2-network system which tries to collapse a self-organizing (possibly multi-level) temporal predictor hierarchy into a single recurrent net. Experiments show that the system can require less computation per time step *and* much less training sequences than the conventional training algorithms for recurrent nets.

2.5.4 Learning to Devide and Conquer 2 - Reinforcement Learning: A Recurrent Sub-goal Generator for Reinforcement Learning and Planning

Previous reinforcement learning algorithms for trajectory generation require too many training sequences. One reason for this is that previous algorithms do not at all learn 'to divide and conquer'. We focus on the case where *many* start-goal trajectories have already been learned [38]. For this case we show how a novel 3-network system can quickly learn to *compose* previously learned trajectories to create plans for solving new tasks. The heart of the system is a recurrent module which *learns without a teacher* to generate sequences of sub-goals to reach new goals.

2.5.5 Adaptive Curiosity for On–Line State Space Exploration

Currently neural 'adaptive critics' are tested versus neural approaches to system identification for sequential adaptive control in non-stationary environments. The test bed is the USIS simulation environment for industrial robots. A by-product of this research is the concept of Adaptive Curiosity for On–Line State Space Exploration [40]. Previous approaches to learning internal world models do not model the *reliability* of the world model's predictions in uncertain environments and use inefficient random search for selecting training examples. This paper describes a better method: A 4-network reinforcement learning system is described which tries to maximize *the expectation of the temporal derivative of the adaptive assumed reliability of future predictions*. The system is 'curious' in the sense that it actively tries to provoke situations for which it *learned to expect to learn* something about the environment. Experiments demonstrate that the method can be clearly faster than conventional model-building strategies.

2.6 Qualitative Representation of Temporal and Spatial Knowledge and its Applications

Our goal in the part of the project at the TU München has been to develop representations of time and space that retain the main properties of their respective domains. In the case of space, in particular, these are "uniqueness" properties of objects and places, as well as spatial neighborhoods and conceptual neighborhoods of spatial relations [11, 12]. The representation allows different degrees of granularity and abstraction and is able to handle fuzzy, incomplete and perhaps globally inconsistent knowledge. Furthermore, knowledge is represented qualitatively, that is using comparative relations among objects. These relations, in turn, are represented using analogical knowledge structures ("abstract maps" [18]), that inherently reflect the structure of the represented domain.

We are also interested in the cognitive aspects of these representations. The internal concepts of the representation and the corresponding cognitive concepts of the user should be equivalent. Furthermore, only knowledge typically available in real situations should be represented.

Qualitative representations of temporal and spatial knowledge describe events and objects only as precisely as required to identify them in a given environment (and not as precisely as required to reconstruct them). The advantage of this context-oriented approach is that an appropriate level of abstraction can be found depending on the task at hand. Similar mechanisms can be used to aid in the interpretation of natural language input, where only those interpretations that make sense in the given context need to be considered. We apply these principles to the mapping between specific quantities and qualitative dimensions of space.

The role of qualitative representations (and of AI-methods in general) in a neural control project is not obvious, but nevertheless important:

- They provide a common representational framework to guide the development of particular neural control applications, in particular in those areas that require a robust representation which goes beyond the subsymbolic level, such as the representation of space.

- They facilitate the communication among partners involved in the control process.

- Finally, AI methods are also vital to close the gap between neural-based basic level tasks (such as for example word recognition) and higher level tasks (such as for example user-friendly natural language interfaces).

3 Neural Control

3.1 Identification and Control of Complex Systems by means of Neural Networks

In the last three decades considerable progress has been made in the development of methods for the adaptive identification and control of linear plants. These methods have been successfully used in process-control and robotics. By contrast, design methods for dealing with nonlinear systems have not reached suffcient maturity to find wide application. Because of their flexibility, robustness and general applicability, neural networks offer an extremely promising instrument for modelling highdimensional nonlinear systems. Further, network training methods used initially to identify a system may be extended to provide for adaptive adjustment of the model to changes in system parameters and environmental variables.

Assuming that a conventional regulator already exists for a system, it may be not necessary to identify a complete model for the plant, rather will be possible to initially use the output of a conventional regulator as signal for the adaption algorithm of a neural network. The neural regulator is then designed so that its signals gradually replace those of the conventional one over time as the network learns the characteristics of the system. This regulator, having the advantage of being able to achieve a better fit on the nonlinear elements of the plant in its adaption process and to take a large number of additional signals into account, should be able to achieve a higher degree of precision in process control than is possible with conventional methods.

At Siemens, currently we work on a concept to improve the control of a system in reference to standard industrial regulators. Here, the plant would be run initially at reduced speed as the neural regulator adjusts itself to replace the conventional regulator. At this stage, the network has only been trained to serve the same function as the existing system, but this under consideration of all coupling effects. It is assumed that this will lead to a smoother control of the system. In the next stage, the speed is increased. Since the network has not been trained under these circumstances, this will lead to a residual error that must be regulated out by the conventional system until the network has the opportunity to observe and adapt itself to the high speed environment. By iteratively repeating this process it should be possible to extend the application range of the neural regulator into regions of high speed process control in which a one-dimensional linear regulator would be incapable of fulfilling its design function.

3.2 Applicability of Neural Nets to Control Tasks

In the joint project the applicability of neural nets with respect to control tasks will be investigated. In addition to neurons with sigmoid transfer functions those implying other suitable non-linearities and local response behaviour are to be taken into account. Questions concerning the convergence characteristics and the optimal training sets for the identification of control plants and adaption of controllers are to be clarified in this context, too.

An example particularly relevant for practical applications is represented by the self-learning improvement of sensory feedback in robots without an explicit dynamical model. This kind of work will be on the three-stage learning concept SLC as developped at DLR [27, 28] and in particular aims at the automatic refinement of force controls e.g. in contour following tasks.

The main advantage of such an approach compared to adaptive systems with model identification (MIAS) lies in the applicability to structurally unknown non-linear plants on one side, and on the other side the model is only used within the limits of its precision. This implies that heavily disturbed plants or plants, the states of which are not completely defined by model inputs, do not pose a problem; thus a rudimentary model is sufficient.

In total the learning scheme consists of 3 stages. The lowest, the controller, is trained on the basis of examples for optimal performance. The teacher's information, i.e. the nominal control commands depending on the controller's inputs are provided by the second stage.

The second stage considers control differences as generated with an a priori chosen controller and corrects the issued control commands in a way so that the control differences disappear. Only a crude plant information is needed for this; it is taken from the plant model, i.e. from the third stage.

Up to now among the three stages modelling, optimization and controller improvement the model and the controller have been realized by trainable associative memories; they were originally derived from the CMAC (cerebellar model articulation controller) of J. ALBUS [1], but meanwhile they are better characterized as a tabular knowledge base, and they are now to be replaced by neural nets.

'Learning by showing and observing' is - especially in the framework of telerobotic concepts for the teleoperation of space robots - an approach pursued in DLR for many years. This terminology does not primarily mean the storage of robot positions and paths as given in classical teach-in, but more the storage and classification of nominal sensory patterns and reference to them in the repetition phase.

As special examples neural nets are not only supposed to help in learning assembly and compliant motion tasks by simulating the non-linear mappings between force-torque- patterns and optimal compliant behaviour; there are also learning procedures envisioned, where the operator using a 6 degree-of-freedom control ball (together with local sensory feedback at the robot gripper) guides the robot through a task, while classification of situations as well as mapping of sensor-values to robot moves are to be trained via neural nets.

Similar concepts make up the basis for learning the (contact less) grasping of objects with two- and multi-finger-grippers. The goal direction here is to show the robot the optimal grasping position, let it registrate the relevant nominal sensory patterns (particularly based on the fusion of stereo and laser range images) and then train (by motions around the object) the mapping between non-nominal sensory patterns and non-nominal relative positions/orientations, so that after training these deviations become immediately transparent. The big advantage of such an approach lies in the fact that by this sensor-based relative reference to the environment all system errors are compensated, e.g. errors in the coordinate-transformation als well as in the camera characteristics (calibration becomes superfluous) etc.

For new light-weight-robots with torque interface as they are presently developped at DLR, the complex, nonlinear and computationally consumptive inverse dynamic model is to be trained by neural nets in order to achieve high path accuracy at high motion speed. In this context hybrid concepts are of particular interest, i.e. for example gross motion control via neural nets, fine motion control via classical techniques.

3.3   Neural-Based Voiced-Activated Robot Control

Within the unified concept of neural-based robot control, a voiced-activated man-machine interface will be integrated. The latter comprises a speech dialogue with command recognition by a dedicated connectionist structure and replay of announcements or questions for user guidance.

Speech is the most common type of human communication and also provides a convenient way to interact with any kind of equipment, e.g., a robot, a microscope or a telecom terminal. Apart from a carefully designed user guidance, however, reliable performance even in noise-corrupted industrial enviroment is crucial for the success of voice-activated man-machine interfaces and thus for an increasing acceptance and popularity.

As is documented by recent results, artificial neural networks yield high accuracy in pattern classification. Particularly in the area of speech recognition, achievements are encouraging. Consequently, the present objective is to exploit the inherent features of neural-based paradigms and develop them further when aiming at high robustness against the impact of environmental noise as well as the common variability in pronounciation by different speakers and even by one person in successive utterance of the same word.

In this way, it is aimed at providing the basis for a broad area of applications for connectionist mechanisms in automatic speech processing.

The objective of this partial project within NERES is to develop and test methods for neural-based voice control of a robot by spoken command words. For evaluation, selected algorithms will be implemented on a generic hardware module, which has recently been developed at the SEL Research Center for universal use in speech processing tasks, such as voice recognition, coding (compression) and synthesis. For coding and replay of announcements, available algorithms will be used, whereas recognition paradigms are to be developed. The speech processing device will be connected to the robot by a specific interface. The result is the demonstration system as sketched in the diagram below.

SEL Generic HW Module

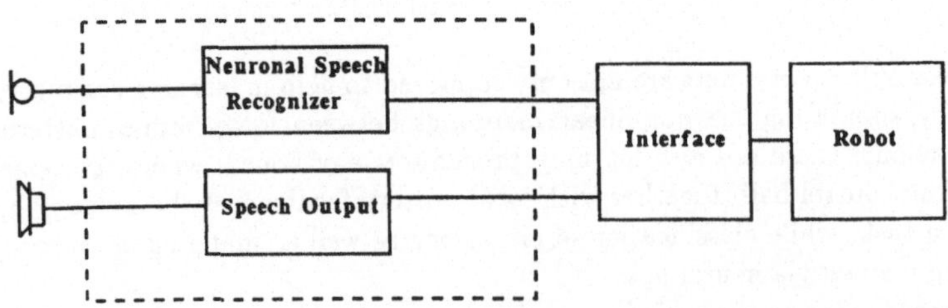

To introduce neural-based recognition, connectionist structures for whole-word classification are to be developed, specified to the features

- speaker-independent and -adaptive recognition of command words,

- rejection of utterances not included in the vocabulary,

- robustness against environmental noise.

In order to differentiate between up to 50 words and to realize speaker adaption, known algorithms [8, 26, 15] are re-investigated and optimized. Apart from such multi-layered neural architectures, further models are to be studied and/or newly conceptualized.

Essential for high user acceptance is the incorporation of an optimally adapted rejection threshold for words not previously trained by the network. Hitherto this topic has not been dealt with in the literature. From recent original work [15], approaches evolved to realize rejection by continuously-valued output functions with probability-related statements derived thereof.

With respect to noise in word recognition, no fundamental investigations have been conducted yet, except for tests over telephone lines [9, 14]. It is to be studied in how far connectionist structures other than perceptron-like ones are suited for this task. To conclude, a comparative evaluation of neural and conventional methods for speech recognition is considered.

As was indicated above, those algorithms selected as best in the simulations will be implemented on generic speech processing device and integrated into the dialogue with the user. Finally, a system optimization is conducted.

The feasibility of such a comprehensive neural approach to robot control will be demonstrated by a man-machine-dialogue for learning and realizing the seizing and assembling of objects. This conveniently replaces cumbersome pushing key sequences on a terminal. In addition, acoustical feedback about the current system status can be obtained at any time.

References

[1] J.S. Albus. A New Approach to Manipulator Control: The Cerebellar Model Articulaton Controller (CMAC). *Transactions of the ASME, Journal of Dynamic Systems, Measurement, and Control*: 221-227, Sept. 1975.

[2] S. Annulova, J. Cuellar, K. U. Höffgen, and H. U. Simon. Probably almost optimal neural classifiers. In preparation.

[3] H. Asada. Teaching and Learning of Compliance Using Neurol Nets: Representation and Generation of Nonlinear Compliance. *1990 IEEE Int. Conf. Robotics and Automation*, Cincinnati, May 13-18, 1990.

[4] E. B. Baum. The perceptron algorithm is fast for non–malicious distributions. *Neural Computation*, 2:249–261, 1990.

[5] E. B. Baum. Polynomial time algorithms for learning neural nets. In M. A. Fulk and J. Case, editors, *Proc. of the 3rd Annual Workshop on Computational Learning Theory*, 258–273, San Mateo, California, Aug. 1990. Morgan Kaufmann.

[6] E. B. Baum and D. Haussler. What size net gives valid generalization? *Neural Computation1*, 1:151–160, 1989.

[7] A. Blumer, A. Ehrenfeucht, D. Haussler, and M. K. Warmuth. Learnability and the Vapnik–Chervonenkis dimension. *Journal of the Association on Computing Machinery*, 36(4):929–965, Oct. 1989.

[8] L. Bottou, J.S. Liénard. Multispeaker Digit Recognition. *Intl. Conf. on Connectionism in Perspective*, Zürich, 38–44, 1988.

[9] M. Codogno, R. Gemello, F. Mana, P. Demichelis, P. Laface, E. Piccolo. ESPRIT Project 2059 "Pygmalion". Final Report on Task 4.3, 1990.

[10] W. Finnoff, H.G. Zimmermann. Reducing complexity and improving generalization in neural networks by mixed strategies. Submitted to NIPS 91.

[11] C. Freksa. Qualitative spatial reasoning. In Mark and Frank [30].

[12] C. Freksa. Temporal reasoning based on semi-intervals. *Technical Report TR-90-016, ICSI, Berkeley, CA*, April 1990.

[13] P. Fischer, S. Pölt, and H. U. Simon. Probably almost bayes decisions. In *Proc. of the 4th Annual Workshop on Computational Learning Theory*, San Mateo, California, Aug. 1991. To appear.

[14] H. Hackbarth, M. Immendörfer. Speaker-dependent isolated word recognition by artifical neural networks. *Proc. VERBA 90 Intl. Conf. on Speech Technol.*, 91–98, 1990.

[15] H. Hackbarth, J. Mantel. Neural subnet assembly for recognition from medium-sized vocabularies. *ICANN-91 Neurocomputing Conf., Helsinki*, 1991 (accepted).

[16] S.J. Hanson, L.Y. Pratt. Comparing biases for minimal network construction with back-propagation. *Advances in Neural Information Processing I, D. S. Touretzky, Ed., Morgan Kaufman*, 177-185, 1989.

[17] D. Haussler. Generalizing the pac model for neural net and other learning applications. Research Report UCSC–CRL–89–30, University of California Santa Cruz, Sept. 1989.

[18] D. Hernández. Relative Representation of Spatial Knowledge: The 2-D Case. In Mark and Frank [30]

[19] G. E. Hinton. Connectionist learning procedures. *Artificial Intelligence*, 40:185–235, 1989.

[20] J. Hollatz, B. Schürmann. The "Detailed Balance" Net: A Stable Asymmetric Artificial Neural System for Unsupervised Learning. *Proceedings of the IEEE International Conference on Neural Networks, San Diego Vol. III*, 453-459, 1990.

[21] R. Hofmann, M. Röscheisen, V. Tresp. Parsimonious Networks of Locally-Tuned Units. Submitted to NIPS 91.

[22] B. Huberman, D. Rumelhart, A. Weigand. Generalization by weight elimination with application to forecasting. *Advances in Neural Information Processing III, Ed. R. P. Lippman and J. Moody*, Morgan Kaufmann, 1991.

[23] E. Karnin. A simple procedure for pruning back-propagation trained neural networks. *IEEE Trans. on Neural Networks, 1.2*, 239-242, June 1990.

[24] M. Kearns, M. Li, L. Pitt, and L. Valiant. Recent results on boolean concept learning. In *Workshop on Machine Learning*, Irvine, 1987.

[25] M. J. Kearns and R. E. Shapire. Eficient distribution–free learning of probabilistic concepts. In *Proc. of the 31st Symposium on Foundations of Computer Science*. IEEE Computer Society, Oct. 1990. To appear.

[26] A. Krause, H. Hackbarth. Scaly artificial neural networks for speaker-independent recognition of isolated words. *Proc. IEEE ICASSP 91*, 21–24, 1989.

[27] F. Lange. A Learning Concept for Improving Robot Force Control, IFAC Symposium on Robot Control. Karlsruhe, Oct. 1988.

[28] F. Lange. Schätzung und Darstellung von mehrdimensionalen Abbildungen, DLR-Mitteilung. DLR-Mitt. 90-06.

[29] Y. Le Cun, J.S. Denker, S.A. Solla. Optimal Brain Damage. *in: D.S. Touretzky (ed.), Neural Information Processing Systems*, Morgan Kaufmann, 598-605, 1990.

[30] D.M. Mark, A.U. Frank, editors. *Cognitive and Linguistic Aspects of Geographic Space*. NATO Advanced Studies Institute. Kluwer, Dordrecht, 1990.

[31] S. Miesbach. Effective Gradient Computation for Continuous and Discrete Time–Dependent Neural Networks. Submitted to IJCANN-91, Singapore.

[32] J. Moody, C. Darken. Fast learning in networks of locally-tuned processing units. *Neural Computation, Vol. 1*, 281-294, 1989.

[33] M.C. Mozer, P. Smolensky. Skeletonization: A Technique for Trimming the Fat from a Network via Relevance Assessment. *in: D.S. Touretzky (ed.), Neural Information Processing Systems*, Morgan Kaufmann, 107–115, 1989.

[34] K.S. Narendra, K. Parthasarathy. Identification and Control of Dynamical Systems Using Neural Networks. *IEEE Transactions on Neural Networks, Vol.1, No.1*, 4–27, 1990.

[35] T. Poggio, F. Girosi. Networks for approximation and learning. *Proceedings of the IEEE Vol. 78*, 1481 - 1497, 1990.

[36] U. Ramacher, B. Schürmann. Unified Description of Neural Algorithms for Time-Independent Pattern Recognition. *in: U. Ramacher, U. Rückert (ed.), VLSI Design of Neural Networks*, Kluwer Academic Publishers, 255-270, 1990.

[37] J.H. Schmidhuber. Learning to Control Fast-Weight Memories: An Alternative to Recurrent Nets. Technical Report FKI-147-91, Institut für Informatik, Technische Universität München, 1990.

[38] J.H. Schmidhuber. Learning to Generate Sub-Goals for Action Sequences. Proceedings ICANN 91, Elsevier Science Publishers B.V., 1991, to appear.

[39] J.H. Schmidhuber. Neural Sequence Chunkers. Technical Report FKI-148-91, Institut für Informatik, Technische Universität München, 1991.

[40] J.H. Schmidhuber. Adaptive Curiosity and Adaptive Confidence. Technical Report FKI-149-91, Institut für Informatik, Technische Universität München, 1991.

[41] J.H. Schmidhuber. An $O(n^3)$ Learning Algorithm for Fully Recurrent Networks. Technical Report FKI-151-91, Institut für Informatik, Technische Universität München, 1991.

[42] B. Schürmann, J. Hollatz, D. Gawronska. Recurrent and Feedforward Multi Layer Perceptrons in Comparison. Submitted to NIPS 91.

[43] H. U. Simon. Algorithmisches Lernen auf der Basis empirischer Daten. In *Tagungsband des 4'ten int. GI–Kongresses über wissensbasierte Systeme*, Oct. 1991. These Proceedings.

[44] L. G. Valiant. A theory of the learnable. *Communications of the ACM*, 27(11):1134–1142, Nov. 1984.

Liste der Autoren

Band 246: Th. Bräunl, Massiv parallele Programmierung mit dem Parallaxis–Modell. XII, 168 Seiten. 1990

Band 247: H. Krumm, Funktionelle Analyse von Kommunikationsprotokollen. IX, 122 Seiten. 1990.

Band 248: G. Moerkotte, Inkonsistenzen in deduktiven Datenbanken. VIII, 141 Seiten. 1990.

Band 249: P. A. Gloor, N. A. Streitz (Hrsg.), Hypertext und Hypermedia. IX, 302 Seiten. 1990.

Band 250: H. W. Meuer (Hrsg.), SUPERCOMPUTER '90. Mannheim, Juni 1990. Proceedings. VIII, 209 Seiten. 1990.

Band 251: H. Marburger (Hrsg.), GWAI-90. 14th German Workshop on Artificial Intelligence. Eringerfeld, September 1990. Proceedings. X, 333 Seiten. 1990.

Band 252: G. Dorffner (Hrsg.), Konnektionismus in Artificial Intelligence und Kognitionsforschung. 6. Österreichische Artificial-Intelligence-Tagung (KONNAI), Salzburg, September 1990. Proceedings. VIII, 246 Seiten. 1990.

Band 253: W. Ameling (Hrsg.), ASST '90. 7. Aachener Symposium für Signaltheorie. Aachen, September 1990. Proceedings. XI, 332 Seiten. 1990.

Band 254: R. E. Großkopf (Hrsg.), Mustererkennung 1990. 12. DAGM-Symposium, Oberkochen-Aalen, September 1990. Proceedings. XXI, 686 Seiten. 1990.

Band 255: B. Reusch, (Hrsg.), Rechnergestützter Entwurf und Architektur mikroelektronischer Systeme. GME/GI/ITG-Fachtagung, Dortmund, Oktober 1990. Proceedings. X, 298 Seiten. 1990.

Band 256: W. Pillmann, A. Jaeschke (Hrsg.), Informatik für den Umweltschutz. 5. Symposium, Wien, September 1990. Proceedings. XV, 864 Seiten. 1990.

Band 257: A. Reuter (Hrsg.), GI-20. Jahrestagung I. Stuttgart, Oktober 1990. Proceedings. XVIII, 602 Seiten. 1990.

Band 258: A. Reuter (Hrsg.), GI-20. Jahrestagung II. Stuttgart, Oktober 1990. Proceedings. XVIII, 602 Seiten. 1990.

Band 259: H.-J. Friemel, G. Müller-Schönberger, A. Schütt (Hrsg.), Forum '90 Wissenschaft und Technik. Trier, Oktober 1990. Proceedings. XI, 532 Seiten. 1990.

Band 260: B. J. Frommherz, Ein Roboteraktionsplanungssystem. XI, 134 Seiten. 1990.

Band 261: W. Zimmermann, Automatische Komplexitätsanalyse funktionaler Programme. VII, 194 Seiten. 1990.

Band 262: W. Gerth, P. Baacke (Hrsg.), PEARL 90 - Workshop über Realzeitsysteme. 11. Fachtagung, Boppard, November 1990. Proceedings. X, 187 Seiten. 1990.

Band 263: H. Eckhardt, Entwurfstransaktionen für modulare Objektsysteme. VIII, 144 Seiten. 1990.

Band 264: T. Härder, H. Wedekind, G. Zimmermann (Hrsg.), Entwurf und Betrieb verteilter Systeme. Fachtagung, Dagstuhl, September 1990. Proceedings. XII, 283 Seiten. 1990.

Band 265: U. Herrmann, Mehrbenutzerkontrolle in Nicht-Standard-Datenbanksystemen. VIII, 183 Seiten. 1991.

Band 266: R. Cunis, A. Günter, H. Strecker (Hrsg.), Das PLAKON-Buch. VIII, 279 Seiten. 1991

Band 267: W. Effelsberg, H. W. Meuer, G. Müller (Hrsg.), Kommunikation in verteilten Systemen. GI/ITG-Fachtagung, Mannheim, Februar 1991. Proceedings. X, 589 Seiten. 1991.

Band 268: J. Raczkowsky, Multisensordatenverarbeitung in der Robotik. X, 168 Seiten. 1991.

Band 269: G. Hommel (Hrsg.), Prozeßrechensysteme '91. Berlin, Februar 1991. Proceedings. XIV, 449 Seiten. 1991.

Band 270: H.-J. Appelrath (Hrsg.), Datenbanksysteme in Büro, Technik und Wissenschaft. GI-Fachtagung, Kaiserslautern, März 1991. Proceedings. XIII, 507 Seiten. 1991.

Band 271: A. Pfitzmann, E. Raubold (Hrsg.), VIS '91, Verläßliche Informationssysteme. GI-Fachtagung, Darmstadt, März 1991. Proceedings. VIII, 355 Seiten. 1991.

Band 272: R. Grebe, C. Ziemann, Parallele Datenverarbeitung mit dem Transputer. Aachen, September 1990. Proceedings. X, 300 Seiten 1991.

Band 273: M. Timm (Hrsg.), Requirements Engineering '91. VIII, 208 Seiten. 1991.

Band 274: R. Denzer, H. Hagen, K.-H. Kutschke (Hrsg.), Visualisierung von Umweltdaten. Workshop, Rostock, November 1990. Proceedings. VII, 97 Seiten. 1991.

Band 276: H. Maurer (Hrsg.), Hypertext / Hypermedia '91. Tagung der GI, SI und OCG, Graz, Mai 1991. Proceedings. VIII, 299 Seiten. 1991.

Band 277: U. Borgolte, Flexible, realzeitfähige Kollisionsvermeidung in Mehrroboter-Systemen. XIII, 105 Seiten. 1991.

Band 278: H. W. Meuer (Hrsg.), SUPERCOMPUTER '91. Proceedings. VIII, 266 Seiten. 1991.

Band 279: G. Schwichtenberg (Hrsg.), Organisation und Betrieb von Informationssystemen. 9. GI – Fachgespräch über Rechenzentren, Dortmund, März 1991. Proceedings. IX, 337 Seiten. 1991.

Band 280: B. Westfechtel, Revisions- und Konsistenzkontrolle in einer integrierten Softwareentwicklungsumgebung. X, 321 Seiten. 1991.

Band 281: W. Emde, Modellbildung, Wissensrevision und Wissensrepräsentation im Maschinellen Lernen. XI, 204 Seiten. 1991.

Band 282: P. Buchholz, Die strukturierte Analyse Markovscher Modelle. VII, 192 Seiten 1991.

Band 283: M. Dal Cin, W. Hohl (Hrsg.), Fault-Tolerant Computing Systems. 5th International GI/ITG/GMA Conference, Nürnberg, September 1991. Proceedings. XII, 425 Seiten. 1991.

Band 284: R. Stadler, Ausführbare Spezifikation von Directory-Systemen in einer logischen Sprache. X, 142 Seiten. 1991.

Band 285: T. Christaller (Hrsg.), GWAI-91. 15. Fachtagung für Künstliche Intelligenz, Bonn, September 1991. IX, 273 Seiten. 1991.

Band 286: A. Lehmann, F. Lehmann (Hrsg.), Messung, Modellierung und Bewertung von Rechensystemen. 6. GI/ITG-Fachtagung, Neubiberg, September 1991. Proceedings. VIII, 338 Seiten. 1991.

Band 287: H. Kaindl (Hrsg.), 7. Österreichische Artificial-Intelligence-Tagung, Wien, September 1991. Proceedings. VIII, 180 Seiten. 1991.

Band 288: G. Helm, Symbolische und konnektionistische Modelle der menschlichen Informationsverarbeitung. X, 161 Seiten. 1991.

Band 289: N. Fuhr (Hrsg.), Information Retrieval. GI/GMD-Workshop, Darmstadt, Juni 1991. Proceedings. VII, 162 Seiten. 1991.

Band 290: B. Radig (Hrsg.), Mustererkennung 1991. 13. DAGM-Symposium, München, Oktober 1991. Proceedings. XVIII, 584 Seiten. 1991.

Band 291: W. Brauer, D. Hernández (Hrsg.) Verteilte künstliche Intelligenz und kooperatives Arbeiten. 4. Internationaler GI-Kongreß, München, Oktober 1991. Proceedings. IX, 546 Seiten. 1991.

Band 292: P. Gorny (Hrsg.), Informatik und Schule 1991. GI-Fachtagung, Oldenburg, Oktober 1991. Proceedings. IX, 335 Seiten. 1991.

Band 293: J. Encarnação (Hrsg.) Telekommunikation und multimediale Anwendungen der Informatik. GI-21. Jahrestagung, Darmstadt, Oktober 1991. Proceedings. XII, 710 Seiten. 1991.